C# 2012 FOR PROGRAMMERS
FIFTH EDITION
DEITEL® DEVELOPER SERIES

The publisher offers excellent discounts on this book when ordered in quantity for bulk purchases or special sales, which may include electronic versions and/or custom covers and content particular to your business, training goals, marketing focus, and branding interests. For more information, please contact:

U. S. Corporate and Government Sales
(800) 382-3419
corpsales@pearsontechgroup.com

For sales outside the U. S., please contact:

International Sales
international@pearsoned.com

Visit us on the Web: informit.com/ph

Library of Congress Cataloging-in-Publication Data

On file

© 2014 Pearson Education, Inc.

ISBN-13: 978-0-13-344057-7
ISBN-10: 0-13-344057-5

Text printed in the United States at Edwards Brothers Malloy in Ann Arbor, Michigan.
First printing, September 2013

C# 2012 FOR PROGRAMMERS
FIFTH EDITION
DEITEL® DEVELOPER SERIES

Paul Deitel

Deitel & Associates, Inc.

Harvey Deitel

Deitel & Associates, Inc.

PRENTICE
HALL

Upper Saddle River, NJ • Boston • Indianapolis • San Francisco
New York • Toronto • Montreal • London • Munich • Paris • Madrid
Capetown • Sydney • Tokyo • Singapore • Mexico City

Trademarks

To our review team

Shay Friedman
Octavio Hernandez
Stephen Hustedde
José Antonio González Seco
Shawn Weisfeld

We are grateful for your guidance and expertise.

Paul and Harvey Deitel

Contents

3   Introduction to C# Apps   46

4   Introduction to Classes, Objects, Methods and `strings`   72

5   Control Statements: Part 1   101

9 Introduction to LINQ and the List Collection   239

10 Classes and Objects: A Deeper Look   256

13 Exception Handling: A Deeper Look   358

14 Graphical User Interfaces with Windows Forms: Part 1   386

18 Generics   557

19 Collections   577

20 Databases and LINQ   607

21 Web App Development with ASP.NET   649

22 XML and LINQ to XML   695

25 Building a Windows Phone 8 App   808

Preface

"Live in fragments no longer, only connect."
—Edgar Morgan Forster

Welcome to Visual C#® 2012 and the world of Microsoft® Windows® and Internet and web programming with Microsoft's .NET platform. Please read the book's back cover and inside back cover—these concisely capture the book's essence. In this Preface we provide more details.

We focus on software engineering best practices. At the heart of the book is the Deitel signature "live-code approach"—concepts are presented in the context of complete working programs, rather than in code snippets. Each complete code example is accompanied by live sample executions. All the source code is available at

```
www.deitel.com/books/cs2012fp/
```

If you have questions as you read the book, we're easy to reach at deitel@deitel.com—we'll respond promptly. For book updates, visit www.deitel.com/books/cs2012fp, join our social media communities on Facebook (www.deitel.com/DeitelFan), Twitter (@deitel), Google+ (gplus.to/deitel) and LinkedIn (bit.ly/DeitelLinkedIn), and subscribe to the *Deitel® Buzz Online* newsletter (www.deitel.com/newsletter/subscribe.html).

Visual C#® 2012, the Visual Studio® 2012 IDE, .NET 4.5, Windows® 7 and Windows® 8

The new Visual C# 2012 and its associated technologies motivated us to write *C# 2012 for Programmers, 5/e.* These are some of the key features of this new edition:

- *Use with Windows 7, Windows 8 or both.* The book is designed so that you can continue to use Windows 7 now and begin to evolve to Windows 8, if you like, or you can move right to Windows 8. All of the code examples in Chapters 1–22 and 26–33 were tested on *both* Windows 7 and Windows 8. The code examples for the Windows-8-specific chapters—Chapter 23 (Windows 8 UI and XAML), Chapter 24 (Windows 8 Graphics and Multimedia) and Chapter 25 (Building a Windows Phone 8 App)—were tested *only* on Windows 8, because Visual Studio Express 2012 for Windows 8 and Visual Studio Express 2012 for Windows Phone run only on Windows 8.

- *C# and Visual C#.* The C# language has been standardized internationally by ECMA and ISO (the standards document is available free of charge at bit.ly/ECMA334). This enables other implementations of the language besides Microsoft's Visual C#, such as Mono (www.mono-project.com), which runs on Linux systems, iOS (for Apple's iPhone, iPad and iPod Touch), Google's Android and Windows.

- *Modular multi-GUI treatment with Windows Forms, Windows 8 UI and WPF.* The book features three different GUI treatments, starting with Windows Forms GUI; later chapters contain treatments of the new Windows 8 UI (user interface) and WPF GUI. Windows 8 UI apps are called *Windows Store apps.* In Chapter 23, you'll learn how to create and test Windows Store apps.

- *Modular treatment of graphics and multimedia with Windows 8 and WPF.* The book features chapters on both the new Windows 8 Graphics and Multimedia (Chapter 24) and WPF Graphics and Multimedia (Chapter 31).

- *Database with LINQ to Entities.* In the previous edition of this book, we discussed LINQ (Language Integrated Query) to SQL (Microsoft's SQL Server database system). Microsoft stopped further development on LINQ to SQL in 2008 in favor of the newer and more robust LINQ to Entities and the ADO.NET Entity Framework, which we've switched to in this edition.

- *SQL Server database.* We use Microsoft's free SQL Server Express 2012 (which installs with the free Visual Studio Express 2012 for Windows Desktop) to present the fundamentals of database programming. Chapters 20–21 and 27 use database and LINQ capabilities to build an address-book desktop app, a web-based guestbook app, a bookstore app and an airline reservation system app.

- *ASP.NET 4.5.* Microsoft's .NET server-side technology, ASP.NET, enables you to create robust, scalable web-based apps. In Chapter 21, you'll build several apps, including a web-based guestbook that uses ASP.NET and the ADO.NET Entity Framework to store data in a database and display data in a web page. The chapter also discusses the IIS Express web server for testing your web apps on your local computer.

- *Building a Windows Phone 8 App.* Windows Phone 8 is Microsoft's latest smartphone operating system. It features multi-touch support for touchpads and touchscreen devices, enhanced security features and more. In Chapter 25, you'll build a complete working Windows Phone 8 app and test it on the Windows Phone emulator; we discuss how to upload apps to the Windows Phone Store.

- *Building a Windows Azure™ Cloud Computing App.* Windows Azure is a cloud computing platform that allows you to develop, manage and distribute your apps in the cloud. Chapter 29 shows you how to build a Windows Azure app that can store data in the cloud. You'll test your app on the Windows Azure Storage Emulator.

- *Asynchronous programming with* **async** *and* **await***.* Asynchronous programming is simplified in C# 2012 with the new *async* and *await* capabilities. We introduce asynchronous programming with async and await in Chapter 26. To take advantage of multicore architecture you need to write applications that can process tasks asynchronously. Asynchronous programming is a technique for writing apps containing tasks that can execute asynchronously, which can improve app performance and GUI responsiveness in apps with long-running or compute-intensive tasks.

Object-Oriented Programming

- *Early-objects approach.* The basic concepts and terminology of object technology are introduced in Chapter 1. In Chapter 2, Dive Into® Visual Studio 2012 Express for Windows Desktop, you'll *visually* manipulate objects, such as labels and images. In Chapter 3, Introduction to C# Apps, you'll write C# *program code* that manipulates *existing* objects. You'll develop your first *customized* classes and objects in Chapter 4.

- *A clear, example-driven presentation of classes, objects, inheritance, polymorphism and interfaces.*

- *Case study: Using the UML to develop an object-oriented design and C# implementation of an Automated Teller Machine (ATM).* The UML™ (Unified Modeling Language™) is the industry-standard graphical language for modeling object-oriented systems. We introduce the UML in the early chapters. Chapters 32 and 33 include a case study on object-oriented design using the UML. We design and implement the software for a simple automated teller machine. We analyze a typical *requirements document* that specifies the system to be built. We determine the *classes* needed to implement that system, the *attributes* the classes need to have, the *behaviors* the classes need to exhibit and we specify how the classes must *interact* with one another to meet the system requirements. From the design we produce a complete working C# implementation. Readers often report a "light bulb moment"—the case study helps them "tie it all together" and understand object orientation more deeply.

- *Multiple programming paradigms.* We discuss *structured programming*, *object-oriented programming*, *generic programming* and some *functional programming*.

Other Features

- *We use LINQ to query files, databases, XML and collections.* The introductory LINQ to Objects chapter (Chapter 9) will get you started using LINQ technology early. Later in the book, we take a deeper look, using LINQ to Entities (Chapters 20–21 and 27) and LINQ to XML (Chapters 22 and 26).

- *Local type inference.* When you initialize a local variable in its declaration, you can omit the variable's type—the compiler *infers* it from the initializer value.

- *Object initializers.* For new objects, you can use object initializer syntax (similar to array initializer syntax) to assign values to the new object's public properties and public instance variables.

- *We emphasize the IDE's* **IntelliSense** *feature* that helps you write code faster and with fewer errors.

- *Files and strings.*

- *Generics and collections.*

- *Integrated exception handling.* We introduce exception handling early (Chapter 8, Arrays) to watch for attempts to access array elements outside the array's bounds. Chapter 10, Classes and Objects: A Deeper Look, shows how to indicate an exception when a member function receives an invalid argument. We cover the complete details of exception handling in Chapter 13, Exception Handling: A Deeper Look.

- *C# XML capabilities.* Extensible Markup Language (XML) is pervasive in the software-development industry and throughout the .NET platform. In Chapter 22, we introduce XML syntax and programmatically manipulate the elements of an XML document using LINQ to XML. XAML is an XML vocabulary that's used to describe graphical user interfaces, graphics and multimedia. We discuss XAML in Chapters 23–24 and 30–31.

- *Web app development with ASP.NET 4.5 and ASP.NET Ajax.* Chapter 27 extends Chapter 21's ASP.NET discussion with a case study on building a password-protected, web-based bookstore app. Also, we introduce in Chapter 27 ASP.NET Ajax controls and use them to add Ajax functionality to web apps to give them a look and feel similar to that of desktop apps.

- *Windows Communication Foundation (WCF) web services.* Web services enable you to package app functionality in a manner that turns the web into a library of *reusable* services. Chapter 28 includes a case study on building a math question generator web service that's called by a math tutor app.

- *WPF (Windows Presentation Foundation) GUI, graphics and multimedia.* Chapters 30–31 provide an introduction to Windows Presentation Foundation (WPF)—a XAML-based Microsoft framework that preceded Windows 8 UI and integrates GUI, graphics and multimedia capabilities. WPF was designed as a replacement for Windows Forms GUI technologies. We implement a painting app, a text editor, a color chooser, a book-cover viewer, a television video player, various animations, and speech synthesis and recognition apps.

Training Approach

C# 2012 for Programmers, 5/e stresses program clarity and concentrates on building well-engineered software.

Live-Code Approach. The book includes hundreds of "live-code" examples—each new concept is presented in the context of a complete working C# app that is immediately followed by one or more actual executions showing the program's inputs and outputs. We include a broad range of example programs selected from computer science, business, simulation, game playing, graphics, multimedia and many other areas.

Syntax Shading. For readability, we syntax shade the code, similar to the way most integrated-development environments and code editors syntax color the code. Our syntax-shading conventions are:

```
comments appear like this
keywords appear like this in bold black
constants and literal values appear like this
all other code appears in non-bold black
```

Code Highlighting. We place gray rectangles around each program's key code segments.

Using Fonts for Emphasis. We place the key terms and the index's page reference for each defining occurrence in ***bold italic*** text for easier reference. We emphasize on-screen components in the **bold Helvetica** font (e.g., the **File** menu) and emphasize C# program text in the Lucida font (e.g., int x = 5).

Web Access. All of the source-code examples can be downloaded from:

```
www.deitel.com/books/cs2012fp
```

Objectives. Each chapter begins with a list of chapter objectives.

Programming Tips. The book includes hundreds of programming tips and practices that represent the best we've gleaned from a combined eight decades of programming and teaching experience.

Good Programming Practice

The Good Programming Practices *call attention to techniques that will help you produce programs that are clearer, more understandable and more maintainable.*

Common Programming Error

Pointing out these Common Programming Errors *reduces the likelihood that you'll make them.*

Error-Prevention Tip

These tips contain suggestions for exposing and removing bugs from your programs; many of the tips describe aspects of C# that prevent bugs from getting into programs in the first place.

Performance Tip

These tips highlight opportunities for making your programs run faster or minimizing the amount of memory that they occupy.

Portability Tip

The Portability Tips *help you write code that will run on a variety of platforms.*

Software Engineering Observation

The Software Engineering Observations *highlight architectural and design issues that affect the construction of software systems, especially large-scale systems.*

Look-and-Feel Observation

These observations help you design attractive, user-friendly graphical user interfaces that conform to industry norms.

Obtaining the Software Used in This Book

We wrote the code examples in *C# 2012 for Programmers, 5/e* using Microsoft's *free* Visual Studio Express 2012 products, including:

- Visual Studio Express 2012 for Windows Desktop (Chapters 1–20, 22, 26, 29 and 30–33), which includes Visual C# and other Microsoft development tools. This runs on Windows 7 *and* 8.

- Visual Studio Express 2012 for Web (Chapters 21 and 27–28

- Visual Studio Express 2012 for Windows 8 (Chapters 23–24)

- Visual Studio Express 2012 for Windows Phone (Chapter 25)

Each of these is available for download at

```
www.microsoft.com/visualstudio/eng/products/
       visual-studio-express-products
```

C# 2012 Fundamentals: Parts I, II, III and IV, Second Edition LiveLessons Video Training

Our *C# 2012 Fundamentals: Parts I, II, III and IV* LiveLessons video training shows you what you need to know to start building robust, powerful software with C# 2012. It includes approximately 40 hours of expert training synchronized with *C# 2012 for Programmers, 5/e*. For additional information about Deitel LiveLessons video products available on Safari Books Online and other electronic channels, visit

```
www.deitel.com/livelessons
```

or contact us at deitel@deitel.com.

Acknowledgments

We'd like to thank Abbey Deitel and Barbara Deitel of Deitel & Associates, Inc. for long hours devoted to this project. Abbey co-authored this Preface and Chapter 1 and she and Barbara painstakingly researched the new capabilities of Visual C# 2012, .NET 4.5, Windows 8, Windows Phone 8, Windows Azure and other key topics.

We're fortunate to have worked on this project with the dedicated publishing professionals at Prentice Hall/Pearson. We appreciate the extraordinary efforts and mentorship of our friend and professional colleague Mark L. Taub, Editor-in-Chief of Pearson Technology Group. Carole Snyder did a great job recruiting distinguished members of the C# community to review the manuscript and managing the review process. Chuti Prasertsith designed the cover with creativity and precision. John Fuller does a superb job managing the production of all of our Deitel Developer Series books and LiveLessons video products.

Reviewers

We wish to acknowledge the efforts of the reviewers whose constructive criticisms helped us shape the recent editions of this content. They scrutinized the text and the programs and provided countless suggestions for improving the presentation: Shay Friedman (Microsoft Visual C# MVP), Octavio Hernandez (Microsoft Certified Solutions Developer), Stephen Hustedde (South Mountain College), José Antonio González Seco (Parliament of Andalusia, Spain), Shawn Weisfeld (Microsoft MVP and President and Founder of UserGroup.tv), Huanhui Hu (Microsoft Corporation), Narges Kasiri (Oklahoma State University), Charles Liu (University of Texas at San Antonio), Dr. Hamid R. Nemati

(The University of North Carolina at Greensboro), Jeffrey P. Scott (Blackhawk Technical College), Douglas B. Bock (MCSD.NET, Southern Illinois University Edwardsville), Dan Crevier (Microsoft), Amit K. Ghosh (University of Texas at El Paso), Marcelo Guerra Hahn (Microsoft), Kim Hamilton (Software Design Engineer at Microsoft and co-author of *Learning UML 2.0*), James Edward Keysor (Florida Institute of Technology), Helena Kotas (Microsoft), Chris Lovett (Software Architect at Microsoft), Bashar Lulu (INETA Country Leader, Arabian Gulf), John McIlhinney (Spatial Intelligence; Microsoft MVP 2008 Visual Developer, Visual Basic), Ged Mead (Microsoft Visual Basic MVP, DevCity.net), Anand Mukundan (Architect, Polaris Software Lab Ltd.), Timothy Ng (Microsoft), Akira Onishi (Microsoft), Joe Stagner (Senior Program Manager, Developer Tools & Platforms), Erick Thompson (Microsoft), Jesús Ubaldo Quevedo-Torrero (University of Wisconsin–Parkside, Department of Computer Science) and Zijiang Yang (Western Michigan University).

As you read the book, we'd sincerely appreciate your comments, criticisms and suggestions for improving the text. Please address all correspondence to:

```
deitel@deitel.com
```

We'll respond promptly. We really enjoyed writing this book—we hope you enjoy reading it!

Paul Deitel
Harvey Deitel

About the Authors

Paul Deitel, CEO and Chief Technical Officer of Deitel & Associates, Inc., is a graduate of MIT, where he studied Information Technology. Through Deitel & Associates, Inc., he has delivered hundreds of programming courses to industry clients, including Cisco, IBM, Siemens, Sun Microsystems, Dell, Fidelity, NASA at the Kennedy Space Center, the National Severe Storm Laboratory, White Sands Missile Range, Rogue Wave Software, Boeing, SunGard Higher Education, Nortel Networks, Puma, iRobot, Invensys and many more. He and his co-author, Dr. Harvey M. Deitel, are the world's best-selling programming-language textbook/professional book/video authors.

Paul was named as a Microsoft® Most Valuable Professional (MVP) for C# in 2012. According to Microsoft, "the Microsoft MVP Award is an annual award that recognizes exceptional technology community leaders worldwide who actively share their high quality, real world expertise with users and Microsoft."

2012/2013 C# MVP

Dr. Harvey Deitel, Chairman and Chief Strategy Officer of Deitel & Associates, Inc., has 52 years of experience in the computer field. Dr. Deitel earned B.S. and M.S. degrees in Electrical Engineering from MIT and a Ph.D. in Mathematics from Boston University, all with an emphasis in Computer Science. In the 1960s, through Advanced Computer Techniques and Computer Usage Corporation, he worked on the teams building various IBM operating systems. In the 1970s, he built commercial software systems and more recently committed to a career in Computer Science education. He has extensive college teaching experience, including earning tenure and serving as the Chairman of the Computer Science Department at Boston College before founding Deitel & Associates, Inc., in 1991 with his son, Paul Deitel. The Deitels' publications have earned international recognition, with translations published in Chinese, Korean, Japanese, German, Russian, Spanish, French, Polish, Italian, Portuguese, Greek, Urdu and Turkish. Dr. Deitel has delivered hundreds of programming courses to corporate, academic, government and military clients.

Deitel® Dive-Into® Series Corporate Training

Deitel & Associates, Inc., founded by Paul Deitel and Harvey Deitel, is an internationally recognized authoring and corporate training organization, specializing in computer programming languages, object technology, mobile app development and Internet and web software technology. The company's clients include many of the world's largest companies, government agencies, branches of the military, and academic institutions. The company offers instructor-led training courses delivered at client sites worldwide on major programming languages and platforms, including Visual C#®, Visual Basic®, C++, Visual C++®, C, Java™, XML®, Python®, object technology, Internet and web programming, Android app development, Objective-C and iOS app development and a growing list of additional programming and software development courses.

Through its 37-year publishing partnership with Prentice Hall/Pearson, Deitel & Associates, Inc., publishes leading-edge programming professional books, college textbooks and LiveLessons video courses. Deitel & Associates, Inc. and the authors can be reached at:

```
deitel@deitel.com
```

To learn more about Deitel's *Dive-Into® Series* Corporate Training curriculum, visit:

```
www.deitel.com/training
```

To request a proposal for worldwide on-site, instructor-led training at your organization, e-mail deitel@deitel.com.

Individuals wishing to purchase Deitel books and LiveLessons video training can do so through www.deitel.com. Bulk orders by corporations, the government, the military and academic institutions should be placed directly with Pearson. For more information, visit

```
www.informit.com/store/sales.aspx
```

Before You Begin

This section contains information you should review before using this book and instructions to ensure that your computer is set up properly for use with this book.

Font and Naming Conventions

We use fonts to distinguish between features, such as menu names, menu items, and other elements that appear in the program-development environment. Our convention is to emphasize IDE features in a sans-serif bold **Helvetica** font (for example, **Properties** window) and to emphasize program text in a sans-serif Lucida font (for example, bool x = true).

Software

This book uses the following software:

- Microsoft Visual Studio Express 2012 for Windows Desktop
- Microsoft Visual Studio Express 2012 for Web (Chapters 21 and 27–28)
- Microsoft Visual Studio Express 2012 for Windows 8 (Chapters 23–24)
- Microsoft Visual Studio Express 2012 for Windows Phone (Chapter 25)

Each is available free for download at www.microsoft.com/express. The Express Editions are fully functional, and there's no time limit for using the software.

Hardware and Software Requirements for the Visual Studio 2012 Express Editions

To install and run the Visual Studio 2012 Express Editions, ensure that your system meets the minimum requirements specified at:

www.microsoft.com/visualstudio/eng/products/compatibility

Microsoft Visual Studio Express 2012 for Windows 8 works *only* on Windows 8.

Viewing File Extensions

Several screenshots in *C# 2012 for Programmers, 5/e* display file names with file-name extensions (e.g., .txt, .cs or .png). Your system's settings may need to be adjusted to display file-name extensions. Follow these steps to configure your Windows 7 computer:

1. In the **Start** menu, select **All Programs**, then **Accessories**, then **Windows Explorer**.
2. Press *Alt* to display the menu bar, then select **Folder Options...** from **Windows Explorer**'s **Tools** menu.
3. In the dialog that appears, select the **View** tab.
4. In the **Advanced settings:** pane, uncheck the box to the left of the text **Hide extensions for known file types**. [*Note*: If this item is already unchecked, no action needs to be taken.]
5. Click **OK** to apply the setting and close the dialog.

Follow these steps to configure your Windows 8 computer:

1. On the **Start** screen, click the **Desktop** tile to switch to the desktop.

2. On the task bar, click the **File Explorer** icon to open the **File Explorer**.

3. Click the **View** tab, then ensure that the **File name extensions** checkbox is checked.

Obtaining the Code Examples

The examples for *C# 2012 for Programmers, 5/e* are available for download at

> www.deitel.com/books/cs2012fp/

If you're not already registered at our website, go to www.deitel.com and click the **Register** link below our logo in the upper-left corner of the page. Fill in your information. There's no charge to register, and we do not share your information with anyone. We send you only account-management e-mails unless you register separately for our free e-mail newsletter at www.deitel.com/newsletter/subscribe.html. *You must enter a valid e-mail address.* After registering, you'll receive a confirmation e-mail with your verification code. Click the link in the confirmation email to go to www.deitel.com and sign in.

Next, go to www.deitel.com/books/cs2012fp/. Click the **Examples** link to download the ZIP archive file to your computer. Write down the location where you save the file—most browsers will save the file into your Downloads folder.

Throughout the book, steps that require you to access our example code on your computer assume that you've extracted the examples from the ZIP file and placed them at C:\Examples. You can extract them anywhere you like, but if you choose a different location, you'll need to update our steps accordingly. You can extract the ZIP archive file's contents using tools such as WinZip (www.winzip.com), 7-zip (www.7-zip.org) or the built-in capabilities of **Windows Explorer** on Window 7 or **File Explorer** on Windows 8.

Visual Studio Theme

Visual Studio 2012 has a **Dark** theme (the default) and a **Light** theme. The screen captures shown in this book use the **Light** theme, which is more readable in print. If you'd like to switch to the **Light** theme, in the **TOOLS** menu, select **Options...** to display the **Options** dialog. In the left column, select **Environment**, then select **Light** under **Color theme**. Keep the **Options** dialog open for the next step.

Displaying Line Numbers and Configuring Tabs

Next, you'll change the settings so that your code matches that of this book. To have the IDE display line numbers, expand the **Text Editor** node in the left pane then select **All Languages**. On the right, check the **Line numbers** checkbox. Next, expand the C# node in the left pane and select **Tabs**. Make sure that the option **Insert spaces** is selected. Enter **3** for both the **Tab size** and **Indent size** fields. Any new code you add will now use three spaces for each level of indentation. Click **OK** to save your settings.

Miscellaneous Notes

- Some people like to change the workspace layout in the development tools. You can return the tools to their default layouts by selecting **Window > Reset Window Layout**.

- Many of the menu items we use in the book have corresponding icons shown with each menu item in the menus. Many of the icons also appear on one of the toolbars at the top of the development environment. As you become familiar with these icons, you can use the toolbars to help speed up your development time. Similarly, many of the menu items have keyboard shortcuts (also shown with each menu item in the menus) for accessing commands quickly.

You are now ready to begin your Visual C# studies with *C# 2012 for Programmers, 5/e*. We hope you enjoy the book!

1

Introduction

Objectives

In this chapter you'll:

- Review the history of the Visual C# programming language and the Windows operating system.

- Learn what cloud computing with Windows Azure is.

- Learn the basics of object technology.

- Understand the parts that Windows 8, .NET 4.5, Visual Studio 2012 and Visual C# 2012 play in the Visual C# ecosystem.

- Test-drive a Visual C# 2012 drawing app.

1.1 Introduction

Welcome to Visual C# 2012 which, from this point forward, we'll refer to simply as C#.[1] C# is a powerful computer programming language that's appropriate for building substantial information systems.

We'll focus on *object-oriented programming*—today's key programming methodology that's enhancing programmer productivity, and reducing software development costs. You'll create many *software objects* that model both abstract and real-world *things*. And you'll build C# apps for a variety of environments including the *desktop*—and new to this edition of the book—mobile devices like *smartphones* and *tablets*, and even *"the cloud."*

1.2 Object Technology

C# is an object-oriented programming language. In this section we'll introduce the basics of object technology.

Building software quickly, correctly and economically remains an elusive goal at a time when demands for new and more powerful software are soaring. **Objects**, or more precisely the *classes* objects come from, are essentially *reusable* software components. There are date objects, time objects, audio objects, video objects, automobile objects, people objects, etc. Almost any *noun* can be reasonably represented as a software object in terms of *attributes* (e.g., name, color and size) and *behaviors* (e.g., calculating, moving and communicating). Software developers have discovered that using a modular, object-oriented design and implementation approach can make software-development groups much more productive than was possible with earlier techniques—object-oriented programs are often easier to understand, correct and modify.

---

1.   The name C#, pronounced "C-sharp," is based on the musical # notation for "sharp" notes.

The Automobile as an Object

Let's begin with a simple analogy. Suppose you want to *drive a car and make it go faster by pressing its accelerator pedal*. What must happen before you can do this? Well, before you can drive a car, someone has to *design* it. A car typically begins as engineering drawings, similar to the *blueprints* that describe the design of a house. These drawings include the design for an accelerator pedal. The pedal *hides* from the driver the complex mechanisms that actually make the car go faster, just as the brake pedal hides the mechanisms that slow the car, and the steering wheel hides the mechanisms that turn the car. This enables people with little or no knowledge of how engines, braking and steering mechanisms work to drive a car easily.

Before you can drive a car, it must be *built* from the engineering drawings that describe it. A completed car has an *actual* accelerator pedal to make the car go faster, but even that's not enough—the car won't accelerate on its own (we hope), so the driver must *press* the pedal to accelerate the car.

Methods and Classes

Let's use our car example to introduce some key object-oriented programming concepts. Performing a task in a program requires a **method**. The method houses the program statements that actually perform the task. It *hides* these statements from its user, just as a car's accelerator pedal hides from the driver the mechanisms of making the car go faster. In object-oriented programming languages, we create a program unit called a **class** to house the set of methods that perform the class's tasks. For example, a class that represents a bank account might contain one method to *deposit* money to an account, another to *withdraw* money from an account and a third to *inquire* what the account's current balance is. A class that represents a car might contain methods for accelerating, braking and turning. A class is similar in concept to a car's engineering drawings, which house the design of an accelerator pedal, steering wheel, and so on.

Making Objects from Classes

Just as someone has to *build a car* from its engineering drawings before you can actually drive a car, you must *build an object* from a class before a program can perform the tasks that the class's methods define. The process of doing this is called *instantiation*. An object is then referred to as an **instance** of its class.

Reuse

Just as a car's engineering drawings can be *reused* many times to build many cars, you can *reuse* a class many times to build many objects. Reuse of existing classes when building new classes and programs saves time and effort. Reuse also helps you build more reliable and effective systems, because existing classes and components often have gone through extensive *testing* (to locate problems), *debugging* (to correct those problems) and *performance tuning*. Just as the notion of *interchangeable parts* was crucial to the Industrial Revolution, reusable classes are crucial to the software revolution that's been spurred by object technology.

Software Engineering Observation 1.1

Use a building-block approach to creating your programs. Avoid reinventing the wheel— use existing pieces wherever possible. This software reuse is a key benefit of object-oriented programming.

Messages and Method Calls

When you drive a car, pressing its gas pedal sends a *message* to the car to perform a task—that is, to go faster. Similarly, you *send messages to an object*. Each message is implemented as a **method call** that tells a method of the object to perform its task. For example, a program might call a particular bank-account object's *deposit* method to increase the account's balance.

Attributes and Instance Variables

A car, besides having capabilities to accomplish tasks, also has *attributes*, such as its color, its number of doors, the amount of gas in its tank, its current speed and its record of total miles driven (i.e., its odometer reading). Like its capabilities, the car's attributes are represented as part of its design in its engineering diagrams (which, for example, include an odometer and a fuel gauge). As you drive an actual car, these attributes are carried along with the car. Every car maintains its *own* attributes. For example, each car knows how much gas is in its own gas tank, but *not* how much is in the tanks of *other* cars.

An object, similarly, has attributes that it carries along as it's used in a program. These attributes are specified as part of the object's class. For example, a bank-account object has a *balance attribute* that represents the amount of money in the account. Each bank-account object knows the balance in the account it represents, but *not* the balances of the *other* accounts in the bank. Attributes are specified by the class's **instance variables**.

Encapsulation

Classes **encapsulate** (i.e., wrap) attributes and methods into objects—an object's attributes and operations are intimately related. Objects may communicate with one another, but they're normally not allowed to know how other objects are implemented—implementation details are *hidden* within the objects themselves. This **information hiding**, as we'll see, is crucial to good software engineering.

Inheritance

A new class of objects can be created quickly and conveniently by **inheritance**—the new class absorbs the characteristics of an existing class, possibly customizing them and adding unique characteristics of its own. In our car analogy, an object of class "convertible" certainly *is an* object of the more *general* class "automobile," but more *specifically*, the roof can be raised or lowered.

Object-Oriented Analysis and Design (OOAD)

Soon you'll be writing programs in C#. Perhaps, like many programmers, you'll simply turn on your computer and start typing. This approach may work for small programs (like the ones we present in the early chapters of this book), but what if you were asked to create a software system to control thousands of automated teller machines for a major bank? Or suppose you were assigned to work on a team of thousands of software developers building the next U.S. air traffic control system? For projects so large and complex, you should not simply sit down and start writing programs.

To create the best solutions, you should follow a detailed **analysis** process for determining your project's **requirements** (i.e., defining *what* the system is supposed to do) and developing a **design** that satisfies them (i.e., deciding *how* the system should do it). Ideally, you'd go through this process and carefully review the design (and have your design reviewed by other software professionals) before writing any code. If this process involves analyzing and designing your system from an object-oriented point of view, it's called an **object-oriented analysis and design (OOAD) process**. Languages like C# are object oriented. Programming in such a language, called **object-oriented programming (OOP)**, allows you to implement an object-oriented design as a working system.

The UML (Unified Modeling Language)
Though many different OOAD processes exist, a single graphical language for communicating the results of *any* OOAD process—known as the *Unified Modeling Language (UML)*—is now the most widely used graphical scheme for modeling object-oriented systems. We present our first simple UML diagrams in Chapters 4 and 5, then use them in our deeper treatment of object-oriented programming through Chapter 12. In our optional ATM Software Engineering Case Study in Chapters 32–33 we present a simple subset of the UML's features as we guide you through a simple object-oriented design experience.

1.3 C#

In 2000, Microsoft announced the **C#** programming language. C# has roots in the C, C++ and Java programming languages. It has similar capabilities to Java and is appropriate for the most demanding app-development tasks, especially for building today's large-scale enterprise apps, and web-based, mobile and "cloud"-based apps.

1.3.1 Object-Oriented Programming

C# is *object oriented*—we've discussed the basics of object technology and will present a rich treatment of object-oriented programming throughout the book. C# has access to the powerful **.NET Framework Class Library**—a vast collection of prebuilt classes that enable you to develop apps quickly (Fig. 1.1). We'll say more about .NET in Section 1.4.

Some key capabilities in the .NET Framework Class Library	
Database	Debugging
Building web apps	Multithreading
Graphics	File processing
Input/output	Security
Computer networking	Web communication
Permissions	Graphical user interface
Mobile	Data structures
String processing	

Fig. 1.1 | Some key capabilities in the .NET Framework Class Library.

1.3.2 Event-Driven Programming

C# is **event driven**. You'll write programs that respond to user-initiated **events** such as mouse clicks, keystrokes, timer expirations and—new in Visual C# 2012—*touches* and *finger swipes*—gestures that are widely used on smartphones and tablets.

1.3.3 Visual Programming

Microsoft's Visual C# is a *visual programming language*—in addition to writing program statements to build portions of your apps, you'll also use Visual Studio's graphical user interface (GUI) to conveniently drag and drop predefined objects like *buttons* and *textboxes* into place on your screen, and label and resize them. Visual Studio will write much of the GUI code for you.

1.3.4 An International Standard; Other C# Implementations

C# has been standardized internationally. This enables other implementations of the language besides Microsoft's Visual C#, such as Mono (www.mono-project.com) that runs on Linux systems, iOS (for Apple's iPhone, iPad and iPod touch), Google's Android and Windows. You can find the C# standard document at:

> www.ecma-international.org/publications/standards/Ecma-334.htm

1.3.5 Internet and Web Programming

Today's apps can be written with the aim of communicating among the world's computers. As you'll see, this is the focus of Microsoft's .NET strategy. In Chapters 21, 27 and 28, you'll build web-based apps with C# and Microsoft's **ASP.NET** technology.

1.3.6 Introducing async/await

In most programming today, each task in a program must finish executing before the next task can begin. This is called *synchronous programming* and is the style we use for most of this book. C# also allows *asynchronous programming* in which multiple tasks can be performed at the *same* time. Asynchronous programming can help you make your apps more responsive to user interactions, such as mouse clicks and keystrokes, among many other uses.

Asynchronous programming in previous versions of Visual C# was difficult and error prone. Visual C# 2012's new *async* and *await* capabilities simplify asynchronous programming, because the compiler hides much of the associated complexity from the developer. In Chapter 26, we'll provide a brief introduction to asynchronous programming with async and await.

1.4 Microsoft's .NET

In 2000, Microsoft announced its **.NET initiative** (www.microsoft.com/net), a broad vision for using the Internet and the web in the development, engineering, distribution and use of software. Rather than forcing you to use a single programming language, .NET permits you to create apps in *any* .NET-compatible language (such as C#, Visual Basic, Visual C++ and many others). Part of the initiative includes Microsoft's ASP.NET technology.

1.4.1 .NET Framework

The .NET Framework executes apps and contains the .NET Framework **Class Library**, which provides many capabilities that you'll use to build substantial C# apps quickly and easily. The .NET Framework Class Library has *thousands* of valuable *prebuilt* classes that have been tested and tuned to maximize performance. You'll learn how to create your own classes, but you should *re-use* the .NET Framework classes whenever possible to speed up the software development process, while enhancing the quality and performance of the software you develop.

1.4.2 Common Language Runtime

The **Common Language Runtime (CLR)**, another key part of the .NET Framework, executes .NET programs and provides functionality to make them easier to develop and debug. The CLR is a **virtual machine (VM)**—software that manages the execution of programs and hides from them the underlying operating system and hardware. The source code for programs that are executed and managed by the CLR is called *managed code*. The CLR provides various services to managed code, such as integrating software components written in different .NET languages, error handling between such components, enhanced security, automatic memory management and more. Unmanaged-code programs do not have access to the CLR's services, which makes unmanaged code more difficult to write.[2] Managed code is compiled into machine-specific instructions in the following steps:

1. First, the code is compiled into **Microsoft Intermediate Language** (MSIL). Code converted into MSIL from other languages and sources can be woven together by the CLR—this allows programmers to work in their preferred .NET programming language. The MSIL for an app's components is placed into the app's *executable file*—the file that causes the computer to perform the app's tasks.

2. When the app executes, another compiler (known as the **just-in-time compiler** or **JIT compiler**) in the CLR translates the MSIL in the executable file into machine-language code (for a particular platform).

3. The machine-language code executes on that platform.

1.4.3 Platform Independence

If the .NET Framework exists and is installed for a platform, that platform can run *any* .NET program. The ability of a program to run without modification across multiple platforms is known as **platform independence**. Code written once can be used on another type of computer without modification, saving time and money. In addition, software can target a wider audience. Previously, companies had to decide whether converting their programs to different platforms—a process called **porting**—was worth the cost. With .NET, porting programs is no longer an issue, at least once .NET itself has been made available on the platforms.

1.4.4 Language Interoperability

The .NET Framework provides a high level of **language interoperability**. Because software components written in different .NET languages (such as C# and Visual Basic) are all compiled into MSIL, the components can be combined to create a single unified program. Thus, MSIL allows the .NET Framework to be **language independent**.

---

2. msdn.microsoft.com/en-us/library/8bs2ecf4.aspx.

The .NET Framework Class Library can be used by any .NET language. .NET 4.5, which was released in 2012, includes several improvements and new features to make your apps faster and more responsive. It also features **.NET for Windows Store Apps**—a subset of .NET that's used to create Windows 8 UI (user interface) style apps.

1.5 Microsoft's Windows® Operating System

Microsoft's Windows is the most widely used desktop operating system worldwide. **Operating systems** are software systems that make using computers more convenient for users, developers and system administrators. They provide *services* that allow each app to execute safely, efficiently and *concurrently* (i.e., in parallel) with other apps. Other popular desktop operating systems include Linux and Mac OS X. Popular *mobile operating systems* used in smartphones and tablets include Microsoft's Windows Phone, Google's Android, Apple's iOS (for iPhone, iPad and iPod Touch devices) and BlackBerry OS. Figure 1.2 presents the evolution of the Windows operating system.

Version	Description
Windows in the 1990s	In the mid-1980s, Microsoft developed the **Windows operating system** based on a graphical user interface with buttons, textboxes, menus and other graphical elements. The various versions released throughout the 1990s were intended for personal computing. Microsoft entered the corporate operating systems market with the 1993 release of *Windows NT.*
Windows XP and Windows Vista	*Windows XP* was released in 2001 and combined Microsoft's corporate and consumer operating system lines. It remains popular today—according to a 2012 Netmarketshare study, it's used on more than 40% of Windows computers (netmarketshare.com/operating-system-market-share.aspx?qprid=10&qpcustomd=0). *Windows Vista*, released in 2007, offered the attractive new Aero user interface, many powerful enhancements and new apps and enhanced security. But Vista never caught on—today, it has "only" six percent of the total desktop operating systems market share (that's still a pretty significant number; netmarketshare.com/operating-system-market-share.aspx?qprid=10&qpcustomd=0).
Windows 7	*Windows 7*, now the most widely used version of Windows, includes enhancements to the Aero user interface, faster startup times, further refinement of Vista's security features, touch-screen with multi-touch support, and more. Windows 7 had a 44% market share, and overall, Windows (including Windows 7, Windows XP and Windows Vista) had over 90% of the desktop operating system market share worldwide (netmarketshare.com/operating-system-market-share.aspx?qprid=10&qpcustomd=0). The core chapters of this book use Windows 7, Visual Studio 2012 and Visual C# 2012.

Fig. 1.2 | The evolution of the Windows operating system. (Part 1 of 2.)

Version	Description
Windows 8 for Desktops and Tablets	**Windows 8**, released in 2012 provides a similar **platform** (the underlying system on which apps run) and *user experience* across a wide range of devices including personal computers, smartphones, tablets *and* the Xbox Live online game service. The new look-and-feel features a Start screen with *tiles* that represent each app, similar to that of *Windows Phone*—Microsoft's operating system for smartphones. Windows 8 features *multi-touch* support for *touch-pads* and *touchscreen* devices, enhanced security features and more.
Windows 8 UI (User Interface)	Visual C# 2012 supports the new Windows 8 UI (previously called "Metro") which has a clean look-and-feel with minimal distractions to the user. Windows 8 apps feature a *chromeless window*—there's no longer a border around the window with the typical interface elements such as title bars and menus. These elements are *hidden*, allowing apps to fill the *entire* screen, which is particularly helpful on smaller screens such as tablets and smartphones. The interface elements are displayed in the *app bar* when the user *swipes* the top or bottom of the screen by holding down the mouse button, moving the mouse in the swipe direction and releasing the mouse button; this can be done with a *finger swipe* on a touchscreen device. We discuss Windows 8 and the Windows 8 UI in Chapter 23 and Windows Phone 8 in Chapter 25.

Fig. 1.2 | The evolution of the Windows operating system. (Part 2 of 2.)

Windows Store
You can sell Windows 8 UI desktop and tablet apps or offer them for free in the Windows Store. The fee to become a registered Windows Store developer is $49 for individuals and $99 for companies. For Windows 8 UI apps, Microsoft retains 30% of the purchase price and distributes 70% to you, up to $25,000. If revenues for your app exceed that amount, Microsoft will retain 20% of the purchase price and distribute 80% to you.

The Windows Store offers several business models for monetizing your app. You can charge the full price for your app before download, with prices starting at $1.49. You can also offer a time-limited trial or feature-limited trial that allows users to try the app before purchasing the full version, sell virtual goods (such as additional app features) using in-app purchases and more. To learn more about the Windows Store and monetizing your apps, visit msdn.microsoft.com/en-us/library/windows/apps/br229519.aspx.

1.6 Windows Phone 8 for Smartphones

Windows Phone 8 is a pared down version of Windows 8 designed for *smartphones*. These are *resource-constrained devices*—they have less memory and processor power than desktop computers, and limited battery life. Windows Phone 8 has the *same* core operating systems services as Windows 8, including a common file system, security, networking, media and Internet Explorer 10 (IE10) web browser technology. However, Windows Phone 8 has *only* the features necessary for smartphones, allowing them to run efficiently, minimizing the burden on the device's resources.

New to this edition of the book, you'll use Visual C# 2012 to develop your own Windows Phone 8 apps. Just as the Objective-C programming language has increased in popularity due to iOS app development for iPhone, iPad and iPod touch, Visual C# 2012 is sure to become even more popular as the demand for Windows Phones increases. International Data Corporation (IDC) predicts that Windows Phone will have over 19% of the smartphone market share by 2016, second only to Android and ahead of Apple's iPhone.[3] You'll learn how to develop Windows Phone apps in Chapter 25.

1.6.1 Selling Your Apps in the Windows Phone Marketplace

You can sell your own Windows Phone apps in the **Windows Phone Marketplace** (www.windowsphone.com/marketplace), similar to other app commerce platforms such as Apple's App Store, Google Play (formerly Android Market), Facebook's App Center and the Windows Store. You can also earn money by making your apps free for download and selling *virtual goods* (e.g., additional content, game levels, e-gifts and add-on features) using *in-app purchase*.

1.6.2 Free vs. Paid Apps

A recent study by Gartner found that 89% of all mobile apps are free, and that number is likely to increase to 93% by 2016, at which point in-app purchases will account for over 40% of mobile app revenues.[4] Paid Windows Phone 8 apps range in price from $1.49 (which is higher than the $0.99 starting price for apps in Google Play and Apple's App Store) to $999.99. The average price for mobile apps is approximately $1.50 to $3, depending on the platform. For Windows Phone apps, Microsoft retains 30% of the purchase price and distributes 70% to you. At the time of this writing, there were over 100,000 apps in the Windows Phone Marketplace.[5]

1.6.3 Testing Your Windows Phone Apps

You can test your phone apps on the Windows Phone Emulator that Microsoft provides with the Windows Phone 8 SDK (software development kit). To test your apps on a Windows phone and to sell your apps or distribute your free apps through the Windows Phone Marketplace, you'll need to join the *Windows Phone Dev Center*. There's an annual fee of $99; the program is *free* to MSDN subscribers. The website includes development tools, sample code, tips for selling your apps, design guidelines and more. To join the Windows Phone Dev Center and submit apps, visit dev.windowsphone.com/en-us/downloadsdk.

---

3.   www.idc.com/getdoc.jsp?containerId=prUS23523812.
4.   techcrunch.com/2012/09/11/free-apps/.
5.   windowsteamblog.com/windows_phone/b/windowsphone/archive/2012/06/20/announcing-windows-phone-8.aspx.

1.7 Windows Azure™ and Cloud Computing

Cloud computing allows you to use software and data stored in the "cloud"—i.e., accessed on remote computers (or servers) via the Internet and available on demand—rather than having it stored on your desktop, notebook computer or mobile device. Cloud computing gives you the flexibility to increase or decrease computing resources to meet your resource needs at any given time, making it more cost effective than purchasing expensive hardware to ensure that you have enough storage and processing power at their occasional peak levels. Using cloud computing services also saves money by shifting the burden of *managing* these apps to the service provider. New to this edition of the book, in Chapter 29 you'll use Microsoft's **Windows Azure**—a cloud computing platform that allows you to develop, manage and distribute your apps in the cloud. With Windows Azure, your apps can store their data in the cloud so that the data is available at all times from any of your desktop computer and mobile devices. You can sign up for a free 90-day trial of Windows Azure at `www.windowsazure.com/en-us/pricing/free-trial/`.

1.8 Visual Studio Express 2012 Integrated Development Environment

C# programs are created using Microsoft's Visual Studio—a collection of software tools called an **Integrated Development Environment (IDE)**. The **Visual Studio 2012 Express** IDE enables you to *write, run, test* and *debug* C# programs quickly and conveniently. It also supports Microsoft's Visual Basic, Visual C++ and F# programming languages. Most of this book's examples were built using *Visual Studio Express 2012 for Windows Desktop*, which runs on both Windows 7 and Windows 8. The Windows 8 UI and Windows 8 Graphics and Multimedia chapters require *Visual Studio Express 2012 for Windows 8*.

1.9 Painter Test-Drive in Visual Studio Express 2012 for Windows Desktop

[*Note:* This test-drive can be performed on a computer running either Windows 7 or Windows 8. The steps shown here are for Windows 7. We discuss running an app on Windows 8 in Section 1.10.]

You'll now use *Visual Studio Express 2012 for Windows Desktop* to "test-drive" an existing app that enables you to draw on the screen using the mouse. The **Painter** app—which you'll build in a later chapter—allows you to choose among several brush sizes and colors. The elements and functionality you see in this app are typical of what you'll learn to program in this text. The following steps walk you through test-driving the app.

Step 1: Checking Your Setup
Confirm that you've set up your computer and the software properly by reading the book's Before You Begin section that follows the Preface.

Step 2: Locating the Painter App's Directory
Open a Windows Explorer window and navigate to C:\examples\ch01\win7testdrive. (We assume you placed the examples in the C:\examples folder.) Double click the Painter folder to view its contents (Fig. 1.3), then double click the Painter.sln file to open the app's solution in Visual Studio. An app's *solution* contains all of the app's *code files*, *supporting files* (such as *images, videos, data files*, etc.) and configuration information. We'll discuss the contents of a solution in more detail in the next chapter.

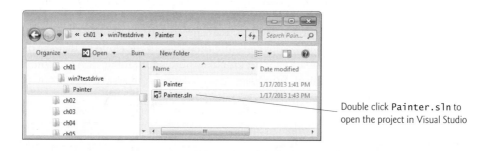

Double click Painter.sln to open the project in Visual Studio

Fig. 1.3 | Contents of C:\examples\ch01\win7testdrive\Painter.

Depending on your system configuration, Windows Explorer might not display file name extensions. To display them (like .sln in Fig. 1.3):

1. In Windows Explorer, type *Alt + t* to display the **Tools** menu, then select **Folder options....**

2. Select the **View** tab in the **Folder Options** dialog.

3. Locate the checkbox **Hide extensions for known file types** and ensure that it's unchecked.

4. Click **OK** to dismiss the **Folder Options** dialog.

Step 3: Running the Painter App
To see the running **Painter** app, click the **Start** (▶) button (Fig. 1.4) or press the *F5* key. Figure 1.5 shows the executing app.

Figure 1.5 labels several of the app's graphical elements—called **controls**. These include GroupBoxes, RadioButtons, Buttons and a Panel. These controls and many others are discussed throughout the text. The app allows you to draw with a **Black, Red, Blue** or **Green** brush of **Small, Medium** or **Large** size. As you drag the mouse on the white Panel, the app draws circles of the specified color and size at the mouse pointer's current position. The slower you drag the mouse, the closer the circles will be. Thus, dragging slowly draws a continuous line (as in Fig. 1.6) and dragging quickly draws individual circles with space in between. You can also **Undo** your previous operation or **Clear** the drawing to start from scratch by pressing the Buttons below the RadioButtons in the GUI. By using existing *controls*—which are *objects*—you can create powerful apps much faster than if you had to write all the code yourself. This is a key benefit of *software reuse.*

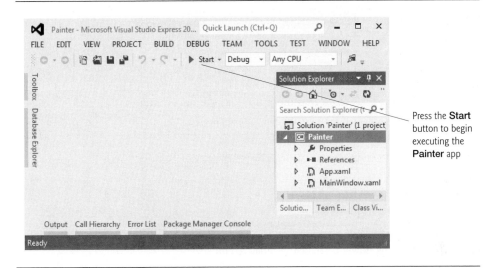

Press the **Start** button to begin executing the **Painter** app

Fig. 1.4 | Running the **Painter** app.

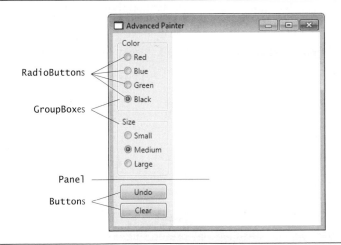

Fig. 1.5 | **Painter** app running in Windows 7.

The brush's properties, selected in the RadioButtons labeled **Black** and **Medium**, are *default settings*—the initial settings you see when you first run the app. Programmers include default settings to provide *reasonable* choices that the app will use if the user *does not* change the settings. Default settings also provide visual cues for users to choose their own settings. Now you'll choose your own settings as a user of this app.

Step 4: Changing the Brush Color
Click the RadioButton labeled **Red** to change the brush color, then click the RadioButton labeled **Small** to change the brush size. Position the mouse over the white Panel, then drag the mouse to draw with the brush. Draw flower petals, as shown in Fig. 1.6.

Fig. 1.6 | Drawing flower petals with a small red brush.

Step 5: Changing the Brush Color and Size
Click the **Green** RadioButton to change the brush color. Then, click the **Large** RadioButton to change the brush size. Draw grass and a flower stem, as shown in Fig. 1.7.

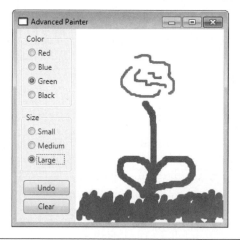

Fig. 1.7 | Drawing the flower stem and grass with a large green brush.

Step 6: Finishing the Drawing
Click the **Blue** and **Medium** RadioButtons. Draw raindrops, as shown in Fig. 1.8, to complete the drawing.

Step 7: Stopping the App
When you run an app from Visual Studio, you can terminate it by clicking the stop button (⬛) on the Visual Studio toolbar or by clicking the close box (❌) on the running app's window.

Fig. 1.8 | Drawing rain drops with a medium blue brush.

Now that you've completed the test-drive, you're ready to begin developing C# apps. In Chapter 2, Dive Into® Visual Studio, you'll use Visual Studio to create your first C# program using *visual programming* techniques. As you'll see, Visual Studio will generate for you the code that builds the app's GUI. In Chapter 3, Introduction to C# Apps, you'll begin writing C# programs containing conventional program code that you write.

1.10 Painter Test-Drive in Visual Studio Express 2012 for Windows 8

[*Note:* This test-drive can be performed *only* on a computer running Windows 8.] You'll now use Visual Studio to "test-drive" an existing Windows 8 UI app that enables you to draw on the screen using the mouse. The **Painter** app—which you'll build in a later chapter—allows you to choose among several brush sizes and colors. The elements and functionality you see in this app are typical of what you'll learn to program in this text. The following steps walk you through test-driving the app.

Step 1: Checking Your Setup
Confirm that you've set up your computer and the software properly by reading the book's Before You Begin section that follows the Preface.

Step 2: Switching to the Windows 8 Desktop
Click the **Desktop** tile in the Windows 8 **Start** screen to switch to the desktop.

Step 3: Locating the Painter App's Directory
Click the **File Explorer** ( ) icon in the task bar to open a **File Explorer** window, then locate the C:\examples\ch01\win8testdrive folder. (We assume you placed the examples in the C:\examples folder.) Double click the Painter folder to view its contents (Fig. 1.9), then double click the Painter.sln file to open the app's solution in Visual Studio. An app's *solution* contains all of the app's *code files*, *supporting files* (such as *images*, *videos*, *data*

files, etc.) and configuration information. We'll discuss the contents of a solution in more detail in the next chapter. [*Note:* Depending on your system configuration, the **File Explorer** window might not display file name extensions. To display file name extensions (like .sln in Fig. 1.9), click the **View** tab in the **File Explorer** window, then ensure that **File name extensions** is selected.]

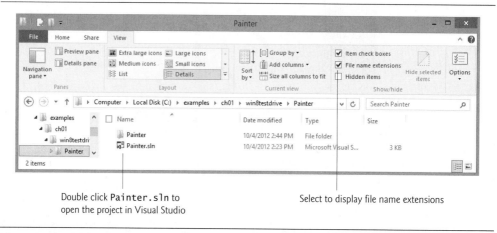

Double click `Painter.sln` to open the project in Visual Studio

Select to display file name extensions

Fig. 1.9 | Contents of C:\examples\ch01\win8testdrive\Painter.

Step 4: Running the Painter App

Windows 8 UI apps normally occupy the *full* screen, though you can also *snap* apps to a 320-pixel-wide area at the left or right of the screen to see two apps side-by-side. To see the running **Painter** app, you can install it on the Windows 8 **Start** screen and execute it by selecting **Local Machine** (Fig. 1.10) then clicking the **Start Debugging** (▶) button or pressing the *F5* key. Once you install the app on the **Start** screen, you can also run it by clicking its **Start** screen tile. Figure 1.11 shows the executing app. Later chapters will discuss the **Simulator** and **Remote Machine** options shown in Fig. 1.10 for running apps.

Fig. 1.10 | Selecting the **Local Machine** for running the **Painter** app.

Figure 1.11 labels several of the app's graphical elements—called **controls**. These include `TextBlocks`, `RadioButtons`, `Buttons` and a `Canvas`. These controls and many others are discussed throughout the text. The app allows you to draw with a **Black**, **Red**,

Fig. 1.11 | **Painter** app running in Windows 8.

Blue or **Green** brush of **Small**, **Medium** or **Large** size. As you drag the mouse on the white Canvas (an object used for drawing), the app draws circles of the specified color and size at the mouse pointer's current position. The slower you drag the mouse, the closer the circles will be. Thus, dragging slowly draws a continuous line (as in Fig. 1.12) and dragging quickly draws individual circles with space in between (as you can see with some of the rain drops in Fig. 1.14). You can also **Undo** your previous operation or **Clear** the drawing to start from scratch by pressing the Buttons below the RadioButtons in the GUI. By using existing *controls*—which are *objects*—you can create powerful apps much faster than if you had to write all the code yourself. This is a key benefit of *software reuse*.

The brush's properties, selected in the RadioButtons labeled **Black** and **Small**, are *default settings*—the initial settings you see when you first run the app. Programmers include default settings to provide *reasonable* choices that the app will use if the user *does not* change the settings. Default settings also provide visual cues for users to choose their own settings. Now you'll choose your own settings as a user of this app.

Step 5: Changing the Brush Color
Click the RadioButton labeled **Red** to change the brush color. Position the mouse over the white Canvas, then drag the mouse to draw with the brush. Draw flower petals, as shown in Fig. 1.12.

Step 6: Changing the Brush Color and Size
Click the RadioButton labeled **Green** to change the brush color again. Then, click the RadioButton labeled **Large** to change the brush size. Draw grass and a flower stem, as shown in Fig. 1.13.

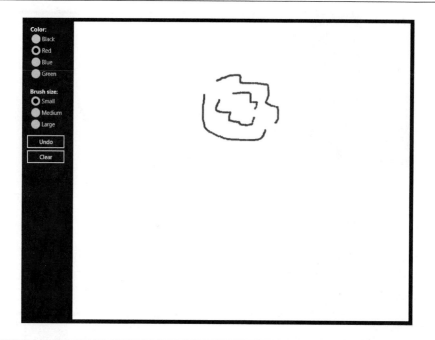

Fig. 1.12 | Drawing flower petals with a small red brush.

Fig. 1.13 | Drawing the flower stem and grass with a large green brush.

Step 7: Finishing the Drawing

Click the **Blue** and **Medium** RadioButtons. Draw raindrops, as shown in Fig. 1.14, to complete the drawing.

Fig. 1.14 | Drawing rain drops with a medium blue brush.

Step 8: Stopping the App

When you run an app from Visual Studio, you can terminate it by clicking the stop button (■) on the Visual Studio toolbar. Typically, when you're done using a Windows 8 UI app like **Painter**, you don't terminate the app. Instead you simply run another app. Windows 8 *suspends* the execution of the previous app you were running, but keeps it in memory in case you decide to *return* to the app. Windows may decide to terminate a suspended app to free up memory for executing other apps. To explicitly shut down a Windows 8 UI app, simply drag from the top of the screen to the bottom or press *Alt + F4*.

Now that you've completed the test-drive, you're ready to begin developing C# apps. In Chapter 2, Dive Into® Visual Studio, you'll use Visual Studio to create your first C# program using *visual programming* techniques. As you'll see, Visual Studio will generate for you the code that builds the app's GUI. In Chapter 3, Introduction to C# Apps, you'll begin writing C# programs containing conventional program code that you write.

2

Dive Into® Visual Studio Express 2012 for Windows Desktop

Objectives

In this chapter you'll:

- Learn the basics of the Visual Studio Express 2012 for Windows Desktop Integrated Development Environment (IDE) for writing, running and debugging your apps.

- Use Visual Studio's help features.

- Learn key commands contained in the IDE's menus and toolbars.

- Understand the purpose of the various kinds of windows in the Visual Studio Express 2012 for Windows Desktop IDE.

- Understand what visual app development is and how it simplifies and speeds app development.

- Use visual app development to create, compile and execute a simple Visual C# app that displays text and an image.

2.1 Introduction

Visual Studio 2012 is Microsoft's Integrated Development Environment (IDE) for creating, running and debugging apps (also called applications) written in various .NET programming languages. This chapter provides an overview of the Visual Studio 2012 IDE and shows how to create a simple Visual C# app by dragging and dropping predefined building blocks into place—a technique known as **visual app development.**

2.2 Overview of the Visual Studio Express 2012 IDE

There are several versions of Visual Studio available. Most of this book's examples are based on the **Visual Studio Express 2012 for Windows Desktop**. See the Before You Begin section that follows the Preface for information on installing the software. Our screen captures and discussions focus on Visual Studio Express 2012 for Windows Desktop. The examples will work on full versions of Visual Studio as well—though some options, menus and instructions might differ. From this point forward, we'll refer to the Visual Studio Express 2012 for Windows Desktop IDE simply as "Visual Studio" or "the IDE." We assume that you're familiar with Windows.

Introduction to Microsoft Visual Studio Express 2012 for Windows Desktop
We use the > character to indicate the selection of a *menu item* from a *menu*. For example, we use the notation **FILE > Open File...** to indicate that you should select the **Open File...** menu item from the **FILE** menu.

   To start the IDE, select **Start > All Programs > Microsoft Visual Studio 2012 Express > VS Express for Desktop** (on Windows 8, click the **VS for Desktop** tile on the **Start** screen. Once the Express Edition begins execution, the **Start Page** displays (Fig. 2.1). Depending on your version of Visual Studio, your **Start Page** may look different. The **Start Page** contains a list of links to Visual Studio resources and web-based resources. At any time, you can return to the **Start Page** by selecting **VIEW > Start Page**. [*Note:* Visual Studio supports both a *dark theme* (with dark window backgrounds and light text) and a *light theme* (with light window backgrounds and dark text). We use the light theme throughout this book. The Before You Begin section after the Preface explains how to set this option.]

Links on the Start Page
The **Start Page** links are organized into two columns. The left column's **Start** section contains options that enable you to start building new apps or to continue working on existing

ones. The **Recent** section contains links to projects you've recently created or modified. You can also create new projects or open existing ones by clicking the links in the **Start** section.

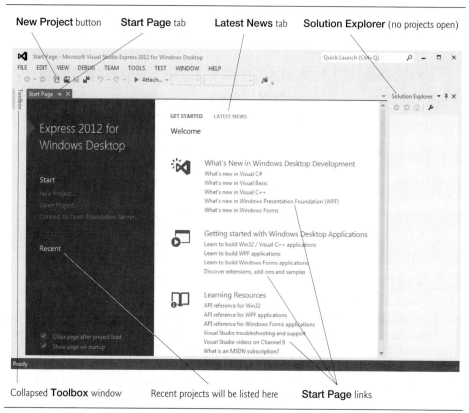

Fig. 2.1 | **Start Page** in Visual Studio Express 2012 for Windows Desktop.

The right column contains two tabs—**GET STARTED** (selected by default) and **LATEST NEWS**. The links in the **GET STARTED** tab provide information about the programming languages supported by Visual Studio and various learning resources. An Internet connection is required for the IDE to access most of this information.

The **LATEST NEWS** tab includes an **Enable RSS Feed** button. Once you click this button, the IDE will display links to the latest Visual Studio developments (such as updates and bug fixes) and to information on advanced app-development topics. To access more extensive information on Visual Studio, you can browse the **MSDN** (**Microsoft Developer Network**) Library at

```
msdn.microsoft.com/en-us/library/default.aspx
```

The MSDN site contains articles, downloads and tutorials on technologies of interest to Visual Studio developers. You can also browse the web from the IDE by selecting **VIEW > Other Windows > Web Browser**. To request a web page, type its URL into the location bar (Fig. 2.2) and press the *Enter* key—your computer, of course, must be connected to the Internet. The web page that you wish to view appears as another tab in the IDE (Fig. 2.2).

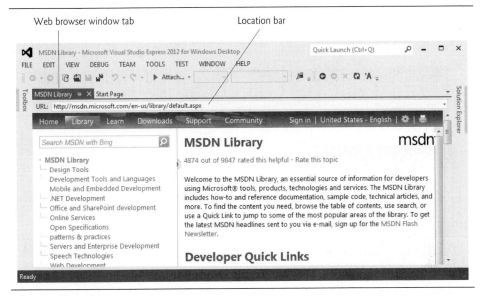

Fig. 2.2 | **MSDN Library** web page in Visual Studio.

Creating a New Project

To begin app development in Visual C#, you must create a new project or open an existing one. You select **FILE > New Project...** to create a new project or **FILE > Open Project...** to open an existing one. From the **Start Page**'s **Start** section, you can also click the links **New Project...** or **Open Project....** A **project** is a group of related files, such as the Visual C# code and any images that might make up an app. Visual Studio organizes apps into projects and **solutions**, which contain one or more projects. Multiple-project solutions are used to create large-scale apps. Most apps we create in this book consist of a solution containing a single project.

New Project *Dialog and Project Templates*

When you select **FILE > New Project...** or click the **New Project...** link on the **Start Page**, the **New Project** dialog (Fig. 2.3) displays. **Dialogs** are windows that facilitate user–computer communication.

Visual Studio provides several **templates** (Fig. 2.3)—the *project types* users can create in Visual C# and other languages. The templates include Windows Forms apps, WPF apps and others—full versions of Visual Studio provide many additional templates. In this chapter, you'll build a **Windows Forms Application**. A **Windows Forms app** is an app that executes within a Windows operating system (such as Windows 7 or Windows 8) and typically has a **graphical user interface** (**GUI**)—users interact with this *visual* part of the app. Windows apps include Microsoft software products like Microsoft Word, Internet Explorer and Visual Studio, software products created by other vendors, and customized software that you and other app developers create. You'll create many Windows apps in this text.

By default, Visual Studio assigns the name **WindowsFormsApplication1** to a new **Windows Forms Application** project and solution (Fig. 2.3). Select **Windows Forms Application**, then click **OK** to display the IDE in **Design** view (Fig. 2.4), which contains the features that enable you to create an app's GUI.

Visual C# **Windows Forms**
Application (selected)

Default project name
(provided by Visual Studio)

Description of selected project
(provided by Visual Studio)

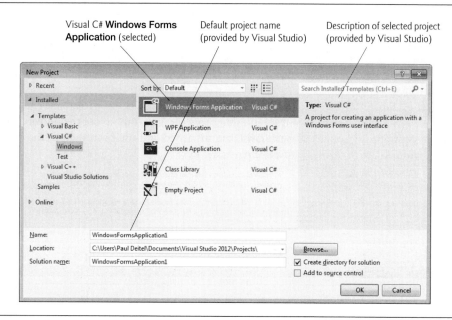

Fig. 2.3 | New Project dialog.

Menu in the
menu bar

Active tab
(highlighted)

Form

Solution
Explorer window

Properties
window

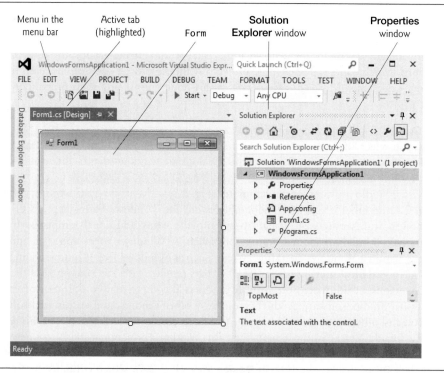

Fig. 2.4 | Design view of the IDE.

Forms and Controls

The rectangle in the **Design** area titled **Form1** (called a **Form**) represents the main window of the Windows Forms app that you're creating. Visual C# apps can have multiple Forms (windows)—however, most apps you'll create in this text will use only one Form. You'll learn how to customize the Form by adding GUI **controls**—in this example, you'll add a Label and a PictureBox (as you'll see in Fig. 2.20). A **Label** typically contains descriptive text (for example, "Welcome to Visual C#!"), and a **PictureBox** displays an image. Visual Studio has many preexisting controls and other components you can use to build and customize your apps. Many of these controls are discussed and used throughout the book. Other controls are available from third parties.

In this chapter, you'll work with preexisting controls from the .NET Framework Class Library. As you place controls on the Form, you'll be able to modify their properties (discussed in Section 2.4). For example, Fig. 2.5 shows where the Form's title can be modified and Fig. 2.6 shows a dialog in which a control's font properties can be modified.

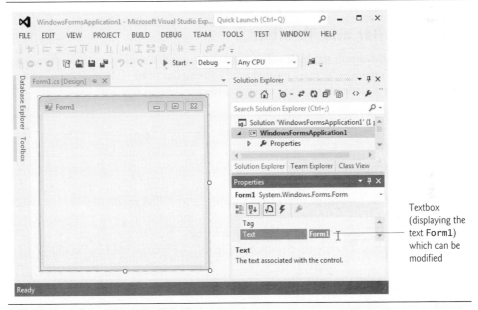

Fig. 2.5 | Textbox control for modifying a property in the Visual Studio IDE.

Collectively, the Form and controls make up the app's GUI. Users enter data into the app by typing at the keyboard, by clicking the mouse buttons and in a variety of other ways. Apps use the GUI to display instructions and other information for users to view. For example, the **New Project** dialog in Fig. 2.3 presents a GUI where the user clicks the mouse button to select a template type, then inputs a project name from the keyboard (the figure is still showing the default project name **WindowsFormsApplication1** supplied by Visual Studio).

Each open document's name is listed on a tab. To view a document when multiple documents are open, click its tab. The **active tab** (the tab of the currently displayed document) is highlighted (for example, **Form1.cs [Design]** in Fig. 2.4).

Fig. 2.6 | Dialog for modifying a control's font properties.

2.3 Menu Bar and Toolbar

Commands for managing the IDE and for developing, maintaining and executing apps are contained in menus, which are located on the **menu bar** of the IDE (Fig. 2.7). The set of menus displayed depends on what you're currently doing in the IDE.

| FILE | EDIT | VIEW | PROJECT | BUILD | DEBUG | TEAM | FORMAT | TOOLS | TEST | WINDOW | HELP |

Fig. 2.7 | Visual Studio menu bar.

Menus contain groups of related commands (also called menu items) that, when selected, cause the IDE to perform specific actions—for example, open a window, save a file, print a file and execute an app. For example, new projects are created by selecting **FILE > New Project...**. The menus depicted in Fig. 2.7 are summarized in Fig. 2.8.

Menu	Description
FILE	Contains commands for opening, closing, adding and saving projects, as well as printing project data and exiting Visual Studio.
EDIT	Contains commands for editing apps, such as cut, copy, paste, undo, redo, delete, find and select.
VIEW	Contains commands for displaying IDE windows (for example, **Solution Explorer**, **Toolbox**, **Properties** window) and for adding toolbars to the IDE.
PROJECT	Contains commands for managing projects and their files.
BUILD	Contains options for turning your app into an executable program.

Fig. 2.8 | Summary of Visual Studio menus that are displayed when a Form is in **Design** view. (Part 1 of 2.)

Menu	Description
DEBUG	Contains commands for compiling, debugging (that is, identifying and correcting problems in apps) and running apps.
TEAM	Allows you to connect to a Team Foundation Server—used by development teams that typically have multiple people working on the same app.
FORMAT	Contains commands for arranging and modifying a Form's controls. The **Format** menu appears *only* when a GUI component is selected in **Design** view.
TOOLS	Contains commands for accessing additional IDE tools and options for customizing the IDE.
TEST	Contains options for performing various types of automated testing on your app.
WINDOW	Contains commands for hiding, opening, closing and displaying IDE windows.
HELP	Contains commands for accessing the IDE's help features.

Fig. 2.8 | Summary of Visual Studio menus that are displayed when a Form is in **Design** view. (Part 2 of 2.)

You can access many common menu commands from the **toolbar** (Fig. 2.9), which contains **icons** that graphically represent commands. By default, the standard toolbar is displayed when you run Visual Studio for the first time—it contains icons for the most commonly used commands, such as opening a file, adding an item to a project, saving files and running apps (Fig. 2.9). The icons that appear on the standard toolbar may vary, depending on the version of Visual Studio you're using. Some commands are initially disabled (grayed out or unavailable to use). These commands are enabled by Visual Studio only when they're necessary. For example, Visual Studio enables the command for *saving* a file once you begin *editing* a file.

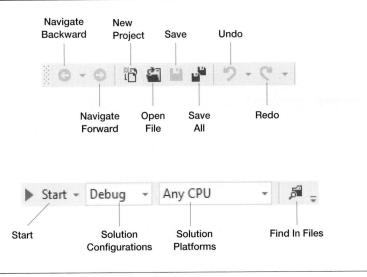

Fig. 2.9 | Standard Visual Studio toolbar.

You can customize which toolbars are displayed by selecting **VIEW > Toolbars** then selecting a toolbar from the list in Fig. 2.10. Each toolbar you select is displayed with the other toolbars at the top of the Visual Studio window. You move a toolbar by dragging its handle (⠿) at the left side of the toolbar. To execute a command via the toolbar, click its icon.

Fig. 2.10 | List of toolbars that can be added to the top of the IDE.

It can be difficult to remember what each toolbar icon represents. *Hovering* the mouse pointer over an icon highlights it and, after a brief pause, displays a description of the icon called a tool tip (Fig. 2.11). **Tool tips** help you become familiar with the IDE's features and serve as useful reminders for each toolbar icon's functionality.

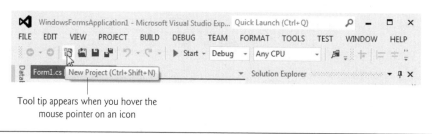

Tool tip appears when you hover the
mouse pointer on an icon

Fig. 2.11 | Tool tip demonstration.

2.4 Navigating the Visual Studio IDE

The IDE provides windows for accessing project files and customizing controls. This section introduces several windows that you'll use frequently when developing Visual C# apps. Each of the IDE's windows can be accessed by selecting its name in the **VIEW** menu.

Auto-Hide
Visual Studio provides a space-saving feature called **auto-hide**. When auto-hide is enabled for a window, a tab containing the window's name appears along either the left, right or bottom edge of the IDE window (Fig. 2.12). Clicking the name of an auto-hidden window displays that window (Fig. 2.13). Clicking the name again (or clicking outside) hides the window. To "pin down" a window (that is, to disable auto-hide and keep the window open), click the pin icon. When auto-hide is enabled, the pin icon is horizontal (icon, Fig. 2.13)—when a window is "pinned down," the pin icon is vertical (icon, Fig. 2.14).

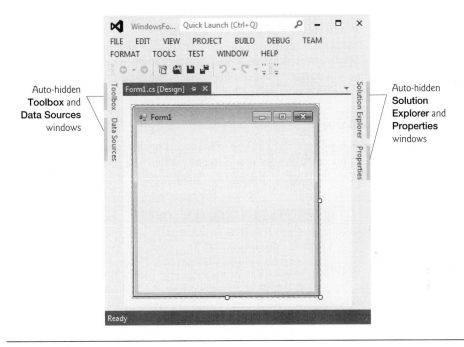

Fig. 2.12 | Auto-hide feature demonstration.

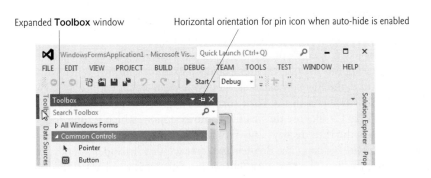

Fig. 2.13 | Displaying the hidden **Toolbox** window when auto-hide is enabled.

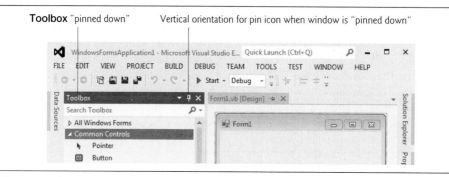

Fig. 2.14 | Disabling auto-hide—"pinning down" a window.

The next few sections cover three of Visual Studio's main windows—the **Solution Explorer**, the **Properties** window and the **Toolbox**. These windows display project information and include tools that help you build your apps.

2.4.1 Solution Explorer

The **Solution Explorer** window (Fig. 2.15) provides access to all of a solution's files. If it's not shown in the IDE, select **VIEW > Solution Explorer**. When you open a new or existing solution, the **Solution Explorer** displays the solution's contents.

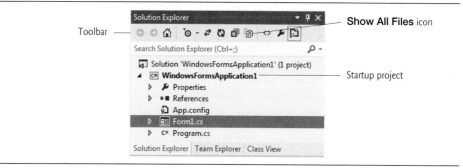

Fig. 2.15 | **Solution Explorer** window with an open project.

The solution's **startup project** is the one that runs when you select **DEBUG > Start Debugging** (or press the *F5* key). For a single-project solution like the examples in this book, the startup project is the only project (in this case, **WindowsFormsApplication1**). The startup project's name appears in bold text in the **Solution Explorer** window. When you create an app for the first time, the **Solution Explorer** window appears as shown in Fig. 2.15. The Visual C# file that corresponds to the Form shown in Fig. 2.4 is named Form1.cs (selected in Fig. 2.15). Visual C# files use the .cs file-name extension, which is short for "C#."

By default, the IDE displays only files that you may need to edit—other files that the IDE generates are hidden. The **Solution Explorer** window includes a toolbar that contains several icons. Clicking the **Show All Files icon** (Fig. 2.15) displays all the solution's files, including those generated by the IDE. Clicking the arrows to the left of an node *expands* or *collapses* that nodes. Try clicking the arrow to the left of **References** to display items grouped under that heading (Fig. 2.16). Click the arrow again to collapse the tree. Other Visual Studio windows also use this convention.

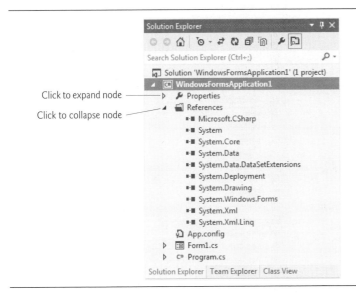

Fig. 2.16 | **Solution Explorer** with the **References** node expanded.

2.4.2 Toolbox

To display the **Toolbox** window, select **VIEW > Toolbox**. The **Toolbox** contains the controls used to customize Forms (Fig. 2.17). With visual app development, you can "drag and drop" controls onto the Form and the IDE will write the code that creates the controls for you. This is faster and simpler than writing this code yourself. Just as you do not need to know how to build an engine to drive a car, you do not need to know how to build controls to use them. *Reusing* preexisting controls saves time and money when you develop apps. You'll use the **Toolbox** when you create your first app later in the chapter.

The **Toolbox** groups the prebuilt controls into categories—**All Windows Forms**, **Common Controls**, **Containers**, **Menus & Toolbars**, **Data**, **Components**, **Printing**, **Dialogs**, **WPF Interoperability**, **Visual Basic PowerPacks** and **General** are listed in Fig. 2.17. Again, note the use of arrows, which can expand or collapse a group of controls. We discuss many of the **Toolbox**'s controls and their functionality throughout the book.

2.4.3 Properties Window

If the **Properties** window is not displayed below the **Solution Explorer**, select **VIEW > Properties Window** to display it. The **Properties window** contains the properties for the currently selected Form, control or file in the IDE. **Properties** specify information about the Form or control, such as its size, color and position. Each Form or control has its own set of properties—a property's description is displayed at the bottom of the **Properties** window whenever that property is selected.

Figure 2.18 shows Form1's **Properties** window. The left column lists the Form's properties—the right column displays the current value of each property. You can sort the

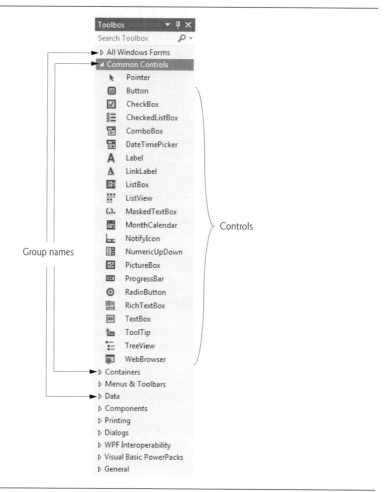

Fig. 2.17 │ **Toolbox** window displaying controls for the **Common Controls** group.

properties either *alphabetically* (by clicking the **Alphabetical icon**) or *categorically* (by clicking the **Categorized icon**). Depending on the size of the **Properties** window, some of the properties may be hidden from view on the screen. You can scroll through the list of properties by **dragging** the **scrollbox** up or down inside the **scrollbar**, or by clicking the arrows at the top and bottom of the scrollbar. We show how to set individual properties later in this chapter.

The **Properties** window is crucial to visual app development—it allows you to modify a control's properties visually, without writing code. You can see which properties are available for modification and, in many cases, can learn the range of acceptable values for a given property. The **Properties** window displays a brief description of the selected property, helping you understand its purpose. A property can be set quickly using this window, and no code needs to be written.

At the top of the **Properties** window is the **component selection drop-down list**, which allows you to select the Form or control whose properties you wish to display in the **Proper-**

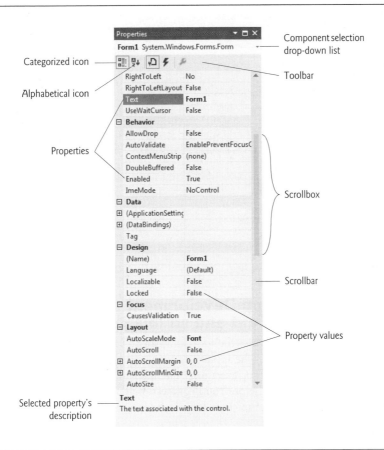

Fig. 2.18 | **Properties** window.

ties window. Using the component selection drop-down list is an alternative way to display a Form's or control's properties without clicking the actual Form or control in the GUI.

2.5 Using Help

Microsoft provides extensive help documentation via the **HELP** menu. Using **HELP** is an excellent way to get information quickly about Visual Studio, Visual C# and more.

Context-Sensitive Help

Visual Studio provides **context-sensitive help** pertaining to the "current content" (that is, the items around the location of the mouse cursor). To use context-sensitive help, click an item, then press the *F1* key. The help documentation is displayed in a web browser window. To return to the IDE, either close the browser window or select the IDE's icon in your Windows task bar. Figure 2.19 shows the help page for a Form's **Text** property. You can view this help by selecting the Form, clicking its **Text** property in the **Properties** window and pressing the *F1* key.

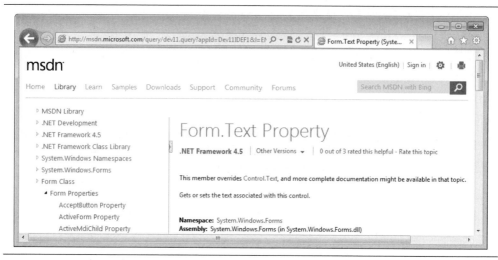

Fig. 2.19 | Using context-sensitive help.

2.6 Using Visual App Development to Create a Simple App that Displays Text and an Image

Next, we create an app that displays the text "Welcome to Visual C#!" and an image of the Deitel & Associates bug mascot. The app consists of a Form that uses a Label and a Picture-Box. Figure 2.20 shows the final app executing. The app and the bug image are available with this chapter's examples. See the Before You Begin section following the Preface for download instructions. We assume the examples are located at C:\examples on your computer.

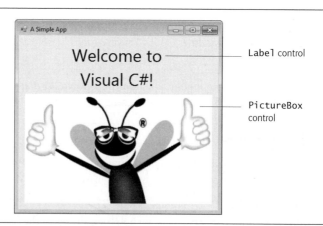

Fig. 2.20 | Simple app executing.

You won't write a single line of code. Instead, you'll use visual app development techniques. Visual Studio processes your actions (such as mouse clicking, dragging and dropping) to generate app code. Chapter 3 begins our discussion of writing app code. Throughout the book, you produce increasingly substantial and powerful apps that usually include a combination of code written by you and code generated by Visual Studio. The generated code can be difficult for novices to understand—but you'll rarely need to look at it.

Visual app development is useful for building GUI-intensive apps that require a significant amount of user interaction. To create, save, run and terminate this first app, perform the following steps:

1. *Closing the open project.* If the project you were working with earlier in this chapter is still open, close it by selecting **FILE > Close Solution**.

2. *Creating the new project.* To create a new Windows Forms app, select **FILE > New Project...** to display the **New Project** dialog (Fig. 2.21). Select **Windows Forms Application**. Name the project **ASimpleApp**, specify the **Location** where you want to save it (we used the default location) and click **OK**. As you saw earlier in this chapter, when you first create a new Windows Forms app, the IDE opens in **Design** view (that is, the app is being designed and is not executing).

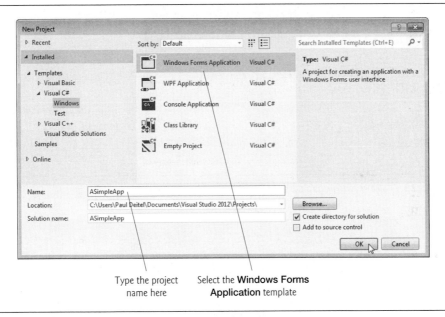

Type the project   Select the **Windows Forms**
name here   **Application** template

Fig. 2.21 | New Project dialog.

3. *Setting the text in the Form's title bar.* The text in the Form's title bar is determined by the Form's **Text property** (Fig. 2.22). If the **Properties** window is not open, select **VIEW > Properties Window**. Click anywhere in the Form to display the Form's properties in the **Properties** window. In the textbox to the right of the Text property, type "A Simple App", as in Fig. 2.22. Press the *Enter* key—the Form's title bar is updated immediately (Fig. 2.23).

4. *Resizing the Form.* Click and drag one of the Form's enabled **sizing handles** (the small white squares that appear around the Form, as shown in Fig. 2.23). Using the mouse, select the bottom-right sizing handle and drag it down and to the right to make the Form larger (Fig. 2.24).

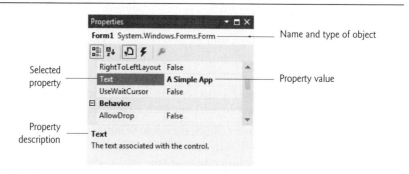

Fig. 2.22 | Setting the Form's Text property in the **Properties** window.

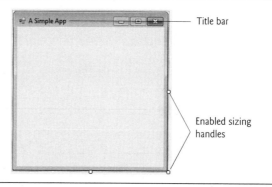

Fig. 2.23 | Form with enabled sizing handles.

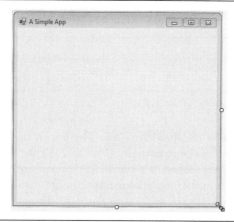

Fig. 2.24 | Resized Form.

5. *Changing the Form's background color.* The **BackColor property** specifies a Form's or control's background color. Clicking BackColor in the **Properties** win-

dow causes a down-arrow button to appear next to the value of the property (Fig. 2.25). When clicked, the down-arrow button displays other options, which vary depending on the property. In this case, the arrow displays tabs for **Custom**, **Web** and **System** (the default). Click the **Custom** tab to display the **palette** (a grid of colors). Select the box that represents light blue. Once you select the color, the palette closes and the Form's background color changes to light blue (Fig. 2.26).

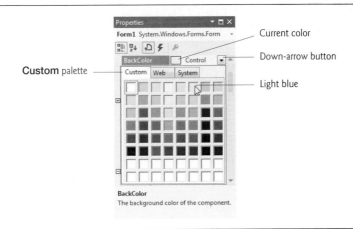

Fig. 2.25 | Changing the Form's BackColor property.

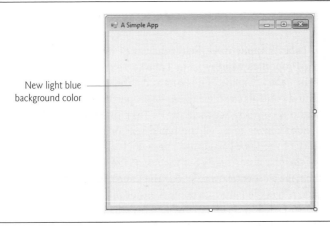

Fig. 2.26 | Form with new BackColor property applied.

6. *Adding a Label control to the Form.* If the **Toolbox** is *not* already open, select **VIEW > Toolbox** to display the set of controls you'll use for creating your apps. For the type of app we're creating in this chapter, the typical controls we use are located in either the **All Windows Forms** group of the **Toolbox** or the **Common Controls** group. If either group name is collapsed, expand it by clicking the arrow to the left of the group name (the **All Windows Forms** and **Common Controls** groups are shown in Fig. 2.17). Next, double click the Label control in the **Toolbox**.

This action causes a Label to appear in the upper-left corner of the Form (Fig. 2.27). [*Note:* If the Form is behind the **Toolbox**, you may need to hide the **Toolbox** to see the Label.] Although double clicking any **Toolbox** control places the control on the Form, you also can "drag" controls from the **Toolbox** to the Form—you may prefer dragging the control because you can position it wherever you want. The Label displays the text **label1** by default. When you add a Label to the Form, the IDE sets the Label's BackColor property to the Form's BackColor. You can change the Label's background color by changing its BackColor property.

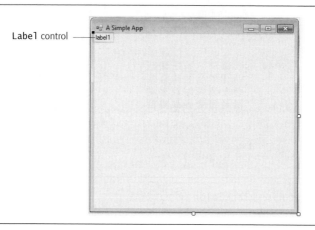

Label control

Fig. 2.27 | Adding a Label to the Form.

7. *Customizing the Label's appearance.* Select the Label by clicking it. Its properties now appear in the **Properties** window. The Label's Text property determines the text (if any) that the Label displays. The Form and Label each have their own Text property—Forms and controls can have the *same* property names (such as BackColor, Text, etc.) without conflict. Set the Label's Text property to Welcome to Visual C#!. The Label resizes to fit all the typed text on one line. By default, the **AutoSize property** of the Label is set to True, which allows the Label to update its size to fit all of the text if necessary. Set the AutoSize property to False so that you can resize the Label on your own. Resize the Label (using the sizing handles) so that the text fits. Move the Label to the top center of the Form by dragging it or by using the keyboard's left and right arrow keys to adjust its position (Fig. 2.28). Alternatively, when the Label is selected, you can center the Label control horizontally by selecting **FORMAT > Center In Form > Horizontally**.

8. *Setting the Label's font size.* To change the font type and appearance of the Label's text, select the value of the **Font property**, which causes an **ellipsis button** to appear next to the value (Fig. 2.29). When the ellipsis button is clicked, a dialog that provides additional values—in this case, the **Font dialog** (Fig. 2.30)—is displayed. You can select the font name (the font options may be different, depending on your system), font style (**Regular, Italic, Bold,** etc.) and font size (**16, 18, 20,** etc.) in this dialog. The **Sample** text shows the selected font settings.

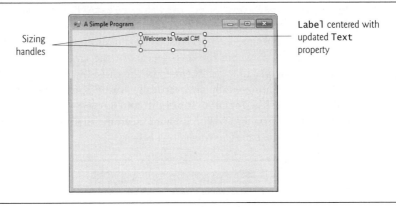

Sizing
handles

Label centered with
updated **Text**
property

Fig. 2.28 | GUI after the Form and Label have been customized.

Under **Font**, select **Segoe UI**, Microsoft's recommended font for user interfaces. Under **Size**, select **24** points and click **OK**. If the Label's text does not fit on a single line, it *wraps* to the next line. Resize the Label so that the words "Welcome to" appear on the Label's first line and the words "Visual C#!" appear on the second line. Re-center the Label horizontally.

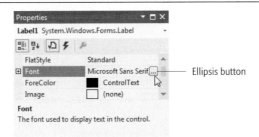

Ellipsis button

Fig. 2.29 | **Properties** window displaying the Label's **Font** property.

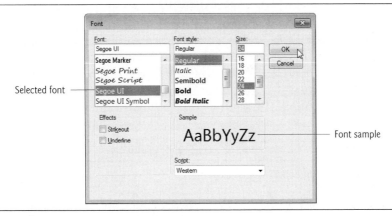

Selected font

Font sample

Fig. 2.30 | **Font** dialog for selecting fonts, styles and sizes.

9. *Aligning the* Label's *text.* Select the Label's **TextAlign** property, which determines how the text is aligned within the Label. A three-by-three grid of buttons representing alignment choices is displayed (Fig. 2.31). The position of each button corresponds to where the text appears in the Label. For this app, set the TextAlign property to MiddleCenter in the three-by-three grid—this selection centers the text horizontally and vertically within the Label. The other Text-Align values, such as TopLeft, TopRight, and BottomCenter, can be used to position the text anywhere within a Label. Certain alignment values may require that you resize the Label to fit the text better.

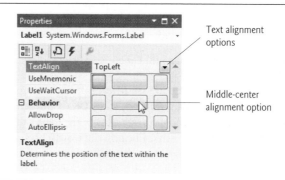

Fig. 2.31 | Centering the Label's text.

10. *Adding a* PictureBox *to the Form.* The PictureBox control displays images. The process involved in this step is similar to that of *Step 6*, in which we added a Label to the Form. Locate the PictureBox in the **Toolbox** (Fig. 2.17) and double click it to add it to the Form. When the PictureBox appears, move it underneath the Label, either by dragging it or by using the arrow keys (Fig. 2.32).

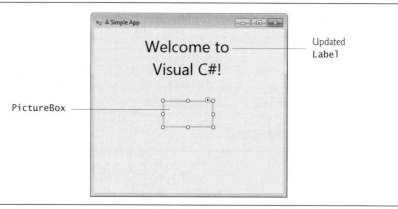

Fig. 2.32 | Inserting and aligning a PictureBox.

11. *Inserting an image.* Click the PictureBox to display its properties in the **Properties** window (Fig. 2.33). Locate and select the **Image property**, which displays a

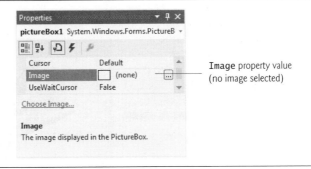

Fig. 2.33 | Image property of the `PictureBox`.

preview of the selected image or **(none)** if no image is selected. Click the ellipsis button (or the **Choose Image...** link above the property description) to display the **Select Resource** dialog (Fig. 2.34), which is used to import files, such as images, for use in an app. Click the **Import...** button to browse for an image to insert, select the image file and click **OK**. We used bug.png from this chapter's examples folder. The image is previewed in the **Select Resource** dialog (Fig. 2.35). Click **OK** to use the image. Supported image formats include PNG (Portable Network Graphics), GIF (Graphic Interchange Format), JPEG (Joint Photographic Experts Group) and BMP (Windows bitmap). To scale the image to the `Picture-Box`'s size, change the **SizeMode property** to **StretchImage** (Fig. 2.36). Resize the `PictureBox`, making it larger (Fig. 2.37).

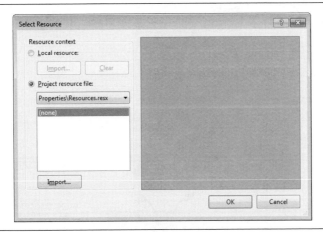

Fig. 2.34 | Select Resource dialog to select an image for the `PictureBox`.

12. *Saving the project.* Select **FILE > Save All** to save the entire solution. The solution file (which has the filename extension .sln) contains the name and location of its project, and the project file (which has the filename extension .csproj) contains the names and locations of all the files in the project. If you want to reopen your project at a later time, simply open its .sln file.

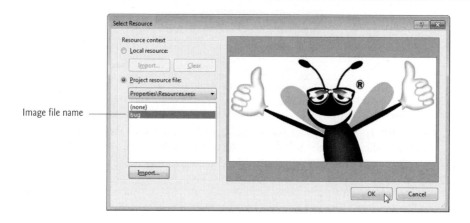

Image file name

Fig. 2.35 | **Select Resource** dialog displaying a preview of selected image.

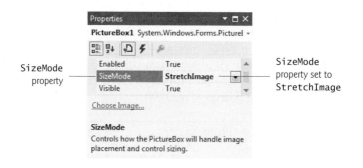

SizeMode property

SizeMode property set to StretchImage

Fig. 2.36 | Scaling an image to the size of the `PictureBox`.

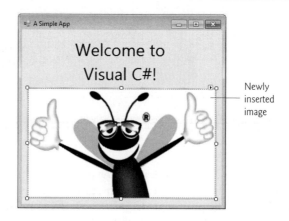

Newly inserted image

Fig. 2.37 | `PictureBox` displaying an image.

13. ***Running the project.*** Recall that up to this point we have been working in the IDE design mode (that is, the app being created is not executing). In **run mode**, the app is executing, and you can interact with only a few IDE features—features that are not available are disabled (grayed out). The text **Form1.cs [Design]** in the project tab (Fig. 2.38) means that we're designing the Form *visually* rather than *programmatically.* If we had been writing code, the tab would have contained only the text **Form1.cs**. If there is an asterisk (*) at the end of the text in the tab, the file has been changed and should be saved. Select **DEBUG > Start Debugging** to execute the app (or you can press the *F5* key). Figure 2.39 shows the IDE in run mode (indicated by the title-bar text **ASimpleApp (Running) – Microsoft Visual Studio Express 2012 for Windows Desktop**). Many toolbar icons and menus are disabled, since they cannot be used while the app is running. The running app appears in a separate window outside the IDE as shown in the lower-right portion of Fig. 2.39.

Fig. 2.38 | Debugging a solution.

14. ***Terminating execution.*** Click the running app's close box (the [×] in the top-right corner of the running app's window). This action stops the app's execution and returns the IDE to design mode. You can also select **DEBUG > Stop Debugging** to terminate the app.

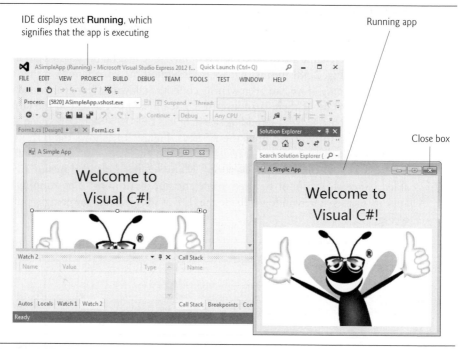

Fig. 2.39 | IDE in run mode, with the running app in the foreground.

2.7 Wrap-Up

In this chapter, we introduced key features of the Visual Studio IDE. You visually designed a working Visual C# app without writing a single line of code. Visual C# app development is a mixture of the two styles: Visual app development allows you to develop GUIs easily and avoid tedious GUI programming. "Conventional" programming (which we introduce in Chapter 3) allows you to specify the behavior of your apps.

You created a Visual C# Windows Forms app with one Form. You worked with the IDE's **Solution Explorer, Toolbox** and **Properties** windows, which are essential to developing Visual C# apps. We also demonstrated context-sensitive help, which displays help topics related to selected controls or text.

You used visual app development to design an app's GUI quickly and easily, by dragging and dropping controls (a Label and a PictureBox) onto a Form or by double clicking controls in the **Toolbox**.

You used the **Properties** window to set a Form's Text and BackColor properties. You learned that Label controls display text and that PictureBoxes display images. You displayed text in a Label and added an image to a PictureBox. You also worked with the Label's AutoSize, TextAlign and Font properties and the PictureBox's Image and Size-Mode properties.

In the next chapter, we discuss "nonvisual," or "conventional," programming—you'll create your first apps with Visual C# code that you write, instead of having Visual Studio write the code.

2.8 Web Resources

Please take a moment to visit each of these sites.

`msdn.microsoft.com/vstudio`

This site is the home page for Microsoft Visual Studio. The site includes news, documentation, downloads and other resources.

`msdn.microsoft.com/en-us/vstudio/hh341490.aspx`

This site provides information on the newest release of Visual C#, including downloads, community information and resources.

`social.msdn.microsoft.com/Forums/en-US/csharpgeneral/threads`

This site provides access to the Microsoft Visual C# forums, which you can use to get your Visual C# language and IDE questions answered.

`msdn.microsoft.com/en-us/magazine/default.aspx`

This is the Microsoft Developer Network Magazine site. This site provides articles and code on many Visual C# and .NET app development topics. There is also an archive of past issues.

3

Introduction to C# Apps

Objectives

In this chapter you'll:

- Input data from the keyboard and output data to the screen.

- Declare and use data of various types.

- Use arithmetic operators.

- Write decision-making statements.

- Use relational and equality operators.

3.1 Introduction

We now introduce C# app programming. Most of the C# apps you'll study in this book process information and display results. In this chapter, we introduce **console apps**—these input and output text in a *console window*, which in Windows is known as the **Command Prompt**.

We begin with several examples that simply display messages on the screen. We then demonstrate an app that obtains two numbers from a user, calculates their sum and displays the result. You'll perform various arithmetic calculations and save the results for later use. Many apps contain logic that makes *decisions*—the last example in this chapter demonstrates decision-making fundamentals by comparing numbers and then displaying messages based on the comparison results. For example, the app displays a message indicating that two numbers are equal only if they have the same value.

3.2 A Simple C# App: Displaying a Line of Text

Let's consider a simple app that displays a line of text. The app and its output are shown in Fig. 3.1, which illustrates several important C# language features. Each program we present in this book includes line numbers, which are *not* part of actual C# code. In the Before You Begin section that follows the Preface, we show how to display line numbers for your C# code. We'll soon see that line 10 does the real work of the app—namely, displaying the phrase `Welcome to C# Programming!` on the screen. Let's now do a code walkthrough of the app.

Comments
Line 1

```
// Fig. 3.1: Welcome1.cs
```

begins with `//`, indicating that the remainder of the line is a **comment**. You'll insert comments to document your apps and improve their readability. The C# compiler ignores comments, so they do *not* cause the computer to perform any action when the app is run. We begin every app with a comment indicating the figure number and the name of the file in which the app is stored.

A comment that begins with `//` is called a **single-line comment**, because it terminates at the end of the line on which it appears. A `//` comment also can begin in the middle of a line and continue until the end of that line (as in lines 7, 11 and 12).

```
1   // Fig. 3.1: Welcome1.cs
2   // Text-displaying app.
3   using System;
4
5   public class Welcome1
6   {
7      // Main method begins execution of C# app
8      public static void Main( string[] args )
9      {
10        Console.WriteLine( "Welcome to C# Programming!" );
11     } // end Main
12  } // end class Welcome1
```

```
Welcome to C# Programming!
```

Fig. 3.1 | Text-displaying app.

Delimited comments such as

```
/* This is a delimited comment.
   It can be split over many lines */
```

can be split over several lines. This type of comment begins with the delimiter /* and ends with the delimiter */. All text between the delimiters is ignored by the compiler.

Common Programming Error 3.1
Forgetting one of the delimiters of a delimited comment is a syntax error.

Line 2

```
// Text-displaying app.
```

is a single-line comment that describes the purpose of the app.

using **Directive**
Line 3

```
using System;
```

is a **using directive** that tells the compiler where to look for a class that's used in this app. A great strength of Visual C# is its rich set of predefined classes that you can *reuse* rather than "reinventing the wheel." These classes are organized under **namespaces**—named collections of related classes. Collectively, .NET's namespaces are referred to as the **.NET Framework Class Library**. Each using directive identifies a namespace containing predefined classes that a C# app should be able to use. The using directive in line 3 indicates that this example intends to use classes from the System namespace, which contains the predefined Console class (discussed shortly) used in line 10, and many other useful classes.

Error-Prevention Tip 3.1
Forgetting to include a using directive for a namespace that contains a class used in your app typically results in a compilation error, containing a message such as "The name 'Console' does not exist in the current context."

For each new .NET class we use, we indicate the namespace in which it's located. This information is important, because it helps you locate descriptions of each class in the **.NET documentation**. A web-based version of this documentation can be found at

> `msdn.microsoft.com/en-us/library/ms229335.aspx`

This can also be accessed via the **Help** menu. You can click the name of any .NET class or method, then press the *F1* key to get more information. Finally, you can learn about the contents of a given namespace by going to

> `msdn.microsoft.com/`*namespace*

So, `msdn.microsoft.com/System` takes you to namespace `System`'s documentation.

Blank Lines and Whitespace

Line 4 is simply a *blank line*. Blank lines and space characters make code easier to read, and together with tab characters are known as **whitespace**. Space characters and tabs are known specifically as **whitespace characters**. Whitespace is ignored by the compiler.

Class Declaration

Line 5

> `public class Welcome1`

begins a **class declaration** for the class `Welcome1`. Every app consists of at least one class declaration that's defined by you. These are known as **user-defined classes**. The **class keyword** introduces a class declaration and is immediately followed by the **class name** (`Welcome1`). Keywords (sometimes called **reserved words**) are reserved for use by C# and are always spelled with all lowercase letters. The complete list of C# keywords is shown in Fig. 3.2.

C# Keywords and contextual keywords				
abstract	as	base	bool	break
byte	case	catch	char	checked
class	const	continue	decimal	default
delegate	do	double	else	enum
event	explicit	extern	false	finally
fixed	float	for	foreach	goto
if	implicit	in	int	interface
internal	is	lock	long	namespace
new	null	object	operator	out
override	params	private	protected	public
readonly	ref	return	sbyte	sealed
short	sizeof	stackalloc	static	string
struct	switch	this	throw	true
try	typeof	uint	ulong	unchecked
unsafe	ushort	using	virtual	void
volatile	while			

Fig. 3.2 | C# keywords and contextual keywords. (Part 1 of 2.)

C# Keywords and contextual keywords				
Contextual Keywords				
add	alias	ascending	async	await
by	descending	dynamic	equals	from
get	global	group	into	join
let	on	orderby	partial	remove
select	set	value	var	where
yield				

Fig. 3.2 | C# keywords and contextual keywords. (Part 2 of 2.)

Class Name Convention

By convention, all class names begin with a capital letter and capitalize the first letter of each word they include (e.g., SampleClassName). This convention is known as **upper camel casing**. A class name is an **identifier**—a series of characters consisting of letters, digits and underscores (_) that does not begin with a digit and does not contain spaces. Some valid identifiers are Welcome1, identifier, _value and m_inputField1. The name 7button is *not* a valid identifier because it begins with a digit, and the name input field is *not* a valid identifier because it contains a space. Normally, an identifier that does not begin with a capital letter is not the name of a class. C# is **case sensitive**—that is, uppercase and lowercase letters are distinct, so a1 and A1 are different (but both valid) identifiers.[1]

Good Programming Practice 3.1

By convention, always begin a class name's identifier with a capital letter and start each subsequent word in the identifier with a capital letter.

Common Programming Error 3.2

C# is case sensitive. Not using the proper uppercase and lowercase letters for an identifier normally causes a compilation error.

public Class

In Chapters 3–9, every class we define begins with the keyword **public**. For now, we'll simply require this keyword. You'll learn more about classes in Chapter 10. When you save your public class declaration in a file, the file name is usually the class name followed by the .cs file-name extension. For our app, the file name is Welcome1.cs.

Good Programming Practice 3.2

By convention, a file that contains a single public class should have a name that's identical to the class name (plus the .cs extension) in both spelling and capitalization.

---

1. Identifiers may also be preceded by the @ character. This indicates that a word should be interpreted as an identifier, even if it's a keyword (e.g., @int). This allows C# code to use code written in other .NET languages where an identifier might have the same name as a C# keyword. The **contextual keywords** in Fig. 3.2 can be used as identifiers outside the contexts in which they're keywords, but for clarity this is not recommended.

Body of a Class Declaration

A **left brace** (in line 6 in Fig. 3.1), {, begins the **body** of every class declaration. A corresponding **right brace** (in line 12), }, must end each class declaration. Lines 7–11 are indented. This indentation is a *spacing convention*. We define each spacing convention as a *Good Programming Practice*.

Good Programming Practice 3.3

Indent the entire body of each class declaration one "level" of indentation between the left and right braces that delimit the body of the class. This format emphasizes the class declaration's structure and makes it easier to read. You can let the IDE format your code by selecting Edit > Advanced > Format Document.

Common Programming Error 3.3

It's a syntax error if braces do not occur in matching pairs.

Main Method

Line 7

```
// Main method begins execution of C# app
```

is a comment indicating the purpose of lines 8–11 of the app. Line 8

```
public static void Main( string[] args )
```

is the starting point of every app. The **parentheses** after the identifier Main indicate that it's an app building block called a **method**. Class declarations normally contain one or more methods. Method names usually follow the same capitalization conventions used for class names. For each app, one of the methods in a class *must* be called Main (which is typically defined as shown in line 8); otherwise, the app will not execute. Methods are able to perform tasks and return information when they complete their tasks. Keyword **void** (line 8) indicates that this method will *not* return any information after it completes its task. Later, we'll see that many methods do return information. You'll learn more about methods in Chapters 4 and 7. We discuss the contents of Main's parentheses in Chapter 8. For now, simply mimic Main's first line in your apps.

Body of a Method Declaration

The left brace in line 9 begins the **body of the method declaration**. A corresponding right brace must end the method's body (line 11). Line 10 in the body of the method is indented between the braces.

Displaying a Line of Text

Line 10

```
Console.WriteLine( "Welcome to C# Programming!" );
```

instructs the computer to **perform an action**—namely, to display the **string** of characters between the double quotation marks, which *delimit* the string. A string is sometimes called a **character string**, a **message** or a **string literal**. We refer to them simply as strings. Whitespace characters in strings are *not* ignored by the compiler.

Class **Console** provides **standard input/output** capabilities that enable apps to read and display text in the console window from which the app executes. The **Console.Write-Line method** displays a line of text in the console window. The string in the parentheses in line 10 is the **argument** to the method. Method Console.WriteLine performs its task by displaying its argument in the console window. When Console.WriteLine completes its task, it positions the **screen cursor** (the blinking symbol indicating where the next character will be displayed) at the beginning of the next line in the console window. This movement of the cursor is similar to what happens when a user presses the *Enter* key while typing in a text editor—the cursor moves to the beginning of the next line in the file.

Statements
The entire line 10, including Console.WriteLine, the parentheses, the argument "Welcome to C# Programming!" in the parentheses and the **semicolon (;)**, is called a **statement**. Most statements end with a semicolon. When the statement in line 10 executes, it displays the message Welcome to C# Programming! in the console window. A method is typically composed of one or more statements that perform the method's task.

Matching Left ({) and Right (}) Braces
You may find it difficult when reading or writing an app to match the left and right braces ({ and }) that delimit the body of a class declaration or a method declaration. To help, you can include a comment after each closing right brace (}) that ends a method declaration and after each closing right brace that ends a class declaration. For example, line 11

```
} // end Main
```

specifies the closing right brace of method Main, and line 12

```
} // end class Welcome1
```

specifies the closing right brace of class Welcome1. Each of these comments indicates the method or class that the right brace terminates. Visual Studio can help you locate matching braces in your code. Simply place the cursor immediately in front of the left brace or immediately after the right brace, and Visual Studio will highlight both.

3.3 Creating a Simple App in Visual Studio

Now that we've presented our first console app (Fig. 3.1), we provide a step-by-step explanation of how to create, compile and execute it using Visual Studio 2012 Express for Windows Desktop, which we'll refer to simply as Visual Studio from this point forward.

Creating the Console App
After opening Visual Studio, select **FILE > New Project…** to display the **New Project** dialog (Fig. 3.3). At the left side of the dialog, under **Installed > Templates > Visual C#** select the **Windows** category, then in the middle of the dialog select the **Console Application** template. In the dialog's **Name** field, type Welcome1, then click **OK** to create the project. By default, the project's folder will be placed in your account's Documents folder under Visual Studio 2012\Projects. The IDE now contains the open console app, as shown in Fig. 3.4. The editor window already contains some code provided by the IDE. Some of

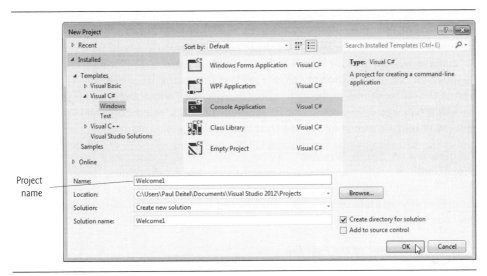

Project name

Fig. 3.3 | Creating a **Console Application** with the **New Project** dialog.

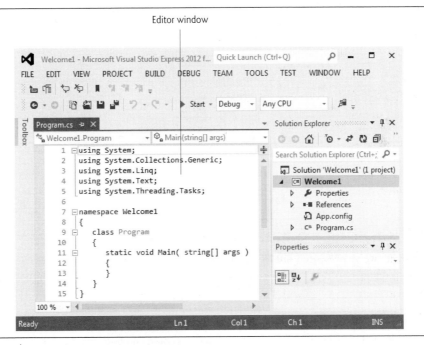

Fig. 3.4 | IDE with an open console app.

this code is similar to that of Fig. 3.1. Some is not, and uses features that we have not yet discussed. The IDE inserts this extra code to help organize the app and to provide access to some common classes in the .NET Framework Class Library—at this point in the book, this code is neither required nor relevant to the discussion of this app; delete all of it.

The code coloring scheme used by the IDE is called **syntax-color highlighting** and helps you visually differentiate app elements. For example, keywords appear in blue and comments appear in green. We syntax-shade our code similarly—bold for keywords, gray for comments, bold gray for literals and constants, and black for other text. One example of a literal is the string passed to `Console.WriteLine` in line 10 of Fig. 3.1. You can customize the colors shown in the code editor by selecting **Tools > Options...**. This displays the **Options** dialog. Then expand the **Environment** node and select **Fonts and Colors**. Here you can change the colors for various code elements.

Configuring the Editor Window
Visual Studio provides many ways to personalize your coding experience. In the Before You Begin section that follows the Preface, we show how to configure the IDE to display line numbers at the left side of the editor window and how to specify indent sizes that match our code examples.

Changing the Name of the App File
For the apps we create in this book, we change the default name of the source-code file (i.e., `Program.cs`) to a more descriptive name. To rename the file, click `Program.cs` in the **Solution Explorer** window. This displays the app file's properties in the **Properties** window (Fig. 3.5). Change the **File Name property** to `Welcome1.cs` and press *Enter*.

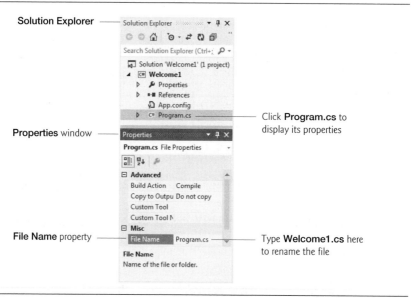

Fig. 3.5 | Renaming the program file in the **Properties** window.

Writing Code and Using IntelliSense
In the editor (Fig. 3.4), replace the IDE-generated code with the code in Fig. 3.1. As you begin typing `Console` (line 10), an *IntelliSense* window is displayed (Fig. 3.6(a)). As you type, *IntelliSense* lists various items that start with or contain the letters you've typed so far. *IntelliSense* also displays a tool tip containing a description of the first matching item. You can

a) *IntelliSense* window displayed as you type

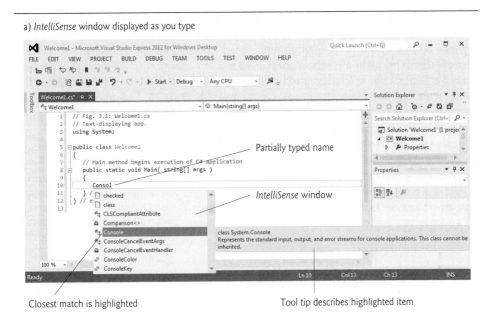

Closest match is highlighted   Tool tip describes highlighted item

b) *IntelliSense* window showing method names that start with `Write`

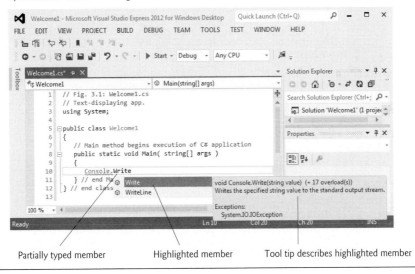

Partially typed member   Highlighted member   Tool tip describes highlighted member

Fig. 3.6 | *IntelliSense.*

either type the complete item name (e.g., `Console`), double click the item name in the member list or press the *Tab* key to complete the name. Once the complete name is provided, the *IntelliSense* window closes. While the *IntelliSense* window is displayed, pressing the *Ctrl* key makes the window transparent so you can see the code behind the window.

When you type the dot (.) after `Console`, the *IntelliSense* window reappears and shows only the members of class `Console` that can be used on the right of the dot (Fig. 3.6(b)). When you type the open parenthesis character, (, after `Console.WriteLine`, the *Parameter*

Info window is displayed (Fig. 3.7). This window contains information about the method's parameters. A class can define several methods that have the *same* name, as long as they have *different* numbers and/or types of parameters—a concept known as *overloaded methods*. These methods normally all perform similar tasks. The *Parameter Info* window indicates how many versions of the selected method are available and provides up and down arrows for scrolling through the different versions. For example, there are 19 versions of the `WriteLine` method—we use one of these in our app. The *Parameter Info* window is one of many features provided by the IDE to facilitate app development. In the next several chapters, you'll learn more about the information displayed in these windows. The *Parameter Info* window is especially helpful when you want to see the different ways in which a method can be used. From the code in Fig. 3.1, we already know that we intend to display one string with `WriteLine`, so, because you know exactly which version of `WriteLine` you want to use, you can simply close the *Parameter Info* window by pressing the *Esc* key.

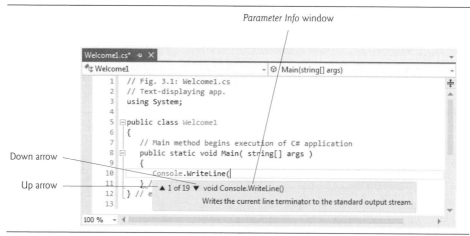

Fig. 3.7 | *Parameter Info* window.

Saving the App
After you type the app's code, select **FILE > Save All** to save the project.

Compiling and Running the App
You're now ready to compile and execute your app. Depending on the project's type, the compiler may compile the code into files with the **.exe (executable) extension**, the **.dll (dynamically linked library) extension** or one of several other extensions. Such files are called **assemblies** and are the packaging units for compiled C# code. These assemblies contain the Microsoft Intermediate Language (MSIL) code for the app.

To compile the app, select **BUILD > Build Solution**. If the app contains no syntax errors, this will create an executable file (named `Welcome1.exe`, in one of the project's subdirectories). To execute it, type *Ctrl + F5*, which invokes the `Main` method (Fig. 3.1). If you attempt to run the app before building it, the IDE will build the app first, then run it only if there are no compilation errors. The statement in line 10 of `Main` displays `Welcome to C# Programming!`. Figure 3.8 shows the results of executing this app, displayed in a console (**Command Prompt**) window. Leave the app's project open in Visual Studio; we'll go back to it later in

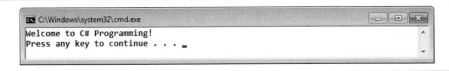

Fig. 3.8 | Executing the app shown in Fig. 3.1.

this section. [*Note:* The console window normally has a black background and white text. We reconfigured it to have a white background and black text for readability. If you'd like to do this, click the ■ icon in the upper-left corner of the console window, then select **Properties**. You can change the colors in the **Colors** tab of the dialog that appears.]

Syntax Errors, Error Messages and the Error List Window

Go back to the app in Visual Studio. As you type code, the IDE responds either by applying syntax-color highlighting or by generating a **syntax error**, which indicates a violation of Visual C#'s rules for creating correct apps. Syntax errors occur for various reasons, such as missing parentheses and misspelled keywords.

When a syntax error occurs, the IDE underlines the location of the error with a red squiggly line and provides a description of it in the **Error List** window (Fig. 3.9). If the

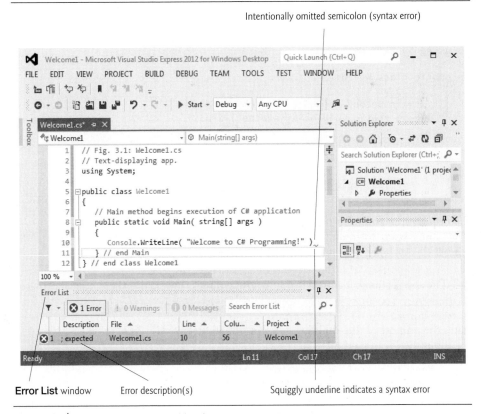

Fig. 3.9 | Syntax error indicated by the IDE.

Error List window is not visible in the IDE, select **VIEW > Error List** to display it. In Figure 3.9, we intentionally omitted the semicolon at the end of the statement in line 10. The error message indicates that the semicolon is missing. You can double click an error message in the **Error List** to jump to the error's location in the code.

> **Error-Prevention Tip 3.2**
> *One syntax error can lead to multiple entries in the* **Error List** *window. Each error that you address could eliminate several subsequent error messages when you recompile your app. So when you see an error you know how to fix, correct it and recompile—this may make several other errors disappear.*

3.4 Modifying Your Simple C# App

This section continues our introduction to C# programming with two examples that modify the example of Fig. 3.1.

Displaying a Single Line of Text with Multiple Statements
Class `Welcome2`, shown in Fig. 3.10, uses two statements to produce the same output as that shown in Fig. 3.1. From this point forward, we highlight the new and key features in each code listing, as shown in lines 10–11 of Fig. 3.10.

```
 1    // Fig. 3.10: Welcome2.cs
 2    // Displaying one line of text with multiple statements.
 3    using System;
 4
 5    public class Welcome2
 6    {
 7       // Main method begins execution of C# app
 8       public static void Main( string[] args )
 9       {
10          Console.Write( "Welcome to " );
11          Console.WriteLine( "C# Programming!" );
12       } // end Main
13    } // end class Welcome2
```

```
Welcome to C# Programming!
```

Fig. 3.10 | Displaying one line of text with multiple statements.

The app is almost identical to Fig. 3.1. We discuss the changes here. Line 2

```
    // Displaying one line of text with multiple statements.
```

states the purpose of this app. Line 5 begins the `Welcome2` class declaration.
Lines 10–11 of method `Main`

```
    Console.Write( "Welcome to " );
    Console.WriteLine( "C# Programming!" );
```

display one line of text in the console window. The first statement uses `Console`'s method **Write** to display a string. Unlike `WriteLine`, after displaying its argument, `Write` does *not* position the screen cursor at the beginning of the next line in the console window—the next character the app displays will appear immediately after the last character that `Write` displays. Thus, line 11 positions the first character in its argument (the letter "C") immediately *after* the last character that line 10 displays (the space character before the string's closing double-quote character). Each `Write` statement resumes displaying characters from where the last `Write` statement displayed its last character.

Displaying Multiple Lines of Text with a Single Statement

A single statement can display multiple lines by using newline characters, which indicate to `Console` methods `Write` and `WriteLine` when they should position the screen cursor to the beginning of the next line in the console window. Like space characters and tab characters, newline characters are whitespace characters. The app of Fig. 3.11 outputs four lines of text, using newline characters to indicate when to begin each new line.

```
1   // Fig. 3.11: Welcome3.cs
2   // Displaying multiple lines with a single statement.
3   using System;
4
5   public class Welcome3
6   {
7      // Main method begins execution of C# app
8      public static void Main( string[] args )
9      {
10        Console.WriteLine( "Welcome\nto\nC#\nProgramming!" );
11     } // end Main
12  } // end class Welcome3
```

```
Welcome
to
C#
Programming!
```

Fig. 3.11 | Displaying multiple lines with a single statement.

Most of the app is identical to the apps of Fig. 3.1 and Fig. 3.10, so we discuss only the changes here. Line 2

```
// Displaying multiple lines with a single statement.
```

states the purpose of this app. Line 5 begins the `Welcome3` class declaration.
Line 10

```
Console.WriteLine( "Welcome\nto\nC#\nProgramming!" );
```

displays four separate lines of text in the console window. Normally, the characters in a string are displayed exactly as they appear in the double quotes. Note, however, that the two characters \ and n (repeated three times in the statement) do *not* appear on the screen. The **backslash** (\) is called an **escape character**. It indicates to C# that a "special character" is in the string. When a backslash appears in a string of characters, C# combines the next character with the backslash to form an **escape sequence.** The escape sequence \n represents the **newline character.** When a newline character appears in a string being output with `Console` methods, the newline character causes the screen cursor to move to the beginning of the next line in the console window. Figure 3.12 lists several common escape sequences and describes how they affect the display of characters in the console window.

Escape sequence	Description
\n	Newline. Positions the screen cursor at the beginning of the next line.
\t	Horizontal tab. Moves the screen cursor to the next tab stop.
\"	Double quote. Used to place a double-quote character (") in a string—e.g., `Console.Write( "\"in quotes\"" );` displays `"in quotes"`.
\r	Carriage return. Positions the screen cursor at the beginning of the current line—does not advance the cursor to the next line. Any characters output after the carriage return overwrite the characters previously output on that line.
\\	Backslash. Used to place a backslash character in a string.

Fig. 3.12 | Some common escape sequences.

3.5 Formatting Text with Console.Write and Console.WriteLine

`Console` methods `Write` and `WriteLine` also have the capability to display formatted data. Figure 3.13 outputs the strings `"Welcome to"` and `"C# Programming!"` with `WriteLine`.

```
1   // Fig. 3.13: Welcome4.cs
2   // Displaying multiple lines of text with string formatting.
3   using System;
4
5   public class Welcome4
6   {
7      // Main method begins execution of C# app
8      public static void Main( string[] args )
9      {
10         Console.WriteLine( "{0}\n{1}", "Welcome to", "C# Programming!" );
11      } // end Main
12   } // end class Welcome4
```

```
Welcome to
C# Programming!
```

Fig. 3.13 | Displaying multiple lines of text with string formatting.

Line 10

```
Console.WriteLine( "{0}\n{1}", "Welcome to", "C# Programming!" );
```

calls method `Console.WriteLine` to display the app's output. The method call specifies three arguments. When a method requires multiple arguments, the arguments are separated with **commas** (,)—this is known as a **comma-separated list**.

Good Programming Practice 3.4

Place a space after each comma (,) in an argument list to make apps more readable.

Most statements end with a semicolon (;). Therefore, line 10 represents only one statement. Large statements can be split over many lines, but there are some restrictions.

Common Programming Error 3.4

Splitting a statement in the middle of an identifier or a string is a syntax error.

Format Strings and Format Items

Method `WriteLine`'s first argument is a **format string** that may consist of **fixed text** and **format items**. Fixed text is output by `WriteLine`, as in Fig. 3.1. Each format item is a placeholder for a value. Format items also may include optional formatting information.

Format items are enclosed in curly braces and contain characters that tell the method which argument to use and how to format it. For example, the format item `{0}` is a *placeholder* for the first additional argument (because C# starts counting from 0), `{1}` is a *placeholder* for the second, and so on. The format string in line 10 specifies that `WriteLine` should output two arguments and that the first one should be followed by a newline character. So this example substitutes `"Welcome to"` for the `{0}` and `"C# Programming!"` for the `{1}`. The output shows that two lines of text are displayed. Because braces in a formatted string normally indicate a placeholder for text substitution, you must type two left braces (`{{`) or two right braces (`}}`) to insert a single left or right brace into a formatted string, respectively. We introduce additional formatting features as they're needed in our examples.

3.6 Another C# App: Adding Integers

Our next app reads (or inputs) two **integers** (whole numbers, like –22, 7, 0 and 1024) typed by a user at the keyboard, computes the sum of the values and displays the result. This app must keep track of the numbers supplied by the user for the calculation later in the app. Apps remember numbers and other data in the computer's memory and access that data through app elements called **variables**. The app of Fig. 3.14 demonstrates these concepts. In the sample output, we highlight data the user enters at the keyboard in bold.

```
 1   // Fig. 3.14: Addition.cs
 2   // Displaying the sum of two numbers input from the keyboard.
 3   using System;
 4
 5   public class Addition
 6   {
 7      // Main method begins execution of C# app
 8      public static void Main( string[] args )
 9      {
10         int number1; // declare first number to add
11         int number2; // declare second number to add
12         int sum; // declare sum of number1 and number2
```

Fig. 3.14 | Displaying the sum of two numbers input from the keyboard. (Part 1 of 2.)

```
13
14          Console.Write( "Enter first integer: " ); // prompt user
15          // read first number from user
16          number1 = Convert.ToInt32( Console.ReadLine() );
17
18          Console.Write( "Enter second integer: " ); // prompt user
19          // read second number from user
20          number2 = Convert.ToInt32( Console.ReadLine() );
21
22          sum = number1 + number2; // add numbers
23
24          Console.WriteLine( "Sum is {0}", sum ); // display sum
25       } // end Main
26    } // end class Addition
```

```
Enter first integer: 45
Enter second integer: 72
Sum is 117
```

Fig. 3.14 | Displaying the sum of two numbers input from the keyboard. (Part 2 of 2.)

Comments
Lines 1–2

```
// Fig. 3.14: Addition.cs
// Displaying the sum of two numbers input from the keyboard.
```

state the figure number, file name and purpose of the app.

Class Addition
Line 5

```
public class Addition
```

begins the declaration of class Addition. Remember that the body of each class declaration starts with an opening left brace (line 6) and ends with a closing right brace (line 26).

Function Main
The app begins execution with Main (lines 8–25). The left brace (line 9) marks the beginning of Main's body, and the corresponding right brace (line 25) marks the end of Main's body. Method Main is indented one level within the body of class Addition and the code in the body of Main is indented another level for readability.

Declaring Variable number1
Line 10

```
int number1; // declare first number to add
```

is a **variable declaration statement** that specifies the name (number1) and type of a variable (int) used in this app. Variables are typically declared with a **name** and a **type** before they're used. A variable's name can be any valid identifier. A variable's type specifies what kind of information is stored at that location in memory and how much space should be set aside to store that value. Like other statements, declaration statements end with a semicolon (;).

Type **int**

The declaration in line 10 specifies that the variable named number1 is of type **int**—it will hold **integer** values (whole numbers such as 7, -11, 0 and 31914). The range of values for an int is –2,147,483,648 (int.MinValue) to +2,147,483,647 (int.MaxValue). We'll soon discuss types **float**, **double** and **decimal**, for specifying real numbers, and type **char**, for specifying characters. Real numbers contain decimal points, as in 3.4, 0.0 and -11.19. Variables of type float and double store approximations of real numbers in memory. Variables of type decimal store real numbers precisely (to 28–29 significant digits), so decimal variables are often used with *monetary calculations*. Variables of type char represent individual characters, such as an uppercase letter (e.g., A), a digit (e.g., 7), a special character (e.g., * or %) or an escape sequence (e.g., the newline character, \n). Types such as int, float, double, decimal and char are often called **simple types**. Simple-type names are keywords and must appear in all lowercase letters. Appendix B summarizes the characteristics of the simple types (bool, byte, sbyte, char, short, ushort, int, uint, long, ulong, float, double and decimal).

Declaring Variables **number2** *and* **sum**

The variable declaration statements at lines 11–12

```
int number2; // declare second number to add
int sum; // declare sum of number1 and number2
```

similarly declare variables number2 and sum to be of type int.

Variable declaration statements can be split over several lines, with the variable names separated by commas (i.e., a comma-separated list of variable names). Several variables of the same type may be declared in one declaration or in multiple declarations. For example, lines 10–12 can also be written as follows:

```
int number1, // declare first number to add
    number2, // declare second number to add
    sum; // declare sum of number1 and number2
```

Good Programming Practice 3.5

Declare each variable on a separate line. This format allows a comment to be easily inserted next to each declaration.

Good Programming Practice 3.6

By convention, variable-name identifiers begin with a lowercase letter, and every word in the name after the first word begins with a capital letter. This naming convention is known as **lower camel casing**.

Prompting the User for Input

Line 14

```
Console.Write( "Enter first integer: " ); // prompt user
```

uses Console.Write to display the message "Enter first integer: ". This message is called a **prompt** because it directs the user to take a specific action.

*Reading a Value into Variable **number1***
Line 16

```
number1 = Convert.ToInt32( Console.ReadLine() );
```

works in two steps. First, it calls the Console's **ReadLine** method, which waits for the user to type a string of characters at the keyboard and press the *Enter* key. As we mentioned, some methods perform a task then return the result of that task. In this case, ReadLine returns the text the user entered. Then, the string is used as an argument to class **Convert**'s **ToInt32** method, which converts this sequence of characters into data of type int. In this case, method ToInt32 returns the int representation of the user's input.

Possible Erroneous User Input
Technically, the user can type anything as the input value. ReadLine will accept it and pass it off to the ToInt32 method. This method assumes that the string contains a valid integer value. In this app, if the user types a noninteger value, a runtime logic error called an *exception* will occur and the app will terminate. C# offers a technology called *exception handling* that will help you make your apps more robust by enabling them to handle exceptions and continue executing. We introduce exception handling in Section 8.4, then use it again in Chapter 10. We take a deeper look at exception handling in Chapter 13.

Assigning a Value to a Variable
In line 16, the result of the call to method ToInt32 (an int value) is placed in variable number1 by using the **assignment operator**, =. The statement is read as "number1 gets the value returned by Convert.ToInt32." Operator = is a **binary operator**, because it works on two pieces of information. These are known as its **operands**—in this case, the operands are number1 and the result of the method call Convert.ToInt32. Everything to the right of the assignment operator, =, is always evaluated *before* the assignment is performed.

Good Programming Practice 3.7
Place spaces on either side of a binary operator to make the code more readable.

*Prompting the User for Input and Reading a Value into Variable **number2***
Line 18

```
Console.Write( "Enter second integer: " ); // prompt user
```

prompts the user to enter the second integer. Line 20

```
number2 = Convert.ToInt32( Console.ReadLine() );
```

reads a second integer and assigns it to the variable number2.

*Summing the **number1** and **number2***
Line 22

```
sum = number1 + number2; // add numbers
```

calculates the sum of number1 and number2 and assigns the result to variable sum by using the assignment operator, =. The statement is read as "sum gets the value of number1 + number2." Most calculations are performed in assignment statements. When number1 + number2 is encountered, the values stored in the variables are used in the calculation. The addition operator is a binary operator—its two **operands** are number1 and number2. Portions of statements that contain calculations are called **expressions**. In fact, an expression is any portion of a statement that has a value associated with it. For example, the value of the expression number1 + number2 is the sum of the numbers. Similarly, the value of the expression Console.ReadLine() is the string of characters typed by the user.

Displaying the sum
After the calculation has been performed, line 24

```
Console.WriteLine( "Sum is {0}", sum ); // display sum
```

uses method Console.WriteLine to display the sum. The format item {0} is a placeholder for the first argument after the format string. Other than the {0} format item, the remaining characters in the format string are all *fixed* text. So method WriteLine displays "Sum is ", followed by the value of sum (in the position of the {0} format item) and a newline.

Performing Calculations in Output Statements
Calculations can also be performed inside output statements. We could have combined the statements in lines 22 and 24 into the statement

```
Console.WriteLine( "Sum is {0}", ( number1 + number2 ) );
```

The parentheses around the expression number1 + number2 are not required—they're included for clarity to emphasize that the value of the expression number1 + number2 is output in the position of the {0} format item.

3.7 Arithmetic

Most apps perform arithmetic calculations. The **arithmetic operators** are summarized in Fig. 3.15. Note the various special symbols not used in algebra. The **asterisk** (*) indicates multiplication, and the **percent sign** (%) is the **remainder operator** (called *modulus* in some languages), which we'll discuss shortly. The arithmetic operators in Fig. 3.15 are binary operators—for example, the expression f + 7 contains the binary operator + and the two operands f and 7.

C# operation	Arithmetic operator	Algebraic expression	C# expression
Addition	+	$f + 7$	f + 7
Subtraction	–	$p - c$	p - c
Multiplication	*	$b \cdot m$	b * m
Division	/	x / y or $\dfrac{x}{y}$ or $x \div y$	x / y
Remainder	%	$r \bmod s$	r % s

Fig. 3.15 | Arithmetic operators.

If both operands of the division operator (/) are integers, **integer division** is performed and the result is an integer—for example, the expression 7 / 4 evaluates to 1, and the expression 17 / 5 evaluates to 3. Any fractional part in integer division is simply *truncated* (i.e., discarded)—*no rounding* occurs. C# provides the remainder operator, %, which yields the remainder after division. The expression x % y yields the remainder after x is divided by y. Thus, 7 % 4 yields 3, and 17 % 5 yields 2. This operator is most commonly used with integer operands but can also be used with floats, doubles, and decimals.

Arithmetic Expressions in Straight-Line Form

Arithmetic expressions must be written in **straight-line form** to facilitate entering apps into the computer. Thus, expressions such as "a divided by b" must be written as a / b, so that all constants, variables and operators appear in a straight line. The following algebraic notation is not acceptable to compilers:

$$\frac{a}{b}$$

Parentheses for Grouping Subexpressions

Parentheses are used to group terms in C# expressions in the same manner as in algebraic expressions. For example, to multiply a times the quantity b + c, we write

```
a * ( b + c )
```

If an expression contains **nested parentheses**, such as

```
( ( a + b ) * c )
```

the expression in the *innermost* set of parentheses (a + b in this case) is evaluated first.

Rules of Operator Precedence

C# applies the operators in arithmetic expressions in a precise sequence determined by the following **rules of operator precedence**, which are generally the same as those followed in algebra (Fig. 3.16). These rules enable C# to apply operators in the correct order.[2]

Operators	Operations	Order of evaluation (associativity)
Evaluated first		
*	Multiplication	If there are several operators of this type,
/	Division	they're evaluated from left to right.
%	Remainder	
Evaluated next		
+	Addition	If there are several operators of this type,
–	Subtraction	they're evaluated from left to right.

Fig. 3.16 | Precedence of arithmetic operators.

---

2. We discuss simple examples here to explain the order of evaluation of expressions. More subtle order of evaluation issues occur in complex expressions. For more information, see the following blog posts from Eric Lippert: blogs.msdn.com/ericlippert/archive/2008/05/23/precedence-vs-associativity-vs-order.aspx and blogs.msdn.com/oldnewthing/archive/2007/08/14/4374222.aspx.

When we say that operators are applied from left to right, we're referring to their **associativity**. You'll see that some operators associate from right to left. Figure 3.16 summarizes these rules of operator precedence. The table will be expanded as additional operators are introduced. Appendix A provides the complete operator precedence chart.

3.8 Decision Making: Equality and Relational Operators

A **condition** is an expression that can be either **true** or **false**. This section introduces a simple version of C#'s **if statement** that allows an app to make a **decision** based on the value of a condition. For example, the condition "grade is greater than or equal to 60" determines whether a student passed a test. If the condition in an if statement is true, the body of the if statement executes. If the condition is false, the body does *not* execute. We'll see an example shortly.

Conditions in if statements can be formed by using the **equality operators** (== and !=) and **relational operators** (>, <, >= and <=) summarized in Fig. 3.17. The two equality operators (== and !=) each have the same level of precedence, the relational operators (>, <, >= and <=) each have the same level of precedence, and the equality operators have lower precedence than the relational operators. They all associate from left to right.

Common Programming Error 3.5

Confusing the equality operator, ==, with the assignment operator, =, can cause a logic error or a syntax error. The equality operator should be read as "is equal to," and the assignment operator should be read as "gets" or "gets the value of." To avoid confusion, some programmers read the equality operator as "double equals" or "equals equals."

Standard algebraic equality and relational operators	C# equality or relational operator	Sample C# condition	Meaning of C# condition
Relational operators			
>	>	x > y	x is greater than y
<	<	x < y	x is less than y
≥	>=	x >= y	x is greater than or equal to y
≤	<=	x <= y	x is less than or equal to y
Equality operators			
=	==	x == y	x is equal to y
≠	!=	x != y	x is not equal to y

Fig. 3.17 | Relational and equality operators.

Using the if Statement

Figure 3.18 uses six if statements to compare two integers entered by the user. If the condition in any of these if statements is true, the assignment statement associated with that if statement executes. The app uses class Console to prompt for and read two lines of text from the user, extracts the integers from that text with the ToInt32 method of class Convert, and stores them in variables `number1` and `number2`. Then the app compares the numbers and displays the results of the comparisons that are true.

```csharp
1   // Fig. 3.18: Comparison.cs
2   // Comparing integers using if statements, equality operators
3   // and relational operators.
4   using System;
5
6   public class Comparison
7   {
8      // Main method begins execution of C# app
9      public static void Main( string[] args )
10     {
11        int number1; // declare first number to compare
12        int number2; // declare second number to compare
13
14        // prompt user and read first number
15        Console.Write( "Enter first integer: " );
16        number1 = Convert.ToInt32( Console.ReadLine() );
17
18        // prompt user and read second number
19        Console.Write( "Enter second integer: " );
20        number2 = Convert.ToInt32( Console.ReadLine() );
21
22        if ( number1 == number2 )
23           Console.WriteLine( "{0} == {1}", number1, number2 );
24
25        if ( number1 != number2 )
26           Console.WriteLine( "{0} != {1}", number1, number2 );
27
28        if ( number1 < number2 )
29           Console.WriteLine( "{0} < {1}", number1, number2 );
30
31        if ( number1 > number2 )
32           Console.WriteLine( "{0} > {1}", number1, number2 );
33
34        if ( number1 <= number2 )
35           Console.WriteLine( "{0} <= {1}", number1, number2 );
36
37        if ( number1 >= number2 )
38           Console.WriteLine( "{0} >= {1}", number1, number2 );
39     } // end Main
40  } // end class Comparison
```

```
Enter first integer: 42
Enter second integer: 42
42 == 42
42 <= 42
42 >= 42
```

Fig. 3.18 | Comparing integers using `if` statements, equality operators and relational operators. (Part 1 of 2.)

```
Enter first integer: 1000
Enter second integer: 2000
1000 != 2000
1000 < 2000
1000 <= 2000
```

```
Enter first integer: 2000
Enter second integer: 1000
2000 != 1000
2000 > 1000
2000 >= 1000
```

Fig. 3.18 | Comparing integers using if statements, equality operators and relational operators. (Part 2 of 2.)

Class *Comparison*

The declaration of class Comparison begins at line 6

```
public class Comparison
```

The class's Main method (lines 9–39) begins the execution of the app.

Variable Declarations
Lines 11–12

```
int number1; // declare first number to compare
int number2; // declare second number to compare
```

declare the int variables used to store the values entered by the user.

Reading the Inputs from the User
Lines 14–16

```
// prompt user and read first number
Console.Write( "Enter first integer: " );
number1 = Convert.ToInt32( Console.ReadLine() );
```

prompt the user to enter the first integer and input the value. The input value is stored in variable number1. Lines 18–20

```
// prompt user and read second number
Console.Write( "Enter second integer: " );
number2 = Convert.ToInt32( Console.ReadLine() );
```

perform the same task, except that the input value is stored in variable number2.

Comparing Numbers
Lines 22–23

```
if ( number1 == number2 )
    Console.WriteLine( "{0} == {1}", number1, number2 );
```

compare the values of the variables number1 and number2 to determine whether they're equal. An if statement always begins with keyword if, followed by a condition in parentheses. An if statement expects *one* statement in its body. Line 23 executes only if the numbers stored in variables number1 and number2 are equal (i.e., the condition is true). The if statements in lines 25–26, 28–29, 31–32, 34–35 and 37–38 compare number1 and number2 with the operators !=, <, >, <= and >=, respectively. If the condition in any of the if statements is true, the corresponding body statement executes.

No Semicolon at the End of the First Line of an **if** *Statement*
There's no semicolon (;) at the end of the first line of each if statement. Such a semicolon would result in a logic error at execution time. For example,

```
if ( number1 == number2 ); // logic error
    Console.WriteLine( "{0} == {1}", number1, number2 );
```

would actually be interpreted by C# as

```
if ( number1 == number2 )
    ; // empty statement
Console.WriteLine( "{0} == {1}", number1, number2 );
```

where the semicolon in the line by itself—called the **empty statement**—is the statement to execute if the condition in the if statement is true. When the empty statement executes, no task is performed in the app. The app then continues with the output statement, which always executes, regardless of whether the condition is true or false, because the output statement is not part of the if statement.

Whitespace
Note the use of whitespace in Fig. 3.18. Recall that whitespace characters, such as tabs, newlines and spaces, are normally ignored by the compiler. So statements may be split over several lines and may be spaced according to your preferences without affecting the meaning of an app. It's incorrect to split identifiers, strings, and multicharacter operators (like >=). Ideally, statements should be kept small, but this is not always possible.

Good Programming Practice 3.8
Place no more than one statement per line in an app. This format enhances readability.

Good Programming Practice 3.9
A lengthy statement can be spread over several lines. If a single statement must be split across lines, choose breaking points that make sense, such as after a comma in a comma-separated list, or after an operator in a lengthy expression. If a statement is split across two or more lines, indent all subsequent lines until the end of the statement.

Precedence and Associativity of the Operators We've Discussed So Far
Figure 3.19 shows the precedence of the operators introduced in this chapter. The operators are shown from top to bottom in decreasing order of precedence. All these operators, with the exception of the assignment operator, =, associate from left to right. Addition is left associative, so an expression like x + y + z is evaluated as if it had been written as (x + y) + z. The assignment operator, =, associates from right to left, so an expression like x = y = 0 is

evaluated as if it had been written as x = (y = 0), which, as you'll soon see, first assigns the value 0 to variable y then assigns the result of that assignment, 0, to x.

Operators				Associativity	Type
*	/	%		left to right	multiplicative
+	−			left to right	additive
<	<=	>	>=	left to right	relational
==	!=			left to right	equality
=				right to left	assignment

Fig. 3.19 | Precedence and associativity of operations discussed so far.

3.9 Wrap-Up

You learned many important features of C# in this chapter. First you learned how to display data on the screen in a **Command Prompt** using the Console class's Write and WriteLine methods. Next, we showed how to use format strings and format items to create formatted output strings. You learned how to input data from the keyboard using the Console class's ReadLine method. We discussed how to perform calculations using C#'s arithmetic operators. Finally, you made decisions using the if statement and the relational and equality operators. As you'll see in Chapter 4, C# apps typically contain just a few lines of code in method Main—these statements normally create the objects that perform the work of the app. You'll implement your own classes and use objects of those classes in apps.

4

Introduction to Classes, Objects, Methods and **string**s

Objectives

In this chapter you'll:

- Declare a class and use it to create an object.
- Implement a class's behaviors as methods.
- Implement a class's attributes as instance variables and properties.
- Use **string** objects.
- Call an object's methods to make them perform their tasks.
- Understand the differences between instance variables of a class and local variables of a method.
- Use a constructor to initialize an object's data.

4.1 Introduction

In this chapter, we begin by explaining the concept of classes using a real-world example. Then we present five complete working apps to demonstrate how to create and use your own classes. The first four begin our case study on developing a grade book class that instructors can use to maintain student test scores. The last example introduces the type decimal and uses it to declare monetary amounts in the context of a bank account class that maintains a customer's balance.

4.2 Classes, Objects, Methods, Properties and Instance Variables

Let's begin with a simple analogy to help you understand classes and their contents. Suppose you want to drive a car and make it go faster by pressing down on its accelerator pedal. What must happen before you can do this? Well, before you can drive a car, someone has to design it. A car typically begins as engineering drawings, similar to the blueprints used to design a house. These engineering drawings include the design for an accelerator pedal to make the car go faster. The pedal "hides" the complex mechanisms that actually make the car go faster, just as the brake pedal "hides" the mechanisms that slow the car and the steering wheel "hides" the mechanisms that turn the car. This enables people with little or no knowledge of how engines work to drive a car easily.

Unfortunately, you can't drive the engineering drawings of a car. Before you can drive a car, it must be built from the engineering drawings that describe it. A completed car will have an actual accelerator pedal to make the car go faster, but even that's not enough—the car will not accelerate on its own, so the driver must press the accelerator pedal.

Methods

Now let's use our car example to introduce the key programming concepts of this section. Performing a task in an app requires a method. The **method** describes the mechanisms that actually perform its tasks. The method hides from its user the complex tasks that it performs, just as the accelerator pedal of a car hides from the driver the complex mechanisms of making the car go faster.

Classes

In C#, we begin by creating an app unit called a **class** to house (among other things) a method, just as a car's engineering drawings house (among other things) the design of an accelerator pedal. In a class, you provide one or more methods that are designed to perform the class's tasks. For example, a class that represents a bank account might contain one method to deposit money in an account, another to withdraw money from an account and a third to inquire what the current account balance is.

Objects

Just as you cannot drive an engineering drawing of a car, you cannot "drive" a class. Just as someone has to build a car from its engineering drawings before you can actually drive it, you must build an **object** of a class before you can make an app perform the tasks the class describes. That's one reason C# is known as an object-oriented programming language.

Method Calls

When you drive a car, pressing its gas pedal sends a message to the car to perform a task—make the car go faster. Similarly, you send **messages** to an object—each message is known as a **method call** and tells the called method of the object to perform its task.

Attributes

Thus far, we've used the car analogy to introduce classes, objects and methods. In addition to a car's capabilities, it also has many **attributes**, such as its color, the number of doors, the amount of gas in its tank, its current speed and its total miles driven (i.e., its odometer reading). Like the car's capabilities, these attributes are represented as part of a car's design in its engineering drawings. As you drive a car, these attributes are always associated with the car. Every car maintains its own attributes. For example, each car knows how much gas is in its own gas tank, but not how much is in the tanks of other cars. Similarly, an object has attributes that are carried with the object as it's used in an app. These attributes are specified as part of the object's class. For example, a bank-account object has a balance attribute that represents the amount of money in the account. Each bank-account object knows the balance in the account it represents, but not the balances of the other accounts in the bank. Attributes are specified by the class's **instance variables**.

Properties, get Accessors and set Accessors

Notice that these attributes are not necessarily accessible directly. The car manufacturer does not want drivers to take apart the car's engine to observe the amount of gas in its tank. Instead, the driver can check the fuel gauge on the dashboard. The bank does not want its customers to walk into the vault to count the amount of money in an account. Instead, the customers talk to a bank teller or check personalized online bank accounts. Similarly, you do not need to have access to an object's instance variables in order to use them. You should use the **properties** of an object. Properties contain **get accessors** for reading the values of variables, and **set accessors** for storing values into them.

4.3 Declaring a Class with a Method and Instantiating an Object of a Class

We begin with an example that consists of classes GradeBook (Fig. 4.1) and GradeBook-Test (Fig. 4.2). Class GradeBook (declared in file GradeBook.cs) will be used to display a message on the screen (Fig. 4.2) welcoming the instructor to the grade-book app. Class GradeBookTest (declared in the file GradeBookTest.cs) is a testing class in which the Main method will create and use an object of class GradeBook. By convention, we declare classes GradeBook and GradeBookTest in separate files, such that each file's name matches the name of the class it contains.

To start, select **File > New Project...** to open the **New Project** dialog, then create a GradeBook **Console Application**. Rename the Program.cs file to GradeBook.cs. Delete all the code provided automatically by the IDE and replace it with the code in Fig. 4.1.

```
1   // Fig. 4.1: GradeBook.cs
2   // Class declaration with one method.
3   using System;
4
5   public class GradeBook
6   {
7      // display a welcome message to the GradeBook user
8      public void DisplayMessage()
9      {
10        Console.WriteLine( "Welcome to the Grade Book!" );
11     } // end method DisplayMessage
12  } // end class GradeBook
```

Fig. 4.1 | Class declaration with one method.

Class *GradeBook*

The GradeBook **class declaration** (Fig. 4.1) contains a DisplayMessage method (lines 8–11) that displays a message on the screen. Line 10 of the class displays the message. Recall that a class is like a blueprint—we need to make an object of this class and call its method to get line 10 to execute and display its message—we do this in Fig. 4.2.

The class declaration begins in line 5. The keyword public is an **access modifier**. Access modifiers determine the accessibility of an object's properties and methods to other methods in an app. For now, we simply declare every class public. Every class declaration contains keyword class followed by the class's name. Every class's body is enclosed in a pair of left and right braces ({ and }), as in lines 6 and 12 of class GradeBook.

Declaration of Method *DisplayMessage*

In Chapter 3, each class we declared had only a Main method. Class GradeBook also has one method—DisplayMessage (lines 8–11). Recall that Main is a special method that's always called automatically when you execute an app. Most methods do *not* get called automatically. As you'll soon see, you must call method DisplayMessage to tell it to perform its task.

The method declaration begins with keyword public to indicate that the method is "available to the public"—that is, it can be called from outside the class declaration's body by methods of other classes. Keyword void—known as the method's **return type**—indicates that this method will *not* return (i.e., give back) any information to its **calling method** when it completes its task. When a method that specifies a return type other than void is called and completes its task, the method returns a result to its calling method. For example, when you go to an automated teller machine (ATM) and request your account balance, you expect the ATM to give you back a value that represents your balance. If you have a method Square that returns the square of its argument, you'd expect the statement

```
int result = Square( 2 );
```

to return 4 from method `Square` and assign 4 to variable `result`. If you have a method `Maximum` that returns the largest of three integer arguments, you'd expect the statement

```
int biggest = Maximum( 27, 114, 51 );
```

to return the value 114 from method `Maximum` and assign the value to variable `biggest`. You've already used methods that return information—for example, in Chapter 3 you used `Console` method `ReadLine` to input a string typed by the user at the keyboard. When `ReadLine` inputs a value, it *returns* that value for use in the app.

Method Name

The name of the method, `DisplayMessage`, follows the return type (line 8). Generally, methods are named as *verbs* or *verb phrases* while classes are named as *nouns*. By convention, method names begin with an uppercase first letter, and all subsequent words in the name begin with an uppercase letter. This naming convention is referred to as upper camel case. The parentheses after the method name indicate that this is a method. An empty set of parentheses, as shown in line 8, indicates that this method does *not* require additional information to perform its task. Line 8 is commonly referred to as the **method header**. Every method's body is delimited by left and right braces, as in lines 9 and 11.

Method Body

The body of a method contains statements that perform the method's task. In this case, the method contains one statement (line 10) that displays the message `"Welcome to the Grade Book!"`, followed by a newline in the console window. After this statement executes, the method has completed its task.

Using Class **GradeBook**

Next, we'd like to use class `GradeBook` in an app. As you learned in Chapter 3, method `Main` begins the execution of every app. Class `GradeBook` cannot begin an app because it does not contain `Main`. This was not a problem in Chapter 3, because every class you declared had a `Main` method. To fix this problem for the `GradeBook`, we must either declare a separate class that contains a `Main` method or place a `Main` method in class `GradeBook`. To help you prepare for the larger apps you'll encounter later in this book and in industry, we use a separate class (`GradeBookTest` in this example) containing method `Main` to test each new class we create in this chapter.

Adding a Class to a Visual C# Project

For each example in this chapter, you'll add a class to your console app. To do this, right click the project name in the **Solution Explorer** and select **Add > New Item...** from the pop-up menu. In the **Add New Item** dialog that appears, select **Code File**, enter the name of your new file (`GradeBookTest.cs`) then click **Add**. A new blank file will be added to your project. Add the code from Fig. 4.2 to this file.

Class **GradeBookTest**

The `GradeBookTest` class declaration (Fig. 4.2) contains the `Main` method that controls our app's execution. Any class that contains a `Main` method (as shown in line 6) can be used to execute an app. This class declaration begins in line 3 and ends in line 14. The class contains only a `Main` method, which is typical of many classes that simply begin an app's execution.

```
 1   // Fig. 4.2: GradeBookTest.cs
 2   // Create a GradeBook object and call its DisplayMessage method.
 3   public class GradeBookTest
 4   {
 5      // Main method begins program execution
 6      public static void Main( string[] args )
 7      {
 8         // create a GradeBook object and assign it to myGradeBook
 9         GradeBook myGradeBook = new GradeBook();
10
11         // call myGradeBook's DisplayMessage method
12         myGradeBook.DisplayMessage();
13      } // end Main
14   } // end class GradeBookTest
```

```
Welcome to the Grade Book!
```

Fig. 4.2 | Create a GradeBook object and call its DisplayMessage method.

Main Method

Lines 6–13 declare method Main. A key part of enabling the method Main to begin the app's execution is the static keyword (line 6), which indicates that Main is a static method. A static method is special because it can be called without first creating an object of the class (in this case, GradeBookTest) in which the method is declared. We explain static methods in Chapter 7, Methods: A Deeper Look.

Creating a GradeBook Object

In this app, we'd like to call class GradeBook's DisplayMessage method to display the welcome message in the console window. Typically, you cannot call a method that belongs to another class until you create an object of that class, as shown in line 9. We begin by declaring variable myGradeBook. The variable's type is GradeBook—the class we declared in Fig. 4.1. Each new class you create becomes a new *type* in C# that can be used to declare variables and create objects. New class types will be accessible to all classes in the same project. You can declare new class types as needed; this is one reason why C# is known as an **extensible language**.

Variable myGradeBook (line 9) is initialized with the result of the **object-creation expression** new GradeBook(). The new operator creates a new object of the class specified to the right of the keyword (i.e., GradeBook). The parentheses to the right of the GradeBook are required. As you'll learn in Section 4.10, those parentheses in combination with a class name represent a call to a constructor, which is similar to a method, but is used only at the time an object is created to initialize the object's data. In that section you'll see that data can be placed in parentheses to specify initial values for the object's data. For now, we simply leave the parentheses empty.

Calling the GradeBook Object's DisplayMessage Method

We can now use myGradeBook to call its method DisplayMessage. Line 12 calls the method DisplayMessage (lines 8–11 of Fig. 4.1) using variable myGradeBook followed by a **member access (.) operator**, the method name DisplayMessage and an empty set of parentheses. This call causes the `DisplayMessage` method to perform its task. This method call differs from the method calls in Chapter 3 that displayed information in a console window—each of those method calls provided arguments that specified the data to display. At the beginning of line 12 (Fig. 4.2), "`myGradeBook.`" indicates that `Main` should use the `GradeBook` object that was created in line 9. The empty parentheses in line 8 of Fig. 4.1 indicate that method `DisplayMessage` does not require additional information to perform its task. For this reason, the method call (line 12 of Fig. 4.2) specifies an empty set of parentheses after the method name to indicate that no arguments are being passed to method `DisplayMessage`. When method `DisplayMessage` completes its task, method `Main` continues executing at line 13. This is the end of method `Main`, so the app terminates.

*UML Class Diagram for Class **GradeBook***
Figure 4.3 presents a **UML class diagram** for class `GradeBook` of Fig. 4.1. Recall from Section 1.2 that the UML is a graphical language used by programmers to represent their object-oriented systems in a standardized manner. In the UML, each class is modeled in a class diagram as a rectangle with three compartments. The top compartment contains the name of the class centered horizontally in boldface type. The middle compartment contains the class's attributes, which correspond to instance variables and properties in C#. In Fig. 4.3, the middle compartment is empty because the version of class `GradeBook` in Fig. 4.1 does not have any attributes. The bottom compartment contains the class's operations, which correspond to methods in C#. The UML models operations by listing the operation name followed by a set of parentheses. Class `GradeBook` has one method, `DisplayMessage`, so the bottom compartment of Fig. 4.3 lists one operation with this name. Method `DisplayMessage` does not require additional information to perform its tasks, so there are empty parentheses following `DisplayMessage` in the class diagram, just as they appeared in the method's declaration in line 8 of Fig. 4.1. The plus sign (+) in front of the operation name indicates that `DisplayMessage` is a public operation in the UML (i.e., a `public` method in C#). The plus sign is sometimes called the **public visibility symbol**. We'll often use UML class diagrams to summarize a class's attributes and operations.

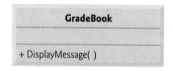

Fig. 4.3 | UML class diagram indicating that class `GradeBook` has a `public` `DisplayMessage` operation.

4.4 Declaring a Method with a Parameter

In our car analogy from Section 4.2, we discussed the fact that pressing a car's gas pedal sends a message to the car to perform a task—make the car go faster. But how fast should the car accelerate? As you know, the farther down you press the pedal, the faster the car accelerates. So the message to the car actually includes both the task to be performed and additional information that helps the car perform the task. This additional information is known as a **parameter**—the value of the parameter helps the car determine how fast to accelerate. Similarly, a method can require one or more parameters that represent additional information it needs to perform its task. A method call supplies values—called arguments—for each of the method's parameters. For example, the Console.WriteLine method requires an argument that specifies the data to be displayed in a console window. Similarly, to make a deposit into a bank account, a Deposit method specifies a parameter that represents the deposit amount. When the Deposit method is called, an argument value representing the deposit amount is assigned to the method's parameter. The method then makes a deposit of that amount, by increasing the account's balance.

Our next example declares class GradeBook (Fig. 4.4) with a DisplayMessage method that displays the course name as part of the welcome message. (See the sample execution in Fig. 4.5.) The new DisplayMessage method requires a parameter that represents the course name to output.

```
1   // Fig. 4.4: GradeBook.cs
2   // Class declaration with a method that has a parameter.
3   using System;
4
5   public class GradeBook
6   {
7      // display a welcome message to the GradeBook user
8      public void DisplayMessage( string courseName )
9      {
10         Console.WriteLine( "Welcome to the grade book for\n{0}!",
11            courseName );
12      } // end method DisplayMessage
13   } // end class GradeBook
```

Fig. 4.4 | Class declaration with a method that has a parameter.

```
1   // Fig. 4.5: GradeBookTest.cs
2   // Create a GradeBook object and pass a string to
3   // its DisplayMessage method.
4   using System;
5
6   public class GradeBookTest
7   {
8      // Main method begins program execution
9      public static void Main( string[] args )
10     {
11         // create a GradeBook object and assign it to myGradeBook
12         GradeBook myGradeBook = new GradeBook();
13
14         // prompt for and input course name
15         Console.WriteLine( "Please enter the course name:" );
16         string nameOfCourse = Console.ReadLine(); // read a line of text
17         Console.WriteLine(); // output a blank line
18
```

Fig. 4.5 | Create GradeBook object and pass a string to its DisplayMessage method. (Part 1 of 2.)

```
19          // call myGradeBook's DisplayMessage method
20          // and pass nameOfCourse as an argument
21          myGradeBook.DisplayMessage( nameOfCourse );
22      } // end Main
23   } // end class GradeBookTest
```

```
Please enter the course name:
CS101 Introduction to C# Programming

Welcome to the grade book for
CS101 Introduction to C# Programming!
```

Fig. 4.5 | Create `GradeBook` object and pass a `string` to its `DisplayMessage` method. (Part 2 of 2.)

Before discussing the new features of class `GradeBook`, let's see how the new class is used from the `Main` method of class `GradeBookTest` (Fig. 4.5). Line 12 creates an object of class `GradeBook` and assigns it to variable `myGradeBook`. Line 15 prompts the user to enter a course name. Line 16 reads the name from the user and assigns it to the variable `nameOfCourse`, using `Console` method `ReadLine` to perform the input. The user types the course name and presses *Enter* to submit the course name to the app. Pressing *Enter* inserts a newline character at the end of the characters typed by the user. Method `ReadLine` reads characters typed by the user until the newline character is encountered, then returns a `string` containing the characters up to, but not including, the newline. The newline character is *discarded*.

Line 21 calls `myGradeBook`'s `DisplayMessage` method. The variable `nameOfCourse` in parentheses is the argument that's passed to method `DisplayMessage` so that the method can perform its task. Variable `nameOfCourse`'s value in `Main` becomes the value of method `DisplayMessage`'s parameter `courseName` in line 8 of Fig. 4.4. When you execute this app, notice that method `DisplayMessage` outputs as part of the welcome message the name you type (Fig. 4.5).

Software Engineering Observation 4.1

Normally, objects are created with new. One exception is a string literal that's contained in quotes, such as "hello". String literals are string objects that are implicitly created by C# the first time they appear in the code.

More on Arguments and Parameters

When you declare a method, you must specify in the method's declaration whether the method requires data to perform its task. To do so, you place additional information in the method's **parameter list**, which is located in the parentheses that follow the method name. The parameter list may contain any number of parameters, including none at all. Each parameter is declared as a variable with a type and identifier in the parameter list. Empty parentheses following the method name (as in Fig. 4.1, line 8) indicate that a method does not require any parameters. In Fig. 4.4, `DisplayMessage`'s parameter list (line 8) declares that the method requires one parameter. Each parameter must specify a type and an identifier. In this case, the type `string` and the identifier `courseName` indicate that method `DisplayMessage` requires a `string` to perform its task. At the time the method is called, the argument value in the call is assigned to the corresponding parameter (in this case, `courseName`) in the method header. Then, the method body uses the parameter `courseName` to access the value. Lines 10–11 of Fig. 4.4 display parameter `courseName`'s value, using the `{0}` format item in `WriteLine`'s first argument. The parameter variable's name (Fig. 4.4, line 8) can be the same or different from the argument variable's name (Fig. 4.5, line 21).

A method can specify multiple parameters by separating each parameter from the next with a comma. The number of arguments in a method call must match the number of required parameters in the parameter list of the called method's declaration. Also, the types of the arguments in the method call must be consistent with the types of the corresponding parameters in the method's declaration. (As you'll see in subsequent chapters, an argument's type and its corresponding parameter's type are *not* always required to be identical.) In our example, the method call passes one argument of type `string` (`nameOfCourse` is declared as a `string` in line 16 of Fig. 4.5), and the method declaration specifies one parameter of type `string` (line 8 in Fig. 4.4). So the type of the argument in the method call exactly matches the type of the parameter in the method header.

Common Programming Error 4.1

A compilation error occurs if the number of arguments in a method call does not match the number of required parameters in the method declaration.

Common Programming Error 4.2

A compilation error occurs if the types of the arguments in a method call are not consistent with the types of the corresponding parameters in the method declaration.

Updated UML Class Diagram for Class **GradeBook**

The UML class diagram of Fig. 4.6 models class `GradeBook` of Fig. 4.4. Like Fig. 4.4, this `GradeBook` class contains `public` operation `DisplayMessage`. However, this version of `DisplayMessage` has a parameter. The UML models a parameter a bit differently from C# by listing the parameter name, followed by a colon and the parameter type in the parentheses following the operation name. The UML has several data types that are similar to the C# types. For example, UML types `String` and `Integer` correspond to C# types `string` and `int`, respectively. Unfortunately, the UML does not provide types that correspond to every C# type. For this reason, and to avoid confusion between UML types and C# types, *we use only C# types in our UML diagrams.* Class `Gradebook`'s method `Display-Message` (Fig. 4.4) has a `string` parameter named `courseName`, so Fig. 4.6 lists the parameter `courseName : string` between the parentheses following `DisplayMessage`.

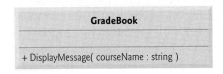

GradeBook
+ DisplayMessage(courseName : string)

Fig. 4.6 | UML class diagram indicating that class `GradeBook` has a public `DisplayMessage` operation with a `courseName` parameter of type `string`.

Notes on using Directives
Notice the `using` directive in Fig. 4.5 (line 4). This indicates to the compiler that the app uses classes in the `System` namespace, like the `Console` class. Why do we need a `using` directive to use class `Console`, but not class `GradeBook`? There's a special relationship between classes that are compiled in the same project, like classes `GradeBook` and `GradeBookTest`. By default, such classes are considered to be in the same namespace. A `using` directive is not required when one class in a namespace uses another in the same namespace—such as when class `GradeBookTest` uses class `GradeBook`. For simplicity, our examples in this chapter do not declare a namespace. Any classes that are not *explicitly* placed in a namespace are *implicitly* placed in the so-called **global namespace**.

Actually, the `using` directive in line 4 is not required if we always refer to class `Console` as `System.Console`, which includes the full namespace and class name. This is known as the class's **fully qualified class name**. For example, line 15 could be written as

```
System.Console.WriteLine( "Please enter the course name:" );
```

Most C# programmers consider using fully qualified names to be cumbersome, and instead prefer to use `using` directives.

4.5 Instance Variables and Properties

In Chapter 3, we declared all of an app's variables in the `Main` method. Variables declared in the body of a method are known as **local variables** and can be used only in that method. When a method terminates, the values of its local variables are lost. Recall from Section 4.2 that an object has attributes that are carried with it as it's used in an app. Such attributes exist before a method is called on an object and after the method completes execution.

Attributes are represented as variables in a class declaration. Such variables are called **fields** and are declared *inside* a class declaration but *outside* the bodies of the class's method declarations. When each object of a class maintains its own copy of an attribute, the field that represents the attribute is also known as an instance variable—each object (instance) of the class has a separate instance of the variable. In Chapter 10, we discuss another type of field called a `static` variable, where all objects of the same class share one variable.

A class normally contains one or more properties that manipulate the attributes that belong to a particular object of the class. The example in this section demonstrates a `GradeBook` class that contains a `courseName` instance variable to represent a particular `GradeBook` object's course name, and a `CourseName` property to manipulate `courseName`.

GradeBook Class with an Instance Variable and a Property
In our next app (Figs. 4.7–4.8), class `GradeBook` (Fig. 4.7) maintains the course name as an instance variable so that it can be used or modified at any time during an app's execution. The class also contains one method—`DisplayMessage` (lines 24–30)—and one property—`CourseName` (line 11–21). Recall from Chapter 2 that properties are used to manipulate an object's *attributes*. For example, in that chapter, we used a `Label`'s `Text` property to specify the text to display on the `Label`. In this example, we use a property in code rather than in the **Properties** window of the IDE. To do this, we first declare a property as a member of the `GradeBook` class. As you'll soon see, the `GradeBook`'s `CourseName` property can be used to store a course name in a `GradeBook` (in instance variable `course-`

Name) or retrieve the GradeBook's course name (from instance variable courseName). Method DisplayMessage—which now specifies no parameters—still displays a welcome message that includes the course name. However, the method now uses the CourseName property to obtain the course name from instance variable courseName.

```csharp
1    // Fig. 4.7: GradeBook.cs
2    // GradeBook class that contains a private instance variable, courseName,
3    // and a public property to get and set its value.
4    using System;
5
6    public class GradeBook
7    {
8       private string courseName; // course name for this GradeBook
9
10      // property to get and set the course name
11      public string CourseName
12      {
13         get
14         {
15            return courseName;
16         } // end get
17         set
18         {
19            courseName = value;
20         } // end set
21      } // end property CourseName
22
23      // display a welcome message to the GradeBook user
24      public void DisplayMessage()
25      {
26         // use property CourseName to get the
27         // name of the course that this GradeBook represents
28         Console.WriteLine( "Welcome to the grade book for\n{0}!",
29            CourseName ); // display property CourseName
30      } // end method DisplayMessage
31   } // end class GradeBook
```

Fig. 4.7 | GradeBook class that contains a private instance variable, courseName, and a public property to get and set its value.

A typical instructor teaches more than one course, each with its own course name. Line 8 declares courseName as a variable of type string. Line 8 is a declaration for an instance variable, because the variable is declared in the class's body (lines 7–31) but outside the bodies of the class's method (lines 24–30) and property (lines 11–21). Every instance (i.e., object) of class GradeBook contains one copy of each instance variable. For example, if there are two GradeBook objects, each object has its own copy of courseName. All the methods and properties of class GradeBook can directly manipulate its instance variable courseName, but it's considered good practice for methods of a class to use that class's properties to manipulate instance variables (as we do in line 29 of method DisplayMessage). The software engineering reasons for this will soon become clear.

Access Modifiers *public* and *private*

Most instance-variable declarations are preceded with the keyword `private` (as in line 8). Like `public`, keyword `private` is an access modifier. Variables, properties or methods declared with access modifier `private` are accessible *only* to members (such as properties and methods) of the class in which they're declared. Thus, variable `courseName` can be used *only* in property `CourseName` and method `DisplayMessage` of class `GradeBook`.

Software Engineering Observation 4.2

Precede every field and method declaration with an access modifier. Generally, instance variables should be declared `private` and methods and properties should be declared `public`. If the access modifier is omitted before a member of a class, the member is implicitly declared `private`. We'll see that it's appropriate to declare certain methods `private`, if they will be accessed only by other methods of the class.

Software Engineering Observation 4.3

Declaring the instance variables of a class as `private` and the methods and properties of the class as `public` facilitates debugging, because problems with data manipulations are localized to the class's methods and properties, since the `private` instance variables are accessible only to these methods and properties.

Declaring instance variables with access modifier `private` is known as **information hiding** (or **encapsulation**). When an app creates (instantiates) an object of class Grade-Book, variable `courseName` is encapsulated (hidden) in the object and can be accessed only by members of the object's class.

Setting and Getting the Values of *private* Instance Variables

How can we allow a program to manipulate a class's `private` instance variables but ensure that they remain in a valid state? We need to provide *controlled* ways for programmers to "get" (i.e., retrieve) the value in an instance variable and "set" (i.e., modify) the value in an instance variable. Although you can define methods like `GetCourseName` and `SetCourse-Name`, C# properties provide a more elegant solution. Next, we show how to declare and use properties.

GradeBook Class with a Property

The `GradeBook` class's `CourseName` **property declaration** is located in lines 11–21 of Fig. 4.7. The property begins in line 11 with an access modifier (in this case, `public`), followed by the type that the property represents (`string`) and the property's name (`Course-Name`). Properties use the *same* naming conventions as methods and classes.

Properties contain **accessors** that handle the details of returning and modifying data. A property declaration can contain a `get` accessor, a `set` accessor or both. The `get` accessor (lines 13–16) enables a client to read the value of `private` instance variable `courseName`; the `set` accessor (lines 17–20) enables a client to modify `courseName`.

After defining a property, you can use it like a variable in your code. For example, you can assign a value to a property using the = (assignment) operator. This executes the property's `set` accessor to set the value of the corresponding instance variable. Similarly, referencing the property to use its value (for example, to display it on the screen) executes the code in the property's `get` accessor to obtain the corresponding *instance variable's* value. We show

how to use properties shortly. By convention, we name each property with the capitalized name of the instance variable that it manipulates (e.g., CourseName is the property that represents instance variable courseName)—C# is case sensitive, so these are distinct identifiers.

get and set Accessors

Let us look more closely at property CourseName's get and set accessors (Fig. 4.7). The get accessor (lines 13–16) begins with the identifier **get** and its body is delimited by braces. The accessor's body contains a **return statement**, which consists of the keyword **return** followed by an expression. The expression's value is returned to the client code that uses the property. In this example, the value of courseName is returned when the property CourseName is referenced. For example, in the following statement

```
string theCourseName = gradeBook.CourseName;
```

the expression gradeBook.CourseName (where gradeBook is an object of class GradeBook) executes property CourseName's get accessor, which returns the value of instance variable courseName. That value is then stored in variable theCourseName. Property CourseName can be used *as simply as if it were an instance variable.* The property notation allows the client to think of the property as the underlying data. Again, the client cannot directly manipulate instance variable courseName because it's private.

The set accessor (lines 17–20) begins with the identifier **set** and its body is delimited by braces. When the property CourseName appears in an assignment statement, as in

```
gradeBook.CourseName = "CS100 Introduction to Computers";
```

the text "CS100 Introduction to Computers" is assigned to the set accessor's contextual keyword named **value** and the set accessor executes. Note that value is *implicitly* declared and initialized in the set accessor—it's a compilation error to declare a local variable value in this body. Line 19 stores the contents of value in instance variable courseName. A set accessor does not return any data when it completes its task.

The statements inside the property in lines 15 and 19 (Fig. 4.7) each access courseName even though it was declared outside the property. We can use instance variable courseName in the methods and properties of class GradeBook, because courseName is an instance variable of the class.

Using Property CourseName in Method DisplayMessage

Method DisplayMessage (lines 24–30 of Fig. 4.7) does not receive any parameters. Lines 28–29 output a welcome message that includes the value of instance variable courseName. We do not reference courseName directly. Instead, we access property CourseName (line 29), which executes the property's get accessor, returning the value of courseName.

GradeBookTest Class That Demonstrates Class GradeBook

Class GradeBookTest (Fig. 4.8) creates a GradeBook object and demonstrates property CourseName. Line 11 creates a GradeBook object and assigns it to local variable myGradeBook. Lines 14–15 display the initial course name using the object's CourseName property—this executes the property's get accessor, which returns the value of courseName.

The first line of the output shows an empty name (marked by single quotes, ''). Unlike local variables, which are not automatically initialized, every field has a **default initial value**—a value provided by C# when you do not specify the initial value. Thus, fields are *not* required to be explicitly initialized before they're used in an app—unless they must be initialized to values *other* than their default values. The default value for an instance variable of type `string` (like courseName) is null. When you display a `string` variable that contains the value null, no text is displayed on the screen.

```
1   // Fig. 4.8: GradeBookTest.cs
2   // Create and manipulate a GradeBook object.
3   using System;
4
5   public class GradeBookTest
6   {
7      // Main method begins program execution
8      public static void Main( string[] args )
9      {
10        // create a GradeBook object and assign it to myGradeBook
11        GradeBook myGradeBook = new GradeBook();
12
13        // display initial value of CourseName
14        Console.WriteLine( "Initial course name is: '{0}'\n",
15           myGradeBook.CourseName );
16
17        // prompt for and read course name
18        Console.WriteLine( "Please enter the course name:" );
19        myGradeBook.CourseName = Console.ReadLine(); // set CourseName
20        Console.WriteLine(); // output a blank line
21
22        // display welcome message after specifying course name
23        myGradeBook.DisplayMessage();
24     } // end Main
25  } // end class GradeBookTest
```

```
Initial course name is: ''

Please enter the course name:
CS101 Introduction to C# Programming

Welcome to the grade book for
CS101 Introduction to C# Programming!
```

Fig. 4.8 | Create and manipulate a GradeBook object.

Line 18 prompts the user to enter a course name. Line 19 assigns the course name entered by the user to object myGradeBook's CourseName property. When a value is assigned to CourseName, the value specified (which is returned by ReadLine in this case) is assigned to implicit parameter value of CourseName's set accessor (lines 17–20, Fig. 4.7). Then parameter value is assigned by the set accessor to instance variable courseName (line 19 of Fig. 4.7). Line 20 (Fig. 4.8) displays a blank line, then line 23 calls myGradeBook's DisplayMessage method to display the welcome message containing the course name.

4.6 UML Class Diagram with a Property

Figure 4.9 contains an updated UML class diagram for the version of class GradeBook in Fig. 4.7. We model properties in the UML as attributes—the property (in this case,

CourseName) is listed as a *public* attribute—as indicated by the plus (+) sign—preceded by the word "property" in **guillemets** (« and »). Using descriptive words in guillemets (called **stereotypes** in the UML) helps distinguish properties from other attributes and operations. The UML indicates the type of the property by placing a colon and a type after the property name. The get and set accessors of the property are implied, so they're not listed in the UML diagram. Class GradeBook also contains one public method Display-Message, so the class diagram lists this operation in the third compartment. Recall that the plus (+) sign is the public visibility symbol.

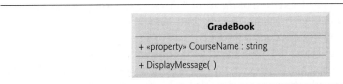

Fig. 4.9 | UML class diagram indicating that class GradeBook has a public CourseName property of type string and one public method.

A class diagram helps you design a class, so it's not required to show every implementation detail of the class. Since an instance variable that's manipulated by a property is really an implementation detail of that property, our class diagram does *not* show the courseName instance variable. A programmer implementing the GradeBook class based on this class diagram would create the instance variable courseName as part of the implementation process (as we did in Fig. 4.7).

In some cases, you may find it necessary to model the private instance variables of a class. Like properties, instance variables are attributes of a class and are modeled in the *middle* compartment of a class diagram. The UML represents instance variables as attributes by listing the attribute name, followed by a colon and the attribute type. To indicate that an attribute is private, a class diagram would list the **private visibility symbol**—a minus sign (-)—before the attribute's name. For example, the instance variable course-Name in Fig. 4.7 would be modeled as "- courseName : string" to indicate that it's a private attribute of type string.

4.7 Software Engineering with Properties and set and get Accessors

Using properties as described earlier in this chapter would seem to *violate* the notion of private data. Although providing a property with get and set accessors may appear to be the same as making its corresponding instance variable public, this is *not* the case. A public instance variable can be read or written by any property or method in the program. If an instance variable is private, the client code can access the instance variable only *indirectly* through the class's non-private properties or methods. This allows the class to *control* the manner in which the data is set or returned. For example, get and set accessors can translate between the format of the data stored in the private instance variable and the format of the data preferred by the client.

Validation

Consider a `Clock` class that represents the time of day as a `private int` instance variable `time`, containing the number of seconds since midnight. Suppose the class provides a `Time` property of type `string` to manipulate this instance variable. Although `get` accessors typically return data *exactly* as it's stored in an object, they need *not* expose the data in this "raw" format. When a client refers to a `Clock` object's `Time` property, the property's `get` accessor could use instance variable `time` to determine the number of hours, minutes and seconds since midnight, then return the time as a `string` of the form `"hh:mm:ss"` in which `hh` represents the hour, `mm` the minute and `ss` the second. Similarly, suppose a `Clock` object's `Time` property is assigned a `string` of the form `"hh:mm:ss"`. Using the `string` capabilities presented in Chapter 16, and the method `Convert.ToInt32` presented in Section 3.6, the `Time` property's `set` accessor can convert this `string` to an `int` number of seconds since midnight and store the result in the `Clock` object's `private` instance variable `time`. The `Time` property's `set` accessor can also provide **data-validation** capabilities that scrutinize attempts to modify the instance variable's value to ensure that the value it receives represents a valid time (e.g., `"12:30:45"` is valid but `"42:85:70"` is not). We demonstrate data validation in Section 4.11. So, although a property's accessors enable clients to manipulate `private` data, they carefully control those manipulations, and the object's `private` data remains safely *encapsulated* (i.e., hidden) in the object. This is not possible with `public` instance variables, which can easily be set by clients to *invalid* values.

Manipulating Data within a Class Via the Class's Properties

Properties of a class should also be used by the class's own methods to manipulate the class's `private` instance variables, even though the methods can directly access the `private` instance variables. Accessing an instance variable via a property's accessors—as in the body of method `DisplayMessage` (Fig. 4.7, lines 28–29)—creates a more robust class that's easier to maintain and less likely to malfunction. If we decide to change the representation of instance variable `courseName` in some way, the declaration of method `DisplayMessage` does not require modification—only the bodies of property `CourseName`'s `get` and `set` accessors that directly manipulate the instance variable will need to change. For example, suppose we want to represent the course name as two *separate* instance variables—`courseNumber` (e.g., `"CS101"`) and `courseTitle` (e.g., `"Introduction to C# Programming"`). The `DisplayMessage` method can still use property `CourseName`'s `get` accessor to obtain the full course name to display as part of the welcome message. In this case, the `get` accessor would need to build and return a `string` containing the `courseNumber`, followed by the `courseTitle`. Method `DisplayMessage` would continue to display the complete course title "CS101 Introduction to C# Programming," because it's unaffected by the change to the class's instance variables.

4.8 Auto-Implemented Properties

In Fig. 4.7, we created a `GradeBook` class with a `private courseName` instance variable and a `public` property `CourseName` to enable client code to access the `courseName`. When you look at the `CourseName` property's definition (Fig. 4.7, lines 11–21), notice that the `get` accessor simply returns `private` instance variable `courseName`'s value and the `set` accessor simply assigns a value to the instance variable—no other logic appears in the accessors. For such cases, C# provides **automatically implemented properties** (also known as **auto-**

implemented properties). With an auto-implemented property, the C# compiler creates a `private` instance variable, and the `get` and `set` accessors for returning and modifying the `private` instance variable. Unlike a user-defined property, an auto-implemented property, must have *both* a `get` and a `set` accessor. This enables you to implement the property trivially, which is handy when you're first designing a class. If you later decide to include other logic in the `get` or `set` accessors, you can simply modify the property's implementation. To use an auto-implemented property in the `GradeBook` class of Fig. 4.7, you can replace the `private` instance variable at line 8 and the property at lines 11–21 with the following code:

```
public string CourseName { get; set; }
```

Code Snippets for Auto-Implemented Properties

The IDE has a feature called **code snippets** that allows you to insert *predefined code templates* into your source code. One such snippet enables you to insert a `public` auto-implemented property by typing the word "prop" in the code window and pressing the *Tab* key twice. Certain pieces of the inserted code are highlighted for you to easily change the property's type and name. You can press the *Tab* key to move from one highlighted piece of text to the next in the inserted code. By default, the new property's type is `int` and its name is MyProperty. To get a list of all available code snippets, type *Ctrl + k, Ctrl + x*. This displays the **Insert Snippet** window in the code editor. You can navigate through the Visual C# snippet folders with the mouse to see the snippets. This feature can also be accessed by *right clicking* in the source code editor and selecting the **Insert Snippet...** menu item.

4.9 Value Types vs. Reference Types

Types in C# are divided into two categories—**value types** and **reference types**.

Value Types

C#'s simple types (like `int` and `double`) are all value types. A variable of a value type simply contains a *value* of that type. For example, Fig. 4.10 shows an `int` variable named `count` that contains the value 7.

```
int count = 7;
```

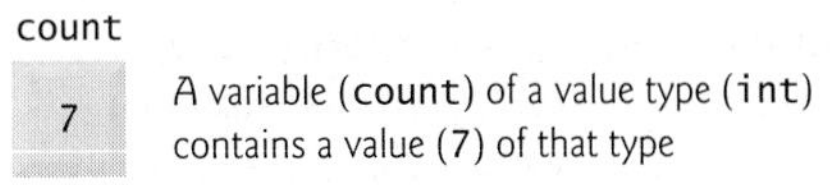

count

7	A variable (`count`) of a value type (`int`) contains a value (7) of that type

Fig. 4.10 | Value-type variable.

Reference Types

By contrast, a reference-type variable (sometimes called a **reference**) contains the *address* of a location in memory where the data referred to by that variable is stored. Such a variable is said to **refer to an object** in the program. Line 11 of Fig. 4.8 creates a `GradeBook` object, places it in memory and stores the object's reference in variable myGradeBook of type GradeBook as shown in Fig. 4.11. The `GradeBook` object is shown with its courseName instance variable.

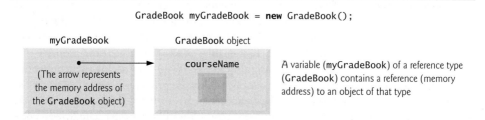

Fig. 4.11 | Reference-type variable.

Reference-Type Instance Variables Initialized to null

Reference-type instance variables (such as `myGradeBook` in Fig. 4.11) are initialized by default to the value **null**. `string` is a reference type. For this reason, `string` variable `course-Name` is shown in Fig. 4.11 with an empty box representing the `null`-valued variable. A `string` variable with the value `null` is *not* an empty string, which is represented by `""` or `string.Empty`. The value `null` represents a reference that does *not* refer to an object. The empty string is a `string` object with *no* characters in it.

Using a Variable That Refers to an Object to Send Messages to the Object

A client of an object must use a variable that refers to the object to **invoke** (i.e., call) the object's methods and access the object's properties. In Fig. 4.8, the statements in `Main` use variable `myGradeBook`, which contains the `GradeBook` object's reference, to send *messages* to the `GradeBook` object. These messages are calls to methods (like `DisplayMessage`) or references to properties (like `CourseName`) that enable the program to interact with `Grade-Book` objects. For example, the statement (in line 19 of Fig. 4.8)

```
myGradeBook.CourseName = Console.ReadLine(); // set CourseName
```

uses the reference `myGradeBook` to set the course name by assigning a value to property `CourseName`. This sends a message to the `GradeBook` object to invoke the `CourseName` property's `set` accessor. The message includes as an argument the value read from the user's input (in this case, `"CS101 Introduction to C# Programming"`) that `CourseName`'s `set` accessor requires to perform its task. The `set` accessor uses this information to set the `courseName` instance variable. In Section 7.16, we discuss value types and reference types in detail.

> ### Software Engineering Observation 4.4
>
> *A variable's declared type (e.g., `int`, `double` or `GradeBook`) indicates whether the variable is of a value type or a reference type. If a variable's type is not one of the simple types (Appendix B), or an `enum` or a `struct` type (which we discuss in Section 7.10 and Chapter 16, respectively), then it's a reference type. For example, `Account account1` indicates that `account1` is a variable that can refer to an `Account` object.*

4.10 Initializing Objects with Constructors

As mentioned in Section 4.5, when a `GradeBook` (Fig. 4.7) object is created, its instance variable `courseName` is initialized to `null` by default. This is also true of the `private` instance variable that the compiler creates for the auto-implemented `CourseName` property discussed in Section 4.8. What if you want to provide a course name when you create a

GradeBook object? Each class can provide a **constructor** that can be used to *initialize* an object of a class when the object is created. In fact, C# requires a constructor call for *every* object that's created. The new operator calls the class's constructor to perform the initialization. The constructor call is indicated by the class name, followed by parentheses. For example, line 11 of Fig. 4.8 first uses new to create a GradeBook object. The empty parentheses after "new GradeBook()" indicate a call *without arguments* to the class's constructor. The compiler provides a **public default constructor** with *no* parameters in any class that does not *explicitly* define a constructor, so *every* class has a constructor. The default constructor does *not* modify the default values of the instance variables.

Custom Initialization with Constructors

When you declare a class, you can provide your own constructor (or several, as you'll see in Chapter 10) to specify custom initialization for objects of your class. For example, you might want to specify a course name for a GradeBook object when the object is created, as in

```
GradeBook myGradeBook =
    new GradeBook( "CS101 Introduction to C# Programming" );
```

In this case, the argument "CS101 Introduction to C# Programming" is passed to the GradeBook object's constructor and used to initialize the CourseName. Each time you create a *new* GradeBook object, you can provide a *different* course name. The preceding statement requires that the class provide a constructor with a string parameter. Figure 4.12 contains a modified GradeBook class with such a constructor.

```
1   // Fig. 4.12: GradeBook.cs
2   // GradeBook class with a constructor to initialize the course name.
3   using System;
4
5   public class GradeBook
6   {
7      // auto-implemented property CourseName implicitly created an
8      // instance variable for this GradeBook's course name
9      public string CourseName { get; set; }
10
11     // constructor initializes auto-implemented property
12     // CourseName with string supplied as argument
13     public GradeBook( string name )
14     {
15        CourseName = name; // set CourseName to name
16     } // end constructor
17
18     // display a welcome message to the GradeBook user
19     public void DisplayMessage()
20     {
21        // use auto-implemented property CourseName to get the
22        // name of the course that this GradeBook represents
23        Console.WriteLine( "Welcome to the grade book for\n{0}!",
24           CourseName );
25     } // end method DisplayMessage
26  } // end class GradeBook
```

Fig. 4.12 | GradeBook class with a constructor to initialize the course name.

Declaring a Constructor

Lines 13–16 declare the constructor for class `GradeBook`. *A constructor must have the same name as its class.* Like a method, a constructor specifies in its parameter list the data it requires to perform its task. When you use `new` to create an object, you place this data in the parentheses that follow the class name. Unlike a method, a constructor doesn't specify a return type, not even `void`. Line 13 indicates that class `GradeBook`'s constructor has a parameter called `name` of type `string`. In line 15, the `name` passed to the constructor is used to initialize auto-implemented property `CourseName` via its `set` accessor.

Initializing GradeBook Objects with a Custom Constructor

Figure 4.13 demonstrates initializing `GradeBook` objects using this constructor. Lines 12–13 create and initialize a `GradeBook` object. The constructor of class `GradeBook` is called with the argument `"CS101 Introduction to C# Programming"` to initialize the course name. The *object-creation expression* to the right of = in lines 12–13 returns a reference to the new object, which is assigned to variable `gradeBook1`. Lines 14–15 repeat this process for another `GradeBook` object, this time passing the argument `"CS102 Data Structures in C#"` to initialize the course name for `gradeBook2`. Lines 18–21 use each object's `Course-Name` property to obtain the course names and show that they were indeed initialized when the objects were created. In Section 4.5, you learned that each instance (i.e., object) of a class contains its own copy of the class's instance variables. The output confirms that each `GradeBook` maintains its own course name.

```
1    // Fig. 4.13: GradeBookTest.cs
2    // GradeBook constructor used to specify the course name at the
3    // time each GradeBook object is created.
4    using System;
5
6    public class GradeBookTest
7    {
8       // Main method begins program execution
9       public static void Main( string[] args )
10      {
11         // create GradeBook object
12         GradeBook gradeBook1 = new GradeBook( // invokes constructor
13            "CS101 Introduction to C# Programming" );
14         GradeBook gradeBook2 = new GradeBook( // invokes constructor
15            "CS102 Data Structures in C#" );
16
17         // display initial value of courseName for each GradeBook
18         Console.WriteLine( "gradeBook1 course name is: {0}",
19            gradeBook1.CourseName );
20         Console.WriteLine( "gradeBook2 course name is: {0}",
21            gradeBook2.CourseName );
22      } // end Main
23   } // end class GradeBookTest
```

Fig. 4.13 | GradeBook constructor used to specify the course name at the time each GradeBook object is created. (Part 1 of 2.)

```
gradeBook1 course name is: CS101 Introduction to C# Programming
gradeBook2 course name is: CS102 Data Structures in C#
```

Fig. 4.13 | GradeBook constructor used to specify the course name at the time each GradeBook object is created. (Part 2 of 2.)

Normally, constructors are declared public. If a class does not *explicitly* define a constructor, the class's instance variables are initialized to their default values—0 for numeric types, false for type bool and null for reference types. If you declare any constructors for a class, C# will *not* create a default constructor for that class.

Error-Prevention Tip 4.1

Unless default initialization of your class's instance variables is acceptable, provide a constructor to ensure that your class's instance variables are initialized with meaningful values when each new object of your class is created.

*Adding the Constructor to Class **GradeBook**'s UML Class Diagram*
The UML class diagram of Fig. 4.14 models class GradeBook of Fig. 4.12, which has a constructor that has a name parameter of type string. Like operations, the UML models constructors in the third compartment of a class in a class diagram. To distinguish a constructor from a class's operations, the UML places the word "constructor" between guillemets (« and ») before the constructor's name. It's customary to list constructors before other operations in the third compartment.

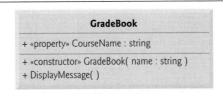

Fig. 4.14 | UML class diagram indicating that class GradeBook has a constructor with a name parameter of type string.

4.11 Floating-Point Numbers and Type decimal

In our next app, we depart temporarily from our GradeBook case study to declare a class called Account that maintains a bank account's balance. Most account balances are not whole numbers (such as 0, –22 and 1024), rather they're numbers that include a decimal point, such as 99.99 or –20.15. For this reason, class Account represents the account balance as a real number. C# provides three simple types for storing real numbers—float, **double**, and decimal. Types float and double are called **floating-point** types. The primary difference between them and decimal is that decimal variables store a limited range of real numbers *precisely*, whereas floating-point variables store only *approximations* of real numbers, but across a much greater range of values. Also, double variables can store numbers with larger magnitude and finer detail (i.e., more digits to the right of the decimal point—also known as the number's **precision**) than `float` variables. A key use of type `decimal` is representing *monetary amounts*.

Real-Number Precision and Storage Requirements

Variables of type `float` represent **single-precision floating-point numbers** and have *seven* significant digits. Variables of type `double` represent **double-precision floating-point numbers**. These require twice as much storage as `float` variables and provide 15–16 significant digits—approximately double the precision of `float` variables. Variables of type `decimal` require twice as much storage as `double` variables and provide 28–29 significant digits. In some apps, even variables of type `double` and `decimal` will be inadequate—such apps are beyond the scope of this book.

Most programmers represent floating-point numbers with type `double`. In fact, C# treats *all* real numbers you type in an app's source code (such as `7.33` and `0.0975`) as `double` values by default. Such values in the source code are known as **floating-point literals**. To type a **decimal literal**, you must type the letter "M" or "m" (which stands for "money") at the end of a real number (for example, `7.33M` is a decimal literal rather than a `double`). Integer literals are implicitly converted into type `float`, `double` or `decimal` when they're assigned to a variable of one of these types. See Appendix B for the ranges of values for `float`s, `double`s, `decimal`s and all the other simple types.

Although floating-point numbers are not always 100% precise, they have numerous applications. For example, when we speak of a "normal" body temperature of 98.6, we do not need to be precise to a large number of digits. When we read the temperature on a thermometer as 98.6, it may actually be 98.5999473210643. Calling this number simply 98.6 is fine for most applications involving body temperatures. Due to the imprecise nature of floating-point numbers, type `decimal` is preferred over the floating-point types whenever the calculations need to be exact, as with monetary calculations. In cases where approximation is enough, `double` is preferred over type `float` because `double` variables can represent floating-point numbers more accurately. For this reason, we use type `decimal` throughout the book for monetary amounts and type `double` for other real numbers.

Real numbers also arise as a result of division. In conventional arithmetic, for example, when we divide 10 by 3, the result is 3.3333333…, with the sequence of 3s repeating *infinitely*. The computer allocates only a fixed amount of space to hold such a value, so clearly the stored floating-point value can be only an approximation.

 Common Programming Error 4.3
Using floating-point numbers in a manner that assumes they're represented precisely can lead to logic errors.

Account Class with an Instance Variable of Type `decimal`

Our next app (Figs. 4.15–4.16) contains a simple class named `Account` (Fig. 4.15) that maintains the balance of a bank account. A typical bank services *many* accounts, each with its *own* balance, so line 7 declares an instance variable named `balance` of type `decimal`. Variable `balance` is an *instance variable* because it's declared *in* the body of the class (lines 6–36) but *outside* the class's method and property declarations (lines 10–13, 16–19 and 22–35). Every instance (i.e., object) of class `Account` contains its own copy of `balance`.

```
 1   // Fig. 4.15: Account.cs
 2   // Account class with a constructor to
 3   // initialize instance variable balance.
 4
 5   public class Account
 6   {
 7      private decimal balance; // instance variable that stores the balance
 8
 9      // constructor
10      public Account( decimal initialBalance )
11      {
12         Balance = initialBalance; // set balance using property
13      } // end Account constructor
14
15      // credit (add) an amount to the account
16      public void Credit( decimal amount )
17      {
18         Balance = Balance + amount; // add amount to balance
19      } // end method Credit
20
21      // a property to get and set the account balance
22      public decimal Balance
23      {
24         get
25         {
26            return balance;
27         } // end get
28         set
29         {
30            // validate that value is greater than or equal to 0;
31            // if it is not, balance is left unchanged
32            if ( value >= 0 )
33               balance = value;
34         } // end set
35      } // end property Balance
36   } // end class Account
```

Fig. 4.15 | Account class with a constructor to initialize instance variable `balance`.

Account *Class Constructor*

Class `Account` contains a constructor, a method, and a property. Since it's common for someone opening an account to place money in the account immediately, the constructor (lines 10–13) receives a parameter `initialBalance` of type `decimal` that represents the account's starting balance. Line 12 assigns `initialBalance` to the property `Balance`, invoking `Balance`'s `set` accessor to initialize the instance variable `balance`.

Account *Method* `Credit`

Method `Credit` (lines 16–19) doesn't return data when it completes its task, so its return type is `void`. The method receives one parameter named `amount`—a `decimal` value that's added to the property `Balance`. Line 18 uses both the `get` and `set` accessors of `Balance`. The expression `Balance + amount` invokes property `Balance`'s `get` accessor to obtain the current value of instance variable `balance`, then adds `amount` to it. We then assign the result to instance variable `balance` by invoking the `Balance` property's `set` accessor (thus replacing the prior `balance` value).

Account *Property* `Balance`

Property `Balance` (lines 22–35) provides a `get` accessor, which allows clients of the class (i.e., other classes that use this class) to obtain the value of a particular `Account` object's `balance`. The property has type `decimal` (line 22). `Balance` also provides an enhanced `set` accessor.

In Section 4.5, we introduced properties whose `set` accessors allow clients of a class to modify the value of a `private` instance variable. In Fig. 4.7, class `GradeBook` defines property `CourseName`'s set accessor to assign the value received in its parameter `value` to instance variable `courseName` (line 19). This `CourseName` property does *not* ensure that `courseName` contains only *valid* data.

The app of Figs. 4.15–4.16 enhances the `set` accessor of class `Account`'s property `Balance` to perform this validation (also known as **validity checking**). Line 32 (Fig. 4.15) ensures that value is nonnegative. If the value is greater than or equal to 0, the amount stored in `value` is assigned to instance variable `balance` in line 33. Otherwise, `balance` is left unchanged.

AccountTest *Class to Use Class* Account

Class `AccountTest` (Fig. 4.16) creates two `Account` objects (lines 10–11) and initializes them respectively with `50.00M` and `-7.53M` (the decimal literals representing the real numbers 50.00 and -7.53). The `Account` constructor (lines 10–13 of Fig. 4.15) references property `Balance` to initialize `balance`. In previous examples, the benefit of referencing the property in the constructor was not evident. Now, however, the constructor takes advantage of the validation provided by the `set` accessor of the `Balance` property. The constructor simply assigns a value to `Balance` rather than duplicating the `set` accessor's validation code. When line 11 of Fig. 4.16 passes an initial balance of -7.53 to the Account constructor, the constructor passes this value to the `set` accessor of property `Balance`, where the actual initialization occurs. This value is less than 0, so the `set` accessor does *not* modify `balance`, leaving this instance variable with its default value of 0.

```
 1    // Fig. 4.16: AccountTest.cs
 2    // Create and manipulate Account objects.
 3    using System;
 4
 5    public class AccountTest
 6    {
 7       // Main method begins execution of C# app
 8       public static void Main( string[] args )
 9       {
10          Account account1 = new Account( 50.00M ); // create Account object
11          Account account2 = new Account( -7.53M ); // create Account object
12
13          // display initial balance of each object using a property
14          Console.WriteLine( "account1 balance: {0:C}",
15             account1.Balance ); // display Balance property
```

Fig. 4.16 | Create and manipulate `Account` objects. (Part 1 of 2.)

```
16          Console.WriteLine( "account2 balance: {0:C}\n",
17              account2.Balance ); // display Balance property
18
19          decimal depositAmount; // deposit amount read from user
20
21          // prompt and obtain user input
22          Console.Write( "Enter deposit amount for account1: " );
23          depositAmount = Convert.ToDecimal( Console.ReadLine() );
24          Console.WriteLine( "adding {0:C} to account1 balance\n",
25              depositAmount );
26          account1.Credit( depositAmount ); // add to account1 balance
27
28          // display balances
29          Console.WriteLine( "account1 balance: {0:C}",
30              account1.Balance );
31          Console.WriteLine( "account2 balance: {0:C}\n",
32              account2.Balance );
33
34          // prompt and obtain user input
35          Console.Write( "Enter deposit amount for account2: " );
36          depositAmount = Convert.ToDecimal( Console.ReadLine() );
37          Console.WriteLine( "adding {0:C} to account2 balance\n",
38              depositAmount );
39          account2.Credit( depositAmount ); // add to account2 balance
40
41          // display balances
42          Console.WriteLine( "account1 balance: {0:C}", account1.Balance );
43          Console.WriteLine( "account2 balance: {0:C}", account2.Balance );
44      } // end Main
45  } // end class AccountTest
```

```
account1 balance: $50.00
account2 balance: $0.00

Enter deposit amount for account1: 49.99
adding $49.99 to account1 balance

account1 balance: $99.99
account2 balance: $0.00

Enter deposit amount for account2: 123.21
adding $123.21 to account2 balance

account1 balance: $99.99
account2 balance: $123.21
```

Fig. 4.16 | Create and manipulate Account objects. (Part 2 of 2.)

Lines 14–17 in Fig. 4.16 output the balance in each Account by using the Account's Balance property. When Balance is used for account1 (line 15), the value of account1's balance is returned by the get accessor in line 26 of Fig. 4.15 and displayed by the Console.WriteLine statement (Fig. 4.16, lines 14–15). Similarly, when property Balance is called for account2 from line 17, the value of the account2's balance is returned from line

26 of Fig. 4.15 and displayed by the `Console.WriteLine` statement (Fig. 4.16, lines 16–17). The balance of `account2` is 0 because the constructor ensured that the account could not begin with a negative balance. The value is output by `WriteLine` with the format item `{0:C}`, which formats the account balance as a monetary amount. The `:` after the 0 indicates that the next character represents a **format specifier**, and the C format specifier after the `:` specifies a monetary amount (C is for currency). The cultural settings on the user's machine determine the format for displaying monetary amounts. For example, in the United States, 50 displays as `$50.00`. In Germany, 50 displays as `50,00` e. [*Note:* Change the Command Prompt's font to Lucida Console for the e symbol to display correctly.] Figure 4.17 lists a few other format specifiers in addition to C.

Format specifier	Description
C or c	Formats the string as currency. Displays an appropriate currency symbol ($ in the U.S.) next to the number. Separates digits with an appropriate *separator character* (comma in the U.S.) and sets the number of decimal places to two by default.
D or d	Formats the string as a whole number (integer types only). Displays number as an integer.
N or n	Formats the string with a thousands separator and a default of two decimal places.
E or e	Formats the number using scientific notation with a default of six decimal places.
F or f	Formats the string with a fixed number of decimal places (two by default).
G or g	Formats the number normally with decimal places or using scientific notation, depending on context. If a format item does not contain a format specifier, format G is assumed implicitly.
X or x	Formats the string as hexadecimal.

Fig. 4.17 | `string` format specifiers.

Line 19 of Fig. 4.16 declares local variable `depositAmount` to store each deposit amount entered by the user. Unlike the instance variable `balance` in class `Account`, the local variable `depositAmount` in `Main` is *not* initialized to 0 by default. Also, *a local variable can be used only in the method in which it's declared.* However, this variable does not need to be initialized here because its value will be determined by the user's input. *The compiler does not allow a local variable's value to be read until it's initialized.*

Line 22 prompts the user to enter a deposit amount for `account1`. Line 23 obtains the input from the user by calling the `Console` class's `ReadLine` method, then passing the `string` entered by the user to the `Convert` class's **ToDecimal** method, which returns the `decimal` value in this `string`. Lines 24–25 display the deposit amount. Line 26 calls object `account1`'s `Credit` method and supplies `depositAmount` as the method's argument. When the method is called, the argument's value is assigned to parameter `amount` of method `Credit` (lines 16–19 of Fig. 4.15), then method `Credit` adds that value to the `balance` (line 18 of Fig. 4.15). Lines 29–32 (Fig. 4.16) output the balances of both `Accounts` again to show that *only* `account1`'s balance changed.

Line 35 prompts the user to enter a deposit amount for `account2`. Line 36 obtains the input from the user by calling method `Console.ReadLine`, and passing the return value to the Convert class's ToDecimal method. Lines 37–38 display the deposit amount. Line 39 calls object account2's Credit method and supplies depositAmount as the method's argument, then method Credit adds that value to the balance. Finally, lines 42–43 output the balances of both Accounts again to show that *only* account2's balance changed.

set and get Accessors with Different Access Modifiers

By default, the get and set accessors of a property have the *same* access as the property—for example, for a public property, the accessors are public. It's possible to declare the get and set accessors with *different* access modifiers. In this case, one of the accessors must implicitly have the *same* access as the property and the other must be declared with a *more restrictive* access modifier than the property. For example, in a public property, the get accessor might be public and the set accessor might be private. We demonstrate this feature in Section 10.7.

Error-Prevention Tip 4.2

The benefits of data integrity are not automatic simply because instance variables are made private*—you must provide appropriate validity checking and report the errors.*

Error-Prevention Tip 4.3

set accessors that set the values of private *data should verify that the intended new values are proper; if they're not, the* set *accessors should leave the instance variables unchanged and indicate an error. We demonstrate how to indicate errors in Chapter 10.*

UML Class Diagram for Class Account

The UML class diagram in Fig. 4.18 models class Account of Fig. 4.15. The diagram models the Balance property as a UML attribute of type decimal (because the corresponding C# property had type decimal). The diagram models class Account's constructor with a parameter initialBalance of type decimal in the third compartment of the class. The diagram models operation Credit in the third compartment with an amount parameter of type decimal (because the corresponding method has an amount parameter of C# type decimal).

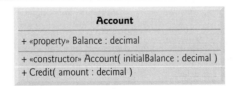

Account
+ «property» Balance : decimal
+ «constructor» Account(initialBalance : decimal)
+ Credit(amount : decimal)

Fig. 4.18 | UML class diagram indicating that class Account has a public Balance property of type decimal, a constructor and a method.

4.12 Wrap-Up

In this chapter, we presented the basic object-oriented concepts of classes, objects, methods, instance variables, properties and constructors—these will be used in most substantial C# apps you create. We showed how to declare instance variables of a class to maintain data for each object of the class, how to declare methods that operate on that data, and how to declare properties to obtain and set that data. We demonstrated how to call a method to tell it to perform its task and how to pass information to methods as arguments. We discussed the difference between a local variable of a method and an instance variable of a class and that only instance variables are initialized automatically. We discussed the difference between a value type and a reference type. You saw how to create auto-implemented properties and how to use a class's constructor to specify the initial values for an object's instance variables. We discussed some of the differences between value types and reference types, and explained the value types `float`, `double` and `decimal` for storing real numbers.

We showed how the UML can be used to create class diagrams that model the constructors, methods, properties and attributes of classes. You learned the value of declaring instance variables `private` and using `public` properties to manipulate them. For example, we demonstrated how `set` accessors in properties can be used to validate an object's data and ensure that the object is maintained in a consistent state. In the next chapter we introduce control statements, which specify the order in which an app's actions are performed.

5

Control Statements: Part 1

Objectives

In this chapter you'll:

- Use the if and if...else selection statements to choose between actions.
- Use the while statement to execute statements repeatedly.
- Use counter-controlled repetition and sentinel-controlled repetition.
- Use the increment, decrement and compound assignment operators.

5.1 Introduction

In this chapter, we introduce C#'s if, if...else and while statements. We devote a portion of this chapter (and Chapters 6 and 8) to further developing the GradeBook class. In particular, we add a member function to the GradeBook class that uses control statements to calculate the average of a set of student grades. Another example demonstrates additional ways to combine control statements. We introduce C#'s assignment, increment and decrement operators. These additional operators abbreviate and simplify many program statements.

5.2 Control Structures

Normally, statements execute one after the other in the order in which they're written. This process is called **sequential execution**. Various C# statements enable you to specify that the next statement to execute is *not* necessarily the next one in sequence. This is called **transfer of control**.

During the 1960s, it became clear that the indiscriminate use of transfers of control was the root of much difficulty experienced by software development groups. The blame was pointed at the **goto statement** (used in most programming languages of the time), which allows you to specify a transfer of control to one of a wide range of possible destinations in an app (creating what is often called "spaghetti code"). The notion of so-called **structured programming** became almost synonymous with "goto elimination." We recommend that you avoid C#'s goto statement.

Research[1] had demonstrated that apps could be written *without* goto statements. The challenge of the era for programmers was to shift their styles to "goto-less programming." Not until the 1970s did programmers start taking *structured programming* seriously. The results were impressive because *structured* apps were clearer, easier to debug and modify, and more likely to be bug free in the first place.

Bohm and Jacopini's work demonstrated that all apps could be written in terms of only three control structures—the **sequence structure**, the **selection structure** and the **repetition structure**. When we introduce C#'s implementations of control structures, we'll refer to them in the terminology of the *C# Language Specification* as "control statements."

---

1. Böhm, C., and G. Jacopini, "Flow Diagrams, Turing Machines, and Languages with Only Two Formation Rules," *Communications of the ACM*, Vol. 9, No. 5, May 1966, pp. 366–371.

Sequence Structure in C#

The *sequence structure* is built into C#. Unless directed otherwise, the computer executes C# statements one after the other in the order in which they're written—that is, in sequence. The UML **activity diagram** in Fig. 5.1 illustrates a typical sequence structure in which two calculations are performed in order. C# lets you have as many actions as you want in a sequence structure.

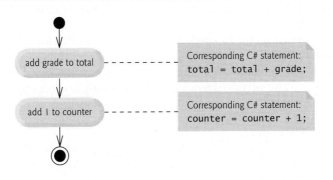

Fig. 5.1 | Sequence structure activity diagram.

An activity diagram models the **workflow** (also called the **activity**) of a portion of a software system. Such workflows may include a portion of an algorithm, such as the sequence structure in Fig. 5.1. Activity diagrams are composed of special-purpose symbols, such as **action-state symbols** (rectangles with their left and right sides replaced with arcs curving outward), **diamonds** and **small circles**. These symbols are connected by **transition arrows**, which represent the *flow* of the activity—that is, the *order* in which the actions should occur.

Activity diagrams help you develop and represent algorithms and they can clearly show how control structures operate. Consider the activity diagram for the sequence structure in Fig. 5.1. It contains two **action states** that represent actions to perform. Each action state contains an **action expression**—for example, "add grade to total" or "add 1 to counter"—that specifies an action to perform. Other actions might include calculations or input–output operations. The arrows in the activity diagram represent **transitions**, which indicate the order in which the actions occur. The portion of the app that implements the activities illustrated by the diagram in Fig. 5.1 first adds grade to total, then adds 1 to counter.

The **solid circle** at the top of the diagram represents the activity's **initial state**—the beginning of the workflow *before* the app performs the modeled actions. The **solid circle surrounded by a hollow circle** that appears at the bottom of the diagram represents the **final state**—the end of the workflow after the app performs its actions.

Figure 5.1 also includes rectangles with the upper-right corners folded over. These are UML **notes** (like comments in C#) that describe the purpose of symbols in the diagram. Figure 5.1 uses UML notes to show the C# code associated with each action state in the activity diagram. A **dotted line** connects each note with the element that the note describes.

Activity diagrams normally do *not* show the C# code that implements the activity. We use notes for this purpose here to illustrate how the diagram relates to C# code.

Selection Structures in C#

C# has three types of selection structures, which from this point forward we shall refer to as **selection statements**. The **if** statement either performs (selects) an action if a condition is *true* or skips the action if the condition is *false*. The **if...else** statement performs an action if a condition is *true* or performs a different action if the condition is *false*. The switch statement (Chapter 6) performs one of many different actions, depending on the value of an expression.

The if statement is called a **single-selection statement** because it selects or ignores a single action (or, as we'll soon see, a single group of actions). The if...else statement is called a **double-selection statement** because it selects between *two* different actions (or groups of actions). The switch statement is called a **multiple-selection statement** because it selects among *many* different actions (or groups of actions).

Repetition Structures in C#

C# provides four repetition structures, which from this point forward we shall refer to as **repetition statements** (also called **iteration statements**). Repetition statements enable apps to perform statements repeatedly, depending on the value of a **loop-continuation condition**. The repetition statements are the while, do...while, for and foreach statements. (Chapter 6 presents the do...while and for statements. Chapter 8 discusses the foreach statement.) The while, for and foreach statements perform the action (or group of actions) in their bodies *zero or more times*—if the loop-continuation condition is initially *false*, the action (or group of actions) will not execute. The do...while statement performs the action (or group of actions) in its body one or more times. The words if, else, switch, while, do, for and foreach are C# keywords.

Summary of Control Statements in C#

C# has only three kinds of structured control statements: the *sequence statement*, *selection statement* (three types) and *repetition statement* (four types). We combine as many of each type of statement as necessary to make the program flow and work as required. As with the sequence statement in Fig. 5.1, we can model each control statement as an activity diagram. Each diagram contains one initial state and one final state that represent a control statement's entry point and exit point, respectively. **Single-entry/single-exit control statements** make it easy to build apps—the control statements are "attached" to one another by connecting the exit point of one to the entry point of the next. This procedure is similar to the way in which a child stacks building blocks, so we call it **control-statement stacking**. You'll see that there's only one other way in which control statements may be connected: **control-statement nesting**, in which one control statement appears *inside* another. Thus, algorithms in C# apps are constructed from only three kinds of structured control statements, combined in only two ways. This is the essence of simplicity.

5.3 if Single-Selection Statement

Apps use selection statements to choose among alternative courses of action. For example, suppose that the passing grade on an exam is 60. The statement

```
if ( grade >= 60 )
    Console.WriteLine( "Passed" );
```

determines whether the *condition* grade >= 60 is true or false. If the condition is *true*, "Passed" is output, and the next statement in order is performed. If the condition is *false*, the output statement is ignored, and the next statement in order is performed.

Figure 5.2 illustrates the single-selection if statement. This activity diagram contains what is perhaps the most important symbol in an activity diagram—the diamond, or **decision symbol**, which indicates that a *decision* is to be made. The workflow will continue along a path determined by *one* of the symbol's two associated **guard conditions**—one must be *true* and the other *false*. Each transition arrow emerging from a decision symbol has a guard condition (specified in square brackets next to the transition arrow). If a guard condition is *true*, the workflow enters the action state to which the transition arrow points. In Fig. 5.2, if grade >= 60, the app displays "Passed" then transitions to the final state of this activity. If grade < 60, the app immediately transitions to the final state without displaying a message.

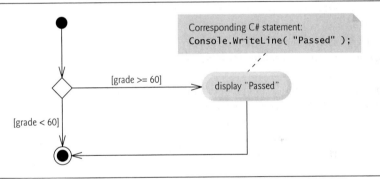

Corresponding C# statement:
```
Console.WriteLine( "Passed" );
```

[grade >= 60]   display "Passed"

[grade < 60]

Fig. 5.2 | if single-selection statement UML activity diagram.

The if statement is a *single-entry/single-exit* control statement. You'll see that the activity diagrams for the remaining control statements also contain initial states, transition arrows, action states that indicate actions to perform and decision symbols (with associated guard conditions) that indicate decisions to be made, and final states. This is consistent with the **action/decision model of programming** we've been emphasizing.

5.4 if...else Double-Selection Statement

The if single-selection statement performs an indicated action *only* when the condition is true; otherwise, the action is skipped. The if...else double-selection statement allows you to specify an action to perform when the condition is *true* and a different action when the condition is *false*. For example, the statement

```
if ( grade >= 60 )
    Console.WriteLine( "Passed" );
else
    Console.WriteLine( "Failed" );
```

outputs "Passed" if the grade is greater than or equal to 60, or "Failed" otherwise. In either case, after output occurs, the next pseudocode statement in sequence is performed.

Figure 5.3 illustrates the flow of control in the if...else statement.

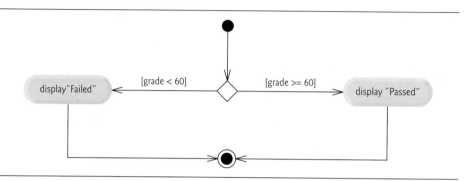

Fig. 5.3 | if...else double-selection statement UML activity diagram.

Conditional Operator (?:)

C# provides the **conditional operator (?:)**, which can be used in place of an if...else statement like the one diagrammed in Fig. 5.3. This is C#'s only **ternary operator**—this means that it takes three operands. Together, the operands and the ?: symbols form a **conditional expression**. The first operand (to the left of the ?) is a **boolean** expression (i.e., an expression that evaluates to a bool-type value—**true** or **false**), the second operand (between the ? and :) is the value of the conditional expression if the boolean expression is true and the third operand (to the right of the :) is the value of the conditional expression if the boolean expression is false. For example, the statement

```
Console.WriteLine( grade >= 60 ? "Passed" : "Failed" );
```

displays the value of WriteLine's conditional-expression argument. The conditional expression in the preceding statement evaluates to the string "Passed" if the boolean expression grade >= 60 is true and evaluates to the string "Failed" if the boolean expression is false. Thus, this statement with the conditional operator performs essentially the same function as the if...else statement shown earlier in this section, in which the boolean expression grade >= 60 was used as the if...else statement's condition. Actually, every control statement's condition *must* evaluate to the bool-type value true or false. You'll see that conditional expressions can be used in some situations where if...else statements cannot.

 Good Programming Practice 5.1

When a conditional expression is inside a larger expression, it's good practice to parenthesize the conditional expression for clarity. Adding parentheses may also prevent operator-precedence problems that could cause syntax errors.

Nested if...else Statements

An app can test multiple cases by placing if...else statements *inside* other if...else statements to create **nested if...else statements**. For example, the following nested if...else statement displays A for exam grades greater than or equal to 90, B for grades in the range 80 to 89, C for grades in the range 70 to 79, D for grades in the range 60 to 69 and F for all other grades:

```
if ( grade >= 90 )
    Console.WriteLine( "A" );
else
    if ( grade >= 80 )
        Console.WriteLine( "B" );
    else
        if ( grade >= 70 )
            Console.WriteLine( "C" );
        else
            if ( grade >= 60 )
                Console.WriteLine( "D" );
            else
                Console.WriteLine( "F" );
```

If grade is greater than or equal to 90, the first four conditions will be true, but *only* the statement in the if-part of the first if...else statement will execute. After that statement executes, the else-part of the "outermost" if...else statement is skipped. Many C# programmers prefer to write the preceding if...else statement as

```
if ( grade >= 90 )
    Console.WriteLine( "A" );
else if ( grade >= 80 )
    Console.WriteLine( "B" );
else if ( grade >= 70 )
    Console.WriteLine( "C" );
else if ( grade >= 60 )
    Console.WriteLine( "D" );
else
    Console.WriteLine( "F" );
```

The two forms are identical except for the spacing and indentation, which the compiler ignores. The latter form is popular because it avoids deep indentation of the code to the right—such indentation can leave little room on a line of code, forcing lines to be split and decreasing the readability of your code.

Dangling-*else* Problem

The C# compiler always associates an else with the *immediately preceding* if unless told to do otherwise by the placement of braces ({ and }). This behavior can lead to what is referred to as the **dangling-else problem**. For example,

```
if ( x > 5 )
    if ( y > 5 )
        Console.WriteLine( "x and y are > 5" );
else
    Console.WriteLine( "x is <= 5" );
```

appears to indicate that if x is greater than 5, the nested if statement determines whether y is also greater than 5. If so, the string "x and y are > 5" is output. Otherwise, it appears that if x is *not* greater than 5, the else part of the if...else outputs the string "x is <= 5".

Beware! This nested if...else statement does *not* execute as it appears. The compiler actually interprets the statement as

```
if ( x > 5 )
    if ( y > 5 )
        Console.WriteLine( "x and y are > 5" );
    else
        Console.WriteLine( "x is <= 5" );
```

in which the body of the first if is a nested if...else. The outer if statement tests whether x is greater than 5. If so, execution continues by testing whether y is also greater than 5. If the second condition is true, the proper string—"x and y are > 5"—is displayed. However, if the second condition is false, the string "x is <= 5" is displayed, even though we know that x is greater than 5.

To force the nested if...else statement to execute as it was originally intended, we must write it as follows:

```
if ( x > 5 )
{
    if ( y > 5 )
        Console.WriteLine( "x and y are > 5" );
}
else
    Console.WriteLine( "x is <= 5" );
```

The braces ({}) indicate to the compiler that the second if statement is in the body of the first if and that the else is associated with the *first* if.

Blocks

The if statement expects only one statement in its body. To include *several* statements in the body of an if (or the body of an else for an if...else statement), enclose the statements in braces ({ and }). A set of statements contained within a pair of braces is called a **block**. A block can be placed anywhere in an app that a single statement can be placed.

The following example includes a block in the else-part of an if...else statement:

```
if ( grade >= 60 )
    Console.WriteLine( "Passed" );
else
{
    Console.WriteLine( "Failed" );
    Console.WriteLine( "You must take this course again." );
}
```

In this case, if grade is less than 60, the app executes *both* statements in the body of the else and displays

```
Failed.
You must take this course again.
```

Note the braces surrounding the two statements in the else clause. These braces are important. Without the braces, the statement

```
Console.WriteLine( "You must take this course again." );
```

would be outside the body of the else-part of the if...else statement and would execute regardless of whether the grade was less than 60.

5.5 while Repetition Statement

A **repetition statement** allows you to specify that an app should repeat an action while some condition remains true. As an example of C#'s **while repetition statement**, consider a code segment designed to find the first power of 3 larger than 100. When the following while statement finishes executing, product contains the result:

```
int product = 3;
while ( product <= 100 )
    product = 3 * product;
```

When this while statement begins execution, the value of variable product is 3. Each repetition of the while statement multiplies product by 3, so product takes on the subsequent values 9, 27, 81 and 243 successively. When variable product becomes 243, the while statement condition—product <= 100—becomes false. This terminates the repetition, so the final value of product is 243. At this point, execution continues with the next statement after the while statement.

Common Programming Error 5.1

Not providing in the body of a while statement an action that eventually causes the condition in the while to become false normally results in an infinite loop, in which the loop never terminates.

while Repetition Statement Activity Diagram

The activity diagram in Fig. 5.4 illustrates the flow of control for the preceding while statement. This diagram also introduces the UML's **merge symbol**. The UML represents *both* the merge and decision symbols as diamonds. The merge symbol joins two flows of activity into one. In this diagram, the merge symbol joins the transitions from the initial state and the action state, so they both flow into the decision that determines whether the loop should begin (or continue) executing. The decision and merge symbols can be distinguished by the number of "incoming" and "outgoing" transition arrows. A decision symbol has one transition arrow pointing to the diamond and two or more transition arrows pointing out from the diamond to indicate possible transitions from that point. Each tran-

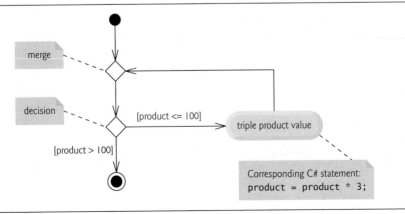

Fig. 5.4 | while repetition statement UML activity diagram.

sition arrow pointing out of a decision symbol has a guard condition. A merge symbol has *two or more* transition arrows pointing to the diamond and *only one* transition arrow pointing from the diamond, to indicate multiple activity flows merging to continue the activity. None of the transition arrows associated with a merge have guard conditions.

Figure 5.4 clearly shows the repetition of the while statement discussed earlier in this section. The transition arrow emerging from the action state points back to the merge, from which program flow transitions back to the decision that's tested at the beginning of each repetition of the loop. The loop continues to execute until the guard condition product > 100 becomes true. Then the while statement exits (reaches its final state), and control passes to the next statement in sequence in the app.

5.6 Counter-Controlled Repetition

Consider the following problem statement:

> *A class of 10 students took a quiz. The grades (integers in the range 0 to 100) for this quiz are available to you. Determine the class average on the quiz.*

The class average is equal to the sum of the grades divided by the number of students. The app must input each grade, keep track of the total of all grades input, perform the averaging calculation and display the result.

Counter-Controlled Repetition

We use **counter-controlled repetition** to input the grades one at a time. This technique uses a variable called a **counter** (or **control variable**) to control the number of times a set of statements will execute. Counter-controlled repetition is often called **definite repetition**, because the number of repetitions is known *before* the loop begins executing. In this example, repetition terminates when the counter exceeds 10. This section presents a version of class GradeBook (Fig. 5.5) that implements the algorithm in a C# method. The section then presents an app (Fig. 5.6) that demonstrates the algorithm in action.

Implementing Counter-Controlled Repetition in Class *GradeBook*

Class GradeBook (Fig. 5.5) contains a constructor (lines 12–15) that assigns a value to the instance variable created by auto-implemented property CourseName in line 9. Lines 18–23 declare method DisplayMessage. Lines 26–52 declare method DetermineClassAverage, which implements the class-averaging algorithm.

```
1   // Fig. 5.5: GradeBook.cs
2   // GradeBook class that solves the class-average problem using
3   // counter-controlled repetition.
4   using System;
5
6   public class GradeBook
7   {
8      // auto-implemented property CourseName
9      public string CourseName { get; set; }
```

Fig. 5.5 | GradeBook class that solves the class-average problem using counter-controlled repetition. (Part 1 of 2.)

```
10
11      // constructor initializes CourseName property
12      public GradeBook( string name )
13      {
14         CourseName = name; // set CourseName to name
15      } // end constructor
16
17      // display a welcome message to the GradeBook user
18      public void DisplayMessage()
19      {
20         // property CourseName gets the name of the course
21         Console.WriteLine( "Welcome to the grade book for\n{0}!\n",
22            CourseName );
23      } // end method DisplayMessage
24
25      // determine class average based on 10 grades entered by user
26      public void DetermineClassAverage()
27      {
28         int total; // sum of the grades entered by user
29         int gradeCounter; // number of the grade to be entered next
30         int grade; // grade value entered by the user
31         int average; // average of the grades
32
33         // initialization phase
34         total = 0; // initialize the total
35         gradeCounter = 1; // initialize the loop counter
36
37         // processing phase
38         while ( gradeCounter <= 10 ) // loop 10 times
39         {
40            Console.Write( "Enter grade: " ); // prompt the user
41            grade = Convert.ToInt32( Console.ReadLine() ); // read grade
42            total = total + grade; // add the grade to total
43            gradeCounter = gradeCounter + 1; // increment the counter by 1
44         } // end while
45
46         // termination phase
47         average = total / 10; // integer division yields integer result
48
49         // display total and average of grades
50         Console.WriteLine( "\nTotal of all 10 grades is {0}", total );
51         Console.WriteLine( "Class average is {0}", average );
52      } // end method DetermineClassAverage
53   } // end class GradeBook
```

Fig. 5.5 | GradeBook class that solves the class-average problem using counter-controlled repetition. (Part 2 of 2.)

Method *DetermineClassAverage*

Lines 28–31 declare local variables total, gradeCounter, grade and average to be of type int. In this example, variable total accumulates the sum of the grades entered and grade-Counter counts the number of grades entered. Variable grade stores the most recent grade value entered (line 41). Variable average stores the average grade.

The declarations (in lines 28–31) appear in method DetermineClassAverage's body. Variables declared in a method body are *local* variables and can be used only from the line of their declaration to the closing right brace of the block in which they're declared. A local variable's declaration *must* appear before the variable is used in that method. A local variable cannot be accessed *outside* the block in which it's declared.

In the versions of class GradeBook in this chapter, we read and process a set of grades. The averaging calculation is performed in method DetermineClassAverage using local variables—we do not preserve any information about student grades in instance variables of the class. In later versions of the class (in Chapter 8), we store the grades using an instance variable that refers to an array. This will allow a GradeBook object to perform various calculations on the same set of grades without requiring the user to enter the grades multiple times.

We say that a variable is **definitely assigned** when it's guaranteed to be assigned a value before the variable is used. Notice that each local variable declared in lines 28–31 is definitely assigned before it's used in calculations. The assignments (in lines 34–35) initialize total to 0 and gradeCounter to 1. Variables grade and average (for the user input and calculated average, respectively) need not be initialized here—their values are assigned as they're input or calculated later in the method.

Common Programming Error 5.2

Using the value of a local variable before it's definitely assigned results in a compilation error. All local variables must be definitely assigned before their values are used in expressions.

Line 38 indicates that the while statement should continue looping (also called **iterating**) as long as the value of gradeCounter is less than or equal to 10. While this condition remains true, the while statement repeatedly executes the statements between the braces that delimit its body (lines 39–44).

Line 40 displays the prompt "Enter grade: " in the console window. Line 41 reads the grade entered by the user and assigns it to variable grade. Then line 42 adds the new grade entered by the user to the total and assigns the result to total, which replaces its previous value.

Line 43 adds 1 to gradeCounter to indicate that the app has processed a grade and is ready to input the next grade from the user. Incrementing gradeCounter eventually causes gradeCounter to exceed 10. At that point the while loop terminates, because its condition (line 38) becomes false.

When the loop terminates, line 47 performs the averaging calculation and assigns its result to the variable average. Line 50 uses Console's WriteLine method to display the text "Total of all 10 grades is " followed by variable total's value. Line 51 then displays the text "Class average is " followed by variable average's value. Method DetermineClassAverage returns control to the calling method (i.e., Main in GradeBookTest of Fig. 5.6) after reaching line 52.

Class *GradeBookTest*

Class GradeBookTest (Fig. 5.6) creates an object of class GradeBook (Fig. 5.5) and demonstrates its capabilities. Lines 9–10 of Fig. 5.6 create a new GradeBook object and assign it to variable myGradeBook. The string in line 10 is passed to the GradeBook constructor (lines 12–15 of Fig. 5.5). Line 12 (Fig. 5.6) calls myGradeBook's DisplayMessage method to display a welcome message to the user. Line 13 then calls myGradeBook's DetermineClassAverage method to allow the user to enter 10 grades, for which the method then calculates and displays the average.

```
1   // Fig. 5.6: GradeBookTest.cs
2   // Create GradeBook object and invoke its DetermineClassAverage method.
3   public class GradeBookTest
4   {
5      public static void Main( string[] args )
6      {
7         // create GradeBook object myGradeBook and
8         // pass course name to constructor
9         GradeBook myGradeBook = new GradeBook(
10           "CS101 Introduction to C# Programming" );
11
12        myGradeBook.DisplayMessage(); // display welcome message
13        myGradeBook.DetermineClassAverage(); // find average of 10 grades
14     } // end Main
15  } // end class GradeBookTest
```

```
Welcome to the grade book for
CS101 Introduction to C# Programming!

Enter grade: 88
Enter grade: 79
Enter grade: 95
Enter grade: 100
Enter grade: 48
Enter grade: 88
Enter grade: 92
Enter grade: 83
Enter grade: 90
Enter grade: 85

Total of all 10 grades is 848
Class average is 84
```

Fig. 5.6 | Create GradeBook object and invoke its DetermineClassAverage method.

Notes on Integer Division and Truncation

The averaging calculation performed by method DetermineClassAverage in response to the method call at line 13 in Fig. 5.6 produces an integer result. The app's output indicates that the sum of the grade values in the sample execution is 848, which, when divided by 10, should yield the floating-point number 84.8. However, the result of the calculation total / 10 (line 47 of Fig. 5.5) is the integer 84, because total and 10 are *both* integers. Dividing two integers results in **integer division**—any fractional part of the calculation is lost (i.e., **truncated**, not rounded). We'll see how to obtain a floating-point result from the averaging calculation in the next section.

5.7 Sentinel-Controlled Repetition

Let us generalize Section 5.6's class-average problem. Consider the following problem:

> *Develop a class-averaging app that processes grades for an arbitrary number of students each time it's run.*

In the previous class-average example, the problem statement specified the number of students, so the number of grades (10) was known in advance. In this example, no indication is given of how many grades the user will enter during the app's execution. The app must process an *arbitrary* number of grades. How can it determine when to *stop* the input of grades? How will it know *when* to calculate and display the class average?

One way to solve this problem is to use a special value called a **sentinel value** (also called a **signal value**, a **dummy value** or a **flag value**) to indicate "end of data entry." This is called **sentinel-controlled repetition.** The user enters grades until all *legitimate* grades have been entered. The user then types the sentinel value to indicate that no more grades will be entered. Sentinel-controlled repetition is often called **indefinite repetition** because the number of repetitions is *not* known by the app before the loop begins executing.

Clearly, a sentinel value must be chosen that *cannot* be confused with an acceptable input value. Grades on a quiz are nonnegative integers, so –1 is an acceptable sentinel value for this problem. Thus, a run of the class-average app might process a stream of inputs such as 95, 96, 75, 74, 89 and –1. The app would then compute and display the class average for the grades 95, 96, 75, 74 and 89. Since –1 is the sentinel value, it should not enter into the averaging calculation.

Common Programming Error 5.3

Choosing a sentinel value that's also a legitimate data value is a logic error.

*Implementing Sentinel-Controlled Repetition in Class **GradeBook***

Figure 5.7 shows the C# class GradeBook containing method DetermineClassAverage. Although each grade is an integer, the averaging calculation is likely to produce a number with a decimal point—in other words, a real number or floating-point number. The type int cannot represent such a number, so this class uses type double to do so.

```
1   // Fig. 5.7: GradeBook.cs
2   // GradeBook class that solves the class-average problem using
3   // sentinel-controlled repetition.
4   using System;
5
6   public class GradeBook
7   {
8      // auto-implemented property CourseName
9      public string CourseName { get; set; }
10
11     // constructor initializes the CourseName property
12     public GradeBook( string name )
13     {
14        CourseName = name; // set CourseName to name
15     } // end constructor
16
```

Fig. 5.7 | GradeBook class that solves the class-average problem using sentinel-controlled repetition. (Part I of 2.)

```
17      // display a welcome message to the GradeBook user
18      public void DisplayMessage()
19      {
20         Console.WriteLine( "Welcome to the grade book for\n{0}!\n",
21            CourseName );
22      } // end method DisplayMessage
23
24      // determine the average of an arbitrary number of grades
25      public void DetermineClassAverage()
26      {
27         int total; // sum of grades
28         int gradeCounter; // number of grades entered
29         int grade; // grade value
30         double average; // number with decimal point for average
31
32         // initialization phase
33         total = 0; // initialize total
34         gradeCounter = 0; // initialize loop counter
35
36         // processing phase
37         // prompt for and read a grade from the user
38         Console.Write( "Enter grade or -1 to quit: " );
39         grade = Convert.ToInt32( Console.ReadLine() );
40
41         // loop until sentinel value is read from the user
42         while ( grade != -1 )
43         {
44            total = total + grade; // add grade to total
45            gradeCounter = gradeCounter + 1; // increment counter
46
47            // prompt for and read the next grade from the user
48            Console.Write( "Enter grade or -1 to quit: " );
49            grade = Convert.ToInt32( Console.ReadLine() );
50         } // end while
51
52         // termination phase
53         // if the user entered at least one grade...
54         if ( gradeCounter != 0 )
55         {
56            // calculate the average of all the grades entered
57            average = ( double ) total / gradeCounter;
58
59            // display the total and average (with two digits of precision)
60            Console.WriteLine( "\nTotal of the {0} grades entered is {1}",
61               gradeCounter, total );
62            Console.WriteLine( "Class average is {0:F}", average );
63         } // end if
64         else // no grades were entered, so output error message
65            Console.WriteLine( "No grades were entered" );
66      } // end method DetermineClassAverage
67   } // end class GradeBook
```

Fig. 5.7 | GradeBook class that solves the class-average problem using sentinel-controlled repetition. (Part 2 of 2.)

In this example, we see that control statements may be *stacked* on top of one another (in sequence) just as a child stacks building blocks. The `while` statement (lines 42–50) is followed in sequence by an `if...else` statement (lines 54–65). Much of the code in this app is identical to the code in Fig. 5.5, so we concentrate on the new features and issues.

Line 30 declares `double` variable `average`. This variable allows us to store the calculated class average as a floating-point number. Line 34 initializes `gradeCounter` to 0, because no grades have been entered yet. Remember that this app uses sentinel-controlled repetition to input the grades from the user. To keep an accurate record of the number of grades entered, the app increments `gradeCounter` only when the user inputs a valid grade value.

Program Logic for Sentinel-Controlled Repetition vs. Counter-Controlled Repetition
Compare the program logic for sentinel-controlled repetition in this app with that for counter-controlled repetition in Fig. 5.5. In counter-controlled repetition, each repetition of the `while` statement (e.g., lines 38–44 of Fig. 5.5) reads a value from the user, for the specified number of repetitions. In sentinel-controlled repetition, the app reads the first value (lines 38–39 of Fig. 5.7) before reaching the `while`. This value determines whether the app's flow of control should enter the body of the `while`. If the condition of the `while` is `false`, the user entered the sentinel value, so the body of the `while` does *not* execute (because no grades were entered). If, on the other hand, the condition is `true`, the body begins execution, and the loop adds the `grade` value to the `total` (line 44) and adds 1 to `grade-Counter` (line 45). Then lines 48–49 in the loop's body input the next value from the user. Next, program control reaches the closing right brace of the body at line 50, so execution continues with the test of the `while`'s condition (line 42).

The condition uses the most recent `grade` input by the user to determine whether the loop's body should execute again. The value of variable `grade` is always input from the user immediately before the app tests the `while` condition. This allows the app to determine whether the value just input is the sentinel value *before* the app processes that value (i.e., adds it to the `total`). If the sentinel value is input, the loop terminates; the app does *not* add -1 to the `total`.

Good Programming Practice 5.2

In a sentinel-controlled loop, the prompts requesting data entry should explicitly remind the user of the sentinel value.

Notice the `while` statement's block in Fig. 5.7 (lines 43–50). Without the braces, the loop would consider its body to be *only* the first statement, which adds the `grade` to the `total`. The last three statements in the block would fall outside the loop's body, causing the computer to interpret the code incorrectly as follows:

```
while ( grade != -1 )
   total = total + grade; // add grade to total
gradeCounter = gradeCounter + 1; // increment counter

// prompt for input and read next grade from user
Console.Write( "Enter grade or -1 to quit: " );
grade = Convert.ToInt32( Console.ReadLine() );
```

The preceding code would cause an *infinite loop* if the user did not enter the sentinel -1 at line 39 (before the `while` statement).

Error-Prevention Tip 5.1

Omitting the braces that delimit a block can lead to logic errors, such as infinite loops. To prevent this problem, some programmers enclose the body of every control statement in braces even if the body contains only a single statement.

After the loop terminates, the if...else statement at lines 54–65 executes. The condition at line 54 determines whether any grades were input. If none were input, the else part (lines 64–65) of the if...else statement executes and displays the message "No grades were entered", and the method returns control to the calling method.

Explicitly and Implicitly Converting Between Simple Types

If at least one grade was entered, line 57 calculates the average of the grades. Recall from Fig. 5.5 that integer division yields an integer result. Even though variable average is declared as a double (line 30), the calculation

```
average = total / gradeCounter;
```

loses the division's fractional part before the result is assigned to average. This occurs because total and gradeCounter are *both* integers, and integer division yields an integer result. To perform a floating-point calculation with integer values, we must *temporarily* treat these values as floating-point numbers for use in the calculation. C# provides the **unary cast operator** to accomplish this task. Line 57 uses the **(double)** cast operator—which has higher precedence than the arithmetic operators—to create a *temporary* floating-point copy of its operand total (which appears to the right of the operator). Using a cast operator in this manner is called **explicit conversion**. The value stored in total is still an integer.

The calculation now consists of a floating-point value (the temporary double version of total) divided by the integer gradeCounter. C# knows how to evaluate only arithmetic expressions in which the operands' types are *identical*. To ensure that the operands are of the same type, C# performs an operation called **promotion** (or **implicit conversion**) on selected operands. For example, in an expression containing values of the types int and double, the int values are promoted to double values for use in the expression. In this example, the value of gradeCounter is promoted to type double, then floating-point division is performed and the result of the calculation is assigned to average. As long as the (double) cast operator is applied to *any* variable in the calculation, the calculation will yield a double result.

Common Programming Error 5.4

A cast operator can be used to convert between simple numeric types, such as int and double, and between related reference types (as we discuss in Chapter 12, OOP: Polymorphism, Interfaces and Operator Overloading). Casting to the wrong type may cause compilation or runtime errors.

Cast operators are available for all simple types. We'll discuss cast operators for reference types in Chapter 12. The cast operator is formed by placing parentheses around the name of a type. This operator is a **unary operator** (i.e., an operator that takes only one operand). In Chapter 3, we studied the binary arithmetic operators. C# also supports unary versions of the plus (+) and minus (–) operators, so you can write expressions like +5 or -7. Cast operators associate from right to left and have the same precedence as other unary operators, such as unary + and unary -. This precedence is one level higher than that of the **multiplicative operators** *, / and %. (See the operator precedence chart in Appendix A.) We indicate the cast operator with the notation (*type*) in our precedence charts, to indicate that any type name can be used to form a cast operator.

Line 62 outputs the class average. In this example, we decided that we'd like to display the class average *rounded to the nearest hundredth* and output the average with exactly two digits to the right of the decimal point. The format specifier F in WriteLine's format item (line 62) indicates that variable average's value should be displayed as a real number. By default, numbers output with F have two digits to the right of the decimal point. The number of decimal places to the right of the decimal point is also known as the number's **precision**. Any floating-point value output with F will be rounded to the hundredths position—for example, 123.457 will be rounded to 123.46, and 27.333 will be rounded to 27.33. In this app, the three grades entered during the sample execution of class Grade-BookTest (Fig. 5.8) total 263, which yields the average 87.66666.... The format item rounds the average to the hundredths position, and the average is displayed as 87.67.

```
1    // Fig. 5.8: GradeBookTest.cs
2    // Create GradeBook object and invoke its DetermineClassAverage method.
3    public class GradeBookTest
4    {
5       public static void Main( string[] args )
6       {
7          // create GradeBook object myGradeBook and
8          // pass course name to constructor
9          GradeBook myGradeBook = new GradeBook(
10             "CS101 Introduction to C# Programming" );
11
12         myGradeBook.DisplayMessage(); // display welcome message
13         myGradeBook.DetermineClassAverage(); // find average of grades
14      } // end Main
15   } // end class GradeBookTest
```

```
Welcome to the grade book for
CS101 Introduction to C# Programming!

Enter grade or -1 to quit: 96
Enter grade or -1 to quit: 88
Enter grade or -1 to quit: 79
Enter grade or -1 to quit: -1

Total of the 3 grades entered is 263
Class average is 87.67
```

Fig. 5.8 | Create GradeBook object and invoke its DetermineClassAverage method.

5.8 Nested Control Statements

We've seen that control statements can be *stacked* on top of one another (in sequence). In this case study, we examine the only other structured way control statements can be connected, namely, by **nesting** one control statement within another.

Consider the following problem statement:

A college offers a course that prepares students for the state licensing exam for real estate brokers. Last year, 10 of the students who completed this course took the exam. The college wants to know how well its students did on the exam. You've been asked to write an app to summarize the results. You've been given a list of these 10 students. Next to each name is written a 1 if the student passed the exam or a 2 if the student failed.

Your app should analyze the results of the exam as follows:

1. *Input each test result (i.e., a 1 or a 2). Display the message "Enter result" on the screen each time the app requests another test result.*

2. *Count the number of test results of each type.*

3. *Display a summary of the test results indicating the number of students who passed and the number who failed.*

4. *If more than eight students passed the exam, display the message "Bonus to instructor!"*

After reading the problem statement, we make the following observations:

1. The app must process test results for 10 students. A *counter-controlled loop* can be used because the number of test results is known in advance.

2. Each test result has a numeric value—either a 1 or a 2. Each time the app reads a test result, the app must determine whether the number is a 1 or a 2. We test for a 1 in our algorithm. If the number is not a 1, we assume that it's a 2.

3. Two counters are used to keep track of the exam results—one to count the number of students who passed the exam and one to count the number of students who failed the exam.

4. After the app has processed all the results, it must determine whether more than eight students passed the exam.

Class *Analysis*

This example (Fig. 5.9) contains only *one* class, with method Main performing all the class's work. In this chapter and in Chapter 4, you've seen examples consisting of *two* classes—one class containing methods that perform useful tasks and one containing method Main, which creates an object of the other class and calls its methods. Occasionally, when it makes no sense to try to create a reusable class, we'll use a mechanical example contained entirely within the Main method of a single class.

Lines 10–13 of Fig. 5.9 declare the variables that method Main uses to process the examination results. Several of these declarations use C#'s ability to incorporate variable initialization into declarations (passes is assigned 0, failures is assigned 0 and student-Counter is assigned 1).

The while statement (lines 16–30) loops 10 times. During each repetition, the loop inputs and processes one exam result. Notice that the if...else statement (lines 23–26) for processing each result is *nested* in the while statement. If the result is 1, the if...else statement increments passes; otherwise, it *assumes* the result is 2 and increments failures. Line 29 increments studentCounter before the loop condition is tested again at line 16. After 10 values have been input, the loop terminates and line 33 displays the number of passes and the number of failures. Lines 36–37 determine whether more than eight students passed the exam and, if so, outputs the message "Bonus to instructor!".

```csharp
1   // Fig. 5.9: Analysis.cs
2   // Analysis of examination results, using nested control statements.
3   using System;
4
5   public class Analysis
6   {
7      public static void Main( string[] args )
8      {
9         // initialize variables in declarations
10        int passes = 0; // number of passes
11        int failures = 0; // number of failures
12        int studentCounter = 1; // student counter
13        int result; // one exam result from user
14
15        // process 10 students using counter-controlled repetition
16        while ( studentCounter <= 10 )
17        {
18           // prompt user for input and obtain a value from the user
19           Console.Write( "Enter result (1 = pass, 2 = fail): " );
20           result = Convert.ToInt32( Console.ReadLine() );
21
22           // if...else nested in while
23           if ( result == 1 ) // if result 1,
24              passes = passes + 1; // increment passes
25           else // else result is not 1, so
26              failures = failures + 1; // increment failures
27
28           // increment studentCounter so loop eventually terminates
29           studentCounter = studentCounter + 1;
30        } // end while
31
32        // termination phase; prepare and display results
33        Console.WriteLine( "Passed: {0}\nFailed: {1}", passes, failures );
34
35        // determine whether more than 8 students passed
36        if ( passes > 8 )
37           Console.WriteLine( "Bonus to instructor!" );
38     } // end Main
39  } // end class Analysis
```

```
Enter result (1 = pass, 2 = fail): 1
Enter result (1 = pass, 2 = fail): 2
Enter result (1 = pass, 2 = fail): 1
Enter result (1 = pass, 2 = fail): 1
Enter result (1 = pass, 2 = fail): 1
Enter result (1 = pass, 2 = fail): 1
Enter result (1 = pass, 2 = fail): 1
Enter result (1 = pass, 2 = fail): 1
Enter result (1 = pass, 2 = fail): 1
Enter result (1 = pass, 2 = fail): 1
Passed: 9
Failed: 1
Bonus to instructor!
```

Fig. 5.9 | Analysis of examination results, using nested control statements. (Part I of 2.)

```
Enter result (1 = pass, 2 = fail): 1
Enter result (1 = pass, 2 = fail): 2
Enter result (1 = pass, 2 = fail): 2
Enter result (1 = pass, 2 = fail): 2
Enter result (1 = pass, 2 = fail): 1
Enter result (1 = pass, 2 = fail): 1
Enter result (1 = pass, 2 = fail): 1
Enter result (1 = pass, 2 = fail): 1
Enter result (1 = pass, 2 = fail): 2
Enter result (1 = pass, 2 = fail): 2
Passed: 5
Failed: 5
```

Fig. 5.9 | Analysis of examination results, using nested control statements. (Part 2 of 2.)

Figure 5.9 shows the input and output from two sample executions of the app. During the first sample execution, the condition at line 36 is true—more than eight students passed the exam, so the app outputs a message indicating that the instructor should receive a bonus.

Error-Prevention Tip 5.2

Initializing local variables when they're declared helps you avoid compilation errors that might arise from attempts to use uninitialized data. While C# does not require that local-variable initializations be incorporated into declarations, it does require that local variables be initialized before their values are used in an expression.

5.9 Compound Assignment Operators

C# provides several **compound assignment operators** for abbreviating assignment expressions. Any statement of the form

>   *variable* = *variable operator expression*;

where *operator* is one of the binary operators +, -, *, / or % (or others we discuss later in the text) can be written in the form

>   *variable operator*= *expression*;

For example, you can abbreviate the statement

>   c = c + 3;

with the **addition compound assignment operator, +=,** as

>   c += 3;

The += operator adds the value of the expression on the right of the operator to the value of the variable on the left of the operator and stores the result in the variable on the left of the operator. Thus, the assignment expression c += 3 adds 3 to c. Figure 5.10 shows the arithmetic compound assignment operators, sample expressions using the operators and explanations of what the operators do.

Assignment operator	Sample expression	Explanation	Assigns
Assume: **int** c = 3, d = 5, e = 4, f = 6, g = 12;			
+=	c += 7	c = c + 7	10 to c
-=	d -= 4	d = d - 4	1 to d
*=	e *= 5	e = e * 5	20 to e
/=	f /= 3	f = f / 3	2 to f
%=	g %= 9	g = g % 9	3 to g

Fig. 5.10 | Arithmetic compound assignment operators.

5.10 Increment and Decrement Operators

C# provides two unary operators for adding 1 to or subtracting 1 from the value of a numeric variable. These are the unary **increment operator**, **++**, and the unary **decrement operator**, **--**, respectively, which are summarized in Fig. 5.11. An app can increment by 1 the value of a variable called c using the increment operator, ++, rather than the expression c = c + 1 or c += 1. An increment or decrement operator that's prefixed to (placed *before*) a variable is referred to as the **prefix increment operator** or **prefix decrement operator**, respectively. An increment or decrement operator that's postfixed to (placed *after*) a variable is referred to as the **postfix increment operator** or **postfix decrement operator**, respectively.

Operator	Called	Sample expression	Explanation
++	prefix increment	++a	Increments a by 1 and uses the new value of a in the expression in which a resides.
++	postfix increment	a++	Increments a by 1, but uses the original value of a in the expression in which a resides.
--	prefix decrement	--b	Decrements b by 1 and uses the new value of b in the expression in which b resides.
--	postfix decrement	b--	Decrements b by 1 but uses the original value of b in the expression in which b resides.

Fig. 5.11 | Increment and decrement operators.

Incrementing (or decrementing) a variable with an *increment* (or decrement) operator causes it to be incremented (or decremented) by 1. For a *prefix increment* (or decrement) operator, the variable's *new* value is used in the expression in which the variable appears. For a *postfix increment* (or decrement) operator, the variable's *original* value is used in the expression in which the variable appears.

Figure 5.12 demonstrates the difference between the prefix increment and postfix increment versions of the ++ increment operator. The decrement operator (--) works sim-

ilarly. In this example, we simply want to show the mechanics of the ++ operator, so we
use only one class declaration containing method Main.

```
1   // Fig. 5.12: Increment.cs
2   // Prefix increment and postfix increment operators.
3   using System;
4
5   public class Increment
6   {
7      public static void Main( string[] args )
8      {
9         int c;
10
11        // demonstrate postfix increment operator
12        c = 5; // assign 5 to c
13        Console.WriteLine( c ); // display 5
14        Console.WriteLine( c++ ); // increment c and display 5
15        Console.WriteLine( c ); // display 6
16
17        Console.WriteLine(); // skip a line
18
19        // demonstrate prefix increment operator
20        c = 5; // assign 5 to c
21        Console.WriteLine( c ); // display 5
22        Console.WriteLine( ++c ); // increment c and display 6
23        Console.WriteLine( c ); // display 6 again
24     } // end Main
25  } // end class Increment
```

```
5
5
6

5
6
6
```

Fig. 5.12 | Prefix increment and postfix increment operators.

Line 12 initializes the variable c to 5, and line 13 outputs c's initial value. Line 14 outputs the value of the expression c++. This expression performs the postfix increment operation on the variable c, so even though c's value is incremented, c's *original* value (5) is
output. Thus, line 14 outputs c's initial value (5) again. Line 15 outputs c's new value (6)
to prove that the variable's value was indeed incremented in line 14.

Line 20 resets c's value to 5, and line 21 outputs c's value. Line 22 outputs the value
of the expression ++c. This expression performs the prefix increment operation on c, so its
value is incremented and the *new* value (6) is output. Line 23 outputs c's value again to
show that the value of c is still 6 after line 22 executes.

The arithmetic compound assignment operators and the increment and decrement
operators can be used to simplify statements. For example, the three assignment statements in Fig. 5.9 (lines 24, 26 and 29)

```
passes = passes + 1;
failures = failures + 1;
studentCounter = studentCounter + 1;
```

can be written more concisely with compound assignment operators as

```
passes += 1;
failures += 1;
studentCounter += 1;
```

and even more concisely with prefix increment operators as

```
++passes;
++failures;
++studentCounter;
```

or with postfix increment operators as

```
passes++;
failures++;
studentCounter++;
```

When incrementing or decrementing a variable in a statement by itself, the prefix increment and postfix increment forms have the *same* result, and the prefix decrement and postfix decrement forms have the *same* result. It's only when a variable appears in the context of a larger expression that the prefix increment and postfix increment have *different* results (and similarly for the prefix decrement and postfix decrement).

Common Programming Error 5.5

Attempting to use the increment or decrement operator on an expression other than one to which a value can be assigned is a syntax error. For example, writing ++(x + 1) is a syntax error, because (x + 1) is not an expression to which a value can be assigned.

Precedence and Associativity of the Operators We've Discussed So Far

Figure 5.13 shows the precedence and associativity of the operators we've introduced to this point. The operators are shown from top to bottom in decreasing order of precedence. The second column describes the associativity of the operators at each level of precedence. The conditional operator (?:); the unary operators prefix increment (++), prefix decrement (--), plus (+) and minus (-); the cast operators; and the assignment operators =, +=, -=, *=, /= and %= associate from right to left. All the other operators in the operator precedence chart in Fig. 5.13 associate from left to right. The third column names the groups of operators.

Operators					Associativity	Type
.	new	++*(postfix)*	--*(postfix)*		left to right	highest precedence
++	--	+	-	*(type)*	right to left	unary prefix
*	/	%			left to right	multiplicative
+	-				left to right	additive
<	<=	>	>=		left to right	relational

Fig. 5.13 | Precedence and associativity of the operators discussed so far. (Part 1 of 2.)

Operators	Associativity	Type
== !=	left to right	equality
?:	right to left	conditional
= += -= *= /= %=	right to left	assignment

Fig. 5.13 | Precedence and associativity of the operators discussed so far. (Part 2 of 2.)

5.11 Simple Types

The table in Appendix B lists the 13 **simple types** in C#. Like its predecessor languages C and C++, C# requires *all* variables to have a type. For this reason, C# is referred to as a **strongly typed language**.

In C and C++, you frequently have to write separate versions of apps to support different computer platforms, because the simple types are *not* guaranteed to be identical from computer to computer. For example, an int value on one machine might be represented by 16 bits (2 bytes) of storage, while an int value on another machine might be represented by 32 bits (4 bytes) of storage. In C#, int values are always 32 bits (4 bytes). In fact, *all* C# numeric types have fixed sizes, as is shown in Appendix B.

Each type in Appendix B is listed with its size in bits (there are eight bits to a byte) and its range of values. Because the designers of C# want it to be maximally portable, they use internationally recognized standards for both character formats (Unicode; for more information, see Appendix F, Unicode®) and floating-point numbers (IEEE 754; for more information, visit grouper.ieee.org/groups/754/).

Recall from Section 4.5 that variables of *simple types* declared *outside* of a method as fields of a class are automatically assigned default values unless explicitly initialized. Instance variables of types char, byte, sbyte, short, ushort, int, uint, long, ulong, float, double, and decimal are all given the value 0 by default. Instance variables of type bool are given the value false by default. Similarly, reference-type instance variables are initialized by default to the value null.

5.12 Wrap-Up

We demonstrated the if single-selection statement, the if...else double-selection statement and the while repetition statement. We used control-statement stacking to compute the total and the average of a set of student grades with counter- and sentinel-controlled repetition, and we used control-statement nesting to analyze and make decisions based on a set of exam results. We introduced C#'s compound assignment, unary cast, conditional (?:), increment and decrement operators. Finally, we discussed the simple types. In Chapter 6, we continue our discussion of control statements, introducing the for, do...while and switch statements.

6

Control Statements: Part 2

Objectives

In this chapter you'll:

- Use counter-controlled repetition.

- Use the **for** and **do...while** repetition statements.

- Use the **switch** multiple selection statement.

- Use the **break** and **continue** statements to alter the flow of control.

- Use the logical operators to form complex conditional expressions.

6.1 Introduction

In this chapter, we introduce several of C#'s remaining control statements. (The foreach statement is introduced in Chapter 8.) The control statements we study here and in Chapter 5 are helpful in building and manipulating objects.

Through a series of short examples using while and for, we explore the essentials of counter-controlled repetition. We create a version of class GradeBook that uses a switch statement to count the number of A, B, C, D and F grade equivalents in a set of numeric grades entered by the user. We introduce the break and continue program-control statements. We discuss C#'s logical operators, which enable you to use more complex conditional expressions in control statements.

6.2 Essentials of Counter-Controlled Repetition

This section uses the while **repetition statement** to formalize the elements required to perform counter-controlled repetition. Counter-controlled repetition requires

1. a **control variable** (or loop counter)

2. the **initial value** of the control variable

3. the **increment** (or **decrement**) by which the control variable is modified each time through the loop (also known as each **iteration of the loop**)

4. the **loop-continuation condition** that determines whether to continue looping.

To see these elements of counter-controlled repetition, consider the app of Fig. 6.1, which uses a loop to display the numbers from 1 through 10.

```
1   // Fig. 6.1: WhileCounter.cs
2   // Counter-controlled repetition with the while repetition statement.
3   using System;
4
5   public class WhileCounter
6   {
7      public static void Main( string[] args )
8      {
9         int counter = 1; // declare and initialize control variable
10
11        while ( counter <= 10 ) // loop-continuation condition
12        {
13           Console.Write( "{0}  ", counter );
14           ++counter; // increment control variable
15        } // end while
```

Fig. 6.1 | Counter-controlled repetition with the while repetition statement. (Part 1 of 2.)

```
16
17          Console.WriteLine(); // output a newline
18      } // end Main
19  } // end class WhileCounter
```

```
1  2  3  4  5  6  7  8  9  10
```

Fig. 6.1 | Counter-controlled repetition with the `while` repetition statement. (Part 2 of 2.)

In method `Main` (lines 7–18), the elements of counter-controlled repetition are defined in lines 9, 11 and 14. Line 9 declares the control variable (`counter`) as an `int`, reserves space for it in memory and sets its initial value to 1.

Line 13 in the `while` statement displays control variable `counter`'s value during each iteration of the loop. Line 14 increments the control variable by 1 for each iteration of the loop. The loop-continuation condition in the `while` (line 11) tests whether the value of the control variable is less than or equal to 10 (the final value for which the condition is `true`). The app performs the body of this `while` even when the control variable is 10. The loop terminates when the control variable exceeds 10 (i.e., `counter` becomes 11).

Error-Prevention Tip 6.1

Because floating-point values may be approximate, controlling loops with floating-point variables may result in imprecise counter values and inaccurate termination tests. Control counting loops with integers.

The app in Fig. 6.1 can be made more concise by initializing `counter` to 0 in line 9 and incrementing `counter` in the `while` condition with the prefix increment operator as follows:

```
while ( ++counter <= 10 ) // loop-continuation condition
    Console.Write( "{0}  ", counter );
```

This code saves a statement (and eliminates the need for braces around the loop's body), because the `while` condition performs the increment before testing the condition. (Recall from Section 5.10 that the precedence of `++` is higher than that of `<=`.) Code written in such a condensed fashion might be more difficult to read, debug, modify and maintain.

Software Engineering Observation 6.1

"Keep it simple" is good advice for most of the code you'll write.

6.3 for Repetition Statement

Section 6.2 presented the essentials of counter-controlled repetition. The `while` statement can be used to implement *any* counter-controlled loop. C# also provides the **for repetition statement**, which specifies the elements of counter-controlled-repetition in a single line of code. In general, counter-controlled repetition should be implemented with a `for` statement. Figure 6.2 reimplements the app in Fig. 6.1 using the `for` statement.

When the `for` statement (lines 11–12) begins executing, control variable `counter` is declared and initialized to 1. (Recall from Section 6.2 that the first two elements of counter-controlled repetition are the *control variable* and its *initial value*.) Next, the app checks the

```
 1   // Fig. 6.2: ForCounter.cs
 2   // Counter-controlled repetition with the for repetition statement.
 3   using System;
 4
 5   public class ForCounter
 6   {
 7      public static void Main( string[] args )
 8      {
 9         // for statement header includes initialization,
10         // loop-continuation condition and increment
11         for ( int counter = 1; counter <= 10; ++counter )
12            Console.Write( "{0}  ", counter );
13
14         Console.WriteLine(); // output a newline
15      } // end Main
16   } // end class ForCounter
```

```
1  2  3  4  5  6  7  8  9  10
```

Fig. 6.2 | Counter-controlled repetition with the **for** repetition statement.

loop-continuation condition, counter <= 10, which is between the two required semicolons. The initial value of counter is 1, so the condition initially is true. Therefore, the body statement (line 12) displays control variable counter's value, which is 1. Next, the app increments counter in the expression ++counter, which appears to the right of the second semicolon. Then the loop-continuation test is performed again to determine whether the app should continue with the next iteration of the loop. At this point, the control-variable value is 2, so the condition is still true—and the app performs the body statement again (i.e., the next iteration of the loop). This process continues until the numbers 1 through 10 have been displayed and the counter's value becomes 11, causing the loop-continuation test to fail and repetition to terminate (after 10 repetitions of the loop body at line 12). Then the app performs the first statement after the for—in this case, line 14.

Fig. 6.2 uses (in line 11) the loop-continuation condition counter <= 10. If you incorrectly specified counter < 10 as the condition, the loop would iterate only nine times—a common logic error called an **off-by-one error**.

Figure 6.3 takes a closer look at the for statement in Fig. 6.2. The for's first line (including the keyword for and everything in parentheses after for)—line 11 in Fig. 6.2—is sometimes called the **for statement header**, or simply the **for header**. The for header "does it all"—it specifies each of the items needed for counter-controlled repetition with a control variable. If there's more than one statement in the body of the for, braces are required to define the body of the loop.

The general format of the for statement is

> **for** (*initialization*; *loopContinuationCondition*; *increment*)
>   *statement*

where the *initialization* expression names the loop's control variable and provides its initial value, the *loopContinuationCondition* is the condition that determines whether looping should continue and the *increment* modifies the control variable's value (whether an increment or decrement), so that the loop-continuation condition eventually becomes false. The

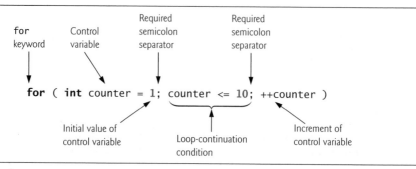

Fig. 6.3 | for statement header components.

two semicolons in the for header are required. We don't include a semicolon after *statement*, because the semicolon is already assumed to be included in the notion of a *statement*.

In most cases, the for statement can be represented with an equivalent while statement as follows:

```
initialization;

while ( loopContinuationCondition )
{
    statement
    increment;
}
```

In Section 6.7, we discuss a case in which a for statement cannot be represented with a while statement like the one above.

Typically, for statements are used for counter-controlled repetition, and while statements are used for sentinel-controlled repetition. However, while and for can each be used for either repetition type.

If the *initialization* expression in the for header declares the control variable (i.e., the control variable's type is specified before the variable name, as in Fig. 6.2), the control variable can be used *only* in that for statement—it will not exist outside it. This restricted use of the name of the control variable is known as the variable's **scope**. The scope of a variable defines where it can be used in an app. For example, a local variable can be used only in the method that declares the variable and *only* from the point of declaration through the end of the block in which the variable has been declared. Scope is discussed in detail in Chapter 7, Methods: A Deeper Look.

Common Programming Error 6.1

When a for statement's control variable is declared in the initialization section of the for's header, using the control variable after the for's body is a compilation error.

All three expressions in a for header are *optional*. If the *loopContinuationCondition* is omitted, C# assumes that it's *always true*, thus creating an *infinite loop*. You can omit the *initialization* expression if the app initializes the control variable *before* the loop—in this case, the scope of the control variable will *not* be limited to the loop. You can omit the *increment* expression if the app calculates the increment with statements in the loop's body or if no increment is needed. The increment expression in a for acts as if it were a standalone statement at the end of the for's body. Therefore, the expressions

```
counter = counter + 1
counter += 1
++counter
counter++
```

are equivalent increment expressions in a for statement.

Performance Tip 6.1

There's a slight performance advantage to using the prefix increment operator, but if you choose the postfix increment operator because it seems more natural (as in a for header), optimizing compilers will generate code that uses the more efficient form anyway.

The initialization, loop-continuation condition and increment portions of a for statement can contain arithmetic expressions. For example, assume that x = 2 and y = 10; if x and y are not modified in the body of the loop, then the statement

```
for ( int j = x; j <= 4 * x * y; j += y / x )
```

is equivalent to the statement

```
for ( int j = 2; j <= 80; j += 5 )
```

The increment of a for statement may also be *negative*, in which case it's actually a *decrement*, and the loop counts downward.

If the loop-continuation condition is initially false, the app does *not* execute the for statement's body. Instead, execution proceeds with the statement following the for.

Figure 6.4 shows the activity diagram of the for statement in Fig. 6.2. The diagram makes it clear that initialization occurs *only once* before the loop-continuation test is evaluated the first time, and that incrementing occurs *each* time through the loop after the body statement executes.

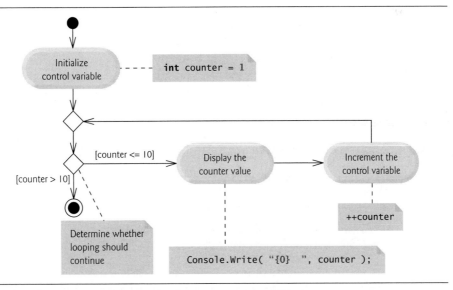

Fig. 6.4 | UML activity diagram for the for statement in Fig. 6.2.

6.4 Examples Using the for Statement

The following examples show techniques for varying the control variable in a for statement. In each case, we write the appropriate for header. Note the change in the relational operator for loops that decrement the control variable.

a) Vary the control variable from 1 to 100 in increments of 1.

```
for ( int i = 1; i <= 100; ++i )
```

b) Vary the control variable from 100 to 1 in decrements of 1.

```
for ( int i = 100; i >= 1; --i )
```

c) Vary the control variable from 7 to 77 in increments of 7.

```
for ( int i = 7; i <= 77; i += 7 )
```

d) Vary the control variable from 20 to 2 in decrements of 2.

```
for ( int i = 20; i >= 2; i -= 2 )
```

e) Vary the control variable over the sequence 2, 5, 8, 11, 14, 17, 20.

```
for ( int i = 2; i <= 20; i += 3 )
```

f) Vary the control variable over the sequence 99, 88, 77, 66, 55, 44, 33, 22, 11, 0.

```
for ( int i = 99; i >= 0; i -= 11 )
```

Common Programming Error 6.2

Not using the proper relational operator in the loop-continuation condition of a loop that counts downward (e.g., using i <= 1 instead of i >= 1 in a loop counting down to 1) is a logic error.

App: Summing the Even Integers from 2 to 20

We now consider two sample apps that demonstrate simple uses of for. The app in Fig. 6.5 uses a for statement to sum the even integers from 2 to 20 and store the result in an int variable called total.

```
 1   // Fig. 6.5: Sum.cs
 2   // Summing integers with the for statement.
 3   using System;
 4
 5   public class Sum
 6   {
 7      public static void Main( string[] args )
 8      {
 9         int total = 0; // initialize total
10
11         // total even integers from 2 through 20
12         for ( int number = 2; number <= 20; number += 2 )
13            total += number;
14
```

Fig. 6.5 | Summing integers with the for statement. (Part 1 of 2.)

```
15              Console.WriteLine( "Sum is {0}", total ); // display results
16          } // end Main
17      } // end class Sum
```

```
Sum is 110
```

Fig. 6.5 | Summing integers with the for statement. (Part 2 of 2.)

The *initialization* and *increment* expressions can be *comma-separated lists* that enable you to use *multiple* initialization expressions or *multiple* increment expressions. For example, you could merge the body of the for statement in lines 12–13 of Fig. 6.5 into the increment portion of the for header by using a comma as follows:

```
for ( int number = 2; number <= 20; total += number, number += 2 )
    ; // empty statement
```

We prefer *not* complicating for headers in this manner.

App: Compound-Interest Calculations

The next app uses the for statement to compute compound interest. Consider the following problem:

> *A person invests $1,000 in a savings account yielding 5% interest, compounded yearly. Assuming that all the interest is left on deposit, calculate and display the amount of money in the account at the end of each year for 10 years. Use the following formula to determine the amounts:*
>
> $$a = p\,(1 + r)^n$$
>
> *where*
>
> p is the original amount invested (i.e., the principal)
> r is the annual interest rate (e.g., use 0.05 for 5%)
> n is the number of years
> a is the amount on deposit at the end of the nth year.

This problem involves a loop that performs the indicated calculation for each of the 10 years the money remains on deposit. The solution is the app shown in Fig. 6.6. Lines 9–11 in method Main declare decimal variables amount and principal, and double variable rate. Lines 10–11 also initialize principal to 1000 (i.e., $1000.00) and rate to 0.05. C# treats real-number constants like 0.05 as type double. Similarly, C# treats whole-number constants like 7 and 1000 as type int. When principal is initialized to 1000, the value 1000 of type int is *promoted* to a decimal type *implicitly*—no cast is required.

```
1   // Fig. 6.6: Interest.cs
2   // Compound-interest calculations with for.
3   using System;
4
5   public class Interest
6   {
```

Fig. 6.6 | Compound-interest calculations with for. (Part 1 of 2.)

```
 7        public static void Main( string[] args )
 8        {
 9           decimal amount; // amount on deposit at end of each year
10           decimal principal = 1000; // initial amount before interest
11           double rate = 0.05; // interest rate
12
13           // display headers
14           Console.WriteLine( "Year{0,20}", "Amount on deposit" );
15
16           // calculate amount on deposit for each of ten years
17           for ( int year = 1; year <= 10; ++year )
18           {
19              // calculate new amount for specified year
20              amount = principal *
21                 ( ( decimal ) Math.Pow( 1.0 + rate, year ) );
22
23              // display the year and the amount
24              Console.WriteLine( "{0,4}{1,20:C}", year, amount );
25           } // end for
26        } // end Main
27     } // end class Interest
```

```
Year    Amount on deposit
   1            $1,050.00
   2            $1,102.50
   3            $1,157.63
   4            $1,215.51
   5            $1,276.28
   6            $1,340.10
   7            $1,407.10
   8            $1,477.46
   9            $1,551.33
  10            $1,628.89
```

Fig. 6.6 | Compound-interest calculations with for. (Part 2 of 2.)

Line 14 outputs the headers for the app's two columns of output. The first column displays the year, and the second displays the amount on deposit at the end of that year. We use the format item {0,20} to output the string "Amount on deposit". The integer 20 after the comma indicates that the value output should be displayed with a **field width** of 20—that is, WriteLine displays the value with at least 20 character positions. If the value to be output is *less than* 20 character positions wide (17 characters in this example), the value is **right justified** in the field by default (in this case the value is preceded by three blanks). If the year value to be output were *more* than four character positions wide, the field width would be *extended to the right* to accommodate the entire value—this would push the amount field to the right, upsetting the neat columns of our tabular output. To indicate that output should be **left justified**, simply use a *negative* field width.

The for statement (lines 17–25) executes its body 10 times, varying control variable year from 1 to 10 in increments of 1. This loop terminates when control variable year becomes 11. (year corresponds to *n* in the problem statement.)

Classes provide methods that perform common tasks on objects. In fact, most methods must be called on a specific object. For example, to output a greeting in Fig. 4.2, we called method `DisplayMessage` on the `myGradeBook` object. Many classes also provide methods that perform common tasks and cannot be called on objects—they *must* be called using a class name. Such methods are called **static methods**. For example, C# does not include an exponentiation operator, so the designers of C#'s `Math` class defined `static` method `Pow` for raising a value to a power. You can call a `static` method by specifying the class name followed by the member access (.) operator and the method name, as in

> *ClassName*.*MethodName*(*arguments*)

`Console` methods `Write` and `WriteLine` are `static` methods. In Chapter 7, you'll learn how to implement `static` methods in your own classes.

We use `static` method `Pow` of class `Math` to perform the compound interest calculation in Fig. 6.6. `Math.Pow(x, y)` calculates the value of *x* raised to the *y*th power. The method receives two `double` arguments and returns a `double` value. Lines 20–21 perform the calculation $a = p(1 + r)^n$, where *a* is the amount, *p* is the principal, *r* is the rate and *n* is the year. Notice that, in this calculation, we need to multiply a `decimal` value (`principal`) by a `double` value (the return value of `Math.Pow`). C# will not implicitly convert `double` to a `decimal` type, or vice versa, because of the *possible loss of information* in either conversion, so line 21 contains a (`decimal`) cast operator that explicitly converts the `double` return value of `Math.Pow` to a `decimal`.

After each calculation, line 24 outputs the year and the amount on deposit at the end of that year. The year is output in a field width of four characters (as specified by `{0,4}`). The amount is output as a currency value with the format item `{1,20:C}`. The number 20 in the format item indicates that the value should be output *right justified* with a field width of 20 characters. The format specifier `C` indicates that the number should be formatted as currency.

We declared the variables `amount` and `principal` to be of type `decimal` rather than `double`. Recall that we introduced type `decimal` for monetary calculations in Section 4.11. We also use `decimal` in Fig. 6.6 for this purpose. You may be curious as to why we do this. We're dealing with fractional parts of dollars and thus need a type that allows decimal points in its values. Unfortunately, floating-point numbers of type `double` (or `float`) can cause trouble in monetary calculations. Two `double` dollar amounts stored in the machine could be 14.234 (which would normally be rounded to 14.23 for display purposes) and 18.673 (which would normally be rounded to 18.67 for display purposes). When these amounts are added, they produce the internal sum 32.907, which would normally be rounded to 32.91 for display purposes. Thus, your output could appear as

```
   14.23
 + 18.67
 -------
   32.91
```

but a person adding the individual numbers as displayed would expect the sum to be 32.90. You've been warned! For people who work with programming languages that do not support a type for precise monetary calculations,

Error-Prevention Tip 6.2

Do not use variables of type `double` (or `float`) to perform precise monetary calculations; use type `decimal` instead. The imprecision of floating-point numbers can cause errors that will result in incorrect monetary values.

The body of the for statement contains the calculation 1.0 + rate, which appears as an argument to the Math.Pow method. In fact, this calculation produces the same result each time through the loop, so repeating the calculation in every iteration of the loop is wasteful.

Performance Tip 6.2

In loops, avoid calculations for which the result never changes—such calculations should typically be placed before the loop. Optimizing compilers will typically place such calculations outside loops in the compiled code.

6.5 do...while Repetition Statement

The **do...while repetition statement** is similar to the while statement. In the while, the app tests the loop-continuation condition, *before* executing the loop's body. If the condition is false, the body *never* executes. The do...while statement tests the loop-continuation condition *after* executing the loop's body; therefore, the body always executes *at least once*. When a do...while statement terminates, execution continues with the next statement in sequence. Figure 6.7 uses a do...while (lines 11–15) to output the numbers 1–10.

```
1   // Fig. 6.7: DoWhileTest.cs
2   // do...while repetition statement.
3   using System;
4
5   public class DoWhileTest
6   {
7      public static void Main( string[] args )
8      {
9         int counter = 1; // initialize counter
10
11         do
12         {
13            Console.Write( "{0}   ", counter );
14            ++counter;
15         } while ( counter <= 10 ); // end do...while
16
17         Console.WriteLine(); // outputs a newline
18      } // end Main
19   } // end class DoWhileTest
```

```
1 2 3 4 5 6 7 8 9 10
```

Fig. 6.7 | do...while repetition statement.

Line 9 declares and initializes control variable counter. Upon entering the do...while statement, line 13 outputs counter's value, and line 14 increments counter. Then the app evaluates the loop-continuation test at the *bottom* of the loop (line 15). If the condition is true, the loop continues from the first body statement (line 13). If the condition is false, the loop terminates, and the app continues with the next statement after the loop.

Figure 6.8 contains the UML activity diagram for the do...while statement. This diagram makes it clear that the loop-continuation condition is not evaluated until *after* the loop performs the action state *at least once*. Compare this activity diagram with that of the while statement (Fig. 5.4). It's not necessary to use braces in the do...while repetition statement if there's only one statement in the body. However, most programmers include the braces to avoid confusion between the while and do...while statements. For example,

> **while** (*condition*)

is normally the first line of a while statement. A do...while statement with no braces around a single-statement body appears as:

> **do**
>   *statement*
> **while** (*condition*);

which can be confusing. A reader may misinterpret the last line—while(*condition*);—as a while statement containing an empty statement (the semicolon by itself). To avoid confusion, a do...while statement with one body statement can be written as follows:

> **do**
> {
>   *statement*
> } **while** (*condition*);

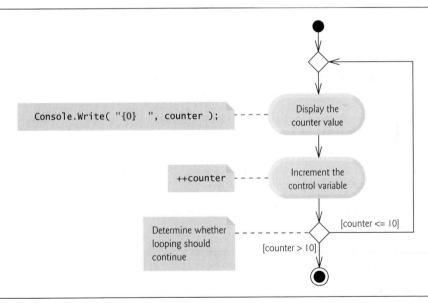

Fig. 6.8 | do...while repetition statement UML activity diagram.

6.6 switch Multiple-Selection Statement

We discussed the if single-selection statement and the if...else double-selection statement in Chapter 5. C# provides the **switch multiple-selection** statement to perform different actions based on the possible values of an expression. Each action is associated with the value of a **constant integral expression** or a **constant string expression** that the variable or expression on which the switch is based may assume. A constant integral expression is any expression involving character and integer constants that evaluates to an integer value—i.e., values of type sbyte, byte, short, ushort, int, uint, long, ulong and char, or a constant from an enum type (enum is discussed in Section 7.10). A constant string expression is any expression composed of string literals that always results in the same string.

GradeBook Class with *switch* Statement to Count A, B, C, D and F Grades.

Figure 6.9 contains an enhanced version of the GradeBook class introduced in Chapter 4 and further developed in Chapter 5. This version of the class not only calculates the average of a set of numeric grades entered by the user, but uses a switch statement to determine whether each grade is the equivalent of an A, B, C, D or F, then increments the appropriate grade counter. The class also displays a summary of the number of students who received each grade. Figure 6.10 shows sample input and output of the GradeBookTest app that uses class GradeBook to process a set of grades.

```
1   // Fig. 6.9: GradeBook.cs
2   // GradeBook class that uses a switch statement to count letter grades.
3   using System;
4
5   public class GradeBook
6   {
7      private int total; // sum of grades
8      private int gradeCounter; // number of grades entered
9      private int aCount; // count of A grades
10     private int bCount; // count of B grades
11     private int cCount; // count of C grades
12     private int dCount; // count of D grades
13     private int fCount; // count of F grades
14
15     // automatic property CourseName
16     public string CourseName { get; set; }
17
18     // constructor initializes automatic property CourseName;
19     // int instance variables are initialized to 0 by default
20     public GradeBook( string name )
21     {
22        CourseName = name; // set CourseName to name
23     } // end constructor
24
25     // display a welcome message to the GradeBook user
26     public void DisplayMessage()
27     {
28        // CourseName gets the name of the course
29        Console.WriteLine( "Welcome to the grade book for\n{0}!\n",
30           CourseName );
31     } // end method DisplayMessage
32
33     // input arbitrary number of grades from user
34     public void InputGrades()
35     {
36        int grade; // grade entered by user
```

Fig. 6.9 | GradeBook class that uses a switch statement to count letter grades. (Part 1 of 3.)

```
37          string input; // text entered by the user
38
39          Console.WriteLine( "{0}\n{1}",
40             "Enter the integer grades in the range 0-100.",
41             "Type <Ctrl> z and press Enter to terminate input:" );
42
43          input = Console.ReadLine(); // read user input
44
45          // loop until user enters the end-of-file indicator (<Ctrl> z)
46          while ( input != null )
47          {
48             grade = Convert.ToInt32( input ); // read grade off user input
49             total += grade; // add grade to total
50             ++gradeCounter; // increment number of grades
51
52             // call method to increment appropriate counter
53             IncrementLetterGradeCounter( grade );
54
55             input = Console.ReadLine(); // read user input
56          } // end while
57       } // end method InputGrades
58
59       // add 1 to appropriate counter for specified grade
60       private void IncrementLetterGradeCounter( int grade )
61       {
62          // determine which grade was entered
63          switch ( grade / 10 )
64          {
65             case 9: // grade was in the 90s
66             case 10: // grade was 100
67                ++aCount; // increment aCount
68                break; // necessary to exit switch
69             case 8: // grade was between 80 and 89
70                ++bCount; // increment bCount
71                break; // exit switch
72             case 7: // grade was between 70 and 79
73                ++cCount; // increment cCount
74                break; // exit switch
75             case 6: // grade was between 60 and 69
76                ++dCount; // increment dCount
77                break; // exit switch
78             default: // grade was less than 60
79                ++fCount; // increment fCount
80                break; // exit switch
81          } // end switch
82       } // end method IncrementLetterGradeCounter
83
84       // display a report based on the grades entered by the user
85       public void DisplayGradeReport()
86       {
87          Console.WriteLine( "\nGrade Report:" );
88
```

Fig. 6.9 | GradeBook class that uses a switch statement to count letter grades. (Part 2 of 3.)

```
89              // if user entered at least one grade...
90              if ( gradeCounter != 0 )
91              {
92                 // calculate average of all grades entered
93                 double average = ( double ) total / gradeCounter;
94
95                 // output summary of results
96                 Console.WriteLine( "Total of the {0} grades entered is {1}",
97                    gradeCounter, total );
98                 Console.WriteLine( "Class average is {0:F}", average );
99                 Console.WriteLine( "{0}A: {1}\nB: {2}\nC: {3}\nD: {4}\nF: {5}",
100                   "Number of students who received each grade:\n",
101                   aCount, // display number of A grades
102                   bCount, // display number of B grades
103                   cCount, // display number of C grades
104                   dCount, // display number of D grades
105                   fCount ); // display number of F grades
106             } // end if
107             else // no grades were entered, so output appropriate message
108                Console.WriteLine( "No grades were entered" );
109         } // end method DisplayGradeReport
110     } // end class GradeBook
```

Fig. 6.9 | GradeBook class that uses a `switch` statement to count letter grades. (Part 3 of 3.)

Instance Variables

Class GradeBook (Fig. 6.9) declares instance variables total (line 7) and gradeCounter (line 8), which keep track of the sum of the grades entered by the user and the number of grades entered, respectively. Lines 9–13 declare counter variables for each grade category. Class GradeBook maintains total, gradeCounter and the five letter-grade counters as instance variables so that they can be used or modified in any of the class's methods.

Property CourseName, Method DisplayMessage and the Constructor

Like earlier versions of the class, class GradeBook declares automatic property CourseName (line 16) and method DisplayMessage (lines 26–31) to display a welcome message to the user. The class also contains a constructor (lines 20–23) that initializes the course name. The constructor sets only the course name—the remaining seven instance variables are ints and are initialized to 0 by default.

Methods InputGrades and DisplayGradeReport

Class GradeBook contains three additional methods—InputGrades, IncrementLetterGradeCounter and DisplayGradeReport. Method InputGrades (lines 34–57) reads an arbitrary number of integer grades from the user using sentinel-controlled repetition and updates instance variables total and gradeCounter. Method InputGrades calls method IncrementLetterGradeCounter (lines 60–82) to update the appropriate letter-grade counter for each grade entered. Class GradeBook also contains method DisplayGradeReport (lines 85–109), which outputs a report containing the total of all grades entered, the average of the grades and the number of students who received each letter grade. Let's examine these methods in more detail.

Lines 36–37 in method InputGrades declare variables grade and input, which will first store the user's input as a string (in the variable input), then convert it to an int to store in the variable grade. Lines 39–41 prompt the user to enter integer grades and to type *Ctrl + z*, then press *Enter* to terminate the input. The notation *Ctrl + z* means to simultaneously press both the *Ctrl* key and the *z* key when typing in a **Command Prompt**. *Ctrl + z* is the Windows key sequence for typing the **end-of-file indicator**. This is one way to inform an app that there's no more data to input. If *Ctrl + z* is entered while the app is awaiting input with a ReadLine method, null is returned. (The end-of-file indicator is a system-dependent keystroke combination. On many non-Windows systems, end-of-file is entered by typing *Ctrl + d*.) In Chapter 17, Files and Streams, we'll see how the end-of-file indicator is used when an app reads its input from a file. Windows typically displays the characters ^Z in a **Command Prompt** when the end-of-file indicator is typed, as shown in the output of Fig. 6.10.

Line 43 uses the ReadLine method to get the first line that the user entered and store it in variable input. The while statement (lines 46–56) processes this user input. The condition at line 46 checks whether the value of input is null. The Console class's ReadLine method returns null only if the user typed an end-of-file indicator. As long as the end-of-file indicator has not been typed, input will not be null, and the condition will pass.

Line 48 converts the string in input to an int type. Line 49 adds grade to total. Line 50 increments gradeCounter. The class's DisplayGradeReport method uses these variables to compute the average of the grades. Line 53 calls the class's IncrementLetterGradeCounter method (declared in lines 60–82) to increment the appropriate letter-grade counter, based on the numeric grade entered.

Method *IncrementLetterGradeCounter*

Method IncrementLetterGradeCounter contains a switch statement (lines 63–81) that determines which counter to increment. In this example, we assume that the user enters a valid grade in the range 0–100. A grade in the range 90–100 represents A, 80–89 represents B, 70–79 represents C, 60–69 represents D and 0–59 represents F. The switch statement consists of a block that contains a sequence of **case labels** and an optional **default label**. These are used in this example to determine which counter to increment based on the grade.

The *switch* Statement

When control reaches the switch statement, the app evaluates the expression in the parentheses (grade / 10) following keyword switch—this is called the **switch expression**. The app attempts to match the value of the switch expression with one of the case labels. The switch expression in line 63 performs integer division, which *truncates* the fractional part of the result. Thus, when we divide any value in the range 0–100 by 10, the result is always a value from 0 to 10. We use several of these values in our case labels. For example, if the user enters the integer 85, the switch expression evaluates to int value 8. If a match occurs between the switch expression and a case (case 8: at line 69), the app executes the statements for that case. For the integer 8, line 70 increments bCount, because a grade in the 80s is a B. The **break statement** (line 71) causes program control to proceed with the first statement after the switch—in this app, we reach the end of method IncrementLetterGradeCounter's body, so control returns to line 55 in method InputGrades (the first line after the call to IncrementLetterGradeCounter). This line uses the ReadLine method to read the next line entered by the user and assign it to the variable input. Line 56 marks the end of the body of the while statement that inputs grades (lines 46–56), so control flows to the while's condition (line 46) to determine whether the loop should continue executing based on the value just assigned to the variable input.

Consecutive *case Labels*

The cases in our switch explicitly test for the values 10, 9, 8, 7 and 6. Note the case labels at lines 65–66 that test for the values 9 and 10 (both of which represent the grade A). Listing case labels consecutively in this manner with no statements between them enables the cases to perform the same set of statements—when the switch expression evaluates to 9 or 10, the statements in lines 67–68 execute. The switch statement does not provide a mechanism for testing ranges of values, so every value to be tested must be listed in a separate case label. Each case can have multiple statements. The switch statement differs from other control statements in that it does *not* require braces around multiple statements in each case.

No *"Fall Through"* in the C# *switch Statement*

In C, C++, and many other programming languages that use the switch statement, the break statement *is not* required at the end of a case. Without break statements, each time a match occurs in the switch, the statements for that case and subsequent cases execute until a break statement or the end of the switch is encountered. This is often referred to as "falling through" to the statements in subsequent cases. This leads to logic errors when you forget the break statement. C# is different from other programming languages—after the statements in a case, you're required to include a statement that terminates the case, such as a break, a return or a throw; otherwise, a compilation error occurs (We discuss the throw statement in Chapter 13, Exception Handling: A Deeper Look.)

The *default Case*

If *no match* occurs between the switch expression's value and a case label, the statements after the default label (lines 79–80) execute. We use the default label in this example to process all switch-expression values that are less than 6—that is, all failing grades. If no match occurs and the switch does *not* contain a default label, program control simply continues with the first statement (if there's one) after the switch statement.

GradeBookTest *Class That Demonstrates Class GradeBook*

Class GradeBookTest (Fig. 6.10) creates a GradeBook object (lines 10–11). Line 13 invokes the object's DisplayMessage method to output a welcome message to the user. Line 14 invokes the object's InputGrades method to read a set of grades from the user and keep track of the sum of all the grades entered and the number of grades. Recall that method InputGrades also calls method IncrementLetterGradeCounter to keep track of the number of students who received each letter grade. Line 15 invokes method DisplayGradeReport of class GradeBook, which outputs a report based on the grades entered. Line 90 of class GradeBook (Fig. 6.9) determines whether the user entered at least one grade—this avoids dividing by zero. If so, line 93 calculates the average of the grades. Lines 96–105 then output the total of all the grades, the class average and the number of students who received each letter grade. If no grades were entered, line 108 outputs an appropriate message. The output in Fig. 6.10 shows a sample grade report based on 9 grades.

```
 1   // Fig. 6.10: GradeBookTest.cs
 2   // Create GradeBook object, input grades and display grade report.
 3
 4   public class GradeBookTest
 5   {
 6      public static void Main( string[] args )
 7      {
 8         // create GradeBook object myGradeBook and
 9         // pass course name to constructor
10         GradeBook myGradeBook = new GradeBook(
11            "CS101 Introduction to C# Programming" );
12
13         myGradeBook.DisplayMessage(); // display welcome message
14         myGradeBook.InputGrades(); // read grades from user
15         myGradeBook.DisplayGradeReport(); // display report based on grades
16      } // end Main
17   } // end class GradeBookTest
```

```
Welcome to the grade book for
CS101 Introduction to C# Programming!

Enter the integer grades in the range 0-100.
Type <Ctrl> z and press Enter to terminate input:
99
92
45
100
57
63
76
14
92
^Z

Grade Report:
Total of the 9 grades entered is 638
Class average is 70.89
Number of students who received each grade:
A: 4
B: 0
C: 1
D: 1
F: 3
```

Fig. 6.10 | Create GradeBook object, input grades and display grade report.

Class GradeBookTest (Fig. 6.10) does not directly call GradeBook method IncrementLetterGradeCounter (lines 60–82 of Fig. 6.9). This method is used exclusively by method InputGrades of class GradeBook to update the appropriate letter-grade counter as each new grade is entered by the user. Method IncrementLetterGradeCounter exists solely to support the operations of class GradeBook's other methods and thus is declared private. Members of a class declared with access modifier private can be accessed only by members of the class in which the private members are declared. When a private member is a method, it's commonly referred to as a **utility method** or **helper method**, because it can be called *only* by other members of that class and is used to support the operation of those other members.

switch *Statement UML Activity Diagram*

Figure 6.11 shows the UML activity diagram for the general switch statement. Every set of statements after a case label normally ends its execution with a break or return statement to terminate the switch statement after processing the case. Typically, you'll use break statements. Figure 6.11 emphasizes this by including break statements in the activity diagram. The diagram makes it clear that the break statement at the end of a case causes control to exit the switch statement immediately.

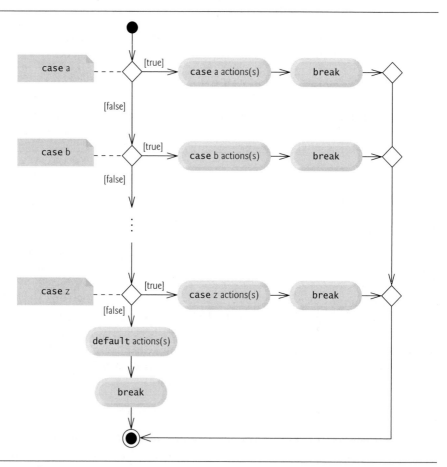

Fig. 6.11 | switch multiple-selection statement UML activity diagram with break statements.

Good Programming Practice 6.1

Although each case *and the* default *label in a* switch *can occur in any order, place the* default *label last for clarity.*

When using the switch statement, remember that the expression after each case can be only a *constant integral expression* or a *constant string expression*—that is, any combination of constants that evaluates to a constant value of an integral or string type. An integer constant is simply an integer value (e.g., –7, 0 or 221). In addition, you can use **character constants**—specific characters in single quotes, such as 'A', '7' or '$'—which represent the integer values of characters. (Appendix C shows the integer values of the characters in the ASCII character set, which is a popular subset of the Unicode character set used by C#.) A *string constant* (or *string literal*) is a sequence of characters in double quotes, such as "Welcome to C# Programming!". For strings, you can also use null.

The expression in each case also can be a **constant**—a value which does not change for the entire app. Constants are declared with the keyword const (discussed in Chapter 7). C# also has a feature called *enumerations*, which we also present in Chapter 7. Enumeration constants can also be used in case labels. In Chapter 12, we present a more elegant way to implement switch logic—we use the technique of *polymorphism* to create apps that are often clearer, easier to maintain and easier to extend than apps using switch logic.

6.7 break and continue Statements

In addition to selection and repetition statements, C# provides statements break and continue to alter the flow of control. The preceding section showed how break can be used to terminate a switch statement's execution. This section discusses how to use break to terminate any repetition statement.

break *Statement*

The break statement, when executed in a while, for, do...while, switch, or foreach, causes immediate exit from that statement. Execution typically continues with the first statement after the control statement—you'll see that there are other possibilities as you learn about additional statement types in C#. Common uses of the break statement are to escape early from a repetition statement or to skip the remainder of a switch (as in Fig. 6.9). Figure 6.12 demonstrates a break statement exiting a for.

When the if nested at line 13 in the for statement (lines 11–17) determines that count is 5, the break statement at line 14 executes. This terminates the for statement, and the app proceeds to line 19 (immediately after the for statement), which displays a message indicating the value of the control variable when the loop terminated. The loop fully executes its body only four times instead of 10 because of the break.

```
1   // Fig. 6.12: BreakTest.cs
2   // break statement exiting a for statement.
3   using System;
4
5   public class BreakTest
6   {
7      public static void Main( string[] args )
8      {
9         int count; // control variable also used after loop terminates
10
```

Fig. 6.12 | break statement exiting a for statement. (Part 1 of 2.)

```
11              for ( count = 1; count <= 10; ++count ) // loop 10 times
12              {
13                 if ( count == 5 ) // if count is 5,
14                    break; // terminate loop
15
16                 Console.Write( "{0} ", count );
17              } // end for
18
19              Console.WriteLine( "\nBroke out of loop at count = {0}", count );
20           } // end Main
21        } // end class BreakTest
```

```
1 2 3 4
Broke out of loop at count = 5
```

Fig. 6.12 | break statement exiting a for statement. (Part 2 of 2.)

continue Statement

The **continue statement**, when executed in a while, for, do...while, or foreach, skips the remaining statements in the loop body and proceeds with the next iteration of the loop. In while and do...while statements, the app evaluates the loop-continuation test *immediately after* the continue statement executes. In a for statement, the increment expression normally executes next, then the app evaluates the loop-continuation test.

Figure 6.13 uses the continue statement in a for to skip the statement at line 14 when the nested if (line 11) determines that the value of count is 5. When the continue statement executes, program control continues with the increment of the control variable in the for statement (line 9).

```
1   // Fig. 6.13: ContinueTest.cs
2   // continue statement terminating an iteration of a for statement.
3   using System;
4
5   public class ContinueTest
6   {
7      public static void Main( string[] args )
8      {
9         for ( int count = 1; count <= 10; ++count ) // loop 10 times
10        {
11           if ( count == 5 ) // if count is 5,
12              continue; // skip remaining code in loop
13
14           Console.Write( "{0} ", count );
15        } // end for
16
17        Console.WriteLine( "\nUsed continue to skip displaying 5" );
18     } // end Main
19  } // end class ContinueTest
```

Fig. 6.13 | continue statement terminating an iteration of a for statement. (Part 1 of 2.)

```
1 2 3 4 6 7 8 9 10
Used continue to skip displaying 5
```

Fig. 6.13 | `continue` statement terminating an iteration of a `for` statement. (Part 2 of 2.)

In Section 6.3, we stated that the `while` statement can be used in most cases in place of `for`. One exception occurs when the increment expression in the `while` *follows* a `continue` statement. In this case, the increment does not execute before the app evaluates the repetition-continuation condition, so the `while` does *not* execute in the same manner as the `for`.

Software Engineering Observation 6.2

There's a tension between achieving quality software engineering and achieving the best-performing software. Often, one of these goals is achieved at the expense of the other. For all but the most performance-intensive situations, apply the following rule: First, make your code simple and correct; then make it fast, but only if necessary.

6.8 Logical Operators

The `if`, `if...else`, `while`, `do...while` and `for` statements each require a condition to determine how to continue an app's flow of control. So far, we've studied only **simple conditions**, such as `count <= 10`, `number != sentinelValue` and `total > 1000`. Simple conditions are expressed in terms of the relational operators `>`, `<`, `>=` and `<=`, and the equality operators `==` and `!=`. Each expression tests only one condition. To test *multiple* conditions in the process of making a decision, we performed these tests in separate statements or in nested `if` or `if...else` statements. Sometimes, control statements require more complex conditions to determine an app's flow of control.

C# provides **logical operators** to enable you to form more complex conditions by combining simple conditions. The logical operators are `&&` (conditional AND), `||` (conditional OR), `&` (boolean logical AND), `|` (boolean logical inclusive OR), `^` (boolean logical exclusive OR) and `!` (logical negation).

Conditional AND (&&) Operator

Suppose that we wish to ensure at some point in an app that two conditions are *both* true before we choose a certain path of execution. In this case, we can use the **&&** (**conditional AND**) operator, as follows:

```
if ( gender == 'F' && age >= 65 )
    ++seniorFemales;
```

This `if` statement contains two simple conditions. The condition `gender == 'F'` determines whether a person is female. The condition `age >= 65` might be evaluated to determine whether a person is a senior citizen. The `if` statement considers the combined condition

```
gender == 'F' && age >= 65
```

which is true if and only if *both* simple conditions are true. If the combined condition is true, the `if` statement's body increments `seniorFemales` by 1. If either or both of the simple conditions are false, the app skips the increment. Some programmers find that the preceding combined condition is more readable when redundant parentheses are added, as in:

```
( gender == 'F' ) && ( age >= 65 )
```

The table in Fig. 6.14 summarizes the && operator. The table shows all four possible combinations of false and true values for *expression1* and *expression2*. Such tables are called **truth tables**. C# evaluates all expressions that include relational operators, equality operators or logical operators to bool values—which are either true or false.

expression1	expression2	expression1 && expression2
false	false	false
false	true	false
true	false	false
true	true	true

Fig. 6.14 | && (conditional AND) operator truth table.

Conditional OR (||) Operator

Now suppose we wish to ensure that *either or both* of two conditions are true before we choose a certain path of execution. In this case, we use the **||** (**conditional OR**) operator, as in the following app segment:

```
if ( ( semesterAverage >= 90 ) || ( finalExam >= 90 ) )
    Console.WriteLine ( "Student grade is A" );
```

This statement also contains two simple conditions. The condition semesterAverage >= 90 is evaluated to determine whether the student deserves an A in the course because of a solid performance throughout the semester. The condition finalExam >= 90 is evaluated to determine whether the student deserves an A in the course because of an outstanding performance on the final exam. The if statement then considers the combined condition

```
( semesterAverage >= 90 ) || ( finalExam >= 90 )
```

and awards the student an A if either or both of the simple conditions are true. The only time the message "Student grade is A" is *not* displayed is when *both* of the simple conditions are *false*. Figure 6.15 is a truth table for operator conditional OR (||). Operator && has a higher precedence than operator ||. Both operators associate from left to right.

expression1	expression2	expression1 || expression2
false	false	false
false	true	true
true	false	true
true	true	true

Fig. 6.15 | || (conditional OR) operator truth table.

Short-Circuit Evaluation of Complex Conditions

The parts of an expression containing && or || operators are evaluated *only* until it's known whether the condition is true or false. Thus, evaluation of the expression

```
( gender == 'F' ) && ( age >= 65 )
```

stops immediately if gender is not equal to 'F' (i.e., at that point, it's certain that the entire expression is false) and continues *only* if gender *is* equal to 'F' (i.e., the entire expression could still be true if the condition age >= 65 is true). This feature of conditional AND and conditional OR expressions is called **short-circuit evaluation**.

Common Programming Error 6.3

In expressions using operator &&, a condition—which we refer to as the dependent condition—may require another condition to be true for the evaluation of the dependent condition to be meaningful. In this case, the dependent condition should be placed after the other one, or an error might occur. For example, in the expression (i != 0) && (10 / i == 2), the second condition must appear after the first condition, or a divide-by-zero error might occur.

Boolean Logical AND (&) and Boolean Logical OR (|) Operators

The **boolean logical AND (&)** and **boolean logical inclusive OR** (|) operators work identically to the && (conditional AND) and || (conditional OR) operators, with one exception—the boolean logical operators *always* evaluate both of their operands (i.e., they do *not* perform short-circuit evaluation). Therefore, the expression

```
( gender == 'F' ) & ( age >= 65 )
```

evaluates age >= 65 regardless of whether gender is equal to 'F'. This is useful if the right operand of the boolean logical AND or boolean logical inclusive OR operator has a required **side effect**—such as, a modification of a variable's value. For example, the expression

```
( birthday == true ) | ( ++age >= 65 )
```

guarantees that the condition ++age >= 65 will be evaluated. So, age is incremented in the preceding expression, *regardless* of whether the overall expression is true or false.

Boolean Logical Exclusive OR (^)

A complex condition containing the **boolean logical exclusive OR** (^) operator (also called the **logical XOR operator**) is true *if and only if one of its operands is* true *and the other is* false. If both operands are true or both are false, the entire condition is false. Figure 6.16 is a truth table for the boolean logical exclusive OR operator (^). This operator is also guaranteed to evaluate *both* of its operands.

expression1	expression2	expression1 ^ expression2
false	false	false
false	true	true
true	false	true
true	true	false

Fig. 6.16 | ^ (boolean logical exclusive OR) operator truth table.

Logical Negation (!) Operator

The **!** (**logical negation** or **not**) operator enables you to "reverse" the meaning of a condition. Unlike the logical operators &&, ||, &, | and ∧, which are *binary* operators that combine two conditions, the logical negation operator is a *unary* operator that has only a single condition as an operand. The logical negation operator is placed before a condition to choose a path of execution if the original condition (without the logical negation operator) is false, as in the code segment

```
if ( ! ( grade == sentinelValue ) )
    Console.WriteLine( "The next grade is {0}", grade );
```

which executes the WriteLine call *only if* grade is not equal to sentinelValue. The parentheses around the condition grade == sentinelValue are needed because the logical negation operator has a higher precedence than the equality operator.

In most cases, you can avoid using logical negation by expressing the condition differently with an appropriate relational or equality operator. For example, the previous statement may also be written as follows:

```
if ( grade != sentinelValue )
    Console.WriteLine( "The next grade is {0}", grade );
```

This flexibility can help you express a condition in a more convenient manner. Figure 6.17 is a truth table for the logical negation operator.

expression	!expression
false	true
true	false

Fig. 6.17 | ! (logical negation) operator truth table.

Logical Operators Example

Figure 6.18 demonstrates the logical operators and boolean logical operators by producing their truth tables. The output shows the expression that was evaluated and the bool result of that expression. Lines 10–14 produce the truth table for && (conditional AND). Lines 17–21 produce the truth table for || (conditional OR). Lines 24–28 produce the truth table for & (boolean logical AND). Lines 31–36 produce the truth table for | (boolean logical inclusive OR). Lines 39–44 produce the truth table for ∧ (boolean logical exclusive OR). Lines 47–49 produce the truth table for ! (logical negation).

```
1   // Fig. 6.18: LogicalOperators.cs
2   // Logical operators.
3   using System;
4
5   public class LogicalOperators
6   {
```

Fig. 6.18 | Logical operators. (Part 1 of 3.)

```
7      public static void Main( string[] args )
8      {
9         // create truth table for && (conditional AND) operator
10        Console.WriteLine( "{0}\n{1}: {2}\n{3}: {4}\n{5}: {6}\n{7}: {8}\n",
11           "Conditional AND (&&)", "false && false", ( false && false ),
12           "false && true", ( false && true ),
13           "true && false", ( true && false ),
14           "true && true", ( true && true ) );
15
16        // create truth table for || (conditional OR) operator
17        Console.WriteLine( "{0}\n{1}: {2}\n{3}: {4}\n{5}: {6}\n{7}: {8}\n",
18           "Conditional OR (||)", "false || false", ( false || false ),
19           "false || true", ( false || true ),
20           "true || false", ( true || false ),
21           "true || true", ( true || true ) );
22
23        // create truth table for & (boolean logical AND) operator
24        Console.WriteLine( "{0}\n{1}: {2}\n{3}: {4}\n{5}: {6}\n{7}: {8}\n",
25           "Boolean logical AND (&)", "false & false", ( false & false ),
26           "false & true", ( false & true ),
27           "true & false", ( true & false ),
28           "true & true", ( true & true ) );
29
30        // create truth table for | (boolean logical inclusive OR) operator
31        Console.WriteLine( "{0}\n{1}: {2}\n{3}: {4}\n{5}: {6}\n{7}: {8}\n",
32           "Boolean logical inclusive OR (|)",
33           "false | false", ( false | false ),
34           "false | true", ( false | true ),
35           "true | false", ( true | false ),
36           "true | true", ( true | true ) );
37
38        // create truth table for ^ (boolean logical exclusive OR) operator
39        Console.WriteLine( "{0}\n{1}: {2}\n{3}: {4}\n{5}: {6}\n{7}: {8}\n",
40           "Boolean logical exclusive OR (^)",
41           "false ^ false", ( false ^ false ),
42           "false ^ true", ( false ^ true ),
43           "true ^ false", ( true ^ false ),
44           "true ^ true", ( true ^ true ) );
45
46        // create truth table for ! (logical negation) operator
47        Console.WriteLine( "{0}\n{1}: {2}\n{3}: {4}",
48           "Logical negation (!)", "!false", ( !false ),
49           "!true", ( !true ) );
50     } // end Main
51  } // end class LogicalOperators
```

```
Conditional AND (&&)
false && false: False
false && true: False
true && false: False
true && true: True
```

Fig. 6.18 | Logical operators. (Part 2 of 3.)

```
Conditional OR (||)
false || false: False
false || true: True
true || false: True
true || true: True

Boolean logical AND (&)
false & false: False
false & true: False
true & false: False
true & true: True

Boolean logical inclusive OR (|)
false | false: False
false | true: True
true | false: True
true | true: True

Boolean logical exclusive OR (^)
false ^ false: False
false ^ true: True
true ^ false: True
true ^ true: False

Logical negation (!)
!false: True
!true: False
```

Fig. 6.18 | Logical operators. (Part 3 of 3.)

Figure 6.19 shows the precedence and associativity of the C# operators introduced so far. The operators are shown from top to bottom in decreasing order of precedence.

Operators	Associativity	Type
. new ++*(postfix)* --*(postfix)*	left to right	highest precedence
++ -- + - ! *(type)*	right to left	unary prefix
* / %	left to right	multiplicative
+ -	left to right	additive
< <= > >=	left to right	relational
== !=	left to right	equality
&	left to right	boolean logical AND
^	left to right	boolean logical exclusive OR
|	left to right	boolean logical inclusive OR
&&	left to right	conditional AND
||	left to right	conditional OR
?:	right to left	conditional
= += -= *= /= %=	right to left	assignment

Fig. 6.19 | Precedence/associativity of the operators discussed so far.

6.9 Wrap-Up

Chapter 5 discussed the if, if...else and while control statements. In this chapter, we discussed the for, do...while and switch control statements. (We'll discuss the foreach statement in Chapter 8.) You saw that any algorithm can be developed using combinations of sequence (i.e., statements listed in the order in which they should execute), the three selection statements—if, if...else and switch—and the four repetition statements—while, do...while, for and foreach. You saw that the for and do...while statements are simply more convenient ways to express certain types of repetition. Similarly, we showed that the switch statement is a convenient notation for multiple selection, rather than using nested if...else statements. We discussed how you can combine various control statements by stacking and nesting them. We showed how to use the break and continue statements to alter the flow of control in repetition statements. You used the logical operators, which enable you to form more complex conditional expressions in control statements. In Chapter 7, we examine methods in greater depth.

7

Methods: A Deeper Look

Objectives

In this chapter you'll:

- Learn how **static** methods and variables are associated with classes rather than objects.

- Learn how the method call/return mechanism is supported by the method-call stack.

- Use random-number generation to implement game-playing apps.

- Learn how the visibility of declarations is limited to specific parts of apps.

- Create overloaded methods.

- Use optional and named parameters.

- Use recursive methods.

- Pass method arguments by value and by reference.

7.1 Introduction

Most computer apps that solve real-world problems are much larger than the apps presented in this book's first few chapters. Experience has shown that the best way to develop and maintain a large app is to construct it from small, simple pieces. For this purpose, we introduced methods in Chapter 4. In this chapter we study methods in more depth.

You'll see that it's possible for certain methods, called static methods, to be called without the need for an object of the class to exist. You'll learn how C# is able to keep track of which method is currently executing, how value-type and reference-type arguments are passed to methods, how local variables of methods are maintained in memory and how a method knows where to return after it completes execution.

We discuss **simulation** techniques with random-number generation and develop a version of the casino dice game called craps that uses most of the programming techniques you've learned to this point in the book. In addition, you'll see how to declare constant values and you'll write recursive methods—methods that call themselves.

Many of the classes you'll use or create will have more than one method of the same name. This technique, called *method overloading*, is used to implement methods that perform similar tasks but with different types and/or different numbers of arguments.

7.2 Packaging Code in C#

Common ways of packaging code are properties, methods, classes and namespaces. C# apps are written by combining new properties, methods and classes that you write with predefined properties, methods and classes available in the .NET Framework Class Library and in various other class libraries. Related classes are often grouped into namespaces and compiled into class libraries so that they can be reused in other apps. You'll learn how to create your own namespaces and class libraries in Chapter 15. The Framework Class Library provides many *predefined* classes that contain methods for performing common mathematical calculations, string manipulations, character manipulations, input/output operations, database operations, networking operations, file processing, error checking, web-app development and more.

Software Engineering Observation 7.1

Don't try to "reinvent the wheel." When possible, reuse Framework Class Library classes and methods (msdn.microsoft.com/en-us/library/ms229335.aspx). This reduces app development time, avoids introducing programming errors and contributes to good app performance.

7.3 static Methods, static Variables and Class Math

Although most methods execute on specific objects in response to method calls, this is not always the case. Sometimes a method performs a task that does *not* depend on the contents of any object. Such a method applies to the class in which it's declared as a whole and is known as a static method. It's not uncommon for a class to contain a group of static methods to perform common tasks. For example, recall that we used static method Pow of class Math to raise a value to a power in Fig. 6.6. To declare a method as static, place the keyword static before the return type in the method's declaration. You call any static method by specifying the name of the class in which the method is declared, followed by the member access (.) operator and the method name, as in

> *ClassName*.*MethodName*(*arguments*)

We use various methods of the Math class here to present the concept of static methods. Class Math (from the System namespace) provides a collection of methods that enable you to perform common mathematical calculations. For example, you can calculate the square root of 900.0 with the static method call

```
Math.Sqrt( 900.0 )
```

The preceding expression evaluates to 30.0. Method Sqrt takes an argument of type double and returns a result of type double. To output the value of the preceding method call in the console window, you might write the statement

```
Console.WriteLine( Math.Sqrt( 900.0 ) );
```

In this statement, the value that Sqrt returns becomes the argument to method WriteLine. We did not create a Math object before calling method Sqrt. Also, *all* of Math's methods are static—therefore, each is called by preceding the name of the method with the class name Math and the member access (.) operator. Similarly, Console method WriteLine is a static method of class Console, so we invoke the method by preceding its name with the class name Console and the member access (.) operator. Figure 7.1 summarizes several Math class methods. In the figure, *x* and *y* are of type double.

Method	Description	Example
Abs(*x*)	absolute value of *x*	Abs(23.7) is 23.7 Abs(0.0) is 0.0 Abs(-23.7) is 23.7

Fig. 7.1 | Math class methods. (Part 1 of 2.)

Method	Description	Example
Ceiling(x)	rounds x to the smallest integer not less than x	Ceiling(9.2) is 10.0 Ceiling(-9.8) is -9.0
Cos(x)	trigonometric cosine of x (x in radians)	Cos(0.0) is 1.0
Exp(x)	exponential method e^x	Exp(1.0) is 2.71828 Exp(2.0) is 7.38906
Floor(x)	rounds x to the largest integer not greater than x	Floor(9.2) is 9.0 Floor(-9.8) is -10.0
Log(x)	natural logarithm of x (base e)	Log(Math.E) is 1.0 Log(Math.E * Math.E) is 2.0
Max(x, y)	larger value of x and y	Max(2.3, 12.7) is 12.7 Max(-2.3, -12.7) is -2.3
Min(x, y)	smaller value of x and y	Min(2.3, 12.7) is 2.3 Min(-2.3, -12.7) is -12.7
Pow(x, y)	x raised to the power y (i.e., x^y)	Pow(2.0, 7.0) is 128.0 Pow(9.0, 0.5) is 3.0
Sin(x)	trigonometric sine of x (x in radians)	Sin(0.0) is 0.0
Sqrt(x)	square root of x	Sqrt(900.0) is 30.0
Tan(x)	trigonometric tangent of x (x in radians)	Tan(0.0) is 0.0

Fig. 7.1 | Math class methods. (Part 2 of 2.)

Math Class Constants *PI and E*

Class Math also declares two static double constants that represent commonly used mathematical values: **Math.PI** and **Math.E**. The constant Math.PI (3.14159265358979323846) is the ratio of a circle's circumference to its diameter. Math.E (2.7182818284590452354) is the base value for natural logarithms (calculated with static Math method Log). These constants are declared in class Math with the modifiers public and const. Making them public allows other programmers to use these variables in their own classes. A constant is declared with the keyword **const**—its value cannot be changed after the constant is declared. Both PI and E are declared const. Because these constants are static, you can access them via the class name Math and the member access (.) operator, just like class Math's methods.

Recall from Section 4.5 that when each object of a class maintains its own copy of an attribute, the variable that represents the attribute is also known as an *instance variable*—each object (instance) of the class has a separate instance of the variable. There are also variables for which each object of a class does *not* have a separate instance of the variable. That's the case with static variables. When objects of a class containing static variables are created, all the objects of that class share one copy of the class's static variables. Together the static variables and instance variables represent the **fields** of a class.

Common Programming Error 7.1

Every constant declared in a class, but not inside a method of the class is implicitly static, so it's a syntax error to declare such a constant with keyword static explicitly.

Why Is Method Main Declared static?

Why must Main be declared static? During app *startup*, when *no objects* of the class have been created, the Main method must be called to begin program execution. Main is sometimes called the app's **entry point**. Declaring Main as static allows the execution environment to invoke Main without creating an instance of the class. Method Main is often declared with the header:

```
public static void Main( string args[] )
```

When you execute your app from the command line, you type the app name, as in

AppName argument1 argument2 …

In the preceding command, *argument1* and *argument2* are the **command-line arguments** to the app that specify a list of strings (separated by spaces) the execution environment will pass to the Main method of your app. Such arguments might be used to specify options (e.g., a file name) to run the app. As you'll learn in Chapter 8, your app can access its command-line arguments (via the args parameter) and use them to customize the app.

Additional Comments about Method Main

Apps that do not take command-line arguments may omit the string[] args parameter. The public keyword may also be omitted. In addition, you can declare Main with return type int (instead of void) to enable Main to return an error code. A Main method declared with any one of these headers can be used as the app's entry point—but you can declare only one Main method in each class.

Most earlier examples had one class that contained only Main, and some examples had a second class that was used by Main to create and manipulate objects. Actually, *any* class can contain a Main method. In fact, each of our two-class examples could have been implemented as one class. For example, in the app in Figs. 6.9 and 6.10, method Main (lines 6–16 of Fig. 6.10) could have been taken as is and placed in class GradeBook (Fig. 6.9). The app results would have been identical to those of the two-class version. You can place a Main method in every class you declare. Some programmers take advantage of this to build a small test app into each class they declare. However, if you declare more than one Main method among the classes of your project, you'll need to indicate to the IDE which one you would like to be the *app's* entry point. You can do this by selecting **PROJECT > [ProjectName] Properties...** (where **[ProjectName]** is the name of your project) and selecting the class containing the Main method that should be the entry point from the **Startup object** list box.

7.4 Declaring Methods with Multiple Parameters

We now consider how to write your own methods with multiple parameters. The app in Fig. 7.2 uses a user-defined method called Maximum to determine and return the largest of *three* double values. When the app begins execution, the Main method (lines 8–22) executes. Line 18 calls method Maximum (lines 25–38) to determine and return the largest of the three double values. At the end of this section, we'll discuss the use of operator + in line 21.

The public and static Keywords

Method Maximum's declaration begins with keyword public to indicate that the method is "available to the public"—it can be called from methods of other classes. The keyword

```csharp
1   // Fig. 7.2: MaximumFinder.cs
2   // User-defined method Maximum.
3   using System;
4
5   public class MaximumFinder
6   {
7      // obtain three floating-point values and determine maximum value
8      public static void Main( string[] args )
9      {
10        // prompt for and input three floating-point values
11        Console.WriteLine( "Enter three floating-point values,\n" +
12           "  pressing 'Enter' after each one: " );
13        double number1 = Convert.ToDouble( Console.ReadLine() );
14        double number2 = Convert.ToDouble( Console.ReadLine() );
15        double number3 = Convert.ToDouble( Console.ReadLine() );
16
17        // determine the maximum value
18        double result = Maximum( number1, number2, number3 );
19
20        // display maximum value
21        Console.WriteLine( "Maximum is: " + result );
22     } // end Main
23
24     // returns the maximum of its three double parameters
25     public static double Maximum( double x, double y, double z )
26     {
27        double maximumValue = x; // assume x is the largest to start
28
29        // determine whether y is greater than maximumValue
30        if ( y > maximumValue )
31           maximumValue = y;
32
33        // determine whether z is greater than maximumValue
34        if ( z > maximumValue )
35           maximumValue = z;
36
37        return maximumValue;
38     } // end method Maximum
39  } // end class MaximumFinder
```

```
Enter three floating-point values,
  pressing 'Enter' after each one:
2.22
3.33
1.11
Maximum is: 3.33
```

Fig. 7.2 | User-defined method Maximum.

static enables the Main method (another static method) to call Maximum as shown in line 18 without qualifying the method name with the class name MaximumFinder—static methods in the *same* class can call each other directly. Any other class that uses Maximum must fully qualify the method name with the class name.

Method `Maximum`

Consider the declaration of method `Maximum` (lines 25–38). Line 25 indicates that the method returns a `double` value, that the method's name is `Maximum` and that the method requires *three* `double` parameters (x, y and z) to accomplish its task. There must be one argument in the method call for each *required* parameter in the method declaration. Also, each argument must be *consistent* with the type of the corresponding parameter. For example, a parameter of type `double` can receive values like 7.35 (a `double`), 22 (an `int`) or –0.03456 (a `double`), but not `strings` like "hello". Section 7.7 discusses the argument types that can be provided in a method call for each parameter of a simple type.

Common Programming Error 7.2

Declaring method parameters of the same type as `double x, y` instead of `double x, double y` is a syntax error—a type is required for each parameter in the parameter list.

Logic of Determining the Maximum Value

To determine the maximum value, we begin with the assumption that parameter x contains the largest value, so line 27 declares local variable `maximumValue` and initializes it with the value of parameter x. Of course, it's possible that parameter y or z contains the largest value, so we must compare each of these values with `maximumValue`. The `if` statement at lines 30–31 determines whether y is greater than `maximumValue`. If so, line 31 assigns y to `maximumValue`. The `if` statement at lines 34–35 determines whether z is greater than `maximumValue`. If so, line 35 assigns z to `maximumValue`. At this point, the largest of the three values resides in `maximumValue`, so line 37 returns that value to line 18. When program control returns to the point in the app where `Maximum` was called, `Maximum`'s parameters x, y and z are no longer accessible. Methods can return *at most one* value; the returned value can be a value type that contains one or more values (implemented as a `struct`) or a reference to an object that contains one or more values.

When to Declare Variables as Fields of a Class

Variable `result` is a local variable in method `Main` because it's declared in the *block* that represents the method's body. Variables should be declared as fields of a class (i.e., as either instance variables or `static` variables of the class) *only* if they're required for use in more than one method of the class or if the app should save their values between calls to a given method.

Implementing Method `Maximum` by Reusing Method `Math.Max`

Recall from Fig. 7.1 that class `Math` has a `Max` method that can determine the larger of two values. The entire body of our maximum method could also be implemented with nested calls to `Math.Max`, as follows:

```
return Math.Max( x, Math.Max( y, z ) );
```

The leftmost call to `Math.Max` specifies arguments x and `Math.Max( y, z )`. Before any method can be called, the .NET runtime evaluates *all* its arguments to determine their values. If an argument is a method call, the method call must be performed to determine its return value. So, in the preceding statement, `Math.Max( y, z )` is evaluated first to determine the maximum of y and z. Then the result is passed as the second argument to the other call to `Math.Max`, which returns the larger of its two arguments. Using `Math.Max` in this manner is a good example of *software reuse*—we find the largest of three values by reusing Math.Max, which finds the larger of two values. Note how concise this code is compared to lines 27–37 of Fig. 7.2.

Assembling Strings with String Concatenation

C# allows string objects to be created by assembling smaller strings into larger strings using operator + (or the compound assignment operator +=). This is known as **string concatenation**. When both operands of operator + are string objects, operator + creates a new string object in which a copy of the characters of the *right* operand is placed at the end of a copy of the characters in the *left* operand. For example, the expression "hello " + "there" creates the string "hello there" without disturbing the original strings.

In line 21 of Fig. 7.2, the expression "Maximum is: " + result uses operator + with operands of types string and double. Every value of a simple type in C# has a string representation. When one of the + operator's operands is a string, the other is implicitly converted to a string, then the two are *concatenated*. In line 21, the double value is *implicitly* converted to its string representation and placed at the end of the string "Maximum is: ". If there are any trailing zeros in a double value, these will be *discarded* when the number is converted to a string. Thus, the number 9.3500 would be represented as 9.35 in the resulting string.

Anything Can Be Converted to a *string*

For values of simple types used in string concatenation, the values are converted to strings. If a bool is concatenated with a string, the bool is converted to the string "True" or "False" (each is capitalized). All objects have a ToString method that returns a string representation of the object. When an object is concatenated with a string, the object's ToString method is called *implicitly* to obtain the string representation of the object. If the object is null, an *empty string* is written.

Outputting *strings* with Format Items

Line 21 of Fig. 7.2 could also be written using string formatting as

```
Console.WriteLine( "Maximum is: {0}", result );
```

As with string concatenation, using a format item to substitute an object into a string *implicitly* calls the object's ToString method to obtain the object's string representation. You'll learn more about method ToString in Chapter 8.

Breaking a Large *string* Literal into Smaller *strings*

When a large string literal is typed into an app's source code, you can break that string into several smaller strings and place them on multiple lines for readability. The strings can be reassembled using either string concatenation or string formatting. We discuss the details of strings in Chapter 16.

 Common Programming Error 7.3

It's a syntax error to break a string literal across multiple lines in an app. If a string does not fit on one line, split the string into several smaller strings and use concatenation to form the desired string. C# also provides so-called verbatim string literals, which are preceded by the @ character. Such literals can be split over multiple lines and the characters in the literal, including whitespace, are processed exactly as they appear in the literal.

Common Programming Error 7.4

Confusing the + operator used for string concatenation with the + operator used for addition can lead to strange results. The + operator is left-associative. For example, if integer variable y has the value 5, the expression "y + 2 = " + y + 2 results in the string "y + 2 = 52", not "y + 2 = 7", because first the value of y (5) is concatenated with the string "y + 2 = ", then the value 2 is concatenated with the new larger string "y + 2 = 5". The expression "y + 2 = " + (y + 2) produces the desired result "y + 2 = 7".

7.5 Notes on Declaring and Using Methods

You've seen three ways to call a method:

1. Using a method name by itself to call a method of the *same* class—such as `Maximum(number1, number2, number3)` in line 18 of Fig. 7.2.

2. Using a variable that contains a reference to an object, followed by the member access (.) operator and the method name to call a non-`static` method of the referenced object—such as the method call in line 13 of Fig. 6.10, `myGradeBook.DisplayMessage()`, which calls a method of class `GradeBook` from the `Main` method of `GradeBookTest`.

3. Using the class name and the member access (.) operator to call a `static` method of a class—such as `Convert.ToDouble(Console.ReadLine())` in lines 13–15 of Fig. 7.2 or `Math.Sqrt(900.0)` in Section 7.3.

There are three ways to return control to the statement that calls a method. If the method's return type is `void` (that is, it does not return a result), control returns when the method-ending right brace is reached or when the statement

```
return;
```

is executed. If the method returns a result, the statement

```
return expression;
```

evaluates the *expression*, then returns the result (and control) to the caller.

Common Programming Error 7.5

Declaring a method outside the body of a class declaration or inside the body of another method is a syntax error.

Common Programming Error 7.6

Redeclaring a method parameter as a local variable in the method's body is a compilation error.

Common Programming Error 7.7

Forgetting to return a value from a method that should return one is a compilation error. If a return type other than `void` is specified, the method must use a `return` statement to return a value and that value must be consistent with the method's return type. Returning a value from a method whose return type has been declared `void` is a compilation error.

A static method can call *only* other static methods of the same class directly (i.e., using the method name by itself) and can manipulate *only* static variables in the same class directly. To access the class's non-static members, a static method must use a reference to an object of the class. Recall that static methods relate to a class as a whole, whereas non-static methods are associated with a specific instance (object) of the class and may manipulate the instance variables of that object. Many objects of a class, each with its own copies of the instance variables, may exist at the same time. Suppose a static method were to invoke a non-static method directly. How would the method know which object's instance variables to manipulate? What would happen if no objects of the class existed at the time the non-static method was invoked? Thus, C# does not allow a static method to access non-static members of the same class directly.

7.6 Method-Call Stack and Activation Records

To understand how C# performs method calls, we first need to consider a data structure (i.e., collection of related data items) known as a **stack**. You can think of a stack as analogous to a pile of dishes. When a dish is placed on the pile, it's normally placed at the top (referred to as **pushing** the dish onto the stack). Similarly, when a dish is removed from the pile, it's always removed from the top (referred to as **popping** the dish off the stack). Stacks are known as **last-in, first-out (LIFO) data structures**—the last item pushed (inserted) on the stack is the first item popped off (removed from) the stack.

When an app calls a method, the called method must know how to return to its caller, so the return address of the calling method is *pushed* onto the **program-execution stack** (sometimes referred to as the **method-call stack**). If a series of method calls occurs, the successive return addresses are *pushed* onto the stack in last-in, first-out order so that each method can return to its caller.

The program-execution stack also contains the *memory for the local variables* used in each invocation of a method during an app's execution. This data, stored as a portion of the program-execution stack, is known as the **activation record** or **stack frame** of the method call. When a method call is made, the activation record for it is pushed onto the program-execution stack. When the method returns to its caller, the activation record for this method call is *popped* off the stack, and those local variables are no longer known to the app. If a local variable holding a reference to an object is the only variable in the app with a reference to that object, when the activation record containing that local variable is popped off the stack, the object can no longer be accessed by the app and will eventually be deleted from memory during *garbage collection*—we'll discuss garbage collection in Section 10.8.

Of course, the amount of memory in a computer is finite, so only a certain amount of memory can be used to store activation records on the program-execution stack. If more method calls occur than can have their activation records stored on the program-execution stack, a fatal error known as a **stack overflow** occurs.

7.7 Argument Promotion and Casting

Another important feature of method calls is **argument promotion**—implicitly converting an argument's value to the type that the method expects to receive (if possible) in its corresponding parameter. For example, an app can call Math method Sqrt with an integer argument even though the method expects to receive a double argument. The statement

```
Console.WriteLine( Math.Sqrt( 4 ) );
```

correctly evaluates Math.Sqrt(4) and displays the value 2.0. Sqrt's parameter list causes C# to convert the int value 4 to the double value 4.0 before passing the value to Sqrt. Such conversions may lead to compilation errors if C#'s **promotion rules** are not satisfied. The promotion rules specify which conversions are allowed—that is, which conversions can be performed *without losing data*. In the Sqrt example above, an int is converted to a double without changing its value. However, converting a double to an int *truncates* the fractional part of the double value—thus, part of the value is lost. Also, double variables can hold values much larger (and much smaller) than int variables, so assigning a double to an int can cause a loss of information when the double value doesn't fit in the int. Converting large integer types to small integer types (e.g., long to int) can also result in changed values.

Promotion Rules

The promotion rules apply to expressions containing values of two or more simple types and to simple-type values passed as arguments to methods. Each value is promoted to the appropriate type in the expression. (Actually, the expression uses a *temporary* copy of each value—the types of the original values remain unchanged.) Figure 7.3 lists the simple types alphabetically and the types to which each can be promoted. Values of all simple types can also be implicitly converted to type object.

Type	Conversion types
bool	no possible implicit conversions to other simple types
byte	ushort, short, uint, int, ulong, long, decimal, float or double
char	ushort, int, uint, long, ulong, decimal, float or double
decimal	no possible implicit conversions to other simple types
double	no possible implicit conversions to other simple types
float	double
int	long, decimal, float or double
long	decimal, float or double
sbyte	short, int, long, decimal, float or double
short	int, long, decimal, float or double
uint	ulong, long, decimal, float or double
ulong	decimal, float or double
ushort	uint, int, ulong, long, decimal, float or double

Fig. 7.3 | Implicit conversions between simple types.

Sometimes Explicit Casts Are Required

By default, C# does not allow you to implicitly convert values between simple types if the target type cannot represent the value of the original type (e.g., the int value 2000000 cannot be represented as a short, and any floating-point number with digits after its decimal point cannot be represented in an integer type such as long, int or short). Therefore, to prevent a compilation error in cases where information may be lost due to an implicit conversion between simple types, the compiler requires you to use a *cast operator* to *force* the conversion. This enables you to "take control" from the compiler. You essentially say, "I know this conversion might cause loss of information, but for my purposes here, that's fine." Suppose you create a method Square that calculates the square of an integer and thus requires an int argument. To call Square with the whole part of a double argument named doubleValue, you'd write Square((int) doubleValue). This method call explicitly casts (converts) the value of doubleValue to an integer for use in method Square. Thus, if doubleValue's value is 4.5, the method receives the value 4 and returns 16, not 20.25 (which does, unfortunately, result in the loss of information).

Common Programming Error 7.8

Converting a simple-type value to a value of another simple type may change the value if the promotion is not allowed. For example, converting a floating-point value to an integral value may introduce truncation errors (loss of the fractional part) in the result.

7.8 The .NET Framework Class Library

Many predefined classes are grouped into categories of related classes called *namespaces*. Together, these namespaces are referred to as the .NET Framework Class Library.

Throughout the text, using directives allow us to use library classes from the Framework Class Library without specifying their fully qualified names. For example, an app includes the declaration

    using System;

in order to use the class names from the System namespace without fully qualifying their names. This allows you to use the **unqualified class name** Console, rather than the fully qualified class name System.Console, in your code. A strength of C# is the large number of classes in the namespaces of the .NET Framework Class Library. Some key Framework Class Library namespaces are described in Fig. 7.4, which represents only a small portion of the reusable classes in the .NET Framework Class Library.

Namespace	Description
System.Windows.Forms	Contains the classes required to create and manipulate GUIs. (Various classes in this namespace are discussed in Chapter 14, Graphical User Interfaces with Windows Forms: Part 1, and Chapter 15, Graphical User Interfaces with Windows Forms: Part 2.)
System.Windows.Controls System.Windows.Input System.Windows.Media System.Windows.Shapes	Contain the classes of the Windows Presentation Foundation for GUIs, 2-D and 3-D graphics, multimedia and animation. (See Chapter 30, GUI with Windows Presentation Foundation and Chapter 31, WPF Graphics and Multimedia.)

Fig. 7.4 | .NET Framework Class Library namespaces (a subset). (Part 1 of 2.)

Namespace	Description
`System.Linq`	Contains the classes that support Language Integrated Query (LINQ). (See Chapter 9, Introduction to LINQ and the `List` Collection, and several other chapters throughout the book.)
`System.Data.Entity`	Contains the classes for manipulating data in databases (i.e., organized collections of data), including support for LINQ to Entities. (See Chapter 20, Databases and LINQ.)
`System.IO`	Contains the classes that enable programs to input and output data. (See Chapter 17, Files and Streams.)
`System.Web`	Contains the classes used for creating and maintaining web apps, which are accessible over the Internet. (See Chapter 21, Web App Development with ASP.NET.)
`System.Xml`	Contains the classes for creating and manipulating XML data. Data can be read from or written to XML files. (See Chapter 22, XML and LINQ to XML.)
`System.Xml.Linq`	Contains the classes that support Language Integrated Query (LINQ) for XML documents. (See Chapter 22, XML and LINQ to XML, and several other chapters throughout the book.)
`System.Collections` `System.Collections.Generic`	Contain the classes that define data structures for maintaining collections of data. (See Chapter 19, Collections.)
`System.Text`	Contains classes that enable programs to manipulate characters and strings. (See Chapter 16, Strings and Characters: A Deeper Look.)

Fig. 7.4 | .NET Framework Class Library namespaces (a subset). (Part 2 of 2.)

The .NET Framework Class Library also contains namespaces for complex graphics, advanced graphical user interfaces, printing, advanced networking, security, database processing, multimedia, accessibility (for people with disabilities) and many other capabilities—over 200 namespaces in all.

Locating Additional Information About a .NET Class's Methods
You can locate additional information about a .NET class's methods in the *.NET Framework Class Library* reference (msdn.microsoft.com/en-us/library/ms229335.aspx). When you visit this site, you'll see an alphabetical listing of all the namespaces in the Framework Class Library. Locate the namespace and click its link to see an alphabetical listing of all its classes, with a brief description of each. Click a class's link to see a more complete description of the class. Click the **Methods** link in the left-hand column to see a listing of the class's methods.

Good Programming Practice 7.1

The online .NET Framework documentation is easy to search and provides many details about each class. As you learn each class in this book, you should review the class in the online documentation for additional information.

7.9 Case Study: Random-Number Generation

In this and the next section, we develop a nicely structured game-playing app with multiple methods. The app uses most of the control statements presented thus far in the book and introduces several new programming concepts.

There's something in the air of a casino that invigorates people—from the high rollers at the plush mahogany-and-felt craps tables to the quarter poppers at the one-armed bandits. It's the *element of chance*, the possibility that luck will convert a pocketful of money into a mountain of wealth. The element of chance can be introduced in an app via an object of class Random (of namespace System). Objects of class **Random** can produce random byte, int and double values. In the next several examples, we use objects of class Random to produce random numbers.

Creating a Random Number Generator Object
A new random-number generator object can be created as follows:

```
Random randomNumbers = new Random();
```

The random-number generator object can then be used to generate random byte, int and double values—we discuss only random int values here.

Generating a Random Integer
Consider the following statement:

```
int randomValue = randomNumbers.Next();
```

Method **Next** of class Random generates a random int value in the range 0 to +2,147,483,646, inclusive. If the Next method truly produces values at random, then every value in that range should have an equal chance (or probability) of being chosen each time method Next is called. The values returned by Next are actually **pseudorandom numbers**—a sequence of values produced by a complex mathematical calculation. The calculation uses the current time of day (which, of course, changes constantly) to **seed** the random-number generator such that each execution of an app yields a different sequence of random values.

Scaling the Range of Random Numbers Produced
The range of values produced directly by method Next often differs from the range of values required in a particular C# app. For example, an app that simulates coin tossing might require only 0 for "heads" and 1 for "tails." An app that simulates the rolling of a six-sided die might require random integers in the range 1–6. A video game that randomly predicts the next type of spaceship (out of four possibilities) that will fly across the horizon might require random integers in the range 1–4. For cases like these, class Random provides other versions of method Next. One receives an int argument and returns a value from 0 up to, but not including, the argument's value. For example, you might use the statement

```
int randomValue = randomNumbers.Next( 6 );
```

which returns 0, 1, 2, 3, 4 or 5. The argument 6—called the **scaling factor**—represents the number of unique values that Next should produce (in this case, six—0, 1, 2, 3, 4 and 5). This manipulation is called **scaling** the range of values produced by Random method Next.

Shifting the Range of Random Numbers Produced
Suppose we wanted to simulate a six-sided die that has the numbers 1–6 on its faces, not 0–5. Scaling the range of values alone is not enough. So we **shift** the range of numbers produced. We could do this by adding a **shifting value**—in this case 1—to the result of method Next, as in

```
face = 1 + randomNumbers.Next( 6 );
```

The shifting value (1) specifies the first value in the desired set of random integers. The preceding statement assigns to face a random integer in the range 1–6.

Combining Shifting and Scaling
The third alternative of method Next provides a more intuitive way to express both shifting and scaling. This method receives two int arguments and returns a value from the first argument's value up to, but not including, the second argument's value. We could use this method to write a statement equivalent to our previous statement, as in

```
face = randomNumbers.Next( 1, 7 );
```

Rolling a Six-Sided Die
To demonstrate random numbers, let's develop an app that simulates 20 rolls of a six-sided die and displays each roll's value. Figure 7.5 shows two sample outputs, which confirm that the results of the preceding calculation are integers in the range 1–6 and that each run of the app can produce a *different* sequence of random numbers. The using directive (line 3) enables us to use class Random without fully qualifying its name. Line 9 creates the Random object randomNumbers to produce random values. Line 16 executes 20 times in a loop to roll the die. The if statement (lines 21–22) starts a new line of output after every five numbers, so the results will be presented on multiple lines.

```
1   // Fig. 7.5: RandomIntegers.cs
2   // Shifted and scaled random integers.
3   using System;
4
5   public class RandomIntegers
6   {
7      public static void Main( string[] args )
8      {
9         Random randomNumbers = new Random(); // random-number generator
10        int face; // stores each random integer generated
11
12        // loop 20 times
13        for ( int counter = 1; counter <= 20; counter++ )
14        {
15           // pick random integer from 1 to 6
16           face = randomNumbers.Next( 1, 7 );
17
18           Console.Write( "{0}  ", face ); // display generated value
19
```

Fig. 7.5 | Shifted and scaled random integers. (Part 1 of 2.)

```
20              // if counter is divisible by 5, start a new line of output
21              if ( counter % 5 == 0 )
22                 Console.WriteLine();
23           } // end for
24        } // end Main
25     } // end class RandomIntegers
```

```
3   3   3   1   1
2   1   2   4   2
2   3   6   2   5
3   4   6   6   1
```

```
6   2   5   1   3
5   2   1   6   5
4   1   6   1   3
3   1   4   3   4
```

Fig. 7.5 | Shifted and scaled random integers. (Part 2 of 2.)

Rolling a Six-Sided Die 6,000,000 Times

To show that the numbers produced by Next occur with approximately equal likelihood, let's simulate 6,000,000 rolls of a die (Fig. 7.6). Each integer from 1 to 6 should appear approximately 1,000,000 times.

```
1    // Fig. 7.6: RollDie.cs
2    // Roll a six-sided die 6,000,000 times.
3    using System;
4
5    public class RollDie
6    {
7       public static void Main( string[] args )
8       {
9          Random randomNumbers = new Random(); // random-number generator
10
11         int frequency1 = 0; // count of 1s rolled
12         int frequency2 = 0; // count of 2s rolled
13         int frequency3 = 0; // count of 3s rolled
14         int frequency4 = 0; // count of 4s rolled
15         int frequency5 = 0; // count of 5s rolled
16         int frequency6 = 0; // count of 6s rolled
17
18         int face; // stores most recently rolled value
19
20         // summarize results of 6,000,000 rolls of a die
21         for ( int roll = 1; roll <= 6000000; ++roll )
22         {
23            face = randomNumbers.Next( 1, 7 ); // number from 1 to 6
24
```

Fig. 7.6 | Roll a six-sided die 6,000,000 times. (Part 1 of 2.)

```
25              // determine roll value 1-6 and increment appropriate counter
26              switch ( face )
27              {
28                 case 1:
29                    ++frequency1; // increment the 1s counter
30                    break;
31                 case 2:
32                    ++frequency2; // increment the 2s counter
33                    break;
34                 case 3:
35                    ++frequency3; // increment the 3s counter
36                    break;
37                 case 4:
38                    ++frequency4; // increment the 4s counter
39                    break;
40                 case 5:
41                    ++frequency5; // increment the 5s counter
42                    break;
43                 case 6:
44                    ++frequency6; // increment the 6s counter
45                    break;
46              } // end switch
47           } // end for
48
49        Console.WriteLine( "Face\tFrequency" ); // output headers
50        Console.WriteLine(
51           "1\t{0}\n2\t{1}\n3\t{2}\n4\t{3}\n5\t{4}\n6\t{5}", frequency1,
52           frequency2, frequency3, frequency4, frequency5, frequency6 );
53     } // end Main
54  } // end class RollDie
```

Face	Frequency
1	999147
2	1001249
3	999929
4	1000301
5	1000294
6	999080

Face	Frequency
1	1000538
2	1002700
3	1000294
4	997662
5	999507
6	999299

Fig. 7.6 | Roll a six-sided die 6,000,000 times. (Part 2 of 2.)

As the two sample outputs show, the values produced by method Next enable the app to realistically simulate rolling a six-sided die. The app uses nested control statements (the switch is nested inside the for) to determine the number of times each side of the die occurred. The for statement (lines 21–47) iterates 6,000,000 times. During each iteration, line 23 produces a random value from 1 to 6. This face value is then used as the switch expression (line 26) in the switch statement (lines 26–46). Based on the face value, the switch statement increments one of the six counter variables during each iteration of the loop. (In Section 8.4, we show an elegant way to replace the entire switch statement in this app with a single statement.) The switch statement has no default label because we have a case label for every possible die value that the expression in line 23 can produce. Run the app several times and observe the results. You'll see that every time you execute this app, it produces different results.

7.9.1 Scaling and Shifting Random Numbers

Previously, we demonstrated the statement

```
face = randomNumbers.Next( 1, 7 );
```

which simulates the rolling of a six-sided die. This statement always assigns to variable face an integer in the range $1 \le$ face < 7. The width of this range (i.e., the number of consecutive integers in the range) is 6, and the starting number in the range is 1. Referring to the preceding statement, we see that the width of the range is determined by the difference between the two integers passed to Random method Next, and the starting number of the range is the value of the first argument. We can generalize this result as

```
number = randomNumbers.Next( shiftingValue, shiftingValue + scalingFactor );
```

where *shiftingValue* specifies the first number in the desired range of consecutive integers and *scalingFactor* specifies how many numbers are in the range.

It's also possible to choose integers at random from sets of values *other* than ranges of consecutive integers. For this purpose, it's simpler to use the version of the Next method that takes only *one* argument. For example, to obtain a random value from the sequence 2, 5, 8, 11 and 14, you could use the statement

```
number = 2 + 3 * randomNumbers.Next( 5 );
```

In this case, randomNumberGenerator.Next(5) produces values in the range 0–4. Each value produced is multiplied by 3 to produce a number in the sequence 0, 3, 6, 9 and 12. We then add 2 to that value to *shift* the range of values and obtain a value from the sequence 2, 5, 8, 11 and 14. We can generalize this result as

```
number = shiftingValue +
         differenceBetweenValues * randomNumbers.Next( scalingFactor );
```

where *shiftingValue* specifies the first number in the desired range of values, *differenceBetweenValues* represents the difference between consecutive numbers in the sequence and *scalingFactor* specifies how many numbers are in the range.

7.9.2 Random-Number Repeatability for Testing and Debugging

As we mentioned earlier in this section, the methods of class Random actually generate pseudorandom numbers based on complex mathematical calculations. Repeatedly calling any of Random's methods produces a sequence of numbers that appears to be random. The calculation that produces the pseudorandom numbers uses the time of day as a **seed value** to change the sequence's starting point. Each new Random object seeds itself with a value based on the computer system's clock at the time the object is created, enabling each execution of an app to produce a *different* sequence of random numbers.

When debugging an app, it's sometimes useful to repeat the *same* sequence of pseudorandom numbers during each execution of the app. This repeatability enables you to prove that your app is working for a specific sequence of random numbers before you test the app with different sequences of random numbers. When repeatability is important, you can create a Random object as follows:

```
Random randomNumbers = new Random( seedValue );
```

The seedValue argument (type int) seeds the random-number calculation. If the *same* seedValue is used every time, the Random object produces the *same* sequence of random numbers.

7.10 Case Study: A Game of Chance; Introducing Enumerations

One popular game of chance is the dice game known as "craps," which is played in casinos and back alleys throughout the world. The rules of the game are straightforward:

> *You roll two dice. Each die has six faces, which contain one, two, three, four, five and six spots, respectively. After the dice have come to rest, the sum of the spots on the two upward faces is calculated. If the sum is 7 or 11 on the first throw, you win. If the sum is 2, 3 or 12 on the first throw (called "craps"), you lose (i.e., "the house" wins). If the sum is 4, 5, 6, 8, 9 or 10 on the first throw, that sum becomes your "point." To win, you must continue rolling the dice until you "make your point" (i.e., roll that same point value). You lose by rolling a 7 before making your point.*

The app in Fig. 7.7 simulates the game of craps, using methods to define the logic of the game. The Main method (lines 24–70) calls the static RollDice method (lines 73–85) as needed to roll the two dice and compute their sum. The four sample outputs show winning on the first roll, losing on the first roll, winning on a subsequent roll and losing on a subsequent roll, respectively. Variable randomNumbers (line 8) is declared static so it can be created once during the program's execution and used in method RollDice.

```
1   // Fig. 7.7: Craps.cs
2   // Craps class simulates the dice game craps.
3   using System;
4
5   public class Craps
6   {
7      // create random-number generator for use in method RollDice
8      private static Random randomNumbers = new Random();
9
10     // enumeration with constants that represent the game status
11     private enum Status { CONTINUE, WON, LOST }
12
```

Fig. 7.7 | Craps class simulates the dice game craps. (Part 1 of 3.)

```
13      // enumeration with constants that represent common rolls of the dice
14      private enum DiceNames
15      {
16         SNAKE_EYES = 2,
17         TREY = 3,
18         SEVEN = 7,
19         YO_LEVEN = 11,
20         BOX_CARS = 12
21      }
22
23      // plays one game of craps
24      public static void Main( string[] args )
25      {
26         // gameStatus can contain CONTINUE, WON or LOST
27         Status gameStatus = Status.CONTINUE;
28         int myPoint = 0; // point if no win or loss on first roll
29
30         int sumOfDice = RollDice(); // first roll of the dice
31
32         // determine game status and point based on first roll
33         switch ( ( DiceNames ) sumOfDice )
34         {
35            case DiceNames.SEVEN: // win with 7 on first roll
36            case DiceNames.YO_LEVEN: // win with 11 on first roll
37               gameStatus = Status.WON;
38               break;
39            case DiceNames.SNAKE_EYES: // lose with 2 on first roll
40            case DiceNames.TREY: // lose with 3 on first roll
41            case DiceNames.BOX_CARS: // lose with 12 on first roll
42               gameStatus = Status.LOST;
43               break;
44            default: // did not win or lose, so remember point
45               gameStatus = Status.CONTINUE; // game is not over
46               myPoint = sumOfDice; // remember the point
47               Console.WriteLine( "Point is {0}", myPoint );
48               break;
49         } // end switch
50
51         // while game is not complete
52         while ( gameStatus == Status.CONTINUE ) // game not WON or LOST
53         {
54            sumOfDice = RollDice(); // roll dice again
55
56            // determine game status
57            if ( sumOfDice == myPoint ) // win by making point
58               gameStatus = Status.WON;
59            else
60               // lose by rolling 7 before point
61               if ( sumOfDice == ( int ) DiceNames.SEVEN )
62                  gameStatus = Status.LOST;
63         } // end while
64
```

Fig. 7.7 | Craps class simulates the dice game craps. (Part 2 of 3.)

```
65          // display won or lost message
66          if ( gameStatus == Status.WON )
67              Console.WriteLine( "Player wins" );
68          else
69              Console.WriteLine( "Player loses" );
70       } // end Main
71
72       // roll dice, calculate sum and display results
73       public static int RollDice()
74       {
75          // pick random die values
76          int die1 = randomNumbers.Next( 1, 7 ); // first die roll
77          int die2 = randomNumbers.Next( 1, 7 ); // second die roll
78
79          int sum = die1 + die2; // sum of die values
80
81          // display results of this roll
82          Console.WriteLine( "Player rolled {0} + {1} = {2}",
83              die1, die2, sum );
84          return sum; // return sum of dice
85       } // end method RollDice
86    } // end class Craps
```

```
Player rolled 2 + 5 = 7
Player wins
```

```
Player rolled 2 + 1 = 3
Player loses
```

```
Player rolled 2 + 4 = 6
Point is 6
Player rolled 3 + 1 = 4
Player rolled 5 + 5 = 10
Player rolled 6 + 1 = 7
Player loses
```

```
Player rolled 4 + 6 = 10
Point is 10
Player rolled 1 + 3 = 4
Player rolled 1 + 3 = 4
Player rolled 2 + 3 = 5
Player rolled 4 + 4 = 8
Player rolled 6 + 6 = 12
Player rolled 4 + 4 = 8
Player rolled 4 + 5 = 9
Player rolled 2 + 6 = 8
Player rolled 6 + 6 = 12
Player rolled 6 + 4 = 10
Player wins
```

Fig. 7.7 | Craps class simulates the dice game craps. (Part 3 of 3.)

Method RollDice

In the rules of the game, the player must roll two dice on the first roll and must do the same on all subsequent rolls. We declare method RollDice (lines 73–85) to roll the dice and compute and display their sum. Method RollDice is declared once, but it's called from two places (lines 30 and 54) in method Main, which contains the logic for one complete game of craps. Each time it's called, RollDice returns the sum of the dice, so the return type int is indicated in the method header (line 73). Although lines 76 and 77 look the same (except for the die names), they do not necessarily produce the same result. Each of these statements produces a random value in the range 1–6. Variable randomNumbers (used in lines 76 and 77) is *not* declared in the method. Rather it's declared as a private static variable of the class and initialized in line 8. This enables us to create one Random object that's reused in each call to RollDice.

Method Main's Local Variables

The game is reasonably involved. The player may win or lose on the first roll or may win or lose on any subsequent roll. Method Main (lines 24–70) uses local variable gameStatus (line 27) to keep track of the overall game status, local variable myPoint (line 28) to store the "point" if the player does not win or lose on the first roll and local variable sumOfDice (line 30) to maintain the sum of the dice for the most recent roll. Variable myPoint is initialized to 0 to ensure that the app will compile. If you do not initialize myPoint, the compiler issues an error, because myPoint is not assigned a value in every case of the switch statement—thus, the app could try to use myPoint before it's definitely assigned a value. By contrast, gameStatus does not require initialization because it's assigned a value in every branch of the switch statement—thus, it's guaranteed to be initialized before it's used. However, as good programming practice, we initialize it anyway.

enum Type Status

Local variable gameStatus is declared to be of a new type called Status, which we declared in line 11. Type Status is declared as a private member of class Craps, because Status will be used only in that class. Status is a user-defined type called an **enumeration**, which declares a set of *constants* represented by identifiers. An enumeration is introduced by the keyword **enum** and a type name (in this case, Status). As with a class, braces ({ and }) delimit the body of an enum declaration. Inside the braces is a comma-separated list of **enumeration constants**. The enum constant names must be *unique*, but the value associated with each constant need not be.

Variables of type Status should be assigned only one of the three constants declared in the enumeration. When the game is won, the app sets local variable gameStatus to Status.WON (lines 37 and 58). When the game is lost, the app sets local variable gameStatus to Status.LOST (lines 42 and 62). Otherwise, the app sets local variable gameStatus to Status.CONTINUE (line 45) to indicate that the dice must be rolled again.

Good Programming Practice 7.2

Using enumeration constants (like Status.WON, Status.LOST and Status.CONTINUE) rather than literal integer values (such as 0, 1 and 2) can make code easier to read and maintain.

The First Roll

Line 30 in method Main calls RollDice, which picks two random values from 1 to 6, displays the value of the first die, the value of the second die and the sum of the dice, and returns the sum of the dice. Method Main next enters the switch statement at lines 33–49, which uses the sumOfDice value from line 30 to determine whether the game has been won or lost, or whether it should continue with another roll.

DiceNames Enumeration

The sums of the dice that would result in a win or loss on the first roll are declared in the DiceNames enumeration in lines 14–21. These are used in the cases of the switch statement. The identifier names use casino parlance for these sums. Notice that in the Dice-Names enumeration, a value is explicitly assigned to each identifier name. When the enum is declared, each constant in the enum declaration is a constant value of type int. If you do not assign a value to an identifier in the enum declaration, the compiler will do so. If the first enum constant is unassigned, the compiler gives it the value 0. If any other enum constant is unassigned, the compiler gives it a value one higher than that of the preceding enum constant. For example, in the Status enumeration, the compiler implicitly assigns 0 to Status.WON, 1 to Status.CONTINUE and 2 to Status.LOST.

Underlying Type of an **enum**

You could also declare an enum's underlying type to be byte, sbyte, short, ushort, int, uint, long or ulong by writing

```
private enum MyEnum : typeName { Constant1, Constant2, ... }
```

where *typeName* represents one of the integral simple types.

Comparing an Integral Type to an **enum** *Constant*

If you need to compare a simple integral type value to the underlying value of an enumeration constant, you must use a cast operator to make the two types match. In the switch statement at lines 33–49, we use the cast operator to convert the int value in sumOfDice to type DiceNames and compare it to each of the constants in DiceNames. Lines 35–36 determine whether the player won on the first roll with SEVEN (7) or YO_LEVEN (11). Lines 39–41 determine whether the player lost on the first roll with SNAKE_EYES (2), TREY (3) or BOX_CARS (12). After the first roll, if the game is not over, the default case (lines 44–48) saves sumOfDice in myPoint (line 46) and displays the point (line 47).

Additional Rolls of the Dice

If we're still trying to "make our point" (i.e., the game is continuing from a prior roll), the loop in lines 52–63 executes. Line 54 rolls the dice again. If sumOfDice matches myPoint in line 57, line 58 sets gameStatus to Status.WON, and the loop terminates because the game is complete. In line 61, we use the cast operator (int) to obtain the underlying value of DiceNames.SEVEN so that we can compare it to sumOfDice. If sumOfDice is equal to SEVEN (7), line 62 sets gameStatus to Status.LOST, and the loop terminates because the game is over. When the game completes, lines 66–69 display a message indicating whether the player won or lost, and the app terminates.

Summary of the **Craps** *Example*

Note the use of the various program-control mechanisms we've discussed. The Craps class uses two methods—Main and RollDice (called twice from Main)—and the switch, while, if...else and nested if control statements. Also, notice that we use multiple case labels in the switch statement to execute the same statements for sums of SEVEN and YO_LEVEN (lines 35–36) and for sums of SNAKE_EYES, TREY and BOX_CARS (lines 39–41). To easily create a switch statement with all possible values for an enum type, you can use the switch code snippet. Type switch in the C# code then press *Tab* twice. If you specify a variable of an enum type in the switch statement's expression and press *Enter*, a case for each enum constant will be generated automatically.

7.11 Scope of Declarations

You've seen declarations of C# entities, such as classes, methods, properties, variables and parameters. Declarations introduce names that can be used to refer to such C# entities. The **scope** of a declaration is the portion of the app that can refer to the declared entity by its unqualified name. Such an entity is said to be "in scope" for that portion of the app. This section introduces several important scope issues. The basic scope rules are as follows:

1. The scope of a parameter declaration is the body of the method in which the declaration appears.

2. The scope of a local-variable declaration is from the point at which the declaration appears to the end of the block containing the declaration.

3. The scope of a local-variable declaration that appears in the initialization section of a for statement's header is the body of the for statement and the other expressions in the header.

4. The scope of a method, property or field of a class is the entire body of the class. This enables non-static methods and properties of a class to use any of the class's fields, methods and properties, regardless of the order in which they're declared. Similarly, static methods and properties can use any of the static members of the class.

Any block may contain variable declarations. If a local variable or parameter in a method has the same name as a field, the field is hidden until the block terminates. A compilation error occurs if a *nested block* in a method contains a variable with the same name as a local variable in an *outer block* of the method. In Chapter 10, we discuss how to access hidden fields. The app in Fig. 7.8 demonstrates scoping issues with fields and local variables.

```
1   // Fig. 7.8: Scope.cs
2   // Scope class demonstrates static and local variable scopes.
3   using System;
4
5   public class Scope
6   {
7       // static variable that's accessible to all methods of this class
8       private static int x = 1;
```

Fig. 7.8 | Scope class demonstrates static and local variable scopes. (Part I of 3.)

```
 9
10      // Main creates and initializes local variable x
11      // and calls methods UseLocalVariable and UseStaticVariable
12      public static void Main( string[] args )
13      {
14         int x = 5; // method's local variable x hides static variable x
15
16         Console.WriteLine( "local x in method Main is {0}", x );
17
18         // UseLocalVariable has its own local x
19         UseLocalVariable();
20
21         // UseStaticVariable uses class Scope's static variable x
22         UseStaticVariable();
23
24         // UseLocalVariable reinitializes its own local x
25         UseLocalVariable();
26
27         // class Scope's static variable x retains its value
28         UseStaticVariable();
29
30         Console.WriteLine( "\nlocal x in method Main is {0}", x );
31      } // end Main
32
33      // create and initialize local variable x during each call
34      public static void UseLocalVariable()
35      {
36         int x = 25; // initialized each time UseLocalVariable is called
37
38         Console.WriteLine(
39            "\nlocal x on entering method UseLocalVariable is {0}", x );
40         ++x; // modifies this method's local variable x
41         Console.WriteLine(
42            "local x before exiting method UseLocalVariable is {0}", x );
43      } // end method UseLocalVariable
44
45      // modify class Scope's static variable x during each call
46      public static void UseStaticVariable()
47      {
48         Console.WriteLine( "\nstatic variable x on entering {0} is {1}",
49            "method UseStaticVariable", x );
50         x *= 10; // modifies class Scope's static variable x
51         Console.WriteLine( "static variable x before exiting {0} is {1}",
52            "method UseStaticVariable", x );
53      } // end method UseStaticVariable
54   } // end class Scope
```

```
local x in method Main is 5

local x on entering method UseLocalVariable is 25
local x before exiting method UseLocalVariable is 26
```

Fig. 7.8 | Scope class demonstrates static and local variable scopes. (Part 2 of 3.)

```
static variable x on entering method UseStaticVariable is 1
static variable x before exiting method UseStaticVariable is 10

local x on entering method UseLocalVariable is 25
local x before exiting method UseLocalVariable is 26

static variable x on entering method UseStaticVariable is 10
static variable x before exiting method UseStaticVariable is 100

local x in method Main is 5
```

Fig. 7.8 | Scope class demonstrates static and local variable scopes. (Part 3 of 3.)

 Error-Prevention Tip 7.1
Use different names for fields and local variables to help prevent subtle logic errors that occur when a method is called and a local variable of the method hides a field of the same name in the class.

Line 8 declares and initializes the static variable x to 1. This static variable is *hidden* in any block (or method) that declares local variable named x. Method Main (lines 12–31) declares local variable x (line 14) and initializes it to 5. This local variable's value is output to show that static variable x (whose value is 1) is hidden in method Main. The app declares two other methods—UseLocalVariable (lines 34–43) and UseStaticVariable (lines 46–53)—that each take no arguments and do not return results. Method Main calls each method twice (lines 19–28). Method UseLocalVariable declares local variable x (line 36). When UseLocalVariable is first called (line 19), it creates local variable x and initializes it to 25 (line 36), outputs the value of x (lines 38–39), increments x (line 40) and outputs the value of x again (lines 41–42). When UseLocalVariable is called a second time (line 25), it re-creates local variable x and reinitializes it to 25, so the output of each UseLocalVariable call is identical.

Method UseStaticVariable does not declare any local variables. Therefore, when it refers to x, static variable x (line 8) of the class is used. When method UseStaticVariable is first called (line 22), it outputs the value (1) of static variable x (lines 48–49), multiplies the static variable x by 10 (line 50) and outputs the value (10) of static variable x again (lines 51–52) before returning. The next time method UseStaticVariable is called (line 28), the static variable has its modified value, 10, so the method outputs 10, then 100. Finally, in method Main, the app outputs the value of local variable x again (line 30) to show that none of the method calls modified Main's local variable x, because the methods all referred to variables named x in other scopes.

7.12 Method Overloading

Methods of the same name can be declared in the same class, as long as they have different sets of parameters (determined by the number, types and order of the parameters). This is called **method overloading**. When an **overloaded method** is called, the C# compiler selects the appropriate method by examining the number, types and order of the arguments in the call. Method overloading is commonly used to create several methods with the *same name* that perform the same or similar tasks, but on *different types* or *different numbers of arguments*.

For example, Math methods Min and Max (summarized in Section 7.3) are overloaded with 11 versions. These find the minimum and maximum, respectively, of two values of each of the 11 numeric simple types. Our next example demonstrates declaring and invoking overloaded methods. You'll see examples of overloaded constructors in Chapter 10.

Declaring Overloaded Methods

In class MethodOverload (Fig. 7.9), we include two overloaded versions of a method called Square—one that calculates the square of an int (and returns an int) and one that calculates the square of a double (and returns a double). Although these methods have the same name and similar parameter lists and bodies, you can think of them simply as *different* methods. It may help to think of the method names as "Square of int" and "Square of double," respectively.

```
1   // Fig. 7.9: MethodOverload.cs
2   // Overloaded method declarations.
3   using System;
4
5   public class MethodOverload
6   {
7      // test overloaded square methods
8      public static void Main( string[] args )
9      {
10        Console.WriteLine( "Square of integer 7 is {0}", Square( 7 ) );
11        Console.WriteLine( "Square of double 7.5 is {0}", Square( 7.5 ) );
12     } // end Main
13
14     // square method with int argument
15     public static int Square( int intValue )
16     {
17        Console.WriteLine( "Called square with int argument: {0}",
18           intValue );
19        return intValue * intValue;
20     } // end method Square with int argument
21
22     // square method with double argument
23     public static double Square( double doubleValue )
24     {
25        Console.WriteLine( "Called square with double argument: {0}",
26           doubleValue );
27        return doubleValue * doubleValue;
28     } // end method Square with double argument
29  } // end class MethodOverload
```

```
Called square with int argument: 7
Square of integer 7 is 49
Called square with double argument: 7.5
Square of double 7.5 is 56.25
```

Fig. 7.9 | Overloaded method declarations.

Line 10 in Main invokes method Square with the argument 7. Literal integer values are treated as type int, so the method call in line 10 invokes the version of Square at lines 15–

20 that specifies an int parameter. Similarly, line 11 invokes method Square with the argument 7.5. Literal real-number values are treated as type double, so the method call in line 11 invokes the version of Square at lines 23–28 that specifies a double parameter. Each method first outputs a line of text to prove that the proper method was called in each case.

Notice that the overloaded methods in Fig. 7.9 perform the same calculation, but with two different types. C#'s generics feature provides a mechanism for writing a single "generic method" that can perform the same tasks as an entire set of overloaded methods. We discuss generic methods in Chapter 18.

Distinguishing Between Overloaded Methods

The compiler distinguishes overloaded methods by their **signature**—a combination of the method's name and the number, types and order of its parameters. The signature also includes the way those parameters are passed, which can be modified by the ref and out keywords (discussed in Section 7.16). If the compiler looked only at method names during compilation, the code in Fig. 7.9 would be *ambiguous*—the compiler would not know how to distinguish between the Square methods (lines 15–20 and 23–28). Internally, the compiler uses signatures to determine whether a class's methods are unique in that class.

For example, in Fig. 7.9, the compiler will use the method signatures to distinguish between the "Square of int" method (the Square method that specifies an int parameter) and the "Square of double" method (the Square method that specifies a double parameter). If Method1's declaration begins as

```
void Method1( int a, float b )
```

then that method will have a different signature than the method declared beginning with

```
void Method1( float a, int b )
```

The *order* of the parameter types is important—the compiler considers the preceding two Method1 headers to be distinct.

Return Types of Overloaded Methods

In discussing the logical names of methods used by the compiler, we did not mention the return types of the methods. This is because method *calls* cannot be distinguished by return type. The app in Fig. 7.10 illustrates the compiler errors generated when two methods have the *same* signature but *different* return types. Overloaded methods can have the *same* or *different* return types if the methods have *different* parameter lists. Also, overloaded methods need not have the same number of parameters.

Common Programming Error 7.9

Declaring overloaded methods with identical parameter lists is a compilation error regardless of whether the return types are different.

```
1   // Fig. 7.10: MethodOverload.cs
2   // Overloaded methods with identical signatures
3   // cause compilation errors, even if return types are different.
```

Fig. 7.10 | Overloaded methods with identical signatures cause compilation errors, even if return types are different. (Part 1 of 2.)

```
 4   public class MethodOverloadError
 5   {
 6      // declaration of method Square with int argument
 7      public int Square( int x )
 8      {
 9         return x * x;
10      } // end method Square
11
12      // second declaration of method Square with int argument
13      // causes compilation error even though return types are different
14      public double Square( int y )
15      {
16         return y * y;
17      } // end method Square
18   } // end class MethodOverloadError
```

Error List					
▼ ▾ ❌ 1 Error ⚠ 0 Warnings ⓘ 0 Messages			Search Error List		𝒫 ▾
Description		File ▲	Line ▲	Column ▲	Project ▲
❌ 1	Type 'MethodOverloadError' already defines a member called 'Square' with the same parameter types	MethodOverloadError.cs	14	25	MethodOverloadError

Fig. 7.10 | Overloaded methods with identical signatures cause compilation errors, even if return types are different. (Part 2 of 2.)

7.13 Optional Parameters

Methods can have **optional parameters** that allow the calling method to *vary the number of arguments* to pass. An optional parameter specifies a **default value** that's assigned to the parameter if the optional argument is omitted.

You can create methods with one or more optional parameters. *All optional parameters must be placed to the right of the method's non-optional parameters*—that is, at the end of the parameter list.

Common Programming Error 7.10
Declaring a non-optional parameter to the right of an optional one is a compilation error.

When a parameter has a default value, the caller has the *option* of passing that particular argument. For example, the method header

```
public int Power( int baseValue, int exponentValue = 2)
```

specifies an optional second parameter. Any call to Power must pass at least an argument for the parameter baseValue, or a compilation error occurs. Optionally, a second argument (for the exponentValue parameter) can be passed to Power. Consider the following calls to Power:

```
Power()
Power(10)
Power(10, 3)
```

The first call generates a compilation error because this method requires a minimum of one argument. The second call is valid because one argument (10) is being passed—the optional exponentValue is not specified in the method call. The last call is also valid—10 is passed as the required argument and 3 is passed as the optional argument.

In the call that passes only one argument (10), parameter exponentValue defaults to 2, which is the default value specified in the method's header. Each optional parameter must specify a default value by using an equal (=) sign followed by the value. For example, the header for Power sets 2 as exponentValue's default value.

Figure 7.11 demonstrates an optional parameter. The program calculates the result of raising a base value to an exponent. Method Power (lines 15–23) specifies that its second parameter is optional. In method DisplayPowers, lines 10–11 call method Power. Line 10 calls the method without the optional second argument. In this case, the compiler provides the second argument, 2, using the default value of the optional argument, which is not visible to you in the call.

```vb
 1    // Fig. 7.11: Power.vb
 2    // Optional argument demonstration with method Power.
 3    using System;
 4
 5    class CalculatePowers
 6    {
 7       // call Power with and without optional arguments
 8       public static void Main( string[] args )
 9       {
10          Console.WriteLine( "Power(10) = {0}", Power( 10 ) ) ;
11          Console.WriteLine( "Power(2, 10) = {0}", Power( 2, 10 ) );
12       } // end Main
13
14       // use iteration to calculate power
15       public int Power( int baseValue, int exponentValue = 2 )
16       {
17          int result = 1; // initialize total
18
19          for ( int i = 1; i <= exponentValue; i++ )
20             result *= baseValue;
21
22          return result;
23       } // end method Power
24    } // end class CalculatePowers
```

```
Power(10) = 100
Power(2, 10) = 1024
```

Fig. 7.11 | Optional argument demonstration with method Power.

7.14 Named Parameters

Normally, when calling a method that has optional parameters, the argument values—in order—are assigned to the parameters from left to right in the parameter list. Consider a Time class that stores the time of day in 24-hour clock format as int values representing the hour (0–23), minute (0–59) and second (0–59). Such a class might provide a SetTime method with optional parameters like

```csharp
public void SetTime( int hour = 0, int minute = 0, int second = 0 )
```

In the preceding method header, all three of SetTime's parameters are optional. Assuming that we have a Time object named t, we can call SetTime as follows:

```
t.SetTime(); // sets the time to 12:00:00 AM
t.SetTime( 12 ); // sets the time to 12:00:00 PM
t.SetTime( 12, 30 ); // sets the time to 12:30:00 PM
t.SetTime( 12, 30, 22 ); // sets the time to 12:30:22 PM
```

In the first call, no arguments are specified, so the compiler assigns 0 to each parameter. In the second call, the compiler assigns the argument, 12, to the first parameter, hour, and assigns default values of 0 to the minute and second parameters. In the third call, the compiler assigns the two arguments, 12 and 30, to the parameters hour and minute, respectively, and assigns the default value 0 to the parameter second. In the last call, the compiler assigns the three arguments, 12, 30 and 22, to the parameters hour, minute and second, respectively.

What if you wanted to specify only arguments for the hour and second? You might think that you could call the method as follows:

```
t.SetTime( 12, , 22 ); // COMPILATION ERROR
```

Unlike some programming languages, C# doesn't allow you to skip an argument as shown in the preceding statement. C# provides a feature called **named parameters**, which enable you to call methods that receive optional parameters by providing *only* the optional arguments you wish to specify. To do so, you explicitly specify the parameter's name and value—separated by a colon (:)—in the argument list of the method call. For example, the preceding statement can be implemented as follows:

```
t.SetTime( hour: 12, second: 22 ); // sets the time to 12:00:22
```

In this case, the compiler assigns parameter hour the argument 12 and parameter second the argument 22. The parameter minute is not specified, so the compiler assigns it the default value 0. It's also possible to specify the arguments *out of order* when using named parameters. The arguments for the required parameters must always be supplied.

7.15 Recursion

The apps we've discussed thus far are generally structured as methods that call one another in a disciplined, hierarchical manner. For some problems, however, it's useful to have a method call itself. A **recursive method** is a method that calls itself, either *directly* or *indirectly through another method*.

We consider recursion conceptually first. Then we examine an app containing a recursive method. Recursive problem-solving approaches have a number of elements in common. When a recursive method is called to solve a problem, it actually is capable of solving *only* the simplest case(s), or **base case(s)**. If the method is called with a base case, it returns a result. If the method is called with a more complex problem, it divides the problem into two conceptual pieces: a piece that the method knows how to do and a piece that it does not know how to do. To make recursion feasible, the latter piece must resemble the original problem, but be a slightly simpler or slightly smaller version of it. Because this new problem looks like the original problem, the method calls a fresh copy (or several fresh copies) of itself to work on the smaller problem; this is referred to as a

recursive call and is also called the **recursion step**. The recursion step normally includes a return statement, because its result will be combined with the portion of the problem the method knew how to solve to form a result that will be passed back to the original caller.

The recursion step executes while the original call to the method is still active (i.e., while it has not finished executing). The recursion step can result in many more recursive calls, as the method divides each new subproblem into two conceptual pieces. For the recursion to *terminate* eventually, each time the method calls itself with a slightly simpler version of the original problem, the sequence of smaller and smaller problems must converge on the base case. At that point, the method recognizes the base case and returns a result to the previous copy of the method. A sequence of returns ensues until the original method call returns the result to the caller. This process sounds complex compared with the conventional problem solving we've performed to this point.

Recursive Factorial Calculations

As an example of recursion concepts at work, let's write a recursive app to perform a popular mathematical calculation. Consider the factorial of a nonnegative integer n, written $n!$ (and pronounced "n factorial"), which is the product

$n \cdot (n-1) \cdot (n-2) \cdot \dots \cdot 1$

1! is equal to 1 and 0! is defined to be 1. For example, 5! is the product $5 \cdot 4 \cdot 3 \cdot 2 \cdot 1$, which is equal to 120.

The factorial of an integer, number, greater than or equal to 0 can be calculated iteratively (nonrecursively) using the for statement as follows:

```
factorial = 1;
for ( int counter = number; counter >= 1; --counter )
    factorial *= counter;
```

A recursive declaration of the factorial method is arrived at by observing the following relationship:

$n! = n \cdot (n-1)!$

For example, 5! is clearly equal to $5 \cdot 4!$, as is shown by the following equations:

```
5! = 5 · 4 · 3 · 2 · 1
5! = 5 · (4 · 3 · 2 · 1)
5! = 5 · (4!)
```

The evaluation of 5! would proceed as shown in Fig. 7.12. Figure 7.12(a) shows how the succession of recursive calls proceeds until 1! is evaluated to be 1, which terminates the recursion. Figure 7.12(b) shows the values returned from each recursive call to its caller until the value is calculated and returned.

Figure 7.13 uses recursion to calculate and display the factorials of the integers from 0 to 10. The recursive method Factorial (lines 16–24) first tests to determine whether a terminating condition (line 19) is true. If number is less than or equal to 1 (the base case), Factorial returns 1, no further recursion is necessary and the method returns. If number is greater than 1, line 23 expresses the problem as the product of number and a recursive call to Factorial evaluating the factorial of number - 1, which is a slightly simpler problem than the original calculation, Factorial(number).

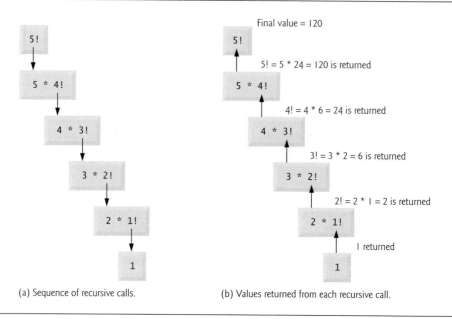

(a) Sequence of recursive calls.   (b) Values returned from each recursive call.

Fig. 7.12 | Recursive evaluation of 5!.

```
1   // Fig. 7.13: FactorialTest.cs
2   // Recursive Factorial method.
3   using System;
4
5   public class FactorialTest
6   {
7      public static void Main( string[] args )
8      {
9         // calculate the factorials of 0 through 10
10        for ( long counter = 0; counter <= 10; ++counter )
11           Console.WriteLine( "{0}! = {1}",
12              counter, Factorial( counter ) );
13     } // end Main
14
15     // recursive declaration of method Factorial
16     public static long Factorial( long number )
17     {
18        // base case
19        if ( number <= 1 )
20           return 1;
21        // recursion step
22        else
23           return number * Factorial( number - 1 );
24     } // end method Factorial
25  } // end class FactorialTest
```

Fig. 7.13 | Recursive Factorial method. (Part 1 of 2.)

```
0!  = 1
1!  = 1
2!  = 2
3!  = 6
4!  = 24
5!  = 120
6!  = 720
7!  = 5040
8!  = 40320
9!  = 362880
10! = 3628800
```

Fig. 7.13 | Recursive `Factorial` method. (Part 2 of 2.)

Method `Factorial` (lines 16–24) receives a parameter of type `long` and returns a result of type `long`. As you can see in Fig. 7.13, factorial values become large quickly. We chose type `long` (which can represent relatively large integers) so that the app could calculate factorials greater than 20!. Unfortunately, the `Factorial` method produces large values so quickly that factorial values soon exceed even the maximum value that can be stored in a `long` variable. Due to the restrictions on the integral types, variables of type `float`, `double` or `decimal` might ultimately be needed to calculate factorials of larger numbers. This situation points to a weakness in many programming languages—the languages are *not easily extended* to handle the unique requirements of various apps. As you know, C# allows you to create a type that supports arbitrarily large integers if you wish. For example, you could create a `HugeInteger` class that would enable an app to calculate the factorials of arbitrarily large numbers. You can also use the new type `BigInteger` from the .NET Framework's class library.

Common Programming Error 7.11

*Either omitting the base case or writing the recursion step incorrectly so that it does not converge on the base case will cause **infinite recursion**, eventually exhausting memory. This error is analogous to the problem of an infinite loop in an iterative (nonrecursive) solution.*

7.16 Passing Arguments: Pass-by-Value vs. Pass-by-Reference

Two ways to pass arguments to functions in many programming languages are **pass-by-value** and **pass-by-reference**. When an argument is passed by *value* (the default in C#), a *copy* of its value is made and passed to the called function. Changes to the copy do *not* affect the original variable's value in the caller. This prevents the accidental side effects that so greatly hinder the development of correct and reliable software systems. Each argument that's been passed in the programs in this chapter so far has been passed by value. When an argument is passed by *reference*, the caller gives the method the ability to access and modify the caller's original variable.

> ### Software Engineering Observation 7.2
> *Pass-by-reference can weaken security, because the called function can corrupt the caller's data.*

To pass an object by reference into a method, simply provide as an argument in the method call the variable that refers to the object. Then, in the method body, reference the object using the parameter name. The parameter refers to the original object in memory, so the called method can access the original object directly.

Previously, we discussed the difference between *value types* and *reference types*. A major difference between them is that *value-type variables store values*, so specifying a value-type variable in a method call passes a *copy* of that variable's value to the method. *Reference-type variables store references to objects*, so specifying a reference-type variable as an argument passes the method a copy of the actual reference that refers to the object. Even though the reference itself is passed by value, the method can still use the reference it receives to interact with—and possibly modify—the original object. Similarly, when returning information from a method via a `return` statement, the method returns a copy of the value stored in a value-type variable or a copy of the reference stored in a reference-type variable. When a reference is returned, the calling method can use that reference to interact with the referenced object.

ref *and* out *Parameters*

What if you would like to pass a variable by reference so the called method can modify the variable's value? To do this, C# provides keywords **ref** and **out**. Applying the `ref` keyword to a parameter declaration allows you to pass a variable to a method *by reference*—the called method will be able to *modify the original variable in the caller*. The `ref` keyword is used for variables that already have been initialized in the calling method. When a method call contains an uninitialized variable as an argument to a `ref` parameter, the compiler generates an error. Preceding a parameter with keyword out creates an **output parameter**. This indicates to the compiler that the argument will be passed into the called method *by reference* and that the called method will assign a value to the original variable in the caller. If the method does *not* assign a value to the output parameter in *every* possible path of execution, the compiler generates an error. This also prevents the compiler from generating an error message for an *uninitialized variable* that's passed as an argument to a method. A method can return only one value to its caller via a return statement, but can return many values by specifying multiple output (`ref` and/or `out`) parameters.

You can also pass a reference-type variable by reference, which allows you to modify it so that it refers to a new object. Passing a reference by reference is a tricky but powerful technique that we discuss in Section 8.8.

Demonstrating ref, out *and Value Parameters*

The app in Fig. 7.14 uses the `ref` and `out` keywords to manipulate integer values. The class contains three methods that calculate the square of an integer. Method `SquareRef` (lines 37–40) multiplies its parameter x by itself and assigns the new value to x. Square-Ref's parameter is declared as ref int, which indicates that the argument passed to this method must be an integer that's passed by reference. Because the argument is passed by reference, the assignment at line 39 modifies the original argument's value in the caller.

Method SquareOut (lines 44–48) assigns its parameter the value 6 (line 46), then squares that value. SquareOut's parameter is declared as out int, which indicates that the argument passed to this method must be an integer that's passed by reference and that the argument does not need to be initialized in advance.

```
1   // Fig. 7.14: ReferenceAndOutputParameters.cs
2   // Reference, output and value parameters.
3   using System;
4
5   class ReferenceAndOutputParameters
6   {
7      // call methods with reference, output and value parameters
8      public static void Main( string[] args )
9      {
10        int y = 5; // initialize y to 5
11        int z; // declares z, but does not initialize it
12
13        // display original values of y and z
14        Console.WriteLine( "Original value of y: {0}", y );
15        Console.WriteLine( "Original value of z: uninitialized\n" );
16
17        // pass y and z by reference
18        SquareRef( ref y ); // must use keyword ref
19        SquareOut( out z ); // must use keyword out
20
21        // display values of y and z after they're modified by
22        // methods SquareRef and SquareOut, respectively
23        Console.WriteLine( "Value of y after SquareRef: {0}", y );
24        Console.WriteLine( "Value of z after SquareOut: {0}\n", z );
25
26        // pass y and z by value
27        Square( y );
28        Square( z );
29
30        // display values of y and z after they're passed to method Square
31        // to demonstrate that arguments passed by value are not modified
32        Console.WriteLine( "Value of y after Square: {0}", y );
33        Console.WriteLine( "Value of z after Square: {0}", z );
34     } // end Main
35
36     // uses reference parameter x to modify caller's variable
37     static void SquareRef( ref int x )
38     {
39        x = x * x; // squares value of caller's variable
40     } // end method SquareRef
```

Fig. 7.14 | Reference, output and value parameters. (Part 1 of 2.)

```
41
42        // uses output parameter x to assign a value
43        // to an uninitialized variable
44        static void SquareOut( out int x )
45        {
46           x = 6; // assigns a value to caller's variable
47           x = x * x; // squares value of caller's variable
48        } // end method SquareOut
49
50        // parameter x receives a copy of the value passed as an argument,
51        // so this method cannot modify the caller's variable
52        static void Square( int x )
53        {
54           x = x * x;
55        } // end method Square
56     } // end class ReferenceAndOutputParameters
```

```
Original value of y: 5
Original value of z: uninitialized

Value of y after SquareRef: 25
Value of z after SquareOut: 36

Value of y after Square: 25
Value of z after Square: 36
```

Fig. 7.14 | Reference, output and value parameters. (Part 2 of 2.)

Method Square (lines 52–55) multiplies its parameter x by itself and assigns the new value to x. When this method is called, a *copy* of the argument is passed to the parameter x. Thus, even though parameter x is modified in the method, the original value in the caller is *not* modified.

Method Main (lines 8–34) invokes methods SquareRef, SquareOut and Square. We begin by initializing variable y to 5 and declaring, but *not* initializing, variable z. Lines 18–19 call methods SquareRef and SquareOut. Notice that when you pass a variable to a method with a reference parameter, you must precede the argument with the same keyword (ref or out) that was used to declare the reference parameter. Lines 23–24 display the values of y and z after the calls to SquareRef and SquareOut. Notice that y has been changed to 25 and z has been set to 36.

Lines 27–28 call method Square with y and z as arguments. In this case, both variables are passed by *value*—only *copies* of their values are passed to Square. As a result, the values of y and z remain 25 and 36, respectively. Lines 32–33 output the values of y and z to show that they were *not* modified.

Common Programming Error 7.12

The ref and out arguments in a method call must match the parameters specified in the method declaration; otherwise, a compilation error occurs.

Software Engineering Observation 7.3

By default, value types are passed by value. Objects are not passed to methods; rather, references to objects are passed to methods. The references themselves are passed by value. When a method receives a reference to an object, the method can manipulate the object directly, but the reference value cannot be changed to refer to a new object. In Section 8.8, you'll see that references also can be passed by reference.

7.17 Wrap-Up

In this chapter, we discussed the difference between non-static and static methods, and we showed how to call static methods by preceding the method name with the name of the class in which it appears and the member access (.) operator. You saw that the Math class in the .NET Framework Class Library provides many static methods to perform mathematical calculations. We presented several commonly used Framework Class Library namespaces. You learned how to use operator + to perform string concatenations. You also learned how to declare constant values in two ways—with the const keyword and with enum types. We demonstrated simulation techniques and used class Random to generate sets of random numbers. We discussed the scope of fields and local variables in a class. You saw how to overload methods in a class by providing methods with the same name but different signatures. You learned how to use optional and named parameters. We discussed how recursive methods call themselves, breaking larger problems into smaller subproblems until eventually the original problem is solved. You learned the differences between value types and reference types with respect to how they're passed to methods, and how to use the ref and out keywords to pass arguments by reference.

In Chapter 8, you'll learn how to maintain lists and tables of data in arrays. You'll see a more elegant implementation of the app that rolls a die 6,000,000 times and two enhanced versions of our GradeBook case study. You'll also learn how to access an app's command-line arguments that are passed to method Main when a console app begins execution.

8

Arrays; Introduction to Exception Handling

Objectives

In this chapter you'll:

- Use arrays to store data in and retrieve data from lists and tables of values.

- Declare arrays, initialize arrays and refer to individual elements of arrays.

- Use **foreach** to iterate through arrays.

- Use exception handling to process runtime problems.

- Use implicitly typed local variables.

- Pass arrays to methods.

- Declare and manipulate multidimensional arrays.

- Write methods that use variable-length argument lists.

- Read command-line arguments into an app.

Outline

8.1 Introduction

This chapter introduces the important topic of **data structures**—collections of related data items. **Arrays** are data structures consisting of related data items of the *same* type. Arrays are *fixed-length* entities—they remain the same length once they're created, although an array variable may be reassigned such that it refers to a new array of a different length.

After discussing how arrays are declared, created and initialized, we present examples that demonstrate several common array manipulations. We use arrays to simulate shuffling and dealing playing cards. The chapter demonstrates C#'s remaining structured control statement—the `foreach` repetition statement—which provides a concise notation for accessing data in arrays (and other data structures, as you'll see in Chapter 9 and later in the book). We enhance the `GradeBook` case study using arrays to enable the class to store a set of grades and analyze student grades from multiple exams.

8.2 Arrays

An array is a group of variables (called **elements**) containing values that all have the *same type*. Recall that types are divided into two categories—*value types* and *reference types*. Arrays are reference types. As you'll see, what we typically think of as an array is actually a reference to an array object. The elements of an array can be either value types or reference types, including other arrays. To refer to a particular element in an array, we specify the *name* of the reference to the array and the *position number* of the element in the array, which is known as the element's **index**.

Figure 8.1 shows a logical representation of an integer array called c containing sample values. This array contains 12 elements. An app refers to any one of these elements with an **array-access expression** that includes the name of the array, followed by the index of the particular element in **square brackets** (`[]`). The first element in every array has **index zero** and is sometimes called the **zeroth element**. Thus, the elements of array c are c[0], c[1], c[2] and so on. The highest index in array c is 11, which is one less than the number of elements in the array, because indices begin at 0. Array names follow the same conventions as other variable names.

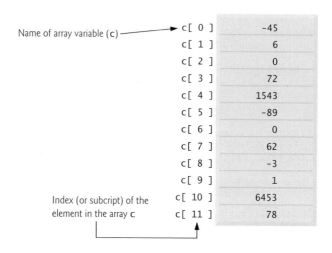

Fig. 8.1 | A 12-element array.

An index must be a nonnegative integer and can be an expression. For example, if we assume that variable a is 5 and variable b is 6, then the statement

```
c[ a + b ] += 2;
```

adds 2 to array element c[11]. An indexed array name is an array-access expression. Such expressions can be used on the left side of an assignment (i.e., as an *lvalue*) to place a new value into an array element. The array index must be a value of type int, uint, long or ulong, or a value of a type that can be implicitly promoted to one of these types.

Let's examine array c in Fig. 8.1 more closely. The **name** of the variable that references the array is c. Every array instance knows its own length and provides access to this information with the Length property. For example, the expression c.Length uses array c's Length property to determine the length of the array (that is, 12). The Length property of an array *cannot* be changed, because it does not provide a set accessor. The array's 12 elements are referred to as c[0], c[1], c[2], ..., c[11]. Referring to elements *outside* of this range, such as c[-1] or c[12], is a runtime error (as we'll demonstrate in Fig. 8.8). The value of c[0] is -45, the value of c[1] is 6, the value of c[2] is 0, the value of c[7] is 62 and the value of c[11] is 78. To calculate the sum of the values contained in the first three elements of array c and store the result in variable sum, we would write

```
sum = c[ 0 ] + c[ 1 ] + c[ 2 ];
```

To divide the value of c[6] by 2 and assign the result to the variable x, we would write

```
x = c[ 6 ] / 2;
```

8.3 Declaring and Creating Arrays

Arrays occupy space in memory. Since they're objects, they're created with keyword new. To create an array object, you specify the type and the number of array elements as part of an **array-creation expression** that uses keyword new. Such an expression returns a reference that can be stored in an array variable. The following declaration and array-creation expression create an array object containing 12 int elements and store the array's reference in variable c:

```
int[] c = new int[ 12 ];
```

This expression can be used to create the array shown in Fig. 8.1 (but not the initial values in the array—we'll show how to initialize the elements of an array momentarily). This task also can be performed as follows:

```
int[] c; // declare the array variable
c = new int[ 12 ]; // create the array; assign to array variable
```

In the declaration, the square brackets following the type int indicate that c is a variable that will refer to an array of ints (i.e., c will store a reference to an array object). In the assignment statement, the array variable c receives the reference to a new array object of 12 int elements. The number of elements can also be specified as an expression that's calculated at execution time. When an array is created, each element of the array receives a default value—0 for the numeric simple-type elements, false for bool elements and null for references. As we'll soon see, we can provide specific, nondefault initial element values when we create an array.

Common Programming Error 8.1
In the declaration of a variable that will refer to an array, specifying the number of elements in the square brackets (e.g., int[12] c;) is a syntax error.

An app can create several arrays in a single declaration. The following statement reserves 100 elements for string array b and 27 elements for string array x:

```
string[] b = new string[ 100 ], x = new string[ 27 ];
```

In this statement, string[] applies to each variable. For readability and ease of commenting, we prefer to split the preceding statement into two statements, as in:

```
string[] b = new string[ 100 ]; // create string array b
string[] x = new string[ 27 ]; // create string array x
```

An app can declare variables that will refer to arrays of value-type elements or reference-type elements. For example, every element of an int array is an int *value*, and every element of a string array is a *reference* to a string object.

Resizing an Array
Though arrays are fixed-length entities, you can use the static Array method Resize, which takes two arguments—the array to be resized and the new length—to create a new array with the specified length. This method copies the contents of the old array into the new array and sets the variable it receives as its first argument to reference the new array. For example, consider the following statements:

```
int[] newArray = new int[ 5 ];
Array.Resize( ref newArray, 10 );
```

The variable newArray initially refers to a five-element array. The resize method sets newArray to refer to a new 10-element array. If the new array is *smaller* than the old array, any content that cannot fit into the new array is *truncated without warning*.

8.4 Examples Using Arrays

This section presents several examples that demonstrate declaring arrays, creating arrays, initializing arrays and manipulating array elements.

8.4.1 Creating and Initializing an Array

The app of Fig. 8.2 uses keyword new to create an array of five int elements that are initially 0 (the default for int variables).

```
1   // Fig. 8.2: InitArray.cs
2   // Creating an array.
3   using System;
4
5   public class InitArray
6   {
7      public static void Main( string[] args )
8      {
9         int[] array; // declare array named array
10
11        // create the space for array and initialize to default zeros
12        array = new int[ 5 ]; // 5 int elements
13
14        Console.WriteLine( "{0}{1,8}", "Index", "Value" ); // headings
15
16        // output each array element's value
17        for ( int counter = 0; counter < array.Length; ++counter )
18           Console.WriteLine( "{0,5}{1,8}", counter, array[ counter ] );
19     } // end Main
20  } // end class InitArray
```

```
Index   Value
    0       0
    1       0
    2       0
    3       0
    4       0
```

Fig. 8.2 | Creating an array.

Line 9 declares array—a variable capable of referring to an array of int elements. Line 12 creates the five-element array object and assigns its reference to variable array. Line 14 outputs the column headings. The first column contains the index (0–4) of each array element, and the second column contains the default value (0) of each array element right justified in a field width of 8.

The for statement in lines 17–18 outputs the index number (represented by counter) and the value (represented by array[counter]) of each array element. The loop-control variable counter is initially 0—index values start at 0, so using zero-based counting allows the loop to access *every* element of the array. The for statement's loop-continuation condition uses the property array.Length (line 17) to obtain the length of the array. In this example, the length of the array is 5, so the loop continues executing as long as the value of control variable counter is less than 5. The highest index value of a five-element array is 4, so using the less-than operator in the loop-continuation condition guarantees that the loop does not attempt to access an element beyond the end of the array (i.e., during the *final* iteration of the loop, counter is 4). We'll soon see what happens when an *out-of-range index* is encountered at execution time.

8.4.2 Using an Array Initializer

An app can create an array and initialize its elements with an **array initializer**, which is a comma-separated list of expressions (called an **initializer list**) enclosed in braces. In this case, the array length is determined by the number of elements in the initializer list. For example, the declaration

```
int[] n = { 10, 20, 30, 40, 50 };
```

creates a five-element array with index values 0, 1, 2, 3 and 4. Element n[0] is initialized to 10, n[1] is initialized to 20 and so on. This statement does *not* require new to create the array object. When the compiler encounters an array initializer list, it counts the number of initializers in the list to determine the array's size, then sets up the appropriate new operation "behind the scenes." The app in Fig. 8.3 initializes an integer array with 10 values (line 10) and displays the array in tabular format. The code for displaying the array elements (lines 15–16) is identical to that in Fig. 8.2 (lines 17–18).

```
 1   // Fig. 8.3: InitArray.cs
 2   // Initializing the elements of an array with an array initializer.
 3   using System;
 4
 5   public class InitArray
 6   {
 7      public static void Main( string[] args )
 8      {
 9         // initializer list specifies the value for each element
10         int[] array = { 32, 27, 64, 18, 95, 14, 90, 70, 60, 37 };
11
12         Console.WriteLine( "{0}{1,8}", "Index", "Value" ); // headings
13
14         // output each array element's value
15         for ( int counter = 0; counter < array.Length; ++counter )
16            Console.WriteLine( "{0,5}{1,8}", counter, array[ counter ] );
17      } // end Main
18   } // end class InitArray
```

Fig. 8.3 | Initializing the elements of an array with an array initializer. (Part 1 of 2.)

Index	Value
0	32
1	27
2	64
3	18
4	95
5	14
6	90
7	70
8	60
9	37

Fig. 8.3 | Initializing the elements of an array with an array initializer. (Part 2 of 2.)

8.4.3 Calculating a Value to Store in Each Array Element

Some apps calculate the value to be stored in each array element. The app in Fig. 8.4 creates a 10-element array and assigns to each element one of the even integers from 2 to 20 (2, 4, 6, ..., 20). Then the app displays the array in tabular format. The for statement at lines 13–14 calculates an array element's value by multiplying the current value of the for loop's control variable counter by 2, then adding 2.

Line 9 uses the modifier **const** to declare the constant ARRAY_LENGTH, whose value is 10. Constants must be initialized when they're declared and cannot be modified thereafter. We declare constants with *all capital letters by convention* to make them stand out in the code.

```csharp
1   // Fig. 8.4: InitArray.cs
2   // Calculating values to be placed into the elements of an array.
3   using System;
4
5   public class InitArray
6   {
7      public static void Main( string[] args )
8      {
9         const int ARRAY_LENGTH = 10; // create a named constant
10        int[] array = new int[ ARRAY_LENGTH ]; // create array
11
12        // calculate value for each array element
13        for ( int counter = 0; counter < array.Length; ++counter )
14           array[ counter ] = 2 + 2 * counter;
15
16        Console.WriteLine( "{0}{1,8}", "Index", "Value" ); // headings
17
18        // output each array element's value
19        for ( int counter = 0; counter < array.Length; ++counter )
20           Console.WriteLine( "{0,5}{1,8}", counter, array[ counter ] );
21     } // end Main
22  } // end class InitArray
```

Fig. 8.4 | Calculating values to be placed into the elements of an array. (Part 1 of 2.)

```
Index    Value
  0        2
  1        4
  2        6
  3        8
  4       10
  5       12
  6       14
  7       16
  8       18
  9       20
```

Fig. 8.4 | Calculating values to be placed into the elements of an array. (Part 2 of 2.)

Common Programming Error 8.2

Assigning a value to a named constant after it's been initialized is a compilation error.

Common Programming Error 8.3

Attempting to declare a named constant without initializing it is a compilation error.

Good Programming Practice 8.1

Constants also are called named constants. Apps using constants often are more readable than those that use literal values (e.g., 10)—a named constant such as ARRAY_LENGTH *clearly indicates its purpose, whereas a literal value could have different meanings based on the context in which it's used. Another advantage to using named constants is that if the value of the constant must be changed, the change is necessary only in the declaration, thus reducing the cost of maintaining the code.*

Good Programming Practice 8.2

Defining the size of an array as a constant variable instead of a literal constant makes code clearer. This technique eliminates so-called magic numbers. For example, repeatedly mentioning the size 10 in array-processing code for a 10-element array gives the number 10 an artificial significance and can be confusing when the program includes other 10s that have nothing to do with the array size.

8.4.4 Summing the Elements of an Array

Often, the elements of an array represent a series of values to be used in a calculation. For example, if the elements of an array represent exam grades, an instructor may wish to total the elements and use that total to calculate the class average for the exam. The GradeBook examples later in the chapter (Fig. 8.15 and Fig. 8.20) use this technique.

```
1   // Fig. 8.5: SumArray.cs
2   // Computing the sum of the elements of an array.
3   using System;
4
```

Fig. 8.5 | Computing the sum of the elements of an array. (Part 1 of 2.)

```
 5   public class SumArray
 6   {
 7      public static void Main( string[] args )
 8      {
 9         int[] array = { 87, 68, 94, 100, 83, 78, 85, 91, 76, 87 };
10         int total = 0;
11
12         // add each element's value to total
13         for ( int counter = 0; counter < array.Length; ++counter )
14            total += array[ counter ];
15
16         Console.WriteLine( "Total of array elements: {0}", total );
17      } // end Main
18   } // end class SumArray
```

```
Total of array elements: 849
```

Fig. 8.5 | Computing the sum of the elements of an array. (Part 2 of 2.)

The app in Fig. 8.5 sums the values contained in a 10-element integer array. The app creates and initializes the array at line 9. The for statement performs the calculations. [*Note:* The values supplied as array initializers are often read into an app, rather than specified in an initializer list. For example, an app could input the values from a user or from a file on disk (as discussed in Chapter 17, Files and Streams). Reading the data into an app makes the app more *reusable*, because it can be used with *different* sets of data.]

8.4.5 Using Bar Charts to Display Array Data Graphically

Many apps present data to users in a graphical manner. For example, numeric values are often displayed as bars in a bar chart. In such a chart, longer bars represent proportionally larger numeric values. One simple way to display numeric data graphically is with a bar chart that shows each numeric value as a bar of asterisks (*).

An instructor might graph the number of grades in each of several categories to visualize the grade distribution for an exam. Suppose the grades on an exam were 87, 68, 94, 100, 83, 78, 85, 91, 76 and 87. There was one grade of 100, two grades in the 90s, four grades in the 80s, two grades in the 70s, one grade in the 60s and no grades below 60. Our next app (Fig. 8.6) stores this grade distribution data in an array of 11 elements, each corresponding to a category of grades. For example, array[0] indicates the number of grades in the range 0–9, array[7] the number of grades in the range 70–79 and array[10] the number of 100 grades. The two versions of class GradeBook later in the chapter (Figs. 8.15 and 8.20) contain code that calculates these grade frequencies based on a set of grades. For now, we manually create array by examining the set of grades and initializing the elements of array to the number of values in each range (line 9).

```
1   // Fig. 8.6: BarChart.cs
2   // Bar chart displaying app.
3   using System;
4
```

Fig. 8.6 | Bar chart displaying app. (Part 1 of 2.)

```
5   public class BarChart
6   {
7      public static void Main( string[] args )
8      {
9         int[] array = { 0, 0, 0, 0, 0, 0, 1, 2, 4, 2, 1 }; // distribution
10
11        Console.WriteLine( "Grade distribution:" );
12
13        // for each array element, output a bar of the chart
14        for ( int counter = 0; counter < array.Length; ++counter )
15        {
16           // output bar labels ( "00-09: ", ..., "90-99: ", "100: " )
17           if ( counter == 10 )
18              Console.Write( "  100: " );
19           else
20              Console.Write( "{0:D2}-{1:D2}: ",
21                 counter * 10, counter * 10 + 9 );
22
23           // display bar of asterisks
24           for ( int stars = 0; stars < array[ counter ]; ++stars )
25              Console.Write( "*" );
26
27           Console.WriteLine(); // start a new line of output
28        } // end outer for
29     } // end Main
30  } // end class BarChart
```

```
Grade distribution:
00-09:
10-19:
20-29:
30-39:
40-49:
50-59:
60-69: *
70-79: **
80-89: ****
90-99: **
  100: *
```

Fig. 8.6 | Bar chart displaying app. (Part 2 of 2.)

The app reads the numbers from the array and graphs the information as a bar chart. Each grade range is followed by a bar of asterisks indicating the number of grades in that range. To label each bar, lines 17–21 output a grade range (e.g., "70-79: ") based on the current value of counter. When counter is 10, line 18 outputs " 100: " to align the colon with the other bar labels. When counter is not 10, line 20 uses the format items {0:D2} and {1:D2} to output the label of the grade range. The format specifier D indicates that the value should be formatted as an integer, and the number after the D indicates how many digits this formatted integer must contain. The 2 indicates that values with fewer than two digits should begin with a **leading 0**.

The nested for statement (lines 24–25) outputs the bars. Note the loop-continuation condition at line 24 (stars < array[counter]). Each time the app reaches the inner for, the loop counts from 0 up to one less than array[counter], thus using a value in array to determine the number of asterisks to display. In this example, array[0]–array[5] contain 0s because no students received a grade below 60. Thus, the app displays no asterisks next to the first six grade ranges.

8.4.6 Using the Elements of an Array as Counters

Sometimes, apps use counter variables to summarize data, such as the results of a survey. In Fig. 7.6, we used separate counters in our die-rolling app to track the number of times each face of a six-sided die appeared as the app rolled the die 6,000,000 times. An array version of the app in Fig. 7.6 is shown in Fig. 8.7.

```
1   // Fig. 8.7: RollDie.cs
2   // Roll a six-sided die 6,000,000 times.
3   using System;
4
5   public class RollDie
6   {
7      public static void Main( string[] args )
8      {
9         Random randomNumbers = new Random(); // random-number generator
10        int[] frequency = new int[ 7 ]; // array of frequency counters
11
12        // roll die 6,000,000 times; use die value as frequency index
13        for ( int roll = 1; roll <= 6000000; ++roll )
14           ++frequency[ randomNumbers.Next( 1, 7 ) ];
15
16        Console.WriteLine( "{0}{1,10}", "Face", "Frequency" );
17
18        // output each array element's value
19        for ( int face = 1; face < frequency.Length; ++face )
20           Console.WriteLine( "{0,4}{1,10}", face, frequency[ face ] );
21     } // end Main
22  } // end class RollDie
```

```
Face Frequency
   1    999924
   2   1000939
   3   1001249
   4    998454
   5   1000233
   6    999201
```

Fig. 8.7 | Roll a six-sided die 6,000,000 times.

The app uses array frequency (line 10) to count the occurrences of each side of the die. *The single statement in line 14 of this app replaces lines 26–46 of Fig. 7.6.* Line 14 uses the random value to determine which frequency element to increment during each iteration of the loop. The calculation in line 14 produces random numbers from 1 to 6, so array frequency must be large enough to store six counters. We use a seven-element array in which we ignore frequency[0]—it's more logical to have the face value 1 increment frequency[1] than frequency[0]. Thus, each face value is used as an index for array frequency. We also replaced lines 50–52 of Fig. 7.6 by looping through array frequency to output the results (Fig. 8.7, lines 19–20).

8.4.7 Using Arrays to Analyze Survey Results; Introduction to Exception Handling

Our next example uses arrays to summarize data collected in a survey. Consider the following problem statement:

> *Twenty students were asked to rate on a scale of 1 to 5 the quality of the food in the student cafeteria, with 1 being "awful" and 5 being "excellent." Place the 20 responses in an integer array and determine the frequency of each rating.*

This is a typical array-processing app (Fig. 8.8). We wish to summarize the number of responses of each type (that is, 1–5). Array responses (lines 10–11) is a 20-element integer array containing the students' survey responses. The last value in the array is intentionally an incorrect response (14). When a C# program executes, array element indices are checked for *validity*—all indices must be greater than or equal to 0 and less than the length of the array. Any attempt to access an element *outside* that range of indices results in a runtime error that's known as an IndexOutOfRangeException. At the end of this section, we'll discuss the invalid response value, demonstrate array **bounds checking** and introduce C#'s exception-handling mechanism, which can be used to detect and handle an IndexOutOfRangeException.

```
1   // Fig. 8.8: StudentPoll.cs
2   // Poll analysis app.
3   using System;
4
5   public class StudentPoll
6   {
7      public static void Main( string[] args )
8      {
9         // student response array (more typically, input at run time)
10        int[] responses = { 1, 2, 5, 4, 3, 5, 2, 1, 3, 3, 1, 4, 3, 3, 3,
11           2, 3, 3, 2, 14 };
12        int[] frequency = new int[ 6 ]; // array of frequency counters
13
14        // for each answer, select responses element and use that value
15        // as frequency index to determine element to increment
16        for ( int answer = 0; answer < responses.Length; ++answer )
17        {
18           try
19           {
20              ++frequency[ responses[ answer ] ];
21           } // end try
22           catch ( IndexOutOfRangeException ex )
23           {
24              Console.WriteLine( ex.Message );
25              Console.WriteLine( "   responses({0}) = {1}\n",
26                 answer, responses[ answer ] );
27           } // end catch
28        } // end for
```

Fig. 8.8 | Poll analysis app. (Part 1 of 2.)

```
29
30              Console.WriteLine( "{0}{1,10}", "Rating", "Frequency" );
31
32              // output each array element's value
33              for ( int rating = 1; rating < frequency.Length; ++rating )
34                  Console.WriteLine( "{0,6}{1,10}", rating, frequency[ rating ] );
35          } // end Main
36      } // end class StudentPoll
```

```
Index was outside the bounds of the array.
    responses(19) = 14

Rating Frequency
    1       3
    2       4
    3       8
    4       2
    5       2
```

Fig. 8.8 | Poll analysis app. (Part 2 of 2.)

The *frequency* Array
We use the *six-element* array frequency (line 12) to count the number of occurrences of each response. Each element is used as a counter for one of the possible types of survey responses—frequency[1] counts the number of students who rated the food as 1, frequency[2] counts the number of students who rated the food as 2, and so on.

Summarizing the Results
The for statement (lines 16–28) reads the responses from the array responses one at a time and increments one of the counters frequency[1] to frequency[5]; we ignore frequency[0] because the survey responses are limited to the range 1–5. The key statement in the loop appears in line 20. This statement increments the appropriate frequency counter as determined by the value of responses[answer].

Let's step through the first few iterations of the for statement:

- When the counter answer is 0, responses[answer] is the value of responses[0] (that is, 1—see line 10). In this case, frequency[responses[answer]] is interpreted as frequency[1], and the counter frequency[1] is incremented by one. To evaluate the expression, we begin with the value in the *innermost* set of brackets (answer, currently 0). The value of answer is plugged into the expression, and the next set of brackets (responses[answer]) is evaluated. That value is used as the index for the frequency array to determine which counter to increment (in this case, frequency[1]).

- The next time through the loop answer is 1, responses[answer] is the value of responses[1] (that is, 2—see line 10), so frequency[responses[answer]] is interpreted as frequency[2], causing frequency[2] to be incremented.

- When answer is 2, responses[answer] is the value of responses[2] (that is, 5—see line 10), so frequency[responses[answer]] is interpreted as frequency[5], causing frequency[5] to be incremented, and so on.

Regardless of the number of responses processed in the survey, only a six-element array (in which we *ignore* element zero) is required to summarize the results, because all the correct response values are between 1 and 5, and the index values for a six-element array are 0–5. In the output in Fig. 8.8, the frequency column summarizes only 19 of the 20 values in the responses array—the last element of the array responses contains an *incorrect* response that was *not* counted.

Exception Handling: Processing the Incorrect Response

An **exception** indicates a problem that occurs while a program executes. The name "exception" suggests that the problem occurs infrequently—if the "rule" is that a statement normally executes correctly, then the problem represents the "exception to the rule." **Exception handling** enables you to create **fault-tolerant programs** that can resolve (or handle) exceptions. In many cases, this allows a program to continue executing as if no problems were encountered. For example, the **Student Poll** app still displays results (Fig. 8.8), even though one of the responses was out of range. More severe problems might prevent a program from continuing normal execution, instead requiring the program to notify the user of the problem, then terminate. When the runtime or a method detects a problem, such as an invalid array index or an invalid method argument, it **throws** an exception—that is, an exception occurs.

The *try* Statement

To handle an exception, place any code that might throw an exception in a **try statement** (lines 18–27). The **try block** (lines 18–21) contains the code that might *throw* an exception, and the **catch block** (lines 22–27) contains the code that *handles* the exception if one occurs. You can have many catch blocks to handle different types of exceptions that might be thrown in the corresponding try block. When line 20 correctly increments an element of the frequency array, lines 22–27 are ignored. The braces that delimit the bodies of the try and catch blocks are required.

Executing the *catch* Block

When the program encounters the value 14 in the responses array, it attempts to add 1 to frequency[14], which does *not* exist—the frequency array has only six elements. Because array bounds checking is performed at *execution time*, the Common Language Runtime generates an exception—specifically line 20 throws an **IndexOutOfRangeException** to notify the program of this problem. At this point the try block *terminates* and the catch block begins executing—if you declared any variables in the try block, they're now *out of scope* and are *not accessible* in the catch block.

The catch block declares a type (IndexOutOfRangeException) and an exception parameter (ex). The catch block can handle exceptions of the specified type. Inside the catch block, you can use the parameter's identifier to interact with a caught exception object.

Error-Prevention Tip 8.1

When writing code to access an array element, ensure that the array index remains greater than or equal to 0 and less than the length of the array. This helps prevent IndexOutOf-RangeExceptions in your program.

Message *Property of the Exception Parameter*

When lines 22–27 *catch* the exception, the program displays a message indicating the problem that occurred. Line 24 uses the exception object's **Message property** to get the error message that's stored in the exception object and display it. Once the message is displayed in this example, the exception is considered handled and the program continues with the next statement after the catch block's closing brace. In this example, the end of the for statement is reached (line 28), so the program continues with the increment of the control variable in line 16. We use exception handling again in Chapter 10 and Chapter 13 presents a deeper look at exception handling.

8.5 Case Study: Card Shuffling and Dealing Simulation

So far, this chapter's examples have used arrays of value-type elements. This section uses random-number generation and an *array of reference-type elements*—namely, *objects* representing playing cards—to develop a class that simulates card shuffling and dealing. This class can then be used to implement apps that play card games.

We first develop class Card (Fig. 8.9), which represents a playing card that has a face (e.g., "Ace", "Deuce", "Three", …, "Jack", "Queen", "King") and a suit (e.g., "Hearts", "Diamonds", "Clubs", "Spades"). Next, we develop class DeckOfCards (Fig. 8.10), which creates a deck of 52 playing cards in which each element is a Card object. Then we build an app (Fig. 8.11) that uses class DeckOfCards's card shuffling and dealing capabilities.

Class **Card**

Class Card (Fig. 8.9) contains two string instance variables—face and suit—that are used to store references to the *face value* and *suit name* for a specific Card. The constructor for the class (lines 9–13) receives two strings that it uses to initialize face and suit. Method ToString (lines 16–19) creates a string consisting of the face of the card, the string " of " and the suit of the card. Recall from Chapter 7 that the + operator can be used to concatenate (i.e., combine) several strings to form one larger string. Card's ToString method can be invoked *explicitly* to obtain a string representation of a Card object (e.g., "Ace of Spades"). The ToString method of an object is called *implicitly* in many cases when the object is used where a string is expected (e.g., when WriteLine outputs the object or when the object is *concatenated* to a string using the + operator). For this behavior to occur, ToString must be declared with the header exactly as shown in line 16 of Fig. 8.9. We'll explain the purpose of the override keyword in more detail when we discuss inheritance in Chapter 11.

```
1   // Fig. 8.9: Card.cs
2   // Card class represents a playing card.
3   public class Card
4   {
5       private string face; // face of card ("Ace", "Deuce", ...)
6       private string suit; // suit of card ("Hearts", "Diamonds", ...)
7
```

Fig. 8.9 | Card class represents a playing card. (Part 1 of 2.)

```
8        // two-parameter constructor initializes card's face and suit
9        public Card( string cardFace, string cardSuit )
10       {
11          face = cardFace; // initialize face of card
12          suit = cardSuit; // initialize suit of card
13       } // end two-parameter Card constructor
14
15       // return string representation of Card
16       public override string ToString()
17       {
18          return face + " of " + suit;
19       } // end method ToString
20    } // end class Card
```

Fig. 8.9 | Card class represents a playing card. (Part 2 of 2.)

Class *DeckOfCards*

Class DeckOfCards (Fig. 8.10) declares an instance-variable named deck that will refer to an array of Card objects (line 7). Like simple-type array variable declarations, the declaration of a variable for an array of objects (e.g., Card[] deck) includes the type of the elements in the array, followed by square brackets and the name of the array variable. Class DeckOfCards also declares int instance variable currentCard (line 8), representing the next Card to be dealt from the deck array, and named constant NUMBER_OF_CARDS (line 9), indicating the number of Cards in the deck (52).

```
1     // Fig. 8.10: DeckOfCards.cs
2     // DeckOfCards class represents a deck of playing cards.
3     using System;
4
5     public class DeckOfCards
6     {
7        private Card[] deck; // array of Card objects
8        private int currentCard; // index of next Card to be dealt (0-51)
9        private const int NUMBER_OF_CARDS = 52; // constant number of Cards
10       private Random randomNumbers; // random-number generator
11
12       // constructor fills deck of Cards
13       public DeckOfCards()
14       {
15          string[] faces = { "Ace", "Deuce", "Three", "Four", "Five", "Six",
16             "Seven", "Eight", "Nine", "Ten", "Jack", "Queen", "King" };
17          string[] suits = { "Hearts", "Diamonds", "Clubs", "Spades" };
18
19          deck = new Card[ NUMBER_OF_CARDS ]; // create array of Card objects
20          currentCard = 0; // set currentCard so deck[ 0 ] is dealt first
21          randomNumbers = new Random(); // create random-number generator
22
```

Fig. 8.10 | DeckOfCards class represents a deck of playing cards. (Part 1 of 2.)

```
23        // populate deck with Card objects
24        for ( int count = 0; count < deck.Length; ++count )
25           deck[ count ] =
26              new Card( faces[ count % 13 ], suits[ count / 13 ] );
27     } // end DeckOfCards constructor
28
29     // shuffle deck of Cards with one-pass algorithm
30     public void Shuffle()
31     {
32        // after shuffling, dealing should start at deck[ 0 ] again
33        currentCard = 0; // reinitialize currentCard
34
35        // for each Card, pick another random Card and swap them
36        for ( int first = 0; first < deck.Length; ++first )
37        {
38           // select a random number between 0 and 51
39           int second = randomNumbers.Next( NUMBER_OF_CARDS );
40
41           // swap current Card with randomly selected Card
42           Card temp = deck[ first ];
43           deck[ first ] = deck[ second ];
44           deck[ second ] = temp;
45        } // end for
46     } // end method Shuffle
47
48     // deal one Card
49     public Card DealCard()
50     {
51        // determine whether Cards remain to be dealt
52        if ( currentCard < deck.Length )
53           return deck[ currentCard++ ]; // return current Card in array
54        else
55           return null; // indicate that all Cards were dealt
56     } // end method DealCard
57  } // end class DeckOfCards
```

Fig. 8.10 | DeckOfCards class represents a deck of playing cards. (Part 2 of 2.)

Class *DeckOfCards: Constructor*

The class's constructor instantiates the deck array (line 19) to be of size NUMBER_OF_CARDS. When first created, the elements of the deck array are null by default, so the constructor uses a for statement (lines 24–26) to fill the deck array with Cards. The for statement initializes control variable count to 0 and loops while count is less than deck.Length, causing count to take on each integer value from 0 to 51 (the indices of the deck array). Each Card is instantiated and initialized with two strings—one from the faces array (which contains the strings "Ace" through "King") and one from the suits array (which contains the strings "Hearts", "Diamonds", "Clubs" and "Spades"). The calculation count % 13 always results in a value from 0 to 12 (the 13 indices of the faces array in lines 15–16), and the calculation count / 13 always results in a value from 0 to 3 (the four indices of the suits array in line 17). When the deck array is initialized, it contains the Cards with faces "Ace" through "King" in order for each suit.

Class *DeckOfCards: Shuffle Method*

Method Shuffle (lines 30–46) shuffles the Cards in the deck. The method loops through all 52 Cards (array indices 0 to 51). For each Card, a number between 0 and 51 is picked randomly to select another Card. Next, the current Card object and the randomly selected Card object are swapped in the array. This exchange is performed by the three assignments in lines 42–44. The extra variable temp temporarily stores one of the two Card objects being swapped. *The swap cannot be performed with only the two statements*

```
deck[ first ] = deck[ second ];
deck[ second ] = deck[ first ];
```

If deck[first] is the "Ace" of "Spades" and deck[second] is the "Queen" of "Hearts", then after the first assignment, both array elements contain the "Queen" of "Hearts", and the "Ace" of "Spades" is lost—hence, the extra variable temp is needed. After the for loop terminates, the Card objects are randomly ordered. Only 52 swaps are made in a single pass of the entire array, and the array of Card objects is shuffled.

Recommendation: *Use an Unbiased Shuffling Algorithm*

It's recommended that you use a so-called unbiased shuffling algorithm for real card games. Such an algorithm ensures that all possible shuffled card sequences are equally likely to occur. A popular unbiased shuffling algorithm is the Fisher-Yates algorithm— en.wikipedia.org/wiki/Fisher%E2%80%93Yates_shuffle. This page also shows how to implement the algorithm in several programming languages.

Class *DeckOfCards: DealCard Method*

Method DealCard (lines 49–56) deals one Card in the array. Recall that currentCard indicates the index of the next Card to be dealt (i.e., the Card at the top of the deck). Thus, line 52 compares currentCard to the length of the deck array. If the deck is not empty (i.e., currentCard is less than 52), line 53 returns the top Card and increments current-Card to prepare for the next call to DealCard—otherwise, null is returned.

Shuffling and Dealing Cards

The app of Fig. 8.11 demonstrates the card shuffling and dealing capabilities of class Deck-OfCards (Fig. 8.10). Line 10 creates a DeckOfCards object named myDeckOfCards. Recall that the DeckOfCards constructor creates the deck with the 52 Card objects in order by suit and face. Line 11 invokes myDeckOfCards's Shuffle method to rearrange the Card objects. The for statement in lines 14–20 deals all 52 Cards in the deck and displays them in four columns of 13 Cards each. Line 16 deals and displays a Card object by invoking myDeckOf-Cards's DealCard method. When Console.Write outputs a Card with string formatting, the Card's ToString method (declared in lines 16–19 of Fig. 8.9) is invoked implicitly. Because the field width is *negative*, the result is output *left* justified in a field of width 19.

```
1   // Fig. 8.11: DeckOfCardsTest.cs
2   // Card shuffling and dealing app.
3   using System;
4
```

Fig. 8.11 | Card shuffling and dealing app. (Part 1 of 2.)

```
 5  public class DeckOfCardsTest
 6  {
 7     // execute app
 8     public static void Main( string[] args )
 9     {
10        DeckOfCards myDeckOfCards = new DeckOfCards();
11        myDeckOfCards.Shuffle(); // place Cards in random order
12
13        // display all 52 Cards in the order in which they are dealt
14        for ( int i = 0; i < 52; ++i )
15        {
16           Console.Write( "{0,-19}", myDeckOfCards.DealCard() );
17
18           if ( ( i + 1 ) % 4 == 0 )
19              Console.WriteLine();
20        } // end for
21     } // end Main
22  } // end class DeckOfCardsTest
```

```
Eight of Clubs        Ten of Clubs          Ten of Spades         Four of Spades
Ace of Spades         Jack of Spades        Three of Spades       Seven of Spades
Three of Diamonds     Five of Clubs         Eight of Spades       Five of Hearts
Ace of Hearts         Ten of Hearts         Deuce of Hearts       Deuce of Clubs
Jack of Hearts        Nine of Spades        Four of Hearts        Seven of Clubs
Queen of Spades       Seven of Diamonds     Five of Diamonds      Ace of Clubs
Four of Clubs         Ten of Diamonds       Jack of Clubs         Six of Diamonds
Eight of Diamonds     King of Hearts        Three of Clubs        King of Spades
King of Diamonds      Six of Spades         Deuce of Spades       Five of Spades
Queen of Clubs        King of Clubs         Queen of Hearts       Seven of Hearts
Ace of Diamonds       Deuce of Diamonds     Four of Diamonds      Nine of Clubs
Queen of Diamonds     Jack of Diamonds      Six of Hearts         Nine of Diamonds
Nine of Hearts        Three of Hearts       Six of Clubs          Eight of Hearts
```

Fig. 8.11 | Card shuffling and dealing app. (Part 2 of 2.)

8.6 foreach Statement

In previous examples, we demonstrated how to use counter-controlled for statements to iterate through the elements in an array. In this section, we introduce the **foreach state-ment**, which iterates through the elements of an entire array or collection. This section discusses how to use the foreach statement to loop through an array. We show how to use it with collections in Chapter 19. The syntax of a foreach statement is:

> **foreach** (*type identifier* **in** *arrayName*)
>   *statement*

where *type* and *identifier* are the type and name (e.g., int number) of the **iteration variable**, and *arrayName* is the array through which to iterate. The type of the iteration variable must be consistent with the type of the elements in the array. As the next example illustrates, the iteration variable represents successive values in the array on successive iterations of the foreach statement.

Figure 8.12 uses the foreach statement (lines 13–14) to calculate the sum of the integers in an array of student grades. The type specified is int, because array contains int values—therefore, the loop will select one int value from the array during each iteration. The foreach statement iterates through successive values in the array one by one. The foreach header can be read concisely as "for each iteration, assign the next element of array to int variable number, then execute the following statement." Thus, for each iteration, identifier number represents the next int value in the array. Lines 13–14 are equivalent to the following counter-controlled repetition used in lines 13–14 of Fig. 8.5 to total the integers in array:

```
for ( int counter = 0; counter < array.Length; ++counter )
    total += array[ counter ];
```

Common Programming Error 8.4

The foreach statement's iteration variable can be used only to access array elements—it cannot be used to modify elements. Any attempt to change the value of the iteration variable in the body of a foreach statement will cause a compilation error.

```
1   // Fig. 8.12: ForEachTest.cs
2   // Using the foreach statement to total integers in an array.
3   using System;
4
5   public class ForEachTest
6   {
7      public static void Main( string[] args )
8      {
9         int[] array = { 87, 68, 94, 100, 83, 78, 85, 91, 76, 87 };
10        int total = 0;
11
12        // add each element's value to total
13        foreach ( int number in array )
14           total += number;
15
16        Console.WriteLine( "Total of array elements: {0}", total );
17     } // end Main
18  } // end class ForEachTest
```

```
Total of array elements: 849
```

Fig. 8.12 | Using the foreach statement to total integers in an array.

The foreach statement can be used in place of the for statement whenever code looping through an array does not require access to the counter indicating the index of the current array element. For example, totaling the integers in an array requires access only to the element values—the index of each element is irrelevant. However, if an app must use a counter for some reason other than simply to loop through an array (e.g., to display an index number next to each array element value, as in the examples earlier in this chapter), use the for statement.

8.7 Passing Arrays and Array Elements to Methods

To pass an array argument to a method, specify the name of the array *without any brackets*. For example, if hourlyTemperatures is declared as

```
double[] hourlyTemperatures = new double[ 24 ];
```

then the method call

```
ModifyArray( hourlyTemperatures );
```

passes the reference of array hourlyTemperatures to method ModifyArray. Every array object "knows" its own length (and makes it available via its Length property). Thus, when we pass an array object's reference to a method, we need not pass the array length as an additional argument.

Specifying an Array Parameter

For a method to receive an array reference through a method call, the method's parameter list must specify an array parameter. For example, the method header for method Modify-Array might be written as

```
void ModifyArray( double[] b )
```

indicating that ModifyArray receives the reference of an array of doubles in parameter b. The method call passes array hourlyTemperature's reference, so when the called method uses the array variable b, it refers to the same array object as hourlyTemperatures in the calling method.

Pass-By-Value vs. Pass-By-Reference

When an argument to a method is an entire array or an individual array element of a reference type, the called method receives a *copy of the reference*. However, when an argument to a method is an individual array element of a value type, the called method receives a *copy of the element's value*. To pass an individual array element to a method, use the indexed name of the array as an argument in the method call. If you want to pass a value-type array element to a method by reference, you must use the ref keyword as shown in Section 7.16.

Figure 8.13 demonstrates the difference between passing an entire array and passing a value-type array element to a method. The foreach statement at lines 17–18 outputs the five elements of array (an array of int values). Line 20 invokes method ModifyArray, passing array as an argument. Method ModifyArray (lines 37–41) receives a *copy* of array's *reference* and uses the reference to multiply each of array's elements by 2. To prove that array's elements (in Main) were modified, the foreach statement at lines 24–25 outputs the five elements of array again. As the output shows, method ModifyArray doubled the value of each element.

```
1   // Fig. 8.13: PassArray.cs
2   // Passing arrays and individual array elements to methods.
3   using System;
4
```

Fig. 8.13 | Passing arrays and individual array elements to methods. (Part 1 of 3.)

```
5   public class PassArray
6   {
7      // Main creates array and calls ModifyArray and ModifyElement
8      public static void Main( string[] args )
9      {
10         int[] array = { 1, 2, 3, 4, 5 };
11
12         Console.WriteLine(
13            "Effects of passing reference to entire array:\n" +
14            "The values of the original array are:" );
15
16         // output original array elements
17         foreach ( int value in array )
18            Console.Write( "   {0}", value );
19
20         ModifyArray( array ); // pass array reference
21         Console.WriteLine( "\n\nThe values of the modified array are:" );
22
23         // output modified array elements
24         foreach ( int value in array )
25            Console.Write( "   {0}", value );
26
27         Console.WriteLine(
28            "\n\nEffects of passing array element value:\n" +
29            "array[3] before ModifyElement: {0}", array[ 3 ] );
30
31         ModifyElement( array[ 3 ] ); // attempt to modify array[ 3 ]
32         Console.WriteLine(
33            "array[3] after ModifyElement: {0}", array[ 3 ] );
34      } // end Main
35
36      // multiply each element of an array by 2
37      public static void ModifyArray( int[] array2 )
38      {
39         for ( int counter = 0; counter < array2.Length; ++counter )
40            array2[ counter ] *= 2;
41      } // end method ModifyArray
42
43      // multiply argument by 2
44      public static void ModifyElement( int element )
45      {
46         element *= 2;
47         Console.WriteLine(
48            "Value of element in ModifyElement: {0}", element );
49      } // end method ModifyElement
50   } // end class PassArray
```

```
Effects of passing reference to entire array:
The values of the original array are:
   1   2   3   4   5

The values of the modified array are:
   2   4   6   8   10
```

Fig. 8.13 | Passing arrays and individual array elements to methods. (Part 2 of 3.)

```
Effects of passing array element value:
array[3] before ModifyElement: 8
Value of element in ModifyElement: 16
array[3] after ModifyElement: 8
```

Fig. 8.13 | Passing arrays and individual array elements to methods. (Part 3 of 3.)

Figure 8.13 next demonstrates that when a copy of an individual value-type array element is passed to a method, modifying the copy in the called method does *not* affect the original value of that element in the calling method's array. To show the value of array[3] before invoking method ModifyElement, lines 27–29 output the value of array[3], which is 8. Line 31 calls method ModifyElement and passes array[3] as an argument. Remember that array[3] is actually one int value (8) in array. Therefore, the app passes a copy of the value of array[3]. Method ModifyElement (lines 44–49) multiplies the value received as an argument by 2, stores the result in its parameter element, then outputs the value of element (16). Since method parameters, like local variables, cease to exist when the method in which they're declared completes execution, the method parameter element is destroyed when method ModifyElement terminates. Thus, when the app returns control to Main, lines 32–33 output the unmodified value of array[3] (i.e., 8).

8.8 Passing Arrays by Value and by Reference

In C#, a variable that "stores" an object, such as an array, does not actually store the object itself. Instead, such a variable stores a *reference* to the object. The distinction between reference-type variables and value-type variables raises some subtle issues that you must understand to create secure, stable programs.

As you know, when an app passes an argument to a method, the called method receives a *copy* of that argument's value. Changes to the *local copy* in the called method do *not* affect the original variable in the caller. If the argument is of a *reference* type, the method makes a *copy* of the *reference*, not a *copy* of the actual object that's referenced. The local copy of the reference also refers to the original object, which means that changes to the object in the called method affect the original object.

Performance Tip 8.1

Passing references to arrays and other objects makes sense for performance reasons. If arrays were passed by value, a copy of each element would be passed. For large, frequently passed arrays, this would waste time and consume considerable storage for the copies of the arrays.

In Section 7.16, you learned that C# allows variables to be passed by reference with keyword ref. You can also use keyword ref to pass a *reference-type variable* by reference, which allows the called method to modify the original variable in the caller and make that variable refer to a different object. This is a subtle capability, which, if misused, can lead to problems. For instance, when a reference-type object like an array is passed with ref, the called method actually gains control over the *reference itself*, allowing the called method to replace the original reference in the caller with a reference to a different object, or even with null. Such behavior can lead to *unpredictable effects*, which can be disastrous in mission-critical apps. The app in Fig. 8.14 demonstrates the subtle difference between passing a reference by value and passing a reference by reference with keyword ref.

```
1   // Fig. 8.14: ArrayReferenceTest.cs
2   // Testing the effects of passing array references
3   // by value and by reference.
4   using System;
5
6   public class ArrayReferenceTest
7   {
8      public static void Main( string[] args )
9      {
10        // create and initialize firstArray
11        int[] firstArray = { 1, 2, 3 };
12
13        // copy the reference in variable firstArray
14        int[] firstArrayCopy = firstArray;
15
16        Console.WriteLine(
17           "Test passing firstArray reference by value" );
18
19        Console.Write( "\nContents of firstArray " +
20           "before calling FirstDouble:\n\t" );
21
22        // display contents of firstArray
23        for ( int i = 0; i < firstArray.Length; ++i )
24           Console.Write( "{0} ", firstArray[ i ] );
25
26        // pass variable firstArray by value to FirstDouble
27        FirstDouble( firstArray );
28
29        Console.Write( "\n\nContents of firstArray after " +
30           "calling FirstDouble\n\t" );
31
32        // display contents of firstArray
33        for ( int i = 0; i < firstArray.Length; ++i )
34           Console.Write( "{0} ", firstArray[ i ] );
35
36        // test whether reference was changed by FirstDouble
37        if ( firstArray == firstArrayCopy )
38           Console.WriteLine(
39              "\n\nThe references refer to the same array" );
40        else
41           Console.WriteLine(
42              "\n\nThe references refer to different arrays" );
43
44        // create and initialize secondArray
45        int[] secondArray = { 1, 2, 3 };
46
47        // copy the reference in variable secondArray
48        int[] secondArrayCopy = secondArray;
49
50        Console.WriteLine( "\nTest passing secondArray " +
51           "reference by reference" );
```

Fig. 8.14 | Passing an array reference by value and by reference. (Part 1 of 3.)

```
52
53        Console.Write( "\nContents of secondArray " +
54           "before calling SecondDouble:\n\t" );
55
56        // display contents of secondArray before method call
57        for ( int i = 0; i < secondArray.Length; ++i )
58           Console.Write( "{0} ", secondArray[ i ] );
59
60        // pass variable secondArray by reference to SecondDouble
61        SecondDouble( ref secondArray );
62
63        Console.Write( "\n\nContents of secondArray " +
64           "after calling SecondDouble:\n\t" );
65
66        // display contents of secondArray after method call
67        for ( int i = 0; i < secondArray.Length; ++i )
68           Console.Write( "{0} ", secondArray[ i ] );
69
70        // test whether reference was changed by SecondDouble
71        if ( secondArray == secondArrayCopy )
72           Console.WriteLine(
73              "\n\nThe references refer to the same array" );
74        else
75           Console.WriteLine(
76              "\n\nThe references refer to different arrays" );
77     } // end Main
78
79     // modify elements of array and attempt to modify reference
80     public static void FirstDouble( int[] array )
81     {
82        // double each element's value
83        for ( int i = 0; i < array.Length; ++i )
84           array[ i ] *= 2;
85
86        // create new object and assign its reference to array
87        array = new int[] { 11, 12, 13 };
88     } // end method FirstDouble
89
90     // modify elements of array and change reference array
91     // to refer to a new array
92     public static void SecondDouble( ref int[] array )
93     {
94        // double each element's value
95        for ( int i = 0; i < array.Length; ++i )
96           array[ i ] *= 2;
97
98        // create new object and assign its reference to array
99        array = new int[] { 11, 12, 13 };
100    } // end method SecondDouble
101 } // end class ArrayReferenceTest
```

Fig. 8.14 | Passing an array reference by value and by reference. (Part 2 of 3.)

```
Test passing firstArray reference by value

Contents of firstArray before calling FirstDouble:
       1 2 3

Contents of firstArray after calling FirstDouble
       2 4 6

The references refer to the same array

Test passing secondArray reference by reference

Contents of secondArray before calling SecondDouble:
       1 2 3

Contents of secondArray after calling SecondDouble:
       11 12 13

The references refer to different arrays
```

Fig. 8.14 | Passing an array reference by value and by reference. (Part 3 of 3.)

Lines 11 and 14 declare two integer array variables, firstArray and firstArrayCopy. Line 11 initializes firstArray with the values 1, 2 and 3. The assignment statement at line 14 copies the reference stored in firstArray to variable firstArrayCopy, causing these variables to reference the same array object. We make the copy of the reference so that we can determine later whether reference firstArray gets overwritten. The for statement at lines 23–24 displays the contents of firstArray before it's passed to method FirstDouble (line 27) so that we can verify that the called method indeed changes the array's contents.

Method FirstDouble

The for statement in method FirstDouble (lines 83–84) multiplies the values of all the elements in the array by 2. Line 87 creates a new array containing the values 11, 12 and 13, and assigns the array's reference to parameter array in an attempt to overwrite reference firstArray in the caller—this, of course, does not happen, because the reference was passed by value. After method FirstDouble executes, the for statement at lines 33–34 displays the contents of firstArray, demonstrating that the values of the elements have been changed by the method. The if...else statement at lines 37–42 uses the == operator to compare references firstArray (which we just attempted to overwrite) and firstArray-Copy. The expression in line 37 evaluates to true if the operands of operator == reference the same object. In this case, the object represented by firstArray is the array created in line 11—not the array created in method FirstDouble (line 87)—so the original reference stored in firstArray was not modified.

Method SecondDouble

Lines 45–76 perform similar tests, using array variables secondArray and second-ArrayCopy, and method SecondDouble (lines 92–100). Method SecondDouble performs the same operations as FirstDouble, but receives its array argument using keyword ref. In this case, the reference stored in secondArray after the method call is a reference to the array created in line 99 of SecondDouble, demonstrating that a variable passed with keyword ref can be modified by the called method so that the variable in the caller actually points to a *different* object—in this case, an array created in SecondDouble. The if...else statement in lines 71–76 confirms that secondArray and secondArrayCopy no longer refer to the same array.

Software Engineering Observation 8.1

When a method receives a reference-type parameter by value, a copy of the object's reference is passed. This prevents a method from overwriting references passed to that method. In the vast majority of cases, protecting the caller's reference from modification is the desired behavior. If you encounter a situation where you truly want the called procedure to modify the caller's reference, pass the reference-type parameter using keyword ref—but, again, such situations are rare.

Software Engineering Observation 8.2

In C#, references to objects (including arrays) are passed to called methods. A called method receiving a reference to an object in a caller can interact with, and possibly change, the caller's object.

8.9 Case Study: GradeBook Using an Array to Store Grades

This section further evolves class GradeBook, introduced in Chapter 4 and expanded in Chapters 5–6. Recall that this class represents a grade book used by an instructor to store and analyze a set of student grades. Previous versions of the class process a set of grades entered by the user, but do not maintain the individual grade values in instance variables of the class. Thus, repeat calculations require the user to re-enter the same grades. One way to solve this problem would be to store each grade entered in an individual instance of the class. For example, we could create instance variables grade1, grade2, ..., grade10 in class GradeBook to store 10 student grades. However, the code to total the grades and determine the class average would be cumbersome, and the class would not be able to process any more than 10 grades at a time. In this section, we solve this problem by storing grades in an array.

*Storing Student Grades in an Array in Class **GradeBook***
The version of class GradeBook (Fig. 8.15) presented here uses an array of integers to store the grades of several students on a single exam. This eliminates the need to repeatedly input the same set of grades. Variable grades (which will refer to an array of ints) is declared as an instance variable in line 7—therefore, each GradeBook object maintains its own set of grades. The class's constructor (lines 14–18) has two parameters—the name of the course and an array of grades. When an app (e.g., class GradeBookTest in Fig. 8.16) creates a GradeBook object, the app passes an existing int array to the constructor, which assigns the array's reference to instance variable grades (line 17). The size of array grades is determined by the class that passes the array to the constructor. Thus, a GradeBook object can process a variable number of grades—as many as are in the array in the caller. The grade values in the passed array could have been input from a user at the keyboard or read from a file on disk (as discussed in Chapter 17). In our test app, we simply initialize an array with a set of grade values (Fig. 8.16, line 9). Once the grades are stored in instance

variable grades of class GradeBook, all the class's methods can access the eleme
grades as needed to perform various calculations.

```csharp
1   // Fig. 8.15: GradeBook.cs
2   // Grade book using an array to store test grades.
3   using System;
4
5   public class GradeBook
6   {
7      private int[] grades; // array of student grades
8
9      // auto-implemented property CourseName
10     public string CourseName { get; set; }
11
12     // two-parameter constructor initializes
13     // auto-implemented property CourseName and grades array
14     public GradeBook( string name, int[] gradesArray )
15     {
16        CourseName = name; // set CourseName to name
17        grades = gradesArray; // initialize grades array
18     } // end two-parameter GradeBook constructor
19
20     // display a welcome message to the GradeBook user
21     public void DisplayMessage()
22     {
23        // auto-implemented property CourseName gets the name of course
24        Console.WriteLine( "Welcome to the grade book for\n{0}!\n",
25           CourseName );
26     } // end method DisplayMessage
27
28     // perform various operations on the data
29     public void ProcessGrades()
30     {
31        // output grades array
32        OutputGrades();
33
34        // call method GetAverage to calculate the average grade
35        Console.WriteLine( "\nClass average is {0:F}", GetAverage() );
36
37        // call methods GetMinimum and GetMaximum
38        Console.WriteLine( "Lowest grade is {0}\nHighest grade is {1}\n",
39           GetMinimum(), GetMaximum() );
40
41        // call OutputBarChart to display grade distribution chart
42        OutputBarChart();
43     } // end method ProcessGrades
44
45     // find minimum grade
46     public int GetMinimum()
47     {
48        int lowGrade = grades[ 0 ]; // assume grades[ 0 ] is smallest
49
```

Fig. 8.15 | Grade book using an array to store test grades. (Part 1 of 3.)

```
50        // loop through grades array
51        foreach ( int grade in grades )
52        {
53            // if grade lower than lowGrade, assign it to lowGrade
54            if ( grade < lowGrade )
55                lowGrade = grade; // new lowest grade
56        } // end for
57
58        return lowGrade; // return lowest grade
59    } // end method GetMinimum
60
61    // find maximum grade
62    public int GetMaximum()
63    {
64        int highGrade = grades[ 0 ]; // assume grades[ 0 ] is largest
65
66        // loop through grades array
67        foreach ( int grade in grades )
68        {
69            // if grade greater than highGrade, assign it to highGrade
70            if ( grade > highGrade )
71                highGrade = grade; // new highest grade
72        } // end for
73
74        return highGrade; // return highest grade
75    } // end method GetMaximum
76
77    // determine average grade for test
78    public double GetAverage()
79    {
80        int total = 0; // initialize total
81
82        // sum grades for one student
83        foreach ( int grade in grades )
84            total += grade;
85
86        // return average of grades
87        return ( double ) total / grades.Length;
88    } // end method GetAverage
89
90    // output bar chart displaying grade distribution
91    public void OutputBarChart()
92    {
93        Console.WriteLine( "Grade distribution:" );
94
95        // stores frequency of grades in each range of 10 grades
96        int[] frequency = new int[ 11 ];
97
98        // for each grade, increment the appropriate frequency
99        foreach ( int grade in grades )
100           ++frequency[ grade / 10 ];
101
```

Fig. 8.15 | Grade book using an array to store test grades. (Part 2 of 3.)

```
102          // for each grade frequency, display bar in chart
103          for ( int count = 0; count < frequency.Length; ++count )
104          {
105             // output bar label ( "00-09: ", ..., "90-99: ", "100: " )
106             if ( count == 10 )
107                Console.Write( "  100: " );
108             else
109                Console.Write( "{0:D2}-{1:D2}: ",
110                   count * 10, count * 10 + 9 );
111
112             // display bar of asterisks
113             for ( int stars = 0; stars < frequency[ count ]; ++stars )
114                Console.Write( "*" );
115
116             Console.WriteLine(); // start a new line of output
117          } // end outer for
118       } // end method OutputBarChart
119
120       // output the contents of the grades array
121       public void OutputGrades()
122       {
123          Console.WriteLine( "The grades are:\n" );
124
125          // output each student's grade
126          for ( int student = 0; student < grades.Length; ++student )
127             Console.WriteLine( "Student {0,2}: {1,3}",
128                student + 1, grades[ student ] );
129       } // end method OutputGrades
130    } // end class GradeBook
```

Fig. 8.15 | Grade book using an array to store test grades. (Part 3 of 3.)

Method *ProcessGrades*

Method ProcessGrades (lines 29–43) contains a series of method calls that result in the output of a report summarizing the grades. Line 32 calls method OutputGrades to display the contents of array grades. Lines 126–128 in method OutputGrades use a for statement to output the student grades. A for statement, rather than a foreach, must be used in this case, because lines 127–128 use counter variable student's value to output each grade next to a particular student number (see Fig. 8.16). Although array indices start at 0, an instructor would typically number students starting at 1. Thus, lines 127–128 output student + 1 as the student number to produce grade labels "Student 1: ", "Student 2: " and so on.

Method *GetAverage*

Method ProcessGrades next calls method GetAverage (line 35) to obtain the average of the grades in the array. Method GetAverage (lines 78–88) uses a foreach statement to total the values in array grades before calculating the average. The iteration variable in the foreach's header (e.g., int grade) indicates that for each iteration, int variable grade takes on a value in array grades. The averaging calculation in line 87 uses grades.Length to determine the number of grades being averaged.

Methods GetMinimum and GetMaximum

Lines 38–39 in method ProcessGrades call methods GetMinimum and GetMaximum to determine the lowest and highest grades of any student on the exam, respectively. Each of these methods uses a foreach statement to loop through array grades. Lines 51–56 in method GetMinimum loop through the array, and lines 54–55 compare each grade to lowGrade. If a grade is less than lowGrade, lowGrade is set to that grade. When line 58 executes, lowGrade contains the lowest grade in the array. Method GetMaximum (lines 62–75) works the same way as method GetMinimum.

Method OutputBarChart

Finally, line 42 in method ProcessGrades calls method OutputBarChart to display a distribution chart of the grade data, using a technique similar to that in Fig. 8.6. In that example, we manually calculated the number of grades in each category (i.e., 0–9, 10–19, …, 90–99 and 100) by simply looking at a set of grades. In this example, lines 99–100 use a technique similar to that in Figs. 8.7 and 8.8 to calculate the frequency of grades in each category. Line 96 declares variable frequency and initializes it with an array of 11 ints to store the frequency of grades in each grade category. For each grade in array grades, lines 99–100 increment the appropriate element of the frequency array. To determine which element to increment, line 100 divides the current grade by 10, using integer division. For example, if grade is 85, line 100 increments frequency[8] to update the count of grades in the range 80–89. Lines 103–117 next display the bar chart (see Fig. 8.6) based on the values in array frequency. Like lines 24–25 of Fig. 8.6, lines 113–114 of Fig. 8.15 use a value in array frequency to determine the number of asterisks to display in each bar.

Class GradeBookTest That Demonstrates Class GradeBook

The app of Fig. 8.16 creates an object of class GradeBook (Fig. 8.15) using int array gradesArray (declared and initialized in line 9). Lines 11–12 pass a course name and gradesArray to the GradeBook constructor. Line 13 displays a welcome message, and line 14 invokes the GradeBook object's ProcessGrades method. The output reveals the summary of the 10 grades in myGradeBook.

```
1   // Fig. 8.16: GradeBookTest.cs
2   // Create a GradeBook object using an array of grades.
3   public class GradeBookTest
4   {
5      // Main method begins app execution
6      public static void Main( string[] args )
7      {
8         // one-dimensional array of student grades
9         int[] gradesArray = { 87, 68, 94, 100, 83, 78, 85, 91, 76, 87 };
10
11        GradeBook myGradeBook = new GradeBook(
12           "CS101 Introduction to C# Programming", gradesArray );
13        myGradeBook.DisplayMessage();
14        myGradeBook.ProcessGrades();
15     } // end Main
16  } // end class GradeBookTest
```

Fig. 8.16 | Create a GradeBook object using an array of grades. (Part 1 of 2.)

```
Welcome to the grade book for
CS101 Introduction to C# Programming!

The grades are:

Student  1:  87
Student  2:  68
Student  3:  94
Student  4: 100
Student  5:  83
Student  6:  78
Student  7:  85
Student  8:  91
Student  9:  76
Student 10:  87

Class average is 84.90
Lowest grade is 68
Highest grade is 100

Grade distribution:
00-09:
10-19:
20-29:
30-39:
40-49:
50-59:
60-69: *
70-79: **
80-89: ****
90-99: **
  100: *
```

Fig. 8.16 | Create a `GradeBook` object using an array of grades. (Part 2 of 2.)

Software Engineering Observation 8.3

A test harness (or test app) is responsible for creating an object of the class being tested and providing it with data. This data could come from any of several sources. Test data can be placed directly into an array with an array initializer, it can come from the user at the keyboard or it can come from a file (as you'll see in Chapter 17). After passing this data, typically through the class's constructor, to instantiate the object, the test harness should call the object to test its methods and manipulate its data. Gathering data in the test harness like this allows the class to manipulate data from several sources.

8.10 Multidimensional Arrays

Multidimensional arrays with two dimensions are often used to represent **tables of values** consisting of information arranged in **rows** and **columns**. To identify a particular table element, we must specify *two* indices. By convention, the first identifies the element's row and the second its column. Arrays that require two indices to identify a particular element are called **two-dimensional arrays**. (Multidimensional arrays can have more than two dimensions, but such arrays are beyond the scope of this book.) C# supports two types of two-dimensional arrays—**rectangular arrays** and **jagged arrays**.

Rectangular Arrays

Rectangular arrays are used to represent tables of information in the form of rows and columns, where each row has the same number of columns. Figure 8.17 illustrates a rectangular array named a containing three rows and four columns—a three-by-four array. In general, an array with *m* rows and *n* columns is called an **m-by-n array**.

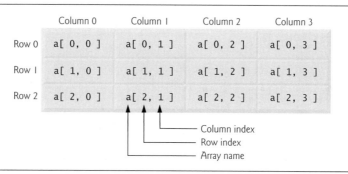

Fig. 8.17 | Rectangular array with three rows and four columns.

Array-Access Expression for a Two-Dimensional Rectangular Array

Every element in array a is identified in Fig. 8.17 by an array-access expression of the form a[*row*, *column*]; a is the name of the array, and *row* and *column* are the indices that uniquely identify each element in array a by row and column number. The names of the elements in row 0 all have a first index of 0, and the names of the elements in column 3 all have a second index of 3.

Array Initializer for a Two-Dimensional Rectangular Array

Like one-dimensional arrays, multidimensional arrays can be initialized with array initializers in declarations. A rectangular array b with two rows and two columns could be declared and initialized with **nested array initializers** as follows:

```
int[ , ] b = { { 1, 2 }, { 3, 4 } };
```

The initializer values are grouped by row in braces. So 1 and 2 initialize b[0, 0] and b[0, 1], respectively, and 3 and 4 initialize b[1, 0] and b[1, 1], respectively. The compiler counts the number of nested array initializers (represented by sets of two inner braces within the outer braces) in the initializer list to determine the number of rows in array b. The compiler counts the initializer values in the nested array initializer for a row to determine the number of columns (two) in that row. The compiler will generate an error if the number of initializers in each row is not the same, because every row of a rectangular array must have the *same* length.

Jagged Arrays

A jagged array is maintained as a one-dimensional array in which each element refers to a one-dimensional array. The manner in which jagged arrays are represented makes them quite flexible, because the lengths of the rows in the array need *not* be the same. For example, jagged arrays could be used to store a single student's exam grades across multiple classes, where the number of exams may vary from class to class.

Array Initializer for a Two-Dimensional Jagged Array

We can access the elements in a jagged array by an array-access expression of the form *arrayName*[*row*][*column*]—similar to the array-access expression for rectangular arrays, but with a separate set of square brackets for each dimension. A jagged array with three rows of different lengths could be declared and initialized as follows:

```
int[][] jagged = { new int[] { 1, 2 },
                   new int[] { 3 },
                   new int[] { 4, 5, 6 } };
```

In this statement, 1 and 2 initialize jagged[0][0] and jagged[0][1], respectively; 3 initializes jagged[1][0]; and 4, 5 and 6 initialize jagged[2][0], jagged[2][1] and jagged[2][2], respectively. Therefore, array jagged in the preceding declaration is actually composed of four separate one-dimensional arrays—one that represents the rows, one containing the values in the first row ({1, 2}), one containing the value in the second row ({3}) and one containing the values in the third row ({4, 5, 6}). Thus, array jagged itself is an array of three elements, each a reference to a one-dimensional array of int values.

Diagram of a Two-Dimensional Jagged Array in Memory

Observe the differences between the array-creation expressions for rectangular arrays and for jagged arrays. Two sets of square brackets follow the type of jagged, indicating that this is an array of int arrays. Furthermore, in the array initializer, C# requires the keyword new to create an array object for each row. Figure 8.18 illustrates the array reference jagged after it's been declared and initialized.

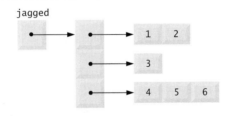

Fig. 8.18 | Jagged array with three rows of different lengths.

Creating Two-Dimensional Arrays with Array-Creation Expressions

A rectangular array can be created with an array-creation expression. For example, the following lines declare variable b and assign it a reference to a three-by-four rectangular array:

```
int[ , ] b;
b = new int[ 3, 4 ];
```

In this case, we use the literal values 3 and 4 to specify the number of rows and number of columns, respectively, but this is *not* required—apps can also use variables and expressions to specify array dimensions. As with one-dimensional arrays, the elements of a rectangular array are initialized when the array object is created.

A jagged array cannot be completely created with a single array-creation expression. The following statement is a syntax error:

```
int[][] c = new int[ 2 ][ 5 ]; // error
```

Instead, each one-dimensional array in the jagged array must be initialized separately. A jagged array can be created as follows:

```
int[][] c;
c = new int[ 2 ][ ]; // create 2 rows
c[ 0 ] = new int[ 5 ]; // create 5 columns for row 0
c[ 1 ] = new int[ 3 ]; // create 3 columns for row 1
```

The preceding statements create a jagged array with two rows. Row 0 has five columns, and row 1 has three columns.

Two-Dimensional Array Example: Displaying Element Values

Figure 8.19 demonstrates initializing rectangular and jagged arrays with array initializers and using nested for loops to **traverse** the arrays (i.e., visit every element of each array). Class InitArray's Main method creates two arrays. Line 12 uses nested array initializers to initialize variable rectangular with an array in which row 0 has the values 1, 2 and 3, and row 1 has the values 4, 5 and 6. Lines 17–19 uses nested initializers of different lengths to initialize variable jagged. In this case, the initializer uses the keyword new to create a one-dimensional array for each row. Row 0 is initialized to have two elements with values 1 and 2, respectively. Row 1 is initialized to have one element with value 3. Row 2 is initialized to have three elements with the values 4, 5 and 6, respectively.

```
 1   // Fig. 8.19: InitArray.cs
 2   // Initializing rectangular and jagged arrays.
 3   using System;
 4
 5   public class InitArray
 6   {
 7      // create and output rectangular and jagged arrays
 8      public static void Main( string[] args )
 9      {
10         // with rectangular arrays,
11         // every row must be the same length.
12         int[ , ] rectangular = { { 1, 2, 3 }, { 4, 5, 6 } };
13
14         // with jagged arrays,
15         // we need to use "new int[]" for every row,
16         // but every row does not need to be the same length.
17         int[][] jagged = { new int[] { 1, 2 },
18                            new int[] { 3 },
19                            new int[] { 4, 5, 6 } };
20
21         OutputArray( rectangular ); // displays array rectangular by row
22         Console.WriteLine(); // output a blank line
23         OutputArray( jagged ); // displays array jagged by row
24      } // end Main
25
26      // output rows and columns of a rectangular array
27      public static void OutputArray( int[ , ] array )
28      {
29         Console.WriteLine( "Values in the rectangular array by row are" );
```

Fig. 8.19 | Initializing jagged and rectangular arrays. (Part 1 of 2.)

```
30
31          // loop through array's rows
32          for ( int row = 0; row < array.GetLength( 0 ); ++row )
33          {
34              // loop through columns of current row
35              for ( int column = 0; column < array.GetLength( 1 ); ++column )
36                  Console.Write( "{0}  ", array[ row, column ] );
37
38              Console.WriteLine(); // start new line of output
39          } // end outer for
40      } // end method OutputArray
41
42      // output rows and columns of a jagged array
43      public static void OutputArray( int[][] array )
44      {
45          Console.WriteLine( "Values in the jagged array by row are" );
46
47          // loop through each row
48          foreach ( int[] row in array )
49          {
50              // loop through each element in current row
51              foreach ( int element in row )
52                  Console.Write( "{0}  ", element );
53
54              Console.WriteLine(); // start new line of output
55          } // end outer foreach
56      } // end method OutputArray
57  } // end class InitArray
```

```
Values in the rectangular array by row are
1  2  3
4  5  6

Values in the jagged array by row are
1  2
3
4  5  6
```

Fig. 8.19 | Initializing jagged and rectangular arrays. (Part 2 of 2.)

Overloaded Method OutputArray

Method OutputArray has been overloaded with two versions. The first version (lines 27–40) specifies the array parameter as int[,] array to indicate that it takes a rectangular array. The second version (lines 43–56) takes a jagged array, because its array parameter is listed as int[][] array.

Method OutputArray for Rectangular Arrays

Line 21 invokes method OutputArray with argument rectangular, so the version of OutputArray at lines 27–40 is called. The nested for statement (lines 32–39) outputs the rows of a rectangular array. The loop-continuation condition of each for statement (lines 32 and 35) uses the rectangular array's GetLength method to obtain the length of each dimension. Dimensions are numbered starting from 0, so the method call GetLength(0) on array returns the size of the first dimension of the array (the number of rows), and the call GetLength(1) returns the size of the second dimension (the number of columns).

Method *OutputArray for Jagged Arrays*

Line 23 invokes method OutputArray with argument jagged, so the version of Output-Array at lines 43–56 is called. The nested foreach statement (lines 48–55) outputs the rows of a jagged array. The inner foreach statement (lines 51–52) iterates through each element in the current row of the array. This allows the loop to determine the exact number of columns in each row. Since the jagged array is created as an array of arrays, we can use nested foreach statements to output the elements in the console window. The outer loop iterates through the elements of array, which are references to one-dimensional arrays of int values that represent each row. The inner loop iterates through the elements of the current row. A foreach statement can also iterate through all the elements in a rectangular array. In this case, foreach iterates through all the rows and columns starting from row 0, as if the elements were in a one-dimensional array.

Common Multidimensional-Array Manipulations Performed with **for** Statements

Many common array manipulations use for statements. As an example, the following for statement sets all the elements in row 2 of rectangular array a in Fig. 8.17 to 0:

```
for ( int column = 0; column < a.GetLength( 1 ); ++column )
    a[ 2, column ] = 0;
```

We specified row 2; therefore, we know that the first index is always 2 (0 is the first row, and 1 is the second row). This for loop varies only the second index (i.e., the **column index**). The preceding for statement is equivalent to the assignment statements

```
a[ 2, 0 ] = 0;
a[ 2, 1 ] = 0;
a[ 2, 2 ] = 0;
a[ 2, 3 ] = 0;
```

The following nested for statement totals the values of all the elements in array a:

```
int total = 0;
for ( int row = 0; row < a.GetLength( 0 ); ++row )
{
    for ( int column = 0; column < a.GetLength( 1 ); ++column )
        total += a[ row, column ];
} // end outer for
```

These nested for statements total the array elements one row at a time. The outer for statement begins by setting the row index to 0 so that row 0's elements can be totaled by the inner for statement. The outer for then increments row to 1 so that row 1's elements can be totaled. Then the outer for increments row to 2 so that row 2's elements can be totaled. The variable total can be displayed when the outer for statement terminates. In the next example, we show how to process a rectangular array in a more concise manner using foreach statements.

8.11 Case Study: GradeBook Using a Rectangular Array

In Section 8.9, we presented class GradeBook (Fig. 8.15), which used a one-dimensional array to store student grades on a single exam. In most courses, students take several exams.

Instructors are likely to want to analyze grades across the entire course, both for a single student and for the class as a whole.

Storing Student Grades in a Rectangular Array in Class **GradeBook**

Figure 8.20 contains a version of class GradeBook that uses a rectangular array grades to store the grades of a number of students on multiple exams. Each row of the array represents a single student's grades for the entire course, and each column represents the grades for the whole class on one of the exams the students took during the course. An app such as Grade-BookTest (Fig. 8.21) passes the array as an argument to the GradeBook constructor. In this example, we use a 10-by-3 array containing 10 students' grades on three exams. Five methods perform array manipulations to process the grades. Each method is similar to its counterpart in the earlier one-dimensional-array version of class GradeBook (Fig. 8.15). Method GetMinimum (lines 44–58 in Fig. 8.20) determines the lowest grade of any student for the semester. Method GetMaximum (lines 61–75) determines the highest grade of any student for the semester. Method GetAverage (lines 78–90) determines a particular student's semester average. Method OutputBarChart (lines 93–122) outputs a bar chart of the distribution of all student grades for the semester. Method OutputGrades (lines 125–149) outputs the two-dimensional array in tabular format, along with each student's semester average.

```csharp
1   // Fig. 8.20: GradeBook.cs
2   // Grade book using a rectangular array to store grades.
3   using System;
4
5   public class GradeBook
6   {
7      private int[ , ] grades; // rectangular array of student grades
8
9      // auto-implemented property CourseName
10     public string CourseName { get; set; }
11
12     // two-parameter constructor initializes
13     // auto-implemented property CourseName and grades array
14     public GradeBook( string name, int[ , ] gradesArray )
15     {
16        CourseName = name; // set CourseName to name
17        grades = gradesArray; // initialize grades array
18     } // end two-parameter GradeBook constructor
19
20     // display a welcome message to the GradeBook user
21     public void DisplayMessage()
22     {
23        // auto-implemented property CourseName gets the name of course
24        Console.WriteLine( "Welcome to the grade book for\n{0}!\n",
25           CourseName );
26     } // end method DisplayMessage
27
28     // perform various operations on the data
29     public void ProcessGrades()
30     {
```

Fig. 8.20 | Grade book using a rectangular array to store grades. (Part 1 of 4.)

```
31          // output grades array
32          OutputGrades();
33
34          // call methods GetMinimum and GetMaximum
35          Console.WriteLine( "\n{0} {1}\n{2} {3}\n",
36             "Lowest grade in the grade book is", GetMinimum(),
37             "Highest grade in the grade book is", GetMaximum() );
38
39          // output grade distribution chart of all grades on all tests
40          OutputBarChart();
41       } // end method ProcessGrades
42
43       // find minimum grade
44       public int GetMinimum()
45       {
46          // assume first element of grades array is smallest
47          int lowGrade = grades[ 0, 0 ];
48
49          // loop through elements of rectangular grades array
50          foreach ( int grade in grades )
51          {
52             // if grade less than lowGrade, assign it to lowGrade
53             if ( grade < lowGrade )
54                lowGrade = grade;
55          } // end foreach
56
57          return lowGrade; // return lowest grade
58       } // end method GetMinimum
59
60       // find maximum grade
61       public int GetMaximum()
62       {
63          // assume first element of grades array is largest
64          int highGrade = grades[ 0, 0 ];
65
66          // loop through elements of rectangular grades array
67          foreach ( int grade in grades )
68          {
69             // if grade greater than highGrade, assign it to highGrade
70             if ( grade > highGrade )
71                highGrade = grade;
72          } // end foreach
73
74          return highGrade; // return highest grade
75       } // end method GetMaximum
76
77       // determine average grade for particular student
78       public double GetAverage( int student )
79       {
80          // get the number of grades per student
81          int amount = grades.GetLength( 1 );
82          int total = 0; // initialize total
83
```

Fig. 8.20 | Grade book using a rectangular array to store grades. (Part 2 of 4.)

```
84          // sum grades for one student
85          for ( int exam = 0; exam < amount; ++exam )
86             total += grades[ student, exam ];
87
88          // return average of grades
89          return ( double ) total / amount;
90       } // end method GetAverage
91
92       // output bar chart displaying overall grade distribution
93       public void OutputBarChart()
94       {
95          Console.WriteLine( "Overall grade distribution:" );
96
97          // stores frequency of grades in each range of 10 grades
98          int[] frequency = new int[ 11 ];
99
100         // for each grade in GradeBook, increment the appropriate frequency
101         foreach ( int grade in grades )
102         {
103            ++frequency[ grade / 10 ];
104         } // end foreach
105
106         // for each grade frequency, display bar in chart
107         for ( int count = 0; count < frequency.Length; ++count )
108         {
109            // output bar label ( "00-09: ", ..., "90-99: ", "100: " )
110            if ( count == 10 )
111               Console.Write( "  100: " );
112            else
113               Console.Write( "{0:D2}-{1:D2}: ",
114                  count * 10, count * 10 + 9 );
115
116            // display bar of asterisks
117            for ( int stars = 0; stars < frequency[ count ]; ++stars )
118               Console.Write( "*" );
119
120            Console.WriteLine(); // start a new line of output
121         } // end outer for
122      } // end method OutputBarChart
123
124      // output the contents of the grades array
125      public void OutputGrades()
126      {
127         Console.WriteLine( "The grades are:\n" );
128         Console.Write( "              " ); // align column heads
129
130         // create a column heading for each of the tests
131         for ( int test = 0; test < grades.GetLength( 1 ); ++test )
132            Console.Write( "Test {0}  ", test + 1 );
133
134         Console.WriteLine( "Average" ); // student average column heading
135
```

Fig. 8.20 | Grade book using a rectangular array to store grades. (Part 3 of 4.)

```
136            // create rows/columns of text representing array grades
137            for ( int student = 0; student < grades.GetLength( 0 ); ++student )
138            {
139               Console.Write( "Student {0,2}", student + 1 );
140
141               // output student's grades
142               for ( int grade = 0; grade < grades.GetLength( 1 ); ++grade )
143                  Console.Write( "{0,8}", grades[ student, grade ] );
144
145               // call method GetAverage to calculate student's average grade;
146               // pass row number as the argument to GetAverage
147               Console.WriteLine( "{0,9:F}", GetAverage( student ) );
148            } // end outer for
149         } // end method OutputGrades
150      } // end class GradeBook
```

Fig. 8.20 | Grade book using a rectangular array to store grades. (Part 4 of 4.)

Processing a Two-Dimensional Array with a foreach Statement

Methods GetMinimum, GetMaximum and OutputBarChart each loop through array grades using the foreach statement—for example, the foreach statement from method GetMinimum (lines 50–55). To find the lowest overall grade, this foreach statement iterates through rectangular array grades and compares each element to variable lowGrade. If a grade is less than lowGrade, lowGrade is set to that grade.

When the foreach statement traverses the elements of array grades, it looks at each element of the first row in order by index, then each element of the second row in order by index and so on. The foreach statement in lines 50–55 traverses the elements of grade in the same order as the following equivalent code, expressed with nested for statements:

```
for ( int row = 0; row < grades.GetLength( 0 ); ++row )
   for ( int column = 0; column < grades.GetLength( 1 ); ++column )
   {
      if ( grades[ row, column ] < lowGrade )
         lowGrade = grades[ row, column ];
   }
```

When the foreach statement completes, lowGrade contains the lowest grade in the rectangular array. Method GetMaximum works similarly to method GetMinimum.

Method OutputBarChart

Method OutputBarChart (lines 93–122) displays the grade distribution as a bar chart. The syntax of the foreach statement (lines 101–104) is identical for one-dimensional and two-dimensional arrays.

Method OutputGrades

Method OutputGrades (lines 125–149) uses nested for statements to output values of the array grades, in addition to each student's semester average. The output in Fig. 8.21 shows the result, which resembles the tabular format of an instructor's physical grade book. Lines 131–132 (in Fig. 8.20) display the column headings for each test. We use the for statement rather than the foreach statement here so that we can identify each test with a number. Similarly, the for statement in lines 137–148 first outputs a row label using a counter variable to identify each student (line 139). Although array indices start at 0, lines 132 and 139 output test + 1 and student + 1, respectively, to produce test and student numbers starting at 1 (see Fig. 8.21). The inner for statement in lines 142–143 uses the outer for statement's counter variable student to loop through a specific row of array grades and output each student's test grade. Finally, line 147 obtains each student's semester average by passing the row index of grades (i.e., student) to method GetAverage.

Method *GetAverage*
Method GetAverage (lines 78–90) takes one argument—the row index for a particular student. When line 147 calls GetAverage, the argument is int value student, which specifies the particular row of rectangular array grades. Method GetAverage calculates the sum of the array elements on this row, divides the total by the number of test results and returns the floating-point result as a double value (line 89).

Class *GradeBookTest* That Demonstrates Class *GradeBook*
The app in Fig. 8.21 creates an object of class GradeBook (Fig. 8.20) using the two-dimensional array of ints that gradesArray references (Fig. 8.21, lines 9–18). Lines 20–21 pass a course name and gradesArray to the GradeBook constructor. Lines 22–23 then invoke myGradeBook's DisplayMessage and ProcessGrades methods to display a welcome message and obtain a report summarizing the students' grades for the semester, respectively.

```
1   // Fig. 8.21: GradeBookTest.cs
2   // Create a GradeBook object using a rectangular array of grades.
3   public class GradeBookTest
4   {
5      // Main method begins app execution
6      public static void Main( string[] args )
7      {
8         // rectangular array of student grades
9         int[ , ] gradesArray = { { 87, 96, 70 },
10                                 { 68, 87, 90 },
11                                 { 94, 100, 90 },
12                                 { 100, 81, 82 },
13                                 { 83, 65, 85 },
14                                 { 78, 87, 65 },
15                                 { 85, 75, 83 },
16                                 { 91, 94, 100 },
17                                 { 76, 72, 84 },
18                                 { 87, 93, 73 } };
19
20         GradeBook myGradeBook = new GradeBook(
21            "CS101 Introduction to C# Programming", gradesArray );
22         myGradeBook.DisplayMessage();
23         myGradeBook.ProcessGrades();
24      } // end Main
25   } // end class GradeBookTest
```

```
Welcome to the grade book for
CS101 Introduction to C# Programming!
```

Fig. 8.21 | Create a GradeBook object using a rectangular array of grades. (Part 1 of 2.)

```
The grades are:

            Test 1  Test 2  Test 3  Average
Student  1      87      96      70    84.33
Student  2      68      87      90    81.67
Student  3      94     100      90    94.67
Student  4     100      81      82    87.67
Student  5      83      65      85    77.67
Student  6      78      87      65    76.67
Student  7      85      75      83    81.00
Student  8      91      94     100    95.00
Student  9      76      72      84    77.33
Student 10      87      93      73    84.33

Lowest grade in the grade book is 65
Highest grade in the grade book is 100

Overall grade distribution:
00-09:
10-19:
20-29:
30-39:
40-49:
50-59:
60-69: ***
70-79: ******
80-89: ***********
90-99: *******
  100: ***
```

Fig. 8.21 | Create a GradeBook object using a rectangular array of grades. (Part 2 of 2.)

8.12 Variable-Length Argument Lists

Variable-length argument lists allow you to create methods that receive an arbitrary number of arguments. A one-dimensional array-type argument preceded by the keyword **params** in a method's parameter list indicates that the method receives a variable number of arguments with the type of the array's elements. This use of a params modifier can occur only in the last entry of the parameter list. While you can use method overloading and array passing to accomplish much of what is accomplished with variable-length argument lists, using the params modifier is more concise.

Figure 8.22 demonstrates method Average (lines 8–17), which receives a variable-length sequence of doubles (line 8). C# treats the variable-length argument list as a one-dimensional array whose elements are all of the same type. Hence, the method body can manipulate the parameter numbers as an array of doubles. Lines 13–14 use the foreach loop to walk through the array and calculate the total of the doubles in the array. Line 16 accesses numbers.Length to obtain the size of the numbers array for use in the averaging calculation. Lines 31, 33 and 35 in Main call method Average with two, three and four arguments, respectively. Method Average has a variable-length argument list, so it can average as many double arguments as the caller passes. The output reveals that each call to method Average returns the correct value.

Common Programming Error 8.5
The params modifier may be used only with the last parameter of the parameter list.

```csharp
1   // Fig. 8.22: ParamArrayTest.cs
2   // Using variable-length argument lists.
3   using System;
4
5   public class ParamArrayTest
6   {
7      // calculate average
8      public static double Average( params double[] numbers )
9      {
10        double total = 0.0; // initialize total
11
12        // calculate total using the foreach statement
13        foreach ( double d in numbers )
14           total += d;
15
16        return total / numbers.Length;
17     } // end method Average
18
19     public static void Main( string[] args )
20     {
21        double d1 = 10.0;
22        double d2 = 20.0;
23        double d3 = 30.0;
24        double d4 = 40.0;
25
26        Console.WriteLine(
27           "d1 = {0:F1}\nd2 = {1:F1}\nd3 = {2:F1}\nd4 = {3:F1}\n",
28           d1, d2, d3, d4 );
29
30        Console.WriteLine( "Average of d1 and d2 is {0:F1}",
31           Average( d1, d2 ) );
32        Console.WriteLine( "Average of d1, d2 and d3 is {0:F1}",
33           Average( d1, d2, d3 ) );
34        Console.WriteLine( "Average of d1, d2, d3 and d4 is {0:F1}",
35           Average( d1, d2, d3, d4 ) );
36     } // end Main
37  } // end class ParamArrayTest
```

```
d1 = 10.0
d2 = 20.0
d3 = 30.0
d4 = 40.0

Average of d1 and d2 is 15.0
Average of d1, d2 and d3 is 20.0
Average of d1, d2, d3 and d4 is 25.0
```

Fig. 8.22 | Using variable-length argument lists.

8.13 Using Command-Line Arguments

On many systems, it's possible to pass arguments from the command line (these are known as **command-line arguments**) to an app by including a parameter of type string[] (i.e., an array of strings) in the parameter list of Main, exactly as we've done in every app in the book. By convention, this parameter is named args (Fig. 8.23, line 7). When an app is executed from the **Command Prompt**, the execution environment passes the command-line arguments that appear after the app name to the app's Main method as strings in the one-dimensional array args. The number of arguments passed from the command line is obtained by accessing the array's Length property. For example, the command "MyApp a b" passes two command-line arguments to app MyApp. Command-line arguments are separated by whitespace, not commas. When the preceding command executes, the Main method entry point receives the two-element array args (i.e., args.Length is 2) in which args[0] contains the string "a" and args[1] contains the string "b". Common uses of command-line arguments include passing options and file names to apps.

```
 1   // Fig. 8.23: InitArray.cs
 2   // Using command-line arguments to initialize an array.
 3   using System;
 4
 5   public class InitArray
 6   {
 7      public static void Main( string[] args )
 8      {
 9         // check number of command-line arguments
10         if ( args.Length != 3 )
11            Console.WriteLine(
12               "Error: Please re-enter the entire command, including\n" +
13               "an array size, initial value and increment." );
14         else
15         {
16            // get array size from first command-line argument
17            int arrayLength = Convert.ToInt32( args[ 0 ] );
18            int[] array = new int[ arrayLength ]; // create array
19
20            // get initial value and increment from command-line argument
21            int initialValue = Convert.ToInt32( args[ 1 ] );
22            int increment = Convert.ToInt32( args[ 2 ] );
23
24            // calculate value for each array element
25            for ( int counter = 0; counter < array.Length; ++counter )
26               array[ counter ] = initialValue + increment * counter;
27
28            Console.WriteLine( "{0}{1,8}", "Index", "Value" );
29
30            // display array index and value
31            for ( int counter = 0; counter < array.Length; ++counter )
32               Console.WriteLine( "{0,5}{1,8}", counter, array[ counter ] );
33         } // end else
34      } // end Main
35   } // end class InitArray
```

Fig. 8.23 | Using command-line arguments to initialize an array. (Part 1 of 2.)

```
C:\Examples\ch08\fig08_23>InitArray.exe
Error: Please re-enter the entire command, including
an array size, initial value and increment.
```

```
C:\Examples\ch08\fig08_23>InitArray.exe 5 0 4
Index    Value
   0        0
   1        4
   2        8
   3       12
   4       16
```

```
C:\Examples\ch08\fig08_23>InitArray.exe 10 1 2
Index    Value
   0        1
   1        3
   2        5
   3        7
   4        9
   5       11
   6       13
   7       15
   8       17
   9       19
```

Fig. 8.23 | Using command-line arguments to initialize an array. (Part 2 of 2.)

Figure 8.23 uses three command-line arguments to initialize an array. When the app executes, if args.Length is not 3, the app displays an error message and terminates (lines 10–13). Otherwise, lines 16–32 initialize and display the array based on the values of the command-line arguments.

The command-line arguments become available to Main as strings in args. Line 17 gets args[0]—a string that specifies the array size—and converts it to an int value, which the app uses to create the array in line 18. The static method ToInt32 of class Convert converts its string argument to an int.

Lines 21–22 convert the args[1] and args[2] command-line arguments to int values and store them in initialValue and increment, respectively. Lines 25–26 calculate the value for each array element.

The first sample execution indicates that the app received an insufficient number of command-line arguments. The second sample execution uses command-line arguments 5, 0 and 4 to specify the size of the array (5), the value of the first element (0) and the increment of each value in the array (4), respectively. The corresponding output indicates that these values create an array containing the integers 0, 4, 8, 12 and 16. The output from the third sample execution illustrates that the command-line arguments 10, 1 and 2 produce an array whose 10 elements are the nonnegative odd integers from 1 to 19.

Specifying Command-Line Arguments in Visual Studio
We ran this example from a Command Prompt. You can also supply command-line arguments in the IDE. Right click the project's **Properties** node in the **Solution Explorer**, then

select **Open**. Select the **Debug** tab, then enter the arguments in the text box labeled **Command line arguments**.

8.14 Wrap-Up

This chapter began our discussion of data structures, exploring the use of arrays to store data in and retrieve data from lists and tables of values. The chapter examples demonstrated how to declare array variables, initialize arrays and refer to individual elements of arrays. The chapter introduced the `foreach` statement as an additional means (besides the `for` statement) for iterating through arrays. We showed how to pass arrays to methods and how to declare and manipulate multidimensional arrays. Finally, the chapter showed how to write methods that use variable-length argument lists and how to read arguments passed to an app from the command line.

We continue our coverage of data structures in Chapter 9, where we discuss the `List` collection, which is a dynamically resizable array-based collection. We introduce Language Integrated Query (LINQ), which enables you to write expressions that can retrieve information from a wide variety of data sources, such as arrays. You'll see how to search, sort and filter data using LINQ.

Introduction to LINQ and the **List** Collection

In this chapter you'll:

- Learn basic LINQ concepts.
- Query an array using LINQ.
- Learn basic .NET collections concepts.
- Create and use a generic **List** collection.
- Query a generic **List** collection using LINQ.

9.1 Introduction

Chapter 8 introduced arrays—simple data structures used to store items of a specific type. Although commonly used, arrays have limited capabilities. For instance, you must specify an array's size, and if at execution time, you wish to modify it, you must do so manually by creating a new array or by using class Array's Resize method, which incurs the overhead of creating a new array and copying the existing elements into the new array for you.

In this chapter, we introduce a set of *prepackaged* data structures—the .NET Framework's *collection* classes—that offer greater capabilities than traditional arrays. They're reusable, reliable, powerful and efficient and have been carefully designed and tested to ensure correctness and good performance. This chapter focuses on the List collection. A List is similar to an array but provides additional functionality, such as **dynamic resizing**—a List can increase its size when items are added to it and decrease its size when items are removed. We use the List collection to implement several examples similar to those used in the preceding chapter.

Large amounts of data that need to persist beyond an app's execution are typically stored in a *database*—an organized collection of data. (We discuss databases in detail in Chapter 20.) A *database management system (DBMS)* provides mechanisms for storing, organizing, retrieving and modifying data in the database. A language called SQL—pronounced "sequel"—is the international standard used to perform **queries** (i.e., to request information that satisfies given criteria) and to manipulate data. For years, programs accessing a relational database passed SQL queries to the database management system, then processed the results. This chapter introduces C#'s new **LINQ (Language Integrated Query)** capabilities. LINQ allows you to write **query expressions**, similar to SQL queries, that retrieve information from a *variety* of data sources, not just databases. We use **LINQ to Objects** in this chapter to query arrays and Lists, selecting elements that satisfy a set of conditions—this is known as **filtering**. Figure 9.1 shows where and how we use LINQ throughout the book.

Chapter	Used to
Chapter 9, Introduction to LINQ and the List Collection	Query arrays and Lists.
Chapter 16, Strings and Characters: A Deeper Look	Select GUI controls in a Windows Forms app

Fig. 9.1 | LINQ usage throughout the book. (Part 1 of 2.)

Chapter	Used to
Chapter 17, Files and Streams	Search a directory and manipulate text files.
Chapter 20, Databases and LINQ	Retrieve information from a database.
Chapter 21, Web App Development with ASP.NET	Retrieve information from a database to be used in a web-based app.
Chapter 22, XML and LINQ to XML	Query an XML document.
Chapter 28, Web Services	Query and update a database. Process XML returned by WCF services.

Fig. 9.1 | LINQ usage throughout the book. (Part 2 of 2.)

LINQ Providers

The syntax of LINQ is built into C#, but LINQ queries may be used in many different contexts because of libraries known as *providers*. A **LINQ provider** is a set of classes that implement LINQ operations and enable programs to interact with *data sources* to perform tasks such as *sorting*, *grouping* and *filtering* elements.

In this book, we discuss *LINQ to Entities* and *LINQ to XML*, which allow you to query databases and XML documents using LINQ. These providers, along with *LINQ to Objects*, mentioned above, are included with C# and the .NET Framework. There are many providers that are more specialized, allowing you to interact with a specific website or data format. Many LINQ providers are available. Be sure to check out the open source site `codeplex.com`. Simply search for "LINQ providers" on the site.

9.2 Querying an Array of `int` Values Using LINQ

Figure 9.2 demonstrates querying an array of integers using LINQ. Repetition statements that *filter* arrays focus on the process of getting the results—iterating through the elements and checking whether they satisfy the desired criteria. LINQ specifies the conditions that selected elements must satisfy. This is known as **declarative programming**—as opposed to **imperative programming** (which we've been doing so far) in which you specify the actual steps to perform a task. The query in lines 20–22 specifies that the results should consist of all the `int`s in the `values` array that are greater than 4. It *does not* specify *how* those results are obtained—the C# compiler generates all the necessary code, which is one of the great strengths of LINQ. To use *LINQ to Objects*, you must import the `System.Linq` namespace (line 4).

```
1   // Fig. 9.2: LINQWithSimpleTypeArray.cs
2   // LINQ to Objects using an int array.
3   using System;
4   using System.Linq;
5
```

Fig. 9.2 | LINQ to Objects using an `int` array. (Part 1 of 3.)

```
 6   class LINQWithSimpleTypeArray
 7   {
 8      public static void Main( string[] args )
 9      {
10         // create an integer array
11         int[] values = { 2, 9, 5, 0, 3, 7, 1, 4, 8, 5 };
12
13         // display original values
14         Console.Write( "Original array:" );
15         foreach ( var element in values )
16            Console.Write( " {0}", element );
17
18         // LINQ query that obtains values greater than 4 from the array
19         var filtered =
20            from value in values
21            where value > 4
22            select value;
23
24         // display filtered results
25         Console.Write( "\nArray values greater than 4:" );
26         foreach ( var element in filtered )
27            Console.Write( " {0}", element );
28
29         // use orderby clause to original values in ascending order
30         var sorted =
31            from value in values
32            orderby value
33            select value;
34
35         // display sorted results
36         Console.Write( "\nOriginal array, sorted:" );
37         foreach ( var element in sorted )
38            Console.Write( " {0}", element );
39
40         // sort the filtered results into descending order
41         var sortFilteredResults =
42            from value in filtered
43            orderby value descending
44            select value;
45
46         // display the sorted results
47         Console.Write(
48            "\nValues greater than 4, descending order (separately):" );
49         foreach ( var element in sortFilteredResults )
50            Console.Write( " {0}", element );
51
52         // filter original array and sort results in descending order
53         var sortAndFilter =
54            from value in values
55            where value > 4
56            orderby value descending
57            select value;
58
```

Fig. 9.2 | LINQ to Objects using an int array. (Part 2 of 3.)

```
59            // display the filtered and sorted results
60            Console.Write(
61               "\nValues greater than 4, descending order (one query):" );
62            foreach ( var element in sortAndFilter )
63               Console.Write( " {0}", element );
64
65            Console.WriteLine();
66         } // end Main
67      } // end class LINQWithSimpleTypeArray
```

```
Original array: 2 9 5 0 3 7 1 4 8 5
Array values greater than 4: 9 5 7 8 5
Original array, sorted: 0 1 2 3 4 5 5 7 8 9
Values greater than 4, descending order (separately): 9 8 7 5 5
Values greater than 4, descending order (one query): 9 8 7 5 5
```

Fig. 9.2 | LINQ to Objects using an `int` array. (Part 3 of 3.)

The *from* Clause and Implicitly Typed Local Variables

A LINQ query begins with a **from clause** (line 20), which specifies a **range variable** (`value`) and the data source to query (`values`). The range variable represents each item in the data source (one at a time), much like the control variable in a `foreach` statement. We do *not* specify the range variable's type. Since it's assigned one element at a time from the array `values`, which is an `int` array, the compiler determines that the range variable `value` should be of type `int`. This is a C# feature called **implicitly typed local variables**, which enables the compiler to *infer* a local variable's type based on the context in which it's used.

Introducing the range variable in the `from` clause at the beginning of the query allows the IDE to provide *IntelliSense* while you write the rest of the query. The IDE knows the range variable's type, so when you enter the range variable's name followed by a dot (.) in the code editor, the IDE can display the range variable's methods and properties.

The *var* Keyword and Implicitly Typed Local Variables

You can also declare a local variable and let the compiler *infer* the variable's type based on the variable's *initializer*. To do so, the **var keyword** is used in place of the variable's type when declaring the variable. Consider the declaration

```
var x = 7;
```

Here, the compiler *infers* that the variable x should be of type `int`, because the compiler assumes that whole-number values, like 7, are of type `int`. Similarly, in the declaration

```
var y = -123.45;
```

the compiler *infers* that y should be of type `double`, because the compiler assumes that floating-point number values, like -123.45, are of type `double`. Typically, implicitly typed local variables are used for more complex types, such as the collections of data returned by LINQ queries. We use this feature in lines 19, 30, 41 and 53 to let the compiler determine the type of each variable that stores the results of a LINQ query. We also use this feature to declare the control variable in the `foreach` statements at lines 15–16, 26–27, 37–38, 49–50 and 62–63. In each case, the compiler infers that the control variable is of type `int` because the array `values` and the LINQ query results all contain `int` values.

The *where* Clause

If the condition in the **where clause** (line 21) evaluates to true, the element is *selected*—i.e., it's included in the results. Here, the ints in the array are included only if they're greater than 4. An expression that takes an element of a collection and returns true or false by testing a condition on that element is known as a **predicate**.

The *select* Clause

For each item in the data source, the **select clause** (line 22) determines what value appears in the results. In this case, it's the int that the range variable currently represents. A LINQ query typically ends with a select clause.

Iterating Through the Results of the LINQ Query

Lines 26–27 use a foreach statement to display the query results. As you know, a foreach statement can iterate through the contents of an array, allowing you to process each element in the array. Actually, the foreach statement can iterate through the contents of arrays, collections and the results of LINQ queries. The foreach statement in lines 26–27 iterates over the query result filtered, displaying each of its items.

LINQ vs. Repetition Statements

It would be simple to display the integers greater than 4 using a repetition statement that tests each value before displaying it. However, this would intertwine the code that selects elements and the code that displays them. With LINQ, these are kept separate, making the code easier to understand and maintain.

The *orderby* Clause

The **orderby clause** (line 32) sorts the query results in *ascending* order. Lines 43 and 56 use the **descending** modifier in the orderby clause to sort the results in *descending* order. An **ascending** modifier also exists but isn't normally used, because it's the default. Any value that can be compared with other values of the same type may be used with the orderby clause. A value of a *simple type* (e.g., int) can always be compared to another value of the *same* type; we'll say more about comparing values of *reference types* in Chapter 12.

The queries in lines 42–44 and 54–57 generate the same results, but in different ways. The first query uses LINQ to sort the results of the query from lines 20–22. The second query uses both the where and orderby clauses. Because queries can operate on the results of other queries, it's possible to build a query one step at a time, and pass the results of queries between methods for further processing.

More on Implicitly Typed Local Variables

Implicitly typed local variables can also be used to initialize arrays *without* explicitly giving their type. For example, the following statement creates an array of int values:

```
var array = new[] { 32, 27, 64, 18, 95, 14, 90, 70, 60, 37 };
```

Note that there are no square brackets on the left side of the assignment operator, and that new[] is used to specify that the variable is an array.

An Aside: Interface *IEnumerable<T>*

As we mentioned, the foreach statement can iterate through the contents of *arrays, collections* and *LINQ query results*. Actually, foreach iterates over any so-called IEnumerable<T> object, which just happens to be what most LINQ queries return.

IEnumerable<T> is an **interface**. Interfaces define and standardize the ways in which people and systems can interact with one another. For example, the controls on a radio serve as an *interface* between radio users and the radio's internal components. The controls allow users to perform a limited set of *operations* (e.g., changing the station, adjusting the volume, and choosing between AM and FM), and different radios may implement the controls in different ways (e.g., using push buttons, dials or voice commands). The interface specifies *what* operations a radio permits users to perform but does not specify *how* the operations are implemented. Similarly, the interface between a driver and a car with a manual transmission includes the steering wheel, the gear shift, the clutch, the gas pedal and the brake pedal. This same interface is found in nearly all manual-transmission cars, enabling someone who knows how to drive one manual-transmission car to drive another.

Software objects also communicate via interfaces. A C# interface describes a set of members that can be called on an object—to tell the object, for example, to perform some task or return some piece of information. The IEnumerable<T> interface describes the functionality of any object that can be iterated over and thus offers members to access each element. A class that implements an interface must define each member in the interface with a signature identical to the one in the interface definition. Implementing an interface is like signing a contract with the compiler that states, "I will declare *all* the members specified by the interface." Chapter 12 covers use of interfaces in more detail, as well as how to define your own interfaces.

Arrays are IEnumerable<T> objects, so a foreach statement can iterate over an array's elements. Similarly, each LINQ query returns an IEnumerable<T> object. Therefore, you can use a foreach statement to iterate over the results of any LINQ query. The notation <T> indicates that the interface is a *generic* interface that can be used with any type of data (for example, ints, strings or Employees). You'll learn more about the <T> notation in Section 9.4. You'll learn more about interfaces in Section 12.7.

9.3 Querying an Array of Employee Objects Using LINQ

LINQ is not limited to querying arrays of simple types such as ints. It can be used with most data types, including strings and user-defined classes. It cannot be used when a query does not have a defined meaning—for example, you cannot use orderby on objects that are not *comparable*. Comparable types in .NET are those that implement the IComparable interface, which is discussed in Section 18.4. All built-in types, such as string, int and double implement IComparable. Figure 9.3 presents the Employee class. Figure 9.4 uses LINQ to query an array of Employee objects.

```
1   // Fig. 9.3: Employee.cs
2   // Employee class with FirstName, LastName and MonthlySalary properties.
3   public class Employee
4   {
5      private decimal monthlySalaryValue; // monthly salary of employee
6
7      // auto-implemented property FirstName
8      public string FirstName { get; set; }
9
```

Fig. 9.3 | Employee class. (Part 1 of 2.)

```
10       // auto-implemented property LastName
11       public string LastName { get; set; }
12
13       // constructor initializes first name, last name and monthly salary
14       public Employee( string first, string last, decimal salary )
15       {
16          FirstName = first;
17          LastName = last;
18          MonthlySalary = salary;
19       } // end constructor
20
21       // property that gets and sets the employee's monthly salary
22       public decimal MonthlySalary
23       {
24          get
25          {
26             return monthlySalaryValue;
27          } // end get
28          set
29          {
30             if ( value >= 0M ) // if salary is nonnegative
31             {
32                monthlySalaryValue = value;
33             } // end if
34          } // end set
35       } // end property MonthlySalary
36
37       // return a string containing the employee's information
38       public override string ToString()
39       {
40          return string.Format( "{0,-10} {1,-10} {2,10:C}",
41             FirstName, LastName, MonthlySalary );
42       } // end method ToString
43    } // end class Employee
```

Fig. 9.3 | Employee class. (Part 2 of 2.)

```
1    // Fig. 9.4: LINQWithArrayOfObjects.cs
2    // LINQ to Objects using an array of Employee objects.
3    using System;
4    using System.Linq;
5
6    public class LINQWithArrayOfObjects
7    {
8       public static void Main( string[] args )
9       {
10          // initialize array of employees
11          Employee[] employees = {
12             new Employee( "Jason", "Red", 5000M ),
13             new Employee( "Ashley", "Green", 7600M ),
14             new Employee( "Matthew", "Indigo", 3587.5M ),
```

Fig. 9.4 | LINQ to Objects using an array of Employee objects. (Part 1 of 3.)

```
15          new Employee( "James", "Indigo", 4700.77M ),
16          new Employee( "Luke", "Indigo", 6200M ),
17          new Employee( "Jason", "Blue", 3200M ),
18          new Employee( "Wendy", "Brown", 4236.4M ) }; // end init list
19
20      // display all employees
21      Console.WriteLine( "Original array:" );
22      foreach ( var element in employees )
23          Console.WriteLine( element );
24
25      // filter a range of salaries using && in a LINQ query
26      var between4K6K =
27          from e in employees
28          where e.MonthlySalary >= 4000M && e.MonthlySalary <= 6000M
29          select e;
30
31      // display employees making between 4000 and 6000 per month
32      Console.WriteLine( string.Format(
33          "\nEmployees earning in the range {0:C}-{1:C} per month:",
34          4000, 6000 ) );
35      foreach ( var element in between4K6K )
36          Console.WriteLine( element );
37
38      // order the employees by last name, then first name with LINQ
39      var nameSorted =
40          from e in employees
41          orderby e.LastName, e.FirstName
42          select e;
43
44      // header
45      Console.WriteLine( "\nFirst employee when sorted by name:" );
46
47      // attempt to display the first result of the above LINQ query
48      if ( nameSorted.Any() )
49          Console.WriteLine( nameSorted.First() );
50      else
51          Console.WriteLine( "not found" );
52
53      // use LINQ to select employee last names
54      var lastNames =
55          from e in employees
56          select e.LastName;
57
58      // use method Distinct to select unique last names
59      Console.WriteLine( "\nUnique employee last names:" );
60      foreach ( var element in lastNames.Distinct() )
61          Console.WriteLine( element );
62
63      // use LINQ to select first and last names
64      var names =
65          from e in employees
66          select new { e.FirstName, Last = e.LastName };
67
```

Fig. 9.4 | LINQ to Objects using an array of Employee objects. (Part 2 of 3.)

```
68              // display full names
69              Console.WriteLine( "\nNames only:" );
70              foreach ( var element in names )
71                  Console.WriteLine( element );
72
73              Console.WriteLine();
74          } // end Main
75      } // end class LINQWithArrayOfObjects
```

```
Original array:
Jason        Red          $5,000.00
Ashley       Green        $7,600.00
Matthew      Indigo       $3,587.50
James        Indigo       $4,700.77
Luke         Indigo       $6,200.00
Jason        Blue         $3,200.00
Wendy        Brown        $4,236.40

Employees earning in the range $4,000.00-$6,000.00 per month:
Jason        Red          $5,000.00
James        Indigo       $4,700.77
Wendy        Brown        $4,236.40

First employee when sorted by name:
Jason        Blue         $3,200.00

Unique employee last names:
Red
Green
Indigo
Blue
Brown

Names only:
{ FirstName = Jason, Last = Red }
{ FirstName = Ashley, Last = Green }
{ FirstName = Matthew, Last = Indigo }
{ FirstName = James, Last = Indigo }
{ FirstName = Luke, Last = Indigo }
{ FirstName = Jason, Last = Blue }
{ FirstName = Wendy, Last = Brown }
```

Fig. 9.4 | LINQ to Objects using an array of Employee objects. (Part 3 of 3.)

Accessing the Properties of a LINQ Query's Range Variable

Line 28 of Fig. 9.4 shows a where clause that accesses the properties of the *range variable*. In this example, the compiler infers that the range variable is of type Employee based on its knowledge that employees was defined as an array of Employee objects (lines 11–18). Any bool expression can be used in a where clause. Line 28 uses the conditional AND (&&) operator to combine conditions. Here, only employees that have a salary between $4,000 and $6,000 per month, inclusive, are included in the query result, which is displayed in lines 35–36.

Sorting a LINQ Query's Results By Multiple Properties

Line 41 uses an orderby clause to sort the results according to *multiple* properties—specified in a comma-separated list. In this query, the employees are sorted alphabetically by last name. Each group of Employees that have the same last name is then sorted within the group by first name.

Any, *First* and *Count Extension Methods*

Line 48 introduces the query result's **Any** method, which returns true if there's at least one element, and false if there are no elements. The query result's **First** method (line 49) returns the first element in the result. You should check that the query result is not empty (line 48) *before* calling First.

We've not specified the class that defines methods First and Any. Your intuition probably tells you they're methods declared in the IEnumerable<T> interface, but they aren't. They're actually *extension methods*—such methods can be used to enhance a class's capabilities without modifying the class's definition. The LINQ extension methods can be used as if they were methods of IEnumerable<T>.

LINQ defines many more extension methods, such as **Count**, which returns the number of elements in the results. Rather than using Any, we could have checked that Count was nonzero, but it's more efficient to determine whether there's at least one element than to count all the elements. The LINQ query syntax is actually transformed by the compiler into extension method calls, with the results of one method call used in the next. It's this design that allows queries to be run on the results of previous queries, as it simply involves passing the result of a method call to another method.

Selecting a Property of an Object

Line 56 uses the select clause to select the range variable's LastName property rather than the range variable itself. This causes the results of the query to consist of only the last names (as strings), instead of complete Employee objects. Lines 60–61 display the unique last names. The **Distinct extension method** (line 60) removes duplicate elements, causing all elements in the result to be unique.

Creating New Types in the *select* Clause of a LINQ Query

The last LINQ query in the example (lines 65–66) selects the properties FirstName and LastName. The syntax

```
new { e.FirstName, Last = e.LastName }
```

creates a new object of an **anonymous type** (a type with no name), which the compiler generates for you based on the properties listed in the curly braces ({}). In this case, the anonymous type consists of properties for the first and last names of the selected Employee. The LastName property is assigned to the property Last in the select clause. This shows how you can specify a new name for the selected property. If you don't specify a new name, the property's original name is used—this is the case for FirstName in this example. The preceding query is an example of a **projection**—it performs a transformation on the data. In this case, the transformation creates new objects containing only the FirstName and Last properties. Transformations can also manipulate the data. For example, you could give all employees a 10% raise by multiplying their MonthlySalary properties by 1.1.

When creating a new anonymous type, you can select any number of properties by specifying them in a comma-separated list within the curly braces ({}) that delineate the anonymous type definition. In this example, the compiler automatically creates a new class having properties FirstName and Last, and the values are copied from the Employee objects. These selected properties can then be accessed when iterating over the results. Implicitly typed local variables allow you to use *anonymous types* because you do not have to explicitly state the type when declaring such variables.

When the compiler creates an anonymous type, it automatically generates a ToString method that returns a string representation of the object. You can see this in the program's output—it consists of the property names and their values, enclosed in braces. Anonymous types are discussed in more detail in Chapter 20.

9.4 Introduction to Collections

The .NET Framework Class Library provides several classes, called *collections*, used to store groups of related objects. These classes provide efficient methods that organize, store and retrieve your data *without* requiring knowledge of how the data is being *stored*. This reduces app development time.

You've used arrays to store sequences of objects. Arrays do *not* automatically change their size at execution time to accommodate additional elements—you must do so manually by creating a new array or by using the Array class's Resize method.

The collection class **List<T>** (from namespace System.Collections.Generic) provides a convenient solution to this problem. The T is a placeholder—when declaring a new List, replace it with the type of elements that you want the List to hold. This is similar to specifying the type when declaring an array. For example,

```
List< int > list1;
```

declares list1 as a List collection that can store only int values, and

```
List< string > list2;
```

declares list2 as a List of strings. Classes with this kind of placeholder that can be used with any type are called **generic classes**. Generic classes and additional generic collection classes are discussed in Chapters 18 and 19, respectively. Figure 19.2 provides a table of collection classes. Figure 9.5 shows some common methods and properties of class List<T>.

Method or property	Description
Add	Adds an element to the end of the List.
Capacity	Property that gets or sets the number of elements a List can store without resizing.
Clear	Removes all the elements from the List.
Contains	Returns true if the List contains the specified element and false otherwise.
Count	Property that returns the number of elements stored in the List.
IndexOf	Returns the index of the first occurrence of the specified value in the List.
Insert	Inserts an element at the specified index.
Remove	Removes the first occurrence of the specified value.

Fig. 9.5 | Some methods and properties of class List<T>. (Part 1 of 2.)

Method or property	Description
RemoveAt	Removes the element at the specified index.
RemoveRange	Removes a specified number of elements starting at a specified index.
Sort	Sorts the List.
TrimExcess	Sets the Capacity of the List to the number of elements the List currently contains (Count).

Fig. 9.5 | Some methods and properties of class List<T>. (Part 2 of 2.)

Figure 9.6 demonstrates dynamically resizing a List object. The Add and Insert methods add elements to the List (lines 13–14). The **Add** method *appends* its argument to the end of the List. The **Insert** method inserts a new element at the specified position. The first argument is an index—as with arrays, collection indices start at zero. The second argument is the value that's to be inserted at the specified index. The indices of elements at the specified index and above *increase* by one. This is usually slower than adding an element to the end of the List.

```
 1   // Fig. 9.6: ListCollection.cs
 2   // Generic List<T> collection demonstration.
 3   using System;
 4   using System.Collections.Generic;
 5
 6   public class ListCollection
 7   {
 8      public static void Main( string[] args )
 9      {
10         // create a new List of strings
11         List< string > items = new List< string >();
12
13         items.Add( "red" ); // append an item to the List
14         items.Insert( 0, "yellow" ); // insert the value at index 0
15
16         // display the colors in the list
17         Console.Write(
18            "Display list contents with counter-controlled loop:" );
19         for ( int i = 0; i < items.Count; i++ )
20            Console.Write( " {0}", items[ i ] );
21
22         // display colors using foreach
23         Console.Write(
24            "\nDisplay list contents with foreach statement:" );
25         foreach ( var item in items )
26            Console.Write( " {0}", item );
27
28         items.Add( "green" ); // add "green" to the end of the List
29         items.Add( "yellow" ); // add "yellow" to the end of the List
30
```

Fig. 9.6 | Generic List<T> collection demonstration. (Part 1 of 2.)

```
31      // display the List
32      Console.Write( "\nList with two new elements:" );
33      foreach ( var item in items )
34         Console.Write( " {0}", item );
35
36      items.Remove( "yellow" ); // remove the first "yellow"
37
38      // display the List
39      Console.Write( "\nRemove first instance of yellow:" );
40      foreach ( var item in items )
41         Console.Write( " {0}", item );
42
43      items.RemoveAt( 1 ); // remove item at index 1
44
45      // display the List
46      Console.Write( "\nRemove second list element (green):" );
47      foreach ( var item in items )
48         Console.Write( " {0}", item );
49
50      // check if a value is in the List
51      Console.WriteLine( "\n\"red\" is {0}in the list",
52         items.Contains( "red" ) ? string.Empty : "not " );
53
54      // display number of elements in the List
55      Console.WriteLine( "Count: {0}", items.Count );
56
57      // display the capacity of the List
58      Console.WriteLine( "Capacity: {0}", items.Capacity );
59   } // end Main
60   } // end class ListCollection
```

```
Display list contents with counter-controlled loop: yellow red
Display list contents with foreach statement: yellow red
List with two new elements: yellow red green yellow
Remove first instance of yellow: red green yellow
Remove second list element (green): red yellow
"red" is in the list
Count: 2
Capacity: 4
```

Fig. 9.6 | Generic List<T> collection demonstration. (Part 2 of 2.)

Lines 19–20 display the items in the List. The **Count** property returns the number of elements currently in the List. Lists can be indexed like arrays by placing the index in square brackets after the List variable's name. The indexed List expression can be used to modify the element at the index. Lines 25–26 output the List by using a foreach statement. More elements are then added to the List, and it's displayed again (lines 28–34).

The **Remove** method is used to remove the *first* element with a specific value (line 36). If no such element is in the List, Remove does nothing. A similar method, **RemoveAt**, removes the element at the specified index (line 43). When an element is removed through either of these methods, the indices of all elements above that index *decrease* by one—the opposite of the Insert method.

Line 52 uses the **Contains** method to check if an item is in the List. The Contains method returns true if the element is found in the List, and false otherwise. The method compares its argument to each element of the List in order until the item is found, so using Contains on a large List is *inefficient*.

Lines 55 and 58 display the List's Count and Capacity. Recall that the Count property (line 55) indicates the number of items in the List. The **Capacity** property (line 58) indicates how many items the List can hold without having to grow. When the List grows, it must create a larger internal array and copy each element to the new array. This is a time-consuming operation. It would be inefficient for the List to grow each time an element is added. Instead, the List grows only when an element is added *and* the Count and Capacity properties are equal—there's no space for the new element.

9.5 Querying a Generic Collection Using LINQ

You can use LINQ to Objects to query Lists just as arrays. In Fig. 9.7, a List of strings is converted to uppercase and searched for those that begin with "R".

```
1   // Fig. 9.7: LINQWithListCollection.cs
2   // LINQ to Objects using a List< string >.
3   using System;
4   using System.Linq;
5   using System.Collections.Generic;
6
7   public class LINQWithListCollection
8   {
9      public static void Main( string[] args )
10     {
11        // populate a List of strings
12        List< string > items = new List< string >();
13        items.Add( "aQua" ); // add "aQua" to the end of the List
14        items.Add( "RusT" ); // add "RusT" to the end of the List
15        items.Add( "yElLow" ); // add "yElLow" to the end of the List
16        items.Add( "rEd" ); // add "rEd" to the end of the List
17
18        // convert all strings to uppercase; select those starting with "R"
19        var startsWithR =
20           from item in items
21           let uppercaseString = item.ToUpper()
22           where uppercaseString.StartsWith( "R" )
23           orderby uppercaseString
24           select uppercaseString;
25
26        // display query results
27        foreach ( var item in startsWithR )
28           Console.Write( "{0} ", item );
29
30        Console.WriteLine(); // output end of line
```

Fig. 9.7 | LINQ to Objects using a List<string>. (Part I of 2.)

```
31
32          items.Add( "rUbY" ); // add "rUbY" to the end of the List
33          items.Add( "SaFfRon" ); // add "SaFfRon" to the end of the List
34
35          // display updated query results
36          foreach ( var item in startsWithR )
37             Console.Write( "{0} ", item );
38
39          Console.WriteLine(); // output end of line
40       } // end Main
41    } // end class LINQWithListCollection
```

```
RED RUST
RED RUBY RUST
```

Fig. 9.7 | LINQ to Objects using a List<string>. (Part 2 of 2.)

Line 21 uses LINQ's **let clause** to create a new range variable. This is useful if you need to store a temporary result for use later in the LINQ query. Typically, let declares a new range variable to which you assign the result of an expression that operates on the query's original range variable. In this case, we use string method **ToUpper** to convert each item to uppercase, then store the result in the new range variable uppercaseString. We then use the new range variable uppercaseString in the where, orderby and select clauses. The where clause (line 22) uses string method **StartsWith** to determine whether uppercaseString starts with the character "R". Method StartsWith performs a case-sensitive comparison to determine whether a string starts with the string received as an argument. If uppercaseString starts with "R", method StartsWith returns true, and the element is included in the query results. More powerful string matching can be done using the *regular-expression* capabilities introduced in Chapter 16, Strings and Characters: A Deeper Look.

The query is created only once (lines 20–24), yet iterating over the results (lines 27–28 and 36–37) gives two different lists of colors. This demonstrates LINQ's **deferred execution**—the query executes *only* when you access the results—such as iterating over them or using the Count method—*not* when you define the query. This allows you to create a query once and execute it many times. Any changes to the data source are reflected in the results each time the query executes.

There may be times when you do not want this behavior, and want to retrieve a collection of the results immediately. LINQ provides extension methods ToArray and ToList for this purpose. These methods execute the query on which they're called and give you the results as an array or List<T>, respectively. These methods can also improve efficiency if you'll be iterating over the same results multiple times, as you execute the query only once.

Collection Initializers

C# has a feature called **collection initializers**, which provide a convenient syntax (similar to *array initializers*) for initializing a collection. For example, lines 12–16 of Fig. 9.7 could be replaced with the following statement:

```
List< string > items =
   new List< string > { "aQua", "RusT", "yElLow", "rEd" };
```

9.6 Wrap-Up

This chapter introduced LINQ (Language Integrated Query), a powerful feature for querying data. We showed how to filter an array or collection using LINQ's where clause, and how to sort the query results using the orderby clause. We used the select clause to select specific properties of an object, and the let clause to introduce a new range variable to make writing queries more convenient. The StartsWith method of class string was used to filter strings starting with a specified character or series of characters. We used several LINQ extension methods to perform operations not provided by the query syntax—the Distinct method to remove duplicates from the results, the Any method to determine if the results contain any items, and the First method to retrieve the first element in the results.

We introduced the List<T> generic collection, which provides all the functionality of arrays, along with other useful capabilities such as dynamic resizing. We used method Add to append new items to the end of the List, method Insert to insert new items into specified locations in the List, method Remove to remove the first occurrence of a specified item, method RemoveAt to remove an item at a specified index and method Contains to determine if an item was in the List. We used property Count to get the number of items in the List, and property Capacity to determine the size the List can hold without growing. We use more advanced features of LINQ in later chapters. In Chapter 10 we take a deeper look at classes and objects.

9.7 Deitel LINQ Resource Center

We've created a LINQ Resource Center (www.deitel.com/LINQ/) that contains many links to additional information, including blogs by Microsoft LINQ team members, books, sample chapters, FAQs, tutorials, videos, webcasts and more.

10

Classes and Objects: A Deeper Look

Objectives

In this chapter you'll:

- Understand encapsulation and data hiding.

- Use composition to allow a class to have references to objects of other classes as members.

- Throw an exception to indicate that an argument is out of range.

- Use keyword `this`.

- Use `static` variables and methods.

- Use `readonly` fields.

- Take advantage of C#'s memory-management features.

- Use the IDE's **Class View** and **Object Browser** windows.

- Use object initializers to create an object and initialize it in the same statement.

10.1 Introduction

In this chapter, we take a deeper look at building classes, controlling access to members of a class and creating constructors. We discuss *composition*—a capability that allows a class to have references to objects of other classes as members. We reexamine the use of properties. The chapter also discusses static class members and readonly instance variables in detail. We investigate issues such as software reusability, data abstraction and encapsulation. We also discuss several miscellaneous topics related to defining classes.

10.2 Time Class Case Study

Time1 *Class Declaration*

Our first example consists of classes Time1 (Fig. 10.1) and Time1Test (Fig. 10.2). Class Time1 represents the time of day. Class Time1Test's Main method creates an object of class Time1 and invokes its methods. The output of this app appears in Fig. 10.2. [Note: C# has the type DateTime for date and time manipulations. Our time examples are for *demonstration* purposes—you do not need to create your own types for dates and times.]

Class Time1 contains three private instance variables of type int (Fig. 10.1, lines 7–9)—hour, minute and second—that represent the time in universal-time format (24-hour clock format, in which hours are in the range 0–23). Class Time1 contains public methods SetTime (lines 13–25), ToUniversalString (lines 28–32) and ToString (lines 35–40). These are the **public services** or the **public interface** that this class provides to its clients.

```csharp
1   // Fig. 10.1: Time1.cs
2   // Time1 class declaration maintains the time in 24-hour format.
3   using System; // namespace containing ArgumentOutOfRangeException
4
5   public class Time1
6   {
7       private int hour; // 0 - 23
8       private int minute; // 0 - 59
9       private int second; // 0 - 59
```

Fig. 10.1 | Time1 class declaration maintains the time in 24-hour format. (Part 1 of 2.)

```
10
11      // set a new time value using universal time; throw an
12      // exception if the hour, minute or second is invalid
13      public void SetTime( int h, int m, int s )
14      {
15         // validate hour, minute and second
16         if ( ( h >= 0 && h < 24 ) && ( m >= 0 && m < 60 ) &&
17            ( s >= 0 && s < 60 ) )
18         {
19            hour = h;
20            minute = m;
21            second = s;
22         } // end if
23         else
24            throw new ArgumentOutOfRangeException();
25      } // end method SetTime
26
27      // convert to string in universal-time format (HH:MM:SS)
28      public string ToUniversalString()
29      {
30         return string.Format( "{0:D2}:{1:D2}:{2:D2}",
31            hour, minute, second );
32      } // end method ToUniversalString
33
34      // convert to string in standard-time format (H:MM:SS AM or PM)
35      public override string ToString()
36      {
37         return string.Format( "{0}:{1:D2}:{2:D2} {3}",
38            ( ( hour == 0 || hour == 12 ) ? 12 : hour % 12 ),
39            minute, second, ( hour < 12 ? "AM" : "PM" ) );
40      } // end method ToString
41   } // end class Time1
```

Fig. 10.1 | `Time1` class declaration maintains the time in 24-hour format. (Part 2 of 2.)

In this example, class `Time1` does not declare a constructor, so the class has a default constructor that's supplied by the compiler. Each instance variable implicitly receives the default value 0 for an `int`. When instance variables are declared in the class body, they can be initialized using the same initialization syntax as a local variable.

Method SetTime and Throwing Exceptions

Method `SetTime` (lines 13–25) is a `public` method that declares three `int` parameters and uses them to set the time. Lines 16–17 test each argument to determine whether the value is in the proper range, and, if so, lines 19–21 assign the values to the `hour`, `minute` and `second` instance variables. The hour value (line 13) must be greater than or equal to 0 and less than 24, because universal-time format represents hours as integers from 0 to 23 (e.g., 1 PM is hour 13 and 11 PM is hour 23; midnight is hour 0 and noon is hour 12). Similarly, both `minute` and `second` values must be greater than or equal to 0 and less than 60. For values outside these ranges, `SetTime` **throws an exception** of type **`ArgumentOutOfRangeException`** (lines 23–24), which notifies the client code that an invalid argument was passed to the method. As you learned in Chapter 8, you can use `try…catch` to catch exceptions and attempt to recover from them, which we'll do in Fig. 10.2. The **throw statement** (line

24) creates a new object of type `ArgumentOutOfRangeException`. The parentheses following the class name indicate a call to the `ArgumentOutOfRangeException` constructor. After the exception object is created, the `throw` statement immediately terminates method `Set-Time` and the exception is returned to the code that attempted to set the time.

Method *ToUniversalString*

Method `ToUniversalString` (lines 28–32) takes no arguments and returns a `string` in universal-time format, consisting of six digits—two for the hour, two for the minute and two for the second. For example, if the time were 1:30:07 PM, method `ToUniversal-String` would return `13:30:07`. The `return` statement (lines 30–31) uses `static` method **Format** of class `string` to return a `string` containing the formatted hour, minute and second values, each with two digits and, where needed, a leading 0 (specified with the D2 format specifier—which pads the integer with *leading 0s* if it has less than two digits). Method `Format` is similar to the `string` formatting in method `Console.Write`, except that `Format` returns a formatted `string` rather than displaying it in a console window. The formatted `string` is returned by method `ToUniversalString`.

Method *ToString*

Method `ToString` (lines 35–40) takes no arguments and returns a `string` in standard-time format, consisting of the hour, minute and second values separated by colons and followed by an AM or PM indicator (e.g., `1:27:06 PM`). Like method `ToUniversalString`, method `ToString` uses `static string` method `Format` to format the minute and second as two-digit values with leading 0s, if necessary. Line 38 uses a conditional operator (`?:`) to determine the value for hour in the string—if the hour is 0 or 12 (AM or PM), it appears as 12—otherwise, it appears as a value from 1 to 11. The conditional operator in line 39 determines whether AM or PM will be returned as part of the `string`.

Recall from Section 7.4 that all objects in C# have a `ToString` method that returns a `string` representation of the object. We chose to return a `string` containing the time in standard-time format. Method `ToString` is called *implicitly* when an object's value is output with a format item in a call to `Console.Write`. Remember that to enable objects to be converted to their `string` representations, we need to declare method `ToString` with keyword `override`—the reason for this will become clear when we discuss *inheritance* in Chapter 11.

Using Class *Time1*

As you learned in Chapter 4, each class you declare represents a new *type* in C#. Therefore, after declaring class `Time1`, we can use it as a type in declarations such as

```
Time1 sunset; // sunset can hold a reference to a Time1 object
```

The `Time1Test` app class (Fig. 10.2) uses class `Time1`. Line 10 creates a `Time1` object and assigns it to local variable `time`. Operator new invokes class `Time1`'s *default constructor*, since `Time1` does not declare any constructors. Lines 13–17 output the time, first in universal-time format (by invoking time's `ToUniversalString` method in line 14), then in standard-time format (by explicitly invoking time's `ToString` method in line 16) to confirm that the `Time1` object was initialized properly. Line 20 invokes method `SetTime` of the `time` object to change the time. Then lines 21–25 output the time again in both formats to confirm that the time was set correctly.

```
1    // Fig. 10.2: Time1Test.cs
2    // Time1 object used in an app.
3    using System;
4
5    public class Time1Test
6    {
7       public static void Main( string[] args )
8       {
9          // create and initialize a Time1 object
10         Time1 time = new Time1(); // invokes Time1 constructor
11
12         // output string representations of the time
13         Console.Write( "The initial universal time is: " );
14         Console.WriteLine( time.ToUniversalString() );
15         Console.Write( "The initial standard time is: " );
16         Console.WriteLine( time.ToString() );
17         Console.WriteLine(); // output a blank line
18
19         // change time and output updated time
20         time.SetTime( 13, 27, 6 );
21         Console.Write( "Universal time after SetTime is: " );
22         Console.WriteLine( time.ToUniversalString() );
23         Console.Write( "Standard time after SetTime is: " );
24         Console.WriteLine( time.ToString() );
25         Console.WriteLine(); // output a blank line
26
27         // attempt to set time with invalid values
28         try
29         {
30            time.SetTime( 99, 99, 99 );
31         } // end try
32         catch ( ArgumentOutOfRangeException ex )
33         {
34            Console.WriteLine( ex.Message + "\n" );
35         } // end catch
36
37         // display time after attempt to set invalid values
38         Console.WriteLine( "After attempting invalid settings:" );
39         Console.Write( "Universal time: " );
40         Console.WriteLine( time.ToUniversalString() );
41         Console.Write( "Standard time: " );
42         Console.WriteLine( time.ToString() );
43      } // end Main
44   } // end class Time1Test
```

```
The initial universal time is: 00:00:00
The initial standard time is: 12:00:00 AM

Universal time after SetTime is: 13:27:06
Standard time after SetTime is: 1:27:06 PM

Specified argument was out of the range of valid values.
```

Fig. 10.2 | Time1 object used in an app. (Part 1 of 2.)

```
After attempting invalid settings:
Universal time: 13:27:06
Standard time: 1:27:06 PM
```

Fig. 10.2 | Time1 object used in an app. (Part 2 of 2.)

Calling **Time** *Method* **SetTime** *with Invalid Values*

To illustrate that method SetTime validates its arguments, line 30 calls method SetTime with invalid arguments of 99 for the hour, minute and second. This statement is placed in a try block (lines 28–31) in case SetTime throws an ArgumentOutOfRangeException, which it will do since the arguments are all invalid. When this occurs, the exception is caught at lines 32–35 and the exception's Message property is displayed. Lines 38–42 output the time again in both formats to confirm that SetTime did not change the time when invalid arguments were supplied.

Notes on the **Time1** *Class Declaration*

Consider several issues of class design with respect to class Time1. The instance variables hour, minute and second are each declared private. The actual data representation used within the class is of no concern to the class's clients. For example, it would be perfectly reasonable for Time1 to represent the time internally as the number of seconds since midnight or the number of minutes and seconds since midnight. Clients could use the same public methods and properties to get the same results without being aware of this. (As an exercise, you can represent the time as the number of seconds since midnight and show that indeed no change is visible to the clients of the class.)

Software Engineering Observation 10.1

Classes simplify programming because the client can use only the public *members exposed by the class. Such members are usually client oriented rather than implementation oriented. Clients are neither aware of, nor involved in, a class's implementation. Clients generally care about* what *the class does but not* how *the class does it. Clients do, of course, care that the class operates correctly and efficiently.*

Software Engineering Observation 10.2

Interfaces change less frequently than implementations. When an implementation changes, implementation-dependent code must change accordingly. Hiding the implementation reduces the possibility that other app parts become dependent on class-implementation details.

10.3 Controlling Access to Members

The access modifiers public and private control access to a class's variables, methods and properties. (In Chapter 11, we'll introduce the additional access modifier protected.) As we stated in Section 10.2, the primary purpose of public methods is to present to the class's clients a view of the services the class provides (that is, the class's public interface). Clients of the class need not be concerned with how the class accomplishes its tasks. For this reason, a class's private variables, properties and methods (i.e., the class's implementation details) are not directly accessible to the class's clients.

Figure 10.3 demonstrates that private class members are not directly accessible outside the class. Lines 9–11 attempt to directly access private instance variables hour, minute and second of Time1 object time. When this app is compiled, the compiler generates error messages stating that these private members are not accessible. [*Note:* This app uses the Time1 class from Fig. 10.1.]

```
1   // Fig. 10.3: MemberAccessTest.cs
2   // Private members of class Time1 are not accessible outside the class.
3   public class MemberAccessTest
4   {
5      public static void Main( string[] args )
6      {
7         Time1 time = new Time1(); // create and initialize Time1 object
8
9         time.hour = 7; // error: hour has private access in Time1
10        time.minute = 15; // error: minute has private access in Time1
11        time.second = 30; // error: second has private access in Time1
12     } // end Main
13  } // end class MemberAccessTest
```

	Description	File ▲	Line ▲	Column ▲	Project ▲
❌ 1	'Time1.hour' is inaccessible due to its protection level	MemberAccessTest.cs	9	12	MemberAccessTest
❌ 2	'Time1.minute' is inaccessible due to its protection level	MemberAccessTest.cs	10	12	MemberAccessTest
❌ 3	'Time1.second' is inaccessible due to its protection level	MemberAccessTest.cs	11	12	MemberAccessTest

Fig. 10.3 | Private members of class Time1 are not accessible outside the class.

Notice that members of a class—for instance, properties, methods and instance variables—do not need to be *explicitly* declared private. If a class member is not declared with an access modifier, it has private access *by default*. For clarity, we always explicitly declare private members.

10.4 Referring to the Current Object's Members with the this Reference

Every object can access a *reference to itself* with keyword **this** (also called the **this reference**). When a non-static method is called for a particular object, the method's body *implicitly* uses keyword this to refer to the object's instance variables and other methods. As you'll see in Fig. 10.4, you can also use keyword this *explicitly* in a non-static method's body. Section 10.5 shows a more interesting use of keyword this. Section 10.9 explains why keyword this *cannot* be used in a static method.

We now demonstrate implicit and explicit use of the this reference to enable class ThisTest's Main method to display the private data of a class SimpleTime object (Fig. 10.4). For the sake of brevity, we declare two classes in one file—class ThisTest is declared in lines 5–12, and class SimpleTime is declared in lines 15–48.

```
 I   // Fig. 10.4: ThisTest.cs
 2   // this used implicitly and explicitly to refer to members of an object.
 3   using System;
 4
 5   public class ThisTest
 6   {
 7      public static void Main( string[] args )
 8      {
 9         SimpleTime time = new SimpleTime( 15, 30, 19 );
10         Console.WriteLine( time.BuildString() );
11      } // end Main
12   } // end class ThisTest
13
14   // class SimpleTime demonstrates the "this" reference
15   public class SimpleTime
16   {
17      private int hour; // 0-23
18      private int minute; // 0-59
19      private int second; // 0-59
20
21      // if the constructor uses parameter names identical to
22      // instance-variable names, the "this" reference is
23      // required to distinguish between names
24      public SimpleTime( int hour, int minute, int second )
25      {
26         this.hour = hour; // set "this" object's hour instance variable
27         this.minute = minute; // set "this" object's minute
28         this.second = second; // set "this" object's second
29      } // end SimpleTime constructor
30
31      // use explicit and implicit "this" to call ToUniversalString
32      public string BuildString()
33      {
34         return string.Format( "{0,24}: {1}\n{2,24}: {3}",
35            "this.ToUniversalString()", this.ToUniversalString(),
36            "ToUniversalString()", ToUniversalString() );
37      } // end method BuildString
38
39      // convert to string in universal-time format (HH:MM:SS)
40      public string ToUniversalString()
41      {
42         // "this" is not required here to access instance variables,
43         // because method does not have local variables with same
44         // names as instance variables
45         return string.Format( "{0:D2}:{1:D2}:{2:D2}",
46            this.hour, this.minute, this.second );
47      } // end method ToUniversalString
48   } // end class SimpleTime
```

```
this.ToUniversalString(): 15:30:19
    ToUniversalString(): 15:30:19
```

Fig. 10.4 | this used implicitly and explicitly to refer to members of an object.

Class SimpleTime declares three private instance variables—hour, minute and second (lines 17–19). The constructor (lines 24–29) receives three int arguments to initialize a SimpleTime object. For the constructor we used parameter names that are identical to the class's instance-variable names (lines 17–19). We don't recommend this practice, but we intentionally did it here to hide the corresponding instance variables so that we could illustrate explicit use of the this reference. Recall from Section 7.11 that if a method contains a local variable with the *same* name as a field, within that method the name refers to the local variable rather than the field. In this case, the parameter *hides* the field in the method's scope. However, the method can use the this reference to refer to the hidden instance variable explicitly, as shown in lines 26–28 for SimpleTime's hidden instance variables.

Method BuildString (lines 32–37) returns a string created by a statement that uses the this reference explicitly and implicitly. Line 35 uses the this reference *explicitly* to call method ToUniversalString. Line 36 uses the this reference *implicitly* to call the same method. Programmers typically do not use the this reference explicitly to reference other methods in the current object. Also, line 46 in method ToUniversalString explicitly uses the this reference to access each instance variable. This is not necessary here, because the method does *not* have any local variables that hide the instance variables of the class.

Common Programming Error 10.1

It's often a logic error when a method contains a parameter or local variable that has the same name as an instance variable of the class. In such a case, use reference this if you wish to access the instance variable of the class—otherwise, the method parameter or local variable will be referenced.

Error-Prevention Tip 10.1

Avoid method-parameter names or local-variable names that conflict with field names. This helps prevent subtle, hard-to-locate bugs.

Class ThisTest (lines 5–12) demonstrates class SimpleTime. Line 9 creates an instance of class SimpleTime and invokes its constructor. Line 10 invokes the object's BuildString method, then displays the results.

Performance Tip 10.1

C# conserves memory by maintaining only one copy of each method per class—this method is invoked by every object of the class. Each object, on the other hand, has its own copy of the class's instance variables (i.e., non-static variables). Each non-static method of the class implicitly uses the this reference to determine the specific object of the class to manipulate.

10.5 Time Class Case Study: Overloaded Constructors

Next, we demonstrate a class with several **overloaded constructors** that enable objects of that class to be conveniently initialized in different ways. To overload constructors, simply provide multiple constructor declarations with different signatures.

Class *Time2* with Overloaded Constructors

By default, instance variables hour, minute and second of class Time1 (Fig. 10.1) are initialized to their default values of 0—midnight in universal time. Class Time1 doesn't enable the class's clients to initialize the time with specific nonzero values. Class Time2 (Fig. 10.5) contains overloaded constructors. In this app, one constructor invokes the other constructor, which in turn calls SetTime to set the hour, minute and second. The compiler invokes the appropriate Time2 constructor by matching the number and types of the arguments specified in the constructor call with the number and types of the parameters specified in each constructor declaration.

```csharp
1   // Fig. 10.5: Time2.cs
2   // Time2 class declaration with overloaded constructors.
3   using System; // for class ArgumentOutOfRangeException
4
5   public class Time2
6   {
7      private int hour; // 0 - 23
8      private int minute; // 0 - 59
9      private int second; // 0 - 59
10
11     // constructor can be called with zero, one, two or three arguments
12     public Time2( int h = 0, int m = 0, int s = 0 )
13     {
14        SetTime( h, m, s ); // invoke SetTime to validate time
15     } // end Time2 three-argument constructor
16
17     // Time2 constructor: another Time2 object supplied as an argument
18     public Time2( Time2 time )
19        : this( time.Hour, time.Minute, time.Second ) { }
20
21     // set a new time value using universal time; ensure that
22     // the data remains consistent by setting invalid values to zero
23     public void SetTime( int h, int m, int s )
24     {
25        Hour = h; // set the Hour property
26        Minute = m; // set the Minute property
27        Second = s; // set the Second property
28     } // end method SetTime
29
30     // property that gets and sets the hour
31     public int Hour
32     {
33        get
34        {
35           return hour;
36        } // end get
37        set
38        {
39           if ( value >= 0 && value < 24 )
40              hour = value;
41           else
42              throw new ArgumentOutOfRangeException(
43                 "Hour", value, "Hour must be 0-23" );
44        } // end set
45     } // end property Hour
```

Fig. 10.5 | Time2 class declaration with overloaded constructors. (Part 1 of 2.)

```
46
47      // property that gets and sets the minute
48      public int Minute
49      {
50         get
51         {
52            return minute;
53         } // end get
54         set
55         {
56            if ( value >= 0 && value < 60 )
57               minute = value;
58            else
59               throw new ArgumentOutOfRangeException(
60                  "Minute", value, "Minute must be 0-59" );
61         } // end set
62      } // end property Minute
63
64      // property that gets and sets the second
65      public int Second
66      {
67         get
68         {
69            return second;
70         } // end get
71         set
72         {
73            if ( value >= 0 && value < 60 )
74               second = value;
75            else
76               throw new ArgumentOutOfRangeException(
77                  "Second", value, "Second must be 0-59" );
78         } // end set
79      } // end property Second
80
81      // convert to string in universal-time format (HH:MM:SS)
82      public string ToUniversalString()
83      {
84         return string.Format(
85            "{0:D2}:{1:D2}:{2:D2}", Hour, Minute, Second );
86      } // end method ToUniversalString
87
88      // convert to string in standard-time format (H:MM:SS AM or PM)
89      public override string ToString()
90      {
91         return string.Format( "{0}:{1:D2}:{2:D2} {3}",
92            ( ( Hour == 0 || Hour == 12 ) ? 12 : Hour % 12 ),
93            Minute, Second, ( Hour < 12 ? "AM" : "PM" ) );
94      } // end method ToString
95   } // end class Time2
```

Fig. 10.5 | Time2 class declaration with overloaded constructors. (Part 2 of 2.)

Class *Time2's Parameterless Constructor*

Lines 12–15 declare a constructor with three *default parameters*. This constructor is also considered to be the class's **parameterless constructor** because you can call the constructor without arguments and the compiler will automatically provide the default parameter values. This constructor can also be called with one argument for the hour, two arguments for the hour and minute, or three arguments for the hour, minute and second. This constructor calls SetTime to set the time.

Common Programming Error 10.2

A constructor can call methods of its class. Be aware that the instance variables might not yet be initialized, because the constructor is in the process of initializing the object. Using instance variables before they have been initialized properly is a logic error.

Class *Time2's Constructor That Receives a Reference to Another Time2 Object*

Lines 18–19 declare a Time2 constructor that receives a reference to a Time2 object. In this case, the values from the Time2 argument are passed to the three-parameter constructor at lines 12–15 to initialize the hour, minute and second. In this constructor, we use this in a manner that's allowed *only* in the constructor's header. In line 19, the usual constructor header is followed by a colon (:), then the keyword this. The this reference is used in method-call syntax (along with the three int arguments) to invoke the Time2 constructor that takes three int arguments (lines 12–15). The constructor passes the values of the time argument's Hour, Minute and Second properties to set the hour, minute and second of the Time2 object being constructed. Additional initialization code can be placed in this constructor's body and it will execute after the other constructor is called.

Constructor Initializers

The use of the this reference as shown in line 19 is called a **constructor initializer**. Constructor initializers are a popular way to reuse initialization code provided by one of the class's constructors rather than defining similar code in another constructor's body. This syntax makes the class easier to maintain, because one constructor *reuses* the other. If we needed to change how objects of class Time2 are initialized, only the constructor at lines 12–15 would need to be modified. Even that constructor might not need modification— it simply calls the SetTime method to perform the actual initialization, so it's possible that the changes the class might require would be localized to this method.

Line 19 could have directly accessed instance variables hour, minute and second of the constructor's time argument with the expressions time.hour, time.minute and time.second—even though they're declared as private variables of class Time2.

Software Engineering Observation 10.3

When one object of a class has a reference to another object of the same class, the first object can access all the second object's data and methods (including those that are private).

Class *Time2's SetTime Method*

Method SetTime (lines 23–28) invokes the set accessors of the new properties Hour (lines 31–45), Minute (lines 48–62) and Second (lines 65–79), which ensure that the value supplied for hour is in the range 0 to 23 and that the values for minute and second are each in the range 0 to 59. If a value is out of range, each set accessor throws an ArgumentOutOf-

RangeException (lines 42–43, 59–60 and 76–77). In this example, we use the Argument-OutOfRangeException constructor that receives three arguments—the name of the item that was out of range, the value that was supplied for that item and an error message.

*Notes Regarding Class **Time2**'s Methods, Properties and Constructors*

Time2's properties are accessed throughout the class's body. Method SetTime assigns values to properties Hour, Minute and Second in lines 25–27, and methods ToUniversal-String and ToString use properties Hour, Minute and Second in line 85 and lines 92–93, respectively. These methods could have accessed the class's private data directly. However, consider changing the representation of the time from three int values (requiring 12 bytes of memory) to a single int value representing the total number of seconds that have elapsed since midnight (requiring only 4 bytes of memory). If we make such a change, only the bodies of the methods that access the private data directly would need to change—in particular, the individual properties Hour, Minute and Second. There would be no need to modify the bodies of methods SetTime, ToUniversalString or ToString, because they do not access the private data directly. Designing the class in this manner reduces the likelihood of programming errors when altering the class's implementation.

Similarly, each constructor could be written to include a copy of the appropriate statements from method SetTime. Doing so may be slightly more efficient, because the extra constructor call and the call to SetTime are eliminated. However, duplicating statements in multiple methods or constructors makes changing the class's internal data representation more difficult and error-prone. Having one constructor call the other or even call SetTime directly requires any changes to SetTime's implementation to be made only once.

Software Engineering Observation 10.4

When implementing a method of a class, using the class's properties to access the class's private data simplifies code maintenance and reduces the likelihood of errors.

*Using Class **Time2**'s Overloaded Constructors*

Class Time2Test (Fig. 10.6) creates six Time2 objects (lines 9–13 and 42) to invoke the overloaded Time2 constructors. Lines 9–13 demonstrate passing arguments to the Time2 constructors. C# invokes the appropriate overloaded constructor by matching the number and types of the arguments specified in the constructor call with the number and types of the parameters specified in each constructor declaration. Lines 9–12 each invoke the constructor at lines 12–15 of Fig. 10.5. Line 9 of Fig. 10.6 invokes the constructor with no arguments, which causes the compiler to supply the default value 0 for each of the three parameters. Line 10 invokes the constructor with one argument that represents the hour—the compiler supplies the default value 0 for the minute and second. Line 11 invokes the constructor with two arguments that represent the hour and minute—the compiler supplies the default value 0 for the second. Line 12 invoke the constructor with values for all three parameters. Line 13 invokes the constructor at lines 18–19 of Fig. 10.5. Lines 16–37 display the string representation of each initialized Time2 object to confirm that each was initialized properly.

Line 42 attempts to intialize t6 by creating a new Time2 object and passing three invalid values to the constructor. When the constructor attempts to use the invalid hour value to initialize the object's Hour property, an ArgumentOutOfRangeException occurs. We catch this exception at line 44 and display its Message property, which results in the last three lines of the output in Fig. 10.6. Because we used the three-argument Argument-

OutOfRangeException constructor when the exception object was created, the exception's Message property also includes the *information about the out-of-range value.*

```csharp
1   // Fig. 10.6: Time2Test.cs
2   // Overloaded constructors used to initialize Time2 objects.
3   using System;
4
5   public class Time2Test
6   {
7      public static void Main( string[] args )
8      {
9         Time2 t1 = new Time2(); // 00:00:00
10        Time2 t2 = new Time2( 2 ); // 02:00:00
11        Time2 t3 = new Time2( 21, 34 ); // 21:34:00
12        Time2 t4 = new Time2( 12, 25, 42 ); // 12:25:42
13        Time2 t5 = new Time2( t4 ); // 12:25:42
14        Time2 t6; // initialized later in the program
15
16        Console.WriteLine( "Constructed with:\n" );
17        Console.WriteLine( "t1: all arguments defaulted" );
18        Console.WriteLine( "   {0}", t1.ToUniversalString() ); // 00:00:00
19        Console.WriteLine( "   {0}\n", t1.ToString() ); // 12:00:00 AM
20
21        Console.WriteLine(
22           "t2: hour specified; minute and second defaulted" );
23        Console.WriteLine( "   {0}", t2.ToUniversalString() ); // 02:00:00
24        Console.WriteLine( "   {0}\n", t2.ToString() ); // 2:00:00 AM
25
26        Console.WriteLine(
27           "t3: hour and minute specified; second defaulted" );
28        Console.WriteLine( "   {0}", t3.ToUniversalString() ); // 21:34:00
29        Console.WriteLine( "   {0}\n", t3.ToString() ); // 9:34:00 PM
30
31        Console.WriteLine( "t4: hour, minute and second specified" );
32        Console.WriteLine( "   {0}", t4.ToUniversalString() ); // 12:25:42
33        Console.WriteLine( "   {0}\n", t4.ToString() ); // 12:25:42 PM
34
35        Console.WriteLine( "t5: Time2 object t4 specified" );
36        Console.WriteLine( "   {0}", t5.ToUniversalString() ); // 12:25:42
37        Console.WriteLine( "   {0}", t5.ToString() ); // 12:25:42 PM
38
39        // attempt to initialize t6 with invalid values
40        try
41        {
42           t6 = new Time2( 27, 74, 99 ); // invalid values
43        } // end try
44        catch ( ArgumentOutOfRangeException ex )
45        {
46           Console.WriteLine( "\nException while initializing t6:" );
47           Console.WriteLine( ex.Message );
48        } // end catch
49     } // end Main
50  } // end class Time2Test
```

Fig. 10.6 | Overloaded constructors used to initialize Time2 objects. (Part 1 of 2.)

```
Constructed with:

t1: all arguments defaulted
    00:00:00
    12:00:00 AM

t2: hour specified; minute and second defaulted
    02:00:00
    2:00:00 AM

t3: hour and minute specified; second defaulted
    21:34:00
    9:34:00 PM

t4: hour, minute and second specified
    12:25:42
    12:25:42 PM

t5: Time2 object t4 specified
    12:25:42
    12:25:42 PM

Exception while initializing t6:
hour must be 0-23
Parameter name: hour
Actual value was 27.
```

Fig. 10.6 | Overloaded constructors used to initialize Time2 objects. (Part 2 of 2.)

10.6 Default and Parameterless Constructors

Every class *must* have at least one constructor. Recall from Section 4.10 that if you do not provide any constructors in a class's declaration, the compiler creates a *default constructor* that takes no arguments when it's invoked. In Section 11.4.1, you'll learn that the default constructor implicitly performs a special task.

The compiler will *not* create a default constructor for a class that *explicitly* declares at least one constructor. In this case, if you want to be able to invoke the constructor with no arguments, you must declare a *parameterless constructor*—as in line 12 of Fig. 10.5. Like a default constructor, a parameterless constructor is invoked with *empty parentheses*. The Time2 parameterless constructor explicitly initializes a Time2 object by passing to SetTime 0 for each parameter. If we omit the parameterless constructor, clients of this class would not be able to create a Time2 object with the expression new Time2().

Common Programming Error 10.3

If a class has constructors, but none of the public constructors are parameterless constructors, and an attempt is made to call a parameterless constructor to initialize an object of the class, a compilation error occurs. A constructor can be called with no arguments only if the class does not have any constructors (in which case the default constructor is called) or if the class has a parameterless constructor.

10.7 Composition

A class can have references to objects of other classes as members. This is called **composition** and is sometimes referred to as a *has-a* relationship. For example, an object of class AlarmClock needs to know the current time *and* the time when it's supposed to sound its alarm, so it's reasonable to include *two* references to Time objects in an AlarmClock object.

> **Software Engineering Observation 10.5**
> *One form of software reuse is composition, in which a class contains references to other objects. A class can have a property of its own type—for example, a* Person *class could have a* Mom *property of type* Person.

Class **Date**

Our example of composition contains three classes—Date (Fig. 10.7), Employee (Fig. 10.8) and EmployeeTest (Fig. 10.9). Class Date (Fig. 10.7) declares instance variables month and day (lines 7–8) and *auto-implemented property* Year (line 11) to represent a date. The constructor receives three int parameters. Line 17 invokes the set accessor of property Month (lines 24–38) to validate the month—if the value is out-of-range the accessor throws an exception. Line 18 uses property Year to set the year. Since Year is an *auto-implemented property*, we're assuming in this example that the value for Year is correct. Line 19 uses property Day (lines 41–63), which validates and assigns the value for day based on the current month and Year (by using properties Month and Year in turn to obtain the values of month and Year). The *order of initialization is important*, because the set accessor of property Day validates the value for day based on the assumption that month and Year are correct. Line 53 determines whether the day is correct based on the number of days in the particular Month. If the day is not correct, lines 56–57 determine whether the Month is February, the day is 29 and the Year is a leap year. Otherwise, if the parameter value does not contain a correct value for day, the set accessor throws an exception. Line 20 in the constructor outputs the this reference as a string. Since this is a reference to the current Date object, the object's ToString method (lines 66–69) is called *implicitly* to obtain the object's string representation.

```
1   // Fig. 10.7: Date.cs
2   // Date class declaration.
3   using System;
4
5   public class Date
6   {
7      private int month; // 1-12
8      private int day; // 1-31 based on month
9
10     // auto-implemented property Year
11     public int Year { get; private set; }
12
13     // constructor: use property Month to confirm proper value for month;
14     // use property Day to confirm proper value for day
15     public Date( int theMonth, int theDay, int theYear )
16     {
17        Month = theMonth; // validate month
```

Fig. 10.7 | Date class declaration. (Part 1 of 2.)

```
18          Year = theYear; // could validate year
19          Day = theDay; // validate day
20          Console.WriteLine( "Date object constructor for date {0}", this );
21       } // end Date constructor
22
23       // property that gets and sets the month
24       public int Month
25       {
26          get
27          {
28             return month;
29          } // end get
30          private set // make writing inaccessible outside the class
31          {
32             if ( value > 0 && value <= 12 ) // validate month
33                month = value;
34             else // month is invalid
35                throw new ArgumentOutOfRangeException(
36                   "Month", value, "Month must be 1-12" );
37          } // end set
38       } // end property Month
39
40       // property that gets and sets the day
41       public int Day
42       {
43          get
44          {
45             return day;
46          } // end get
47          private set // make writing inaccessible outside the class
48          {
49             int[] daysPerMonth = { 0, 31, 28, 31, 30, 31, 30,
50                                    31, 31, 30, 31, 30, 31 };
51
52             // check if day in range for month
53             if ( value > 0 && value <= daysPerMonth[ Month ] )
54                day = value;
55             // check for leap year
56             else if ( Month == 2 && value == 29 &&
57                ( Year % 400 == 0 || ( Year % 4 == 0 && Year % 100 != 0 ) ) )
58                day = value;
59             else // day is invalid
60                throw new ArgumentOutOfRangeException(
61                   "Day", value, "Day out of range for current month/year" );
62          } // end set
63       } // end property Day
64
65       // return a string of the form month/day/year
66       public override string ToString()
67       {
68          return string.Format( "{0}/{1}/{2}", Month, Day, Year );
69       } // end method ToString
70    } // end class Date
```

Fig. 10.7 | Date class declaration. (Part 2 of 2.)

Class Date's private set Accessors

Class Date uses access modifiers to ensure that *clients* of the class must use the appropriate methods and properties to access private data. In particular, the properties Year, Month and Day declare private set accessors (lines 11, 30 and 47, respectively) to restrict the use of the set accessors to members of the class. We declare these private for the same reasons that we declare the instance variables private—to simplify code maintenance and control access to the class's data. Although the constructor, method and properties in class Date still have all the advantages of using the set accessors to perform validation, clients of the class must use the class's constructor to initialize the data in a Date object. The get accessors of properties Year, Month and Day are *implicitly* declared public because their properties are declared public—when there's no access modifier before a get or set accessor, the accessor inherits the access modifier *preceding* the property name.

Class Employee

Class Employee (Fig. 10.8) has public auto-implemented properties FirstName, Last-Name, BirthDate and HireDate. BirthDate and HireDate (lines 7–8) manipulate Date objects, demonstrating that *a class can have references to objects of other classes as members.* This, of course, is also true of the properties FirstName and LastName, which manipulate String objects. The Employee constructor (lines 11–18) takes four parameters—first, last, dateOfBirth and dateOfHire. The objects referenced by parameters dateOfBirth and dateOfHire are assigned to the Employee object's BirthDate and HireDate properties, respectively. When class Employee's ToString method is called, it returns a string containing the string representations of the two Date objects. Each of these strings is obtained with an *implicit* call to the Date class's ToString method.

```
 1   // Fig. 10.8: Employee.cs
 2   // Employee class with references to other objects.
 3   public class Employee
 4   {
 5      public string FirstName { get; private set; }
 6      public string LastName { get; private set; }
 7      public Date BirthDate { get; private set; }
 8      public Date HireDate { get; private set; }
 9
10      // constructor to initialize name, birth date and hire date
11      public Employee( string first, string last,
12         Date dateOfBirth, Date dateOfHire )
13      {
14         firstName = first;
15         lastName = last;
16         birthDate = dateOfBirth;
17         hireDate = dateOfHire;
18      } // end Employee constructor
19
20      // convert Employee to string format
21      public override string ToString()
22      {
```

Fig. 10.8 | Employee class with references to other objects. (Part I of 2.)

```
23          return string.Format( "{0}, {1}  Hired: {2}  Birthday: {3}",
24            lastName, firstName, hireDate, birthDate );
25       } // end method ToString
26    } // end class Employee
```

Fig. 10.8 | Employee class with references to other objects. (Part 2 of 2.)

Class *EmployeeTest*

Class EmployeeTest (Fig. 10.9) creates two Date objects (lines 9–10) to represent an Employee's birthday and hire date, respectively. Line 11 creates an Employee and initializes its instance variables by passing to the constructor two strings (representing the Employee's first and last names) and two Date objects (representing the birthday and hire date). Line 13 *implicitly* invokes the Employee's ToString method to display the values of its instance variables and demonstrate that the object was initialized properly.

```
 1   // Fig. 10.9: EmployeeTest.cs
 2   // Composition demonstration.
 3   using System;
 4
 5   public class EmployeeTest
 6   {
 7      public static void Main( string[] args )
 8      {
 9         Date birth = new Date( 7, 24, 1949 );
10         Date hire = new Date( 3, 12, 1988 );
11         Employee employee = new Employee( "Bob", "Blue", birth, hire );
12
13         Console.WriteLine( employee );
14      } // end Main
15   } // end class EmployeeTest
```

```
Date object constructor for date 7/24/1949
Date object constructor for date 3/12/1988
Blue, Bob  Hired: 3/12/1988  Birthday: 7/24/1949
```

Fig. 10.9 | Composition demonstration.

10.8 Garbage Collection and Destructors

Every object you create uses various system resources, such as memory. In many programming languages, these system resources are reserved for the object's use until they're explicitly released by the programmer. If all the references to the object that manages the resource are lost before the resource is explicitly released, the app can no longer access the resource to release it. This is known as a **resource leak**.

We need a disciplined way to give resources back to the system when they're no longer needed, thus avoiding resource leaks. The Common Language Runtime (CLR) performs automatic memory management by using a **garbage collector** to *reclaim* the memory occupied by objects that are no longer in use, so the memory can be used for other objects. When there are no more references to an object, the object becomes **eligible for destruction**. Every object has a special member, called a **destructor**, that's invoked by the garbage collector to perform **termination housekeeping** on an object before the garbage collector reclaims the object's memory. A destructor is declared like a parameterless constructor, except that its name is the class name, preceded by a tilde (~), and it has no access modifier in its header. After the garbage collector calls the object's destructor, the object becomes **eligible for garbage collection**. The memory for such an object can be reclaimed by the garbage collector.

Memory leaks, which are common in other languages such as C and C++ (because memory is *not* automatically reclaimed in those languages), are less likely in C# (but some can still happen in subtle ways). Other types of resource leaks can occur. For example, an app could open a file on disk to modify its contents. If the app does not close the file, no other app can modify (or possibly even use) the file until the app that opened it terminates.

A problem with the garbage collector is that it doesn't guarantee that it will perform its tasks at a specified time. Therefore, the garbage collector may call the destructor any time after the object becomes eligible for destruction, and may reclaim the memory any time after the destructor executes. In fact, it's possible that neither will happen before the app terminates. Thus, it's unclear whether, or when, the destructor will be called. For this reason, destructors are rarely used.

Software Engineering Observation 10.6

A class that uses resources, such as files on disk, should provide a method to eventually release the resources. Many Framework Class Library classes provide Close *or* Dispose *methods for this purpose. Section 13.6 introduces the* Dispose *method, which is then used in many later examples.* Close *methods are typically used with objects that are associated with files (Chapter 17) and other types of so-called streams of data.*

10.9 static Class Members

Every object has its *own* copy of all the instance variables of the class. In certain cases, only one copy of a particular variable should be *shared* by all objects of a class. A **static variable** is used in such cases. A static variable represents **classwide information**—all objects of the class share the *same* piece of data. The declaration of a static variable begins with the keyword static.

Let's motivate static data with an example. Suppose that we have a video game with Martians and other space creatures. Each Martian tends to be brave and willing to attack other space creatures when it's aware that there are at least four other Martians present. If fewer than five Martians are present, each Martian becomes cowardly. Thus each Martian needs to know the martianCount. We could endow class Martian with martianCount as an instance variable. If we do this, every Martian will have a separate copy of the instance variable, and every time we create a new Martian, we'll have to update the instance variable martianCount in every Martian. This wastes space on redundant copies, wastes time updating the separate copies and is error prone. Instead, we declare martianCount to be static, making martianCount classwide data. Every Martian can access the martianCount, but only one copy of the static martianCount is maintained. This saves space. We save time by having the Martian constructor increment the static martianCount—there's *only one copy*, so we do not have to increment separate copies of martianCount for each Martian object.

Software Engineering Observation 10.7

Use a static variable when all objects of a class must share the same copy of the variable.

The scope of a `static` variable is the body of its class. A class's `public static` members can be accessed by qualifying the member name with the class name and the member access (`.`) operator, as in `Math.PI`. A class's `private static` class members can be accessed *only* through the methods and properties of the class. Actually, `static` class members exist even when *no* objects of the class exist—they're available as soon as the class is loaded into memory at execution time. To access a `private static` member from outside its class, a `public static` method or property can be provided.

Common Programming Error 10.4

It's a compilation error to access or invoke a static member by referencing it through an instance of the class, like a non-static member.

Software Engineering Observation 10.8

Static variables, methods and properties exist, and can be used, even if no objects of that class have been instantiated.

Class *Employee*

Our next app declares two classes—`Employee` (Fig. 10.10) and `EmployeeTest` (Fig. 10.11). Class `Employee` declares `private static` auto-implemented property `Count`. We declare `Count`'s `set` accessor `private`, because we don't want clients of the class to be able to modify the property's value. The compiler automatically creates a `private static` variable that property `Count` will manage. If a `static` variable is not initialized, the compiler assigns a default value to the variable—in this case, the `static` variable for the auto-implemented `Count` property is initialized to 0, the default value for type `int`. Property `Count` maintains a count of the number of objects of class `Employee` that have been created.

When `Employee` objects exist, `Count` can be used in any method of an `Employee` object—this example increments `Count` in the constructor (Fig. 10.10, line 22). Client code can access the `Count` with the expression `Employee.Count`, which evaluates to the number of `Employee` objects that have been created.

```
1   // Fig. 10.10: Employee.cs
2   // Static variable used to maintain a count of the number of
3   // Employee objects that have been created.
4   using System;
5
6   public class Employee
7   {
8      public static int Count { get; private set; } // objects in memory
9
10     // read-only auto-implemented property FirstName
11     public string FirstName { get; private set; }
```

Fig. 10.10 | `static` property used to maintain a count of the number of `Employee` objects that have been created. (Part 1 of 2.)

```
12
13      // read-only auto-implemented property LastName
14      public string LastName { get; private set; }
15
16      // initialize employee, add 1 to static Count and
17      // output string indicating that constructor was called
18      public Employee( string first, string last )
19      {
20         FirstName = first;
21         LastName = last;
22         ++Count; // increment static count of employees
23         Console.WriteLine( "Employee constructor: {0} {1}; Count = {2}",
24            FirstName, LastName, Count );
25      } // end Employee constructor
26   } // end class Employee
```

Fig. 10.10 | static property used to maintain a count of the number of Employee objects that have been created. (Part 2 of 2.)

Class *EmployeeTest*

EmployeeTest method Main (Fig. 10.11) instantiates two Employee objects (lines 14–15). When each object's constructor is invoked, lines 20–21 of Fig. 10.10 assign the Employee's first name and last name to properties FirstName and LastName. These two statements do *not* make copies of the original string arguments. Actually, string objects in C# are **immutable**—they *cannot* be modified after they're created. Therefore, it's safe to have many references to one string. This is *not* normally the case for objects of most other classes. If string objects are immutable, you might wonder why we're able to use operators + and += to concatenate string objects. String-concatenation operations actually result in a *new* string object containing the concatenated values. The original string objects are *not* modified.

```
1    // Fig. 10.11: EmployeeTest.cs
2    // Static member demonstration.
3    using System;
4
5    public class EmployeeTest
6    {
7       public static void Main( string[] args )
8       {
9          // show that Count is 0 before creating Employees
10          Console.WriteLine( "Employees before instantiation: {0}",
11             Employee.Count );
12
13          // create two Employees; Count should become 2
14          Employee e1 = new Employee( "Susan", "Baker" );
15          Employee e2 = new Employee( "Bob", "Blue" );
16
17          // show that Count is 2 after creating two Employees
18          Console.WriteLine( "\nEmployees after instantiation: {0}",
19             Employee.Count );
```

Fig. 10.11 | static member demonstration. (Part 1 of 2.)

```
20
21          // get names of Employees
22          Console.WriteLine( "\nEmployee 1: {0} {1}\nEmployee 2: {2} {3}\n",
23             e1.FirstName, e1.LastName,
24             e2.FirstName, e2.LastName );
25
26          // in this example, there is only one reference to each Employee,
27          // so the following statements cause the CLR to mark each
28          // Employee object as being eligible for garbage collection
29          e1 = null; // mark object referenced by e1 as no longer needed
30          e2 = null; // mark object referenced by e2 as no longer needed
31       } // end Main
32    } // end class EmployeeTest
```

```
Employees before instantiation: 0
Employee constructor: Susan Baker; Count = 1
Employee constructor: Bob Blue; Count = 2

Employees after instantiation: 2

Employee 1: Susan Baker
Employee 2: Bob Blue
```

Fig. 10.11 | static member demonstration. (Part 2 of 2.)

Lines 18–19 of Fig. 10.11 display the updated Count. When Main has finished using the two Employee objects, references e1 and e2 are set to null at lines 29–30, so they no longer refer to the objects that were instantiated in lines 14–15. The objects become *eligible for destruction* because there are *no more references to them* in the app. After the objects' destructors are called, the objects become *eligible for garbage collection.*

Eventually, the garbage collector might reclaim the memory for these objects (or the operating system will reclaim the memory when the app terminates). C# does not guarantee when, or even whether, the garbage collector will execute. When the garbage collector does run, it's possible that no objects or only a subset of the eligible objects will be collected.

A method declared static cannot access non-static class members directly, because a static method can be called even when *no* objects of the class exist. For the same reason, the this reference cannot be used in a static method—the this reference must refer to a *specific object* of the class, and when a static method is called, there might *not* be any objects of its class in memory.

10.10 readonly Instance Variables

The **principle of least privilege** is fundamental to good software engineering. In the context of an app, the principle states that *code should be granted the amount of privilege and access needed to accomplish its designated task, but no more.* Let's see how this principle applies to instance variables.

Some instance variables need to be modifiable, and some do not. In Section 8.4, we used keyword const for declaring constants. These constants must be initialized to a constant value when they're declared. Suppose, however, we want to initialize in the object's constructor a constant belonging to a specific object of the class. C# provides keyword **readonly** to specify that an instance variable of an object is *not* modifiable and that any attempt to modify it after the object is constructed is an error. For example,

```
private readonly int INCREMENT;
```

declares `readonly` instance variable INCREMENT of type `int`. Like constants, `readonly` variables are declared with all capital letters by convention. Although `readonly` instance variables can be initialized when they're declared, this isn't required. Readonly variables should be initialized *by each* of the class's constructors. Each constructor can assign values to a `readonly` instance variable multiple times—the variable doesn't become unmodifiable until *after* the constructor completes execution. If a constructor does not initialize the `readonly` variable, the variable receives the same default value as any other instance variable (0 for numeric simple types, `false` for `bool` type and `null` for reference types), and the compiler generates a warning.

Software Engineering Observation 10.9

Declaring an instance variable as `readonly` helps enforce the principle of least privilege. If an instance variable should not be modified after the object is constructed, declare it to be `readonly` to prevent modification.

Members that are declared as `const` must be assigned values at compile time. Therefore, `const` members can be initialized *only* with other constant values, such as integers, `string` literals, characters and other `const` members. Constant members with values that cannot be determined at compile time must be declared with keyword `readonly`, so they can be initialized at *execution time*. Variables that are `readonly` can be initialized with more complex expressions, such as an array initializer or a method call that returns a value or a reference to an object.

Common Programming Error 10.5

Attempting to modify a `readonly` instance variable anywhere but in its declaration or the object's constructors is a compilation error.

Error-Prevention Tip 10.2

Attempts to modify a `readonly` instance variable are caught at compilation time rather than causing execution-time errors. It's always preferable to get bugs out at compile time, if possible, rather than allowing them to slip through to execution time (where studies have found that repairing bugs is often much more costly).

Software Engineering Observation 10.10

If a `readonly` instance variable is initialized to a constant only in its declaration, it's not necessary to have a separate copy of the instance variable for every object of the class. The variable should be declared `const` instead. Constants declared with `const` are implicitly `static`, so there will only be one copy for the entire class.

10.11 Data Abstraction and Encapsulation

Classes normally *hide* the details of their implementation from their clients. This is called **information hiding**. As an example, let's consider the **stack data structure** introduced in

Section 7.6. Recall that a stack is a **last-in, first-out (LIFO)** data structure—the *last* item pushed (inserted) on the stack is the *first* item popped (removed) off the stack.

Data Abstraction

Stacks can be implemented with arrays and with other data structures, such as linked lists. A client of a stack class need not be concerned with the stack's implementation. The client knows only that when data items are placed in the stack, they'll be recalled in last-in, first-out order. The client cares about *what* functionality a stack offers, not about *how* that functionality is implemented. This concept is referred to as **data abstraction**. Even if you know the details of a class's implementation, you shouldn't write code that depends on these details as they may later change. This enables a particular class (such as one that implements a stack and its *push* and *pop* operations) to be replaced with another version—perhaps one that runs faster or uses less memory—without affecting the rest of the system. As long as the `public` services of the class do not change (i.e., every original method still has the same name, return type and parameter list in the new class declaration), the rest of the system is not affected.

Abstract Data Types (ADTs)

Earlier non-object-oriented programming languages like C emphasize actions. In these languages, data exists to support the actions that apps must take. Data is "less interesting" than actions. Data is "crude." Only a few simple types exist, and it's difficult for programmers to create their own types. C# and the object-oriented style of programming elevate the importance of data. The primary activities of object-oriented programming in C# are creating types (e.g., classes) and expressing the interactions among objects of those types. To create languages that emphasize data, the programming-languages community needed to formalize some notions about data. The formalization we consider here is the notion of **abstract data types (ADTs)**, which improve the app-development process.

Consider the type `int`, which most people associate with an integer in mathematics. Actually, an `int` is an *abstract representation of an integer*. Unlike mathematical integers, computer `int`s are *fixed* in size. Type `int` in C# is limited to the range –2,147,483,648 to +2,147,483,647. If the result of a calculation falls *outside* this range, an error occurs, and the computer responds in some appropriate manner. It might produce an incorrect result, such as a value too large to fit in an `int` variable—commonly called **arithmetic overflow**. It also might throw an exception, called an `OverflowException`. *Mathematical* integers do not have this problem. Therefore, the computer `int` is only an *approximation* of the real-world integer. Simple types like `int`, `double`, and `char` are all examples of abstract data types—*representations of real-world concepts to some satisfactory level of precision within a computer system.*

An ADT actually captures two notions: a **data representation** and the **operations** that can be performed on that data. For example, in C#, an `int` contains an integer value (data) and provides addition, subtraction, multiplication, division and remainder operations—division by zero is *undefined*.

Software Engineering Observation 10.11

Programmers create types through the class mechanism. Although the language is easy to extend via new types, you cannot alter the base language itself.

Queue Abstract Data Type

Another ADT we discuss is a **queue**, which is similar to a "waiting line." Computer systems use many queues internally. A queue offers well-understood behavior to its clients: Clients place items in a queue one at a time via an *enqueue* operation, then retrieve them one at a time via a *dequeue* operation. A queue returns items in **first-in, first-out (FIFO)** order—the first item inserted in a queue is the first removed. Conceptually, a queue can become infinitely long, but real queues are finite.

The queue hides an internal data representation that keeps track of the items currently waiting in line. The clients are not concerned about the implementation of the queue—they simply depend on the queue to operate "as advertised." When a client enqueues an item, the queue should accept that item and place it in some kind of internal FIFO data structure. Similarly, when the client wants the next item from the front of the queue, the queue should remove the item from its internal representation and deliver it in FIFO order—the item that has been in the queue the *longest* should be returned by the next dequeue operation.

The queue ADT guarantees the integrity of its internal data structure. Clients cannot manipulate this data structure directly—only the queue ADT has access to its internal data. Clients are able to perform only allowable operations on the data representation—the ADT rejects operations that its public interface does not provide.

10.12 Class View and Object Browser

Now that we have introduced key concepts of object-oriented programming, we present two features that Visual Studio provides to facilitate the design of object-oriented apps—**Class View** and **Object Browser**.

Using the Class View Window

The **Class View** displays the fields, methods and properties for all classes in a project. Select **VIEW > Class View** to display the **Class View** as a tab in the same position within the IDE as the **Solution Explorer**. Figure 10.12 shows the **Class View** for the Time1 project of Fig. 10.1 (class Time1) and Fig. 10.2 (class Time1Test). The view follows a hierarchical structure, positioning the project name (Time1) as the *root* and including a series of nodes that represent the classes, variables, methods and properties in the project. If a ▷ appears to the left of a node, that node can be *expanded* to show other nodes. If a ◢ appears to the left of a node, that node can be *collapsed*. According to the **Class View**, project Time1 contains class Time1 and class Time1Test as children. When class Time1 is selected, the class's members appear in the lower half of the window. Class Time1 contains methods SetTime, ToString and ToUniversalString (indicated by purple boxes, ◉) and instance variables hour, minute and second (indicated by blue boxes, ◕ₐ). The lock icons to the right of the blue box icons for the instance variables specify that the variables are private. Both class Time1 and class Time1Test contain the **Base Types** node. If you expand this node, you'll see class Object in each case, because each class *inherits* from class System.Object (discussed in Chapter 11).

Using the Object Browser

Visual Studio's **Object Browser** lists all classes in the .NET library. You can use the **Object Browser** to learn about the functionality provided by a specific class. To open the **Object**

Fig. 10.12 | **Class View** of class Time1 (Fig. 10.1) and class Time1Test (Fig. 10.2).

Browser, select **VIEW > Object Browser**. Figure 10.13 depicts the **Object Browser** when the user navigates to the Math class in namespace System. To do this, we expanded the node for mscorlib (Microsoft Core Library) in the upper-left pane of the **Object Browser**, then expanded its subnode for System. [*Note:* The most common classes from the System namespace, such as System.Math, are in mscorlib.]

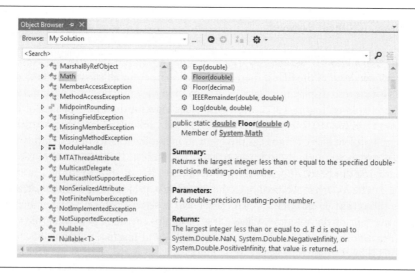

Fig. 10.13 | **Object Browser** for class Math.

The **Object Browser** lists all methods provided by class Math in the upper-right frame—this offers you "instant access" to information regarding the functionality of various objects. If you click the name of a member in the upper-right frame, a description of that member appears in the lower-right frame. The **Object Browser** can be a quick mechanism to learn about a class or one of its methods. You can also view the complete description of a class or a method in the online documentation by selecting the type or member in the **Object Browser** and pressing *F1*.

10.13 **Object Initializers**

Visual C# provides **object initializers** that allow you to create an object and initialize its public properties (and public instance variables, if any) in the same statement. This can be useful when a class does not provide an appropriate constructor to meet your needs, but does provide properties that you can use to manipulate the class's data. The following statements demonstrate object initializers using the class Time2 from Fig. 10.5.

```
// create a Time2 object and initialize its properties
Time2 aTime = new Time2 { Hour = 14, Minute = 30, Second = 12 };

// create a Time2 object and initialize only its Minute property
Time2 anotherTime = new Time2 { Minute = 45 };
```

The first statement creates a Time2 object (aTime), initializes it with class Time2's constructor that can be called with no arguments, then uses an object initializer to set its Hour, Minute and Second properties. Notice that new Time2 is immediately followed by an **object-initializer list**—a comma-separated list in curly braces ({ }) of properties and their values. Each property name can appear only *once* in the object-initializer list. The object initializer executes the property initializers in the order in which they appear.

The second statement creates a new Time2 object (anotherTime), initializes it with class Time2's constructor that can be called with no arguments, then sets only its Minute property using an object initializer. When the Time2 constructor is called with no arguments, it initializes the time to midnight. The object initializer then sets each specified property to the supplied value. In this case, the Minute property is set to 45. The Hour and Second properties retain their default values, because no values are specified for them in the object initializer.

10.14 **Wrap-Up**

In this chapter, we discussed additional class concepts. The Time class case study presented a complete class declaration consisting of private data, overloaded public constructors for initialization flexibility, properties for manipulating the class's data and methods that returned string representations of a Time object in two different formats. You learned that every class can declare a ToString method that returns a string representation of an object of the class and that this method is invoked *implicitly* when an object of a class is output as a string or concatenated with a string.

You learned that the this reference is used implicitly in a class's non-static methods to access the class's instance variables and other non-static methods. You saw explicit uses of the this reference to access the class's members (including hidden fields) and learned how to use keyword this in a constructor to call another constructor of the class.

You saw that composition enables a class to have references to objects of other classes as members. You learned about C#'s garbage-collection capability and how it reclaims the memory of objects that are no longer used. We explained the motivation for static variables in a class and demonstrated how to declare and use static variables and methods in your own classes. You also learned how to declare and initialize readonly variables.

We also showed how to use Visual Studio's **Class View** and **Object Browser** windows to navigate the classes of the Framework Class Library and your own apps to discover information about those classes. Finally, you learned how to initialize an object's properties as you create it with an object-initializer list.

In the next chapter, you'll learn about inheritance. You'll see that all classes in C# are related directly or indirectly to the `object` class and begin to understand how inheritance enables you to build more powerful apps faster.

Object-Oriented Programming: Inheritance

Objectives

In this chapter you'll:

- Learn how inheritance promotes software reusability.

- Create a derived class that inherits attributes and behaviors from a base class.

- Use access modifier **protected** to give derived-class methods access to base-class members.

- Access base-class members with **base**.

- Understand how constructors are used in inheritance hierarchies.

- Learn the methods of class **object**, the direct or indirect base class of all classes.

11.1 Introduction

This chapter continues our discussion of object-oriented programming (OOP) by introducing one of its primary features—**inheritance**, a form of *software reuse* in which a new class is created by absorbing an existing class's members and enhancing them with new or modified capabilities. Inheritance lets you save time during app development by reusing proven and debugged high-quality software. This also increases the likelihood that a system will be implemented effectively.

The existing class from which a new class inherits members is called the **base class**, and the new class is the **derived class.** Each derived class can become the base class for future derived classes.

A derived class normally adds its own fields and methods. Therefore, it's more *specific* than its base class and represents a more specialized group of objects. Typically, the derived class exhibits the behaviors of its base class and additional ones that are specific to itself.

The **direct base class** is the base class from which the derived class explicitly inherits. An **indirect base class** is any class above the direct base class in the **class hierarchy**, which defines the inheritance relationships among classes. The class hierarchy begins with class **object** (which is the C# alias for System.Object in the Framework Class Library), which *every* class directly or indirectly **extends** (or "inherits from"). Section 11.7 lists the methods of class object, which *every* other class inherits. In the case of **single inheritance**, a class is derived from one *direct* base class. C# supports only single inheritance. In Chapter 12, OOP: Polymorphism, Interfaces and Operator Overloading, we explain how you can use interfaces to realize many of the benefits of multiple inheritance while avoiding the associated problems.

Experience in building software systems indicates that significant amounts of code deal with closely related special cases. When you're preoccupied with special cases, the details can obscure the big picture. With object-oriented programming, you can, when appropriate, focus on the commonalities among objects in the system rather than the special cases.

We distinguish between the *is-a* **relationship** and the *has-a* **relationship**. *Is-a* represents inheritance. In an *is-a* relationship, an object of a derived class can also be treated as an object of its base class. For example, a car *is a* vehicle, and a truck *is a* vehicle. By contrast, *has-a* represents composition (see Chapter 10). In a *has-a* relationship, an object contains as members references to other objects. For example, a car *has a* steering wheel, and a car object *has a* reference to a steering-wheel object.

New classes can inherit from classes in **class libraries**. Organizations develop their own class libraries and can take advantage of others available worldwide. Some day, most new software likely will be constructed from **standardized reusable components**, just as automobiles and most computer hardware are constructed today. This will facilitate the development of more powerful, abundant and economical software.

11.2 Base Classes and Derived Classes

Often, an object of one class *is an* object of another class as well. For example, in geometry, a rectangle *is a* quadrilateral (as are squares, parallelograms and trapezoids). Thus, class `Rectangle` can be said to inherit from class `Quadrilateral`. In this context, class `Quadrilateral` is a *base class* and class `Rectangle` is a *derived class*. A rectangle *is a* specific type of quadrilateral, but it's incorrect to claim that every quadrilateral *is a* rectangle—the quadrilateral could be a parallelogram or some other shape. Figure 11.1 lists several simple examples of base classes and derived classes—base classes tend to be more *general*, and derived classes tend to be more *specific*.

Base class	Derived classes
Student	GraduateStudent, UndergraduateStudent
Shape	Circle, Triangle, Rectangle
Loan	CarLoan, HomeImprovementLoan, MortgageLoan
Employee	Faculty, Staff, HourlyWorker, CommissionWorker
BankAccount	CheckingAccount, SavingsAccount

Fig. 11.1 | Inheritance examples.

Because every derived-class object *is an* object of its base class, and one base class can have *many* derived classes, the set of objects represented by a base class is typically larger than the set of objects represented by any of its derived classes. For example, the base class `Vehicle` represents all vehicles—cars, trucks, boats, bicycles and so on. By contrast, derived class `Car` represents a smaller, more specific subset of vehicles.

Inheritance relationships form treelike hierarchical structures (Figs. 11.2 and 11.3). A base class exists in a hierarchical relationship with its derived classes. When classes participate in inheritance relationships, they become "affiliated" with other classes. A class becomes either a base class, supplying members to other classes, or a derived class, inheriting its members from another class. Sometimes, a class is *both* a base and a derived class.

Let us develop a sample class hierarchy, also called an **inheritance hierarchy** (Fig. 11.2). The UML class diagram of Fig. 11.2 shows a university community that has many types of members, including employees, students and alumni. Employees are either faculty members or staff members. Faculty members are either administrators (such as deans and department chairpersons) or teachers. The hierarchy could contain many other classes. For example, students can be graduate or undergraduate students. Undergraduate students can be freshmen, sophomores, juniors or seniors.

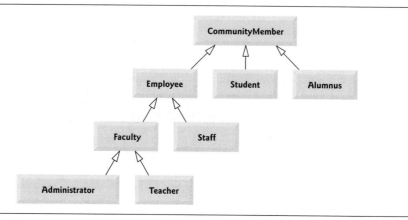

Fig. 11.2 | UML class diagram showing an inheritance hierarchy for university CommunityMembers.

Each arrow with a *hollow triangular arrowhead* in the hierarchy diagram represents an *is-a* relationship. As we follow the arrows, we can state, for instance, that "an Employee *is a* CommunityMember" and "a Teacher *is a* Faculty member." CommunityMember is the *direct* base class of Employee, Student and Alumnus and is an *indirect* base class of all the other classes in the diagram. Starting from the bottom, you can follow the arrows and apply the *is-a* relationship up to the topmost base class. For example, an Administrator *is a* Faculty member, *is an* Employee and *is a* CommunityMember.

Now consider the Shape hierarchy in Fig. 11.3, which begins with base class Shape. This class is extended by derived classes TwoDimensionalShape and ThreeDimensionalShape—a Shape is either a TwoDimensionalShape or a ThreeDimensionalShape. The third level of this hierarchy contains specific TwoDimensionalShapes and ThreeDimensionalShapes. We can follow the arrows from the bottom to the topmost base class in this hierarchy to identify the *is-a* relationships. For instance, a Triangle *is a* TwoDimensionalShape and *is a* Shape, while a Sphere *is a* ThreeDimensionalShape and *is a* Shape. This hierarchy could contain many other classes. For example, ellipses and trapezoids also are TwoDimensionalShapes.

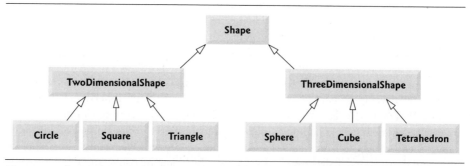

Fig. 11.3 | UML class diagram showing an inheritance hierarchy for Shapes.

Not every class relationship is an inheritance relationship. In Chapter 10 we discussed the *has-a* relationship, in which classes have members that are references to objects of other classes. Such relationships create classes by *composition* of existing classes. For example, given the classes `Employee`, `BirthDate` and `TelephoneNumber`, it's improper to say that an `Employee` *is a* `BirthDate` or that an `Employee` *is a* `TelephoneNumber`. However, an `Employee` *has a* `BirthDate`, and an `Employee` *has a* `TelephoneNumber`.

It's possible to treat base-class objects and derived-class objects similarly—their commonalities are expressed in the base class's members. Objects of all classes that extend a common base class can be treated as objects of that base class—such objects have an *is-a* relationship with the base class. However, *base-class objects cannot be treated as objects of their derived classes*. For example, all cars are vehicles, but not all vehicles are cars (other vehicles could be trucks, planes, bicycles, etc.). This chapter and Chapter 12 consider many examples of *is-a* relationships.

A derived class can customize methods it inherits from its base class. In such cases, the derived class can **override** (redefine) the base-class method with an appropriate implementation, as we'll see often in the chapter's code examples.

11.3 protected Members

Chapter 10 discussed access modifiers `public` and `private`. A class's `public` members are accessible wherever the app has a reference to an object of that class or one of its derived classes. A class's `private` members are accessible *only* within the class itself. A base class's `private` members *are* inherited by its derived classes, but are *not* directly accessible by derived-class methods and properties. In this section, we introduce access modifier `protected`. Using `protected` access offers an intermediate level of access between `public` and `private`. A base class's `protected` members can be accessed by members of that base class *and* by members of its derived classes.

All non-`private` base-class members retain their original access modifier when they become members of the derived class—`public` members of the base class become `public` members of the derived class, and `protected` members of the base class become `protected` members of the derived class.

Derived-class methods can refer to `public` and `protected` members inherited from the base class simply by using the member names. When a derived-class method overrides a base-class method, the base-class version can be accessed from the derived class by preceding the base-class method name with the keyword `base` and the member access (.) operator. We discuss accessing overridden members of the base class in Section 11.4.

Software Engineering Observation 11.1

Properties and methods of a derived class cannot directly access `private` members of the base class. A derived class can change the state of `private` base-class fields only through non-`private` methods and properties provided in the base class.

Software Engineering Observation 11.2

Declaring `private` fields in a base class helps you test, debug and correctly modify systems. If a derived class could access its base class's `private` fields, classes that inherit from that derived class could access the fields as well. This would propagate access to what should be `private` fields, and the benefits of information hiding would be lost.

11.4 Relationship between Base Classes and Derived Classes

In this section, we use an inheritance hierarchy containing types of employees in a company's payroll app to discuss the relationship between a base class and its derived classes. In this company, *commission employees* (who will be represented as objects of a base class) are paid a percentage of their sales, while *base-salaried commission employees* (who will be represented as objects of a derived class) receive a base salary *plus* a percentage of their sales.

We divide our discussion of the relationship between commission employees and base-salaried commission employees into five examples:

1. The first creates class CommissionEmployee, which directly inherits from class object and declares as private instance variables a first name, last name, social security number, commission rate and gross (i.e., total) sales amount.

2. The second declares class BasePlusCommissionEmployee, which also directly inherits from object and declares as private instance variables a first name, last name, social security number, commission rate, gross sales amount *and* base salary. We create the class by writing *every* line of code the class requires—we'll soon see that it's more efficient to create this class by inheriting from CommissionEmployee.

3. The third declares a separate BasePlusCommissionEmployee class that extends class CommissionEmployee (i.e., a BasePlusCommissionEmployee *is a* CommissionEmployee who also has a base salary). We show that base-class methods must be explicitly declared virtual if they're to be overridden by methods in derived classes. BasePlusCommissionEmployee attempts to access class CommissionEmployee's private members, but this results in compilation errors because a derived class *cannot* access its base class's private instance variables.

4. The fourth shows that if base class CommissionEmployee's instance variables are declared as protected, a BasePlusCommissionEmployee class that inherits from class CommissionEmployee can access that data directly. For this purpose, we declare class CommissionEmployee with protected instance variables.

5. The fifth example demonstrates *best practice* by setting the CommissionEmployee instance variables back to private in class CommissionEmployee to enforce good software engineering. Then we show how a separate BasePlusCommissionEmployee class, which inherits from class CommissionEmployee, can use CommissionEmployee's public methods to manipulate CommissionEmployee's private instance variables.

11.4.1 Creating and Using a CommissionEmployee Class

We begin by declaring class CommissionEmployee (Fig. 11.4). Line 5 begins the class declaration. The colon (:) followed by class name object at the end of the declaration header indicates that class CommissionEmployee *extends* (i.e., *inherits from*) class object (System.Object in the Framework Class Library). C# programmers use inheritance to create classes from existing classes. In fact, *every* class in C# (except object) extends an existing class. Because class CommissionEmployee extends class object, class CommissionEmployee inherits the methods of class object—class object has no fields. Every C# class directly or indirectly inherits object's methods. If a class does not specify that it inherits from another class, the new class *implicitly* inherits from object. For this reason, you typically do *not* include ": object" in your code—we do so in this example for demonstration purposes.

```csharp
1   // Fig. 11.4: CommissionEmployee.cs
2   // CommissionEmployee class represents a commission employee.
3   using System;
4
5   public class CommissionEmployee : object
6   {
7      private string firstName;
8      private string lastName;
9      private string socialSecurityNumber;
10     private decimal grossSales; // gross weekly sales
11     private decimal commissionRate; // commission percentage
12
13     // five-parameter constructor
14     public CommissionEmployee( string first, string last, string ssn,
15        decimal sales, decimal rate )
16     {
17        // implicit call to object constructor occurs here
18        firstName = first;
19        lastName = last;
20        socialSecurityNumber = ssn;
21        GrossSales = sales; // validate gross sales via property
22        CommissionRate = rate; // validate commission rate via property
23     } // end five-parameter CommissionEmployee constructor
24
25     // read-only property that gets commission employee's first name
26     public string FirstName
27     {
28        get
29        {
30           return firstName;
31        } // end get
32     } // end property FirstName
33
34     // read-only property that gets commission employee's last name
35     public string LastName
36     {
37        get
38        {
39           return lastName;
40        } // end get
41     } // end property LastName
42
43     // read-only property that gets
44     // commission employee's social security number
45     public string SocialSecurityNumber
46     {
47        get
48        {
49           return socialSecurityNumber;
```

Fig. 11.4 | CommissionEmployee class represents a commission employee. (Part 1 of 2.)

```
50          } // end get
51       } // end property SocialSecurityNumber
52
53       // property that gets and sets commission employee's gross sales
54       public decimal GrossSales
55       {
56          get
57          {
58             return grossSales;
59          } // end get
60          set
61          {
62             if ( value >= 0 )
63                grossSales = value;
64             else
65                throw new ArgumentOutOfRangeException(
66                   "GrossSales", value, "GrossSales must be >= 0" );
67          } // end set
68       } // end property GrossSales
69
70       // property that gets and sets commission employee's commission rate
71       public decimal CommissionRate
72       {
73          get
74          {
75             return commissionRate;
76          } // end get
77          set
78          {
79             if ( value > 0 && value < 1 )
80                commissionRate = value;
81             else
82                throw new ArgumentOutOfRangeException( "CommissionRate",
83                   value, "CommissionRate must be > 0 and < 1" );
84          } // end set
85       } // end property CommissionRate
86
87       // calculate commission employee's pay
88       public decimal Earnings()
89       {
90          return commissionRate * grossSales;
91       } // end method Earnings
92
93       // return string representation of CommissionEmployee object
94       public override string ToString()
95       {
96          return string.Format(
97             "{0}: {1} {2}\n{3}: {4}\n{5}: {6:C}\n{7}: {8:F2}",
98             "commission employee", FirstName, LastName,
99             "social security number", SocialSecurityNumber,
100            "gross sales", GrossSales, "commission rate", CommissionRate );
101      } // end method ToString
102   } // end class CommissionEmployee
```

Fig. 11.4 | CommissionEmployee class represents a commission employee. (Part 2 of 2.)

CommissionEmployee Class Overview

CommissionEmployee's public services include a constructor (lines 14–23), methods Earnings (lines 88–91) and ToString (lines 94–101), and the public properties (lines 26–85) for manipulating the class's instance variables firstName, lastName, socialSecurityNumber, grossSales and commissionRate (declared in lines 7–11). Each of its instance variable is private, so objects of other classes cannot directly access these variables. Declaring instance variables as private and providing public properties to manipulate and validate them helps enforce good software engineering. The set accessors of properties GrossSales and CommissionRate, for example, *validate* their arguments before assigning the values to instance variables grossSales and commissionRate, respectively.

CommissionEmployee Constructor

Constructors are *not* inherited, so class CommissionEmployee does not inherit class object's constructor. However, class CommissionEmployee's constructor calls class object's constructor *implicitly*. In fact, before executing the code in its own body, the derived class's constructor calls its direct base class's constructor, either explicitly or implicitly (if no constructor call is specified), to ensure that the instance variables inherited from the base class are initialized properly. The syntax for calling a base-class constructor *explicitly* is discussed in Section 11.4.3. If the code does not include an *explicit* call to the base-class constructor, the compiler generates an *implicit* call to the base class's *default* or *parameterless* constructor. The comment in line 17 indicates where the implicit call to the base class object's default constructor is made (you do not write the code for this call). Class object's default (empty) constructor does nothing. Even if a class does not have constructors, the default constructor that the compiler implicitly declares for the class will call the base class's default or parameterless constructor. Class object is the *only* class that does not have a base class.

After the implicit call to object's constructor occurs, lines 18–22 in the constructor assign values to the class's instance variables. We do *not* validate the values of arguments first, last and ssn before assigning them to the corresponding instance variables. We certainly could validate the first and last names—perhaps by ensuring that they're of a reasonable length. Similarly, a social security number could be validated to ensure that it contains nine digits, with or without dashes (e.g., 123-45-6789 or 123456789).

CommissionEmployee Method Earnings

Method Earnings (lines 88–91) calculates a CommissionEmployee's earnings. Line 90 multiplies the commissionRate by the grossSales and returns the result.

CommissionEmployee Method ToString

Method ToString (lines 94–101) is special—it's one of the methods that *every* class inherits directly or indirectly from class object, which is the *root* of the C# class hierarchy. Section 11.7 summarizes class object's methods. Method ToString returns a string representing an object. It's called *implicitly* by an app whenever an object must be converted to a string representation, such as in Console's Write method or string method Format using a format item. Class object's ToString method returns a string that includes the name of the object's class. It's primarily a placeholder that can be (and typically should be) *overridden* by a derived class to specify an appropriate string representation of the data in a derived class object. Method ToString of class CommissionEmployee overrides (redefines) class object's ToString method. When invoked, CommissionEmployee's ToString method uses string method Format to return a string containing information about the Commission-Employee. Line 97 uses the format specifier C (in "{6:C}") to format grossSales as currency and the format specifier F2 (in "{8:F2}") to format the commissionRate with two digits of precision to the right of the decimal point. To override a base-class method, a derived class must declare a method with keyword **override** and with the *same signature* (method name, number of parameters and parameter types) *and* return type as the base-class method—object's ToString method takes *no* parameters and returns type string, so CommissionEmployee declares ToString with the same parameter list and return type.

Common Programming Error 11.1

It's a compilation error to override a method with one that has a different access modifier. Overriding a method with a more restrictive access modifier would break the is-a relationship. If a public method could be overridden as a protected or private method, the derived-class objects would not be able to respond to the same method calls as base-class objects. Once a method is declared in a base class, the method must have the same access modifier for all that class's direct and indirect derived classes.

Class CommissionEmployeeTest

Figure 11.5 tests class CommissionEmployee. Lines 10–11 create a CommissionEmployee object and invoke its constructor (lines 14–23 of Fig. 11.4) to initialize it. We append the M suffix to the gross sales amount and the commission rate to indicate that the compiler should treat these as decimal literals, rather than doubles. Lines 16–22 use Commission-Employee's properties to retrieve the object's instance-variable values for output. Line 23 outputs the amount calculated by the Earnings method. Lines 25–26 invoke the set accessors of the object's GrossSales and CommissionRate properties to change the values of instance variables grossSales and commissionRate. Lines 28–29 output the string representation of the updated CommissionEmployee. When an object is output using a format item, the object's ToString method is invoked *implicitly* to obtain the object's string representation. Line 30 outputs the earnings again.

```
1   // Fig. 11.5: CommissionEmployeeTest.cs
2   // Testing class CommissionEmployee.
3   using System;
4
5   public class CommissionEmployeeTest
6   {
7      public static void Main( string[] args )
8      {
9         // instantiate CommissionEmployee object
10        CommissionEmployee employee = new CommissionEmployee( "Sue",
11           "Jones", "222-22-2222", 10000.00M, .06M );
12
13        // display CommissionEmployee data
14        Console.WriteLine(
15           "Employee information obtained by properties and methods: \n" );
16        Console.WriteLine( "First name is {0}", employee.FirstName );
17        Console.WriteLine( "Last name is {0}", employee.LastName );
```

Fig. 11.5 | Testing class CommissionEmployee. (Part 1 of 2.)

```
18            Console.WriteLine( "Social security number is {0}",
19               employee.SocialSecurityNumber );
20            Console.WriteLine( "Gross sales are {0:C}", employee.GrossSales );
21            Console.WriteLine( "Commission rate is {0:F2}",
22               employee.CommissionRate );
23            Console.WriteLine( "Earnings are {0:C}", employee.Earnings() );
24
25            employee.GrossSales = 5000.00M; // set gross sales
26            employee.CommissionRate = .1M; // set commission rate
27
28            Console.WriteLine( "\n{0}:\n\n{1}",
29               "Updated employee information obtained by ToString", employee );
30            Console.WriteLine( "earnings: {0:C}", employee.Earnings() );
31      } // end Main
32   } // end class CommissionEmployeeTest
```

```
Employee information obtained by properties and methods:

First name is Sue
Last name is Jones
Social security number is 222-22-2222
Gross sales are $10,000.00
Commission rate is 0.06
Earnings are $600.00

Updated employee information obtained by ToString:

commission employee: Sue Jones
social security number: 222-22-2222
gross sales: $5,000.00
commission rate: 0.10
earnings: $500.00
```

Fig. 11.5 | Testing class CommissionEmployee. (Part 2 of 2.)

11.4.2 Creating a BasePlusCommissionEmployee Class without Using Inheritance

We now discuss the second part of our introduction to inheritance by declaring and testing the (completely new and independent) class BasePlusCommissionEmployee (Fig. 11.6), which contains a first name, last name, social security number, gross sales amount, commission rate *and* base salary—"Base" in the class name stands for "base salary" not base class. Class BasePlusCommissionEmployee's public services include a BasePlusCommissionEmployee constructor (lines 16–26), methods Earnings (lines 113–116) and ToString (lines 119–127), and public properties (lines 30–110) for the class's private instance variables firstName, lastName, socialSecurityNumber, grossSales, commissionRate and baseSalary (declared in lines 8–13). These variables, properties and methods encapsulate all the necessary features of a base-salaried commission employee. Note the similarity between this class and class CommissionEmployee (Fig. 11.4)—in this example, *we do not yet exploit that similarity.*

Class BasePlusCommissionEmployee does *not* specify that it extends object with the syntax ": object" in line 6, so the class *implicitly* extends object. Also, like class CommissionEmployee's constructor (lines 14–23 of Fig. 11.4), class BasePlusCommissionEmployee's constructor invokes class object's default constructor *implicitly*, as noted in the comment in line 19 of Fig. 11.6.

```
1   // Fig. 11.6: BasePlusCommissionEmployee.cs
2   // BasePlusCommissionEmployee class represents an employee that receives
3   // a base salary in addition to a commission.
4   using System;
5
6   public class BasePlusCommissionEmployee
7   {
8      private string firstName;
9      private string lastName;
10     private string socialSecurityNumber;
11     private decimal grossSales; // gross weekly sales
12     private decimal commissionRate; // commission percentage
13     private decimal baseSalary; // base salary per week
14
15     // six-parameter constructor
16     public BasePlusCommissionEmployee( string first, string last,
17        string ssn, decimal sales, decimal rate, decimal salary )
18     {
19        // implicit call to object constructor occurs here
20        firstName = first;
21        lastName = last;
22        socialSecurityNumber = ssn;
23        GrossSales = sales; // validate gross sales via property
24        CommissionRate = rate; // validate commission rate via property
25        BaseSalary = salary; // validate base salary via property
26     } // end six-parameter BasePlusCommissionEmployee constructor
27
28     // read-only property that gets
29     // BasePlusCommissionEmployee's first name
30     public string FirstName
31     {
32        get
33        {
34           return firstName;
35        } // end get
36     } // end property FirstName
37
38     // read-only property that gets
39     // BasePlusCommissionEmployee's last name
40     public string LastName
41     {
42        get
43        {
44           return lastName;
45        } // end get
46     } // end property LastName
47
```

Fig. 11.6 | BasePlusCommissionEmployee class represents an employee that receives a base salary in addition to a commission. (Part 1 of 3.)

```
48        // read-only property that gets
49        // BasePlusCommissionEmployee's social security number
50        public string SocialSecurityNumber
51        {
52           get
53           {
54              return socialSecurityNumber;
55           } // end get
56        } // end property SocialSecurityNumber
57
58        // property that gets and sets
59        // BasePlusCommissionEmployee's gross sales
60        public decimal GrossSales
61        {
62           get
63           {
64              return grossSales;
65           } // end get
66           set
67           {
68              if ( value >= 0 )
69                 grossSales = value;
70              else
71                 throw new ArgumentOutOfRangeException(
72                    "GrossSales", value, "GrossSales must be >= 0" );
73           } // end set
74        } // end property GrossSales
75
76        // property that gets and sets
77        // BasePlusCommissionEmployee's commission rate
78        public decimal CommissionRate
79        {
80           get
81           {
82              return commissionRate;
83           } // end get
84           set
85           {
86              if ( value > 0 && value < 1 )
87                 commissionRate = value;
88              else
89                 throw new ArgumentOutOfRangeException( "CommissionRate",
90                    value, "CommissionRate must be > 0 and < 1" );
91           } // end set
92        } // end property CommissionRate
93
94        // property that gets and sets
95        // BasePlusCommissionEmployee's base salary
96        public decimal BaseSalary
97        {
98           get
99           {
```

Fig. 11.6 | BasePlusCommissionEmployee class represents an employee that receives a base salary in addition to a commission. (Part 2 of 3.)

```
100                return baseSalary;
101          } // end get
102          set
103          {
104             if ( value >= 0 )
105                baseSalary = value;
106             else
107                throw new ArgumentOutOfRangeException( "BaseSalary",
108                   value, "BaseSalary must be >= 0" );
109          } // end set
110       } // end property BaseSalary
111
112       // calculate earnings
113       public decimal Earnings()
114       {
115          return baseSalary + ( commissionRate * grossSales );
116       } // end method Earnings
117
118       // return string representation of BasePlusCommissionEmployee
119       public override string ToString()
120       {
121          return string.Format(
122             "{0}: {1} {2}\n{3}: {4}\n{5}: {6:C}\n{7}: {8:F2}\n{9}: {10:C}",
123             "base-salaried commission employee", firstName, lastName,
124             "social security number", socialSecurityNumber,
125             "gross sales", grossSales, "commission rate", commissionRate,
126             "base salary", baseSalary );
127       } // end method ToString
128    } // end class BasePlusCommissionEmployee
```

Fig. 11.6 | BasePlusCommissionEmployee class represents an employee that receives a base salary in addition to a commission. (Part 3 of 3.)

Class BasePlusCommissionEmployee's Earnings method (lines 113–116) computes the earnings of a base-salaried commission employee. Line 115 adds the employee's base salary to the product of the commission rate and the gross sales, and returns the result.

Class BasePlusCommissionEmployee overrides object method ToString to return a string containing the BasePlusCommissionEmployee's information (lines 119–127). Once again, we use format specifier C to format the gross sales and base salary as currency and format specifier F2 to format the commission rate with two digits of precision to the right of the decimal point (line 122).

Class BasePlusCommissionEmployeeTest

Figure 11.7 tests class BasePlusCommissionEmployee. Lines 10–12 instantiate a Base-PlusCommissionEmployee object and pass "Bob", "Lewis", "333-33-3333", 5000.00M, .04M and 300.00M to the constructor as the first name, last name, social security number, gross sales, commission rate and base salary, respectively. Lines 17–25 use BasePlusCommissionEmployee's properties and methods to retrieve the values of the object's instance variables and calculate the earnings for output. Line 27 invokes the object's BaseSalary property to *change* the base salary. Property BaseSalary's set accessor (Fig. 11.6, lines 102–109) ensures that instance variable baseSalary is not assigned a negative value, because an employee's base salary cannot be negative. Lines 29–30 of Fig. 11.7 invoke the object's ToString method *implicitly* to get the object's string representation.

```
 1   // Fig. 11.7: BasePlusCommissionEmployeeTest.cs
 2   // Testing class BasePlusCommissionEmployee.
 3   using System;
 4
 5   public class BasePlusCommissionEmployeeTest
 6   {
 7      public static void Main( string[] args )
 8      {
 9         // instantiate BasePlusCommissionEmployee object
10         BasePlusCommissionEmployee employee =
11            new BasePlusCommissionEmployee( "Bob", "Lewis",
12            "333-33-3333", 5000.00M, .04M, 300.00M );
13
14         // display BasePlusCommissionEmployee's data
15         Console.WriteLine(
16            "Employee information obtained by properties and methods: \n" );
17         Console.WriteLine( "First name is {0}", employee.FirstName );
18         Console.WriteLine( "Last name is {0}", employee.LastName );
19         Console.WriteLine( "Social security number is {0}",
20            employee.SocialSecurityNumber );
21         Console.WriteLine( "Gross sales are {0:C}", employee.GrossSales );
22         Console.WriteLine( "Commission rate is {0:F2}",
23            employee.CommissionRate );
24         Console.WriteLine( "Earnings are {0:C}", employee.Earnings() );
25         Console.WriteLine( "Base salary is {0:C}", employee.BaseSalary );
26
27         employee.BaseSalary = 1000.00M; // set base salary
28
29         Console.WriteLine( "\n{0}:\n\n{1}",
30            "Updated employee information obtained by ToString", employee );
31         Console.WriteLine( "earnings: {0:C}", employee.Earnings() );
32      } // end Main
33   } // end class BasePlusCommissionEmployeeTest
```

```
Employee information obtained by properties and methods:

First name is Bob
Last name is Lewis
Social security number is 333-33-3333
Gross sales are $5,000.00
Commission rate is 0.04
Earnings are $500.00
Base salary is $300.00

Updated employee information obtained by ToString:

base-salaried commission employee: Bob Lewis
social security number: 333-33-3333
gross sales: $5,000.00
commission rate: 0.04
base salary: $1,000.00
earnings: $1,200.00
```

Fig. 11.7 | Testing class BasePlusCommissionEmployee.

Much of the code for class BasePlusCommissionEmployee (Fig. 11.6) is similar, if not identical, to the code for class CommissionEmployee (Fig. 11.4). For example, in class Base-PlusCommissionEmployee, private instance variables firstName and lastName and properties FirstName and LastName are identical to those of class CommissionEmployee. Classes CommissionEmployee and BasePlusCommissionEmployee also both contain private instance variables socialSecurityNumber, commissionRate and grossSales, as well as properties to manipulate these variables. In addition, the BasePlusCommissionEmployee constructor is almost identical to that of class CommissionEmployee, except that Base-PlusCommissionEmployee's constructor also sets the baseSalary. The other additions to class BasePlusCommissionEmployee are private instance variable baseSalary and property BaseSalary. Class BasePlusCommissionEmployee's Earnings method is nearly identical to that of class CommissionEmployee, except that BasePlusCommissionEmployee's also adds the baseSalary. Similarly, class BasePlusCommissionEmployee's ToString method is nearly identical to that of class CommissionEmployee, except that BasePlusCommissionEmployee's ToString also formats the value of instance variable baseSalary as currency.

We literally *copied* the code from class CommissionEmployee and *pasted* it into class BasePlusCommissionEmployee, then modified class BasePlusCommissionEmployee to include a base salary and methods and properties that manipulate the base salary. This "copy-and-paste" approach is often error prone and time consuming. Worse yet, it can spread many physical copies of the same code throughout a system, creating a code-maintenance nightmare. Is there a way to "absorb" the members of one class in a way that makes them part of other classes without copying code? In the next several examples we answer this question, using a more elegant approach to building classes—namely, *inheritance*.

Error-Prevention Tip 11.1

Copying and pasting code from one class to another can spread errors across multiple source-code files. To avoid duplicating code (and possibly errors) in situations where you want one class to "absorb" the members of another class, use inheritance rather than the "copy-and-paste" approach.

Software Engineering Observation 11.3

With inheritance, the common members of all the classes in the hierarchy are declared in a base class. When changes are required for these common features, you need to make the changes only in the base class—derived classes then inherit the changes. Without inheritance, changes would need to be made to all the source-code files that contain a copy of the code in question.

11.4.3 Creating a CommissionEmployee– BasePlusCommissionEmployee Inheritance Hierarchy

Now we declare class BasePlusCommissionEmployee (Fig. 11.8), which extends class CommissionEmployee (Fig. 11.4). A BasePlusCommissionEmployee object *is a* CommissionEmployee (because inheritance passes on the capabilities of class CommissionEmployee), but class BasePlusCommissionEmployee also has instance variable baseSalary (Fig. 11.8, line 7). The colon (:) in line 5 of the class declaration indicates inheritance. As a derived class, BasePlusCommissionEmployee inherits the members of class CommissionEmployee and can access those members that are non-private. The constructor of class CommissionEmployee is *not* inherited. Thus, the public services of BasePlusCommissionEmployee include its constructor (lines 11–16), public methods and properties inherited from class Commission-Employee, property BaseSalary (lines 20–34), method Earnings (lines 37–41) and method ToString (lines 44–53).

```
1   // Fig. 11.8: BasePlusCommissionEmployee.cs
2   // BasePlusCommissionEmployee inherits from class CommissionEmployee.
3   using System;
4
5   public class BasePlusCommissionEmployee : CommissionEmployee
6   {
7      private decimal baseSalary; // base salary per week
8
9      // six-parameter derived-class constructor
10     // with call to base class CommissionEmployee constructor
11     public BasePlusCommissionEmployee( string first, string last,
12        string ssn, decimal sales, decimal rate, decimal salary )
13        : base( first, last, ssn, sales, rate )
14     {
15        BaseSalary = salary; // validate base salary via property
16     } // end six-parameter BasePlusCommissionEmployee constructor
17
18     // property that gets and sets
19     // BasePlusCommissionEmployee's base salary
20     public decimal BaseSalary
21     {
22        get
23        {
24           return baseSalary;
25        } // end get
26        set
27        {
28           if ( value >= 0 )
29              baseSalary = value;
30           else
31              throw new ArgumentOutOfRangeException( "BaseSalary",
32                 value, "BaseSalary must be >= 0" );
33        } // end set
34     } // end property BaseSalary
35
36     // calculate earnings
37     public override decimal Earnings()
38     {
39        // not allowed: commissionRate and grossSales private in base class
40        return baseSalary + ( commissionRate * grossSales );
41     } // end method Earnings
42
43     // return string representation of BasePlusCommissionEmployee
44     public override string ToString()
45     {
```

Fig. 11.8 | BasePlusCommissionEmployee inherits from class CommissionEmployee. (Part 1 of 2.)

```
46          // not allowed: attempts to access private base-class members
47          return string.Format(
48             "{0}: {1} {2}\n{3}: {4}\n{5}: {6:C}\n{7}: {8:F2}\n{9}: {10:C}",
49             "base-salaried commission employee", firstName, lastName,
50             "social security number", socialSecurityNumber,
51             "gross sales", grossSales, "commission rate", commissionRate,
52             "base salary", baseSalary );
53       } // end method ToString
54    } // end class BasePlusCommissionEmployee
```

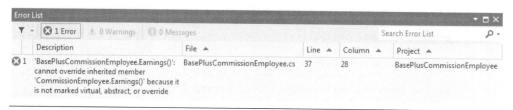

Fig. 11.8 | `BasePlusCommissionEmployee` inherits from class `CommissionEmployee`. (Part 2 of 2.)

A Derived Class's Constructor Must Call Its Base Class's Constructor

Each derived-class constructor *must* implicitly or explicitly call its base-class constructor to ensure that the instance variables inherited from the base class are initialized properly. `Base-PlusCommissionEmployee`'s six-parameter constructor explicitly calls class `CommissionEmployee`'s five-parameter constructor to initialize the `CommissionEmployee` portion of a `BasePlusCommissionEmployee` object—that is, the instance variables `firstName`, `lastName`, `socialSecurityNumber`, `grossSales` and `commissionRate`. Line 13 in the header of `Base-PlusCommissionEmployee`'s six-parameter constructor invokes the `CommissionEmployee`'s five-parameter constructor (declared at lines 14–23 of Fig. 11.4) by using a *constructor initializer*. In Section 10.5, we used constructor initializers with keyword `this` to call overloaded constructors in the *same* class. In line 13 of Fig. 11.8, we use a constructor initializer with keyword **base** to invoke the base-class constructor. The arguments `first`, `last`, `ssn`, `sales` and `rate` are used to initialize base-class members `firstName`, `lastName`, `socialSecurity-Number`, `grossSales` and `commissionRate`, respectively. If `BasePlusCommissionEmployee`'s constructor did not invoke `CommissionEmployee`'s constructor explicitly, C# would attempt to invoke class `CommissionEmployee`'s parameterless or default constructor *implicitly*—but the class does *not* have such a constructor, so the compiler would issue an error. When a base class contains a parameterless constructor, you can use `base()` in the constructor initializer to call that constructor explicitly, but this is rarely done.

Common Programming Error 11.2

A compilation error occurs if a derived-class constructor calls one of its base-class constructors with arguments that do not match the number and types of parameters specified in one of the base-class constructor declarations.

BasePlusCommissionEmployee Method Earnings

Lines 37–41 of Fig. 11.8 declare method `Earnings` using keyword `override` to override the `CommissionEmployee`'s `Earnings` method, as we did with method `ToString` in previous examples. Line 37 causes a compilation error indicating that we cannot override the base class's Earnings method because it was not explicitly "marked virtual, abstract, or override." The **virtual** and **abstract** keywords indicate that a base-class method can be overridden in derived classes. (As you'll learn in Section 12.4, abstract methods are *implicitly virtual*.) The override modifier declares that a derived-class method overrides a virtual or abstract base-class method. This modifier also *implicitly* declares the derived-class method virtual and allows it to be overridden in derived classes further down the inheritance hierarchy.

If we add the keyword virtual to method Earnings' declaration in Fig. 11.4 and recompile, other compilation errors appear (Fig. 11.9). The compiler generates additional errors for line 40 of Fig. 11.8 because base class CommissionEmployee's instance variables commissionRate and grossSales are private—derived class BasePlusCommissionEmployee's methods are not allowed to access base class CommissionEmployee's private instance variables. The compiler issues additional errors at lines 49–51 of BasePlusCommissionEmployee's ToString method for the same reason. The errors in BasePlusCommissionEmployee could have been prevented by using the public properties inherited from class CommissionEmployee. For example, line 40 could have invoked the get accessors of properties CommissionRate and GrossSales to access CommissionEmployee's private instance variables commissionRate and grossSales, respectively. Lines 49–51 also could have used appropriate properties to retrieve the values of the base class's instance variables.

	Description	File ▲	Line ▲	Column ▲	Project ▲
⊗ 1	'CommissionEmployee.commissionRate' is inaccessible due to its protection level	BasePlusCommissionEmployee.cs	40	29	BasePlusCommissionEmployee
⊗ 2	'CommissionEmployee.grossSales' is inaccessible due to its protection level	BasePlusCommissionEmployee.cs	40	46	BasePlusCommissionEmployee
⊗ 3	'CommissionEmployee.firstName' is inaccessible due to its protection level	BasePlusCommissionEmployee.cs	49	47	BasePlusCommissionEmployee
⊗ 4	'CommissionEmployee.lastName' is inaccessible due to its protection level	BasePlusCommissionEmployee.cs	49	58	BasePlusCommissionEmployee
⊗ 5	'CommissionEmployee.socialSecurityNumber' is inaccessible due to its protection level	BasePlusCommissionEmployee.cs	50	36	BasePlusCommissionEmployee
⊗ 6	'CommissionEmployee.grossSales' is inaccessible due to its protection level	BasePlusCommissionEmployee.cs	51	25	BasePlusCommissionEmployee
⊗ 7	'CommissionEmployee.commissionRate' is inaccessible due to its protection level	BasePlusCommissionEmployee.cs	51	56	BasePlusCommissionEmployee

Fig. 11.9 | Compilation errors generated by BasePlusCommissionEmployee (Fig. 11.8) after declaring the Earnings method in Fig. 11.4 with keyword virtual.

11.4.4 CommissionEmployee–BasePlusCommissionEmployee Inheritance Hierarchy Using protected Instance Variables

To enable class BasePlusCommissionEmployee to directly access base-class instance variables firstName, lastName, socialSecurityNumber, grossSales and commissionRate, we can declare those members as protected in the base class. As we discussed in Section 11.3, a base class's protected members *are* inherited by all derived classes of that base class. Class CommissionEmployee in this example is a modification of the version from Fig. 11.4 that declares its instance variables firstName, lastName, socialSecurityNumber, grossSales and commissionRate as protected rather than private. We also declare the Earnings method virtual as in

> **public virtual decimal** Earnings()

so that BasePlusCommissionEmployee can override the method. The rest of the class declaration in this example is identical to that of Fig. 11.4. The complete source code for class CommissionEmployee is included in this example's project.

public vs. protected Data

We could have declared base class CommissionEmployee's instance variables firstName, lastName, socialSecurityNumber, grossSales and commissionRate as public to enable derived class BasePlusCommissionEmployee to access the base-class instance variables. However, declaring public instance variables is poor software engineering, because it allows unrestricted access to the instance variables, greatly increasing the chance of errors. With protected instance variables, the derived class gets access to the instance variables, but classes that are not derived from the base class cannot access its variables directly.

Class BasePlusCommissionEmployee

Class BasePlusCommissionEmployee (Fig. 11.10) in this example extends the version of class CommissionEmployee with protected data rather than the one with private data in Fig. 11.4. Each BasePlusCommissionEmployee object inherits CommissionEmployee's protected instance variables firstName, lastName, socialSecurityNumber, grossSales and commissionRate—all these variables are now protected members of BasePlusCommissionEmployee. As a result, the compiler does *not* generate errors when compiling line 40 of method Earnings and lines 48–50 of method ToString. If another class extends BasePlusCommissionEmployee, the new derived class also inherits the protected members.

Class BasePlusCommissionEmployee does *not* inherit class CommissionEmployee's constructor. However, class BasePlusCommissionEmployee's six-parameter constructor (lines 12–17) calls class CommissionEmployee's five-parameter constructor with a constructor initializer. BasePlusCommissionEmployee's six-parameter constructor must *explicitly* call the five-parameter constructor of class CommissionEmployee, because CommissionEmployee does *not* provide a parameterless constructor that could be invoked implicitly.

```
1   // Fig. 11.10: BasePlusCommissionEmployee.cs
2   // BasePlusCommissionEmployee inherits from CommissionEmployee and has
3   // access to CommissionEmployee's protected members.
4   using System;
5
6   public class BasePlusCommissionEmployee : CommissionEmployee
7   {
8      private decimal baseSalary; // base salary per week
9
```

Fig. 11.10 | BasePlusCommissionEmployee inherits from CommissionEmployee and has access to CommissionEmployee's protected members. (Part 1 of 2.)

```
10    // six-parameter derived-class constructor
11    // with call to base class CommissionEmployee constructor
12    public BasePlusCommissionEmployee( string first, string last,
13       string ssn, decimal sales, decimal rate, decimal salary )
14       : base( first, last, ssn, sales, rate )
15    {
16       BaseSalary = salary; // validate base salary via property
17    } // end six-parameter BasePlusCommissionEmployee constructor
18
19    // property that gets and sets
20    // BasePlusCommissionEmployee's base salary
21    public decimal BaseSalary
22    {
23       get
24       {
25          return baseSalary;
26       } // end get
27       set
28       {
29          if ( value >= 0 )
30             baseSalary = value;
31          else
32             throw new ArgumentOutOfRangeException( "BaseSalary",
33                value, "BaseSalary must be >= 0" );
34       } // end set
35    } // end property BaseSalary
36
37    // calculate earnings
38    public override decimal Earnings()
39    {
40       return baseSalary + ( commissionRate * grossSales );
41    } // end method Earnings
42
43    // return string representation of BasePlusCommissionEmployee
44    public override string ToString()
45    {
46       return string.Format(
47          "{0}: {1} {2}\n{3}: {4}\n{5}: {6:C}\n{7}: {8:F2}\n{9}: {10:C}",
48          "base-salaried commission employee", firstName, lastName,
49          "social security number", socialSecurityNumber,
50          "gross sales", grossSales, "commission rate", commissionRate,
51          "base salary", baseSalary );
52    } // end method ToString
53 } // end class BasePlusCommissionEmployee
```

Fig. 11.10 | BasePlusCommissionEmployee inherits from CommissionEmployee and has access to CommissionEmployee's protected members. (Part 2 of 2.)

Class *BasePlusCommissionEmployeeTest*

Figure 11.11 uses a BasePlusCommissionEmployee object to perform the *same* tasks that Fig. 11.7 performed on the version of the class from Fig. 11.6. The outputs of the two apps are identical. Although we declared the version of the class in Fig. 11.6 without using inheritance and declared the version in Fig. 11.10 using inheritance, both classes provide the same functionality. The source code in Fig. 11.10 (which is 53 lines) is considerably *shorter* than the version in Fig. 11.6 (which is 128 lines), because the new class inherits most of its functionality from CommissionEmployee, whereas the version in Fig. 11.6 inherits only class object's functionality. Also, there's now only *one* copy of the commission-employee functionality declared in class CommissionEmployee. This makes the code easier to maintain, modify and debug, because the code related to a commission employee exists *only* in class CommissionEmployee.

```
1   // Fig. 11.11: BasePlusCommissionEmployee.cs
2   // Testing class BasePlusCommissionEmployee.
3   using System;
4
5   public class BasePlusCommissionEmployeeTest
6   {
7      public static void Main( string[] args )
8      {
9         // instantiate BasePlusCommissionEmployee object
10        BasePlusCommissionEmployee basePlusCommissionEmployee =
11           new BasePlusCommissionEmployee( "Bob", "Lewis",
12           "333-33-3333", 5000.00M, .04M, 300.00M );
13
14        // display BasePlusCommissionEmployee's data
15        Console.WriteLine(
16           "Employee information obtained by properties and methods: \n" );
17        Console.WriteLine( "First name is {0}",
18           basePlusCommissionEmployee.FirstName );
19        Console.WriteLine( "Last name is {0}",
20           basePlusCommissionEmployee.LastName );
21        Console.WriteLine( "Social security number is {0}",
22           basePlusCommissionEmployee.SocialSecurityNumber );
23        Console.WriteLine( "Gross sales are {0:C}",
24           basePlusCommissionEmployee.GrossSales );
25        Console.WriteLine( "Commission rate is {0:F2}",
26           basePlusCommissionEmployee.CommissionRate );
27        Console.WriteLine( "Earnings are {0:C}",
28           basePlusCommissionEmployee.Earnings() );
29        Console.WriteLine( "Base salary is {0:C}",
30           basePlusCommissionEmployee.BaseSalary );
31
32        basePlusCommissionEmployee.BaseSalary = 1000.00M; // set base salary
33
34        Console.WriteLine( "\n{0}:\n\n{1}",
35           "Updated employee information obtained by ToString",
36           basePlusCommissionEmployee );
37        Console.WriteLine( "earnings: {0:C}",
38           basePlusCommissionEmployee.Earnings() );
39     } // end Main
40  } // end class BasePlusCommissionEmployeeTest
```

Fig. 11.11 | Testing class BasePlusCommissionEmployee. (Part 1 of 2.)

```
Employee information obtained by properties and methods:

First name is Bob
Last name is Lewis
Social security number is 333-33-3333
Gross sales are $5,000.00
Commission rate is 0.04
Earnings are $500.00
Base salary is $300.00

Updated employee information obtained by ToString:

base-salaried commission employee: Bob Lewis
social security number: 333-33-3333
gross sales: $5,000.00
commission rate: 0.04
base salary: $1,000.00
earnings: $1,200.00
```

Fig. 11.11 | Testing class `BasePlusCommissionEmployee`. (Part 2 of 2.)

Problems with **protected** *Instance Variables*

In this example, we declared base-class instance variables as `protected` so that derived classes could access them. Inheriting `protected` instance variables enables you to directly access the variables in the derived class *without* invoking the `set` or `get` accessors of the corresponding property, thus violating encapsulation. In most cases, it's better to use `private` instance variables to encourage proper software engineering. Your code will be easier to maintain, modify and debug.

Using `protected` instance variables creates several potential problems. First, since the derived-class object can set an inherited variable's value directly *without* using a property's set accessor, a derived-class object can assign an *invalid* value to the variable. For example, if we were to declare `CommissionEmployee`'s instance variable `grossSales` as `protected`, a derived-class object (e.g., `BasePlusCommissionEmployee`) could then assign a *negative* value to `grossSales`. The second problem with using `protected` instance variables is that derived-class methods are more likely to be written to *depend* on the base class's data implementation. In practice, derived classes should depend only on the base-class *services* (i.e., non-`private` methods and properties) and *not* on the base-class data implementation. With `protected` instance variables in the base class, we may need to modify all the derived classes of the base class if the base-class implementation changes. For example, if for some reason we were to change the names of instance variables `firstName` and `lastName` to `first` and `last`, then we would have to do so for all occurrences in which a derived class directly references base-class instance variables `firstName` and `lastName`. In such a case, the software is said to be **fragile** or **brittle**, because a small change in the base class can "break" derived-class implementation. You should be able to *change* the base-class *implementation* while still providing the *same services* to the derived classes. Of course, if the base-class services change, we must reimplement our derived classes.

Software Engineering Observation 11.4

Declaring base-class instance variables private *(as opposed to* protected*) enables the base-class implementation of these instance variables to change without affecting derived-class implementations.*

II.4.5 CommissionEmployee–BasePlusCommissionEmployee Inheritance Hierarchy Using private Instance Variables

We now reexamine our hierarchy once more, this time using the best software engineering practices. Class CommissionEmployee (Fig. 11.12) declares instance variables firstName, lastName, socialSecurityNumber, grossSales and commissionRate as private (lines 7–11) and provides public properties FirstName, LastName, SocialSecurityNumber, GrossSales and CommissionRate for manipulating these values. Methods Earnings (lines 88–91) and ToString (lines 94–101) use the class's *properties* to obtain the values of its instance variables. If we decide to change the instance-variable names, the Earnings and ToString declarations will *not* require modification—only the bodies of the properties that directly manipulate the instance variables will need to change. These changes occur solely within the base class—no changes to the derived class are needed. Localizing the effects of changes like this is a good software engineering practice. Derived class BasePlusCommissionEmployee (Fig. 11.13) inherits from CommissionEmployee's and can access the private base-class members via the inherited public properties.

```
1    // Fig. 11.12: CommissionEmployee.cs
2    // CommissionEmployee class represents a commission employee.
3    using System;
4
5    public class CommissionEmployee
6    {
7       private string firstName;
8       private string lastName;
9       private string socialSecurityNumber;
10      private decimal grossSales; // gross weekly sales
11      private decimal commissionRate; // commission percentage
12
13      // five-parameter constructor
14      public CommissionEmployee( string first, string last, string ssn,
15         decimal sales, decimal rate )
16      {
17         // implicit call to object constructor occurs here
18         firstName = first;
19         lastName = last;
20         socialSecurityNumber = ssn;
21         GrossSales = sales; // validate gross sales via property
22         CommissionRate = rate; // validate commission rate via property
23      } // end five-parameter CommissionEmployee constructor
24
25      // read-only property that gets commission employee's first name
26      public string FirstName
27      {
28         get
29         {
30            return firstName;
31         } // end get
32      } // end property FirstName
33
```

Fig. II.12 | CommissionEmployee class represents a commission employee. (Part I of 3.)

```
34        // read-only property that gets commission employee's last name
35        public string LastName
36        {
37           get
38           {
39              return lastName;
40           } // end get
41        } // end property LastName
42
43        // read-only property that gets
44        // commission employee's social security number
45        public string SocialSecurityNumber
46        {
47           get
48           {
49              return socialSecurityNumber;
50           } // end get
51        } // end property SocialSecurityNumber
52
53        // property that gets and sets commission employee's gross sales
54        public decimal GrossSales
55        {
56           get
57           {
58              return grossSales;
59           } // end get
60           set
61           {
62              if ( value >= 0 )
63                 grossSales = value;
64              else
65                 throw new ArgumentOutOfRangeException(
66                    "GrossSales", value, "GrossSales must be >= 0" );
67           } // end set
68        } // end property GrossSales
69
70        // property that gets and sets commission employee's commission rate
71        public decimal CommissionRate
72        {
73           get
74           {
75              return commissionRate;
76           } // end get
77           set
78           {
79              if ( value > 0 && value < 1 )
80                 commissionRate = value;
81              else
82                 throw new ArgumentOutOfRangeException( "CommissionRate",
83                    value, "CommissionRate must be > 0 and < 1" );
84           } // end set
85        } // end property CommissionRate
86
```

Fig. 11.12 | `CommissionEmployee` class represents a commission employee. (Part 2 of 3.)

```
87      // calculate commission employee's pay
88      public virtual decimal Earnings()
89      {
90         return CommissionRate * GrossSales;
91      } // end method Earnings
92
93      // return string representation of CommissionEmployee object
94      public override string ToString()
95      {
96         return string.Format(
97            "{0}: {1} {2}\n{3}: {4}\n{5}: {6:C}\n{7}: {8:F2}",
98            "commission employee", FirstName, LastName,
99            "social security number", SocialSecurityNumber,
100           "gross sales", GrossSales, "commission rate", CommissionRate );
101     } // end method ToString
102 } // end class CommissionEmployee
```

Fig. 11.12 | CommissionEmployee class represents a commission employee. (Part 3 of 3.)

Class BasePlusCommissionEmployee (Fig. 11.13) has several changes to its method implementations that distinguish it from the version in Fig. 11.10. Methods Earnings (Fig. 11.13, lines 39–42) and ToString (lines 45–49) each invoke property BaseSalary's get accessor to obtain the base-salary value, rather than accessing baseSalary directly. If we decide to rename instance variable baseSalary, only the body of property BaseSalary will need to change.

```
1     // Fig. 11.13: BasePlusCommissionEmployee.cs
2     // BasePlusCommissionEmployee inherits from CommissionEmployee and has
3     // access to CommissionEmployee's private data via
4     // its public properties.
5     using System;
6
7     public class BasePlusCommissionEmployee : CommissionEmployee
8     {
9        private decimal baseSalary; // base salary per week
10
11       // six-parameter derived class constructor
12       // with call to base class CommissionEmployee constructor
13       public BasePlusCommissionEmployee( string first, string last,
14          string ssn, decimal sales, decimal rate, decimal salary )
15          : base( first, last, ssn, sales, rate )
16       {
17          BaseSalary = salary; // validate base salary via property
18       } // end six-parameter BasePlusCommissionEmployee constructor
19
20       // property that gets and sets
21       // BasePlusCommissionEmployee's base salary
22       public decimal BaseSalary
23       {
```

Fig. 11.13 | BasePlusCommissionEmployee inherits from CommissionEmployee and has access to CommissionEmployee's private data via its public properties. (Part 1 of 2.)

```
24          get
25          {
26             return baseSalary;
27          } // end get
28          set
29          {
30             if ( value >= 0 )
31                baseSalary = value;
32             else
33                throw new ArgumentOutOfRangeException( "BaseSalary",
34                   value, "BaseSalary must be >= 0" );
35          } // end set
36       } // end property BaseSalary
37
38       // calculate earnings
39       public override decimal Earnings()
40       {
41          return BaseSalary + base.Earnings();
42       } // end method Earnings
43
44       // return string representation of BasePlusCommissionEmployee
45       public override string ToString()
46       {
47          return string.Format( "base-salaried {0}\nbase salary: {1:C}",
48             base.ToString(), BaseSalary );
49       } // end method ToString
50    } // end class BasePlusCommissionEmployee
```

Fig. 11.13 | BasePlusCommissionEmployee inherits from CommissionEmployee and has access to CommissionEmployee's private data via its public properties. (Part 2 of 2.)

BasePlusCommissionEmployee *Method Earnings*

Class BasePlusCommissionEmployee's Earnings method (Fig. 11.13, lines 39–42) overrides class CommissionEmployee's Earnings method (Fig. 11.12, lines 88–91) to calculate the earnings of a BasePlusCommissionEmployee. The new version obtains the portion of the employee's earnings based on commission alone by calling CommissionEmployee's Earnings method with the expression base.Earnings() (Fig. 11.13, line 41), then adds the base salary to this value to calculate the total earnings of the employee. Note the syntax used to invoke an overridden base-class method from a derived class—place the keyword base and the member access (.) operator before the base-class method name. This method invocation is a good software engineering practice—by having BasePlusCommissionEmployee's Earnings method invoke CommissionEmployee's Earnings method to calculate part of a BasePlusCommissionEmployee object's earnings, we avoid duplicating the code and reduce code-maintenance problems.

Common Programming Error 11.3

When a base-class method is overridden in a derived class, the derived-class version often calls the base-class version to do a portion of the work. Failure to prefix the base-class method name with the keyword base and the member access (.) operator when referencing the base class's method from the derived-class version causes the derived-class method to call itself, creating infinite recursion.

BasePlusCommissionEmployee Method ToString

Similarly, BasePlusCommissionEmployee's ToString method (Fig. 11.13, lines 45–49) overrides CommissionEmployee's (Fig. 11.12, lines 94–101) to return a string representation that's appropriate for a base-salaried commission employee. The new version creates part of BasePlusCommissionEmployee string representation (i.e., the string "commission employee" and the values of CommissionEmployee's private instance variables) by calling CommissionEmployee's ToString method with the expression base.ToString() (Fig. 11.13, line 48). The derived class's ToString method then outputs the remainder of the object's string representation (i.e., the base salary).

Class BasePlusCommissionEmployeeTest

Figure 11.14 performs the same manipulations on a BasePlusCommissionEmployee object as did Figs. 11.7 and 11.11. Although each "base-salaried commission employee" class behaves identically, the BasePlusCommissionEmployee in this example is the best engineered. *By using inheritance and by using properties that hide the data and ensure consistency, we have efficiently and effectively constructed a well-engineered class.*

```
1   // Fig. 11.14: BasePlusCommissionEmployeeTest.cs
2   // Testing class BasePlusCommissionEmployee.
3   using System;
4
5   public class BasePlusCommissionEmployeeTest
6   {
7      public static void Main( string[] args )
8      {
9         // instantiate BasePlusCommissionEmployee object
10        BasePlusCommissionEmployee employee =
11           new BasePlusCommissionEmployee( "Bob", "Lewis",
12           "333-33-3333", 5000.00M, .04M, 300.00M );
13
14        // display BasePlusCommissionEmployee's data
15        Console.WriteLine(
16           "Employee information obtained by properties and methods: \n" );
17        Console.WriteLine( "First name is {0}", employee.FirstName );
18        Console.WriteLine( "Last name is {0}", employee.LastName );
19        Console.WriteLine( "Social security number is {0}",
20           employee.SocialSecurityNumber );
21        Console.WriteLine( "Gross sales are {0:C}", employee.GrossSales );
22        Console.WriteLine( "Commission rate is {0:F2}",
23           employee.CommissionRate );
24        Console.WriteLine( "Earnings are {0:C}", employee.Earnings() );
25        Console.WriteLine( "Base salary is {0:C}", employee.BaseSalary );
26
27        employee.BaseSalary = 1000.00M; // set base salary
28
29        Console.WriteLine( "\n{0}:\n\n{1}",
30           "Updated employee information obtained by ToString", employee );
31        Console.WriteLine( "earnings: {0:C}", employee.Earnings() );
32     } // end Main
33  } // end class BasePlusCommissionEmployeeTest
```

Fig. 11.14 | Testing class BasePlusCommissionEmployee. (Part 1 of 2.)

```
Employee information obtained by properties and methods:

First name is Bob
Last name is Lewis
Social security number is 333-33-3333
Gross sales are $5,000.00
Commission rate is 0.04
Earnings are $500.00
Base salary is $300.00

Updated employee information obtained by ToString:

base-salaried commission employee: Bob Lewis
social security number: 333-33-3333
gross sales: $5,000.00
commission rate: 0.04
base salary: $1,000.00
earnings: $1,200.00
```

Fig. 11.14 | Testing class `BasePlusCommissionEmployee`. (Part 2 of 2.)

In this section, you saw an evolutionary set of examples that was carefully designed to teach key capabilities for good software engineering with inheritance. You learned how to create a derived class using inheritance, how to use `protected` base-class members to enable a derived class to access inherited base-class instance variables and how to override base-class methods to provide versions that are more appropriate for derived-class objects. In addition, you applied effective software engineering techniques from Chapter 4, Chapter 10 and this chapter to create classes that are easy to maintain, modify and debug.

11.5 Constructors in Derived Classes

As we explained in the preceding section, instantiating a derived-class object begins a chain of constructor calls. The derived-class constructor, before performing its own tasks, invokes its direct base class's constructor either explicitly (via a constructor initializer with the `base` reference) or implicitly (calling the base class's default constructor or parameterless constructor). Similarly, if the base class is derived from another class (as every class except `object` is), the base-class constructor invokes the constructor of the next class up in the hierarchy, and so on. The *last* constructor called in the chain is always the constructor for class `object`. The original derived-class constructor's body finishes executing last. Each base class's constructor manipulates the base-class instance variables that the derived-class object inherits. For example, consider again the `CommissionEmployee`–`BasePlusCommissionEmployee` hierarchy from Figs. 11.12 and 11.13. When an app creates a `BasePlusCommissionEmployee` object, the `BasePlusCommissionEmployee` constructor is called. That constructor immediately calls `CommissionEmployee`'s constructor, which in turn immediately calls `object`'s constructor implicitly. Class `object`'s constructor has an empty body, so it immediately returns control to `CommissionEmployee`'s constructor, which then initializes the `private` instance variables of `CommissionEmployee` that are part of the `BasePlusCommissionEmployee` object. When `CommissionEmployee`'s constructor completes execution, it returns control to `BasePlusCommissionEmployee`'s constructor, which initializes the `BasePlusCommissionEmployee` object's `baseSalary`.

11.6 Software Engineering with Inheritance

This section discusses customizing existing software with inheritance. When a new class extends an existing class, the new class inherits the members of the existing class. We can customize the new class to meet our needs by including additional members and by overriding base-class members. Doing this does *not* require the derived-class programmer to change the base class's source code. C# simply requires access to the compiled base-class code, so it can compile and execute any app that uses or extends the base class. This powerful capability is attractive to independent software vendors (ISVs), who can develop proprietary classes for sale or license and make them available to users in class libraries. Users then can derive new classes from these library classes rapidly, without accessing the ISVs' proprietary source code.

Software Engineering Observation 11.5

Although inheriting from a class does not require access to the class's source code, developers often insist on seeing the source code to understand how the class is implemented. They may, for example, want to ensure that they're extending a class that performs well and is implemented securely.

People experienced with large-scale software projects in industry projects say that effective software reuse improves the software-development process. Object-oriented programming facilitates software reuse, potentially shortening development time. The availability of substantial and useful class libraries helps deliver the maximum benefits of software reuse through inheritance.

Software Engineering Observation 11.6

At the design stage in an object-oriented system, the designer often finds that certain classes are closely related. The designer should "factor out" common members and place them in a base class. Then the designer should use inheritance to develop derived classes, specializing them with capabilities beyond those inherited from the base class.

Software Engineering Observation 11.7

Declaring a derived class does not affect its base class's source code. Inheritance preserves the integrity of the base class.

Reading derived-class declarations can be confusing, because inherited members are not declared explicitly in the derived classes, but are nevertheless present in them. A similar problem exists in documenting derived-class members.

11.7 Class object

As we discussed earlier in this chapter, all classes inherit directly or indirectly from the object class (System.Object in the Framework Class Library), so its seven methods are inherited by *all* classes. Figure 11.15 summarizes object's methods. You can learn more about object's methods at:

msdn.microsoft.com/en-us/library/system.object.aspx

Method	Description
Equals	This method compares two objects for equality and returns `true` if they're equal and `false` otherwise. It takes any object as an argument. When objects of a particular class must be compared for equality, the class should override method `Equals` to compare the *contents* of the two objects. The following website explains the requirements for a properly overridden `Equals` method: `http://bit.ly/OverridingEqualsCSharp`
Finalize	This method cannot be explicitly declared or called. When a class contains a destructor, the compiler implicitly renames it to override the `protected` method `Finalize`, which is called *only* by the garbage collector before it reclaims an object's memory. The garbage collector is not guaranteed to reclaim an object, thus it's *not* guaranteed that an object's `Finalize` method will execute. When a derived class's `Finalize` method executes, it performs its task, then invokes the base class's `Finalize` method. In general, you should avoid using `Finalize`.
GetHashCode	A hashtable data structure relates objects, called *keys*, to corresponding objects, called *values*. We discuss `Hashtable` in Chapter 19, Collections. When a value is initially inserted in a hashtable, the key's `GetHashCode` method is called. The value returned is used by the hashtable to determine the location at which to insert the corresponding value. The key's hashcode is also used by the hashtable to locate the key's corresponding value.
GetType	Every object knows its own type at execution time. Method `GetType` (used in Section 12.5) returns an object of class `Type` (namespace `System`) that contains information about the object's type, such as its class name (obtained from `Type` property `FullName`).
Memberwise-Clone	This `protected` method, which takes no arguments and returns an `object` reference, makes a copy of the object on which it's called. The implementation of this method performs a **shallow copy**—instance-variable values in one object are copied into another object of the same type. For reference types, only the references are copied.
Reference-Equals	This `static` method receives two `object` references and returns `true` if they're the same instance or if they're `null` references. Otherwise, it returns `false`.
ToString	This method (introduced in Section 7.4) returns a `string` representation of an object. The default implementation of this method returns the namespace followed by a dot and the class name of the object's class.

Fig. 11.15 | `object` methods that are inherited directly or indirectly by all classes.

11.8 Wrap-Up

This chapter introduced inheritance—the ability to create classes by absorbing an existing class's members and enhancing them with new capabilities. You learned the notions of base classes and derived classes and created a derived class that inherits members from a base class. The chapter introduced access modifier `protected`; derived-class members can access `protected` base-class members. You learned how to access base-class members with base. You also saw how constructors are used in inheritance hierarchies. Finally, you learned about the methods of class object, the direct or indirect base class of *all* classes.

In Chapter 12, we build on our discussion of inheritance by introducing polymorphism—an object-oriented concept that enables us to write apps that handle, in a more general manner, objects of a wide variety of classes related by inheritance. After studying Chapter 12, you'll be familiar with classes, objects, encapsulation, inheritance and polymorphism—the most essential aspects of object-oriented programming.

OOP: Polymorphism, Interfaces and Operator Overloading

12.1 Introduction

We now continue our study of object-oriented programming by explaining and demonstrating **polymorphism** with inheritance hierarchies. Polymorphism enables us to *program in the general* rather than *program in the specific*. In particular, polymorphism enables us to write apps that process objects that share the *same* base class in a class hierarchy as if they were all objects of the base class.

Let's consider a polymorphism example. Suppose we create an app that simulates moving several types of animals for a biological study. Classes Fish, Frog and Bird represent the types of animals under investigation. Imagine that each class extends base class Animal, which contains a method Move and maintains an animal's current location as *x*–*y*–*z* coordinates. Each derived class implements method Move. Our app maintains an array of references to objects of the various Animal-derived classes. To simulate an animal's movements, the app sends each object the *same* message once per second—namely, Move. Each specific type of Animal responds to a Move message in a unique way—a Fish might swim three feet, a Frog might jump five feet and a Bird might fly 10 feet. The app issues the Move message to each animal object *generically*, but each object modifies its *x*–*y*–*z* coordinates appropriately for its *specific* type of movement. Relying on each object to "do the right thing" in response to the *same* method call is the key concept of polymorphism. The *same* message (in this case, Move) sent to a *variety* of objects has *many forms* of results—hence the term polymorphism.

Systems Are Easy to Extend

With polymorphism, we can design and implement systems that are easily *extensible*—new classes can be added with little or no modification to the general portions of the app, as long as the new classes are part of the inheritance hierarchy that the app processes generically. The only parts of an app that must be altered to accommodate new classes are those that require direct knowledge of the new classes that you add to the hierarchy. For example, if we extend class Animal to create class Tortoise (which might respond to a Move message by crawling one inch), we need to write only the Tortoise class and the part of the simulation that instantiates a Tortoise object. The portions of the simulation that process each Animal generically can remain the *same*.

This chapter has several parts. First, we discuss common examples of polymorphism. We then provide a live-code example demonstrating polymorphic behavior. As you'll soon see, you'll use base-class references to manipulate both base-class objects *and* derived-class objects polymorphically.

Polymorphic Employee Inheritance Hierarchy

We then present a case study that revisits the Employee hierarchy of Section 11.4.5. We develop a simple payroll app that polymorphically calculates the weekly pay of several different types of employees using each employee's Earnings method. Though the earnings of each type of employee are calculated in a specific way, polymorphism allows us to process the employees "in the general." In the case study, we enlarge the hierarchy to include two new classes—SalariedEmployee (for people paid a fixed weekly salary) and HourlyEmployee (for people paid an hourly salary and "time-and-a-half" for overtime). We declare a *common set of functionality* for all the classes in the updated hierarchy in an *abstract* class, Employee (Section 12.5.1), from which classes SalariedEmployee, HourlyEmployee and CommissionEmployee *inherit directly* and class BasePlusCommissionEmployee *inherits indirectly*. As you'll soon see, when we invoke each employee's Earnings method via a base-class Employee reference, the correct earnings calculation is performed due to C#'s polymorphic capabilities.

Determining the Type of an Object at Execution Time

Occasionally, when performing polymorphic processing, we need to program "in the specific." Our Employee case study demonstrates that an app can determine the type of an object at *execution* time and act on that object accordingly. In the case study, we use these capabilities to determine whether a particular employee object *is a* BasePlusCommissionEmployee. If so, we increase that employee's base salary by 10%.

Interfaces

The chapter continues with an introduction to C# interfaces. An interface describes a set of methods and properties that can be called on an object, but does *not* provide *concrete* implementations for them. You can declare classes that **implement** (i.e., provide *concrete* implementations for the methods and properties of) one or more interfaces. Each interface member must be defined for *all* the classes that implement the interface. Once a class implements an interface, all objects of that class have an *is-a* relationship with the interface type, and all objects of the class are *guaranteed* to provide the functionality described by the interface. This is true of all *derived* classes of that class as well.

Interfaces are particularly useful for assigning common functionality to possibly *unrelated* classes. This allows objects of unrelated classes to be processed polymorphically—

objects of classes that implement the *same* interface can respond to the *same* method calls. To demonstrate creating and using interfaces, we modify our payroll app to create a general accounts-payable app that can calculate payments due for the earnings of company employees and for invoice amounts to be billed for purchased goods. As you'll see, interfaces enable polymorphic capabilities similar to those enabled by inheritance.

Operator Overloading

This chapter ends with an introduction to operator overloading. In previous chapters, we declared our own classes and used methods to perform tasks on objects of those classes. Operator overloading allows us to define the behavior of the built-in operators, such as +, – and <, when used on objects of our own classes. This provides a much more convenient notation than calling methods for performing certain tasks on objects.

12.2 Polymorphism Examples

Let's consider several additional examples of polymorphism.

Quadrilateral *Inheritance Hierarchy*

If class Rectangle is derived from class Quadrilateral (a four-sided shape), then a Rectangle *is a* more specific version of a Quadrilateral. Any operation (e.g., calculating the perimeter or the area) that can be performed on a Quadrilateral object can also be performed on a Rectangle object. These operations also can be performed on other Quadrilaterals, such as Squares, Parallelograms and Trapezoids. The polymorphism occurs when an app invokes a method through a base-class variable—at execution time, the correct derived-class version of the method is called, based on the type of the referenced object. You'll see a simple code example that illustrates this process in Section 12.3.

Video Game **SpaceObject** *Inheritance Hierarchy*

As another example, suppose we design a video game that manipulates objects of many different types, including objects of classes Martian, Venusian, Plutonian, SpaceShip and LaserBeam. Imagine that each class inherits from the common base class SpaceObject, which contains method Draw. Each derived class implements this method. A screen-manager app maintains a collection (e.g., a SpaceObject array) of references to objects of the various classes. To refresh the screen, the screen manager periodically sends each object the *same message*—namely, Draw. However, each object responds in a unique way. For example, a Martian object might *draw itself* in red with the appropriate number of antennae. A SpaceShip object might *draw itself* as a bright silver flying saucer. A LaserBeam object might *draw itself* as a bright red beam across the screen. Again, the *same message* (in this case, Draw) sent to a variety of objects has *many forms* of results.

A polymorphic screen manager might use polymorphism to facilitate adding new classes to a system with minimal modifications to the system's code. Suppose we want to add Mercurian objects to our video game. To do so, we must build a Mercurian class that extends SpaceObject and provides its own Draw method implementation. When objects of class Mercurian appear in the SpaceObject collection, the screen-manager code invokes method Draw, exactly as it does for every other object in the collection, *regardless of its type*, so the new Mercurian objects simply "plug right in" without any modification of the screen-manager code by the programmer. Thus, without modifying the system (other than to build new classes and modify the code that creates new objects), you can use polymorphism to include additional types that might not have been envisioned when the system was created.

Software Engineering Observation 12.1

Polymorphism promotes extensibility: Software that invokes polymorphic behavior is independent of the object types to which messages are sent. New object types that can respond to existing method calls can be incorporated into a system without requiring modification of the base system. Only client code that instantiates new objects must be modified to accommodate new types.

12.3 Demonstrating Polymorphic Behavior

Section 11.4 created a commission-employee class hierarchy, in which class BasePlusCommissionEmployee inherited from class CommissionEmployee. The examples in that section manipulated CommissionEmployee and BasePlusCommissionEmployee objects by using references to them to invoke their methods. We aimed base-class references at base-class objects and derived-class references at derived-class objects. These assignments are natural and straightforward—base-class references are intended to refer to base-class objects, and derived-class references are intended to refer to derived-class objects. However, other assignments are possible.

In the next example, we aim a base-class reference at a derived-class object. We then show how invoking a method on a derived-class object via a base-class reference can invoke the derived-class functionality—*the type of the actual referenced object, not the type of the reference, determines which method is called.* This demonstrates the key concept that a derived-class object can be treated as an object of its base class, which enables various interesting manipulations. An app can create an array of base-class references that refer to objects of many derived-class types. This is allowed because each derived-class object *is an* object of its base class. For instance, we can assign the reference of a BasePlusCommissionEmployee object to a base-class CommissionEmployee variable because a BasePlusCommissionEmployee *is a* CommissionEmployee—so we can treat a BasePlusCommissionEmployee as a CommissionEmployee.

A base-class object is not an object of any of its derived classes. For example, we cannot directly assign the reference of a CommissionEmployee object to a derived-class BasePlusCommissionEmployee variable, because a CommissionEmployee *is not* a BasePlusCommissionEmployee—a CommissionEmployee does not, for example, have a baseSalary instance variable and does not have a BaseSalary property. The *is-a* relationship applies from a derived class to its direct and indirect base classes, but not vice versa.

The compiler allows the assignment of a base-class reference to a derived-class variable *if* we explicitly cast the base-class reference to the derived-class type—a technique we discuss in greater detail in Section 12.5.6. Why would we ever want to perform such an assignment? *A base-class reference can be used to invoke only the methods declared in the base class*—attempting to invoke a derived-class-only method through a base-class reference results in a compilation error. If an app needs to perform a derived-class-specific operation on a derived-class object referenced by a base-class variable, the app must first cast the base-class reference to a derived-class reference through a technique known as **downcasting**. This enables the app to invoke derived-class methods that are not in the base class. We present an example of downcasting in Section 12.5.6.

Figure 12.1 demonstrates three ways to use base-class and derived-class variables to store references to base-class and derived-class objects. The first two are straightforward—as in Section 11.4, we assign a base-class reference to a base-class variable, and we assign a derived class reference to a derived-class variable. Then we demonstrate the relationship between derived classes and base classes (i.e., the *is-a* relationship) by assigning a derived-class reference to a base-class variable. [*Note:* This app uses classes CommissionEmployee and BasePlusCommissionEmployee from Fig. 11.12 and Fig. 11.13, respectively.]

```
1   // Fig. 12.1: PolymorphismTest.cs
2   // Assigning base-class and derived-class references to base-class and
3   // derived-class variables.
4   using System;
5
6   public class PolymorphismTest
7   {
8      public static void Main( string[] args )
9      {
10        // assign base-class reference to base-class variable
11        CommissionEmployee commissionEmployee = new CommissionEmployee(
12           "Sue", "Jones", "222-22-2222", 10000.00M, .06M );
13
14        // assign derived-class reference to derived-class variable
15        BasePlusCommissionEmployee basePlusCommissionEmployee =
16           new BasePlusCommissionEmployee( "Bob", "Lewis",
17           "333-33-3333", 5000.00M, .04M, 300.00M );
18
19        // invoke ToString and Earnings on base-class object
20        // using base-class variable
21        Console.WriteLine( "{0} {1}:\n\n{2}\n{3}: {4:C}\n",
22           "Call CommissionEmployee's ToString and Earnings methods ",
23           "with base-class reference to base class object",
24           commissionEmployee.ToString(),
25           "earnings", commissionEmployee.Earnings() );
26
27        // invoke ToString and Earnings on derived-class object
28        // using derived-class variable
29        Console.WriteLine( "{0} {1}:\n\n{2}\n{3}: {4:C}\n",
30           "Call BasePlusCommissionEmployee's ToString and Earnings ",
31           "methods with derived class reference to derived-class object",
32           basePlusCommissionEmployee.ToString(),
33           "earnings", basePlusCommissionEmployee.Earnings() );
34
35        // invoke ToString and Earnings on derived-class object
36        // using base-class variable
37        CommissionEmployee commissionEmployee2 =
38           basePlusCommissionEmployee;
39        Console.WriteLine( "{0} {1}:\n\n{2}\n{3}: {4:C}",
40           "Call BasePlusCommissionEmployee's ToString and Earnings ",
41           "with base class reference to derived-class object",
```

Fig. 12.1 | Assigning base-class and derived-class references to base-class and derived-class variables. (Part 1 of 2.)

```
42                  commissionEmployee2.ToString(), "earnings",
43                  commissionEmployee2.Earnings() );
44      } // end Main
45   } // end class PolymorphismTest
```

```
Call CommissionEmployee's ToString and Earnings methods with base class ref-
erence to base class object:

commission employee: Sue Jones
social security number: 222-22-2222
gross sales: $10,000.00
commission rate: 0.06
earnings: $600.00

Call BasePlusCommissionEmployee's ToString and Earnings methods with derived
class reference to derived class object:

base-salaried commission employee: Bob Lewis
social security number: 333-33-3333
gross sales: $5,000.00
commission rate: 0.04
base salary: $300.00
earnings: $500.00

Call BasePlusCommissionEmployee's ToString and Earnings methods with base
class reference to derived class object:

base-salaried commission employee: Bob Lewis
social security number: 333-33-3333
gross sales: $5,000.00
commission rate: 0.04
base salary: $300.00
earnings: $500.00
```

Fig. 12.1 | Assigning base-class and derived-class references to base-class and derived-class variables. (Part 2 of 2.)

In Fig. 12.1, lines 11–12 create a new CommissionEmployee object and assign its reference to a CommissionEmployee variable. Lines 15–17 create a new BasePlus-CommissionEmployee object and assign its reference to a BasePlusCommissionEmployee variable. These assignments are *natural*—for example, a CommissionEmployee variable's primary purpose is to hold a reference to a CommissionEmployee object. Lines 21–25 use the reference commissionEmployee to invoke methods ToString and Earnings. Because commissionEmployee refers to a CommissionEmployee object, *base class* Commission-Employee's version of the methods are called. Similarly, lines 29–33 use the reference basePlusCommissionEmployee to invoke the methods ToString and Earnings on the BasePlusCommissionEmployee object. This invokes *derived class* BasePlusCommission-Employee's version of the methods.

Lines 37–38 then assign the reference to derived-class object basePlusCommission-Employee to a base-class CommissionEmployee variable, which lines 39–43 use to invoke methods ToString and Earnings. *A base-class variable that contains a reference to a derived-class object and is used to call a virtual method actually calls the overriding derived-class ver-*

sion of the method. Hence, `commissionEmployee2.ToString()` in line 42 actually calls *derived* class `BasePlusCommissionEmployee`'s `ToString` method. The compiler allows this "crossover" because an object of a derived class *is an* object of its base class (but not vice versa). When the compiler encounters a `virtual` method call made through a variable, the compiler checks the *variable's* class type to determine if the method can be called. If that class contains the proper method declaration (or inherits one), the compiler allows the call to be compiled. At execution time, *the type of the object to which the variable refers* determines the actual method to use.

12.4 Abstract Classes and Methods

When we think of a class type, we assume that apps will create objects of that type. In some cases, however, it's useful to declare *classes for which you never intend to instantiate objects.* Such classes are called **abstract classes**. Because they're used only as base classes in inheritance hierarchies, we refer to them as **abstract base classes**. These classes *cannot* be used to instantiate objects, because, as you'll soon see, abstract classes are *incomplete*—derived classes must define the "missing pieces." We demonstrate abstract classes in Section 12.5.1.

Purpose of an Abstract Class

The purpose of an abstract class is primarily to provide an appropriate base class from which other classes can inherit, and thus *share a common design.* In the `Shape` hierarchy of Fig. 11.3, for example, derived classes inherit the notion of what it means to be a `Shape`—common attributes such as `location`, `color` and `borderThickness`, and behaviors such as `Draw`, `Move`, `Resize` and `ChangeColor`. Classes that can be used to instantiate objects are called **concrete classes**. Such classes provide implementations of *every* method they declare (some of the implementations can be inherited). For example, we could derive concrete classes `Circle`, `Square` and `Triangle` from abstract base class `TwoDimensionalShape`. Similarly, we could derive concrete classes `Sphere`, `Cube` and `Tetrahedron` from abstract base class `ThreeDimensionalShape`. Abstract base classes are *too general* to create real objects—they specify only what is common among derived classes. We need to be more *specific* before we can create objects. For example, if you send the `Draw` message to abstract class `TwoDimensionalShape`, the class knows that two-dimensional shapes should be drawable, but it does *not* know what *specific* shape to draw, so it cannot implement a real `Draw` method. *Concrete* classes provide the *specifics* that make it reasonable to instantiate objects.

Client Code That Uses Only Abstract Base-Class Types

Not all inheritance hierarchies contain abstract classes. However, you'll often write client code that uses only abstract base-class types to reduce client code's dependencies on a range of specific derived-class types. For example, you can write a method with a parameter of an abstract base-class type. When called, such a method can be passed an object of any concrete class that directly or indirectly extends the base class specified as the parameter's type.

Multiple Levels of Abstract Base-Class Types in a Hierarchy

Abstract classes sometimes constitute several levels of the hierarchy. For example, the `Shape` hierarchy of Fig. 11.3 begins with *abstract* class `Shape`. On the next level of the hierarchy are two more *abstract* classes, `TwoDimensionalShape` and `ThreeDimensionalShape`. The next level of the hierarchy declares *concrete* classes for TwoDimensionalShapes (Circle, Square and Triangle) and for ThreeDimensionalShapes (Sphere, Cube and Tetrahedron).

Creating an Abstract Class

You make a class abstract by declaring it with the keyword **abstract**. An abstract class normally contains one or more **abstract methods**. An abstract method is one with keyword abstract in its declaration, as in

```
public abstract void Draw(); // abstract method
```

Abstract methods are implicitly virtual and do not provide implementations. A class that contains abstract methods must be declared as an abstract class *even* if it contains some concrete (non-abstract) methods. Each *concrete* derived class of an abstract base class also must provide concrete implementations of the base class's abstract methods. We show an example of an abstract class with an abstract method in Fig. 12.4.

Abstract Properties

Properties can also be declared abstract or virtual, then overridden in derived classes with the override keyword, just like methods. This allows an abstract base class to specify common properties of its derived classes. Abstract property declarations have the form:

```
public abstract PropertyType MyProperty
{
    get;
    set;
} // end abstract property
```

The semicolons after the get and set keywords indicate that we provide *no implementation* for these accessors. An abstract property omits implementations for the get accessor and/or the set accessor. Concrete derived classes *must* provide implementations for *every* accessor declared in the abstract property. When both get and set accessors are specified, every concrete derived class must implement both. If one accessor is omitted, the derived class is *not* allowed to implement that accessor. Doing so causes a compilation error.

Constructors and **static** Methods Cannot be Abstract

Constructors and static methods *cannot* be declared abstract. Constructors are not inherited, so an abstract constructor could never be implemented. Similarly, derived classes cannot override static methods, so an abstract static method could never be implemented.

Software Engineering Observation 12.2

An abstract class declares common attributes and behaviors of the various classes that inherit from it, either directly or indirectly, in a class hierarchy. An abstract class typically contains one or more abstract methods or properties that concrete derived classes must override. The instance variables, concrete methods and concrete properties of an abstract class are subject to the normal rules of inheritance.

Common Programming Error 12.1

Attempting to instantiate an object of an abstract class is a compilation error.

> **Common Programming Error 12.2**
>
> *Failure to implement a base class's abstract methods and properties in a derived class is a compilation error unless the derived class is also declared* abstract.

Declaring Variables of Abstract Base-Class Types

Although we cannot instantiate objects of abstract base classes, you'll soon see that we *can* use abstract base classes to declare variables that can hold references to objects of *any* concrete classes *derived* from those abstract classes. Apps typically use such variables to manipulate derived-class objects polymorphically. Also, you can use abstract base-class names to invoke static methods declared in those abstract base classes.

Polymorphism and Device Drivers

Polymorphism is particularly effective for implementing so-called *layered software systems*. In operating systems, for example, each type of physical device could operate quite differently from the others. Even so, common commands can read or write data from and to the devices. For each device, the operating system uses a piece of software called a *device driver* to control all communication between the system and the device. The write message sent to a device driver object needs to be interpreted *specifically* in the context of that driver and how it manipulates a specific device. However, the write call itself really is no different from the write to any other device in the system: Place some number of bytes from memory onto that device. An object-oriented operating system might use an abstract base class to provide an "interface" appropriate for all device drivers. Then, through inheritance from that abstract base class, derived classes are formed that all behave similarly. The device-driver methods are declared as abstract methods in the abstract base class. The implementations of these abstract methods are provided in the derived classes that correspond to the specific types of device drivers. New devices are always being developed, often long after the operating system has been released. When you buy a new device, it comes with a device driver provided by the device vendor. The device is immediately operational after you connect it to your computer and install the device driver. This is another elegant example of how polymorphism makes systems *extensible*.

12.5 Case Study: Payroll System Using Polymorphism

This section reexamines the CommissionEmployee-BasePlusCommissionEmployee hierarchy that we explored in Section 11.4. Now we use an abstract method and polymorphism to perform payroll calculations based on the type of employee. We create an enhanced employee hierarchy to solve the following problem:

> *A company pays its employees on a weekly basis. The employees are of four types: Salaried employees are paid a fixed weekly salary regardless of the number of hours worked, hourly employees are paid by the hour and receive "time-and-a-half" overtime pay for all hours worked in excess of 40 hours, commission employees are paid a percentage of their sales, and salaried-commission employees receive a base salary plus a percentage of their sales. For the current pay period, the company has decided to reward salaried-commission employees by adding 10% to their base salaries. The company wants to implement an app that performs its payroll calculations polymorphically.*

We use abstract class Employee to represent the general concept of an employee. The classes that extend Employee are SalariedEmployee, CommissionEmployee and Hourly-Employee. Class BasePlusCommissionEmployee—which extends CommissionEmployee—represents the last employee type. The UML class diagram in Fig. 12.2 shows the inheritance hierarchy for our polymorphic employee payroll app. Abstract class Employee is *italicized*, as per the convention of the UML.

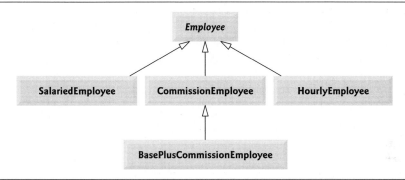

Fig. 12.2 | Employee hierarchy UML class diagram.

Abstract base class Employee declares the "interface" to the hierarchy—that is, the set of members that an app can invoke on all Employee objects. We use the term "interface" here in a general sense to refer to the various ways apps can communicate with objects of any Employee derived class. Be careful not to confuse the general notion of an "interface" with the formal notion of a C# interface, the subject of Section 12.7. Each employee, regardless of the way his or her earnings are calculated, has a first name, a last name and a social security number, so those pieces of data appear in abstract base class Employee.

The following subsections implement the Employee class hierarchy. Section 12.5.1 implements abstract base class Employee. Sections 12.5.2–12.5.5 each implement one of the concrete classes. Section 12.5.6 implements a test app that builds objects of all these classes and processes those objects polymorphically.

12.5.1 Creating Abstract Base Class Employee

Class Employee (Fig. 12.4) provides methods Earnings and ToString, in addition to the auto-implemented properties that manipulate Employee's data. An Earnings method certainly applies generically to all employees. But each earnings calculation depends on the employee's class. So we declare Earnings as abstract in base class Employee, because a default implementation does not make sense for that method—there's not enough information to determine what amount Earnings should return. Each derived class overrides Earnings with a specific implementation. To calculate an employee's earnings, the app assigns a reference to the employee's object to a base class Employee variable, then invokes the Earnings method on that variable. We maintain an array of Employee variables, each of which holds a reference to an Employee object (of course, there *cannot* be Employee objects because Employee is an *abstract* class—because of inheritance, however, all objects of all derived classes of Employee may nevertheless be thought of as Employee objects). The app iterates through the array and calls method Earnings for each Employee object. These method calls are processed polymorphically. Including Earnings as an abstract method in Employee *forces* every directly derived *concrete* class of Employee to override Earnings with a method that performs an appropriate pay calculation.

Method ToString in class Employee returns a string containing the employee's first name, last name and social security number. Each derived class of Employee overrides method ToString to create a string representation of an object of that class containing the employee's type (e.g., "salaried employee:"), followed by the rest of the employee's information.

The diagram in Fig. 12.3 shows each of the five classes in the hierarchy down the left side and methods Earnings and ToString across the top. For each class, the diagram shows the desired results of each method. [*Note:* We do not list base class Employee's properties because they're not overridden in any of the derived classes—each of these properties is inherited and used "as is" by each of the derived classes.]

	Earnings	ToString
Employee	abstract	*firstName lastName* social security number: *SSN*
Salaried-Employee	weeklySalary	salaried employee: *firstName lastName* social security number: *SSN* weekly salary: *weeklysalary*

Hourly-Employee	*If hours <= 40*
	    wage * hours
	If hours > 40
	    40 * wage +
	    (hours - 40) *
	    wage * 1.5
		hourly employee: *firstName lastName*
		social security number: *SSN*
		hourly wage: *wage*
		hours worked: *hours*

Commission-Employee	commissionRate * grossSales	commission employee: *firstName lastName* social security number: *SSN* gross sales: *grossSales* commission rate: *commissionRate*
BasePlus-Commission-Employee	(commissionRate * grossSales) + baseSalary	base salaried commission employee: *firstName lastName* social security number: *SSN* gross sales: *grossSales* commission rate: *commissionRate* base salary: *baseSalary*

Fig. 12.3 | Polymorphic interface for the Employee hierarchy classes.

Class *Employee*

Let's consider class Employee's declaration (Fig. 12.4). The class includes a constructor that takes the first name, last name and social security number as arguments (lines 15–20); properties with public get accessors for obtaining the first name, last name and social security number (lines 6, 9 and 12, respectively); method ToString (lines 23–27), which uses properties to return the string representation of the Employee; and abstract method

Earnings (line 30), which *must* be implemented by *concrete* derived classes. The Employee constructor does not validate the social security number in this example. Normally, such validation should be provided.

```
 1   // Fig. 12.4: Employee.cs
 2   // Employee abstract base class.
 3   public abstract class Employee
 4   {
 5      // read-only property that gets employee's first name
 6      public string FirstName { get; private set; }
 7
 8      // read-only property that gets employee's last name
 9      public string LastName { get; private set; }
10
11      // read-only property that gets employee's social security number
12      public string SocialSecurityNumber { get; private set; }
13
14      // three-parameter constructor
15      public Employee( string first, string last, string ssn )
16      {
17         FirstName = first;
18         LastName = last;
19         SocialSecurityNumber = ssn;
20      } // end three-parameter Employee constructor
21
22      // return string representation of Employee object, using properties
23      public override string ToString()
24      {
25         return string.Format( "{0} {1}\nsocial security number: {2}",
26            FirstName, LastName, SocialSecurityNumber );
27      } // end method ToString
28
29      // abstract method overridden by derived classes
30      public abstract decimal Earnings(); // no implementation here
31   } // end abstract class Employee
```

Fig. 12.4 | Employee abstract base class.

Why did we declare Earnings as an abstract method? As explained earlier, it simply does not make sense to provide an implementation of this method in class Employee. We cannot calculate the earnings for a *general* Employee—we first must know the *specific* Employee type to determine the appropriate earnings calculation. By declaring this method abstract, we indicate that each *concrete* derived class *must* provide an appropriate Earnings implementation and that an app will be able to use base-class Employee variables to invoke method Earnings polymorphically for *any* type of Employee.

12.5.2 Creating Concrete Derived Class SalariedEmployee

Class SalariedEmployee (Fig. 12.5) extends class Employee (line 5) and overrides Earnings (lines 34–37), which makes SalariedEmployee a concrete class. The class includes a constructor (lines 10–14) that takes a first name, a last name, a social security number and a weekly salary as arguments; property WeeklySalary (lines 17–31) to manipulate instance variable weeklySalary, including a set accessor that ensures we assign only nonnegative values to weeklySalary; method Earnings (lines 34–37) to calculate a SalariedEmployee's earnings; and method ToString (lines 40–44), which returns a string including the employee's type, namely, "salaried employee: ", followed by employee-specific information produced by base class Employee's ToString method and SalariedEmployee's WeeklySalary property. Class SalariedEmployee's constructor passes the first name, last name and social security number to the Employee constructor (line 11) via a constructor initializer to initialize the base class's data. Method Earnings overrides Employee's abstract method Earnings to provide a concrete implementation that returns the SalariedEmployee's weekly salary. If we do not implement Earnings, class SalariedEmployee must be declared abstract—otherwise, a compilation error occurs (and, of course, we want SalariedEmployee to be a concrete class).

```csharp
 1   // Fig. 12.5: SalariedEmployee.cs
 2   // SalariedEmployee class that extends Employee.
 3   using System;
 4
 5   public class SalariedEmployee : Employee
 6   {
 7      private decimal weeklySalary;
 8
 9      // four-parameter constructor
10      public SalariedEmployee( string first, string last, string ssn,
11         decimal salary ) : base( first, last, ssn )
12      {
13         WeeklySalary = salary; // validate salary via property
14      } // end four-parameter SalariedEmployee constructor
15
16      // property that gets and sets salaried employee's salary
17      public decimal WeeklySalary
18      {
19         get
20         {
21            return weeklySalary;
22         } // end get
23         set
24         {
25            if ( value >= 0 ) // validation
26               weeklySalary = value;
27            else
28               throw new ArgumentOutOfRangeException( "WeeklySalary",
29                  value, "WeeklySalary must be >= 0" );
30         } // end set
31      } // end property WeeklySalary
32
33      // calculate earnings; override abstract method Earnings in Employee
34      public override decimal Earnings()
35      {
36         return WeeklySalary;
37      } // end method Earnings
```

Fig. 12.5 | SalariedEmployee class that extends Employee. (Part 1 of 2.)

```
38
39       // return string representation of SalariedEmployee object
40       public override string ToString()
41       {
42          return string.Format( "salaried employee: {0}\n{1}: {2:C}",
43             base.ToString(), "weekly salary", WeeklySalary );
44       } // end method ToString
45    } // end class SalariedEmployee
```

Fig. 12.5 | SalariedEmployee class that extends Employee. (Part 2 of 2.)

SalariedEmployee method ToString (lines 40–44) overrides Employee's version. If class SalariedEmployee did *not* override ToString, SalariedEmployee would have inherited the Employee version. In that case, SalariedEmployee's ToString method would simply return the employee's full name and social security number, which does not adequately represent a SalariedEmployee. To produce a complete string representation of a SalariedEmployee, the derived class's ToString method returns "salaried employee: ", followed by the base-class Employee-specific information (i.e., first name, last name and social security number) obtained by invoking the base class's ToString (line 43)—this is a nice example of code reuse. The string representation of a SalariedEmployee also contains the employee's weekly salary, obtained by using the class's WeeklySalary property.

12.5.3 Creating Concrete Derived Class HourlyEmployee

Class HourlyEmployee (Fig. 12.6) also extends class Employee (line 5). The class includes a constructor (lines 11–17) that takes as arguments a first name, a last name, a social security number, an hourly wage and the number of hours worked. Lines 20–34 and 37–51 declare properties Wage and Hours for instance variables wage and hours, respectively. The set accessor in property Wage ensures that wage is nonnegative, and the set accessor in property Hours ensures that hours is in the range 0–168 (the total number of hours in a week) inclusive. The class overrides method Earnings (lines 54–60) to calculate an HourlyEmployee's earnings and method ToString (lines 63–68) to return the employee's string representation. The HourlyEmployee constructor, similarly to the SalariedEmployee constructor, passes the first name, last name and social security number to the base-class Employee constructor (line 13) to initialize the base class's data. Also, method ToString calls base-class method ToString (line 67) to obtain the Employee-specific information (i.e., first name, last name and social security number).

```
1    // Fig. 12.6: HourlyEmployee.cs
2    // HourlyEmployee class that extends Employee.
3    using System;
4
5    public class HourlyEmployee : Employee
6    {
7       private decimal wage; // wage per hour
8       private decimal hours; // hours worked for the week
9
```

Fig. 12.6 | HourlyEmployee class that extends Employee. (Part 1 of 3.)

```csharp
10     // five-parameter constructor
11     public HourlyEmployee( string first, string last, string ssn,
12        decimal hourlyWage, decimal hoursWorked )
13        : base( first, last, ssn )
14     {
15        Wage = hourlyWage; // validate hourly wage via property
16        Hours = hoursWorked; // validate hours worked via property
17     } // end five-parameter HourlyEmployee constructor
18
19     // property that gets and sets hourly employee's wage
20     public decimal Wage
21     {
22        get
23        {
24           return wage;
25        } // end get
26        set
27        {
28           if ( value >= 0 ) // validation
29              wage = value;
30           else
31              throw new ArgumentOutOfRangeException( "Wage",
32                 value, "Wage must be >= 0" );
33        } // end set
34     } // end property Wage
35
36     // property that gets and sets hourly employee's hours
37     public decimal Hours
38     {
39        get
40        {
41           return hours;
42        } // end get
43        set
44        {
45           if ( value >= 0 && value <= 168 ) // validation
46              hours = value;
47           else
48              throw new ArgumentOutOfRangeException( "Hours",
49                 value, "Hours must be >= 0 and <= 168" );
50        } // end set
51     } // end property Hours
52
53     // calculate earnings; override Employee's abstract method Earnings
54     public override decimal Earnings()
55     {
56        if ( Hours <= 40 ) // no overtime
57           return Wage * Hours;
58        else
59           return ( 40 * Wage ) + ( ( Hours - 40 ) * Wage * 1.5M );
60     } // end method Earnings
61
```

Fig. 12.6 | HourlyEmployee class that extends Employee. (Part 2 of 3.)

```
62      // return string representation of HourlyEmployee object
63      public override string ToString()
64      {
65         return string.Format(
66            "hourly employee: {0}\n{1}: {2:C}; {3}: {4:F2}",
67            base.ToString(), "hourly wage", Wage, "hours worked", Hours );
68      } // end method ToString
69   } // end class HourlyEmployee
```

Fig. 12.6 | HourlyEmployee class that extends Employee. (Part 3 of 3.)

12.5.4 Creating Concrete Derived Class CommissionEmployee

Class CommissionEmployee (Fig. 12.7) extends class Employee (line 5). The class includes a constructor (lines 11–16) that takes a first name, a last name, a social security number, a sales amount and a commission rate; properties (lines 19–33 and 36–50) for instance variables grossSales and commissionRate, respectively; method Earnings (lines 53–56) to calculate a CommissionEmployee's earnings; and method ToString (lines 59–64), which returns the employee's string representation. The CommissionEmployee's constructor also passes the first name, last name and social security number to the Employee constructor (line 12) to initialize Employee's data. Method ToString calls base-class method ToString (line 62) to obtain the Employee-specific information (i.e., first name, last name and social security number).

```
1    // Fig. 12.7: CommissionEmployee.cs
2    // CommissionEmployee class that extends Employee.
3    using System;
4
5    public class CommissionEmployee : Employee
6    {
7       private decimal grossSales; // gross weekly sales
8       private decimal commissionRate; // commission percentage
9
10      // five-parameter constructor
11      public CommissionEmployee( string first, string last, string ssn,
12         decimal sales, decimal rate ) : base( first, last, ssn )
13      {
14         GrossSales = sales; // validate gross sales via property
15         CommissionRate = rate; // validate commission rate via property
16      } // end five-parameter CommissionEmployee constructor
17
18      // property that gets and sets commission employee's gross sales
19      public decimal GrossSales
20      {
21         get
22         {
23            return grossSales;
24         } // end get
25         set
26         {
```

Fig. 12.7 | CommissionEmployee class that extends Employee. (Part 1 of 2.)

```
27            if ( value >= 0 )
28               grossSales = value;
29            else
30               throw new ArgumentOutOfRangeException(
31                  "GrossSales", value, "GrossSales must be >= 0" );
32         } // end set
33      } // end property GrossSales
34
35      // property that gets and sets commission employee's commission rate
36      public decimal CommissionRate
37      {
38         get
39         {
40            return commissionRate;
41         } // end get
42         set
43         {
44            if ( value > 0 && value < 1 )
45               commissionRate = value;
46            else
47               throw new ArgumentOutOfRangeException( "CommissionRate",
48                  value, "CommissionRate must be > 0 and < 1" );
49         } // end set
50      } // end property CommissionRate
51
52      // calculate earnings; override abstract method Earnings in Employee
53      public override decimal Earnings()
54      {
55         return CommissionRate * GrossSales;
56      } // end method Earnings
57
58      // return string representation of CommissionEmployee object
59      public override string ToString()
60      {
61         return string.Format( "{0}: {1}\n{2}: {3:C}\n{4}: {5:F2}",
62            "commission employee", base.ToString(),
63            "gross sales", GrossSales, "commission rate", CommissionRate );
64      } // end method ToString
65   } // end class CommissionEmployee
```

Fig. 12.7 | CommissionEmployee class that extends Employee. (Part 2 of 2.)

12.5.5 Creating Indirect Concrete Derived Class BasePlusCommissionEmployee

Class BasePlusCommissionEmployee (Fig. 12.8) extends class CommissionEmployee (line 5) and therefore is an *indirect* derived class of class Employee. Class BasePlusCommission-Employee has a constructor (lines 10–15) that takes as arguments a first name, a last name, a social security number, a sales amount, a commission rate and a base salary. It then passes the first name, last name, social security number, sales amount and commission rate to the CommissionEmployee constructor (line 12) to initialize the base class's data. BasePlusCom-missionEmployee also contains property BaseSalary (lines 19–33) to manipulate instance variable baseSalary. Method Earnings (lines 36–39) calculates a BasePlusCommission-Employee's earnings. Line 38 in method Earnings calls base class CommissionEmployee's Earnings method to calculate the commission-based portion of the employee's earnings. Again, this shows the benefits of code reuse. BasePlusCommissionEmployee's ToString method (lines 42–46) creates a string representation of a BasePlusCommissionEmployee that contains "base-salaried", followed by the string obtained by invoking base class CommissionEmployee's ToString method (another example of code reuse), then the base salary. The result is a string beginning with "base-salaried commission employee", followed by the rest of the BasePlusCommissionEmployee's information. Recall that CommissionEmployee's ToString method obtains the employee's first name, last name and social security number by invoking the ToString method of *its* base class (i.e., Employee)—a further demonstration of code reuse. BasePlusCommissionEmployee's ToString initiates a *chain of method calls* that spans all three levels of the Employee hierarchy.

```csharp
1    // Fig. 12.8: BasePlusCommissionEmployee.cs
2    // BasePlusCommissionEmployee class that extends CommissionEmployee.
3    using System;
4
5    public class BasePlusCommissionEmployee : CommissionEmployee
6    {
7       private decimal baseSalary; // base salary per week
8
9       // six-parameter constructor
10      public BasePlusCommissionEmployee( string first, string last,
11         string ssn, decimal sales, decimal rate, decimal salary )
12         : base( first, last, ssn, sales, rate )
13      {
14         BaseSalary = salary; // validate base salary via property
15      } // end six-parameter BasePlusCommissionEmployee constructor
16
17      // property that gets and sets
18      // base-salaried commission employee's base salary
19      public decimal BaseSalary
20      {
21         get
22         {
23            return baseSalary;
24         } // end get
25         set
26         {
27            if ( value >= 0 )
28               baseSalary = value;
29            else
30               throw new ArgumentOutOfRangeException( "BaseSalary",
31                  value, "BaseSalary must be >= 0" );
32         } // end set
33      } // end property BaseSalary
34
```

Fig. 12.8 | BasePlusCommissionEmployee class that extends CommissionEmployee. (Part 1 of 2.)

```
35        // calculate earnings; override method Earnings in CommissionEmployee
36        public override decimal Earnings()
37        {
38           return BaseSalary + base.Earnings();
39        } // end method Earnings
40
41        // return string representation of BasePlusCommissionEmployee object
42        public override string ToString()
43        {
44           return string.Format( "base-salaried {0}; base salary: {1:C}",
45              base.ToString(), BaseSalary );
46        } // end method ToString
47     } // end class BasePlusCommissionEmployee
```

Fig. 12.8 | BasePlusCommissionEmployee class that extends CommissionEmployee. (Part 2 of 2.)

12.5.6 Polymorphic Processing, Operator is and Downcasting

To test our Employee hierarchy, the app in Fig. 12.9 creates an object of each of the four concrete classes SalariedEmployee, HourlyEmployee, CommissionEmployee and BasePlusCommissionEmployee. The app manipulates these objects, first via variables of each object's own type, then polymorphically, using an array of Employee variables. While processing the objects polymorphically, the app increases the base salary of each BasePlusCommissionEmployee by 10% (this, of course, requires determining the object's type at *execution* time). Finally, the app polymorphically determines and outputs the type of each object in the Employee array. Lines 10–20 create objects of each of the four concrete Employee derived classes. Lines 24–32 output the string representation and earnings of each of these objects. Each object's ToString method is called *implicitly* by WriteLine when the object is output as a string with format items.

Assigning Derived-Class Objects to Base-Class References
Line 35 declares employees and assigns it an array of four Employee variables. Lines 38–41 assign a SalariedEmployee object, an HourlyEmployee object, a CommissionEmployee object and a BasePlusCommissionEmployee object to employees[0], employees[1], employees[2] and employees[3], respectively. Each assignment is allowed, because a SalariedEmployee *is an* Employee, an HourlyEmployee *is an* Employee, a CommissionEmployee *is an* Employee and a BasePlusCommissionEmployee *is an* Employee. Therefore, we can assign the references of SalariedEmployee, HourlyEmployee, CommissionEmployee and BasePlusCommissionEmployee objects to base-class Employee variables, even though Employee is an *abstract* class.

```
1     // Fig. 12.9: PayrollSystemTest.cs
2     // Employee hierarchy test app.
3     using System;
4
5     public class PayrollSystemTest
6     {
```

Fig. 12.9 | Employee hierarchy test app. (Part 1 of 4.)

```csharp
 7    public static void Main( string[] args )
 8    {
 9       // create derived-class objects
10       SalariedEmployee salariedEmployee =
11          new SalariedEmployee( "John", "Smith", "111-11-1111", 800.00M );
12       HourlyEmployee hourlyEmployee =
13          new HourlyEmployee( "Karen", "Price",
14          "222-22-2222", 16.75M, 40.0M );
15       CommissionEmployee commissionEmployee =
16          new CommissionEmployee( "Sue", "Jones",
17          "333-33-3333", 10000.00M, .06M );
18       BasePlusCommissionEmployee basePlusCommissionEmployee =
19          new BasePlusCommissionEmployee( "Bob", "Lewis",
20          "444-44-4444", 5000.00M, .04M, 300.00M );
21
22       Console.WriteLine( "Employees processed individually:\n" );
23
24       Console.WriteLine( "{0}\nearned: {1:C}\n",
25          salariedEmployee, salariedEmployee.Earnings() );
26       Console.WriteLine( "{0}\nearned: {1:C}\n",
27          hourlyEmployee, hourlyEmployee.Earnings() );
28       Console.WriteLine( "{0}\nearned: {1:C}\n",
29          commissionEmployee, commissionEmployee.Earnings() );
30       Console.WriteLine( "{0}\nearned: {1:C}\n",
31          basePlusCommissionEmployee,
32          basePlusCommissionEmployee.Earnings() );
33
34       // create four-element Employee array
35       Employee[] employees = new Employee[ 4 ];
36
37       // initialize array with Employees of derived types
38       employees[ 0 ] = salariedEmployee;
39       employees[ 1 ] = hourlyEmployee;
40       employees[ 2 ] = commissionEmployee;
41       employees[ 3 ] = basePlusCommissionEmployee;
42
43       Console.WriteLine( "Employees processed polymorphically:\n" );
44
45       // generically process each element in array employees
46       foreach ( Employee currentEmployee in employees )
47       {
48          Console.WriteLine( currentEmployee ); // invokes ToString
49
50          // determine whether element is a BasePlusCommissionEmployee
51          if ( currentEmployee is BasePlusCommissionEmployee )
52          {
53             // downcast Employee reference to
54             // BasePlusCommissionEmployee reference
55             BasePlusCommissionEmployee employee =
56                ( BasePlusCommissionEmployee ) currentEmployee;
57
58             employee.BaseSalary *= 1.10M;
```

Fig. 12.9 | Employee hierarchy test app. (Part 2 of 4.)

```
59              Console.WriteLine(
60                 "new base salary with 10% increase is: {0:C}",
61                 employee.BaseSalary );
62           } // end if
63
64           Console.WriteLine(
65              "earned {0:C}\n", currentEmployee.Earnings() );
66        } // end foreach
67
68        // get type name of each object in employees array
69        for ( int j = 0; j < employees.Length; j++ )
70           Console.WriteLine( "Employee {0} is a {1}", j,
71              employees[ j ].GetType() );
72     } // end Main
73  } // end class PayrollSystemTest
```

```
Employees processed individually:

salaried employee: John Smith
social security number: 111-11-1111
weekly salary: $800.00
earned: $800.00

hourly employee: Karen Price
social security number: 222-22-2222
hourly wage: $16.75; hours worked: 40.00
earned: $670.00

commission employee: Sue Jones
social security number: 333-33-3333
gross sales: $10,000.00
commission rate: 0.06
earned: $600.00

base-salaried commission employee: Bob Lewis
social security number: 444-44-4444
gross sales: $5,000.00
commission rate: 0.04; base salary: $300.00
earned: $500.00


Employees processed polymorphically:

salaried employee: John Smith
social security number: 111-11-1111
weekly salary: $800.00
earned $800.00

hourly employee: Karen Price
social security number: 222-22-2222
hourly wage: $16.75; hours worked: 40.00
earned $670.00
```

Fig. 12.9 | `Employee` hierarchy test app. (Part 3 of 4.)

```
commission employee: Sue Jones
social security number: 333-33-3333
gross sales: $10,000.00
commission rate: 0.06
earned $600.00

base-salaried commission employee: Bob Lewis
social security number: 444-44-4444
gross sales: $5,000.00
commission rate: 0.04; base salary: $300.00
new base salary with 10% increase is: $330.00
earned $530.00

Employee 0 is a SalariedEmployee
Employee 1 is a HourlyEmployee
Employee 2 is a CommissionEmployee
Employee 3 is a BasePlusCommissionEmployee
```

Fig. 12.9 | Employee hierarchy test app. (Part 4 of 4.)

Polymorphically Processing Employees

Lines 46–66 iterate through array employees and invoke methods ToString and Earnings with Employee variable currentEmployee, which is assigned the reference to a different Employee during each iteration. The output illustrates that the appropriate methods for each class are indeed invoked. All calls to virtual methods ToString and Earnings are resolved at *execution* time, based on the type of the object to which currentEmployee refers. This process is known as **dynamic binding** or **late binding**. For example, line 48 *implicitly* invokes method ToString of the object to which currentEmployee refers. Only the methods of class Employee can be called via an Employee variable—and Employee includes class object's methods, such as ToString. (Section 11.7 discussed the methods that all classes inherit from class object.) A base-class reference can be used to invoke only methods of the base class.

Giving BasePlusCommissionEmployees 10% Raises

We perform special processing on BasePlusCommissionEmployee objects—as we encounter them, we increase their base salary by 10%. When processing objects polymorphically, we typically do not need to worry about the *specifics*, but to adjust the base salary, we do have to determine the specific type of each Employee object at execution time. Line 51 uses the is operator to determine whether a particular Employee object's type is BasePlusCommissionEmployee. The condition in line 51 is true if the object referenced by currentEmployee *is a* BasePlusCommissionEmployee. This would also be true for any object of a BasePlusCommissionEmployee derived class (if there were any), because of the *is-a* relationship a derived class has with its base class. Lines 55–56 *downcast* currentEmployee from type Employee to type BasePlusCommissionEmployee—this cast is allowed only if the object has an *is-a* relationship with BasePlusCommissionEmployee. The condition at line 51 ensures that this is the case. This cast is *required* if we are to use derived class BasePlusCommissionEmployee's BaseSalary property on the current Employee object—*attempting to invoke a derived-class-only method directly on a base class reference is a compilation error.*

Common Programming Error 12.3

Assigning a base-class variable to a derived-class variable (without an explicit downcast) is a compilation error.

Software Engineering Observation 12.3

If at execution time the reference to a derived-class object has been assigned to a variable of one of its direct or indirect base classes, it's acceptable to cast the reference stored in that base-class variable back to a reference of the derived-class type. Before performing such a cast, use the is *operator to ensure that the object is indeed an object of an appropriate derived-class type.*

When *downcasting* an object, an InvalidCastException (of namespace *System*) occurs if at execution time the object does not have an *is a* relationship with the type specified in the cast operator. An object can be cast only to its own type or to the type of one of its base classes. You can avoid a potential InvalidCastException by using the **as** operator to perform a downcast rather than a cast operator. For example, in the statement

```
BasePlusCommissionEmployee employee =
    currentEmployee as BasePlusCommissionEmployee;
```

employee is assigned a reference to an object that *is a* BasePlusCommissionEmployee, or the value null if currentEmployee is not a BasePlusCommissionEmployee. You can then compare employee with null to determine whether the cast succeeded.

If the is expression in line 51 is true, the if statement (lines 51–62) performs the special processing required for the BasePlusCommissionEmployee object. Using BasePlusCommissionEmployee variable employee, line 58 accesses the derived-class-only property BaseSalary to retrieve and update the employee's base salary with the 10% raise.

Lines 64–65 invoke method Earnings on currentEmployee, which calls the appropriate derived-class object's Earnings method polymorphically. Obtaining the earnings of the SalariedEmployee, HourlyEmployee and CommissionEmployee polymorphically in lines 64–65 produces the same result as obtaining these employees' earnings individually in lines 24–29. However, the earnings amount obtained for the BasePlusCommissionEmployee in lines 64–65 is higher than that obtained in lines 30–32, due to the 10% increase in its base salary.

Every Object Knows Its Own Type

Lines 69–71 display each employee's type as a string. Every object knows its own type and can access this information through method **GetType**, which all classes inherit from class object. Method GetType returns an object of class Type (of namespace System), which contains information about the object's type, including its class name, the names of its methods, and the name of its base class. Line 71 invokes method GetType on the object to get its runtime class (i.e., a Type object that represents the object's type). Then method ToString is *implicitly* invoked on the object returned by GetType. The Type class's ToString method returns the class name.

Avoiding Compilation Errors with Downcasting

In the previous example, we avoid several compilation errors by *downcasting* an Employee variable to a BasePlusCommissionEmployee variable in lines 55–56. If we remove the cast operator (BasePlusCommissionEmployee) from line 56 and attempt to assign Employee variable `currentEmployee` directly to `BasePlusCommissionEmployee` variable `employee`, we receive a "Cannot implicitly convert type" compilation error. This error indicates that the attempt to assign the reference of base-class object `currentEmployee` to derived-class variable `employee` is *not* allowed without an appropriate cast operator. The compiler prevents this assignment, because a `CommissionEmployee` is *not* a `BasePlusCommission-Employee`—again, the *is-a* relationship applies only between the derived class and its base classes, not vice versa.

Similarly, if lines 58 and 61 use base-class variable `currentEmployee`, rather than derived-class variable `employee`, to use derived-class-only property `BaseSalary`, we receive an "'Employee' does not contain a definition for 'BaseSalary'" compilation error on each of these lines. *Attempting to invoke derived-class-only methods on a base-class reference is not allowed.* While lines 58 and 61 execute only if `is` in line 51 returns `true` to indicate that `currentEmployee` has been assigned a reference to a `BasePlusCommissionEmployee` object, we *cannot* attempt to use derived-class `BasePlusCommissionEmployee` property `BaseSalary` with base-class `Employee` reference `currentEmployee`. The compiler would generate errors in lines 58 and 61, because `BaseSalary` is not a base-class member and cannot be used with a base-class variable. Although the actual method that's called depends on the object's type at execution time, *a variable can be used to invoke only those methods that are members of that variable's type*, which the compiler verifies. Using a base-class `Employee` variable, we can invoke only methods and properties found in class `Employee`—methods `Earnings` and `ToString`, and properties `FirstName`, `LastName` and `SocialSecurity-Number`—and method methods inherited from class `object`.

12.5.7 Summary of the Allowed Assignments Between Base-Class and Derived-Class Variables

Now that you've seen a complete app that processes diverse derived-class objects polymorphically, we summarize what you can and cannot do with base-class and derived-class objects and variables. Although a derived-class object also *is a* base-class object, the two are nevertheless different. As discussed previously, derived-class objects can be treated as if they were base-class objects. However, the derived class can have additional derived-class-only members. For this reason, assigning a base-class reference to a derived-class variable is *not* allowed without an *explicit* cast—such an assignment would leave the derived-class members *undefined* for a base-class object.

We've discussed four ways to assign base-class and derived-class references to variables of base-class and derived-class types:

1. *Assigning a base-class reference to a base-class variable* is straightforward.

2. *Assigning a derived-class reference to a derived-class variable* is straightforward.

3. *Assigning a derived-class reference to a base-class variable* is safe, because the derived-class object *is an* object of its base class. However, this reference can be used to refer *only* to base-class members. If this code refers to derived-class-only members through the base-class variable, the compiler reports errors.

4. *Attempting to assign a base-class reference to a derived-class variable* is a compilation error. To avoid this error, the base-class reference must be cast to a derived-class type explicitly or must be converted using the `as` operator. At execution time, if the object to which the reference refers is *not* a derived-class object, an exception will

occur (unless you use the as operator). The is operator can be used to ensure that such a cast is performed *only* if the object is a derived-class object.

12.6 sealed Methods and Classes

Only methods declared virtual, override or abstract can be *overridden* in derived classes. A method declared **sealed** in a base class *cannot* be overridden in a derived class. Methods that are declared private are implicitly sealed, because it's impossible to override them in a derived class (though the derived class can declare a new method with the same signature as the private method in the base class). Methods that are declared static also are implicitly sealed, because static methods cannot be overridden either. A derived-class method declared both override and sealed can override a base-class method, but cannot be overridden in derived classes further down the inheritance hierarchy.

A sealed method's declaration can never change, so all derived classes use the same method implementation, and calls to sealed methods (and non-virtual methods) are resolved at *compile time*—this is known as **static binding**. Since the compiler knows that sealed methods cannot be overridden, it can often *optimize* code by removing calls to sealed methods and replacing them with the expanded code of their declarations at each method-call location—a technique known as **inlining the code**.

Performance Tip 12.1

The compiler can decide to inline a sealed method call and will do so for small, simple sealed methods. Inlining does not violate encapsulation or information hiding, but does improve performance, because it eliminates the overhead of making a method call.

A class that's declared sealed *cannot* be a base class (i.e., a class cannot extend a sealed class). All methods in a sealed class are implicitly sealed. Class string is a sealed class. This class cannot be extended, so apps that use strings can rely on the functionality of string objects as specified in the Framework Class Library.

Common Programming Error 12.4

Attempting to declare a derived class of a sealed class is a compilation error.

12.7 Case Study: Creating and Using Interfaces

Our next example (Figs. 12.11–12.15) reexamines the payroll system of Section 12.5. Suppose that the company involved wishes to perform several accounting operations in a single accounts-payable app—in addition to calculating the payroll earnings that must be paid to each employee, the company must also calculate the payment due on each of several invoices (i.e., bills for goods purchased). Though applied to unrelated things (i.e., employees and invoices), both operations have to do with calculating some kind of payment amount. For an employee, the payment refers to the employee's earnings. For an invoice, the payment refers to the total cost of the goods listed on the invoice. Can we calculate such different things as the payments due for employees and invoices polymorphically in a single app? Is there a capability that requires that *unrelated* classes implement a set of common methods (e.g., a method that calculates a payment amount)? *Interfaces* offer exactly this capability.

Standardized Interactions

Interfaces define and standardize the ways in which people and systems can interact with one another. For example, the controls on a radio serve as an interface between a radio's users and its internal components. The controls allow users to perform a limited set of operations (e.g., changing the station, adjusting the volume, choosing between AM and FM), and different radios may implement the controls in different ways (e.g., using push buttons, dials, voice commands). The interface specifies *what* operations a radio must permit users to perform but does not specify *how* they're performed. Similarly, the interface between a driver and a car with a manual transmission includes the steering wheel, the gear shift, the clutch pedal, the gas pedal and the brake pedal. This same interface is found in nearly all manual-transmission cars, enabling someone who knows how to drive one particular manual-transmission car to drive just about any other. The components of each car may look a bit different, but the *general* purpose is the same—to allow people to drive the car.

Interfaces in Software

Software objects also communicate via interfaces. A C# interface describes a set of methods and properties that can be called on an object—to tell it, for example, to perform some task or return some piece of information. The next example introduces an interface named `IPayable` that describes the functionality of any object that must be capable of being paid and thus must offer a method to determine the proper payment amount due. An **interface declaration** begins with the keyword **interface** and can contain only abstract methods, abstract properties, abstract indexers (not covered in this book) and abstract events (events are discussed in Chapter 14, Graphical User Interfaces with Windows Forms: Part 1.) All interface members are *implicitly* declared both `public` and `abstract`. In addition, each interface can extend one or more other interfaces to create a more elaborate interface that other classes can implement.

Common Programming Error 12.5

It's a compilation error to declare an interface member `public` or `abstract` explicitly, because they're redundant in interface-member declarations. It's also a compilation error to specify any implementation details, such as concrete method declarations, in an interface.

Implementing an Interface

To use an interface, a class must specify that it **implements** the interface by listing the interface after the colon (`:`) in the class declaration. This is the *same* syntax used to indicate inheritance from a base class. A concrete class implementing the interface must declare each member of the interface with the signature specified in the interface declaration. A class that implements an interface but does *not* implement all its members is an abstract class—it must be declared `abstract` and must contain an `abstract` declaration for each unimplemented member of the interface. Implementing an interface is like signing a contract with the compiler that states, "I will provide an implementation for all the members specified by the interface, or I will declare them `abstract`."

Common Programming Error 12.6

Failing to define or declare any member of an interface in a class that implements the interface results in a compilation error.

Common Methods for Unrelated Classes

An interface is typically used when *unrelated* classes need to *share* common methods. This allows objects of unrelated classes to be processed polymorphically—objects of classes that implement the same interface can respond to the *same* method calls. You can create an interface that describes the desired functionality, then implement this interface in any classes requiring that functionality. For example, in the accounts-payable app developed in this section, we implement interface IPayable in any class that must be able to calculate a payment amount (e.g., Employee, Invoice).

Interfaces vs. Abstract Classes

An interface often is used in place of an abstract class when there's no default implementation to inherit—that is, no fields and no default method implementations. Like abstract classes, interfaces are typically public types, so they're normally declared in files by themselves with the same name as the interface and the .cs file-name extension.

12.7.1 Developing an IPayable Hierarchy

To build an app that can determine payments for employees and invoices alike, we first create an interface named IPayable. Interface IPayable contains method GetPayment-Amount that returns a decimal amount to be paid for an object of any class that implements the interface. Method GetPaymentAmount is a general-purpose version of method Earnings of the Employee hierarchy—method Earnings calculates a payment amount specifically for an Employee, while GetPaymentAmount can be applied to a broad range of *unrelated* objects. After declaring interface IPayable, we introduce class Invoice, which implements interface IPayable. We then modify class Employee such that it also implements interface IPayable. Finally, we update Employee derived class SalariedEmployee to "fit" into the IPayable hierarchy (i.e., we rename SalariedEmployee method Earnings as GetPaymentAmount).

Good Programming Practice 12.1

By convention, the name of an interface begins with I. This helps distinguish interfaces from classes, improving code readability.

Good Programming Practice 12.2

When declaring a method in an interface, choose a name that describes the method's purpose in a general manner, because the method may be implemented by a broad range of unrelated classes.

Classes Invoice and Employee both represent things for which the company must be able to calculate a payment amount. Both classes implement IPayable, so an app can invoke method GetPaymentAmount on Invoice objects and Employee objects alike. This enables the polymorphic processing of Invoices and Employees required for our company's accounts-payable app.

UML Diagram Containing an Interface

The UML class diagram in Fig. 12.10 shows the interface and class hierarchy used in our accounts-payable app. The hierarchy begins with interface IPayable. The UML distinguishes an interface from a class by placing the word "interface" in guillemets (« and ») above the interface name. The UML expresses the relationship between a class and an interface through a **realization**. A class is said to "realize," or implement, an interface. A class diagram models a realization as a dashed arrow with a *hollow arrowhead* pointing from the implementing class to the interface. The diagram in Fig. 12.10 indicates that classes Invoice and Employee each realize (i.e., implement) interface IPayable. As in the class diagram of Fig. 12.2, class Employee appears in italics, indicating that it's an abstract class. Concrete class SalariedEmployee extends Employee and inherits its base class's realization relationship with interface IPayable.

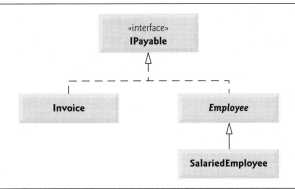

Fig. 12.10 │ IPayable interface and class hierarchy UML class diagram.

12.7.2 Declaring Interface IPayable

The declaration of interface IPayable begins in Fig. 12.11 at line 3. Interface IPayable contains public abstract method GetPaymentAmount (line 5). The method cannot be *explicitly* declared public or abstract. Interfaces can have *any* number of members and interface methods can have parameters.

```
1   // Fig. 12.11: IPayable.cs
2   // IPayable interface declaration.
3   public interface IPayable
4   {
5      decimal GetPaymentAmount(); // calculate payment; no implementation
6   } // end interface IPayable
```

Fig. 12.11 │ IPayable interface declaration.

12.7.3 Creating Class Invoice

We now create class Invoice (Fig. 12.12) to represent a simple invoice that contains billing information for one kind of part. The class contains properties PartNumber (line 11), PartDescription (line 14), Quantity (lines 27–41) and PricePerItem (lines 44–58) that indicate the part number, the description of the part, the quantity of the part ordered and the price per item. Class Invoice also contains a constructor (lines 17–24) and a ToString method (lines 61–67) that returns a string representation of an Invoice object. The set accessors of properties Quantity and PricePerItem ensure that quantity and pricePerItem are assigned only nonnegative values.

```
1   // Fig. 12.12: Invoice.cs
2   // Invoice class implements IPayable.
3   using System;
4
5   public class Invoice : IPayable
6   {
7      private int quantity;
8      private decimal pricePerItem;
9
10     // property that gets and sets the part number on the invoice
11     public string PartNumber { get; set; }
12
13     // property that gets and sets the part description on the invoice
14     public string PartDescription { get; set; }
15
16     // four-parameter constructor
17     public Invoice( string part, string description, int count,
18        decimal price )
19     {
20        PartNumber = part;
21        PartDescription = description;
22        Quantity = count; // validate quantity via property
23        PricePerItem = price; // validate price per item via property
24     } // end four-parameter Invoice constructor
25
26     // property that gets and sets the quantity on the invoice
27     public int Quantity
28     {
29        get
30        {
31           return quantity;
32        } // end get
33        set
34        {
35           if ( value >= 0 ) // validate quantity
36              quantity = value;
37           else
38              throw new ArgumentOutOfRangeException( "Quantity",
39                 value, "Quantity must be >= 0" );
40        } // end set
41     } // end property Quantity
42
43     // property that gets and sets the price per item
44     public decimal PricePerItem
45     {
46        get
47        {
48           return pricePerItem;
49        } // end get
50        set
51        {
52           if ( value >= 0 ) // validate price
53              quantity = value;
```

Fig. 12.12 | Invoice class implements IPayable. (Part 1 of 2.)

```
54              else
55                  throw new ArgumentOutOfRangeException( "PricePerItem",
56                      value, "PricePerItem must be >= 0" );
57          } // end set
58      } // end property PricePerItem
59
60      // return string representation of Invoice object
61      public override string ToString()
62      {
63          return string.Format(
64              "{0}: \n{1}: {2} ({3}) \n{4}: {5} \n{6}: {7:C}",
65              "invoice", "part number", PartNumber, PartDescription,
66              "quantity", Quantity, "price per item", PricePerItem );
67      } // end method ToString
68
69      // method required to carry out contract with interface IPayable
70      public decimal GetPaymentAmount()
71      {
72          return Quantity * PricePerItem; // calculate total cost
73      } // end method GetPaymentAmount
74  } // end class Invoice
```

Fig. 12.12 | `Invoice` class implements `IPayable`. (Part 2 of 2.)

Line 5 indicates that class `Invoice` implements interface `IPayable`. Like all classes, class `Invoice` also implicitly inherits from class `object`. *C# does not allow derived classes to inherit from more than one base class, but it does allow a class to inherit from a base class and implement* any *number of interfaces.* All objects of a class that implement multiple interfaces have the *is-a* relationship with each implemented interface type. To implement more than one interface, use a comma-separated list of interface names after the colon (:) in the class declaration, as in:

> **public class** *ClassName* : *BaseClassName*, *FirstInterface*, *SecondInterface*, ...

When a class inherits from a base class and implements one or more interfaces, the class declaration *must* list the base-class name *before* any interface names.

Class `Invoice` implements the one method in interface `IPayable`—method `GetPaymentAmount` is declared in lines 70–73. The method calculates the amount required to pay the invoice. The method multiplies the values of `quantity` and `pricePerItem` (obtained through the appropriate properties) and returns the result (line 72). This method satisfies the implementation requirement for the method in interface `IPayable`—we've fulfilled the *interface contract* with the compiler.

12.7.4 Modifying Class `Employee` to Implement Interface `IPayable`

We now modify class `Employee` to implement interface `IPayable`. Figure 12.13 contains the modified `Employee` class. This class declaration is identical to that of Fig. 12.4 with two exceptions. First, line 3 of Fig. 12.13 indicates that class `Employee` now implements interface `IPayable`. Because of this, we renamed `Earnings` to `GetPaymentAmount` throughout the Employee hierarchy. As with method `Earnings` in Fig. 12.4, however, it does not make sense to implement method `GetPaymentAmount` in class `Employee`, because we cannot calculate the earnings payment owed to a *general* Employee—first, we must know the *specific* type of Employee. In Fig. 12.4, we declared method Earnings as abstract for this reason, and as a result, class Employee had to be declared abstract. This forced each Employee derived class to override Earnings with a concrete implementation. [*Note:* Though we renamed Earnings to GetPaymentAmount, in class Employee we could have defined GetPaymentAmount and had it call Earnings. Then the other Employee hierarchy classes would not need to change.]

```csharp
1   // Fig. 12.13: Employee.cs
2   // Employee abstract base class.
3   public abstract class Employee : IPayable
4   {
5      // read-only property that gets employee's first name
6      public string FirstName { get; private set; }
7
8      // read-only property that gets employee's last name
9      public string LastName { get; private set; }
10
11     // read-only property that gets employee's social security number
12     public string SocialSecurityNumber { get; private set; }
13
14     // three-parameter constructor
15     public Employee( string first, string last, string ssn )
16     {
17        FirstName = first;
18        LastName = last;
19        SocialSecurityNumber = ssn;
20     } // end three-parameter Employee constructor
21
22     // return string representation of Employee object
23     public override string ToString()
24     {
25        return string.Format( "{0} {1}\nsocial security number: {2}",
26           FirstName, LastName, SocialSecurityNumber );
27     } // end method ToString
28
29     // Note: We do not implement IPayable method GetPaymentAmount here, so
30     // this class must be declared abstract to avoid a compilation error.
31     public abstract decimal GetPaymentAmount();
32  } // end abstract class Employee
```

Fig. 12.13 | Employee abstract base class.

In Fig. 12.13, we handle this situation the same way. Recall that when a class implements an interface, the class makes a contract with the compiler stating that the class either will implement *each* of the methods in the interface *or* will declare them abstract. If the latter option is chosen, we must also declare the class abstract. As we discussed in Section 12.4, any concrete derived class of the abstract class must implement the abstract methods of the base class. If the derived class does not do so, it too must be declared abstract. As indicated by the comments in lines 29–30 of Fig. 12.13, class Employee does not implement method GetPaymentAmount, so the class is declared abstract.

12.7.5 Modifying Class SalariedEmployee for Use with IPayable

Figure 12.14 contains a modified version of class SalariedEmployee that extends Employee and implements method GetPaymentAmount. This version of SalariedEmployee is identical to that of Fig. 12.5 with the exception that the version here implements method GetPaymentAmount (lines 35–38) instead of method Earnings. The two methods contain the *same* functionality but have different names. Recall that the IPayable version of the method has a more general name to be applicable to possibly disparate classes. The remaining Employee derived classes (e.g., HourlyEmployee, CommissionEmployee and BasePlusCommissionEmployee) also must be modified to contain method GetPaymentAmount in place of Earnings to reflect the fact that Employee now implements IPayable. We leave these modifications to you as an exercise and use only SalariedEmployee in our test app in this section.

```
1   // Fig. 12.14: SalariedEmployee.cs
2   // SalariedEmployee class that extends Employee.
3   using System;
4
5   public class SalariedEmployee : Employee
6   {
7      private decimal weeklySalary;
8
9      // four-parameter constructor
10     public SalariedEmployee( string first, string last, string ssn,
11        decimal salary ) : base( first, last, ssn )
12     {
13        WeeklySalary = salary; // validate salary via property
14     } // end four-parameter SalariedEmployee constructor
15
16     // property that gets and sets salaried employee's salary
17     public decimal WeeklySalary
18     {
19        get
20        {
21           return weeklySalary;
22        } // end get
23        set
24        {
25           if ( value >= 0 ) // validation
26              weeklySalary = value;
27           else
28              throw new ArgumentOutOfRangeException( "WeeklySalary",
29                 value, "WeeklySalary must be >= 0" );
30        } // end set
31     } // end property WeeklySalary
32
33     // calculate earnings; implement interface IPayable method
34     // that was abstract in base class Employee
35     public override decimal GetPaymentAmount()
36     {
37        return WeeklySalary;
38     } // end method GetPaymentAmount
```

Fig. 12.14 | SalariedEmployee class that extends Employee. (Part 1 of 2.)

```
39
40     // return string representation of SalariedEmployee object
41     public override string ToString()
42     {
43        return string.Format( "salaried employee: {0}\n{1}: {2:C}",
44           base.ToString(), "weekly salary", WeeklySalary );
45     } // end method ToString
46  } // end class SalariedEmployee
```

Fig. 12.14 | SalariedEmployee class that extends Employee. (Part 2 of 2.)

When a class implements an interface, the same *is-a* relationship provided by inheritance applies. Class Employee implements IPayable, so we can say that an Employee *is an* IPayable, as are any classes that extend Employee. As such, SalariedEmployee objects are IPayable objects. An object of a class that implements an interface may be thought of as an object of the interface type. Objects of any classes derived from the class that implements the interface can also be thought of as objects of the interface type. Thus, just as we can assign the reference of a SalariedEmployee object to a base-class Employee variable, we can assign the reference of a SalariedEmployee object to an interface IPayable variable. Invoice implements IPayable, so an Invoice object also *is an* IPayable object, and we can assign the reference of an Invoice object to an IPayable variable.

Software Engineering Observation 12.4

Inheritance and interfaces are similar in their implementation of the is-a relationship. An object of a class that implements an interface may be thought of as an object of that interface type. An object of any derived classes of a class that implements an interface also can be thought of as an object of the interface type.

Software Engineering Observation 12.5

The is-a relationship that exists between base classes and derived classes, and between interfaces and the classes that implement them, holds when passing an object to a method. When a method parameter receives an argument of a base class or interface type, the method polymorphically processes the object received as an argument.

12.7.6 Using Interface IPayable to Process Invoices and Employees Polymorphically

PayableInterfaceTest (Fig. 12.15) illustrates that interface IPayable can be used to process a set of Invoices and Employees polymorphically in a single app. Line 10 declares payableObjects and assigns it an array of four IPayable variables. Lines 13–14 assign the references of Invoice objects to the first two elements of payableObjects. Lines 15–18 assign the references of SalariedEmployee objects to the remaining two elements of payableObjects. These assignments are allowed because an Invoice *is an* IPayable, a SalariedEmployee *is an* Employee and an Employee *is an* IPayable. Lines 24–29 use a foreach statement to process each IPayable object in payableObjects polymorphically, displaying the object as a string, along with the payment due. Lines 27–28 implicitly invokes method ToString off an IPayable interface reference, even though ToString is not declared in interface IPayable—all references (including those of interface types) refer to objects that extend object and therefore have a ToString method. Line 28 invokes IPayable method GetPaymentAmount to obtain the payment amount for each object in payableObjects, regardless of the actual type of the object. The output reveals that the method calls in lines 27–28 invoke the appropriate class's implementation of methods ToString and GetPaymentAmount. For instance, when currentPayable refers to an Invoice during the first iteration of the foreach loop, class Invoice's ToString and GetPaymentAmount methods execute.

Software Engineering Observation 12.6

All methods of class object can be called by using a reference of an interface type—the reference refers to an object, and all objects inherit the methods of class object.

```
1   // Fig. 12.15: PayableInterfaceTest.cs
2   // Tests interface IPayable with disparate classes.
3   using System;
4
5   public class PayableInterfaceTest
6   {
7      public static void Main( string[] args )
8      {
9         // create four-element IPayable array
10         IPayable[] payableObjects = new IPayable[ 4 ];
11
12         // populate array with objects that implement IPayable
13         payableObjects[ 0 ] = new Invoice( "01234", "seat", 2, 375.00M );
14         payableObjects[ 1 ] = new Invoice( "56789", "tire", 4, 79.95M );
15         payableObjects[ 2 ] = new SalariedEmployee( "John", "Smith",
16            "111-11-1111", 800.00M );
17         payableObjects[ 3 ] = new SalariedEmployee( "Lisa", "Barnes",
18            "888-88-8888", 1200.00M );
19
20         Console.WriteLine(
21            "Invoices and Employees processed polymorphically:\n" );
22
23         // generically process each element in array payableObjects
24         foreach ( var currentPayable in payableObjects )
25         {
26            // output currentPayable and its appropriate payment amount
27            Console.WriteLine( "{0}\npayment due: {1:C}\n",
28               currentPayable, currentPayable.GetPaymentAmount() );
29         } // end foreach
30      } // end Main
31   } // end class PayableInterfaceTest
```

```
Invoices and Employees processed polymorphically:

invoice:
part number: 01234 (seat)
quantity: 2
price per item: $375.00
payment due: $750.00
```

Fig. 12.15 | Tests interface IPayable with disparate classes. (Part 1 of 2.)

```
invoice:
part number: 56789 (tire)
quantity: 4
price per item: $79.95
payment due: $319.80

salaried employee: John Smith
social security number: 111-11-1111
weekly salary: $800.00
payment due: $800.00

salaried employee: Lisa Barnes
social security number: 888-88-8888
weekly salary: $1,200.00
payment due: $1,200.00
```

Fig. 12.15 | Tests interface IPayable with disparate classes. (Part 2 of 2.)

12.7.7 Common Interfaces of the .NET Framework Class Library

In this section, we overview several common interfaces defined in the .NET Framework Class Library. These interfaces are implemented and used in the same manner as those you create (e.g., interface IPayable in Section 12.7.2). The Framework Class Library's interfaces enable you to extend many important aspects of C# with your own classes. Figure 12.16 overviews several commonly used Framework Class Library interfaces.

Interface	Description
IComparable	As you learned in Chapter 3, C# contains several comparison operators (e.g., <, <=, >, >=, ==, !=) that allow you to compare simple-type values. In Section 12.8 you'll see that these operators can be defined to compare two objects. Interface IComparable can also be used to allow objects of a class that implements the interface to be compared to one another. The interface contains one method, CompareTo, that compares the object that calls the method to the object passed as an argument to the method. Classes must implement CompareTo to return a value indicating whether the object on which it's invoked is less than (negative integer return value), equal to (0 return value) or greater than (positive integer return value) the object passed as an argument, using any criteria you specify. For example, if class Employee implements IComparable, its CompareTo method could compare Employee objects by their earnings amounts. Interface IComparable is commonly used for ordering objects in a collection such as an array. We use IComparable in Chapter 18, Generics, and Chapter 19, Collections.
IComponent	Implemented by any class that represents a component, including Graphical User Interface (GUI) controls (such as buttons or labels). Interface IComponent defines the behaviors that components must implement. We discuss IComponent and many GUI controls that implement this interface in Chapter 14, Graphical User Interfaces with Windows Forms: Part 1, and Chapter 15, Graphical User Interfaces with Windows Forms: Part 2.

Fig. 12.16 | Common interfaces of the .NET Framework Class Library. (Part 1 of 2.)

Interface	Description
IDisposable	Implemented by classes that must provide an explicit mechanism for *releasing* resources. Some resources can be used by only one program at a time. In addition, some resources, such as files on disk, are unmanaged resources that, unlike memory, cannot be released by the garbage collector. Classes that implement interface IDisposable provide a Dispose method that can be called to explicitly release resources. We discuss IDisposable briefly in Chapter 13, Exception Handling: A Deeper Look. You can learn more about this interface at msdn.microsoft.com/en-us/library/system.idisposable.aspx. The MSDN article *Implementing a Dispose Method* at msdn.microsoft.com/en-us/library/fs2xkftw.aspx discusses the proper implementation of this interface in your classes.
IEnumerator	Used for iterating through the elements *of a collection* (such as an array) one element at a time. Interface IEnumerator contains method MoveNext to move to the next element in a collection, method Reset to move to the position before the first element and property Current to return the object at the current location. We use IEnumerator in Chapter 19.

Fig. 12.16 | Common interfaces of the .NET Framework Class Library. (Part 2 of 2.)

12.8 Operator Overloading

Object manipulations are accomplished by sending *messages* (in the form of method calls) to the objects. This method-call notation is cumbersome for certain kinds of classes, especially mathematical classes. For these classes, it would be convenient to use C#'s rich set of built-in operators to specify object manipulations. In this section, we show how to enable these operators to work with class objects—via a process called **operator overloading**.

You can overload most operators to make them sensitive to the context in which they're used. Some operators are overloaded more frequently than others, especially the various arithmetic operators, such as + and -, where operator notation often is more natural. Figures 12.17 and 12.18 provide an example of using operator overloading with a ComplexNumber class. For a list of overloadable operators, see msdn.microsoft.com/en-us/library/8edha89s.aspx.

Class *ComplexNumber*
Class ComplexNumber (Fig. 12.17) overloads the plus (+), minus (-) and multiplication (*) operators to enable programs to add, subtract and multiply instances of class ComplexNumber using common mathematical notation. Lines 9 and 12 define properties for the Real and Imaginary components of the complex number.

```
1   // Fig. 12.17: ComplexNumber.cs
2   // Class that overloads operators for adding, subtracting
3   // and multiplying complex numbers.
4   using System;
```

Fig. 12.17 | Class that overloads operators for adding, subtracting and multiplying complex numbers. (Part 1 of 2.)

```
5
6    public class ComplexNumber
7    {
8       // read-only property that gets the real component
9       public double Real { get; private set; }
10
11      // read-only property that gets the imaginary component
12      public double Imaginary { get; private set; }
13
14      // constructor
15      public ComplexNumber( double a, double b )
16      {
17         Real = a;
18         Imaginary = b;
19      } // end constructor
20
21      // return string representation of ComplexNumber
22      public override string ToString()
23      {
24         return string.Format( "({0} {1} {2}i)",
25            Real, ( Imaginary < 0 ? "-" : "+" ), Math.Abs( Imaginary ) );
26      } // end method ToString
27
28      // overload the addition operator
29      public static ComplexNumber operator+ (
30         ComplexNumber x, ComplexNumber y )
31      {
32         return new ComplexNumber( x.Real + y.Real,
33            x.Imaginary + y.Imaginary );
34      } // end operator +
35
36      // overload the subtraction operator
37      public static ComplexNumber operator- (
38         ComplexNumber x, ComplexNumber y )
39      {
40         return new ComplexNumber( x.Real - y.Real,
41            x.Imaginary - y.Imaginary );
42      } // end operator -
43
44      // overload the multiplication operator
45      public static ComplexNumber operator* (
46         ComplexNumber x, ComplexNumber y )
47      {
48         return new ComplexNumber(
49            x.Real * y.Real - x.Imaginary * y.Imaginary,
50            x.Real * y.Imaginary + y.Real * x.Imaginary );
51      } // end operator *
52   } // end class ComplexNumber
```

Fig. 12.17 | Class that overloads operators for adding, subtracting and multiplying complex numbers. (Part 2 of 2.)

Lines 29–34 overload the plus operator (+) to perform addition of ComplexNumbers. Keyword **operator**, followed by an operator symbol, indicates that a method overloads the specified operator. Methods that overload binary operators must take two arguments. The *first* argument is the *left* operand, and the *second* argument is the *right* operand. Class ComplexNumber's overloaded plus operator takes two ComplexNumber references as arguments and returns a ComplexNumber that represents the sum of the arguments. This method is marked public and static, which is required for overloaded operators. The body of the method (lines 32–33) performs the addition and returns the result as a new Complex-Number. Notice that we do *not* modify the contents of either of the original operands passed as arguments x and y. This matches our intuitive sense of how this operator should behave—adding two numbers does not modify either of the original numbers. Lines 37–51 provide similar overloaded operators for subtracting and multiplying ComplexNumbers.

Software Engineering Observation 12.7

Overload operators to perform the same function or similar functions on class objects as the operators perform on objects of simple types. Avoid nonintuitive use of operators.

Software Engineering Observation 12.8

At least one parameter of an overloaded operator method must be a reference to an object of the class in which the operator is overloaded. This prevents you from changing how operators work on simple types.

Class *ComplexNumber*

Class ComplexTest (Fig. 12.18) demonstrates the overloaded ComplexNumber operators +, - and *. Lines 14–27 prompt the user to enter two complex numbers, then use this input to create two ComplexNumbers and assign them to variables x and y.

```
1   // Fig. 12.18: ComplexTest.cs
2   // Overloading operators for complex numbers.
3   using System;
4
5   public class ComplexTest
6   {
7      public static void Main( string[] args )
8      {
9         // declare two variables to store complex numbers
10        // to be entered by user
11        ComplexNumber x, y;
12
13        // prompt the user to enter the first complex number
14        Console.Write( "Enter the real part of complex number x: " );
15        double realPart = Convert.ToDouble( Console.ReadLine() );
16        Console.Write(
17           "Enter the imaginary part of complex number x: " );
18        double imaginaryPart = Convert.ToDouble( Console.ReadLine() );
19        x = new ComplexNumber( realPart, imaginaryPart );
20
21        // prompt the user to enter the second complex number
22        Console.Write( "\nEnter the real part of complex number y: " );
23        realPart = Convert.ToDouble( Console.ReadLine() );
```

Fig. 12.18 | Overloading operators for complex numbers. (Part 1 of 2.)

```
24          Console.Write(
25             "Enter the imaginary part of complex number y: " );
26          imaginaryPart = Convert.ToDouble( Console.ReadLine() );
27          y = new ComplexNumber( realPart, imaginaryPart );
28
29          // display the results of calculations with x and y
30          Console.WriteLine();
31          Console.WriteLine( "{0} + {1} = {2}", x, y, x + y );
32          Console.WriteLine( "{0} - {1} = {2}", x, y, x - y );
33          Console.WriteLine( "{0} * {1} = {2}", x, y, x * y );
34       } // end method Main
35    } // end class ComplexTest
```

```
Enter the real part of complex number x: 2
Enter the imaginary part of complex number x: 4

Enter the real part of complex number y: 4
Enter the imaginary part of complex number y: -2

(2 + 4i) + (4 - 2i) = (6 + 2i)
(2 + 4i) - (4 - 2i) = (-2 + 6i)
(2 + 4i) * (4 - 2i) = (16 + 12i)
```

Fig. 12.18 | Overloading operators for complex numbers. (Part 2 of 2.)

Lines 31–33 add, subtract and multiply x and y with the overloaded operators, then output the results. In line 31, we perform the addition by using the plus operator with ComplexNumber operands x and y. Without operator overloading, the expression x + y wouldn't make sense—the compiler wouldn't know how two objects of class Complex-Number should be added. This expression makes sense here because we've defined the plus operator for two ComplexNumbers in lines 29–34 of Fig. 12.17. When the two Complex-Numbers are "added" in line 31 of Fig. 12.18, this invokes the operator+ declaration, passing the left operand as the first argument and the right operand as the second argument. When we use the subtraction and multiplication operators in lines 32–33, their respective overloaded operator declarations are invoked similarly.

Each calculation's result is a reference to a new ComplexNumber object. When this new object is passed to the Console class's WriteLine method, its ToString method (Fig. 12.17, lines 22–26) is implicitly invoked. Line 31 of Fig. 12.18 could be rewritten to explicitly invoke the ToString method of the object created by the overloaded plus operator, as in:

```
Console.WriteLine( "{0} + {1} = {2}", x, y, ( x + y ).ToString() );
```

12.9 Wrap-Up

This chapter introduced polymorphism—the ability to process objects that share the same base class in a class hierarchy as if they were all objects of the base class. The chapter discussed how polymorphism makes systems extensible and maintainable, then demonstrated how to use overridden methods to effect polymorphic behavior. We introduced the notion of an abstract class, which allows you to provide an appropriate base class from which other classes can inherit. You learned that an abstract class can declare abstract methods that each derived class must implement to become a concrete class, and that an app can use variables of an abstract class to invoke derived class implementations of abstract methods polymorphically. You also learned how to determine an object's type at execution time. We showed how to create `sealed` methods and classes. The chapter discussed declaring and implementing an interface as another way to achieve polymorphic behavior, often among objects of different classes. Finally, you learned how to define the behavior of the built-in operators on objects of your own classes with operator overloading.

You should now be familiar with classes, objects, encapsulation, inheritance, interfaces and polymorphism—the most essential aspects of object-oriented programming. Next, we take a deeper look at using exception handling to deal with runtime errors.

13

Exception Handling: A Deeper Look

Objectives

In this chapter you'll:

- Learn what exceptions are and how they're handled.

- Learn when to use exception handling.

- Use `try` blocks to delimit code in which exceptions might occur.

- Use `catch` blocks to specify exception handlers.

- Use the `finally` block to release resources.

- Learn about the .NET exception class hierarchy.

- Learn various `Exception` properties.

- Create user-defined exceptions.

13.1 Introduction

In this chapter, we take a deeper look at **exception handling**. As you know from Section 8.4, an **exception** indicates that a problem occurred during a program's execution. The name "exception" comes from the fact that, although the problem can occur, it occurs infrequently. As we showed in Section 8.4 and in Chapter 10, exception handling enables you to create apps that can handle exceptions—in many cases allowing a program to continue executing as if no problems were encountered. More severe problems may prevent a program from continuing normal execution, instead requiring the program to notify the user of the problem, then terminate in a controlled manner. The features presented in this chapter enable you to write clear, **robust** and more **fault-tolerant programs** (i.e., programs that are able to deal with problems that may arise and continue executing). The style and details of C# exception handling are based in part on the work of Andrew Koenig and Bjarne Stroustrup. "Best practices" for exception handling in Visual C# are specified in the Visual Studio documentation.[1]

After reviewing exception-handling concepts and basic exception-handling techniques, we overview .NET's exception-handling class hierarchy. Programs typically *request* and *release* resources (such as files on disk) during program execution. Often, the supply of these resources is limited, or the resources can be used by only one program at a time. We demonstrate a part of the exception-handling mechanism that enables a program to use a resource, then *guarantee* that it will be released for use by other programs, even if an exception occurs. We show several properties of class System.Exception (the base class of all exception classes) and discuss how you can create and use your own exception classes.

A Note About the Version of Visual Studio Used in This Chapter

In earlier versions of Visual Studio, all versions included a useful tool known as the *Exception Assistant* that we'll discuss in Section 13.3.3. Unfortunately, this tool is *not* part of the various Visual Studio Express 2012 editions (at the time of this writing). For this reason, we used Visual Studio Professional 2012 in this chapter. If you have only Visual Studio Express 2012 for Windows Desktop, the programs in this chapter will still execute. Start-

---

1. "Best Practices for Handling Exceptions [C#]," *.NET Framework Developer's Guide*, Visual Studio .NET Online Help. Available at msdn.microsoft.com/en-us/library/seyhszts.aspx.

ing in the next section, we'll discuss the differences between the IDE versions when you run a program with **DEBUG > Start Debugging** and exceptions occur.

13.2 Example: Divide by Zero without Exception Handling

Let's revisit what happens when errors arise in a console app that does not use exception handling. Figure 13.1 inputs two integers from the user, then divides the first integer by the second using integer division to obtain an int result. In this example, an exception is **thrown** (i.e., an exception occurs) when a method detects a problem and is unable to handle it.

```
1   // Fig. 13.1: DivideByZeroNoExceptionHandling.cs
2   // Integer division without exception handling.
3   using System;
4
5   class DivideByZeroNoExceptionHandling
6   {
7      static void Main()
8      {
9         // get numerator
10        Console.Write( "Please enter an integer numerator: " );
11        int numerator = Convert.ToInt32( Console.ReadLine() );
12
13        // get denominator
14        Console.Write( "Please enter an integer denominator: " );
15        int denominator = Convert.ToInt32( Console.ReadLine() );
16
17        // divide the two integers, then display the result
18        int result = numerator / denominator;
19        Console.WriteLine( "\nResult: {0:D} / {1:D} = {2:D}",
20           numerator, denominator, result );
21     } // end Main
22  } // end class DivideByZeroNoExceptionHandling
```

```
Please enter an integer numerator: 100
Please enter an integer denominator: 7

Result: 100 / 7 = 14
```

```
Please enter an integer numerator: 100
Please enter an integer denominator: 0

Unhandled Exception: System.DivideByZeroException:
   Attempted to divide by zero.
   at DivideByZeroNoExceptionHandling.Main()
      in C:\examples\ch13\Fig13_01\DivideByZeroNoExceptionHandling\
      DivideByZeroNoExceptionHandling\
      DivideByZeroNoExceptionHandling.cs:line 18
```

Fig. 13.1 | Integer division without exception handling. (Part 1 of 2.)

```
Please enter an integer numerator: 100
Please enter an integer denominator: hello

Unhandled Exception: System.FormatException:
   Input string was not in a correct format.
   at System.Number.StringToNumber(String str, NumberStyles options,
      NumberBuffer& number, NumberFormatInfo info, Boolean parseDecimal)
   at System.Number.ParseInt32(String s, NumberStyles style,
      NumberFormatInfo info)
   at DivideByZeroNoExceptionHandling.Main()
      in C:\examples\ch13\Fig13_01\DivideByZeroNoExceptionHandling\
      DivideByZeroNoExceptionHandling\
      DivideByZeroNoExceptionHandling.cs:line 15
```

Fig. 13.1 | Integer division without exception handling. (Part 2 of 2.)

Running the App

In most of our examples, an app appears to run the same with or without debugging. As we discuss shortly, the example in Fig. 13.1 might cause exceptions, depending on the user's input. If you run this app in Visual Studio Express 2012 for Windows Desktop using the **DEBUG > Start Debugging** menu option and an exception occurs, the IDE displays a dialog like the one below:

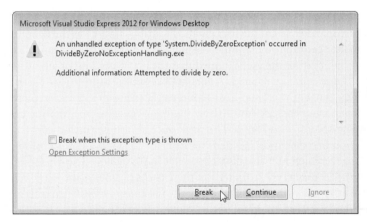

You can click the **Break** button to pause the program at the line where the exception occurred, allowing you to analyze the program's state and debug the program. For this example, we do not wish to debug the app; we simply want to see what happens when errors arise. For this reason, we executed this app with **DEBUG > Start Without Debugging** If an exception occurs during execution, a dialog appears indicating that the app "has stopped working." You can simply click **Close the Program** to terminate the app. An error message describing the exception that occurred is displayed in the output window. We formatted the error messages in Fig. 13.1 for readability.

Successful Execution

The first sample execution shows a successful division.

Attempting to Divide By Zero

In the second, the user enters 0 as the denominator. Several lines of information are displayed in response to the invalid input. This information—known as a **stack trace**—includes the exception class's name (System.DivideByZeroException) in a message indicating the problem that occurred and the path of execution that led to the exception, method by method. Stack traces help you debug a program. The first line of the error message specifies that a DivideByZeroException occurred. When a program divides an integer by 0, the CLR throws a **DivideByZeroException** (namespace System). The text after the exception name, "Attempted to divide by zero," indicates why this exception occurred. Division by zero is not allowed in integer arithmetic.[2]

Each "at" line in a stack trace indicates a line of code in the particular method that was executing when the exception occurred. The "at" line contains the namespace, class and method in which the exception occurred (DivideByZeroNoExceptionHandling.Main), the location and name of the file containing the code (C:\examples\ch13\Fig13_01\DivideByZeroNoExceptionHandling\DivideByZeroNoExceptionHandling\DivideByZeroNoExceptionHandling.cs) and the line number (:line 18) where the exception occurred. In this case, the stack trace indicates that the DivideByZeroException occurred when the program was executing line 18 of method Main. The first "at" line in the stack trace indicates the exception's **throw point**—the initial point at which the exception occurred (i.e., line 18 in Main). This information makes it easy for you to see which method call caused the exception, and what method calls were made to get to that point in the program.

Attempting to Enter a Non-Integer Value for the Denominator

In the third sample execution, the user enters the string "hello" as the denominator. This causes a FormatException, and another stack trace is displayed. Our earlier examples that read numeric values from the user assumed that the user would input an integer value, but a noninteger value could be entered. A **FormatException** (namespace System) occurs, for example, when Convert method ToInt32 receives a string that does not represent a valid integer. Starting from the last "at" line in the stack trace, we see that the exception was detected in line 15 of method Main. The stack trace also shows the other methods that led to the exception being thrown. To perform its task, Convert.ToInt32 calls method Number.ParseInt32, which in turn calls Number.StringToNumber. The throw point occurs in Number.StringToNumber, as indicated by the first "at" line in the stack trace. Method Convert.ToInt32 is *not in the stack trace* because the compiler *optimized* this call out of the code—all it does forward its arguments to Number.ParseInt32.

Program Termination Due to an Unhandled Exception

In the sample executions in Fig. 13.1, the program terminates when an *unhandled* exception occurs and a stack trace is displayed. This does not always happen—sometimes a program may continue executing even though an exception has occurred and a stack trace has been displayed. In such cases, the app may produce incorrect results. The next section demonstrates how to handle exceptions to enable the program to run to normal completion.

---

2. Division by zero with floating-point values *is* allowed and results in the value infinity—represented by either constant **Double.PositiveInfinity** or constant **Double.NegativeInfinity**, depending on whether the numerator is positive or negative. These values are displayed as Infinity or -Infinity. If *both* the numerator and denominator are *zero*, the result of the calculation is the constant **Double.NaN** ("not a number"), which is returned when a calculation's result is *undefined*.

13.3 Example: Handling DivideByZeroExceptions and FormatExceptions

Now, let's consider a simple example of exception handling. The app in Fig. 13.2 uses exception handling to process any DivideByZeroExceptions and FormatExceptions that might arise. The app reads two integers from the user (lines 18–21). Assuming that the user provides integers as input and does not specify 0 as the denominator for the division, line 25 performs the division and lines 28–29 display the result. However, if the user inputs a noninteger value or supplies 0 as the denominator, an exception occurs. This program demonstrates how to **catch** and **handle** such exceptions—in this case, displaying an error message and allowing the user to enter another set of values.

```
1   // Fig. 13.2: DivideByZeroExceptionHandling.cs
2   // FormatException and DivideByZeroException handlers.
3   using System;
4
5   class DivideByZeroExceptionHandling
6   {
7      static void Main( string[] args )
8      {
9         bool continueLoop = true; // determines whether to keep looping
10
11        do
12        {
13           // retrieve user input and calculate quotient
14           try
15           {
16              // Convert.ToInt32 generates FormatException
17              // if argument cannot be converted to an integer
18              Console.Write( "Enter an integer numerator: " );
19              int numerator = Convert.ToInt32( Console.ReadLine() );
20              Console.Write( "Enter an integer denominator: " );
21              int denominator = Convert.ToInt32( Console.ReadLine() );
22
23              // division generates DivideByZeroException
24              // if denominator is 0
25              int result = numerator / denominator;
26
27              // display result
28              Console.WriteLine( "\nResult: {0} / {1} = {2}",
29                 numerator, denominator, result );
30              continueLoop = false;
31           } // end try
32           catch ( FormatException formatException )
33           {
34              Console.WriteLine( "\n" + formatException.Message );
35              Console.WriteLine(
36                 "You must enter two integers. Please try again.\n" );
37           } // end catch
38           catch ( DivideByZeroException divideByZeroException )
39           {
```

Fig. 13.2 | FormatException and DivideByZeroException handlers. (Part 1 of 2.)

```
40                    Console.WriteLine( "\n" + divideByZeroException.Message );
41                    Console.WriteLine(
42                       "Zero is an invalid denominator. Please try again.\n" );
43                 } // end catch
44              } while ( continueLoop ); // end do...while
45           } // end Main
46        } // end class DivideByZeroExceptionHandling
```

```
Please enter an integer numerator: 100
Please enter an integer denominator: 7

Result: 100 / 7 = 14
```

```
Enter an integer numerator: 100
Enter an integer denominator: 0

Attempted to divide by zero.
Zero is an invalid denominator. Please try again.

Enter an integer numerator: 100
Enter an integer denominator: 7

Result: 100 / 7 = 14
```

```
Enter an integer numerator: 100
Enter an integer denominator: hello

Input string was not in a correct format.
You must enter two integers. Please try again.

Enter an integer numerator: 100
Enter an integer denominator: 7

Result: 100 / 7 = 14
```

Fig. 13.2 | FormatException and DivideByZeroException handlers. (Part 2 of 2.)

Sample Outputs

Before we discuss the details of the program, let's consider the sample outputs in Fig. 13.2. The first sample output shows a successful calculation in which the user enters the numerator 100 and the denominator 7. The result (14) is an int, because integer division always yields an int result. The second sample output demonstrates the result of an attempt to divide by zero. In integer arithmetic, the CLR tests for division by zero and generates a DivideByZeroException if the denominator is zero. The program detects the exception and displays an error message indicating the attempt to divide by zero. The last sample output depicts the result of inputting a non-int value—in this case, the user enters "hello" as the denominator. The program attempts to convert the input strings to ints using method Convert.ToInt32 (lines 19 and 21). If an argument cannot be converted to an int, the method throws a FormatException. The program catches the exception and displays an error message indicating that the user must enter two ints.

Another Way to Convert Strings to Integers

Another way to validate the input is to use the **Int32.TryParse** method, which converts a string to an int value if possible. All of the numeric types have TryParse methods. The method requires two arguments—one is the string to parse and the other is the variable in which the converted value is to be stored. The method returns a bool value that's true only if the string was parsed successfully. If the string could not be converted, the value 0 is assigned to the second argument, which is passed by reference so its value can be modified in the calling method. Method TryParse can be used to validate input in code rather than allowing the code to throw an exception—this technique is generally preferred.

13.3.1 Enclosing Code in a try Block

Now we consider the user interactions and flow of control that yield the results shown in the sample output windows. Lines 14–31 define a **try block** enclosing the code that might throw exceptions, as well as the code that's skipped when an exception occurs. For example, the program should not display a new result (lines 28–29) unless the calculation in line 25 completes successfully.

The user inputs values that represent the numerator and denominator. The two statements that read the ints (lines 19 and 21) call method Convert.ToInt32 to convert strings to int values. This method throws a FormatException if it cannot convert its string argument to an int. If lines 19 and 21 convert the values properly (i.e., no exceptions occur), then line 25 divides the numerator by the denominator and assigns the result to variable result. If denominator is 0, line 25 causes the CLR to throw a DivideByZero-Exception. If line 25 does not cause an exception to be thrown, then lines 28–29 display the result of the division.

13.3.2 Catching Exceptions

Exception-handling code appears in a **catch block**. In general, when an exception occurs in a try block, a corresponding catch block *catches* the exception and *handles* it. The try block in this example is followed by two catch blocks—one that handles a Format-Exception (lines 32–37) and one that handles a DivideByZeroException (lines 38–43). A catch block specifies an exception parameter representing the exception that the catch block can handle. The catch block can use the parameter's identifier (which you choose) to interact with a caught exception object. If there's no need to use the exception object in the catch block, the exception parameter's identifier can be omitted. The type of the catch's parameter is the type of the exception that the catch block handles. Optionally, you can include a catch block that does *not* specify an exception type—such a catch block (known as a **general catch clause**) catches all exception types. At least one catch block and/or a **finally block** (discussed in Section 13.5) must immediately follow a try block.

In Fig. 13.2, the first catch block catches FormatExceptions (thrown by method Convert.ToInt32), and the second catch block catches DivideByZeroExceptions (thrown by the CLR). If an exception occurs, the program executes only the first matching catch block. Both exception handlers in this example display an error-message dialog. After either catch block terminates, program control continues with the first statement after the last catch block (the end of the method, in this example). We'll soon take a deeper look at how this flow of control works in exception handling.

13.3.3 Uncaught Exceptions

An **uncaught exception** (or **unhandled exception**) is an exception for which there's no matching catch block. You saw the results of uncaught exceptions in the second and third outputs of Fig. 13.1. Recall that when exceptions occur in that example, the app terminates early (after displaying the exception's stack trace). The result of an uncaught exception depends on how you execute the program—Fig. 13.1 demonstrated the results of an uncaught exception when an app is executed using **DEBUG > Start Without Debugging**. If you run the app from a non-Express version of Visual Studio by using **DEBUG > Start Debugging** and the runtime environment detects an uncaught exception, the app pauses, and the **Exception Assistant** window appears containing:

- a line pointing from the Exception Assistant to the line of code that caused the exception
- the type of the exception
- **Troubleshooting tips** with links to helpful information on what might have caused the exception and how to handle it
- links to view or copy the complete exception details

Figure 13.3 shows the Exception Assistant that's displayed if the user attempts to divide by zero in the app of Fig. 13.1.

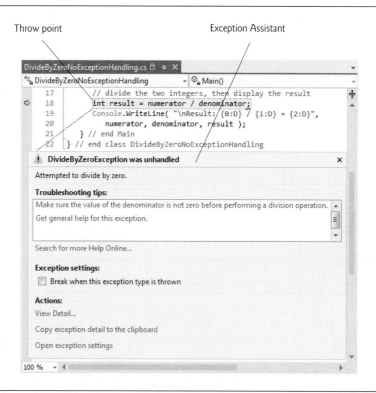

Fig. 13.3 | Exception Assistant.

13.3.4 Termination Model of Exception Handling

Recall that the point in the program at which an exception occurs is called the *throw point*—this is an important location for debugging purposes (as we demonstrate in Section 13.7). If an exception occurs in a `try` block (such as a `FormatException` being thrown as a result of the code in lines 19 and 21 in Fig. 13.2), the `try` block terminates immediately, and program control transfers to the first of the following `catch` blocks in which the exception parameter's type matches that of the thrown exception. In Fig. 13.2, the first `catch` block catches `FormatExceptions` (which occur if input of an invalid type is entered); the second `catch` block catches `DivideByZeroExceptions` (which occur if an attempt is made to divide by zero). After the exception is handled, program control does *not* return to the throw point because the `try` block has *exited* (which also causes any of its local variables to go out of scope). Rather, control resumes after the last `catch` block. This is known as the **termination model of exception handling**. [*Note:* Some languages use the **resumption model of exception handling**, in which, after an exception is handled, control resumes just after the throw point.]

If no exceptions occur in the `try` block, the program of Fig. 13.2 successfully completes the `try` block by ignoring the `catch` blocks in lines 32–37 and 38–43, and passing line 43. Then the program executes the first statement following the `try` and `catch` blocks. In this example, the program reaches the end of the `do...while` loop (line 44), so the method terminates, and the program awaits the next user interaction.

The `try` block and its corresponding `catch` and `finally` blocks together form a **try statement**. It's important not to confuse the terms "try block" and "try statement"—the term "try block" refers to the block of code following the keyword `try` (but before any `catch` or `finally` blocks), while the term "try statement" includes all the code from the opening `try` keyword to the end of the last `catch` or `finally` block. This includes the `try` block, as well as any associated `catch` blocks and `finally` block.

When a `try` block terminates, local variables defined in the block go out of scope. If a `try` block terminates due to an exception, the CLR searches for the first `catch` block that can process the type of exception that occurred. The CLR locates the matching `catch` by comparing the type of the thrown exception to each `catch`'s parameter type. A match occurs if the types are identical or if the thrown exception's type is a derived class of the `catch`'s parameter type. Once an exception is matched to a `catch` block, the code in that block executes and the other `catch` blocks in the `try` statement are ignored.

13.3.5 Flow of Control When Exceptions Occur

In the third sample output of Fig. 13.2, the user inputs `hello` as the denominator. When line 21 executes, `Convert.ToInt32` cannot convert this `string` to an `int`, so the method throws a `FormatException` object to indicate that the method was unable to convert the `string` to an `int`. When the exception occurs, the `try` block exits (terminates). Next, the CLR attempts to locate a matching `catch` block. A match occurs with the `catch` block in line 32, so the exception handler displays the exception's `Message` property (to retrieve the error message associated with the exception) and the program ignores all other exception handlers following the `try` block. Program control then continues with line 44.

Common Programming Error 13.1

Specifying a comma-separated list of parameters in a `catch` block is a syntax error. A catch block can have at most one parameter.

In the second sample output of Fig. 13.2, the user inputs 0 as the denominator. When the division in line 25 executes, a `DivideByZeroException` occurs. Once again, the `try` block terminates, and the program attempts to locate a matching `catch` block. In this case, the first `catch` block does not match—the exception type in the catch-handler declaration is not the same as the type of the thrown exception, and `FormatException` is not a base class of `DivideByZeroException`. Therefore the program continues to search for a matching `catch` block, which it finds in line 38. Line 40 displays the exception's `Message` property. Again, program control then continues with line 44.

13.4 .NET Exception Hierarchy

In C#, the exception-handling mechanism allows only objects of class **Exception** (namespace `System`) and its derived classes to be thrown and caught. Note, however, that C# programs may interact with software components written in other .NET languages (such as C++) that do not restrict exception types. The general `catch` clause can be used to catch such exceptions.

This section overviews several of the .NET Framework's exception classes and focuses exclusively on exceptions that derive from class `Exception`. In addition, we discuss how to determine whether a particular method throws exceptions.

13.4.1 Class SystemException

Class `Exception` (namespace `System`) is the base class of .NET's exception class hierarchy. An important derived class is **SystemException**. The CLR generates `SystemException`s. Many of these can be avoided if apps are coded properly. For example, if a program attempts to access an **out-of-range array index**, the CLR throws an exception of type **IndexOutOfRangeException** (a derived class of `SystemException`). Similarly, an exception occurs when a program uses a reference-type variable to call a method when the reference has a value of `null`. This causes a **NullReferenceException** (another derived class of `SystemException`). You saw earlier in this chapter that a `DivideByZeroException` occurs in integer division when a program attempts to divide by zero.

Other exceptions thrown by the CLR include **OutOfMemoryException**, **StackOverflowException** and **ExecutionEngineException**, which are thrown when something goes wrong that causes the CLR to become unstable. Sometimes such exceptions cannot even be caught. It's best to simply log such exceptions (using a tool such as Apache's *log4net*—`logging.apache.org/log4net/`), then terminate your app.

A benefit of the exception class hierarchy is that a `catch` block can catch exceptions of a particular type or—because of the *is-a* relationship of inheritance—can use a base-class type to catch exceptions in a hierarchy of related exception types. For example, Section 13.3.2 discussed the `catch` block with no parameter, which catches exceptions of all types (including those that are not derived from `Exception`). A `catch` block that specifies a parameter of type `Exception` can catch all exceptions that derive from `Exception`, because `Exception` is the base class of all exception classes. The advantage of this approach is that the exception handler can access the caught exception's information via the parameter in the `catch`. We'll say more about accessing exception information in Section 13.7.

Using inheritance with exceptions enables a `catch` block to catch related exceptions using a concise notation. A set of exception handlers could catch each derived-class exception type individually, but catching the base-class exception type is more concise. However, this technique makes sense *only* if the handling behavior is the same for a base class and all derived classes. Otherwise, catch each derived-class exception individually.

Common Programming Error 13.2

The compiler issues an error if a catch *block that catches a base-class exception is placed before a* catch *block for any of that class's derived-class types. In this case, the base-class* catch *block would catch all base-class and derived-class exceptions, so the derived-class exception handler would never execute.*

13.4.2 Determining Which Exceptions a Method Throws

How do we determine that an exception might occur in a program? For methods contained in the .NET Framework classes, read the detailed descriptions of the methods in the online documentation. If a method throws an exception, its description contains a section called **Exceptions** that specifies the types of exceptions the method throws and briefly describes what causes them. For an example, search for "Convert.ToInt32 method" in the Visual Studio online documentation. The **Exceptions** section of this method's web page indicates that method Convert.ToInt32 throws two exception types—FormatException and OverflowException—and describes the reason why each might occur. [*Note:* You can also find this information in the **Object Browser** described in Section 10.12.]

Software Engineering Observation 13.1

If a method throws exceptions, statements that invoke the method directly or indirectly should be placed in try *blocks, and those exceptions should be caught and handled.*

It's more difficult to determine when the CLR throws exceptions. Such information appears in the *C# Language Specification* (available from bit.ly/CSharp4Spec). This document defines C#'s syntax and specifies cases in which exceptions are thrown.

13.5 **finally** Block

Programs frequently request and release resources dynamically (i.e., at execution time). For example, a program that reads a file from disk first makes a file-open request (as we'll see in Chapter 17, Files and Streams). If that request succeeds, the program reads the contents of the file. Operating systems typically prevent more than one program from manipulating a file at once. Therefore, when a program finishes processing a file, the program should close the file (i.e., release the resource) so other programs can use it. If the file is not closed, a **resource leak** occurs. In such a case, the file resource is not available to other programs.

In programming languages such as C and C++, in which the programmer is responsible for dynamic memory management, the most common type of resource leak is a **memory leak**. A memory leak occurs when a program allocates memory (as C# programmers do via keyword new), but does not deallocate the memory when it's no longer needed. Normally, this is *not* an issue in C#, because the CLR performs *garbage collection* of memory that's no longer needed by an executing program (Section 10.8). However, other kinds of resource leaks (such as unclosed files) can occur.

Error-Prevention Tip 13.1

The CLR does not completely eliminate memory leaks. The CLR will not garbage collect an object until the program contains no more references to that object, and even then there may be a delay until the memory is required. Thus, memory leaks can occur if you inadvertently keep references to unwanted objects.

Moving Resource-Release Code to a `finally` Block

Exceptions often occur when an app processes resources that require explicit release. For example, a program that processes a file might receive `IOExceptions` during the processing. For this reason, file-processing code normally appears in a try block. Regardless of whether a program experiences exceptions while processing a file, the program should close the file when it's no longer needed. Suppose a program places all resource-request and resource-release code in a try block. If no exceptions occur, the try block executes normally and releases the resources after using them. However, if an exception occurs, the try block may exit *before* the resource-release code can execute. We could duplicate all the resource-release code in each of the catch blocks, but this would make the code more difficult to modify and maintain. We could also place the resource-release code after the try statement; however, if the try block terminated due to a return statement or an exception occurred, code following the try statement would never execute.

To address these problems, C#'s exception-handling mechanism provides the `finally` block, which is guaranteed to execute regardless of whether the try block executes successfully or an exception occurs. This makes the `finally` block an ideal location in which to place resource-release code for resources that are acquired and manipulated in the corresponding try block. If the try block executes successfully, the `finally` block executes immediately after the try block terminates. If an exception occurs in the try block, the `finally` block executes immediately after a catch block completes. If the exception is not caught by a catch block associated with the try block, or if a catch block associated with the try block throws an exception itself, the `finally` block executes before the exception is processed by the next enclosing try block, which could be in the calling method. By placing the resource-release code in a `finally` block, we ensure that even if the program terminates due to an uncaught exception, the resource will be deallocated. Local variables in a try block cannot be accessed in the corresponding `finally` block. For this reason, variables that must be accessed in both a try block, and its corresponding `finally` block should be declared before the try block.

Error-Prevention Tip 13.2

A `finally` block typically contains code to release resources acquired in the corresponding try block, which makes the `finally` block an effective mechanism for eliminating resource leaks.

Performance Tip 13.1

As a rule, resources should be released as soon as they're no longer needed in a program. This makes them available for reuse promptly.

If one or more catch blocks follow a try block, the `finally` block is optional. However, if no catch blocks follow a try block, a `finally` block must appear immediately after the try block. If any catch blocks follow a try block, the `finally` block (if there is one) appears *after* the last catch block. Only whitespace and comments can separate the blocks in a try statement.

Demonstrating the finally Block

The app in Fig. 13.4 demonstrates that the finally block *always* executes, regardless of whether an exception occurs in the corresponding try block. The app consists of method Main (lines 8–47) and four other methods that Main invokes to demonstrate finally. These methods are DoesNotThrowException (lines 50–67), ThrowExceptionWithCatch (lines 70–89), ThrowExceptionWithoutCatch (lines 92–108) and ThrowException-CatchRethrow (lines 111–136).

```csharp
1   // Fig. 13.4: UsingExceptions.cs
2   // Using finally blocks.
3   // finally blocks always execute, even when no exception occurs.
4   using System;
5
6   class UsingExceptions
7   {
8      static void Main()
9      {
10        // Case 1: No exceptions occur in called method
11        Console.WriteLine( "Calling DoesNotThrowException" );
12        DoesNotThrowException();
13
14        // Case 2: Exception occurs and is caught in called method
15        Console.WriteLine( "\nCalling ThrowExceptionWithCatch" );
16        ThrowExceptionWithCatch();
17
18        // Case 3: Exception occurs, but is not caught in called method
19        // because there is no catch block.
20        Console.WriteLine( "\nCalling ThrowExceptionWithoutCatch" );
21
22        // call ThrowExceptionWithoutCatch
23        try
24        {
25           ThrowExceptionWithoutCatch();
26        } // end try
27        catch
28        {
29           Console.WriteLine( "Caught exception from " +
30              "ThrowExceptionWithoutCatch in Main" );
31        } // end catch
32
33        // Case 4: Exception occurs and is caught in called method,
34        // then rethrown to caller.
35        Console.WriteLine( "\nCalling ThrowExceptionCatchRethrow" );
36
37        // call ThrowExceptionCatchRethrow
38        try
39        {
```

Fig. 13.4 | finally blocks always execute, even when no exception occurs. (Part 1 of 4.)

```
40                ThrowExceptionCatchRethrow();
41          } // end try
42          catch
43          {
44             Console.WriteLine( "Caught exception from " +
45                "ThrowExceptionCatchRethrow in Main" );
46          } // end catch
47       } // end method Main
48
49       // no exceptions thrown
50       static void DoesNotThrowException()
51       {
52          // try block does not throw any exceptions
53          try
54          {
55             Console.WriteLine( "In DoesNotThrowException" );
56          } // end try
57          catch
58          {
59             Console.WriteLine( "This catch never executes" );
60          } // end catch
61          finally
62          {
63             Console.WriteLine( "finally executed in DoesNotThrowException" );
64          } // end finally
65
66          Console.WriteLine( "End of DoesNotThrowException" );
67       } // end method DoesNotThrowException
68
69       // throws exception and catches it locally
70       static void ThrowExceptionWithCatch()
71       {
72          // try block throws exception
73          try
74          {
75             Console.WriteLine( "In ThrowExceptionWithCatch" );
76             throw new Exception( "Exception in ThrowExceptionWithCatch" );
77          } // end try
78          catch ( Exception exceptionParameter )
79          {
80             Console.WriteLine( "Message: " + exceptionParameter.Message );
81          } // end catch
82          finally
83          {
84             Console.WriteLine(
85                "finally executed in ThrowExceptionWithCatch" );
86          } // end finally
87
88          Console.WriteLine( "End of ThrowExceptionWithCatch" );
89       } // end method ThrowExceptionWithCatch
90
```

Fig. 13.4 | finally blocks always execute, even when no exception occurs. (Part 2 of 4.)

```
91    // throws exception and does not catch it locally
92    static void ThrowExceptionWithoutCatch()
93    {
94       // throw exception, but do not catch it
95       try
96       {
97          Console.WriteLine( "In ThrowExceptionWithoutCatch" );
98          throw new Exception( "Exception in ThrowExceptionWithoutCatch" );
99       } // end try
100      finally
101      {
102         Console.WriteLine( "finally executed in " +
103            "ThrowExceptionWithoutCatch" );
104      } // end finally
105
106      // unreachable code; logic error
107      Console.WriteLine( "End of ThrowExceptionWithoutCatch" );
108   } // end method ThrowExceptionWithoutCatch
109
110   // throws exception, catches it and rethrows it
111   static void ThrowExceptionCatchRethrow()
112   {
113      // try block throws exception
114      try
115      {
116         Console.WriteLine( "In ThrowExceptionCatchRethrow" );
117         throw new Exception( "Exception in ThrowExceptionCatchRethrow" );
118      } // end try
119      catch ( Exception exceptionParameter )
120      {
121         Console.WriteLine( "Message: " + exceptionParameter.Message );
122
123         // rethrow exception for further processing
124         throw;
125
126         // unreachable code; logic error
127      } // end catch
128      finally
129      {
130         Console.WriteLine( "finally executed in " +
131            "ThrowExceptionCatchRethrow" );
132      } // end finally
133
134      // any code placed here is never reached
135      Console.WriteLine( "End of ThrowExceptionCatchRethrow" );
136   } // end method ThrowExceptionCatchRethrow
137 } // end class UsingExceptions
```

```
Calling DoesNotThrowException
In DoesNotThrowException
finally executed in DoesNotThrowException
End of DoesNotThrowException
```

Fig. 13.4 | finally blocks always execute, even when no exception occurs. (Part 3 of 4.)

```
Calling ThrowExceptionWithCatch
In ThrowExceptionWithCatch
Message: Exception in ThrowExceptionWithCatch
finally executed in ThrowExceptionWithCatch
End of ThrowExceptionWithCatch

Calling ThrowExceptionWithoutCatch
In ThrowExceptionWithoutCatch
finally executed in ThrowExceptionWithoutCatch
Caught exception from ThrowExceptionWithoutCatch in Main

Calling ThrowExceptionCatchRethrow
In ThrowExceptionCatchRethrow
Message: Exception in ThrowExceptionCatchRethrow
finally executed in ThrowExceptionCatchRethrow
Caught exception from ThrowExceptionCatchRethrow in Main
```

Fig. 13.4 | `finally` blocks always execute, even when no exception occurs. (Part 4 of 4.)

Line 12 of `Main` invokes method `DoesNotThrowException`. This method's `try` block outputs a message (line 55). Because the `try` block does *not* throw any exceptions, program control ignores the `catch` block (lines 57–60) and executes the `finally` block (lines 61–64), which outputs a message. At this point, program control continues with the first statement after the close of the `finally` block (line 66), which outputs a message indicating that the end of the method has been reached. Then, program control returns to `Main`.

Throwing Exceptions Using the `throw` Statement
Line 16 of `Main` invokes method `ThrowExceptionWithCatch` (lines 70–89), which begins in its `try` block (lines 73–77) by outputting a message. Next, the `try` block creates an `Exception` object and uses a **throw statement** to throw it (line 76). Executing the `throw` statement indicates that a problem has occurred in the code. As you've seen in earlier chapters, you can throw exceptions by using the `throw` statement. Just as with exceptions thrown by the Framework Class Library's methods and the CLR, this indicates to client apps that an error has occurred. A `throw` statement specifies an object to be thrown. The operand of a `throw` statement can be of type `Exception` or of any type derived from class `Exception`.

The `string` passed to the constructor becomes the exception object's error message. When a `throw` statement in a `try` block executes, the `try` block *exits immediately*, and program control continues with the first matching `catch` block (lines 78–81) following the `try` block. In this example, the type thrown (`Exception`) matches the type specified in the `catch`, so line 80 outputs a message indicating the exception that occurred. Then, the `finally` block (lines 82–86) executes and outputs a message. At this point, program control continues with the first statement after the close of the `finally` block (line 88), which outputs a message indicating that the end of the method has been reached. Program control then returns to `Main`. In line 80, we use the exception object's `Message` property to retrieve the error message associated with the exception (i.e., the message passed to the `Exception` constructor). Section 13.7 discusses several properties of class `Exception`.

Lines 23–31 of `Main` define a `try` statement in which `Main` invokes method `ThrowExceptionWithoutCatch` (lines 92–108). The `try` block enables `Main` to catch any exceptions thrown by `ThrowExceptionWithoutCatch`. The `try` block in lines 95–99 of

ThrowExceptionWithoutCatch begins by outputting a message. Next, the try block throws an Exception (line 98) and exits immediately.

Normally, program control would continue at the first catch following this try block. However, this try block does not have any catch blocks. Therefore, the exception is not caught in method ThrowExceptionWithoutCatch. Program control proceeds to the finally block (lines 100–104), which outputs a message. At this point, program control returns to Main—any statements appearing after the finally block (e.g., line 107) do not execute. In this example, such statements could cause logic errors, because the exception thrown in line 98 is not caught. In Main, the catch block in lines 27–31 catches the exception and displays a message indicating that the exception was caught in Main.

Rethrowing Exceptions

Lines 38–46 of Main define a try statement in which Main invokes method Throw-ExceptionCatchRethrow (lines 111–136). The try statement enables Main to catch any exceptions thrown by ThrowExceptionCatchRethrow. The try statement in lines 114–132 of ThrowExceptionCatchRethrow begins by outputting a message. Next, the try block throws an Exception (line 117). The try block *exits immediately*, and program control continues at the first catch (lines 119–127) following the try block. In this example, the type thrown (Exception) matches the type specified in the catch, so line 121 outputs a message indicating where the exception occurred. Line 124 uses the throw statement to **rethrow** the exception. This indicates that the catch block performed partial processing of the exception and now is throwing the exception again (in this case, back to the method Main) for further processing. In general, it's considered better practice to throw a new exception and pass the original one to the new exception's constructor. This maintains all of the stack-trace information from the original exception. Rethrowing an exception loses the original exception's stack-trace information.

You can also rethrow an exception with a version of the throw statement which takes an operand that's the reference to the exception that was caught. It's important to note, however, that this form of throw statement *resets the throw point*, so the original throw point's stack-trace information is *lost*. Section 13.7 demonstrates using a throw statement with an operand from a catch block. In that section, you'll see that after an exception is caught, you can create and throw a different type of exception object from the catch block and you can include the original exception as part of the new exception object. Class library designers often do this to *customize* the exception types thrown from methods in their class libraries or to provide additional debugging information.

The exception handling in method ThrowExceptionCatchRethrow does not complete, because the throw statement in line 124 immediately terminates the catch block—if there were any code between line 124 and the end of the block, it would not execute. When line 124 executes, method ThrowExceptionCatchRethrow terminates and returns control to Main. Once again, the finally block (lines 128–132) executes and outputs a message before control returns to Main. When control returns to Main, the catch block in lines 42–46 catches the exception and displays a message indicating that the exception was caught. Then the program terminates.

Returning After a finally Block

The next statement to execute after a finally block terminates depends on the exception-handling state. If the try block successfully completes, or if a catch block catches and handles an exception, the program continues its execution with the next statement after the fi-nally block. However, if an exception is not caught, or if a catch block rethrows an exception, program control continues in the next enclosing try block. The enclosing try could be in the calling method or in one of its callers. It also is possible to nest a try statement in a try block; in such a case, the outer try statement's catch blocks would process any exceptions that were not caught in the inner try statement. If a try block executes and has a corresponding finally block, the finally block executes even if the try block terminates due to a return statement. The return occurs after the execution of the finally block.

Common Programming Error 13.3

If an uncaught exception is awaiting processing when the finally block executes, and the finally block throws a new exception that's not caught in the finally block, the first exception is lost, and the new exception is passed to the next enclosing try block.

Error-Prevention Tip 13.3

When placing code that can throw an exception in a finally block, always enclose the code in a try statement that catches the appropriate exception types. This prevents the loss of any uncaught and rethrown exceptions that occur before the finally block executes.

Software Engineering Observation 13.2

Do not place try blocks around every statement that might throw an exception—this can make programs difficult to read. Instead, place one try block around a significant portion of code, and follow this try block with catch blocks that handle each possible exception. Then follow the catch blocks with a single finally block. Use separate try blocks to distinguish between multiple statements that can throw the same exception type.

13.6 The using Statement

Typically resource-release code should be placed in a finally block to ensure that a resource is released, *regardless* of whether there were exceptions when the resource was used in the corresponding try block. An alternative notation—the **using** statement (not to be confused with the using directive for using namespaces)—simplifies writing code in which you obtain a resource, use the resource in a try block and release the resource in a corresponding finally block. For example, a file-processing app (Chapter 17) could process a file with a using statement to ensure that the file is closed properly when it's no longer needed. The resource must be an object that implements the IDisposable interface and therefore has a Dispose method. The general form of a using statement is

```
using ( ExampleClass exampleObject = new ExampleClass() )
{
    exampleObject.SomeMethod();
}
```

where ExampleClass is a class that implements the IDisposable interface. This code creates an object of type ExampleClass and uses it in a statement, then calls its Dispose method to release any resources used by the object. The using statement implicitly places the code in its body in a try block with a corresponding finally block that calls the object's Dispose method. For instance, the preceding brief code segment is equivalent to

```
{
    ExampleClass exampleObject = new ExampleClass();
    try
    {
        exampleObject.SomeMethod();
    }
    finally
    {
        if ( exampleObject != null )
            ( ( IDisposable ) exampleObject ).Dispose();
    }
}
```

The if statement ensures that exampleObject still references an object; otherwise, a Null-ReferenceException might occur.

13.7 Exception Properties

As we discussed in Section 13.4, exception types derive from class Exception, which has several properties. These frequently are used to formulate error messages indicating a caught exception. Two important properties are Message and **StackTrace**. Property Message stores the error message associated with an Exception object. This message can be a default message associated with the exception type or a customized message passed to an Exception object's constructor when the Exception object is thrown. Property Stack-Trace contains a string that represents the **method-call stack**. Recall that the runtime environment at all times keeps a list of open method calls that have been made but have not yet returned. The StackTrace represents the series of methods that have not finished processing at the time the exception occurs. If the debugging information that's generated by the compiler for the method is accessible to the IDE, the stack trace also includes line numbers; the first line number indicates the *throw point*, and subsequent line numbers indicate the locations from which the methods in the stack trace were called. The IDE creates PDB files to maintain the debugging information for your projects.

Property *InnerException*

Another property used frequently is **InnerException**. Typically, class library programmers "wrap" exception objects caught in their code so that they then can throw new exception types that are specific to their libraries. For example, a programmer implementing an accounting system might have some account-number processing code in which account numbers are input as strings but represented as ints in the code. Recall that a program can convert strings to int values with Convert.ToInt32, which throws a FormatException when it encounters an invalid number format. When an invalid account-number format occurs, the accounting-system programmer might wish to employ a different error message than the default message supplied by FormatException or might wish to indicate a new exception type, such as InvalidAccountNumberFormatException. In such cases, you'd provide code to catch the FormatException, then create an appropriate type of Exception object in the catch block and pass the original exception as one of the constructor arguments. The original exception object becomes the InnerException of the new exception object. When an InvalidAccountNumberFormatException occurs in code that uses the accounting system library, the catch block that catches the exception can obtain a reference to the original exception via property InnerException. So the exception indicates *both* that the user specified an invalid account number and that the number format was invalid. If the InnerException property is null, this indicates that the exception was not caused by another exception.

*Other **Exception** Properties*

Class Exception provides other properties, including **HelpLink**, **Source** and **TargetSite**. Property HelpLink specifies the location of the help file that describes the problem that occurred. This property is null if no such file exists. Property Source specifies the name of the app or object that caused the exception. Property TargetSite specifies the method where the exception originated.

*Demonstrating **Exception** Properties and Stack Unwinding*

Our next example (Fig. 13.5) demonstrates properties Message, StackTrace and Inner-Exception of class Exception. In addition, the example introduces **stack unwinding**—when an exception is thrown but not caught in a particular scope, the method-call stack is "unwound," and an attempt is made to catch the exception in the next outer try block. We keep track of the methods on the call stack as we discuss property StackTrace and the stack-unwinding mechanism. To see the proper stack trace, you should execute this program using steps similar to those presented in Section 13.2.

```
1   // Fig. 13.5: Properties.cs
2   // Stack unwinding and Exception class properties.
3   // Demonstrates using properties Message, StackTrace and InnerException.
4   using System;
5
6   class Properties
7   {
8      static void Main()
9      {
10        // call Method1; any Exception generated is caught
11        // in the catch block that follows
12        try
13        {
14           Method1();
15        } // end try
16        catch ( Exception exceptionParameter )
17        {
18           // output the string representation of the Exception, then output
19           // properties Message, StackTrace and InnerException
20           Console.WriteLine( "exceptionParameter.ToString: \n{0}\n",
21              exceptionParameter );
22           Console.WriteLine( "exceptionParameter.Message: \n{0}\n",
23              exceptionParameter.Message );
24           Console.WriteLine( "exceptionParameter.StackTrace: \n{0}\n",
25              exceptionParameter.StackTrace );
26           Console.WriteLine( "exceptionParameter.InnerException: \n{0}\n",
27              exceptionParameter.InnerException );
28        } // end catch
29     } // end method Main
```

Fig. 13.5 | Stack unwinding and Exception class properties. (Part 1 of 3.)

```
30
31      // calls Method2
32      static void Method1()
33      {
34         Method2();
35      } // end method Method1
36
37      // calls Method3
38      static void Method2()
39      {
40         Method3();
41      } // end method Method2
42
43      // throws an Exception containing an InnerException
44      static void Method3()
45      {
46         // attempt to convert string to int
47         try
48         {
49            Convert.ToInt32( "Not an integer" );
50         } // end try
51         catch ( FormatException formatExceptionParameter )
52         {
53            // wrap FormatException in new Exception
54            throw new Exception( "Exception occurred in Method3",
55               formatExceptionParameter );
56         } // end catch
57      } // end method Method3
58   } // end class Properties
```

```
exceptionParameter.ToString:
System.Exception: Exception occurred in Method3 --->
System.FormatException: Input string was not in a correct format.
   at System.Number.StringToNumber(String str, NumberStyles options,
      NumberBuffer& number, NumberFormatInfo info, Boolean parseDecimal)
   at System.Number.ParseInt32(String s, NumberStyles style,
      NumberFormatInfo info)
   at Properties.Method3() in C:\examples\ch13\Fig13_05\Properties\
      Properties\Properties.cs:line 49
   --- End of inner exception stack trace ---
   at Properties.Method3() in C:\examples\ch13\Fig13_05\Properties\
      Properties\Properties.cs:line 54
   at Properties.Method2() in C:\examples\ch13\Fig13_05\Properties\
      Properties\Properties.cs:line 40
   at Properties.Method1() in C:\examples\ch13\Fig13_05\Properties\
      Properties\Properties.cs:line 34
   at Properties.Main() in C:\examples\ch13\Fig13_05\Properties\
      Properties\Properties.cs:line 14

exceptionParameter.Message:
Exception occurred in Method3

exceptionParameter.StackTrace:
   at Properties.Method3() in C:\examples\ch13\Fig13_05\Properties\
      Properties\Properties.cs:line 54
```

Fig. 13.5 | Stack unwinding and Exception class properties. (Part 2 of 3.)

```
    at Properties.Method2() in C:\examples\ch13\Fig13_05\Properties\
       Properties\Properties.cs:line 40
    at Properties.Method1() in C:\examples\ch13\Fig13_05\Properties\
       Properties\Properties.cs:line 34
    at Properties.Main() in C:\examples\ch13\Fig13_05\Properties\
       Properties\Properties.cs:line 14

exceptionParameter.InnerException:
System.FormatException: Input string was not in a correct format.
    at System.Number.StringToNumber(String str, NumberStyles options,
       NumberBuffer& number, NumberFormatInfo info, Boolean parseDecimal)
    at System.Number.ParseInt32(String s, NumberStyles style,
       NumberFormatInfo info)
    at Properties.Method3() in C:\examples\ch13\Fig13_05\Properties\
       Properties\Properties.cs:line 49
```

Fig. 13.5 | Stack unwinding and `Exception` class properties. (Part 3 of 3.)

Program execution begins with Main, which becomes the first method on the method-call stack. Line 14 of the try block in Main invokes Method1 (declared in lines 32–35), which becomes the second method on the stack. If Method1 throws an exception, the catch block in lines 16–28 handles the exception and outputs information about the exception that occurred. Line 34 of Method1 invokes Method2 (lines 38–41), which becomes the third method on the stack. Then line 40 of Method2 invokes Method3 (lines 44–57), which becomes the fourth method on the stack.

At this point, the method-call stack (from top to bottom) for the program is:

```
Method3
Method2
Method1
Main
```

The method called *most recently* (Method3) appears at the *top* of the stack; the *first* method called (Main) appears at the *bottom*. The try statement (lines 47–56) in Method3 invokes method Convert.ToInt32 (line 49), which attempts to convert a string to an int. At this point, Convert.ToInt32 becomes the fifth and final method on the call stack.

Throwing an *Exception* with an *InnerException*

Because the argument to Convert.ToInt32 is not in int format, line 49 throws a FormatException that's caught in line 51 of Method3. The exception terminates the call to Convert.ToInt32, so the method is *unwound* (i.e., removed) from the method-call stack. The catch block in Method3 then creates and throws an Exception object. The first argument to the Exception constructor is the custom error message for our example, "Exception occurred in Method3." The second argument is the InnerException—the FormatException that was caught. The StackTrace for this new exception object reflects the point at which the exception was thrown (lines 54–55). Now Method3 terminates, because the exception thrown in the catch block is not caught in the method body. Thus, control returns to the statement that invoked Method3 in the prior method in the call stack (Method2). This *unwinds* Method3 from the method-call stack.

When control returns to line 40 in Method2, the CLR determines that line 40 is not in a try block. Therefore the exception cannot be caught in Method2, and Method2 terminates. This *unwinds* Method2 from the call stack and returns control to line 34 in Method1.

Here again, line 34 is not in a try block, so Method1 cannot catch the exception. The method terminates and is *unwound* from the call stack, returning control to line 14 in Main, which *is* located in a try block. The try block in Main exits and the catch block (lines 16–28) catches the exception. The catch block uses properties Message, Stack-Trace and InnerException to create the output. Stack unwinding continues until a catch block catches the exception or the program terminates.

Displaying Information About the **Exception**
The first block of output (which we reformatted for readability) in Fig. 13.5 contains the exception's string representation, which is returned from an *implicit* call to method To-String. The string begins with the name of the exception class followed by the Message property value. The next four items present the stack trace of the InnerException object. The remainder of the block of output shows the StackTrace for the exception thrown in Method3. The StackTrace represents the state of the method-call stack at the throw point of the exception, rather than at the point where the exception eventually is caught. Each StackTrace line that begins with "at" represents a method on the call stack. These lines indicate the method in which the exception occurred, the file in which the method resides and the line number of the throw point in the file. The inner-exception information includes the *inner-exception stack trace*.

Error-Prevention Tip 13.4

When catching and rethrowing an exception, provide additional debugging information in the rethrown exception. To do so, create an Exception *object containing more specific debugging information, then pass the original caught exception to the new exception object's constructor to initialize the* InnerException *property.*

The next block of output (two lines) simply displays the Message property's value (Exception occurred in Method3) of the exception thrown in Method3.

The third block of output displays the StackTrace property of the exception thrown in Method3. This StackTrace property contains the stack trace starting from line 54 in Method3, because that's the point at which the Exception object was created and thrown. The stack trace *always* begins from the exception's throw point.

Finally, the last block of output displays the string representation of the Inner-Exception property, which includes the namespace and class name of the exception object, as well as its Message and StackTrace properties.

13.8 User-Defined Exception Classes

In many cases, you can use existing exception classes from the .NET Framework Class Library to indicate exceptions that occur in your programs. In some cases, however, you might wish to create new exception classes specific to the problems that occur in your programs. **User-defined exception classes** should derive directly or indirectly from class Exception of namespace System. When you create code that throws exceptions, they should be well documented, so that other developers who use your code will know how to handle them.

Good Programming Practice 13.1

Associating each type of malfunction with an appropriately named exception class improves program clarity.

Software Engineering Observation 13.3

Before creating a user-defined exception class, investigate the existing exceptions in the .NET Framework Class Library to determine whether an appropriate exception type already exists.

Class *NegativeNumberException*

Figures 13.6–13.7 demonstrate a user-defined exception class. NegativeNumberException (Fig. 13.6) represents exceptions that occur when a program performs an illegal operation on a negative number, such as attempting to calculate its square root.

```
 1   // Fig. 13.6: NegativeNumberException.cs
 2   // NegativeNumberException represents exceptions caused by
 3   // illegal operations performed on negative numbers.
 4   using System;
 5
 6   class NegativeNumberException : Exception
 7   {
 8      // default constructor
 9      public NegativeNumberException()
10         : base( "Illegal operation for a negative number" )
11      {
12         // empty body
13      } // end default constructor
14
15      // constructor for customizing error message
16      public NegativeNumberException( string messageValue )
17         : base( messageValue )
18      {
19         // empty body
20      } // end one-argument constructor
21
22      // constructor for customizing the exception's error
23      // message and specifying the InnerException object
24      public NegativeNumberException( string messageValue,
25         Exception inner )
26         : base( messageValue, inner )
27      {
28         // empty body
29      } // end two-argument constructor
30   } // end class NegativeNumberException
```

Fig. 13.6 | NegativeNumberException represents exceptions caused by illegal operations performed on negative numbers.

According to Microsoft's document on "Best Practices for Handling Exceptions" (bit.ly/ExceptionsBestPractices), user-defined exceptions should typically extend class Exception, have a class name that ends with "Exception" and define three constructors: a *parameterless constructor*; a *constructor that receives a* `string` *argument* (the error message); and a *constructor that receives a* `string` *argument and an* `Exception` *argument* (the error message and the inner-exception object). Defining these three constructors makes your exception class more flexible, allowing other programmers to easily use and extend it.

NegativeNumberExceptions most frequently occur during arithmetic operations, so it seems logical to derive class `NegativeNumberException` from class `ArithmeticException`. However, class `ArithmeticException` derives from class `SystemException`—the category of exceptions thrown by the CLR. Per Microsoft's best practices for exception handling, *user-defined exception classes should inherit from* `Exception` *rather than* `SystemException`. In this case, we could have used the built-in `ArgumentException` class, which is recommended in the best practices for invalid argument values. We create our own exception type here simply for demonstration purposes.

Class *NegativeNumberException*

Class `SquareRootTest` (Fig. 13.7) demonstrates our user-defined exception class. The app enables the user to input a numeric value, then invokes method `SquareRoot` (lines 40–48) to calculate the square root of that value. To perform this calculation, `SquareRoot` invokes class `Math`'s `Sqrt` method, which receives a `double` value as its argument. Normally, if the argument is *negative*, method `Sqrt` returns NaN. In this program, we'd like to *prevent* the user from calculating the square root of a negative number. If the numeric value that the user enters is negative, method `SquareRoot` throws a `NegativeNumberException` (lines 44–45). Otherwise, `SquareRoot` invokes class `Math`'s method `Sqrt` to compute the square root (line 47).

When the user inputs a value, the `try` statement (lines 14–34) attempts to invoke `SquareRoot` using the value input by the user. If the user input is not a number, a `FormatException` occurs, and the `catch` block in lines 25–29 processes the exception. If the user inputs a negative number, method `SquareRoot` throws a `NegativeNumberException` (lines 44–45); the `catch` block in lines 30–34 catches and handles this type of exception.

```
 1   // Fig. 13.7: SquareRootTest.cs
 2   // Demonstrating a user-defined exception class.
 3   using System;
 4
 5   class SquareRootTest
 6   {
 7      static void Main( string[] args )
 8      {
 9         bool continueLoop = true;
10
11         do
12         {
13            // catch any NegativeNumberException thrown
14            try
15            {
16               Console.Write(
17                  "Enter a value to calculate the square root of: " );
18               double inputValue = Convert.ToDouble( Console.ReadLine() );
```

Fig. 13.7 | Demonstrating a user-defined exception class. (Part 1 of 2.)

```
19              double result = SquareRoot( inputValue );
20
21              Console.WriteLine( "The square root of {0} is {1:F6}\n",
22                  inputValue, result );
23              continueLoop = false;
24          } // end try
25          catch ( FormatException formatException )
26          {
27              Console.WriteLine( "\n" + formatException.Message );
28              Console.WriteLine( "Please enter a double value.\n" );
29          } // end catch
30          catch ( NegativeNumberException negativeNumberException )
31          {
32              Console.WriteLine( "\n" + negativeNumberException.Message );
33              Console.WriteLine( "Please enter a non-negative value.\n" );
34          } // end catch
35          } while ( continueLoop );
36      } // end Main
37
38      // computes square root of parameter; throws
39      // NegativeNumberException if parameter is negative
40      public static double SquareRoot( double value )
41      {
42          // if negative operand, throw NegativeNumberException
43          if ( value < 0 )
44              throw new NegativeNumberException(
45                  "Square root of negative number not permitted" );
46          else
47              return Math.Sqrt( value ); // compute square root
48      } // end method SquareRoot
49  } // end class SquareRootTest
```

```
Enter a value to calculate the square root of: 30
The square root of 30 is 5.477226
```

```
Enter a value to calculate the square root of: hello

Input string was not in a correct format.
Please enter a double value.

Enter a value to calculate the square root of: 25
The square root of 25 is 5.000000
```

```
Enter a value to calculate the square root of: -2

Square root of negative number not permitted
Please enter a non-negative value.

Enter a value to calculate the square root of: 2
The square root of 2 is 1.414214
```

Fig. 13.7 | Demonstrating a user-defined exception class. (Part 2 of 2.)

13.9 Wrap-Up

In this chapter, you learned how to use exception handling to deal with errors in an app. We demonstrated that exception handling enables you to remove error-handling code from the "main line" of the program's execution. You saw exception handling in the context of a divide-by-zero example. You learned how to use `try` blocks to enclose code that may throw an exception, and how to use `catch` blocks to deal with exceptions that may arise. We explained the termination model of exception handling, in which, after an exception is handled, program control does not return to the throw point. We discussed several important classes of the .NET Exception hierarchy, including `Exception` (from which user-defined exception classes are derived) and `SystemException`. Next you learned how to use the `finally` block to release resources whether or not an exception occurs, and how to throw and rethrow exceptions with the `throw` statement. We showed how the `using` statement can be used to automate the process of releasing a resource. You then learned how to obtain information about an exception using Exception properties `Message`, `StackTrace` and `InnerException`, and method `ToString`. You learned how to create your own exception classes. In the next two chapters, we present an in-depth treatment of graphical user interfaces. In these chapters and throughout the rest of the book, we use exception handling to make our examples more robust, while demonstrating new features of the language.

14

Graphical User Interfaces with Windows Forms: Part 1

Objectives

In this chapter you'll:

- Learn design principles of graphical user interfaces (GUIs).
- Create graphical user interfaces.
- Process events in response to user interactions with GUI controls.
- Learn the namespaces that contain the classes for GUI controls and event handling.
- create and manipulate various controls.
- Add descriptive ToolTips to GUI controls.
- Process mouse and keyboard events.

14.1 Introduction

A graphical user interface (GUI) allows a user to interact *visually* with a program. A GUI (pronounced "GOO-ee") gives a program a distinctive "look" and "feel."

Look-and-Feel Observation 14.1

Consistent user interfaces enable a user to learn new apps more quickly because the apps have the same "look" and "feel."

As an example of a GUI, consider Fig. 14.1, which shows a Visual Studio Express window containing various GUI controls. Near the top, there's a *menu bar* containing the menus **FILE**, **EDIT**, **VIEW**, **PROJECT**, **BUILD**, **DEBUG**, **TEAM**, **TOOLS**, **TEST**, **WINDOW**, and **HELP**. Below that is a *tool bar* of buttons, each with a defined task, such as creating a new

Button   Tab   Menu   Title bar   Menu bar   Tool bar

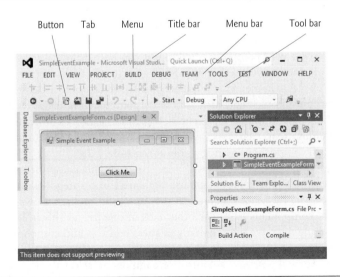

Fig. 14.1 | GUI controls in the Visual Studio Express 2012 for Windows Desktop window.

project or opening an existing one. Below that is a *tab* representing a currently open file—this *tabbed view* allows users to switch between the open files. These controls form a user-friendly interface through which you have been interacting with the IDE.

GUIs are built from *GUI controls* (which are sometimes called **components** or **widgets**—short for **window gadgets**). GUI controls are *objects* that can display information on the screen or enable users to interact with an app via the mouse, keyboard or some other form of input (such as voice commands). Several common GUI controls are listed in Fig. 14.2—in the sections that follow and in Chapter 15, we discuss each of these in detail. Chapter 15 explores the features and properties of additional GUI controls.

Control	Description
Label	Displays *images* or *uneditable text*.
TextBox	Enables the user to *enter data via the keyboard*. It can also be used to *display editable or uneditable text*.
Button	Triggers an *event* when clicked with the mouse.
CheckBox	Specifies an option that can be *selected* (checked) or *unselected* (not checked).
ComboBox	Provides a *drop-down list* of items from which the user can make a *selection* either by clicking an item in the list or by typing in a box.
ListBox	Provides a *list* of items from which the user can make a *selection* by clicking one or more items.
Panel	A *container* in which controls can be placed and organized.
NumericUpDown	Enables the user to select from a *range* of numeric input values.

Fig. 14.2 | Some basic GUI controls.

14.2 Windows Forms

Windows Forms is one library that can be used to create GUIs—you'll also learn about *Windows 8 UI* and *Windows Presentation Foundation* in later chapters. A Form is a graphical element that appears on your computer's desktop; it can be a dialog, a window or an **MDI window (multiple document interface window)**—discussed in Chapter 15. A *component* is an instance of a class that implements the **IComponent** interface, which defines the behaviors that components must implement, such as how the component is loaded. A *control*, such as a Button or Label, has a graphical representation at runtime. Some components lack graphical representations (e.g., class Timer of namespace System.Windows.Forms—see Chapter 15). Such components are not visible at run time.

Figure 14.3 displays the Windows Forms controls and components from the C# **Toolbox**. The controls and components are organized into categories by functionality. Selecting the category **All Windows Forms** at the top of the **Toolbox** allows you to view all the controls and components from the other tabs in one list (as shown in Fig. 14.3). In this chapter and the next, we discuss many of these controls and components. To add a control or component to a Form, select that control or component from the **Toolbox** and drag it onto the Form. To *deselect* a control or component, select the **Pointer** item in the **Toolbox** (the icon at the top of the list). When the **Pointer** item is selected, you cannot accidentally add a new control to the Form.

Fig. 14.3 | Components and controls for Windows Forms.

When there are several windows on the screen, the **active window** is the *frontmost* and has a *highlighted title bar*. A window becomes the active window when the user clicks somewhere inside it. The active window is said to "have the **focus**." For example, in Visual Studio the active window is the **Toolbox** when you're selecting an item from it, or the **Properties** window when you're editing a control's properties.

A Form is a **container** for controls and components. When you drag items from the **Toolbox** onto the Form, Visual Studio generates code that creates the object and sets its basic properties. This code is updated when the control or component's properties are modified in the IDE. Removing a control or component from the Form *deletes* the corresponding generated code. The IDE maintains the generated code in a separate file using **partial classes**—classes that are split among multiple files and assembled into a single class by the compiler. You could write this code yourself, but it's much easier to allow Visual Studio to handle the details. We introduced visual programming concepts in Chapter 2. In this chapter and the next, we use visual programming to build more substantial GUIs.

Each control or component we present in this chapter is located in namespace System.Windows.Forms. To create a Windows Forms app, you generally create a Windows Form, set its properties, add controls to the Form, set their properties and implement event handlers (methods) that respond to events generated by the controls. Figure 14.4 lists common Form properties, common methods and a common event.

When we create controls and event handlers, Visual Studio generates much of the GUI-related code. In visual programming, the IDE maintains GUI-related code and you write the bodies of the *event handlers* to indicate what actions the program should take when particular *events* occur.

Form properties, methods and an event	Description
Common Properties	
AcceptButton	Default Button that's clicked for you when you press *Enter*.
AutoScroll	bool value (false by default) that allows or disallows *scrollbars* when needed.
CancelButton	Button that's clicked when the *Escape* key is pressed.
FormBorderStyle	*Border style* for the Form (Sizable by default).
Font	Font of text displayed on the Form, and the *default font* for controls added to the Form.
Text	Text in the Form's title bar.
Common Methods	
Close	Closes a Form and *releases all resources*, such as the memory used for the Form's contents. A closed Form cannot be reopened.
Hide	Hides a Form, but does *not* destroy the Form or release its resources.
Show	Displays a *hidden* Form.
Common Event	
Load	Occurs before a Form is displayed to the user. You'll learn about events and event-handling in the next section.

Fig. 14.4 | Common Form properties, methods and an event.

14.3 Event Handling

Normally, a user interacts with an app's GUI to indicate the tasks that the app should perform. For example, when you write an e-mail in an e-mail app, clicking the **Send** button tells the app to send the e-mail to the specified e-mail addresses. GUIs are **event driven**. When the user interacts with a GUI component, the interaction—known as an **event**—drives the program to perform a task. Common events (user interactions) that might cause an app to perform a task include *clicking* a Button, *typing* in a TextBox, *selecting* an item from a menu, *closing* a window and *moving* the mouse. All GUI controls have events associated with them. Objects of other types can also have associated events as well. A method that performs a task in response to an event is called an **event handler**, and the overall process of responding to events is known as **event handling**.

14.3.1 A Simple Event-Driven GUI

The Form in the app of Fig. 14.5 contains a Button that a user can click to display a MessageBox. In line 6, notice the namespace declaration, which is inserted for every class you create. We've been removing these from earlier simple examples because they were unnecessary. Namespaces organize groups of related classes. Each class's name is actually a combination of its namespace name, a dot (.) and the class name. This is known as the class's **fully qualified class name**. You can use the class's **simple name** (the unqualified class name—SimpleEventExample) in the app. Each class name is *scoped* to the namespace in which it's defined. If you were to reuse this class in another app, you'd use the fully qualified name or write a using directive so that you could refer to the class by its simple name. We'll use namespaces like this in Chapters 15 and 19. If another namespace also contains a class with the same name, the fully qualified class names can be used to distinguish between the classes in the app and prevent a **name conflict** (also called a **name collision**).

```
 1   // Fig. 14.5: SimpleEventExampleForm.cs
 2   // Simple event handling example.
 3   using System;
 4   using System.Windows.Forms;
 5
 6   namespace SimpleEventExample
 7   {
 8      // Form that shows a simple event handler
 9      public partial class SimpleEventExampleForm : Form
10      {
11         // default constructor
12         public SimpleEventExampleForm()
13         {
14            InitializeComponent();
15         } // end constructor
16
17         // handles click event of Button clickButton
18         private void clickButton_Click( object sender, EventArgs e )
19         {
20            MessageBox.Show( "Button was clicked." );
21         } // end method clickButton_Click
22      } // end class SimpleEventExampleForm
23   } // end namespace SimpleEventExample
```

Fig. 14.5 | Simple event-handling example.

Renaming the Form1.cs *File*
Using the techniques presented in Chapter 2, create a Form containing a Button. First, create a new Windows Forms app. Next, rename the Form1.cs file to SimpleEventExampleForm.cs in the **Solution Explorer**. Click the Form in the designer, then use the **Properties** window to set the Form's Text property to "Simple Event Example". Set the Form's Font property to Segoe UI, 9pt. To do so, select the Font property in the **Properties** window, then click the *ellipsis (...) button* in the property's value field to display a font dialog.

Adding a Button *to the* Form
Drag a Button from the **Toolbox** onto the Form. In the **Properties** window for the Button, set the (Name) property to clickButton and the Text property to Click Me. You'll notice that we use a convention in which each variable name we create for a control ends with

the control's type. For example, in the variable name clickButton, "Button" is the control's type.

Adding an Event Handler for the **Button's** Click Event

When the user clicks the Button in this example, we want the app to respond by displaying a MessageBox. To do this, you must create an *event handler* for the Button's *Click event*. You can create this event handler by double clicking the Button on the Form, which declares the following *empty* event handler in the program code:

```
private void clickButton_Click( object sender, EventArgs e )
{
}
```

By convention, the IDE names the event-handler method as *objectName_eventName* (e.g., clickButton_Click). The clickButton_Click event handler *executes* when the user *clicks* the clickButton control.

Event Handler Parameters

Each event handler receives two parameters when it's called. The first—an object reference typically named sender—is a reference to the *object that generated the event*. The second is a reference to an EventArgs object (or an object of an EventArgs derived class), which is typically named e. This object contains additional information about the event that occurred. EventArgs is the *base class* of all classes that represent event information.

Displaying a **MessageBox**

To display a MessageBox in response to the event, insert the statement

```
MessageBox.Show( "Button was clicked." );
```

in the event handler's body. The resulting event handler appears in lines 18–21 of Fig. 14.5. When you execute the app and click the Button, a MessageBox appears displaying the text "Button was clicked".

14.3.2 Auto-Generated GUI Code

Visual Studio places the *auto-generated* GUI code in the Designer.cs file of the Form (SimpleEventExampleForm.Designer.cs in this example). You can open this file by expanding the node in the **Solution Explorer** window for the file you're currently working in (SimpleEventExampleForm.cs) and double clicking the file name that ends with Designer.cs. Figs. 14.6 and 14.7 show this file's contents. The IDE collapses the code in lines 23–57 of Fig. 14.7 by default—you can click the + icon next to line 23 to *expand* the code, then click the − icon next to that line to *collapse* it.

Now that you have studied classes and objects in detail, this code will be easier to understand. Since this code is created and maintained by Visual Studio, you generally don't need to look at it. In fact, you do not need to understand most of the code shown here to build GUI apps. However, we now take a closer look to help you understand how GUI apps work.

The auto-generated code that defines the GUI is actually part of the Form's *class*—in this case, SimpleEventExampleForm. Line 3 of Fig. 14.6 (and line 9 of Fig. 14.5) uses the partial modifier, which allows this class to be split among multiple files, including the

SimpleEventExampleForm.Designer.cs | SimpleEventExampleForm.cs

SimpleEventExample.SimpleEventExampleForm | components

```
namespace SimpleEventExample
{
   partial class SimpleEventExampleForm
   {
      /// <summary>
      /// Required designer variable.
      /// </summary>
      private System.ComponentModel.IContainer components = null;

      /// <summary>
      /// Clean up any resources being used.
      /// </summary>
      /// <param name="disposing">true if managed resources should be disposed; othe
      protected override void Dispose( bool disposing )
      {
         if ( disposing && ( components != null ) )
         {
            components.Dispose();
         }
         base.Dispose( disposing );
      }
```

100 %

Fig. 14.6 | First half of the Visual Studio generated code file.

SimpleEventExampleForm.Designer.cs | SimpleEventExampleForm.cs [Design]

SimpleEventExample.SimpleEventExampleForm | components

```
23       #region Windows Form Designer generated code
24
25       /// <summary>
26       /// Required method for Designer support - do not modify
27       /// the contents of this method with the code editor.
28       /// </summary>
29       private void InitializeComponent()
30       {
31          this.clickButton = new System.Windows.Forms.Button();
32          this.SuspendLayout();
33          //
34          // clickButton
35          //
36          this.clickButton.Location = new System.Drawing.Point(104, 37);
37          this.clickButton.Name = "clickButton";
38          this.clickButton.Size = new System.Drawing.Size(75, 23);
39          this.clickButton.TabIndex = 0;
40          this.clickButton.Text = "Click Me";
41          this.clickButton.UseVisualStyleBackColor = true;
42          this.clickButton.Click += new System.EventHandler(this.clickButton_Click);
43          //
44          // SimpleEventExampleForm
45          //
46          this.AutoScaleDimensions = new System.Drawing.SizeF(7F, 15F);
47          this.AutoScaleMode = System.Windows.Forms.AutoScaleMode.Font;
48          this.ClientSize = new System.Drawing.Size(282, 97);
49          this.Controls.Add(this.clickButton);
50          this.Font = new System.Drawing.Font("Segoe UI", 9F, System.Drawing.FontStyl
51          this.Name = "SimpleEventExampleForm";
52          this.Text = "Simple Event Example";
53          this.ResumeLayout(false);
54
55       }
56
57       #endregion
58
59       private System.Windows.Forms.Button clickButton;
60    }
61 }
```

100 %

Fig. 14.7 | Second half of the Visual Studio generated code file.

files that contain auto-generated code and those in which you write your own code. Line 59 of Fig. 14.7 declares the `clickButton` that we created in **Design** mode. It's declared as an instance variable of class SimpleEventExampleForm. By default, all variable declarations for controls created through C#'s *design window* have a private access modifier. The code also includes the *Dispose method* for *releasing resources* (Fig. 14.6, lines 14–21) and method InitializeComponent (Fig. 14.7, lines 29–55), which contains the code that creates the Button, then sets some of the Button's and the Form's properties. The property values correspond to the values set in the **Properties** window for each control. Visual Studio adds comments to the code that it generates, as in lines 33–35. Line 42 was generated when we created the event handler for the Button's Click event.

Method InitializeComponent is called when the Form is created, and establishes such properties as the Form title, the Form size, control sizes and text. Visual Studio also uses the code in this method to create the GUI you see in design view. Changing the code in InitializeComponent may prevent Visual Studio from displaying the GUI properly.

Error-Prevention Tip 14.1

*The code generated by building a GUI in **Design** mode is not meant to be modified directly, which is why this code is placed in a separate file. Modifying this code can prevent the GUI from being displayed correctly in **Design** mode and might cause an app to function incorrectly. In **Design** mode, modify control properties only through the **Properties** window.*

14.3.3 Delegates and the Event-Handling Mechanism

The control that generates an event is known as the **event sender**. An event-handling method—known as the *event handler*—responds to a particular event that a control generates. When the event occurs, the event sender calls its event handler to perform a task (i.e., to "handle the event").

The .NET event-handling mechanism allows you to choose your own names for event-handling methods. However, each event-handling method must declare the proper parameters to receive information about the event that it handles. Since you can choose your own method names, an event sender such as a Button cannot know in advance which method will respond to its events. So, we need a mechanism to indicate which method is the event handler for an event.

Delegates

Event handlers are connected to a control's events via special objects called **delegates**. A delegate type declaration specifies the signature of a method—in event handling, the signature specifies the return type and arguments for an event handler. GUI controls have predefined delegates that correspond to every event they can generate. For example, the delegate for a Button's Click event is of type EventHandler (namespace System). The online help documentation declares this type as follows:

```
public delegate void EventHandler( object sender, EventArgs e );
```

This uses the **delegate** keyword to declare a delegate type named EventHandler, which can hold references to methods that return void and receive two parameters—one of type object (the *event sender*) and one of type EventArgs. If you compare the delegate declaration with clickButton_Click's first line (Fig. 14.5, line 18), you'll see that this event handler returns void and receives the parameters specified by the EventHandler delegate. The preceding declaration actually creates an entire class for you. The details of this special class's declaration are handled by the compiler.

Indicating the Method that a Delegate Should Call
An *event sender* calls a delegate object like a method. Since each event handler is declared as a delegate, the event sender can simply call the appropriate delegate when an event occurs—a Button calls the EventHandler delegate that corresponds to its Click event in response to a click. The delegate's job is to invoke the appropriate method. To enable the clickButton_Click method to be called, Visual Studio assigns clickButton_Click to the click Button's Click EventHandler delegate, as shown in line 42 of Fig. 14.7. This code is added by Visual Studio when you double click the Button control in **Design** mode. The expression

```
new System.EventHandler(this.clickButton_Click);
```

creates an EventHandler delegate object and initializes it with the clickButton_Click method. Line 42 uses the += operator to *add* the delegate to the Button's Click EventHandler delegate. This indicates that clickButton_Click will respond when a user clicks the Button. The += operator is overloaded by the delegate class that's created by the compiler.

Multicast Delegates
You can actually specify that several different methods should be invoked in response to an event by adding other delegates to the Button's Click event with statements similar to line 42 of Fig. 14.7. Event delegates are **multicast**—they represent a *set of delegate objects* that all have the *same signature*. *Multicast delegates* enable several methods to be called in response to a single event. When an event occurs, the event sender calls *every* method referenced by the multicast delegate. This is known as **event multicasting**. Event delegates derive from class **MulticastDelegate**, which derives from class **Delegate** (both from namespace System). For most cases, you'll specify only one event handler for a particular event on a control.

14.3.4 Another Way to Create Event Handlers

For the GUI app in Fig. 14.5, you double clicked the Button control on the Form to create its event handler. This technique creates an event handler for a control's **default event**—the event that's most frequently used with that control. Controls can generate many different events, and each one can have its own event handler. For instance, your app can also provide an event handler for a Button's MouseHover event, which occurs when the mouse pointer remains positioned over the Button for a short period of time. We now discuss how to create an event handler for an event that's not a control's default event.

Using the Properties Window to Create Event Handlers
You can create additional event handlers through the **Properties** window. If you select a control on the Form, then click the **Events** icon (the lightning bolt icon in Fig. 14.8) in the **Properties** window, all the events for that control are listed in the window. You can double click an event's name to display in the editor an existing event handler for that event, or to create the event handler if it does not yet exist in your code. You can also select an event, then use the drop-down list to its right to choose an existing method that should be used as the event handler for that event. The methods that appear in this drop-down list are the Form class's methods that have the proper signature to be an event handler for the selected event. You can return to viewing the properties of a control by selecting the **Properties** icon (Fig. 14.8).

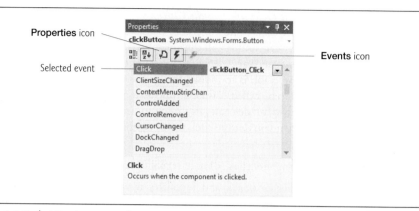

Fig. 14.8 | Viewing events for a `Button` control in the **Properties** window.

A single method can handle events from multiple controls. For example, the `Click` events of three `Button`s could all be handled by the same method. You can specify an event handler for multiple events by selecting multiple controls (by dragging over them or holding *Shift* and clicking each) and selecting a single method in the **Properties** window's **Events** tab. If you create a new event handler this way, you should rename it appropriately. You could also select each control individually and specify the same method for each one's event.

14.3.5 Locating Event Information

Read the Visual Studio documentation to learn about the different events raised by each control. To do this, select a control in the IDE and press the *F1* key to display that control's online help (Fig. 14.9). The web page that's displayed contains basic information

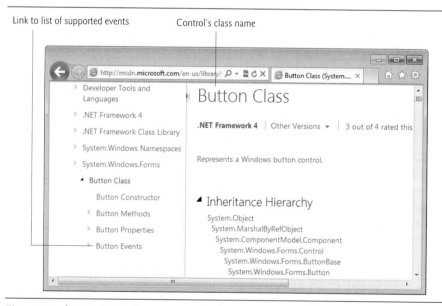

Fig. 14.9 | Link to list of `Button` events.

about the control's class. In the left column of the page are several links to more information about the class—**Button Constructor, Button Methods, Button Properties** and **Button Events.** This list may vary by class. Each link displays a subset of the class's members. Click the link to the list of events for that control (**Button Events** in this case) to display the supported events for that control.

Next, click the name of an event to view its description and examples of its use. We selected the Click event to display the information in Fig. 14.10. The Click event is a member of class Control, an indirect base class of class Button. The **Remarks** section of the page discusses the details of the selected event. Alternatively, you could use the **Object Browser** to look up this information in the System.Windows.Forms namespace. The **Object Browser** shows only the members *originally* defined in a given class. The Click event is originally defined in class Control and inherited into Button. For this reason, you must look at class Control in the **Object Browser** to see the documentation for the Click event. See Section 10.12 for more information regarding the **Object Browser**.

Event argument class   Event name   Event type

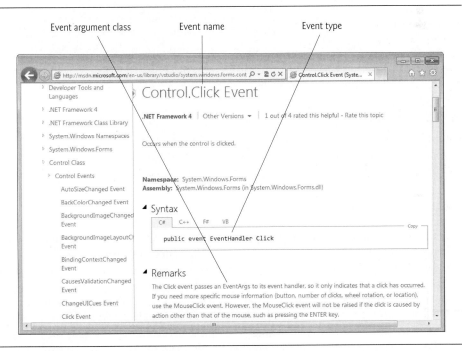

Fig. 14.10 | Click event details.

14.4 Control Properties and Layout

This section overviews properties that are common to many controls. Controls derive from class **Control** (namespace System.Windows.Forms). Figure 14.11 lists some of class Control's properties and methods. The properties shown here can be set for many controls. For example, the Text property specifies the text that appears on a control. The location of this text varies depending on the control. In a Form, the text appears in the title bar, but the text of a Button appears on its face.

Class `Control` properties and methods	Description
Common Properties	
`BackColor`	The control's background color.
`BackgroundImage`	The control's background image.
`Enabled`	Specifies whether the control is *enabled* (i.e., if the user can interact with it). Typically, portions of a *disabled* control appear "grayed out" as a visual indication to the user that the control is disabled.
`Focused`	Indicates whether the control *has the focus* (only available at runtime).
`Font`	The `Font` used to display the control's text.
`ForeColor`	The control's foreground color. This usually determines the color of the text in the `Text` property.
`TabIndex`	The *tab order* of the control. When the *Tab* key is pressed, the focus transfers between controls based on the tab order. You can set this order.
`TabStop`	If `true`, then a user can give focus to this control via the *Tab* key.
`Text`	The text associated with the control. The location and appearance of the text vary depending on the type of control.
`Visible`	Indicates whether the control is visible.
Common Methods	
`Hide`	Hides the control (sets the `Visible` property to `false`).
`Select`	*Acquires the focus.*
`Show`	Shows the control (sets the `Visible` property to `true`).

Fig. 14.11 | Class `Control` properties and methods.

The **Select** method transfers the focus to a control and makes it the **active control**. When you press the *Tab* key in an executing Windows Forms app, controls *receive the focus* in the order specified by their **TabIndex** property. This property is set by Visual Studio based on the order in which controls are added to a Form, but you can change the *tabbing order* using **VIEW > Tab Order**. TabIndex is helpful for users who enter information in many controls, such as a set of TextBoxes that represent a user's name, address and telephone number. The user can enter information, then quickly select the next control by pressing the *Tab* key.

The **Enabled** property indicates whether the user can interact with a control to generate an event. Often, if a control is *disabled*, it's because an option is unavailable to the user at that time. For example, text editor apps often disable the "paste" command until the user copies some text. In most cases, a disabled control's text appears in gray (rather than in black). You can also hide a control from the user without disabling the control by setting the `Visible` property to `false` or by calling method `Hide`. In each case, the control still exists but is not visible on the Form.

Anchoring and Docking

You can use anchoring and docking to specify the layout of controls inside a container (such as a Form). **Anchoring** causes controls to remain at a fixed distance from the sides of the container even when the container is resized. Anchoring enhances the user experience. For example, if the user expects a control to appear in a particular corner of the app, anchoring ensures that the control will always be in that corner—even if the user *resizes* the Form. **Docking** attaches a control to a container such that the control stretches across an entire side or fills an entire area. For example, a button docked to the top of a container stretches across the entire top of that container, regardless of the width of the container.

When a window (or other type of *parent container* like a Panel) is resized, anchored controls are moved (and possibly resized) so that the distance from the sides to which they're anchored does not vary. By default, most controls are anchored to the top-left corner of the Form. To see the effects of anchoring a control, create a simple Windows Forms app that contains two Buttons. Anchor one control to the right and bottom sides by setting the **Anchor** property as shown in Fig. 14.12. Leave the other control with its default anchoring (top, left). Execute the app and enlarge the Form. Notice that the Button anchored to the bottom-right corner is always the same distance from the Form's bottom-right corner (Fig. 14.13), but that the other control stays its original distance from the top-left corner of the Form.

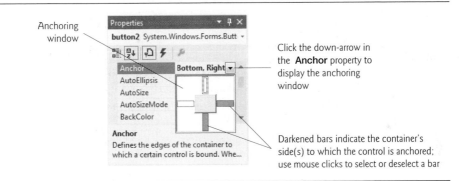

Fig. 14.12 | Manipulating the **Anchor** property of a control.

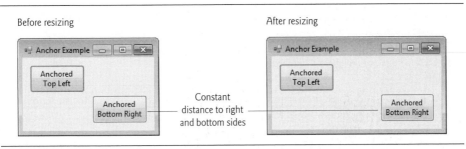

Fig. 14.13 | Anchoring demonstration.

Sometimes, it's desirable for a control to span an entire side of the Form, even when the Form is resized. For example, a control such as a status bar typically should remain at the bottom of the Form. Docking allows a control to *span an entire side* (left, right, top or bottom) of its parent container or to *fill the entire container*. When the parent control is resized, the docked control resizes as well. In Fig. 14.14, a Button is docked at the top of the Form (spanning the top portion). When the Form is resized, the Button is resized to the Form's new width. Forms have a **Padding** property that specifies the distance between the docked controls and the Form edges. This property specifies four values (one for each side), and each value is set to 0 by default. Some common control layout properties are summarized in Fig. 14.15.

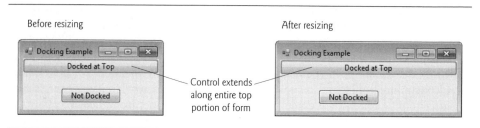

Fig. 14.14 | Docking a Button to the top of a Form.

Control layout properties	Description
Anchor	Causes a control to remain at a fixed distance from the side(s) of the container even when the container is resized.
Dock	Allows a control to span one side of its container or to fill the remaining space in the container.
Padding	Sets the space between a container's edges and docked controls. The default is 0, causing the control to appear flush with the container's sides.
Location	Specifies the location (as a set of coordinates) of the upper-left corner of the control, in relation to its container's upper-left corner.
Size	Specifies the size of the control in pixels as a Size object, which has properties Width and Height.
MinimumSize, MaximumSize	Indicates the minimum and maximum size of a Control, respectively.

Fig. 14.15 | Control layout properties.

The Anchor and Dock properties of a Control are set with respect to the Control's parent container, which could be a Form or another parent container (such as a Panel; discussed in Section 14.6). The minimum and maximum Form (or other Control) sizes can be set via properties **MinimumSize** and **MaximumSize**, respectively. Both are of type **Size**, which has properties **Width** and **Height** to specify the size of the Form. Properties MinimumSize and MaximumSize allow you to design the GUI layout for a given size range. The user cannot make a Form smaller than the size specified by property MinimumSize and cannot make a Form larger than the size specified by property MaximumSize. To set a Form to a *fixed* size (where the Form cannot be resized by the user), set its minimum and maximum size to the same value.

Using Visual Studio To Edit a GUI's Layout

Visual Studio helps you with GUI layout. When you drag a control across a Form, blue **snap lines** appear to help you position the control with respect to others (Fig. 14.16) and the Form's edges. This feature makes the control you're dragging appear to "snap into place" alongside other controls. Visual Studio also provides the **FORMAT** menu, which contains options for modifying your GUI's layout. The **FORMAT** menu does not appear in the IDE unless you select one or more controls in design view. When you select multiple controls, you can align them with the **FORMAT** menu's **Align** submenu. The **FORMAT** menu also enables you to modify the space between controls or to center a control on the Form.

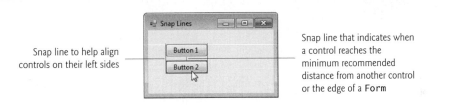

Snap line to help align controls on their left sides

Snap line that indicates when a control reaches the minimum recommended distance from another control or the edge of a Form

Fig. 14.16 | Snap lines for aligning controls.

14.5 Labels, TextBoxes and Buttons

Labels provide text information (as well as optional images) and are defined with class **Label** (a derived class of **Control**). A **Label** displays text that the *user cannot directly modify*. A **Label**'s text can be changed programmatically by modifying the **Label**'s **Text** property. Figure 14.17 lists common **Label** properties.

Common Label properties	Description
Font	The font of the text on the Label.
Text	The text on the Label.
TextAlign	The alignment of the Label's text on the control—horizontally (left, center or right) and vertically (top, middle or bottom). The default is top, left.

Fig. 14.17 | Common Label properties.

A **textbox** (class **TextBox**) is an area in which either text can be displayed by a program or the user can type text via the keyboard. A **password TextBox** is a TextBox that hides the information entered by the user. As the user types characters, the password TextBox masks the user input by displaying a password character. If you set the property **UseSystemPasswordChar** to **true**, the TextBox becomes a password TextBox. Users often encounter both types of TextBoxes, when logging into a computer or website—the username TextBox allows users to input their usernames; the password TextBox allows users to enter their passwords. Figure 14.18 lists the common properties and a common event of TextBoxes.

TextBox properties and an event	Description
Common Properties	
AcceptsReturn	If true in a multiline TextBox, pressing *Enter* in the TextBox creates a new line. If false (the default), pressing *Enter* is the same as pressing the default Button on the Form. The default Button is the one assigned to a Form's AcceptButton property.
Multiline	If true, the TextBox can span multiple lines. The default value is false.
ReadOnly	If true, the TextBox has a gray background, and its text cannot be edited. The default value is false.
ScrollBars	For multiline textboxes, this property indicates which scrollbars appear (None—the default, Horizontal, Vertical or Both).
Text	The TextBox's text content.
UseSystem-PasswordChar	When true, the TextBox becomes a password TextBox, and the system-specified character masks each character the user types.
Common Event	
TextChanged	Generated when the text changes in a TextBox (i.e., when the user adds or deletes characters). When you double click the TextBox control in **Design** mode, an empty event handler for this event is generated.

Fig. 14.18 | TextBox properties and an event.

A button is a control that the user clicks to trigger a specific action or to select an option in a program. As you'll see, a program can use several types of buttons, such as **checkboxes** and **radio buttons**. All the button classes derive from class **ButtonBase** (namespace System.Windows.Forms), which defines common button features. In this section, we discuss class Button, which typically enables a user to issue a command to an app. Figure 14.19 lists common properties and a common event of class Button.

Button properties and an event	Description
Common Properties	
Text	Specifies the text displayed on the Button face.
FlatStyle	Modifies a Button's appearance—Flat (for the Button to display without a three-dimensional appearance), Popup (for the Button to appear flat until the user moves the mouse pointer over the Button), Standard (three-dimensional) and System, where the Button's appearance is controlled by the operating system. The default value is Standard.
Common Event	
Click	Generated when the user clicks the Button. When you double click a Button in design view, an empty event handler for this event is created.

Fig. 14.19 | Button properties and an event.

Figure 14.20 uses a TextBox, a Button and a Label. The user enters text into a password box and clicks the Button, causing the text input to be displayed in the Label. Normally, we would not display this text—the purpose of password TextBoxes is to hide the text being entered by the user. When the user clicks the **Show Me** Button, this app retrieves the text that the user typed in the password TextBox and displays it in a Label.

```csharp
1   // Fig. 14.20: LabelTextBoxButtonTestForm.cs
2   // Using a TextBox, Label and Button to display
3   // the hidden text in a password TextBox.
4   using System;
5   using System.Windows.Forms;
6
7   namespace LabelTextBoxButtonTest
8   {
9      // Form that creates a password TextBox and
10     // a Label to display TextBox contents
11     public partial class LabelTextBoxButtonTestForm : Form
12     {
13        // default constructor
14        public LabelTextBoxButtonTestForm()
15        {
16           InitializeComponent();
17        } // end constructor
18
19        // display user input in Label
20        private void displayPasswordButton_Click(
21           object sender, EventArgs e )
22        {
23           // display the text that the user typed
24           displayPasswordLabel.Text = inputPasswordTextBox.Text;
25        } // end method displayPasswordButton_Click
26     } // end class LabelTextBoxButtonTestForm
27  } // end namespace LabelTextBoxButtonTest
```

Fig. 14.20 | Program to display hidden text in a password box.

First, create the GUI by dragging the controls (a TextBox, a Button and a Label) onto the Form. Once the controls are positioned, change their names in the **Properties** window from the default values—textBox1, button1 and label1—to the more descriptive displayPasswordLabel, displayPasswordButton and inputPasswordTextBox. The (Name) property in the **Properties** window enables us to change the variable name for a control. Visual Studio creates the necessary code and places it in method InitializeComponent of the partial class in the file LabelTextBoxButtonTestForm.Designer.cs.

We set displayPasswordButton's Text property to "Show Me" and clear the Text of displayPasswordLabel so that it's blank when the program begins executing. The BorderStyle property of displayPasswordLabel is set to Fixed3D, giving our Label a three-dimensional appearance. We also changed its TextAlign property to MiddleLeft so that the Label's text is displayed centered between its top and bottom. The password character for inputPasswordTextBox is determined by the user's system settings when you set UseSystemPasswordChar to true.

We create an event handler for displayPasswordButton by double clicking this control in **Design** mode. We added line 24 to the event handler's body. When the user clicks the **Show Me** Button in the executing app, line 24 obtains the text entered by the user in inputPasswordTextBox and displays the text in displayPasswordLabel.

14.6 GroupBoxes and Panels

GroupBoxes and **Panels** arrange controls on a GUI. GroupBoxes and Panels are typically used to group several controls of similar functionality or several controls that are related in a GUI. All of the controls in a GroupBox or Panel move together when the GroupBox or Panel is moved. Furthermore, a GroupBoxes and Panels can also be used to show or hide a set of controls at once. When you modify a container's Visible property, it toggles the visibility of all the controls within it.

The primary difference between these two controls is that GroupBoxes can display a caption (i.e., text) and do *not* include scrollbars, whereas Panels can include scrollbars and do not include a caption. GroupBoxes have thin borders by default; Panels can be set so that they also have borders by changing their BorderStyle property. Figures 14.21–14.22 list the common properties of GroupBoxes and Panels, respectively.

 Look-and-Feel Observation 14.2
Panels and GroupBoxes can contain other Panels and GroupBoxes for more complex layouts.

GroupBox properties	Description
Controls	The set of controls that the GroupBox contains.
Text	Specifies the caption text displayed at the top of the GroupBox.

Fig. 14.21 | GroupBox properties.

Panel properties	Description
AutoScroll	Indicates whether scrollbars appear when the Panel is too small to display all of its controls. The default value is false.
BorderStyle	Sets the border of the Panel. The default value is None; other options are Fixed3D and FixedSingle.
Controls	The set of controls that the Panel contains.

Fig. 14.22 | Panel properties.

Look-and-Feel Observation 14.3

You can organize a GUI by anchoring and docking controls inside a GroupBox or Panel. The GroupBox or Panel then can be anchored or docked inside a Form. This divides controls into functional "groups" that can be arranged easily.

To create a GroupBox, drag its icon from the **Toolbox** onto a Form. Then, drag new controls from the **Toolbox** into the GroupBox. These controls are added to the GroupBox's **Controls** property and become part of the GroupBox. The GroupBox's Text property specifies the caption at the top of the GroupBox.

To create a Panel, drag its icon from the **Toolbox** onto the Form. You can then add controls directly to the Panel by dragging them from the **Toolbox** onto the Panel. To enable the scrollbars, set the Panel's AutoScroll property to true. If the Panel is resized and cannot display all of its controls, scrollbars appear (Fig. 14.23). The scrollbars can be used to view *all* the controls in the Panel—at design time *and* at execution time. In Fig. 14.23, we set the Panel's BorderStyle property to FixedSingle so that you can see the Panel in the Form.

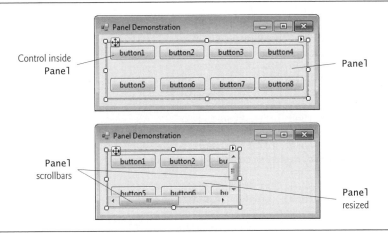

Fig. 14.23 | Creating a Panel with scrollbars.

Look-and-Feel Observation 14.4

Use Panels with scrollbars to avoid cluttering a GUI and to reduce the GUI's size.

The program in Fig. 14.24 uses a GroupBox and a Panel to arrange Buttons. When these Buttons are clicked, their event handlers change the text on a Label.

```
1   // Fig. 14.24: GroupBoxPanelExampleForm.cs
2   // Using GroupBoxes and Panels to arrange Buttons.
3   using System;
4   using System.Windows.Forms;
```

Fig. 14.24 | Using GroupBoxes and Panels to arrange Buttons. (Part 1 of 2.)

```
5
6   namespace GroupBoxPanelExample
7   {
8      // Form that displays a GroupBox and a Panel
9      public partial class GroupBoxPanelExampleForm : Form
10     {
11        // default constructor
12        public GroupBoxPanelExampleForm()
13        {
14           InitializeComponent();
15        } // end constructor
16
17        // event handler for Hi Button
18        private void hiButton_Click( object sender, EventArgs e )
19        {
20           messageLabel.Text = "Hi pressed"; // change text in Label
21        } // end method hiButton_Click
22
23        // event handler for Bye Button
24        private void byeButton_Click( object sender, EventArgs e )
25        {
26           messageLabel.Text = "Bye pressed"; // change text in Label
27        } // end method byeButton_Click
28
29        // event handler for Far Left Button
30        private void leftButton_Click( object sender, EventArgs e )
31        {
32           messageLabel.Text = "Far left pressed"; // change text in Label
33        } // end method leftButton_Click
34
35        // event handler for Far Right Button
36        private void rightButton_Click( object sender, EventArgs e )
37        {
38           messageLabel.Text = "Far right pressed"; // change text in Label
39        } // end method rightButton_Click
40     } // end class GroupBoxPanelExampleForm
41  } // end namespace GroupBoxPanelExample
```

Fig. 14.24 | Using GroupBoxes and Panels to arrange Buttons. (Part 2 of 2.)

The mainGroupBox has two Buttons—hiButton (which displays the text **Hi**) and bye-Button (which displays the text **Bye**). The Panel (named mainPanel) also has two Buttons, leftButton (which displays the text **Far Left**) and rightButton (which displays the text **Far Right**). The mainPanel has its AutoScroll property set to true, allowing scrollbars to appear when the contents of the Panel require more space than the Panel's visible area. The Label (named messageLabel) is initially blank. To add controls to mainGroupBox or mainPanel, Visual Studio calls method Add of each container's Controls property. This code is placed in the partial class located in the file GroupBoxPanelExample.Designer.cs.

The event handlers for the four Buttons are located in lines 18–39. Lines 20, 26, 32 and 38 change the text of messageLabel to indicate which Button the user pressed.

14.7 CheckBoxes and RadioButtons

C# has two types of **state buttons** that can be in the on/off or true/false states—**CheckBoxes** and **RadioButtons**. Like class Button, classes CheckBox and RadioButton are derived from class ButtonBase.

CheckBoxes

A CheckBox is a small square that either is blank or contains a check mark. When the user clicks a CheckBox to select it, a check mark appears in the box. If the user clicks the Check-Box again to deselect it, the check mark is removed. You can also configure a CheckBox to toggle between three states (*checked*, *unchecked* and *indeterminate*) by setting its **Three-State** property to true. Any number of CheckBoxes can be selected at a time. A list of common CheckBox properties and events appears in Fig. 14.25.

CheckBox properties and events	Description
Common Properties	
Appearance	By default, this property is set to Normal, and the CheckBox displays as a traditional checkbox. If it's set to Button, the CheckBox displays as a Button that looks pressed when the CheckBox is checked.
Checked	Indicates whether the CheckBox is *checked* (contains a check mark) or unchecked (blank). This property returns a bool value. The default is false (*unchecked*).
CheckState	Indicates whether the CheckBox is *checked* or *unchecked* with a value from the CheckState enumeration (Checked, Unchecked or Indeterminate). Indeterminate is used when it's unclear whether the state should be Checked or Unchecked. When CheckState is set to Indeterminate, the CheckBox is usually shaded.
Text	Specifies the text displayed to the right of the CheckBox.
ThreeState	When this property is true, the CheckBox has three states—*checked, unchecked* and *indeterminate*. By default, this property is false and the CheckBox has only two states—*checked* and *unchecked*.
Common Events	
CheckedChanged	Generated when the Checked or CheckState property changes. This is a CheckBox's default event. When a user double clicks the CheckBox control in design view, an empty event handler for this event is generated.
CheckStateChanged	Generated when the Checked or CheckState property changes.

Fig. 14.25 | CheckBox properties and events.

The program in Fig. 14.26 allows the user to select CheckBoxes to change a Label's font style. The event handler for one CheckBox applies bold and the event handler for the other applies italic. If both CheckBoxes are selected, the font style is set to bold and italic. Initially, neither CheckBox is checked.

```csharp
1   // Fig. 14.26: CheckBoxTestForm.cs
2   // Using CheckBoxes to toggle italic and bold styles.
3   using System;
4   using System.Drawing;
5   using System.Windows.Forms;
6
7   namespace CheckBoxTest
8   {
9      // Form contains CheckBoxes to allow the user to modify sample text
10     public partial class CheckBoxTestForm : Form
11     {
12        // default constructor
13        public CheckBoxTestForm()
14        {
15           InitializeComponent();
16        } // end constructor
17
18        // toggle the font style between bold and
19        // not bold based on the  current setting
20        private void boldCheckBox_CheckedChanged(
21           object sender, EventArgs e )
22        {
23           outputLabel.Font = new Font( outputLabel.Font,
24              outputLabel.Font.Style ^ FontStyle.Bold );
25        } // end method boldCheckBox_CheckedChanged
26
27        // toggle the font style between italic and
28        // not italic based on the current setting
29        private void italicCheckBox_CheckedChanged(
30           object sender, EventArgs e )
31        {
32           outputLabel.Font = new Font( outputLabel.Font,
33              outputLabel.Font.Style ^ FontStyle.Italic );
34        } // end method italicCheckBox_CheckedChanged
35     } // end class CheckBoxTestForm
36  } // end namespace CheckBoxTest
```

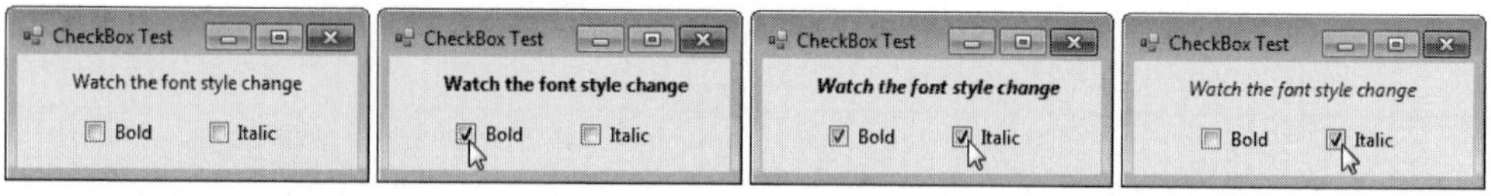

Fig. 14.26 | Using CheckBoxes to change font styles.

The boldCheckBox has its Text property set to Bold. The italicCheckBox has its Text property set to Italic. The Text property of outputLabel is set to Watch the font style change. After creating the controls, we define their event handlers. Double clicking the CheckBoxes at design time creates empty CheckedChanged event handlers.

To change a Label's font style, set its Font property to a new **Font object** (lines 23–24 and 32–33). Class Font is in the System.Drawing namespace. The Font constructor that we use here takes the current font and new style as arguments. The first argument—output-Label.Font—uses outputLabel's original font name and size. The style is specified with a member of the **FontStyle enumeration**, which contains Regular, Bold, Italic, Strikeout and Underline. (The Strikeout style displays text with a line through it.) A Font object's **Style** property is read-only, so it can be set only when the Font object is created.

Combining Font Styles with Bitwise Operators

Styles can be combined via **bitwise operators**—operators that perform manipulation on bits of information. Recall from Chapter 1 that all data is represented in the computer as combinations of 0s and 1s. Each 0 or 1 represents a bit. The FontStyle (namespace System.Drawing) is represented as a set of bits that are selected in a way that allows us to combine different FontStyle elements to create compound styles, using bitwise operators. These styles are *not mutually exclusive*, so we can combine different styles and remove them without affecting the combination of previous FontStyle elements. We can combine these various font styles, using either the *logical OR (|) operator* or the *logical exclusive OR (∧) operator* (also called XOR). When the *logical OR operator* is applied to two bits, if at least one bit of the two has the value 1, then the result is 1. Combining styles using the *logical OR operator* works as follows. Assume that FontStyle.Bold is represented by bits 01 and that FontStyle.Italic is represented by bits 10. When we use the *logical OR (|)* to combine the styles, we obtain the bits 11.

```
01   =   Bold
10   =   Italic
--
11   =   Bold and Italic
```

The *logical OR operator* helps create style combinations. However, what happens if we want to *undo* a style combination, as we did in Fig. 14.26?

The *logical exclusive OR operator* enables us to combine styles and to *undo* existing style settings. When *logical exclusive OR* is applied to two bits, if both bits have the same value, then the result is 0. If both bits are different, then the result is 1.

Combining styles using *logical exclusive OR* works as follows. Assume, again, that FontStyle.Bold is represented by bits 01 and that FontStyle.Italic is represented by bits 10. When we use *logical exclusive OR (∧)* on both styles, we obtain the bits 11.

```
01   =   Bold
10   =   Italic
--
11   =   Bold and Italic
```

Now, suppose that we would like to *remove* the FontStyle.Bold style from the previous combination of FontStyle.Bold and FontStyle.Italic. The easiest way to do so is to reapply the *logical exclusive OR (∧) operator* to the compound style and Font-Style.Bold.

```
11   =   Bold and Italic
01   =   Bold
--
10   =   Italic
```

This is a simple example. The advantages of using bitwise operators to combine FontStyle values become more evident when we consider that there are five FontStyle values (Bold, Italic, Regular, Strikeout and Underline), resulting in 16 FontStyle combinations. Using bitwise operators to combine font styles greatly reduces the amount of code required to check all possible font combinations.

In Fig. 14.26, we need to set the FontStyle so that the text appears in bold if it was not bold originally, and vice versa. Line 24 uses the *bitwise logical exclusive OR operator* to do this. If outputLabel.Font.Style is bold, then the resulting style is not bold. If the text is originally italic, the resulting style is bold and italic, rather than just bold. The same applies for FontStyle.Italic in line 33.

If we didn't use bitwise operators to compound FontStyle elements, we'd have to test for the current style and change it accordingly. In boldCheckBox_CheckedChanged, we could test for the regular style and make it bold, test for the bold style and make it regular, test for the italic style and make it bold italic and test for the italic bold style and make it italic. This is cumbersome because, for every new style we add, we double the number of combinations. Adding a CheckBox for underline would require testing eight additional styles. Adding a CheckBox for strikeout would require testing 16 additional styles.

RadioButtons

Radio buttons (defined with class RadioButton) are similar to CheckBoxes in that they also have two states—**selected** and **not selected** (also called **deselected**). However, RadioButtons normally appear as a **group**, in which only one RadioButton can be selected at a time. Selecting one RadioButton in the group forces all the others to be deselected. Therefore, RadioButtons are used to represent a set of **mutually exclusive** options (i.e., a set in which multiple options *cannot* be selected at the same time).

Look-and-Feel Observation 14.5

Use RadioButtons when the user should choose only one option in a group. Use Check-Boxes when the user should be able to choose multiple options in a group.

All RadioButtons added to a container become part of the same group. To divide RadioButtons into several groups, they must be added to *separate* containers, such as GroupBoxes or Panels. The common properties and a common event of class RadioButton are listed in Fig. 14.27.

RadioButton properties and an event	Description
Common Properties	
Checked	Indicates whether the RadioButton is checked.
Text	Specifies the RadioButton's text.
Common Event	
CheckedChanged	Generated every time the RadioButton is checked or unchecked. When you double click a RadioButton control in design view, an empty event handler for this event is generated.

Fig. 14.27 | RadioButton properties and an event.

Software Engineering Observation 14.1

Forms, GroupBoxes, and Panels can act as logical groups for RadioButtons. The RadioButtons within each group are mutually exclusive to each other, but not to RadioButtons in different logical groups.

The program in Fig. 14.28 uses RadioButtons to enable users to select options for a MessageBox. After selecting the desired attributes, the user presses the **Display** Button to display the MessageBox. A Label in the lower-left corner shows the result of the MessageBox (i.e., which Button the user clicked—**Yes**, **No**, **Cancel**, etc.).

```
 1   // Fig. 14.28: RadioButtonsTestForm.cs
 2   // Using RadioButtons to set message window options.
 3   using System;
 4   using System.Windows.Forms;
 5
 6   namespace RadioButtonsTest
 7   {
 8      // Form contains several RadioButtons--user chooses one
 9      // from each group to create a custom MessageBox
10      public partial class RadioButtonsTestForm : Form
11      {
12         // create variables that store the user's choice of options
13         private MessageBoxIcon iconType;
14         private MessageBoxButtons buttonType;
15
16         // default constructor
17         public RadioButtonsTestForm()
18         {
19            InitializeComponent();
20         } // end constructor
21
22         // change Buttons based on option chosen by sender
23         private void buttonType_CheckedChanged(
24            object sender, EventArgs e )
25         {
26            if ( sender == okRadioButton ) // display OK Button
27               buttonType = MessageBoxButtons.OK;
28
29            // display OK and Cancel Buttons
30            else if ( sender == okCancelRadioButton )
31               buttonType = MessageBoxButtons.OKCancel;
32
33            // display Abort, Retry and Ignore Buttons
34            else if ( sender == abortRetryIgnoreRadioButton )
35               buttonType = MessageBoxButtons.AbortRetryIgnore;
36
37            // display Yes, No and Cancel Buttons
38            else if ( sender == yesNoCancelRadioButton )
39               buttonType = MessageBoxButtons.YesNoCancel;
40
```

Fig. 14.28 | Using RadioButtons to set message-window options. (Part 1 of 4.)

```
41          // display Yes and No Buttons
42          else if ( sender == yesNoRadioButton )
43             buttonType = MessageBoxButtons.YesNo;
44
45          // only one option left--display Retry and Cancel Buttons
46          else
47             buttonType = MessageBoxButtons.RetryCancel;
48       } // end method buttonType_CheckedChanged
49
50       // change Icon based on option chosen by sender
51       private void iconType_CheckedChanged( object sender, EventArgs e )
52       {
53          if ( sender == asteriskRadioButton ) // display asterisk Icon
54             iconType = MessageBoxIcon.Asterisk;
55
56          // display error Icon
57          else if ( sender == errorRadioButton )
58             iconType = MessageBoxIcon.Error;
59
60          // display exclamation point Icon
61          else if ( sender == exclamationRadioButton )
62             iconType = MessageBoxIcon.Exclamation;
63
64          // display hand Icon
65          else if ( sender == handRadioButton )
66             iconType = MessageBoxIcon.Hand;
67
68          // display information Icon
69          else if ( sender == informationRadioButton )
70             iconType = MessageBoxIcon.Information;
71
72          // display question mark Icon
73          else if ( sender == questionRadioButton )
74             iconType = MessageBoxIcon.Question;
75
76          // display stop Icon
77          else if ( sender == stopRadioButton )
78             iconType = MessageBoxIcon.Stop;
79
80          // only one option left--display warning Icon
81          else
82             iconType = MessageBoxIcon.Warning;
83       } // end method iconType_CheckedChanged
84
85       // display MessageBox and Button user pressed
86       private void displayButton_Click( object sender, EventArgs e )
87       {
88          // display MessageBox and store
89          // the value of the Button that was pressed
90          DialogResult result = MessageBox.Show(
91             "This is your Custom MessageBox.", "Custom MessageBox",
92             buttonType, iconType );
93
```

Fig. 14.28 | Using RadioButtons to set message-window options. (Part 2 of 4.)

```
 94            // check to see which Button was pressed in the MessageBox
 95            // change text displayed accordingly
 96            switch (result)
 97            {
 98               case DialogResult.OK:
 99                  displayLabel.Text = "OK was pressed.";
100                  break;
101               case DialogResult.Cancel:
102                  displayLabel.Text = "Cancel was pressed.";
103                  break;
104               case DialogResult.Abort:
105                  displayLabel.Text = "Abort was pressed.";
106                  break;
107               case DialogResult.Retry:
108                  displayLabel.Text = "Retry was pressed.";
109                  break;
110               case DialogResult.Ignore:
111                  displayLabel.Text = "Ignore was pressed.";
112                  break;
113               case DialogResult.Yes:
114                  displayLabel.Text = "Yes was pressed.";
115                  break;
116               case DialogResult.No:
117                  displayLabel.Text = "No was pressed.";
118                  break;
119            } // end switch
120         } // end method displayButton_Click
121      } // end class RadioButtonsTestForm
122   } // end namespace RadioButtonsTest
```

a) GUI for testing **RadioButtons**

b) **AbortRetryIgnore** button type

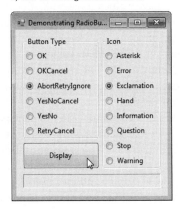

Fig. 14.28 | Using RadioButtons to set message-window options. (Part 3 of 4.)

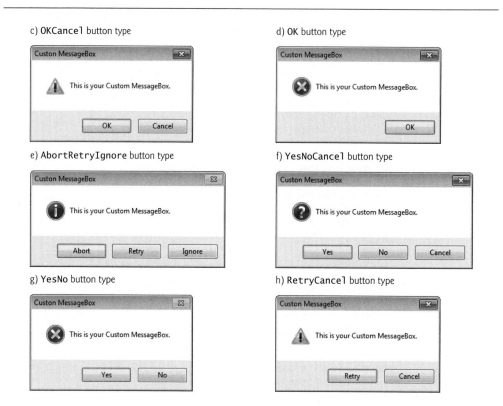

c) OKCancel button type d) OK button type

e) AbortRetryIgnore button type f) YesNoCancel button type

g) YesNo button type h) RetryCancel button type

Fig. 14.28 | Using RadioButtons to set message-window options. (Part 4 of 4.)

We store the user's choices in iconType and buttonType (declared in lines 13–14). Object iconType is of type MessageBoxIcon, and can have values Asterisk, Error, Exclamation, Hand, Information, None, Question, Stop and Warning. The sample output shows only Error, Exclamation, Information and Question icons.

Object buttonType is of type MessageBoxButtons, and can have values Abort-RetryIgnore, OK, OKCancel, RetryCancel, YesNo and YesNoCancel. The name indicates the options that are presented to the user in the MessageBox. The sample output windows show MessageBoxes for all of the MessageBoxButtons enumeration values.

We created two GroupBoxes, one for each set of enumeration values. The GroupBox captions are **Button Type** and **Icon**. The GroupBoxes contain RadioButtons for the corresponding enumeration options, and the RadioButtons' Text properties are set appropriately. Because the RadioButtons are grouped, only one RadioButton can be selected from each GroupBox. There's also a Button (displayButton) labeled **Display**. When a user clicks this Button, a customized MessageBox is displayed. A Label (displayLabel) displays which Button the user pressed within the MessageBox.

The event handler for the RadioButtons handles the CheckedChanged event of each RadioButton. When a RadioButton contained in the **Button Type** GroupBox is checked, the corresponding event handler sets buttonType to the appropriate value. Lines 23–48 contain the event handling for these RadioButtons. Similarly, when the user checks the

RadioButtons belonging to the **Icon** GroupBox, the corresponding event handler associated with these events (lines 51–83) sets iconType to the appropriate value.

The Click event handler for displayButton (lines 86–120) creates a MessageBox (lines 90–92). The MessageBox options are specified with the values stored in iconType and buttonType. When the user clicks one of the MessageBox's buttons, the result of the message box is returned to the app. This result is a value from the **DialogResult** enumeration that contains Abort, Cancel, Ignore, No, None, OK, Retry or Yes. The switch statement in lines 96–119 tests for the result and sets displayLabel.Text appropriately.

14.8 PictureBoxes

A PictureBox displays an image. The image can be one of several formats, such as bitmap, PNG (Portable Network Graphics), GIF (Graphics Interchange Format) and JPEG. A PictureBox's Image property specifies the image that's displayed, and the SizeMode property indicates how the image is displayed (Normal, StretchImage, Autosize, CenterImage or Zoom). Figure 14.29 describes common PictureBox properties and a common event.

Figure 14.30 uses a PictureBox named imagePictureBox to display one of three bitmap images—image0.bmp, image1.bmp or image2.bmp. These images are provided in the Images subdirectory of this chapter's examples directory. Whenever a user clicks the **Next Image** Button, the image changes to the next image in sequence. When the last image is displayed and the user clicks the **Next Image** Button, the first image is displayed again.

PictureBox properties and an event	Description
Common Properties	
Image	Sets the image to display in the PictureBox.
SizeMode	Enumeration that controls image sizing and positioning. Values are Normal (default), StretchImage, AutoSize, CenterImage, and Zoom. Normal places the image in the PictureBox's top-left corner, and CenterImage puts the image in the middle. These two options truncate the image if it's too large. StretchImage resizes the image to fit in the PictureBox. AutoSize resizes the PictureBox to hold the image. Zoom resizes the image to to fit the PictureBox but maintains the original aspect ratio.
Common Event	
Click	Occurs when the user clicks a control. When you double click this control in the designer, an event handler is generated for this event.

Fig. 14.29 | PictureBox properties and an event.

```
1   // Fig. 14.30: PictureBoxTestForm.cs
2   // Using a PictureBox to display images.
3   using System;
```

Fig. 14.30 | Using a PictureBox to display images. (Part 1 of 2.)

```
 4    using System.Drawing;
 5    using System.Windows.Forms;
 6
 7    namespace PictureBoxTest
 8    {
 9       // Form to display different images when PictureBox is clicked
10       public partial class PictureBoxTestForm : Form
11       {
12          private int imageNum = -1; // determines which image is displayed
13
14          // default constructor
15          public PictureBoxTestForm()
16          {
17             InitializeComponent();
18          } // end constructor
19
20          // change image whenever Next Button is clicked
21          private void nextButton_Click( object sender, EventArgs e )
22          {
23             imageNum = ( imageNum + 1 ) % 3; // imageNum cycles from 0 to 2
24
25             // retrieve image from resources and load into PictureBox
26             imagePictureBox.Image = ( Image )
27                ( Properties.Resources.ResourceManager.GetObject(
28                string.Format( "image{0}", imageNum ) ) );
29          } // end method nextButton_Click
30       } // end class PictureBoxTestForm
31    } // end namespace PictureBoxTest
```

Fig. 14.30 | Using a PictureBox to display images. (Part 2 of 2.)

Using Resources Programmatically

In this example, we added the images to the project as **resources**. This causes the compiler to embed the images in the app's executable file and enables the app to access the images through the project's Properties namespace. By embedding the images in the app, you don't need to worry about wrapping the images with the app when you move it to another location or computer.

If you're creating a new project, use the following steps to add images to the project as resources:

1. After creating your project, right click the project's **Properties** node in the **Solution Explorer** and select **Open** to display the project's properties.

2. From the tabs on the left, click the **Resources** tab.

3. At the top of the **Resources** tab, click the down arrow next to **Add Resource** and select **Add Existing File...** to display the **Add existing file to resources** dialog.

4. Locate the image files you wish to add as resources and click the **Open** button. We provided three sample images in the Images folder with this chapter's examples.

5. Save your project.

The files now appear in a folder named **Resources** in the **Solution Explorer**. We'll use this technique in most examples that use images going forward.

A project's resources are stored in its **Resources** class (of the project's Properties namespace). The Resources class contains a **ResourceManager** object for interacting with the resources programmatically. To access an image, you can use the method **GetObject**, which takes as an argument the resource name as it appears in the **Resources** tab (e.g., "image0") and returns the resource as an Object. Lines 27–28 invoke GetObject with the result of the expression

```
string.Format( "image{0}", imageNum )
```

which builds the name of the resource by placing the index of the next picture (imageNum, which was obtained earlier in line 23) at the end of the word "image". You must convert this Object to type Image (namespace System.Drawing) to assign it to the PictureBox's Image property (line 26).

The Resources class also provides direct access to the resources you define with expressions of the form Resources.*resourceName*, where *resourceName* is the name you provided to the resource when you created it. When using such an expression, the resource returned already has the appropriate type. For example, Properties.Resources.image0 is an Image object representing the first image.

14.9 ToolTips

In Chapter 2, we demonstrated *tool tips*—the helpful text that appears when the mouse hovers over an item in a GUI. Recall that the tool tips displayed in Visual Studio help you become familiar with the IDE's features and serve as useful reminders for each toolbar icon's functionality. Many programs use tool tips to remind users of each control's purpose. For example, Microsoft Word has tool tips that help users determine the purpose of the app's icons. This section demonstrates how to use the **ToolTip component** to add tool tips to your apps. Figure 14.31 describes common properties and a common event of class ToolTip.

ToolTip properties and an event	Description
Common Properties	
AutoPopDelay	The amount of time (in milliseconds) that the tool tip appears while the mouse is over a control.
InitialDelay	The amount of time (in milliseconds) that a mouse must hover over a control before a tool tip appears.
ReshowDelay	The amount of time (in milliseconds) between which two different tool tips appear (when the mouse is moved from one control to another).
Common Event	
Draw	Raised when the tool tip is displayed. This event allows programmers to modify the appearance of the tool tip.

Fig. 14.31 | ToolTip properties and an event.

When you add a ToolTip component from the **Toolbox**, it appears in the **component tray**—the region below the Form in **Design** mode. Once a ToolTip is added to a Form, a new property appears in the **Properties** window for the Form's other controls. This property appears in the **Properties** window as **ToolTip on**, followed by the name of the ToolTip component. For instance, if our Form's ToolTip were named helpfulToolTip, you would set a control's **ToolTip on helpfulToolTip** property value to specify the control's tool tip text. Figure 14.32 demonstrates the ToolTip component. For this example, we create a GUI containing two Labels, so we can demonstrate different tool tip text for each Label. To make the sample outputs clearer, we set the BorderStyle property of each Label to FixedSingle, which displays a solid border. Since there's no event-handling code in this example, we do not show you the code for the Form class.

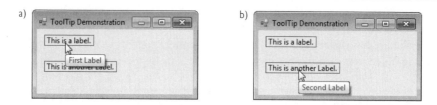

Fig. 14.32 | Demonstrating the ToolTip component.

In this example, we named the ToolTip component labelsToolTip. Figure 14.33 shows the ToolTip in the component tray. We set the tool tip text for the first Label to "First Label" and the tool tip text for the second Label to "Second Label". Figure 14.34 demonstrates setting the tool tip text for the first Label.

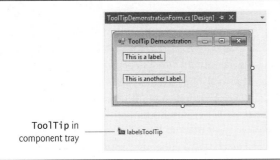

ToolTip in
component tray

Fig. 14.33 | Demonstrating the component tray.

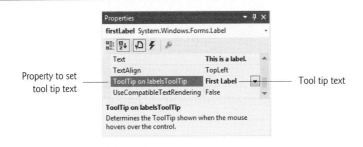

Property to set
tool tip text

Tool tip text

Fig. 14.34 | Setting a control's tool tip text.

14.10 NumericUpDown Control

At times, you'll want to restrict a user's input choices to a specific *range of numeric values*. This is the purpose of the **NumericUpDown control**. This control appears as a TextBox, with two small Buttons on the right side—one with an up arrow and one with a down arrow. By default, a user can type numeric values into this control as if it were a TextBox or click the up and down arrows to increase or decrease the value in the control, respectively. The largest and smallest values in the range are specified with the **Maximum** and **Minimum** properties, respectively (both of type decimal). The **Increment** property (also of type decimal) specifies by how much the current value changes when the user clicks the arrows. Property **DecimalPlaces** specifies the number of decimal places that the control should display as an integer. Figure 14.35 describes common NumericUpDown properties and an event.

NumericUpDown properties and an event	Description
Common Properties	
DecimalPlaces	Specifies how many decimal places to display in the control.
Increment	Specifies by how much the current number in the control changes when the user clicks the control's up and down arrows.

Fig. 14.35 | NumericUpDown properties and an event. (Part 1 of 2.)

NumericUpDown properties and an event	Description
Maximum	Largest value in the control's range.
Minimum	Smallest value in the control's range.
UpDownAlign	Modifies the alignment of the up and down Buttons on the NumericUpDown control. This property can be used to display these Buttons either to the left or to the right of the control.
Value	The numeric value currently displayed in the control.
Common Event	
ValueChanged	This event is raised when the value in the control is changed. This is the default event for the NumericUpDown control.

Fig. 14.35 | NumericUpDown properties and an event. (Part 2 of 2.)

Figure 14.36 demonstrates a NumericUpDown control in a GUI that calculates interest rate. The calculations performed in this app are similar to those in Fig. 6.6. TextBoxes are used to input the principal and interest rate amounts, and a NumericUpDown control is used to input the number of years for which we want to calculate interest.

```
 1   // Fig. 14.36: InterestCalculatorForm.cs
 2   // Demonstrating the NumericUpDown control.
 3   using System;
 4   using System.Windows.Forms;
 5
 6   namespace NumericUpDownTest
 7   {
 8      public partial class InterestCalculatorForm : Form
 9      {
10         // default constructor
11         public InterestCalculatorForm()
12         {
13            InitializeComponent();
14         } // end constructor
15
16         private void calculateButton_Click(
17            object sender, EventArgs e )
18         {
19            // declare variables to store user input
20            decimal principal; // store principal
21            double rate; // store interest rate
22            int year; // store number of years
23            decimal amount; // store amount
24            string output; // store output
25
26            // retrieve user input
27            principal = Convert.ToDecimal( principalTextBox.Text );
```

Fig. 14.36 | Demonstrating the NumericUpDown control. (Part 1 of 2.)

```
28          rate = Convert.ToDouble( interestTextBox.Text );
29          year = Convert.ToInt32( yearUpDown.Value );
30
31          // set output header
32          output = "Year\tAmount on Deposit\r\n";
33
34          // calculate amount after each year and append to output
35          for ( int yearCounter = 1; yearCounter <= year; ++yearCounter )
36          {
37             amount =  principal *
38                ( ( decimal ) Math.Pow( ( 1 + rate / 100 ), yearCounter ) );
39             output += ( yearCounter + "\t" +
40                string.Format( "{0:C}", amount ) + "\r\n" );
41          } // end for
42
43          displayTextBox.Text = output; // display result
44       } // end method calculateButton_Click
45    } // end class InterestCalculatorForm
46 } // end namespace NumericUpDownTest
```

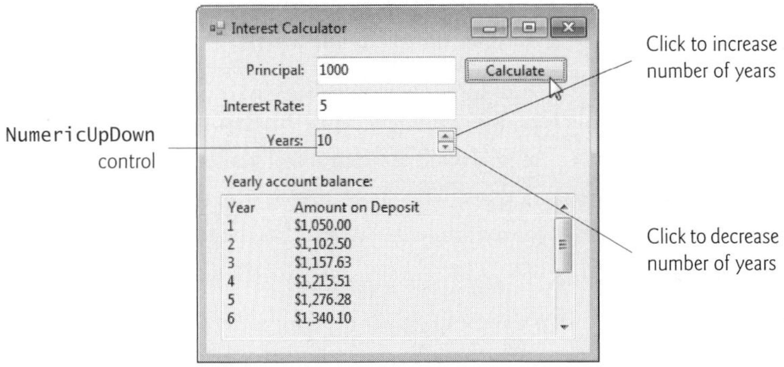

Fig. 14.36 | Demonstrating the NumericUpDown control. (Part 2 of 2.)

For the NumericUpDown control named yearUpDown, we set the Minimum property to 1 and the Maximum property to 10. We left the Increment property set to 1, its default value. These settings specify that users can enter a number of years in the range 1 to 10 in increments of 1. If we had set the Increment to 0.5, we could also input values such as 1.5 or 2.5. If you don't modify the DecimalPlaces property (0 by default), 1.5 and 2.5 display as 2 and 3, respectively. We set the NumericUpDown's **ReadOnly property** to true to indicate that the user cannot type a number into the control to make a selection. Thus, the user must click the up and down arrows to modify the value in the control. By default, the ReadOnly property is set to false. The output for this app is displayed in a multiline read-only TextBox with a vertical scrollbar, so the user can scroll through the entire output.

14.11 Mouse-Event Handling

This section explains how to handle **mouse events**, such as **clicks** and **moves**, which are generated when the user interacts with a control via the mouse. Mouse events can be handled for any control that derives from class `System.Windows.Forms.Control`. For most mouse events, information about the event is passed to the event-handling method through an object of class **MouseEventArgs**, and the delegate used to create the mouse-event handlers is **MouseEventHandler**. Each mouse-event-handling method for these events requires an `object` and a MouseEventArgs object as arguments.

Class MouseEventArgs contains information related to the mouse event, such as the mouse pointer's *x*- and *y*-coordinates, the mouse button pressed (Right, Left or Middle) and the number of times the mouse was clicked. The *x*- and *y*-coordinates of the MouseEventArgs object are relative to the control that generated the event—i.e., point (0,0) represents the upper-left corner of the control where the mouse event occurred. Several common mouse events and event arguments are described in Fig. 14.37.

Mouse events and event arguments	
Mouse Events with Event Argument of Type EventArgs	
MouseEnter	Mouse cursor enters the control's boundaries.
MouseHover	Mouse cursor hovers within the control's boundaries.
MouseLeave	Mouse cursor leaves the control's boundaries.
Mouse Events with Event Argument of Type MouseEventArgs	
MouseDown	Mouse button is pressed while the mouse cursor is within a control's boundaries.
MouseMove	Mouse cursor is moved while in the control's boundaries.
MouseUp	Mouse button is released when the cursor is over the control's boundaries.
MouseWheel	Mouse wheel is moved while the control has the focus.
Class MouseEventArgs Properties	
Button	Specifies which mouse button was pressed (Left, Right, Middle or None).
Clicks	The number of times that the mouse button was clicked.
X	The *x*-coordinate within the control where the event occurred.
Y	The *y*-coordinate within the control where the event occurred.

Fig. 14.37 | Mouse events and event arguments.

Figure 14.38 uses mouse events to draw on a Form. Whenever the user *drags* the mouse (i.e., moves the mouse while a mouse button is pressed), small circles appear on the Form at the position where each mouse event occurs during the drag operation.

```
1   // Fig. 14.38: PainterForm.cs
2   // Using the mouse to draw on a Form.
3   using System;
4   using System.Drawing;
5   using System.Windows.Forms;
6
7   namespace Painter
8   {
```

Fig. 14.38 | Using the mouse to draw on a Form. (Part 1 of 2.)

```
 9      // creates a Form that's a drawing surface
10      public partial class PainterForm : Form
11      {
12         bool shouldPaint = false; // determines whether to paint
13
14         // default constructor
15         public PainterForm()
16         {
17            InitializeComponent();
18         } // end constructor
19
20         // should paint when mouse button is pressed down
21         private void PainterForm_MouseDown(
22            object sender, MouseEventArgs e )
23         {
24            // indicate that user is dragging the mouse
25            shouldPaint = true;
26         } // end method PainterForm_MouseDown
27
28         // stop painting when mouse button is released
29         private void PainterForm_MouseUp( object sender, MouseEventArgs e )
30         {
31            // indicate that user released the mouse button
32            shouldPaint = false;
33         } // end method PainterForm_MouseUp
34
35         // draw circle whenever mouse moves with its button held down
36         private void PainterForm_MouseMove(
37            object sender, MouseEventArgs e )
38         {
39            if ( shouldPaint ) // check if mouse button is being pressed
40            {
41               // draw a circle where the mouse pointer is present
42               using ( Graphics graphics = CreateGraphics() )
43               {
44                  graphics.FillEllipse(
45                     new SolidBrush( Color.BlueViolet ), e.X, e.Y, 4, 4 );
46               } // end using; calls graphics.Dispose()
47            } // end if
48         } // end method PainterForm_MouseMove
49      } // end class PainterForm
50   } // end namespace Painter
```

Fig. 14.38 | Using the mouse to draw on a Form. (Part 2 of 2.)

In line 12, the program declares variable shouldPaint, which determines whether to draw on the Form. We want the program to draw only while the mouse button is pressed (i.e., held down). Thus, when the user clicks or holds down a mouse button, the system generates a MouseDown event, and the event handler (lines 21–26) sets shouldPaint to true. When the user releases the mouse button, the system generates a MouseUp event, shouldPaint is set to false in the PainterForm_MouseUp event handler (lines 29–33) and the program stops drawing. Unlike MouseMove events, which occur continuously as the user moves the mouse, the system generates a MouseDown event only when a mouse button is first *pressed* and generates a MouseUp event only when a mouse button is *released*.

Whenever the mouse moves over a control, the MouseMove event for that control occurs. Inside the PainterForm_MouseMove event handler (lines 36–48), the program draws only if shouldPaint is true (i.e., a mouse button is pressed). In the using statement, line 42 calls inherited Form method CreateGraphics to create a **Graphics** object that allows the program to draw on the Form. Class Graphics provides methods that draw various shapes. For example, lines 44–45 use method **FillEllipse** to draw a circle. The first parameter to method FillEllipse in this case is an object of class **SolidBrush**, which specifies the solid color that will fill the shape. The color is provided as an argument to class SolidBrush's constructor. Type **Color** contains numerous predefined color constants—we selected Color.BlueViolet. FillEllipse draws an oval in a bounding rectangle that's specified by the *x*- and *y*-coordinates of its upper-left corner, its width and its height—the final four arguments to the method. The *x*- and *y*-coordinates represent the location of the mouse event and can be taken from the mouse-event arguments (e.X and e.Y). To draw a circle, we set the width and height of the bounding rectangle so that they're equal—in this example, both are 4 pixels. Graphics, SolidBrush and Color are all part of the namespace System.Drawing. Recall from Chapter 13 that the using statement automatically calls Dispose on the object that was created in the parentheses following keyword using. This is important because Graphics objects are a limited resource. Calling Dispose on a Graphics object ensures that its resources are returned to the system for reuse.

14.12 Keyboard-Event Handling

Key events occur when keyboard keys are pressed and released. Such events can be handled for any control that inherits from System.Windows.Forms.Control. There are three key events—KeyPress, KeyUp and KeyDown. The **KeyPress** event occurs when the user presses a key that represents an ASCII character. The specific key can be determined with property **KeyChar** of the event handler's **KeyPressEventArgs** argument. ASCII is a 128-character set of alphanumeric symbols, a full listing of which can be found in Appendix C.

The KeyPress event does *not* indicate whether **modifier keys** (e.g., *Shift*, *Alt* and *Ctrl*) were pressed when a key event occurred. If this information is important, the **KeyUp** or **KeyDown** events can be used. The **KeyEventArgs** argument for each of these events contains information about modifier keys. Figure 14.39 lists important key event information. Several properties return values from the **Keys enumeration**, which provides constants that specify the various keys on a keyboard. Like the FontStyle enumeration (Section 14.7), the Keys enumeration is represented with a set of bits, so the enumeration's constants can be combined with the bitwise operators to indicate *multiple keys* pressed at the same time.

Keyboard events and event arguments	
Key Events with Event Arguments of Type `KeyEventArgs`	
KeyDown	Generated when a key is initially pressed.
KeyUp	Generated when a key is released.
Key Event with Event Argument of Type `KeyPressEventArgs`	
KeyPress	Generated when a key is pressed. Raised after `KeyDown` and before `KeyUp`.
Class `KeyPressEventArgs` *Properties*	
KeyChar	Returns the ASCII character for the key pressed.
Class `KeyEventArgs` *Properties*	
Alt	Indicates whether the *Alt* key was pressed.
Control	Indicates whether the *Ctrl* key was pressed.
Shift	Indicates whether the *Shift* key was pressed.
KeyCode	Returns the key code for the key as a value from the `Keys` enumeration. This does not include modifier-key information. It's used to test for a specific key.
KeyData	Returns the key code for a key combined with modifier information as a `Keys` value. This property contains all information about the pressed key.
KeyValue	Returns the key code as an `int`, rather than as a value from the `Keys` enumeration. This property is used to obtain a numeric representation of the pressed key. The `int` value is known as a Windows virtual key code.
Modifiers	Returns a `Keys` value indicating any pressed modifier keys (*Alt*, *Ctrl* and *Shift*). This property is used to determine modifier-key information only.

Fig. 14.39 | Keyboard events and event arguments.

Figure 14.40 demonstrates the use of the key-event handlers to display a key pressed by a user. The program is a `Form` with two `Label`s that displays the pressed key on one `Label` and modifier key information on the other.

```
 1   // Fig. 14.40: KeyDemo.cs
 2   // Displaying information about the key the user pressed.
 3   using System;
 4   using System.Windows.Forms;
 5
 6   namespace KeyDemo
 7   {
 8      // Form to display key information when key is pressed
 9      public partial class KeyDemo : Form
10      {
11         // default constructor
12         public KeyDemo()
13         {
```

Fig. 14.40 | Demonstrating keyboard events. (Part 1 of 2.)

```
14              InitializeComponent();
15         } // end constructor
16
17         // display the character pressed using KeyChar
18         private void KeyDemo_KeyPress(
19            object sender, KeyPressEventArgs e )
20         {
21            charLabel.Text = "Key pressed: " + e.KeyChar;
22         } // end method KeyDemo_KeyPress
23
24         // display modifier keys, key code, key data and key value
25         private void KeyDemo_KeyDown( object sender, KeyEventArgs e )
26         {
27            keyInfoLabel.Text =
28               "Alt: " + ( e.Alt ? "Yes" : "No" ) + '\n' +
29               "Shift: " + ( e.Shift ? "Yes" : "No" ) + '\n' +
30               "Ctrl: " + ( e.Control ? "Yes" : "No" ) + '\n' +
31               "KeyCode: " + e.KeyCode + '\n' +
32               "KeyData: " + e.KeyData + '\n' +
33               "KeyValue: " + e.KeyValue;
34         } // end method KeyDemo_KeyDown
35
36         // clear Labels when key released
37         private void KeyDemo_KeyUp( object sender, KeyEventArgs e )
38         {
39            charLabel.Text = "";
40            keyInfoLabel.Text = "";
41         } // end method KeyDemo_KeyUp
42      } // end class KeyDemo
43   } // end namespace KeyDemo
```

a) *H pressed*   b) *F7 pressed*   c) *$ pressed*   d) *Tab pressed*

Key Demo	Key Demo	Key Demo	Key Demo
Key pressed: H		Key pressed: $	Key pressed:
Alt: No	Alt: No	Alt: No	Alt: No
Shift: Yes	Shift: No	Shift: Yes	Shift: No
Ctrl: No	Ctrl: No	Ctrl: No	Ctrl: No
KeyCode: H	KeyCode: F7	KeyCode: D4	KeyCode: Tab
KeyData: H, Shift	KeyData: F7	KeyData: D4, Shift	KeyData: Tab
KeyValue: 72	KeyValue: 118	KeyValue: 52	KeyValue: 9

Fig. 14.40 | Demonstrating keyboard events. (Part 2 of 2.)

Control charLabel displays the character value of the key pressed, whereas keyInfo-
Label displays information relating to the pressed key. Because the KeyDown and KeyPress
events convey different information, the Form (KeyDemo) handles both.

The KeyPress event handler (lines 18–22) accesses the KeyChar property of the Key-
PressEventArgs object. This returns the pressed key as a char, which we then display in
charLabel (line 21). If the pressed key is not an ASCII character, then the KeyPress event
will not occur, and charLabel will not display any text. ASCII is a common encoding

format for letters, numbers, punctuation marks and other characters. It does not support keys such as the **function keys** (like *F1*) or the modifier keys (*Alt, Ctrl* and *Shift*).

The KeyDown event handler (lines 25–34) displays information from its KeyEventArgs object. The event handler tests for the *Alt, Shift* and *Ctrl* keys by using the Alt, Shift and Control properties, each of which returns a bool value—true if the corresponding key is pressed and false otherwise. The event handler then displays the KeyCode, KeyData and KeyValue properties.

The KeyCode property returns a Keys enumeration value (line 31). The KeyCode property returns the pressed key, but does not provide any information about modifier keys. Thus, both a capital and a lowercase "a" are represented as the *A* key.

The KeyData property (line 32) also returns a Keys enumeration value, but this property includes data about modifier keys. Thus, if "A" is input, the KeyData shows that both the *A* key and the *Shift* key were pressed. Lastly, KeyValue (line 33) returns an int representing a pressed key. This int is the **key code**. The key code is useful when testing for non-ASCII keys like *F12*.

The KeyUp event handler (lines 37–41) clears both Labels when the key is released. As we can see from the output, non-ASCII keys are not displayed in charLabel, because the KeyPress event is not generated. For example, charLabel does not display any text when you press the *F7* or *Tab* keys, as shown in Fig. 14.40(b) and (d). However, the Key-Down event still is generated, and keyInfoLabel displays information about the key that's pressed. The Keys enumeration can be used to test for specific keys by comparing the Key-Code of the pressed key to values in the Keys enumeration.

Software Engineering Observation 14.2

To cause a control to react when a particular key is pressed (such as Enter*), handle a key event and test for the pressed key. To cause a* Button *to be clicked when the* Enter *key is pressed on a Form, set the Form's* AcceptButton *property.*

By default, a keyboard event is handled by the control that currently has the focus. Sometimes it's appropriate to have the Form handle these events. This can be accomplished by setting the Form's KeyPreview property to true, which makes the Form receive keyboard events before they're passed to another control. For example, a key press would raise the Form's KeyPress, even if a control within the Form has the focus instead of the Form itself.

14.13 Wrap-Up

This chapter introduced several common GUI controls. We discussed event handling in detail, and showed how to create event handlers. We showed how delegates are used to connect event handlers to the events of specific controls. You learned how to use a control's properties and Visual Studio to specify the layout of your GUI. We then demonstrated several controls, beginning with Labels, Buttons and TextBoxes. You learned how to use GroupBoxes and Panels to organize other controls. We then demonstrated CheckBoxes and RadioButtons, which are state buttons that allow users to select among several options. We displayed images in PictureBox controls, displayed helpful text on a GUI with ToolTip components and specified a range of numeric input values for users with a NumericUpDown control. We then demonstrated how to handle mouse and keyboard events. The next chapter introduces additional GUI controls. You'll learn how to add menus to your GUIs and create Windows Forms apps that display multiple Forms.

15

Graphical User Interfaces with Windows Forms: Part 2

Objectives

In this chapter you'll:

- Create menus, tabbed windows and multiple document interface (MDI) programs.

- Use the `ListView` and `TreeView` controls for displaying information.

- Create hyperlinks using the `LinkLabel` control.

- Display lists of information in `ListBox`, `CheckedListBox` and `ComboBox` controls.

- Input dates with the `MonthCalendar` control.

- Input date and time data with the `DateTimePicker` control.

- Create custom controls.

15.1 Introduction

This chapter continues our study of Windows Forms GUIs. We start with menus, which present users with logically organized commands (or options). We show how to develop menus with the tools provided by Visual Studio. Next, we discuss how to input and display dates and times using the `MonthCalendar` and `DateTimePicker` controls. We also introduce `LinkLabel`s—powerful GUI components that enable the user to access one of several destinations, such as a file on the current machine or a web page, simply by clicking the mouse.

We demonstrate how to manipulate a list of values via a `ListBox` and how to combine several checkboxes in a `CheckedListBox`. We also create drop-down lists using `ComboBoxes` and display data hierarchically with a `TreeView` control. You'll learn two other important GUI elements—tab controls and multiple document interface (MDI) windows. These components enable you to create real-world programs with sophisticated GUIs.

Visual Studio provides many GUI components, several of which are discussed in this (and the previous) chapter. You can also design custom controls and add them to the **ToolBox**, as we demonstrate in this chapter's last example. The techniques presented here form the groundwork for creating more substantial GUIs and custom controls.

15.2 Menus

Menus provide groups of related commands for Windows Forms apps. Although these commands depend on the program, some—such as **Open** and **Save**—are common to many apps. Menus are an integral part of GUIs, because they organize commands without "cluttering" the GUI.

In Fig. 15.1, an expanded menu from the Visual C# IDE lists various commands (called **menu items**), plus **submenus** (menus within a menu). The top-level menus appear in the left portion of the figure, whereas any submenus or menu items are displayed to the right. The menu that contains a menu item is called that menu item's **parent menu**. A menu item that contains a submenu is considered to be the parent of that submenu.

Menus can have *Alt* key shortcuts (also called **access shortcuts**, **keyboard shortcuts** or **hotkeys**), which are accessed by pressing *Alt* and the underlined letter—for example, *Alt* + *F* typically expands the **File** menu. Menu items can have shortcut keys as well (combinations of *Ctrl, Shift, Alt, F1, F2,* letter keys, and so on). Some menu items display checkmarks, usually indicating that multiple options on the menu can be selected at once.

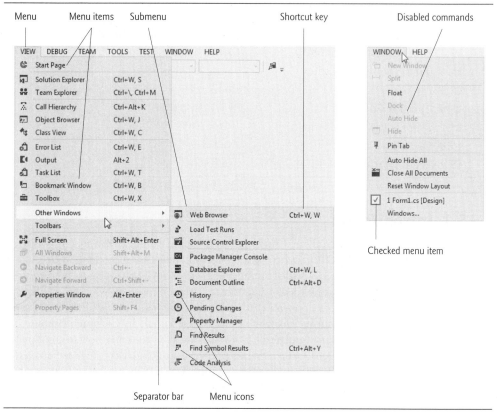

Fig. 15.1 | Menus, submenus and menu items.

To create a menu, open the **Toolbox** and drag a **MenuStrip** control onto the Form. This creates a menu bar across the top of the Form (below the title bar) and places a MenuStrip icon in the component tray. To select the MenuStrip, click this icon. You can now use **Design** mode to create and edit menus for your app. Menus, like other controls, have properties and events, which can be accessed through the **Properties** window.

To add menu items to the menu, click the **Type Here** TextBox (Fig. 15.2) and type the menu item's name. This action adds an entry to the menu of type **ToolStripMenuItem**. After you press the *Enter* key, the menu item name is added to the menu. Then more **Type Here** TextBoxes appear, allowing you to add items underneath or to the side of the original menu item (Fig. 15.3).

To create an access shortcut, type an ampersand (&) before the character to be underlined. For example, to create the **File** menu item with the letter **F** underlined, type &File. To display an ampersand, type &&. To add other shortcut keys (e.g., *Ctrl + F9*) for menu items, set the **ShortcutKeys** property of the appropriate ToolStripMenuItems. To do this, select the down arrow to the right of this property in the **Properties** window. In the window that appears (Fig. 15.4), use the CheckBoxes and drop-down list to select the shortcut keys. When you're finished, click elsewhere on the screen. You can hide the shortcut keys by setting property **ShowShortcutKeys** to false, and you can modify how the shortcut keys are displayed in the menu item by modifying property **ShortcutKeyDisplayString**.

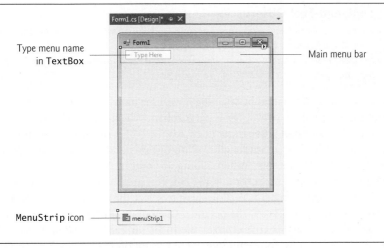

Fig. 15.2 | Editing menus in Visual Studio.

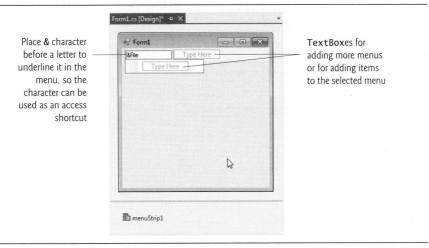

Fig. 15.3 | Adding ToolStripMenuItems to a MenuStrip.

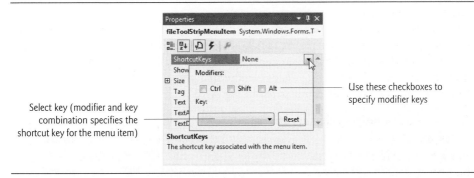

Fig. 15.4 | Setting a menu item's shortcut keys.

Look-and-Feel Observation 15.1

Buttons can have access shortcuts. Place the & symbol immediately before the desired character in the Button's text. To press the button by using its access key in the running app, the user presses Alt *and the underlined character. If the underline is not visible when the app runs, press the* Alt *key to display the underlines.*

You can remove a menu item by selecting it with the mouse and pressing the *Delete* key. Menu items can be grouped logically by **separator bars**, which are inserted by right clicking the menu and selecting **Insert > Separator** or by typing "-" for the text of a menu item.

In addition to text, Visual Studio allows you to easily add TextBoxes and ComboBoxes (drop-down lists) as menu items. When adding an item in **Design** mode, you may have noticed that before you enter text for a new item, you're provided with a drop-down list. Clicking the down arrow (Fig. 15.5) allows you to select the type of item to add—**Menu-Item** (of type ToolStripMenuItem, the default), **ComboBox** (of type ToolStripComboBox) and **TextBox** (of type ToolStripTextBox). We focus on ToolStripMenuItems. [*Note:* If you view this drop-down list for menu items that are not on the top level, a fourth option appears, allowing you to insert a separator bar.]

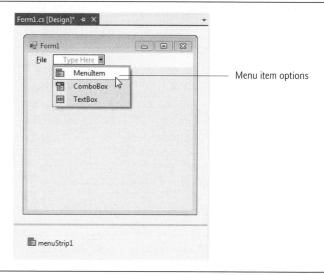

Menu item options

Fig. 15.5 | Menu-item options.

ToolStripMenuItems generate a **Click** event when selected. To create an empty Click event handler, double click the menu item in **Design** mode. Common actions in response to these events include displaying dialogs and setting properties. Common menu properties and a common event are summarized in Fig. 15.6.

Look-and-Feel Observation 15.2

It's a convention to place an ellipsis (...) after the name of a menu item (e.g., **Save As...**) *that requires the user to provide more information—typically through a dialog. A menu item that produces an immediate action without prompting the user for more information (e.g.,* **Save**) *should not have an ellipsis following its name.*

MenuStrip and ToolStripMenuItem properties and an event	Description
MenuStrip Properties	
RightToLeft	Causes text to display from right to left. This is useful for languages that are read from right to left.
ToolStripMenuItem Properties	
Checked	Indicates whether a menu item is checked. The default value is false, meaning that the menu item is unchecked.
CheckOnClick	Indicates that a menu item should appear checked or unchecked as it is clicked.
ShortcutKey-DisplayString	Specifies text that should appear beside a menu item for a shortcut key. If left blank, the key names are displayed. Otherwise, the text in this property is displayed for the shortcut key.
ShortcutKeys	Specifies the shortcut key for the menu item (e.g., *<Ctrl>-F9* is equivalent to clicking a specific item).
ShowShortcutKeys	Indicates whether a shortcut key is shown beside menu item text. The default is true, which displays the shortcut key.
Text	Specifies the menu item's text. To create an *Alt* access shortcut, precede a character with & (e.g., &File to specify a menu named **File** with the letter **F** underlined).
Common ToolStripMenuItem Event	
Click	Generated when an item is clicked or a shortcut key is used. This is the default event when the menu is double clicked in the designer.

Fig. 15.6 | MenuStrip and ToolStripMenuItem properties and an event.

Class MenuTestForm (Fig. 15.7) creates a simple menu on a Form. The Form has a top-level **File** menu with menu items **About** (which displays a MessageBox) and **Exit** (which terminates the program). The program also includes a **Format** menu, which contains menu items that change the format of the text on a Label. The **Format** menu has submenus **Color** and **Font**, which change the color and font of the text on a Label.

Create the GUI
To create this GUI, begin by dragging the MenuStrip from the **ToolBox** onto the Form. Then use **Design** mode to create the menu structure shown in the sample outputs. The **File** menu (fileToolStripMenuItem) has menu items **About** (aboutToolStripMenuItem) and **Exit** (exitToolStripMenuItem); the **Format** menu (formatToolStripMenuItem) has two submenus. The first submenu, **Color** (colorToolStripMenuItem), contains menu items **Black** (blackToolStripMenuItem), **Blue** (blueToolStripMenuItem), **Red** (redToolStripMenuItem) and **Green** (greenToolStripMenuItem). The second submenu, **Font** (fontToolStripMenuItem), contains menu items **Times New Roman** (timesToolStripMenuItem), **Courier** (courierToolStripMenuItem), **Comic Sans** (comicToolStripMenuItem), a separator bar (dashToolStripMenuItem), **Bold** (boldToolStripMenuItem) and **Italic** (italicToolStripMenuItem).

```
1   // Fig. 15.7: MenuTestForm.cs
2   // Using Menus to change font colors and styles.
3   using System;
4   using System.Drawing;
5   using System.Windows.Forms;
6
7   namespace MenuTest
8   {
9      // our Form contains a Menu that changes the font color
10     // and style of the text displayed in Label
11     public partial class MenuTestForm : Form
12     {
13        // constructor
14        public MenuTestForm()
15        {
16           InitializeComponent();
17        } // end constructor
18
19        // display MessageBox when About ToolStripMenuItem is selected
20        private void aboutToolStripMenuItem_Click(
21           object sender, EventArgs e )
22        {
23           MessageBox.Show( "This is an example\nof using menus.", "About",
24              MessageBoxButtons.OK, MessageBoxIcon.Information );
25        } // end method aboutToolStripMenuItem_Click
26
27        // exit program when Exit ToolStripMenuItem is selected
28        private void exitToolStripMenuItem_Click(
29           object sender, EventArgs e )
30        {
31           Application.Exit();
32        } // end method exitToolStripMenuItem_Click
33
34        // reset checkmarks for Color ToolStripMenuItems
35        private void ClearColor()
36        {
37           // clear all checkmarks
38           blackToolStripMenuItem.Checked = false;
39           blueToolStripMenuItem.Checked = false;
40           redToolStripMenuItem.Checked = false;
41           greenToolStripMenuItem.Checked = false;
42        } // end method ClearColor
43
44        // update Menu state and color display black
45        private void blackToolStripMenuItem_Click(
46           object sender, EventArgs e )
47        {
48           // reset checkmarks for Color ToolStripMenuItems
49           ClearColor();
50
51           // set color to Black
52           displayLabel.ForeColor = Color.Black;
```

Fig. 15.7 | Menus for changing text font and color. (Part 1 of 4.)

```
53            blackToolStripMenuItem.Checked = true;
54         } // end method blackToolStripMenuItem_Click
55
56         // update Menu state and color display blue
57         private void blueToolStripMenuItem_Click(
58            object sender, EventArgs e )
59         {
60            // reset checkmarks for Color ToolStripMenuItems
61            ClearColor();
62
63            // set color to Blue
64            displayLabel.ForeColor = Color.Blue;
65            blueToolStripMenuItem.Checked = true;
66         } // end method blueToolStripMenuItem_Click
67
68         // update Menu state and color display red
69         private void redToolStripMenuItem_Click(
70            object sender, EventArgs e )
71         {
72            // reset checkmarks for Color ToolStripMenuItems
73            ClearColor();
74
75            // set color to Red
76            displayLabel.ForeColor = Color.Red;
77            redToolStripMenuItem.Checked = true;
78         } // end method redToolStripMenuItem_Click
79
80         // update Menu state and color display green
81         private void greenToolStripMenuItem_Click(
82            object sender, EventArgs e )
83         {
84            // reset checkmarks for Color ToolStripMenuItems
85            ClearColor();
86
87            // set color to Green
88            displayLabel.ForeColor = Color.Green;
89            greenToolStripMenuItem.Checked = true;
90         } // end method greenToolStripMenuItem_Click
91
92         // reset checkmarks for Font ToolStripMenuItems
93         private void ClearFont()
94         {
95            // clear all checkmarks
96            timesToolStripMenuItem.Checked = false;
97            courierToolStripMenuItem.Checked = false;
98            comicToolStripMenuItem.Checked = false;
99         } // end method ClearFont
100
101         // update Menu state and set Font to Times New Roman
102         private void timesToolStripMenuItem_Click(
103            object sender, EventArgs e )
104         {
105            // reset checkmarks for Font ToolStripMenuItems
```

Fig. 15.7 | Menus for changing text font and color. (Part 2 of 4.)

```
106             ClearFont();
107
108             // set Times New Roman font
109             timesToolStripMenuItem.Checked = true;
110             displayLabel.Font = new Font( "Times New Roman", 14,
111                 displayLabel.Font.Style );
112         } // end method timesToolStripMenuItem_Click
113
114         // update Menu state and set Font to Courier
115         private void courierToolStripMenuItem_Click(
116             object sender, EventArgs e )
117         {
118             // reset checkmarks for Font ToolStripMenuItems
119             ClearFont();
120
121             // set Courier font
122             courierToolStripMenuItem.Checked = true;
123             displayLabel.Font = new Font( "Courier", 14,
124                 displayLabel.Font.Style );
125         } // end method courierToolStripMenuItem_Click
126
127         // update Menu state and set Font to Comic Sans MS
128         private void comicToolStripMenuItem_Click(
129             object sender, EventArgs e )
130         {
131             // reset checkmarks for Font ToolStripMenuItems
132             ClearFont();
133
134             // set Comic Sans font
135             comicToolStripMenuItem.Checked = true;
136             displayLabel.Font = new Font( "Comic Sans MS", 14,
137                 displayLabel.Font.Style );
138         } // end method comicToolStripMenuItem_Click
139
140         // toggle checkmark and toggle bold style
141         private void boldToolStripMenuItem_Click(
142             object sender, EventArgs e )
143         {
144             // toggle checkmark
145             boldToolStripMenuItem.Checked = !boldToolStripMenuItem.Checked;
146
147             // use Xor to toggle bold, keep all other styles
148             displayLabel.Font = new Font( displayLabel.Font,
149                 displayLabel.Font.Style ^ FontStyle.Bold );
150         } // end method boldToolStripMenuItem_Click
151
152         // toggle checkmark and toggle italic style
153         private void italicToolStripMenuItem_Click(
154             object sender, EventArgs e )
155         {
156             // toggle checkmark
157             italicToolStripMenuItem.Checked =
158                 !italicToolStripMenuItem.Checked;
```

Fig. 15.7 | Menus for changing text font and color. (Part 3 of 4.)

```
159
160                 // use Xor to toggle italic, keep all other styles
161                 displayLabel.Font = new Font( displayLabel.Font,
162                    displayLabel.Font.Style ^ FontStyle.Italic );
163          } // end method italicToolStripMenuItem_Click
164       } // end class MenuTestForm
165    } // end namespace MenuTest
```

a) Initial GUI

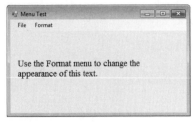

b) Selecting the **Bold** menu item

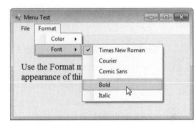

c) GUI after text set to bold

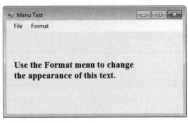

d) Selecting the **Red** menu item

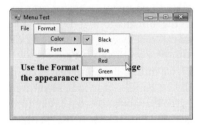

e) GUI after text set to **Red**

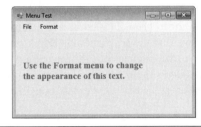

f) Dialog displayed by selecting **File > About**

Fig. 15.7 | Menus for changing text font and color. (Part 4 of 4.)

Handling the **Click** *Events for the* **About** *and* **Exit** *Menu Items*
The **About** menu item in the **File** menu displays a MessageBox when clicked (lines 20–25). The **Exit** menu item closes the app through static method **Exit** of class **Application** (line 31). Class Application's static methods control program execution. Method Exit causes our app to terminate.

Color Submenu Events
We made the items in the **Color** submenu (**Black**, **Blue**, **Red** and **Green**) mutually exclusive—the user can select *only one* at a time (we explain how we did this shortly). To indicate that a menu item is selected, we will set each **Color** menu item's **Checked** property to true. This causes a check to appear to the left of a menu item.

Each **Color** menu item has its own `Click` event handler. The method handler for color **Black** is `blackToolStripMenuItem_Click` (lines 45–54). Similarly, the event handlers for colors **Blue**, **Red** and **Green** are `blueToolStripMenuItem_Click` (lines 57–66), `redTool-StripMenuItem_Click` (lines 69–78) and `greenToolStripMenuItem_Click` (lines 81–90), respectively. Each **Color** menu item must be *mutually exclusive*, so each event handler calls method `ClearColor` (lines 35–42) before setting its corresponding `Checked` property to `true`. Method `ClearColor` sets the `Checked` property of each color `ToolStripMenuItem` to `false`, effectively preventing more than one menu item from being selected at a time. In the designer, we initially set the **Black** menu item's `Checked` property to `true`, because at the start of the program, the text on the `Form` is black.

Software Engineering Observation 15.1

The mutual exclusion of menu items is not enforced by the `MenuStrip`, *even when the* `Checked` *property is* `true`. *You must program this behavior.*

Font Submenu Events

The **Font** menu contains three menu items for fonts (**Courier**, **Times New Roman** and **Comic Sans**) and two menu items for font styles (**Bold** and **Italic**). We added a separator bar between the font and font-style menu items to indicate that these are separate options. A `Font` object can specify only one font at a time but can *set multiple styles at once* (e.g., a font can be both *bold* and italic). We set the font menu items to display checks. As with the **Color** menu, we must enforce mutual exclusion of these items in our event handlers.

Event handlers for font menu items **Times New Roman**, **Courier** and **Comic Sans** are `timesToolStripMenuItem_Click` (lines 102–112), `courierToolStripMenuItem_Click` (lines 115–125) and `comicToolStripMenuItem_Click` (lines 128–138), respectively. These event handlers are similar to those of the **Color** menu items. Each clears the `Checked` properties for all font menu items by calling method `ClearFont` (lines 93–99), then sets the `Checked` property of the menu item that raised the event to `true`. This enforces the mutual exclusion of the font menu items. In the designer, we initially set the **Times New Roman** menu item's `Checked` property to `true`, because this is the original font for the text on the `Form`. The event handlers for the **Bold** and **Italic** menu items (lines 141–163) use the bitwise logical exclusive OR (^) operator to combine font styles, as we discussed in Chapter 14.

15.3 `MonthCalendar` Control

Many apps must perform date and time calculations. The .NET Framework provides two controls that allow an app to retrieve date and time information—the `MonthCalendar` and `DateTimePicker` (Section 15.4) controls.

The **`MonthCalendar`** (Fig. 15.8) control displays a monthly calendar on the `Form`. The user can select a date from the currently displayed month or can use the provided arrows to navigate to another month. When a date is selected, it is highlighted. Multiple dates can be selected by clicking dates on the calendar while holding down the *Shift* key. The default event for this control is the **DateChanged** event, which is generated when a new date is selected. Properties are provided that allow you to modify the appearance of the calendar, how many dates can be selected at once, and the minimum date and maximum date that may be selected. `MonthCalendar` properties and a common `MonthCalendar` event are summarized in Fig. 15.9.

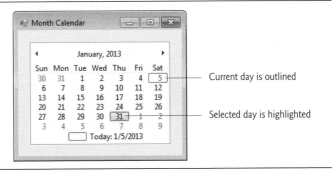

Current day is outlined

Selected day is highlighted

Fig. 15.8 | MonthCalendar control.

MonthCalendar properties and an event	Description
MonthCalendar Properties	
FirstDayOfWeek	Sets which day of the week is the first displayed for each week in the calendar.
MaxDate	The last date that can be selected.
MaxSelectionCount	The maximum number of dates that can be selected at once.
MinDate	The first date that can be selected.
MonthlyBoldedDates	An array of dates that will displayed in bold in the calendar.
SelectionEnd	The last of the dates selected by the user.
SelectionRange	The dates selected by the user.
SelectionStart	The first of the dates selected by the user.
Common MonthCalendar Event	
DateChanged	Generated when a date is selected in the calendar.

Fig. 15.9 | MonthCalendar properties and an event.

15.4 DateTimePicker Control

The **DateTimePicker** control (see output of Fig. 15.11) is similar to the MonthCalendar control but displays the calendar when a *down arrow* is selected. The DateTimePicker can be used to retrieve date and time information from the user. A DateTimePicker's **Value** property stores a DateTime object, which always contains both date and time information. You can retrieve the date information from the DateTime object by using property **Date**, and you can retrieve only the time information by using the **TimeOfDay** property.

The DateTimePicker is also more customizable than a MonthCalendar control—more properties are provided to edit the look and feel of the drop-down calendar. Property **Format** specifies the user's selection options using the **DateTimePickerFormat** enumeration. The values in this enumeration are Long (displays the date in long format, as in **Thursday, July 10, 2013**), Short (displays the date in short format, as in **7/10/2013**), Time (displays a time value, as in **5:31:02 PM**) and Custom (indicates that a custom format will be used). If value `Custom` is used, the display in the `DateTimePicker` is specified using property **CustomFormat**. The default event for this control is **ValueChanged**, which occurs when the selected value (whether a date or a time) is changed. `DateTimePicker` properties and a common event are summarized in Fig. 15.10.

DateTimePicker properties and an event	Description
DateTimePicker Properties	
`CalendarForeColor`	Sets the text color for the calendar.
`CalendarMonthBackground`	Sets the calendar's background color.
`CustomFormat`	Sets the custom format string for the date and/or time displayed in the control.
`Format`	Sets the format of the date and/or time used for the date and/or time displayed in the control.
`MaxDate`	The maximum date and time that can be selected.
`MinDate`	The minimum date and time that can be selected.
`ShowCheckBox`	Indicates if a `CheckBox` should be displayed to the left of the selected date and time.
`ShowUpDown`	Indicates whether the control displays up and down `Buttons`. Helpful when the `DateTimePicker` is used to select a time—the `Buttons` can be used to increase or decrease hour, minute and second.
`Value`	The data selected by the user.
Common DateTimePicker Event	
`ValueChanged`	Generated when the `Value` property changes, including when the user selects a new date or time.

Fig. 15.10 | `DateTimePicker` properties and an event.

Figure 15.11 demonstrates using a `DateTimePicker` to select an item's drop-off time. Many companies use such functionality—several online DVD rental companies specify the day a movie is sent out and the estimated time that it will arrive at your home. The user selects a drop-off day, then an estimated arrival date is displayed. The date is always two days after drop-off, three days if a Sunday is reached (mail is not delivered on Sunday).

```
1   // Fig. 15.11: DateTimePickerForm.cs
2   // Using a DateTimePicker to select a drop-off time.
3   using System;
4   using System.Windows.Forms;
5
6   namespace DateTimePickerTest
7   {
```

Fig. 15.11 | Demonstrating `DateTimePicker`. (Part 1 of 3.)

```
8      // Form lets user select a drop-off date using a DateTimePicker
9      // and displays an estimated delivery date
10     public partial class DateTimePickerForm : Form
11     {
12        // constructor
13        public DateTimePickerForm()
14        {
15           InitializeComponent();
16        } // end constructor
17
18        private void dateTimePickerDropOff_ValueChanged(
19           object sender, EventArgs e )
20        {
21           DateTime dropOffDate = dateTimePickerDropOff.Value;
22
23           // add extra time when items are dropped off around Sunday
24           if ( dropOffDate.DayOfWeek == DayOfWeek.Friday ||
25              dropOffDate.DayOfWeek == DayOfWeek.Saturday ||
26              dropOffDate.DayOfWeek == DayOfWeek.Sunday )
27
28              //estimate three days for delivery
29              outputLabel.Text =
30                 dropOffDate.AddDays( 3 ).ToLongDateString();
31           else
32              // otherwise estimate only two days for delivery
33              outputLabel.Text =
34                 dropOffDate.AddDays( 2 ).ToLongDateString();
35        } // end method dateTimePickerDropOff_ValueChanged
36
37        private void DateTimePickerForm_Load( object sender, EventArgs e )
38        {
39           // user cannot select days before today
40           dateTimePickerDropOff.MinDate = DateTime.Today;
41
42           // user can only select days up to one year in the future
43           dateTimePickerDropOff.MaxDate = DateTime.Today.AddYears( 1 );
44        } // end method DateTimePickerForm_Load
45     } // end class DateTimePickerForm
46  } // end namespace DateTimePickerTest
```

a) GUI when app first executes shows current date   b) Selecting a drop-off date

Fig. 15.11 | Demonstrating DateTimePicker. (Part 2 of 3.)

c) GUI after selecting drop-off date

d) GUI showing current and selected dates

Fig. 15.11 | Demonstrating `DateTimePicker`. (Part 3 of 3.)

The `DateTimePicker` (`dropOffDateTimePicker`) has its `Format` property set to `Long`, so the user can select just a date in this app. When the user selects a date, the `ValueChanged` event occurs. The event handler for this event (lines 18–35) first retrieves the selected date from the `DateTimePicker`'s `Value` property (line 21). Lines 24–26 use the `DateTime` structure's **`DayOfWeek`** property to determine the day of the week on which the selected date falls. The day values are represented using the **`DayOfWeek`** enumeration. Lines 29–30 and 33–34 use `DateTime`'s **`AddDays`** method to increase the date by three days or two days, respectively. The resulting date is then displayed in `Long` format using method **`ToLongDateString`**.

In this app, we do not want the user to be able to select a drop-off day before the current day, or one that's more than a year into the future. To enforce this, we set the `DateTimePicker`'s **`MinDate`** and **`MaxDate`** properties when the `Form` is loaded (lines 40 and 43). Property `Today` returns the current day, and method **`AddYears`** (with an argument of 1) is used to specify a date one year in the future.

Let's take a closer look at the output. This app begins by displaying the current date (Fig. 15.11(a)). In Fig. 15.11(b), we selected the 18th of January. In Fig. 15.11(c), the estimated arrival date is displayed as the 21st of January. Figure 15.11(d) shows that the 18th, after it is selected, is highlighted in the calendar.

15.5 LinkLabel Control

The **`LinkLabel`** control displays *links* to other resources, such as files or web pages (Fig. 15.12). A `LinkLabel` appears as underlined text (colored blue by default). When the mouse moves over the link, the pointer changes to a hand; this is similar to the behavior of a hyperlink in a web page. The link can change color to indicate whether it is not yet visited, previously visited or active (the mouse is over the link). When clicked, the `LinkLabel` generates a **`LinkClicked`** event (see Fig. 15.13). Class `LinkLabel` is derived from class `Label` and therefore inherits all of class `Label`'s functionality.

LinkLabel on a Form

Hand image displays when mouse moves over LinkLabel

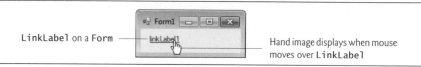

Fig. 15.12 | LinkLabel control in running program.

Look-and-Feel Observation 15.3

A LinkLabel is the preferred control for indicating that the user can click a link to jump to a resource such as a web page, though other controls can perform similar tasks.

LinkLabel properties and an event	Description
Common Properties	
ActiveLinkColor	Specifies the color of the active link when the user is in the process of clicking the link. The default color (typically red) is set by the system.
LinkArea	Specifies which portion of text in the LinkLabel is part of the link.
LinkBehavior	Specifies the link's behavior, such as how the link appears when the mouse is placed over it.
LinkColor	Specifies the original color of the link before it's been visited. The default color (typically blue) is set by the system.
LinkVisited	If true, the link appears as though it has been visited (its color is changed to that specified by property VisitedLinkColor). The default value is false.
Text	Specifies the control's text.
UseMnemonic	If true, the & character in the Text property acts as a shortcut (similar to the *Alt* shortcut in menus).
VisitedLinkColor	Specifies the color of a visited link. The default color (typically purple) is set by the system.
Common Event (Event arguments LinkLabelLinkClickedEventArgs)	
LinkClicked	Generated when the link is clicked. This is the default event when the control is double clicked in **Design** mode.

Fig. 15.13 | LinkLabel properties and an event.

Class LinkLabelTestForm (Fig. 15.14) uses three LinkLabels to link to the C: drive, the Deitel website (www.deitel.com) and the Notepad app, respectively. The Text properties of the LinkLabel's cDriveLinkLabel, deitelLinkLabel and notepadLinkLabel describe each link's purpose.

```
1   // Fig. 15.14: LinkLabelTestForm.cs
2   // Using LinkLabels to create hyperlinks.
3   using System;
4   using System.Windows.Forms;
5
6   namespace LinkLabelTest
7   {
8      // Form using LinkLabels to browse the C:\ drive,
9      // load a web page and run Notepad
10     public partial class LinkLabelTestForm : Form
11     {
```

Fig. 15.14 | LinkLabels used to link to a drive, a web page and an app. (Part 1 of 3.)

```
12          // constructor
13          public LinkLabelTestForm()
14          {
15             InitializeComponent();
16          } // end constructor
17
18          // browse C:\ drive
19          private void cDriveLinkLabel_LinkClicked( object sender,
20             LinkLabelLinkClickedEventArgs e )
21          {
22             // change LinkColor after it has been clicked
23             driveLinkLabel.LinkVisited = true;
24
25             System.Diagnostics.Process.Start( @"C:\" );
26          } // end method cDriveLinkLabel_LinkClicked
27
28          // load www.deitel.com in web browser
29          private void deitelLinkLabel_LinkClicked( object sender,
30             LinkLabelLinkClickedEventArgs e )
31          {
32             // change LinkColor after it has been clicked
33             deitelLinkLabel.LinkVisited = true;
34
35             System.Diagnostics.Process.Start( "http://www.deitel.com" );
36          } // end method deitelLinkLabel_LinkClicked
37
38          // run app Notepad
39          private void notepadLinkLabel_LinkClicked( object sender,
40             LinkLabelLinkClickedEventArgs e )
41          {
42             // change LinkColor after it has been clicked
43             notepadLinkLabel.LinkVisited = true;
44
45             // program called as if in run
46             // menu and full path not needed
47             System.Diagnostics.Process.Start( "notepad" );
48          } // end method notepadLinkLabel_LinkClicked
49       } // end class LinkLabelTestForm
50    } // end namespace LinkLabelTest
```

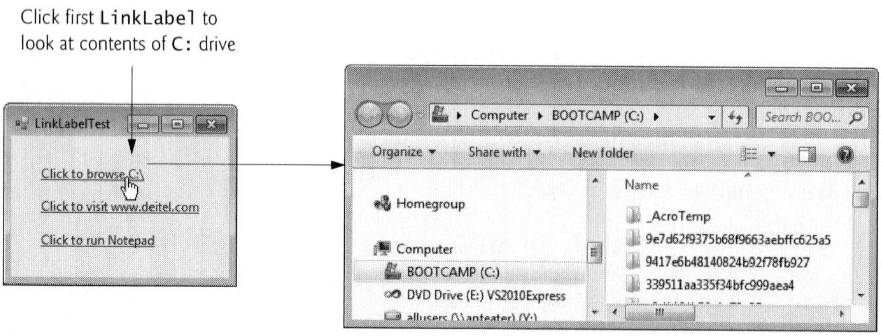

Click first LinkLabel to
look at contents of C: drive

Fig. 15.14 | LinkLabels used to link to a drive, a web page and an app. (Part 2 of 3.)

Click second `LinkLabel`
to go to Deitel website

Click on third `LinkLabel`
to open Notepad

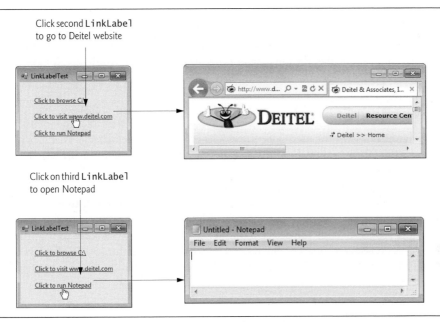

Fig. 15.14 | `LinkLabel`s used to link to a drive, a web page and an app. (Part 3 of 3.)

The event handlers for the `LinkLabel`s call method **Start** of class **Process** (namespace **System.Diagnostics**), which allows you to execute other programs, or load documents or web sites from an app. Method `Start` can take one argument, the file to open, or two arguments, the app to run and its command-line arguments. Method `Start`'s arguments can be in the same form as if they were provided for input to the Windows **Run** command (**Start > Run...**). For apps that are known to Windows, full path names are not needed, and the file extension often can be omitted. To open a file of a type that Windows recognizes (and knows how to handle), simply use the file's full path name. For example, if you a pass the method a `.docx` file, Windows will open it in Microsoft Word (or whatever program is registered to open `.docx` files, if any). The Windows operating system must be able to use the app associated with the given file's extension to open the file.

The event handler for `cDriveLinkLabel`'s `LinkClicked` event browses the C: drive (lines 19–26). Line 23 sets the `LinkVisited` property to `true`, which changes the link's color from blue to purple (the `LinkVisited` colors can be configured through the **Properties** window in Visual Studio). The event handler then passes `@"C:\"` to method `Start` (line 25), which opens a **Windows Explorer** window. The `@` symbol that we placed before `"C:\"` indicates that all characters in the `string` should be interpreted literally—this is known as a **verbatim string**. Thus, the backslash within the `string` is not considered to be the first character of an escape sequence. This simplifies `string`s that represent directory paths, since you do not need to use `\\` for each `\` character in the path.

The event handler for `deitelLinkLabel`'s `LinkClicked` event (lines 29–36) opens the web page `www.deitel.com` in the user's default web browser. We achieve this by passing the web-page address as a `string` (line 35), which opens the web page in a new web browser window or tab. Line 33 sets the `LinkVisited` property to `true`.

The event handler for notepadLinkLabel's LinkClicked event (lines 39–48) opens the Notepad app. Line 43 sets the LinkVisited property to true so that the link appears as a visited link. Line 47 passes the argument "notepad" to method Start, which runs notepad.exe. In line 47, neither the full path nor the .exe extension is required—Windows automatically recognizes the argument given to method Start as an executable file.

15.6 ListBox Control

The **ListBox** control allows the user to view and select from multiple items in a list. ListBoxes are static GUI entities, which means that users cannot directly edit the list of items. The user can be provided with TextBoxes and Buttons with which to specify items to be added to the list, but the actual additions must be performed in code. The **CheckedListBox** control (Section 15.7) extends a ListBox by including CheckBoxes next to each item in the list. This allows users to place checks on multiple items at once, as is possible with CheckBox controls. (Users also can select multiple items from a ListBox by setting the ListBox's **SelectionMode** property, which is discussed shortly.) Figure 15.15 displays a ListBox and a CheckedListBox. In both controls, scrollbars appear if the number of items exceeds the ListBox's viewable area.

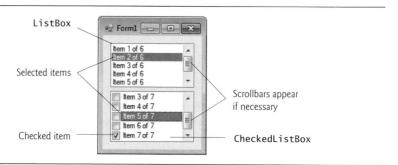

Fig. 15.15 | ListBox and CheckedListBox on a Form.

Figure 15.16 lists common ListBox properties and methods and a common event. The SelectionMode property determines the number of items that can be selected. This property has the possible values None, One, MultiSimple and MultiExtended (from the **SelectionMode** enumeration)—the differences among these settings are explained in Fig. 15.16. The **SelectedIndexChanged** event occurs when the user selects a new item.

ListBox properties, methods and an event	Description
Common Properties	
Items	The collection of items in the ListBox.
MultiColumn	Indicates whether the ListBox can display multiple columns. Multiple columns eliminate vertical scrollbars from the display.

Fig. 15.16 | ListBox properties, methods and an event. (Part 1 of 2.)

ListBox properties, methods and an event	Description
SelectedIndex	Returns the index of the selected item. If no items have been selected, the property returns -1. If the user selects multiple items, this property returns only one of the selected indices. If multiple items are selected, use property SelectedIndices.
SelectedIndices	Returns a collection containing the indices for all selected items.
SelectedItem	Returns a reference to the selected item. If multiple items are selected, it can return any of the selected items.
SelectedItems	Returns a collection of the selected item(s).
SelectionMode	Determines the number of items that can be selected and the means through which multiple items can be selected. Values None, One (the default), MultiSimple (multiple selection allowed) or Multi-Extended (multiple selection allowed using a combination of arrow keys or mouse clicks and *Shift* and *Ctrl* keys).
Sorted	Indicates whether items are sorted *alphabetically*. Setting this property's value to true sorts the items. The default value is false.
Common Methods	
ClearSelected	Deselects every item.
GetSelected	Returns true if the item at the specified index is selected.
Common Event	
SelectedIndexChanged	Generated when the selected index changes. This is the default event when the control is double clicked in the designer.

Fig. 15.16 | ListBox properties, methods and an event. (Part 2 of 2.)

Both the ListBox and CheckedListBox have properties Items, SelectedItem and SelectedIndex. Property **Items** returns a collection of the list items. *Collections* are a common way to manage lists of objects in the .NET framework. Many .NET GUI components (e.g., ListBoxes) use collections to expose lists of internal objects (e.g., items in a ListBox). We discuss collections further in Chapter 19. The collection returned by property Items is represented as an object of type ListBox.ObjectCollection. Property **SelectedItem** returns the ListBox's currently selected item. If the user can select multiple items, use collection **SelectedItems** to return all the selected items as a ListBox.SelectedObject-Colection. Property **SelectedIndex** returns the index of the selected item—if there could be more than one, use property **SelectedIndices**, which returns a ListBox.SelectedIndexColection. If no items are selected, property SelectedIndex returns -1. Method **GetSelected** takes an index and returns true if the corresponding item is selected.

Adding Items to *ListBoxes* and *CheckedListBoxes*
To add items to a ListBox or to a CheckedListBox, we must add objects to its Items collection. This can be accomplished by calling method Add to add a string to the ListBox's or CheckedListBox's Items collection. For example, we could write

```
myListBox.Items.Add( myListItem );
```

to add string *myListItem* to ListBox *myListBox*. To add multiple objects, you can either call method Add multiple times or call method AddRange to add an array of objects. Classes ListBox and CheckedListBox each call the submitted object's ToString method to determine the Label for the corresponding object's entry in the list. This allows you to add different objects to a ListBox or a CheckedListBox that later can be returned through properties SelectedItem and SelectedItems.

Alternatively, you can add items to ListBoxes and CheckedListBoxes visually by examining the Items property in the **Properties** window. Clicking the ellipsis button opens the **String Collection Editor**, which contains a text area for adding items; each item appears on a separate line (Fig. 15.17). Visual Studio then writes code to add these strings to the Items collection inside method InitializeComponent.

Fig. 15.17 | String Collection Editor.

Figure 15.18 uses class ListBoxTestForm to add, remove and clear items from ListBox displayListBox. Class ListBoxTestForm uses TextBox inputTextBox to allow the user to type in a new item. When the user clicks the **Add** Button, the new item appears in displayListBox. Similarly, if the user selects an item and clicks **Remove**, the item is deleted. When clicked, **Clear** deletes all entries in displayListBox. The user terminates the app by clicking **Exit**.

The addButton_Click event handler (lines 20–24) calls method Add of the Items collection in the ListBox. This method takes a string as the item to add to displayListBox. In this case, the string used is the user input from the inputTextBox (line 22). After the item is added, inputTextBox.Text is cleared (line 23).

```
1    // Fig. 15.18: ListBoxTestForm.cs
2    // Program to add, remove and clear ListBox items
3    using System;
4    using System.Windows.Forms;
5
6    namespace ListBoxTest
7    {
8       // Form uses a TextBox and Buttons to add,
9       // remove, and clear ListBox items
10      public partial class ListBoxTestForm : Form
11      {
```

Fig. 15.18 | Program that adds, removes and clears ListBox items. (Part 1 of 3.)

```
12          // constructor
13          public ListBoxTestForm()
14          {
15             InitializeComponent();
16          } // end constructor
17
18          // add new item to ListBox (text from input TextBox)
19          // and clear input TextBox
20          private void addButton_Click( object sender, EventArgs e )
21          {
22             displayListBox.Items.Add( inputTextBox.Text );
23             inputTextBox.Clear();
24          } // end method addButton_Click
25
26          // remove item if one is selected
27          private void removeButton_Click( object sender, EventArgs e )
28          {
29             // check whether item is selected; if so, remove
30             if ( displayListBox.SelectedIndex != -1 )
31                displayListBox.Items.RemoveAt(
32                   displayListBox.SelectedIndex );
33          } // end method removeButton_Click
34
35          // clear all items in ListBox
36          private void clearButton_Click( object sender, EventArgs e )
37          {
38             displayListBox.Items.Clear();
39          } // end method clearButton_Click
40
41          // exit app
42          private void exitButton_Click( object sender, EventArgs e )
43          {
44             Application.Exit();
45          } // end method exitButton_Click
46       } // end class ListBoxTestForm
47    } // end namespace ListBoxTest
```

a) GUI after adding **Dog**, **Cat** and **Chicken** and before adding **Cow**

b) GUI after adding **Cow** and before deleting **Chicken**

Fig. 15.18 | Program that adds, removes and clears ListBox items. (Part 2 of 3.)

c) GUI after deleting **Chicken**

d) GUI after clearing the `ListBox`

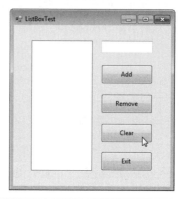

Fig. 15.18 | Program that adds, removes and clears `ListBox` items. (Part 3 of 3.)

The `removeButton_Click` event handler (lines 27–33) uses method `RemoveAt` to remove an item from the `ListBox`. Event handler `removeButton_Click` first uses property `SelectedIndex` to determine which index is selected. If `SelectedIndex` is not –1 (i.e., an item is selected), lines 31–32 remove the item that corresponds to the selected index.

The `clearButton_Click` event handler (lines 36–39) calls method `Clear` of the `Items` collection (line 38). This removes all the entries in `displayListBox`. Finally, event handler `exitButton_Click` (lines 42–45) terminates the app by calling method `Application.Exit` (line 44).

15.7 CheckedListBox Control

The `CheckedListBox` control derives from `ListBox` and displays a `CheckBox` with each item. Items can be added via methods `Add` and `AddRange` or through the **String Collection Editor**. `CheckedListBox`es allow multiple items to be checked, but item selection is more restrictive. The only values for the `SelectionMode` property are `None` and `One`. `One` allows a single selection, whereas `None` allows no selections. Because an item must be selected to be checked, you must set the `SelectionMode` to be `One` if you wish to allow users to check items. Thus, toggling property `SelectionMode` between `One` and `None` effectively switches between enabling and disabling the user's ability to check list items. Common properties, a method and an event of `CheckedListBox`es appear in Fig. 15.19.

Common Programming Error 15.1

*The IDE displays an error message if you attempt to set the `SelectionMode` property to `MultiSimple` or `MultiExtended` in the **Properties** window of a `CheckedListBox`. If this value is set programmatically, a runtime error occurs.*

Event **ItemCheck** occurs whenever a user checks or unchecks a `CheckedListBox` item. Event-argument properties `CurrentValue` and `NewValue` return `CheckState` values for the current and new state of the item, respectively. A comparison of these values allows you to determine whether the `CheckedListBox` item was checked or unchecked. The `CheckedListBox` control retains the `SelectedItems` and `SelectedIndices` properties (it inherits

CheckedListBox properties, a method and an event	Description
Common Properties	*(All the ListBox properties, methods and events are inherited by CheckedListBox.)*
CheckedItems	Accessible only at runtime. Returns the collection of items that are checked as a CheckedListBox.CheckedItemCollection. This is distinct from the selected item, which is highlighted (but not necessarily checked). There can be at most one selected item at any given time.
CheckedIndices	Accessible only at runtime. Returns indices for all checked items as a CheckedListBox.CheckedIndexCollection.
CheckOnClick	When true and the user clicks an item, the item is both selected and checked or unchecked. By default, this property is false, which means that the user must select an item, then click it again to check or uncheck it.
SelectionMode	Determines whether items can be selected and checked. The possible values are One (the default; allows multiple checks to be placed) or None (does not allow any checks to be placed).
Common Method	
GetItemChecked	Takes an index and returns true if the corresponding item is checked.
Common Event (Event arguments ItemCheckEventArgs)	
ItemCheck	Generated when an item is checked or unchecked.
ItemCheckEventArgs Properties	
CurrentValue	Indicates whether the current item is checked or unchecked. Possible values are Checked, Unchecked and Indeterminate.
Index	Returns the zero-based index of the item that changed.
NewValue	Specifies the new state of the item.

Fig. 15.19 | CheckedListBox properties, a method and an event.

them from class ListBox). However, it also includes properties CheckedItems and CheckedIndices, which return information about the checked items and indices.

In Fig. 15.20, class CheckedListBoxTestForm uses a CheckedListBox and a ListBox to display a user's selection of books. The CheckedListBox allows the user to select multiple titles. In the **String Collection Editor**, items were added for some Deitel books: C, C++, Java™, Internet & WWW, VB 2012, Visual C++ and Visual C# 2012 (the abbreviation HTP stands for "How to Program"). The ListBox (named displayListBox) displays the user's selection. In the screenshots accompanying this example, the CheckedListBox appears to the left, the ListBox on the right.

When the user checks or unchecks an item in itemCheckedListBox, an ItemCheck event occurs and event handler itemCheckedListBox_ItemCheck (lines 19–31) executes. An if...else statement (lines 27–30) determines whether the user checked or unchecked an item in the CheckedListBox. Line 27 uses the NewValue property to determine whether

```
1    // Fig. 15.20: CheckedListBoxTestForm.cs
2    // Using a CheckedListBox to add items to a display ListBox
3    using System;
4    using System.Windows.Forms;
5
6    namespace CheckedListBoxTest
7    {
8       // Form uses a checked ListBox to add items to a display ListBox
9       public partial class CheckedListBoxTestForm : Form
10      {
11         // constructor
12         public CheckedListBoxTestForm()
13         {
14            InitializeComponent();
15         } // end constructor
16
17         // item checked or unchecked
18         // add or remove from display ListBox
19         private void itemCheckedListBox_ItemCheck(
20            object sender, ItemCheckEventArgs e )
21         {
22            // obtain reference of selected item
23            string item = itemCheckedListBox.SelectedItem.ToString();
24
25            // if item checked, add to ListBox
26            // otherwise remove from ListBox
27            if ( e.NewValue == CheckState.Checked )
28               displayListBox.Items.Add( item );
29            else
30               displayListBox.Items.Remove( item );
31         } // end method itemCheckedListBox_ItemCheck
32      } // end class CheckedListBoxTestForm
33   } // end namespace CheckedListBoxTest
```

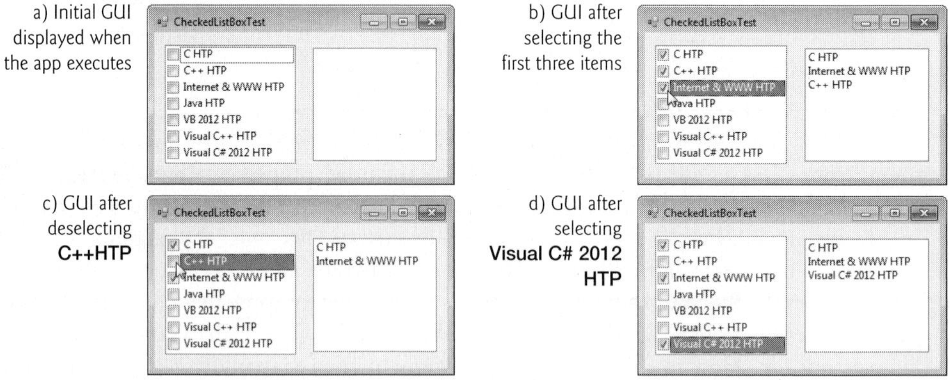

a) Initial GUI displayed when the app executes

b) GUI after selecting the first three items

c) GUI after deselecting C++HTP

d) GUI after selecting Visual C# 2012 HTP

Fig. 15.20 | CheckedListBox and ListBox used in an app to display a user selection.

the item is being checked (CheckState.Checked). If the user checks an item, line 28 adds the checked entry to the ListBox displayListBox. If the user unchecks an item, line 30 removes the corresponding item from displayListBox. This event handler was created by selecting the CheckedListBox in **Design** mode, viewing the control's events in the **Properties** window and double clicking the ItemCheck event. The default event for a CheckedListBox is a SelectedIndexChanged event.

15.8 ComboBox Control

The **ComboBox** control combines TextBox features with a **drop-down list**—a GUI component that contains a list from which a value can be selected. A ComboBox usually appears as a TextBox with a down arrow to its right. By default, the user can enter text into the TextBox or click the down arrow to display a list of predefined items. If a user chooses an element from this list, that element is displayed in the TextBox. If the list contains more elements than can be displayed in the drop-down list, a *scrollbar* appears. The maximum number of items that a drop-down list can display at one time is set by property **MaxDropDownItems**. Figure 15.21 shows a sample ComboBox in three different states.

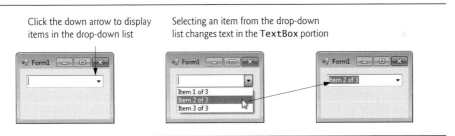

Fig. 15.21 | ComboBox demonstration.

As with the ListBox control, you can add objects to collection Items programmatically, using methods Add and AddRange, or visually, with the **String Collection Editor**. Figure 15.22 lists common properties and a common event of class ComboBox.

Look-and-Feel Observation 15.4

Use a ComboBox to save space on a GUI. A disadvantage is that, unlike with a ListBox, the user cannot see available items without expanding the drop-down list.

ComboBox properties and an event	Description
Common Properties	
DropDownStyle	Determines the type of ComboBox. Value Simple means that the text portion is editable and the list portion is always visible. Value DropDown (the default) means that the text portion is editable but the user must click an arrow button to see the list portion. Value DropDownList means that the text portion is not editable and the user must click the arrow button to see the list portion.
Items	The collection of items in the ComboBox control.

Fig. 15.22 | ComboBox properties and an event. (Part 1 of 2.)

ComboBox properties and an event	Description
MaxDropDownItems	Specifies the maximum number of items (between 1 and 100) that the drop-down list can display. If the number of items exceeds the maximum number of items to display, a scrollbar appears.
SelectedIndex	Returns the index of the selected item, or -1 if none are selected.
SelectedItem	Returns a reference to the selected item.
Sorted	Indicates whether items are sorted alphabetically. Setting this property's value to true sorts the items. The default is false.
Common Event	
SelectedIndexChanged	Generated when the selected index changes (such as when a different item is selected). This is the default event when control is double clicked in the designer.

Fig. 15.22 | ComboBox properties and an event. (Part 2 of 2.)

Property **DropDownStyle** determines the type of ComboBox and is represented as a value of the **ComboBoxStyle** enumeration, which contains values Simple, DropDown and DropDownList. Option Simple does not display a drop-down arrow. Instead, a scrollbar appears next to the control, allowing the user to select a choice from the list. The user also can type in a selection. Style DropDown (the default) displays a drop-down list when the down arrow is clicked (or the down arrow key is pressed). The user can type a new item in the ComboBox. The last style is DropDownList, which displays a drop-down list but does not allow the user to type in the TextBox.

The ComboBox control has properties **Items** (a collection), **SelectedItem** and **SelectedIndex**, which are similar to the corresponding properties in ListBox. There can be at most one selected item in a ComboBox. If no items are selected, then SelectedIndex is -1. When the selected item changes, a **SelectedIndexChanged** event occurs.

Class ComboBoxTestForm (Fig. 15.23) allows users to select a shape to draw—circle, ellipse, square or pie (in both filled and unfilled versions)—by using a ComboBox. The ComboBox in this example is uneditable, so the user cannot type in the TextBox.

Look-and-Feel Observation 15.5

Make lists (such as ComboBoxes) editable only if the app is designed to accept user-submitted elements. Otherwise, the user might try to enter a custom item that's improper for the purposes of your app.

```
1   // Fig. 15.23: ComboBoxTestForm.cs
2   // Using ComboBox to select a shape to draw.
3   using System;
4   using System.Drawing;
5   using System.Windows.Forms;
```

Fig. 15.23 | ComboBox used to draw a selected shape. (Part 1 of 3.)

```
6
7    namespace ComboBoxTest
8    {
9       // Form uses a ComboBox to select different shapes to draw
10      public partial class ComboBoxTestForm : Form
11      {
12         // constructor
13         public ComboBoxTestForm()
14         {
15            InitializeComponent();
16         } // end constructor
17
18         // get index of selected shape, draw shape
19         private void imageComboBox_SelectedIndexChanged(
20            object sender, EventArgs e )
21         {
22            // create graphics object, Pen and SolidBrush
23            Graphics myGraphics = base.CreateGraphics();
24
25            // create Pen using color DarkRed
26            Pen myPen = new Pen( Color.DarkRed );
27
28            // create SolidBrush using color DarkRed
29            SolidBrush mySolidBrush = new SolidBrush( Color.DarkRed );
30
31            // clear drawing area, setting it to color white
32            myGraphics.Clear( Color.White );
33
34            // find index, draw proper shape
35            switch ( imageComboBox.SelectedIndex )
36            {
37               case 0: // case Circle is selected
38                  myGraphics.DrawEllipse( myPen, 50, 50, 150, 150 );
39                  break;
40               case 1: // case Rectangle is selected
41                  myGraphics.DrawRectangle( myPen, 50, 50, 150, 150 );
42                  break;
43               case 2: // case Ellipse is selected
44                  myGraphics.DrawEllipse( myPen, 50, 85, 150, 115 );
45                  break;
46               case 3: // case Pie is selected
47                  myGraphics.DrawPie( myPen, 50, 50, 150, 150, 0, 45 );
48                  break;
49               case 4: // case Filled Circle is selected
50                  myGraphics.FillEllipse( mySolidBrush, 50, 50, 150, 150 );
51                  break;
52               case 5: // case Filled Rectangle is selected
53                  myGraphics.FillRectangle( mySolidBrush, 50, 50, 150,
54                     150 );
55                  break;
56               case 6: // case Filled Ellipse is selected
57                  myGraphics.FillEllipse( mySolidBrush, 50, 85, 150, 115 );
58                  break;
```

Fig. 15.23 | ComboBox used to draw a selected shape. (Part 2 of 3.)

```
59                      case 7: // case Filled Pie is selected
60                          myGraphics.FillPie( mySolidBrush, 50, 50, 150, 150, 0,
61                              45 );
62                          break;
63                  } // end switch
64
65                  myGraphics.Dispose(); // release the Graphics object
66          } // end method imageComboBox_SelectedIndexChanged
67      } // end class ComboBoxTestForm
68  } // end namespace ComboBoxTest
```

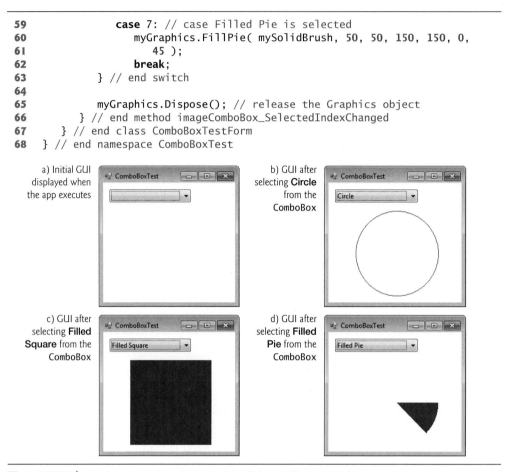

a) Initial GUI displayed when the app executes

b) GUI after selecting **Circle** from the ComboBox

c) GUI after selecting **Filled Square** from the ComboBox

d) GUI after selecting **Filled Pie** from the ComboBox

Fig. 15.23 | ComboBox used to draw a selected shape. (Part 3 of 3.)

After creating ComboBox imageComboBox, make it uneditable by setting its DropDown-Style to DropDownList in the **Properties** window. Next, add items Circle, Square, Ellipse, Pie, Filled Circle, Filled Square, Filled Ellipse and Filled Pie to the Items collection using the **String Collection Editor**. Whenever the user selects an item from imageComboBox, a SelectedIndexChanged event occurs and event handler imageCombo-Box_SelectedIndexChanged (lines 19–66) executes. Lines 23–29 create a Graphics object, a Pen and a SolidBrush, which are used to draw on the Form. The Graphics object (line 23) allows a pen or brush to draw on a component, using one of several Graphics methods. The Pen object (line 26) is used by methods DrawEllipse, DrawRectangle and DrawPie (lines 38, 41, 44 and 47) to draw the outlines of their corresponding shapes. The SolidBrush object (line 29) is used by methods FillEllipse, FillRectangle and FillPie (lines 50, 53–54, 57 and 60–61) to fill their corresponding solid shapes. Line 32 colors the entire Form White, using Graphics method **Clear**.

The app draws a shape based on the selected item's index. The switch statement (lines 35–63) uses imageComboBox.SelectedIndex to determine which item the user selected. Graphics method **DrawEllipse** (line 38) takes a Pen, and the *x*- and *y*-coordinates of the upper-left corner, the width and height of the bounding box (i.e., rectangular area) in which the ellipse will be displayed. The origin of the coordinate system is in the upper-left corner of the Form; the *x*-coordinate increases to the right, and the *y*-coordinate increases downward. A circle is a special case of an ellipse (with the width and height equal). Line 38 draws a circle. Line 44 draws an ellipse that has different values for width and height.

Class Graphics method **DrawRectangle** (line 41) takes a Pen, the *x*- and *y*-coordinates of the upper-left corner and the width and height of the rectangle to draw. Method **DrawPie** (line 47) draws a pie as a portion of an ellipse. The ellipse is bounded by a rectangle. Method DrawPie takes a Pen, the *x*- and *y*-coordinates of the upper-left corner of the rectangle, its width and height, the start angle (in degrees) and the sweep angle (in degrees) of the pie. Angles increase clockwise. The **FillEllipse** (lines 50 and 57), **Fill-Rectangle** (line 53–54) and **FillPie** (line 60–61) methods are similar to their unfilled counterparts, except that they take a Brush (e.g., SolidBrush) instead of a Pen. Some of the drawn shapes are illustrated in the screenshots of Fig. 15.23.

15.9 TreeView Control

The **TreeView** control displays **nodes** hierarchically in a **tree**. Traditionally, nodes are objects that contain values and can refer to other nodes. A **parent node** contains **child nodes**, and the child nodes can be parents to other nodes. Two child nodes that have the same parent node are considered **sibling nodes**. A tree is a collection of nodes, usually organized in a *hierarchical* manner. The first parent node of a tree is the **root** node (a TreeView can have multiple roots). For example, the file system of a computer can be represented as a tree. The top-level directory (perhaps C:) would be the root, each subfolder of C: would be a child node and each child folder could have its own children. TreeView controls are useful for displaying hierarchical information, such as the file structure that we just mentioned. Figure 15.24 displays a sample TreeView control on a Form.

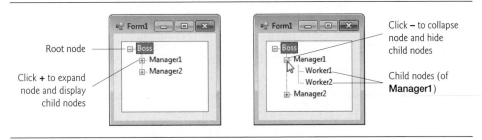

Fig. 15.24 | TreeView displaying a sample tree.

A parent node can be expanded or collapsed by clicking the plus box or minus box to its left. Nodes without children do not have these boxes.

The nodes in a TreeView are instances of class **TreeNode**. Each TreeNode has a **Nodes** collection (type **TreeNodeCollection**), which contains a list of other TreeNodes—known as its children. The Parent property returns a reference to the parent node (or null if the node is a root node). Figures 15.25 and 15.26 list the common properties of TreeViews and TreeNodes, common TreeNode methods and a common TreeView event.

TreeView properties and an event	Description
Common Properties	
CheckBoxes	Indicates whether CheckBoxes appear next to nodes. A value of true displays CheckBoxes. The default value is false.
ImageList	Specifies an ImageList object containing the node icons. An **ImageList** object is a collection that contains Image objects.
Nodes	Returns the collection of TreeNodes in the control as a TreeNodeCollection. It contains methods Add (adds a TreeNode object), Clear (deletes the entire collection) and Remove (deletes a specific node). Removing a parent node deletes all of its children.
SelectedNode	The selected node.
*Common Event (Event arguments **TreeViewEventArgs**)*	
AfterSelect	Generated after selected node changes. This is the default event when the control is double clicked in the designer.

Fig. 15.25 | TreeView properties and an event.

TreeNode properties and methods	Description
Common Properties	
Checked	Indicates whether the TreeNode is checked (CheckBoxes property must be set to true in the parent TreeView).
FirstNode	Specifies the first node in the Nodes collection (i.e., the first child in the tree).
FullPath	Indicates the path of the node, starting at the root of the tree.
ImageIndex	Specifies the index in the TreeView's ImageList of the image shown when the node is deselected.
LastNode	Specifies the last node in the Nodes collection (i.e., the last child in the tree).
NextNode	Next sibling node.
Nodes	Collection of TreeNodes contained in the current node (i.e., all the children of the current node). It contains methods Add (adds a TreeNode object), Clear (deletes the entire collection) and Remove (deletes a specific node). Removing a parent node deletes all of its children.
PrevNode	Previous sibling node.
SelectedImageIndex	Specifies the index in the TreeView's ImageList of the image to use when the node is selected.
Text	Specifies the TreeNode's text.
Common Methods	
Collapse	Collapses a node.

Fig. 15.26 | TreeNode properties and methods. (Part 1 of 2.)

TreeNode properties and methods	Description
Expand	Expands a node.
ExpandAll	Expands all the children of a node.
GetNodeCount	Returns the number of child nodes.

Fig. 15.26 | TreeNode properties and methods. (Part 2 of 2.)

To add nodes to the TreeView visually, click the ellipsis next to the Nodes property in the **Properties** window. This opens the **TreeNode Editor** (Fig. 15.27), which displays an empty tree representing the TreeView. There are Buttons to create a root and to add or delete a node. To the right are the properties of the current node. Here you can rename the node.

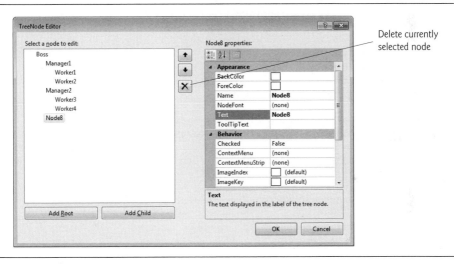

Fig. 15.27 | TreeNode Editor.

To add nodes programmatically, first create a root node. Create a new TreeNode object and pass it a string to display. Then call method Add to add this new TreeNode to the TreeView's Nodes collection. Thus, to add a root node to TreeView *myTreeView*, write

> *myTreeView*.Nodes.Add(**new** TreeNode(*rootLabel*));

where *myTreeView* is the TreeView to which we are adding nodes, and *rootLabel* is the text to display in *myTreeView*. To add children to a root node, add new TreeNodes to its Nodes collection. We select the appropriate root node from the TreeView by writing

> *myTreeView*.Nodes[*myIndex*]

where *myIndex* is the root node's index in *myTreeView*'s Nodes collection. We add nodes to child nodes through the same process by which we added root nodes to *myTreeView*. To add a child to the root node at index *myIndex*, write

> *myTreeView*.Nodes[*myIndex*].Nodes.Add(**new** TreeNode(*ChildLabel*));

Class TreeViewDirectoryStructureForm (Fig. 15.28) uses a TreeView to display the contents of a directory chosen by the user. A TextBox and a Button are used to specify the directory. First, enter the full path of the directory you want to display. Then click the Button to set the specified directory as the root node in the TreeView. Each subdirectory of this directory becomes a child node. This layout is similar to that used in **Windows Explorer**. Folders can be expanded or collapsed by clicking the plus or minus boxes that appear to their left.

When the user clicks the enterButton, all the nodes in directoryTreeView are cleared (line 68). Then, if the directory exists (line 73), the path entered in inputTextBox is used to create the root node. Line 76 adds the directory to directoryTreeView as the root node, and lines 79–80 call method PopulateTreeView (lines 21–62), which takes a directory (a string) and a parent node. Method PopulateTreeView then creates child nodes corresponding to the subdirectories of the directory it receives as an argument.

```
1    // Fig. 15.28: TreeViewDirectoryStructureForm.cs
2    // Using TreeView to display directory structure.
3    using System;
4    using System.Windows.Forms;
5    using System.IO;
6
7    namespace TreeViewDirectoryStructure
8    {
9       // Form uses TreeView to display directory structure
10      public partial class TreeViewDirectoryStructureForm : Form
11      {
12         string substringDirectory; // store last part of full path name
13
14         // constructor
15         public TreeViewDirectoryStructureForm()
16         {
17            InitializeComponent();
18         } // end constructor
19
20         // populate current node with subdirectories
21         public void PopulateTreeView(
22            string directoryValue, TreeNode parentNode )
23         {
24            // array stores all subdirectories in the directory
25            string[] directoryArray =
26               Directory.GetDirectories( directoryValue );
27
28            // populate current node with subdirectories
29            try
30            {
31               // check to see if any subdirectories are present
32               if ( directoryArray.Length != 0 )
33               {
34                  // for every subdirectory, create new TreeNode,
35                  // add as a child of current node and recursively
36                  // populate child nodes with subdirectories
```

Fig. 15.28 | TreeView used to display directories. (Part 1 of 3.)

```
37                    foreach ( string directory in directoryArray )
38                    {
39                       // obtain last part of path name from the full path
40                       // name by calling the GetFileNameWithoutExtension
41                       // method of class Path
42                       substringDirectory =
43                          Path.GetFileNameWithoutExtension( directory );
44
45                       // create TreeNode for current directory
46                       TreeNode myNode = new TreeNode( substringDirectory );
47
48                       // add current directory node to parent node
49                       parentNode.Nodes.Add( myNode );
50
51                       // recursively populate every subdirectory
52                       PopulateTreeView( directory, myNode );
53                    } // end foreach
54                 } // end if
55              } //end try
56
57              // catch exception
58              catch ( UnauthorizedAccessException )
59              {
60                 parentNode.Nodes.Add( "Access denied" );
61              } // end catch
62           } // end method PopulateTreeView
63
64           // handles enterButton click event
65           private void enterButton_Click( object sender, EventArgs e )
66           {
67              // clear all nodes
68              directoryTreeView.Nodes.Clear();
69
70              // check if the directory entered by user exists
71              // if it does, then fill in the TreeView,
72              // if not, display error MessageBox
73              if ( Directory.Exists( inputTextBox.Text ) )
74              {
75                 // add full path name to directoryTreeView
76                 directoryTreeView.Nodes.Add( inputTextBox.Text );
77
78                 // insert subfolders
79                 PopulateTreeView(
80                    inputTextBox.Text, directoryTreeView.Nodes[ 0 ] );
81              }
82              // display error MessageBox if directory not found
83              else
84                 MessageBox.Show( inputTextBox.Text + " could not be found.",
85                    "Directory Not Found", MessageBoxButtons.OK,
86                    MessageBoxIcon.Error );
87           } // end method enterButton_Click
88        } // end class TreeViewDirectoryStructureForm
89     } // end namespace TreeViewDirectoryStructure
```

Fig. 15.28 | TreeView used to display directories. (Part 2 of 3.)

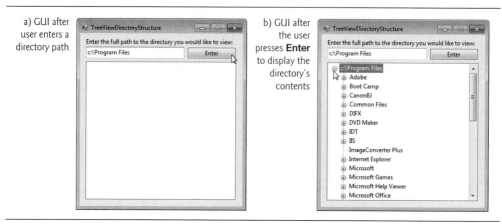

a) GUI after user enters a directory path

b) GUI after the user presses **Enter** to display the directory's contents

Fig. 15.28 | TreeView used to display directories. (Part 3 of 3.)

Method PopulateTreeView (lines 21–62) obtains a list of subdirectories, using method **GetDirectories** of class Directory (namespace System.IO) in lines 25–26. Method GetDirectories takes a string (the current directory) and returns an array of strings (the subdirectories). If a directory is not accessible for security reasons, an UnauthorizedAccessException is thrown. Lines 58–61 catch this exception and add a node containing "Access denied" instead of displaying the subdirectories.

If there are accessible subdirectories, lines 42–43 use method GetFileNameWithoutExtension of class Path to increase readability by shortening the full path name to just the directory name. The **Path** class provides functionality for working with strings that are file or directory paths. Next, each string in the directoryArray is used to create a new child node (line 46). We use method Add (line 49) to add each child node to the parent. Then method PopulateTreeView is called recursively on every subdirectory (line 52), which eventually populates the TreeView with the entire directory structure. Our recursive algorithm may cause a delay when the program loads large directories. However, once the folder names are added to the appropriate Nodes collection, they can be expanded and collapsed without delay. In the next section, we present an alternate algorithm to solve this problem.

15.10 ListView Control

The **ListView** control is similar to a ListBox in that both display lists from which the user can select one or more items (an example of a ListView can be found in Fig. 15.31). ListView is more versatile and can display items in different formats. For example, a ListView can display icons next to the list items (controlled by its SmallImageList, LargeImageList or StateImageList properties) and show the details of items in columns. Property **MultiSelect** (a bool) determines whether multiple items can be selected. CheckBoxes can be included by setting property **CheckBoxes** (a bool) to true, making the ListView's appearance similar to that of a CheckedListBox. The **View** property specifies the layout of the ListBox. Property **Activation** determines the method by which the user selects a list item. The details of these properties and the ItemActivate event are explained in Fig. 15.29.

ListView allows you to define the images used as icons for ListView items. To display images, an ImageList component is required. Create one by dragging it to a Form from the

ListView properties and events	Description
Common Properties	
Activation	Determines how the user activates an item. This property takes a value in the ItemActivation enumeration. Possible values are OneClick (single-click activation), TwoClick (double-click activation, item changes color when selected) and Standard (the default; double-click activation, item does not change color).
CheckBoxes	Indicates whether items appear with CheckBoxes. true displays CheckBoxes. The default is false.
LargeImageList	Specifies the ImageList containing large icons for display.
Items	Returns the collection of ListViewItems in the control.
MultiSelect	Determines whether multiple selection is allowed. The default is true, which enables multiple selection.
SelectedItems	Returns the collection of selected items as a ListView.SelectedListView-ItemCollection.
SmallImageList	Specifies the ImageList containing small icons for display.
View	Determines appearance of ListViewItems. Possible values are LargeIcon (the default; large icon displayed, items can be in multiple columns), SmallIcon (small icon displayed, items can be in multiple columns), List (small icons displayed, items appear in a single column), Details (like List, but multiple columns of information can be displayed per item) and Tile (large icons displayed, information provided to right of icon).
Common Events	
Click	Generated when an item is clicked. This is the default event.
ItemActivate	Generated when an item in the ListView is activated (clicked or double clicked). Does not contain the specifics of which item is activated—you can use SelectedItems or SelectedIndices to determine this.

Fig. 15.29 | ListView properties and events.

ToolBox. Then, select the **Images** property in the **Properties** window to display the **Image Collection Editor** (Fig. 15.30). Here you can browse for images that you wish to add to the ImageList, which contains an array of Images. Adding images this way embeds them into the app (like resources), so they do not need to be included separately with the published app. They're not however part of the project. In this example, we added images to the ImageList programmatically rather than using the **Image Collection Editor** so that we could use image resources. After creating an empty ImageList, add the file and folder icon images (provided with this chapter's examples) to the project as resources. Next, set property SmallImageList of the ListView to the new ImageList object. Property **SmallImageList** specifies the image list for the small icons. Property **LargeImageList** sets the ImageList for large icons. The items in a ListView are each of type **ListViewItem**. Icons for the ListView items are selected by setting the item's **ImageIndex** property to the appropriate index.

Class ListViewTestForm (Fig. 15.31) displays files and folders in a ListView, along with small icons representing each file or folder. If a file or folder is inaccessible because of

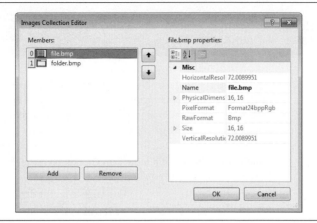

Fig. 15.30 | Image Collection Editor window for an `ImageList` component.

permission settings, a `MessageBox` appears. The program scans the contents of the directory as it browses, rather than indexing the entire drive at once.

Method *ListViewTestForm_Load*

Method `ListViewTestForm_Load` (lines 114–123) handles the Form's Load event. When the app loads, the folder and file icon images are added to the Images collection of `file-FolderImageList` (lines 117–118). Since the `ListView`'s `SmallImageList` property is set to this `ImageList`, the `ListView` can display these images as icons for each item. Because the folder icon was added first, it has array index 0, and the file icon has array index 1. The app also loads its home directory (obtained at line 14) into the `ListView` when it first loads (line 121) and displays the directory path (line 122).

```
1   // Fig. 15.31: ListViewTestForm.cs
2   // Displaying directories and their contents in ListView.
3   using System;
4   using System.Windows.Forms;
5   using System.IO;
6
7   namespace ListViewTest
8   {
9      // Form contains a ListView which displays
10     // folders and files in a directory
11     public partial class ListViewTestForm : Form
12     {
13        // store current directory
14        string currentDirectory = Directory.GetCurrentDirectory();
15
16        // constructor
17        public ListViewTestForm()
18        {
19           InitializeComponent();
20        } // end constructor
```

Fig. 15.31 | `ListView` displaying files and folders. (Part 1 of 4.)

```
21
22          // browse directory user clicked or go up one level
23          private void browserListView_Click( object sender, EventArgs e )
24          {
25             // ensure an item is selected
26             if ( browserListView.SelectedItems.Count != 0 )
27             {
28                // if first item selected, go up one level
29                if ( browserListView.Items[ 0 ].Selected )
30                {
31                   // create DirectoryInfo object for directory
32                   DirectoryInfo directoryObject =
33                      new DirectoryInfo( currentDirectory );
34
35                   // if directory has parent, load it
36                   if ( directoryObject.Parent != null )
37                   {
38                      LoadFilesInDirectory(
39                         directoryObject.Parent.FullName );
40                   } // end if
41                } // end if
42
43                // selected directory or file
44                else
45                {
46                   // directory or file chosen
47                   string chosen = browserListView.SelectedItems[ 0 ].Text;
48
49                   // if item selected is directory, load selected directory
50                   if ( Directory.Exists(
51                      Path.Combine( currentDirectory, chosen ) ) )
52                   {
53                      LoadFilesInDirectory(
54                         Path.Combine( currentDirectory, chosen ) );
55                   } // end if
56                } // end else
57
58                // update displayLabel
59                displayLabel.Text = currentDirectory;
60             } // end if
61          } // end method browserListView_Click
62
63          // display files/subdirectories of current directory
64          public void LoadFilesInDirectory( string currentDirectoryValue )
65          {
66             // load directory information and display
67             try
68             {
69                // clear ListView and set first item
70                browserListView.Items.Clear();
71                browserListView.Items.Add( "Go Up One Level" );
72
```

Fig. 15.31 | ListView displaying files and folders. (Part 2 of 4.)

```
73                      // update current directory
74                      currentDirectory = currentDirectoryValue;
75                      DirectoryInfo newCurrentDirectory =
76                         new DirectoryInfo( currentDirectory );
77
78                      // put files and directories into arrays
79                      DirectoryInfo[] directoryArray =
80                         newCurrentDirectory.GetDirectories();
81                      FileInfo[] fileArray = newCurrentDirectory.GetFiles();
82
83                      // add directory names to ListView
84                      foreach ( DirectoryInfo dir in directoryArray )
85                      {
86                         // add directory to ListView
87                         ListViewItem newDirectoryItem =
88                            browserListView.Items.Add( dir.Name );
89
90                         newDirectoryItem.ImageIndex = 0;  // set directory image
91                      } // end foreach
92
93                      // add file names to ListView
94                      foreach ( FileInfo file in fileArray )
95                      {
96                         // add file to ListView
97                         ListViewItem newFileItem =
98                            browserListView.Items.Add( file.Name );
99
100                        newFileItem.ImageIndex = 1;  // set file image
101                     } // end foreach
102                  } // end try
103
104               // access denied
105               catch ( UnauthorizedAccessException )
106               {
107                  MessageBox.Show( "Warning: Some files may not be " +
108                     "visible due to permission settings",
109                     "Attention", 0, MessageBoxIcon.Warning );
110               } // end catch
111            } // end method LoadFilesInDirectory
112
113            // handle load event when Form displayed for first time
114            private void ListViewTestForm_Load( object sender, EventArgs e )
115            {
116               // add icon images to ImageList
117               fileFolderImageList.Images.Add( Properties.Resources.folder );
118               fileFolderImageList.Images.Add( Properties.Resources.file );
119
120               // load current directory into browserListView
121               LoadFilesInDirectory( currentDirectory );
122               displayLabel.Text = currentDirectory;
123            } // end method ListViewTestForm_Load
124         } // end class ListViewTestForm
125      } // end namespace ListViewTest
```

Fig. 15.31 | ListView displaying files and folders. (Part 3 of 4.)

a) GUI showing app's default folder

b) GUI showing the contents of the c:\Users directoy

c) Dialog that appears if you try to access a directory for which you do not have permission

Fig. 15.31 | ListView displaying files and folders. (Part 4 of 4.)

Method LoadFilesInDirectory

The LoadFilesInDirectory method (lines 64–111) populates browserListView with the directory passed to it (currentDirectoryValue). It clears browserListView and adds the element "Go Up One Level". When the user clicks this element, the program attempts to move up one level (we see how shortly). The method then creates a DirectoryInfo object initialized with the string currentDirectory (lines 75–76). If permission is not given to browse the directory, an exception is thrown (and caught in line 105). Method LoadFilesInDirectory works differently from method PopulateTreeView in the previous program (Fig. 15.28). Instead of loading all the folders on the hard drive, method LoadFilesInDirectory loads only the folders in the current directory.

Class **DirectoryInfo** (namespace System.IO) enables us to browse or manipulate the directory structure easily. Method **GetDirectories** (line 80) returns an array of DirectoryInfo objects containing the subdirectories of the current directory. Similarly, method **GetFiles** (line 81) returns an array of class **FileInfo** objects containing the files in the current directory. Property **Name** (of both class DirectoryInfo and class FileInfo) contains only the directory or file name, such as temp instead of C:\myfolder\temp. To access the full name, use property **FullName**.

Lines 84–91 and lines 94–101 iterate through the subdirectories and files of the current directory and add them to `browserListView`. Lines 90 and 100 set the `ImageIndex` properties of the newly created items. If an item is a directory, we set its icon to a directory icon (index 0); if an item is a file, we set its icon to a file icon (index 1).

Method `browserListView_Click`

Method `browserListView_Click` (lines 23–61) responds when the user clicks control `browserListView`. Line 26 checks whether anything is selected. If a selection has been made, line 29 determines whether the user chose the first item in `browserListView`. The first item in `browserListView` is always **Go Up One Level**; if it's selected, the program attempts to go up a level. Lines 32–33 create a `DirectoryInfo` object for the current directory. Line 36 tests property `Parent` to ensure that the user is not at the root of the directory tree. Property **Parent** indicates the parent directory as a `DirectoryInfo` object; if no parent directory exists, `Parent` returns the value `null`. If a parent directory does exist, lines 38–39 pass the parent directory's full name to `LoadFilesInDirectory`.

If the user did not select the first item in `browserListView`, lines 44–56 allow the user to continue navigating through the directory structure. Line 47 creates `string chosen` and assigns it the text of the selected item (the first item in collection `SelectedItems`). Lines 50–51 determine whether the user selected a valid directory (rather than a file). Using the `Combine` method of class `Path`, the program combines `strings currentDirectory` and `chosen` to form the new directory path. The `Combine` method automatically adds a backslash (\), if necessary, between the two pieces. This value is passed to the **Exists** method of class `Directory`. Method `Exists` returns `true` if its `string` parameter is a valid directory. If so, the program passes the `string` to method `LoadFilesInDirectory` (lines 53–54). Finally, `displayLabel` is updated with the new directory (line 59).

This program loads quickly, because it indexes only the files in the current directory. A small delay may occur when a new directory is loaded. In addition, changes in the directory structure can be shown by reloading a directory. The previous program (Fig. 15.28) may have a large initial delay, as it loads an entire directory structure. This type of trade-off is typical in the software world.

Software Engineering Observation 15.2

When designing apps that run for long periods of time, you might choose a large initial delay to improve performance throughout the rest of the program. However, in apps that run for only short periods, developers often prefer fast initial loading times and small delays after each action.

15.11 TabControl Control

The **TabControl** creates tabbed windows, such as those in Visual Studio (Fig. 15.32). This enables you to specify more information in the same space on a `Form` and group displayed data logically. `TabControls` contain **TabPage** objects, which are similar to `Panels` and `GroupBoxes` in that `TabPages` also can contain controls. You first add controls to the `TabPage` objects, then add the `TabPages` to the `TabControl`. Only one `TabPage` is displayed at a time. To add objects to the `TabPage` and the `TabControl`, write

```
myTabPage.Controls.Add( myControl );
myTabControl.TabPages.Add( myTabPage );
```

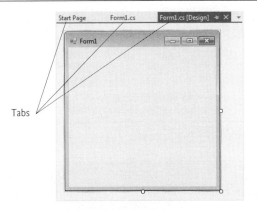

Fig. 15.32 | Tabbed windows in Visual Studio.

The preceding statements call method Add of the Controls collection and method Add of the TabPages collection. The example adds TabControl *myControl* to TabPage *myTabPage*, then adds *myTabPage* to *myTabControl*. Alternatively, we can use method AddRange to add an array of TabPages or controls to a TabControl or TabPage, respectively. Figure 15.33 depicts a sample TabControl.

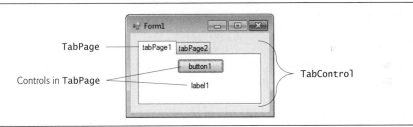

Fig. 15.33 | TabControl with TabPages example.

You can add TabControls visually by dragging and dropping them onto a Form in **Design** mode. To add TabPages in **Design** mode, click the top of the TabControl, open its *smart tasks menu* and select **Add Tab** (Fig. 15.34). Alternatively, click the **TabPages** property in the **Properties** window and add tabs in the dialog that appears. To change a tab label, set the **Text** property of the TabPage. Clicking the tabs selects the TabControl—to select the TabPage, click the control area underneath the tabs. You can add controls to the TabPage by dragging and dropping items from the **ToolBox**. To view different TabPages, click the appropriate tab (in either design or run mode). Common properties and a common event of TabControls are described in Fig. 15.35.

Each TabPage generates a Click event when its tab is clicked. Event handlers for this event can be created by double clicking the body of the TabPage.

Class UsingTabsForm (Fig. 15.36) uses a TabControl to display various options relating to the text on a label (**Color, Size** and **Message**). The last TabPage displays an **About** message, which describes the use of TabControls.

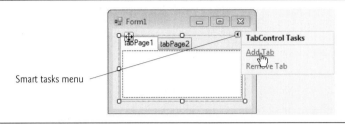

Fig. 15.34 | TabPages added to a TabControl.

TabControl properties and an event	Description
Common Properties	
ImageList	Specifies images to be displayed on tabs.
ItemSize	Specifies the tab size.
Multiline	Indicates whether multiple rows of tabs can be displayed.
SelectedIndex	Index of the selected TabPage.
SelectedTab	The selected TabPage.
TabCount	Returns the number of tab pages.
TabPages	Returns the collection of TabPages within the TabControl as a TabControl.TabPageCollection.
Common Event	
SelectedIndexChanged	Generated when SelectedIndex changes (i.e., another TabPage is selected).

Fig. 15.35 | TabControl properties and an event.

```
 1   // Fig. 15.36: UsingTabsForm.cs
 2   // Using TabControl to display various font settings.
 3   using System;
 4   using System.Drawing;
 5   using System.Windows.Forms;
 6
 7   namespace UsingTabs
 8   {
 9      // Form uses Tabs and RadioButtons to display various font settings
10      public partial class UsingTabsForm : Form
11      {
12         // constructor
13         public UsingTabsForm()
14         {
15            InitializeComponent();
16         } // end constructor
```

Fig. 15.36 | TabControl used to display various font settings. (Part 1 of 3.)

```
17
18        // event handler for Black RadioButton
19        private void blackRadioButton_CheckedChanged(
20           object sender, EventArgs e )
21        {
22           displayLabel.ForeColor = Color.Black; // change color to black
23        } // end method blackRadioButton_CheckedChanged
24
25        // event handler for Red RadioButton
26        private void redRadioButton_CheckedChanged(
27           object sender, EventArgs e )
28        {
29           displayLabel.ForeColor = Color.Red; // change color to red
30        } // end method redRadioButton_CheckedChanged
31
32        // event handler for Green RadioButton
33        private void greenRadioButton_CheckedChanged(
34           object sender, EventArgs e )
35        {
36           displayLabel.ForeColor = Color.Green; // change color to green
37        } // end method greenRadioButton_CheckedChanged
38
39        // event handler for 12 point RadioButton
40        private void size12RadioButton_CheckedChanged(
41           object sender, EventArgs e )
42        {
43           // change font size to 12
44           displayLabel.Font = new Font( displayLabel.Font.Name, 12 );
45        } // end method size12RadioButton_CheckedChanged
46
47        // event handler for 16 point RadioButton
48        private void size16RadioButton_CheckedChanged(
49           object sender, EventArgs e )
50        {
51           // change font size to 16
52           displayLabel.Font = new Font( displayLabel.Font.Name, 16 );
53        } // end method size16RadioButton_CheckedChanged
54
55        // event handler for 20 point RadioButton
56        private void size20RadioButton_CheckedChanged(
57           object sender, EventArgs e )
58        {
59           // change font size to 20
60           displayLabel.Font = new Font( displayLabel.Font.Name, 20 );
61        } // end method size20RadioButton_CheckedChanged
62
63        // event handler for Hello! RadioButton
64        private void helloRadioButton_CheckedChanged(
65           object sender, EventArgs e )
66        {
67           displayLabel.Text = "Hello!"; // change text to Hello!
68        } // end method helloRadioButton_CheckedChanged
69
```

Fig. 15.36 | TabControl used to display various font settings. (Part 2 of 3.)

```
70              // event handler for Goodbye! RadioButton
71              private void goodbyeRadioButton_CheckedChanged(
72                 object sender, EventArgs e )
73              {
74                 displayLabel.Text = "Goodbye!"; // change text to Goodbye!
75              } // end method goodbyeRadioButton_CheckedChanged
76           } // end class UsingTabsForm
77        } // end namespace UsingTabs
```

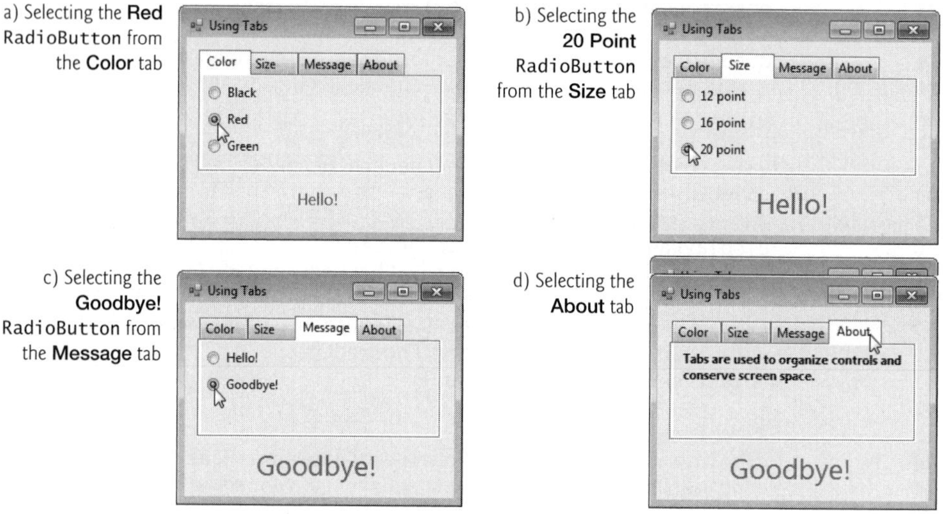

a) Selecting the **Red** RadioButton from the **Color** tab

b) Selecting the **20 Point** RadioButton from the **Size** tab

c) Selecting the **Goodbye!** RadioButton from the **Message** tab

d) Selecting the **About** tab

Fig. 15.36 | TabControl used to display various font settings. (Part 3 of 3.)

The textOptionsTabControl and the colorTabPage, sizeTabPage, messageTabPage and aboutTabPage are created in the designer (as described previously). The colorTabPage contains three RadioButtons for the colors black (blackRadioButton), red (redRadioButton) and green (greenRadioButton). This TabPage is displayed in Fig. 15.36(a). The CheckedChanged event handler for each RadioButton updates the color of the text in displayLabel (lines 22, 29 and 36). The sizeTabPage (Fig. 15.36(b)) has three RadioButtons, corresponding to font sizes 12 (size12RadioButton), 16 (size16RadioButton) and 20 (size20RadioButton), which change the font size of displayLabel—lines 44, 52 and 60, respectively. The messageTabPage (Fig. 15.36(c)) contains two RadioButtons for the messages **Hello!** (helloRadioButton) and **Goodbye!** (goodbyeRadioButton). The two RadioButtons determine the text on displayLabel (lines 67 and 74, respectively). The aboutTabPage (Fig. 15.36(d)) contains a Label (messageLabel) describing the purpose of TabControls.

Software Engineering Observation 15.3

A TabPage can act as a container for a single logical group of RadioButtons, enforcing their mutual exclusivity. To place multiple RadioButton groups inside a single TabPage, you should group RadioButtons within Panels or GroupBoxes contained within the TabPage.

15.12 Multiple Document Interface (MDI) Windows

In previous chapters, we have built only **single document interface** (SDI) apps. Such programs (including Microsoft's Notepad and Paint) can support only one open window or document at a time. SDI apps usually have limited abilities—Paint and Notepad, for example, have limited image- and text-editing features. To edit *multiple* documents, the user must execute another instance of the SDI app.

Many complex apps are **multiple document interface** (MDI) programs, which allow users to edit multiple documents at once (e.g., Microsoft Office products). MDI programs also tend to be more complex—Paint Shop Pro and Photoshop have a greater number of image-editing features than does Paint.

An MDI program's main window is called the **parent window**, and each window inside the app is referred to as a **child window**. Although an MDI app can have many child windows, each has only one parent window. Furthermore, a maximum of one child window can be active at once. Child windows cannot be parents themselves and cannot be moved outside their parent. Otherwise, a child window behaves like any other window (with regard to closing, minimizing, resizing, and so on). A child window's functionality can differ from that of other child windows of the parent. For example, one child window might allow the user to edit images, another might allow the user to edit text and a third might display network traffic graphically, but all could belong to the same MDI parent. Figure 15.37 depicts a sample MDI app with two child windows.

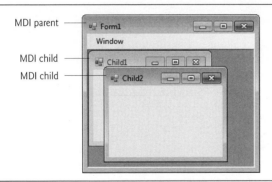

Fig. 15.37 | MDI parent window and MDI child windows.

To create an MDI Form, create a new Form and set its **IsMdiContainer** property to true. The Form changes appearance, as in Fig. 15.38. Next, create a child Form class to be added to the Form. To do this, right click the project in the **Solution Explorer**, select **Project > Add Windows Form...** and name the file. Edit the Form as you like. To add the child Form to the parent, we must create a new child Form object, set its **MdiParent** property to the parent Form and call the child Form's Show method. In general, to add a child Form to a parent, write

```
ChildFormClass childForm = New ChildFormClass();
childForm.MdiParent = parentForm;
childForm.Show();
```

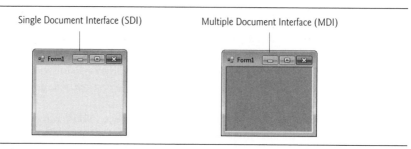

Fig. 15.38 | SDI and MDI forms.

In most cases, the parent Form creates the child, so the *parentForm* reference is this. The code to create a child usually lies inside an event handler, which creates a new window in response to a user action. Menu selections (such as **File**, followed by a submenu option of **New**, followed by a submenu option of **Window**) are common techniques for creating new child windows.

Class Form property **MdiChildren** returns an array of child Form references. This is useful if the parent window wants to check the status of all its children (for example, ensuring that all are saved before the parent closes). Property **ActiveMdiChild** returns a reference to the active child window; it returns null if there are no active child windows. Other features of MDI windows are described in Fig. 15.39.

MDI Form properties, a method and an event	Description
Common MDI Child Properties	
IsMdiChild	Indicates whether the Form is an MDI child. If true, Form is an MDI child (read-only property).
MdiParent	Specifies the MDI parent Form of the child.
Common MDI Parent Properties	
ActiveMdiChild	Returns the Form that's the currently active MDI child (returns null if no children are active).
IsMdiContainer	Indicates whether a Form can be an MDI parent. If true, the Form can be an MDI parent. The default value is false.
MdiChildren	Returns the MDI children as an array of Forms.
Common Method	
LayoutMdi	Determines the display of child forms on an MDI parent. The method takes as a parameter an MdiLayout enumeration with possible values ArrangeIcons, Cascade, TileHorizontal and TileVertical. Figure 15.42 depicts the effects of these values.
Common Event	
MdiChildActivate	Generated when an MDI child is closed or activated.

Fig. 15.39 | MDI parent and MDI child properties, a method and an event.

Child windows can be minimized, maximized and closed independently of the parent window. Figure 15.40 shows two images: one containing two minimized child windows and a second containing a maximized child window. When the parent is minimized or closed, the child windows are minimized or closed as well. Notice that the title bar in Fig. 15.40(b) is **Form1 - [Child1]**. When a child window is maximized, its title-bar text is inserted into the parent window's title bar. When a child window is minimized or maximized, its title bar displays a restore icon, which can be used to return the child window to its previous size (its size before it was minimized or maximized).

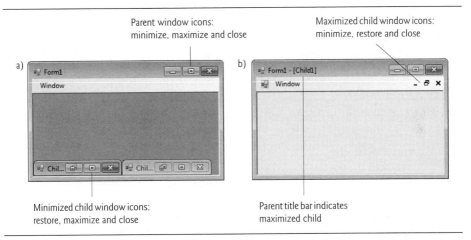

Fig. 15.40 | Minimized and maximized child windows.

C# provides a property that helps track which child windows are open in an MDI container. Property **MdiWindowListItem** of class MenuStrip specifies which menu, if any, displays a list of open child windows that the user can select to bring the corresponding window to the foreground. When a new child window is opened, an entry is added to the end of the list (Fig. 15.41). If ten or more child windows are open, the list includes the option **More Windows...**, which allows the user to select a window from a list in a dialog.

Good Programming Practice 15.1

When creating MDI apps, include a menu that displays a list of the open child windows. This helps the user select a child window quickly, rather than having to search for it in the parent window.

MDI containers allow you to organize the placement of its child windows. The child windows in an MDI app can be arranged by calling method **LayoutMdi** of the parent Form. Method LayoutMdi takes an **MdiLayout** enumeration, which can have values ArrangeIcons, Cascade, TileHorizontal and TileVertical. **Tiled windows** completely fill the parent and do *not* overlap; such windows can be arranged horizontally (value TileHorizontal) or vertically (value TileVertical). **Cascaded windows** (value Cascade) overlap—each is the same size and displays a visible title bar, if possible. Value ArrangeIcons arranges the icons for any minimized child windows. If minimized windows are scattered around the parent window, value ArrangeIcons orders them neatly at the bottom-left corner of the parent window. Figure 15.42 illustrates the values of the MdiLayout enumeration.

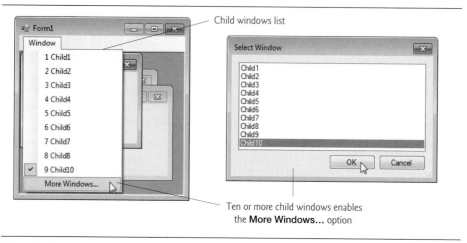

Fig. 15.41 | MenuStrip property MdiWindowListItem example.

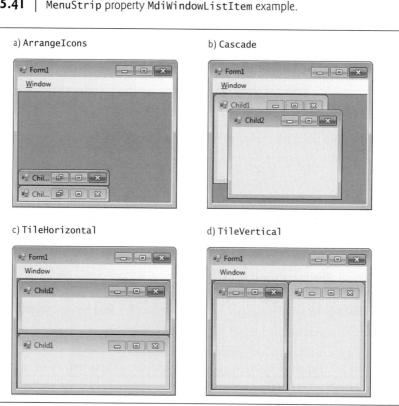

a) ArrangeIcons

b) Cascade

c) TileHorizontal

d) TileVertical

Fig. 15.42 | MdiLayout enumeration values.

Class UsingMDIForm (Fig. 15.43) demonstrates MDI windows. Class UsingMDIForm uses three instances of child Form ChildForm (Fig. 15.44), each containing a PictureBox that displays an image. The parent MDI Form contains a menu enabling users to create and arrange child Forms.

*MDI Parent **Form***

Figure 15.43 presents class UsingMDIForm—the app's MDI parent Form. This Form, which
is created first, contains two top-level menus. The first of these menus, **File** (fileTool-
StripMenuItem), contains both an **Exit** item (exitToolStripMenuItem) and a **New** submenu (newToolStripMenuItem) consisting of items for each type of child window. The
second menu, **Window** (windowToolStripMenuItem), provides options for laying out the
MDI children, plus a list of the active MDI children.

```
 1   // Fig. 15.43: UsingMDIForm.cs
 2   // Demonstrating use of MDI parent and child windows.
 3   using System;
 4   using System.Windows.Forms;
 5
 6   namespace UsingMDI
 7   {
 8      // Form demonstrates the use of MDI parent and child windows
 9      public partial class UsingMDIForm : Form
10      {
11         // constructor
12         public UsingMDIForm()
13         {
14            InitializeComponent();
15         } // end constructor
16
17         // create Lavender Flowers image window
18         private void lavenderToolStripMenuItem_Click(
19            object sender, EventArgs e )
20         {
21            // create new child
22            ChildForm child = new ChildForm(
23               "Lavender Flowers", "lavenderflowers" );
24            child.MdiParent = this; // set parent
25            child.Show(); // display child
26         } // end method lavenderToolStripMenuItem_Click
27
28         // create Purple Flowers image window
29         private void purpleToolStripMenuItem_Click(
30            object sender, EventArgs e )
31         {
32            // create new child
33            ChildForm child = new ChildForm(
34               "Purple Flowers", "purpleflowers" );
35            child.MdiParent = this; // set parent
36            child.Show(); // display child
37         } // end method purpleToolStripMenuItem_Click
38
39         // create Yellow Flowers image window
40         private void yellowToolStripMenuItem_Click(
41            object sender, EventArgs e )
42         {
```

Fig. 15.43 | MDI parent-window class. (Part 1 of 3.)

```
43              // create new child
44              Child child = new ChildForm(
45                  "Yellow Flowers", "yellowflowers" );
46              child.MdiParent = this; // set parent
47              child.Show(); // display child
48          } // end method yellowToolStripMenuItem_Click
49
50          // exit app
51          private void exitToolStripMenuItem_Click(
52              object sender, EventArgs e )
53          {
54              Application.Exit();
55          } // end method exitToolStripMenuItem_Click
56
57          // set Cascade layout
58          private void cascadeToolStripMenuItem_Click(
59              object sender, EventArgs e )
60          {
61              this.LayoutMdi( MdiLayout.Cascade );
62          } // end method cascadeToolStripMenuItem_Click
63
64          // set TileHorizontal layout
65          private void tileHorizontalToolStripMenuItem_Click(
66              object sender, EventArgs e )
67          {
68              this.LayoutMdi( MdiLayout.TileHorizontal );
69          } // end method tileHorizontalToolStripMenuItem
70
71          // set TileVertical layout
72          private void tileVerticalToolStripMenuItem_Click(
73              object sender, EventArgs e )
74          {
75              this.LayoutMdi( MdiLayout.TileVertical );
76          } // end method tileVerticalToolStripMenuItem_Click
77      } // end class UsingMDIForm
78  } // end namespace UsingMDI
```

a) Selecting the **Lavender Flowers** menu item

b) **Lavender Flowers** ChildForm window displayed

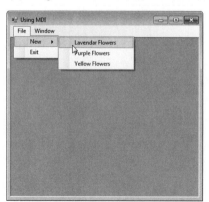

Fig. 15.43 | MDI parent-window class. (Part 2 of 3.)

c) Selecting the **Cascade** menu item

d) Cascaded child windows in an MDI window

Fig. 15.43 | MDI parent-window class. (Part 3 of 3.)

In the **Properties** window, we set the Form's IsMdiContainer property to true, making the Form an MDI parent. In addition, we set the MenuStrip's MdiWindowListItem property to windowToolStripMenuItem. This enables the **Window** menu to contain the list of child MDI windows.

The **Cascade** menu item (cascadeToolStripMenuItem) has an event handler (cascadeToolStripMenuItem_Click, lines 58–62) that arranges the child windows in a cascading manner. The event handler calls method LayoutMdi with the argument Cascade from the MdiLayout enumeration (line 61).

The **Tile Horizontal** menu item (tileHorizontalToolStripMenuItem) has an event handler (tileHorizontalToolStripMenuItem_Click, lines 65–69) that arranges the child windows in a horizontal manner. The event handler calls method LayoutMdi with the argument TileHorizontal from the MdiLayout enumeration (line 68).

Finally, the **Tile Vertical** menu item (tileVerticalToolStripMenuItem) has an event handler (tileVerticalToolStripMenuItem_Click, lines 72–76) that arranges the child windows in a vertical manner. The event handler calls method LayoutMdi with the argument TileVertical from the MdiLayout enumeration (line 75).

MDI Child *Form*
At this point, the app is still incomplete—we must define the MDI child class. To do this, right click the project in the **Solution Explorer** and select **Add > Windows Form....** Then name the new class in the dialog as ChildForm (Fig. 15.44). Next, we add a PictureBox (displayPictureBox) to ChildForm. In ChildForm's constructor, line 16 sets the title-bar text. Lines 19–21 retrieve the appropriate image resource, cast it to an Image and set displayPictureBox's Image property. The images that are used can be found in the Images subfolder of this chapter's examples directory.

After the MDI child class is defined, the parent MDI Form (Fig. 15.43) can create new child windows. The event handlers in lines 18–48 create a new child Form corresponding to the menu item clicked. Lines 22–23, 33–34 and 44–45 create new instances of ChildForm. Lines 24, 35 and 46 set each Child's MdiParent property to the parent Form. Lines 25, 36 and 47 call method Show to display each child Form.

```
 1   // Fig. 15.44: ChildForm.cs
 2   // Child window of MDI parent.
 3   using System;
 4   using System.Drawing;
 5   using System.Windows.Forms;
 6
 7   namespace UsingMDI
 8   {
 9      public partial class ChildForm : Form
10      {
11         public ChildForm( string title, string resourceName )
12         {
13            // Required for Windows Form Designer support
14            InitializeComponent();
15
16            Text = title; // set title text
17
18            // set image to display in PictureBox
19            displayPictureBox.Image =
20               ( Image ) ( Properties.Resources.ResourceManager.GetObject(
21                  resourceName );
22         } // end constructor
23      } // end class ChildForm
24   } // end namespace UsingMDI
```

Fig. 15.44 | MDI child `ChildForm`.

15.13 Visual Inheritance

Chapter 11 discussed how to create classes by inheriting from other classes. We have also used inheritance to create Forms that display a GUI, by deriving our new Form classes from class System.Windows.Forms.Form. This is an example of **visual inheritance**. The derived Form class contains the functionality of its Form base class, including any base-class properties, methods, variables and controls. The derived class also inherits all visual aspects—such as sizing, component layout, spacing between GUI components, colors and fonts—from its base class.

Visual inheritance enables you to achieve visual consistency across apps. For example, you could define a base Form that contains a product's logo, a specific background color, a predefined menu bar and other elements. You then could use the base Form throughout an app for uniformity and branding. You can also create controls that inherit from other controls. For example, you might create a custom UserControl (discussed in Section 15.14) that's derived from an existing control.

Creating a Base Form

Class VisualInheritanceBaseForm (Fig. 15.45) derives from Form. The output depicts the workings of the program. The GUI contains two Labels with text **Bugs, Bugs, Bugs** and **Copyright 2014, by Deitel & Associates, Inc.**, as well as one Button displaying the text **Learn More**. When a user presses the **Learn More** Button, method learnMoreButton_Click (lines 18–24) is invoked. This method displays a MessageBox that provides some informative text.

```
 1   // Fig. 15.45: VisualInheritanceBaseForm.cs
 2   // Base Form for use with visual inheritance.
 3   using System;
 4   using System.Windows.Forms;
 5
 6   namespace VisualInheritanceBase
 7   {
 8      // base Form used to demonstrate visual inheritance
 9      public partial class VisualInheritanceBaseForm : Form
10      {
11         // constructor
12         public VisualInheritanceForm()
13         {
14            InitializeComponent();
15         } // end constructor
16
17         // display MessageBox when Button is clicked
18         private void learnMoreButton_Click( object sender, EventArgs e )
19         {
20            MessageBox.Show(
21               "Bugs, Bugs, Bugs is a product of deitel.com",
22               "Learn More", MessageBoxButtons.OK,
23               MessageBoxIcon.Information );
24         } // end method learnMoreButton_Click
25      } // end class VisualInheritanceBaseForm
26   } // end namespace VisualInheritanceBase
```

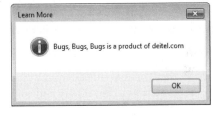

Fig. 15.45 | Class VisualInheritanceBaseForm, which inherits from class Form, contains a Button (**Learn More**).

Steps for Declaring and Using a Reusable Class

Before a Form (or any class) can be used in multiple apps, it must be placed in a class library to make it reusable. The steps for creating a reusable class are:

1. Declare a public class. If the class is not public, it can be used only by other classes in the same assembly—that is, compiled into the same DLL or EXE file.

2. Choose a namespace name and add a namespace declaration to the source-code file for the reusable class declaration.

3. Compile the class into a class library.

4. Add a reference to the class library in an app.

5. Use the class.

Let's take a look at these steps in the context of this example:

Step 1: Creating a **public** Class

For *Step 1* in this discussion, we use the `public class VisualInheritanceBaseForm` declared in Fig. 15.45. By default, every new `Form` class you create is declares as a public class.

Step 2: Adding the **namespace** Declaration

For *Step 2*, we use the `namespace` declaration that was created for us by the IDE. By default, every new class you define is placed in a `namespace` with the same name as the project. In almost every example in the text, we've seen that classes from preexisting libraries, such as the .NET Framework Class Library, can be imported into a C# app. Each class belongs to a namespace that contains a group of related classes. As apps become more complex, namespaces help you manage the complexity of app components. Class libraries and namespaces also facilitate software reuse by enabling apps to add classes from other namespaces (as we've done in most examples). We removed the namespace declarations in earlier chapters because they were not necessary.

Placing a class inside a `namespace` declaration indicates that the class is part of the specified namespace. The `namespace` name is part of the fully qualified class name, so the name of class `VisualInheritanceTestForm` is actually `VisualInheritanceBase.VisualInheritanceBaseForm`. You can use this fully qualified name in your apps, or you can write a `using` directive and use the class's simple name (the unqualified class name—`VisualInheritanceBaseForm`) in the app. If another namespace also contains a class with the same name, the fully qualified class names can be used to distinguish between the classes in the app and prevent a name conflict (also called a name collision).

Step 3: Compiling the Class Library

To allow other `Form`s to inherit from `VisualInheritanceForm`, we must package `VisualInheritanceForm` as a class library and compile it into a **.dll file**. Such as file is known as a **dynamically linked library**—a way to package classes that you can reference from other apps. Right click the project name in the **Solution Explorer** and select **Properties**, then choose the **Application** tab. In the **Output type** drop-down list, change **Windows Application** to **Class Library**. Building the project produces the `.dll`. You can configure a project to be a class library when you first create it by selecting the **Class Library** template in the **New Project** dialog. [*Note:* A class library cannot execute as a stand-alone app. The screen captures in Fig. 15.45 were taken before changing the project to a class library.]

Step 4: Adding a Reference to the Class Library

Once the class is compiled and stored in the class library file, the library can be referenced from any app by indicating to the Visual C# Express IDE where to find the class library file. To visually inherit from `VisualInheritanceBaseForm`, first create a new Windows app. Right-click the project name in the **Solution Explorer** window and select **Add Reference...** from the pop-up menu that appears. The dialog box that appears will contain a list of class libraries from the .NET Framework. Some class libraries, like the one containing the `System` namespace, are so common that they're added to your app by the IDE. The ones in this list are not.

In the **Reference Manager** dialog box, click **Browse** then click the **Browse...** button. When you build a class library, Visual C# places the `.dll` file in the project's `bin\Debug` or `bin\Release` folder, depending on whether the **Solution Configurations** drop-down list in the IDE's toolbar is set to **Debug** or **Release**. In the **Browse** tab, you can navigate to the directory containing the class library file you created in *Step 3*, as shown in Fig. 15.46. Select the `.dll` file and click **OK**.

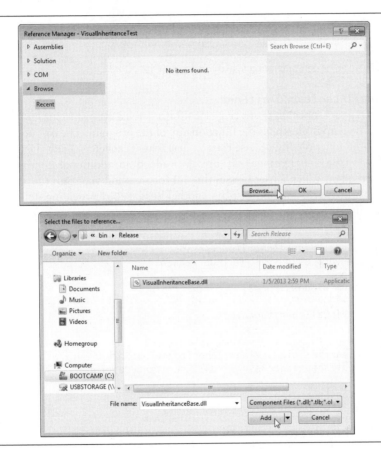

Fig. 15.46 | Using the **Reference Manager** dialog to browse for a DLL.

Step 5: Using the Class—Deriving From a Base *Form*

Open the file that defines the new app's GUI and modify the line that defines the class to indicate that the app's `Form` should inherit from class `VisualInheritanceBaseForm`. The class-declaration line should now appear as follows:

```
public partial class VisualInhertianceTestForm :
    VisualInheritanceBase.VisualInheritanceBaseForm
```

Unless you specify namespace `VisualInheritanceBase` in a using directive, you must use the fully qualified name `VisualInheritanceBase.VisualInheritanceBaseForm`. In **Design** view, the new app's `Form` should now display the controls inherited from the base `Form` (Fig. 15.47). We can now add more components to the `Form`.

Fig. 15.47 | Form demonstrating visual inheritance.

Class *VisualInheritanceTestForm*

Class VisualInheritanceTestForm (Fig. 15.48) is a derived class of VisualInheritance-BaseForm. The output illustrates the functionality of the program. The components, their layouts and the functionality of base class VisualInheritanceBaseForm (Fig. 15.45) are inherited by VisualInheritanceTestForm. We added an additional Button with text **About this Program**. When a user presses this Button, method aboutButton_Click (lines 19–25) is invoked. This method displays another MessageBox providing different informative text (lines 21–24).

```
1   // Fig. 15.48: VisualInheritanceTestForm.cs
2   // Derived Form using visual inheritance.
3   using System;
4   using System.Windows.Forms;
5
6   namespace VisualInheritanceTest
7   {
8      // derived form using visual inheritance
9      public partial class VisualInheritanceTestForm :
10        VisualInheritanceBase.VisualInheritanceBaseForm
11     {
12        // constructor
13        public VisualInheritanceTestForm()
14        {
15           InitializeComponent();
16        } // end constructor
17
18        // display MessageBox when Button is clicked
19        private void aboutButton_Click(object sender, EventArgs e)
20        {
21           MessageBox.Show(
22              "This program was created by Deitel & Associates.",
23              "About This Program", MessageBoxButtons.OK,
24              MessageBoxIcon.Information );
25        } // end method aboutButton_Click
26     } // end class VisualInheritanceTestForm
27  } // end namespace VisualInheritanceTest
```

Fig. 15.48 | Class VisualInheritanceTestForm, which inherits from class VisualInheritanceBaseForm, contains an additional Button. (Part 1 of 2.)

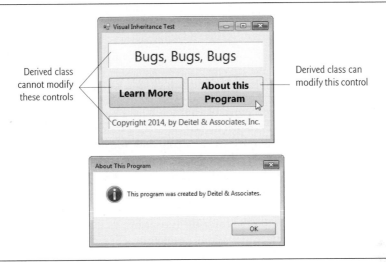

Fig. 15.48 | Class `VisualInheritanceTestForm`, which inherits from class `VisualInheritanceBaseForm`, contains an additional `Button`. (Part 2 of 2.)

If a user clicks the **Learn More** button, the event is handled by the base-class event handler `learnMoreButton_Click`. Because `VisualInheritanceBaseForm` uses a private access modifier to declare its controls, `VisualInheritanceTestForm` cannot modify the controls inherited from class `VisualInheritanceBaseForm` visually or programmatically. The IDE displays a small icon at the top left of the visually inherited controls to indicate that they're inherited and cannot be altered.

15.14 **User-Defined Controls**

The .NET Framework allows you to create **custom controls**. These custom controls appear in the user's **Toolbox** and can be added to `Forms`, `Panels` or `GroupBoxes` in the same way that we add `Buttons`, `Labels` and other predefined controls. The simplest way to create a custom control is to derive a class from an existing control, such as a `Label`. This is useful if you want to add functionality to an existing control, rather than replacing it with one that provides the desired functionality. For example, you can create a new type of `Label` that behaves like a normal `Label` but has a different appearance. You accomplish this by inheriting from class `Label` and overriding method `OnPaint`.

Method `OnPaint`
All controls have an **`OnPaint`** method, which the system calls when a component must be redrawn (such as when the component is resized). The method receives a **`PaintEventArgs`** object, which contains graphics information—property **`Graphics`** is the graphics object used to draw, and property **`ClipRectangle`** defines the rectangular boundary of the control. Whenever the system raises a `Paint` event to draw the control on the screen, the control catches the event and calls its `OnPaint` method. The base class's `OnPaint` should be called explicitly from an overridden `OnPaint` implementation before executing custom-

paint code. In most cases, you want to do this to ensure that the original painting code executes in addition to the code you define in the custom control's class.

Creating New Controls

To create a new control composed of existing controls, use class **UserControl**. Controls added to a custom control are called **constituent controls**. For example, a programmer could create a UserControl composed of a Button, a Label and a TextBox, each associated with some functionality (for example, the Button setting the Label's text to that contained in the TextBox). The UserControl acts as a container for the controls added to it. The UserControl contains constituent controls, but it does not determine how these constituent controls are displayed. To control the appearance of each constituent control, you can handle each control's Paint event or override OnPaint. Both the Paint event handler and OnPaint are passed a PaintEventArgs object, which can be used to draw graphics (lines, rectangles, and so on) on the constituent controls.

Using another technique, a programmer can create a brand-new control by inheriting from class Control. This class does not define any specific behavior; that's left to you. Instead, class Control handles the items associated with all controls, such as events and sizing handles. Method OnPaint should contain a call to the base class's OnPaint method, which calls the Paint event handlers. You add code that draws custom graphics inside the overridden OnPaint method. This technique allows for the greatest flexibility but also requires the most planning. All three approaches are summarized in Fig. 15.49.

Custom-control techniques and PaintEventArgs properties	Description
Custom-Control Techniques	
Inherit from Windows Forms control	You can do this to add functionality to a preexisting control. If you override method OnPaint, call the base class's OnPaint method. You only can add to the original control's appearance, not redesign it.
Create a UserControl	You can create a UserControl composed of multiple preexisting controls (e.g., to combine their functionality). You place drawing code in a Paint event handler or overridden OnPaint method.
Inherit from class Control	Define a brand new control. Override method OnPaint, then call base-class method OnPaint and include methods to draw the control. With this method you can customize control appearance and functionality.
PaintEventArgs Properties	
Graphics	The control's graphics object, which is used to draw on the control.
ClipRectangle	Specifies the rectangle indicating the boundary of the control.

Fig. 15.49 | Custom-control creation.

Clock Control
We create a "clock" control in Fig. 15.50. This is a UserControl composed of a Label and a Timer—whenever the Timer raises an event (once per second in this example), the Label is updated to reflect the current time.

```
1   // Fig. 15.50: ClockUserControl.cs
2   // User-defined control with a timer and a Label.
3   using System;
4   using System.Windows.Forms;
5
6   namespace ClockExample
7   {
8      // UserControl that displays the time on a Label
9      public partial class ClockUserControl : UserControl
10     {
11        // constructor
12        public ClockUserControl()
13        {
14           InitializeComponent();
15        } // end constructor
16
17        // update Label at every tick
18        private void clockTimer_Tick(object sender, EventArgs e)
19        {
20           // get current time (Now), convert to string
21           displayLabel.Text = DateTime.Now.ToLongTimeString();
22        } // end method clockTimer_Tick
23     } // end class ClockUserControl
24  } // end namespace ClockExample
```

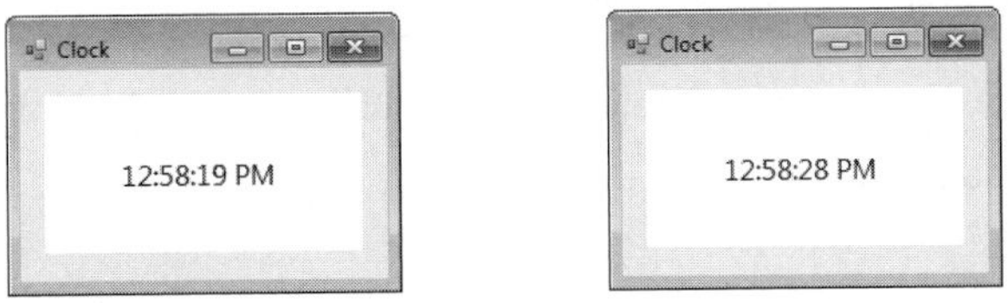

Fig. 15.50 | UserControl-defined clock.

Timers
Timers (System.Windows.Forms namespace) are non-visual components that generate **Tick** events at a set interval. This interval is set by the Timer's **Interval** property, which defines the number of milliseconds (thousandths of a second) between events. By default, timers are disabled and do not generate events.

Adding a User Control
This app contains a user control (ClockUserControl) and a Form that displays the user control. Create a Windows app, then create a UserControl class by selecting **Project > Add User Control...** This displays a dialog from which we can select the type of item to add—user controls are already selected. We then name the file (and the class) ClockUserControl. Our empty ClockUserControl is displayed as a grey rectangle.

Designing the User Control

You can treat this control like a Windows Form, meaning that you can add controls using the **ToolBox** and set properties using the **Properties** window. However, instead of creating an app, you're simply creating a new control composed of other controls. Add a Label (displayLabel) and a Timer (clockTimer) to the UserControl. Set the Timer interval to 1000 milliseconds and set displayLabel's text with each Tick event (lines 18–22). To generate events, clockTimer must be enabled by setting property Enabled to true in the **Properties** window.

Structure **DateTime** (namespace System) contains property **Now**, which returns the current time. Method **ToLongTimeString** converts Now to a string containing the current hour, minute and second (along with AM or PM, depending on your locale). We use this to set the time in displayLabel in line 21.

Once created, our clock control appears as an item in the **ToolBox** in the section titled *ProjectName* **Components**, where *ProjectName* is your project's name. *You may need to switch to the app's Form before the item appears in the ToolBox.* To use the control, simply drag it to the Form and run the Windows app. We gave the ClockUserControl object a white background to make it stand out in the Form. Figure 15.50 shows the output of Clock, which contains our ClockUserControl. There are no event handlers in Clock, so we show only the code for ClockUserControl.

Sharing Custom Controls with Other Developers

Visual Studio allows you to share custom controls with other developers. To create a User-Control that can be exported to other solutions, do the following:

1. Create a new **Class Library** project.

2. Delete Class1.cs, initially provided with the app.

3. Right click the project in the **Solution Explorer** and select **Add > User Control...**. In the dialog that appears, name the user-control file and click **Add**.

4. Inside the project, add controls and functionality to the UserControl (Fig. 15.51).

Fig. 15.51 | Custom-control creation.

5. Build the project. Visual Studio creates a .dll file for the UserControl in the output directory (bin/Release or bin/Release). The file is not executable; class libraries are used to define classes that are reused in other executable apps.

6. Create a new Windows app.

7. In the new Windows app, right click the **ToolBox** and select **Choose Items...**. In the **Choose Toolbox Items** dialog that appears, click **Browse...**. Browse for the .dll file from the class library created in *Steps 1–5*. The item will then appear in

the **Choose Toolbox Items** dialog (Fig. 15.52). If it's not already checked, check this item. Click **OK** to add the item to the **Toolbox**. This control can now be added to the Form as if it were any other control.

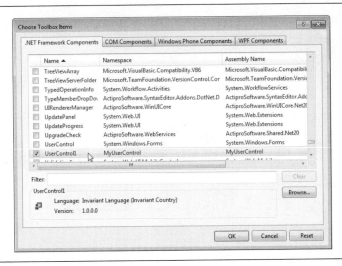

Fig. 15.52 | Custom control added to the **ToolBox**.

15.15 Wrap-Up

Many of today's commercial apps provide GUIs that are easy to use and manipulate. Because of this demand for user-friendly GUIs, the ability to design sophisticated GUIs is an essential programming skill. Visual Studio's IDE makes GUI development quick and easy. In Chapters 14 and 15, we presented basic Windows Forms GUI development techniques. In Chapter 15, we demonstrated how to create menus, which provide users easy access to an app's functionality. You learned the DateTimePicker and MonthCalendar controls, which allow users to input date and time values. We demonstrated LinkLabels, which are used to link the user to an app or a web page. You used several controls that provide lists of data to the user—ListBoxes, CheckedListBoxes and ListViews. We used the ComboBox control to create drop-down lists, and the TreeView control to display data in hierarchical form. We then introduced complex GUIs that use tabbed windows and multiple document interfaces. The chapter concluded with demonstrations of visual inheritance and creating custom controls. In Chapter 16, we introduce string and character processing.

16

Strings and Characters:
A Deeper Look

Objectives

In this chapter you'll:

- Create and manipulate immutable character-string objects of class `string` and mutable character-string objects of class `StringBuilder`.

- Use various methods of classes `string` and `StringBuilder`.

- Manipulate character objects of `struct Char`.

- Use regular-expression classes `Regex` and `Match`.

16.1 Introduction

This chapter introduces the .NET Framework Class Library's string- and character-processing capabilities and demonstrates how to use regular expressions to search for patterns in text. The techniques it presents can be employed in text editors, word processors, page-layout software, computerized typesetting systems and other kinds of text-processing software. Previous chapters presented some basic string-processing capabilities. Now we discuss in detail the text-processing capabilities of class string and type char from the System namespace and class StringBuilder from the System.Text namespace.

We begin with an overview of the fundamentals of characters and strings in which we discuss *character constants* and *string literals*. We then provide examples of class string's many constructors and methods. The examples demonstrate how to determine the *length* of strings, *copy* strings, *access individual characters* in strings, *search* strings, obtain *substrings* from larger strings, *compare* strings, *concatenate* strings, *replace characters* in strings and convert strings to uppercase or lowercase letters.

Next, we introduce class StringBuilder, which is used to build strings dynamically. We demonstrate StringBuilder capabilities for determining and specifying the *size* of a StringBuilder, as well as *appending*, *inserting*, *removing* and *replacing* characters in a StringBuilder object. We then introduce the character-testing methods of struct Char that enable a program to determine whether a character is a digit, a letter, a lowercase letter, an uppercase letter, a punctuation mark or a symbol other than a punctuation mark. Such methods are useful for validating individual characters in user input. In addition, type Char provides methods for *converting* a character to *uppercase or lowercase*.

We provide an online section that discusses *regular expressions*. We present classes Regex and Match from the System.Text.RegularExpressions namespace as well as the symbols that are used to form regular expressions. We then demonstrate how to *find patterns* in a string, *match entire strings to patterns*, *replace characters* in a string that match a pattern and *split strings* at delimiters specified as a pattern in a regular expression.

16.2 Fundamentals of Characters and Strings

Characters are the fundamental building blocks of C# source code. Every program is composed of characters that, when grouped together meaningfully, create a sequence that the compiler interprets as instructions describing how to accomplish a task. A program also can contain **character constants**. A character constant is a character that's represented as an integer value, called a *character code*. For example, the integer value 122 corresponds to the character constant 'z'. The integer value 10 corresponds to the newline character '\n'. Character constants are established according to the **Unicode character set**, an international character set that contains many more symbols and letters than does the ASCII character set (listed in Appendix C). To learn more about Unicode, see Appendix F.

A string is a series of characters treated as a unit. These characters can be uppercase letters, lowercase letters, digits and various **special characters**: +, -, *, /, $ and others. A string is an object of class `string` in the `System` namespace.[1] We write **string literals**, also called **string constants**, as sequences of characters in double quotation marks, as follows:

```
"John Q. Doe"
"9999 Main Street"
"Waltham, Massachusetts"
"(201) 555-1212"
```

A declaration can assign a `string` literal to a `string` reference. The declaration

```
string color = "blue";
```

initializes the `string color` to refer to the `string` literal object `"blue"`.

Performance Tip 16.1

If there are multiple occurrences of the same `string` literal object in an app, a single copy of it will be referenced from each location in the program that uses that `string` literal. It's possible to share the object in this manner, because `string` literal objects are implicitly constant. Such sharing conserves memory.

Verbatim Strings

On occasion, a `string` will contain multiple *backslash characters* (this often occurs in the name of a file). To avoid excessive backslash characters, it's possible to exclude escape sequences and interpret all the characters in a `string` literally, using the @ character to create what's known as a **verbatim string**. Backslashes within the double quotation marks following the @ character are not considered escape sequences. Often this simplifies programming and makes the code easier to read. For example, consider the string "C:\MyFolder\MySubFolder\MyFile.txt" with the following assignment:

```
string file = "C:\\MyFolder\\MySubFolder\\MyFile.txt";
```

Using the *verbatim string syntax*, the assignment can be altered to

```
string file = @"C:\MyFolder\MySubFolder\MyFile.txt";
```

This approach also has the advantage of allowing string literals to span multiple lines by preserving all newlines, spaces and tabs.

---

1. C# provides the `string` keyword as an alias for class `String`. In this book, we use the term `string`.

16.3 string **Constructors**

Class string provides eight constructors for initializing strings in various ways. Figure 16.1 demonstrates three of the constructors.

```
1   // Fig. 16.1: StringConstructor.cs
2   // Demonstrating string class constructors.
3   using System;
4
5   class StringConstructor
6   {
7      public static void Main( string[] args )
8      {
9         // string initialization
10        char[] characterArray =
11           { 'b', 'i', 'r', 't', 'h', ' ', 'd', 'a', 'y' };
12        string originalString = "Welcome to C# programming!";
13        string string1 = originalString;
14        string string2 = new string( characterArray );
15        string string3 = new string( characterArray, 6, 3 );
16        string string4 = new string( 'C', 5 );
17
18        Console.WriteLine( "string1 = " + "\"" + string1 + "\"\n" +
19           "string2 = " + "\"" + string2 + "\"\n" +
20           "string3 = " + "\"" + string3 + "\"\n" +
21           "string4 = " + "\"" + string4 + "\"\n" );
22     } // end Main
23  } // end class StringConstructor
```

```
string1 = "Welcome to C# programming!"
string2 = "birth day"
string3 = "day"
string4 = "CCCCC"
```

Fig. 16.1 | string constructors.

Lines 10–11 allocate the char array characterArray, which contains nine characters. Lines 12–16 declare the strings originalString, string1, string2, string3 and string4. Line 12 assigns string literal "Welcome to C# programming!" to string reference originalString. Line 13 sets string1 to reference the same string literal.

Line 14 assigns to string2 a new string, using the string constructor with a character array argument. The new string contains a copy of the array's characters.

Line 15 assigns to string3 a new string, using the string constructor that takes a char array and two int arguments. The second argument specifies the starting index position (the *offset*) from which characters in the array are to be copied. The third argument specifies the number of characters (the *count*) to be copied from the specified starting position in the array. The new string contains a copy of the specified characters in the array. If the specified offset or count indicates that the program should access an element outside the bounds of the character array, an ArgumentOutOfRangeException is thrown.

Line 16 assigns to string4 a new string, using the string constructor that takes as arguments a character and an int specifying the number of times to repeat that character in the string.

Software Engineering Observation 16.1

In most cases, it's not necessary to make a copy of an existing string. All strings are immutable—their character contents cannot be changed after they're created. Also, if there are one or more references to a string (or any object for that matter), the object cannot be reclaimed by the garbage collector.

16.4 string Indexer, Length Property and CopyTo Method

The app in Fig. 16.2 presents the string *indexer*, which facilitates the retrieval of any character in the string, and the string property Length, which returns the length of the string. The string method CopyTo copies a specified number of characters from a string into a char array.

```
1   // Fig. 16.2: StringMethods.cs
2   // Using the indexer, property Length and method CopyTo
3   // of class string.
4   using System;
5
6   class StringMethods
7   {
8      public static void Main( string[] args )
9      {
10        string string1 = "hello there";
11        char[] characterArray = new char[ 5 ];
12
13        // output string1
14        Console.WriteLine( "string1: \"" + string1 + "\"" );
15
16        // test Length property
17        Console.WriteLine( "Length of string1: " + string1.Length );
18
19        // loop through characters in string1 and display reversed
20        Console.Write( "The string reversed is: " );
21
22        for ( int i = string1.Length - 1; i >= 0; --i )
23           Console.Write( string1[ i ] );
24
25        // copy characters from string1 into characterArray
26        string1.CopyTo( 0, characterArray, 0, characterArray.Length );
27        Console.Write( "\nThe character array is: " );
28
29        for ( int i = 0; i < characterArray.Length; ++i )
30           Console.Write( characterArray[ i ] );
31
32        Console.WriteLine( "\n" );
33     } // end Main
34  } // end class StringMethods
```

Fig. 16.2 | string indexer, Length property and CopyTo method. (Part 1 of 2.)

```
string1: "hello there"
Length of string1: 11
The string reversed is: ereht olleh
The character array is: hello
```

Fig. 16.2 | string indexer, Length property and CopyTo method. (Part 2 of 2.)

This app determines the length of a string, displays its characters in reverse order and copies a series of characters from the string to a character array. Line 17 uses string property Length to determine the number of characters in string1. Like arrays, strings always know their own size.

Lines 22–23 write the characters of string1 in reverse order using the string indexer. The string indexer treats a string as an array of chars and returns each character at a specific position in the string. The indexer receives an integer argument as the *position number* and returns the character at that position. As with arrays, the first element of a string is considered to be at position 0.

Common Programming Error 16.1

Attempting to access a character that's outside a string's bounds results in an Index-OutOfRangeException.

Line 26 uses string method CopyTo to copy the characters of string1 into a character array (characterArray). The first argument given to method CopyTo is the index from which the method begins copying characters in the string. The second argument is the character array into which the characters are copied. The third argument is the index specifying the starting location at which the method begins placing the copied characters into the character array. The last argument is the number of characters that the method will copy from the string. Lines 29–30 output the char array contents one character at a time.

16.5 Comparing strings

The next two examples demonstrate various methods for *comparing* strings. To understand how one string can be "greater than" or "less than" another, consider the process of alphabetizing a series of last names. The reader would, no doubt, place "Jones" before "Smith", because the first letter of "Jones" comes before the first letter of "Smith" in the alphabet. The alphabet is more than just a set of 26 letters—it's an ordered list of characters in which each letter occurs in a specific position. For example, Z is more than just a letter of the alphabet; it's specifically the twenty-sixth letter of the alphabet. Computers can order characters alphabetically because they're represented internally as numeric codes and those codes are ordered according to the alphabet so, for example, 'a' is less than 'b'—see Appendix C.

*Comparing Strings with **Equals**, **CompareTo** and the Equality Operator (==)*
Class string provides several ways to compare strings. The app in Fig. 16.3 demonstrates the use of method Equals, method CompareTo and the equality operator (==).

The condition in line 21 uses string method Equals to compare string1 and literal string "hello" to determine whether they're equal. Method Equals (inherited from object and overridden in string) tests two strings for equality (i.e., checks whether the strings have *identical contents*). The method returns true if the objects are equal and false otherwise. In this case, the condition returns `true`, because `string1` references string literal object `"hello"`. Method `Equals` uses word sorting rules that depend on your system's currently selected culture. Comparing `"hello"` with `"HELLO"` would return `false`, because the lowercase letters are different from the those of corresponding uppercase letters.

```
1   // Fig. 16.3: StringCompare.cs
2   // Comparing strings
3   using System;
4
5   class StringCompare
6   {
7      public static void Main( string[] args )
8      {
9         string string1 = "hello";
10        string string2 = "good bye";
11        string string3 = "Happy Birthday";
12        string string4 = "happy birthday";
13
14        // output values of four strings
15        Console.WriteLine( "string1 = \"" + string1 + "\"" +
16           "\nstring2 = \"" + string2 + "\"" +
17           "\nstring3 = \"" + string3 + "\"" +
18           "\nstring4 = \"" + string4 + "\"\n" );
19
20        // test for equality using Equals method
21        if ( string1.Equals( "hello" ) )
22           Console.WriteLine( "string1 equals \"hello\"" );
23        else
24           Console.WriteLine( "string1 does not equal \"hello\"" );
25
26        // test for equality with ==
27        if ( string1 == "hello" )
28           Console.WriteLine( "string1 equals \"hello\"" );
29        else
30           Console.WriteLine( "string1 does not equal \"hello\"" );
31
32        // test for equality comparing case
33        if ( string.Equals( string3, string4 ) ) // static method
34           Console.WriteLine( "string3 equals string4" );
35        else
36           Console.WriteLine( "string3 does not equal string4" );
37
38        // test CompareTo
39        Console.WriteLine( "\nstring1.CompareTo( string2 ) is " +
40           string1.CompareTo( string2 ) + "\n" +
41           "string2.CompareTo( string1 ) is " +
42           string2.CompareTo( string1 ) + "\n" +
43           "string1.CompareTo( string1 ) is " +
44           string1.CompareTo( string1 ) + "\n" +
45           "string3.CompareTo( string4 ) is " +
46           string3.CompareTo( string4 ) + "\n" +
```

Fig. 16.3 | `string` test to determine equality. (Part 1 of 2.)

```
47          "string4.CompareTo( string3 ) is " +
48          string4.CompareTo( string3 ) + "\n\n" );
49    } // end Main
50  } // end class StringCompare
```

```
string1 = "hello"
string2 = "good bye"
string3 = "Happy Birthday"
string4 = "happy birthday"

string1 equals "hello"
string1 equals "hello"
string3 does not equal string4

string1.CompareTo( string2 ) is 1
string2.CompareTo( string1 ) is -1
string1.CompareTo( string1 ) is 0
string3.CompareTo( string4 ) is 1
string4.CompareTo( string3 ) is -1
```

Fig. 16.3 | string test to determine equality. (Part 2 of 2.)

The condition in line 27 uses the *overloaded equality operator (==)* to compare string string1 with the literal string "hello" for equality. In C#, the equality operator also compares the contents of two strings. Thus, the condition in the if statement evaluates to true, because the values of string1 and "hello" are equal.

Line 33 tests whether string3 and string4 are equal to illustrate that comparisons are indeed case sensitive. Here, static method Equals is used to compare the values of two strings. "Happy Birthday" does not equal "happy birthday", so the condition of the if statement fails, and the message "string3 does not equal string4" is output (line 36).

Lines 40–48 use string method CompareTo to compare strings. Method CompareTo returns 0 if the strings are equal, a negative value if the string that invokes CompareTo is less than the string that's passed as an argument and a positive value if the string that invokes CompareTo is greater than the string that's passed as an argument.

Notice that CompareTo considers string3 to be greater than string4. The only difference between these two strings is that string3 contains two uppercase letters in positions where string4 contains lowercase letters—the uppercase version of a letter has a lower numeric code than the corresponding lowercase letter (e.g., 'A' is 65 and 'a' is 97).

Determining Whether a String Begins or Ends with a Specified String
Figure 16.4 shows how to test whether a string instance begins or ends with a given string. Method StartsWith determines whether a string instance starts with the string text passed to it as an argument. Method EndsWith determines whether a string instance ends with the string text passed to it as an argument. Class StringStartEnd's Main method defines an array of strings (called strings), which contains "started", "starting", "ended" and "ending". The remainder of method Main tests the elements of the array to determine whether they start or end with a particular set of characters.

Line 13 uses method StartsWith, which takes a string argument. The condition in the if statement determines whether the string at index i of the array starts with the characters "st". If so, the method returns true, and strings[i] is output along with a message.

Line 21 uses method EndsWith to determine whether the string at index i of the array ends with the characters "ed". If so, the method returns true, and strings[i] is displayed along with a message.

```
 1   // Fig. 16.4: StringStartEnd.cs
 2   // Demonstrating StartsWith and EndsWith methods.
 3   using System;
 4
 5   class StringStartEnd
 6   {
 7      public static void Main( string[] args )
 8      {
 9         string[] strings = { "started", "starting", "ended", "ending" };
10
11         // test every string to see if it starts with "st"
12         for ( int i = 0; i < strings.Length; i++ )
13            if ( strings[ i ].StartsWith( "st" ) )
14               Console.WriteLine( "\"" + strings[ i ] + "\"" +
15                  " starts with \"st\"" );
16
17         Console.WriteLine();
18
19         // test every string to see if it ends with "ed"
20         for ( int i = 0; i < strings.Length; i++ )
21            if ( strings[ i ].EndsWith( "ed" ) )
22               Console.WriteLine( "\"" + strings[ i ] + "\"" +
23                  " ends with \"ed\"" );
24
25         Console.WriteLine();
26      } // end Main
27   } // end class StringStartEnd
```

```
"started" starts with "st"
"starting" starts with "st"

"started" ends with "ed"
"ended" ends with "ed"
```

Fig. 16.4 | StartsWith and EndsWith methods.

16.6 Locating Characters and Substrings in strings

In many apps, it's necessary to search for a character or set of characters in a string. For example, a programmer creating a word processor would want to provide capabilities for searching through documents. The app in Fig. 16.5 demonstrates some of the many versions of string methods IndexOf, IndexOfAny, LastIndexOf and LastIndexOfAny, which search for a specified character or substring in a string. We perform all searches in this example on the string letters (initialized with "abcdefghijklmabcdefghijklm") located in method Main of class StringIndexMethods.

Lines 14, 16 and 18 use method IndexOf to locate the first occurrence of a character or substring in a string. If it finds a character, IndexOf returns the index of the specified

```
1   // Fig. 16.5: StringIndexMethods.cs
2   // Using string-searching methods.
3   using System;
4
5   class StringIndexMethods
6   {
7       public static void Main( string[] args )
8       {
9           string letters = "abcdefghijklmabcdefghijklm";
10          char[] searchLetters = { 'c', 'a', '$' };
11
12          // test IndexOf to locate a character in a string
13          Console.WriteLine( "First 'c' is located at index " +
14             letters.IndexOf( 'c' ) );
15          Console.WriteLine( "First 'a' starting at 1 is located at index " +
16             letters.IndexOf( 'a', 1 ) );
17          Console.WriteLine( "First '$' in the 5 positions starting at 3 " +
18             "is located at index " + letters.IndexOf( '$', 3, 5 ) );
19
20          // test LastIndexOf to find a character in a string
21          Console.WriteLine( "\nLast 'c' is located at index " +
22             letters.LastIndexOf( 'c' ) );
23          Console.WriteLine( "Last 'a' up to position 25 is located at " +
24             "index " + letters.LastIndexOf( 'a', 25 ) );
25          Console.WriteLine( "Last '$' in the 5 positions ending at 15 " +
26             "is located at index " + letters.LastIndexOf( '$', 15, 5 ) );
27
28          // test IndexOf to locate a substring in a string
29          Console.WriteLine( "\nFirst \"def\" is located at index " +
30             letters.IndexOf( "def" ) );
31          Console.WriteLine( "First \"def\" starting at 7 is located at " +
32             "index " + letters.IndexOf( "def", 7 ) );
33          Console.WriteLine( "First \"hello\" in the 15 positions " +
34             "starting at 5 is located at index " +
35             letters.IndexOf( "hello", 5, 15 ) );
36
37          // test LastIndexOf to find a substring in a string
38          Console.WriteLine( "\nLast \"def\" is located at index " +
39             letters.LastIndexOf( "def" ) );
40          Console.WriteLine( "Last \"def\" up to position 25 is located " +
41             "at index " + letters.LastIndexOf( "def", 25 ) );
42          Console.WriteLine( "Last \"hello\" in the 15 positions " +
43             "ending at 20 is located at index " +
44             letters.LastIndexOf( "hello", 20, 15 ) );
45
46          // test IndexOfAny to find first occurrence of character in array
47          Console.WriteLine( "\nFirst 'c', 'a' or '$' is " +
48             "located at index " + letters.IndexOfAny( searchLetters ) );
49          Console.WriteLine("First 'c', 'a' or '$' starting at 7 is " +
50             "located at index " + letters.IndexOfAny( searchLetters, 7 ) );
51          Console.WriteLine( "First 'c', 'a' or '$' in the 5 positions " +
52             "starting at 7 is located at index " +
53             letters.IndexOfAny( searchLetters, 7, 5 ) );
```

Fig. 16.5 | Searching for characters and substrings in strings. (Part 1 of 2.)

```
54
55          // test LastIndexOfAny to find last occurrence of character
56          // in array
57          Console.WriteLine( "\nLast 'c', 'a' or '$' is " +
58             "located at index " + letters.LastIndexOfAny( searchLetters ) );
59          Console.WriteLine( "Last 'c', 'a' or '$' up to position 1 is " +
60             "located at index " +
61             letters.LastIndexOfAny( searchLetters, 1 ) );
62          Console.WriteLine( "Last 'c', 'a' or '$' in the 5 positions " +
63             "ending at 25 is located at index " +
64             letters.LastIndexOfAny( searchLetters, 25, 5 ) );
65       } // end Main
66    } // end class StringIndexMethods
```

```
First 'c' is located at index 2
First 'a' starting at 1 is located at index 13
First '$' in the 5 positions starting at 3 is located at index -1

Last 'c' is located at index 15
Last 'a' up to position 25 is located at index 13
Last '$' in the 5 positions ending at 15 is located at index -1

First "def" is located at index 3
First "def" starting at 7 is located at index 16
First "hello" in the 15 positions starting at 5 is located at index -1

Last "def" is located at index 16
Last "def" up to position 25 is located at index 16
Last "hello" in the 15 positions ending at 20 is located at index -1

First 'c', 'a' or '$' is located at index 0
First 'c', 'a' or '$' starting at 7 is located at index 13
First 'c', 'a' or '$' in the 5 positions starting at 7 is located at index -1

Last 'c', 'a' or '$' is located at index 15
Last 'c', 'a' or '$' up to position 1 is located at index 0
Last 'c', 'a' or '$' in the 5 positions ending at 25 is located at index -1
```

Fig. 16.5 | Searching for characters and substrings in `string`s. (Part 2 of 2.)

character in the `string`; otherwise, `IndexOf` returns –1. The expression in line 16 uses a version of method `IndexOf` that takes two arguments—the character to search for and the starting index at which the search of the `string` should begin. The method does not examine any characters that occur prior to the starting index (in this case, 1). The expression in line 18 uses another version of method `IndexOf` that takes three arguments—the character to search for, the index at which to start searching and the number of characters to search.

Lines 22, 24 and 26 use method `LastIndexOf` to locate the last occurrence of a character in a `string`. Method `LastIndexOf` performs the search from the end of the `string` to the beginning of the `string`. If it finds the character, `LastIndexOf` returns the index of the specified character in the `string`; otherwise, `LastIndexOf` returns –1. There are three versions of method `LastIndexOf`. The expression in line 22 uses the version that takes as an argument the character for which to search. The expression in line 24 uses the version that takes two arguments—the character for which to search and the highest index from which to begin searching backward for the character. The expression in line 26 uses a third version of method `LastIndexOf` that takes three arguments—the character for which to search, the starting index from which to start searching backward and the number of characters (the portion of the `string`) to search.

Lines 29–44 use versions of `IndexOf` and `LastIndexOf` that take a `string` instead of a character as the first argument. These versions of the methods perform identically to those described above except that they search for sequences of characters (or substrings) that are specified by their `string` arguments.

Lines 47–64 use methods `IndexOfAny` and `LastIndexOfAny`, which take an array of characters as the first argument. These versions of the methods also perform identically to those described above, except that they return the index of the first occurrence of any of the characters in the character-array argument.

Common Programming Error 16.2

In the overloaded methods `LastIndexOf` and `LastIndexOfAny` that take three parameters, the second argument must be greater than or equal to the third. This might seem counterintuitive, but remember that the search moves from the end of the string toward the start of the string.

16.7 Extracting Substrings from strings

Class `string` provides two `Substring` methods, which create a new `string` by copying part of an existing `string`. Each method returns a new `string`. The app in Fig. 16.6 demonstrates the use of both methods.

```
1   // Fig. 16.6: SubString.cs
2   // Demonstrating the string Substring method.
3   using System;
4
5   class SubString
6   {
7      public static void Main( string[] args )
8      {
9         string letters = "abcdefghijklmabcdefghijklm";
10
11        // invoke Substring method and pass it one parameter
12        Console.WriteLine( "Substring from index 20 to end is \"" +
13           letters.Substring( 20 ) + "\"" );
14
15        // invoke Substring method and pass it two parameters
16        Console.WriteLine( "Substring from index 0 of length 6 is \"" +
17           letters.Substring( 0, 6 ) + "\"" );
18     } // end method Main
19  } // end class SubString
```

```
Substring from index 20 to end is "hijklm"
Substring from index 0 of length 6 is "abcdef"
```

Fig. 16.6 | Substrings generated from strings.

The statement in line 13 uses the Substring method that takes one int argument. The argument specifies the starting index from which the method copies characters in the original string. The substring returned contains a copy of the characters from the starting index to the end of the string. If the index specified in the argument is outside the bounds of the string, the program throws an ArgumentOutOfRangeException.

The second version of method Substring (line 17) takes two int arguments. The first argument specifies the starting index from which the method copies characters from the original string. The second argument specifies the length of the substring to copy. The substring returned contains a copy of the specified characters from the original string. If the supplied length of the substring is too large (i.e., the substring tries to retrieve characters past the end of the original string), an ArgumentOutOfRangeException is thrown.

16.8 Concatenating strings

The + operator is not the only way to perform string concatenation. The static method Concat of class string (Fig. 16.7) concatenates two strings and returns a new string containing the combined characters from both original strings. Line 16 appends the characters from string2 to the end of a copy of string1, using method Concat. The statement in line 16 does not modify the original strings.

```
 1   // Fig. 16.7: SubConcatenation.cs
 2   // Demonstrating string class Concat method.
 3   using System;
 4
 5   class StringConcatenation
 6   {
 7      public static void Main( string[] args )
 8      {
 9         string string1 = "Happy ";
10         string string2 = "Birthday";
11
12         Console.WriteLine( "string1 = \"" + string1 + "\"\n" +
13            "string2 = \"" + string2 + "\"" );
14         Console.WriteLine(
15            "\nResult of string.Concat( string1, string2 ) = " +
16            string.Concat( string1, string2 ) );
17         Console.WriteLine( "string1 after concatenation = " + string1 );
18      } // end Main
19   } // end class StringConcatenation
```

```
string1 = "Happy "
string2 = "Birthday"

Result of string.Concat( string1, string2 ) = Happy Birthday
string1 after concatenation = Happy
```

Fig. 16.7 | Concat static method.

16.9 Miscellaneous `string` Methods

Class `string` provides several methods that return modified copies of `strings`. The app in Fig. 16.8 demonstrates the use of these methods, which include `string` methods `Replace`, `ToLower`, `ToUpper` and `Trim`.

```
1   // Fig. 16.8: StringMethods2.cs
2   // Demonstrating string methods Replace, ToLower, ToUpper, Trim,
3   // and ToString.
4   using System;
5
6   class StringMethods2
7   {
8      public static void Main( string[] args )
9      {
10         string string1 = "cheers!";
11         string string2 = "GOOD BYE ";
12         string string3 = "   spaces   ";
13
14         Console.WriteLine( "string1 = \"" + string1 + "\"\n" +
15            "string2 = \"" + string2 + "\"\n" +
16            "string3 = \"" + string3 + "\"" );
17
18         // call method Replace
19         Console.WriteLine(
20            "\nReplacing \"e\" with \"E\" in string1: \"" +
21            string1.Replace( 'e', 'E' ) + "\"" );
22
23         // call ToLower and ToUpper
24         Console.WriteLine( "\nstring1.ToUpper() = \"" +
25            string1.ToUpper() + "\"\nstring2.ToLower() = \"" +
26            string2.ToLower() + "\"" );
27
28         // call Trim method
29         Console.WriteLine( "\nstring3 after trim = \"" +
30            string3.Trim() + "\"" );
31
32         Console.WriteLine( "\nstring1 = \"" + string1 + "\"" );
33      } // end Main
34   } // end class StringMethods2
```

```
string1 = "cheers!"
string2 = "GOOD BYE "
string3 = "   spaces   "

Replacing "e" with "E" in string1: "chEErs!"

string1.ToUpper() = "CHEERS!"
string2.ToLower() = "good bye "

string3 after trim = "spaces"

string1 = "cheers!"
```

Fig. 16.8 | `string` methods `Replace`, `ToLower`, `ToUpper` and `Trim`.

Line 21 uses string method Replace to return a new string, replacing every occurrence in string1 of character 'e' with 'E'. Method Replace takes two arguments—a char for which to search and another char with which to replace all matching occurrences of the first argument. The original string remains unchanged. If there are no occurrences of the first argument in the string, the method returns the original string. An overloaded version of this method allows you to provide two strings as arguments.

The string method ToUpper generates a new string (line 25) that replaces any *lowercase* letters in string1 with their *uppercase* equivalents. The method returns a new string containing the converted string; the original string remains *unchanged*. If there are no characters to convert, the original string is returned. Line 26 uses string method ToLower to return a new string in which any *uppercase* letters in string2 are replaced by their *lowercase* equivalents. The original string is *unchanged*. As with ToUpper, if there are *no* characters to convert to lowercase, method ToLower returns the *original* string.

Line 30 uses string method Trim to remove all *whitespace characters* that appear at the beginning and end of a string. Without otherwise altering the original string, the method returns a new string that contains the string, but *omits* leading and trailing *whitespace* characters. This method is particularly useful for retrieving user input (i.e., via a TextBox). Another version of method Trim takes a character array and returns a copy of the string that does not begin or end with any of the characters in the array argument.

16.10 Class StringBuilder

The string class provides many capabilities for processing strings. However a string's contents can *never* change. Operations that seem to concatenate strings are in fact creating new strings—the += operator creates a new string and assigns its reference to the variable on the left of the += operator.

The next several sections discuss the features of class StringBuilder (namespace System.Text), used to create and manipulate dynamic string information—i.e., *mutable* strings. Every StringBuilder can store a certain number of characters that's specified by its capacity. Exceeding the capacity of a StringBuilder causes the capacity to expand to accommodate the additional characters. As we'll see, members of class StringBuilder, such as methods Append and AppendFormat, can be used for *concatenation* like the operators + and += for class string. StringBuilder is particularly useful for manipulating in place a large number of strings, as it's much more efficient than creating individual immutable strings.

Performance Tip 16.2

Objects of class string are immutable (i.e., constant strings), whereas objects of class StringBuilder are mutable. C# can perform certain optimizations involving strings (such as the sharing of one string among multiple references), because it knows these objects will not change.

Class StringBuilder provides six overloaded constructors. Class StringBuilderConstructor (Fig. 16.9) demonstrates three of these overloaded constructors.

Line 10 employs the no-parameter StringBuilder constructor to create a StringBuilder that contains no characters and has an implementation-specific *default initial capacity*. Line 11 uses the StringBuilder constructor that takes an int argument to create a StringBuilder that contains no characters and has the *initial capacity* specified in the int argument (i.e., 10). Line 12 uses the StringBuilder constructor that takes a string argument to create a StringBuilder containing the characters of the string argument—the initial capacity might differ from the string's size. Lines 14–16 implicitly use StringBuilder method ToString to obtain string representations of the StringBuilders' contents.

```
1   // Fig. 16.9: StringBuilderConstructor.cs
2   // Demonstrating StringBuilder class constructors.
3   using System;
4   using System.Text;
5
6   class StringBuilderConstructor
7   {
8      public static void Main( string[] args )
9      {
10        StringBuilder buffer1 = new StringBuilder();
11        StringBuilder buffer2 = new StringBuilder( 10 );
12        StringBuilder buffer3 = new StringBuilder( "hello" );
13
14        Console.WriteLine( "buffer1 = \"" + buffer1 + "\"" );
15        Console.WriteLine( "buffer2 = \"" + buffer2 + "\"" );
16        Console.WriteLine( "buffer3 = \"" + buffer3 + "\"" );
17     } // end Main
18  } // end class StringBuilderConstructor
```

```
buffer1 = ""
buffer2 = ""
buffer3 = "hello"
```

Fig. 16.9 | StringBuilder class constructors.

16.11 Length and Capacity Properties, EnsureCapacity Method and Indexer of Class StringBuilder

Class StringBuilder provides the Length and Capacity properties to return the number of characters currently in a StringBuilder and the number of characters that a StringBuilder can store without allocating more memory, respectively. These properties also can increase or decrease the length or the capacity of the StringBuilder. Method EnsureCapacity allows you to reduce the number of times that a StringBuilder's capacity must be increased. The method ensures that the StringBuilder's capacity is at least the specified value. The program in Fig. 16.10 demonstrates these methods and properties.

```
1   // Fig. 16.10: StringBuilderFeatures.cs
2   // Demonstrating some features of class StringBuilder.
3   using System;
4   using System.Text;
5
6   class StringBuilderFeatures
7   {
```

Fig. 16.10 | StringBuilder size manipulation. (Part 1 of 2.)

```
 8    public static void Main( string[] args )
 9    {
10       StringBuilder buffer =
11          new StringBuilder( "Hello, how are you?" );
12
13       // use Length and Capacity properties
14       Console.WriteLine( "buffer = " + buffer +
15          "\nLength = " + buffer.Length +
16          "\nCapacity = " + buffer.Capacity );
17
18       buffer.EnsureCapacity( 75 ); // ensure a capacity of at least 75
19       Console.WriteLine( "\nNew capacity = " +
20          buffer.Capacity );
21
22       // truncate StringBuilder by setting Length property
23       buffer.Length = 10;
24       Console.Write( "\nNew length = " +
25          buffer.Length + "\nbuffer = " );
26
27       // use StringBuilder indexer
28       for ( int i = 0; i < buffer.Length; ++i )
29          Console.Write( buffer[ i ] );
30
31       Console.WriteLine( "\n" );
32    } // end Main
33 } // end class StringBuilderFeatures
```

```
buffer = Hello, how are you?
Length = 19
Capacity = 19
New capacity = 75
New length = 10
buffer = Hello, how
```

Fig. 16.10 | StringBuilder size manipulation. (Part 2 of 2.)

The program contains one StringBuilder, called buffer. Lines 10–11 of the program use the StringBuilder constructor that takes a string argument to instantiate the StringBuilder and initialize its value to "Hello, how are you?". Lines 14–16 output the content, length and capacity of the StringBuilder.

Line 18 expands the capacity of the StringBuilder to a minimum of 75 characters. If new characters are added to a StringBuilder so that its length exceeds its capacity, the capacity *grows* to accommodate the additional characters in the same manner as if method EnsureCapacity had been called.

Line 23 uses property Length to set the length of the StringBuilder to 10—this does *not* change the Capacity. If the specified length is less than the current number of characters in the StringBuilder, the contents of the StringBuilder are *truncated* to the specified length. If the specified length is greater than the number of characters currently in the StringBuilder, null characters (that is, '\0' characters) are appended to the StringBuilder until the total number of characters in the StringBuilder is equal to the specified length.

16.12 Append and AppendFormat Methods of Class StringBuilder

Class StringBuilder provides 19 overloaded Append methods that allow various types of values to be added to the end of a StringBuilder. The Framework Class Library provides versions for each of the simple types and for character arrays, strings and objects. (Remember that method ToString produces a string representation of any object.) Each method takes an argument, converts it to a string and appends it to the StringBuilder. Figure 16.11 demonstrates the use of several Append methods.

```
1   // Fig. 16.11: StringBuilderAppend.cs
2   // Demonstrating StringBuilder Append methods.
3   using System;
4   using System.Text;
5
6   class StringBuilderAppend
7   {
8      public static void Main( string[] args )
9      {
10        object objectValue = "hello";
11        string stringValue = "good bye";
12        char[] characterArray = { 'a', 'b', 'c', 'd', 'e', 'f' };
13        bool booleanValue = true;
14        char characterValue = 'Z';
15        int integerValue = 7;
16        long longValue = 1000000;
17        float floatValue = 2.5F; // F suffix indicates that 2.5 is a float
18        double doubleValue = 33.333;
19        StringBuilder buffer = new StringBuilder();
20
21        // use method Append to append values to buffer
22        buffer.Append( objectValue );
23        buffer.Append( "  " );
24        buffer.Append( stringValue );
25        buffer.Append( "  " );
26        buffer.Append( characterArray );
27        buffer.Append( "  ");
28        buffer.Append( characterArray, 0, 3 );
29        buffer.Append( "  " );
30        buffer.Append( booleanValue );
31        buffer.Append( "  " );
32        buffer.Append( characterValue );
33        buffer.Append( "  " );
34        buffer.Append( integerValue );
35        buffer.Append( "  " );
36        buffer.Append( longValue );
37        buffer.Append( "  " );
38        buffer.Append( floatValue );
39        buffer.Append( "  " );
40        buffer.Append( doubleValue );
41
```

Fig. 16.11 | Append methods of StringBuilder. (Part 1 of 2.)

```
42            Console.WriteLine( "buffer = " + buffer.ToString() + "\n" );
43         } // end Main
44      } // end class StringBuilderAppend
```

```
buffer = hello   good bye   abcdef   abc   True   Z   7   1000000   2.5   33.333
```

Fig. 16.11 | Append methods of `StringBuilder`. (Part 2 of 2.)

Lines 22–40 use 10 different overloaded `Append` methods to attach the string representations of objects created in lines 10–18 to the end of the `StringBuilder`.

Class `StringBuilder` also provides method `AppendFormat`, which converts a `string` to a specified format, then appends it to the `StringBuilder`. The example in Fig. 16.12 demonstrates the use of this method.

```
 1   // Fig. 16.12: StringBuilderAppendFormat.cs
 2   // Demonstrating method AppendFormat.
 3   using System;
 4   using System.Text;
 5
 6   class StringBuilderAppendFormat
 7   {
 8      public static void Main( string[] args )
 9      {
10         StringBuilder buffer = new StringBuilder();
11
12         // formatted string
13         string string1 = "This {0} costs: {1:C}.\n";
14
15         // string1 argument array
16         object[] objectArray = new object[ 2 ];
17
18         objectArray[ 0 ] = "car";
19         objectArray[ 1 ] = 1234.56;
20
21         // append to buffer formatted string with argument
22         buffer.AppendFormat( string1, objectArray );
23
24         // formatted string
25         string string2 = "Number:{0:d3}.\n" +
26            "Number right aligned with spaces:{0, 4}.\n" +
27            "Number left aligned with spaces:{0, -4}.";
28
29         // append to buffer formatted string with argument
30         buffer.AppendFormat( string2, 5 );
31
32         // display formatted strings
33         Console.WriteLine( buffer.ToString() );
34      } // end Main
35   } // end class StringBuilderAppendFormat
```

Fig. 16.12 | `StringBuilder`'s `AppendFormat` method. (Part 1 of 2.)

```
This car costs: $1,234.56.
Number:005.
Number right aligned with spaces:    5.
Number left aligned with spaces:5    .
```

Fig. 16.12 | StringBuilder's AppendFormat method. (Part 2 of 2.)

Line 13 creates a string that contains formatting information. The information enclosed in braces specifies how to format a specific piece of data. Format items have the form {X[,Y][:FormatString]}, where X is the number of the argument to be formatted, counting from zero. Y is an optional argument, which can be positive or negative, indicating how many characters should be in the result. If the resulting string is less than the number Y, it will be padded with spaces to make up for the difference. A positive integer aligns the string to the right; a negative integer aligns it to the left. The optional Format-String applies a particular format to the argument—currency, decimal or scientific, among others. In this case, "{0}" means the first argument will be displayed. "{1:C}" specifies that the second argument will be formatted as a *currency* value.

Line 22 shows a version of AppendFormat that takes two parameters—a string specifying the format and an array of objects to serve as the arguments to the format string. The argument referred to by "{0}" is in the object array at index 0.

Lines 25–27 define another string used for formatting. The first format "{0:d3}", specifies that the first argument will be formatted as a three-digit decimal, meaning that any number having fewer than three digits will have leading zeros placed in front to make up the difference. The next format, "{0, 4}", specifies that the formatted string should have four characters and be right aligned. The third format, "{0, -4}", specifies that the formatted string should be aligned to the left.

Line 30 uses a version of AppendFormat that takes two parameters—a string containing a format and an object to which the format is applied. In this case, the object is the number 5. The output of Fig. 16.12 displays the result of applying these two versions of AppendFormat with their respective arguments.

16.13 Insert, Remove and Replace Methods of Class StringBuilder

Class StringBuilder provides 18 overloaded Insert methods to allow various types of data to be inserted at any position in a StringBuilder. The class provides versions for each of the simple types and for character arrays, strings and objects. Each method takes its second argument, converts it to a string and inserts the string into the StringBuilder in front of the character in the position specified by the first argument. The index specified by the first argument must be greater than or equal to 0 and less than the length of the StringBuilder; otherwise, the program throws an ArgumentOutOfRangeException.

Class StringBuilder also provides method Remove for deleting any portion of a StringBuilder. Method Remove takes two arguments—the index at which to begin deletion and the number of characters to delete. The sum of the starting index and the number of characters to be deleted must always be less than the length of the StringBuilder; otherwise, the program throws an ArgumentOutOfRangeException. The Insert and Remove methods are demonstrated in Fig. 16.13.

```
 1   // Fig. 16.13: StringBuilderInsertRemove.cs
 2   // Demonstrating methods Insert and Remove of the
 3   // StringBuilder class.
 4   using System;
 5   using System.Text;
 6
 7   class StringBuilderInsertRemove
 8   {
 9      public static void Main( string[] args )
10      {
11         object objectValue = "hello";
12         string stringValue = "good bye";
13         char[] characterArray = { 'a', 'b', 'c', 'd', 'e', 'f' };
14         bool booleanValue = true;
15         char characterValue = 'K';
16         int integerValue = 7;
17         long longValue = 10000000;
18         float floatValue = 2.5F; // F suffix indicates that 2.5 is a float
19         double doubleValue = 33.333;
20         StringBuilder buffer = new StringBuilder();
21
22         // insert values into buffer
23         buffer.Insert( 0, objectValue );
24         buffer.Insert( 0, "  " );
25         buffer.Insert( 0, stringValue );
26         buffer.Insert( 0, "  " );
27         buffer.Insert( 0, characterArray );
28         buffer.Insert( 0, "  " );
29         buffer.Insert( 0, booleanValue );
30         buffer.Insert( 0, "  " );
31         buffer.Insert( 0, characterValue );
32         buffer.Insert( 0, "  " );
33         buffer.Insert( 0, integerValue );
34         buffer.Insert( 0, "  " );
35         buffer.Insert( 0, longValue );
36         buffer.Insert( 0, "  " );
37         buffer.Insert( 0, floatValue );
38         buffer.Insert( 0, "  " );
39         buffer.Insert( 0, doubleValue );
40         buffer.Insert( 0, "  " );
41
42         Console.WriteLine( "buffer after Inserts: \n" + buffer + "\n" );
43
44         buffer.Remove( 10, 1 ); // delete 2 in 2.5
45         buffer.Remove( 4, 4 );  // delete .333 in 33.333
46
47         Console.WriteLine( "buffer after Removes:\n" + buffer );
48      } // end Main
49   } // end class StringBuilderInsertRemove
```

```
buffer after Inserts:
  33.333  2.5  10000000  7  K  True  abcdef  good bye  hello
```

Fig. 16.13 | StringBuilder text insertion and removal. (Part 1 of 2.)

```
buffer after Removes:
   33   .5   10000000   7   K   True   abcdef   good bye   hello
```

Fig. 16.13 | StringBuilder text insertion and removal. (Part 2 of 2.)

Another useful method included with StringBuilder is Replace. Replace searches for a specified string or character and *substitutes* another string or character in its place. Figure 16.14 demonstrates this method.

```
1   // Fig. 16.14: StringBuilderReplace.cs
2   // Demonstrating method Replace.
3   using System;
4   using System.Text;
5
6   class StringBuilderReplace
7   {
8      public static void Main( string[] args )
9      {
10        StringBuilder builder1 =
11           new StringBuilder( "Happy Birthday Jane" );
12        StringBuilder builder2 =
13           new StringBuilder( "goodbye greg" );
14
15        Console.WriteLine( "Before replacements:\n" +
16           builder1.ToString() + "\n" + builder2.ToString() );
17
18        builder1.Replace( "Jane", "Greg" );
19        builder2.Replace( 'g', 'G', 0, 5 );
20
21        Console.WriteLine( "\nAfter replacements:\n" +
22           builder1.ToString() + "\n" + builder2.ToString() );
23      } // end Main
24   } // end class StringBuilderReplace
```

```
Before Replacements:
Happy Birthday Jane
good bye greg

After replacements:
Happy Birthday Greg
Goodbye greg
```

Fig. 16.14 | StringBuilder text replacement.

Line 18 uses method Replace to replace all instances of "Jane" with the "Greg" in builder1. Another overload of this method takes two characters as parameters and *replaces* each occurrence of the first character with the second. Line 19 uses an overload of Replace that takes four parameters, of which the first two can both be characters or both be strings and the second two are ints. The method replaces all instances of the first character with the second character (or the first string with the second), beginning at the index specified by the first int and continuing for a count specified by the second int. Thus, in this case,

Replace looks through only five characters, starting with the character at index 0. As the output illustrates, this version of Replace replaces g with G in the word "good", but not in "greg". This is because the gs in "greg" are not in the range indicated by the int arguments (i.e., between indexes 0 and 4).

16.14 Char Methods

C# provides a concept called a **struct** (short for "structure") that's similar to a class. Although structs and classes are comparable, structs represent value types. Like classes, structs can have methods and properties, and can use the access modifiers public and private. Also, struct members are accessed via the *member access operator (.)*.

The simple types are actually aliases for struct types. For instance, an int is defined by struct System.Int32, a long by System.Int64 and so on. All struct types derive from class **ValueType**, which derives from object. Also, all struct types are implicitly sealed, so they do not support virtual or abstract methods, and their members cannot be declared protected or protected internal.

In the struct **System.Char**,[2] which is the struct for characters, most methods are static, take at least one character argument and perform either a test or a manipulation on the character. We present several of these methods in the next example. Figure 16.15 demonstrates static methods that test characters to determine whether they're of a specific character type and static methods that perform case conversions on characters.

```
1   // Fig. 16.15: StaticCharMethods.cs
2   // Demonstrates static character-testing and case-conversion methods
3   // from Char struct
4   using System;
5
6   class StaticCharMethods
7   {
8      static void Main( string[] args )
9      {
10        Console.Write( "Enter a character: " );
11        char character = Convert.ToChar( Console.ReadLine() );
12
13        Console.WriteLine( "is digit: {0}", Char.IsDigit( character ) );
14        Console.WriteLine( "is letter: {0}", Char.IsLetter( character )  );
15        Console.WriteLine( "is letter or digit: {0}",
16           Char.IsLetterOrDigit( character ) );
17        Console.WriteLine( "is lower case: {0}",
18           Char.IsLower( character ) );
19        Console.WriteLine( "is upper case: {0}",
20           Char.IsUpper( character ) );
21        Console.WriteLine( "to upper case: {0}",
22           Char.ToUpper( character ) );
23        Console.WriteLine( "to lower case: {0}",
24           Char.ToLower( character ) );
```

Fig. 16.15 | Char's static character-testing and case-conversion methods. (Part 1 of 3.)

2. Just as keyword string is an alias for class String, keyword char is an alias for struct Char. In this text, we use the term Char when calling a static method of struct Char and the term char elsewhere.

```
25          Console.WriteLine( "is punctuation: {0}",
26              Char.IsPunctuation( character ) );
27          Console.WriteLine( "is symbol: {0}", Char.IsSymbol( character ) );
28      } // end Main
29  } // end class StaticCharMethods
```

```
Enter a character: A
is digit: False
is letter: True
is letter or digit: True
is lower case: False
is upper case: True
to upper case: A
to lower case: a
is punctuation: False
is symbol: False
```

```
Enter a character: 8
is digit: True
is letter: False
is letter or digit: True
is lower case: False
is upper case: False
to upper case: 8
to lower case: 8
is punctuation: False
is symbol: False
```

```
Enter a character: @
is digit: False
is letter: False
is letter or digit: False
is lower case: False
is upper case: False
to upper case: @
to lower case: @
is punctuation: True
is symbol: False
```

```
Enter a character: m
is digit: False
is letter: True
is letter or digit: True
is lower case: True
is upper case: False
to upper case: M
to lower case: m
is punctuation: False
is symbol: False
```

Fig. 16.15 | Char's static character-testing and case-conversion methods. (Part 2 of 3.)

```
Enter a character: +
is digit: False
is letter: False
is letter or digit: False
is lower case: False
is upper case: False
to upper case: +
to lower case: +
is punctuation: False
is symbol: True
```

Fig. 16.15 | Char's `static` character-testing and case-conversion methods. (Part 3 of 3.)

After the user enters a character, lines 13–27 analyze it. Line 13 uses Char method `IsDigit` to determine whether `character` is defined as a digit. If so, the method returns `true`; otherwise, it returns `false` (note again that `bool` values are output capitalized). Line 14 uses Char method `IsLetter` to determine whether character `character` is a letter. Line 16 uses Char method `IsLetterOrDigit` to determine whether character `character` is a letter or a digit.

Line 18 uses Char method `IsLower` to determine whether character `character` is a *lowercase* letter. Line 20 uses Char method `IsUpper` to determine whether character `character` is an *uppercase* letter. Line 22 uses Char method `ToUpper` to convert character `character` to its *uppercase* equivalent. The method returns the converted character if the character has an uppercase equivalent; otherwise, the method returns its *original* argument. Line 24 uses Char method `ToLower` to convert character `character` to its *lowercase* equivalent. The method returns the converted character if the character has a lowercase equivalent; otherwise, the method returns its *original* argument.

Line 26 uses Char method `IsPunctuation` to determine whether `character` is a punctuation mark, such as "!", ":" or ")". Line 27 uses Char method `IsSymbol` to determine whether character `character` is a symbol, such as "+", "=" or "^".

Structure type Char also contains other methods not shown in this example. Many of the `static` methods are similar—for instance, `IsWhiteSpace` is used to determine whether a certain character is a whitespace character (e.g., newline, tab or space). The `struct` also contains several `public` instance methods; many of these, such as methods `ToString` and `Equals`, are methods that we have seen before in other classes. This group includes method `CompareTo`, which is used to compare one character value with another.

16.15 (Online) Introduction to Regular Expressions

This online section is available via the book's website. In this section, we introduce **regular expressions**—specially formatted strings used to find patterns in text. They can be used to ensure that data is in a particular format. For example, a U.S. zip code must consist of five digits, or five digits followed by a dash followed by four more digits. Compilers use regular expressions to *validate* program syntax. If the program code does *not* match the regular expression, the compiler indicates that there's a syntax error. We discuss classes Regex and Match from the System.Text.RegularExpressions namespace as well as the symbols used to form regular expressions. We then demonstrate how to find patterns in a string, match entire strings to patterns, replace characters in a string that match a pattern and split strings at delimiters specified as a pattern in a regular expression.

16.16 Wrap-Up

In this chapter, you learned about the Framework Class Library's string- and character-processing capabilities. We overviewed the fundamentals of characters and strings. You saw how to determine the length of strings, copy strings, access the individual characters in strings, search strings, obtain substrings from larger strings, compare strings, concatenate strings, replace characters in strings and convert strings to uppercase or lowercase letters.

We showed how to use class `StringBuilder` to build strings dynamically. You learned how to determine and specify the size of a `StringBuilder` object, and how to append, insert, remove and replace characters in a `StringBuilder` object. We then introduced the character-testing methods of type `Char` that enable a program to determine whether a character is a digit, a letter, a lowercase letter, an uppercase letter, a punctuation mark or a symbol other than a punctuation mark, and the methods for converting a character to uppercase or lowercase.

In the online `Regex` section, we discussed classes `Regex`, `Match` and `MatchCollection` from namespace `System.Text.RegularExpressions` and the symbols that are used to form regular expressions. You learned how to find patterns in a `string` and match entire `strings` to patterns with `Regex` methods `Match` and `Matches`, how to replace characters in a `string` with `Regex` method `Replace` and how to split `strings` at delimiters with `Regex` method `Split`. In the next chapter, you'll learn how to read data from and write data to files.

17

Files and Streams

Objectives

In this chapter you'll:

- Create, read, write and update files.

- Use classes `File` and `Directory` to obtain information about files and directories on your computer.

- Use LINQ to search through directories.

- Become familiar with sequential-access file processing.

- Use classes `FileStream`, `StreamReader` and `StreamWriter` to read text from and write text to files.

- Use classes `FileStream` and `BinaryFormatter` to read objects from and write objects to files.

17.1 Introduction

Variables and arrays offer only *temporary* storage of data—the data is lost when a local variable "goes out of scope" or when the program terminates. By contrast, **files** (and databases, which we cover in Chapter 20) are used for long-term retention of large amounts of data, even after the program that created the data terminates. Data maintained in files often is called **persistent data**. Computers store files on **secondary storage devices**, such as magnetic disks, optical disks, flash memory and magnetic tapes. In this chapter, we explain how to create, update and process data files in C# programs.

We begin with an overview of the data hierarchy from bits to files. Next, we overview some of the Framework Class Library's file-processing classes. We then present examples that show how you can determine information about the files and directories on your computer. The remainder of the chapter shows how to write to and read from *text files* that are *human readable* and binary files that store entire objects in binary format.

17.2 Data Hierarchy

Ultimately, all data items that computers process are reduced to combinations of 0s and 1s. This occurs because it's simple and economical to build electronic devices that can assume two stable states—one state represents 0 and the other represents 1. It's remarkable that the impressive functions performed by computers involve only the most fundamental manipulations of 0s and 1s.

Bits

The smallest data item that computers support is called a **bit** (short for "**binary digit**"—a digit that can assume one of *two* values). Each bit can assume either the value 0 or the value 1. Computer circuitry performs various simple **bit manipulations**, such as examining the value of a bit, setting the value of a bit and reversing a bit (from 1 to 0 or from 0 to 1).

Characters

Programming with data in the low-level form of bits is cumbersome. It's preferable to program with data in forms such as **decimal digits** (i.e., 0, 1, 2, 3, 4, 5, 6, 7, 8 and 9), **letters** (i.e., A–Z and a–z) and **special symbols** (i.e., $, @, %, &, *, (,), -, +, ", :, ?, / and many others). Digits, letters and special symbols are referred to as **characters**. The set of all characters used to write programs and represent data items on a particular computer is called that computer's **character set**. Because computers can process only 0s and 1s, every character in a computer's character set is represented as a pattern of 0s and 1s. **Bytes** are composed of eight bits. C# uses the **Unicode® character set** (www.unicode.org). Programmers create programs and data items with characters; computers manipulate and process these characters as patterns of bits.

Fields
Just as characters are composed of bits, fields are composed of characters. A **field** is a group of characters that conveys meaning. For example, a field consisting of uppercase and lowercase letters can represent a person's name.

Data items processed by computers form a **data hierarchy** (Fig. 17.1), in which data items become larger and more complex in structure as we progress from bits to characters to fields to larger data aggregates.

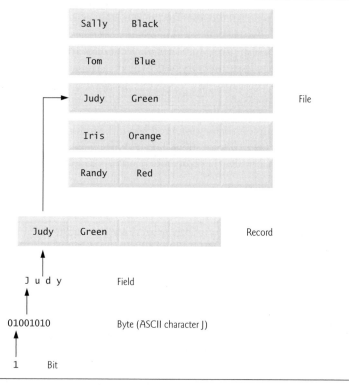

Fig. 17.1 | Data hierarchy.

Records and Files
Typically, a **record** (which can be represented as a class) is composed of several related fields. In a payroll system, for example, a record for a particular employee might include the following fields:

1. Employee identification number
2. Name

3. Address

4. Hourly pay rate

5. Number of exemptions claimed

6. Year-to-date earnings

7. Amount of taxes withheld

In the preceding example, each field is associated with the same employee. A file is a group of related records.[1] A company's payroll file normally contains one record for each employee. A payroll file for a small company might contain only 22 records, whereas one for a large company might contain 100,000. It's not unusual for a company to have many files, some containing millions, billions or even trillions of characters of information.

Record Key

To facilitate the retrieval of specific records from a file, at least one field in each record is chosen as a **record key**, which identifies a record as belonging to a particular person or entity and distinguishes that record from all others. For example, in a payroll record, the employee identification number normally would be the record key.

Sequential Files

There are many ways to organize records in a file. A common organization is called a **sequential file,** in which records typically are stored in order by a *record-key field*. In a payroll file, records usually are placed in order by employee identification number. The first employee record in the file contains the lowest employee identification number, and subsequent records contain increasingly higher ones.

Databases

Most businesses use many different files to store data. For example, a company might have payroll files, accounts-receivable files (listing money due from clients), accounts-payable files (listing money due to suppliers), inventory files (listing facts about all the items handled by the business) and many other files. Related data are often stored in a **database.** A collection of programs designed to create and manage databases is called a **database management system (DBMS).** We discuss databases in Chapter 20.

17.3 Files and Streams

C# views each file as a sequential **stream** of bytes (Fig. 17.2). Each file ends either with an **end-of-file marker** or at a specific byte number that's recorded in a system-maintained administrative data structure. When a file is opened, an object is created and a stream is associated with the object. When a console app executes, the runtime environment creates three stream objects that are accessible via properties `Console.Out`, `Console.In` and `Console.Error`, respectively. These objects use streams to facilitate communication between a program and a particular file or device. `Console.In` refers to the **standard input stream object**, which

---

1. Generally, a file can contain arbitrary data in arbitrary formats. In some operating systems, a file is viewed as nothing more than a collection of bytes, and any organization of the bytes in a file (such as organizing the data into records) is a view created by the app programmer.

enables a program to input data from the keyboard. Console.Out refers to the **standard output stream object**, which enables a program to output data to the screen. Console.Error refers to the **standard error stream object**, which enables a program to output error messages to the screen. We've been using Console.Out and Console.In in our console apps, Console methods Write and WriteLine use Console.Out to perform output, and Console methods Read and ReadLine use Console.In to perform input.

Fig. 17.2 | C#'s view of an *n*-byte file.

There are many file-processing classes in the Framework Class Library. The **System.IO namespace** includes stream classes such as **StreamReader** (for text input from a file), **StreamWriter** (for text output to a file) and **FileStream** (for both input from and output to a file). These stream classes inherit from abstract classes **TextReader**, **TextWriter** and Stream, respectively. Actually, properties Console.In and Console.Out are of type TextReader and TextWriter, respectively. The system creates objects of TextReader and TextWriter derived classes to initialize Console properties Console.In and Console.Out.

Abstract class **Stream** provides functionality for representing streams as bytes. Classes FileStream, **MemoryStream** and **BufferedStream** (all from namespace System.IO) inherit from class Stream. Class FileStream can be used to write data to and read data from files. Class MemoryStream enables the transfer of data directly to and from memory—this is much faster than reading from and writing to external devices. Class BufferedStream uses **buffering** to transfer data to or from a stream. Buffering is an I/O performance-enhancement technique, in which each output operation is directed to a region in memory, called a **buffer**, that's large enough to hold the data from *many* output operations. Then actual transfer to the output device is performed in one large **physical output operation** each time the buffer fills. The output operations directed to the output buffer in memory often are called **logical output operations**. Buffering can also be used to speed input operations by initially reading more data than is required into a buffer, so subsequent reads get data from high-speed memory rather than a slower external device.

In this chapter, we use key stream classes to implement file-processing programs that create and manipulate sequential-access files.

17.4 Classes File and Directory

Information is stored in files, which are organized in directories (also called folders). Classes File and Directory enable programs to manipulate files and directories on disk. Class **File** can determine information about files and can be used to open files for reading or writing. We discuss techniques for writing to and reading from files in subsequent sections.

Figure 17.3 lists several of class File's static methods for manipulating and determining information about files. We demonstrate several of these methods in Fig. 17.5.

static Method	Description
AppendText	Returns a StreamWriter that appends text to an existing file or creates a file if one does not exist.
Copy	Copies a file to a new file.
Create	Creates a file and returns its associated FileStream.
CreateText	Creates a text file and returns its associated StreamWriter.
Delete	Deletes the specified file.
Exists	Returns true if the specified file exists and false otherwise.
GetCreationTime	Returns a DateTime object representing when the file was created.
GetLastAccessTime	Returns a DateTime object representing when the file was last accessed.
GetLastWriteTime	Returns a DateTime object representing when the file was last modified.
Move	Moves the specified file to a specified location.
Open	Returns a FileStream associated with the specified file and equipped with the specified read/write permissions.
OpenRead	Returns a read-only FileStream associated with the specified file.
OpenText	Returns a StreamReader associated with the specified file.
OpenWrite	Returns a write FileStream associated with the specified file.

Fig. 17.3 | File class static methods (partial list).

Class **Directory** provides capabilities for manipulating directories. Figure 17.4 lists some of class Directory's static methods for directory manipulation. Figure 17.5 demonstrates several of these methods, as well. The **DirectoryInfo** object returned by method **CreateDirectory** contains information about a directory. Much of the information contained in class DirectoryInfo also can be accessed via the methods of class Directory.

static Method	Description
CreateDirectory	Creates a directory and returns its associated DirectoryInfo object.
Delete	Deletes the specified directory.
Exists	Returns true if the specified directory exists and false otherwise.
GetDirectories	Returns a string array containing the names of the subdirectories in the specified directory.
GetFiles	Returns a string array containing the names of the files in the specified directory.
GetCreationTime	Returns a DateTime object representing when the directory was created.
GetLastAccessTime	Returns a DateTime object representing when the directory was last accessed.
GetLastWriteTime	Returns a DateTime object representing when items were last written to the directory.
Move	Moves the specified directory to a specified location.

Fig. 17.4 | Directory class static methods.

Demonstrating Classes *File* and *Directory*

Class FileTestForm (Fig. 17.5) uses File and Directory methods to access file and directory information. The Form contains the inputTextBox, in which the user enters a file or directory name. For each key that the user presses while typing in the TextBox, the program calls inputTextBox_KeyDown (lines 19–75). If the user presses the *Enter* key (line 22), this method displays either the file's or directory's contents, depending on the text the user input. (If the user does not press the *Enter* key, this method returns without displaying any content.) Line 28 uses File method Exists to determine whether the user-specified text is the name of an existing file. If so, line 31 invokes private method GetInformation (lines 79–97), which calls File methods GetCreationTime (line 88), GetLastWriteTime (line 92) and GetLastAccessTime (line 96) to access file information. When method GetInformation returns, line 38 instantiates a StreamReader for reading text from the file. The StreamReader constructor takes as an argument a string containing the name and path of the file to open. Line 40 calls StreamReader method ReadToEnd to read the entire contents of the file as a string, then appends the string to outputTextBox. Once the file has been read, the using block terminates and disposes of the corresponding object, which closes the file.

```
1   // Fig. 17.5: FileTestForm.cs
2   // Using classes File and Directory.
3   using System;
4   using System.Windows.Forms;
5   using System.IO;
6
7   namespace FileTest
8   {
9      // displays contents of files and directories
10     public partial class FileTestForm : Form
11     {
12        // parameterless constructor
13        public FileTestForm()
14        {
15           InitializeComponent();
16        } // end constructor
17
18        // invoked when user presses key
19        private void inputTextBox_KeyDown( object sender, KeyEventArgs e )
20        {
21           // determine whether user pressed Enter key
22           if ( e.KeyCode == Keys.Enter )
23           {
24              // get user-specified file or directory
25              string fileName = inputTextBox.Text;
26
27              // determine whether fileName is a file
28              if ( File.Exists( fileName ) )
29              {
30                 // get file's creation date, modification date, etc.
31                 GetInformation( fileName );
32                 StreamReader stream = null; // declare StreamReader
33
```

Fig. 17.5 | Using classes File and Directory. (Part 1 of 3.)

```
34                  // display file contents through StreamReader
35                  try
36                  {
37                     // obtain reader and file contents
38                     using ( stream = new StreamReader( fileName ) )
39                     {
40                        outputTextBox.AppendText( stream.ReadToEnd() );
41                     } // end using
42                  } // end try
43                  catch ( IOException )
44                  {
45                     MessageBox.Show( "Error reading from file",
46                        "File Error", MessageBoxButtons.OK,
47                        MessageBoxIcon.Error );
48                  } // end catch
49               } // end if
50               // determine whether fileName is a directory
51               else if ( Directory.Exists( fileName ) )
52               {
53                  // get directory's creation date,
54                  // modification date, etc.
55                  GetInformation( fileName );
56
57                  // obtain directory list of specified directory
58                  string[] directoryList =
59                     Directory.GetDirectories( fileName );
60
61                  outputTextBox.AppendText( "Directory contents:\n" );
62
63                  // output directoryList contents
64                  foreach ( var directory in directoryList )
65                     outputTextBox.AppendText( directory + "\n" );
66               } // end else if
67               else
68               {
69                  // notify user that neither file nor directory exists
70                  MessageBox.Show( inputTextBox.Text +
71                     " does not exist", "File Error",
72                     MessageBoxButtons.OK, MessageBoxIcon.Error );
73               } // end else
74            } // end if
75         } // end method inputTextBox_KeyDown
76
77         // get information on file or directory,
78         // and output it to outputTextBox
79         private void GetInformation( string fileName )
80         {
81            outputTextBox.Clear();
82
83            // output that file or directory exists
84            outputTextBox.AppendText( fileName + " exists\n" );
85
```

Fig. 17.5 | Using classes File and Directory. (Part 2 of 3.)

```
86              // output when file or directory was created
87              outputTextBox.AppendText( "Created: " +
88                 File.GetCreationTime( fileName ) + "\n" );
89
90              // output when file or directory was last modified
91              outputTextBox.AppendText( "Last modified: " +
92                 File.GetLastWriteTime( fileName ) + "\n" );
93
94              // output when file or directory was last accessed
95              outputTextBox.AppendText( "Last accessed: " +
96                 File.GetLastAccessTime( fileName ) + "\n" );
97           } // end method GetInformation
98        } // end class FileTestForm
99     } // end namespace FileTest
```

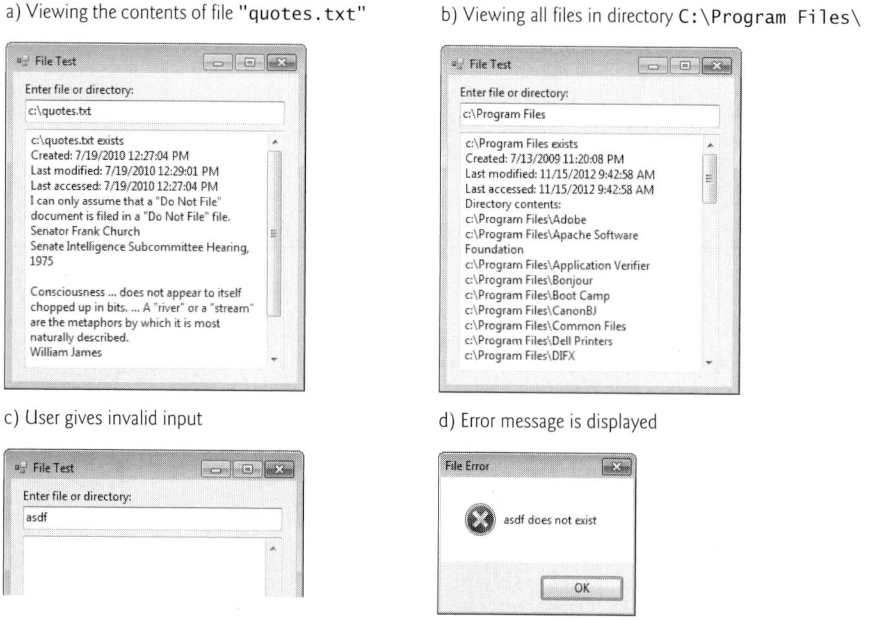

a) Viewing the contents of file `"quotes.txt"`   b) Viewing all files in directory `C:\Program Files\`

c) User gives invalid input   d) Error message is displayed

Fig. 17.5 | Using classes `File` and `Directory`. (Part 3 of 3.)

If line 28 determines that the user-specified text is not a file, line 51 determines whether it's a directory using `Directory` method **Exists**. If the user specified an *existing* directory, line 55 invokes method GetInformation to access the directory information. Line 59 calls `Directory` method **GetDirectories** to obtain a `string` array containing the names of the subdirectories in the specified directory. Lines 64–65 display each element in the `string` array. Note that, if line 51 determines that the user-specified text is *not* a directory name, lines 70–72 notify the user (via a `MessageBox`) that the name the user entered does not exist as a file or directory.

Searching Directories with LINQ
We now consider another example that uses file- and directory-manipulation capabilities. Class `LINQToFileDirectoryForm` (Fig. 17.6) uses LINQ with classes `File`, `Path` and

Directory to report the number of files of each file type that exist in the specified directory path. The program also serves as a "clean-up" utility—when it finds a file that has the .bak file-name extension (i.e., a *backup* file), the program displays a MessageBox asking the user whether that file should be removed, then responds appropriately to the user's input. This example also uses *LINQ to Objects* to help delete the backup files.

When the user clicks **Search Directory**, the program invokes searchButton_Click (lines 25–65), which searches recursively through the directory path specified by the user. If the user inputs text in the TextBox, line 29 calls Directory method Exists to determine whether that text is a valid directory. If it's not, lines 32–33 notify the user of the error.

```
1   // Fig. 17.6: LINQToFileDirectoryForm.cs
2   // Using LINQ to search directories and determine file types.
3   using System;
4   using System.Collections.Generic;
5   using System.Linq;
6   using System.Windows.Forms;
7   using System.IO;
8
9   namespace LINQToFileDirectory
10  {
11     public partial class LINQToFileDirectoryForm : Form
12     {
13        string currentDirectory; // directory to search
14
15        // store extensions found, and number of each extension found
16        Dictionary<string, int> found = new Dictionary<string, int>();
17
18        // parameterless constructor
19        public LINQToFileDirectoryForm()
20        {
21           InitializeComponent();
22        } // end constructor
23
24        // handles the Search Directory Button's Click event
25        private void searchButton_Click( object sender, EventArgs e )
26        {
27           // check whether user specified path exists
28           if ( pathTextBox.Text != string.Empty &&
29              !Directory.Exists( pathTextBox.Text ) )
30           {
31              // show error if user does not specify valid directory
32              MessageBox.Show( "Invalid Directory", "Error",
33                 MessageBoxButtons.OK, MessageBoxIcon.Error );
34           } // end if
35           else
36           {
37              // use current directory if no directory is specified
38              if ( pathTextBox.Text == string.Empty )
39                 currentDirectory = Directory.GetCurrentDirectory();
```

Fig. 17.6 | Using LINQ to search directories and determine file types. (Part 1 of 4.)

```
40              else
41                  currentDirectory = pathTextBox.Text;
42
43              directoryTextBox.Text = currentDirectory; // show directory
44
45              // clear TextBoxes
46              pathTextBox.Clear();
47              resultsTextBox.Clear();
48
49              SearchDirectory( currentDirectory ); // search the directory
50
51              // allow user to delete .bak files
52              CleanDirectory( currentDirectory );
53
54              // summarize and display the results
55              foreach ( var current in found.Keys )
56              {
57                  // display the number of files with current extension
58                  resultsTextBox.AppendText( string.Format(
59                      "* Found {0} {1} files.\r\n",
60                      found[ current ], current ) );
61              } // end foreach
62
63              found.Clear(); // clear results for new search
64          } // end else
65      } // end method searchButton_Click
66
67      // search directory using LINQ
68      private void SearchDirectory( string folder )
69      {
70          // files contained in the directory
71          string[] files = Directory.GetFiles( folder );
72
73          // subdirectories in the directory
74          string[] directories = Directory.GetDirectories( folder );
75
76          // find all file extensions in this directory
77          var extensions =
78              ( from file in files
79                select Path.GetExtension( file ) ).Distinct();
80
81          // count the number of files using each extension
82          foreach ( var extension in extensions )
83          {
84
85              // count the number of files with the extension
86              var extensionCount =
87                  ( from file in files
88                    where Path.GetExtension( file ) == extension
89                    select file ).Count();
90
91
```

Fig. 17.6 | Using LINQ to search directories and determine file types. (Part 2 of 4.)

```
92              // if the Dictionary already contains a key for the extension
93              if ( found.ContainsKey( extension ) )
94                  found[ extension ] += extensionCount; // update the count
95              else
96                  found.Add( extension, extensionCount ); // add new count
97          } // end foreach
98
99          // recursive call to search subdirectories
100         foreach ( var subdirectory in directories )
101             SearchDirectory( subdirectory );
102     } // end method SearchDirectory
103
104     // allow user to delete backup files (.bak)
105     private void CleanDirectory( string folder )
106     {
107         // files contained in the directory
108         string[] files = Directory.GetFiles( folder );
109
110         // subdirectories in the directory
111         string[] directories = Directory.GetDirectories( folder );
112
113         // select all the backup files in this directory
114         var backupFiles =
115             from file in files
116             where Path.GetExtension( file ) == ".bak"
117             select file;
118
119         // iterate over all backup files (.bak)
120         foreach ( var backup in backupFiles )
121         {
122             DialogResult result = MessageBox.Show( "Found backup file " +
123                 Path.GetFileName( backup ) + ". Delete?", "Delete Backup",
124                 MessageBoxButtons.YesNo, MessageBoxIcon.Question );
125
126             // delete file if user clicked 'yes'
127             if ( result == DialogResult.Yes )
128             {
129                 File.Delete( backup ); // delete backup file
130                 --found[ ".bak" ]; // decrement count in Dictionary
131
132                 // if there are no .bak files, delete key from Dictionary
133                 if ( found[ ".bak" ] == 0 )
134                     found.Remove( ".bak" );
135             } // end if
136         } // end foreach
137
138         // recursive call to clean subdirectories
139         foreach ( var subdirectory in directories )
140             CleanDirectory( subdirectory );
141     } // end method CleanDirectory
142 } // end class LINQToFileDirectoryForm
143 } // end namespace LINQToFileDirectory
```

Fig. 17.6 | Using LINQ to search directories and determine file types. (Part 3 of 4.)

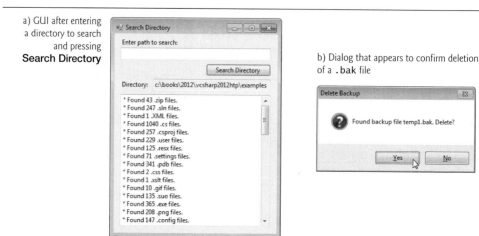

a) GUI after entering a directory to search and pressing **Search Directory**

b) Dialog that appears to confirm deletion of a `.bak` file

Fig. 17.6 | Using LINQ to search directories and determine file types. (Part 4 of 4.)

Method *SearchDirectory*

Lines 38–41 get the current directory (if the user did not specify a path) or the specified directory. Line 49 passes the directory name to *recursive* method SearchDirectory (lines 68–102). Line 71 calls Directory method **GetFiles** to get a string array containing file names in the specified directory. Line 74 calls Directory method GetDirectories to get a string array containing the subdirectory names in the specified directory.

Lines 78–79 use LINQ to get the Distinct file-name extensions in the files array. **Path** method **GetExtension** obtains the extension for the specified file name. For each file-name extension returned by the LINQ query, lines 82–97 determine the number of occurrences of that extension in the files array. The LINQ query at lines 87–89 compares each file-name extension in the files array with the current extension being processed (line 89). All matches are included in the result. We then use LINQ method Count to determine the total number of files that matched the current extension.

Class LINQToFileDirectoryForm uses a Dictionary (declared in line 16) to store each file-name extension and the corresponding number of file names with that extension. A **Dictionary** (namespace System.Collections.Generic) is a collection of *key–value pairs*, in which each *key* has a corresponding *value*. Class Dictionary is a *generic class* like class List (presented in Section 9.4). Line 16 indicates that the Dictionary found contains pairs of strings and ints, which represent the file-name extensions and the number of files with those extensions, respectively. Line 93 uses Dictionary method **ContainsKey** to determine whether the specified file-name extension has been placed in the Dictionary previously. If this method returns true, line 94 adds the extensionCount determined in lines 88–90 to the current total for that extension that's stored in the Dictionary. Otherwise, line 96 uses Dictionary method **Add** to insert a new *key–value pair* into the Dictionary for the new file-name extension and its extensionCount. Lines 100–101 recursively call SearchDirectory for each subdirectory in the current directory.

Method *CleanDirectory*

When method SearchDirectory returns, line 52 calls CleanDirectory (lines 105–141) to search for all files with extension .bak. Lines 108 and 111 obtain the list of file names and list of directory names in the current directory, respectively. The LINQ query in lines 115–117 locates all file names in the current directory that have the .bak extension. Lines 120–136 iterate through the results and ask the user whether each file should be deleted. If the user clicks **Yes** in the dialog, line 129 uses File method **Delete** to remove the file from disk, and line 130 subtracts 1 from the total number of .bak files. If the number of .bak files remaining is 0, line 134 uses Dictionary method **Remove** to delete the key–value pair for .bak files from the Dictionary. Lines 139–140 recursively call CleanDirectory for each subdirectory in the current directory. After each subdirectory has been checked for .bak files, method CleanDirectory returns, and lines 55–61 display the summary of file-name extensions and the number of files with each extension. Line 55 uses Dictionary property **Keys** to get all the keys. Line 60 uses the Dictionary's indexer to get the value for the current key. Finally, line 63 uses Dictionary method **Clear** to delete the contents of the Dictionary.

17.5 Creating a Sequential-Access Text File

C# imposes *no* structure on files. Thus, the concept of a "record" does *not* exist in C# files. This means that you must structure files to meet the requirements of your apps. The next few examples use text and special characters to organize our own concept of a "record."

Class *BankUIForm*

The following examples demonstrate file processing in a bank-account maintenance app. These programs have similar user interfaces, so we created reusable class BankUIForm (Fig. 17.7) to encapsulate a base-class GUI (see the screen capture in Fig. 17.7). Class BankUIForm (part of the BankLibrary project with this chapter's examples) contains four Labels and four TextBoxes. Methods ClearTextBoxes (lines 28–40), SetTextBoxValues (lines 43–64) and GetTextBoxValues (lines 67–78) clear, set the values of and get the values of the text in the TextBoxes, respectively.

```
1   // Fig. 17.7: BankUIForm.cs
2   // A reusable Windows Form for the examples in this chapter.
3   using System;
4   using System.Windows.Forms;
5
6   namespace BankLibrary
7   {
8      public partial class BankUIForm : Form
9      {
10        protected int TextBoxCount = 4; // number of TextBoxes on Form
11
12        // enumeration constants specify TextBox indices
13        public enum TextBoxIndices
14        {
15           ACCOUNT,
16           FIRST,
17           LAST,
18           BALANCE
19        } // end enum
20
```

Fig. 17.7 | Base class for GUIs in our file-processing apps. (Part 1 of 3.)

```
21          // parameterless constructor
22          public BankUIForm()
23          {
24             InitializeComponent();
25          } // end constructor
26
27          // clear all TextBoxes
28          public void ClearTextBoxes()
29          {
30             // iterate through every Control on form
31             foreach ( Control guiControl in Controls )
32             {
33                // determine whether Control is TextBox
34                if ( guiControl is TextBox )
35                {
36                   // clear TextBox
37                   ( ( TextBox ) guiControl ).Clear();
38                } // end if
39             } // end for
40          } // end method ClearTextBoxes
41
42          // set text box values to string-array values
43          public void SetTextBoxValues( string[] values )
44          {
45             // determine whether string array has correct length
46             if ( values.Length != TextBoxCount )
47             {
48                // throw exception if not correct length
49                throw ( new ArgumentException( "There must be " +
50                   ( TextBoxCount ) + " strings in the array" ) );
51             } // end if
52             // set array values if array has correct length
53             else
54             {
55                // set array values to TextBox values
56                accountTextBox.Text =
57                   values[ ( int ) TextBoxIndices.ACCOUNT ];
58                firstNameTextBox.Text =
59                   values[ ( int ) TextBoxIndices.FIRST ];
60                lastNameTextBox.Text = values[ ( int ) TextBoxIndices.LAST ];
61                balanceTextBox.Text =
62                   values[ ( int ) TextBoxIndices.BALANCE ];
63             } // end else
64          } // end method SetTextBoxValues
65
66          // return TextBox values as string array
67          public string[] GetTextBoxValues()
68          {
69             string[] values = new string[ TextBoxCount ];
70
71             // copy TextBox fields to string array
72             values[ ( int ) TextBoxIndices.ACCOUNT ] = accountTextBox.Text;
73             values[ ( int ) TextBoxIndices.FIRST ] = firstNameTextBox.Text;
```

Fig. 17.7 | Base class for GUIs in our file-processing apps. (Part 2 of 3.)

```
74                values[ ( int ) TextBoxIndices.LAST ] = lastNameTextBox.Text;
75                values[ ( int ) TextBoxIndices.BALANCE ] = balanceTextBox.Text;
76
77                return values;
78            } // end method GetTextBoxValues
79        } // end class BankUIForm
80    } // end namespace BankLibrary
```

Fig. 17.7 | Base class for GUIs in our file-processing apps. (Part 3 of 3.)

Using *visual inheritance* (Section 15.13), you can extend this class to create the GUIs for several examples in this chapter. Recall that to reuse class BankUIForm, you must compile the GUI into a class library, then add a reference to the new class library in each project that will reuse it. This library (BankLibrary) is provided with the code for this chapter. You might need to re-add the references to this library in our examples when you copy them to your system, since the library most likely will reside in a different location on your system.

Class *Record*
Figure 17.8 contains class Record that Figs. 17.9, 17.11 and 17.12 use for maintaining the information in each record that's written to or read from a file. This class also belongs to the BankLibrary DLL, so it's located in the same project as class BankUIForm.

```
1    // Fig. 17.8: Record.cs
2    // Class that represents a data record.
3
4    namespace BankLibrary
5    {
6        public class Record
7        {
8            // auto-implemented Account property
9            public int Account { get; set; }
10
11           // auto-implemented FirstName property
12           public string FirstName { get; set; }
13
14           // auto-implemented LastName property
15           public string LastName { get; set; }
```

Fig. 17.8 | Record for sequential-access file-processing apps. (Part 1 of 2.)

```
16
17      // auto-implemented Balance property
18      public decimal Balance { get; set; }
19
20      // parameterless constructor sets members to default values
21      public Record()
22         : this( 0, string.Empty, string.Empty, 0M )
23      {
24      } // end constructor
25
26      // overloaded constructor sets members to parameter values
27      public Record( int accountValue, string firstNameValue,
28         string lastNameValue, decimal balanceValue )
29      {
30         Account = accountValue;
31         FirstName = firstNameValue;
32         LastName = lastNameValue;
33         Balance = balanceValue;
34      } // end constructor
35   } // end class Record
36 } // end namespace BankLibrary
```

Fig. 17.8 | Record for sequential-access file-processing apps. (Part 2 of 2.)

Class Record contains *auto-implemented properties* for instance variables Account, FirstName, LastName and Balance (lines 9–18), which collectively represent all the information for a record. The parameterless constructor (lines 21–24) sets these members by calling the four-argument constructor with 0 for the account number, string.Empty for the first and last name and 0.0M for the balance. The four-argument constructor (lines 27–34) sets these members to the specified parameter values.

Using a Character Stream to Create an Output File

Class CreateFileForm (Fig. 17.9) uses instances of class Record to create a *sequential-access file* that might be used in an accounts-receivable system—i.e., a program that organizes data regarding money owed by a company's credit clients. For each client, the program obtains an account number and the client's first name, last name and balance (i.e., the amount of money that the client owes to the company for previously received goods and services). The data obtained for each client constitutes a record for that client. In this app, the account number is used as the *record key*—files are created and maintained in account-number order. This program assumes that the user enters records in account-number order. However, a comprehensive accounts-receivable system would provide a *sorting* capability, so the user could enter the records in any order.

```
1  // Fig. 17.9: CreateFileForm.cs
2  // Creating a sequential-access file.
3  using System;
4  using System.Windows.Forms;
5  using System.IO;
```

Fig. 17.9 | Creating and writing to a sequential-access file. (Part 1 of 5.)

```
 6   using BankLibrary;
 7
 8   namespace CreateFile
 9   {
10      public partial class CreateFileForm : BankUIForm
11      {
12         private StreamWriter fileWriter; // writes data to text file
13
14         // parameterless constructor
15         public CreateFileForm()
16         {
17            InitializeComponent();
18         } // end constructor
19
20         // event handler for Save Button
21         private void saveButton_Click( object sender, EventArgs e )
22         {
23            // create and show dialog box enabling user to save file
24            DialogResult result; // result of SaveFileDialog
25            string fileName; // name of file containing data
26
27            using ( SaveFileDialog fileChooser = new SaveFileDialog() )
28            {
29               fileChooser.CheckFileExists = false; // let user create file
30               result = fileChooser.ShowDialog();
31               fileName = fileChooser.FileName; // name of file to save data
32            } // end using
33
34            // ensure that user clicked "OK"
35            if ( result == DialogResult.OK )
36            {
37               // show error if user specified invalid file
38               if ( fileName == string.Empty )
39                  MessageBox.Show( "Invalid File Name", "Error",
40                     MessageBoxButtons.OK, MessageBoxIcon.Error );
41               else
42               {
43                  // save file via FileStream if user specified valid file
44                  try
45                  {
46                     // open file with write access
47                     FileStream output = new FileStream( fileName,
48                        FileMode.OpenOrCreate, FileAccess.Write );
49
50                     // sets file to where data is written
51                     fileWriter = new StreamWriter( output );
52
53                     // disable Save button and enable Enter button
54                     saveButton.Enabled = false;
55                     enterButton.Enabled = true;
56                  } // end try
57                  // handle exception if there's a problem opening the file
```

Fig. 17.9 | Creating and writing to a sequential-access file. (Part 2 of 5.)

```
58              catch ( IOException )
59              {
60                 // notify user if file does not exist
61                 MessageBox.Show( "Error opening file", "Error",
62                    MessageBoxButtons.OK, MessageBoxIcon.Error );
63              } // end catch
64           } // end else
65        } // end if
66     } // end method saveButton_Click
67
68     // handler for enterButton Click
69     private void enterButton_Click( object sender, EventArgs e )
70     {
71        // store TextBox values string array
72        string[] values = GetTextBoxValues();
73
74        // Record containing TextBox values to output
75        Record record = new Record();
76
77        // determine whether TextBox account field is empty
78        if ( values[ ( int ) TextBoxIndices.ACCOUNT ] != string.Empty )
79        {
80           // store TextBox values in Record and output it
81           try
82           {
83              // get account-number value from TextBox
84              int accountNumber = Int32.Parse(
85                 values[ ( int ) TextBoxIndices.ACCOUNT ] );
86
87              // determine whether accountNumber is valid
88              if ( accountNumber > 0 )
89              {
90                 // store TextBox fields in Record
91                 record.Account = accountNumber;
92                 record.FirstName = values[ ( int )
93                    TextBoxIndices.FIRST ];
94                 record.LastName = values[ ( int )
95                    TextBoxIndices.LAST ];
96                 record.Balance = Decimal.Parse(
97                    values[ ( int ) TextBoxIndices.BALANCE ] );
98
99                 // write Record to file, fields separated by commas
100                fileWriter.WriteLine(
101                   record.Account + "," + record.FirstName + "," +
102                   record.LastName + "," + record.Balance );
103             } // end if
104             else
105             {
106                // notify user if invalid account number
107                MessageBox.Show( "Invalid Account Number", "Error",
108                   MessageBoxButtons.OK, MessageBoxIcon.Error );
109             } // end else
110          } // end try
```

Fig. 17.9 | Creating and writing to a sequential-access file. (Part 3 of 5.)

```
111          // notify user if error occurs during the output operation
112          catch ( IOException )
113          {
114             MessageBox.Show( "Error Writing to File", "Error",
115                MessageBoxButtons.OK, MessageBoxIcon.Error );
116          } // end catch
117          // notify user if error occurs regarding parameter format
118          catch ( FormatException )
119          {
120             MessageBox.Show( "Invalid Format", "Error",
121                MessageBoxButtons.OK, MessageBoxIcon.Error );
122          } // end catch
123       } // end if
124
125       ClearTextBoxes(); // clear TextBox values
126    } // end method enterButton_Click
127
128    // handler for exitButton Click
129    private void exitButton_Click( object sender, EventArgs e )
130    {
131       // determine whether file exists
132       if ( fileWriter != null )
133       {
134          try
135          {
136             // close StreamWriter and underlying file
137             fileWriter.Close();
138          } // end try
139          // notify user of error closing file
140          catch ( IOException )
141          {
142             MessageBox.Show( "Cannot close file", "Error",
143                MessageBoxButtons.OK, MessageBoxIcon.Error );
144          } // end catch
145       } // end if
146
147       Application.Exit();
148    } // end method exitButton_Click
149 } // end class CreateFileForm
150 } // end namespace CreateFile
```

a) BankUI graphical user interface with three additional controls

Fig. 17.9 | Creating and writing to a sequential-access file. (Part 4 of 5.)

b) Save File dialog

Files and directories

c) Account 100,
"Nancy Brown",
saved with a
balance of -25.54

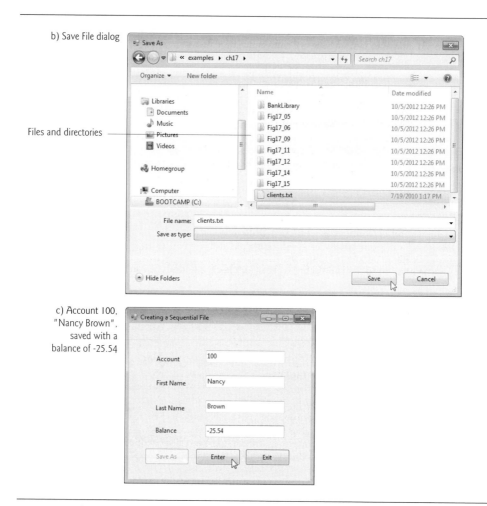

Fig. 17.9 | Creating and writing to a sequential-access file. (Part 5 of 5.)

Class `CreateFileForm` either creates or opens a file (depending on whether one exists), then allows the user to write records to it. The `using` directive in line 6 enables us to use the classes of the `BankLibrary` namespace; this namespace contains class `BankUI-Form`, from which class `CreateFileForm` inherits (line 10). Class `CreateFileForm`'s GUI enhances that of class `BankUIForm` with buttons **Save As**, **Enter** and **Exit**.

Method *saveButton_Click*

When the user clicks the **Save As** button, the program invokes the event handler `saveButton_Click` (lines 21–66). Line 27 instantiates an object of class **SaveFileDialog** (namespace `System.Windows.Forms`). By placing this object in a `using` statement (lines 27–32), we can ensure that the dialog's `Dispose` method is called to release its resources as soon as the program has retrieved user input from it. `SaveFileDialog` objects are used for selecting files (see the second screen in Fig. 17.9). Line 29 indicates that the dialog should not check if the file name specified by the user already exists (this is actually the default).

Line 30 calls SaveFileDialog method ShowDialog to display the dialog. When displayed, a SaveFileDialog prevents the user from interacting with any other window in the program until the user closes the SaveFileDialog by clicking either **Save** or **Cancel**. Dialogs that behave in this manner are called **modal dialogs**. The user selects the appropriate drive, directory and file name, then clicks **Save**. Method **ShowDialog** returns a DialogResult specifying which button (**Save** or **Cancel**) the user clicked to close the dialog. This is assigned to DialogResult variable result (line 30). Line 31 gets the file name from the dialog. Line 35 tests whether the user clicked **OK** by comparing this value to DialogResult.OK. If the values are equal, method saveButton_Click continues.

You can open files to perform text manipulation by creating objects of class FileStream. In this example, we want the file to be opened for *output*, so lines 47–48 create a FileStream object. The FileStream constructor that we use receives three arguments—a string containing the path and name of the file to open, a constant describing how to open the file and a constant describing the file permissions. The constant FileMode.OpenOrCreate (line 48) indicates that the FileStream object should open the file if it *exists* or create the file if it *does not exist*. Note that the contents of an existing file are *overwritten* by the StreamWriter. To *preserve* the original contents of a file, use FileMode.Append. There are other FileMode constants describing how to open files; we introduce these constants as we use them in examples. The constant FileAccess.Write indicates that the program can perform only *write* operations with the FileStream object. There are two other constants for the third constructor parameter—FileAccess.Read for read-only access and FileAccess.ReadWrite for both read and write access. Line 58 catches an **IOException** if there's a problem opening the file or creating the StreamWriter. If so, the program displays an error message (lines 61–62). If no exception occurs, the file is open for writing.

Good Programming Practice 17.1

When opening files, use the FileAccess enumeration to control user access to these files.

Common Programming Error 17.1

Failure to open a file before attempting to use it in a program is a logic error.

Method enterButton_Click

After typing information into each TextBox, the user clicks **Enter**, which calls enterButton_Click (lines 69–126) to save the data from the TextBoxes into the user-specified file. If the user entered a *valid* account number (i.e., an integer greater than zero), lines 91–97 store the TextBox values in an object of type Record (created at line 75). If the user entered *invalid* data in one of the TextBoxes (such as nonnumeric characters in the **Balance** field), the program throws a FormatException. The catch block in lines 118–122 handles such exceptions by notifying the user (via a MessageBox) of the improper format.

If the user entered *valid* data, lines 100–102 write the record to the file by invoking method WriteLine of the StreamWriter object that was created at line 51. Method WriteLine writes a sequence of characters to a file. The StreamWriter object is constructed with a FileStream argument that specifies the file to which the StreamWriter will output text. Class StreamWriter (like most of the classes we discuss in this chapter) belongs to the System.IO namespace.

Method exitButton_Click

When the user clicks **Exit**, exitButton_Click (lines 129–148) executes. Line 137 closes the StreamWriter, which automatically closes the FileStream. Then, line 147 terminates the program. Note that method Close is called in a try block. Method Close throws an IOException if the file or stream cannot be closed properly. In this case, it's important to notify the user that the information in the file or stream might be *corrupted*.

> ### Performance Tip 17.1
> *Close each file explicitly when the program no longer needs to use it. This can reduce resource usage in programs that continue executing long after they finish using a specific file. The practice of explicitly closing files also improves program clarity.*

> ### Performance Tip 17.2
> *Releasing resources explicitly when they're no longer needed makes them immediately available for reuse by other programs, thus improving resource utilization.*

Sample Data

To test the program, we entered information for the accounts shown in Fig. 17.10. The program does not depict how the data records are stored in the file. To verify that the file has been created successfully, we create a program in the next section to read and display the file. Since this is a *text file*, you can actually open it in any *text editor* to see its contents.

Account number	First name	Last name	Balance
100	Nancy	Brown	-25.54
200	Stacey	Dunn	314.33
300	Doug	Barker	0.00
400	Dave	Smith	258.34
500	Sam	Stone	34.98

Fig. 17.10 | Sample data for the program of Fig. 17.9.

17.6 Reading Data from a Sequential-Access Text File

The previous section demonstrated how to create a file for use in sequential-access apps. In this section, we discuss how to read (or retrieve) data sequentially from a file.

Class ReadSequentialAccessFileForm (Fig. 17.11) reads records from the file created by the program in Fig. 17.9, then displays the contents of each record. Much of the code in this example is similar to that of Fig. 17.9, so we discuss only the unique aspects of the app.

```
1   // Fig. 17.11: ReadSequentialAccessFileForm.cs
2   // Reading a sequential-access file.
3   using System;
```

Fig. 17.11 | Reading sequential-access files. (Part 1 of 4.)

```
 4   using System.Windows.Forms;
 5   using System.IO;
 6   using BankLibrary;
 7
 8   namespace ReadSequentialAccessFile
 9   {
10      public partial class ReadSequentialAccessFileForm : BankUIForm
11      {
12         private StreamReader fileReader; // reads data from a text file
13
14         // parameterless constructor
15         public ReadSequentialAccessFileForm()
16         {
17            InitializeComponent();
18         } // end constructor
19
20         // invoked when user clicks the Open button
21         private void openButton_Click( object sender, EventArgs e )
22         {
23            // create and show dialog box enabling user to open file
24            DialogResult result; // result of OpenFileDialog
25            string fileName; // name of file containing data
26
27            using ( OpenFileDialog fileChooser = new OpenFileDialog() )
28            {
29               result = fileChooser.ShowDialog();
30               fileName = fileChooser.FileName; // get specified name
31            } // end using
32
33            // ensure that user clicked "OK"
34            if ( result == DialogResult.OK )
35            {
36               ClearTextBoxes();
37
38               // show error if user specified invalid file
39               if ( fileName == string.Empty )
40                  MessageBox.Show( "Invalid File Name", "Error",
41                     MessageBoxButtons.OK, MessageBoxIcon.Error );
42               else
43               {
44                  try
45                  {
46                     // create FileStream to obtain read access to file
47                     FileStream input = new FileStream(
48                        fileName, FileMode.Open, FileAccess.Read );
49
50                     // set file from where data is read
51                     fileReader = new StreamReader( input );
52
53                     openButton.Enabled = false; // disable Open File button
54                     nextButton.Enabled = true; // enable Next Record button
55                  } // end try
```

Fig. 17.11 | Reading sequential-access files. (Part 2 of 4.)

```
56                       catch ( IOException )
57                       {
58                           MessageBox.Show( "Error reading from file",
59                               "File Error", MessageBoxButtons.OK,
60                               MessageBoxIcon.Error );
61                       } // end catch
62                   } // end else
63               } // end if
64           } // end method openButton_Click
65
66           // invoked when user clicks Next button
67           private void nextButton_Click( object sender, EventArgs e )
68           {
69               try
70               {
71                   // get next record available in file
72                   string inputRecord = fileReader.ReadLine();
73                   string[] inputFields; // will store individual pieces of data
74
75                   if ( inputRecord != null )
76                   {
77                       inputFields = inputRecord.Split( ',' );
78
79                       Record record = new Record(
80                           Convert.ToInt32( inputFields[ 0 ] ), inputFields[ 1 ],
81                           inputFields[ 2 ],
82                           Convert.ToDecimal( inputFields[ 3 ] ) );
83
84                       // copy string-array values to TextBox values
85                       SetTextBoxValues( inputFields );
86                   } // end if
87                   else
88                   {
89                       // close StreamReader and underlying file
90                       fileReader.Close();
91                       openButton.Enabled = true; // enable Open File button
92                       nextButton.Enabled = false; // disable Next Record button
93                       ClearTextBoxes();
94
95                       // notify user if no records in file
96                       MessageBox.Show( "No more records in file", string.Empty,
97                           MessageBoxButtons.OK, MessageBoxIcon.Information );
98                   } // end else
99               } // end try
100              catch ( IOException )
101              {
102                  MessageBox.Show( "Error Reading from File", "Error",
103                      MessageBoxButtons.OK, MessageBoxIcon.Error );
104              } // end catch
105          } // end method nextButton_Click
106      } // end class ReadSequentialAccessFileForm
107  } // end namespace ReadSequentialAccessFile
```

Fig. 17.11 | Reading sequential-access files. (Part 3 of 4.)

a) BankUI graphical user interface with an Open File button

b) OpenFileDialog window

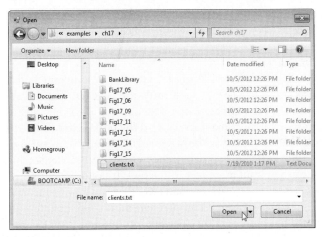

c) Reading account 100

d) User is shown a messagebox when all records have been read

Fig. 17.11 | Reading sequential-access files. (Part 4 of 4.)

Method *openButton_Click*

When the user clicks **Open File**, the program calls event handler openButton_Click (lines 21–64). Line 27 creates an **OpenFileDialog**, and line 29 calls its ShowDialog method to display the **Open** dialog (see the second screenshot in Fig. 17.11). The behavior and GUI for the **Save** and **Open** dialog types are identical, except that **Save** is replaced by **Open**. If the user selects a *valid* file name, lines 47–48 create a FileStream object and assign it to reference input. We pass constant FileMode.Open as the second argument to the FileStream constructor to indicate that the FileStream should open the file if it exists or throw a **FileNot-FoundException** if it does not. (In this example, the FileStream constructor will *not* throw a FileNotFoundException, because the OpenFileDialog is configured to check that the file exists.) In the last example (Fig. 17.9), we wrote text to the file using a FileStream object with *write-only access*. In this example (Fig. 17.11), we specify *read-only access* to the file by passing constant FileAccess.Read as the third argument to the FileStream constructor. This FileStream object is used to create a StreamReader object in line 51. The FileStream object specifies the file from which the StreamReader object will read text.

> **Error-Prevention Tip 17.1**
>
> *Open a file with the* FileAccess.Read *file-open mode if its contents should not be modified. This prevents unintentional modification of the contents.*

Method *nextButton_Click*

When the user clicks the **Next Record** button, the program calls event handler nextButton_Click (lines 67–105), which reads the next record from the user-specified file. (The user must click **Next Record** after opening the file to view the first record.) Line 72 calls StreamReader method ReadLine to read the next record. If an error occurs while reading the file, an IOException is thrown (caught at line 100), and the user is notified (lines 102–103). Otherwise, line 75 determines whether StreamReader method ReadLine returned null (i.e., there's no more text in the file). If not, line 77 uses method **Split** of class string to separate the stream of characters that was read from the file into tokens (strings) that represent the Record's properties—the second argument indicates that the tokens are delimited by commas in this file. These properties are then stored by constructing a Record object using the properties as arguments (lines 79–82). Line 85 displays the Record values in the TextBoxes. If ReadLine returns null, the program closes the StreamReader object (line 90), automatically closing the FileStream object, then notifies the user that there are no more records (lines 96–97).

17.7 Case Study: Credit Inquiry Program

To retrieve data *sequentially* from a file, programs normally start from the *beginning* of the file, reading consecutively until the desired data is found. It sometimes is necessary to process a file *sequentially* several times (from the *beginning* of the file) during the execution of a program. A FileStream object can *reposition* its **file-position pointer** (which contains the byte number of the next byte to be read from or written to the file) to *any* position in the file. When a FileStream object is opened, its *file-position pointer* is set to *byte position 0* (i.e., the *beginning* of the file)

We now present a program that builds on the concepts employed in Fig. 17.11. Class CreditInquiryForm (Fig. 17.12) is a credit-inquiry program that enables a credit manager to search for and display account information for those customers with credit balances (i.e., customers to whom the company owes money), zero balances (i.e., customers who do not owe the company money) and debit balances (i.e., customers who owe the company money for previously received goods and services). We use a RichTextBox in the program to display the account information. RichTextBoxes provide more functionality than regular TextBoxes—for example, RichTextBoxes offer method Find for searching individual strings and method LoadFile for displaying file contents. Classes RichTextBox and TextBox both inherit from abstract class System.Windows.Forms.TextBoxBase. In this example, we chose a RichTextBox, because it displays multiple lines of text by default, whereas a regular TextBox displays only one. Alternatively, we could have specified that a TextBox object display *multiple* lines of text by setting its Multiline property to true.

The program displays buttons that enable a credit manager to obtain credit information. The **Open File** button opens a file for gathering data. The **Credit Balances** button displays a list of accounts that have credit balances, the **Debit Balances** button displays a list of accounts that have debit balances and the **Zero Balances** button displays a list of accounts that have zero balances. The **Done** button exits the app.

```
1   // Fig. 17.12: CreditInquiryForm.cs
2   // Read a file sequentially and display contents based on
3   // account type specified by user ( credit, debit or zero balances ).
4   using System;
5   using System.Windows.Forms;
6   using System.IO;
7   using BankLibrary;
8
9   namespace CreditInquiry
10  {
11     public partial class CreditInquiryForm : Form
12     {
13        private FileStream input; // maintains the connection to the file
14        private StreamReader fileReader; // reads data from text file
15
16        // name of file that stores credit, debit and zero balances
17        private string fileName;
18
19        // parameterless constructor
20        public CreditInquiryForm()
21        {
22           InitializeComponent();
23        } // end constructor
24
25        // invoked when user clicks Open File button
26        private void openButton_Click( object sender, EventArgs e )
27        {
28           // create dialog box enabling user to open file
29           DialogResult result;
30
31           using ( OpenFileDialog fileChooser = new OpenFileDialog() )
32           {
```

Fig. 17.12 | Credit-inquiry program. (Part 1 of 5.)

```
33                    result = fileChooser.ShowDialog();
34                    fileName = fileChooser.FileName;
35                } // end using
36
37                // exit event handler if user clicked Cancel
38                if ( result == DialogResult.OK )
39                {
40                    // show error if user specified invalid file
41                    if ( fileName == string.Empty )
42                        MessageBox.Show( "Invalid File Name", "Error",
43                            MessageBoxButtons.OK, MessageBoxIcon.Error );
44                    else
45                    {
46                        // create FileStream to obtain read access to file
47                        input = new FileStream( fileName,
48                            FileMode.Open, FileAccess.Read );
49
50                        // set file from where data is read
51                        fileReader = new StreamReader( input );
52
53                        // enable all GUI buttons, except for Open File button
54                        openButton.Enabled = false;
55                        creditButton.Enabled = true;
56                        debitButton.Enabled = true;
57                        zeroButton.Enabled = true;
58                    } // end else
59                } // end if
60            } // end method openButton_Click
61
62            // invoked when user clicks credit balances,
63            // debit balances or zero balances button
64            private void getBalances_Click( object sender, System.EventArgs e )
65            {
66                // convert sender explicitly to object of type button
67                Button senderButton = ( Button ) sender;
68
69                // get text from clicked Button, which stores account type
70                string accountType = senderButton.Text;
71
72                // read and display file information
73                try
74                {
75                    // go back to the beginning of the file
76                    input.Seek( 0, SeekOrigin.Begin );
77
78                    displayTextBox.Text = "The accounts are:\r\n";
79
80                    // traverse file until end of file
81                    while ( true )
82                    {
83                        string[] inputFields; // stores individual pieces of data
84                        Record record; // store each Record as file is read
85                        decimal balance; // store each Record's balance
```

Fig. 17.12 | Credit-inquiry program. (Part 2 of 5.)

```
 86
 87                    // get next Record available in file
 88                    string inputRecord = fileReader.ReadLine();
 89
 90                    // when at the end of file, exit method
 91                    if ( inputRecord == null )
 92                       return;
 93
 94                    inputFields = inputRecord.Split( ',' ); // parse input
 95
 96                    // create Record from input
 97                    record = new Record(
 98                       Convert.ToInt32( inputFields[ 0 ] ), inputFields[ 1 ],
 99                       inputFields[ 2 ], Convert.ToDecimal(inputFields[ 3 ]));
100
101                    // store record's last field in balance
102                    balance = record.Balance;
103
104                    // determine whether to display balance
105                    if ( ShouldDisplay( balance, accountType ) )
106                    {
107                       // display record
108                       string output = record.Account + "\t" +
109                          record.FirstName + "\t" + record.LastName + "\t";
110
111                       // display balance with correct monetary format
112                       output += String.Format( "{0:F}", balance ) + "\r\n";
113
114                       // copy output to screen
115                       displayTextBox.AppendText( output );
116                    } // end if
117                 } // end while
118              } // end try
119              // handle exception when file cannot be read
120              catch ( IOException )
121              {
122                 MessageBox.Show( "Cannot Read File", "Error",
123                    MessageBoxButtons.OK, MessageBoxIcon.Error );
124              } // end catch
125           } // end method getBalances_Click
126
127           // determine whether to display given record
128           private bool ShouldDisplay( decimal balance, string accountType )
129           {
130              if ( balance > 0M )
131              {
132                 // display credit balances
133                 if ( accountType == "Credit Balances" )
134                    return true;
135              } // end if
136              else if ( balance < 0M )
137              {
```

Fig. 17.12 | Credit-inquiry program. (Part 3 of 5.)

```
138                // display debit balances
139                if ( accountType == "Debit Balances" )
140                    return true;
141            } // end else if
142            else // balance == 0
143            {
144                // display zero balances
145                if ( accountType == "Zero Balances" )
146                    return true;
147            } // end else
148
149            return false;
150        } // end method ShouldDisplay
151
152        // invoked when user clicks Done button
153        private void doneButton_Click( object sender, EventArgs e )
154        {
155            if ( input != null )
156            {
157                // close file and StreamReader
158                try
159                {
160                    // close StreamReader and underlying file
161                    fileReader.Close();
162                } // end try
163                // handle exception if FileStream does not exist
164                catch ( IOException )
165                {
166                    // notify user of error closing file
167                    MessageBox.Show( "Cannot close file", "Error",
168                        MessageBoxButtons.OK, MessageBoxIcon.Error );
169                } // end catch
170            } // end if
171
172            Application.Exit();
173        } // end method doneButton_Click
174    } // end class CreditInquiryForm
175 } // end namespace CreditInquiry
```

a) GUI when the app first executes

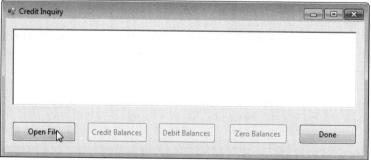

Fig. 17.12 | Credit-inquiry program. (Part 4 of 5.)

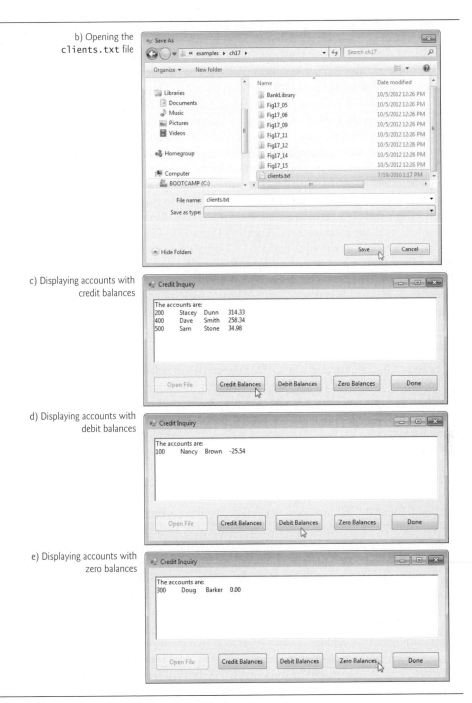

b) Opening the
clients.txt file

c) Displaying accounts with
credit balances

d) Displaying accounts with
debit balances

e) Displaying accounts with
zero balances

Fig. 17.12 | Credit-inquiry program. (Part 5 of 5.)

When the user clicks the **Open File** button, the program calls the event handler
openButton_Click (lines 26–60). Line 31 creates an OpenFileDialog, and line 33 calls its

ShowDialog method to display the **Open** dialog, in which the user selects the file to open. Lines 47–48 create a FileStream object with *read-only file access* and assign it to reference input. Line 51 creates a StreamReader object that we use to read text from the FileStream.

When the user clicks **Credit Balances**, **Debit Balances** or **Zero Balances**, the program invokes method getBalances_Click (lines 64–125). Line 67 casts the sender parameter, which is an object reference to the control that generated the event, to a Button object. Line 70 extracts the Button object's text, which the program uses to determine which type of accounts to display. Line 76 uses FileStream method **Seek** to reset the *file-position pointer* back to the *beginning* of the file. FileStream method Seek allows you to reset the *file-position pointer* by specifying the number of bytes it should be *offset* from the file's *beginning*, *end* or *current* position. The part of the file you want to be *offset* from is chosen using constants from the **SeekOrigin** enumeration. In this case, our stream is offset by 0 bytes from the file's *beginning* (SeekOrigin.Begin). Lines 81–117 define a while loop that uses private method ShouldDisplay (lines 128–150) to determine whether to display each record in the file. The while loop obtains each record by repeatedly calling StreamReader method ReadLine (line 88) and splitting the text into *tokens* (line 94) that are used to initialize object record (lines 97–99). Line 91 determines whether the *file-position pointer* has reached the end of the file, in which case ReadLine returns null. If so, the program returns from method getBalances_Click (line 92).

17.8 Serialization

Section 17.5 demonstrated how to write the individual fields of a Record object to a text file, and Section 17.6 demonstrated how to read those fields from a file and place their values in a Record object in memory. In the examples, Record was used to *aggregate* the information for one record. When the instance variables for a Record were output to a disk file, certain information was lost, such as the type of each value. For instance, if the value "3" is read from a file, there's no way to tell if the value came from an int, a string or a decimal. We have only data, not type information, on disk. If the program that's going to read this data "knows" what object type the data corresponds to, then the data can be read directly into objects of that type. For example, in Fig. 17.11, we know that we are inputting an int (the account number), followed by two strings (the first and last name) and a decimal (the balance). We also know that these values are separated by commas, with only one record on each line. So, we are able to parse the strings and convert the account number to an int and the balance to a decimal. Sometimes it would be easier to read or write entire objects. C# provides such a mechanism, called **object serialization**. A **serialized object** is an object represented as a sequence of bytes that includes the *object's data*, as well as information about the *object's type* and the *types of data stored in the object*. After a *serialized object* has been written to a file, it can be read from the file and **deserialized**—that is, the type information and bytes that represent the object and its data can be used to *recreate* the object in memory.

Class **BinaryFormatter** (namespace **System.Runtime.Serialization.Formatters. Binary**) enables entire objects to be written to or read from a stream. BinaryFormatter method **Serialize** writes an object's representation to a file. BinaryFormatter method **Deserialize** reads this representation from a file and *reconstructs* the original object. Both methods throw a **SerializationException** if an error occurs during *serialization* or *deserialization*. Both methods require a Stream object (e.g., the FileStream) as a parameter so that the BinaryFormatter can access the correct stream.

In Sections 17.9–17.10, we create and manipulate *sequential-access files* using *object serialization*. Object serialization is performed with *byte-based streams*, so the sequential files created and manipulated will be *binary files*. Binary files are not human readable. For this reason, we write a separate app that reads and displays *serialized objects*.

17.9 Creating a Sequential-Access File Using Object Serialization

We begin by creating and writing *serialized objects* to a *sequential-access file*. In this section, we reuse much of the code from Section 17.5, so we focus only on the new features.

Defining the RecordSerializable Class
Let's modify class Record (Fig. 17.8) so that objects of this class can be *serialized*. Class RecordSerializable (Fig. 17.13; part of the BankLibrary project) is marked with the **[Serializable]** attribute (line 7), which indicates to the CLR that RecordSerializable objects can be *serialized*. Classes that represent serializable types must include this attribute in their declarations or must implement *interface* **ISerializable**.

```csharp
 1   // Fig. 17.13: RecordSerializable.cs
 2   // Serializable class that represents a data record.
 3   using System;
 4
 5   namespace BankLibrary
 6   {
 7      [Serializable]
 8      public class RecordSerializable
 9      {
10         // automatic Account property
11         public int Account { get; set; }
12
13         // automatic FirstName property
14         public string FirstName { get; set; }
15
16         // automatic LastName property
17         public string LastName { get; set; }
18
19         // automatic Balance property
20         public decimal Balance { get; set; }
21
22         // default constructor sets members to default values
23         public RecordSerializable()
24            : this( 0, string.Empty, string.Empty, 0M )
25         {
26         } // end constructor
27
28         // overloaded constructor sets members to parameter values
29         public RecordSerializable( int accountValue, string firstNameValue,
30            string lastNameValue, decimal balanceValue )
31         {
32            Account = accountValue;
```

Fig. 17.13 | RecordSerializable class for serializable objects. (Part 1 of 2.)

```
33                  FirstName = firstNameValue;
34                  LastName = lastNameValue;
35                  Balance = balanceValue;
36          } // end constructor
37       } // end class RecordSerializable
38    } // end namespace BankLibrary
```

Fig. 17.13 | `RecordSerializable` class for serializable objects. (Part 2 of 2.)

In a class that's marked with the [Serializable] attribute or that implements interface ISerializable, you must ensure that every instance variable of the class is also *serializable*. All simple-type variables and strings are *serializable*. For variables of *reference types*, you must check the class declaration (and possibly its base classes) to ensure that the type is *serializable*. By default, array objects are serializable. However, if the array contains references to other objects, those objects may or may not be serializable.

Using a Serialization Stream to Create an Output File

Next, we'll create a sequential-access file with *serialization* (Fig. 17.14). To test this program, we used the sample data from Fig. 17.10 to create a file named clients.ser. Since the sample screen captures are the same as Fig. 17.9, they are not shown here. Line 15 creates a BinaryFormatter for writing *serialized objects*. Lines 53–54 open the FileStream to which this program writes the *serialized objects*. The string argument that's passed to the FileStream's constructor represents the name and path of the file to be opened. This specifies the file to which the *serialized objects* will be written.

This program assumes that data is input correctly and in the proper record-number order. Event handler enterButton_Click (lines 72–127) performs the write operation. Line 78 creates a RecordSerializable object, which is assigned values in lines 94–100. Line 103 calls method Serialize to write the RecordSerializable object to the output file. Method Serialize takes the FileStream object as the first argument so that the BinaryFormatter can write its second argument to the correct file. Only one statement is required to write the entire object. If a problem occurs during *serialization*, a SerializationException occurs—we catch this exception in lines 113–117.

In the sample execution for the program in Fig. 17.14, we entered information for five accounts—the same information shown in Fig. 17.10. The program does not show how the data records actually appear in the file. Remember that we are now using *binary files*, which are *not* human readable. To verify that the file was created successfully, the next section presents a program to read the file's contents.

```
1  // Fig. 17.14: CreateFileForm.cs
2  // Creating a sequential-access file using serialization.
3  using System;
4  using System.Windows.Forms;
5  using System.IO;
6  using System.Runtime.Serialization.Formatters.Binary;
7  using System.Runtime.Serialization;
8  using BankLibrary;
9
```

Fig. 17.14 | Sequential file created using serialization. (Part 1 of 4.)

```
10   namespace CreateFile
11   {
12      public partial class CreateFileForm : BankUIForm
13      {
14         // object for serializing RecordSerializables in binary format
15         private BinaryFormatter formatter = new BinaryFormatter();
16         private FileStream output; // stream for writing to a file
17
18         // parameterless constructor
19         public CreateFileForm()
20         {
21            InitializeComponent();
22         } // end constructor
23
24         // handler for saveButton_Click
25         private void saveButton_Click( object sender, EventArgs e )
26         {
27            // create and show dialog box enabling user to save file
28            DialogResult result;
29            string fileName; // name of file to save data
30
31            using ( SaveFileDialog fileChooser = new SaveFileDialog() )
32            {
33               fileChooser.CheckFileExists = false; // let user create file
34
35               // retrieve the result of the dialog box
36               result = fileChooser.ShowDialog();
37               fileName = fileChooser.FileName; // get specified file name
38            } // end using
39
40            // ensure that user clicked "OK"
41            if ( result == DialogResult.OK )
42            {
43               // show error if user specified invalid file
44               if ( fileName == string.Empty )
45                  MessageBox.Show( "Invalid File Name", "Error",
46                     MessageBoxButtons.OK, MessageBoxIcon.Error );
47               else
48               {
49                  // save file via FileStream if user specified valid file
50                  try
51                  {
52                     // open file with write access
53                     output = new FileStream( fileName,
54                        FileMode.OpenOrCreate, FileAccess.Write );
55
56                     // disable Save button and enable Enter button
57                     saveButton.Enabled = false;
58                     enterButton.Enabled = true;
59                  } // end try
60                  // handle exception if there's a problem opening the file
61                  catch ( IOException )
62                  {
```

Fig. 17.14 | Sequential file created using serialization. (Part 2 of 4.)

```
63              // notify user if file could not be opened
64              MessageBox.Show( "Error opening file", "Error",
65                 MessageBoxButtons.OK, MessageBoxIcon.Error );
66           } // end catch
67        } // end else
68     } // end if
69  } // end method saveButton_Click
70
71  // handler for enterButton Click
72  private void enterButton_Click( object sender, EventArgs e )
73  {
74     // store TextBox values string array
75     string[] values = GetTextBoxValues();
76
77     // RecordSerializable containing TextBox values to serialize
78     RecordSerializable record = new RecordSerializable();
79
80     // determine whether TextBox account field is empty
81     if ( values[ ( int ) TextBoxIndices.ACCOUNT ] != string.Empty )
82     {
83        // store TextBox values in RecordSerializable and serialize it
84        try
85        {
86           // get account-number value from TextBox
87           int accountNumber = Int32.Parse(
88              values[ ( int ) TextBoxIndices.ACCOUNT ] );
89
90           // determine whether accountNumber is valid
91           if ( accountNumber > 0 )
92           {
93              // store TextBox fields in RecordSerializable
94              record.Account = accountNumber;
95              record.FirstName = values[ ( int )
96                 TextBoxIndices.FIRST ];
97              record.LastName = values[ ( int )
98                 TextBoxIndices.LAST ];
99              record.Balance = Decimal.Parse( values[
100                ( int ) TextBoxIndices.BALANCE ] );
101
102             // write Record to FileStream ( serialize object )
103             formatter.Serialize( output, record );
104          } // end if
105          else
106          {
107             // notify user if invalid account number
108             MessageBox.Show( "Invalid Account Number", "Error",
109                MessageBoxButtons.OK, MessageBoxIcon.Error );
110          } // end else
111       } // end try
112       // notify user if error occurs in serialization
113       catch ( SerializationException )
114       {
```

Fig. 17.14 | Sequential file created using serialization. (Part 3 of 4.)

```
115                   MessageBox.Show( "Error Writing to File", "Error",
116                      MessageBoxButtons.OK, MessageBoxIcon.Error );
117                } // end catch
118                // notify user if error occurs regarding parameter format
119                catch ( FormatException )
120                {
121                   MessageBox.Show( "Invalid Format", "Error",
122                      MessageBoxButtons.OK, MessageBoxIcon.Error );
123                } // end catch
124             } // end if
125
126             ClearTextBoxes(); // clear TextBox values
127          } // end method enterButton_Click
128
129          // handler for exitButton Click
130          private void exitButton_Click( object sender, EventArgs e )
131          {
132             // determine whether file exists
133             if ( output != null )
134             {
135                // close file
136                try
137                {
138                   output.Close(); // close FileStream
139                } // end try
140                // notify user of error closing file
141                catch ( IOException )
142                {
143                   MessageBox.Show( "Cannot close file", "Error",
144                      MessageBoxButtons.OK, MessageBoxIcon.Error );
145                } // end catch
146             } // end if
147
148             Application.Exit();
149          } // end method exitButton_Click
150       } // end class CreateFileForm
151    } // end namespace CreateFile
```

Fig. 17.14 | Sequential file created using serialization. (Part 4 of 4.)

17.10 Reading and Deserializing Data from a Binary File

The preceding section showed how to create a *sequential-access file* using *object serialization*. In this section, we discuss how to read serialized objects sequentially from a file.

Figure 17.15 reads and displays the contents of the clients.ser file created by the program in Fig. 17.14. The sample screen captures are identical to those of Fig. 17.11, so they are not shown here. Line 15 creates the BinaryFormatter that will be used to read objects. The program opens the file for input by creating a FileStream object (lines 49–50). The name of the file to open is specified as the first argument to the FileStream constructor.

The program reads objects from a file in event handler nextButton_Click (lines 59–92). We use method Deserialize (of the BinaryFormatter created in line 15) to read the data (lines 65–66). Note that we cast the result of Deserialize to type RecordSerializ-

able (line 66)—this cast is necessary, because Deserialize returns a reference of type
object and we need to access properties that belong to class RecordSerializable. If an
error occurs during *deserialization* or the end of the file is reached, a SerializationException is thrown, and the FileStream object is closed (line 82).

```
1    // Fig. 17.15: ReadSequentialAccessFileForm.cs
2    // Reading a sequential-access file using deserialization.
3    using System;
4    using System.Windows.Forms;
5    using System.IO;
6    using System.Runtime.Serialization.Formatters.Binary;
7    using System.Runtime.Serialization;
8    using BankLibrary;
9
10   namespace ReadSequentialAccessFile
11   {
12      public partial class ReadSequentialAccessFileForm : BankUIForm
13      {
14         // object for deserializing RecordSerializable in binary format
15         private BinaryFormatter reader = new BinaryFormatter();
16         private FileStream input; // stream for reading from a file
17
18         // parameterless constructor
19         public ReadSequentialAccessFileForm()
20         {
21            InitializeComponent();
22         } // end constructor
23
24         // invoked when user clicks the Open button
25         private void openButton_Click( object sender, EventArgs e )
26         {
27            // create and show dialog box enabling user to open file
28            DialogResult result; // result of OpenFileDialog
29            string fileName; // name of file containing data
30
31            using ( OpenFileDialog fileChooser = new OpenFileDialog() )
32            {
33               result = fileChooser.ShowDialog();
34               fileName = fileChooser.FileName; // get specified name
35            } // end using
36
37            // ensure that user clicked "OK"
38            if ( result == DialogResult.OK )
39            {
40               ClearTextBoxes();
41
42               // show error if user specified invalid file
43               if ( fileName == string.Empty )
44                  MessageBox.Show( "Invalid File Name", "Error",
45                     MessageBoxButtons.OK, MessageBoxIcon.Error );
46               else
47               {
```

Fig. 17.15 | Sequential file read using deserialization. (Part 1 of 2.)

```
48                    // create FileStream to obtain read access to file
49                    input = new FileStream(
50                       fileName, FileMode.Open, FileAccess.Read );
51
52                    openButton.Enabled = false; // disable Open File button
53                    nextButton.Enabled = true;  // enable Next Record button
54                 } // end else
55              } // end if
56           } // end method openButton_Click
57
58           // invoked when user clicks Next button
59           private void nextButton_Click( object sender, EventArgs e )
60           {
61              // deserialize RecordSerializable and store data in TextBoxes
62              try
63              {
64                 // get next RecordSerializable available in file
65                 RecordSerializable record =
66                    ( RecordSerializable ) reader.Deserialize( input );
67
68                 // store RecordSerializable values in temporary string array
69                 string[] values = new string[] {
70                    record.Account.ToString(),
71                    record.FirstName.ToString(),
72                    record.LastName.ToString(),
73                    record.Balance.ToString()
74                 };
75
76                 // copy string-array values to TextBox values
77                 SetTextBoxValues( values );
78              } // end try
79              // handle exception when there are no RecordSerializables in file
80              catch ( SerializationException )
81              {
82                 input.Close(); // close FileStream
83                 openButton.Enabled = true; // enable Open File button
84                 nextButton.Enabled = false; // disable Next Record button
85
86                 ClearTextBoxes();
87
88                 // notify user if no RecordSerializables in file
89                 MessageBox.Show( "No more records in file", string.Empty,
90                    MessageBoxButtons.OK, MessageBoxIcon.Information );
91              } // end catch
92           } // end method nextButton_Click
93        } // end class ReadSequentialAccessFileForm
94     } // end namespace ReadSequentialAccessFile
```

Fig. 17.15 | Sequential file read using deserialization. (Part 2 of 2.)

17.11 Wrap-Up

In this chapter, you learned how to use file processing to manipulate persistent data. You learned that data is stored in computers as 0s and 1s, and that combinations of these values are used to form bytes, fields, records and eventually files. We overviewed several file-processing classes from the System.IO namespace. You used class File to manipulate files, and classes Directory and DirectoryInfo to manipulate directories. Next, you learned how to use sequential-access file processing to manipulate records in text files. We then discussed the differences between text-file processing and object serialization, and used serialization to store entire objects in and retrieve entire objects from files.

18

Generics

Objectives

In this chapter you'll:

- Create generic methods that perform identical tasks on arguments of different types.

- Create a generic Stack class that can be used to store objects of most types.

- Understand how to overload generic methods with nongeneric methods or with other generic methods.

- Understand the kinds of constraints that can be applied to a type parameter.

- Apply multiple constraints to a type parameter.

18.1 Introduction

Chapter 9 introduced the List generic collection. Before generics were introduced to C#, it was common to implement collections that could store object references. One inconvenient aspect of storing object references occurs when retrieving them from a collection. An app normally needs to process specific types of objects. As a result, the object references obtained from a collection typically need to be *downcast* to an appropriate type to allow the app to process the objects correctly. In addition, data of value types (e.g., int and double) must be *boxed* to be manipulated with object references, which increases the overhead of processing such data. Most importantly, processing all data as type object limits the C# compiler's ability to perform type checking.

Though we can easily create data structures that manipulate any type of data as objects, it would be nice if we could detect type mismatches at compile time—this is known as **compile-time type safety**. For example, if a Stack should store only int values, attempting to push a string onto that Stack should cause a compile-time error. Similarly, a Sort method should be able to compare elements that are all guaranteed to have the same type. If we create type-specific versions of class Stack class and method Sort, the C# compiler would certainly be able to ensure compile-time type safety. However, this would require that we create many copies of the same basic code.

This chapter discusses **generics**, which provide the means to create the general models mentioned above. **Generic methods** enable you to specify, with a *single method declaration, a set of related methods*. **Generic classes** enable you to specify, with a *single class declaration, a set of related classes*. Similarly, **generic interfaces** enable you to specify, with a *single interface declaration, a set of related interfaces*. Generics provide *compile-time type safety*. [*Note:* You can also implement generic structs and delegates.] So far in this book, we've used the generic types List (Chapter 9) and Dictionary (Chapter 17).

We can write a generic method for sorting an array of objects, then invoke the generic method separately with an int array, a double array, a string array and so on, to sort each different type of array. The compiler performs **type checking** to ensure that the array passed to the sorting method contains only elements of the correct type. We can write a single generic Stack class that manipulates a stack of objects, then instantiate Stack objects for a stack of ints, a stack of doubles, a stack of strings and so on. The compiler performs *type checking* to ensure that the Stack stores *only* elements of the correct type.

This chapter presents examples of generic methods and generic classes. It also considers the relationships between generics and other C# features, such as overloading. Chapter 19, Collections, discusses the .NET Framework's generic and nongeneric collections classes. A *collection* is a data structure that maintains a group of related objects or values. The .NET Framework collection classes use generics to allow you to specify the exact types of object that a particular collection will store.

18.2 Motivation for Generic Methods

Overloaded methods are often used to perform similar operations on different types of data. To understand the motivation for generic methods, let's begin with an example (Fig. 18.1) that contains three overloaded DisplayArray methods (lines 23–29, lines 32–38 and lines 41–47). These methods display the elements of an int array, a double array and a char array, respectively. Soon, we'll reimplement this program more concisely and elegantly using a single generic method.

```csharp
1   // Fig. 18.1: OverloadedMethods.cs
2   // Using overloaded methods to display arrays of different types.
3   using System;
4
5   class OverloadedMethods
6   {
7      static void Main( string[] args )
8      {
9         // create arrays of int, double and char
10        int[] intArray = { 1, 2, 3, 4, 5, 6 };
11        double[] doubleArray = { 1.1, 2.2, 3.3, 4.4, 5.5, 6.6, 7.7 };
12        char[] charArray = { 'H', 'E', 'L', 'L', 'O' };
13
14        Console.WriteLine( "Array intArray contains:" );
15        DisplayArray( intArray ); // pass an int array argument
16        Console.WriteLine( "Array doubleArray contains:" );
17        DisplayArray( doubleArray ); // pass a double array argument
18        Console.WriteLine( "Array charArray contains:" );
19        DisplayArray( charArray ); // pass a char array argument
20     } // end Main
21
22     // output int array
23     private static void DisplayArray( int[] inputArray )
24     {
25        foreach ( int element in inputArray )
26           Console.Write( element + " " );
27
28        Console.WriteLine( "\n" );
29     } // end method DisplayArray
30
31     // output double array
32     private static void DisplayArray( double[] inputArray )
33     {
34        foreach ( double element in inputArray )
35           Console.Write( element + " " );
36
37        Console.WriteLine( "\n" );
38     } // end method DisplayArray
```

Fig. 18.1 | Using overloaded methods to display arrays of different types. (Part 1 of 2.)

```
39
40      // output char array
41      private static void DisplayArray( char[] inputArray )
42      {
43         foreach ( char element in inputArray )
44            Console.Write( element + " " );
45
46         Console.WriteLine( "\n" );
47      } // end method DisplayArray
48   } // end class OverloadedMethods
```

```
Array intArray contains:
1 2 3 4 5 6

Array doubleArray contains:
1.1 2.2 3.3 4.4 5.5 6.6 7.7

Array charArray contains:
H E L L O
```

Fig. 18.1 | Using overloaded methods to display arrays of different types. (Part 2 of 2.)

The program begins by declaring and initializing three arrays—six-element int array intArray (line 10), seven-element double array doubleArray (line 11) and five-element char array charArray (line 12). Then, lines 14–19 output the arrays.

When the compiler encounters a method call, it attempts to locate a method declaration that has the *same* method name and parameters that *match* the argument types in the method call. In this example, each DisplayArray call exactly matches one of the Display-Array method declarations. For example, line 15 calls DisplayArray with intArray as its argument. At compile time, the compiler determines argument intArray's type (i.e., int[]), attempts to locate a method named DisplayArray that specifies a single int[] parameter (which it finds at lines 23–29) and sets up a call to that method. Similarly, when the compiler encounters the DisplayArray call at line 17, it determines argument double-Array's type (i.e., double[]), then attempts to locate a method named DisplayArray that specifies a single double[] parameter (which it finds at lines 32–38) and sets up a call to that method. Finally, when the compiler encounters the DisplayArray call at line 19, it determines argument charArray's type (i.e., char[]), then attempts to locate a method named DisplayArray that specifies a single char[] parameter (which it finds at lines 41–47) and sets up a call to that method.

Study each DisplayArray method. Note that the array element type (int, double or char) appears in two locations in each method—the method header (lines 23, 32 and 41) and the foreach statement header (lines 25, 34 and 43). If we replace the element types in each method with a generic name (such as T for "type") then all three methods would look like the one in Fig. 18.2. It appears that if we can replace the array element type in each of the three methods with a single "generic type parameter," then we should be able to declare one DisplayArray method that can display the elements of *any* array. The method in Fig. 18.2 *will not compile*, because its syntax is not correct. We declare a generic Display-Array method with the proper syntax in Fig. 18.3.

```
1    private static void DisplayArray( T[] inputArray )
2    {
3       foreach ( T element in inputArray )
4          Console.Write( element + " " );
5
6       Console.WriteLine( "\n" );
7    } // end method DisplayArray
```

Fig. 18.2 | `DisplayArray` method in which actual type names are replaced by convention with the generic name T. Again, this code will *not* compile.

18.3 Generic-Method Implementation

If the operations performed by several overloaded methods are identical for each argument type, the overloaded methods can be more compactly and conveniently coded using a generic method. You can write a single generic-method declaration that can be called at different times with arguments of different types. Based on the types of the arguments passed to the generic method, the compiler handles each method call appropriately.

Figure 18.3 reimplements the app of Fig. 18.1 using a generic `DisplayArray` method (lines 24–30). Note that the `DisplayArray` method calls in lines 16, 18 and 20 are identical to those of Fig. 18.1, the outputs of the two apps are identical and the code in Fig. 18.3 is 17 lines *shorter* than that in Fig. 18.1. As illustrated in Fig. 18.3, generics enable us to create and test our code once, then *reuse* it for many different types of data. This demonstrates the expressive power of generics.

```
1    // Fig. 18.3: GenericMethod.cs
2    // Using overloaded methods to display arrays of different types.
3    using System;
4    using System.Collections.Generic;
5
6    class GenericMethod
7    {
8       public static void Main( string[] args )
9       {
10          // create arrays of int, double and char
11          int[] intArray = { 1, 2, 3, 4, 5, 6 };
12          double[] doubleArray = { 1.1, 2.2, 3.3, 4.4, 5.5, 6.6, 7.7 };
13          char[] charArray = { 'H', 'E', 'L', 'L', 'O' };
14
15          Console.WriteLine( "Array intArray contains:" );
16          DisplayArray( intArray ); // pass an int array argument
17          Console.WriteLine( "Array doubleArray contains:" );
18          DisplayArray( doubleArray ); // pass a double array argument
19          Console.WriteLine( "Array charArray contains:" );
20          DisplayArray( charArray ); // pass a char array argument
21       } // end Main
22
```

Fig. 18.3 | Using a generic method to display arrays of different types. (Part 1 of 2.)

```
23        // output array of all types
24        private static void DisplayArray< T >( T[] inputArray )
25        {
26            foreach ( T element in inputArray )
27                Console.Write( element + " " );
28
29            Console.WriteLine( "\n" );
30        } // end method DisplayArray
31    } // end class GenericMethod
```

```
Array intArray contains:
1 2 3 4 5 6

Array doubleArray contains:
1.1 2.2 3.3 4.4 5.5 6.6 7.7

Array charArray contains:
H E L L O
```

Fig. 18.3 | Using a generic method to display arrays of different types. (Part 2 of 2.)

Line 24 begins method DisplayArray's declaration. All generic method declarations have a **type-parameter list** delimited by angle brackets (<T> in this example) that follows the method's name. Each type-parameter list contains one or more **type parameters**, separated by commas. A type parameter is an identifier that's used in place of actual type names. The type parameters can be used to declare the return type, the parameter types and the local variable types in a generic method declaration; the type parameters act as placeholders for **type arguments** that represent the types of data that will be passed to the generic method.

A generic method's body is declared like that of any other method. Note that the type-parameter names throughout the method declaration must match those declared in the type-parameter list. For example, line 26 declares element in the foreach statement as type T, which matches the type parameter (T) declared in line 24. Also, a type parameter can be declared *only once* in the type-parameter list but can appear *more than once* in the method's parameter list. Type-parameter names need *not* be unique among different generic methods.

Common Programming Error 18.1

If you forget to include the type-parameter list when declaring a generic method, the compiler will not recognize the type-parameter names when they're encountered in the method. This results in compilation errors.

Method DisplayArray's type-parameter list (line 24) declares type parameter T as the placeholder for the array-element type that DisplayArray will output. Note that T appears in the parameter list as the array-element type (line 24). The foreach statement header (line 26) also uses T as the element type. These are the same two locations where the overloaded DisplayArray methods of Fig. 18.1 specified int, double or char as the element type. The remainder of DisplayArray is identical to the version presented in Fig. 18.1.

Good Programming Practice 18.1

It's recommended that type parameters be specified as individual capital letters. Typically, a type parameter that represents the type of an element in an array (or other collection) is named E for "element" or T for "type."

As in Fig. 18.1, the program of Fig. 18.3 begins by declaring and initializing six-element int array intArray (line 11), seven-element double array doubleArray (line 12) and five-element char array charArray (line 13). Then each array is output by calling DisplayArray (lines 16, 18 and 20)—once with argument intArray, once with argument doubleArray and once with argument charArray.

When the compiler encounters a method call such as line 16, it analyzes the set of methods (both nongeneric and generic) that might match the method call, looking for a method that best matches the call. If there are no matching methods, or if there's more than one best match, the compiler generates an error. If you have any uncertainty on which of your methods will be called, the complete details of method-call resolution can be found in Section 14.5.5.1 of the ECMA C# Language Specification

```
www.ecma-international.org/publications/standards/Ecma-334.htm
```

or Section 7.5.3 of the Microsoft C# Language Specification 4

```
bit.ly/CSharp4Spec
```

In the case of line 16, the compiler determines that the best match occurs if the type parameter T in lines 24 and 26 of method DisplayArray's declaration is replaced with the type of the elements in the method call's argument intArray (i.e., int). Then, the compiler sets up a call to DisplayArray with int as the **type argument** for the type parameter T. This is known as the **type-inferencing** process. The same process is repeated for the calls to method DisplayArray in lines 18 and 20.

Common Programming Error 18.2

If the compiler cannot find a single nongeneric or generic method declaration that's a best match for a method call, or if there are multiple best matches, a compilation error occurs.

You can also use **explicit type arguments** to indicate the exact type that should be used to call a generic function. For example, line 16 could be written as

```
DisplayArray< int >( intArray ); // pass an int array argument
```

The preceding method call explicitly provides the type argument (int) that should be used to replace type parameter T in lines 24 and 26 of the DisplayArray method's declaration.

For each variable declared with a type parameter, the compiler also determines whether the operations performed on such a variable are allowed for all types that the type parameter can assume. The only operation performed on the array elements in this example is to output the string representation of the elements. Line 27 performs an *implicit* boxing conversion for every value-type array element and an *implicit* ToString call on every array element. Since all objects have a ToString method, the compiler is satisfied that line 27 performs a valid operation for any array element.

By declaring DisplayArray as a generic method in Fig. 18.3, we eliminated the need for the overloaded methods of Fig. 18.1, saving 17 lines of code and creating a *reusable* method that can output the string representations of the elements in *any* one-dimensional array, not just arrays of `int`, `double` or `char` elements.

18.4 Type Constraints

In this section, we present a generic `Maximum` method that determines and returns the largest of its three arguments (all of the same type). The generic method in this example uses the type parameter to declare *both* the method's return type *and* its parameters. Normally, when comparing values to determine which one is greater, you would use the > operator. However, this operator is not overloaded for use with every type that's built into the Framework Class Library or that might be defined by extending those types. Generic code is restricted to performing operations that are guaranteed to work for every possible type. Thus, an expression like `variable1 < variable2` is not allowed unless the compiler can ensure that the operator < is provided for every type that will ever be used in the generic code. Similarly, you cannot call a method on a generic-type variable unless the compiler can ensure that all types that will ever be used in the generic code support that method.

IComparable<T> Interface

It's possible to compare two objects of the *same* type if that type implements the generic interface **IComparable<T>** (of namespace `System`). A benefit of implementing interface IComparable<T> is that IComparable<T> objects can be used with the *sorting* and *searching* methods of classes in the `System.Collections.Generic` namespace—we discuss those methods in Chapter 19. The structures in the Framework Class Library that correspond to the simple types *all* implement this interface. For example, the structure for simple type `double` is `Double` and the structure for simple type `int` is `Int32`—both `Double` and `Int32` implement the IComparable<T> interface. Types that implement IComparable<T> must declare a `CompareTo` method for comparing objects. For example, if we have two ints, `int1` and `int2`, they can be compared with the expression:

```
int1.CompareTo( int2 )
```

Method `CompareTo` must return 0 if the objects are equal, a negative integer if `int1` is less than `int2` or a positive integer if `int1` is greater than `int2`. It's the responsibility of the programmer who declares a type that implements IComparable<T> to define method CompareTo such that it compares the contents of two objects of that type and returns the appropriate result.

Specifying Type Constraints

Even though IComparable objects can be compared, they cannot be used with generic code by default, because *not* all types implement interface IComparable<T>. However, we can restrict the types that can be used with a generic method or class to ensure that they meet certain requirements. This feature—known as a **type constraint**—restricts the type of the argument supplied to a particular type parameter. Figure 18.4 declares method `Maximum` (lines 20–34) with a type constraint that requires each of the method's arguments to be of type IComparable<T>. This restriction is important, because *not* all objects can be compared. However, all IComparable<T> objects are guaranteed to have a `CompareTo` method that can be used in method Maximum to determine the largest of its three arguments.

```
 1   // Fig. 18.4: MaximumTest.cs
 2   // Generic method Maximum returns the largest of three objects.
 3   using System;
 4
 5   class MaximumTest
 6   {
 7      public static void Main( string[] args )
 8      {
 9         Console.WriteLine( "Maximum of {0}, {1} and {2} is {3}\n",
10            3, 4, 5, Maximum( 3, 4, 5 ) );
11         Console.WriteLine( "Maximum of {0}, {1} and {2} is {3}\n",
12            6.6, 8.8, 7.7, Maximum( 6.6, 8.8, 7.7 ) );
13         Console.WriteLine( "Maximum of {0}, {1} and {2} is {3}\n",
14            "pear", "apple", "orange",
15            Maximum( "pear", "apple", "orange" ) );
16      } // end Main
17
18      // generic function determines the
19      // largest of the IComparable objects
20      private static T Maximum< T >( T x, T y, T z )
21         where T : IComparable< T >
22      {
23         T max = x; // assume x is initially the largest
24
25         // compare y with max
26         if ( y.CompareTo( max ) > 0 )
27            max = y; // y is the largest so far
28
29         // compare z with max
30         if ( z.CompareTo( max ) > 0 )
31            max = z; // z is the largest
32
33         return max; // return largest object
34      } // end method Maximum
35   } // end class MaximumTest
```

```
Maximum of 3, 4 and 5 is 5

Maximum of 6.6, 8.8 and 7.7 is 8.8

Maximum of pear, apple and orange is pear
```

Fig. 18.4 | Generic method Maximum returns the largest of three objects.

Generic method Maximum uses type parameter T as the return type of the method (line 20), as the type of method parameters x, y and z (line 20), and as the type of local variable max (line 23). Generic method Maximum's **where** clause (after the parameter list in line 21) specifies the type constraint for type parameter T. In this case, the clause where T : IComparable<T> indicates that this method requires the type argument to implement interface IComparable<T>. If no type constraint is specified, the default type constraint is object.

C# provides several kinds of type constraints. A **class constraint** indicates that the type argument must be an object of a specific base class or one of its subclasses. An **interface constraint** indicates that the type argument's class must implement a specific interface. The type constraint in line 21 is an interface constraint, because IComparable<T> is an interface. You can specify that the type argument must be a reference type or a value type by using the **reference-type constraint (class)** or the **value-type constraint (struct)**, respectively. Finally, you can specify a **constructor constraint—new()**—to indicate that the generic code can use operator new to create new objects of the type represented by the type parameter. If a type parameter is specified with a constructor constraint, the type argument's class must provide a public parameterless or default constructor to ensure that objects of the class can be created without passing constructor arguments; otherwise, a compilation error occurs.

It's possible to apply **multiple constraints** to a type parameter. To do so, simply provide a comma-separated list of constraints in the where clause. If you have a class constraint, reference-type constraint or value-type constraint, it must be listed first—only one of these types of constraints can be used for each type parameter. Interface constraints (if any) are listed next. The constructor constraint is listed last (if there is one).

Analyzing the Code
Method Maximum assumes that its first argument (x) is the largest and assigns it to local variable max (line 23). Next, the if statement at lines 26–27 determines whether y is greater than max. The condition invokes y's CompareTo method with the expression y.CompareTo(max). If y is greater than max, then y is assigned to variable max (line 27). Similarly, the statement at lines 30–31 determines whether z is greater than max. If so, line 31 assigns z to max. Then, line 33 returns max to the caller.

In Main (lines 7–16), line 10 calls Maximum with the integers 3, 4 and 5. Generic method Maximum is a match for this call, but its arguments must implement interface IComparable<T> to ensure that they can be compared. Type int is a synonym for struct Int32, which implements interface IComparable<int>. Thus, ints (and other simple types) are valid arguments to method Maximum.

Line 12 passes three double arguments to Maximum. Again, this is allowed because double is a synonym for the Double struct, which implements IComparable<double>. Line 15 passes Maximum three strings, which are also IComparable<string> objects. We intentionally placed the largest value in a different position in each method call (lines 10, 12 and 15) to show that the generic method always finds the maximum value, regardless of its position in the argument list and regardless of the inferred type argument.

18.5 Overloading Generic Methods

A generic method may be **overloaded**. Each overloaded method must have a unique signature (as discussed in Chapter 7). A class can provide two or more generic methods with the *same* name but *different* method parameters. For example, we could provide a second version of generic method DisplayArray (Fig. 18.3) with the additional parameters lowIndex and highIndex that specify the portion of the array to output.

A generic method can be overloaded by nongeneric methods with the same method name. When the compiler encounters a method call, it searches for the method declaration that best matches the method name and the argument types specified in the call. For example, generic method DisplayArray of Fig. 18.3 could be overloaded with a version specific to strings that outputs the strings in tabular format. If the compiler cannot match a method call to either a nongeneric method or a generic method, or if there's ambiguity due to multiple possible matches, the compiler generates an error.

18.6 Generic Classes

The concept of a data structure (e.g., a stack) that contains data elements can be understood independently of the element type it manipulates. A generic class provides a means for describing a class in a type-independent manner. We can then instantiate type-specific versions of the generic class. This capability is an opportunity for software reusability.

With a generic class, you can use a simple, concise notation to indicate the actual type(s) that should be used in place of the class's type parameter(s). At compilation time, the compiler ensures your code's type safety, and the runtime system replaces type parameters with type arguments to enable your client code to interact with the generic class.

One generic Stack class, for example, could be the basis for creating many Stack classes (e.g., "Stack of double," "Stack of int," "Stack of char," "Stack of Employee"). Figure 18.5 presents a generic Stack class declaration. This class should not be confused with the class Stack from namespace System.Collections.Generics. A generic class declaration is similar to a nongeneric class declaration, except that the class name is followed by a type-parameter list (line 5) and, optionally, one or more constraints on its type parameter. Type parameter T represents the element type the Stack will manipulate. As with generic methods, the type-parameter list of a generic class can have one or more type parameters separated by commas. Type parameter T is used throughout the Stack class declaration (Fig. 18.5) to represent the element type. Class Stack declares variable elements as an array of type T (line 8). This array (created at line 21) will store the Stack's elements. [*Note:* This example implements a Stack as an array. As you've seen in Chapter 19, Stacks also are commonly implemented as constrained versions of linked lists.]

```
1   // Fig. 18.5: Stack.cs
2   // Generic class Stack.
3   using System;
4
5   class Stack< T >
6   {
7      private int top; // location of the top element
8      private T[] elements; // array that stores stack elements
9
10     // parameterless constructor creates a stack of the default size
11     public Stack()
12        : this( 10 ) // default stack size
13     {
14        // empty constructor; calls constructor at line 18 to perform init
15     } // end stack constructor
16
17     // constructor creates a stack of the specified number of elements
18     public Stack( int stackSize )
19     {
20        if ( stackSize > 0 ) // validate stackSize
21           elements = new T[ stackSize ]; // create stackSize elements
22        else
23           throw new ArgumentException( "Stack size must be positive." );
```

Fig. 18.5 | Generic class Stack. (Part 1 of 2.)

```
24
25          top = -1; // stack initially empty
26      } // end stack constructor
27
28      // push element onto the stack; if unsuccessful,
29      // throw FullStackException
30      public void Push( T pushValue )
31      {
32          if ( top == elements.Length - 1 ) // stack is full
33              throw new FullStackException( string.Format(
34                  "Stack is full, cannot push {0}", pushValue ) );
35
36          ++top; // increment top
37          elements[ top ] = pushValue; // place pushValue on stack
38      } // end method Push
39
40      // return the top element if not empty,
41      // else throw EmptyStackException
42      public T Pop()
43      {
44          if ( top == -1 ) // stack is empty
45              throw new EmptyStackException( "Stack is empty, cannot pop" );
46
47          --top; // decrement top
48          return elements[ top + 1 ]; // return top value
49      } // end method Pop
50  } // end class Stack
```

Fig. 18.5 | Generic class Stack. (Part 2 of 2.)

Stack *Constructors*

Class Stack has two constructors. The parameterless constructor (lines 11–15) passes the default stack size (10) to the one-argument constructor, using the syntax this (line 12) to invoke another constructor in the same class. The one-argument constructor (lines 18–26) validates the stackSize argument and creates an array of the specified stackSize (if it's greater than 0) or throws an exception, otherwise.

Stack *Method* Push

Method Push (lines 30–38) first determines whether an attempt is being made to push an element onto a full Stack. If so, lines 33–34 throw a FullStackException (declared in Fig. 18.6). If the Stack is not full, line 36 increments the top counter to indicate the new top position, and line 37 places the argument in that location of array elements.

Stack *Method* Pop

Method Pop (lines 42–49) first determines whether an attempt is being made to pop an element from an empty Stack. If so, line 45 throws an EmptyStackException (declared in Fig. 18.7). Otherwise, line 47 decrements the top counter to indicate the new top position, and line 48 returns the original top element of the Stack.

Classes FullStackException (Fig. 18.6) and EmptyStackException (Fig. 18.7) each provide a parameterless constructor, a one-argument constructor of exception classes (as discussed in Section 13.8) and a two-argument constructor for creating a new exception using an existing one. The parameterless constructor sets the default error message while the other two constructors set custom error messages.

```
 1   // Fig. 18.6: FullStackException.cs
 2   // FullStackException indicates a stack is full.
 3   using System;
 4
 5   class FullStackException : Exception
 6   {
 7      // parameterless constructor
 8      public FullStackException() : base( "Stack is full" )
 9      {
10         // empty constructor
11      } // end FullStackException constructor
12
13      // one-parameter constructor
14      public FullStackException( string exception ) : base( exception )
15      {
16         // empty constructor
17      } // end FullStackException constructor
18
19      // two-parameter constructor
20      public FullStackException( string exception, Exception inner )
21         : base( exception, inner )
22      {
23         // empty constructor
24      } // end FullStackException constructor
25   } // end class FullStackException
```

Fig. 18.6 | `FullStackException` indicates a stack is full.

```
 1   // Fig. 18.7: EmptyStackException.cs
 2   // EmptyStackException indicates a stack is empty.
 3   using System;
 4
 5   class EmptyStackException : Exception
 6   {
 7      // parameterless constructor
 8      public EmptyStackException() : base( "Stack is empty" )
 9      {
10         // empty constructor
11      } // end EmptyStackException constructor
12
13      // one-parameter constructor
14      public EmptyStackException( string exception ) : base( exception )
15      {
16         // empty constructor
17      } // end EmptyStackException constructor
18
```

Fig. 18.7 | `EmptyStackException` indicates a stack is empty. (Part I of 2.)

```
19      // two-parameter constructor
20      public EmptyStackException( string exception, Exception inner )
21          : base( exception, inner )
22      {
23          // empty constructor
24      } // end EmptyStackException constructor
25   } // end class EmptyStackException
```

Fig. 18.7 | EmptyStackException indicates a stack is empty. (Part 2 of 2.)

As with generic methods, when a generic class is compiled, the compiler performs type checking on the class's type parameters to ensure that they can be used with the code in the generic class. The constraints determine the operations that can be performed on the type parameters. The runtime system replaces the type parameters with the actual types at runtime. For class Stack (Fig. 18.5), no type constraint is specified, so the default type constraint, object, is used. The scope of a generic class's type parameter is the entire class.

Now, let's consider an app (Fig. 18.8) that uses the Stack generic class. Lines 13–14 declare variables of type Stack<double> (pronounced "Stack of double") and Stack<int> (pronounced "Stack of int"). The types double and int are the Stack's type arguments. The compiler replaces the type parameters in the generic class so that the compiler can perform type checking. Method Main instantiates objects doubleStack of size 5 (line 18) and intStack of size 10 (line 19), then calls methods TestPushDouble (lines 28–48), TestPopDouble (lines 51–73), TestPushInt (lines 76–96) and TestPopInt (lines 99–121) to manipulate the two Stacks in this example.

```
1   // Fig. 18.8: StackTest.cs
2   // Testing generic class Stack.
3   using System;
4
5   class StackTest
6   {
7      // create arrays of doubles and ints
8      private static double[] doubleElements =
9         new double[]{ 1.1, 2.2, 3.3, 4.4, 5.5, 6.6 };
10     private static int[] intElements =
11        new int[]{ 1, 2, 3, 4, 5, 6, 7, 8, 9, 10, 11 };
12
13     private static Stack< double > doubleStack; // stack stores doubles
14     private static Stack< int > intStack; // stack stores int objects
15
16     public static void Main( string[] args )
17     {
18        doubleStack = new Stack< double >( 5 ); // stack of doubles
19        intStack = new Stack< int >( 10 ); // stack of ints
20
21        TestPushDouble(); // push doubles onto doubleStack
22        TestPopDouble(); // pop doubles from doubleStack
23        TestPushInt(); // push ints onto intStack
24        TestPopInt(); // pop ints from intStack
25     } // end Main
```

Fig. 18.8 | Testing generic class Stack. (Part 1 of 4.)

```
26
27        // test Push method with doubleStack
28        private static void TestPushDouble()
29        {
30           // push elements onto stack
31           try
32           {
33              Console.WriteLine( "\nPushing elements onto doubleStack" );
34
35              // push elements onto stack
36              foreach ( var element in doubleElements )
37              {
38                 Console.Write( "{0:F1} ", element );
39                 doubleStack.Push( element ); // push onto doubleStack
40              } // end foreach
41           } // end try
42           catch ( FullStackException exception )
43           {
44              Console.Error.WriteLine();
45              Console.Error.WriteLine( "Message: " + exception.Message );
46              Console.Error.WriteLine( exception.StackTrace );
47           } // end catch
48        } // end method TestPushDouble
49
50        // test Pop method with doubleStack
51        private static void TestPopDouble()
52        {
53           // pop elements from stack
54           try
55           {
56              Console.WriteLine( "\nPopping elements from doubleStack" );
57
58              double popValue; // store element removed from stack
59
60              // remove all elements from stack
61              while ( true )
62              {
63                 popValue = doubleStack.Pop(); // pop from doubleStack
64                 Console.Write( "{0:F1} ", popValue );
65              } // end while
66           } // end try
67           catch ( EmptyStackException exception )
68           {
69              Console.Error.WriteLine();
70              Console.Error.WriteLine( "Message: " + exception.Message );
71              Console.Error.WriteLine( exception.StackTrace );
72           } // end catch
73        } // end method TestPopDouble
74
75        // test Push method with intStack
76        private static void TestPushInt()
77        {
```

Fig. 18.8 | Testing generic class Stack. (Part 2 of 4.)

```
 78            // push elements onto stack
 79            try
 80            {
 81               Console.WriteLine( "\nPushing elements onto intStack" );
 82
 83               // push elements onto stack
 84               foreach ( var element in intElements )
 85               {
 86                  Console.Write( "{0} ", element );
 87                  intStack.Push( element ); // push onto intStack
 88               } // end foreach
 89            } // end try
 90            catch ( FullStackException exception )
 91            {
 92               Console.Error.WriteLine();
 93               Console.Error.WriteLine( "Message: " + exception.Message );
 94               Console.Error.WriteLine( exception.StackTrace );
 95            } // end catch
 96         } // end method TestPushInt
 97
 98         // test Pop method with intStack
 99         private static void TestPopInt()
100         {
101            // pop elements from stack
102            try
103            {
104               Console.WriteLine( "\nPopping elements from intStack" );
105
106               int popValue; // store element removed from stack
107
108               // remove all elements from stack
109               while ( true )
110               {
111                  popValue = intStack.Pop(); // pop from intStack
112                  Console.Write( "{0} ", popValue );
113               } // end while
114            } // end try
115            catch ( EmptyStackException exception )
116            {
117               Console.Error.WriteLine();
118               Console.Error.WriteLine( "Message: " + exception.Message );
119               Console.Error.WriteLine( exception.StackTrace );
120            } // end catch
121         } // end method TestPopInt
122      } // end class StackTest
```

```
Pushing elements onto doubleStack
1.1 2.2 3.3 4.4 5.5 6.6
Message: Stack is full, cannot push 6.6
   at Stack`1.Push(T pushValue) in
      c:\examples\ch18\Fig18_05_08\Stack\Stack\Stack.cs:line 36
   at StackTest.TestPushDouble() in
      c:\examples\ch18\Fig18_05_08\Stack\Stack\StackTest.cs:line 39
```

Fig. 18.8 | Testing generic class Stack. (Part 3 of 4.)

```
Popping elements from doubleStack
5.5 4.4 3.3 2.2 1.1
Message: Stack is empty, cannot pop
   at Stack`1.Pop() in
      c:\examples\ch18\Fig18_05_08\Stack\Stack\Stack.cs:line 47
   at StackTest.TestPopDouble() in
      c:\examples\ch18\Fig18_05_08\Stack\Stack\StackTest.cs:line 63

Pushing elements onto intStack
1 2 3 4 5 6 7 8 9 10 111
Message: Stack is full, cannot push 11
   at Stack`1.Push(T pushValue) in
      c:\examples\ch18\Fig18_05_08\Stack\Stack\Stack.cs:line 36
   at StackTest.TestPushInt() in
      c:\examples\ch18\Fig18_05_08\Stack\Stack\StackTest.cs:line 87

Popping elements from intStack
10 9 8 7 6 5 4 3 2 1
Message: Stack is empty, cannot pop
   at Stack`1.Pop() in
      c:\examples\ch18\Fig18_05_08\Stack\Stack\Stack.cs:line 47
   at StackTest.TestPopInt() in
      c:\examples\ch18\Fig18_05_08\Stack\Stack\StackTest.cs:line 111
```

Fig. 18.8 | Testing generic class Stack. (Part 4 of 4.)

Method *TestPushDouble*

Method TestPushDouble (lines 28–48) invokes method Push to place the double values 1.1, 2.2, 3.3, 4.4 and 5.5 stored in array doubleElements onto doubleStack. The foreach statement terminates when the test program attempts to Push a sixth value onto doubleStack (which is full, because doubleStack can store only five elements). In this case, the method throws a FullStackException (Fig. 18.6) to indicate that the Stack is full. Lines 42–47 catch this exception and display the message and stack-trace information. The stack trace indicates the exception that occurred and shows that Stack method Push generated the exception at line 36 of the file Stack.cs (Fig. 18.5). The trace also shows that method Push was called by StackTest method TestPushDouble at line 39 of StackTest.cs. This information enables you to determine the methods that were on the method-call stack at the time that the exception occurred. Because the program catches the exception, the C# runtime environment considers the exception to have been handled, and the program can continue executing.

Method *TestPopDouble*

Method TestPopDouble (lines 51–73) invokes Stack method Pop in an infinite while loop to remove all the values from the stack. Note in the output that the values are popped off in *last-in, first-out order*—this, of course, is the defining characteristic of stacks. The while loop (lines 61–65) continues until the stack is empty. An EmptyStackException occurs when an attempt is made to pop from the empty stack. This causes the program to proceed to the catch block (lines 67–72) and handle the exception, so the program can continue executing. When the test program attempts to Pop a sixth value, the doubleStack is empty, so method Pop throws an EmptyStackException.

Methods TestPushInt and TestPopInt
Method TestPushInt (lines 76–96) invokes Stack method Push to place values onto int-Stack until it's full. Method TestPopInt (lines 99–121) invokes Stack method Pop to remove values from intStack until it's empty. Again, values pop in last-in, first-out order.

Creating Generic Methods to Test Class Stack< T >
Note that the code in methods TestPushDouble and TestPushInt is almost identical for pushing values onto a Stack<double> or a Stack<int>, respectively. Similarly the code in methods TestPopDouble and TestPopInt is almost identical for popping values from a Stack<double> or a Stack<int>, respectively. This presents another opportunity to use generic methods. Figure 18.9 declares generic method TestPush (lines 33–54) to perform the same tasks as TestPushDouble and TestPushInt in Fig. 18.8—that is, Push values onto a Stack<T>. Similarly, generic method TestPop (lines 57–79) performs the same tasks as TestPopDouble and TestPopInt in Fig. 18.8—that is, Pop values off a Stack<T>.

```
1   // Fig. 18.9: StackTest.cs
2   // Testing generic class Stack.
3   using System;
4   using System.Collections.Generic;
5
6   class StackTest
7   {
8      // create arrays of doubles and ints
9      private static double[] doubleElements =
10        new double[] { 1.1, 2.2, 3.3, 4.4, 5.5, 6.6 };
11     private static int[] intElements =
12        new int[] { 1, 2, 3, 4, 5, 6, 7, 8, 9, 10, 11 };
13
14     private static Stack< double > doubleStack; // stack stores doubles
15     private static Stack< int > intStack; // stack stores int objects
16
17     public static void Main( string[] args )
18     {
19        doubleStack = new Stack< double >( 5 ); // stack of doubles
20        intStack = new Stack< int >( 10 ); // stack of ints
21
22        // push doubles onto doubleStack
23        TestPush( "doubleStack", doubleStack, doubleElements );
24        // pop doubles from doubleStack
25        TestPop( "doubleStack", doubleStack );
26        // push ints onto intStack
27        TestPush( "intStack", intStack, intElements );
28        // pop ints from intStack
29        TestPop( "intStack", intStack );
30     } // end Main
31
32     // test Push method
33     private static void TestPush< T >( string name, Stack< T > stack,
34        IEnumerable< T > elements )
35     {
```

Fig. 18.9 | Testing generic class Stack. (Part 1 of 3.)

```
36          // push elements onto stack
37          try
38          {
39             Console.WriteLine( "\nPushing elements onto " + name );
40
41             // push elements onto stack
42             foreach ( var element in elements )
43             {
44                Console.Write( "{0} ", element );
45                stack.Push( element ); // push onto stack
46             } // end foreach
47          } // end try
48          catch ( FullStackException exception )
49          {
50             Console.Error.WriteLine();
51             Console.Error.WriteLine( "Message: " + exception.Message );
52             Console.Error.WriteLine( exception.StackTrace );
53          } // end catch
54       } // end method TestPush
55
56       // test Pop method
57       private static void TestPop< T >( string name, Stack< T > stack )
58       {
59          // pop elements from stack
60          try
61          {
62             Console.WriteLine( "\nPopping elements from " + name );
63
64             T popValue; // store element removed from stack
65
66             // remove all elements from stack
67             while ( true )
68             {
69                popValue = stack.Pop(); // pop from stack
70                Console.Write( "{0} ", popValue );
71             } // end while
72          } // end try
73          catch ( EmptyStackException exception )
74          {
75             Console.Error.WriteLine();
76             Console.Error.WriteLine( "Message: " + exception.Message );
77             Console.Error.WriteLine( exception.StackTrace );
78          } // end catch
79       } // end TestPop
80    } // end class StackTest
```

```
Pushing elements onto doubleStack
1.1 2.2 3.3 4.4 5.5 6.6
Message: Stack is full, cannot push 6.6
   at Stack`1.Push(T pushValue)
      in c:\examples\ch18\Fig18_09\Stack\Stack\Stack.cs:line 36
   at StackTest.TestPush[T](String name, Stack`1 stack, IEnumerable`1 elements)
      in c:\examples\ch18\Fig18_09\Stack\Stack\StackTest.cs:line 45
```

Fig. 18.9 | Testing generic class Stack. (Part 2 of 3.)

```
Popping elements from doubleStack
5.5 4.4 3.3 2.2 1.1
Message: Stack is empty, cannot pop
   at Stack`1.Pop() in c:\examples\ch18\Fig18_09\Stack\Stack\Stack.cs:line 47
   at StackTest.TestPop[T](String name, Stack`1 stack) in
      c:\examples\ch18\Fig18_09\Stack\Stack\StackTest.cs:line 69

Pushing elements onto intStack
1 2 3 4 5 6 7 8 9 10 11
Message: Stack is full, cannot push 11
   at Stack`1.Push(T pushValue) in
      c:\examples\ch18\Fig18_09\Stack\Stack\Stack.cs:line 36
   at StackTest.TestPush[T](String name, Stack`1 stack, IEnumerable`1 elements)
      in c:\examples\ch18\Fig18_09\Stack\Stack\StackTest.cs:line 45

Popping elements from intStack
10 9 8 7 6 5 4 3 2 1
Message: Stack is empty, cannot pop
   at Stack`1.Pop() in c:\examples\ch18\Fig18_09\Stack\Stack\Stack.cs:line 47
   at StackTest.TestPop[T](String name, Stack`1 stack) in
      c:\examples\ch18\Fig18_09\Stack\Stack\StackTest.cs:line 69
```

Fig. 18.9 | Testing generic class Stack. (Part 3 of 3.)

Method Main (Fig. 18.9, lines 17–30) creates the Stack<double> (line 19) and Stack<int> (line 20) objects. Lines 23–29 invoke generic methods TestPush and TestPop to test the Stack objects.

Generic method TestPush (lines 33–54) uses type parameter T (specified at line 33) to represent the data type stored in the Stack. The generic method takes three arguments—a string that represents the name of the Stack object for output purposes, an object of type Stack<T> and an IEnumerable<T> that contains the elements that will be Pushed onto Stack<T>. Note that the compiler enforces consistency between the type of the Stack and the elements that will be pushed onto the Stack when Push is invoked, which is the type argument of the generic method call. Generic method TestPop (lines 57–79) takes two arguments—a string that represents the name of the Stack object for output purposes and an object of type Stack<T>.

18.7 Wrap-Up

This chapter introduced generics. We discussed how generics ensure compile-time type safety by checking for type mismatches at compile time. You learned that the compiler will allow generic code to compile only if all operations performed on the type parameters in the generic code are supported for all types that could be used with the generic code. You also learned how to declare generic methods and classes using type parameters. We demonstrated how to use a type constraint to specify the requirements for a type parameter—a key component of compile-time type safety. We discussed several kinds of type constraints, including reference-type constraints, value-type constraints, class constraints, interface constraints and constructor constraints. We also discussed how to implement multiple type constraints for a type parameter. Finally, we showed how generics improve code reuse. In the next chapter, we demonstrate the .NET Framework Class Library's collection classes, interfaces and algorithms. Collection classes are pre-built data structures that you can reuse in your apps, saving you time.

19

Collections

Objectives

In this chapter you'll:

- Learn about the nongeneric and generic collections that are provided by the .NET Framework.

- Use class **Array**'s **static** methods to manipulate arrays.

- Use enumerators to "walk through" a collection.

- Use the **foreach** statement with the .NET collections.

- Use nongeneric collection classes **ArrayList**, **Stack**, and **Hashtable**.

- Use generic collections **SortedDictionary** and **LinkedList**.

- Be introduced to covariance and contravariance for generic types.

19.1 Introduction

For the vast majority of apps, there's no need to build custom data structures. Instead, you can use the *prepackaged* data-structure classes provided by the .NET Framework. These classes are known as **collection classes**—they store collections of data. Each instance of one of these classes is a **collection** of items. Some examples of collections are the cards you hold in a card game, the songs stored in your computer, the real-estate records in your local registry of deeds (which map book numbers and page numbers to property owners), and the players on your favorite sports team.

Collection classes enable you to store sets of items by using *existing* data structures, without concern for how they're implemented. This is a nice example of code reuse. Programmers can code faster and expect excellent performance, maximizing execution speed and minimizing memory consumption. In this chapter, we discuss the collection interfaces that list the capabilities of each collection type, the implementation classes and the **enumerators** that "walk through" collections.

The .NET Framework provides several namespaces dedicated to collections. Namespace **System.Collections** contains collections that store references to objects. We included these because there's a large amount of legacy code in industry that uses these collections. Most new apps should use the collections in the **System.Collections.Generic** namespace, which contains generic classes—such as the List<T> and Dictionary<K, V> classes you learned previously—to store collections of specific types. Namespace **System.Collections.Concurrent** contains so-called thread-safe collections for use in multithreaded applications. The **System.Collections.Specialized** namespace contains several collections that support specific types, such as strings and bits. You can learn more about this namespace at msdn.microsoft.com/en-us/library/system.collections.specialized.aspx. The collections in these namespaces provide standardized, reusable components; you do not need to write your own collection classes. These collections are written for broad reuse. They're tuned for rapid execution and for efficient use of memory.

19.2 Collections Overview

All collection classes in the .NET Framework implement some combination of the collection interfaces. These interfaces declare the operations to be performed generically on various types of collections. Figure 19.1 lists some of the interfaces of the .NET Framework collections. All the interfaces in Fig. 19.1 are declared in namespace System.Collections and have generic analogs in namespace System.Collections.Generic. Implementations of these interfaces are provided within the framework. Programmers may also provide implementations specific to their own requirements.

Interface	Description
ICollection	The interface from which interfaces IList and IDictionary inherit. Contains a Count property to determine the size of a collection and a CopyTo method for copying a collection's contents into a traditional array.
IList	An ordered collection that can be manipulated like an array. Provides an indexer for accessing elements with an int index. Also has methods for searching and modifying a collection, including Add, Remove, Contains and IndexOf.
IDictionary	A collection of values, indexed by an arbitrary "key" object. Provides an indexer for accessing elements with an object index and methods for modifying the collection (e.g., Add, Remove). IDictionary property Keys contains the objects used as indices, and property Values contains all the stored objects.
IEnumerable	An object that can be enumerated. This interface contains exactly one method, GetEnumerator, which returns an IEnumerator object (discussed in Section 19.3). ICollection extends IEnumerable, so all collection classes implement IEnumerable directly or indirectly.

Fig. 19.1 | Some common collection interfaces.

Namespaces *System.Collections and System.Collections.Specialized*
In earlier versions of C#, the .NET Framework primarily provided the collection classes in the System.Collections and System.Collections.Specialized namespaces. These classes stored and manipulated object references. You could store any object in a collection. One inconvenient aspect of storing object references occurs when retrieving them from a collection. An app normally needs to process specific types of objects. As a result, the object references obtained from a collection typically need to be downcast to an appropriate type to allow the app to process the objects correctly.

Namespace *System.Collections.Generic*
The .NET Framework also includes the System.Collections.Generic namespace, which uses the generics capabilities we introduced in Chapter 18. Many of these classes are simply generic counterparts of the classes in namespace System.Collections. This means that you can specify the exact type that will be stored in a collection. You receive the benefits of *compile-time type checking*—the compiler ensures that you're using appropriate types with your collection and, if not, issues compile-time error messages. Also, once you specify the type stored in a collection, any item you retrieve from the collection will have the correct type. This *eliminates* the need for *explicit type casts* that can throw InvalidCastExceptions at execution time if the referenced object is not of the appropriate type. This also eliminates the overhead of explicit casting, improving efficiency. Generic collections are especially useful for storing structs, since they eliminate the overhead of boxing and unboxing.

This chapter demonstrates collection classes **Array**, **ArrayList**, **Stack**, **Hashtable**, generic **SortedDictionary**, and generic **LinkedList**—plus built-in array capabilities. Namespace System.Collections provides several other data structures, including **BitArray** (a collection of true/false values), **Queue** and **SortedList** (a collection of *key–value* pairs that are sorted by key and can be accessed either by key or by index). Figure 19.2 summarizes many of the collection classes. We also discuss the IEnumerator interface. Collection classes can create enumerators that allow programmers to walk through the collections. Although these enumerators have different implementations, they all implement the IEnumerator interface so that they can be processed polymorphically. As we'll soon see, the foreach statement is simply a convenient notation for using an enumerator. In the next section, we begin our discussion by examining enumerators and the capabilities for array manipulation. Collection classes directly or indirectly implement ICollection and IEnumerable (or their generic equivalents ICollection<T> and IEnumerable<T> for generic collections).

Class	Implements	Description
System namespace:		
Array	IList	The base class of all conventional arrays. See Section 19.3.
System.Collections namespace:		
ArrayList	IList	Mimics conventional arrays, but will grow or shrink as needed to accommodate the number of elements. See Section 19.4.1.
BitArray	ICollection	A memory-efficient array of bools.
Hashtable	IDictionary	An unordered collection of key–value pairs that can be accessed by key. See Section 19.4.3.
Queue	ICollection	A first-in, first-out collection.
SortedList	IDictionary	A collection of key–value pairs that are sorted by key and can be accessed either by key or by index.
Stack	ICollection	A last-in, first-out collection. See Section 19.4.2.
System.Collections.Generic namespace:		
Dictionary<K, V>	IDictionary<K, V>	A generic, unordered collection of key–value pairs that can be accessed by key. See Section 17.4.
LinkedList<T>	ICollection<T>	A doubly linked list. See Section 19.5.2.
List<T>	IList<T>	A generic ArrayList. Section 9.4.
Queue<T>	ICollection<T>	A generic Queue.
SortedDictionary<K, V>	IDictionary<K, V>	A Dictionary that sorts the data by the keys in a binary tree. See Section 19.5.1.
SortedList<K, V>	IDictionary<K, V>	A generic SortedList.
Stack<T>	ICollection<T>	A generic Stack. See Section 19.4.2.

Fig. 19.2 | Some collection classes of the .NET Framework.

19.3 Class Array and Enumerators

Chapter 8 presented basic array-processing capabilities. All arrays implicitly inherit from abstract base class Array (namespace System); this class defines property Length, which specifies the number of elements in the array. In addition, class Array provides static methods that provide algorithms for processing arrays. Typically, class Array overloads these methods—for example, Array method Reverse can reverse the order of the elements in an entire array or can reverse the elements in a specified range of elements in an array. For a complete list of class Array's static methods visit:

msdn.microsoft.com/en-us/library/system.array.aspx

Figure 19.3 demonstrates several static methods of class Array.

```
 1    // Fig. 19.3: UsingArray.cs
 2    // Array class static methods for common array manipulations.
 3    using System;
 4    using System.Collections;
 5
 6    // demonstrate algorithms of class Array
 7    public class UsingArray
 8    {
 9       private static int[] intValues = { 1, 2, 3, 4, 5, 6 };
10       private static double[] doubleValues = { 8.4, 9.3, 0.2, 7.9, 3.4 };
11       private static int[] intValuesCopy;
12
13       // method Main demonstrates class Array's methods
14       public static void Main( string[] args )
15       {
16          intValuesCopy = new int[ intValues.Length ]; // defaults to zeroes
17
18          Console.WriteLine( "Initial array values:\n" );
19          PrintArrays(); // output initial array contents
20
21          // sort doubleValues
22          Array.Sort( doubleValues );
23
24          // copy intValues into intValuesCopy
25          Array.Copy( intValues, intValuesCopy, intValues.Length );
26
27          Console.WriteLine( "\nArray values after Sort and Copy:\n" );
28          PrintArrays(); // output array contents
29          Console.WriteLine();
30
31          // search for 5 in intValues
32          int result = Array.BinarySearch( intValues, 5 );
33          if ( result >= 0 )
34             Console.WriteLine( "5 found at element {0} in intValues",
35                result );
36          else
37             Console.WriteLine( "5 not found in intValues" );
38
```

Fig. 19.3 | Array class used to perform common array manipulations. (Part 1 of 2.)

```
39          // search for 8763 in intValues
40          result = Array.BinarySearch( intValues, 8763 );
41          if ( result >= 0 )
42             Console.WriteLine( "8763 found at element {0} in intValues",
43                result );
44          else
45             Console.WriteLine( "8763 not found in intValues" );
46       } // end Main
47
48       // output array content with enumerators
49       private static void PrintArrays()
50       {
51          Console.Write( "doubleValues: " );
52
53          // iterate through the double array with an enumerator
54          IEnumerator enumerator = doubleValues.GetEnumerator();
55
56          while ( enumerator.MoveNext() )
57             Console.Write( enumerator.Current + " " );
58
59          Console.Write( "\nintValues: " );
60
61          // iterate through the int array with an enumerator
62          enumerator = intValues.GetEnumerator();
63
64          while ( enumerator.MoveNext() )
65             Console.Write( enumerator.Current + " " );
66
67          Console.Write( "\nintValuesCopy: " );
68
69          // iterate through the second int array with a foreach statement
70          foreach ( var element in intValuesCopy )
71             Console.Write( element + " " );
72
73          Console.WriteLine();
74       } // end method PrintArrays
75    } // end class UsingArray
```

```
Initial array values:

doubleValues: 8.4 9.3 0.2 7.9 3.4
intValues: 1 2 3 4 5 6
intValuesCopy: 0 0 0 0 0 0

Array values after Sort and Copy:

doubleValues: 0.2 3.4 7.9 8.4 9.3
intValues: 1 2 3 4 5 6
intValuesCopy: 1 2 3 4 5 6

5 found at element 4 in intValues
8763 not found in intValues
```

Fig. 19.3 | Array class used to perform common array manipulations. (Part 2 of 2.)

The using directives in lines 3–4 include the namespaces System (for classes Array and Console) and System.Collections (for interface IEnumerator, which we discuss shortly). References to the assemblies for these namespaces are *implicitly* included in every app, so we do not need to add any new references to the project file.

Our test class declares three static array variables (lines 9–11). The first two lines initialize intValues and doubleValues to an int and double array, respectively. static variable intValuesCopy is intended to demonstrate the Array's Copy method, so it's left with the default value null—it does not yet refer to an array.

Line 16 initializes intValuesCopy to an int array with the same length as array intValues. Line 19 calls the PrintArrays method (lines 49–74) to output the initial contents of all three arrays. We discuss the PrintArrays method shortly. We can see from the output of Fig. 19.3 that each element of array intValuesCopy is initialized to the default value 0.

Array Method *Sort*

Line 22 uses static Array method **Sort** to sort array doubleValues. When this method returns, the array contains its original elements sorted in *ascending* order. The elements in the array must implement the IComparable interface.

Array Method *Copy*

Line 25 uses static Array method **Copy** to copy elements from array intValues to array intValuesCopy. The first argument is the array to copy (intValues), the second argument is the destination array (intValuesCopy) and the third argument is an int representing the number of elements to copy (in this case, intValues.Length specifies all elements).

Array Method *BinarySearch*

Lines 32 and 40 invoke static Array method **BinarySearch** to perform binary searches on array intValues. Method BinarySearch receives the *sorted* array in which to search and the key for which to search. The method returns the index in the array at which it finds the key (or a negative number if the key was not found). BinarySearch assumes that it receives a sorted array. Its behavior on an *unsorted* array is *unpredictable*.

Array Method *GetEnumerator* and Interface *IEnumerator*

Method PrintArrays (lines 49–74) uses class Array's methods to loop though each array. The GetEnumerator method (line 54) obtains an enumerator for array doubleValues. Recall that Array implements the **IEnumerable** interface. All arrays inherit implicitly from Array, so both the int[] and double[] array types implement IEnumerable interface method **GetEnumerator**, which returns an enumerator that can *iterate* over the collection. Interface **IEnumerator** (which all enumerators implement) defines methods **MoveNext** and **Reset** and property **Current**. MoveNext moves the enumerator to the next element in the collection. The first call to MoveNext positions the enumerator at the first element of the collection. MoveNext returns true if there's at least one more element in the collection; otherwise, the method returns false. Method Reset positions the enumerator before the first element of the collection. Methods MoveNext and Reset throw an **Invalid-OperationException** if the contents of the collection are modified in any way after the enumerator is created. Property Current returns the object at the current location in the collection.

> **Common Programming Error 19.1**
>
> *If a collection is modified after an enumerator is created for that collection, the enumerator immediately becomes invalid—any methods called on the enumerator after this point throw* `InvalidOperationExceptions`. *For this reason, enumerators are said to be "fail fast."*

When an enumerator is returned by the `GetEnumerator` method in line 54, it's initially positioned *before* the first element in `Array doubleValues`. Then when line 56 calls `MoveNext` in the first iteration of the `while` loop, the enumerator advances to the first element in `doubleValues`. The `while` statement in lines 56–57 loops over each element until the enumerator passes the end of `doubleValues` and `MoveNext` returns `false`. In each iteration, we use the enumerator's `Current` property to obtain and output the current array element. Lines 62–65 iterate over array `intValues`.

Notice that `PrintArrays` is called twice (lines 19 and 28), so `GetEnumerator` is called twice on `doubleValues`. The `GetEnumerator` method (lines 54 and 62) always returns an enumerator positioned *before the first element.* Also notice that the `IEnumerator` property `Current` is read-only. Enumerators *cannot* be used to *modify* the contents of collections, only to obtain the contents.

Iterating Over a Collection with **foreach**

Lines 70–71 use a `foreach` statement to iterate over the collection elements. The `foreach` statement uses an enumerator to accomplish this task. Both loop over the elements of an array one by one in consecutive order. Neither allows you to modify the elements during the iteration. This is not a coincidence. The `foreach` statement implicitly obtains an enumerator via the `GetEnumerator` method and uses the enumerator's `MoveNext` method and `Current` property to traverse the collection, just as we did explicitly in lines 54–57. For this reason, we can use the `foreach` statement to iterate over *any* collection that implements the `IEnumerable` interface—not just arrays. We demonstrate this functionality in the next section when we discuss class `ArrayList`.

Array Methods **Clear**, **CreateInstance**, **IndexOf**, **LastIndexOf** *and* **Reverse**

Other `static Array` methods include **Clear** (to set a range of elements to 0, false or null, as appropriate), **CreateInstance** (to create a new array of a specified type), **IndexOf** (to locate the first occurrence of an object in an array or portion of an array), **LastIndexOf** (to locate the last occurrence of an object in an array or portion of an array) and **Reverse** (to reverse the contents of an array or portion of an array).

19.4 Nongeneric Collections

The `System.Collections` namespace in the .NET Framework Class Library is the primary source for *nongeneric collections*. These classes provide standard implementations of many of data structures that store references of type `object`. In this section, we demonstrate classes `ArrayList`, `Stack` and `Hashtable`.

19.4.1 Class **ArrayList**

In most programming languages, conventional arrays have a *fixed* size—they cannot be changed dynamically to conform to an app's execution-time memory requirements. In some apps, this fixed-size limitation presents a problem. You must choose between using fixed-size arrays that are large enough to store the maximum number of elements the app may require and using dynamic data structures that can grow and shrink the amount of memory required to store data in response to the changing requirements of an app at execution time.

The .NET Framework's **ArrayList** collection class mimics the functionality of conventional arrays and provides dynamic resizing of the collection through the class's methods. At any time, an ArrayList contains a certain number of elements less than or equal to its **capacity**—the number of elements currently *reserved* for the ArrayList. An app can manipulate the capacity with ArrayList property Capacity. New apps should use the generic List<T> class (the generic version of ArrayList) introduced in Chapter 9.

Performance Tip 19.1
As with linked lists, inserting additional elements into an ArrayList whose current size is less than its capacity is a fast operation.

Performance Tip 19.2
It's a slow operation to insert an element into an ArrayList that needs to grow larger to accommodate a new element. An ArrayList that's at its capacity must have its memory reallocated and the existing values copied into it.

Performance Tip 19.3
If storage is at a premium, use method TrimToSize of class ArrayList to trim an Array-List to its exact size. This will optimize an ArrayList's memory use. Be careful—if the app needs to insert additional elements, the process will be slower, because the ArrayList must grow dynamically (trimming leaves no room for growth).

ArrayLists store references to objects. All classes derive from class object, so an ArrayList can contain objects of any type. Figure 19.4 lists some useful methods and properties of class ArrayList.

Method or property	Description
Add	Adds an object to the ArrayList's end and returns an int specifying the index at which the object was added.
Capacity	Property that gets and sets the number of elements for which space is currently reserved in the ArrayList.
Clear	Removes all the elements from the ArrayList.
Contains	Returns true if the specified object is in the ArrayList; otherwise, returns false.
Count	Read-only property that gets the number of elements stored in the ArrayList.
IndexOf	Returns the index of the first occurrence of the specified object in the Array-List.
Insert	Inserts an object at the specified index.

Fig. 19.4 | Some methods and properties of class ArrayList. (Part 1 of 2.)

Method or property	Description
Remove	Removes the first occurrence of the specified object.
RemoveAt	Removes an object at the specified index.
RemoveRange	Removes a specified number of elements starting at a specified index.
Sort	Sorts the ArrayList—the elements must implement IComparable or the overloaded version of Sort that receives a IComparer must be used.
TrimToSize	Sets the Capacity of the ArrayList to the number of elements the ArrayList currently contains (Count).

Fig. 19.4 | Some methods and properties of class ArrayList. (Part 2 of 2.)

Figure 19.5 demonstrates class ArrayList and several of its methods. Class ArrayList belongs to the System.Collections namespace (line 4). Lines 8–11 declare two arrays of strings (colors and removeColors) that we'll use to fill two ArrayList objects. Recall from Section 10.10 that constants must be initialized at compile time, but readonly variables can be initialized at execution time. Arrays are objects created at execution time, so we declare colors and removeColors with readonly—not const—to make them *unmodifiable*. When the app begins execution, we create an ArrayList with an *initial capacity* of one element and store it in variable list (line 16). The foreach statement in lines 19–20 adds the five elements of array colors to list via ArrayList's **Add** method, so list *grows* to accommodate these new elements. Line 24 uses ArrayList's overloaded constructor to create a new ArrayList initialized with the contents of array removeColors, then assigns it to variable removeList. This constructor can initialize the contents of an ArrayList with the elements of any ICollection passed to it. Many of the collection classes have such a constructor. Notice that the constructor call in line 24 performs the task of lines 19–20.

Line 27 calls method DisplayInformation (lines 37–54) to output the contents of the list. This method uses a foreach statement to traverse the elements of an ArrayList. As we discussed in Section 19.3, the foreach statement is a convenient shorthand for calling ArrayList's GetEnumerator method and using an enumerator to *traverse* the elements of the collection. Also, line 40 *infers* that the iteration variable's type is object because class ArrayList is nongeneric and stores references to objects.

```
1    // Fig. 19.5: ArrayListTest.cs
2    // Using class ArrayList.
3    using System;
4    using System.Collections;
5
6    public class ArrayListTest
7    {
8       private static readonly string[] colors =
9          { "MAGENTA", "RED", "WHITE", "BLUE", "CYAN" };
10      private static readonly string[] removeColors =
11          { "RED", "WHITE", "BLUE" };
```

Fig. 19.5 | Using class ArrayList. (Part 1 of 3.)

```
12
13      // create ArrayList, add colors to it and manipulate it
14      public static void Main( string[] args )
15      {
16         ArrayList list = new ArrayList( 1 ); // initial capacity of 1
17
18         // add the elements of the colors array to the ArrayList list
19         foreach ( var color in colors )
20            list.Add( color ); // add color to the ArrayList list
21
22         // add elements in the removeColors array to
23         // the ArrayList removeList with the ArrayList constructor
24         ArrayList removeList = new ArrayList( removeColors );
25
26         Console.WriteLine( "ArrayList: " );
27         DisplayInformation( list ); // output the list
28
29         // remove from ArrayList list the colors in removeList
30         RemoveColors( list, removeList );
31
32         Console.WriteLine( "\nArrayList after calling RemoveColors: " );
33         DisplayInformation( list ); // output list contents
34      } // end Main
35
36      // displays information on the contents of an array list
37      private static void DisplayInformation( ArrayList arrayList )
38      {
39         // iterate through array list with a foreach statement
40         foreach ( var element in arrayList )
41            Console.Write( "{0} ", element ); // invokes ToString
42
43         // display the size and capacity
44         Console.WriteLine( "\nSize = {0}; Capacity = {1}",
45            arrayList.Count, arrayList.Capacity );
46
47         int index = arrayList.IndexOf( "BLUE" );
48
49         if ( index != -1 )
50            Console.WriteLine( "The array list contains BLUE at index {0}.",
51               index );
52         else
53            Console.WriteLine( "The array list does not contain BLUE." );
54      } // end method DisplayInformation
55
56      // remove colors specified in secondList from firstList
57      private static void RemoveColors( ArrayList firstList,
58         ArrayList secondList )
59      {
60         // iterate through second ArrayList like an array
61         for ( int count = 0; count < secondList.Count; ++count )
62            firstList.Remove( secondList[ count ] );
63      } // end method RemoveColors
64   } // end class ArrayListTest
```

Fig. 19.5 | Using class ArrayList. (Part 2 of 3.)

```
ArrayList:
MAGENTA RED WHITE BLUE CYAN
Size = 5; Capacity = 8
The array list contains BLUE at index 3.

ArrayList after calling RemoveColors:
MAGENTA CYAN
Size = 2; Capacity = 8
The array list does not contain BLUE.
```

Fig. 19.5 | Using class `ArrayList`. (Part 3 of 3.)

ArrayList Methods **Count** *and* **Capacity**
We use properties **Count** and **Capacity** (line 45) to display the *current number* and the *maximum number* of elements that can be stored without allocating more memory to the `ArrayList`. The output of Fig. 19.5 indicates that the `ArrayList` has capacity 8.

ArrayList Methods **IndexOf** *and* **Contains**
In line 47, we invoke method **IndexOf** to determine the position of the `string` "BLUE" in `arrayList` and store the result in local variable `index`. `IndexOf` returns -1 if the element is not found. The `if` statement in lines 49–53 checks if `index` is -1 to determine whether `arrayList` contains "BLUE". If it does, we output its index. `ArrayList` also provides method **Contains**, which simply returns `true` if an object is in the `ArrayList`, and `false` otherwise. Method `Contains` is preferred if we do not need the index of the element.

>
> **Performance Tip 19.4**
> *ArrayList methods* IndexOf *and* Contains *each perform a linear search, which is a costly operation for large* ArrayLists. *If the* ArrayList *is sorted, use* ArrayList *method* BinarySearch *to perform a more efficient search. Method* BinarySearch *returns the index of the element, or a negative number if the element is not found.*

ArrayList Method **Remove**
After method `DisplayInformation` returns, we call method `RemoveColors` (lines 57–63) with the two `ArrayLists`. The `for` statement in lines 61–62 iterates over `ArrayList` sec-ondList. Line 62 uses an indexer to access an `ArrayList` element—by following the Ar-rayList reference name with square brackets (`[]`) containing the desired index of the element. An `ArgumentOutOfRangeException` occurs if the specified index is not both greater than 0 and less than the number of elements currently stored in the `ArrayList` (specified by the `ArrayList`'s `Count` property).

We use the indexer to obtain each of `secondList`'s elements, then remove each one from `firstList` with the **Remove** method. This method deletes a specified item from an `ArrayList` by performing a *linear search* and removing (only) the first occurrence of the specified object. All subsequent elements *shift* toward the beginning of the `ArrayList` to fill the emptied position.

After the call to `RemoveColors`, line 33 again outputs the contents of `list`, confirming that the elements of `removeList` were, indeed, removed.

19.4.2 Class Stack

The Stack class implements a stack data structure. We created a test app in Fig. 19.14 to demonstrate the StackInheritance data structure that we developed. We adapt Fig. 19.14 in Fig. 19.6 to demonstrate the .NET Framework collection class Stack. New apps requiring a stack class should use the generic Stack<T> class.

```csharp
 1   // Fig. 19.6: StackTest.cs
 2   // Demonstrating class Stack.
 3   using System;
 4   using System.Collections;
 5
 6   public class StackTest
 7   {
 8      public static void Main( string[] args )
 9      {
10         Stack stack = new Stack(); // create an empty Stack
11
12         // create objects to store in the stack
13         bool aBoolean = true;
14         char aCharacter = '$';
15         int anInteger = 34567;
16         string aString = "hello";
17
18         // use method Push to add items to (the top of) the stack
19         stack.Push( aBoolean );
20         PrintStack( stack );
21         stack.Push( aCharacter );
22         PrintStack( stack );
23         stack.Push( anInteger );
24         PrintStack( stack );
25         stack.Push( aString );
26         PrintStack( stack );
27
28         // check the top element of the stack
29         Console.WriteLine( "The top element of the stack is {0}\n",
30            stack.Peek() );
31
32         // remove items from stack
33         try
34         {
35            while ( true )
36            {
37               object removedObject = stack.Pop();
38               Console.WriteLine( removedObject + " popped" );
39               PrintStack( stack );
40            } // end while
41         } // end try
42         catch ( InvalidOperationException exception )
43         {
```

Fig. 19.6 | Demonstrating class Stack. (Part 1 of 2.)

```
44              // if exception occurs, output stack trace
45              Console.Error.WriteLine( exception );
46          } // end catch
47      } // end Main
48
49      // display the contents of a stack
50      private static void PrintStack( Stack stack )
51      {
52          if ( stack.Count == 0 )
53              Console.WriteLine( "stack is empty\n" ); // the stack is empty
54          else
55          {
56              Console.Write( "The stack is: " );
57
58              // iterate through the stack with a foreach statement
59              foreach ( var element in stack )
60                  Console.Write( "{0} ", element ); // invokes ToString
61
62              Console.WriteLine( "\n" );
63          } // end else
64      } // end method PrintStack
65  } // end class StackTest
```

```
The stack is: True

The stack is: $ True

The stack is: 34567 $ True

The stack is: hello 34567 $ True

The top element of the stack is hello

hello popped
The stack is: 34567 $ True

34567 popped
The stack is: $ True

$ popped
The stack is: True

True popped
stack is empty

System.InvalidOperationException: Stack empty.
   at System.Collections.Stack.Pop()
   at StackTest.Main(String[] args) in
      c:\examples\ch23\fig23_06\StackTest\StackTest\StackTest.cs:line 37
```

Fig. 19.6 | Demonstrating class Stack. (Part 2 of 2.)

The using directive in line 4 allows us to use the Stack class with its unqualified name from the System.Collections namespace. Line 10 creates a Stack. As one might expect, class Stack has methods **Push** and **Pop** to perform the basic stack operations.

Stack *Method Push*
Method Push takes an object as an argument and inserts it at the top of the Stack. If the number of items on the Stack (the Count property) is equal to the capacity at the time of

the Push operation, the Stack *grows* to accommodate more objects. Lines 19–26 use method Push to add four elements (a bool, a char, an int and a string) to the stack and invoke method PrintStack (lines 50–64) after each Push to output the contents of the stack. Notice that this nongeneric Stack class can store only *references* to objects, so each of the value-type items—the bool, the char and the int—is *implicitly boxed* before it's added to the Stack. (Namespace System.Collections.Generic provides a generic Stack class that has many of the same methods and properties used in Fig. 19.6. This version eliminates the overhead of boxing and unboxing simple types.)

Method PrintStack
Method PrintStack (lines 50–64) uses Stack property Count (implemented to fulfill the contract of interface ICollection) to obtain the number of elements in stack. If the stack is not empty (i.e., Count is not equal to 0), we use a foreach statement to iterate over the stack and output its contents by *implicitly* invoking the ToString method of each element. The foreach statement implicitly invokes Stack's GetEnumerator method, which we could have called *explicitly* to traverse the stack via an enumerator.

Stack Method Peek
Method **Peek** returns the value of the *top* stack element but does *not* remove the element from the Stack. We use Peek at line 30 to obtain the *top* object of the Stack, then output that object, *implicitly* invoking the object's ToString method. An InvalidOperationException occurs if the Stack is empty when the app calls Peek. We do *not* need an exception-handling block because we know the stack is *not* empty here.

Stack Method Pop
Method Pop takes no arguments—it removes and returns the object currently on the Stack's top. An infinite loop (lines 35–40) pops objects off the stack and outputs them until the stack is empty. When the app calls Pop on the empty stack, an InvalidOperationException is thrown. The catch block (lines 42–46) outputs the exception, *implicitly* invoking the InvalidOperationException's ToString method to obtain its error message and stack trace.

Common Programming Error 19.2
Attempting to Peek or Pop an empty Stack (a Stack whose Count property is 0) causes an InvalidOperationException.

Stack Method Contains
Although Fig. 19.6 does not demonstrate it, class Stack also has method **Contains**, which returns true if the Stack contains the specified object, and returns false otherwise.

19.4.3 Class Hashtable
When an app creates objects of new or existing types, it needs to manage those objects efficiently. This includes sorting and retrieving objects. Sorting and retrieving information with arrays is efficient if some aspect of your data directly matches the key value and if those keys are *unique* and *tightly packed*. If you have 100 employees with nine-digit social security numbers and you want to store and retrieve employee data by using the social security number as a key, it would nominally require an array with 1,000,000,000 elements, because there are 1,000,000,000 unique nine-digit numbers. If you have an array that large, you

could get high performance storing and retrieving employee records by simply using the social security number as the array index, but it would be a huge waste of memory.

Many apps have this problem—either the keys are of the wrong type (i.e., not nonnegative integers), or they're of the right type but are sparsely spread over a large range.

Hashing

What is needed is a high-speed scheme for converting keys such as social security numbers and inventory part numbers to unique array indices. Then, when an app needs to store something, the scheme could convert the key rapidly to an index and the record of information could be stored at that location in the array. Retrieval occurs the same way—once the app has a key for which it wants to retrieve the data record, the app simply applies the conversion to the key, which produces the array index where the data resides in the array and retrieves the data.

The scheme we describe here is the basis of a technique called **hashing**, in which we store data in a data structure called a **hash table**. Why the name? Because, when we convert a key into an array index, we literally *scramble* the bits, making a "hash" of the number. The number actually has no real significance beyond its usefulness in storing and retrieving this particular data record.

Collisions

A glitch in the scheme occurs when there are **collisions** (i.e., two different keys "hash into" the same cell, or element, in the array). Since we cannot sort two different data records to the *same* space, we need to find an alternative home for all records beyond the first that hash to a particular array index. One scheme for doing this is to "hash again" (i.e., to reapply the hashing transformation to the key to provide a next candidate cell in the array). The hashing process is designed so that with just a few hashes, an available cell will be found.

Another scheme uses one hash to locate the first candidate cell. If the cell is occupied, successive cells are searched linearly until an available cell is found. Retrieval works the same way—the key is hashed once, the resulting cell is checked to determine whether it contains the desired data. If it does, the search is complete. If it does not, successive cells are searched linearly until the desired data is found.

The most popular solution to hash-table collisions is to have each cell of the table be a hash "bucket"—typically, a linked list of all the key–value pairs that hash to that cell. This is the solution that the .NET Framework's **Hashtable** class implements.

Load Factor

The **load factor** affects the performance of hashing schemes. The load factor is the ratio of the number of objects stored in the hash table to the total number of cells of the hash table. As this ratio gets *higher*, the chance of collisions tends to *increase*.

Performance Tip 19.5

*The load factor in a hash table is a classic example of a **space/time trade-off**: By increasing the load factor, we get better memory utilization, but the app runs slower due to increased hashing collisions. By decreasing the load factor, we get better speed because of reduced hashing collisions, but we get poorer memory utilization because a larger portion of the hash table remains empty.*

Recognizing the value of hashing, the .NET Framework provides class Hashtable to enable programmers to easily employ hashing in apps.

This concept is profoundly important in our study of object-oriented programming. Classes *encapsulate* and *hide* complexity (i.e., implementation details) and offer user-friendly interfaces. Crafting classes to do this properly is one of the most valued skills in the field of object-oriented programming.

Hash Function

A **hash function** performs a calculation that determines *where* to place data in the hash table. The hash function is applied to the key in a key–value pair of objects. Class Hashtable can accept any object as a key. For this reason, class object defines method **GetHashCode**, which all objects inherit. Most classes that are candidates to be used as keys in a hash table override this method to provide one that performs efficient hash-code calculations for a specific type. For example, a string has a hash-code calculation that's based on the contents of the string.

Demonstrating **Hashtable**

Figure 19.7 uses a Hashtable to count the number of occurrences of each word in a string. New apps should use generic class Dictionary<K, V> (introduced in Section 17.4) rather than Hashtable.

```
 1   // Fig. 19.7: HashtableTest.cs
 2   // App counts the number of occurrences of each word in a string
 3   // and stores them in a hash table.
 4   using System;
 5   using System.Text.RegularExpressions;
 6   using System.Collections;
 7
 8   public class HashtableTest
 9   {
10      public static void Main( string[] args )
11      {
12         // create hash table based on user input
13         Hashtable table = CollectWords();
14
15         // display hash-table content
16         DisplayHashtable( table );
17      } // end Main
18
19      // create hash table from user input
20      private static Hashtable CollectWords()
21      {
22         Hashtable table = new Hashtable(); // create a new hash table
23
24         Console.WriteLine( "Enter a string: " ); // prompt for user input
25         string input = Console.ReadLine(); // get input
26
```

Fig. 19.7 | App counts the number of occurrences of each word in a string and stores them in a hash table. (Part 1 of 2.)

```
27        // split input text into tokens
28        string[] words = Regex.Split( input, @"\s+" );
29
30        // processing input words
31        foreach ( var word in words )
32        {
33           string wordKey = word.ToLower(); // get word in lowercase
34
35           // if the hash table contains the word
36           if ( table.ContainsKey( wordKey ) )
37           {
38              table[ wordKey ] = ( ( int ) table[ wordKey ] ) + 1;
39           } // end if
40           else
41              // add new word with a count of 1 to hash table
42              table.Add( wordKey, 1 );
43        } // end foreach
44
45        return table;
46     } // end method CollectWords
47
48     // display hash-table content
49     private static void DisplayHashtable( Hashtable table )
50     {
51        Console.WriteLine( "\nHashtable contains:\n{0,-12}{1,-12}",
52           "Key:", "Value:" );
53
54        // generate output for each key in hash table
55        // by iterating through the Keys property with a foreach statement
56        foreach ( var key in table.Keys )
57           Console.WriteLine( "{0,-12}{1,-12}", key, table[ key ] );
58
59        Console.WriteLine( "\nsize: {0}", table.Count );
60     } // end method DisplayHashtable
61  } // end class HashtableTest
```

```
Enter a string:
As idle as a painted ship upon a painted ocean

Hashtable contains:
Key:         Value:
ocean        1
a            2
as           2
ship         1
upon         1
painted      2
idle         1

size: 7
```

Fig. 19.7 | App counts the number of occurrences of each word in a `string` and stores them in a hash table. (Part 2 of 2.)

Lines 4–6 contain using directives for namespaces System (for class Console), System.Text.RegularExpressions (for class Regex) and System.Collections (for class Hashtable). Class HashtableTest declares three static methods. Method CollectWords (lines 20–46) inputs a string and returns a Hashtable in which each value stores the number of times that word appears in the string and the word is used for the key. Method DisplayHashtable (lines 49–60) displays the Hashtable passed to it in column format. The Main method (lines 10–17) simply invokes CollectWords (line 13), then passes the Hashtable returned by CollectWords to DisplayHashtable in line 16.

Method CollectWords

Method CollectWords (lines 20–46) begins by initializing local variable table with a new Hashtable (line 22) that has a default maximum load factor of 1.0. When the Hashtable reaches the specified load factor, the capacity is increased *automatically*. (This implementation detail is invisible to clients of the class.) Lines 24–25 prompt the user and input a string. We use static method Split of class Regex (introduced in the online section of Chapter 16) in line 28 to divide the string by its whitespace characters. This creates an array of "words," which we then store in local variable words.

Hashtable Methods ContainsKey and Add

Lines 31–43 loop over every element of array words. Each word is converted to lowercase with string method **ToLower**, then stored in variable wordKey (line 33). Then line 36 calls Hashtable method **ContainsKey** to determine whether the word is in the hash table (and thus has occurred previously in the string). If the Hashtable does *not* contain an entry for the word, line 42 uses Hashtable method **Add** to create a new entry in the hash table, with the lowercase word as the key and an object containing 1 as the value. *Autoboxing* occurs when the app passes integer 1 to method Add, because the hash table stores both the key and value in references of type object.

Common Programming Error 19.3
Using the Add method to add a key that already exists in the hash table causes an ArgumentException.

Hashtable Indexer

If the word is already a key in the hash table, line 38 uses the Hashtable's indexer to obtain and set the key's associated value (the word count) in the hash table. We first *downcast* the value obtained by the get accessor from an object to an int. This *unboxes* the value so that we can increment it by 1. Then, when we use the indexer's set accessor to assign the key's associated value, the incremented value is *implicitly reboxed* so that it can be stored in the hash table.

Invoking the get accessor of a Hashtable indexer with a key that does *not* exist in the hash table obtains a null reference. Using the set accessor with a key that does not exist in the hash table creates a new entry, as if you had used the Add method.

Method DisplayHashtable

Line 45 returns the hash table to the Main method, which then passes it to method DisplayHashtable (lines 49–60), which displays all the entries. This method uses read-only property **Keys** (line 56) to get an ICollection that contains all the keys. Because ICollection extends IEnumerable, we can use this collection in the foreach statement in lines 56–57 to iterate over the keys of the hash table. This loop accesses and outputs each key and its value in the hash table using the iteration variable and table's get accessor. Each key and its value is displayed in a field width of -12. The *negative field width* indicates that the output is *left justified*. A hash table is not sorted, so the key–value pairs are not displayed in any particular order. Line 59 uses Hashtable property **Count** to get the number of key–value pairs in the Hashtable.

DictionaryEntry and IDictionary

Lines 56–57 could have also used the foreach statement with the Hashtable object itself, instead of using the Keys property. If you use a foreach statement with a Hashtable object, the iteration variable will be of type **DictionaryEntry**. The enumerator of a Hashtable (or any other class that implements **IDictionary**) uses the DictionaryEntry structure to store key–value pairs. This structure provides properties Key and Value for retrieving the key and value of the current element. If you do not need the keys, class Hashtable also provides a read-only **Values** property that gets an ICollection of all the values stored in the Hashtable. We can use this property to iterate through the values stored in the Hashtable without regard for where they're stored.

Problems with Nongeneric Collections

In the word-counting app of Fig. 19.7, our Hashtable stores its keys and data as object references, even though we store only string keys and int values by convention. This results in some awkward code. For example, line 38 was forced to *unbox and box* the int data stored in the Hashtable every time it incremented the count for a particular key. This is inefficient. A similar problem occurs in line 56—the iteration variable of the foreach statement is an object reference. If we need to use any of its string-specific methods, we need an *explicit downcast*.

This can cause subtle bugs. Suppose we decide to improve the readability of Fig. 19.7 by using the indexer's set accessor instead of the Add method to add a key–value pair in line 42, but accidentally type:

```
table[ wordKey ] = wordKey; // initialize to 1
```

This statement will create a new entry with a string key and string value instead of an int value of 1. Although the app will compile correctly, this is clearly incorrect. If a word appears twice, line 38 will try to downcast this string to an int, causing an InvalidCastException at execution time. The error that appears at execution time will indicate that the problem is at line 38, where the exception occurred, *not* at line 42. This makes the error more difficult to find and debug, especially in large apps where the exception may occur in a different file—and even in a different assembly.

19.5 Generic Collections

The System.Collections.Generic namespace contains generic classes that allow us to create collections of specific types. As you saw in Fig. 19.2, many of the classes are simply generic versions of nongeneric collections. A couple of classes implement new data structures. Here, we demonstrate generic collections SortedDictionary and LinkedList.

19.5.1 Generic Class SortedDictionary

A **dictionary** is the general term for a collection of key–value pairs. A hash table is one way to implement a dictionary. The .NET Framework provides several implementations of dictionaries, both generic and nongeneric, all of which implement the IDictionary interface (described in Fig. 19.1). The app in Fig. 19.8 is a modification of Fig. 19.7 that uses the generic class **SortedDictionary**. Generic class SortedDictionary does *not* use a hash table, but instead stores its key–value pairs in a binary search tree. As the class name suggests, the entries in SortedDictionary are sorted in the tree by key. When the key implements generic interface IComparable<T>, the SortedDictionary uses the results of IComparable<T> method CompareTo to sort the keys. Notice that despite these implementation details, we use the same public methods, properties and indexers with classes Hashtable and SortedDictionary in the same ways. In fact, except for the generic-specific syntax, Fig. 19.8 looks remarkably similar to Fig. 19.7. This is the beauty of object-oriented programming.

```
1   // Fig. 19.8: SortedDictionaryTest.cs
2   // App counts the number of occurrences of each word in a string
3   // and stores them in a generic sorted dictionary.
4   using System;
5   using System.Text.RegularExpressions;
6   using System.Collections.Generic;
7
8   public class SortedDictionaryTest
9   {
10      public static void Main( string[] args )
11      {
12         // create sorted dictionary based on user input
13         SortedDictionary< string, int > dictionary = CollectWords();
14
15         // display sorted dictionary content
16         DisplayDictionary( dictionary );
17      } // end Main
18
19      // create sorted dictionary from user input
20      private static SortedDictionary< string, int > CollectWords()
21      {
22         // create a new sorted dictionary
23         SortedDictionary< string, int > dictionary =
24            new SortedDictionary< string, int >();
25
26         Console.WriteLine( "Enter a string: " ); // prompt for user input
27         string input = Console.ReadLine(); // get input
28
29         // split input text into tokens
30         string[] words = Regex.Split( input, @"\s+" );
31
```

Fig. 19.8 | App counts the number of occurrences of each word in a string and stores them in a generic sorted dictionary. (Part 1 of 2.)

```
32          // processing input words
33          foreach ( var word in words )
34          {
35              string wordKey = word.ToLower(); // get word in lowercase
36
37              // if the dictionary contains the word
38              if ( dictionary.ContainsKey( wordKey ) )
39              {
40                  ++dictionary[ wordKey ];
41              } // end if
42              else
43                  // add new word with a count of 1 to the dictionary
44                  dictionary.Add( wordKey, 1 );
45          } // end foreach
46
47          return dictionary;
48      } // end method CollectWords
49
50      // display dictionary content
51      private static void DisplayDictionary< K, V >(
52          SortedDictionary< K, V > dictionary )
53      {
54          Console.WriteLine( "\nSorted dictionary contains:\n{0,-12}{1,-12}",
55              "Key:", "Value:" );
56
57          // generate output for each key in the sorted dictionary
58          // by iterating through the Keys property with a foreach statement
59          foreach ( K key in dictionary.Keys )
60              Console.WriteLine( "{0,-12}{1,-12}", key, dictionary[ key ] );
61
62          Console.WriteLine( "\nsize: {0}", dictionary.Count );
63      } // end method DisplayDictionary
64  } // end class SortedDictionaryTest
```

```
Enter a string:
We few, we happy few, we band of brothers

Sorted dictionary contains:
Key:        Value:
band        1
brothers    1
few,        2
happy       1
of          1
we          3

size: 6
```

Fig. 19.8 | App counts the number of occurrences of each word in a string and stores them in a generic sorted dictionary. (Part 2 of 2.)

Line 6 contains a using directive for the System.Collections.Generic namespace, which contains class SortedDictionary. The generic class SortedDictionary takes two type arguments—the first specifies the type of key (i.e., string) and the second the type of value (i.e., int). We have simply replaced the word Hashtable in line 13 and lines 23–

24 with SortedDictionary<string, int> to create a dictionary of int values keyed with strings. Now, the compiler can check and notify us if we attempt to store an object of the wrong type in the dictionary. Also, because the compiler now knows that the data structure contains int values, there's no longer any need for the *downcast* in line 40. This allows line 40 to use the much more concise prefix increment (++) notation. These changes result in code that can be checked for type safety at compile time.

Static method DisplayDictionary (lines 51–63) has been modified to be completely generic. It takes type parameters K and V. These parameters are used in line 52 to indicate that DisplayDictionary takes a SortedDictionary with keys of type K and values of type V. We use type parameter K again in line 59 as the type of the iteration key. This use of generics is a marvelous example of *code reuse*. If we decide to change the app to count the number of times each character appears in a string, method DisplayDictionary could receive an argument of type SortedDictionary<char, int> without modification. The key–value pairs displayed are now ordered by key, as shown in Fig. 19.8.

Performance Tip 19.6

Because class SortedDictionary keeps its elements sorted in a binary tree, obtaining or inserting a key–value pair takes O(log n) time, which is fast compared to linear searching, then inserting.

Common Programming Error 19.4

Invoking the get accessor of a SortedDictionary indexer with a key that does not exist in the collection causes a **KeyNotFoundException**. *This behavior is different from that of the Hashtable indexer's get accessor, which would return null.*

19.5.2 Generic Class LinkedList

The generic **LinkedList** class is a doubly linked list—we can navigate the list both backward and forward with nodes of generic class **LinkedListNode**. Each node contains property **Value** and read-only properties **Previous** and **Next**. The Value property's type matches LinkedList's single type parameter because it contains the data stored in the node. The Previous property gets a reference to the preceding node in the linked list (or null if the node is the first of the list). Similarly, the Next property gets a reference to the subsequent reference in the linked list (or null if the node is the last of the list). We demonstrate a few linked-list manipulations in Fig. 19.9.

```
1   // Fig. 19.9: LinkedListTest.cs
2   // Using LinkedLists.
3   using System;
4   using System.Collections.Generic;
5
6   public class LinkedListTest
7   {
8       private static readonly string[] colors = { "black", "yellow",
9           "green", "blue", "violet", "silver" };
```

Fig. 19.9 | Using LinkedLists. (Part I of 4.)

```
10      private static readonly string[] colors2 = { "gold", "white",
11         "brown", "blue", "gray" };
12
13      // set up and manipulate LinkedList objects
14      public static void Main( string[] args )
15      {
16         LinkedList< string > list1 = new LinkedList< string >();
17
18         // add elements to first linked list
19         foreach ( var color in colors )
20            list1.AddLast( color );
21
22         // add elements to second linked list via constructor
23         LinkedList< string > list2 = new LinkedList< string >( colors2 );
24
25         Concatenate( list1, list2 ); // concatenate list2 onto list1
26         PrintList( list1 ); // display list1 elements
27
28         Console.WriteLine( "\nConverting strings in list1 to uppercase\n" );
29         ToUppercaseStrings( list1 ); // convert to uppercase string
30         PrintList( list1 ); // display list1 elements
31
32         Console.WriteLine( "\nDeleting strings between BLACK and BROWN\n" );
33         RemoveItemsBetween( list1, "BLACK", "BROWN" );
34
35         PrintList( list1 ); // display list1 elements
36         PrintReversedList( list1 ); // display list in reverse order
37      } // end Main
38
39      // display list contents
40      private static void PrintList< T >( LinkedList< T > list )
41      {
42         Console.WriteLine( "Linked list: " );
43
44         foreach ( T value in list )
45            Console.Write( "{0} ", value );
46
47         Console.WriteLine();
48      } // end method PrintList
49
50      // concatenate the second list on the end of the first list
51      private static void Concatenate< T >( LinkedList< T > list1,
52         LinkedList< T > list2 )
53      {
54         // concatenate lists by copying element values
55         // in order from the second list to the first list
56         foreach ( T value in list2 )
57            list1.AddLast( value ); // add new node
58      } // end method Concatenate
59
60      // locate string objects and convert to uppercase
61      private static void ToUppercaseStrings( LinkedList< string > list )
62      {
```

Fig. 19.9 | Using LinkedLists. (Part 2 of 4.)

```
63          // iterate over the list by using the nodes
64          LinkedListNode< string > currentNode = list.First;
65
66          while ( currentNode != null )
67          {
68             string color = currentNode.Value; // get value in node
69             currentNode.Value = color.ToUpper(); // convert to uppercase
70
71             currentNode = currentNode.Next; // get next node
72          } // end while
73       } // end method ToUppercaseStrings
74
75       // delete list items between two given items
76       private static void RemoveItemsBetween< T >( LinkedList< T > list,
77          T startItem, T endItem )
78       {
79          // get the nodes corresponding to the start and end item
80          LinkedListNode< T > currentNode = list.Find( startItem );
81          LinkedListNode< T > endNode = list.Find( endItem );
82
83          // remove items after the start item
84          // until we find the last item or the end of the linked list
85          while ( ( currentNode.Next != null ) &&
86             ( currentNode.Next != endNode ) )
87          {
88             list.Remove( currentNode.Next ); // remove next node
89          } // end while
90       } // end method RemoveItemsBetween
91
92       // display reversed list
93       private static void PrintReversedList< T >( LinkedList< T > list )
94       {
95          Console.WriteLine( "Reversed List:" );
96
97          // iterate over the list by using the nodes
98          LinkedListNode< T > currentNode = list.Last;
99
100         while ( currentNode != null )
101         {
102            Console.Write( "{0} ", currentNode.Value );
103            currentNode = currentNode.Previous; // get previous node
104         } // end while
105
106         Console.WriteLine();
107      } // end method PrintReversedList
108   } // end class LinkedListTest
```

```
Linked list:
black yellow green blue violet silver gold white brown blue gray

Converting strings in list1 to uppercase
```

Fig. 19.9 | Using LinkedLists. (Part 3 of 4.)

```
Linked list:
BLACK YELLOW GREEN BLUE VIOLET SILVER GOLD WHITE BROWN BLUE GRAY

Deleting strings between BLACK and BROWN

Linked list:
BLACK BROWN BLUE GRAY
Reversed List:
GRAY BLUE BROWN BLACK
```

Fig. 19.9 | Using LinkedLists. (Part 4 of 4.)

The using directive in line 4 allows us to use the LinkedList class by its *unqualified name*. Lines 16–23 create LinkedLists list1 and list2 of strings and fill them with the contents of arrays colors and colors2, respectively. LinkedList is a *generic class* that has one type parameter for which we specify the type argument string in this example (lines 16 and 23).

LinkedList Methods AddLast and AddFirst
We demonstrate two ways to fill the lists. In lines 19–20, we use the foreach statement and method **AddLast** to fill list1. The AddLast method creates a new LinkedListNode (with the given value available via the Value property) and appends this node to the end of the list. There's also an **AddFirst** method that inserts a node at the beginning of the list. Line 23 invokes the constructor that takes an IEnumerable<string> parameter. All arrays *implicitly* inherit from the generic interfaces IList and IEnumerable with the type of the array as the type argument, so the string array colors2 implements IEnumerable<string>. The type parameter of this generic IEnumerable matches the type parameter of the generic LinkedList object. This constructor call copies the contents of the array colors2 to list2.

Methods That Test Class LinkedList
Line 25 calls *generic method* Concatenate (lines 51–58) to append all elements of list2 to the end of list1. Line 26 calls method PrintList (lines 40–48) to output list1's contents. Line 29 calls method ToUppercaseStrings (lines 61–73) to convert each string element to uppercase, then line 30 calls PrintList again to display the modified strings. Line 33 calls method RemoveItemsBetween (lines 76–90) to remove the elements between "BLACK" and "BROWN"—not including either. Line 35 outputs the list again, then line 36 invokes method PrintReversedList (lines 93–107) to display the list in *reverse* order.

Generic Method Concatentate
Generic method Concatenate (lines 51–58) iterates over list2 with a foreach statement and calls method AddLast to append each value to the end of list1. The LinkedList class's enumerator loops over the values of the nodes, not the nodes themselves, so the iteration variable has type T. Notice that this creates a new node in list1 for each node in list2. One LinkedListNode cannot be a member of more than one LinkedList. If you want the same data to belong to more than one LinkedList, you must make a copy of the node for each list to avoid InvalidOperationExceptions.

Generic Method PrintList and Method ToUppercaseStrings
Generic method PrintList (lines 40–48) similarly uses a foreach statement to iterate over the values in a LinkedList, and outputs them. Method ToUppercaseStrings (lines

61–73) takes a linked list of strings and converts each string value to uppercase. This method replaces the strings stored in the list, so we cannot use an enumerator (via a foreach statement) as in the previous two methods. Instead, we obtain the first LinkedList-Node via the First property (line 64), and use a while statement to loop through the list (lines 66–72). Each iteration of the while statement obtains and updates the contents of currentNode via property Value, using string method **ToUpper** to create an uppercase version of string color. At the end of each iteration, we move the current node to the next node in the list by assigning currentNode to the node obtained by its own Next property (line 71). The Next property of the last node of the list gets null, so when the while statement iterates past the end of the list, the loop exits.

Method *ToUppercaseStrings*

It does not make sense to declare ToUppercaseStrings as a generic method, because it uses the string-specific methods of the values in the nodes. Methods PrintList (lines 40–48) and Concatenate (lines 51–58) do not need to use any string-specific methods, so they can be declared with generic type parameters to promote maximal code reuse.

Generic Method *RemoveItemsBetween*

Generic method RemoveItemsBetween (lines 76–90) removes a range of items between two nodes. Lines 80–81 obtain the two "boundary" nodes of the range by using method **Find**. This method performs a linear search on the list and returns the first node that contains a value equal to the passed argument. Method Find returns null if the value is not found. We store the node preceding the range in local variable currentNode and the node following the range in endNode.

Lines 85–89 remove all the elements between currentNode and endNode. On each iteration of the loop, we remove the node following currentNode by invoking method **Remove** (line 88). Method Remove takes a LinkedListNode, splices that node out of the LinkedList, and fixes the references of the surrounding nodes. After the Remove call, currentNode's Next property now gets the node *following* the node just removed, and that node's Previous property now gets currentNode. The while statement continues to loop until there are no nodes left between currentNode and endNode, or until currentNode is the last node in the list. (There's also an overloaded version of method Remove that performs a linear search for the specified value and removes the first node in the list that contains it.)

Method *PrintReversedList*

Method PrintReversedList (lines 93–107) displays the list backward by navigating the nodes manually. Line 98 obtains the last element of the list via the **Last** property and stores it in currentNode. The while statement in lines 100–104 iterates through the list *backward* by moving the currentNode reference to the previous node at the end of each iteration, then exiting when we move past the beginning of the list. Note how similar this code is to lines 64–72, which iterated through the list from the beginning to the end.

19.6 Covariance and Contravariance for Generic Types

C# supports *covariance* and *contravariance* of generic interface and delegate types. We'll consider these concepts in the context of arrays, which have always been covariant and contravariant in C#.

Covariance in Arrays

Recall our Employee class hierarchy from Section 12.5, which consisted of the base class Employee and the derived classes SalariedEmployee, CommissionEmployee and Base-PlusCommissionEmployee. Assuming the declarations

```
SalariedEmployee[] salariedEmployees = {
    new SalariedEmployee( "Bob", "Blue", "111-11-1111", 800M ),
    new SalariedEmployee( "Rachel", "Red", "222-22-2222", 1234M ) };
Employee[] employees;
```

we can write the following statement:

```
employees = salariedEmployees;
```

Even though the array type SalariedEmployee[] does *not* derive from the array type Employee[], the preceding assignment *is* allowed because class SalariedEmployee is a derived class of Employee.

Similarly, suppose we have the following method, which displays the string representation of each Employee in its employees array parameter:

```
void PrintEmployees( Employee[] employees )
```

We can call this method with the array of SalariedEmployees, as in:

```
PrintEmployees( salariedEmployees );
```

and the method will correctly display the string representation of each SalariedEmployee object in the argument array. Assigning an array of a derived-class type to an array variable of a base-class type is an example of **covariance**.

Covariance in Generic Types

Covariance works with several *generic interface and delegate types*, including IEnumerable<T>. Arrays and generic collections implement the IEnumerable<T> interface. Using the salariedEmployees array declared previously, consider the following statement:

```
IEnumerable< Employee > employees = salariedEmployees;
```

Prior to Visual C# 2010, this generated a compilation error. Interface IEnumerable<T> is now covariant, so the preceding statement *is* allowed. If we modify method PrintEmployees as in:

```
void PrintEmployees( IEnumerable< Employee > employees )
```

we can call PrintEmployees with the array of SalariedEmployee objects, because that array implements the interface IEnumerable<SalariedEmployee> and because a SalariedEmployee *is an* Employee and because IEnumerable<T> is covariant. Covariance like this works *only* with *reference* types that are related by a class hierarchy.

Contravariance in Arrays

Previously, we showed that an array of a derived-class type (salariedEmployees) can be assigned to an array variable of a base-class type (employees). Now, consider the following statement, which has *always* worked in C#:

```
SalariedEmployee[] salariedEmployees2 =
    ( SalariedEmployee[] ) employees;
```

Based on the previous statements, we know that the Employee array variable employees currently refers to an array of SalariedEmployees. Using a *cast operator* to assign employees—an array of base-class-type elements—to salariedEmployees2—an array of derived-class-type elements—is an example of *contravariance*. The preceding cast will fail at runtime if employees is *not* an array of SalariedEmployees.

Contravariance in Generic Types

To understand **contravariance** in generic types, consider a SortedSet of SalariedEmployees. Class **SortedSet<T>** maintains a set of objects in sorted order—*no duplicates* are allowed. The objects placed in a SortedSet *must* implement the **IComparable<T> interface**. For classes that *do not* implement this interface, you can still compare their objects using an object that implements the **IComparer<T> interface**. This interface's Compare method compares its two arguments and returns 0 if they're equal, a *negative* integer if the first object is less than the second, or a *positive* integer if the first object is greater than the second.

Our Employee hierarchy classes do *not* implement IComparable<T>. Let's assume we wish to sort Employees by social security number. We can implement the following class to compare *any* two Employees:

```
class EmployeeComparer : IComparer< Employee >
{
    int IComparer< Employee >.Compare( Employee a, Employee b)
    {
        return a.SocialSecurityNumber.CompareTo(
            b.SocialSecurityNumber );
    } // end method Compare
} // end class EmployeeComparer
```

Method Compare returns the result of comparing the two Employees social security numbers using string method CompareTo.

Now consider the following statement, which creates a SortedSet:

```
SortedSet< SalariedEmployee > set =
    new SortedSet< SalariedEmployee >( new EmployeeComparer() );
```

When the type argument does *not* implement IComparable<T>, you must supply an appropriate IComparer<T> object to compare the objects that will be placed in the SortedSet. Since, we're creating a SortedSet of SalariedEmployees, the compiler expects the IComparer<T> object to implement the IComparer<SalariedEmployee>. Instead, we provided an object that implements IComparer<Employee>. The compiler allows us to provide an IComparer for a base-class type where an IComparer for a derived-class type is expected because interface IComparer<T> supports contravariance.

Web Resources

For a list of covariant and contravariant interface types, visit

```
msdn.microsoft.com/en-us/library/dd799517.aspx#VariantList
```

It's also possible to create your own variant types. For information on this, visit

```
msdn.microsoft.com/en-us/library/dd997386.aspx
```

19.7 Wrap-Up

This chapter introduced the .NET Framework collection classes. You learned about the hierarchy of interfaces that many of the collection classes implement. You saw how to use class `Array` to perform array manipulations. You learned that the `System.Collections` and `System.Collections.Generic` namespaces contain many nongeneric and generic collection classes, respectively. We presented the nongeneric classes `ArrayList`, `Stack` and `Hashtable` as well as generic classes `SortedDictionary` and `LinkedList`. In doing so, we discussed data structures in greater depth. We discussed dynamically expandable collections, hashing schemes, and two implementations of a dictionary. You saw the advantages of generic collections over their nongeneric counterparts.

You also learned how to use enumerators to traverse these data structures and obtain their contents. We demonstrated the `foreach` statement with many of the classes of the Framework Class Library, and explained that this works by using enumerators "behind-the-scenes" to traverse the collections.

In Chapter 20, we begin our discussion of databases, which organize data in such a way that the data can be selected and updated quickly. We introduce Structured Query Language (SQL) for writing simple database queries. We then introduce LINQ to Entities, which allows you to write LINQ queries that are automatically converted into SQL queries. These SQL queries are then used to query the database.

20

Databases and LINQ

Objectives

In this chapter you'll:

- Learn about the relational database model.

- Use an ADO.NET Entity Data Model to create classes for interacting with a database via LINQ to Entities.

- Use LINQ to retrieve and manipulate data from a database.

- Add data sources to projects.

- Use the IDE's drag-and-drop capabilities to display database tables in apps.

- Use data binding to move data seamlessly between GUI controls and databases.

- Create Master/Detail views that enable you to select a record and display its details.

20.1 Introduction

A **database** is an organized collection of data. A **database management system** (DBMS) provides mechanisms for storing, organizing, retrieving and modifying data. Today's most popular DBMSs manage *relational databases*, which organize data simply as tables with *rows* and *columns*.

Some popular proprietary DBMSs are Microsoft SQL Server, Oracle, Sybase and IBM DB2. PostgreSQL and MySQL are popular *open-source* DBMSs that can be downloaded and used *freely* by anyone. In this chapter, we use Microsoft's free **SQL Server Express**, which is installed with Visual Studio. It can also be downloaded separately from Microsoft (www.microsoft.com/express/sql).

SQL Server Express
SQL Server Express provides many features of Microsoft's full (fee-based) SQL Server product, but has some limitations, such as a maximum database size of 10GB. A SQL Server Express database file can be easily migrated to a full version of SQL Server—we did this with our deitel.com website once our database became too large for SQL Server Express. You can learn more about the SQL Server versions at bit.ly/SQLServerEditions. The version of SQL Server Express that's bundled with Visual Studio Express 2012 for Windows Desktop is called **SQL Server Express 2012 LocalDB**. It's meant for development and testing of apps on your computer.

Structured Query Language (SQL)
A language called **Structured Query Language** (SQL)—pronounced "sequel"—is an international standard used with relational databases to perform **queries** (that is, to request information that satisfies given criteria) and to manipulate data. For years, programs that accessed a relational database passed SQL queries as strings to the database management system, then processed the results.

LINQ to Entities and the ADO.NET Entity Framework
A logical extension of querying and manipulating data in databases is to perform similar operations on *any* sources of data, such as arrays, collections (like the `Items` collection of a `ListBox`) and files. Chapter 9 introduced *LINQ to Objects* and used it to manipulate data stored in arrays. **LINQ to Entities** allows you to manipulate data stored in a relational database—in our case, a SQL Server Express database. As with LINQ to Objects, the IDE provides *IntelliSense* for your LINQ to Entities queries.

The **ADO.NET Entity Framework** (commonly referred to simply as **EF**) enables apps to interact with data in various forms, including data stored in relational databases. You'll use the ADO.NET Entity Framework and Visual Studio to create a so-called *entity data model* that represents the database, then use LINQ to Entities to manipulate objects in the entity data model. Though you'll manipulate data in a *SQL Server Express* database in this chapter, the ADO.NET Entity Framework works with *most* popular database management systems. Behind the scenes, the ADO.NET Entity Framework generates SQL statements that interact with a database.

This chapter introduces general concepts of relational databases, then implements several database apps using the ADO.NET Entity Framework, LINQ to Entities and the IDE's tools for working with databases. In later chapters, you'll see other practical database and LINQ to Entities apps, such as a web-based guestbook and a web-based bookstore. Databases are at the heart of most "industrial strength" apps.

LINQ to SQL vs. LINQ to Entities
In the previous edition of this book, we discussed LINQ to SQL. Microsoft stopped further development on LINQ to SQL in 2008 in favor of the newer and more powerful LINQ to Entities and the ADO.NET Entity Framework.

Online SQL Introduction
In prior editions of this book, this chapter included an introduction to SQL. We've moved this introduction to the book's website at `www.deitel.com/books/cs2012fp/`, because we now perform all of the database interactions using LINQ.

20.2 Relational Databases

A **relational database** organizes data in **tables**. Figure 20.1 illustrates a sample `Employees` table that might be used in a personnel system. The table stores the attributes of employees. Tables are composed of **rows** (also called **records**) and **columns** (also called **fields**) in which values are stored. This table consists of six rows (one per employee) and five columns (one per attribute). The attributes are the employee's ID, name, department, salary and location. The `ID` column of each row is the table's **primary key**—a column (or group of columns) requiring a *unique* value that cannot be duplicated in other rows. This guarantees that each primary key value can be used to identify *one* row. A primary key composed of two or more columns is known as a **composite key**. Good examples of primary-key columns in other apps are a book's ISBN number in a book information system or a part number in an inventory system—values in each of these columns must be unique. LINQ to Entities *requires every table to have a primary key* to support updating the data in tables. The rows in Fig. 20.1 are displayed in *ascending order* by primary key. But they could be listed in *descending order* or in no particular order at all.

Table Employees

	ID	Name	Department	Salary	Location
	23603	Jones	413	1100	New Jersey
	24568	Kerwin	413	2000	New Jersey
Row	34589	Larson	642	1800	Los Angeles
	35761	Myers	611	1400	Orlando
	47132	Neumann	413	9000	New Jersey
	78321	Stephens	611	8500	Orlando

Primary key   Column

Fig. 20.1 | Employees table sample data.

Each *column* represents a different data *attribute*. Some column values may be duplicated between rows. For example, three different rows in the Employees table's Department column contain the number 413, indicating that these employees work in the same department.

Selecting Data Subsets
You can use LINQ to Entities to define queries that *select subsets* of the data from a table. For example, a program might select data from the Employees table to create a query result that shows where each department is located, in ascending order by Department number (Fig. 20.2).

Department	Location
413	New Jersey
611	Orlando
642	Los Angeles

Fig. 20.2 | Distinct Department and Location data from the Employees table.

20.3 A Books Database

We now consider a simple Books database that stores information about some Deitel books. First, we overview the database's tables. A database's tables, their fields and the relationships among them are collectively known as a **database schema**. The ADO.NET Entity Framework uses a database's schema to define classes that enable you to interact with the database. Sections 20.5–20.7 show how to manipulate the Books database. The database file—Books.mdf—is provided with this chapter's examples. SQL Server database files have the .mdf ("master data file") file-name extension.

***Authors** Table of the **Books** Database*
The database consists of three tables: Authors, Titles and AuthorISBN. The Authors table (described in Fig. 20.3) consists of three columns that maintain each author's unique ID number, first name and last name, respectively. Figure 20.4 contains the data from the Authors table.

Column	Description
AuthorID	Author's ID number in the database. In the Books database, this integer column is defined as an **identity** column, also known as an **autoincremented** column—for each row inserted in the table, the AuthorID value is increased by 1 automatically to ensure that each row has a unique AuthorID. This is the *primary key*.
FirstName	Author's first name (a string).
LastName	Author's last name (a string).

Fig. 20.3 | Authors table of the Books database.

AuthorID	FirstName	LastName
1	Paul	Deitel
2	Harvey	Deitel
3	Abbey	Deitel
4	Dan	Quirk
5	Michael	Morgano

Fig. 20.4 | Data from the Authors table of the Books database.

Titles *Table of the* Books *Database*

The Titles table (described in Fig. 20.5) consists of four columns that maintain information about each book in the database, including its ISBN, title, edition number and copyright year. Figure 20.6 contains the data from the Titles table.

Column	Description
ISBN	ISBN of the book (a string). The table's primary key. ISBN is an abbreviation for "International Standard Book Number"—a numbering scheme that publishers worldwide use to give every book a *unique* identification number.
Title	Title of the book (a string).
EditionNumber	Edition number of the book (an integer).
Copyright	Copyright year of the book (a string).

Fig. 20.5 | Titles table of the Books database.

ISBN	Title	EditionNumber	Copyright
0132151006	Internet & World Wide Web How to Program	5	2012
0132575663	Java How to Program	9	2012

Fig. 20.6 | Data from the Titles table of the Books database. (Part 1 of 2.)

ISBN	Title	EditionNumber	Copyright
013299044X	C How to Program	7	2013
0132990601	Simply Visual Basic 2010	4	2013
0133406954	Visual Basic 2012 How to Program	6	2014
0133379337	Visual C# 2012 How to Program	5	2014
0136151574	Visual C++ 2008 How to Program	2	2008
0133378713	C++ How to Program	9	2014
0132121360	Android for Programmers: An App-Driven Approach	1	2012

Fig. 20.6 | Data from the Titles table of the Books database. (Part 2 of 2.)

AuthorISBN *Table of the* Books *Database*

The AuthorISBN table (described in Fig. 20.7) consists of two columns that maintain ISBNs for each book and their corresponding authors' ID numbers. This table associates authors with their books. The AuthorID column is a **foreign key**—a column in this table that matches the primary-key column in another table (that is, AuthorID in the Authors table). The ISBN column is also a *foreign key*—it matches the primary-key column (that is, ISBN) in the Titles table. A database might consist of many tables. A goal when designing a database is to *minimize* the amount of *duplicated* data among the database's tables. Foreign keys, which are specified when a database table is created in the database, link the data in *multiple* tables. Together the AuthorID and ISBN columns in this table form a *composite primary key*. Every row in this table *uniquely* matches *one* author to *one* book's ISBN. Figure 20.8 contains the data from the AuthorISBN table of the Books database.

Column	Description
AuthorID	The author's ID number, a foreign key to the Authors table.
ISBN	The ISBN for a book, a foreign key to the Titles table.

Fig. 20.7 | AuthorISBN table of the Books database.

AuthorID	ISBN	AuthorID	ISBN
1	0132151006	*(continued)*	
1	0132575663	1	0133379337
1	013299044X	1	0136151574
1	0132990601	1	0133378713
1	0133406954	1	0132121360
(continued)		2	0132151006

Fig. 20.8 | Data from the AuthorISBN table of the Books database. (Part 1 of 2.)

AuthorID	ISBN	AuthorID	ISBN
2	0132575663	*(continued)*	
2	013299044X	2	0132121360
2	0132990601	3	0132151006
2	0133406954	3	0132990601
2	0133379337	3	0132121360
2	0136151574	3	0133406954
2	0133378713	4	0136151574
(continued)		5	0132121360

Fig. 20.8 | Data from the `AuthorISBN` table of the `Books` database. (Part 2 of 2.)

Every foreign-key value must appear as another table's primary-key value so the DBMS can ensure that the foreign key value is valid. For example, the DBMS ensures that the `AuthorID` value for a particular row of the `AuthorISBN` table (Fig. 20.8) is valid by checking that there is a row in the `Authors` table with that `AuthorID` as the primary key.

Foreign keys also allow *related* data in *multiple* tables to be *selected* from those tables—this is known as **joining** the data. There is a **one-to-many relationship** between a primary key and a corresponding foreign key (for example, one author can write many books and one book can be written by many authors). This means that a foreign key can appear *many* times in its own table but only *once* (as the primary key) in another table. For example, the ISBN 0132151006 can appear in several rows of `AuthorISBN` (because this book has several authors) but only once in `Titles`, where ISBN is the primary key.

Entity-Relationship Diagram for the **Books** *Database*
Figure 20.9 is an **entity-relationship (ER) diagram** for the `Books` database. This diagram shows the tables in the database and the relationships among them. The first compartment in each box contains the table's name. The names in italic font are *primary keys*—`AuthorID` in the `Authors` table, `AuthorID` and `ISBN` in the `AuthorISBN` table, and `ISBN` in the `Titles` table. Every row *must* have a value in the primary-key column (or group of columns), and the value of the key must be *unique* in the table; otherwise, the DBMS will report an error. The names `AuthorID` and `ISBN` in the `AuthorISBN` table are both italic—together these form a *composite primary key* for the `AuthorISBN` table.

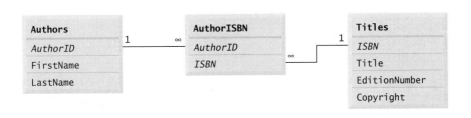

Fig. 20.9 | Entity-relationship diagram for the `Books` database.

The lines connecting the tables in Fig. 20.9 represent the *relationships* among the tables. Consider the line between the Authors and AuthorISBN tables. On the Authors end of the line, there's a 1, and on the AuthorISBN end, an infinity symbol (∞). This indicates a *one-to-many relationship*—for *each* author in the Authors table, there can be an *arbitrary number* of ISBNs for books written by that author in the AuthorISBN table (that is, an author can write *any* number of books). Note that the relationship line links the AuthorID column in the Authors table (where AuthorID is the primary key) to the AuthorID column in the AuthorISBN table (where AuthorID is a foreign key)—the line between the tables links the primary key to the matching foreign key.

The line between the Titles and AuthorISBN tables illustrates a *one-to-many relationship*—one book can be written by many authors. Note that the line between the tables links the primary key ISBN in table Titles to the corresponding foreign key in table AuthorISBN. The relationships in Fig. 20.9 illustrate that the sole purpose of the AuthorISBN table is to provide a **many-to-many relationship** between the Authors and Titles tables—an author can write *many* books, and a book can have *many* authors.

20.4 LINQ to Entities and the ADO.NET Entity Framework

When using the ADO.NET Entity Framework, you interact with the database via classes that the IDE generates from the database schema. You'll initiate this process by adding a new **ADO.NET Entity Data Model** to your project (as you'll see in Section 20.5.1).

Classes Generated in the Entity Data Model

For the Authors and Titles tables in the Books database, the IDE creates two classes *each* in the data model:

- The first class represents a row of the table and contains properties for each column in the table. Objects of this class—called **row objects**—store the data from individual rows of the table. The IDE uses the *singular* version of a table's *plural* name as the row class's name. For the Books database's Authors table, the row class's name is Author, and for the Titles table, it's Title.

- The second class represents the table itself. An object of this class stores a collection of row objects that correspond to all of the rows in the table. The table classes for the Books database are named Authors and Titles.

Once generated, the entity data model classes have full *IntelliSense* support in the IDE. Section 20.7 demonstrates queries that use the relationships among the Books database's tables to join data.

Relationships Between Tables in the Entity Data Model

You'll notice that we did not mention the Books database's AuthorISBN table. Recall that this table links:

- each author in the Authors table to that author's books in the Titles table, and
- each book in the Titles table to the book's authors in the Authors table.

Relationships between tables are taken into account in the entity data model's generated classes. For example, the Author row class contains a **navigation property** named Titles which you can use to get the `Title` objects that represent all the books written by that author. The IDE automatically adds the "s" to "`Title`" to indicate that this property represents a collection of `Title` objects. Similarly, the `Title` row class contains a navigation property named `Authors`, which you can use to get the `Author` objects that represent a given book's authors.

DbContext Class

A **DbContext** (namespace **System.Data.Entity**) manages the data flow between the program and the database. When the IDE generates the *entity data model's* row and table classes, it also creates a derived class of `DbContext` that is specific to the database being manipulated. For the `Books` database, this derived class has properties for the `Authors` and `Titles` tables. As you'll see, these can be used as data sources for manipulating data in LINQ queries and in GUIs. Any changes made to the data managed by the `DbContext` can be saved back to the database using the `DbContext`'s **SaveChanges** method.

IQueryable<T> Interface

LINQ to Entities works through the **IQueryable<T> interface**, which inherits from the interface `IEnumerable<T>` introduced in Chapter 9. When a LINQ to Entities query on an `IQueryable<T>` object executes against the database, the results are loaded into objects of the corresponding entity data model classes for convenient access in your code.

Using Extension Methods to Manipulate IQueryable<T> Objects

Recall that extension methods add functionality to an existing class without modifying the class's source code. In Chapter 9, we introduced several LINQ extension methods, including `First`, `Any`, `Count`, `Distinct`, `ToArray` and `ToList`. These methods, which are defined as `static` methods of class `Enumerable` (namespace `System.Linq`), can be applied to any object that implements the `IEnumerable<T>` interface, such as arrays, collections and the results of LINQ to Objects queries.

In this chapter, we use a combination of the LINQ query syntax and LINQ extension methods to manipulate database contents. The extension methods we use are defined as `static` methods of class **Queryable** (namespace `System.Linq`) and can be applied to any object that implements the `IQueryable<T>` interface—these include various entity data model objects and the results of LINQ to Entities queries.

20.5 Querying a Database with LINQ

In this section, we demonstrate how to *connect* to a database, *query* it and *display* the results of the query. There is little code in this section—the IDE provides *visual programming* tools and *wizards* that simplify accessing data in apps. These tools establish database connections and create the objects necessary to view and manipulate the data through Windows Forms GUI controls—a technique known as **data binding**.

For the examples in Sections 20.5–20.8, we'll create *one* solution that contains *several* projects. One will be a reusable *class library* containing the ADO.NET Entity Data Model for interacting with the `Books` database. The other projects will be Windows Forms apps that use the ADO.NET Entity Data Model in the class library to manipulate the database.

Our first example performs a simple query on the `Books` database from Section 20.3. We retrieve the entire `Authors` table, ordered by the authors' last name, then first name.

We then use data binding to display the data in a **DataGridView**—a control from namespace System.Windows.Forms that can display data from a data source in tabular format. The basic steps we'll perform are:

- Create the ADO.NET entity data model classes for manipulating the database.
- Add the entity data model object that represents the Authors table as a *data source*.
- Drag the Authors table data source onto the **Design** view to create a GUI for displaying the table's data.
- Add code to the Form's code-behind file to allow the app to interact with the database.

The GUI for the program is shown in Fig. 20.10. *All* of the controls in this GUI are automatically generated when we drag a *data source* that represents the Authors table onto the Form in **Design** view. The **BindingNavigator** toolbar at the top of the window is a collection of controls that allow you to navigate through the records in the DataGridView that fills the rest of the window. The BindingNavigator controls also allow you to add records, delete records, modify existing records and save your changes to the database. You can add a new record by pressing the **Add new** (✛) button, then entering the new author's first and last name. You can delete an existing record by selecting an author (either in the DataGridView or via the controls on the BindingNavigator) and pressing the **Delete** (✗) button. You can edit an existing record by clicking the first name or last name field for that record and typing the new value. To save your changes to the database, simply click the **Save Data** (💾) button. Empty values are *not* allowed in the Authors table of the Books database, so if you attempt to save a record that does not contain a value for both the first name and last name an exception occurs.

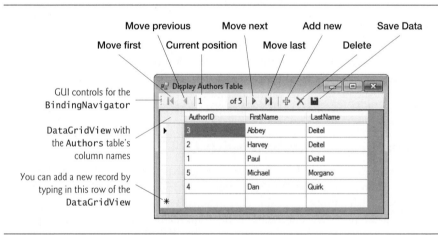

Fig. 20.10 | GUI for the **Display Authors Table** app.

20.5.1 Creating the ADO.NET Entity Data Model Class Library

This section presents the steps required to create the entity data model from an existing database. A *model* describes the data that you'll be manipulating—in our case, the data represented by the tables in the Books database.

Step 1: Creating a Class Library Project for the ADO.NET Entity Data Model
Select **FILE > New Project...** to display the **New Project** dialog, then select **Class Library** from the **Visual C#** templates and name the project BooksExamples. Click **OK** to create the project, then delete the Class1.cs file from the **Solution Explorer**.

Step 2: Adding the ADO.NET Entity Data Model to the Class Library
To interact with the database, you'll add an ADO.NET entity data model to the class library project. This will also configure the **connection** to the database.

1. *Adding the ADO.NET Entity Data Model.* Right click the BooksExamples project in the **Solution Explorer**, then select **Add > New Item...** to display the **Add New Item** dialog (Fig. 20.11). From the **Data** category select **ADO.NET Entity Data Model** and name the model BooksModel.edmx—this file will contain the information about the entity data model you're about to create. Click **Add** to add the entity data model to the class library and display the **Entity Data Model Wizard** dialog.

Fig. 20.11 | Selecting **ADO.NET Entity Data Model** in the **Add New Item** Dialog.

2. *Choosing the Model Contents.* The **Choose Model Contents** step in the **Entity Data Model Wizard** dialog (Fig. 20.12) enables you to specify the entity data model's contents. The model in these examples will consist of data from the Books database, so select **Generate from Database** and click **Next >** to display the **Choose Your Data Connection** step.

3. *Choosing the Data Connection.* In the **Choose Your Data Connection** step, click **New Connection...** to display the **Connection Properties** dialog (Fig. 20.13). (If the **Choose Data Source** dialog box appears, select **Microsoft SQL Server**, then click **OK**.) The **Data source:** TextBox should contain **Microsoft SQL Server Database File (SqlClient)**. (If it does not, click **Change...** to display a dialog where you can change the **Data source**.) Click **Browse...** to locate and select the Books.mdf file in the Databases directory included with this chapter's examples. You can click **Test Connection** to verify that the IDE can connect to the database through

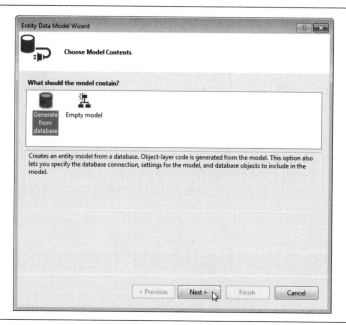

Fig. 20.12 | Entity Data Model Wizard dialog's Choose Model Contents step.

Fig. 20.13 | Connection Properties dialog.

SQL Server Express. Click **OK** to create the connection. Figure 20.14 shows the **Entity connection string** for the Books.mdf database. This string contains the information that the ADO.NET Entity Framework requires to connect to the database at runtime. Click **Next >**. A dialog will appear asking if you'd like to add the database file to your project. Click **Yes** to move to the next step.

Fig. 20.14 | Choose Your Data Connection step *after* selecting `Books.mdf`.

Error-Prevention Tip 20.1
SQL Server Express LocalDB allows only one program at a time to connect to a database file, so ensure that no other program is using the file before connecting to the database.

4. *Choosing the Database Objects to Include in the Model.* In the **Choose Your Database Objects and Settings** step, you'll specify the parts of the database that should be used in the ADO.NET Entity Data Model. Select the **Tables** node as shown in Fig. 20.15, then click **Finish**.

5. *Viewing the Entity Data Model Diagram in the Model Designer.* At this point, the IDE creates the entity data model and displays a diagram (Fig. 20.16) in the *model designer*. The diagram contains **Author** and **Title** *entities*—these represent *authors* and *titles* in the database and the properties of each. Notice that the IDE renamed the `Title` column of the `Titles` table as `Title1` to avoid a naming conflict with the class `Title` that represents a row in the table. The line between the entities indicates a *relationship* between authors and titles—this relationship is implemented in the `Books` database as the `AuthorISBN` table. The asterisk (*) at each end of the line indicates a *many-to-many relationship*—an author can be an author for *many* titles and a title can have *many* authors. The **Navigation Properties** section in the **Author** entity contains the **Titles** property, which connects an author to all titles written by that author. Similarly, the **Navigation Properties** section in the **Title** entity contains the **Authors** property, which connects a title to all of its authors.

6. *Building the Class Library.* Select **BUILD > Build Solution** to build the class library that you'll reuse in the next several examples—this will compile the entity data model classes that were generated by the IDE. When you build the class library,

the IDE generates the classes that you can use to interact with the database. These include a class for each table you selected from the database and a derived class of DbContext named BooksEntities that enables you to programmatically interact with the database. [*Note:* Building the project causes the IDE to execute a script that creates and compiles the entity data model classes. A security warning dialog appears indicating that this script could harm your computer. Click **OK** to allow the script to execute. The warning is intended primarily for cases in which you download from the Internet Visual Studio templates that execute scripts.]

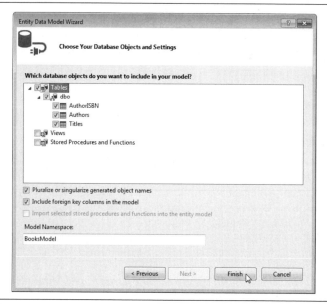

Fig. 20.15 | Selecting the database's tables to include in the ADO.NET Entity Data Model.

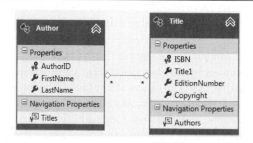

Fig. 20.16 | Entity data model diagram for the **Author** and **Title** entities.

20.5.2 Creating a Windows Forms Project and Configuring It to Use the Entity Data Model

Recall that the next several examples will all be part of *one solution* containing *several projects*—the class library project with our *reusable model* and individual Windows Forms apps for each example. In this section, you'll create a new Windows Forms app and configure it to be able to use the entity data model that you created in the preceding section.

Step 1: Creating the Project
To add a new Windows Forms project to the existing solution:

1. Right click the solution name in **Solution Explorer** and select **Add > New Project...** to display the **Add New Project** dialog.

2. Select **Windows Forms Application**, name the project DisplayTable and click **OK**.

3. Change the name of the Form1.cs source file to DisplayAuthorsTable.cs. The IDE updates the Form's class name to match the source file. Set the Form's **Text** property to Display Authors Table.

4. Configure the solution so that this new project will execute when you select **DEBUG > Start Debugging** (or press *F5*). To do so, right click the DisplayTable project's name in the **Solution Explorer**, then select **Set as Startup Project**.

Step 2: Adding a Reference to the *BooksExamples* Class Library
To use the entity data model classes for data binding, you must first add a *reference* to the class library you created in Section 20.5.1—this allows the new project to use that class library. Each project you create typically contains references to several .NET class libraries (called *assemblies*) by default—for example, a Windows Forms project contains a reference to the System.Windows.Forms library. When you compile a class library, the IDE creates a .dll file (known as an *assembly*) containing the library's components. To add a reference to the class library containing the entity data model's classes:

1. Right click the DisplayTable project's **References** node in the **Solution Explorer** and select **Add Reference....**

2. In the left column of the **Reference Manager** dialog that appears, select **Solution** to display the other projects in this solution, then in center of the dialog select BooksExamples and click **OK**. BooksExamples should now appear in the projects **References** node.

Step 3: Adding References to *System.Data.Entity and EntityFramework*
You'll also need references to the System.Data.Entity and EntityFramework libraries to use the ADO.NET Entity Framework. To add a reference to System.Data.Entity, repeat *Step 2* for adding a reference to the BooksExamples library, but in the left column of the **Reference Manager** dialog that appears, select **Assemblies** then locate System.Data.Entity, ensure that its checkbox is checked and click **OK**. System.Data.Entity should now appear in the projects **References** node.

The EntityFramework library was added by the IDE to the BooksExamples class library project when we created the entity data model, but the EntityFramework library is also required in *each* app that will use the entity data model. To add a reference to the EntityFramework library:

1. Right click the solution name in the **Solution Explorer** and select **Manage NuGet Packages for Solution...** to display the **Manage NuGet Packages** dialog.

2. In the dialog that appears, click **Manage** to display the **Select Projects** dialog, then select the `DisplayTable` project and click **OK**.

3. Click **Close** to close the **Manage NuGet Packages** dialog. `EntityFramework` should now appear in the projects **References** node.

Step 4: Adding the Connection String to the Windows Forms App

Each app that will use the entity data model also requires the *connection string* that tells the Entity Framework how to connect to the database. The connection string is stored in the `BooksExamples` class library's `App.Config` file. In the **Solution Explorer**, open the `Books-Examples` class library's `App.Config` file then copy lines 7–9, which have the format:

```
<connectionStrings>
    Connection string information appears here
</connectionStrings>
```

Next, open the `App.Config` file in the `DisplayTable` project and paste the connection string information *after* the line containing `</entityFramework>` and *before* the line containing `</configuration>`. Save the `App.Config` file.

20.5.3 Data Bindings Between Controls and the Entity Data Model

You'll now use the IDE's drag-and-drop GUI design capabilities to create the GUI for interacting with the `Books` database. You must write a small amount of code to enable the *autogenerated* GUI to interact with the entity data model. You'll now perform the steps to display the contents of the `Authors` table in a GUI.

Step 1: Adding a Data Source for the **Authors** Table

To use the entity data model classes for data binding, you must first add them as a *data source*. To do so:

1. Select **VIEW > Other Windows > Data Sources** to display the **Data Sources** window at the left side of the IDE, then in that window click the **Add New Data Source...** link to display the **Data Source Configuration Wizard**.

2. The Entity Data Model classes are used to create *objects* representing the tables in the database, so we'll use an **Object** data source. In the dialog, select **Object** and click **Next >**. Expand the tree view as shown in Fig. 20.17 and ensure that **Author** is checked. An object of this class will be used as the *data source*.

3. Click **Finish**.

The `Authors` table in the database is now a data source from which a data bound GUI control can obtain data. In the **Data Sources** window (Fig. 20.18), you can see the `Author` class that you added in the previous step. Properties representing columns of the database's `Authors` table should appear below it, as well as a `Titles` navigation property representing the relationship between the database's `Authors` and `Titles` tables.

Step 2: Creating GUI Elements

Next, you'll use the **Design** view to create a `DataGridView` control that can display the `Authors` table's data. To do so:

1. Switch to **Design** view for the `DisplayAuthorsTable` class.

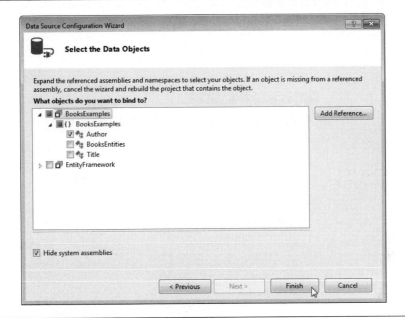

Fig. 20.17 | Selecting the `Author` class as the data source.

Fig. 20.18 | **Data Sources** window showing the `Author` class as a data source.

2. Click the **Author** node in the **Data Sources** window—it should change to a drop-down list. Open the drop-down by clicking the down arrow and ensure that the `DataGridView` option (which is the default) is selected—this is the GUI control that will be used to display and interact with the data.

3. Drag the **Author** node from the **Data Sources** window onto the Form in **Design** view. You'll need to resize the Form to fit the `DataGridView`.

The IDE creates a `DataGridView` (Fig. 20.19) with column names representing *all* the properties for an `Author`, including the `Titles` navigation property. The IDE also creates a **BindingNavigator** that contains Buttons for *moving between entries, adding entries, deleting entries and saving changes to the database*. The IDE also generates a **BindingSource** (`authorBindingSource`), which handles the transfer of data between the *data source* and the *data-bound controls* on the Form. Nonvisual components such as the BindingSource and the non-visual aspects of the BindingNavigator appear in the *component tray*—the gray region below the Form in **Design** view. The IDE names the BindingNavigator and BindingSource (authorBindingNavigator and authorBindingSource, respectively) based on the data source's name (Author). We use the default names for automatically generated components throughout this chapter to show exactly what the IDE creates.

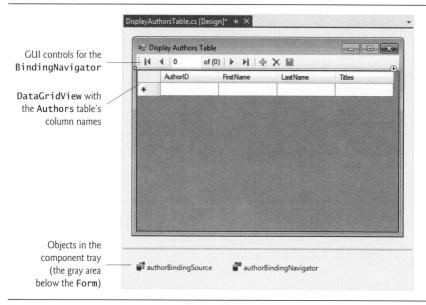

GUI controls for the
BindingNavigator

DataGridView with
the Authors table's
column names

Objects in the
component tray
(the gray area
below the Form)

Fig. 20.19 | Component tray holds nonvisual components in **Design** view.

To make the DataGridView occupy the *entire* window below the BindingNavigator, select the DataGridView, then use the **Properties** window to set the Dock property to Fill. You can stretch the window horizontally to see all the DataGridView columns. We do not use the Titles column in this example, so with the DataGridView selected, click **Edit Columns...** in the **Properties** window to display the **Edit Columns** dialog. Select **Titles** in the **Selected Columns** list, then click **Remove** to remove that column.

Step 3: Connecting the Data Source to the *authorBindingSource*

The final step is to connect the data source to the authorBindingSource, so that the app can interact with the database. Figure 20.20 shows the code needed to *obtain* data from the database and to *save* any changes that the user makes to the data back into the database.

```
1   // Fig. 20.20: DisplayAuthorsTable.cs
2   // Displaying data from a database table in a DataGridView.
3   using System;
4   using System.Data.Entity;
5   using System.Data.Entity.Validation;
```

Fig. 20.20 | Displaying data from a database table in a DataGridView. (Part 1 of 3.)

```
 6   using System.Linq;
 7   using System.Windows.Forms;
 8
 9   namespace DisplayTable
10   {
11       public partial class DisplayAuthorsTable : Form
12       {
13           // constructor
14           public DisplayAuthorsTable()
15           {
16               InitializeComponent();
17           } // end constructor
18
19           // Entity Framework DbContext
20           private BooksExamples.BooksEntities dbcontext =
21               new BooksExamples.BooksEntities();
22
23           // load data from database into DataGridView
24           private void DisplayAuthorsTable_Load( object sender, EventArgs e )
25           {
26               // load Authors table ordered by LastName then FirstName
27               dbcontext.Authors
28                   .OrderBy( author => author.LastName )
29                   .ThenBy( author => author.FirstName )
30                   .Load();
31
32               // specify DataSource for authorBindingSource
33               authorBindingSource.DataSource = dbcontext.Authors.Local;
34           } // end method DisplayAuthorsTable_Load
35
36           // click event handler for the Save Button in the
37           // BindingNavigator saves the changes made to the data
38           private void authorBindingNavigatorSaveItem_Click(
39               object sender, EventArgs e )
40           {
41               Validate(); // validate the input fields
42               authorBindingSource.EndEdit(); // complete current edit, if any
43
44               // try to save changes
45               try
46               {
47                   dbcontext.SaveChanges(); // write changes to database file
48               } // end try
49               catch( DbEntityValidationException )
50               {
51                   MessageBox.Show( "FirstName and LastName must contain values",
52                       "Entity Validation Exception" );
53               } // end catch
54           } // end method authorBindingNavigatorSaveItem_Click
55       } // end class DisplayAuthorsTable
56   } // end namespace DisplayTable
```

Fig. 20.20 | Displaying data from a database table in a DataGridView. (Part 2 of 3.)

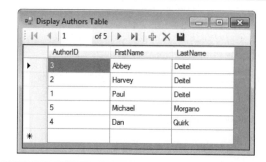

Fig. 20.20 | Displaying data from a database table in a `DataGridView`. (Part 3 of 3.)

Creating the *DbContext Object*

As mentioned in Section 20.4, a DbContext object interacts with the database on the app's behalf. The BooksEntities class (a derived class of DbContext) was automatically generated by the IDE when you created the entity data model classes to access the Books database (Section 20.5.1). Lines 20–21 create an object of this class named dbcontext.

DisplayAuthorsTable_Load Event Handler

You can create the Form's Load event handler (lines 24–34) by double clicking the Form's title bar in **Design** view. In this app, we allow data to move between the DbContext and the database by using LINQ to Entities extension methods to extract data from the Books-Entities's Authors property (lines 27–30), which corresponds to the Authors table in the database. The expression

```
dbcontext.Authors
```

indicates that we wish to get data from the Authors table.

The **OrderBy extension method** call

```
.OrderBy( author => author.LastName )
```

indicates that the rows of the table should be retrieved in ascending order by the authors' last names. The argument to OrderBy is a **lambda expression** that defines a simple, **anonymous method**. A lambda expression begins with a *parameter list*—author in this case, is an object of the Author entity data model class. The lambda expression *infers* the lambda parameter's type from dbcontext.Authors, which contains Author objects. The parameter list is followed by the => **lambda operator** (read as "goes to") and an expression that represents the body of the function. The value produced by the expression—a given author's last name—is implicitly returned by the lambda expression. You do not specify a return type for the lambda expression—the return type is inferred from the return value. As we encounter lambda expressions in this chapter, we'll discuss the syntax we use. You can learn more about lambda expressions at

```
msdn.microsoft.com/en-us/library/bb397687.aspx
```

When there are multiple authors with the *same* last name, we'd like them to be listed in ascending order by first name as well. The **ThenBy extension method** call

```
.ThenBy( author => author.FirstName )
```

enables you to order results by an additional column. This is applied to the Author objects that have already been ordered by last name.

Finally, line 30 calls the **Load extension method** (defined in class **DBExtensions** from the namespace System.Data.Entity). This method executes the LINQ to Entities query and loads the results into memory. This data is tracked by the BookEntities DbContext in local memory so that any changes made to the data can eventually be saved into the database. Lines 27–30 are equivalent to using the following statement:

```
(from author in dbcontext.Authors
 orderby author.LastName, author.FirstName
 select author).Load();
```

Line 33 sets the authorBindingSource's **DataSource property** to the Local property of the dbcontext.Authors object. In this case, the Local property is an ObservableCollection<Author> that represents the query results that were loaded into memory by lines 27–30. When a BindingSource's DataSource property is assigned an **ObservableCollection<T>** (namespace System.Collections.ObjectModel), the GUI that's bound to the BindingSource is notified of any changes to the data so the GUI can be updated accordingly. In addition, changes made by the user to the data in the GUI will be tracked so the DbContext can eventually save those changes to the database.

authorBindingNavigatorSaveItem_Click Event Handler: Saving Modifications to the Database

If the user modifies the data in the DataGridView, we'd also like to save the modifications in the database. By default, the BindingNavigator's **Save Data** Button (💾) is disabled. To enable it, right click this Button's icon in the BindingNavigator and select **Enabled**. Then, double click the icon to create its Click event handler (lines 38–54).

Saving the data entered in the DataGridView back to the database is a three-step process. First, all controls on the form are *validated* (line 41) by calling the DisplayTableForm's inherited Validate method—if any control has an event handler for the Validating event, it executes. You typically handle this event to determine whether a control's contents are valid. Next, line 42 calls **EndEdit** on the authorBindingSource, which forces it to save any pending changes into the BooksEntities model *in memory*. Finally, line 47 calls SaveChanges on the BooksEntities object (dbcontext) to store any changes into the database. We placed this call in a try statement, because the Authors table does not allow empty values for the first name and last name—these rules were configured when we originally created the database. When SaveChanges is called, any changes stored into the Authors table must satisfy the table's rules. If any of the changes do not, a DBEntityValidationException occurs.

20.6 Dynamically Binding Query Results

Now that you've seen how to display an entire database table in a DataGridView, we show how to perform several different queries and display the results in a DataGridView. This app only reads data from the entity data model, so we disabled the buttons in the BindingNavigator that enable the user to add and delete records. Later, we'll explain why we do not support modifying the database in this example.

The **Display Query Results** app (Fig. 20.21) allows the user to select a query from the ComboBox at the bottom of the window, then displays the results of the query.

a) Results of the "All titles" query, which shows the contents of the Titles table ordered by the book titles

b) Results of the "Titles with 2014 copyright" query

c) Results of the "Titles ending with 'How to Program'" query

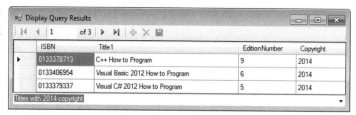

Fig. 20.21 | Sample execution of the **Display Query Results** app.

20.6.1 Creating the Display Query Results GUI

Perform the following steps to build the **Display Query Results** app's GUI.

Step 1: Creating the Project
Perform the steps in Section 20.5.2 to create a new **Windows Forms Application** project named DisplayQueryResult in the same solution as the DisplayTable app. Rename the Form1.cs source file to TitleQueries.cs. Set the Form's **Text** property to Display Query Results. Be sure to set the DisplayQueryResult project as the startup project.

Step 2: Creating a **DataGridView** to Display the **Titles** Table
Follow *Steps 1* and *2* in Section 20.5.3 to create the data source and the DataGridView. For this example, select the Title class (rather than Author) as the data source, and drag the **Title** node from the **Data Sources** window onto the form. Remove the Authors column from the DataGridView as it will not be used in this example.

*Step 3: Adding a **ComboBox** to the **Form***
In **Design** view, add a ComboBox named queriesComboBox below the DataGridView on the Form. Users will select which query to execute from this control. Set the ComboBox's Dock property to Bottom and the DataGridView's Dock property to Fill.

Next, you'll add the names of the queries to the ComboBox. Open the ComboBox's **String Collection Editor** by right clicking the ComboBox and selecting **Edit Items....** You can also access the **String Collection Editor** from the ComboBox's *smart tag menu.* A **smart tag menu** provides you with quick access to common properties you might set for a control (such as the Multiline property of a TextBox), so you can set these properties directly in **Design** view, rather than in the **Properties** window. You can open a control's *smart tag menu* by clicking the small arrowhead (▶) that appears in the control's upper-right corner in **Design** view when the control is selected. In the **String Collection Editor**, add the following three items to queriesComboBox—one for each of the queries we'll create:

1. All titles

2. Titles with 2014 copyright

3. Titles ending with "How to Program"

20.6.2 Coding the **Display Query Results** App
Next you'll create the code for this app (Fig. 20.22).

*Customizing the **Form**'s **Load** Event Handler*
Create the TitleQueries_Load event handler (lines 22–29) by double clicking the title bar in **Design** view. When the Form loads, it should display the complete list of books from the Titles table, sorted by title. Line 24 calls the Load extension method on the BookEntities DbContext's Titles property to load the Titles table's contents into memory. Rather than defining the same LINQ query as in lines 40–41, we can programmatically cause the queriesComboBox_SelectedIndexChanged event handler to execute simply by setting the queriesComboBox's SelectedIndex to 0 (line 28).

```
 1   // Fig. 20.22: TitleQueries.cs
 2   // Displaying the result of a user-selected query in a DataGridView.
 3   using System;
 4   using System.Data.Entity;
 5   using System.Linq;
 6   using System.Windows.Forms;
 7
 8   namespace DisplayQueryResult
 9   {
10      public partial class TitleQueries : Form
11      {
12         public TitleQueries()
13         {
14            InitializeComponent();
15         } // end constructor
16
```

Fig. 20.22 | Displaying the result of a user-selected query in a DataGridView. (Part 1 of 2.)

```
17        // Entity Framework DbContext
18        private BooksExamples.BooksEntities dbcontext =
19           new BooksExamples.BooksEntities();
20
21        // load data from database into DataGridView
22        private void TitleQueries_Load( object sender, EventArgs e )
23        {
24           dbcontext.Titles.Load(); // load Titles table into memory
25
26           // set the ComboBox to show the default query that
27           // selects all books from the Titles table
28           queriesComboBox.SelectedIndex = 0;
29        } // end method TitleQueries_Load
30
31        // loads data into titleBindingSource based on user-selected query
32        private void queriesComboBox_SelectedIndexChanged(
33           object sender, EventArgs e )
34        {
35           // set the data displayed according to what is selected
36           switch ( queriesComboBox.SelectedIndex )
37           {
38              case 0: // all titles
39                 // use LINQ to order the books by title
40                 titleBindingSource.DataSource =
41                    dbcontext.Titles.Local.OrderBy( book => book.Title1 );
42                 break;
43              case 1: // titles with 2014 copyright
44                 // use LINQ to get titles with 2014
45                 // copyright and sort them by title
46                 titleBindingSource.DataSource =
47                    dbcontext.Titles.Local
48                       .Where( book => book.Copyright == "2014" )
49                       .OrderBy( book => book.Title1 );
50                 break;
51              case 2: // titles ending with "How to Program"
52                 // use LINQ to get titles ending with
53                 // "How to Program" and sort them by title
54                 titleBindingSource.DataSource =
55                    dbcontext.Titles.Local
56                       .Where( book =>
57                          book.Title1.EndsWith( "How to Program" ) )
58                       .OrderBy( book => book.Title1 );
59                 break;
60           } // end switch
61
62           titleBindingSource.MoveFirst(); // move to first entry
63        } // end method queriesComboBox_SelectedIndexChanged
64     } // end class TitleQueries
65  } // end namespace DisplayQueryResult
```

Fig. 20.22 | Displaying the result of a user-selected query in a DataGridView. (Part 2 of 2.)

queriesComboBox_SelectedIndexChanged *Event Handler*

Next you must write code that executes the appropriate query each time the user chooses a different item from queriesComboBox. Double click queriesComboBox in **Design** view to generate a queriesComboBox_SelectedIndexChanged event handler (lines 32–63) in the TitleQueries.cs file. In the event handler, add a switch statement (lines 36–60). Each case in the switch will change the titleBindingSource's DataSource property to the results of a query that returns the correct set of data. The data bindings created by the IDE *automatically* update the titleDataGridView *each time* we change its DataSource. The **MoveFirst method** of the BindingSource (line 62) moves to the first row of the result each time a query executes. The results of the queries in lines 40–41, 46–49 and 54–58 are shown in Fig. 20.21(a), (b) and (c), respectively. Because we do not modify the data in this app, each of the queries is performed on the in-memory representation of the Titles table, which is accessible through dbcontext.Titles.Local.

Ordering the Books By Title

Lines 40–41 invoke the OrderBy extension method on dbcontext.Titles.Local to order the Title objects by their Title1 property values. As we mentioned previously, the IDE renamed the Title column of the database's Titles table as Title1 in the generated Title entity data model class to avoid a naming conflict with the class's name. Recall that Local returns an ObservableCollection<T> containing the row objects of the specified table—in this case, Local returns an ObservableCollection<Title>. When you invoke OrderBy on an ObservableCollection<T>, the method returns an IEnumerable<T>. We assign that object to the titleBindingSource's DataSource property. When the DataSource property changes, the DataGridView iterates through the contents of the IEnumerable<T> and displays the data.

Selecting Books with 2014 Copyright

Lines 46–49 filter the titles displayed by using the **Where extension method** with the lambda expression

```
book => book.Copyright == "2014"
```

as an argument. This lambda expression takes one Title object (named book) as its parameter and uses it to check whether the given Title's Copyright property (a string in the database) is equal to 2014. A lambda expression that's used with the Where extension method must return a bool value. Only Title objects for which this lambda expression returns true will be selected. We use OrderBy to order the results by the Title1 property so the books are displayed in ascending order by title. The type of the lambda's book parameter is *inferred* from dbcontext.Titles.Local, which contains Title objects. As soon as the titleBindingSource's DataSource property changes, the DataGridView is updated with the query results.

Selecting Books with Titles That End in "How to Program"

Lines 54–58 filter the titles displayed by using the Where extension method with the lambda expression

```
book => book.Title1.EndsWith( "How to Program" )
```

as an argument. This lambda expression takes one `Title` object (named book) as its parameter and uses it to check whether the given `Title`'s `Title1` property value ends with `"How to Program"`. The expression books.`Title1` returns the `string` stored in that property, then we use the string class's EndsWith method to perform the test. We order the results by the `Title1` property so the books are displayed in ascending order by title.

20.7 Retrieving Data from Multiple Tables with LINQ

In this section, you'll perform LINQ to Entities queries using the LINQ query syntax that was introduced in Chapter 9. In particular, you'll learn how to obtain query results that combine data from multiple tables (Fig. 20.23).

a) List of authors and the ISBNs of the books they've authored; sort the authors by last name then first name

b) List of authors and the titles of the book's they've authored; sort the authors by last name then first name; for a given author, sort the titles alphabetically

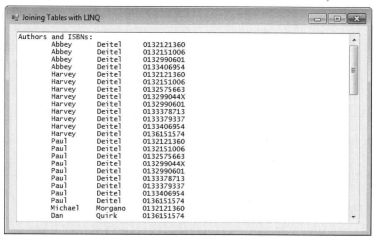

Fig. 20.23 | Outputs from the **Joining Tables with LINQ** app. (Part 1 of 2.)

c) List of titles
grouped by author;
sort the authors by
last name then first
name; for a given
author, sort the titles
alphabetically

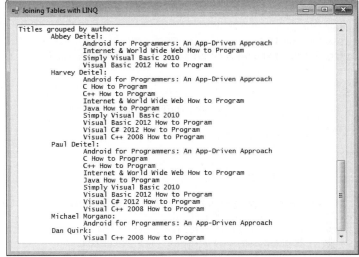

Fig. 20.23 | Outputs from the **Joining Tables with LINQ** app. (Part 2 of 2.)

The **Joining Tables with LINQ** app uses LINQ to Entities to combine and organize data from multiple tables, and shows the results of queries that perform the following tasks:

- Get a list of all the authors and the ISBNs of the books they've authored, sorted by last name then first name (Fig. 20.23(a)).

- Get a list of all the authors and the titles of the books they've authored, sorted by last name then first; for each author sort the titles alphabetically (Fig. 20.23(b)).

- Get a list of all the book titles grouped by author, sorted by last name then first; for a given author sort the titles alphabetically (Fig. 20.23(c)).

GUI for the Joining Tables with LINQ App

For this example (Fig. 20.24–Fig. 20.27), perform the steps in Section 20.5.2 to create a new **Windows Forms Application** project named `JoinQueries` in the same solution as the previous examples. Rename the `Form1.cs` source file to `JoiningTableData.cs`. Set the Form's **Text** property to `Joining Tables with LINQ`. Be sure to set the `JoinQueries` project as the startup project. We set the following properties for the `outputTextBox`:

- **Font** property: Set to `Lucida Console` to display the output in a fixed-width font.

- **Anchor** property: Set to `Top`, `Bottom`, `Left`, `Right` so that you can resize the window and the `outputTextBox` will resize accordingly.

- **Scrollbars** property: Set to `Vertical`, so that you can scroll through the output.

Creating the DbContext

The code uses the entity data model classes to combine data from the tables in the `Books` database and display the relationships between the authors and books in three different ways. We split the code for class `JoiningTableData` into several figures (Figs. 20.24–20.27) for presentation purposes. As in previous examples, the `DbContext` object (Fig. 20.24, lines 19–20) allows the program to interact with the database.

```
 1   // Fig. 20.24: JoiningTableData.cs
 2   // Using LINQ to perform a join and aggregate data across tables.
 3   using System;
 4   using System.Linq;
 5   using System.Windows.Forms;
 6
 7   namespace JoinQueries
 8   {
 9      public partial class JoiningTableData : Form
10      {
11         public JoiningTableData()
12         {
13            InitializeComponent();
14         } // end constructor
15
16         private void JoiningTableData_Load(object sender, EventArgs e)
17         {
18            // Entity Framework DbContext
19            BooksExamples.BooksEntities dbcontext =
20               new BooksExamples.BooksEntities();
21
```

Fig. 20.24 | Creating the `BooksDataContext` for querying the `Books` database.

Combining Author Names with the ISBNs of the Books They've Written

The first query (Fig. 20.25, lines 24–27) *joins* data from two tables and returns a list of author names and the ISBNs representing the books they've written, sorted by `LastName` then `FirstName`. The query takes advantage of the properties in the entity data model classes that were created based on foreign-key relationships between the database's tables. These properties enable you to easily combine data from related rows in multiple tables.

```
22            // get authors and ISBNs of each book they co-authored
23            var authorsAndISBNs =
24               from author in dbcontext.Authors
25               from book in author.Titles
26               orderby author.LastName, author.FirstName
27               select new { author.FirstName, author.LastName, book.ISBN };
28
29            outputTextBox.AppendText( "Authors and ISBNs:" );
30
31            // display authors and ISBNs in tabular format
32            foreach ( var element in authorsAndISBNs )
33            {
34               outputTextBox.AppendText(
35                  String.Format( "\r\n\t{0,-10} {1,-10} {2,-10}",
36                     element.FirstName, element.LastName, element.ISBN ) );
37            } // end foreach
38
```

Fig. 20.25 | Getting a list of authors and the ISBNs of the books they've authored.

The first from clause (line 24) gets each author from the Authors table. The second from clause (line 25) uses the generated Titles property of the Author class to get the ISBNs for the current author. The entity data model uses the foreign-key information stored in the database's AuthorISBN table to get the appropriate ISBNs. The combined result of the two from clauses is a collection of all the authors and the ISBNs of the books they've authored. The two from clauses introduce *two* range variables into the scope of this query—other clauses can access both range variables to combine data from multiple tables. Line 26 orders the results by the author's LastName, then FirstName. Line 27 creates a new anonymous type that contains the FirstName and LastName of an author from the Authors table with the ISBN of a book in the Titles table written by that author.

Anonymous Types

As you know, anonymous types allow you to create simple classes used to store data without writing a class definition. An *anonymous type declaration* (line 27)—known formally as an *anonymous object-creation expression*—is similar to an object initializer (Section 10.13). The anonymous type declaration begins with the keyword new followed by a member-initializer list in braces ({}). No class name is specified after the new keyword. The compiler generates a class definition based on the anonymous object-creation expression. This class contains the properties specified in the member-initializer list—FirstName, LastName and ISBN. All properties of an anonymous type are public. Anonymous type properties are *read-only*—you cannot modify a property's value once the object is created. Each property's type is *inferred* from the values assigned to it. The class definition is generated automatically by the compiler, so you don't know the class's type name (hence the term anonymous type). Thus, you must use *implicitly typed local variables* to store references to objects of anonymous types (e.g., line 32). Though we are not using it here, the compiler defines a ToString method when creating the anonymous type's class definition. The method returns a string in curly braces containing a comma-separated list of *PropertyName = value* pairs. The compiler also provides an Equals method, which compares the properties of the anonymous object that calls the method and the anonymous object that it receives as an argument.

Combining Author Names with the Titles of the Books They've Written

The second query (Fig. 20.26, lines 41–45) gives similar output, but uses the foreign-key relationships to get the title of each book that an author wrote.

```
39          // get authors and titles of each book they co-authored
40          var authorsAndTitles =
41              from book in dbcontext.Titles
42              from author in book.Authors
43              orderby author.LastName, author.FirstName, book.Title1
44              select new { author.FirstName, author.LastName,
45                  book.Title1 };
46
47          outputTextBox.AppendText( "\r\n\r\nAuthors and titles:" );
48
49          // display authors and titles in tabular format
50          foreach ( var element in authorsAndTitles )
51          {
```

Fig. 20.26 | Getting a list of authors and the titles of the books they've authored. (Part 1 of 2.)

```
52                     outputTextBox.AppendText(
53                         String.Format( "\r\n\t{0,-10} {1,-10} {2}",
54                             element.FirstName, element.LastName, element.Title1 ) );
55             } // end foreach
56
```

Fig. 20.26 | Getting a list of authors and the titles of the books they've authored. (Part 2 of 2.)

The first from clause (line 41) gets each book from the Titles table. The second from clause (line 42) uses the generated Authors property of the Title class to get only the authors for the current book. The entity data model uses the foreign-key information stored in the database's AuthorISBN table to get the appropriate authors. The author objects give us access to the names of the current book's authors. The select clause (lines 44–45) uses the author and book range variables introduced earlier in the query to get the FirstName and LastName of each author from the Authors table and the title of each book from the Titles table.

Organizing Book Titles by Author

Most queries return results with data arranged in a relational-style table of rows and columns. The last query (Fig. 20.27, lines 60–66) returns hierarchical results. Each element in the results contains the name of an Author and a list of Titles that the author wrote. The LINQ query does this by using a *nested query* in the select clause. The outer query iterates over the authors in the database. The inner query takes a specific author and retrieves all titles that the author wrote. The select clause (lines 62–66) creates an anonymous type with two properties:

- The property Name (line 62) combines each author's name, separating the first and last names by a space.

- The property Titles (line 63) receives the result of the nested query, which returns the title of each book written by the current author.

In this case, we're providing names for each property in the new anonymous type. When you create an anonymous type, you can specify the name for each property by using the format *name = value*.

```
57             // get authors and titles of each book
58             // they co-authored; group by author
59             var titlesByAuthor =
60                 from author in dbcontext.Authors
61                 orderby author.LastName, author.FirstName
62                 select new { Name = author.FirstName + " " + author.LastName,
63                     Titles =
64                         from book in author.Titles
65                         orderby book.Title1
66                         select book.Title1 };
67
68             outputTextBox.AppendText( "\r\n\r\nTitles grouped by author:" );
69
```

Fig. 20.27 | Getting a list of titles grouped by authors. (Part 1 of 2.)

```
70              // display titles written by each author, grouped by author
71              foreach ( var author in titlesByAuthor )
72              {
73                  // display author's name
74                  outputTextBox.AppendText( "\r\n\t" + author.Name + ":" );
75
76                  // display titles written by that author
77                  foreach ( var title in author.Titles )
78                  {
79                      outputTextBox.AppendText( "\r\n\t\t" + title );
80                  } // end inner foreach
81              } // end outer foreach
82          } // end method JoiningTableData_Load
83      } // end class JoiningTableData
84  } // end namespace JoinQueries
```

Fig. 20.27 | Getting a list of titles grouped by authors. (Part 2 of 2.)

The range variable book in the nested query iterates over the current author's books using in the Titles property. The Title1 property of a given book returns the Title column from that row of the Titles table in the database.

The nested foreach statements (lines 71–81) use the properties of the anonymous type created by the query to output the hierarchical results. The outer loop displays the author's name and the inner loop displays the titles of all the books written by that author.

20.8 Creating a Master/Detail View App

Figure 20.28 demonstrates a so-called **master/detail view**—one part of the GUI (the master) allows you to select an entry, and another part (the details) displays detailed information about that entry. When the app first loads, it displays the name of the first author in the data source and that author's books (Fig. 20.28(a)). When you use the buttons on the Binding-Navigator to change authors, the app displays the details of the books written by the corresponding author (Fig. 20.28(b)). This app only reads data from the entity data model, so we disabled the buttons in the BindingNavigator that enable the user to add and delete records.

a) **Master/Detail** app displaying books for the first author in the data source

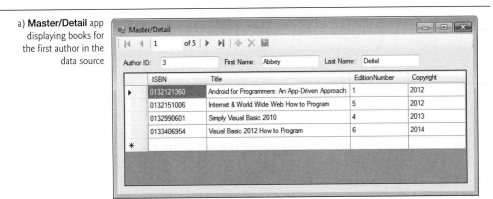

Fig. 20.28 | **Master/Detail** app. (Part 1 of 2.)

b) **Master/Detail** app displaying books for the third author in the data source

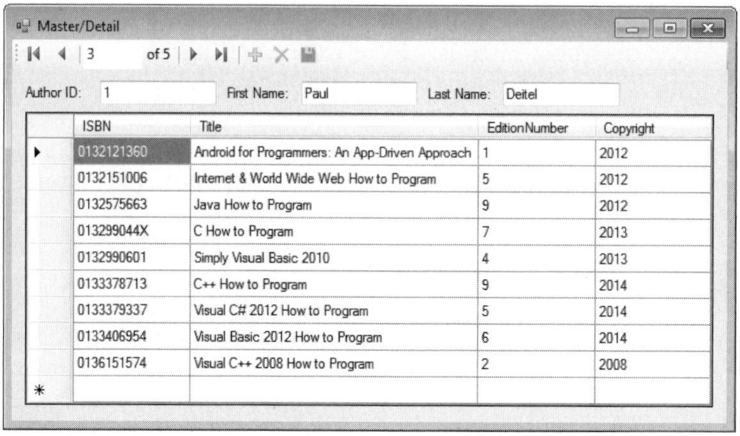

Fig. 20.28 | Master/Detail app. (Part 2 of 2.)

When you run the app, experiment with the BindingNavigator's controls. The DVD-player-like buttons of the BindingNavigator allow you to change the currently displayed row.

20.8.1 Creating the Master/Detail GUI

You've seen that the IDE can automatically generate the BindingSource, BindingNavigator and GUI elements when you drag a data source onto the Form. You'll now use two BindingSources—one for the master list of authors and one for the titles associated with a given author. Both will be generated by the IDE.

Step 1: Creating the Project
Follow the instructions in Section 20.5.2 to create and configure a new **Windows Forms Application** project called MasterDetail. Name the source file Details.cs and set the Form's Text property to **Master/Detail**.

*Step 2: Adding a Data Source for the **Authors** Table*
Follow the steps in Section 20.5.3 to add a data source for the Authors table. Although you'll be displaying records from the Titles table for each author, you do not need to add a data source for that table. The title information will be obtained from the Titles navigation property in the Author entity data model class.

Step 3: Creating GUI Elements
Next, you'll use the **Design** view to create the GUI components by dragging-and-dropping items from the **Data Sources** window onto the Form. In the earlier sections, you dragged an object from the **Data Sources** window to the Form to create a DataGridView. The IDE allows you to specify the type of control(s) that it will create when you drag and drop an object from the **Data Sources** window onto a Form. To do so:

1. Switch to **Design** view for the Details class.

2. Click the **Author** node in the **Data Sources** window—it should change to a drop-down list. Open the drop-down by clicking the down arrow and select the **Details**

option—this indicates that we'd like to generate Label–TextBox pairs that represent each column of the Authors table.

3. Drag the **Author** node from the **Data Sources** window onto the Form in **Design** view. This creates the authorBindingSource, the authorBindingNavigator and the La-bel–TextBox pairs that represent each column in the table. Initially, the controls appear as shown in Fig. 20.29. We rearranged the controls as shown in Fig. 20.28.

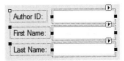

Fig. 20.29 | Details representation of an Author.

4. By default, the Titles navigation property is implemented in the entity data model classes as a HashSet<Title>. To bind the data to GUI controls properly, you must change this to an ObservableCollection<Title>. To do this, expand the class library project's BooksModel.edmx node in the **Solution Explorer**, then expand the BooksModel.tt node and open Author.cs in the editor. Add a using statement for the namespace System.Collections.ObjectModel. Then, in the Author constructor change HashSet to ObservableCollection. Right click the class library project in the **Solution Explorer** and select **Build** to recompile the class.

5. Next, click the **Titles** node that's nested in the **Author** node in the **Data Sources** window—it should change to a drop-down list. Open the drop-down by clicking the down arrow and ensure that the DataGridView option is selected—this is the GUI control that will be used to display the data from the Titles table that corresponds to a given author.

6. Drag the **Titles** node onto the Form in **Design** view. This creates the titlesBind-ingSource and the DataGridView. This control is only for *viewing* data, so set its ReadOnly property to True using the **Properties** window. Because we dragged the **Titles** node from the **Author** node in the **Data Sources** window, the DataGridView will automatically display the books for the currently selected author once we bind the author data to the authorBindingSource.

We used the DataGridView's Anchor property to anchor it to all four sides of the Form. We also set the Form's Size and MinimumSize properties to 550, 300 to set the Form's initial size and minimum size, respectively. The completed GUI is shown in Fig. 20.30.

20.8.2 Coding the Master/Detail App

The code to display an author and the corresponding books (Fig. 20.31) is straightforward. Lines 17–18 create the DbContext. The Form's Load event handler (lines 22–32) orders the Author objects by LastName (line 26) and FirstName (line 27), then loads them into memory (line 28). Next, line 31 assigns dbcontext.Authors.Local to the authorBinding-Source's DataSource property. At this point:

- the BindingNavigator displays the number of Author objects and indicates that the first one in the results is selected,

- the TextBoxes display the currently selected Author's AuthorID, FirstName and LastName property values, and

- the currently selected Author's titles are automatically assigned to the titlesBindingSource's DataSource, which causes the DataGridView to display those titles.

Now, when you use the BindingNavigator to change the selected Author, the corresponding titles are displayed in the DataGridView.

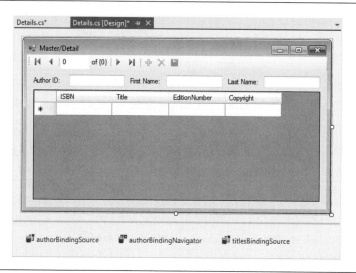

Fig. 20.30 | Finished design of the **Master/Detail** app.

```
 1   // Fig. 20.31: Details.cs
 2   // Using a DataGridView to display details based on a selection.
 3   using System;
 4   using System.Data.Entity;
 5   using System.Linq;
 6   using System.Windows.Forms;
 7
 8   namespace MasterDetail
 9   {
10      public partial class Details : Form
11      {
12         public Details()
13         {
14            InitializeComponent();
15         } // end constructor
16
17         // Entity Framework DbContext
18         BooksExamples.BooksEntities dbcontext =
19            new BooksExamples.BooksEntities();
20
```

Fig. 20.31 | Using a DataGridView to display details based on a selection. (Part 1 of 2.)

```
21            // initialize data sources when the Form is loaded
22            private void Details_Load( object sender, EventArgs e )
23            {
24                // load Authors table ordered by LastName then FirstName
25                dbcontext.Authors
26                    .OrderBy( author => author.LastName )
27                    .ThenBy( author => author.FirstName )
28                    .Load();
29
30                // specify DataSource for authorBindingSource
31                authorBindingSource.DataSource = dbcontext.Authors.Local;
32            } // end method Details_Load
33        } // end class Details
34    } // end namespace MasterDetail
```

Fig. 20.31 | Using a `DataGridView` to display details based on a selection. (Part 2 of 2.)

20.9 Address Book Case Study

Our final example (Fig. 20.32) implements a simple `AddressBook` app that enables users to perform the following tasks on the database `AddressBook.mdf` (which is included in the directory with this chapter's examples):

- Insert new contacts
- Find contacts whose last names begin with the specified letters
- Update existing contacts
- Delete contacts

We populated the database with six fictional contacts.

Rather than displaying a database table in a `DataGridView`, this app presents the details of one contact at a time in several `TextBox`es. The `BindingNavigator` at the top of the window allows you to control which *row* of the table is displayed at any given time. The `BindingNavigator` also allows you to *add* a contact and *delete* a contact—but only

a) Use the `BindingNavigator`'s controls to navigate through the contacts in the database

Fig. 20.32 | Manipulating an address book. (Part 1 of 2.)

b) Type a search `string` in the **Last Name:** TextBox then press **Find** to locate contacts whose last names begin with that `string`; only two names start with "Br" so the `BindingNavigator` indicates two matching records

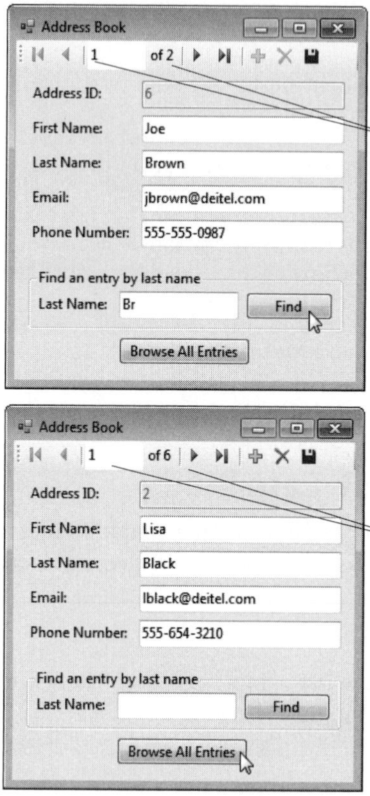

Displaying the first of two matching contacts for the current search

c) Click **Browse All Entries** to clear the search `string` and allow browsing of all contacts in the database

You can now browse through all six contacts

Fig. 20.32 | Manipulating an address book. (Part 2 of 2.)

when browsing the *complete* contact list. When you filter the contacts by last name, the app disables the **Add new** (⊕) and **Delete** (✗) buttons (we'll explain why shortly). Clicking **Browse All Entries** enables these buttons again. Adding a row clears the TextBoxes and sets the TextBox to the right of **Address ID** to zero to indicate that the TextBoxes now represent a new record. When you save a new entry, the **Address ID** field is automatically changed from zero to a unique ID number by the database. No changes are made to the underlying database unless you click the **Save Data** (💾) button.

20.9.1 Creating the Address Book App's GUI

We discuss the app's code momentarily. First you'll set up the entity data model and a Windows Forms app.

Step 1: Creating a Class Library Project for the Entity Data Model

Perform the steps in Section 20.5.1 to create a **Class Library** project named AddressExample that contains an entity data model for the AddressBook.mdf database, which contains only an Addresses table with AddressID, FirstName, LastName, Email and PhoneNumber columns. Name the entity data model AddressModel.edmx. The AddressBook.mdf database is located in the Databases folder with this chapter's examples.

*Step 2: Creating a Windows Forms Application Project for **AddressBook** App*
Perform the steps in Section 20.5.2 to create a new **Windows Forms Application** project named AddressBook in the AddressExample solution. Set the Form's filename to Contacts.cs, then set the Form's **Text** property to Address Book. Set the AddressBook project as the solution's startup project.

*Step 3: Adding the **Address** Object as a Data Source*
Add the entity data model's Address object as a data source, as you did with the Author object in *Step 1* of Section 20.5.3.

Step 4: Displaying the Details of Each Row
In **Design** view, select the **Address** node in the **Data Sources** window. Click the **Address** node's down arrow and select the **Details** option to indicate that the IDE should create a set of Label–TextBox pairs to show the details of a single record at a time.

*Step 5: Dragging the **Address** Data-Source Node to the **Form***
Drag the Address node from the **Data Sources** window to the Form. This automatically creates a BindingNavigator and the Labels and TextBoxes corresponding to the columns of the database table. The fields are placed in alphabetical order. Reorder the components, using **Design** view, so they're in the order shown in Fig. 20.32. You'll also want to change the tab order of the controls. To do so, select **VIEW > Tab Order** then click the TextBoxes from top to bottom in the order they appear in Fig. 20.32.

*Step 5: Making the **AddressID** TextBox **ReadOnly***
The AddressID column of the Addresses table is an *autoincremented identity column*, so users should *not* be allowed to edit the values in this column. Select the TextBox for the AddressID and set its ReadOnly property to True using the **Properties** window.

Step 6: Adding Controls to Allow Users to Specify a Last Name to Locate
While the BindingNavigator allows you to browse the address book, it would be more convenient to be able to find a specific entry by last name. To add this functionality to the app, we must create controls to allow the user to enter a last name and provide event handlers to perform the search.

Add a Label named findLabel, a TextBox named findTextBox, and a Button named findButton. Place these controls in a GroupBox named findGroupBox, then set its Text property to **Find an entry by last name**. Set the Text property of the Label to Last Name: and set the Text property of the Button to Find.

Step 7: Allowing the User to Return to Browsing All Rows of the Database
To allow users to return to browsing all the contacts after searching for contacts with a specific last name, add a Button named browseAllButton below the findGroupBox. Set the Text property of browseAllButton to **Browse All Entries**.

20.9.2 Coding the Address Book App

The Contacts.cs code-behind file is split into several figures (Figs. 20.33–20.37) for presentation purposes.

Method RefreshContacts

As we showed in previous examples, we must connect the addressBindingSource that controls the GUI with the DbContext that interacts with the database. In this example, we declare the AddressEntities DbContext object at line 20 of Fig. 20.33, but create it and initiate the data binding in the RefreshContacts method (lines 23–43), which is called from several other methods in the app. When this method is called, if dbcontext is not null, we call its Dispose method, then create a new AddressEntities DbContext at line 30. We do this so we can re-sort the data in the entity data model. If we maintained one dbcontext.Addresses object in memory for the duration of the program and the user changed a person's last name or first name, the records would still remain in their original order in the dbcontext.Addresses object, even if that order is incorrect. Lines 34–37 order the Address objects by LastName, then FirstName and load the objects into memory. Then line 40 sets the addressBindingSource's DataSource property to dbcontext.Addresses.Local to bind the data in memory to the GUI.

```
 1    // Fig. 20.33: Contact.cs
 2    // Manipulating an address book.
 3    using System;
 4    using System.Data;
 5    using System.Data.Entity;
 6    using System.Data.Entity.Validation;
 7    using System.Linq;
 8    using System.Windows.Forms;
 9
10    namespace AddressBook
11    {
12       public partial class Contacts : Form
13       {
14          public Contacts()
15          {
16             InitializeComponent();
17          } // end constructor
18
19          // Entity Framework DbContext
20          private AddressExample.AddressBookEntities dbcontext = null;
21
22          // fill our addressBindingSource with all rows, ordered by name
23          private void RefreshContacts()
24          {
25             // Dispose old DbContext, if any
26             if ( dbcontext != null )
27                dbcontext.Dispose();
28
29             // create new DbContext so we can reorder records based on edits
30             dbcontext = new AddressExample.AddressBookEntities();
31
32             // use LINQ to order the Addresses table contents
33             // by last name, then first name
```

Fig. 20.33 | Creating the BooksDataContext and defining method RefreshContacts for use in other methods. (Part 1 of 2.)

```
34                 dbcontext.Addresses
35                    .OrderBy( entry => entry.LastName )
36                    .ThenBy( entry => entry.FirstName )
37                    .Load();
38
39                 // specify DataSource for addressBindingSource
40                 addressBindingSource.DataSource = dbcontext.Addresses.Local;
41                 addressBindingSource.MoveFirst(); // go to first result
42                 findTextBox.Clear(); // clear the Find TextBox
43            } // end method RefreshContacts
44
```

Fig. 20.33 | Creating the `BooksDataContext` and defining method `RefreshContacts` for use in other methods. (Part 2 of 2.)

Method *Contacts_Load*

Method `Contacts_Load` (Fig. 20.34) calls `RefreshContacts` (line 48) so that the first record is displayed when the app starts. As before, you create the Load event handler by double clicking the Form's title bar.

```
45            // when the form loads, fill it with data from the database
46            private void Contacts_Load( object sender, EventArgs e )
47            {
48               RefreshContacts(); // fill binding with data from database
49            } // end method Contacts_Load
50
```

Fig. 20.34 | Calling `RefreshContacts` to fill the `TextBox`es when the app loads.

Method *addressBindingNavigatorSaveItem_Click*

Method `addressBindingNavigatorSaveItem_Click` (Fig. 20.35) saves the changes to the database when the `BindingNavigator`'s **Save Data** Button is clicked. (Remember to enable this button.) The `AddressBook` database requires values for the first name, last name, phone number and e-mail. If a field is empty when you attempt to save, a `DbEntityValidationException` exception occurs. We call `RefreshContacts` after saving to re-sort the data and move back to the first element.

```
51            // Click event handler for the Save Button in the
52            // BindingNavigator saves the changes made to the data
53            private void addressBindingNavigatorSaveItem_Click(
54               object sender, EventArgs e )
55            {
56               Validate(); // validate input fields
57               addressBindingSource.EndEdit(); // complete current edit, if any
58
59               // try to save changes
60               try
61               {
```

Fig. 20.35 | Saving changes to the database when the user clicks **Save Data**. (Part 1 of 2.)

```
62                dbcontext.SaveChanges(); // write changes to database file
63            } // end try
64            catch ( DbEntityValidationException )
65            {
66                MessageBox.Show( "Columns cannot be empty",
67                    "Entity Validation Exception" );
68            } // end catch
69
70            RefreshContacts(); // change back to initial unfiltered data
71        } // end method addressBindingNavigatorSaveItem_Click
72
```

Fig. 20.35 | Saving changes to the database when the user clicks **Save Data**. (Part 2 of 2.)

Method findButton_Click

Method findButton_Click (Fig. 20.36) uses LINQ query syntax (lines 79–83) to select only people whose last names start with the characters in the findTextBox. The query sorts the results by last name then first name. In LINQ to Entities, you *cannot* bind a LINQ query's results directly to a BindingSource's DataSource. So, line 86 calls the query object's ToList method to get a List representation of the filtered data and assigns the *List* to the BindingSource's DataSource. When you convert the query result to a List, only changes to *existing* records in the DbContext are tracked by the DbContext—any records that you add or remove while viewing the filtered data would be lost. For this reason we disabled the **Add new** and **Delete** buttons when the data is filtered. When you enter a last name and click **Find**, the BindingNavigator allows the user to browse only the rows containing the matching last names. This is because the data source bound to the Form's controls (the result of the LINQ query) has changed and now contains only a limited number of rows.

```
73        // use LINQ to create a data source that contains only people
74        // with last names that start with the specified text
75        private void findButton_Click( object sender, EventArgs e )
76        {
77            // use LINQ to filter contacts with last names that
78            // start with findTextBox contents
79            var lastNameQuery =
80                from address in dbcontext.Addresses
81                where address.LastName.StartsWith( findTextBox.Text )
82                orderby address.LastName, address.FirstName
83                select address;
84
85            // display matching contacts
86            addressBindingSource.DataSource = lastNameQuery.ToList();
87            addressBindingSource.MoveFirst(); // go to first result
88
89            // don't allow add/delete when contacts are filtered
90            bindingNavigatorAddNewItem.Enabled = false;
91            bindingNavigatorDeleteItem.Enabled = false;
92        } // end method findButton_Click
93
```

Fig. 20.36 | Finding the contacts whose last names begin with a specified String.

Method **browseAllButton_Click**

Method browseAllButton_Click (Fig. 20.37) allows users to return to browsing all the rows after searching for specific rows. Double click browseAllButton to create a Click event handler. The event handler enables the **Add new** and **Delete** buttons then calls RefreshContacts to restore the data source to the full list of people (in sorted order) and clear the findTextBox.

```
94        // reload addressBindingSource with all rows
95        private void browseAllButton_Click( object sender, EventArgs e )
96        {
97           // allow add/delete when contacts are not filtered
98           bindingNavigatorAddNewItem.Enabled = true;
99           bindingNavigatorDeleteItem.Enabled = true;
100          RefreshContacts(); // change back to initial unfiltered data
101       } // end method browseButton_Click
102    } // end class Contacts
103 } // end namespace AddressBook
```

Fig. 20.37 | Allowing the user to browse all contacts.

20.10 Tools and Web Resources

Our LINQ Resource Center at www.deitel.com/LINQ contains many links to additional information, including blogs by Microsoft LINQ team members, sample chapters, tutorials, videos, downloads, FAQs, forums, webcasts and other resource sites.

A useful tool for learning LINQ is LINQPad (www.linqpad.net), which allows you to execute and view the results of any C# or Visual Basic expression, including LINQ queries. It also supports the ADO.NET Entity Framework and LINQ to Entities.

This chapter is meant as an introduction to databases, the ADO.NET Entity Framework and LINQ to Entities. Microsoft's Entity Framework site

    msdn.microsoft.com/en-us/data/aa937723

provides lots of additional information on working with the ADO.NET Entity Framework and LINQ to Entities, including tutorials, videos and more.

20.11 Wrap-Up

This chapter introduced the relational database model, the ADO.NET Entity Framework, LINQ to Entities and the Visual Studio 2012's visual programming tools for working with databases. You examined the contents of a simple Books database and learned about the relationships among the tables in the database. You used LINQ to Entities and the entity data model classes generated by the IDE to retrieve data from, add new data to, delete data from and update data in a SQL Server Express database.

We discussed the entity data model classes automatically generated by the IDE, such as the DbContext class that manages an app's interactions with a database. You learned how to use the IDE's tools to connect to databases and to generate entity data model classes based on an existing database's schema. You then used the IDE's drag-and-drop capabilities to automatically generate GUIs for displaying and manipulating database data.

In the next chapter, we demonstrate how to build web apps using Microsoft's ASP.NET web forms technology, which is similar similar to building Windows Forms apps, but in the context of web pages. We introduce the concept of a three-tier app, which is divided into three pieces that can reside on the same computer or be distributed among separate computers across a network such as the Internet. One of these tiers—the information tier—typically stores data in a database.

21

Web App Development with ASP.NET

Objectives

In this chapter you'll:

- wLearn qeb app development using ASP.NET.

- Handle the events from a Web Form's controls.

- Use validation controls to ensure that data is in the correct format before it's sent from a client to the server.

- Maintain user-specific information.

- Create a data-driven web app using ASP.NET and the ADO.NET Entity Framework.

21.1 Introduction

In this chapter, we introduce **web-app development** with Microsoft's **ASP.NET** technology. Web-based apps create web content for web-browser clients.

We present several examples that demonstrate web-app development using **Web Forms**, **web controls** (also called **ASP.NET server controls**) and Visual C# programming. Web Form files have the filename extension **.aspx** and contain the web page's GUI. You customize Web Forms by adding web controls including labels, textboxes, images, buttons and other GUI components. The Web Form file represents the web page that's sent to the client browser. We often refer to Web Form files as **ASPX files**.

An ASPX file created in Visual Studio has a corresponding class written in a .NET language—we use Visual C# in this book. This class contains event handlers, initialization code, utility methods and other supporting code. The file that contains this class is called the **code-behind file** and provides the ASPX file's programmatic implementation.

Software Used in This Chapter
To develop the code and GUIs in this chapter, we used Microsoft's **Visual Studio Express 2012 for Web**—a free IDE designed for developing ASP.NET web apps. The full version of Visual Studio 2012 includes the functionality of Visual Studio Express 2012 for Web, so the instructions we present in this chapter also apply to Visual Studio 2012. See the Before You Begin section that follows the Preface for additional information on downloading and installing the software for this chapter.

Web App Development with ASP.NET: A Deeper Look
In Chapter 27, Web App Development with ASP.NET: A Deeper Look, we present several additional web-app development topics, including:

- master pages to maintain a uniform look-and-feel across the pages in a web app
- creating password-protected websites with registration and login capabilities

- using the **Web Site Administration Tool** to specify which parts of a website are password protected
- using ASP.NET AJAX to quickly and easily improve the user experience for your web apps, giving them responsiveness comparable to that of desktop apps.

21.2 Web Basics

In this section, we discuss what occurs when a user requests a web page in a browser. In its simplest form, a *web page* is nothing more than an *HTML (HyperText Markup Language) document* (with the extension `.html` or `.htm`) that describes to a web browser the document's content and how to format it.

HTML documents normally contain *hyperlinks* that link to different pages or to other parts of the same page. When the user clicks a hyperlink, a **web server** locates the requested web page and sends it to the user's web browser. Similarly, the user can type the *address of a web page* into the browser's *address field* and press *Enter* to view the specified page.

In this chapter, we develop web apps using visual development techniques that are similar to those you used with Windows `Forms` in Chapters 14–15. To take full advantage of web app development, you'll also want to learn HTML5, CSSS and JavaScript—topics that we cover in our textbook *Internet & World Wide Web How to Program, 5/e*. You can learn more about this book at `deitel.com/books/iw3htp5`.

URIs and URLs

URIs (Uniform Resource Identifiers) identify resources on the Internet. URIs that start with `http://` are called *URLs (Uniform Resource Locators)*. Common URLs refer to files, directories or server-side code that performs tasks such as database lookups, Internet searches and business application processing. If you know the URL of a publicly available resource anywhere on the web, you can enter that URL into a web browser's address field and the browser can access that resource.

Parts of a URL

A URL contains information that directs a browser to the resource that the user wishes to access. Web servers make such resources available to web clients. Popular web servers include Microsoft's Internet Information Services (IIS), Apache's HTTP Server and Nginx.[1]
    Let's examine the components of the URL

```
http://www.deitel.com/books/downloads.html
```

The `http://` indicates that the HyperText Transfer Protocol (HTTP) should be used to obtain the resource. HTTP is the web protocol that enables clients and servers to communicate. Next in the URL is the server's fully qualified **hostname** (`www.deitel.com`)—the name of the web server computer on which the resource resides. This computer is referred to as the **host**, because it houses and maintains resources. The hostname `www.deitel.com` is translated into an **IP (Internet Protocol) address**—a numerical value that uniquely identifies the server on the Internet. A **Domain Name System (DNS) server** maintains a database of hostnames and their corresponding IP addresses, and performs the translations automatically.

---

1. w3techs.com/.

The remainder of the URL (/books/downloads.html) specifies the resource's location (/books) and name (downloads.html) on the web server. The location could represent an actual directory on the web server's file system. For *security* reasons, however, the location is typically a *virtual directory*. The web server translates the virtual directory into a real location on the server, thus hiding the resource's true location.

Making a Request and Receiving a Response

When given a URL, a web browser uses HTTP to retrieve the web page found at that address. Figure 21.1 shows a web browser sending a request to a web server. Figure 21.2 shows the web server responding to that request.

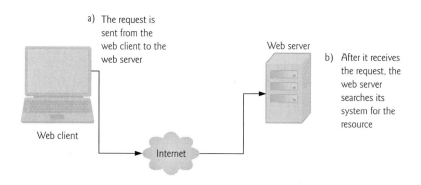

Fig. 21.1 | Client requesting a resource from a web server.

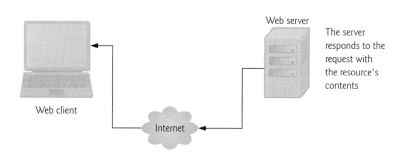

Fig. 21.2 | Client receiving a response from the web server.

21.3 Multitier App Architecture

Web-based apps are **multitier apps** (sometimes referred to as *n*-tier apps). Multitier apps divide functionality into separate **tiers** (that is, logical groupings of functionality). Although tiers can be located on the *same* computer, the tiers of web-based apps commonly reside on *separate* computers for *security* and *scalability*. Figure 21.3 presents the basic architecture of a three-tier web-based app.

Information Tier

The **bottom tier** (also called the **information tier**) maintains the app's data. This tier typically stores data in a relational database management system. For example, a retail store might have a database for storing product information, such as descriptions, prices and quantities in stock. The same database also might contain customer information, such as user names, billing addresses and credit card numbers. This tier can contain multiple databases, which together comprise the data needed for an app.

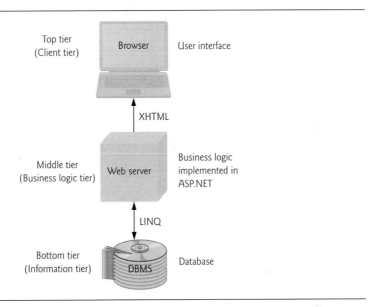

Fig. 21.3 | Three-tier architecture.

Business Logic

The **middle tier** implements **business logic**, **controller logic** and **presentation logic** to control interactions between the app's clients and its data. The middle tier acts as an intermediary between data in the information tier and the app's clients. The middle-tier controller logic processes client requests (such as requests to view a product catalog) and retrieves data from the database. The middle-tier presentation logic then processes data from the information tier and presents the content to the client. Web apps present data to clients as web pages.

Business logic in the middle tier enforces *business rules* and ensures that data is reliable before the server app updates the database or presents the data to users. Business rules dictate how clients can and cannot access app data, and how apps process data. For example, a business rule in the middle tier of a retail store's web-based app might ensure that all product quantities remain positive. A client request to set a negative quantity in the bottom tier's product information database would be rejected by the middle tier's business logic.

Client Tier

The **top tier**, or **client tier**, is the app's user interface, which gathers input and displays output. Users interact directly with the app through the user interface (typically viewed in a web browser), keyboard and mouse. In response to user actions (for example, clicking a hyperlink), the client tier interacts with the middle tier to make requests and to retrieve data from the information tier. The client tier then displays to the user the data retrieved from the middle tier. The client tier *never* directly interacts with the information tier.

21.4 Your First Web App

Our first example displays the web server's time of day in a browser window (Fig. 21.4). When this app executes—that is, a web browser requests the app's web page—the web server executes the app's code, which gets the current time and displays it in a Label. The web server then returns the result to the web browser that made the request, and the web browser *renders* the web page containing the time. We executed this app in both the *Internet Explorer* and *Firefox* web browsers to show you that the web page renders identically in different browsers—the page should look the same in most Web browsers.

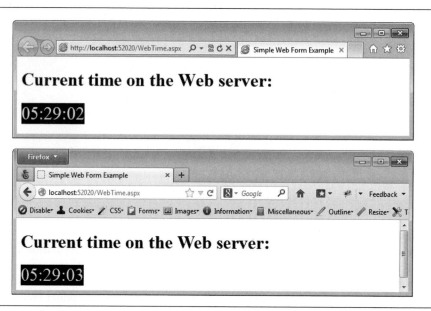

Fig. 21.4 | WebTime web app running in both Internet Explorer and Firefox.

Testing the App in Your Default Web Browser
To test this app in your default web browser, perform the following steps:

1. Open Visual Studio Express For Web.

2. Select **Open Web Site...** from the **FILE** menu.

3. In the **Open Web Site** dialog (Fig. 21.5), ensure that **File System** is selected, then navigate to this chapter's examples, select the WebTime folder and click the **Open Button**.

4. Select WebTime.aspx in the **Solution Explorer**, then type *Ctrl* + *F5* to execute the web app.

Fig. 21.5 | Open Web Site dialog.

Testing the App in a Selected Web Browser

If you wish to execute the app in another web browser, you can copy the web page's address from your default browser's address field and paste it into another browser's address field, or you can perform the following steps:

1. In the **Solution Explorer**, right click WebTime.aspx and select **Browse With...** to display the **Browse With** dialog (Fig. 21.6).

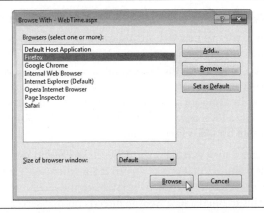

Fig. 21.6 | Selecting another web browser to execute the web app.

2. From the **Browsers** list, select the browser in which you'd like to test the web app and click the **Browse** Button.

If the browser you wish to use is not listed, you can use the **Browse With** dialog to add items to or remove items from the list of web browsers.

21.4.1 Building the WebTime App

Now that you've tested the app, let's create it in Visual Studio Express For Web.

Step 1: Creating the Web Site Project
Select **FILE > New Web Site...** to display the **New Web Site** dialog (Fig. 21.7). In the left column of this dialog, ensure that **Visual C#** is selected, then select **ASP.NET** Empty Web **Site** in the middle column. At the bottom of the dialog you can specify the location and name of the web app.

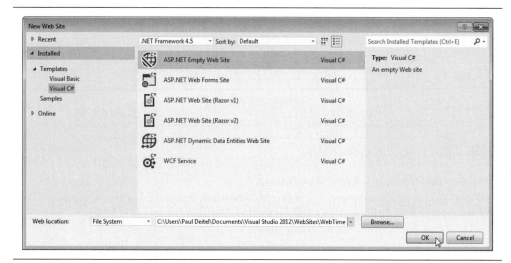

Fig. 21.7 | Creating an **ASP.NET Web Site** in Visual Studio Express For Web.

The **Web location:** ComboBox provides the following options:

- **File System:** Creates a new website for testing on your local computer. Such websites execute on your local machine in **IIS Express** and can be accessed only by web browsers running on the same computer. IIS Express is a version of Microsoft's Internet Information Services (IIS) web server that allows you to test your web apps locally. You can later publish your website to a production IIS web server for access via a local network or the Internet. Each example in this chapter uses the **File System** option, so select it now.

- **HTTP:** Creates a new website on an IIS web server and uses HTTP to allow you to put your website's files on the server. IIS is Microsoft's software that's used to run production websites. If you own a website and have your own web server, you might use this to build a new website directly on that server computer. You must be an Administrator on the computer running IIS to use this option.

- **FTP**: Uses File Transfer Protocol (FTP) to allow you to put your website's files on the server. The server administrator must first create the website on the server for you. FTP is commonly used by so-called "hosting providers" to allow website owners to share a server computer that runs many websites.

Change the name of the web app from WebSite1 to WebTime, then click **OK** to create the website.

Step 2: Adding a Web Form to the Website and Examining the Solution Explorer
A **Web Form** represents one page in a web app—we'll often use the terms "page" and "Web Form" interchangeably. A Web Form contains a web app's GUI. To create the WebTime.aspx Web Form:

1. Right click the project name in the **Solution Explorer** and select **Add > Add New Item...** to display the **Add New Item** dialog (Fig. 21.8).

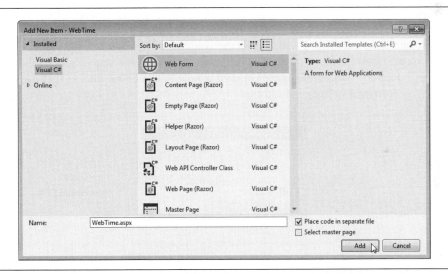

Fig. 21.8 | Adding a new **Web Form** to the website with the **Add New Item** dialog.

2. In the left column, ensure that **Visual C#** is selected, then select **Web Form** in the middle column.

3. In the **Name:** TextBox, change the file name to WebTime.aspx, then click the **Add** Button.

After you add the Web Form, the IDE opens it in **Source** view by default (Fig. 21.9). This view displays the markup for the Web Form. As you become more familiar with ASP.NET and building web sites in general, you might use **Source** view to perform high precision adjustments to your design (in HTML and/or CSS) or to program in the JavaScript language that executes in web browsers. For the purposes of this chapter, we'll keep things simple by working exclusively in **Design** mode. To switch to **Design** mode, you can click the **Design** Button at the bottom of the code editor window.

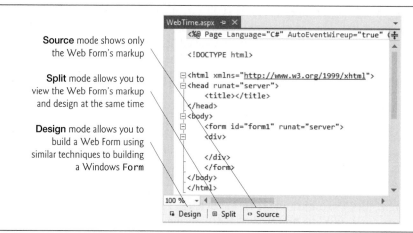

Source mode shows only the Web Form's markup

Split mode allows you to view the Web Form's markup and design at the same time

Design mode allows you to build a Web Form using similar techniques to building a Windows Form

Fig. 21.9 | Web Form in **Source** view.

The Solution Explorer

The **Solution Explorer** (Fig. 21.10) shows the contents of the website. We expanded the node for WebTime.aspx to show you its *code-behind file* WebTime.aspx.cs. Visual Studio Express For Web's **Solution Explorer** contains a **Nest Related Files** button that organizes each Web Form and its code-behind file.

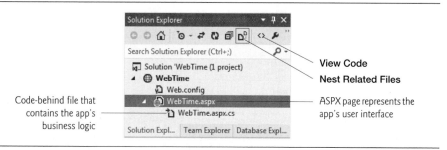

Code-behind file that contains the app's business logic

View Code

Nest Related Files

ASPX page represents the app's user interface

Fig. 21.10 | **Solution Explorer** window for an **Empty Web Site** project after adding the Web Form WebTime.aspx.

If the ASPX file is not open in the IDE, you can open it in **Design** mode by double clicking it in the **Solution Explorer** then selecting the **Design** tab, or by right clicking it in the **Solution Explorer** and selecting **View Designer**. To open the code-behind file in the code editor, you can double click it in the **Solution Explorer** or

- select the ASPX file in the **Solution Explorer**, then click the **View Code** (<>) Button
- right click the ASPX file in the **Solution Explorer**, then select **View Code**
- right click the code-behind file in the **Solution Explorer** and select **Open**

The Toolbox

Figure 21.11 shows the **Toolbox** displayed in the IDE when the project loads. Part (a) displays the beginning of the **Standard** list of web controls, and part (b) displays the remaining web controls and the list of other control groups. We discuss specific controls listed in Fig. 21.11 as they're used throughout the chapter. Many of the controls have similar or identical names to Windows Forms controls presented earlier in the book.

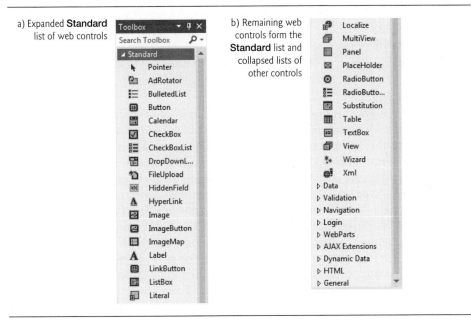

Fig. 21.11 | **Toolbox** in Visual Studio Express For Web.

The Web Forms Designer
Figure 21.12 shows the initial Web Form in **Design** mode. You can drag and drop controls from the **Toolbox** onto the Web Form. You can also type at the current cursor location to add so-called *static text* to the web page. In response to such actions, the IDE generates the appropriate markup in the ASPX file.

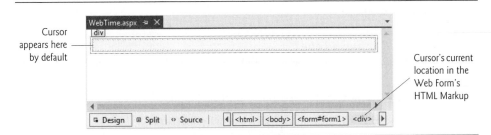

Fig. 21.12 | **Design** mode of the Web Forms Designer.

Step 3: Changing the Title of the Page
Before designing the Web Form's content, you'll change its title to Simple Web Form Example. This title is typically displayed in the web browser's title bar or on the browser tab that is displaying the page (see Fig. 21.4). It's also used by search engines like Google and

Bing when they index real websites for searching. Every page should have a title. To change the title:

1. Ensure that the ASPX file is open in **Design** view.

2. In the **Properties** window's drop-down list, view the Web Form's properties by selecting **DOCUMENT**, which represents the Web Form. A web page is often called a document.

3. Modify the page's `Title` property by setting it to `Simple Web Form Example`.

Designing a Page

Designing a Web Form is similar to designing a Windows Form. To add controls to the page, drag-and-drop them from the **Toolbox** onto the Web Form in **Design** view. The Web Form itself and the control's you add to the Web Form are objects that have properties, methods and events. You can set these properties visually using the **Properties** window, programmatically in the code-behind file or by editing the markup directly in the `.aspx` file. You can also type text directly on a Web Form at the cursor location.

Controls and other elements are placed sequentially on a Web Form one after another in the order in which you drag-and-drop them onto the Web Form. The cursor indicates the insertion point in the page. If you want to position a control between existing text or controls, you can drop the control at a specific position between existing page elements. You can also rearrange controls with drag-and-drop actions in **Design** view. The positions of controls and other elements are relative to the Web Form's upper-left corner. This type of layout is known as *relative positioning* and it allows the browser to move elements and resize them based on the size of the browser window. Relative positioning is the *default*, and we'll use it throughout this chapter.

For precise control over the location and size of elements, you can use absolute positioning in which controls are located exactly where you drop them on the Web Form. If you wish to use absolute positioning:

1. Select **TOOLS > Options....**, to display the **Options** dialog.

2. Expand the **HTML Designer** node, select the **CSS Styling** node and ensure that the checkbox labeled **Change positioning to absolute for controls added using Toolbox, paste or drag and drop** is selected.

Step 4: Adding Text and a Label

You'll now add some text and a Label to the Web Form. Perform the following steps to add the text:

1. Ensure that the Web Form is open in **Design** mode.

2. Type the following text at the current cursor location:

```
Current time on the Web server:
```

3. Select the text you just typed, then select **Heading 1** from the **Block Format** Combo-Box (Fig. 21.13) in the IDE's **Formatting** toolbar. This formats the text as a first-level heading that typically appears in a larger bold font. In more complex pages, headings help you specify the relative importance of parts of the content—like chapters in a book and sections in a chapter.

Block Format ComboBox on the Formatting toolbar

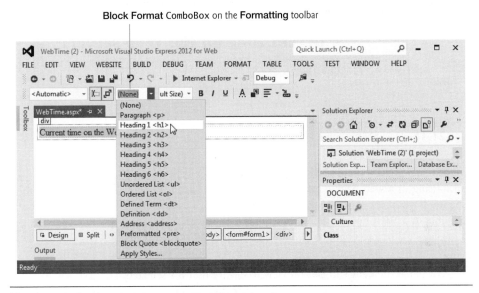

Fig. 21.13 | Changing the text to **Heading 1** heading.

4. Click to the right of the text you just typed and press the *Enter* key to start a new paragraph in the page. The Web Form should now appear as in Fig. 21.14.

The cursor is positioned here after inserting a new paragraph by pressing *Enter*

Fig. 21.14 | `WebTime.aspx` after inserting text and a new paragraph.

5. Next, drag a Label control from the **Toolbox** into the new paragraph or double click the Label control in the **Toolbox** to insert the Label at the current cursor position.

6. Using the **Properties** window, set the Label's (ID) property to `timeLabel`. This specifies the variable name that will be used to *programmatically* change the Label's Text.

7. Because, the Label's Text will be set programmatically, delete the current value of the Label's Text property. When a Label does not contain text, its name is displayed in square brackets in **Design** view (Fig. 21.15) as a placeholder for design and layout purposes. This text is not displayed at execution time.

Label control
currently selected in
Design view

Fig. 21.15 | WebTime.aspx after adding a Label.

Step 5: Formatting the *Label*

Formatting in a web page is performed with *CSS (Cascading Style Sheets)*. The details of CSS are beyond the scope of this book. However, it's easy to use CSS to format text and elements in a Web Form via the tools built into Visual Studio Express For Web. In this example, we'd like to change the Label's *background color* to black, its *foreground color* to yellow and make its *text size* larger. To format the Label, perform the following steps:

1. Click the Label in **Design** view to ensure that it's selected.

2. Select **VIEW > CSS Properties** to display the **CSS Properties** window at the left side of the IDE (Fig. 21.16).

Fig. 21.16 | **CSS Properties** window.

3. Right click below **Applied Rules** and select **New Style...** to display the **New Style** dialog (Fig. 21.17).

4. Type the new style's name in the **Selector:** ComboBox—we chose .timeStyle since this will be the style used to format the time that's displayed in the page. Styles that apply to specific elements must be named with a dot (.) preceding the name. Such a style is called a **CSS class**.

5. Each item you can set in the **New Style** dialog is known as a *CSS attribute*. To change timeLabel's *foreground color*, select the **Font** category from the **Category** list, then select the yellow color swatch for the **color** attribute.

6. Next, change the **font-size** attribute to xx-large.

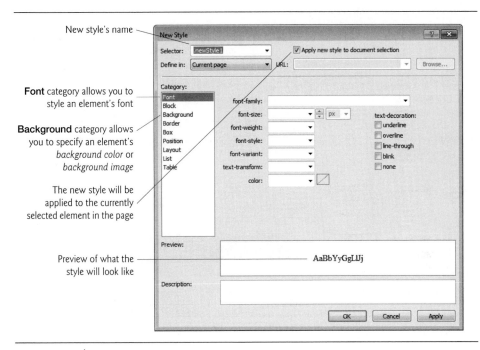

New style's name

Font category allows you to style an element's font

Background category allows you to specify an element's *background color* or *background image*

The new style will be applied to the currently selected element in the page

Preview of what the style will look like

Fig. 21.17 | New Style dialog.

7. To change `timeLabel`'s *background color*, select the **Background** category, then select the black color swatch for the **background-color** attribute.

The **New Style** dialog should now appear as shown in Fig. 21.18. Click the **OK** Button to apply the style to the `timeLabel` so that it appears as shown in Fig. 21.19. Also, notice that the Label's *CssClass property* is now set to `timeStyle` in the **Properties** window.

Step 6: Adding Page Logic

Now that you've designed the GUI, you'll write code in the *code-behind file* to obtain the server's time and display it on the Label. Open `WebTime.aspx.cs` by double clicking it in the **Solution Explorer**. In this example, you'll add an event handler to the code-behind file to handle the Web Form's **Init** event, which occurs when the page is requested by a web browser. The event handler for this event—named **Page_Init**—initializes the page. The only initialization required for this example is to set the `timeLabel`'s Text property to the time on the web server computer. The code-behind file initially contains a `Page_Load` event handler. To create the `Page_Init` event handler, simply rename `Page_Load` as `Page_Init`. Then complete the event handler by inserting the following code in its body:

```
// display the server's current time in timeLabel
timeLabel.Text = DateTime.Now.ToString("hh:mm:ss");
```

Step 7: Setting the Start Page and Running the Program

To ensure that `WebTime.aspx` loads when you execute this app, right click it in the **Solution Explorer** and select **Set As Start Page**. You can now run the program in one of several ways. At the beginning of Fig. 21.4, you learned how to view the Web Form by typing *Ctrl + F5*.

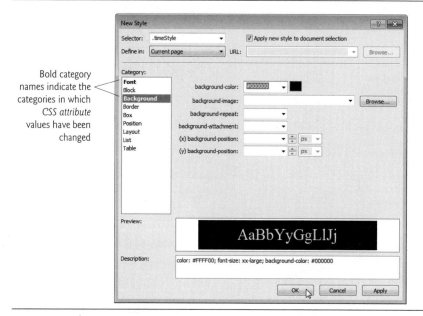

Bold category names indicate the categories in which *CSS attribute values have been changed*

Fig. 21.18 | **New Style** dialog after changing the Label's style.

Fig. 21.19 | **Design** view after changing the Label's style.

You can also right click an ASPX file in the **Solution Explorer** and select **View in Browser**. Both of these techniques execute *IIS Express*, open your *default web browser* and load the page into the browser, thus running the web app. IIS Express stops when you exit Visual Studio Express For Web.

If problems occur when running your app, you can run it in *debug mode* by selecting **DEBUG > Start Debugging**, by clicking the **Start Debugging** Button (▶) or by typing *F5* to view the web page in a web browser with *debugging enabled*. You cannot debug a web app unless debugging is *explicitly* enabled in the app's **Web.config** file—a file that's generated when you create an ASP.NET web app. This file stores the app's configuration settings. You'll rarely need to manually modify Web.config. The first time you select **DEBUG > Start Debugging** in a project, a dialog appears and asks whether you want the IDE to modify the Web.config file to enable debugging. After you click **OK**, the IDE executes the app. You can stop debugging by selecting **DEBUG > Stop Debugging**.

Regardless of how you execute the web app, the IDE will compile the project before it executes. In fact, ASP.NET compiles your web page whenever it changes between HTTP requests. For example, suppose you browse the page, then modify the ASPX file or add code to the code-behind file. When you reload the page, ASP.NET recompiles the page on the server before returning the response to the browser. This important behavior ensures that clients always see the latest version of the page. You can manually compile an entire website by selecting **Build Web Site** from the **DEBUG** menu in Visual Studio Express For Web.

21.4.2 Examining `WebTime.aspx`'s Code-Behind File

Figure 21.20 presents the code-behind file `WebTime.aspx.cs`. Line 5 begins the declaration of class `WebTime`. A class declaration can span multiple source-code files—the separate portions of the class declaration in each file are known as **partial classes**. The **partial modifier** indicates that the code-behind file is part of a larger class. Like Windows Forms apps, the rest of the class's code is generated for you based on your visual interactions to create the app's GUI in **Design** mode. That code is stored in other source code files as partial classes with the same name. The compiler assembles all the partial classes that have the same into a single class declaration.

```
 I    // Fig. 21.20: WebTime.aspx.cs
 2    // Code-behind file for a page that displays the web server's time.
 3    using System;
 4
 5    public partial class WebTime : System.Web.UI.Page
 6    {
 7       // initializes the contents of the page
 8       protected void Page_Init( object sender, EventArgs e )
 9       {
10          // display the server's current time in timeLabel
11          timeLabel.Text = DateTime.Now.ToString( "hh:mm:ss" );
12       } // end method Page_Init
13    } // end class WebTime
```

Fig. 21.20 | Code-behind file for a page that displays the web server's time.

Line 5 indicates that `WebTime` inherits from class **Page** in namespace **System.Web.UI**. This namespace contains classes and controls for building web-based apps. Class `Page` represents the default capabilities of each page in a web app—all pages inherit directly or indirectly from this class.

Lines 8–12 define the `Page_Init` event handler, which initializes the page in response to the page's `Init` event. The only initialization required for this page is to set the `timeLabel`'s `Text` property to the time on the web server computer. The statement in line 11 retrieves the current time (`DateTime.Now`) and formats it as $hh:mm:ss$. For example, 9 AM is formatted as 09:00:00, and 2:30 PM is formatted as 02:30:00. As you'll see, variable `timeLabel` represents an *ASP.NET Label control*. The ASP.NET controls are defined in namespace **System.Web.UI.WebControls**.

21.5 Standard Web Controls: Designing a Form

This section introduces some of the web controls located in the **Standard** section of the **Toolbox** (Fig. 21.11). Figure 21.21 summarizes the controls used in the next example.

Web control	Description
TextBox	Gathers user input and displays text.
Button	Triggers an event when clicked.
HyperLink	Displays a hyperlink.
DropDownList	Displays a drop-down list of choices from which a user can select an item.
RadioButtonList	A group of radio buttons.
Image	Displays images (for example, PNG, GIF and JPG).

Fig. 21.21 │ Commonly used web controls.

A Form Gathering User Input
Figure 21.22 depicts a form for gathering user input. This example does not perform any tasks—that is, no action occurs when the user clicks **Register**. Here we focus on the steps for adding these controls to a Web Form and for setting their properties. Subsequent examples demonstrate how to handle the events of many of these controls. To execute this app:

1. Select **Open Web Site...** from the **FILE** menu.

2. In the **Open Web Site** dialog, ensure that **File System** is selected, then navigate to this chapter's examples, select the WebControls folder and click the **Open** Button.

3. Select WebControls.aspx in the **Solution Explorer**, then type *Ctrl + F5* to execute the web app in your default web browser.

Step 1: Creating the Web Site
To begin, follow the steps in Section 21.4.1 to create an **Empty Web Site** named WebControls, then add a Web Form named WebControls.aspx to the project. Set the document's Title property to "Web Controls Demonstration". Right click WebControls.aspx in the **Solution Explorer** and select **Set As Start Page** to ensure that this page loads when you execute the app.

Step 2: Adding the Images to the Project
The images used in this example are located in the images folder with this chapter's examples. Before you can display this app's images in the Web Form, they must be added to your project. To add the images folder to your project:

1. Open Windows Explorer.

2. Locate and open this chapter's examples folder (ch23).

3. Drag the images folder from Windows Explorer into Visual Studio Express For Web's **Solution Explorer** window and drop the folder on the name of your project.

The IDE will automatically copy the folder and its contents into your project.

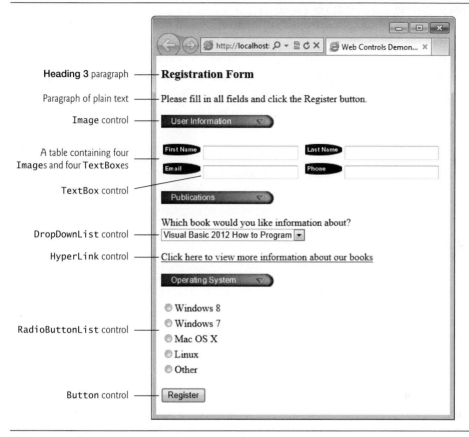

Fig. 21.22 | Web Form that demonstrates web controls.

Step 3: Adding Text and an Image to the Form
Next, you'll begin creating the page. Perform the following steps:

1. First create the page's heading. At the current cursor position on the page, type the text "Registration Form", then use the **Block Format** ComboBox in the IDE's toolbar to change the text to **Heading 3** format.

2. Press *Enter* to start a new paragraph, then type the text "Please fill in all fields and click the Register button.".

3. Press *Enter* to start a new paragraph, then double click the **Image** control in the Toolbox. This control inserts an image into a web page, at the current cursor position. Set the Image's (ID) property to userInformationImage. The **ImageUrl** property specifies the location of the image to display. In the **Properties** window, click the ellipsis for the ImageUrl property to display the **Select Image** dialog. Select the images folder under **Project folders:** to display the list of images. Then select the image user.png.

4. Click **OK** to display the image in **Design** view, then click to the right of the Image and press *Enter* to start a new paragraph.

Step 4: Adding a Table to the Form

Form elements are sometimes placed in tables for layout purposes—like the elements that represent the first name, last name, e-mail and phone information in Fig. 21.22. Next, you'll create a table with two rows and two columns in **Design** mode.

1. Select **Table > Insert Table** to display the **Insert Table** dialog (Fig. 21.23). This dialog allows you to configure the table's options.

2. Under **Size**, ensure that the values of **Rows** and **Columns** are both 2—these are the default values.

3. Click **OK** to close the **Insert Table** dialog and create the table.

By default, the contents of a table cell are aligned *vertically* in the *middle* of the cell.

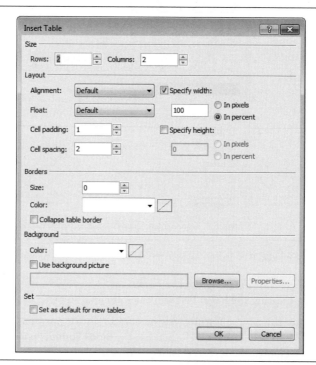

Fig. 21.23 | **Insert Table** dialog.

After creating the table, controls and text can be added to particular cells to create a neatly organized layout. Next, add `Image` and `TextBox` controls to each the four table cells as follows:

1. Click the table cell in the first row and first column of the table, then double click the `Image` control in the **Toolbox**. Set its `(ID)` property to `firstNameImage` and set its `ImageUrl` property to the image `fname.png`.

2. Next, double click the `TextBox` control in the **Toolbox**. Set its `(ID)` property to `firstNameTextBox`. As in Windows Forms, a **TextBox** control allows you to obtain text from the user and display text to the user.

3. Repeat this process in the first row and second column, but set the Image's (ID) property to lastNameImage and its ImageUrl property to the image lname.png, and set the TextBox's (ID) property to lastNameTextBox.

4. Repeat *Steps 1* and *2* in the second row and first column, but set the Image's (ID) property to emailImage and its ImageUrl property to the image email.png, and set the TextBox's (ID) property to emailTextBox.

5. Repeat *Steps 1* and *2* in the second row and second column, but set the Image's (ID) property to phoneImage and its ImageUrl property to the image phone.png, and set the TextBox's (ID) property to phoneTextBox.

Step 5: Creating the Publications *Section of the Page*

This section contains an Image, some text, a DropDownList control and a HyperLink control. Perform the following steps to create this section:

1. Click below the table, then use the techniques you've already learned in this section to add an Image named publicationsImage that displays the publications.png image.

2. Click to the right of the Image, then press *Enter* and type the text "Which book would you like information about?" in the new paragraph.

3. Hold the *Shift* key and press *Enter* to create a new line in the current paragraph, then double click the **DropDownList** control in the **Toolbox**. Set its (ID) property to booksDropDownList. This control is similar to the Windows Forms ComboBox control, but doesn't allow users to type text. When a user clicks the drop-down list, it expands and displays a list from which the user can make a selection.

4. You can add items to the DropDownList using the **ListItem Collection Editor** by clicking the ellipsis next to the DropDownList's Items property in the **Properties** window, or by using the **DropDownList Tasks** smart-tag menu. To open this menu, click the small arrowhead that appears in the upper-right corner of the control in **Design** mode (Fig. 21.24). Visual Studio Express 2012 for Web displays smart-tag menus for many ASP.NET controls to facilitate common tasks. Clicking **Edit Items...** in the **DropDownList Tasks** menu opens the **ListItem Collection Editor**, which allows you to add ListItem elements to the DropDownList. Add items for "Visual Basic 2012 How to Program", "Visual C# 2012 How to Program", "Java

Fig. 21.24 | DropDownList Tasks smart-tag menu.

How to Program" and "C++ How to Program" by clicking the **Add** Button four times. For each item, select it, then set its Text property to one of the four book titles.

5. Click to the right of the DropDownList and press *Enter* to start a new paragraph, then double click the **HyperLink** control in the **Toolbox** to add a hyperlink to the web page. Set its (ID) property to booksHyperLink and its Text property to "Click here to view more information about our books". Set the **NavigateUrl** property to http://www.deitel.com. This specifies the resource or web page that will be requested when the user clicks the HyperLink. Setting the **Target** property to _blank specifies that the requested web page should open in a new tab or browser window. By default, HyperLink controls cause pages to open in the *same* browser window.

Step 6: Completing the Page
Next you'll create the **Operating System** section of the page and the **Register** Button. This section contains a **RadioButtonList** control, which provides a series of radio buttons from which the user can select only one. The **RadioButtonList Tasks** smart-tag menu provides an **Edit Items...** link to open the **ListItem Collection Editor** so that you can create the items in the list. Perform the following steps:

1. Click to the right of the HyperLink control and press *Enter* to create a new paragraph, then add an Image named osImage that displays the os.png image.

2. Click to the right of the Image and press *Enter* to create a new paragraph, then add a RadioButtonList. Set its (ID) property to osRadioButtonList. Use the **ListItem Collection Editor** to add the items shown in Fig. 21.22.

3. Finally, click to the right of the RadioButtonList and press *Enter* to create a new paragraph, then add a **Button**. A Button web control represents a button that triggers an action when clicked. Set its (ID) property to registerButton and its Text property to Register. As stated earlier, clicking the **Register** button in this example does not do anything.

You can now execute the app (*Ctrl + F5*) to see the Web Form in your browser.

21.6 Validation Controls

This section introduces a different type of web control, called a **validation control** or **validator**, which determines whether the *data* in another web control is in the proper *format*. For example, validators can determine whether a user has provided information in a required field or whether a zip-code field contains exactly five digits. Validators provide a mechanism for *validating user input* on the client and the server. When the page is sent to the client, the validator is converted into JavaScript that performs the validation in the client web browser. JavaScript is a scripting language that enhances the functionality of web pages and is typically executed on the client. Unfortunately, some client browsers might not support scripting or the user might disable it. For this reason, you should *always perform validation on the server*. ASP.NET validation controls can function on the *client*, on the *server* or *both*.

Validating Input in a Web Form
The Web Form in Fig. 21.25 prompts the user to enter a name, e-mail address and phone number. A website could use a form like this to collect contact information from visitors.

After the user enters any data, but before the data is sent to the web server, validators ensure that the user *entered a value in each field* and that the e-mail address and phone-number values are in an acceptable format. In this example, (555) 123-4567, 555-123-4567 and 123-4567 are all considered valid phone numbers. Once the data is submitted, the web server responds by displaying a message that repeats the submitted information. A real business app would typically store the submitted data in a database or in a file on the server. We simply send the data back to the client to demonstrate that the server received the data. To execute this app:

1. Select **Open Web Site...** from the **FILE** menu.

2. In the **Open Web Site** dialog, ensure that **File System** is selected, then navigate to this chapter's examples, select the `Validation` folder and click the **Open** Button.

3. Select `Validation.aspx` in the **Solution Explorer**, then type *Ctrl + F5* to execute the web app in your default web browser.

In the sample output:

- Fig. 21.25(a) shows the initial Web Form.

- Fig. 21.25(b) shows the result of submitting the form before typing any data in the TextBoxes.

- Fig. 21.25(c) shows the results after entering data in each TextBox, but specifying an invalid e-mail address and invalid phone number.

- Fig. 21.25(d) shows the results after entering valid values for all three TextBoxes and submitting the form.

Step 1: Creating the Web Site
To begin, follow the steps in Section 21.4.1 to create an **Empty Web Site** named `Validation`, then add a Web Form named `Validation.aspx` to the project. Set the document's `Title` property to `"Demonstrating Validation Controls"`. To ensure that `Validation.aspx` loads when you execute this app, right click it in the **Solution Explorer** and select **Set As Start Page**.

a) Initial Web Form

Fig. 21.25 | Validators in a Web Form that retrieves user contact information. (Part 1 of 2.)

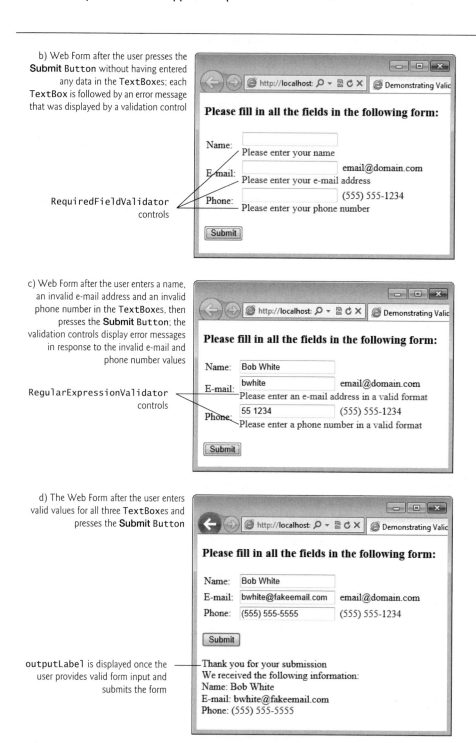

b) Web Form after the user presses the **Submit** Button without having entered any data in the TextBoxes; each TextBox is followed by an error message that was displayed by a validation control

RequiredFieldValidator controls

c) Web Form after the user enters a name, an invalid e-mail address and an invalid phone number in the TextBoxes, then presses the **Submit** Button; the validation controls display error messages in response to the invalid e-mail and phone number values

RegularExpressionValidator controls

d) The Web Form after the user enters valid values for all three TextBoxes and presses the **Submit** Button

outputLabel is displayed once the user provides valid form input and submits the form

Fig. 21.25 | Validators in a Web Form that retrieves user contact information. (Part 2 of 2.)

Step 2: Creating the GUI

To create the page, perform the following steps:

1. Type "Please fill in all the fields in the following form:", then use the **Block Format** ComboBox in the IDE's toolbar to change the text to **Heading 3** format and press *Enter* to create a new paragraph.

2. Insert a three-row and two-column table. You'll add elements to the table momentarily.

3. Click below the table and add a Button. Set its (ID) property to submitButton and its Text property to Submit. By default, a Button control in a Web Form sends the contents of the form back to the server for processing. Select the Button then use the **Block Format** ComboBox in the IDE's toolbar to wrap the Button in a **Paragraph** format—this places additional space above and below the Button.

4. Click to the right of the Button, then press *Enter* to create a new paragraph. Add a Label. Set its (ID) property to outputLabel and clear its Text property—you'll set it *programmatically* when the user clicks the submitButton. Set the outputLabel's **Visible** property to false, so the Label does *not* appear in the client's browser when the page loads for the *first* time. You'll *programmatically* display this Label after the user submits valid data.

Next you'll add text and controls to the table you created in *Step 2* above. Perform the following steps:

1. In the left column, type the text "Name:" in the first row, "E-mail:" in the second row and "Phone:" in the third row.

2. In the right column of the first row, add a TextBox and set its (ID) property to nameTextBox.

3. In the right column of the second row, add a TextBox and set its (ID) property to emailTextBox. Set its TextMode property to Email—this produces an HTML5 e-mail input field when the web page is rendered in the client web browser. Click to the right of the TextBox and type the text "email@domain.com" to show an example of what the user should enter in that TextBox.

4. In the right column of the third row, add a TextBox and set its (ID) property to phoneTextBox. Set its TextMode property to Phone—this produces an HTML5 phone input field when the web page is rendered in the client web browser. Click to the right of the TextBox and type the text "(555) 555-1234" to show an example of what the user should enter in that TextBox.

Step 3: Using RequiredFieldValidator Controls

We use three **RequiredFieldValidator** controls (found in the **Validation** section of the **Toolbox**) to ensure that the name, e-mail address and phone number TextBoxes are *not empty* when the form is submitted. A RequiredFieldValidator makes an *input control* a required field. If such a field is *empty*, validation fails. Add a RequiredFieldValidator as follows:

1. Click to the right of the nameTextBox in the table and press *Enter* to move to the next line.

2. Add a RequiredFieldValidator, set its (ID) to nameRequiredFieldValidator and set the ForeColor property to Red.

3. Set the validator's **ControlToValidate** property to nameTextBox to indicate that this validator verifies the nameTextBox's contents.

4. Set the validator's **ErrorMessage** property to "Please enter your name". This is displayed on the Web Form only if the validation fails.

5. Set the validator's **Display** property to Dynamic, so the validator occupies space on the Web Form only when validation fails. When this occurs, space is allocated dynamically, causing the controls below the validator to shift downward to accommodate the ErrorMessage, as seen in Fig. 21.25(a)–(c).

Repeat these steps to add two more RequiredFieldValidators in the second and third rows of the table. Set their (ID) properties to emailRequiredFieldValidator and phoneRequiredFieldValidator, respectively, and set their ErrorMessage properties to "Please enter your email address" and "Please enter your phone number", respectively.

Step 4: Using RegularExpressionValidator Controls

This example also uses two **RegularExpressionValidator** controls to ensure that the e-mail address and phone number entered by the user are in a valid format. Visual Studio Express 2012 for Web provides several *predefined* regular expressions that you can simply select to take advantage of this powerful validation control. Add a RegularExpressionValidator as follows:

1. Click to the right of the emailRequiredFieldValidator in the second row of the table and add a RegularExpressionValidator, then set its (ID) to emailRegularExpressionValidator and its ForeColor property to Red.

2. Set the ControlToValidate property to emailTextBox to indicate that this validator verifies the emailTextBox's contents.

3. Set the validator's ErrorMessage property to "Please enter an e-mail address in a valid format".

4. Set the validator's Display property to Dynamic, so the validator occupies space on the Web Form only when validation fails.

Repeat the preceding steps to add another RegularExpressionValidator in the third row of the table. Set its (ID) property to phoneRegularExpressionValidator and its ErrorMessage property to "Please enter a phone number in a valid format", respectively.

A RegularExpressionValidator's **ValidationExpression** property specifies the regular expression that validates the ControlToValidate's contents. Clicking the ellipsis next to property ValidationExpression in the **Properties** window displays the **Regular Expression Editor** dialog, which contains a list of **Standard** expressions for phone numbers, zip codes and other formatted information. For the emailRegularExpressionValidator, we selected the standard expression **Internet e-mail address**. If the user enters text in the emailTextBox that does not have the correct format and either clicks in a different text box or attempts to submit the form, the ErrorMessage text is displayed in *red*.

For the phoneRegularExpressionValidator, we selected **U.S. phone number** to ensure that a phone number contains an optional three-digit area code either in parentheses and followed by an optional space or without parentheses and followed by a required hyphen. After an optional area code, a phone number must contain three digits, a hyphen and another four digits. For example, (555) 123-4567, 555-123-4567 and 123-4567 are all valid phone numbers.

Submitting the Web Form's Contents to the Server

If all five validators are successful (that is, each TextBox is filled in, and the e-mail address and phone number provided are valid), clicking the **Submit** button sends the form's data to the server. As shown in Fig. 21.25(d), the server then responds by displaying the submitted data in the outputLabel.

Examining the Code-Behind File for a Web Form That Receives User Input

Figure 21.26 shows the code-behind file for this app. Notice that this code-behind file does not contain any implementation related to the validators. We'll say more about this soon. In this example, we respond to the page's **Load** event to process the data submitted by the user. Like the Init event, the Load event occurs each time the page loads into a web browser—the difference is that on a *postback* you cannot access the posted data in the controls from the Init handler. The event handler for this event is **Page_Load** (lines 8–33). The event handler for the Load event is created for you when you add a new Web Form. To complete the event handler, insert the code from Fig. 21.26.

```
1   // Fig. 21.26: Validation.aspx.cs
2   // Code-behind file for the form demonstrating validation controls.
3   using System;
4
5   public partial class Validation : System.Web.UI.Page
6   {
7      // Page_Load event handler executes when the page is loaded
8      protected void Page_Load( object sender, EventArgs e )
9      {
10         // disable unobtrusive validation
11         UnobtrusiveValidationMode =
12            System.Web.UI.UnobtrusiveValidationMode.None;
13
14         // if this is not the first time the page is loading
15         // (i.e., the user has already submitted form data)
16         if ( IsPostBack )
17         {
18            Validate(); // validate the form
19
20            // if the form is valid
21            if ( IsValid )
22            {
23               // retrieve the values submitted by the user
24               string name = nameTextBox.Text;
25               string email = emailTextBox.Text;
26               string phone = phoneTextBox.Text;
27
```

Fig. 21.26 | Code-behind file for the form demonstrating validation controls. (Part 1 of 2.)

```
28                        // show the the submitted values
29                        outputLabel.Text = "Thank you for your submission<br/>" +
30                            "We received the following information:<br/>";
31                        outputLabel.Text +=
32                            String.Format( "Name: {0}{1}E-mail:{2}{1}Phone:{3}",
33                                name, "<br/>", email, phone);
34                        outputLabel.Visible = true; // display the output message
35                    } // end if
36                } // end if
37            } // end method Page_Load
38        } // end class Validation
```

Fig. 21.26 | Code-behind file for the form demonstrating validation controls. (Part 2 of 2.)

ASP.NET 4.5 Unobtrusive Validation
Prior to ASP.NET 4.5, when you used the validation controls presented in this section, ASP.NET would embed substantial amounts of JavaScript code in a web page to perform the work of the validation controls in the client web browser. ASP.NET 4.5 now uses **unobtrusive validation**, which significantly reduces the amount of JavaScript that gets embedded into the web page—this, in turn, can improve the performance of your website by making pages load faster. When you create an ASP.NET Web Forms website, everything you need for unobtrusive validation is normally configured for you—*unless* you create an *ASP.NET Empty Web Site*, as we've done for the examples in this chapter so far. To enable this app to execute correctly in the web browser, lines 11–12 *disable* unobtrusive validation. In Chapter 27, Web App Development with ASP.NET: A Deeper Look, we'll create a website in which unobtrusive validation is properly enabled.

Differentiating Between the First Request to a Page and a Postback
Web programmers using ASP.NET often design their web pages so that the current page *reloads* when the user *submits* the form; this enables the program to receive input, process it as necessary and display the results in the same page when it's loaded the second time. These pages usually contain a form that, when submitted, sends the values of all the controls to the server and causes the current page to be requested again. This event is known as a **postback**. Line 16 uses the **IsPostBack** property of class Page to determine whether the page is being loaded due to a postback. The first time that the web page is requested, IsPostBack is false, and the page displays only the form for user input. When the postback occurs (from the user clicking **Submit**), IsPostBack is true.

Server-Side Web Form Validation
Server-side Web Form validation must be implemented *programmatically*. Line 18 calls the current Page's **Validate** method to validate the information in the request. This validates the information as specified by the validation controls in the Web Form. Line 21 uses the **IsValid** property of class Page to check whether the validation succeeded. If this property is set to true (that is, validation succeeded and the Web Form is valid), then we display the Web Form's information. Otherwise, the web page loads without any changes, except that any validator that failed now displays its ErrorMessage.

Processing the Data Entered by the User

Lines 24–26 retrieve the values of nameTextBox, emailTextBox and phoneTextBox. When data is posted to the web server, the data that the user entered is accessible to the web app through the web controls' properties. Next, lines 29–33 set outputLabel's Text to display a message that includes the name, e-mail and phone information that was submitted to the server. In lines 29, 30 and 33, notice the use of <br/> rather than \n to start new lines in the outputLabel—
 is the markup for a line break in a web page. Line 34 sets the outputLabel's Visible property to true, so the user can see the thank-you message and submitted data when the page reloads in the client web browser.

21.7 Session Tracking

Originally, critics accused the Internet and e-businesses of failing to provide the customized service typically experienced in "brick-and-mortar" stores. To address this problem, businesses established mechanisms by which they could *personalize* users' browsing experiences, tailoring content to individual users. Businesses can achieve this level of service by tracking each customer's movement through the Internet and combining the collected data with information provided by the consumer, including billing information, personal preferences, interests and hobbies.

Personalization

Personalization makes it possible for businesses to communicate effectively with their customers and also improves users' ability to locate desired products and services. Companies that provide content of particular interest to users can establish relationships with customers and build on those relationships over time. Furthermore, by targeting consumers with personal offers, recommendations, advertisements, promotions and services, businesses create customer loyalty. Websites can use sophisticated technology to allow visitors to customize home pages to suit their individual needs and preferences. Similarly, online shopping sites often store personal information for customers, tailoring notifications and special offers to their interests. Such services encourage customers to visit sites more frequently and make purchases more regularly.

Privacy

A trade-off exists between personalized business service and protection of privacy. Some consumers embrace tailored content, but others fear the possible adverse consequences if the info they provide to businesses is released or collected by tracking technologies. Consumers and privacy advocates ask: What if the business to which we give personal data sells or gives that information to other organizations without our knowledge? What if we do not want our actions on the Internet—a supposedly anonymous medium—to be tracked and recorded by unknown parties? What if unauthorized parties gain access to sensitive private data, such as credit-card numbers or medical history? These are questions that must be addressed by programmers, consumers, businesses and lawmakers alike.

Recognizing Clients

To provide personalized services to consumers, businesses must be able to recognize clients when they request information from a site. As we've discussed, the request–response system on which the web operates is facilitated by HTTP. Unfortunately, HTTP is a *stateless protocol*—it *does not* provide information that would enable web servers to maintain state information regarding particular clients. This means that web servers cannot determine whether a request comes from a particular client or whether the same or different clients generate a series of requests.

To circumvent this problem, sites can provide mechanisms by which they identify individual clients. A *session* represents a unique client on a website. If the client leaves a site and then returns later, the client will still be recognized as the same user. When the user closes the browser, the session typically ends. To help the server distinguish among clients, each client must identify itself to the server. Tracking individual clients is known as **session tracking**. One popular session-tracking technique uses cookies (discussed in Section 21.7.1); another uses ASP.NET's `HttpSessionState` object (used in Section 21.7.2). Additional session-tracking techniques are beyond this book's scope.

21.7.1 Cookies

Cookies provide you with a tool for personalizing web pages. A cookie is a piece of data stored by web browsers in a small text file on the user's computer. A cookie maintains information about the client during and between browser sessions. The first time a user visits the website, the user's computer might receive a cookie from the server; this cookie is then reactivated each time the user revisits that site. The collected information is intended to be an anonymous record containing data that's used to personalize the user's future visits to the site. For example, cookies in a shopping app might store unique identifiers for users. When a user adds items to an online shopping cart or performs another task resulting in a request to the web server, the server receives a cookie containing the user's unique identifier. The server then uses the unique identifier to locate the shopping cart and perform any necessary processing.

In addition to identifying users, cookies also can indicate users' shopping *preferences*. When a Web Form receives a request from a client, the Web Form can examine the cookie(s) it sent to the client during previous communications, identify the user's preferences and immediately display products of interest to the client.

Every HTTP-based interaction between a client and a server includes a header containing information either about the request (when the communication is from the client to the server) or about the response (when the communication is from the server to the client). When a Web Form receives a request, the header includes information such as the request type and any cookies that have been sent previously from the server to be stored on the client machine. When the server formulates its response, the header information contains any cookies the server wants to store on the client computer and other information, such as the type of data in the response.

The **expiration date** of a cookie determines how long the cookie remains on the client's computer. If you do not set an expiration date for a cookie, the web browser maintains the cookie for the duration of the browsing session. Otherwise, the web browser maintains the cookie until the expiration date occurs. Cookies are deleted when they **expire**.

> **Portability Tip 21.1**
> *Users may disable cookies in their web browsers to help ensure their privacy. Such users will experience difficulty using web apps that depend on cookies to maintain state information.*

21.7.2 Session Tracking with `HttpSessionState`

The next web app demonstrates session tracking using class **HttpSessionState**. When you execute this app, the `Options.aspx` page (Fig. 21.27(a)), which is the app's **Start Page**, allows the user to select a programming language from a group of radio buttons. [*Note:* You might need to right click `Options.aspx` in the **Solution Explorer** and select **Set As Start Page** before running this app.] When the user clicks **Submit**, the selection is sent to the web server for processing. The web server uses an `HttpSessionState` object to store the chosen language and the ISBN number for one of our books on that topic. Each user that visits the site has a unique `HttpSessionState` object, so the selections made by one user are maintained separately from all other users. After storing the selection, the server returns the page to the browser (Fig. 21.27(b)) and displays the user's selection and some information about the user's unique session (which we show just for demonstration purposes). The page also includes links that allow the user to choose between selecting another programming language or viewing the `Recommendations.aspx` page (Fig. 21.27(e)), which lists recommended books pertaining to the programming language(s) that the user selected previously. If the user clicks the link for book recommendations, the information stored in the user's unique `HttpSessionState` object is read and used to form the list of recommendations. To test this app:

1. Select **Open Web Site...** from the **FILE** menu.

2. In the **Open Web Site** dialog, ensure that **File System** is selected, then navigate to this chapter's examples, select the `Sessions` folder and click the **Open** Button.

3. Select `Options.aspx` in the **Solution Explorer**, then type *Ctrl + F5* to execute the web app in your default web browser.

a) User selects a language from the `Options.aspx` page, then presses **Submit** to send the selection to the server

b) `Options.aspx` page is updated to hide the controls for selecting a language and to display the user's selection; the user clicks the hyperlink to return to the list of languages and make another selection

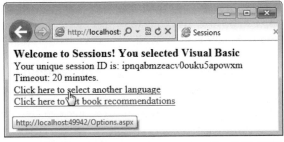

Fig. 21.27 | ASPX file that presents a list of programming languages. (Part 1 of 2.)

c) User selects another
language from the
Options.aspx page, then
presses **Submit** to send the
selection to the server

d) Options.aspx page is
updated to hide the controls for
selecting a language and to
display the user's selection; the
user clicks the hyperlink to get a
list of book recommendations

e) Recommendations.aspx
displays the list of
recommended books based on
the user's selections

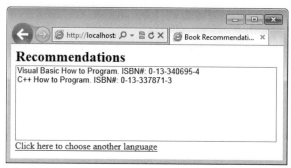

Fig. 21.27 | ASPX file that presents a list of programming languages. (Part 2 of 2.)

Creating the Web Site

To begin, follow the steps in Section 21.4.1 to create an **Empty Web Site** named Sessions, then add two Web Forms named Options.aspx and Recommendations.aspx to the project. Set the Options.aspx document's Title property to "Sessions" and the Recommendations.aspx document's Title property to "Book Recommendations". To ensure that Options.aspx is the first page to load for this app, right click it in the **Solution Explorer** and select **Set As Start Page**.

21.7.3 Options.aspx: Selecting a Programming Language

The Options.aspx page Fig. 21.27(a) contains the following controls arranged *vertically*:

1. A Label with its (ID) property set to promptLabel and its Text property set to "Select a programming language:". We used the techniques shown in *Step 5* of Section 21.4.1 to create a *CSS style* for this label named .labelStyle, and set the style's font-size attribute to large and the font-weight attribute to bold.

2. The user selects a programming language by clicking one of the radio buttons in a RadioButtonList. Each radio button has a Text property and a Value property. The Text property is displayed next to the radio button and the Value property represents a value that's sent to the server when the user selects that radio button and submits the form. In this example, we'll use the Value property to represent the ISBN for the recommended book. Create a RadioButtonList with its (ID) property set to languageList. Use the **ListItem Collection Editor** to add five radio buttons with their Text properties set to Visual Basic, Visual C#, C, C++ and Java, and their Value properties set to 0-13-340695-4, 0-13-337933-7, 0-13-299044-X, 0-13-337871-3 and 0-13-294094-9, respectively.

3. A Button with its (ID) property set to submitButton and its Text property set to Submit. In this example, we'll handle this Button's Click event. You can create its event handler by double clicking the Button in **Design** view.

4. A Label with its (ID) property set to responseLabel and its Text property set to "Welcome to Sessions!". This Label should be placed immediately to the right of the Button so that the Label appears at the top of the page when we hide the preceding controls on the page. Reuse the CSS style you created in *Step 1* by setting this Label's CssClass property to labelStyle.

5. Two more Labels with their (ID) properties set to idLabel and timeoutLabel, respectively. Clear the text in each Label's Text property—you'll set these *programmatically* with information about the current user's session.

6. A HyperLink with its (ID) property set to languageLink and its Text property set to "Click here to choose another language". Set its NavigateUrl property by clicking the ellipsis next to the property in the **Properties** window and selecting Options.aspx from the **Select URL** dialog.

7. A HyperLink with its (ID) property set to recommendationsLink and its Text property set to "Click here to get book recommendations". Set its NavigateUrl property by clicking the ellipsis next to the property in the **Properties** window and selecting Recommendations.aspx from the **Select URL** dialog.

8. Initially, the controls in *Steps 4–7* will not be displayed, so set each control's Visible property to false.

Session Property of a Page

Every ASP.NET Web app includes a user-specific HttpSessionState object, which is accessible through property **Session** of class Page. Throughout this section, we use this property to manipulate the current user's HttpSessionState object. When the user first requests a page in a Web app, a unique HttpSessionState object is created by ASP.NET and assigned to the Page's Session property. The same object is also available to the app's other pages.

Code-Behind File for Options.aspx

Fig. 21.28 presents the code-behind file for the Options.aspx page. When this page is requested, the Page_Load event handler (lines 10–40) executes before the response is sent to the client. Since the first request to a page is *not a postback*, the code in lines 16–38 *does not* execute the first time the page loads.

```
1   // Fig. 23.28: Options.aspx.cs
2   // Processes user's selection of a programming language by displaying
3   // links and writing information in an HttpSessionState object.
4   using System;
5
6   public partial class Options : System.Web.UI.Page
7   {
8      // if postback, hide form and display links to make additional
9      // selections or view recommendations
10     protected void Page_Load( object sender, EventArgs e )
11     {
12        if ( IsPostBack )
13        {
14           // user has submitted information, so display message
15           // and appropriate hyperlinks
16           responseLabel.Visible = true;
17           idLabel.Visible = true;
18           timeoutLabel.Visible = true;
19           languageLink.Visible = true;
20           recommendationsLink.Visible = true;
21
22           // hide other controls used to make language selection
23           promptLabel.Visible = false;
24           languageList.Visible = false;
25           submitButton.Visible = false;
26
27           // if the user made a selection, display it in responseLabel
28           if ( languageList.SelectedItem != null )
29              responseLabel.Text += " You selected " +
30                 languageList.SelectedItem.Text;
31           else
32              responseLabel.Text += " You did not select a language.";
33
34           // display session ID
35           idLabel.Text = "Your unique session ID is: " + Session.SessionID;
36
37           // display the timeout
38           timeoutLabel.Text = "Timeout: " + Session.Timeout + " minutes.";
39        } // end if
40     } // end method Page_Load
41
42     // record the user's selection in the Session
43     protected void submitButton_Click( object sender, EventArgs e )
44     {
45        // if the user made a selection
46        if ( languageList.SelectedItem != null )
47           // add name-value pair to Session
48           Session.Add( languageList.SelectedItem.Text,
49              languageList.SelectedItem.Value );
50     } // end method submitButton_Click
51  } // end class Options
```

Fig. 21.28 | Process user's selection of a programming language by displaying links and writing information in an HttpSessionState object.

Postback Processing

When the user presses **Submit**, a postback occurs. The form is submitted to the server and Page_Load executes. Lines 16–20 display the controls shown in Fig. 21.27(b) and lines 23–25 hide the controls shown in Fig. 21.27(a). Next, lines 28–32 ensure that the user selected a language and, if so, display a message in the responseLabel indicating the selection. Otherwise, the message "You did not select a language" is displayed.

The ASP.NET app contains information about the HttpSessionState object (property Session of the Page object) for the current client. The object's **SessionID** property (displayed in line 35) contains the **unique session ID**—a sequence of random letters and numbers. The *first* time a client connects to the web server, a unique session ID is created for that client and a temporary cookie is written to the client so the server can identify the client on subsequent requests. When the client makes additional requests, the client's session ID from that temporary cookie is compared with the session IDs stored in the web server's memory to retrieve the client's HttpSessionState object. (Since users can disable cookies in their browsers, you can also use cookieless sessions. For more information, see msdn.microsoft.com/en-us/library/aa479314.aspx.) HttpSessionState property **Timeout** (displayed in line 38) specifies the maximum amount of time that an HttpSessionState object can be inactive before it's discarded. By default, if the user does not interact with this web app for 20 minutes, the HttpSessionState object is discarded by the server and a new one will be created if the user interacts with the app again. Figure 21.29 lists some common HttpSessionState properties.

Properties	Description
Count	Specifies the number of key–value pairs in the Session object.
IsNewSession	Indicates whether this is a new session (that is, whether the session was created during loading of this page).
Keys	Returns a collection containing the Session object's keys.
SessionID	Returns the session's unique ID.
Timeout	Specifies the maximum number of minutes during which a session can be inactive (that is, no requests are made) before the session expires. By default, this property is set to 20 minutes.

Fig. 21.29 | HttpSessionState properties.

Method submitButton_Click

We store the user's selection in an HttpSessionState object when the user clicks the **Submit** Button. The submitButton_Click event handler (lines 43–50) adds a key–value pair to the HttpSessionState object for the current user, specifying the language chosen and the ISBN number for a book on that language. The HttpSessionState object is a dictionary—a data structure that stores **key–value pairs**. A program uses the key to store and retrieve the associated value in the dictionary. We covered dictionaries in Chapter 19.

The key–value pairs in an HttpSessionState object are often referred to as **session items**. They're placed in an HttpSessionState object by calling its **Add** method. If the user made a selection (line 46), lines 48–49 get the selection and its corresponding value from the languageList by accessing its SelectedItem's Text and Value properties, respectively, then call HttpSessionState method Add to add this name–value pair as a session item in the HttpSessionState object (Session).

If the app adds a session item that has the same name as an item previously stored in the HttpSessionState object, the session item is replaced—session item names *must* be unique. Another common syntax for placing a session item in the HttpSessionState object is Session[*Name*] = *Value.* For example, we could have replaced lines 48–49 with

```
Session[ languageList.SelectedItem.Text ] =
   languageList.SelectedItem.Value
```

Software Engineering Observation 21.1

A Web Form should not use instance variables to maintain client state information, because each new request or postback is handled by a new instance of the page. Instead, maintain client state information in HttpSessionState objects, because such objects are specific to each client.

Software Engineering Observation 21.2

A benefit of using HttpSessionState objects (rather than cookies) is that they can store any type of object (not just Strings) as attribute values. This provides you with increased flexibility in determining the type of state information to maintain for clients.

21.7.4 Recommendations.aspx: Displaying Recommendations Based on Session Values

After the postback of Options.aspx, the user may request book recommendations. The book-recommendations hyperlink forwards the user to the page Recommendations.aspx (Fig. 21.27(e)) to display the recommendations based on the user's language selections. The page contains the following controls arranged *vertically*:

1. A Label with its (ID) property set to recommendationsLabel and its Text property set to "Recommendations". We created a CSS style for this label named .label-Style, and set the font-size attribute to x-large and the font-weight attribute to bold. (See *Step 5* in Section 21.4.1 for information on creating a CSS style.)

2. A ListBox with its (ID) property set to booksListBox. We created a CSS style for this ListBox named .listBoxStyle. In the **Position** category, we set the width attribute to 450px and the height attribute to 125px. The px indicates that the measurement is in pixels.

3. A HyperLink with its (ID) property set to languageLink and its Text property set to "Click here to choose another language". Set its NavigateUrl property by clicking the ellipsis next to the property in the **Properties** window and selecting Options.aspx from the **Select URL** dialog. When the user clicks this link, the Options.aspx page will be reloaded. Requesting the page in this manner *is not* considered a postback, so the original form in Fig. 21.27(a) will be displayed.

Code-Behind File for Recommendations.aspx

Figure 21.30 presents the *code-behind file* for Recommendations.aspx. Event handler Page_Init (lines 8–28) retrieves the session information. If a user has not selected a language in the Options.aspx page, the HttpSessionState object's **Count** property will be 0 (line 11). This property provides the number of session items contained in a HttpSessionState object. If the Count is 0, then we display the text **No Recommendations** (line 22), hide the ListBox (line 23) and update the Text of the HyperLink back to Options.aspx (line 26).

```
1    // Fig. 23.30: Recommendations.aspx.cs
2    // Creates book recommendations based on a Session object.
3    using System;
4
5    public partial class Recommendations : System.Web.UI.Page
6    {
7        // read Session items and populate ListBox with recommendations
8        protected void Page_Init( object sender, EventArgs e )
9        {
10           // determine whether Session contains any information
11           if ( Session.Count != 0 )
12           {
13               // display Session's name-value pairs
14               foreach ( string keyName in Session.Keys )
15                   booksListBox.Items.Add( keyName +
16                       " How to Program. ISBN#: " + Session[ keyName ] );
17           } // end if
18           else
19           {
20               // if there are no session items, no language was chosen, so
21               // display appropriate message and clear and hide booksListBox
22               recommendationsLabel.Text = "No Recommendations";
23               booksListBox.Visible = false;
24
25               // modify languageLink because no language was selected
26               languageLink.Text = "Click here to choose a language";
27           } // end else
28       } // end method Page_Init
29   } // end class Recommendations
```

Fig. 21.30 | Session data used to provide book recommendations to the user.

If the user chose at least one language, the loop in lines 14–16 iterates through the HttpSessionState object's keys (line 14) by accessing the HttpSessionState's **Keys** property, which returns a collection containing all the keys in the session. Lines 15–16 concatenate the keyName, the String " How to Program. ISBN#: " and the key's corresponding value, which is returned by Session[keyName]. This String is the recommendation that's added to the ListBox.

21.8 Case Study: Database-Driven ASP.NET Guestbook

Many websites allow users to provide feedback about the website in a guestbook. Typically, users click a link on the website's home page to request the guestbook page. This page usually consists of a form that contains fields for the user's name, e-mail address, message/

feedback and so on. Data submitted on the guestbook form is then stored in a database located on the server.

In this section, we create a guestbook Web Form app. The GUI (Fig. 21.31) contains a **GridView** data control, which displays all the entries in the guestbook in tabular format. This control is located in the **Toolbox**'s **Data** section. We explain how to create and configure this data control shortly. The GridView displays **abc** in **Design** mode to indicate data that will be retrieved from a data source at runtime. You'll learn how to create and configure the GridView shortly.

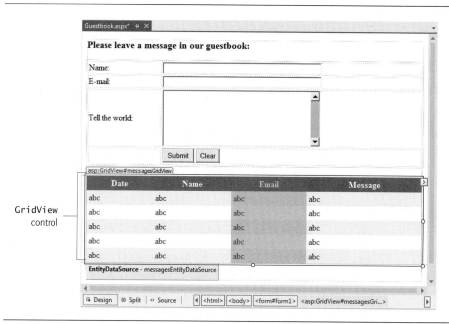

Fig. 21.31 | Guestbook app GUI in **Design** mode.

The Guestbook Database
The app stores the guestbook information in a SQL Server database called Guestbook.mdf located on the web server. (We provide this database in the databases folder with this chapter's examples.) The database contains a single table named Messages.

Testing the App
To test this app:

1. Select **Open Web Site…** from the **FILE** menu.

2. In the **Open Web Site** dialog, ensure that **File System** is selected, then navigate to this chapter's examples, select the Guestbook folder and click the **Open** Button.

3. Select Guestbook.aspx in the **Solution Explorer**, then type *Ctrl* + *F5* to execute the web app in your default web browser.

Figure 21.32(a) shows the user submitting a new entry. Figure 21.32(b) shows the new entry as the last row in the GridView.

a) User enters data for the name, e-mail and message, then presses **Submit** to send the data to the server

b) Server stores the data in the database, then refreshes the `GridView` with the updated data

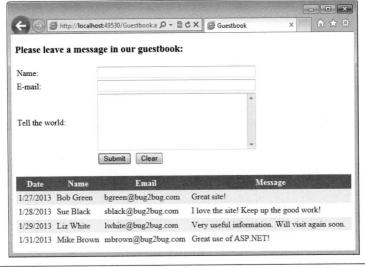

Fig. 21.32 | Sample execution of the **Guestbook** app.

21.8.1 Building a Web Form that Displays Data from a Database

You'll now build this GUI and set up the data binding between the `GridView` control and the database. Many of these steps are similar to those performed in Chapter 20 to access and interact with a database in a Windows app. We discuss the *code-behind file* in Section 21.8.2.

Step 1: Creating the Web Site

To begin, follow the steps in Section 21.4.1 to create an **Empty Web Site** named `Guestbook` then add a Web Form named `Guestbook.aspx` to the project. Set the document's `Title` property to "Guestbook". To ensure that `Guestbook.aspx` loads when you execute this app, right click it in the **Solution Explorer** and select **Set As Start Page**.

Step 2: Creating the Form for User Input

In **Design** mode, add the text `Please leave a message in our guestbook:`, then use the **Block Format** ComboBox in the IDE's toolbar to change the text to **Heading 3** format. Insert a table with four rows and two columns. Place the appropriate text (see Fig. 21.31) in the top three cells in the table's left column. Then place TextBoxes named `nameTextBox`, `emailTextBox` and `messageTextBox` in the top three table cells in the right column. Configure the TextBoxes as follows:

- Select **FORMAT > New Style...** to display the **New Style** dialog. In the **Selector** field, specify `.textBoxWidth` as the new style's name. Select the **Category** named **Position**, then set the **width:** to 300px and click **OK** to create the style and dismiss the dialog. Next set the `CssClass` property for both the `nameTextBox` and `emailTextBox` to `textBoxWidth`. This uses the style to set both TextBoxes to 300 pixels wide.

- Select **FORMAT > New Style...** to display the **New Style** dialog. In the **Selector** field, specify `.textBoxHeight` as the new style's name. Select the **Category** named **Position**, then set the **height:** to 100px and click **OK** to create the style and dismiss the dialog. Next set `messageTextBox`'s `CssClass` property to

```
textBoxWidth textBoxHeight
```

This uses both the `.textBoxWidth` and `.textBoxHeight` styles to set `messageTextBox`'s width to 300 pixels and height to 100 pixels. Also set `messageTextBox`'s `TextMode` property to `MultiLine` so the user can type a message containing multiple lines of text.

Finally, add Buttons named `submitButton` and `clearButton` to the bottom-right table cell. Set the buttons' `Text` properties to `Submit` and `Clear`, respectively. We discuss the buttons' event handlers when we present the code-behind file. You can create these event handlers now by double clicking each Button in **Design** view.

Step 3: Adding a `GridView` Control to the Web Form

Add a `GridView` named `messagesGridView` that will display the guestbook entries. This control is located in the **Toolbox**'s **Data** section. The colors for the `GridView` are specified through the **Auto Format...** link in the **GridView Tasks** *smart-tag menu* that opens when you place the `GridView` on the page. Clicking this link displays an **AutoFormat** dialog with several choices. In this example, we chose **Professional**. We show how to set the `GridView`'s data source (that is, where it gets the data to display in its rows and columns) shortly.

Step 4: Creating the Entity Data Model

Next, you'll add an entity data model to the project. Perform the following steps:

1. Right click the project name in the Solution Explorer and select **Add > Add New Item...** to display the **Add New Item** dialog.

2. Select **ADO.NET Entity Data Model**, change the **Name** to `GuestbookModel.edmx` and click **Add**. A dialog appears asking if you would like to put your new entity data model classes in the `App_Code` folder; click **Yes**. The IDE will create an `App_Code` folder and place the entity data model classes information in that folder. For security reasons, this folder can be accessed only by the web app on the server—clients cannot access this folder over a network.

3. Next, the **Entity Data Model Wizard** dialog appears. Ensure that **Generate from database** is selected so that you can generate the model from the Guestbook.mdf database, then click **Next >**.

4. In the **Entity Data Model Wizard** dialog's **Choose Your Data Connection** step, click **New Connection...** then use the **Connection Properties** dialog to locate the Guestbook.mdf database file (included in the databases folder with this chapter's examples). Click **OK** to create the connection, then click **Next >** to complete the **Choose Your Data Connection** step.

5. A dialog appears asking if you would like to copy the database file into your project. Click **Yes**. The IDE will create an App_Data folder and place the Guestbook.mdf file in that folder. Like the App_Code folder, this folder can be accessed only by the web app on the server.

6. In the **Entity Data Model Wizard** dialog's **Choose Your Database Objects and Settings** step, select the Messages table from the database. By default, the IDE names the model GuestbookModel. Ensure that **Pluralize or singularize generated object names** is checked, keep the other default settings and click **Finish**. The IDE displays the GuestbookModel in the editor, where you can see that a Message has a MessageID, Date, Name, Email and Message1 property. Message1 was renamed from Message by the IDE so that it does not conflict with the entity data model's Message class.

7. Select **BUILD > Build Solution** to ensure that the new entity data model classes are compiled.

Step 5: Binding the GridView to the Messages Table of the Guestbook Database
You can now configure the GridView to display the database's data.

1. In the **GridView Tasks** smart-tag menu, select **<New data source...>** from the **Choose Data Source** ComboBox to display the **Data Source Configuration Wizard** dialog.

2. In this example, we use a **EntityDataSource** control that allows the app to interact with the Guestbook.mdf database. Select **Entity**, then in the **Specify an ID for the data source** field enter messagesEntityDataSource and click **OK** to begin the **Configure Data Source** wizard.

3. In the **Configure ObjectContext** step, select GuestbookEntities in the **Named Connection** ComboBox, then click **Next >**.

4. The **Configure Data Selection** screen (Fig. 21.33) allows you to specify which data the EntityDataSource should retrieve from the data context. The **EntitySetName** drop-down list contains DbContext properties that represent database's tables. For the Guestbook database, select Messages from the drop-down list. In the **Choose the properties in the query result:** pane, ensure that the **Select All** checkbox is selected to indicate that you want to retrieve all the columns in the Messages table.

5. Click **Finish** to complete the wizard. A control named messagesEntityDataSource now appears on the Web Form directly below the GridView. It's represented in **Design** mode as a gray box containing its type and name. It will *not* appear on the web page—the gray box simply provides a way to manipulate the

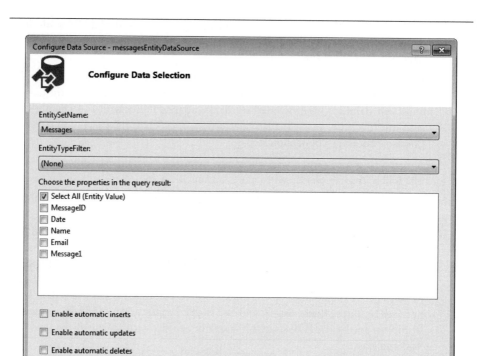

Fig. 21.33 | Configuring the `EntityDataSource`.

control visually through **Design** mode—similar to how the objects in the component tray are used in **Design** mode for a Windows Forms app.

6. Click the `messagesEntityDataSource`, then select **Refresh Schema** from its
   smart-tag menu. The `GridView` updates to display column headers that correspond to the columns in the `Messages` table (Fig. 21.34). The rows each contain
   either a number (which signifies an *autoincremented column*) or **abc** (which indicates string data). The actual data from the `Guestbook.mdf` database file will appear in these rows when you view the ASPX file in a web browser.

Step 6: Customizing the Columns of the Data Source Displayed in the `GridView`
It's not necessary for site visitors to see the `MessageID` column when viewing past guestbook entries—this column is merely a unique primary key required by the `Messages` table
within the database. So, let's modify the `GridView` to prevent this column from displaying
on the Web Form. We'll also modify the column **Message1** to read **Message**.

1. In the **GridView Tasks** *smart tag menu*, click **Edit Columns** to display the **Fields** dialog (Fig. 21.35).

2. Select **MessageID** in the **Selected fields** pane, then click the ⊠ Button. This removes the `MessageID` column from the `GridView`.

EntityDataSource control

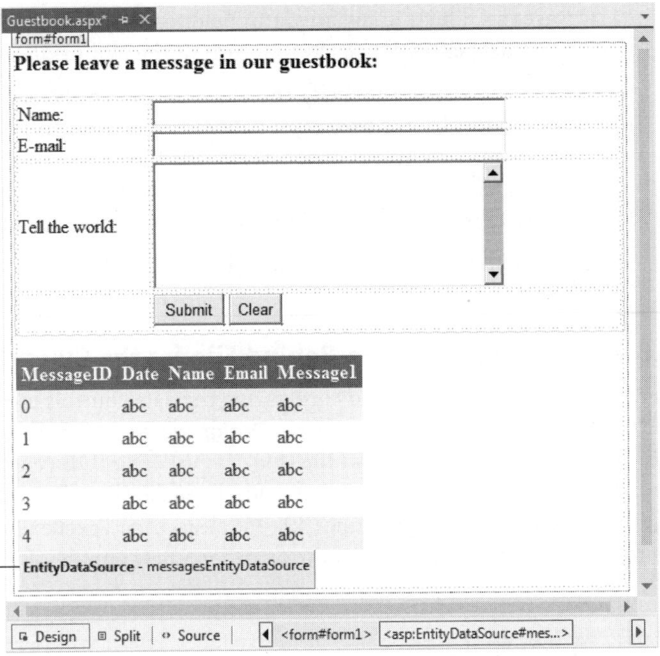

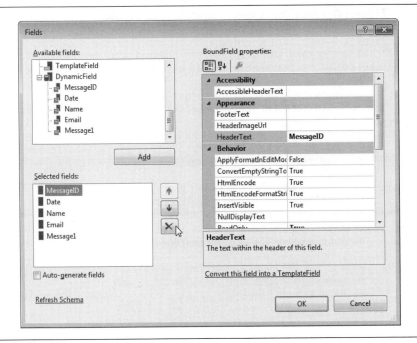

Fig. 21.34 | **Design** mode displaying `EntityDataSource` control for a `GridView`.

Fig. 21.35 | Removing the `MessageID` column from the `GridView`.

3. Select **Message1** in the **Selected fields** pane and change its HeaderText property to Message. The IDE renamed this field to prevent a naming conflict in the entity data model classes. Click **OK** to return to the main IDE window.

4. Next create a style to specify the width of the GridView. Select **FORMAT > New Style...** to display the **New Style** dialog. In the **Selector** field, specify .gridView-Width as the new style's name. Select the **Category** named **Position**, then set the **width:** to 650px and click **OK** to create the style and dismiss the dialog. Next set the CssClass property for the messagesGridView to gridViewWidth.

The GridView should now appear as shown in Fig. 21.31.

21.8.2 Modifying the Code-Behind File for the Guestbook App

After building the Web Form and configuring the data controls used in this example, double click the **Submit** and **Clear** buttons in **Design** view to create their corresponding Click event handlers in the code-behind file (Fig. 21.36). The IDE generates empty event handlers, so we must add the appropriate code to make these buttons work properly. The event handler for clearButton (lines 39–44) clears each TextBox by setting its Text property to an empty string. This resets the form for a new guestbook submission.

```
 1   // Fig. 23.36: Guestbook.aspx.cs
 2   // Code-behind file that defines event handlers for the guestbook.
 3   using System;
 4
 5   public partial class Guestbook : System.Web.UI.Page
 6   {
 7      // Submit Button adds a new guestbook entry to the database,
 8      // clears the form and displays the updated list of guestbook entries
 9      protected void submitButton_Click( object sender, EventArgs e )
10      {
11         // use GuestbookEntities DbContext to add a new message
12         using ( GuestbookEntities dbcontext = new GuestbookEntities() )
13         {
14            // create a new Message to add to the database; Message is
15            // the entity data model class representing a table row
16            Message message = new Message();
17
18            // set new Message's properties
19            message.Date = DateTime.Now.ToShortDateString();
20            message.Name = nameTextBox.Text;
21            message.Email = emailTextBox.Text;
22            message.Message1 = messageTextBox.Text;
23
24            // add new Message to GuestbookEntities DbContext
25            dbcontext.Messages.Add( message );
26            dbcontext.SaveChanges(); // save changes to the database
27         } // end using statement
28
```

Fig. 21.36 | Code-behind file for the guestbook app. (Part 1 of 2.)

```
29          // clear the TextBoxes
30          nameTextBox.Text = String.Empty;
31          emailTextBox.Text = String.Empty;
32          messageTextBox.Text = String.Empty;
33
34          // update the GridView with the new database table contents
35          messagesGridView.DataBind();
36       } // submitButton_Click
37
38       // Clear Button clears the Web Form's TextBoxes
39       protected void clearButton_Click( object sender, EventArgs e )
40       {
41          nameTextBox.Text = String.Empty;
42          emailTextBox.Text = String.Empty;
43          messageTextBox.Text = String.Empty;
44       } // clearButton_Click
45    } // end class Guestbook
```

Fig. 21.36 | Code-behind file for the guestbook app. (Part 2 of 2.)

Lines 9–36 contain submitButton's event-handling code, which adds the user's information to the Guestbook database's Messages table. The using statement in lines 12–27 begins by creating a GuestbookEntities object to interact with the database. Recall that the using statement will call Dispose on this GuestbookEntities object when the using statement terminates. This is a good practice for an ASP.NET web page request, so that we don't maintain a connection to the database beyond the request.

Line 16 creates an object of the entity data model's Message class, which represents a row in the database's Messages table. Lines 19–22 set the new Message object's properties to the values that should be stored in the database. Line 25 calls the Add method of the GuestbookEntities object's Messages property, which represents the Messages table in the database. This adds a new record to the entity data model's representation of the table. Line 26 then saves the changes into the database.

After the data is inserted into the database, lines 30–32 clear the TextBoxes, and line 35 invokes messagesGridView's **DataBind method** to refresh the data that the GridView displays. This causes messagesEntityDataSource (the GridView's data source) to obtain the Messages table's updated data from the database.

21.9 Case Study: ASP.NET AJAX

In Chapter 27, Web App Development with ASP.NET: A Deeper Look, you learn the difference between a traditional web app and an **AJAX (Asynchronous JavaScript and XML) web app**. You also learn how to use **ASP.NET AJAX** to quickly and easily improve the user experience for your web apps, giving them responsiveness comparable to that of desktop apps. To demonstrate ASP.NET AJAX capabilities, you enhance the validation example by displaying the submitted form information without reloading the entire page. The only modifications to this web app appear in Validation.aspx file. You use AJAX-enabled controls to add this feature.

21.10 Case Study: Password-Protected Books Database App

In Chapter 27, Web App Development with ASP.NET: A Deeper Look, we include a web app case study in which a user logs into a password-protected website to view a list of publications by a selected author. The app consists of several pages and provides website registration and login capabilities. You'll learn about ASP.NET master pages, which allow you to specify a common look-and-feel for all the pages in your app. We also introduce the **Web Site Administration Tool** and use it to configure the portions of the app that can be accessed only by users who are logged into the website.

21.11 Wrap-Up

In this chapter, we introduced web-app development using ASP.NET and Visual Studio Express 2012 for Web. We began by discussing the simple HTTP transactions that take place when you request and receive a web page through a web browser. You then learned about the three tiers (that is, the client or top tier, the business logic or middle tier and the information or bottom tier) that comprise most web apps.

Next, we explained the role of ASPX files (that is, Web Form files) and code-behind files, and the relationship between them. We discussed how ASP.NET compiles and executes web apps so that they can be displayed in a web browser. You also learned how to build an ASP.NET web app using Visual Studio Express For Web.

The chapter demonstrated several common ASP.NET web controls used for displaying text and images on a Web Form. We also discussed validation controls, which allow you to ensure that user input on a web page satisfies certain requirements.

We discussed the benefits of maintaining a user's state information across multiple pages of a website. We then demonstrated how you can include such functionality in a web app by using session tracking with `HttpSessionState` objects.

Finally, we built a guestbook app that allows users to submit comments about a website. You learned how to save the user input in a database and how to display past submissions on the web page.

22

XML and LINQ to XML

Objectives

In this chapter you'll:

- Mark up data using XML.

- Specify and validate an XML document's structure.

- Create and use simple XSL style sheets to render XML document data.

- Use the Document Object Model (DOM) to manipulate XML in C# programs.

- Use LINQ to XML to extract and manipulate data from XML documents.

- Create new XML documents using the classes provided by the .NET Framework.

- Work with XML namespaces in your C# code.

- Transform XML documents into XHTML using class `XslCompiledTransform`.

22.1 Introduction

In this chapter, we begin our introduction to XML. The .NET Framework uses XML extensively. Many of the configuration files that Visual Studio creates—such as those that represent project settings—use XML format. XML is also used heavily in serialization, as you'll see in Chapter 28, Web Services. In Chapters 23–25 and Chapters 30–31, you'll also use XAML—an XML *vocabulary* used for creating user interfaces. XAML is also used with Microsoft Silverlight to develop rich Internet applications

In this chapter, you'll learn XML's syntax and how to use XML namespaces. You'll also learn how to create DTDs and schemas to validate your XML documents. Sections 22.7–22.11 demonstrate techniques for working with XML documents in C# applications. Visual C# provides language features and .NET Framework classes for working with XML. **LINQ to XML** provides a convenient way to manipulate data in XML documents using the same LINQ syntax you used on arrays and collections in Chapter 9. LINQ to XML also provides a set of classes for easily navigating and creating XML documents in your code.

22.2 XML Basics

The Extensible Markup Language was developed in 1996 by the **World Wide Web Consortium's (W3C's)** XML Working Group. XML is a widely supported standard for describing data that is commonly used to exchange that data between applications over the Internet. It permits document authors to create markup for virtually any type of information. This enables them to create entirely new markup languages for describing any type of data, such as mathematical formulas, software-configuration instructions, chemical molecular structures, music, news, recipes and financial reports. XML describes data in a way that both human beings and computers can understand.

Figure 22.1 is a simple XML document that describes information for a baseball player. We focus on lines 5–11 to introduce basic XML syntax. You'll learn about the other elements of this document in Section 22.3.

XML documents contain text that represents content (that is, data), such as John (line 6), and **elements** that specify the document's structure, such as firstName (line 6). XML documents delimit elements with **start tags** and **end tags**. A start tag consists of the element name in **angle brackets** (for example, <player> and <firstName> in lines 5 and 6,

```
1   <?xml version = "1.0"?>
2   <!-- Fig. 22.1: player.xml -->
3   <!-- Baseball player structured with XML -->
4
5   <player>
6       <firstName>John</firstName>
7
8       <lastName>Doe</lastName>
9
10      <battingAverage>0.375</battingAverage>
11  </player>
```

Fig. 22.1 | Baseball player structured with XML.

respectively). An end tag consists of the element name preceded by a **forward slash** (/) in angle brackets (for example, </firstName> and </player> in lines 6 and 11, respectively). An element's start and end tags enclose text that represents a piece of data (for example, the firstName of the player—John—in line 6, which is enclosed by the <firstName> start tag and and </firstName> end tag) or other elements (for example, the firstName, lastName, and battingAverage elements in the player element). Every XML document must have exactly one **root element** that contains all the other elements. In Fig. 22.1, player (lines 5–11) is the root element.

Some XML-based markup languages include MathML (for mathematics), VoiceXML™ (for speech), CML (Chemical Markup Language—for chemistry) and XBRL (Extensible Business Reporting Language—for financial data exchange). ODF (Open Document Format—developed by Sun Microsystems) and OOXML (Office Open XML—developed by Microsoft as a replacement for the old proprietary Microsoft Office formats) are two competing standards for electronic office documents such as spreadsheets, presentations, and word processing documents. These markup languages are called XML **vocabularies** and provide a means for describing particular types of data in standardized, structured ways.

Massive amounts of data are currently stored on the Internet in a variety of formats (for example, databases, web pages, text files). Based on current trends, it's likely that much of this data, especially that which is passed between systems, will soon take the form of XML. Organizations see XML as the future of data encoding. Information-technology groups are planning ways to integrate XML into their systems. Industry groups are developing custom XML vocabularies for most major industries that will allow computer-based business applications to communicate in common languages. For example, web services, which we discuss in Chapter 28, allow web-based applications to exchange data seamlessly through standard protocols based on XML. Also, web services are described by an XML vocabulary called WSDL (Web Services Description Language).

The next generation of the Internet and World Wide Web is being built on a foundation of XML, which enables the development of more sophisticated web-based applications. XML allows you to assign meaning to what would otherwise be random pieces of data. As a result, programs can "understand" the data they manipulate. For example, a web browser might view a street address listed on a simple web page as a string of characters without any real meaning. In an XML document, however, this data can be clearly identified (that is, marked up) as an address. A program that uses the document can recognize this data as an address and provide links to a map of that location, driving directions from that location or other location-specific information. Likewise, an application can recognize names of people, dates, ISBN numbers and any other type of XML-encoded data. Based on this data, the application can present users with other related information, providing a richer, more meaningful user experience.

Viewing and Modifying XML Documents

XML documents are portable. Viewing or modifying an XML document—a text file, usually with the `.xml` file-name extension—does not require special software, although many software tools exist, and new ones are frequently released that make it more convenient to develop XML-based applications. Most text editors can open XML documents for viewing and editing. Visual C# Express includes an XML editor that provides *IntelliSense*. The editor also checks that the document is well formed and is valid if a schema (discussed shortly) is present. Also, most web browsers can display an XML document in a formatted manner that shows its structure. We demonstrate this using Internet Explorer in Section 22.3. One important characteristic of XML is that it's both human readable and machine readable.

Processing XML Documents

Processing an XML document requires software called an **XML parser** (or **XML processor**). A parser makes the document's data available to applications. While reading the contents of an XML document, a parser checks that the document follows the syntax rules specified by the W3C's XML Recommendation (www.w3.org/XML). XML syntax requires a single root element, a start tag and end tag for each element and properly nested tags (that is, the end tag for a nested element must appear before the end tag of the enclosing element). Furthermore, XML is case sensitive, so the proper capitalization must be used in elements. A document that conforms to this syntax is a **well-formed XML document**, and is syntactically correct. We present fundamental XML syntax in Section 22.3. If an XML parser can process an XML document successfully, that XML document is well formed. Parsers can provide access to XML-encoded data in well-formed documents only—if a document is not well-formed, the parser will report an error to the user or calling application.

Often, XML parsers are built into software such as Visual Studio or available for download over the Internet. You can find a list of many popular XML parsers at

```
http://en.wikipedia.org/wiki/Category:XML_parsers
```

Validating XML Documents

An XML document can optionally reference a **Document Type Definition (DTD)** or a **W3C XML Schema** (referred to simply as a "schema" for the rest of this book) that defines the XML document's proper structure. When an XML document references a DTD or a schema, some parsers (called **validating parsers**) can use the DTD/schema to check that it has the appropriate structure. If the XML document conforms to the DTD/schema (that is, the document has the appropriate structure), the XML document is **valid**. For example, if in Fig. 22.1 we were referencing a DTD that specifies that a `player` element must have `firstName`, `lastName` and `battingAverage` elements, then omitting the `lastName` element (line 8) would cause the XML document `player.xml` to be invalid. The

XML document would still be well formed, however, because it follows proper XML syntax (that is, it has one root element, and each element has a start and an end tag). By definition, a valid XML document is well formed. Parsers that cannot check for document conformity against DTDs/schemas are **nonvalidating parsers**—they determine only whether an XML document is well formed.

You'll learn more about validation, DTDs and schemas, as well as the key differences between these two types of structural specifications, later in this chapter. For now, schemas are XML documents themselves, whereas DTDs are not. As you'll learn, this difference presents several advantages in using schemas over DTDs.

Software Engineering Observation 22.1

DTDs and schemas are essential for business-to-business (B2B) transactions and mission-critical systems. Validating XML documents ensures that disparate systems can manipulate data structured in standardized ways and prevents errors caused by missing or malformed data.

Formatting and Manipulating XML Documents

XML documents contain only data, not formatting instructions, so applications that process XML documents must decide how to manipulate or display each document's data. For example, a PDA (personal digital assistant) may render an XML document differently than a wireless phone or a desktop computer. You can use **Extensible Stylesheet Language** (**XSL**) to specify rendering instructions for different platforms. We discuss XSL in Section 22.7.

XML-processing programs can also search, sort and manipulate XML data using technologies such as XSL. Some other XML-related technologies are XPath (XML Path Language—a language for accessing parts of an XML document), XSL-FO (XSL Formatting Objects—an XML vocabulary used to describe document formatting) and XSLT (XSL Transformations—a language for transforming XML documents into other documents). We present XSLT and XPath in Section 22.7. We'll also present new C# features that greatly simplify working with XML in your code. With these features, XSLT and similar technologies are not needed while coding in C#, but they remain relevant on platforms where C# and .NET are not available.

22.3 Structuring Data

In Fig. 22.2, we present an XML document that marks up a simple article using XML. The line numbers shown are for reference only and are not part of the XML document.

```
1   <?xml version = "1.0"?>
2   <!-- Fig. 22.2: article.xml -->
3   <!-- Article structured with XML -->
4
5   <article>
6      <title>Simple XML</title>
7
```

Fig. 22.2 | XML used to mark up an article. (Part 1 of 2.)

```
 8          <date>July 24, 2013</date>
 9
10          <author>
11             <firstName>John</firstName>
12             <lastName>Doe</lastName>
13          </author>
14
15          <summary>XML is pretty easy.</summary>
16
17          <content>
18             In this chapter, we present a wide variety of examples that use XML.
19          </content>
20       </article>
```

Fig. 22.2 | XML used to mark up an article. (Part 2 of 2.)

This document begins with an **XML declaration** (line 1), which identifies the document as an XML document. The **version attribute** specifies the XML version to which the document conforms.

Some XML documents also specify an **encoding attribute** in the XML declaration. An encoding specifies how characters are stored in memory and on disk—historically, the way an uppercase "A" was stored on one computer architecture was different than the way it was stored on a different computer architecture. Appendix F discusses Unicode, which specifies encodings that can describe characters in any written language. An introduction to different encodings in XML can be found at the website bit.ly/EncodeXMLData.

Portability Tip 22.1
Documents should include the XML declaration to identify the version of XML used. A document that lacks an XML declaration might be assumed erroneously to conform to the latest version of XML—in which case, errors could result.

Common Programming Error 22.1
Placing whitespace characters before the XML declaration is an error.

XML comments (lines 2–3), which begin with <!-- and end with -->, can be placed almost anywhere in an XML document. XML comments can span to multiple lines—an end marker on each line is not needed; the end marker can appear on a subsequent line, as long as there is exactly one end marker (-->) for each begin marker (<!--). Comments are used in XML for documentation purposes. Line 4 is a blank line. As in a C# program, blank lines, whitespaces and indentation are used in XML to improve readability. Later you'll see that the blank lines are normally ignored by XML parsers.

Common Programming Error 22.2
In an XML document, each start tag must have a matching end tag; omitting either tag is an error. Soon, you'll learn how such errors are detected.

Common Programming Error 22.3

XML is case sensitive. Using different cases for the start-tag and end-tag names for the same element is a syntax error.

In Fig. 22.2, article (lines 5–20) is the root element. The lines that precede the root element (lines 1–4) are the XML **prolog**. In an XML prolog, the XML declaration must appear before the comments and any other markup.

The elements we used in the example do not come from any specific markup language. Instead, we chose the element names and markup structure that best describe our particular data. You can invent whatever elements make sense for the particular data you're dealing with. For example, element title (line 6) contains text that describes the article's title (for example, Simple XML). Similarly, date (line 8), author (lines 10–13), firstName (line 11), lastName (line 12), summary (line 15) and content (lines 17–19) contain text that describes the date, author, the author's first name, the author's last name, a summary and the content of the document, respectively. XML element and attribute names can be of any length and may contain letters, digits, underscores, hyphens and periods. However, they must begin with either a letter or an underscore, and they should not begin with "xml" in any combination of uppercase and lowercase letters (for example, XML, Xml, xMl), as this is reserved for use in the XML standards.

Common Programming Error 22.4

Using a whitespace character in an XML element name is an error.

Good Programming Practice 22.1

XML element names should be meaningful to humans and should not use abbreviations.

XML elements are **nested** to form hierarchies—with the root element at the top of the hierarchy. This allows document authors to create parent/child relationships between data. For example, elements title, date, author, summary and content are nested within article. Elements firstName and lastName are nested within author.

Common Programming Error 22.5

Nesting XML tags improperly is a syntax error—it causes an XML document to not be well-formed. For example, <x><y>hello</x></y> is an error, because the </y> tag must precede the </x> tag.

Any element that contains other elements (for example, article or author) is a **container element**. Container elements also are called **parent elements**. Elements nested inside a container element are **child elements** (or children) of that container element.

Viewing an XML Document in Internet Explorer

The XML document in Fig. 22.2 is simply a text file named article.xml. This document does not contain formatting information for the article. The reason is that XML is a technology for describing the structure of data. Formatting and displaying data from an XML document are application-specific issues. For example, when the user loads article.xml in Internet Explorer (IE), the browser parses and displays the document's data. Internet

Explorer uses a built-in **style sheet** to format the data. The resulting format (Fig. 22.3) is similar to the code listing in Fig. 22.2. In Section 22.7, we show how to create style sheets to transform your XML data into various formats suitable for display.

a) Internet Explorer 10 showing `article.xml` with all nodes expanded

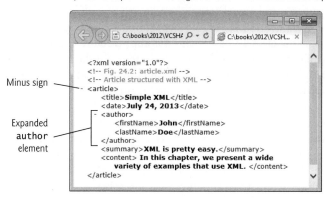

b) Internet Explorer 10 showing `article.xml` with the `author` node collapsed

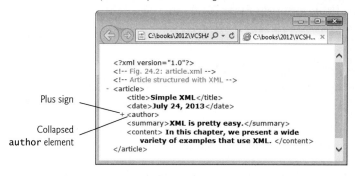

Fig. 22.3 | `article.xml` displayed by Internet Explorer 10 on Windows 7.

Note the minus sign (–) and plus sign (+) in the screenshots of Fig. 22.3. Although these symbols are not part of the XML document, Internet Explorer places them next to every container element. A minus sign indicates that Internet Explorer is displaying the container element's child elements. Clicking the minus sign next to an element collapses that element (that is, causes Internet Explorer to hide the container element's children and replace the minus sign with a plus sign). Conversely, clicking the plus sign next to an element expands that element (that is, causes Internet Explorer to display the container element's children and replace the plus sign with a minus sign). This behavior is similar to viewing the directory structure using Windows Explorer. In fact, a directory structure often is modeled as a series of tree structures, in which the **root** of a tree represents a drive letter (for example, C:), and **nodes** in the tree represent directories. Parsers often store XML data as tree structures to facilitate efficient manipulation.

XML Markup for a Business Letter

Now that we have seen a simple XML document, let's examine a more complex one that marks up a business letter (Fig. 22.4). Again, we begin the document with the XML declaration (line 1) that states the XML version to which the document conforms.

```
1   <?xml version = "1.0"?>
2   <!-- Fig. 22.4: letter.xml -->
3   <!-- Business letter marked up as XML -->
4
5   <!DOCTYPE letter SYSTEM "letter.dtd">
6
7   <letter>
8      <contact type = "sender">
9         <name>Jane Doe</name>
10        <address1>Box 12345</address1>
11        <address2>15 Any Ave.</address2>
12        <city>Othertown</city>
13        <state>Otherstate</state>
14        <zip>67890</zip>
15        <phone>555-4321</phone>
16        <flag gender = "F" />
17     </contact>
18
19     <contact type = "receiver">
20        <name>John Doe</name>
21        <address1>123 Main St.</address1>
22        <address2></address2>
23        <city>Anytown</city>
24        <state>Anystate</state>
25        <zip>12345</zip>
26        <phone>555-1234</phone>
27        <flag gender = "M" />
28     </contact>
29
30     <salutation>Dear Sir:</salutation>
31
32     <paragraph>It is our privilege to inform you about our new database
33        managed with XML. This new system allows you to reduce the
34        load on your inventory list server by having the client machine
35        perform the work of sorting and filtering the data.
36     </paragraph>
37
38     <paragraph>Please visit our website for availability
39        and pricing.
40     </paragraph>
41
42     <closing>Sincerely,</closing>
43     <signature>Ms. Jane Doe</signature>
44  </letter>
```

Fig. 22.4 | Business letter marked up as XML.

Line 5 specifies that this XML document references a DTD. Recall from Section 22.2 that DTDs define the structure of the data for an XML document. For example, a DTD specifies the elements and parent/child relationships between elements permitted in an XML document.

Error-Prevention Tip 22.1

An XML document is not required to reference a DTD, but validating XML parsers can use a DTD to ensure that the document has the proper structure.

Portability Tip 22.2

Validating an XML document helps guarantee that independent developers will exchange data in a standardized form that conforms to the DTD.

The DTD reference (line 5) contains three items: the name of the root element that the DTD specifies (letter); the keyword **SYSTEM** (which denotes an **external DTD**—a DTD declared in a separate file, as opposed to a DTD declared locally in the same file); and the DTD's name and location (that is, letter.dtd in the same directory as the XML document). DTD document file names typically end with the **.dtd** extension. We discuss DTDs and letter.dtd in detail in Section 22.5.

Root element letter (lines 7–44 of Fig. 22.4) contains the child elements contact, contact, salutation, paragraph, paragraph, closing and signature. Besides being placed between tags, data also can be placed in **attributes**—name/value pairs that appear within the angle brackets of start tags. Elements can have any number of attributes (separated by spaces) in their start tags, provided all the attribute names are unique. The first contact element (lines 8–17) has an attribute named type with **attribute value** "sender", which indicates that this contact element identifies the letter's sender. The second contact element (lines 19–28) has attribute type with value "receiver", which indicates that this contact element identifies the letter's recipient. Like element names, attribute names are case sensitive, can be of any length, may contain letters, digits, underscores, hyphens and periods, and must begin with either a letter or an underscore character. A contact element stores various items of information about a contact, such as the contact's name (represented by element name), address (represented by elements address1, address2, city, state and zip), phone number (represented by element phone) and gender (represented by attribute gender of element flag). Element salutation (line 30) marks up the letter's salutation. Lines 32–40 mark up the letter's body using two paragraph elements. Elements closing (line 42) and signature (line 43) mark up the closing sentence and the author's "signature," respectively.

Common Programming Error 22.6

Failure to enclose attribute values in double ("") or single (' ') quotes is a syntax error.

Line 16 introduces the **empty element** flag. An empty element contains no content. However, it may sometimes contain data in the form of attributes. Empty element flag contains an attribute that indicates the gender of the contact (represented by the parent contact element). Document authors can close an empty element either by placing a slash immediately preceding the rightmost angle bracket, as shown in line 16, or by explicitly writing an end tag, as in line 22:

```
<address2></address2>
```

Line 22 can also be written as:

```
<address2/>
```

The `address2` element in line 22 is empty, because there is no second part to this contact's address. However, we must include this element to conform to the structural rules specified in the XML document's DTD—`letter.dtd` (which we present in Section 22.5). This DTD specifies that each `contact` element must have an `address2` child element (even if it's empty). In Section 22.5, you'll learn how DTDs indicate that certain elements are required while others are optional.

22.4 XML Namespaces

XML allows you to create custom elements. This extensibility can result in **naming collisions**—elements with identical names that represent different things—when combining content from multiple sources. For example, we may use the element `book` to mark up data about a Deitel publication. A stamp collector may use the element `book` to mark up data about a book of stamps. Using both of these elements in the same document could create a naming collision, making it difficult to determine which kind of data each element contains.

An XML **namespace** is a collection of element and attribute names. Like C# namespaces, XML namespaces provide a means for document authors to unambiguously refer to elements that have the same name (that is, prevent collisions). For example,

```
<subject>Math</subject>
```

and

```
<subject>Cardiology</subject>
```

use element `subject` to mark up data. In the first case, the subject is something one studies in school, whereas in the second case, the subject is a field of medicine. Namespaces can differentiate these two `subject` elements. For example,

```
<school:subject>Math</school:subject>
```

and

```
<medical:subject>Cardiology</medical:subject>
```

Both `school` and `medical` are **namespace prefixes**. A document author places a namespace prefix and colon (`:`) before an element name to specify the namespace to which that element belongs. Document authors can create their own namespace prefixes using virtually any name except the reserved namespace prefixes `xml` and `xmlns`. In the subsections that follow, we demonstrate how document authors ensure that namespaces are unique.

Common Programming Error 22.7
Attempting to create a namespace prefix named xml in any mixture of uppercase and lowercase letters is a syntax error—the xml namespace is reserved for internal use by XML itself.

Differentiating Elements with Namespaces
Figure 22.5 uses namespaces to differentiate two distinct elements—the `file` element related to a text file and the `file` document related to an image file.

```
 I   <?xml version = "1.0"?>
 2   <!-- Fig. 22.5: namespace.xml -->
 3   <!-- Demonstrating namespaces -->
 4
 5   <text:directory
 6      xmlns:text = "urn:deitel:textInfo"
 7      xmlns:image = "urn:deitel:imageInfo">
 8
 9      <text:file filename = "book.xml">
10         <text:description>A book list</text:description>
11      </text:file>
12
13      <image:file filename = "funny.jpg">
14         <image:description>A funny picture</image:description>
15         <image:size width = "200" height = "100" />
16      </image:file>
17   </text:directory>
```

Fig. 22.5 | XML namespaces demonstration.

Lines 6–7 use the XML-namespace reserved attribute **xmlns** to create two namespace prefixes—text and image. Creating a namespace prefix is similar to using a using statement in C#—it allows you to access XML elements from a given namespace. Each namespace prefix is bound to a series of characters called a **Uniform Resource Identifier** (URI) that uniquely identifies the namespace. Document authors create their own namespace prefixes and URIs. A URI is a way to identify a resource, typically on the Internet. Two popular types of URI are **Uniform Resource Name** (URN) and **Uniform Resource Locator** (URL).

To ensure that namespaces are unique, document authors must provide unique URIs. We chose urn:deitel:textInfo and urn:deitel:imageInfo as URIs. These URIs employ the URN scheme frequently used to identify namespaces. Under this naming scheme, a URI begins with "urn:", followed by a unique series of additional names separated by colons. These URIs are not guaranteed to be unique—the idea is simply that creating a long URI in this way makes it unlikely that two authors will use the same namespace.

Another common practice is to use URLs, which specify the location of a file or a resource on the Internet. For example, http://www.deitel.com is the URL that identifies the home page of the Deitel & Associates website. Using URLs for domains that you own guarantees that the namespaces are unique, because the domain names (for example, www.deitel.com) are guaranteed to be unique. For example, lines 5–7 could be rewritten as

```
<text:directory
   xmlns:text = "http://www.deitel.com/xmlns-text"
   xmlns:image = "http://www.deitel.com/xmlns-image">
```

where URLs related to the Deitel & Associates, Inc. domain name serve as URIs to identify the text and image namespaces. The parser does not visit these URLs, nor do these URLs need to refer to actual web pages. Each simply represents a unique series of characters used to differentiate URI names. In fact, any string can represent a namespace. For example, our image namespace URI could be hgjfkdlsa4556, in which case our prefix assignment would be

```
xmlns:image = "hgjfkdlsa4556"
```

Lines 9–11 use the text namespace prefix for elements file and description. The end tags must also specify the namespace prefix text. Lines 13–16 apply namespace prefix image to the elements file, description and size. Attributes do not require namespace prefixes, because each attribute is already part of an element that specifies the namespace prefix. For example, attribute filename (line 9) is already uniquely identified by being in the context of the filename start tag, which is prefixed with text.

Specifying a Default Namespace
To eliminate the need to place namespace prefixes in each element, document authors may specify a **default namespace** for an element and its children. Figure 22.6 demonstrates using a default namespace (urn:deitel:textInfo) for element directory.

```
1   <?xml version = "1.0"?>
2   <!-- Fig. 22.6: defaultnamespace.xml -->
3   <!-- Using default namespaces -->
4
5   <directory xmlns = "urn:deitel:textInfo"
6      xmlns:image = "urn:deitel:imageInfo">
7
8      <file filename = "book.xml">
9         <description>A book list</description>
10     </file>
11
12     <image:file filename = "funny.jpg">
13        <image:description>A funny picture</image:description>
14        <image:size width = "200" height = "100" />
15     </image:file>
16  </directory>
```

Fig. 22.6 │ Default namespace demonstration.

Line 5 defines a default namespace using attribute xmlns with a URI as its value. Once we define this default namespace, child elements which do not specify a prefix belong to the default namespace. Thus, element file (lines 8–10) is in the default namespace urn:deitel:textInfo. Compare this to lines 9–11 of Fig. 22.5, where we had to prefix the file and description element names with the namespace prefix text.

Common Programming Error 22.8
The default namespace can be overridden at any point in the document with another xmlns attribute. All direct and indirect children of the element with the xmlns attribute use the new default namespace.

The default namespace applies to the directory element and all elements that are not qualified with a namespace prefix. However, we can use a namespace prefix to specify a different namespace for particular elements. For example, the file element in lines 12–15 includes the image namespace prefix, indicating that this element is in the urn:deitel:imageInfo namespace, not the default namespace.

Namespaces in XML Vocabularies
XML-based languages, such as XML Schema and Extensible Stylesheet Language (XSL), often use namespaces to identify their elements. Each vocabulary defines special-purpose elements that are grouped in namespaces. These namespaces help prevent naming collisions between predefined and user-defined elements.

22.5 Document Type Definitions (DTDs)

Document Type Definitions (DTDs) are one of two technologies you can use to specify XML document structure. Section 22.6 presents W3C XML Schema documents, which provide an improved method of specifying XML document structure.

Software Engineering Observation 22.2

XML documents can have many different structures, and for this reason an application cannot be certain whether a particular document it receives is complete, ordered properly, and not missing data. DTDs and schemas (Section 22.6) solve this problem by providing an extensible way to describe XML document structure. Applications should use DTDs or schemas to confirm whether XML documents are valid.

Software Engineering Observation 22.3

Many organizations and individuals are creating DTDs and schemas for a broad range of applications. These collections—called repositories—are available free for download from the web (e.g., www.xml.org, www.oasis-open.org).

Creating a Document Type Definition
Figure 22.4 presented a simple business letter marked up with XML. Recall that line 5 of letter.xml references a DTD—letter.dtd (Fig. 22.7). This DTD specifies the business letter's element types and attributes and their relationships to one another.

```
 1   <!-- Fig. 22.7: letter.dtd     -->
 2   <!-- DTD document for letter.xml -->
 3
 4   <!ELEMENT letter ( contact+, salutation, paragraph+,
 5      closing, signature )>
 6
 7   <!ELEMENT contact ( name, address1, address2, city, state,
 8      zip, phone, flag )>
 9   <!ATTLIST contact type CDATA #IMPLIED>
10
11   <!ELEMENT name ( #PCDATA )>
12   <!ELEMENT address1 ( #PCDATA )>
13   <!ELEMENT address2 ( #PCDATA )>
14   <!ELEMENT city ( #PCDATA )>
15   <!ELEMENT state ( #PCDATA )>
16   <!ELEMENT zip ( #PCDATA )>
17   <!ELEMENT phone ( #PCDATA )>
18   <!ELEMENT flag EMPTY>
19   <!ATTLIST flag gender (M | F) "M">
```

Fig. 22.7 | Document Type Definition (DTD) for a business letter. (Part I of 2.)

```
20
21   <!ELEMENT salutation ( #PCDATA )>
22   <!ELEMENT closing ( #PCDATA )>
23   <!ELEMENT paragraph ( #PCDATA )>
24   <!ELEMENT signature ( #PCDATA )>
```

Fig. 22.7 | Document Type Definition (DTD) for a business letter. (Part 2 of 2.)

A DTD describes the structure of an XML document and enables an XML parser to verify whether an XML document is valid (i.e., whether its elements contain the proper attributes and appear in the proper sequence). DTDs allow users to check document structure and to exchange data in a standardized format. A DTD expresses the set of rules for document structure by specifying what attributes and other elements may appear inside a given element.

Common Programming Error 22.9

For documents validated with DTDs, any document that uses elements, attributes or relationships not explicitly defined by a DTD is an invalid document.

Defining Elements in a DTD

The **ELEMENT element type declaration** in Fig. 22.7, lines 4–5 defines the rules for element letter. In this case, letter contains one or more contact elements, one salutation element, one or more paragraph elements, one closing element and one signature element, in that sequence. The **plus sign (+) occurrence indicator** specifies that the DTD allows one or more occurrences of an element. Other occurrence indicators include the **asterisk (*)**, which indicates an *optional* element that can occur *zero or more* times, and the **question mark (?)**, which indicates an optional element that can occur at most once (i.e., zero or one occurrence). If an element does not have an occurrence indicator, the DTD allows exactly one occurrence.

The contact element type declaration (lines 7–8) specifies that a contact element contains child elements name, address1, address2, city, state, zip, phone and flag—in that order. The DTD requires exactly one occurrence of each of these elements.

Defining Attributes in a DTD

Line 9 uses the **ATTLIST attribute-list declaration** to define an attribute named type for the contact element. Keyword **#IMPLIED** specifies that the type attribute of the contact element is *optional*—a missing type attribute will not invalidate the document. Other keywords that can be used in place of #IMPLIED in an ATTLIST declaration include #REQUIRED and #FIXED. Keyword **#REQUIRED** specifies that the attribute must be present in the element, and keyword **#FIXED** specifies that the attribute (if present) must have the given fixed value. For example,

```
<!ATTLIST address zip CDATA #FIXED "01757">
```

indicates that attribute zip (if present in element address) must have the value 01757 for the document to be valid. If the attribute is not present, then the parser, by default, uses the fixed value that the ATTLIST declaration specifies. You can supply a default value instead of one of these keywords. Doing so makes the attribute optional, but the default value will be used if the attribute's value is not specified.

Character Data vs. Parsed Character Data

Keyword **CDATA** (line 9) specifies that attribute type contains **character data** (i.e., a string). A parser will pass such data to an application without modification.

> **Software Engineering Observation 22.4**
>
> *DTD syntax cannot describe an element's (or attribute's) type. For example, a DTD cannot specify that a particular element or attribute can contain only integer data.*

Keyword **#PCDATA** (line 11) specifies that an element (e.g., name) may contain **parsed character data** (i.e., data that is processed by an XML parser). Elements with parsed character data cannot contain markup characters, such as less than (<), greater than (>) or ampersand (&). The document author should replace any markup character in a #PCDATA element with the character's corresponding **character entity reference**. For example, the character entity reference < should be used in place of the less-than symbol (<), and the character entity reference > should be used in place of the greater-than symbol (>). A document author who wishes to use a literal ampersand should use the entity reference & instead—parsed character data can contain ampersands (&) only for inserting entities. The final two entities defined by XML are ' and ", representing the single (') and double (") quote characters, respectively.

> **Common Programming Error 22.10**
>
> *Using markup characters (e.g., <, > and &) in parsed character data is an error. Use character entity references (e.g., <, > and & instead).*

Defining Empty Elements in a DTD

Line 18 defines an empty element named flag. Keyword **EMPTY** specifies that the element does not contain any data between its start and end tags. Empty elements commonly describe data via attributes. For example, flag's data appears in its gender attribute (line 19). Line 19 specifies that the gender attribute's value must be one of the enumerated values (M or F) enclosed in parentheses and delimited by a vertical bar (|) meaning "or." Line 19 also indicates that gender has a default value of M.

Well-Formed Documents vs. Valid Documents

Recall that a well-formed document is *syntactically correct* (i.e., each start tag has a corresponding end tag, the document contains only one root element, and so on), and a valid document contains the proper elements with the proper attributes in the proper sequence. An XML document cannot be valid unless it's well formed.

Visual Studio can validate XML documents against both DTDs and schemas. You do not have to create a project to use this facility—simply open the XML file in Visual Studio as in Fig. 22.8. If the DTD or schema referenced in the XML document can be retrieved, Visual Studio will automatically validate the XML. If the XML file does not validate, Visual Studio will display a warning just as it does with errors in your C# code. Visit www.w3.org/XML/Schema for a list of additional validation tools.

a) No errors or warnings in the Error List window indicate that this XML document validated properly

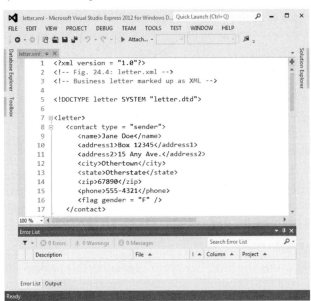

b) The XML document did not validate properly because the value for the **gender** attribute (line 16) as invald

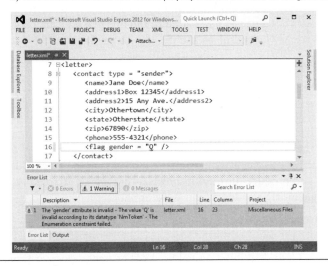

Fig. 22.8 | XML file open in Visual Studio Express 2012 for Windows Desktop.

22.6 W3C XML Schema Documents

In this section, we introduce schemas for specifying XML document structure and validating XML documents. Many developers in the XML community believe that DTDs are not flexible enough to meet today's programming needs. For example, DTDs lack a way of indicating what specific type of data (e.g., numeric, text) an element can contain, and

DTDs are not themselves XML documents, which makes it difficult to manipulate them programmatically. These and other limitations have led to the development of schemas.

Unlike DTDs, schemas use XML syntax and are actually XML documents that programs can manipulate. Like DTDs, schemas are used by validating parsers to validate documents.

In this section, we focus on the W3C's **XML Schema** vocabulary. For the latest information on XML Schema, visit www.w3.org/XML/Schema. For tutorials on XML Schema concepts beyond what we present here, visit www.w3schools.com/schema/default.asp.

A DTD describes an XML document's structure, not the content of its elements. For example,

```
<quantity>5</quantity>
```

contains character data. If the document that contains element `quantity` references a DTD, an XML parser can validate the document to confirm that this element indeed does contain PCDATA content. However, the parser cannot validate that the content is numeric; DTDs do not provide this capability. So, unfortunately, the parser also considers

```
<quantity>hello</quantity>
```

to be valid. An application that uses the XML document containing this markup should test that the data in element `quantity` is numeric and take appropriate action if it's not.

XML Schema enables schema authors to specify that element `quantity`'s data must be numeric or, even more specifically, an integer. A parser validating the XML document against this schema can determine that 5 conforms and `hello` does not. An XML document that conforms to a schema document is **schema valid**, and one that does not conform is **schema invalid**. Schemas are XML documents and can also be validated.

Validating Against an XML Schema Document
Figure 22.9 shows a schema-valid XML document named `book.xml`, and Fig. 22.10 shows the pertinent XML Schema document (`book.xsd`) that defines the structure for `book.xml`. By convention, schemas use the **.xsd** extension. Recall that Visual Studio can perform schema validation if it can locate the schema document. Visual Studio can locate a schema if it's specified in the XML document, is in the same solution or is simply open in Visual Studio at the same time as the XML document. To validate the schema document itself (i.e., `book.xsd`) and produce the output shown in Fig. 22.10, we used an on-line XSV (XML Schema Validator) provided by the W3C at

```
www.w3.org/2001/03/webdata/xsv
```

These tools enforce the W3C's specifications regarding XML Schemas and schema validation. Figure 22.9 contains markup describing several books. The books element (line 5) has the namespace prefix `deitel` (declared in line 5), indicating that the books element is a part of the namespace http://www.deitel.com/booklist.

```
1    <?xml version = "1.0"?>
2    <!-- Fig. 22.9: book.xml -->
3    <!-- Book list marked up as XML -->
```

Fig. 22.9 | Schema-valid XML document describing a list of books. (Part 1 of 2.)

```
 4
 5   <deitel:books xmlns:deitel = "http://www.deitel.com/booklist">
 6      <book>
 7         <title>Visual Basic 2012 How to Program</title>
 8      </book>
 9
10      <book>
11         <title>Visual C# 2012 How to Program, 3/e</title>
12      </book>
13
14      <book>
15         <title>Java How to Program, 7/e</title>
16      </book>
17
18      <book>
19         <title>C++ How to Program, 6/e</title>
20      </book>
21
22      <book>
23         <title>Internet and World Wide Web How to Program, 4/e</title>
24      </book>
25   </deitel:books>
```

Fig. 22.9 | Schema-valid XML document describing a list of books. (Part 2 of 2.)

Creating an XML Schema Document

Figure 22.10 presents the XML Schema document that specifies the structure of book.xml
(Fig. 22.9). This document defines an XML-based language (i.e., a vocabulary) for writing
XML documents about collections of books. The schema defines the elements, attributes
and parent-child relationships that such a document can (or must) include. The schema
also specifies the type of data that these elements and attributes may contain.

```
 1   <?xml version = "1.0"?>
 2   <!-- Fig. 22.10: book.xsd          -->
 3   <!-- Simple W3C XML Schema document -->
 4
 5   <schema xmlns = "http://www.w3.org/2001/XMLSchema"
 6      xmlns:deitel = "http://www.deitel.com/booklist"
 7      targetNamespace = "http://www.deitel.com/booklist">
 8
 9      <element name = "books" type = "deitel:BooksType"/>
10
11      <complexType name = "BooksType">
12         <sequence>
13            <element name = "book" type = "deitel:SingleBookType"
14               minOccurs = "1" maxOccurs = "unbounded"/>
15         </sequence>
16      </complexType>
17
```

Fig. 22.10 | XML Schema document for book.xml. (Part 1 of 2.)

```
18    <complexType name = "SingleBookType">
19       <sequence>
20          <element name = "title" type = "string"/>
21       </sequence>
22    </complexType>
23 </schema>
```

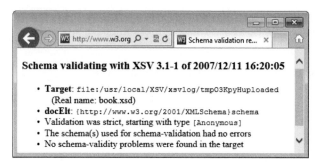

Fig. 22.10 | XML Schema document for `book.xml`. (Part 2 of 2.)

Root element **schema** (Fig. 22.10, lines 5–23) contains elements that define the structure of an XML document such as `book.xml`. Line 5 specifies as the default namespace the standard W3C XML Schema namespace URI—**http://www.w3.org/2001/XMLSchema**. This namespace contains predefined elements (e.g., root element `schema`) that comprise the XML Schema vocabulary—the language used to write an XML Schema document.

Portability Tip 22.3

W3C XML Schema authors specify URI http://www.w3.org/2001/XMLSchema when referring to the XML Schema namespace. This namespace contains predefined elements that comprise the XML Schema vocabulary. Specifying this URI ensures that validation tools correctly identify XML Schema elements and do not confuse them with those defined by document authors.

Line 6 binds the URI `http://www.deitel.com/booklist` to namespace prefix `deitel`. As we discuss momentarily, the schema uses this namespace to differentiate names created by us from names that are part of the XML Schema namespace. Line 7 also specifies `http://www.deitel.com/booklist` as the **targetNamespace** of the schema. This attribute identifies the namespace of the XML vocabulary that this schema defines. The `targetNamespace` of `book.xsd` is the same as the namespace referenced in line 5 of `book.xml` (Fig. 22.9). This is what "connects" the XML document with the schema that defines its structure. When an XML schema validator examines `book.xml` and `book.xsd`, it will recognize that `book.xml` uses elements and attributes from the `http://www.deitel.com/booklist` namespace. The validator also will recognize that this namespace is the one defined in `book.xsd` (i.e., the schema's `targetNamespace`). Thus the validator knows where to look for the structural rules for the elements and attributes used in `book.xml`.

Defining an Element in XML Schema
In XML Schema, the **element** tag (Fig. 22.10, line 9) defines an element to be included in an XML document that conforms to the schema. In other words, `element` specifies the

actual *elements* that can be used to mark up data. Line 9 defines the books element, which we use as the root element in book.xml (Fig. 22.9). Attributes **name** and **type** specify the element's name and type, respectively. An element's type attribute indicates the data type that the element may contain. Possible types include XML Schema–defined types (e.g., string, double) and user-defined types (e.g., BooksType, which is defined in lines 11–16). Figure 22.11 lists several of XML Schema's many built-in types. For a complete list of built-in types, see Section 3 of the specification found at www.w3.org/TR/xmlschema-2.

In this example, books is defined as an element of type deitel:BooksType (line 9). BooksType is a user-defined type (Fig. 22.10, lines 11–16) in the http://www.deitel.com/booklist namespace and therefore must have the namespace prefix deitel. It's not an existing XML Schema type. Two categories of types exist in XML Schema—**simple types** and **complex types**. They differ only in that simple types cannot contain attributes or child elements and complex types can.

A user-defined type that contains attributes or child elements must be defined as a complex type. Lines 11–16 use element **complexType** to define BooksType as a complex type that has a child element named book. The **sequence** element (lines 12–15) allows you to specify the sequential order in which child elements must appear. The **element** (lines 13–14) nested within the complexType element indicates that a BooksType element (e.g., books) can contain child elements named book of type deitel:SingleBookType (defined in lines 18–22). Attribute **minOccurs** (line 14), with value 1, specifies that elements of type BooksType must contain a minimum of one book element. Attribute **maxOccurs** (line 14), with value **unbounded**, specifies that elements of type BooksType may have any number of book child elements. Both of these attributes have default values of 1.

Lines 18–22 define the complex type SingleBookType. An element of this type contains a child element named title. Line 20 defines element title to be of simple type string. Recall that elements of a simple type cannot contain attributes or child elements. The schema end tag (</schema>, line 23) declares the end of the XML Schema document.

A Closer Look at Types in XML Schema

Every element in XML Schema has a type. Types include the *built-in types* provided by XML Schema (Fig. 22.11) or *user-defined types* (e.g., SingleBookType in Fig. 22.10).

Type	Description	Ranges or structures	Examples
string	A character string		hello
boolean	True or false	true, false	true
decimal	A decimal numeral	$i * (10^n)$, where i is an integer and n is an integer that is less than or equal to zero	5, -12, -45.78
float	A floating-point number	$m * (2^e)$, where m is an integer whose absolute value is less than 2^{24} and e is an integer in the range -149 to 104. Plus three additional numbers: positive infinity (INF), negative infinity (-INF) and not-a-number (NaN)	0, 12, -109.375, NaN

Fig. 22.11 | Some XML Schema types. (Part 1 of 2.)

Type	Description	Ranges or structures	Examples
double	A floating-point number	$m * (2^e)$, where m is an integer whose absolute value is less than 2^{53} and e is an integer in the range -1075 to 970. Plus three additional numbers: positive infinity, negative infinity and not-a-number	0, 12, -109.375, NaN
long	A whole number	-9223372036854775808 to 9223372036854775807, inclusive	1234567890, -1234567890
int	A whole number	-2147483648 to 2147483647, inclusive	1234567890, -1234567890
short	A whole number	-32768 to 32767, inclusive	12, -345
date	A date consisting of a year, month and day	yyyy-mm with an optional dd and an optional time zone, where yyyy is four digits long and mm and dd are two digits long. The time zone is specified as +hh:mm or -hh:mm, giving an offset in hours and minutes	2013-07-25+01:00
time	A time consisting of hours, minutes and seconds	hh:mm:ss with an optional time zone, where hh, mm and ss are two digits long	16:30:25-05:00

Fig. 22.11 | Some XML Schema types. (Part 2 of 2.)

Every *simple type* defines a **restriction** on an XML Schema-defined type or a restriction on a user-defined type. Restrictions limit the possible values that an element can hold.

Complex types are divided into two groups—those with **simple content** and those with **complex content**. Both can contain attributes, but only complex content can contain child elements. Complex types with simple content must extend or restrict some other existing type. Complex types with complex content do not have this limitation. We demonstrate complex types with each kind of content in the next example.

XML Schema with Simple and Complext Types
The schema in Fig. 22.12 creates simple types and complex types. The XML document in Fig. 22.13 (laptop.xml) follows the structure defined in Fig. 22.12 to describe parts of a laptop computer. A document such as laptop.xml that conforms to a schema is known as an **XML instance document**—the document is an instance (i.e., example) of the schema.

```
1   <?xml version = "1.0"?>
2   <!-- Fig. 22.12: computer.xsd -->
3   <!-- W3C XML Schema document -->
4
5   <schema xmlns = "http://www.w3.org/2001/XMLSchema"
6      xmlns:computer = "http://www.deitel.com/computer"
7      targetNamespace = "http://www.deitel.com/computer">
```

Fig. 22.12 | XML Schema document defining simple and complex types. (Part 1 of 2.)

```
 8
 9      <simpleType name = "gigahertz">
10         <restriction base = "decimal">
11            <minInclusive value = "2.1"/>
12         </restriction>
13      </simpleType>
14
15      <complexType name = "CPU">
16         <simpleContent>
17            <extension base = "string">
18               <attribute name = "model" type = "string"/>
19            </extension>
20         </simpleContent>
21      </complexType>
22
23      <complexType name = "portable">
24         <all>
25            <element name = "processor" type = "computer:CPU"/>
26            <element name = "monitor" type = "int"/>
27            <element name = "CPUSpeed" type = "computer:gigahertz"/>
28            <element name = "RAM" type = "int"/>
29         </all>
30         <attribute name = "manufacturer" type = "string"/>
31      </complexType>
32
33      <element name = "laptop" type = "computer:portable"/>
34   </schema>
```

Fig. 22.12 | XML Schema document defining simple and complex types. (Part 2 of 2.)

Opening schema Tag

Line 5 (Fig. 22.12) declares the default namespace as the standard XML Schema namespace—any elements without a prefix are assumed to be in the XML Schema namespace. Line 6 binds the namespace prefix computer to the namespace http:// www.deitel.com/computer. Line 7 identifies this namespace as the targetNamespace— the namespace being defined by the current XML Schema document.

simpleType Element gigahertz

To design the XML elements for describing laptop computers, we first create a simple type in lines 9–13 using the **simpleType** element. We name this simpleType gigahertz because it will be used to describe the clock speed of the processor in gigahertz. Simple types are restrictions of a type typically called a **base type**. For this simpleType, line 10 declares the base type as decimal, and we restrict the value to be at least 2.1 by using the **minInclusive** element in line 11.

complexType Element CPU

Next, we declare a complexType named CPU that has **simpleContent** (lines 16–20). Remember that a complex type with simple content can have attributes but not child elements. Also recall that complex types with simple content must extend or restrict some XML Schema type or user-defined type. The **extension** element with attribute **base** (line 17) sets the base type to string. In this complexType, we extend the base type string with an attribute. The **attribute** element (line 18) gives the complexType an attribute of type string named model. Thus an element of type CPU must contain string text (because the base type is string) and may contain a model attribute that is also of type string.

complexType *Element* portable

Last, we define type portable, which is a complexType with complex content (lines 23–31). Such types are allowed to have child elements and attributes. The element **all** (lines 24–29) encloses elements that must each be included once in the corresponding XML instance document. These elements can be included in any order. This complex type holds four elements—processor, monitor, CPUSpeed and RAM. They're given types CPU, int, gigahertz and int, respectively. When using types CPU and gigahertz, we must include the namespace prefix computer, because these user-defined types are part of the computer namespace (http://www.deitel.com/computer)—the namespace defined in the current document (line 7). Also, portable contains an attribute defined in line 30. The attribute element indicates that elements of type portable contain an attribute of type string named manufacturer.

Line 33 declares the actual element that uses the three types defined in the schema. The element is called laptop and is of type portable. We must use the namespace prefix computer in front of portable.

Using the laptop *Element*

We have now created an element named laptop that contains child elements processor, monitor, CPUSpeed and RAM, and an attribute manufacturer. Figure 22.13 uses the laptop element defined in the computer.xsd schema. We used Visual Studio's built-in schema validation to ensure that this XML instance document adheres to the schema's structural rules.

```
1   <?xml version = "1.0"?>
2   <!-- Fig. 22.13: laptop.xml            -->
3   <!-- Laptop components marked up as XML -->
4
5   <computer:laptop xmlns:computer = "http://www.deitel.com/computer"
6      manufacturer = "IBM">
7
8      <processor model = "Centrino">Intel</processor>
9      <monitor>17</monitor>
10     <CPUSpeed>2.4</CPUSpeed>
11     <RAM>256</RAM>
12  </computer:laptop>
```

Fig. 22.13 | XML document using the laptop element defined in computer.xsd.

Line 5 declares namespace prefix computer. The laptop element requires this prefix because it's part of the http://www.deitel.com/computer namespace. Line 6 sets the laptop's manufacturer attribute, and lines 8–11 use the elements defined in the schema to describe the laptop's characteristics.

Automatically Creating Schemas using Visual Studio

Visual Studio includes a tool that allows you to create a schema from an existing XML document, using the document as a template. With an XML document open, select **XML >**

Create Schema to use this feature. A new schema file opens that conforms to the standards of the XML document. You can now save it and add it to the project.

Good Programming Practice 22.2

The schema generated by Visual Studio is a good starting point, but you should refine the restrictions and types it specifies so they're appropriate for your XML documents.

22.7 Extensible Stylesheet Language and XSL Transformations

Extensible Stylesheet Language (XSL) documents specify how programs are to render XML document data. XSL is a group of three technologies—**XSL-FO** (**XSL Formatting Objects**), **XPath** (**XML Path Language**) and **XSLT** (**XSL Transformations**). XSL-FO is a vocabulary for specifying formatting, and XPath is a string-based language of expressions used by XML and many of its related technologies for effectively and efficiently locating structures and data (such as specific elements and attributes) in XML documents.

The third portion of XSL—XSL Transformations (XSLT)—is a technology for transforming XML documents into other documents—i.e., transforming the structure of the XML document data to another structure. XSLT provides elements that define rules for transforming one XML document to produce a different XML document. This is useful when you want to use data in multiple applications or on multiple platforms, each of which may be designed to work with documents written in a particular vocabulary. For example, XSLT allows you to convert a simple XML document to an **XHTML** (**Extensible HyperText Markup Language**) document that presents the XML document's data (or a subset of the data) formatted for display in a web browser. (See Fig. 22.14 for a sample "before" and "after" view of such a transformation.)

Transforming an XML document using XSLT involves two tree structures—the **source tree** (i.e., the XML document to be transformed) and the **result tree** (i.e., the XML document to be created). XPath is used to locate parts of the source-tree document that match **templates** defined in an **XSL style sheet**. When a match occurs (i.e., a node matches a template), the matching template executes and adds its result to the result tree. When there are no more matches, XSLT has transformed the source tree into the result tree. The XSLT does not analyze every node of the source tree; it selectively navigates the source tree using XSLT's `select` and `match` attributes. For XSLT to function, the source tree must be properly structured. Schemas, DTDs and validating parsers can validate document structure before using XPath and XSLTs.

A Simple XSL Example

Figure 22.14 lists an XML document that describes various sports. The output shows the result of the transformation (specified in the XSLT template of Fig. 22.15) rendered by Internet Explorer. Right click with the page open in Internet Explorer and select **View Source** to view the generated XHTML.

To perform transformations, an XSLT processor is required. For a list of some XSLT processors, visit `en.wikipedia.org/wiki/XSL_Transformations`. The XML document shown in Fig. 22.14 is transformed into an XHTML document by Internet Explorer when the document is loaded.

```
 1   <?xml version = "1.0"?>
 2   <?xml-stylesheet type = "text/xsl" href = "sports.xsl"?>
 3
 4   <!-- Fig. 22.14: sports.xml -->
 5   <!-- Sports Database -->
 6
 7   <sports>
 8      <game id = "783">
 9         <name>Cricket</name>
10
11         <paragraph>
12            More popular among Commonwealth nations.
13         </paragraph>
14      </game>
15
16      <game id = "239">
17         <name>Baseball</name>
18
19         <paragraph>
20            More popular in America.
21         </paragraph>
22      </game>
23
24      <game id = "418">
25         <name>Soccer (Futbol)</name>
26
27         <paragraph>
28            Most popular sport in the world.
29         </paragraph>
30      </game>
31   </sports>
```

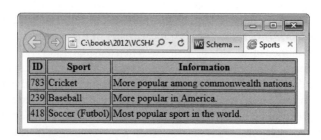

Fig. 22.14 | XML document that describes various sports.

Line 2 (Fig. 22.14) is a **processing instruction (PI)** that references the XSL style sheet sports.xsl (Fig. 22.15). A processing instruction is embedded in an XML document and provides application-specific information to whichever XML processor the application uses. In this particular case, the processing instruction specifies the location of an XSLT document with which to transform the XML document. The characters **<?** and **?>** (Fig. 22.14, line 2) delimit a processing instruction, which consists of a **PI target** (e.g., xml-stylesheet) and a **PI value** (e.g., type = "text/xsl" href = "sports.xsl"). The PI value's type attribute specifies that sports.xsl is a text/xsl file (i.e., a text file containing XSL content). The `href` attribute specifies the name and location of the style sheet to apply—in this case, `sports.xsl` in the current directory.

 Software Engineering Observation 22.5
XSL enables document authors to separate data presentation (specified in XSL documents) from data description (specified in XML documents).

XSL for Transforming `sports.xml`

Figure 22.15 shows the XSL document for transforming the structured data of the XML document of Fig. 22.14 into an XHTML document for presentation. By convention, XSL documents have the file-name extension `.xsl`.

```
 1  <?xml version = "1.0"?>
 2  <!-- Fig. 22.15: sports.xsl -->
 3  <!-- A simple XSLT transformation -->
 4
 5  <!-- reference XSL style sheet URI -->
 6  <xsl:stylesheet version = "1.0"
 7     xmlns:xsl = "http://www.w3.org/1999/XSL/Transform">
 8
 9     <xsl:output method = "xml" omit-xml-declaration = "no"
10        doctype-system =
11           "http://www.w3c.org/TR/xhtml1/DTD/xhtml1-strict.dtd"
12        doctype-public = "-//W3C//DTD XHTML 1.0 Strict//EN"/>
13
14     <xsl:template match = "/"> <!-- match root element -->
15
16     <html xmlns = "http://www.w3.org/1999/xhtml">
17        <head>
18           <title>Sports</title>
19        </head>
20
21        <body>
22           <table border = "1" style = "background-color: turquoise">
23              <thead>
24                 <tr>
25                    <th>ID</th>
26                    <th>Sport</th>
27                    <th>Information</th>
28                 </tr>
29              </thead>
30
31              <!-- insert each name and paragraph element value -->
32              <!-- into a table row. -->
33              <xsl:for-each select = "/sports/game">
34                 <tr>
35                    <td><xsl:value-of select = "@id"/></td>
36                    <td><xsl:value-of select = "name"/></td>
37                    <td><xsl:value-of select = "paragraph"/></td>
38                 </tr>
39              </xsl:for-each>
```

Fig. 22.15 | XSLT that creates elements and attributes in an XHTML document. (Part 1 of 2.)

```
40                    </table>
41                 </body>
42           </html>
43
44        </xsl:template>
45    </xsl:stylesheet>
```

Fig. 22.15 | XSLT that creates elements and attributes in an XHTML document. (Part 2 of 2.)

stylesheet *Start Tag*

Lines 6–7 (Fig. 22.15) begin the XSL style sheet with the **stylesheet** start tag. Attribute **version** specifies the XSLT version to which this document conforms. Line 7 binds namespace prefix **xsl** to the W3C's XSLT URI (i.e., http://www.w3.org/1999/XSL/Transform).

xsl:output *Element*

Lines 9–12 use element **xsl:output** to write an XHTML document type declaration (DOCTYPE) to the result tree (i.e., the XML document to be created). The DOCTYPE identifies XHTML as the type of the resulting document. Attribute method is assigned "xml", which indicates that XML is being output to the result tree. (Recall that XHTML is a type of XML.) Attribute **omit-xml-declaration** specifies whether the transformation should write the XML declaration to the result tree. In this case, we do not want to omit the XML declaration, so we assign to this attribute the value "no". Attributes doctype-system and doctype-public write the DOCTYPE DTD information to the result tree.

xsl:template *Element*

XSLT uses **templates** (i.e., **xsl:template** elements) to describe how to transform particular nodes from the source tree to the result tree. A template is applied to nodes that are specified in the match attribute. Line 14 uses the **match** attribute to select the **document root** (i.e., the conceptual part of the document that contains the root element and everything below it) of the XML source document (i.e., sports.xml). The **XPath character /** (a forward slash) is used as a separator between element names. Recall that XPath is a string-based language used to locate parts of an XML document easily. In XPath, a leading forward slash specifies that we are using **absolute addressing** (i.e., we are starting from the root and defining paths down the source tree). In the XML document of Fig. 22.14, the child nodes of the document root are the two processing-instruction nodes (lines 1–2), the two comment nodes (lines 4–5) and the sports element node (lines 7–31). The template in Fig. 22.15, line 14, matches a node (i.e., the document root), so the contents of the template are now added to the result tree.

xsl:for-each *Element*

The XSLT processor writes the XHTML in lines 16–29 (Fig. 22.15) to the result tree exactly as it appears in the XSL document. Now the result tree consists of the DOCTYPE definition and the XHTML code from lines 16–29. Lines 33–39 use element **xsl:for-each** to iterate through the source XML document, searching for game elements. The xsl:for-each element is similar to C#'s foreach statement. Attribute **select** is an XPath expression that specifies the nodes (called the **node set**) on which the xsl:for-each operates. Again, the first forward slash means that we are using absolute addressing. The forward slash between sports and game indicates that game is a child node of sports. Thus, the xsl:for-each finds game nodes that are children of the sports node. The XML document sports.xml contains only one sports node, which is also the document root element. After finding the elements that match the selection criteria, the xsl:for-each processes each element with the code in lines 34–38 (these lines produce one row in an XHTML table each time they execute) and places the result of lines 34–38 in the result tree.

Line 35 uses element **value-of** to retrieve attribute id's value and place it in a td element in the result tree. The XPath symbol @ specifies that id is an attribute node of the game **context node** (i.e., the current node being processed). Lines 36–37 place the name and paragraph element values in td elements and insert them in the result tree. When an XPath expression has no beginning forward slash, the expression uses **relative addressing**. Omitting the beginning forward slash tells the **xsl:value-of select** statements to search for name and paragraph elements that are children of the context node, not the root node. Owing to the last XPath expression selection, the current context node is game, which indeed has an id attribute, a name child element and a paragraph child element.

Using XSLT to Sort and Format Data

Figure 22.16 presents an XML document (sorting.xml) that marks up information about a book. Several elements of the markup describing the book appear out of order (e.g., the element describing Chapter 3 appears before the element describing Chapter 2). We arranged them this way purposely to demonstrate that the XSL style sheet referenced in line 5 (sorting.xsl) can sort the XML file's data for presentation purposes.

```
 1   <?xml version = "1.0"?>
 2   <!-- Fig. 22.16: sorting.xml -->
 3   <!-- XML document containing book information -->
 4
 5   <?xml-stylesheet type = "text/xsl" href = "sorting.xsl"?>
 6
 7   <book isbn = "999-99999-9-X">
 8      <title>Deitel&apos;s XML Primer</title>
 9
10      <author>
11         <firstName>Jane</firstName>
12         <lastName>Blue</lastName>
13      </author>
14
15      <chapters>
16         <frontMatter>
17            <preface pages = "2" />
18            <contents pages = "5" />
19            <illustrations pages = "4" />
20         </frontMatter>
21
22         <chapter number = "3" pages = "44">Advanced XML</chapter>
23         <chapter number = "2" pages = "35">Intermediate XML</chapter>
24         <appendix number = "B" pages = "26">Parsers and Tools</appendix>
25         <appendix number = "A" pages = "7">Entities</appendix>
26         <chapter number = "1" pages = "28">XML Fundamentals</chapter>
27      </chapters>
```

Fig. 22.16 | XML document containing book information. (Part 1 of 2.)

```
28
29      <media type = "CD" />
30   </book>
```

Fig. 22.16 | XML document containing book information. (Part 2 of 2.)

Figure 22.17 presents an XSL document (sorting.xsl) for transforming sorting.xml (Fig. 22.16) to XHTML. Recall that an XSL document navigates a source tree and builds a result tree. In this example, the source tree is XML, and the output tree is XHTML. Line 14 of Fig. 22.17 matches the root element of the document in Fig. 22.16. Line 15 (Fig. 22.17) outputs an html start tag to the result tree. The <xsl:apply-templates/> element (line 16) specifies that the XSLT processor is to apply the xsl:templates defined in this XSL document to the current node's (i.e., the document root's) children. The content from the applied templates is output in the html element that ends at line 17. Lines 21–86 specify a template that matches element book. The template indicates how to format the information contained in book elements of sorting.xml (Fig. 22.16) as XHTML.

```
 1   <?xml version = "1.0"?>
 2   <!-- Fig. 22.17: sorting.xsl -->
 3   <!-- Transformation of book information into XHTML -->
 4
 5   <xsl:stylesheet version = "1.0" xmlns = "http://www.w3.org/1999/xhtml"
 6      xmlns:xsl = "http://www.w3.org/1999/XSL/Transform">
 7
 8      <!-- write XML declaration and DOCTYPE DTD information -->
 9      <xsl:output method = "xml" omit-xml-declaration = "no"
10         doctype-system = "http://www.w3.org/TR/xhtml11/DTD/xhtml11.dtd"
11         doctype-public = "-//W3C//DTD XHTML 1.1//EN"/>
12
13      <!-- match document root -->
14      <xsl:template match = "/">
15         <html>
16            <xsl:apply-templates/>
17         </html>
18      </xsl:template>
19
20      <!-- match book -->
21      <xsl:template match = "book">
22         <head>
23            <title>ISBN <xsl:value-of select = "@isbn"/> -
24               <xsl:value-of select = "title"/></title>
25         </head>
26
27         <body>
28            <h1 style = "color: blue"><xsl:value-of select = "title"/></h1>
29            <h2 style = "color: blue">by
30               <xsl:value-of select = "author/firstName"/>
31               <xsl:text> </xsl:text>
```

Fig. 22.17 | XSL document that transforms sorting.xml into XHTML. (Part 1 of 3.)

```
32              <xsl:value-of select = "author/lastName"/>
33          </h2>
34
35          <table style = "border-style: groove; background-color: gold">
36
37              <xsl:for-each select = "chapters/frontMatter/*">
38                  <tr>
39                      <td style = "text-align: right">
40                          <xsl:value-of select = "name()"/>
41                      </td>
42
43                      <td>
44                          ( <xsl:value-of select = "@pages"/> pages )
45                      </td>
46                  </tr>
47              </xsl:for-each>
48
49              <xsl:for-each select = "chapters/chapter">
50                  <xsl:sort select = "@number" data-type = "number"
51                      order = "ascending"/>
52                  <tr>
53                      <td style = "text-align: right">
54                          Chapter <xsl:value-of select = "@number"/>
55                      </td>
56
57                      <td>
58                          <xsl:value-of select = "text()"/>
59                          ( <xsl:value-of select = "@pages"/> pages )
60                      </td>
61                  </tr>
62              </xsl:for-each>
63
64              <xsl:for-each select = "chapters/appendix">
65                  <xsl:sort select = "@number" data-type = "text"
66                      order = "ascending"/>
67                  <tr>
68                      <td style = "text-align: right">
69                          Appendix <xsl:value-of select = "@number"/>
70                      </td>
71
72                      <td>
73                          <xsl:value-of select = "text()"/>
74                          ( <xsl:value-of select = "@pages"/> pages )
75                      </td>
76                  </tr>
77              </xsl:for-each>
78          </table>
79
80          <p style = "color: blue">Pages:
81              <xsl:variable name = "pagecount"
82                  select = "sum(chapters//*/@pages)"/>
83              <xsl:value-of select = "$pagecount"/>
```

Fig. 22.17 | XSL document that transforms `sorting.xml` into XHTML. (Part 2 of 3.)

```
84                <br />Media Type: <xsl:value-of select = "media/@type"/></p>
85         </body>
86      </xsl:template>
87   </xsl:stylesheet>
```

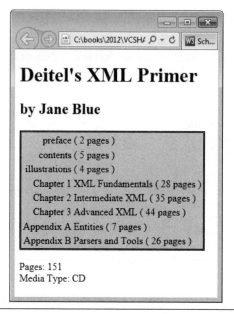

Fig. 22.17 | XSL document that transforms `sorting.xml` into XHTML. (Part 3 of 3.)

Lines 23–24 create the title for the XHTML document. We use the book's ISBN (from attribute `isbn`) and the contents of element `title` to create the string that appears in the browser window's title bar (**ISBN 999-99999-9-X - Deitel's XML Primer**).

Line 28 creates a header element that contains the book's title. Lines 29–33 create a header element that contains the book's author. Because the *context node* (i.e., the node being processed) is `book`, the XPath expression `author/lastName` selects the author's last name, and the expression `author/firstName` selects the author's first name. The **xsl:text** element (line 31) is used to insert literal text. Because XML (and therefore XSLT) ignores whitespace, the author's name would appear as **JaneBlue** without inserting the explicit space.

Line 37 selects each element (indicated by an asterisk) that is a child of element `frontMatter`. Line 40 calls **node-set function name** to retrieve the current node's element name (e.g., `preface`). The current node is the context node specified in the `xsl:for-each` (line 37). Line 44 retrieves the value of the pages attribute of the current node.

Line 49 selects each `chapter` element. Lines 50–51 use element **xsl:sort** to sort chapters by number in *ascending* order. Attribute **select** selects the value of attribute `number` in context node `chapter`. Attribute **data-type**, with value `"number"`, specifies a numeric sort, and attribute **order**, with value `"ascending"`, specifies ascending order. Attribute `data-type` also accepts the value `"text"` (line 65), and attribute `order` also accepts the value `"descending"`. Line 58 uses **node-set function text** to obtain the text between the chapter start and end tags (i.e., the name of the chapter). Line 59 retrieves the value of the pages attribute of the current node. Lines 64–77 perform similar tasks for each appendix.

Lines 81–82 use an **XSL variable** to store the value of the book's total page count and output the page count to the result tree. Such variables cannot be modified after they're initialized. Attribute **name** specifies the variable's name (i.e., pagecount), and attribute select assigns a value to the variable. Function **sum** (line 82) totals the values for all page attribute values. The two slashes between chapters and * indicate a **recursive descent**—the XSLT processor will search for elements that contain an attribute named pages in all descendant nodes of chapters. The XPath expression

```
//*
```

selects all the nodes in an XML document. Line 83 retrieves the value of the newly created XSL variable pagecount by placing a dollar sign in front of its name.

Performance Tip 22.1

Selecting all nodes in a document when it's not necessary slows XSLT processing.

Summary of XSL Style-Sheet Elements

This section's examples used several predefined XSL elements to perform various operations. Figure 22.18 lists commonly used XSL elements. For more information on these elements and XSL in general, see www.w3.org/Style/XSL.

Element	Description
`<xsl:apply-templates>`	Applies the templates of the XSL document to the children of the current node.
`<xsl:apply-templates match = "expression">`	Applies the templates of the XSL document to the children of the nodes matching *expression*. The value of the attribute match (i.e., *expression*) must be an XPath expression that specifies elements.
`<xsl:template>`	Contains rules to apply when a specified node is matched.
`<xsl:value-of select = "expression">`	Selects the value of an XML element or attribute and adds it to the output tree of the transformation. The required select attribute contains an XPath expression.
`<xsl:for-each select = "expression">`	Applies a template to every node selected by the XPath specified by the select attribute.
`<xsl:sort select = "expression">`	Used as a child element of an `<xsl:apply-templates>` or `<xsl:for-each>` element. Sorts the nodes selected by the `<xsl:apply-template>` or `<xsl:for-each>` element so that the nodes are processed in sorted order.
`<xsl:output>`	Has various attributes to define the format (e.g., XML, XHTML), version (e.g., 1.0, 2.0), document type and MIME type of the output document. This tag is a top-level element—it can be used only as a child element of an xsl:stylesheet.
`<xsl:copy>`	Adds the current node to the output tree.

Fig. 22.18 | XSL style-sheet elements.

This section introduced Extensible Stylesheet Language (XSL) and showed how to create XSL transformations to convert XML documents from one format to another. We showed how to transform XML documents to XHTML documents for display in a web browser. In most business applications, XML documents are transferred between business partners and are transformed to other XML vocabularies programmatically. In Section 22.11, we demonstrate how to perform XSL transformations using the XslCompiledTransform class provided by the .NET Framework.

22.8 LINQ to XML: Document Object Model (DOM)

Although an XML document is a text file, retrieving data from the document using traditional sequential file-processing techniques is not practical, especially for adding and removing elements dynamically.

On successfully parsing a document, some XML parsers store document data as *trees* in memory. Figure 22.19 illustrates the tree structure for the document article.xml discussed in Fig. 22.2. This hierarchical tree structure is called a **Document Object Model (DOM) tree**, and an XML parser that creates such a tree is known as a **DOM parser**. DOM gets its name from the conversion of an XML document's tree structure into a tree of objects that are then manipulated using an object-oriented programming language such as C#. Each element name (e.g., article, date, firstName) is represented by a node. A node that contains other nodes (called **child nodes** or children) is called a **parent node** (e.g., author). A parent node can have *many* children, but a child node can have *only one* parent node. Nodes that are *peers* (e.g., firstName and lastName) are called **sibling nodes**. A node's **descendant nodes** include its children, its children's children and so on. A node's **ancestor nodes** include its parent, its parent's parent and so on.

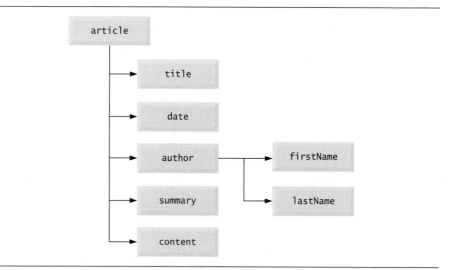

Fig. 22.19 | Tree structure for the document article.xml.

The DOM tree has a single **root node**, which contains all the other nodes in the document. For example, the root node of the DOM tree that represents article.xml

(Fig. 22.2) contains a node for the XML declaration (line 1), two nodes for the comments (lines 2–3) and a node for the XML document's root element article (line 5).

Classes for creating, reading and manipulating XML documents are located in the `System.Xml` namespace, which also contains additional namespaces that provide other XML-related operations.

Reading an XML Document with an XDocument

Namespace **System.Xml.Linq** contains the classes used to manipulate a DOM in .NET. Though LINQ query expressions are not required to use them, the technologies used are collectively referred to as **LINQ to XML**. Previous versions of the .NET Framework used a different DOM implementation in the System.Xml namespace. These classes (such as XmlDocument) should generally be avoided in favor of LINQ to XML. In LINQ to XML, the **XElement** class represents a DOM element node—an XML document is represented by a tree of XElement objects. The **XDocument** class represents an entire XML document. Unlike XElements, XDocuments cannot be nested. Figure 22.20 uses these classes to load the article.xml document (Fig. 22.2) and display its data in a TextBox. The program displays a formatted version of its input XML file. If article.xml were poorly formatted, such as being all on one line, this application would allow you to convert it into a form that is much easier to understand.

To create an XDocument from an existing XML document, we use XDocument's static **Load method**, giving the location of the document as an argument (Fig. 22.20, line 20). The returned XDocument contains a tree representation of the loaded XML file, which is used to navigate the file's contents. The XDocument's **Root property** (line 24) returns an XElement representing the root element of the XML file.

Method PrintElement (lines 28–56) displays an XElement in outputTextBox. Because nested elements should be at different indentation levels, PrintElement takes an int specifying the amount of indentation to use in addition to the XElement it's displaying. Variable indentLevel is passed as an argument to the IndentOutput method (lines 59–63) to add the correct amount of spacing before the begin (line 35) and end (line 55) tags are displayed.

```
 1   // Fig. 22.20: XDocumentTestForm.cs
 2   // Reading an XML document and displaying it in a TextBox.
 3   using System;
 4   using System.Xml.Linq;
 5   using System.Windows.Forms;
 6
 7   namespace XDocumentTest
 8   {
 9      public partial class XDocumentTestForm : Form
10      {
11         public XDocumentTestForm()
12         {
13            InitializeComponent();
14         } // end constructor
```

Fig. 22.20 | Reading an XML document and displaying it in a TextBox. (Part I of 3.)

```
15
16          // read XML document and display its content
17          private void XDocumentTestForm_Load( object sender, EventArgs e )
18          {
19             // load the XML file into an XDocument
20             XDocument xmlFile = XDocument.Load( "article.xml" );
21             int indentLevel = 0; // no indentation for root element
22
23             // print elements recursively
24             PrintElement( xmlFile.Root, indentLevel );
25          } // end method XDocumentTestForm_Load
26
27          // display an element (and its children, if any) in the TextBox
28          private void PrintElement( XElement element, int indentLevel )
29          {
30             // get element name without namespace
31             string name = element.Name.LocalName;
32
33             // display the element's name within its tag
34             IndentOutput( indentLevel ); // indent correct amount
35             outputTextBox.AppendText( '<' + name + ">\n" );
36
37             // check for child elements and print value if none contained
38             if ( element.HasElements )
39             {
40                // print all child elements at the next indentation level
41                foreach ( var child in element.Elements() )
42                   PrintElement( child, indentLevel + 1 );
43             } // end if
44             else
45             {
46                // increase the indentation amount for text elements
47                IndentOutput( indentLevel + 1 );
48
49                // display the text inside this element
50                outputTextBox.AppendText( element.Value.Trim() + '\n' );
51             } // end else
52
53             // display end tag
54             IndentOutput( indentLevel );
55             outputTextBox.AppendText( "</" + name + ">\n" );
56          } // end method PrintElement
57
58          // add the specified amount of indentation to the current line
59          private void IndentOutput( int number )
60          {
61             for ( int i = 0; i < number; ++i )
62                outputTextBox.AppendText( "    " );
63          } // end method IndentOutput
64       } // end class XDocumentTestForm
65    } // end namespace XDocumentTest
```

Fig. 22.20 | Reading an XML document and displaying it in a TextBox. (Part 2 of 3.)

Fig. 22.20 | Reading an XML document and displaying it in a `TextBox`. (Part 3 of 3.)

As you've seen in previous sections, tag and attribute names often have a namespace prefix. Because the full names consist of two parts (the prefix and name), tag and attribute names are stored not simply as `string`s, but as objects of class **XName**. The **Name property** of an `XElement` (line 31) returns an `XName` object containing the tag name and namespace—we are not interested in the namespace for this example, so we retrieve the unqualified name using the `XName`'s **LocalName property**.

`XElement`s with and without children are treated differently in the program—this test is performed using the **HasElements property** (line 38). For `XElement`s with children, we use the **Elements method** (line 41) to obtain the children, then iterate through them and recursively print their children by calling `PrintElement` (line 42). For `XElement`s that do not have children, the text they contain is displayed using the **Value property** (line 50). If used on an element with children, the `Value` property returns all of the text contained within its descendants, with the tags removed. For simplicity, elements with attributes and those with both elements and text as children are not handled. The indentation is increased by one in both cases to allow for proper formatting.

22.9 LINQ to XML Class Hierarchy

As you saw in the previous section, `XElement` objects provide several methods for quickly traversing the DOM tree they represent. LINQ to XML provides many other classes for representing different parts of the tree. Figure 22.21 demonstrates the use of these additional classes to navigate the structure of an XML document and display it in a `TreeView` control. It also shows how to use these classes to get functionality equivalent to the XPath strings introduced in Section 22.7. The file used as a data source (`sports.xml`) is shown in Fig. 22.14.

```
 1    // Fig. 22.21: PathNavigatorForm.cs
 2    // Document navigation using XNode.
 3    using System;
 4    using System.Collections.Generic;
 5    using System.Linq;
 6    using System.Xml; // for XmlNodeType enumeration
 7    using System.Xml.Linq; // for XNode and others
 8    using System.Xml.XPath; // for XPathSelectElements
 9    using System.Windows.Forms;
10
11    namespace PathNavigator
12    {
13       public partial class PathNavigatorForm : Form
14       {
15          private XNode current; // currently selected node
16          private XDocument document; // the document to navigate
17          private TreeNode tree; // TreeNode used by TreeView control
18
19          public PathNavigatorForm()
20          {
21             InitializeComponent();
22          } // end PathNavigatorForm
23
24          // initialize variables and TreeView control
25          private void PathNavigatorForm_Load( object sender, EventArgs e )
26          {
27             document = XDocument.Load( "sports.xml" ); // load sports.xml
28
29             // current node is the entire document
30             current = document;
31
32             // create root TreeNode and add to TreeView
33             tree = new TreeNode( NodeText( current ) );
34             pathTreeView.Nodes.Add( tree ); // add TreeNode to TreeView
35             TreeRefresh(); // reset the tree display
36          } // end method PathNavigatorForm_Load
37
38          // print the elements of the selected path
39          private void locateComboBox_SelectedIndexChanged(
40             object sender, EventArgs e )
41          {
42             // retrieve the set of elements to output
43             switch ( locateComboBox.SelectedIndex )
44             {
45                case 0: // print all sports elements
46                   PrintElements( document.Elements( "sports" ) );
47                   break;
48                case 1: // print all game elements
49                   PrintElements( document.Descendants( "game" ) );
50                   break;
51                case 2: // print all name elements
52                   PrintElements( document.XPathSelectElements( "//name" ) );
53                   break;
```

Fig. 22.21 | Document navigation using XNode. (Part I of 6.)

```
54              case 3: // print all paragraph elements
55                  PrintElements( document.Descendants( "game" )
56                      .Elements( "paragraph" ) );
57                  break;
58              case 4: // print game elements with name element of "Cricket"
59                  // use LINQ to XML to retrieve the correct node
60                  var cricket =
61                      from game in document.Descendants( "game" )
62                      where game.Element( "name" ).Value == "Cricket"
63                      select game;
64                  PrintElements( cricket );
65                  break;
66              case 5: // print all id attributes of game
67                  PrintIDs( document.Descendants( "game" ) );
68                  break;
69          } // end switch
70      } // end method locateComboBox_SelectedIndexChanged
71
72      // traverse to first child
73      private void firstChildButton_Click( object sender, EventArgs e )
74      {
75          // try to convert to an XContainer
76          var container = current as XContainer;
77
78          // if container has children, move to first child
79          if ( container != null && container.Nodes().Any() )
80          {
81              current = container.Nodes().First(); // first child
82
83              // create new TreeNode for this node with correct label
84              var newNode = new TreeNode( NodeText( current ) );
85              tree.Nodes.Add( newNode ); // add node to TreeNode Nodes list
86              tree = newNode; // move current selection to newNode
87              TreeRefresh(); // reset the tree display
88          } // end if
89          else
90          {
91              // current node is not a container or has no children
92              MessageBox.Show( "Current node has no children.", "Warning",
93                  MessageBoxButtons.OK, MessageBoxIcon.Information );
94          } // end else
95      } // end method firstChildButton_Click
96
97      // traverse to node's parent
98      private void parentButton_Click( object sender, EventArgs e )
99      {
100         // if current node is not the root, move to parent
101         if ( current.Parent != null )
102             current = current.Parent; // get parent node
103         else // node is at top level: move to document itself
104             current = current.Document;
105
```

Fig. 22.21 | Document navigation using XNode. (Part 2 of 6.)

```
106              // move TreeView if it is not already at the root
107              if ( tree.Parent != null )
108              {
109                 tree = tree.Parent; // get parent in tree structure
110                 tree.Nodes.Clear(); // remove all children
111                 TreeRefresh(); // reset the tree display
112              } // end if
113           } // end method parentButton_Click
114
115           // traverse to previous node
116           private void previousButton_Click( object sender, EventArgs e )
117           {
118              // if current node is not first, move to previous node
119              if ( current.PreviousNode != null )
120              {
121                 current = current.PreviousNode; // move to previous node
122                 var treeParent = tree.Parent; // get parent node
123                 treeParent.Nodes.Remove( tree ); // delete current node
124                 tree = treeParent.LastNode; // set current display position
125                 TreeRefresh(); // reset the tree display
126              } // end if
127              else // current element is first among its siblings
128              {
129                 MessageBox.Show( "Current node is first sibling.", "Warning",
130                    MessageBoxButtons.OK, MessageBoxIcon.Information );
131              } // end else
132           } // end method previousButton_Click
133
134           // traverse to next node
135           private void nextButton_Click( object sender, EventArgs e )
136           {
137              // if current node is not last, move to next node
138              if ( current.NextNode != null )
139              {
140                 current = current.NextNode; // move to next node
141
142                 // create new TreeNode to display next node
143                 var newNode = new TreeNode( NodeText( current ) );
144                 var treeParent = tree.Parent; // get parent TreeNode
145                 treeParent.Nodes.Add( newNode ); // add to parent node
146                 tree = newNode; // set current position for display
147                 TreeRefresh(); // reset the tree display
148              } // end if
149              else // current node is last among its siblings
150              {
151                 MessageBox.Show( "Current node is last sibling.", "Warning",
152                    MessageBoxButtons.OK, MessageBoxIcon.Information );
153              } // end else
154           } // end method nextButton_Click
155
156           // update TreeView control
157           private void TreeRefresh()
158           {
```

Fig. 22.21 | Document navigation using XNode. (Part 3 of 6.)

```
159              pathTreeView.ExpandAll(); // expand tree node in TreeView
160              pathTreeView.Refresh(); // force TreeView update
161              pathTreeView.SelectedNode = tree; // highlight current node
162          } // end method TreeRefresh
163
164          // print values in the given collection
165          private void PrintElements( IEnumerable< XElement > elements )
166          {
167              locateTextBox.Clear(); // clear the text area
168
169              // display text inside all elements
170              foreach ( var element in elements )
171                  locateTextBox.AppendText( element.Value.Trim() + '\n' );
172          } // end method PrintElements
173
174          // print the ID numbers of all games in elements
175          private void PrintIDs( IEnumerable< XElement > elements )
176          {
177              locateTextBox.Clear(); // clear the text area
178
179              // display "id" attribute of all elements
180              foreach ( var element in elements )
181                  locateTextBox.AppendText(
182                      element.Attribute( "id" ).Value.Trim() + '\n' );
183          } // end method PrintIDs
184
185          // returns text used to represent an element in the tree
186          private string NodeText( XNode node )
187          {
188              // different node types are displayed in different ways
189              switch ( node.NodeType )
190              {
191                  case XmlNodeType.Document:
192                      // display the document root
193                      return "Document root";
194                  case XmlNodeType.Element:
195                      // represent node by tag name
196                      return '<' + ( node as XElement ).Name.LocalName + '>';
197                  case XmlNodeType.Text:
198                      // represent node by text stored in Value property
199                      return ( node as XText ).Value;
200                  case XmlNodeType.Comment:
201                      // represent node by comment text
202                      return ( node as XComment ).ToString();
203                  case XmlNodeType.ProcessingInstruction:
204                      // represent node by processing-instruction text
205                      return ( node as XProcessingInstruction ).ToString();
206                  default:
207                      // all nodes in this example are already covered;
208                      // return a reasonable default value for other nodes
209                      return node.NodeType.ToString();
210              } // end switch
211          } // end method NodeText
```

Fig. 22.21 | Document navigation using XNode. (Part 4 of 6.)

```
212     } // end class PathNavigatorForm
213   } // end namespace PathNavigator
```

a) **Path Navigator** form upon loading

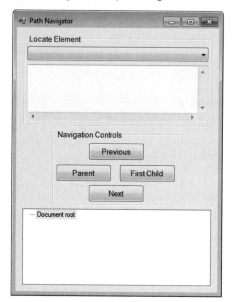

b) The **//name** path is selected

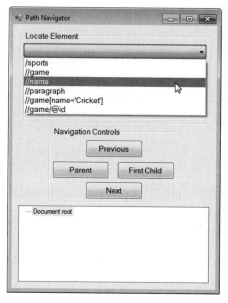

c) The **//name** path displays all **name** elements in the document

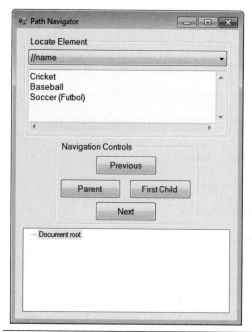

d) The **//game[name='Cricket']** path displays **game** elements with a **name** element containing "Cricket"

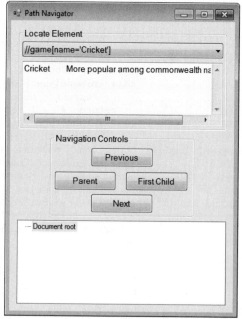

Fig. 22.21 | Document navigation using XNode. (Part 5 of 6.)

e) The **First Child** button expands the tree to show the first element in that group

f) The **Next** button lets you view siblings of the current element

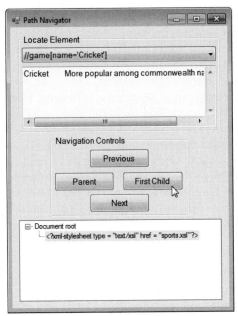

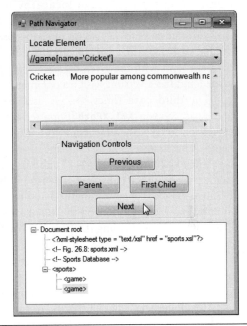

Fig. 22.21 | Document navigation using `XNode`. (Part 6 of 6.)

The interface for this example allows the user to display selected elements in the TextBox, or to navigate through the DOM tree in the lower `TreeView`. Initially, the TextBox is blank, and the `TreeView` is initialized to show the root of the tree. The ComboBox at the top of the `Form` contains XPath expressions. These are not used directly—instead, the example uses the LINQ to XML DOM classes and a LINQ query to retrieve the same results. As in the previous example, the XDocument's `Load` method (line 27) is used to load the contents of the XML file into memory. Instance variable `current`, which points to the current position in the DOM, is initialized to the document itself (line 30). Line 33 creates a `TreeNode` for the `XElement` with the correct text, which is then inserted into the `TreeView` (lines 34–35). The `TreeRefresh` method (lines 157–162) refreshes the `pathTreeView` control so that the user interface updates correctly.

locateComboBox_SelectedIndexChanged Event Handler

The `SelectedIndexChanged` event handler of `locateComboBox` (lines 39–70) fills the TextBox with the elements corresponding to the path the user selected. The first `case` (lines 45–47) uses the `Elements` method of the `XDocument` object document. The `Elements` method is overloaded—one version has no parameter and returns all child elements. The second version returns only elements with the given tag name. Recall from the previous example that `XElement` also has an `Elements` method. This is because the method is actually defined in the **XContainer class**, the base class of `XDocument` and `XElement`. XContainer represents nodes in the DOM tree that can contain other nodes. The results of the call to the method `Elements` are passed to the `PrintElements` method (lines 165–172). The

PrintElements method uses the XElement's Value property (line 171) introduced in the previous example. The Value property returns all text in the current node and its descendants. The text is displayed in locateTextBox.

The second case (lines 48–50) uses the **Descendants method**—another XContainer method common to XElement and XDocument—to get the same results as the XPath double slash (//) operator. In other words, the Descendants method returns all descendant elements with the given tag name, not just direct children. Like Elements, it's overloaded and has a version with no parameter that returns all descendants.

The third case (lines 51–53) uses extension method **XPathSelectElements** from namespace **System.Xml.XPath** (imported at line 8). This method allows you to use an XPath expression to navigate XDocument and XElement objects. It returns an IEnumerable<XElement>. There's also an XPathSelectElement method that returns a single XElement.

The fourth case (lines 54–57) also uses the Descendants method to retrieve all game elements, but it then calls the Elements method to retrieve the child paragraph elements. Because the Descendants method returns an IEnumerable<XElement>, the Elements method is not being called on the XContainer class that we previously stated contains the Elements method. Calling the Elements method in this way is allowed because there's an extension method in the System.Xml.Linq namespace that returns an IEnumerable<XElement> containing the children of all elements in the original collection. To match the interface of the XContainer class, there's also a Descendants extension method, and both have versions that do not take an argument.

In a document where a specific element appears at multiple nesting levels, you may need to use chained calls of the Elements method explicitly to return only the elements in which you are interested. Using the Descendants method in these cases can be a source of subtle bugs—if the XML document's structure changes, your code could silently accept input that the program should not treat as valid. The Descendants method is best used for tags that can appear at any nesting level within the document, such as formatting tags in XHTML, which can occur in many distinct parts of the text.

The fifth case (lines 58–65) retrieves only the game elements with a name element containing "Cricket". To do this, we use a LINQ query (lines 61–63). The Descendants and Element methods return an IEnumerable<XElement>, so they can be used as the subject of a LINQ query. The where clause (line 62) uses the Element method to retrieve all name elements that are children of the game element the range variable represents. The **Element method**, a member of the XContainer class, returns the first child element with the given tag name or null if no such element exists. The where clause uses the Value property to retrieve the text contained in the element. We do not check for Element returning null because we know that all game elements in sports.xml contain name elements.

PrintIDs Method

The PrintIDs method (lines 175–183) displays the id attributes of the XElement objects passed to it—specifically, the game elements in the document (line 67). To do this, it uses the **Attribute method** of the XElement class (line 182). The Attribute method returns an XAttribute object matching the given attribute name or null if no such object exists. The **XAttribute class** represents an XML attribute—it holds the attribute's name and value. Here, we access its Value property to get a string that contains the attribute's value—it can also be used as an *lvalue* to modify the value.

LINQ to XML Class Hierarchy

The Click event handlers for the Buttons in the example are used to update the data displayed in the TreeView. These methods introduce many other classes from the namespace System.Xml.Linq. The entire LINQ to XML class hierarchy is shown in the UML class diagram of Fig. 22.22. XNamespace will be covered in the next section, and **XDocumentType** holds a DTD, which may be defined directly in an XML file rather than externally referenced (as we did in Fig. 22.4, letter.xml).

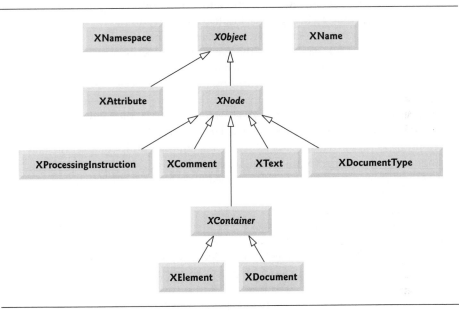

Fig. 22.22 | LINQ to XML class hierarchy diagram.

As you can see from the diagram, the **XNode class** is a common abstract base class of all the node types in an XML document—including elements, text and processing instructions. Because all DOM node classes inherit from XNode, an XNode object can be used to keep track of our current location as we navigate the DOM tree.

firstChildButton_Click Event Handler

The firstChildButton_Click event handler (Fig. 22.21, lines 73–95) uses the as operator to determine whether the current node is an XContainer (line 76). Recall that the as operator attempts to cast the reference to another type, and returns null if it cannot. If current is an XContainer and has children (line 79), we move current to its first child (line 81). These operations use the **Nodes method** of class XContainer, which returns a reference to an object of type IEnumerable<XNode> containing all children of the given XContainer. Line 79 uses the Any extension method introduced in Chapter 9—all of the standard LINQ to Objects methods may be used with the LINQ to XML classes. The event handler then inserts a TreeNode into the TreeView to display the child element that current now references (lines 84–87).

NodeText Method

Line 84 uses the NodeText method (lines 186–211) to determine what text to display in the TreeNode. It uses the **NodeType property**, which returns a value of the **XmlNodeType** **enumeration** from the System.Xml namespace (imported at line 6) indicating the object's node type. Although we call it on an XNode, the NodeType property is actually defined in the **XObject class**. XObject is an abstract base class for all nodes and attributes. The Node- Type property is overridden in the concrete subclasses to return the correct value.

After the node's type has been determined, it's converted to the appropriate type using the as operator, then the correct text is retrieved. For the entire document, it returns the text **Document root** (line 193). For elements, NodeText returns the tag name enclosed in angle brackets (line 196). For text nodes, it uses the contained text. It retrieves this by con- verting the XNode to an XText object—the **XText class** holds the contents of a text node. XText's **Value property** returns the contained text (line 199)—we could also have used its ToString method. Comments, represented by the **XComment class**, are displayed just as they're written in the XML file using the ToString method of XComment (line 202). The ToString methods of all subclasses of XNode return the XML they and their children (if any) represent with proper indentation. The last type handled is processing instructions, stored in the **XProcessingInstruction class** (line 205)—in this example, the only pro- cessing instruction is the XML declaration at the beginning of the file. A default case returning the name of the node type is included for other node types that do not appear in sports.xml (line 209).

Other Button Event Handlers

The event handlers for the other Buttons are structured similarly to firstChild- Button_Click—each moves current and updates the TreeView accordingly. The parentButton_Click method (lines 98–113) ensures that the current node has a parent— that is, it's not at the root of the XDocument—before it tries to move current to the parent (line 102). It uses the **Parent property** of XObject, which returns the parent of the given XObject or null if the parent does not exist. For nodes at the root of the document, in- cluding the root element, XML declaration, header comments and the document itself, Parent with return null. We want to move up to the document root in this case, so we use the **Document property** (also defined in XObject) to retrieve the XDocument represent- ing the document root (line 104). The Document property of an XDocument returns itself. This is consistent with most file systems—attempting to move up a directory from the root will succeed, but not move.

The event handlers for the **Previous** (lines 116–132) and **Next** (lines 135–154) But- tons use the **PreviousNode** (lines 119 and 121) and **NextNode** (lines 138 and 140) prop- erties of XNode, respectively. As their names imply, they return the previous or next sibling node in the tree. If there's no previous or next node, the properties return null.

22.10 LINQ to XML: Namespaces and Creating Documents

As you know, XML namespaces provide a technique for preventing collisions between tag names used for different purposes. LINQ to XML provides the **XNamespace class** to enable creation and manipulation of XML namespaces.

Using LINQ to XML to navigate data already stored in an XML document is a common operation, but sometimes it's necessary to create an XML document from scratch. Figure 22.23 uses these features to update an XML document to a new format and combine the data in it with data from a document already in the new format. Figures 22.24 and 22.25 contain the XML files in the old and new formats, respectively. Figure 22.26 displays the file output by the program.

```
1   // Fig. 22.23: XMLCombine.cs
2   // Transforming an XML document and splicing its contents with another.
3   using System;
4   using System.Linq;
5   using System.Xml.Linq;
6
7   class XMLCombine
8   {
9      // namespaces used in XML files
10     private static readonly XNamespace employeesOld =
11        "http://www.deitel.com/employeesold";
12     private static readonly XNamespace employeesNew =
13        "http://www.deitel.com/employeesnew";
14
15     static void Main( string[] args )
16     {
17        // load files from disk
18        XDocument newDocument = XDocument.Load( "employeesNew.xml" );
19        XDocument oldDocument = XDocument.Load( "employeesOld.xml" );
20
21        // convert from old to new format
22        oldDocument = TransformDocument( oldDocument );
23
24        // combine documents and write to output file
25        SaveFinalDocument( newDocument, oldDocument );
26
27        // tell user we have finished
28        Console.WriteLine( "Documents successfully combined." );
29     } // end Main
30
31     // convert the given XDocument in the old format to the new format
32     private static XDocument TransformDocument( XDocument document )
33     {
34        // use a LINQ query to fill the new XML root with the correct data
35        var newDocumentRoot = new XElement( employeesNew + "employeelist",
36           from employee in document.Root.Elements()
37           select TransformEmployee( employee ) );
38
39        return new XDocument( newDocumentRoot ); // return new document
40     } // end method TransformDocument
41
42     // transform a single employee's data from old to new format
43     private static XElement TransformEmployee( XElement employee )
44     {
```

Fig. 22.23 | Transforming an XML document and splicing its contents with another. (Part 1 of 2.)

```
45        // retrieve values from old-format XML document
46        XNamespace old = employeesOld; // shorter name
47        string firstName = employee.Element( old + "firstname" ).Value;
48        string lastName = employee.Element( old + "lastname" ).Value;
49        string salary = employee.Element( old + "salary" ).Value;
50
51        // return new-format element with the correct data
52        return new XElement( employeesNew + "employee",
53           new XAttribute( "name", firstName + " " + lastName ),
54           new XAttribute( "salary", salary ) );
55     } // end method TransformEmployee
56
57     // take two new-format XDocuments and combine
58     // them into one, then save to output.xml
59     private static void SaveFinalDocument( XDocument document1,
60        XDocument document2 )
61     {
62        // create new root element
63        var root = new XElement( employeesNew + "employeelist" );
64
65        // fill with the elements contained in the roots of both documents
66        root.Add( document1.Root.Elements() );
67        root.Add( document2.Root.Elements() );
68
69        root.Save( "output.xml" ); // save document to file
70     } // end method SaveFinalDocument
71  } // end class XMLCombine
```

Fig. 22.23 | Transforming an XML document and splicing its contents with another. (Part 2 of 2.)

```
1   <?xml version="1.0"?>
2   <!-- Fig. 22.24: employeesOld.xml -->
3   <!-- Sample old-format input for the XMLCombine application. -->
4   <employees xmlns="http://www.deitel.com/employeesold">
5      <employeelisting>
6         <firstname>Christopher</firstname>
7         <lastname>Green</lastname>
8         <salary>1460</salary>
9      </employeelisting>
10     <employeelisting>
11        <firstname>Michael</firstname>
12        <lastname>Red</lastname>
13        <salary>1420</salary>
14     </employeelisting>
15  </employees>
```

Fig. 22.24 | Sample old-format input for the XMLCombine application.

```
1   <?xml version="1.0"?>
2   <!-- Fig. 22.25: employeesNew.xml -->
3   <!-- Sample new-format input for the XMLCombine application. -->
```

Fig. 22.25 | Sample new-format input for the XMLCombine application. (Part 1 of 2.)

```
4   <employeelist xmlns="http://www.deitel.com/employeesnew">
5     <employee name="Jenn Brown" salary="2300"/>
6     <employee name="Percy Indigo" salary="1415"/>
7   </employeelist>
```

Fig. 22.25 | Sample new-format input for the XMLCombine application. (Part 2 of 2.)

```
1   <?xml version="1.0" encoding="utf-8"?>
2   <employeelist xmlns="http://www.deitel.com/employeesnew">
3     <employee name="Jenn Brown" salary="2300" />
4     <employee name="Percy Indigo" salary="1415" />
5     <employee name="Christopher Green" salary="1460" />
6     <employee name="Michael Red" salary="1420" />
7   </employeelist>
```

Fig. 22.26 | XML file generated by XMLCombine (Fig. 22.23).

Lines 10–13 of Fig. 22.23 define XNamespace objects for the two namespaces used in the input XML documents. There's an implicit conversion from string to XNamespace.

The TransformDocument method (lines 32–40) converts an XML document from the old format to the new format. It creates a new XElement newDocumentRoot, passing the desired name and child elements as arguments. It then creates and returns a new XDocument, with newDocumentRoot as its root element.

The first argument (line 35) creates an XName object for the tag name using the XNamespace's overloaded + operator—the XName contains the XNamespace from the left operand and the local name given by the string in the right operand. Recall that you can use XName's LocalName property to access the element's unqualified name. The **Namespace property** gives you access to the contained XNamespace object. The second argument is the result of a LINQ query (lines 36–37), which uses the TransformEmployee method to transform each employeelisting entry in the old format (returned by calling the Elements method on the root of the old document) into an employee entry in the new format. When passed a collection of XElements, the XElement constructor adds all members of the collection as children.

The TransformEmployee method (lines 43–55) reformats the data for one employee. It does this by retrieving the text contained in the child elements of each of the employeelisting entries, then creating a new employee element and returning it. The expressions passed to the Element method use XNamespaces—this is necessary because the elements they're retrieving are in the old namespace. Passing just the tag's local name would cause the Element method to return null, creating a NullReferenceException when the Value property was accessed.

Once we've retrieved the values from the original XML document, we add them as attributes to an employee element. This is done by creating new XAttribute objects with the attribute's name and value, and passing these to the XElement constructor (lines 52–54).

The SaveFinalDocument method (lines 59–70) merges the two documents and saves them to disk. It first creates a new root element in the correct namespace (line 63). Then it adds the employee elements from both documents as children using the **Add method** defined in the XContainer class (lines 66–67). The Add method, like XElement's constructor, will add all elements if passed a collection. After creating and filling the new root, we save it to disk (line 69).

22.11 XSLT with Class XslCompiledTransform

Recall from Section 22.7 that XSL elements define rules for transforming one type of XML document to another type of XML document. We showed how to transform XML documents into XHTML documents and displayed the results in Internet Explorer. The XSLT processor built into Internet Explorer performed the transformations. We now perform a similar task in a C# program.

Performing an XSL Transformation in C# Using the .NET Framework
Figure 22.27 applies the style sheet sports.xsl (Fig. 22.15) to the XML document sports.xml (Fig. 22.14) programmatically. The result of the transformation is written to an XHTML file on disk and displayed in a text box. Figure 22.27(c) shows the resulting XHTML document (sports.html) when you view it in Internet Explorer.

```
1   // Fig. 22.27: TransformTestForm.cs
2   // Applying an XSLT style sheet to an XML Document.
3   using System;
4   using System.IO;
5   using System.Windows.Forms;
6   using System.Xml.Xsl; // contains class XslCompiledTransform
7
8   namespace TransformTest
9   {
10     public partial class TransformTestForm : Form
11     {
12        public TransformTestForm()
13        {
14           InitializeComponent();
15        } // end constructor
16
17        // applies the transformation
18        private XslCompiledTransform transformer;
19
20        // initialize variables
21        private void TransformTestForm_Load( object sender, EventArgs e )
22        {
23           transformer = new XslCompiledTransform(); // create transformer
24
25           // load and compile the style sheet
26           transformer.Load( "sports.xsl" );
27        } // end TransformTestForm_Load
28
29        // transform data on transformButton_Click event
30        private void transformButton_Click( object sender, EventArgs e )
31        {
32           // perform the transformation and store the result in new file
33           transformer.Transform( "sports.xml", "sports.html" );
```

Fig. 22.27 | Applying an XSLT style sheet to an XML document. (Part 1 of 2.)

```
34
35          // read and display the XHTML document's text in a TextBox
36          consoleTextBox.Text = File.ReadAllText( "sports.html" );
37       } // end method transformButton_Click
38    } // end class TransformTestForm
39 } // end namespace TransformTest
```

a) Initial GUI

b) GUI showing transformed raw XHTML

c) Transformed XHTML rendered in Internet Explorer

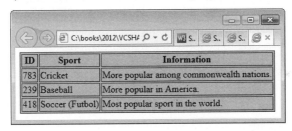

Fig. 22.27 | Applying an XSLT style sheet to an XML document. (Part 2 of 2.)

Line 6 imports the **System.Xml.Xsl** namespace, which contains class **XslCompiledTransform** for applying XSL style sheets to XML documents. Line 18 declares XslCompiledTransform object transformer, which serves as an XSLT processor to transform XML data from one format to another.

In event handler TransformTestForm_Load (lines 21–27), line 23 creates and initializes transformer. Line 26 calls the XslCompiledTransform object's **Load** method, which loads and parses the style sheet that this application uses. This method takes an argument specifying the name and location of the style sheet—sports.xsl (Fig. 22.15) located in the current directory.

The event handler transformButton_Click (lines 30–37) calls the **Transform** method of class XslCompiledTransform to apply the style sheet (sports.xsl) to sports.xml (line 33). This method takes two string arguments—the first specifies the XML file to which the style sheet should be applied, and the second specifies the file in which the result of the transformation should be stored on disk. Thus the Transform method call in line 33 transforms sports.xml to XHTML and writes the result to disk as the file `sports.html`. Figure 22.27(c) shows the new XHTML document rendered in Internet Explorer. The output is identical to that of Fig. 22.14—in the current example, though, the XHTML is stored on disk rather than generated dynamically.

After applying the transformation, the program displays the content of the new file `sports.html` in `consoleTextBox`, as shown in Fig. 22.27(b). Line 36 obtains the text of the file by passing its name to method `ReadAllText` of the `System.IO.File` class, which simplifies file-processing tasks on the local system.

22.12 Wrap-Up

In this chapter, we introduced XML and several related technologies. We discussed how to create DTDs and schemas for specifying and validating the structure of an XML document. We showed how to use various tools to confirm whether XML documents are valid (i.e., conform to a DTD or schema).

You learned how to create and use XSL documents to specify rules for converting XML documents between formats. Specifically, you learned how to format and sort XML data and output it as XHTML for display in a web browser.

The final sections of the chapter presented more advanced uses of XML in C# applications. We demonstrated how to retrieve and display data from an XML document using various .NET classes. We illustrated how a DOM tree represents each element of an XML document as a node in the tree. The chapter also demonstrated loading data from an XML document using the `Load` method of the `XDocument` class. We demonstrated the tools LINQ to XML provides for working with namespaces. Finally, we showed how to use the `XslCompiledTransform` class to perform XSL transformations.

Windows 8 UI and XAML

Objectives

In this chapter you'll:

■ Define Windows Store app GUIs with Windows 8 UI and Extensible Application Markup Language (XAML).

■ Handle Windows 8 UI user-interface events.

■ Customize the look-and-feel of Windows 8 GUIs using styles.

■ Use data binding to display data in Windows 8 UI controls.

■ Be introduced to the Windows Store app lifecycle.

23.1 Introduction

[Note: *Developing and running the apps in this chapter and Chapter 24 requires Windows 8 and Visual Studio Express 2012 for Windows 8 (or a full version of Visual Studio 2012).*]

There are three technologies for building GUIs in Windows—Windows Forms, Windows 8 UI and Windows Presentation Foundation (WPF). In Chapters 14–15, you built GUIs using Windows Forms, which is now considered to be a legacy technology. In this chapter, you'll build GUIs using **Windows 8 UI**—Microsoft's Windows 8 framework for GUI, graphics, animation and multimedia. In Chapter 24, you'll learn how to incorporate graphics, animation, audio and video in Windows 8 UI apps. Windows Presentation Foundation (WPF; Chapters 30–31) was introduced in .NET 3.0 as the replacement for Windows Forms and various graphics and multimedia capabilities. Many of the concepts you'll learn in this chapter originated in WPF.

Windows Store

Apps that use the Windows 8 UI are known as *Windows Store apps* and can be submitted to the Windows Store (`http://www.windowsstore.com/`) as free or for-sale apps. Before an app can appear in the store, it must be *certified*—you can learn more about this at

    http://msdn.microsoft.com/library/windows/apps/bg125379

Extensible Application Markup Language (XAML)

Throughout this chapter, we discuss an important tool for creating Windows Store apps called **XAML** (pronounced "zammel")—**Extensible Application Markup Language**. XAML is an XML vocabulary that can be used to define and arrange GUI controls without any C# code. Because XAML is an XML vocabulary, you should understand the basics of XML before learning XAML and WPF. We introduced XML in Sections 22.2–22.4.

Building a GUI with Windows 8 UI is similar to building a GUI with Windows Forms—you drag-and-drop predefined controls from the **Toolbox** onto the *design area*.

Many Windows 8 UI controls correspond directly to those in Windows Forms. Just as in a Windows Forms app, the functionality is *event driven*. Many of the Windows Forms events you're familiar with are also in Windows 8 UI. A Windows 8 UI Button, for example, functions like a Windows Forms Button, and both raise Click events.

There are several important differences between the two technologies. The Windows 8 UI layout scheme is different. Windows 8 UI properties and events have more capabilities. Most notably, Windows 8 UI allows designers to define the appearance and content of a GUI in XAML without any C# code.

As you build a Windows Store app's GUI visually, the IDE generates XAML. This markup is designed to be readable by both humans and computers, so you can also manually write XAML to define your GUI, and in many cases you will. When you compile your app, a XAML compiler generates code to create and configure controls based on your XAML markup. This technique of defining *what* the GUI should contain without specifying *how* to generate it is an example of **declarative programming**.

XAML allows designers and programmers to work together more efficiently. Without writing any code, a graphic designer can edit the look-and-feel of an app using a design tool, such as Microsoft's Blend for Visual Studio—a XAML graphic design program that is included with full versions of Visual Studio 2012. Even if you're working alone, however, this separation of front-end appearance from back-end logic improves your program's organization and makes it easier to maintain.

Windows 8.1
At time of this writing, Windows 8.1 and Visual Studio 2013 were available as developer previews—even though Windows 8 and Visual Studio 2012 were released only 8 months earlier. Windows 8.1 enhances the Windows 8 operating system and addresses various concerns expressed by users regarding Windows 8, such as the lack of a **Start** button and the requirement to boot to the Windows 8 **Start** screen rather than to the Windows 8 desktop. At Microsoft's 2013 Build Conference (www.buildwindows.com), Microsoft CEO Steve Balmer announced Microsoft's plans for much more frequent software releases, which is now typical of companies (e.g., Apple, Google and many others). To develop this chapter, we used Windows 8 and Visual Studio Express 2012 for Windows 8.

23.2 Welcome App: Introduction to XAML Declarative GUI Programming

A XAML document defines the appearance of a Windows 8 UI app. Figure 23.1 shows a simple XAML document that defines a window that displays Welcome to Windows Store App Development in a **TextBlock**, which is similar to a Label in Windows Forms. We reformatted the XAML generated by the IDE for publication purposes. We discuss the XAML details and how to build this app in following subsections.

```
1   <!-- Fig. 23.1: MainPage.xaml -->
2   <!-- A simple XAML document. -->
3
```

Fig. 23.1 | A simple XAML document. (Part 1 of 2.)

```
 4   <!-- Page control is the root element of the GUI -->
 5   <Page
 6      x:Class="Welcome.MainPage"
 7      xmlns="http://schemas.microsoft.com/winfx/2006/xaml/presentation"
 8      xmlns:x="http://schemas.microsoft.com/winfx/2006/xaml"
 9      xmlns:local="using:Welcome"
10      xmlns:d="http://schemas.microsoft.com/expression/blend/2008"
11      xmlns:mc="http://schemas.openxmlformats.org/markup-compatibility/2006"
12      mc:Ignorable="d">
13
14      <!-- Grid is a layout container -->
15      <Grid
16         Background="{StaticResource ApplicationPageBackgroundThemeBrush}">
17
18         <!-- TextBlock displays text -->
19         <TextBlock HorizontalAlignment="Center" Margin="10"
20            TextWrapping="Wrap" FontSize="96" TextAlignment="Center"
21            Text="Welcome to Windows Store App Development"
22            VerticalAlignment="Center" FontFamily="Global User Interface" />
23      </Grid>
24   </Page>
```

Fig. 23.1 | A simple XAML document. (Part 2 of 2.)

23.2.1 Running the Welcome App

You can test your Windows Store apps three ways by using the drop-down list to the right of **Start Debugging** (Fig. 23.2) on the Visual Studio toolbar:

- *Simulator*—Runs the app in a window that simulates a Windows 8 desktop or tablet computer. The simulator allows you to test capabilities such as rotating a device (orientation), touch input, different screen sizes/resolutions and geolocation (e.g., for maps and other location-aware apps). You can also use the simulator to take screen captures of your app for use in the Windows Store.

- **Local Machine** (the default)—Runs the app directly on the Windows 8 computer that's running Visual Studio.

- **Remote Machine**—Runs the app on a Windows 8 device that's connected to the Windows 8 computer that's running Visual Studio via a network or cable. Windows 8 tablets have various sensors (e.g, GPS, gyroscope, etc.) that are not available on most desktop and laptop computers. Running an app on a remote machine allows you to test these capabilities of your app.

Fig. 23.2 | **Start Debugging** drop-down list on the Visual Studio toolbar.

The screen capture in Fig. 23.1 shows the app running in the Windows 8 simulator. To run the **Welcome** app:

1. Open the `Welcome.sln` file from this chapter's examples folder to load the project into Visual Studio Express 2012 for Windows 8 (or your full version of Visual Studio 2012).

2. Select from the **Start Debugging** drop-down list either **Simulator** or **Local Machine**—whichever item you select is displayed on the toolbar.

3. Click the **Start Debugging** button on the toolbar (or press *F5*) to run the app.

23.2.2 `MainPage.xaml` for the **Welcome** App

A XAML document consists of many *nested elements*, delimited by *start tags* and *end tags*. As with any other XML document, each XAML document must contain a single *root element*. Windows 8 UI **controls** are represented by elements in XAML markup. The root element of the XAML document in Fig. 23.1 is a **Page control** (lines 5–24), which defines the content of the app's page. By default, Windows Store apps use the entire screen. In Windows 8, it's possible to have a maximum of two Windows Store apps on the screen at once. One occupies a column that's 320 pixels wide and as tall as the screen, and the other app occupies the rest. With Windows 8.1, apps must still occupy the screen's height, but they can now be *any* width (the default minimum width is 500 pixels) and there can be more that two apps on the screen at a time.

Page *Element*

A `Page` represents a screen of content and controls in a Windows Store app. The attribute `x:Class` (line 6) of the `Page` start tag (lines 5–12) specifies the name of the class that provides the GUI's functionality. The `x:` signifies that the `Class` attribute is part of the XAML XML vocabulary (discussed in more detail momentarily). A XAML document must have an associated *code-behind file* to handle events. Together, the markup in Main-

`Page.xaml` and its code-behind file represent a derived class of `Page` that defines the `Page`'s GUI and functionality.

`Page` (from namespace **Windows.UI.XAML.Controls**) is a **content control** that may contain only one **layout container**, which arranges other controls in the `Page`. A layout container such as a `Grid` (lines 15–23) can have many *child elements*, including *nested layout containers*, allowing it to arrange many controls in your GUI.

XAML Namespaces

Several XML namespaces (lines 7–11, Fig. 23.1) are automatically defined as attributes of the `Page` element. This enables the XAML compiler to interpret your markup:

- `xmlns="http://schemas.microsoft.com/winfx/2006/xaml/presentation"`
  This default namespace (line 7) defines Windows 8 UI elements and attributes.

- `xmlns:x="http://schemas.microsoft.com/winfx/2006/xaml"`
  Defines XAML language elements and attributes. This namespace is mapped to the prefix x (line 8).

- `xmlns:local="using:Welcome"`
  This namespace give you access in XAML to parts of the `Page` subclass that represents `MainPage.xaml`. This namespace is mapped to the prefix `local` (line 9).

- `xmlns:d="http://schemas.microsoft.com/expression/blend/2008"`
  This namespace defines elements and attributes that are used by the IDE's GUI designer. This namespace is mapped to the prefix d (line 10). Any element or attribute prefixed with d: is ignored when the XAML is loaded at execution time.

- `xmlns:mc="http://schemas.openxmlformats.org/markup-compatibility/2006"`
  This namespace, which is mapped to the prefix mc (line 11), tells the XAML parser which namespaces can be ignored. Line 11 indicates that elements prefixed with d can be ignored.

Grid Element

A **Grid** (from namespace `Windows.UI.XAML.Controls`) is a *flexible, all-purpose layout container* that organizes controls into rows and columns (one row and one column by default). **Layout containers** (discussed in more detail in Section 23.3.1) help you arrange a GUI's controls. Lines 15–23 define a one-cell grid. The **Background** attribute specifies the `Grid`'s background color. By default, the IDE sets this `Grid` element's `Background` to a predefined style named `ApplicationPageBackgroundThemeBrush`. Section 23.3.2 discusses using *predefined styles* in detail. In XAML elements, attributes like `Background` that are *not* qualified with an XML namespace (such as x:) correspond to *properties* of an object.

TextBlock Element

A **TextBlock** (from namespace `Windows.UI.XAML.Controls`; lines 19–22)—similar to the `Label` control in Windows Forms—displays text in a GUI. We specified several `TextBlock` attributes:

- **HorizontalAlignment**—How the `TextBlock` aligns horizontally within the layout container. The options are `Left`, `Center`, `Right` and `Stretch` (which stretches the element to *fill all available horizontal space*; this is the default).

- **Margin**—The number of pixels separating the control from other controls (or the edge of the screen). If you specify one value, it applies to the left, top, right and bottom edges of the control. If you specify two values—as in "10, 20"—the first value applies to the left and right edges, and the second applies to the top and bottom edges. If you specify four values—as in "10, 20, 30, 40"—the values apply to the left, top, right and bottom, respectively.

- **TextWrapping**—Whether the text wraps to multiple lines if it cannot fit within the TextBlock's width. The options are Wrap or NoWrap (the default).

- **FontSize**—The font size measured in pixels. The default size is 11.

- **TextAlignment**—How the text is aligned within the TextBlock. The options are Left (the default), Center, Right and Justify (i.e., aligned both left and right).

- **Text**—The text displayed by the TextBlock.

- **VerticalAlignment**—How the TextBlock is aligned vertically within the layout container. The options are Top, Center, Bottom and Stretch (which stretches the element to *fill all available vertical space*; this is the default).

- **FontFamily**—Specifies the text's font. We used the default font that was set by the IDE.

These attributes correspond to properties of the TextBlock object that's created by the XAML markup in lines 19–22.

23.2.3 Creating the Welcome App's Project

To create a new Windows Store app using Windows 8 UI, open the **New Project** dialog (Fig. 23.3) and select **Templates > Visual C# > Windows Store** from the list of templates.

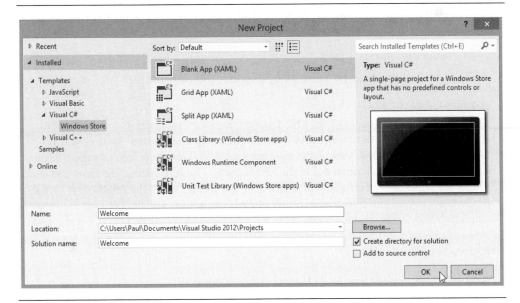

Fig. 23.3 | **New Project** dialog.

You can choose from several project templates, including the ones in Fig. 23.4. For this app, we chose the **Blank App** template. When the project opens in the IDE, the `App.xaml.cs` file is displayed by default. You can close that file for now (we'll discuss it later).

Template	Description
Blank App	A single-page (that is, one screen) app for which you must define your own GUI.
Grid App	A three-page app with predefined layouts and GUI controls. The provided pages allow the user to view a collection of groups of items (e.g., a collection of photo albums) displayed in a grid of rows and columns, view a particular group's details (e.g., a description of one photo album along with a preview of the albums photos) and view a particular item's details (e.g, one photo from a particular photo album). This template also provides support for switching between pages (known as *navigation*) and more.
Split App	A two-page app with predefined layouts and GUI controls. The first page allows the user to view a collection of groups of items displayed in a grid. The second page allows the user to view a particular group *and* a selected item's details. This template also provides support for navigating between pages and more.

Fig. 23.4 | Windows Store app project templates.

Windows Store App Themes

There are two predefined *themes* for Windows Store apps—`Dark` (the default) and `Light`. Microsoft recommends using the `Dark` theme for apps that present mostly images and video and the `Light` theme for apps that display lots of text. In this app, we're displaying only text, so we'll use the `Light` theme. To do so, double click `App.xaml` in the **Solution Explorer**, then add

```
RequestedTheme="Light"
```

to the `application` element's opening tag, then save and close the file.

Design and XAML Views

Double click `MainPage.xaml` in the **Solution Explorer** to open the XAML editor (Fig. 23.5), which has **Design** and **XAML** views. The **Design** view is used for drag-and-drop GUI design and the **XAML** view shows the generated XAML markup. You can also edit the XAML directly (as you'll often do) in the XAML view. The IDE syncs these views and the **Properties** window—when you edit content in the **Design** view, the **XAML** view or the **Properties** window, the IDE automatically updates the others. The bar between the views contains buttons that enable you to show the two views side-by-side (◫), show the two views one above the other (⊟), swap the views (↑↓) and collapse whichever view is on the bottom or right side (⊠).

Setting XAML Indent Size and Displaying Line Numbers

We use *three-space indents* in our code. To ensure that your code appears the same as the book's examples, change the tab spacing for XAML documents to three spaces (the default

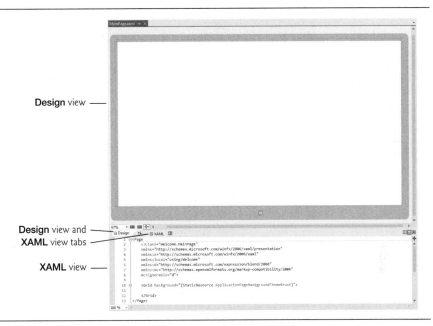

Fig. 23.5 | **Design** and **XAML** views.

is four). Select **Tools > Options** to display the **Options** dialog. In **Text Editor > XAML > Tabs** change the **Tab size** and the **Indent Size** to 3. You should also configure the **XAML** editor to display line numbers by checking the **Line numbers** checkbox in **Text Editor > XAML > General**.

23.2.4 Building the App's GUI

Creating a Windows Store app is similar to creating a Windows Forms app. You can drag-and-drop controls onto the **Design** view. You can also drag them into the **XAML** view. A control's properties can be edited in the **Properties** window or in the **XAML** view.

Because XAML is easy to understand and edit, it's often less difficult to manually edit your XAML markup. In some cases, you *must* manually write XAML markup. Nevertheless, the visual programming tools in Visual Studio are often handy, and we'll point out the situations in which they're useful.

Creating the **TextBlock** *Element and Configuring Its Properties*
To add the TextBlock element, drag a TextBlock from the **Toolbox** and drop it in the **XAML** view between the Grid element's start and end tags, then click the TextBlock element in the **XAML** view to select it. At the top of the **Properties** window for XAML documents (Fig. 23.6), you can specify the variable name of a XAML element. Below that, the window displays the type of the currently selected object in the **Design** or **XAML** view. By default, the selected object's properties are arranged by category. Within each category, the most commonly used properties are displayed. If a down arrow (∨) is displayed you can click it to display more of that category's properties.

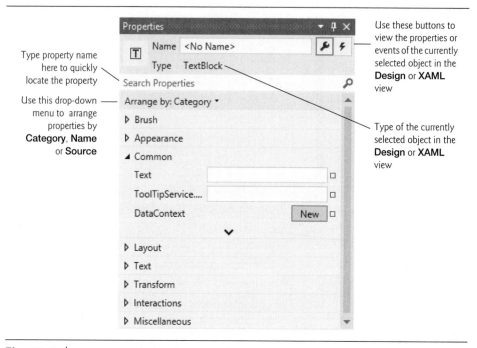

Type property name here to quickly locate the property

Use this drop-down menu to arrange properties by **Category**, **Name** or **Source**

Use these buttons to view the properties or events of the currently selected object in the **Design** or **XAML** view

Type of the currently selected object in the **Design** or **XAML** view

Fig. 23.6 | **Properties** window for XAML documents.

Use the **Properties** window to set the TextBlock's properties to the values in lines 19–22 of Fig. 23.1—as you do, experiment with displaying the properties by **Category** and by **Name**, and use the **Search Properties** box to quickly locate a given property. Below is a list of the properties to set, the category they're located in and the value to specify (we used the default FontFamily set by the IDE, so you do not need to change that property):

- Text (**Common** category)—"Welcome to Windows Store App Development"
- HorizontalAlignment (**Layout** category)—"Center" (click the ☰ button)
- VerticalAlignment (**Layout** category)—"Center" (click the ⵌ button)
- Margin (**Layout** category)—"10" (specify 10 for all four margin values)
- FontSize (**Text** category)—"96"
- TextWrapping (**Text** category)—"Wrap"
- TextAlignment (**Text** category)—"Center"

23.2.5 Overview of Important Project Files and Folders

When you create a Windows Store app, several files and folders are generated and can be viewed in the **Solution Explorer**.

- App.xaml—Defines the Application object and its settings. The most noteworthy element is Application.Resources, which specifies resources, such as common styles that define the GUI's look-and-feel, that should be available to all pages of your app. By default, StandardStyle.xaml (from the project's Common folder) is specified as a resource.

- **App.xaml.cs**—The *code-behind file* for App.xaml specifies app-level event handlers, such as the app's OnLaunched event handler, which ensures that the app's MainPage is displayed when the app starts executing. The file name of the code-behind class is always the file name of the associated XAML document followed by the .cs file-name extension.

- **MainPage.xaml**—Defines the first Page that's loaded in the app. MainPage.xaml.cs is its *code-behind file*, which handles the Page's events.

- **StandardStyles.xaml** (in the Common folder)—Defines styles (discussed in Section 23.3.2) that enable your app's GUI to have the look-and-feel of Windows Store apps.

- **Assets** folder—Typically contains media files, such as images, audio and video files. By default this folder contains four images that are used as logos and a splash screen. We discuss these in Section 23.2.6.

- **Common** folder—Contains files typically used by all Pages in an app, such as the StandardStyles.xaml file.

- **Package.appxmanifest**—Defines various settings for your app, such as the app's display name, logo, splash screen and much more. We discuss this file in Section 23.2.7.

23.2.6 Splash Screen and Logos

When you executed this app, you might have noticed that the Deitel logo was displayed briefly before the app appeared on the screen. This was the app's **splash screen**, which provides a visual indication that the app is loading. The splash screen image is one of four PNG images that are provided by default in the project's Assets folder. These images are described in Fig. 23.7. You can use any image editing tool to edit the default image files provided by the IDE to incorporate your own logo image. We provide the same versions of these four images in all of this chapter's apps. For more details on these and other standard images used in Windows Store apps, see

msdn.microsoft.com/en-us/library/windows/apps/hh846296.aspx

Image	Description
Logo.png	Shown on the app's tile in the **Start** screen.
SmallLogo.png	Displayed with your app's name when your app is shown in Windows 8 search results.
SplashScreen.png	Displayed briefly when your app first loads.
StoreLogo.png	If you post an app to the Windows Store, this image is shown with your app's description and in any Windows Store search results.

Fig. 23.7 | Images provided by default in a Windows Store app project's Assets folder.

23.2.7 `Package.appmanifest`

The app's manifest file `Package.appmanifest` enables you to quickly configure various app settings, such as the app's display name, its logo images and splash screen, the hardware and software capabilities it uses, information for the Windows Store and more. Complete details of the manifest are discussed at

```
msdn.microsoft.com/en-us/library/windows/apps/
    br230259(v=vs.120).aspx
```

Double clicking the `Package.appmanifest` file in the **Solution Explorer** displays the manifest editor. For this app, we made two changes in the **Application UI** tab's **Tile** section, which specifies information for the app's **Start** screen tile. We set the **Foreground text** value to `Dark` and changed the **Background color** to `#FFFFFF`. This causes Windows 8 to display the app's logo and app name on a tile with a white background and the app name in dark text so that it's readable against the white background. By default, the app's tile is displayed with a dark gray background and light text.

23.3 Painter App: Layouts; Event Handling

This section presents our **Painter** app (Fig. 23.8), which allows you to draw by using the mouse, a stylus (a pen like device for touch screens) or your fingers, depending on the type of Windows 8 device that you have. The app draws colored circles in response to your interactions with the drawing area. We use this app to demonstrate how to lay out controls and handle events in Windows Store apps.

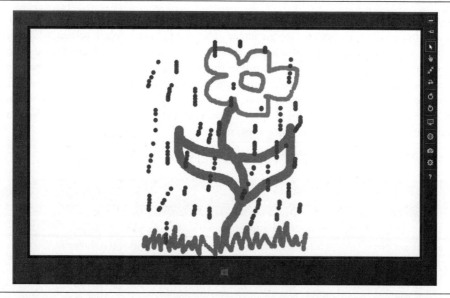

Fig. 23.8 | **Painter** app with a completed drawing running in the Windows 8 simulator.

For this app, we used the **Blank App** template with the default `Dark` theme. In the `Package.appmanifest` file, in addition to the changes we discussed for the **Welcome** app in Section 23.2.7, we also set the **Supported rotations** to **Landscape** and **Landscape-flipped** so that this app can be used only in landscape orientation on tablet devices. Depending on your app's purpose, you may choose to also support **Portrait** and **Portrait-flipped**. For example, apps in which the user reads lots of text are often better in portrait orientation because it's easier to read short lines of text—this is why books and e-readers are designed for portrait orientation.

23.3.1 General Layout Principles

In Windows Forms, a control's size and location are specified explicitly. In Windows 8, apps can execute on a variety of desktop, laptop and tablet computers. Tablets in particular can be held in *portrait* (longer side vertical) or *landscape* (longer side horizontal) orientations, so a Windows Store app's user interface should be able to dynamically adjust based on the device orientation (which can change frequently). For this reason, a control's size is often specified as a range of values, and its location specified relative to those of other controls. This scheme, in which you specify how controls share the available space, is called **flow-based layout**. Its advantage is that it enables your GUIs, if designed properly, to be aesthetically pleasing, no matter the app's width and height on the screen. Likewise, it enables your GUIs to be *resolution independent*.

Size of a Control
Unless necessary, a *control's size should not be defined explicitly*. Doing so often creates a design that looks pleasing when it first loads, but *deteriorates when the app's width and height changes* or the app's *content updates*. Thus, in addition to the Width and Height properties associated with every control, all Windows 8 UI controls have the **MinWidth**, **MinHeight**, **MaxHeight** and **MaxWidth** properties. If the Width and Height properties are both Auto (which is the *default* when they're *not* specified in the XAML code), you can use these minimum and maximum properties to specify a range of acceptable sizes for a control. Its size will *automatically adjust* as the *size of its container changes*.

Position of a Control
A control's position should be specified relative to the *layout container* in which it's included and the other controls in the same container. All controls have three properties for doing this—**Margin**, **HorizontalAlignment** and **VerticalAlignment**. Margin specifies how much space to put around a control's edges. The value of Margin is a comma-separated list of four integers, representing the *left*, *top*, *right* and *bottom margins*. Additionally, you can specify two integers, which it interprets as the left–right and top–bottom margins. If you specify just one integer, it uses the *same* margin on all four sides.

HorizontalAlignment and VerticalAlignment specify how to *align a control within its layout container*. Valid options of HorizontalAlignment are Left, Center, Right and Stretch. Valid options of VerticalAlignment are Top, Center, Bottom and Stretch. Stretch means that the object will *occupy as much space as possible*. For example, if a parent layout container is 100 pixels high and a child control's VerticalAlignment is set to Stretch, then the control will fill the entire 100 pixel height of the layout container.

Layout Containers
Windows 8 UI provides many layout containers. Figure 23.9 lists three of the simpler layout controls that we use in this chapter. These (and many others) are derived from class
`Panel` in the `Windows.UI.Xaml.Control` namespace. A control can have other layout
properties specific to the *layout container* in which it's contained. We'll discuss these as we
examine specific layout containers.

Layout	Description
Grid	Layout is defined by a *grid of rows and columns*, depending on the `RowDefi`-`nitions` and `ColumnDefinitions` properties. Elements are placed into cells.
Canvas	Layout is *coordinate based*. Element positions are defined explicitly by their distance from the Canvas's top and left edges.
StackPanel	Elements are arranged in a *single row or column*, depending on the `Orienta`-`tion` property.

Fig. 23.9 | Common layout containers.

23.3.2 `MainPage.xaml`: Layouts and Controls in the `Painter` App

Figure 23.10 shows the `MainPage.xaml` document and the GUI display of our **Painter** app.
This example uses Windows 8 UI `Buttons` and `RadioButtons`, and several layout controls.
This section focuses on the XAML and Section 23.3.3 discusses the *code-behind file* that
defines the event handlers.

```
 1   <!-- Fig. 23.10: MainPage.xaml -->
 2   <!-- XAML of the Painter app. -->
 3   <Page
 4      x:Class="Painter.MainPage"
 5      xmlns="http://schemas.microsoft.com/winfx/2006/xaml/presentation"
 6      xmlns:x="http://schemas.microsoft.com/winfx/2006/xaml"
 7      xmlns:local="using:Painter"
 8      xmlns:d="http://schemas.microsoft.com/expression/blend/2008"
 9      xmlns:mc="http://schemas.openxmlformats.org/markup-compatibility/2006"
10      mc:Ignorable="d">
11
12      <!-- Defines the AppBar that appears at the bottom of the screen -->
13      <Page.BottomAppBar>
14         <!-- AppBar contains layouts and controls -->
15         <AppBar FontFamily="Global User Interface" IsOpen="True">
16            <!-- AppBar must have one layout element -->
17            <Grid>
18               <!-- StackPanel for left side of AppBar -->
19               <StackPanel Orientation="Horizontal"
20                  HorizontalAlignment="Left" VerticalAlignment="Center">
21
22                  <!-- StackPanel to group Color RadioButtons -->
23                  <StackPanel Orientation="Horizontal" Margin="20,0,20,0">
```

Fig. 23.10 | XAML of the **Painter** app. (Part 1 of 3.)

```
24                           <TextBlock Text="Color:" FontSize="20"
25                               VerticalAlignment="Center"/>
26                           <RadioButton x:Name="blackRadioButton" Content="Black"
27                               GroupName="color" IsChecked="True"
28                               Checked="blackRadioButton_Checked"/>
29                           <RadioButton x:Name="redRadioButton" Content="Red"
30                               GroupName="color" Checked="redRadioButton_Checked"/>
31                           <RadioButton x:Name="blueRadioButton" Content="Blue"
32                               GroupName="color" Checked="blueRadioButton_Checked"/>
33                           <RadioButton x:Name="greenRadioButton" Content="Green"
34                               GroupName="color" Checked="greenRadioButton_Checked"/>
35                       </StackPanel>
36
37                       <!-- StackPanel to group Brush Size RadioButtons -->
38                       <StackPanel Orientation="Horizontal">
39                           <TextBlock Text="Brush Size:" FontSize="20"
40                               VerticalAlignment="Center"/>
41                           <RadioButton x:Name="smallRadioButton" Content="Small"
42                               GroupName="size" IsChecked="True"
43                               Checked="smallRadioButton_Checked"/>
44                           <RadioButton x:Name="mediumRadioButton"
45                               Content="Medium" GroupName="size"
46                               Checked="mediumRadioButton_Checked"/>
47                           <RadioButton x:Name="largeRadioButton" Content="Large"
48                               GroupName="size" Checked="largeRadioButton_Checked"/>
49                       </StackPanel>
50                   </StackPanel>
51
52                   <!-- StackPanel for right side of AppBar -->
53                   <StackPanel Orientation="Horizontal"
54                       HorizontalAlignment="Right">
55                       <Button x:Name="undoButton" Click="undoButton_Click"
56                           Style="{StaticResource UndoAppBarButtonStyle}" />
57                       <Button x:Name="clearButton" Click="clearButton_Click"
58                           Style="{StaticResource DeleteAppBarButtonStyle}" />
59                   </StackPanel>
60               </Grid>
61           </AppBar>
62       </Page.BottomAppBar>
63
64       <!-- Grid layout for the Page's conent -->
65       <Grid
66           Background="{StaticResource ApplicationPageBackgroundThemeBrush}">
67           <!-- Canvas for displaying graphics -->
68           <Canvas x:Name="paintCanvas" Margin="10" Background="White"
69               PointerPressed="paintCanvas_PointerPressed"
70               PointerMoved="paintCanvas_PointerMoved"
71               PointerReleased="paintCanvas_PointerReleased"
72               PointerCanceled="paintCanvas_PointerCanceled"
73               PointerCaptureLost="paintCanvas_PointerCaptureLost"
74               PointerExited="paintCanvas_PointerExited"/>
75       </Grid>
76   </Page>
```

Fig. 23.10 | XAML of the **Painter** app. (Part 2 of 3.)

Fig. 23.10 | XAML of the **Painter** app. (Part 3 of 3.)

Bottom **AppBar**

At the bottom of the **Painter** app is an **AppBar** (lines 13–62) containing the controls that you use to interact with the **Painter** app. Each Page can have AppBars at the top and bottom of the screen for quick access to commands. By default, the AppBars are hidden. You can show them by *swiping from the screen's bottom edge* on a touch screen or by *right clicking* with the mouse on a desktop computer. They're dismissed by interacting with the app's content—in this app's case, by interacting with the drawing area. In this app, we set the AppBar's **IsOpen** attribute to True to indicate that it should be displayed when the app first executes.

Creating an **AppBar**

You create an AppBar by clicking the Page element in the XAML view, then clicking the **New** button to the right of the **BottomAppBar** or **TopAppBar** property in the **Properties** window. This creates a Page.BottomAppBar or Page.TopAppBar element containing an App-Bar control. You can then drag layouts and controls into the AppBar's area in **Design** view or edit the AppBar element's XAML directly in **XAML** view.

Laying Out the **AppBar**

To lay out the AppBar's controls, we added a Grid layout to the AppBar, then added *nested* StackPanel layouts within the Grid—in this case, we edited the XAML directly. A **Stack-Panel** arranges its content either *vertically* or *horizontally*, depending on its **Orientation** value. The default is Vertical, but AppBars are arranged horizontally, so we used Horizontal for each StackPanel (as specified in lines 19, 23, 38 and 53).

The StackPanel at lines 19–50 arranges the controls at the AppBar's left side (Fig. 23.11). We set the StackPanel's HorizontalAlignment property to Left to left align the controls on the AppBar's left side, and set its VerticalAlignment property to Center, which centers the controls vertically within the AppBar.

Fig. 23.11 | Left side of the **Painter** app's AppBar.

The StackPanel at lines 53–59 (of Fig. 23.10) arranges the controls at the AppBar's right side (Fig. 23.12). We set the StackPanel's HorizontalAlignment property to Right, which right aligns the controls on the AppBar's right side.

Fig. 23.12 | Right side of the **Painter** app's AppBar.

RadioButtons

Windows 8 UI **RadioButton**s function as *mutually exclusive options*, just like their Windows Forms counterparts. However, a Windows 8 UI RadioButton does *not* have a Text property. Instead, it's a **ContentControl**, meaning it can have *exactly one child* or *text content*. This makes the control more versatile—for example, it can be labeled by an image or other item. In this app, each RadioButton is labeled by plain text that's specified with the control's **Content property** (for example, line 26 of Fig. 23.10).

Unlike Windows Forms, Windows 8 UI does *not* provide a GroupBox control for maintaining the mutually exclusive relationship between RadioButtons. Instead, this relationship is based on the GroupName property—RadioButtons with the same GroupName are mutually exclusive. Many layouts, including StackPanel, are subclasses of Panel. The StackPanel at lines 23–35 contains a TextBlock and RadioButtons for choosing the *drawing color*. The one at lines 38–49 contains a TextBlock and RadioButtons for choosing the *brush size*. In addition to the GroupName, we set the following properties for each RadioButton in this example:

- **x:Name** (set by the Name property at the top of the **Properties** window)—Specifies the variable name used in C# code to interact with the control programmatically.

- **Content** (**Common** category)—Specifies the text to display (to the right of the RadioButton, by default).

- **Checked**—Specifies the event handler that's called when the user interacts with the control. You can create the event handler either by double clicking the control in **Design** view or by using the **Event handlers** tab (⚡) in the **Properties** window.

For the **Black** and **Small** RadioButtons we also set the **IsChecked property** to True to indicate that those RadioButtons should be *selected* when the app begins executing.

Buttons

A Windows 8 UI **Button** behaves like a Windows Forms Button but is a ContentControl. As such, *a Windows 8 UI Button can display any single element as its content, not just text.* Lines 53–59 define a StackPanel containing two Buttons—an Undo button that removes the last circle that was drawn and a Delete button that removes the entire drawing. For each Button in this example, we set the following properties:

- **x:Name** (set by the Name property at the top of the **Properties** window)—Specifies the variable name used in C# code to interact with the control programmatically.

- **Click**—Specifies the event handler that's called when the user interacts with the control. You can create the event handler either by double clicking the control in **Design** view or by using the **Event handlers** tab (⚡) in the **Properties** window.

- **Style**—Specifies the look-and-feel of the Button, which we discuss below.

Styling the Buttons

Previously, we mentioned that each Windows Store app project also has a Standard-Styles.xaml file (in the project's Common folder) that defines the common look-and-feel of Windows Store apps and their controls. There are many pre-configured AppBar button styles provided in StandardStyles.xaml. To use a style for a Button, you set the **Style** property. Later in this chapter, you'll see how to create your own styles.

To apply a style to a control, you create a **resource binding** between a control's Style property and a Style resource. You create a resource binding in XAML by specifying the resource in a **markup extension**—an expression enclosed in curly braces ({}) of the form {*ResourceType ResourceKey*}. Line 56

```
Style="{StaticResource UndoAppBarButtonStyle}"
```

applies the UndoAppBarButtonStyle, and line 58

```
Style="{StaticResource DeleteAppBarButtonStyle}"
```

applies the DeleteAppBarButtonStyle. These can be created by directly modifying the XAML. You can also click the control's Style property in the **Properties** window, select **Local Resource**, then select **UndoAppBarButtonStyle** or **DeleteAppBarButtonStyle** from the drop-down menu.

There are **static resources** that are applied at initialization time only and **dynamic resources** that are applied every time the resource is modified by the app. To use a style as a static resource, use StaticResource as the type in the markup extension. To use a style as a dynamic resource, use DynamicResource as the type. Styles typically do not change at runtime, so they're normally used as static resources. However, using one as a dynamic resource is sometimes necessary, such as when you wish to enable users to customize a style at runtime.

By default, the AppBar button styles are located in XML comments within the StandardStyles.xaml file. To use these styles you must first *remove them from the comments.* The easiest way to do this is to either locate the comment and remove its delimiters (<!-- and -->) or copy the corresponding Style element and paste it into the file outside the comment's delimiters.

Canvas Control

The painting area of the Painter app is a **Canvas** contained in a one-cell Grid (lines 68–74). A Canvas is a *layout container* that allows you to *position controls* by *defining explicit coordinates* from the Canvas's upper-left corner. For this canvas, we set the following properties:

- **x:Name**—Specifies the variable name used in C# code to interact with the control programmatically.

- **Margin** (**Layout** category)—Specifies the spacing around the Canvas.

- **Background** (**Brush** category)—Specifies the background color of the Canvas.

We also used the **Event handlers** tab (🗲) to create event handlers for the Canvas's PointerPressed, PointerMoved, PointerReleased, PointerCanceled, PointerCaptureLost and PointerExited events, which Section 23.3.3 discusses in detail.

23.3.3 Event Handling

Event handling in Windows 8 UI is similar to Windows Forms event handling. Figure 23.13 shows MainPage.xaml's code-behind file. As in Windows Forms, when you double click a control in **Design** view, the IDE *generates an event handler for that control's primary event*. The IDE also adds an attribute to the control's XAML element specifying the event name and the method name of the event handler that responds to the event. For example, in line 30, the attribute

```
Checked="redRadioButton_Checked"
```

specifies that the redRadioButton's Checked event handler is redRadioButton_Checked.

```
1   // Fig. 23.13: MainPage.xaml.cs
2   // Code-behind for MainPage.xaml.
3   using System;
4   using Windows.UI; // Colors class with predefined colors
5   using Windows.UI.Input; // types related to event handling
6   using Windows.UI.Xaml; // types that support XAML
7   using Windows.UI.Xaml.Controls; // XAML GUI controls and supporting types
8   using Windows.UI.Xaml.Input; // types related to event handling
9   using Windows.UI.Xaml.Media; // graphics and multimedia capabilities
10   using Windows.UI.Xaml.Shapes; // Ellipse class and other shapes
11
12   namespace Painter
13   {
14      public sealed partial class MainPage : Page
15      {
16         private Sizes diameter = Sizes.MEDIUM; // set diameter of circle
17         private Brush brushColor =
18            new SolidColorBrush(Colors.Black); // set the drawing color
19         private bool shouldPaint = false; // specify whether to paint
20
```

Fig. 23.13 | Code-behind for MainPage.xaml. (Part 1 of 4.)

```
21          private enum Sizes // size constants for diameter of the circle
22          {
23             SMALL = 5,
24             MEDIUM = 15,
25             LARGE = 30
26          } // end enum Sizes
27
28          public MainPage()
29          {
30             this.InitializeComponent();
31          } // end constructor
32
33          // paints a circle on the Canvas
34          private void PaintCircle(Brush circleColor, PointerPoint point)
35          {
36             Ellipse newEllipse = new Ellipse(); // create an Ellipse
37
38             newEllipse.Fill = circleColor; // set Ellipse's color
39             newEllipse.Width =
40                Convert.ToInt32(diameter); // set its horizontal diameter
41             newEllipse.Height =
42                Convert.ToInt32(diameter); // set its vertical diameter
43
44             // set the Ellipse's position
45             Canvas.SetTop(newEllipse, point.Position.Y);
46             Canvas.SetLeft(newEllipse, point.Position.X);
47
48             paintCanvas.Children.Add(newEllipse);
49          } // end method PaintCircle
50
51          // user chose red
52          private void redRadioButton_Checked(object sender,
53             RoutedEventArgs e)
54          {
55             brushColor = new SolidColorBrush(Colors.Red);
56          } // end method redRadioButton_Checked
57
58          // user chose blue
59          private void blueRadioButton_Checked(object sender,
60             RoutedEventArgs e)
61          {
62             brushColor = new SolidColorBrush(Colors.Blue);
63          } // end method blueRadioButton_Checked
64
65          // user chose green
66          private void greenRadioButton_Checked(object sender,
67             RoutedEventArgs e)
68          {
69             brushColor = new SolidColorBrush(Colors.Green);
70          } // end method greenRadioButton_Checked
71
```

Fig. 23.13 | Code-behind for MainPage.xaml. (Part 2 of 4.)

```
72          // user chose black
73          private void blackRadioButton_Checked(object sender,
74             RoutedEventArgs e)
75          {
76             brushColor = new SolidColorBrush(Colors.Black);
77          } // end method blackRadioButton_Checked
78
79          // user chose small brush size
80          private void smallRadioButton_Checked(object sender,
81             RoutedEventArgs e)
82          {
83             diameter = Sizes.SMALL;
84          } // end method smallRadioButton_Checked
85
86          // user chose medium brush size
87          private void mediumRadioButton_Checked(object sender,
88             RoutedEventArgs e)
89          {
90             diameter = Sizes.MEDIUM;
91          } // end method mediumRadioButton_Checked
92
93          // user chose large brush size
94          private void largeRadioButton_Checked(object sender,
95             RoutedEventArgs e)
96          {
97             diameter = Sizes.LARGE;
98          } // end method largeRadioButton_Checked
99
100         // remove last ellipse that was added to the paintCanvas
101         private void undoButton_Click(object sender, RoutedEventArgs e)
102         {
103            int count = paintCanvas.Children.Count;
104
105            // if there are any shapes on Canvas remove the last one added
106            if (count > 0)
107               paintCanvas.Children.RemoveAt(count - 1);
108         } // end method undoButton_Click
109
110         // deletes the entire drawing
111         private void deleteButton_Click(object sender, RoutedEventArgs e)
112         {
113            paintCanvas.Children.Clear(); // clear the canvas
114         } // end method deleteButton_Click
115
116         // handles paintCanvas's PointerPressed event
117         private void paintCanvas_PointerPressed(object sender,
118            PointerRoutedEventArgs e)
119         {
120            shouldPaint = true; // the user is drawing
121         } // end method paintCanvas_PointerPressed
122
```

Fig. 23.13 | Code-behind for `MainPage.xaml`. (Part 3 of 4.)

```
123          // handles paintCanvas's PointerMoved event
124          private void paintCanvas_PointerMoved(object sender,
125             PointerRoutedEventArgs e)
126          {
127             if (shouldPaint)
128             {
129                // draw a circle of selected color at current pointer position
130                PointerPoint pointerPosition = e.GetCurrentPoint(paintCanvas);
131                PaintCircle(brushColor, pointerPosition);
132             } // end if
133          } // end method paintCanvas_PointerMoved
134
135          // handles paintCanvas's PointerReleased event
136          private void paintCanvas_PointerReleased(object sender,
137             PointerRoutedEventArgs e)
138          {
139             shouldPaint = false; // the user finished drawing
140          } // end method paintCanvas_PointerReleased
141
142          // handles paintCanvas's PointerCanceled event
143          private void paintCanvas_PointerCanceled(object sender,
144             PointerRoutedEventArgs e)
145          {
146             shouldPaint = false; // the user finished drawing
147          } // end method paintCanvas_PointerCanceled
148
149          // handles paintCanvas's PointerCaptureLost event
150          private void paintCanvas_PointerCaptureLost(object sender,
151             PointerRoutedEventArgs e)
152          {
153             shouldPaint = false; // the user finished drawing
154          } // end method paintCanvas_PointerCaptureLost
155
156          // handles paintCanvas's PointerExited event
157          private void paintCanvas_PointerExited(object sender,
158             PointerRoutedEventArgs e)
159          {
160             shouldPaint = false; // the user finished drawing
161          } // end method paintCanvas_PointerExited
162       } // end class MainPage
163    } // end namespace Painter
```

Fig. 23.13 | Code-behind for `MainPage.xaml`. (Part 4 of 4.)

Instance Variables and *Sizes* enum of Class *MainPage*

Lines 16–19 declare the classes instance variables that maintain the current *brush size* (diameter), the *brush color* (brushColor) and *whether or not the user is currently drawing* (shouldPaint). The Sizes enum (lines 21–26) defines the diameters of the SMALL, MEDIUM and LARGE brush sizes.

Method *PaintCircle*

The Painter app draws by placing colored circles on the Canvas at the pointer position as you *drag the pointer*. The PaintCircle method (lines 34–49) creates the circle by defining an **Ellipse** object (lines 36–42), and positions it using the **Canvas.SetTop** and **Canvas.SetLeft** methods (lines 45–46), which change the Ellipse object's **Canvas.Left** and **Canvas.Top** properties, respectively. These two properties are actually defined by a *different* control than that to which they're applied. In this case, Left and Top are defined by the Canvas but applied to the objects *contained* in the Canvas. Such properties are known as **attached properties**, because they're attached to the child objects.

The Canvas's **Children** property stores a list (of type **UIElementCollection**) of a layout container's child elements that you can manipulate programmatically. You can add an element to the list by calling the **Add** method on the Children property (for example, line 48). The **Undo** and **Delete** Buttons invoke the **RemoveAt** and **Clear** methods on the Children property (lines 107 and 113, respectively) to remove one child and to clear all the children, respectively.

RadioButton Events

Just as with a Windows Forms RadioButton, a Windows 8 UI RadioButton has a Checked event. Lines 52–98 handle the **Checked** event for each of the RadioButtons in this example, which change the color and the size of the circles painted on the Canvas. The event-handler methods look almost identical to how they would look in a Windows Forms app, except that the event-arguments object (e) is a RoutedEventArgs object instead of an EventArgs object.

Button Events

The Button control's **Click** event also functions as in Windows Forms. Lines 101–114 handle the **Undo** and **Delete** Buttons. The **Undo** Button's event handler determines whether the Canvas has any children (i.e., paintCanvas.Children.Count is greater than 0), and if so removes the last child element from the Children collection. The **Delete** Button's event handler clears the entire Children collection, thus deleting the drawing.

User Input Events

Windows 8 UI has built-in support for keyboard and mouse events that's similar to the support in Windows Forms. Because Windows 8 runs on both tablets and desktop computers, some users will interact with your app by touching the screen, some will use a stylus (a pen-like device) and some will use a mouse. In Windows 8 a mouse, a stylus or a finger are known generically as *pointers*, and pointer events enable your apps to respond to these types of input in a uniform manner. Windows 8 also supports keyboard events. For devices that do not have hardware keyboards, "soft" (on-screen) keyboards are displayed when the user must supply keyboard input. The pointer and keyboard events are shown in Fig. 23.14. Handling user interactions in Windows Store apps is discussed in detail at:

> msdn.microsoft.com/en-us/library/windows/apps/hh465397.aspx

Pointer and keyboard events
Pointer Events with an Event Argument of Type **PointerRoutedEventArgs**
PointerEntered   Pointer entered an element's bounds.

Fig. 23.14 | Pointer (touch/mouse) and keyboard events. (Part 1 of 2.)

Pointer and keyboard events	
`PointerExited`	Pointer exited an element's bounds.
`PointerMoved`	Pointer moved within an element's bounds.
`PointerPressed`	Mouse button pressed with the mouse pointer inside an element's bounds or finger/stylus touched an element.
`PointerReleased`	Mouse button released with the mouse pointer inside an element's bounds or finger/stylus removed from an element.
`PointerWheelChanged`	Mouse wheel scrolled.
`PointerCaptureLost`	A pointer can be captured in a `PointerPressed` event handler by calling the control's `CapturePointer` method, at which point only that control can generate pointer events until capture is lost. `PointerCaptureLost` can occur when the pointer moves to another app or when the pointer is released.
`PointerCanceled`	This occurs when a pointer unintentionally makes contact with an element, then the user removes the pointer from that element to cancel the interaction—for example, when the user touches a `Button` then moves the mouse or drags a finger/stylus out of the `Button`'s bounds to indicate that the `Button`'s action should *not* be performed.
Keyboard Events with an Event Argument of Type `KeyRoutedEventArgs`	
KeyDown	Key was pressed.
KeyUp	Key was released.

Fig. 23.14 | Pointer (touch/mouse) and keyboard events. (Part 2 of 2.)

The **Painter** app uses the Canvas's `PointerMoved` event handler (lines 124–133) to paint when `shouldPaint` is `true`. A control's `PointerMoved` event is triggered whenever a *pointer (i.e., finger, stylus or mouse) moves* while *within the boundaries of the control*. Information for the event is passed to the event handler using a **`PointerRoutedEventArgs`** object, which contains pointer-specific information. `PointerRoutedEventArgs` method **`GetCurrentPoint`** (line 130), for example, returns the *current position of the pointer relative to the upper-left corner of the control that triggered the event.*

The app draws only when the user *drags a pointer* on the Canvas—that is, when the user presses and holds a mouse button while moving the mouse or drags a finger or stylus without removing it from the screen. To ensure this, instance variable `shouldPaint` is set to `true` when the Canvas's `PointerPressed` event occurs (handled in lines 117–121).

The app sets `shouldPaint` to `false` for any event that might cause the drag operation to terminate (lines 136–161). In Windows Forms, mouse press and release events occur in pairs; however, according to Microsoft's documentation, this is *not guaranteed* for `PointerPressed` and `PointerReleased` events. For this reason, if your app needs to know when a mouse button is released or a finger/stylus is removed from the screen, Microsoft recommends that you also handle the `PointerCanceled`, `PointerCaptureLost` and `PointerExited` events (lines 143–161).

23.4 CoverViewer App: Data Binding, Data Templates and Styles

The **CoverViewer** app (Fig. 23.15) allows you to browse through book-cover images for several recent Deitel textbooks, by selecting a book from a **ListView control** (similar to the Windows Forms ListBox control) at the app's left side. The large book cover image is then displayed in an **Image control** (similar to a Windows Forms PictureBox control). You can easily adapt this program to display any type of image.

This app demonstrates several new concepts:

- We use a collection of objects as the source of the data that's displayed in the ListView control. Specifying a data source for a ListView (or other control) so that it can automatically display the data is known as **data binding**.

- We customize how the data is displayed in the ListView's items by defining our own Style for the text and using a **DataTemplate** to define how the data should be presented in each ListView's item.

- We use nested Grid layouts with multiple rows and columns to organize the app's GUI.

For this app, we use the **Blank App** template with its default Dark theme. Recall that the Dark theme is recommended for apps that display lots of images and video. This app's images are located in the images folder with the chapter's examples. To add images to a new project, you can simply drag this folder from the **File Explorer** window, into the project's Assets folder in the **Solution Explorer** window.

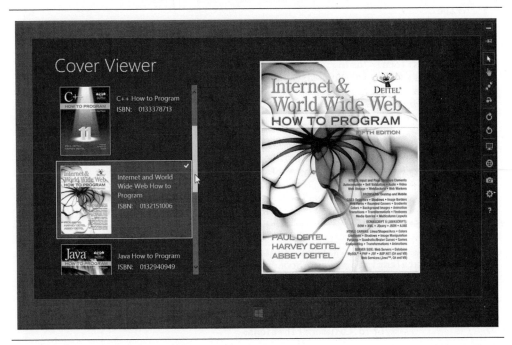

Fig. 23.15 | CoverViewer app running in the Windows 8 simulator.

Class *Book*

Each book in this app is represented by a Book object, which has four string properties:

1. ThumbImage—the path to the small cover image of the book.

2. LargeImage—the path to the large cover image of the book.

3. Title—the title of the book.

4. ISBN—the 10-digit ISBN of the book.

Class Book also contains a constructor that initializes a Book and sets each of its properties. Because this class is straightforward, its full source code is not presented here. You can view it in the IDE by opening the Book.cs file in this example's project. As you'll see in Section 23.4.3, we create a collection of Book objects when this app executes, then use the collection as the data source for the app's ListView.

23.4.1 `MainPage.xaml` for the CoverViewer App

Figure 23.16 presents the **CoverViewer** app's XAML markup. Lines 13–54 (discussed in the next section) define a Style and a DataTemplate in the Page's Page.Resources element—which contains resources that are used only in the current Page. In this section, we present the Page's Grid-based layout (lines 56–89) and show how to bind data to the Image element's Source attribute so that the Image can automatically display the selected book's large cover.

```
 1   <!-- Fig. 23.16: MainPage.xaml -->
 2   <!-- Data binding, data templates and custom styles -->
 3   <Page
 4       x:Class="CoverViewer.MainPage"
 5       xmlns="http://schemas.microsoft.com/winfx/2006/xaml/presentation"
 6       xmlns:x="http://schemas.microsoft.com/winfx/2006/xaml"
 7       xmlns:local="using:CoverViewer"
 8       xmlns:d="http://schemas.microsoft.com/expression/blend/2008"
 9       xmlns:mc="http://schemas.openxmlformats.org/markup-compatibility/2006"
10       mc:Ignorable="d">
11
12       <!-- Define Page's resources -->
13       <Page.Resources>
14          <!-- text style for TextBlocks in the ListView -->
15          <Style x:Key="TextStyle" TargetType="TextBlock"
16             BasedOn="{StaticResource BasicTextStyle}">
17             <Setter Property="TextBlock.FontSize" Value="20" />
18             <Setter Property="TextBlock.TextWrapping" Value="Wrap" />
19          </Style>
20
21          <!-- define data template for displaying Book data in ListView -->
22          <DataTemplate x:Key="BookTemplate">
23             <Grid Margin="10">
24                <Grid.ColumnDefinitions>
25                   <ColumnDefinition Width="auto" />
26                   <ColumnDefinition Width="*" />
27                </Grid.ColumnDefinitions>
```

Fig. 23.16 | Data binding, data templates and custom styles. (Part 1 of 3.)

```
28
29                  <!-- bind book's thumb image to Image element's Source -->
30                  <Border BorderBrush="White" BorderThickness="1">
31                     <Image Grid.Column="0" Source="{Binding Path=ThumbImage}"
32                        Stretch="Uniform" MinHeight="75" MaxHeight="200" />
33                  </Border>
34
35                  <!-- layout the book's title and ISBN text-->
36                  <StackPanel Grid.Column="1" Margin="10">
37                     <!-- bind book's Title to TextBlock's Text -->
38                     <TextBlock Margin="10, 10, 10, 5"
39                        Text="{Binding Path=Title}"
40                        Style="{StaticResource TextStyle}"/>
41
42                     <StackPanel Orientation="Horizontal">
43                        <TextBlock Text="ISBN: " Margin="10, 0, 10, 10"
44                           Style="{StaticResource TextStyle}" />
45
46                        <!-- bind book's ISBN to TextBlock's Text -->
47                        <TextBlock Text="{Binding Path=ISBN}"
48                           Margin="10, 0, 10, 10"
49                           Style="{StaticResource TextStyle}" />
50                     </StackPanel>
51                  </StackPanel>
52               </Grid>
53            </DataTemplate>
54         </Page.Resources>
55
56         <Grid
57            Background="{StaticResource ApplicationPageBackgroundThemeBrush}">
58
59            <!-- define two rows -->
60            <Grid.RowDefinitions>
61               <RowDefinition Height="140"/>
62               <RowDefinition Height="*"/>
63            </Grid.RowDefinitions>
64
65            <!-- define three columns -->
66            <Grid.ColumnDefinitions>
67               <ColumnDefinition Width="70"/>
68               <ColumnDefinition Width="1*"/>
69               <ColumnDefinition Width="2*"/>
70            </Grid.ColumnDefinitions>
71
72            <!-- page title displayed in row 0, column 1-->
73            <TextBlock Grid.Column="1" Text="Cover Viewer"
74               Style="{StaticResource PageHeaderTextStyle}"/>
75
76            <!-- use ListView and data template to display book information -->
77            <ListView x:Name="booksListView" Grid.Row="1" Grid.Column="1"
78               Margin="0,0,0,70" ItemTemplate="{StaticResource BookTemplate}" />
79
```

Fig. 23.16 | Data binding, data templates and custom styles. (Part 2 of 3.)

```
80              <!-- Border around Image -->
81              <Border Grid.Row="0" Grid.Column="2" Grid.RowSpan="2"
82                  HorizontalAlignment="Center" VerticalAlignment="Center"
83                  BorderBrush="White" BorderThickness="5" Margin="70">
84
85                  <!-- bind Image's Source to selected item's full-size image -->
86                  <Image Source="{Binding ElementName=booksListView,
87                      Path=SelectedItem.LargeImage}" />
88              </Border>
89          </Grid>
90      </Page>
```

Fig. 23.16 | Data binding, data templates and custom styles. (Part 3 of 3.)

Grid with Rows and Columns

By default, a Grid layout contains only *one* cell unless you define rows and columns for it. Lines 56–89 define the app's GUI in a Grid layout with two rows and three columns. You define the rows and columns by setting the Grid's **RowDefinitions** and **ColumnDefinitions** properties (located in the **Layout** section of the **Properties** window). These contain collections of **RowDefinition** and **ColumnDefinition** objects, respectively. Because these properties do not take string values, they cannot be specified as attributes in the Grid tag. In such cases, a class's property can be defined in XAML as a *nested element* with the name *ClassName.PropertyName*. For example, the Grid.RowDefinitions element in lines 60–63 sets the Grid's RowDefinitions property and defines two rows—one for the app name at the top of the UI and one for the ListView and Image, as shown in Fig. 23.15. Rows and columns are each indexed from 0.

You can specify the Height of a RowDefinition and the Width of a ColumnDefinition with an *explicit size*, a *relative size (using *)* or Auto. Auto makes the row or column only as big as it needs to be to fit its contents. The setting * specifies the size of a row or column with respect to the Grid's other rows and columns. For example, a column with a Height of 2* would be twice the size of a column that is 1* (or just *). A Grid first allocates its space to the rows and columns whose sizes are defined *explicitly* or determined *automatically*. The remaining space is divided among the other rows and columns. By default, all Widths and Heights are set to *, so every cell in the grid is of *equal size*. In the **CoverViewer** app, the first column (line 67) is 70 pixels wide and the *remaining space* is allocated to the two other columns. The second and third column sizes are specified as 1* and 2*, respectively, so these columns use 1/3 and 2/3 of the remaining space, respectively.

If you click the ellipsis button next to the RowDefinitions or ColumnDefinitions property in the **Properties** window, the **Collection Editor** window (Fig. 23.17) will appear. This tool can be used to add, remove, reorder, and edit the properties of rows and columns in a Grid. In fact, any property that takes a *collection* as a value can be edited in a version of the **Collection Editor** specific to that collection. For example, you could edit the Items property of a ListView to specify predefined ListView items.

Placing Controls in the Grid Using Attached Properties

To indicate a control's location in the Grid, you use the **Grid.Row** and **Grid.Column** attached properties. For the selected control in **Design** or **XAML** view, these appear with the names **Row** and **Column** in the **Layout** section of the **Properties** window.

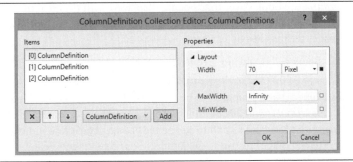

Fig. 23.17 | Collection Editor for a Grid's ColumnDefinitions property.

TextBlock Containing the Page Header

Lines 73–74 define a TextBlock that displays the app name. Many of the *preconfigured Page templates* provided by Visual Studio show a page header that describes the page as a TextBlock in a 140-pixel row at the top of the Page, so we chose to mimic that in the CoverViewer app. StandardStyles.xaml provides the PageHeaderTextStyle (used in line 74) for this text. When defining a control in a Grid, the control is placed in row 0 and column 0 unless you specify otherwise. Since the TextBlock specifies only the Grid.Column attribute with the value 1, the TextBlock is located in row 0 and column 1.

ListView for Displaying a Book's Thumbnail Cover Image, Title and ISBN

Lines 77–78 define the ListView that displays the collection of Books, which appears in row 1 and column 1 of the Grid. The **ItemTemplate** property specifies how each item in the ListView is displayed. By default, items are displayed as text, but you can customize this with a DataTemplate. In this case, the ItemTemplate is a StaticResource named BookTemplate, which we discuss in detail in Section 23.4.2.

Border and Image for Displaying the Selected Book's Large Cover Image

Lines 81–88 define a 5-pixel, white **Border** that contains an Image (lines 86–87) in which the selected Book's large cover image is displayed. The Border is placed in row 0 and column 2, and *spans* both row 0 and row 1, as specified with the attached property **Grid.RowSpan**. Similarly, there is a **Grid.ColumnSpan** property to indicate that a control spans more than one column. The HorizontalAlignment and VerticalAlignment properties (line 82) indicate that this element will be centered within column 2.

Binding the Image's Source Property to the ListView's SelectedItem

Often, an app needs to edit and display data. Windows 8 UI enables GUIs to easily interact with data. A *data binding* is a pointer to data that's represented by a **Binding** object. You can create such bindings to a broad range of data types, including objects, collections, data in XML documents, data in databases and LINQ query results.

Like resource bindings, data bindings can be created declaratively in XAML markup with *markup extensions*. To declare a data binding, you must specify the *data's source*. If it's another element in the XAML markup, you use property **ElementName**; otherwise, you use **Source**. Then, if you're binding to a specific property of a control or other object, you must specify the **Path** to that piece of information.

To *synchronize* the book cover that's being displayed with the currently selected book, we bind the `Image`'s `Source` property to the file location of the currently selected book's large cover image. In lines 86–87

```
<Image Source="{Binding ElementName=booksListView,
    Path=SelectedItem.LargeImage}" />
```

the `Binding`'s `ElementName` property is the name of the selector control, `booksListView`. Each item in this `ListView` is a `Book` object, so the `ListView`'s `SelectedItem` represents one `Book`. Setting the `Binding`'s `Path` to `SelectedItem.LargeImage` indicates the specific `Book` property (`LargeImage`) to use as the `Image`'s `Source`.

Many controls have *built-in support for data binding*, and do *not* require a separate `Binding` object. A `ListView`, for example, has an **ItemsSource** property that specifies the data source of the `ListView`'s items. There is *no need to create a binding*—instead, you can just set the `ItemsSource` property (which we do in Fig. 23.18, line 39) as you would any other property. When you set `ItemsSource` to a collection of data, the objects in the collection automatically become the items in the list.

23.4.2 Defining Styles and Data Templates

Throughout this chapter, we've used various standard `Styles` that are defined in an app's `StandardStyles.xaml` file. One advantage of Windows 8 UI over Windows Forms is that you can *customize the look-and-feel of controls* to meet your app's needs. In addition, many controls that allowed only text content in Windows Forms are `ContentControls` in Windows 8 UI. Such controls can host *any* type of content—including other controls. The caption of a Windows 8 UI `Button`, for example, could be an image or even a video.

In this section, we demonstrate how to use styles to achieve a *uniform look-and-feel*. In Windows Forms, if you want to make all your `Labels` look the same, you have to manually set properties for every `Label`, or copy and paste. To achieve the same result in Windows 8 UI, you can define the properties once as a `Style` and apply the style to each `TextBlock`.

Normally, a `ListView` presents its items as text. This section also introduces *data templates*, which enable you to define how data is presented in a data-bound control. We'll use this capability to display each `Book` object's `ListView` item as a thumbnail image, a title and an ISBN number.

*Defining Styles and Data Templates as **Page** Resources*

Styles and data templates are **Windows 8 UI resources**. A *resource* is an object that is defined for one or more `Pages` of your app and can be *reused* multiple times. Every Windows 8 UI control can hold a collection of resources that can be accessed by any of the control's *nested* elements. If you define a style as a `Page` resource, then any element in the `Page` can use that style. If you define a style as a resource of a layout container, then *only* the elements of the layout container can use that style. You can also define app-level resources for an `Application` object in the `App.xaml` file—the contents of `StandardStyles.xaml` are specified in the `App.xaml` file as app-level resource. These resources can be accessed in any file in the app. A `Page`'s resources are defined in the **Page.Resources** element (lines 13–54, Fig. 23.16).

TextBlock Style

Lines 15–19 (Fig. 23.16) define a **Style** element that's applied to the TextBlocks in our ListView's items. The required x:Key attribute must be set in every Style (or other resource) so that it can be referenced later by other controls. The Style's required attribute **x:TargetType** indicates the type of control that the style can be applied to. The children of a Style element can set properties and define event handlers. A **Setter** element sets a property to a specific value (e.g., line 17, which sets a TextBlock's FontSize property to 20). An **EventSetter** element specifies the method that responds to an event, as in

```
<EventSetter Event="ControlName.EventName" Handler="EventHandlerName"/>
```

The Style in lines 15–19 (named TextStyle) uses two Setters to specify a TextBlock's FontSize and TextWrapping values. Because some of the book titles are long, we set the TextWrapping property to Wrap.

DataTemplate for ListView Items

Lines 22–53 (Fig. 23.16) use a **DataTemplate** element to define how to display *bound data* in the ListView's items. Each book, instead of being displayed as text in a ListView item, is represented by a small thumbnail of its cover image with its title and ISBN text displayed to the right of the image. You apply a *data template* by using a *resource binding*. To apply a data template to items in a ListView, use the **ItemTemplate** property (as in line 78).

A *data template* uses *data bindings* (lines 31, 39 and 47) to specify which data to display. In each case, we can omit the data binding's ElementName property, because the ListView's data source is specified when the app begins executing (as you'll see in Fig. 23.18).

The BookTemplate *data template* arranges controls in a two-column Grid. The left column displays a Border containing an Image and the right column uses nested Stack-Panels to display a Book's Title and ISBN. Line 31 binds the Image's Source to the Book's ThumbImage property, which specifies the location of the thumbnail cover image in the project. The Book's Title and ISBN are displayed to the right of the book using Text-Blocks. The TextBlock in lines 38–40 binds the Book's Title to the Text property. Lines 43–49 display two additional TextBlocks, one that displays ISBN:, and another that's bound to the Book's ISBN.

23.4.3 `MainPage.xaml.cs`: Binding Data to the `ListView`'s `ItemSource`

Figure 23.18 presents the code-behind class for the Cover Viewer. When the Page is created, a collection of six Book objects is initialized (lines 19–37) and set as the ItemsSource of the booksListView, meaning that each item displayed in the ListView is one of the Books.

```
1  // Fig. 23.18: MainPage.xaml.cs
2  // Using data binding
3  using System;
4  using System.Collections.Generic;
5  using Windows.UI.Xaml.Controls;
```

Fig. 23.18 | Using data binding. (Part 1 of 2.)

```
 6
 7   namespace CoverViewer
 8   {
 9      public sealed partial class MainPage : Page
10      {
11         // list of Book objects
12         private List<Book> books = new List<Book>();
13
14         public MainPage()
15         {
16            this.InitializeComponent();
17
18            // add Book objects to the List
19            books.Add(new Book("C How to Program", "013299044X",
20               "assets/images/small/chtp.jpg",
21               "assets/images/large/chtp.jpg"));
22            books.Add(new Book("C++ How to Program", "0133378713",
23               "assets/images/small/cpphtp.jpg",
24               "assets/images/large/cpphtp.jpg"));
25            books.Add(new Book(
26               "Internet and World Wide Web How to Program", "0132151006",
27               "assets/images/small/iw3htp.jpg",
28               "assets/images/large/iw3htp.jpg"));
29            books.Add(new Book("Java How to Program", "0132940949",
30               "assets/images/small/jhtp.jpg",
31               "assets/images/large/jhtp.jpg"));
32            books.Add(new Book("Visual Basic How to Program", "0133406954",
33               "assets/images/small/vbhtp.jpg",
34               "assets/images/large/vbhtp.jpg"));
35            books.Add(new Book("Visual C# How to Program", "0133379337",
36               "assets/images/small/vcshtp.jpg",
37               "assets/images/large/vcshtp.jpg"));
38
39            booksListView.ItemsSource = books; // bind data to the list
40            booksListView.SelectedIndex = 0; // select first item in ListView
41         } // end constructor
42      } // end class MainPage
43   } // end namespace CoverViewer
```

Fig. 23.18 | Using data binding. (Part 2 of 2.)

23.5 App Lifecycle

So far, you've learned how to create GUIs for Windows Store apps. There is much more to Windows Store app development than we've shown here. For example there is a well-defined app lifecycle in which an app at any given time is *not running, running, suspended, terminated* or *closed by the user:*

- An app that's *not running* has not yet been launched by the user.

- An app that's *running* is on the screen so that the user can interact with it.

- An app that's *suspended* is not currently on the screen, so Windows 8 suspends its execution to conserve power and reduce the load on the CPU.

- An app that's *terminated* was shut down by Windows 8—typically to recover resources like memory that are needed by other apps.

- An app that's *closed by the user* was shut down explicitly by the user by swiping from the top of the screen to the bottom.

Various events occur during an app's lifecycle:

- The Suspending event occurs when an app transitions to the *suspended* state—usually because the app is no longer visible on the screen. This typically occurs when the user runs another app.

- The Resuming event occurs when the app transitions from *suspended* to *running*.

The complete details of the Windows Store app lifecycle can be found at

```
msdn.microsoft.com/en-us/library/windows/apps/hh464925.aspx
```

Articles and tutorials about Windows Store app concepts can be found at:

```
msdn.microsoft.com/en-us/library/windows/apps/hh750302.aspx
```

23.6 Wrap-Up

In this chapter, you created several GUI-based apps with Windows 8 UI. You learned how to design a Windows 8 UI GUI with XAML markup and how to give it functionality in a C# code-behind class. We presented various Windows 8 UI layouts, in which we specified a control's size and position relative to other controls. We demonstrated the flexibility Windows 8 UI offers for customizing the look-and-feel of your GUIs with styles and data templates. You learned how to create data-driven GUIs with data bindings. Finally, we overviewed the Windows Store app lifecycle and provided links to resources where you can learn more about Windows Store app development.

Windows 8 UI is not merely a GUI-building platform. Chapter 24 explores some of the many other capabilities of Windows 8 UI, showing you how to incorporate 2D graphics, animation and multimedia into your Windows 8 UI apps.

24

Windows 8 Graphics and Multimedia

Objectives

In this chapter you'll:

- Draw Lines, Rectangles, Ellipses, Polylines and Polygons on Canvas controls.

- Use SolidColorBrushes, ImageBrushes and LinearGradientBrushes to customize the Fill, Foreground or Background of a control.

- Use transforms to reposition or reorient GUI elements.

- Use ControlTemplates to customize the look of a control while maintaining its functionality.

- Use VisualStates and animations to specify how a control's appearance changes as the control's state changes.

- Apply a projection to a control to give it a perspective.

24.1 Introduction

This chapter overviews Windows 8's graphics and multimedia capabilities, including *two-dimensional shapes, transformations and video*. Windows 8 (like WPF in Chapters 30 and 31) integrates graphics and multimedia features that were previously available only in special libraries (such as DirectX). This enables you to use one set of libraries that all use the same XAML and code-behind programming model, rather than several libraries with different programming models. The graphics system in Windows 8 uses your computer's graphics hardware to reduce the load on the CPU.

Windows 8 graphics use *resolution-independent* units of measurement, making apps more uniform and *portable* across devices. The size properties of graphic elements in Windows 8 are measured in **machine-independent pixels**, where one pixel typically represents 1/96 of an inch—however, this depends on the computer's resolution settings—some users set their screens to lower resolutions so that everything appears larger on the screen and some set their screens to higher resolutions to have more screen space to work with. Windows 8 determines the correct size of each graphical element based on the screen size and resolution.

Graphic elements are rendered on screen using a **vector-based** system in which calculations determine how to size and scale each element, allowing graphic elements to be preserved across any rendering size. This produces smoother graphics than the so-called **raster-based** systems, in which the precise pixels are specified for each graphical element. Raster-based graphics tend to degrade in appearance as they're scaled larger. Vector-based graphics appear smooth at any scale. Graphic elements other than images and video are drawn using Windows 8's vector-based system, so they look good at many screen resolutions.

The basic 2-D shapes are `Line`s, `Rectangle`s and `Ellipse`s. Windows 8 also has controls that can be used to create custom shapes or curves. *Brushes* can be used to fill an element with *solid colors, images and gradients,* allowing for unique and interesting visual experiences. Windows 8's robust transform capabilities allow you to further customize GUIs—*transforms* reposition and reorient controls and shapes.

24.2 Basic Shapes

Windows 8 UI has several built-in shapes (namespace `Windows.UI.Xaml.Shapes`). The `BasicShapes` example (Fig. 24.1) displays several `Rectangles`, a `Line` and several `Ellipses`. Each of the apps in this chapter uses the **Blank App** template introduced in Chapter 23. Apps with a white background use the `Light` theme (Section 23.2.3). We generally reformat XAML for clarity.

```
1   <!-- Fig. 24.1: MainPage.xaml -->
2   <!-- Specifying basic shapes in XAML. -->
3   <Page
4       x:Class="BasicShapes.MainPage"
5       xmlns="http://schemas.microsoft.com/winfx/2006/xaml/presentation"
6       xmlns:x="http://schemas.microsoft.com/winfx/2006/xaml"
7       xmlns:local="using:BasicShapes"
8       xmlns:d="http://schemas.microsoft.com/expression/blend/2008"
9       xmlns:mc="http://schemas.openxmlformats.org/markup-compatibility/2006"
10      mc:Ignorable="d">
11
12      <Canvas
13          Background="{StaticResource ApplicationPageBackgroundThemeBrush}">
14          <!-- Rectangle with fill but no stroke -->
15          <Rectangle Canvas.Left="30" Canvas.Top="30" Width="300" Height="180"
16              Fill="Red" />
17
18          <!-- Rectangle with stroke but no fill -->
19          <Rectangle Canvas.Left="350" Canvas.Top="30" Width="300"
20              Height="180" Stroke="Black" StrokeThickness="10"/>
21
22          <!-- Rectangle with stroke and fill -->
23          <Rectangle Canvas.Left="670" Canvas.Top="30" Width="300"
24              Height="180" Stroke="Black" Fill="Red" StrokeThickness="10"/>
25
26          <!-- Line to separate rows of shapes -->
27          <Line X1="30" Y1="225" X2="970" Y2="225" Stroke="Blue"
28              StrokeThickness="10" />
29
30          <!-- Ellipse with fill and no stroke -->
31          <Ellipse Canvas.Left="30" Canvas.Top="240" Width="300" Height="180"
32              Fill="Red" />
33
34          <!-- Ellipse with stroke and no fill -->
35          <Ellipse Canvas.Left="350" Canvas.Top="240" Width="300" Height="180"
36              Stroke="Black" StrokeThickness="10"/>
37
```

Fig. 24.1 | Specifying basic shapes in XAML. (Part 1 of 2.)

```
38        <!-- Ellipse with stroke and fill -->
39        <Ellipse Canvas.Left="670" Canvas.Top="240" Width="300" Height="180"
40           Stroke="Black" Fill="Red" StrokeThickness="10"/>
41     </Canvas>
42  </Page>
```

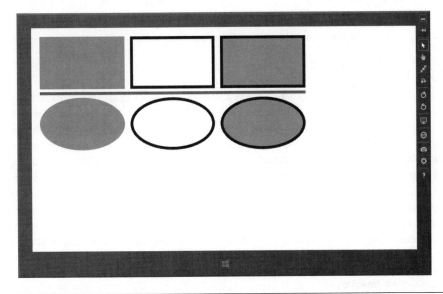

Fig. 24.1 | Specifying basic shapes in XAML. (Part 2 of 2.)

Using the Toolbox vs. Editing the XAML

By default, the **Toolbox** contains only the Rectangle and Ellipse shapes, which you can drag onto the GUI designer, as you did with Windows 8 UI controls in Chapter 23. There are various other shapes—and other less-commonly used controls—that you can add to the **Toolbox**. To do so:

1. Right click in the **General** section at the bottom of the **Toolbox**, then select **Choose Items...** to display the **Choose Toolbox Items** dialog. In the **Windows XAML Components** tab, the items that are *checked* are already displayed in the **Toolbox**.

2. To add any other shape or control, *check* its checkbox, then click **OK**. The new item will appear in the **Toolbox**'s **General** section.

If you'd like the items you add to appear in alphabetical order within the **Toolbox**, you can rearrange the **Toolbox** items by dragging them where you'd like them to appear in the **Toolbox**. You can also edit the XAML directly to create new shapes. Like any other control, you can select a shape in the designer or click its element in the XAML to edit the shape's properties in the **Properties** window.

Changing the Layout from *Grid to Canvas*

For this app, we used the IDE's **Document Outline** window to change the Page's layout from a Grid (the default) to a Canvas. Recall from Section 23.3.1, that a Canvas allows you to specify the exact position of a shape. The **Document Outline** window shows the *nested structure* of a page's layouts and controls and makes it easier to select specific controls to customize them with the **Properties** window. To change the layout:

1. Open the **Document Outline** window by selecting **VIEW > Other Windows > Document Outline.**

2. In the **Document Outline** window, right click the [Grid] node, which represents the Grid layout, and select **Change Layout Type > Canvas** from the popup menu.

24.2.1 Rectangles

The first shape (Fig. 24.1, lines 15–16) uses a **Rectangle** object to create a *filled* rectangle in the window. To specify the Rectangle's location, we set the attached properties Canvas.Left and Canvas.Top to 30. These properties appear as **Left** and **Top** in the **Properties** window's **Layout** section when the Rectangle is selected. We set the Width and Height properties—**Width** and **Height** in the **Properties** window's **Layout** section—to 300 and 180, respectively, to specify the size. To define the color, we set the **Fill** property to Red using **Fill** in the **Properties** window's **Brush** section. You can assign any solid Color or Brush (Section 24.4) to this property. Rectangles also have a **Stroke** property, which defines the color of the *shape's outline* (lines 20 and 24). If either the Fill or the Stroke is *not* specified, that property will be rendered *transparently*. For this reason, the first Rectangle in the window has no outline, while the second has *only* an outline with a *transparent* center. Shape objects have a **StrokeThickness** property which defines the thickness of the outline. The default value for StrokeThickness is one pixel—we used 10 for all Strokes in this app.

24.2.2 Line

A **Line** (lines 27–28) is defined by its two *endpoints*—X1, Y1 and X2, Y2. Lines have a Stroke property that defines the Line's *color*. In this example, the Line's Stroke is set to Blue and its StrokeThickness to 10.

24.2.3 Ellipses

To draw a *circle* or *ellipse*, you can use the **Ellipse** control. An Ellipse's location and size is defined like a Rectangle—with attached properties Canvas.Left and Canvas.Top for the *upper-left* corner, and properties Width and Height for the size (line 31). Together, the Canvas.Left, Canvas.Top, Width and Height of an Ellipse define an invisible *bounding rectangle* in which the Ellipse touches the *center* of each side. To draw a circle, provide the *same* value for the Width and Height. As with Rectangles, having an *unspecified* Fill property for an Ellipse makes the shape's fill *transparent* (lines 35–36).

24.3 Polylines and Polygons

There are two shape controls for drawing *multisided* shapes—**Polyline** and **Polygon**. Polyline draws a series of *connected lines* defined by a set of points, while Polygon does the same but *connects* the start and end points to make a *closed figure*. The app DrawPolygons (Fig. 24.2) displays one Polyline and two Polygons.

```
 1    <!-- Fig. 24.2: MainPage.xaml -->
 2    <!-- Defining Polylines and Polygons in XAML. -->
 3    <Page
 4        x:Class="DrawPolygons.MainPage"
 5        xmlns="http://schemas.microsoft.com/winfx/2006/xaml/presentation"
 6        xmlns:x="http://schemas.microsoft.com/winfx/2006/xaml"
 7        xmlns:local="using:DrawPolygons"
 8        xmlns:d="http://schemas.microsoft.com/expression/blend/2008"
 9        xmlns:mc="http://schemas.openxmlformats.org/markup-compatibility/2006"
10        mc:Ignorable="d">
11
12        <Canvas
13            Background="{StaticResource ApplicationPageBackgroundThemeBrush}">
14            <Polyline Stroke="Black" StrokeThickness="10"
15                Points="50,50 150,700 425,300 200,250"/>
16
17            <Polygon Stroke="Black" StrokeThickness="10"
18                Points="450,50 550,700 825,300 600,250"/>
19
20            <Polygon Fill="Red" Stroke="Black" StrokeThickness="10"
21                Points="850,50 950,700 1225,300 1000,250"/>
22        </Canvas>
23    </Page>
```

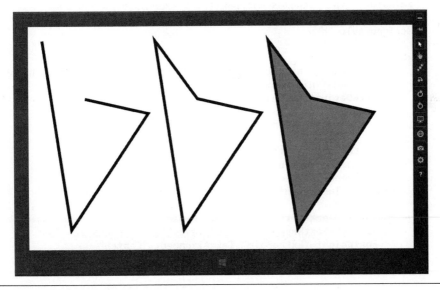

Fig. 24.2 | Defining Polylines and Polygons in XAML.

Embedded in the Canvas are a Polyline (lines 14–15) and two Polygons—one without a Fill (lines 17–18) and one with a Fill (lines 20–21). As you can see, Polyline and Polygon objects have Stroke and StrokeThickness properties like the simple shapes we discussed earlier. Polygons also have the Fill property.

Each Polyline and Polygon object has a **Points property** that we defined directly in the XAML. This property consists of a series of points that are defined as *x-y* coordinates on the Canvas. Each point's *x* and *y* values are separated by a comma, and each point is separated from the next with a space. The Points property is an object of class **PointCollection** (namespace Windows.UI.Xaml.Media) that stores individual Point objects.

24.4 SolidColorBrushes and ImageBrushes

The UsingBrushes app (Fig. 24.3) uses SolidColorBrushes and ImageBrushes to change an element's graphic properties, such as the Fill, Stroke or Background. You'll learn about GradientBrushes in the next section. This app applies brushes to TextBlocks and Ellipses. The image used is provided in the ImagesVideo folder with this chapter's examples. We added it to the project by dragging it from Windows Explorer onto the project's Assets folder in the **Solution Explorer** window.

```
1   <!-- Fig. 24.3: MainWindow.xaml -->
2   <!-- Applying brushes. -->
3   <Page
4      x:Class="UsingBrushes.MainPage"
5      xmlns="http://schemas.microsoft.com/winfx/2006/xaml/presentation"
6      xmlns:x="http://schemas.microsoft.com/winfx/2006/xaml"
7      xmlns:local="using:UsingBrushes"
8      xmlns:d="http://schemas.microsoft.com/expression/blend/2008"
9      xmlns:mc="http://schemas.openxmlformats.org/markup-compatibility/2006"
10     mc:Ignorable="d">
11
12     <Grid
13        Background="{StaticResource ApplicationPageBackgroundThemeBrush}">
14        <Grid.RowDefinitions>
15           <RowDefinition Height="Auto" />
16           <RowDefinition />
17        </Grid.RowDefinitions>
18
19        <Grid.ColumnDefinitions>
20           <ColumnDefinition />
21           <ColumnDefinition />
22        </Grid.ColumnDefinitions>
23
24        <!-- TextBlock with a SolidColorBrush -->
25        <TextBlock TextWrapping="Wrap" Text="Color" FontSize="200"
26           FontWeight="ExtraBold" TextAlignment="Center"
27           VerticalAlignment="Center" HorizontalAlignment="Center"
28           Foreground="Yellow"/>
29
30        <!-- Ellipse with a SolidColorBrush (just a Fill) -->
31        <Ellipse Fill="Yellow" Grid.Row="1" Margin="20"/>
32
33        <!-- TextBlock with an ImageBrush -->
34        <TextBlock TextWrapping="Wrap" Text="Image" FontSize="200"
35           FontWeight="ExtraBold" HorizontalAlignment="Center"
36           VerticalAlignment="Center" Grid.Column="1">
```

Fig. 24.3 | Applying brushes. (Part 1 of 2.)

```
37                <TextBlock.Foreground>
38                   <!-- Flower image as an ImageBrush -->
39                   <ImageBrush ImageSource="Assets/flowers.jpg"
40                      Stretch="UniformToFill"/>
41                </TextBlock.Foreground>
42             </TextBlock>
43
44          <!-- Ellipse with an ImageBrush -->
45          <Ellipse Grid.Row="1" Grid.Column="1" Margin="20">
46             <Ellipse.Fill>
47                <!-- Flower image as an ImageBrush -->
48                <ImageBrush ImageSource="Assets/flowers.jpg"
49                   Stretch="UniformToFill"/>
50             </Ellipse.Fill>
51          </Ellipse>
52       </Grid>
53    </Page>
```

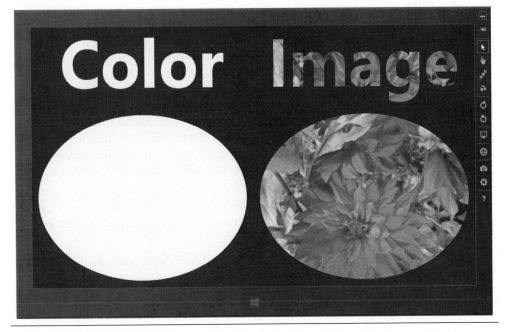

Fig. 24.3 | Applying brushes. (Part 2 of 2.)

SolidColorBrush

A **SolidColorBrush** specifies a solid color to apply to a property. All of the colors specified for the Strokes and Fills in this chapter's previous examples were actually SolidColor-Brushes. For the TextBlock at lines 25–28, the **Foreground** property specifies the text color as a *color name* (Yellow). For the Ellipse at line 31, this is specified with the Fill property. If you're editing the XAML directly, the IDE's *IntelliSense* feature will display a drop-down list of *predefined* color names that you can use.

You may also specify any solid color you like via the **Properties** window's **Brush** section. To do so, click the ■ tab below the **Foreground** property. You can use any *custom* *color* created from a combination of *alpha* (*transparency*), *red, green* and *blue* components called **ARGB values**—each is an integer in the range 0–255 that defines the amount of alpha, red, green and blue in the color, respectively. Custom colors are defined in *hexadecimal (base 16) format* (see Appendix D) in XAML, so the ARGB components are converted to hexadecimal values in the range 00–FF. An alpha value of 0 is *completely transparent* and an alpha value of 255 is *completely opaque*. In the IDE, the alpha is specified as a percentage from 0 to 100, which the IDE then translates into 00–FF.

If you know the hexadecimal value for the exact color you need, you can type it in the textbox that shows the current color's hexadecimal value. Use the format #AARRGGBB. You can see the complete list of predefined colors and their hexadecimal values at

msdn.microsoft.com/en-us/library/system.windows.media.colors.aspx

ImageBrush

An **ImageBrush** paints an image into the property it's assigned to. For instance, the Text-Block with the text "Image" and the Ellipse below it are both filled with the same flower picture. To fill the text, assign the ImageBrush to the Foreground property of the Text-Block. For brushes like ImageBrushes that have more complex settings, nested XAML elements are used to define the brushes and specify the property to which the brushes are assigned, as shown in lines 37–41 for the TextBlock's Foreground property and lines 46–50 for the Ellipse's Fill property.

To specify an ImageBrush for the TextBlock, click the [image] tab below the **Foreground** property, then specify values for the **Stretch** and **ImageSource** properties. In this app, the Stretch value UniformToFill indicates that the image should fill the element in which it's displayed and the original image's **aspect ratio** (that is, the proportion between its width and height) should be maintained. Keeping this ratio at its original value ensures that the video does not look "stretched," though it might be cropped—that is, you'll see only a portion of the image. Other possibilities for Stretch are:

- None—Uses the image at its *original* size. Depending on the image size, it's possible that the image will not fill the area or that only a small portion of the image will be displayed.

- Fill—Resizes the image to the width and height of the area it's filling. This typically changes the image's *aspect ratio*.

- Uniform—Preserves the image's aspect ratio but resizes it to fit the *width or height* of the area it's filling. Some of the area may *not* be filled by the image.

The ImageSource is set to an image file in the project. All of the project's images are displayed in this property's combobox, so you can conveniently select from them.

24.5 GradientBrushes

A **gradient** is a *gradual transition* through two or more colors. Gradients can be applied as the background or fill for various elements. A **LinearGradientBrush** transitions through colors along a *straight* path. The UsingGradients example (Figs. 24.4 and 24.6) displays a gradient across the window. This was created by applying a LinearGradientBrush to a Rectangle's Fill. The gradient starts with white and transitions linearly to black from *left to right*. This app allows you to set the ARGB values of the start and end colors to change the look of the gradient. The values entered in the TextBoxes must be in the range 0–255 for the app to run properly. If you set either color's *alpha* value to less than 255 (as in Fig. 24.4(c)), you'll see the text "Transparency test" in the background, showing that the Rectangle is *semitransparent*. The XAML code for this app is shown in Fig. 24.4.

TextBlock *That's Initially Hidden Behind the Gradient*
Lines 15–17 of Fig. 24.4 define a TextBlock containing the text "Transparency test", which is not visible initially because it's behind a Rectangle containing the gradient, which is completely *opaque*.

```
1    <!-- Fig. 24.4: MainWindow.xaml -->
2    <!-- Defining gradients in XAML. -->
3    <Page
4        x:Class="UsingGradients.MainPage"
5        xmlns="http://schemas.microsoft.com/winfx/2006/xaml/presentation"
6        xmlns:x="http://schemas.microsoft.com/winfx/2006/xaml"
7        xmlns:local="using:UsingGradients"
8        xmlns:d="http://schemas.microsoft.com/expression/blend/2008"
9        xmlns:mc="http://schemas.openxmlformats.org/markup-compatibility/2006"
10       mc:Ignorable="d">
11
12       <Grid
13           Background="{StaticResource ApplicationPageBackgroundThemeBrush}">
14           <!-- TextBlock in the background to show transparency -->
15           <TextBlock TextWrapping="Wrap" Text="Transparency test"
16               FontSize="200" HorizontalAlignment="Center"
17               VerticalAlignment="Center" TextAlignment="Center"/>
18
19           <!-- sample rectangle with linear gradient fill -->
20           <Rectangle>
21               <Rectangle.Fill>
22                   <LinearGradientBrush StartPoint="0,0" EndPoint="1,0">
23                       <GradientStop x:Name="firstStop" Color="White"/>
24                       <GradientStop x:Name="secondStop" Color="Black"
25                           Offset="1"/>
26                   </LinearGradientBrush>
27               </Rectangle.Fill>
28           </Rectangle>
29
30           <!-- Controls for selecting color and transparency -->
31           <StackPanel VerticalAlignment="Top" HorizontalAlignment="Center">
32               <!-- shows which TextBox corresponds with which ARGB value-->
33               <StackPanel Orientation="Horizontal">
34                   <TextBlock TextWrapping="Wrap" Text="Alpha:"
35                       Width="75" Margin="8" FontSize="20"/>
36                   <TextBlock TextWrapping="Wrap" Text="Red:"
37                       Width="75" Margin="8" FontSize="20"/>
38                   <TextBlock TextWrapping="Wrap" Text="Green:"
39                       Width="75" Margin="8" FontSize="20"/>
```

Fig. 24.4 | Defining gradients in XAML. (Part 1 of 3.)

```
40              <TextBlock TextWrapping="Wrap" Text="Blue:"
41                  Width="75" Margin="8" FontSize="20"/>
42          </StackPanel>
43
44          <!-- GUI to select the color of the first GradientStop -->
45          <StackPanel Grid.Row="2" Orientation="Horizontal">
46              <TextBox Name="fromAlpha" TextWrapping="Wrap" Text="255"
47                  Width="75" Margin="8" TextAlignment="Center"
48                  FontSize="20"/>
49              <TextBox Name="fromRed" TextWrapping="Wrap" Text="255"
50                  Width="75" Margin="8" TextAlignment="Center"
51                  FontSize="20"/>
52              <TextBox Name="fromGreen" TextWrapping="Wrap" Text="255"
53                  Width="75" Margin="8" TextAlignment="Center"
54                  FontSize="20"/>
55              <TextBox Name="fromBlue" TextWrapping="Wrap" Text="255"
56                  Width="75" Margin="8" TextAlignment="Center"
57                  FontSize="20"/>
58              <Button Name="startColorButton" Content="Set Start Color"
59                  Width="150" Margin="8" Click="startColorButton_Click"/>
60          </StackPanel>
61
62          <!-- GUI to select the color of second GradientStop -->
63          <StackPanel Grid.Row="3" Orientation="Horizontal">
64              <TextBox Name="toAlpha" TextWrapping="Wrap" Text="255"
65                  Width="75" Margin="8" TextAlignment="Center"
66                  FontSize="20"/>
67              <TextBox Name="toRed" TextWrapping="Wrap" Text="0"
68                  Width="75" Margin="8" TextAlignment="Center"
69                  FontSize="20"/>
70              <TextBox Name="toGreen" TextWrapping="Wrap" Text="0"
71                  Width="75" Margin="8" TextAlignment="Center"
72                  FontSize="20"/>
73              <TextBox Name="toBlue" TextWrapping="Wrap" Text="0"
74                  Width="75" Margin="8" TextAlignment="Center"
75                  FontSize="20"/>
76              <Button Name="endColorButton" Content="Set End Color"
77                  Width="150" Margin="8" Click="endColorButton_Click"/>
78          </StackPanel>
79      </StackPanel>
80  </Grid>
81 </Page>
```

a) Controls for setting the start and end colors

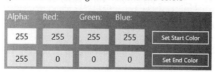

Fig. 24.4 | Defining gradients in XAML. (Part 2 of 3.)

b) The application immediately after it's loaded

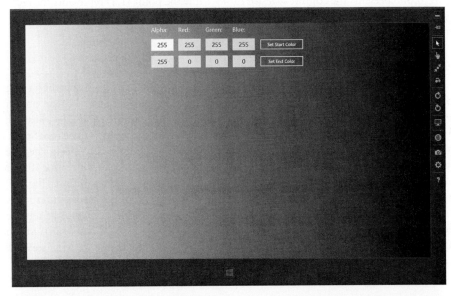

c) The application after changing the start and end colors

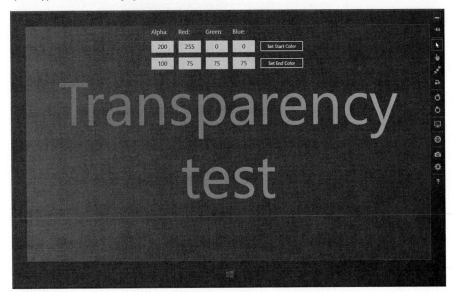

Fig. 24.4 | Defining gradients in XAML. (Part 3 of 3.)

24.5.1 Setting the Rectangle's Fill to a Gradient

The Rectangle with a LinearGradientBrush applied to its Fill is defined in lines 20–28. Line 22 defines the gradient's **StartPoint** and **EndPoint**. You must assign these properties **logical points** that are defined as *x*- and *y*-coordinates with values between 0.0 and 1.0, *inclusive. Logical points* reference locations in the control independent of the actual size. The point (0,0) represents the control's *top-left corner* while the point (1,1) represents the *bottom-right corner*. The point (1,0) used in this example represents the top-right corner. The gradient will transition *linearly* from the start point to the end point.

24.5.2 GradientStops

A gradient's colors are defined by **GradientStop**s (lines 23–25)—each specifies a single color along the gradient. You can define many stops. A GradientStop's **Color** property defines the color you want at that GradientStop's location—lines 23 and 24 indicate that the gradient transitions from white to black. Set the colors of the two GradientStops as shown in Fig. 24.5. A GradientStop's **Offset** property defines where along the linear transition you want the color to appear. In the example we use the default value (0.0) for the first GradientStop's Offset and 1.0 for the other GradientStop's Offset (Fig. 24.4, line 25), indicating that these colors appear at the start and end of the gradient, respectively. You can change the GradientStops' positions by dragging the *thumbs* that represent them on the sample gradient in the **Properties** window (Fig. 24.5). Both GradientStops in this example have x:Name properties (that we added directly in the XAML) so we can interact with them *programmatically* to change their colors.

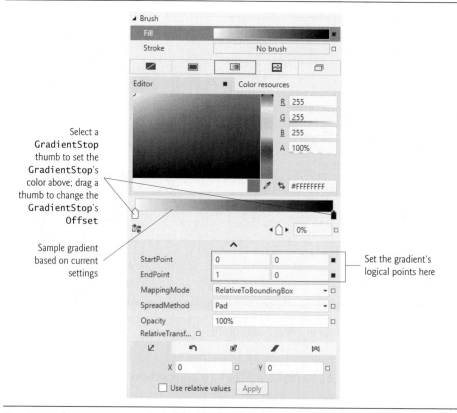

Fig. 24.5 | Brush section of **Properties** window for a Rectangle.

24.5.3 Defining the Gradient in the IDE

To define the gradient, click the Rectangle's **Fill** property's value in the **Properties** window's **Brush** section, then click the ▤ tab below the **Fill** and **Stroke** properties. Set the colors of the GradientStops and the **StartPoint** and **EndPoint** as shown in Fig. 24.5.

24.5.4 Code-Behind File

The code-behind file (Fig. 24.6) responds to the user setting the Colors of the two GradientStops. When the user presses **Set Start Color**, we use the Text properties of the corresponding TextBoxes to obtain the ARGB values and create a new color that we then assign to firstStop's Color property (lines 23–27). Each TextBox's value is converted to a byte by Convert method ToByte—we assume in this example that the user enters a value in the range 0–255 for each color component. Color method FromArgb receives four bytes that specify the alpha, red, green and blue components of a color. Each byte can represent values in the range 0–255. When the user presses **Set End Color**, we do the same for secondStop's Color (lines 35–39).

```csharp
1   // Fig. 24.6: MainPage.xaml.cs
2   // Customizing gradients.
3   using System;
4   using Windows.UI;
5   using Windows.UI.Xaml;
6   using Windows.UI.Xaml.Controls;
7
8   namespace UsingGradients
9   {
10      public sealed partial class MainPage : Page
11      {
12         // constructor
13         public MainPage()
14         {
15            InitializeComponent();
16         } // end constructor
17
18         // change the starting color of the gradient when the user clicks
19         private void startColorButton_Click(object sender,
20            RoutedEventArgs e)
21         {
22            // change the color to use the ARGB values specified by user
23            firstStop.Color = Color.FromArgb(
24               Convert.ToByte(fromAlpha.Text),
25               Convert.ToByte(fromRed.Text),
26               Convert.ToByte(fromGreen.Text),
27               Convert.ToByte(fromBlue.Text));
28         } // end method startColorButton_Click
29
30         // change the ending color of the gradient when the user clicks
31         private void endColorButton_Click(object sender,
32            RoutedEventArgs e)
33         {
```

Fig. 24.6 | Customizing gradients. (Part 1 of 2.)

```
34          // change the color to use the ARGB values specified by user
35          secondStop.Color = Color.FromArgb(
36             Convert.ToByte(toAlpha.Text),
37             Convert.ToByte(toRed.Text),
38             Convert.ToByte(toGreen.Text),
39             Convert.ToByte(toBlue.Text));
40       } // end method endColorButton_Click
41    } // end class MainPage
42 } // end namespace UsingGradients
```

Fig. 24.6 | Customizing gradients. (Part 2 of 2.)

24.6 Transforms

A **transform** can be applied to any UI element to *reposition* or *reorient* the graphic. There are several types of transforms. In this section, we demonstrate the **RotateTransform**, which *rotates* an object around a point by a specified *rotation angle*. Other transforms include:

- **ScaleTransform**—*scales* the object along the *x*-axis and *y*-axis.

- **SkewTransform**—*skews* (or *shears*) the object.

- **TranslateTransform**—*moves* an object to a new location.

You can apply multiple transforms to a control by grouping them in a TransformGroup.

The DrawStars example (Figs. 24.7–24.8) creates a circle of randomly colored stars. The app starts by creating a single Polygon *programmatically*, then makes 18 copies of the star and uses RotateTransforms to place each star around the circle at 20 degree intervals. Figure 24.7 shows the XAML code and a sample output. Lines 13–15 define a Canvas in which the shapes will be displayed. When the Canvas's PointerPressed event occurs, it's event handler recreates the stars with different randomly chosen colors. The code-behind file is shown in Fig. 24.8.

```
 1  <!-- Fig. 24.7: MainWindow.xaml -->
 2  <!-- Transforming a star polygon to display a circle of stars. -->
 3  <Page
 4     x:Class="DrawStars.MainPage"
 5     xmlns="http://schemas.microsoft.com/winfx/2006/xaml/presentation"
 6     xmlns:x="http://schemas.microsoft.com/winfx/2006/xaml"
 7     xmlns:local="using:DrawStars"
 8     xmlns:d="http://schemas.microsoft.com/expression/blend/2008"
 9     xmlns:mc="http://schemas.openxmlformats.org/markup-compatibility/2006"
10     mc:Ignorable="d">
11
12     <!-- Canvas that displays the stars -->
13     <Canvas Name="mainCanvas"
14        Background="{StaticResource ApplicationPageBackgroundThemeBrush}"
15        PointerPressed="mainCanvas_PointerPressed"/>
16  </Page>
```

Fig. 24.7 | Transforming a star polygon to display a circle of stars. (Part 1 of 2.)

Fig. 24.7 | Transforming a star polygon to display a circle of stars. (Part 2 of 2.)

```
1   // Fig. 24.8: MainPage.xaml.cs
2   // Applying transforms to a Polygon.
3   using System;
4   using Windows.Foundation;
5   using Windows.UI;
6   using Windows.UI.Xaml;
7   using Windows.UI.Xaml.Controls;
8   using Windows.UI.Xaml.Input;
9   using Windows.UI.Xaml.Media;
10  using Windows.UI.Xaml.Shapes;
11
12  namespace DrawStars
13  {
14     public sealed partial class MainPage : Page
15     {
16        Random random = new Random(); // for random color values
17        Polygon star = new Polygon(); // used to define star
18
19        // constructor
20        public MainPage()
21        {
22           this.InitializeComponent();
23
24           // determine horizonal center of screen
25           int centerX =
26              Convert.ToInt32(Window.Current.Bounds.Width / 2);
27
28           // set initial star points
29           star.Points.Add(new Point(centerX, 50));
```

Fig. 24.8 | Applying transforms to a Polygon. (Part 1 of 2.)

```
30          star.Points.Add(new Point(centerX + 12, 86));
31          star.Points.Add(new Point(centerX + 44, 86));
32          star.Points.Add(new Point(centerX + 18, 104));
33          star.Points.Add(new Point(centerX + 28, 146));
34          star.Points.Add(new Point(centerX, 122));
35          star.Points.Add(new Point(centerX - 28, 146));
36          star.Points.Add(new Point(centerX - 18, 104));
37          star.Points.Add(new Point(centerX - 44, 86));
38          star.Points.Add(new Point(centerX - 12, 86));
39
40          RotateAndDrawStars(); // draw circle of stars
41       } // end constructor
42
43       // draw circle of stars in random colors
44       private void RotateAndDrawStars()
45       {
46          mainCanvas.Children.Clear(); // remove previous stars
47
48          // create 18 stars
49          for (int count = 0; count < 18; ++count)
50          {
51             Polygon newStar = new Polygon(); // create a polygon object
52
53             // copy star.Points collection into newStar.Points
54             foreach (var point in star.Points)
55                newStar.Points.Add(point);
56
57             byte[] colorValues = new byte[3]; // create a Byte array
58             random.NextBytes(colorValues); // create three random values
59
60             // creates a random color brush
61             newStar.Fill = new SolidColorBrush(Color.FromArgb(
62                255, colorValues[0], colorValues[1], colorValues[2]));
63
64             // apply a rotation to the shape
65             // used to rotate the star
66             RotateTransform rotate = new RotateTransform();
67             rotate.CenterX = Window.Current.Bounds.Width / 2;
68             rotate.CenterY = Window.Current.Bounds.Height / 2;
69             rotate.Angle = count * 20;
70             newStar.RenderTransform = rotate;
71             mainCanvas.Children.Add(newStar);
72          } // end for
73       } // end method RotateAndDrawStars
74
75       // redraws stars in new colors each time user touches the canvas
76       private void mainCanvas_PointerPressed(object sender,
77          PointerRoutedEventArgs e)
78       {
79          RotateAndDrawStars();
80       } // end method mainCanvas_PointerPressed
81    } // end class MainPage
82 } // end namespace DrawStars
```

Fig. 24.8 | Applying transforms to a Polygon. (Part 2 of 2.)

24.6.1 MainPage Instance Variables and Constructor

In the code-behind file, line 17 creates the Polygon that's used to define the initial star shape. The MainPage constructor determines the screen's horizontal center *x*-coordinate (lines 25–26), then adds Point objects (lines 29–38) to Polygon star's Points property—this is the programmatic equivalent of setting the Points property in XAML as we did in Fig. 24.2. Each Point's *x*-coordinate is calculated based on the *x*-coordinate of the screen's horizontal center. These points define the star that appears at the top-center of the screen.

24.6.2 MainPage Method RotateAndDrawStars

Method RotateAndDrawStars (lines 44–73) is called from the constructor and the mainCanvas_PointerPressed event handler. The method replicates the star object 18 times and applies a different RotateTransform to each to get the circle of Polygons shown in the screen capture of Fig. 24.7. Each iteration of the loop creates a new Polygon with the *same* set of points (Fig. 24.8, lines 51–55). To generate the random colors for each star, we use the Random class's **NextBytes** method, which assigns a random value in the range 0–255 to each element in its byte-array argument. Lines 57–58 define a four-element Byte array and pass it to NextBytes. We then set the newStar's Fill to a new SolidColorBrush with 255 for the *alpha* and the three randomly generated bytes as its *red*, *green* and *blue* values (lines 61–62).

24.6.3 Applying a RotateTransform

To apply a rotation to each new Polygon, we set its **RenderTransform** property to a new RotateTransform object (lines 66–70). Lines 67–68 set the RotateTransform's CenterX and CenterY properties, which represent the coordinates of the *point of rotation*—that is, the point around which the shape will rotate. We used the screen's center *x-y* coordinates. Next, line 69 sets the Angle property, which indicates the number of *degrees to rotate*. A *positive* value rotates *clockwise*. Each iteration of the loop in RotateAndDrawStars assigns a new rotation-angle value by multiplying the control variable by 20. After setting newStar's RenderTransform property (line 70), line 71 adds newStar as a child element of mainCanvas so it can be rendered on screen.

24.7 Windows 8 Customization: A Television GUI

In Chapter 23, we introduced styles for customizing the appearance of Windows 8 controls. Now that you have a basic understanding of how to create and manipulate graphics in Windows 8, you'll use **ControlTemplates** to define a control's appearance and to create an app with a graphically sophisticated multimedia GUI (Fig. 24.9). This app models a *television* screen in perspective. The TV can be turned on or off. When it's on, the user can *play*, *pause* and *stop* the TV's video. The video we used (media.mp4) is located with the chapter's examples in the ImagesVideo folder. You should create a Video subfolder in the project's Assets folder, then drag the video file from Windows Explorer into the Video subfolder in the **Solution Explorer** window. We downloaded this public-domain NASA video from

```
www.nasa.gov/multimedia/videogallery
```

Fig. 24.9 | GUI representing a television with video playing.

24.7.1 XAML for the TV GUI

The TV GUI may appear complex, but it's actually just a basic Windows 8 GUI built using standard controls that you've learned previously. Figures 24.10–24.12 present the XAML markup. When the app first loads, the power CheckBox (⏻) at the GUI's bottom-left is colored red to indicate that the power is *off*, and the *play* (▶), *pause* (❚❚) and *stop* (■) RadioButtons at the GUI's bottom-right are gray to indicate that they're *disabled*. When you check the power CheckBox, it becomes green to indicate that the power is *on* and the *play*, *pause* and *stop* RadioButtons turn red to indicate that they're *unchecked*. As you select each RadioButton, it turns green to indicate that it's *checked*. As always, only *one* Radio-Button in the group can be selected at a time.

When we built this app's GUI, we first defined the elements in Fig. 24.12, then implemented the ControlTemplates in Figs. 24.10–24.11 to customize the CheckBox and RadioButton controls.

24.7.2 XAML for the Power CheckBox's ControlTemplate

Figure 24.10 begins MainPage's XAML markup. Within the Page.Resources element (starting at line 12 and spanning Figs. 24.10–24.11) are two ControlTemplates. The one in Fig. 24.10 specifies the look-and-feel of the app's powerCheckBox.

```
1   <!-- Fig. 24.10: MainPage.xaml -->
2   <!-- TV GUI showing the versatility of Windows 8 customization. -->
3   <Page
4      x:Class="TV.MainPage"
5      xmlns="http://schemas.microsoft.com/winfx/2006/xaml/presentation"
6      xmlns:x="http://schemas.microsoft.com/winfx/2006/xaml"
7      xmlns:local="using:TV"
8      xmlns:d="http://schemas.microsoft.com/expression/blend/2008"
9      xmlns:mc="http://schemas.openxmlformats.org/markup-compatibility/2006"
10     mc:Ignorable="d">
11
12     <Page.Resources>
13        <!-- define ControlTemplate for power CheckBox -->
14        <ControlTemplate x:Key="CheckBoxControlTemplate"
15           TargetType="CheckBox">
16           <Grid>
17              <!-- CheckBox checked/unchecked appearance changes -->
18              <VisualStateManager.VisualStateGroups>
19                 <VisualStateGroup x:Name="CheckStates">
20                    <VisualState x:Name="Checked">
21                       <Storyboard>
22                          <ObjectAnimationUsingKeyFrames
23                             Storyboard.TargetProperty="Color"
24                             Storyboard.TargetName="startColor">
25                             <DiscreteObjectKeyFrame KeyTime="0"
26                                Value="LimeGreen"/>
27                          </ObjectAnimationUsingKeyFrames>
28                       </Storyboard>
29                    </VisualState>
30                    <VisualState x:Name="Unchecked" />
31                 </VisualStateGroup>
32              </VisualStateManager.VisualStateGroups>
33
34              <!-- Red circle background for CheckBox -->
35              <Ellipse Stroke="Black" Width="50" Height="50">
36                 <Ellipse.Fill>
37                    <LinearGradientBrush StartPoint="0,0" EndPoint="2,0">
38                       <GradientStop x:Name="startColor" Color="Red"/>
39                       <GradientStop Color="Black" Offset="1"/>
40                    </LinearGradientBrush>
41                 </Ellipse.Fill>
42              </Ellipse>
43
44              <!-- display button image -->
45              <ContentPresenter Content="{TemplateBinding Content}" />
46           </Grid>
47        </ControlTemplate>
48
```

Fig. 24.10 | TV GUI XAML—CheckBoxControlTemplate that specifies the powerCheckBox's custom look-and-feel.

24.7.3 Creating a Basic `ControlTemplate`

You can create a `ControlTemplate` one of several ways:

- You can create a `Page.Resources` element in the XAML and edit the XAML directly.

- You can edit a copy of a control's default `Style`, which contains the control's default `ControlTemplate`. To do this, in **Design** view you'd right-click the control you wish to customize in your GUI, then select **Edit Template > Edit a Copy....** In the dialog that appears, you can specify the `ControlTemplate`'s name (known as its *key*) and where the `ControlTemplate` should be defined. For example, you can define it in the `Page`'s resources to share it among many elements on the `Page`, or in the app's resources to share it across pages in the app.

- You can define a new `ControlTemplate` then edit its content. We used this approach. To do this, right-click the control you wish to customize in your GUI, then select **Edit Template > Create Empty....** In the dialog that appears, specify the name `CheckBoxControlTemplate`. Leave the **This document** radio button selected and ensure that **Page** is selected in the drop-down list. This places the XAML for a basic `ControlTemplate` in your Page's `Page.Resources` element.

24.7.4 Default `ControlTemplate` Markup

The default `ControlTemplate` markup that the IDE generated contains:

- An **x:Key** property (Fig. 24.10, line 14)—the `ControlTemplate` name you specified. This name is used in the `CheckBox` control's definition in Fig. 24.12 to specify which `ControlTemplate` should be applied. As you'll see shortly, because you right-clicked the `CheckBox` to create this `ControlTemplate`, the IDE uses it to change the `CheckBox`'s look and feel.

- A **TargetType** property (Fig. 24.10, line 15)—the type of control that the template can be applied to.

- A nested `Grid` element (Fig. 24.10, starting at line 16)—used to define the control's look and feel.

- A nested **VisualStateManager.VisualGroups** element within the `Grid`—used to specify changes to the control's look and feel due to various events and user interactions, such as when the `CheckBox` is *checked* or *unchecked*. We kept only the items in this element that we needed to customize the `CheckBox` appropriately for this app.

When you place controls in a `ControlTemplate` and select them, you can edit their properties in the **Properties** window or directly in the XAML.

24.7.5 Defining the CheckBox's New Look-And-Feel

The template defines a one-cell `Grid` containing a 50-by-50 `Ellipse` with a red-to-black gradient `Fill` (lines 35–42) on which we display the `CheckBox`'s `Content` property value. Normally this is text that appears next to the checkbox, but this app uses an image instead. Unless otherwise specified, the elements in a one-cell `Grid` are centered horizontally *and* vertically within the `Grid`, so the `CheckBox`'s `Content` value appears centered over the El-

lipse—recall that the element defined later in the XAML is placed on top. Together, the **Ellipse** and image *completely change* the default look-and-feel of a standard **CheckBox**, but the control maintains its ability to be *checked* or *unchecked*.

The **ControlTemplate**'s **ContentPresenter element** (line 45) specifies where the **CheckBox**'s **Content** value should be displayed. The **ContentPresenter**'s **Content** property is set to "**{TemplateBinding Content}**", which indicates that the **CheckBox**'s **Content** value should appear at the **ContentPresenter**'s location in the template.

24.7.6 Using Animation to Change a Control's Look-and-Feel in Response to State Changes

Lines 18–32 specify how the control's appearance should change as the control's state changes—for example, from *checked* to *unchecked*. The **CheckBox** in this app is *unchecked* by default, so it will initially appear as defined by lines 35–42 within the **Grid**. The **VisualStateManager.VisualGroups** element may contain one or more **VisualState-Group** elements that define various control states. For this **CheckBox**, we have one **Visual-StateGroup** that defines two **VisualState** elements—one with the **x:Name** "**Checked**" (lines 20–29) and one with "**Unchecked**" (line 30). These are just two of many **Visual-States** that a **CheckBox** can have—we deleted the others for simplicity in this app. You must use the pre-defined state names (which you can see in the basic **ControlTemplate** when it's first generated) so that the app can look up and apply the correct **VisualState** each time the control's state changes.

The empty **VisualState** element at line 30

```
<VisualState x:Name="Unchecked" />
```

indicates that when the **CheckBox** is *unchecked*, it should return to the default appearance defined by the **ControlTemplate**.

The **VisualState** element at lines 20–29

```
<VisualState x:Name="Checked">
    <Storyboard>
        <ObjectAnimationUsingKeyFrames
            Storyboard.TargetProperty="Color"
            Storyboard.TargetName="startColor">
            <DiscreteObjectKeyFrame KeyTime="0"
                Value="LimeGreen"/>
        </ObjectAnimationUsingKeyFrames>
    </Storyboard>
</VisualState>
```

indicates that when the **CheckBox** is *checked*, the **GradientStop** named **startColor** should have its **Color** property changed to **LimeGreen**. Property value changes are specified in the nested **StoryBoard** element, which is used to perform *animations*. There are many animation capabilities in Windows 8 (**bit.ly/Win8StoryBoard**). Here, we use an **ObjectAnimationUsingKeyFrames** animation, which allows you to change a property of an object to a new value. **StoryBoard.TargetName** specifies the object that will be modified and **Story-Board.TargetProperty** specifies the property to change. Within the **ObjectAnimation-UsingKeyFrames** element, the nested **DiscreteObjectKeyFrame** specifies the new color value (**LimeGreen**) and that the color change should be performed immediately (**KeyTime** is set to 0). You can also specify animations that are performed over a period of time. Some other animation types include animating Points so that you can move an object, animating transitions from one color to another over time and animating numeric values over time—this could be used to animate an object's size changes.

24.7.7 XAML for the Play, Pause and Stop RadioButtons' ControlTemplate

Figure 24.11 presents the ControlTemplate that specifies the look and feel of the app's playRadioButton, pauseRadioButton and stopRadioButton. Most of this markup is similar or identical to that of the CheckBoxControlTemplate in Fig. 24.10. The important differences are in lines 54–81 where we define the VisualStates for the RadioButtons' Normal, Disabled, Checked and Unchecked states using the same animation capabilities as in the CheckBoxControlTemplate.

```
49        <!-- define template for play, pause and stop RadioButtons -->
50        <ControlTemplate x:Key="RadioButtonControlTemplate"
51            TargetType="RadioButton">
52            <Grid>
53                <!-- RadioButton appearance changes -->
54                <VisualStateManager.VisualStateGroups>
55                    <VisualStateGroup x:Name="CommonStates">
56                        <VisualState x:Name="Normal" />
57                        <VisualState x:Name="Disabled">
58                            <Storyboard>
59                                <ObjectAnimationUsingKeyFrames
60                                    Storyboard.TargetProperty="Color"
61                                    Storyboard.TargetName="startColor">
62                                    <DiscreteObjectKeyFrame KeyTime="0"
63                                        Value="LightGray"/>
64                                </ObjectAnimationUsingKeyFrames>
65                            </Storyboard>
66                        </VisualState>
67                    </VisualStateGroup>
68                    <VisualStateGroup x:Name="CheckStates">
69                        <VisualState x:Name="Checked">
70                            <Storyboard>
71                                <ObjectAnimationUsingKeyFrames
72                                    Storyboard.TargetProperty="Color"
73                                    Storyboard.TargetName="startColor">
74                                    <DiscreteObjectKeyFrame KeyTime="0"
75                                        Value="LimeGreen"/>
76                                </ObjectAnimationUsingKeyFrames>
77                            </Storyboard>
78                        </VisualState>
79                        <VisualState x:Name="Unchecked" />
80                    </VisualStateGroup>
81                </VisualStateManager.VisualStateGroups>
82
```

Fig. 24.11 | TV GUI XAML—RadioButtonControlTemplate that specifies the RadioButtons' custom look-and-feel. (Part 1 of 2.)

```
83                  <!-- Red circle background for RadioButtons -->
84                  <Ellipse Name="backgroundEllipse" Stroke="Black"
85                     Width="50" Height="50">
86                     <Ellipse.Fill>
87                        <LinearGradientBrush StartPoint="0,0" EndPoint="2,0">
88                           <GradientStop x:Name="startColor" Color="Red"/>
89                           <GradientStop Color="Black" Offset="1"/>
90                        </LinearGradientBrush>
91                     </Ellipse.Fill>
92                  </Ellipse>
93
94                  <!-- display button image -->
95                  <ContentPresenter Content="{TemplateBinding Content}" />
96               </Grid>
97            </ControlTemplate>
98         </Page.Resources>
99
```

Fig. 24.11 | TV GUI XAML—RadioButtonControlTemplate that specifies the RadioButtons' custom look-and-feel. (Part 2 of 2.)

24.7.8 XAML for the GUI

Figure 24.12 presents the XAML for the app's controls. The main Grid contains a Border object (lines 104–165) that surrounds the entire GUI and defines the TV's size. To make the TV appear as if it's in perspective from a point in the distance, we selected the Border and used the **Properties** windows **Transform** section to specify a **Projection**, which gives an object a 3-D look that's known as a **perspective projection**. The projection is applied to *everything* nested in the Border element. You can also apply such projections to individual controls. For this app, we set the **Projection**'s **Y** value to 20 which created the Border.Projection element in lines 109–111. Try setting the **X** and **Z** values individually in this app's project to see how the *x*- and *z*-axis projections differ from the *y*-axis projection we used here.

```
100      <!-- Grid that defines the GUI -->
101      <Grid
102         Background="{StaticResource ApplicationPageBackgroundThemeBrush}">
103         <!-- define the "TV" -->
104         <Border x:Name="tvBorder" Width="800" Height="540"
105            HorizontalAlignment="Center" VerticalAlignment="Center"
106            Background="Silver">
107
108            <!-- Make the TV look like its in perspective -->
109            <Border.Projection>
110               <PlaneProjection RotationY="20"/>
111            </Border.Projection>
112
113            <!-- Screen within the Border's bounds -->
114            <Grid>
115               <Grid.RowDefinitions>
```

Fig. 24.12 | TV GUI XAML—Grid containing the GUI. (Part 1 of 2.)

```
116                    <RowDefinition />
117                    <RowDefinition Height="Auto" />
118                </Grid.RowDefinitions>
119
120                <!-- define the screen -->
121                <Border Margin="10" Background="Black"
122                    BorderThickness="2" BorderBrush="Silver">
123                    <MediaElement Name="videoMediaElement" AutoPlay="False" />
124                </Border>
125
126                <!-- define the play, pause, and stop buttons -->
127                <StackPanel Grid.Row="1" HorizontalAlignment="Right"
128                    Orientation="Horizontal">
129                    <RadioButton Name="playRadioButton" IsEnabled="False"
130                        Margin="15" Checked="playRadioButton_Checked"
131                        Template="{StaticResource RadioButtonControlTemplate}">
132                        <!-- displayed by ControlTemplate's ContentPresenter -->
133                        <Image Width="40" Height="40"
134                            Source="Assets/Images/play.png" Stretch="Uniform" />
135                    </RadioButton>
136
137                    <RadioButton Name="pauseRadioButton" IsEnabled="False"
138                        Margin="15" Checked="pauseRadioButton_Checked"
139                        Template="{StaticResource RadioButtonControlTemplate}">
140                        <!-- displayed by ControlTemplate's ContentPresenter -->
141                        <Image Width="40" Height="40"
142                            Source="Assets/Images/pause.png" Stretch="Uniform" />
143                    </RadioButton>
144
145                    <RadioButton Name="stopRadioButton" IsEnabled="False"
146                        Margin="15" Checked="stopRadioButton_Checked"
147                        Template="{StaticResource RadioButtonControlTemplate}">
148                        <!-- displayed by ControlTemplate's ContentPresenter -->
149                        <Image Width="40" Height="40"
150                            Source="Assets/Images/stop.png" Stretch="Uniform" />
151                    </RadioButton>
152                </StackPanel>
153
154                <!-- define the power button -->
155                <CheckBox Name="powerCheckBox" Grid.Row="1"
156                    HorizontalAlignment="Left"
157                    Margin="15" Checked="powerCheckBox_Checked"
158                    Unchecked="powerCheckBox_Unchecked"
159                    Template="{StaticResource CheckBoxControlTemplate}">
160                    <!-- displayed by ControlTemplate's ContentPresenter -->
161                    <Image Source="Assets/Images/power.png"
162                        Width="40" Height="40" />
163                </CheckBox>
164            </Grid>
165        </Border>
166    </Grid>
167 </Page>
```

Fig. 24.12 | TV GUI XAML—Grid containing the GUI. (Part 2 of 2.)

Within the Border is a two-row Grid. Lines 121–124 define the first row, which contains a Border with a nested **MediaElement**—used to add audio or video to a Windows 8 app. Before using an audio or video file in your app, add it to your project's Assets folder. In this app, we'll set the MediaElement's **Source** property *programmatically* in response to user interactions.

Lines 127–152 define a horizontal StackPanel containing the *play*, *pause* and *stop* RadioButtons that appear at the right side of the Grid's second row. Each RadioButton's Template property (lines 131, 139 and 147) binds the RadioButton to the RadioButton-ControlTemplate from Fig. 24.11. Nested in each RadioButton element is an Image element (e.g., lines 133–134) that specifies the RadioButton's Content property value—the RadioButtonControlTemplate's ContentPresenter uses this Image on the RadioButton.

Lines 155–163 define the power CheckBox that appears at the left side of the Grid's second row. Line 159 specifies the CheckBox's ControlTemplate.

24.7.9 TV GUI Code-Behind File

Figure 24.13 presents the code-behind file for the TV app. Line 11 declares a Uri that specifies the video played by the MediaElement. The Uri is initialized in the MainPage constructor at line 19. The inherited Page property BaseUri specifies this app's location. The second argument specifies the relative path to the video file within the project's Assets folder.

```
1   // Fig. 24.13: MainPage.xaml.cs
2   // Code-behind file for the TV GUI.
3   using System;
4   using Windows.UI.Xaml;
5   using Windows.UI.Xaml.Controls;
6
7   namespace TV
8   {
9      public sealed partial class MainPage : Page
10     {
11        Uri uri; // Uri for location of video in this project
12
13        // constructor
14        public MainPage()
15        {
16           this.InitializeComponent();
17
18           // set Uri for location of video in this project
19           uri = new Uri(BaseUri, @"Assets\Video\media.mp4");
20        } // end constructor
21
22        // turn "on" the TV
23        private void powerCheckBox_Checked( object sender,
24           RoutedEventArgs e )
25        {
26           // set the videoMediaElement's Source
27           videoMediaElement.Source = uri;
```

Fig. 24.13 | Code-behind file for the TV GUI. (Part 1 of 2.)

```
28
29              // enable play, pause, and stop buttons
30              playRadioButton.IsEnabled = true;
31              pauseRadioButton.IsEnabled = true;
32              stopRadioButton.IsEnabled = true;
33          } // end method powerCheckBox_Checked
34
35          // turn "off" the TV
36          private void powerCheckBox_Unchecked( object sender,
37              RoutedEventArgs e )
38          {
39              // remove the videoMediaElement's source
40              videoMediaElement.Source = null;
41
42              // disable the play, pause, and stop buttons
43              playRadioButton.IsChecked = false;
44              pauseRadioButton.IsChecked = false;
45              stopRadioButton.IsChecked = false;
46              playRadioButton.IsEnabled = false;
47              pauseRadioButton.IsEnabled = false;
48              stopRadioButton.IsEnabled = false;
49          } // end method powerCheckBox_Unchecked
50
51          // play the video
52          private void playRadioButton_Checked( object sender,
53              RoutedEventArgs e )
54          {
55              videoMediaElement.Play();
56          } // end method playRadioButton_Checked
57
58          // pause the video
59          private void pauseRadioButton_Checked( object sender,
60              RoutedEventArgs e )
61          {
62              videoMediaElement.Pause();
63          } // end method pauseRadioButton_Checked
64
65          // stop the video
66          private void stopRadioButton_Checked( object sender,
67              RoutedEventArgs e )
68          {
69              videoMediaElement.Stop();
70          } // end method stopRadioButton_Checked
71      } // end class MainPage
72  } // end namespace TV
```

Fig. 24.13 | Code-behind file for the TV GUI. (Part 2 of 2.)

When the user turns on the TV (i.e., *checks* the powerCheckBox), the event handling method powerCheckBox_Checked (lines 23–33) sets the MediaElement's Source property to the Uri representing the video, then enables the *play*, *pause* and *stop* RadioButtons. When the user turns the TV off (i.e., *unchecks* the powerCheckBox), the event handling method powerCheckBox_Unchecked (lines 36–49) sets the MediaElement's Source property to `null` (which causes the picture to be removed from the screen), then *unchecks* and *disables* the *play*, *pause* and *stop* `RadioButtons`.

Whenever one of the playback-option `RadioButtons` is selected, the corresponding event handler (lines 52–70) calls the `MediaElement`'s `Play`, `Pause` or `Stop` method. The methods that execute these tasks are built into the `MediaElement` control.

24.8 Wrap-Up

This chapter introduced several Windows 8 graphics and multimedia capabilities, including two-dimensional shapes, transformations and video. You learned that Windows 8 graphics uses machine-independent pixels—making apps more portable across devices—and that graphic elements are rendered on screen using a vector-based system in which calculations determine how to size and scale each element so that graphics appear smooth at any scale.

You learned how to create basic shapes such as `Lines`, `Rectangles` and `Ellipses`, and set their `Fill` and `Stroke` properties.

Next, you created an app that displayed a `Polyline` and `Polygons`. These controls allowed you to specify sets of `Points` in `PointCollections`. You specified these `Points` by declaring them in the shapes' XAML markup.

We discussed several types of brushes for customizing an object's `Fill`, `Foreground` and `Background`. We demonstrated `SolidColorBrush` for a single color, `ImageBrush` for an image and the `LinearGradientBrush` for a gradient that transitions between multiple colors.

Next, you programmatically created a `Polygon` and added `Points` to it, then applied a `RotateTransform` to reposition and reorient the polygon around a point on the screen.

Finally, in the television GUI app, you used `ControlTemplates` to completely customize the look of a `CheckBox` and `RadioButtons` while maintaining their normal functionality. You defined `VisualStates` that used animation to specify how a control's look and feel changes for various states. You also used a projection to apply a perspective effect to the TV GUI.

25

Building a Windows Phone 8 App

Objectives

In this chapter you'll:

■ Register for a Windows Phone Dev Center account.

■ Code a complete Windows Phone 8 app.

■ Define an app's GUI with Visual Studio's GUI designer, **Document Outline** and **Properties** windows.

■ Handle Windows Phone 8 user-interface events.

■ Test a Windows Phone 8 app in the emulator on your desktop.

■ Learn how to register a Windows Phone device for testing.

■ Learn how to submit your apps to the Windows Phone Store for sale or free distribution.

■ Learn about other popular app platforms to which you can port your Windows Phone 8 app to reach a broader audience.

25.1 Introduction

In this chapter, you'll develop a simple **Tip Calculator** app for Windows Phone 8 (which from this point forward we'll abbreviate as WP8). This chapter assumes that you're already familiar with the Windows 8 UI and XAML concepts presented in Chapter 23. The WP8 SDK and the emulator used to test your WP8 apps both require 64-bit Windows 8 versions.

WP8—Microsoft's second-generation mobile phone operating system—was released in late 2012. WP8 is a pared down version of Windows 8, designed specifically for smartphones. These are *resource-constrained devices*—they have less memory and processor power than desktop computers, and limited battery life. WP8 has the same core operating systems services as Windows 8, including a common file system, security, networking, media and Internet Explorer 10 (IE10) web browser technology. However, WP8 has *only* the features necessary for smartphones, allowing them to run efficiently, minimizing the burden on the device's resources. Figure 25.1 lists some of the WP8 features.

WP8 developer features

- Support for multiple screen sizes.
- A tile-based user interface.
- Multitasking.
- WebBrowser control based on Internet Explorer 10.

Fig. 25.1 | Some WP8 developer features. (Part 1 of 2.)

> **WP8 developer features**
>
> - Map and navigation controls.
> - Camera and photo APIs.
> - Music and background audio APIs.
> - Speech synthesis and recognition APIs.
> - Bluetooth APIs.
> - VoIP (Voice over IP) APIs for audio and video calls made over an Internet connection.
> - Near Field Communication (NFC) APIs, which enable users to share content between two devices by touching them together (e.g., for making mobile payments, sharing contacts, etc.)
> - Multilingual App Toolkit for Visual Studio 2012 for localizing your apps.
> - In-app purchase for selling virtual goods (e.g., additional game levels, game scenery, ringtones, e-gifts, e-books, videos, music and more).
> - Windows Phone Application Analysis for app monitoring, which allows you to determine the quality and performance of your app and improve it during the development process, rather than after making it available to users.
> - Simulation Dashboard that shows you how your app will respond to network connectivity issues (e.g., a low bandwidth or weak connection), the lock screen, interruptions (e.g., notifications, phone calls) and more.
> - Wallet, which allows you to offer users coupons, memberships, loyalty cards and more that they can collect and store in their Wallet on a WP8 device.
> - And more.

Fig. 25.1 | Some WP8 developer features. (Part 2 of 2.)

25.2 Downloading the Windows Phone 8 SDK

The Windows Phone 8 SDK is included with the Visual Studio 2012 Professional edition or higher. If you do not have a full version of Visual Studio, you can download and install the Windows Phone 8 SDK for free from dev.windowsphone.com/downloadsdk. This will also install Visual Studio Express 2012 for Windows Phone, which includes all the tools you'll need to develop WP8 apps that you can submit to the Windows Phone Store. The WP8 SDK requires 64-bit Windows 8. The complete system requirements are located at:

```
bit.ly/WPSystemRequirements
```

Windows Phone 8 Emulator
The Windows Phone 8 SDK includes Visual Studio Express 2012 for Windows Phone and the **Windows Phone 8 Emulator**, which allows you to test your smartphone apps on your computer. If you're interested in testing your apps on WP8 devices, see Section 25.9. Figure 25.2 lists the WP8 Emulator features. You cannot test app features that use the compass, gyroscope or the vibration controller. For the latest information about the WP8 Emulator including installation, system requirements, features, running your apps in the emulator and more, see

```
bit.ly/WPEmulator
```

Windows Phone 8 Emulator features	
Accelerometer	App lifecycle (transitioning between active
Camera and video (with some limitations)	and dormant state)
GPS	In-app purchase
Language and region settings	Local folder (storage that's used only while
Lock screen	the emulator is running)
Microphone (e.g., for speech recognition)	Memory-constrained devices
Multiple screen resolutions	Multi-touch
NFC	Networking
Screen configuration options	Notifications
Copy and paste	

Fig. 25.2 | Windows Phone 8 Emulator features. (`bit.ly/WP8EmulatorFeatures`)

25.3 Tip Calculator App Introduction

The **Tip Calculator** app (Fig. 25.3(a)) calculates and displays possible tips for a restaurant bill. As you enter each digit of a bill amount by touching the *numeric keypad*, the app calculates and displays the tip amount and total bill (i.e., bill amount + tip) for a 15% tip and a custom tip percentage (18% by default). You can specify a custom tip percentage from 0% to 30% by moving the Slider *thumb*—this updates the custom percentage shown and displays the

a) Initial GUI

b) GUI after user enters the bill total 34.56 and changes the custom tip percentage to 20%

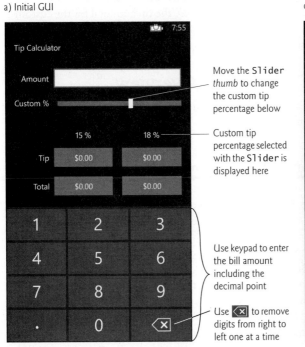

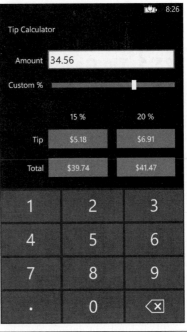

Move the Slider *thumb* to change the custom tip percentage below

Custom tip percentage selected with the Slider is displayed here

Use keypad to enter the bill amount including the decimal point

Use ⟨×⟩ to remove digits from right to left one at a time

Fig. 25.3 | Entering the bill total and calculating the tip.

custom tip and total (Fig. 25.3(b)). We chose 18% as the default custom percentage because many restaurants in the U.S. add this tip percentage for parties of six people or more.

You'll begin by test-driving the app—you'll use it to calculate 15% and custom tips. Then we'll overview the technologies you'll use to create the app. You'll build the app's GUI using Microsoft Visual Studio Express 2012 for Windows Phone, which we'll refer to simply as "the IDE" throughout the rest of the chapter, and the **Document Outline** window. Finally, we'll present the complete C# code for the app and do a detailed code walkthrough.

25.4 Test-Driving the Tip Calculator App

Open and Run the App
Open the **Tip Calculator** app's project (`TipCalculator.sln`) from the ch25 folder with the book's examples. Execute the app in the *WP8 Emulator* by selecting **DEBUG > Start Debugging** or by clicking the ▶ button on the IDE's toolbar.

Enter a Bill Total
Using the numeric keypad, enter the bill amount 34.56 (including the decimal point). If you make a mistake, press the delete (▣) button to erase one *rightmost* digit at a time. The TextBlocks under the **15%** and the custom tip percentage (**18%** by default) labels show the tip amount and the total bill for these tip percentages. All the **Tip** and **Total** TextBlocks update each time you enter or delete a digit.

Select a Custom Tip Percentage
Use the Slider to specify a *custom* tip percentage. Drag the Slider's *thumb* until the custom percentage reads **20%** (Fig. 25.3(b)). As you drag the *thumb*, the tip and total for the custom tip percentage update continuously. By default, the Slider allows you to select values from 0.0 to 10.0—we specified a maximum value of 0.3 (representing a 30% tip) for this app.

25.5 Tip Calculator Technologies Overview

This section introduces the IDE features and WP8 technologies you'll use to build the **Tip Calculator** app. We assume that you're familiar with the Windows 8 UI concepts presented in Chapter 23.

25.5.1 Classes App and PhoneApplicationPage

Unlike many C# apps, WP8 apps *do not have a Main method*. Instead, they have a derived class of Application (namespace System.Windows.Application) that the OS uses to launch an app. This class, named App, is defined by the files App.xaml and App.xaml.cs. As in a Windows Store app, the App class defines app-level event handlers (for events like the Launching, Activated, Deactivated and Closing), app-wide resources and more. The app-level event handlers are defined in class App's code-behind file (App.xaml.cs)—you can add your own code to these event handlers to respond to any of these events.

A WP8 app consists of one or more *pages* that are derived classes of PhoneApplicationPage (namespace Microsoft.Phone.Controls). As in Windows 8 UI, each page's XAML specifies the *controls* that enable the user to interact with the page, and each page's code-behind file defines the page's functionality. You'll build the **Tip Calculator**'s GUI *without* manipulating the XAML directly.

25.5.2 Arranging Controls with Grid

Recall that layouts arrange controls in an GUI. As you did in Chapter 23, you'll use a Grid (namespace System.Windows.Controls) to arrange controls into rows and columns. You'll use the Grid's RowDefinitions and ColumnDefinitions properties to define the rows and columns. You'll also specify two controls that span multiple columns.

25.5.3 Controls

You'll create TextBlocks, Borders, a TextBox and a Slider in this app:

- A **TextBox**—often called a *text field* in other GUI technologies—can display text, but is normally used to receive text input from the user. You'll specify a TextBox that allows only *numeric* input representing the bill amount.
- A **Border** enables you to place a border around a control or group of controls. You'll use Borders in this app to place a filled rectangle of color behind the Text-Blocks that display the calculated tips and totals.
- A **TextBlock** displays text.
- A **Slider** represents a double in the range 0.0–10.0 by default and allows the user to select a number in that range by moving the Slider's *thumb*. You'll customize the Slider so the user can choose a custom tip percentage *only* from the more limited range 0.0 to 0.30 (for tips of 0 to 30%).

25.5.4 IDE Features

You'll use the IDE's GUI designer, **Document Outline** window and **Properties** window to create, organize and customize control properties. The **Document Outline** window shows the *nested structure* of a page's layouts and controls and makes it easier to select specific controls to customize them with the **Properties** window.

25.6 Building the App's GUI

In this section, we'll walk through the precise steps for building the **Tip Calculator**'s GUI. The GUI will not look exactly like Fig. 25.3 until you've completed all the steps.

25.6.1 Grid Introduction

This app uses a Grid (Fig. 25.4) to arrange controls into five *rows* and two *columns*. Rows and columns are indexed from 0, like arrays. Each cell in a Grid can be *empty* or can hold one or more *controls*, including layouts that *contain* other controls. Controls can span *multiple* rows or columns, as shown in row 0 and row 1. As you'll see, you can specify a Grid's number of rows and columns.

Row Heights and Column Widths in a Grid
Each row's *height* and each column's *width* can be specified as an *explicit size*, a *relative size (using *)* or Auto. Auto makes the row or column only as big as it needs to be to fit its contents. The setting * specifies the size of a row or column with respect to the Grid's other rows and columns. For example, a column with a Height of 2* would be twice the size of

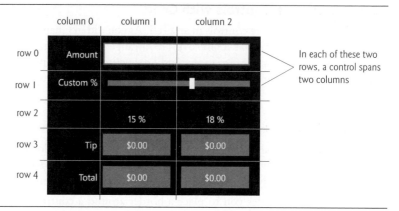

Fig. 25.4 | **Tip Calculator** GUI's `Grid` labeled by its rows and columns.

a column that is 1* (or just *). A `Grid` first allocates its space to the rows and columns that *explicitly* define their sizes or that are configured to allow the layout to *automatically* determine their sizes. The remaining space is divided among the other rows and columns.

In Fig. 25.4, the first column's width is set to `Auto`, so its width is determined by the `TextBlock` containing **Custom %**—the widest control in that column. We did not set the width of the second and third columns, so both columns occupy 50% of the remaining available horizontal space. All of this `Grid`'s rows have their heights set to `Auto`. You'll see how to configure rows and columns in Section 25.6.3—for example, you can specify the exact row and column in which a control is to be placed.

x:Name Property Values for This App's Controls

Figure 25.5 shows the controls' **x:Name** property values—in the **Properties** window, this is represented as the **Name** property. Recall from Chapter 23 that **x:Name** values are used as the control's variable names in your C# code. For clarity, our naming convention is to use the control's class name in the **x:Name** property. In the first and second rows, the `amountTextBox` and `customTipPercentSlider` each span two columns.

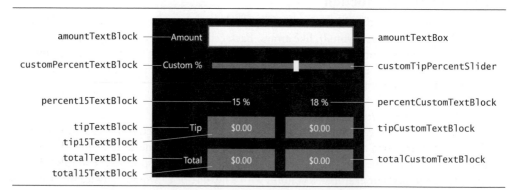

Fig. 25.5 | **Tip Calculator** GUI's components labeled with their **x:Name** property values.

25.6.2 Creating the `TipCalculator` Project

In this section, you'll create a new project for a WP8 app using the **Windows Phone App template** provided by the IDE. This template represents a simple *single-screen app*. There are 10 other templates for various common scenarios found in many types of apps—clicking a given template name shows a preview screen and a brief description of that template's purpose. Each template saves you time by providing capabilities for common app scenarios.

Perform the following steps to create the project:

1. Open Visual Studio Express 2012 for Windows Phone.

2. Select **File > New Project...** to display the **New Project** dialog.

3. In the dialog under **Templates > Visual C#**, select **Windows Phone** to display the list of Windows Phone project templates.

4. Select the **Windows Phone App** template.

5. In the **Name:** field, enter `TipCalculator`.

6. In the **Location:** field, specify where you'd like to save the app's project—you can change this by clicking the **Browse...** button and selecting a folder in the **Project Location** dialog.

7. Leave the default value in the **Solution name:** field—by default, the solution's name is the same as the project's name.

8. Click **OK**.

9. In the **New Windows Phone Application** dialog, ensure that **Windows Phone OS 8.0** is selected, then click **OK**.

The IDE creates and configures the `TipCalculator` project, then displays the app's `MainPage.xaml` file so that you can begin designing your app's GUI. In Fig. 25.6, we collapsed the **Solution Explorer** window and set the GUI designer's **Zoom** to 50% so that the screen capture would fit in the book. The initial GUI provided by the **Windows Phone App** template contains two `TextBlock`s—you'll modify the first and remove the second in the next section.

Device Window

At the left side of the IDE, the **Device** window (**Design > Device Window**) allows you to specify various settings for the GUI designer, including:

- **Orientation**—Allows you to choose between portrait and landscape for the design area.

- **Display**—Allows you to choose the screen resolution for which you're designing the GUI.

- **Theme**—Allows you to choose between the default **Dark** theme with white text and a **Light** theme with dark text.

- **Accent**—Allows you to set the accent color for your app in the GUI designer. Windows phone allows users to chose from one of several accent colors and many controls use the currently selected color so that they have the same look and feel as other apps on the device. The default accent color is **Red** and you can choose other colors to see how your app will appear with each accent color.

Device window GUI designer's **Zoom** GUI designer XAML editor

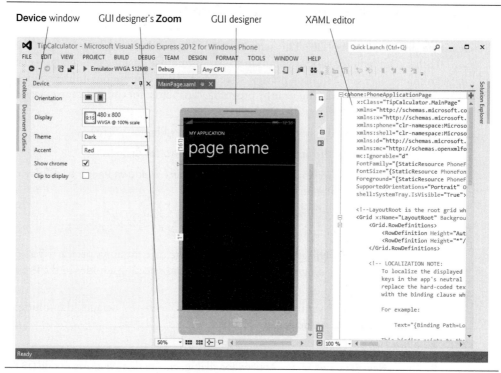

Fig. 25.6 | `TipCalculator` project in the IDE.

25.6.3 Changing the Default GUI

The default `MainPage` layout consists of a `Grid` with two rows—the first row contains a vertically oriented `StackPanel` named `TitlePanel` and the second row contains a `Grid` named `ContentPanel` in which you define the page's GUI. In the `StackPanel` are two `TextBlock`s—one displays **MY APPLICATION** and the other **page name**. In apps with multiple screens, these help provide context to users so they know which app they're using and which page of the app they're interacting with.

Changing the App Name
Change **MY APPLICATION** to **Tip Calculator** by double clicking the text in the designer and typing the new value directly in the designer. You can also select the control in the designer, then change its **Text** property in the **Common** section of the **Properties** window.

Deleting the Page Name
This app has only one screen, so we don't need the page name to provide additional context to the user. For that reason, select the `TextBlock` containing **page name** and delete it.

Specifying Five Rows and Three Columns
Recall that the GUI in Fig. 25.4 consists of five rows and three columns. You'll now use the **Document Outline** window to select the `Grid`, then use the **Properties** window to define

the rows and columns by setting the Grid's **RowDefinitions** and **ColumnDefinitions** properties. Perform the following tasks:

1. Open the **Document Outline** window by selecting **VIEW > Other Windows > Document Outline**.

2. In the **Document Outline** window, expand the LayoutRoot node and select ContentPanel—this is the predefined Grid control (provided when you created the project) in which you'll define the rest of the **Tip Calculator**'s GUI.

3. In the **Properties** window, expand the **Layout** node, then click the **Show advanced properties** (⌄) button to display all of the Grid's layout-related properties.

4. Click the ellipsis button to the right of the **RowDefinitions** property to display the **RowDefinition Collection Editor** dialog Fig. 25.7.

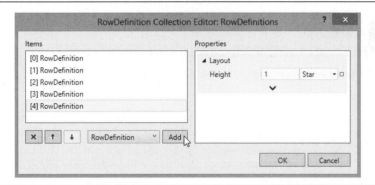

Fig. 25.7 | RowDefinition Collection Editor.

5. To create five rows, click the **Add** button five times to create five **RowDefinitions**—each allows you to specify the **Height** of a Grid row. You can also specify minimum and maximum row heights, though we do not use that in this app.

6. By default each row's **Height** property is set to 1 Star as shown for the last RowDefinition object in Fig. 25.7. One at a time, select each **RowDefinition** and set its height to Auto.

7. Click **OK** to dismiss the dialog.

Repeat the preceding tasks to create three **ColumnDefinition**s for the Grid's **ColumnDefinitions** property by using the **ColumnDefinition Collection Editor** dialog that's displayed when you click the ellipsis button to the right of the **ColumnDefinitions** property. For the first **ColumnDefinition**, set its **Width** to Auto so that the column's **Width** will be based on the widest control in the column. Leave the default **Width** for the other two **ColumnDefinitions**, so that they'll split the remaining horizontal space evenly between them.

25.6.4 Adding the TextBlocks, Borders, a TextBox and a Slider

You'll now build the rest of the GUI in Fig. 25.4. As you add each control to the GUI, immediately use the **Properties** window to set the control's **Name** property using the names shown in Fig. 25.5.

You'll use the **Document Outline** window to add controls to the Grid's rows and columns. The steps refer to the row and column numbers in Fig. 25.4. When working with layouts, it's sometimes difficult to see the layout's *nested structure* and to place controls in the correct locations by dragging them onto the GUI designer. The **Document Outline** window makes these tasks easier because it clearly shows the GUI's nested structure. As you'll soon see, you can reorder controls by dragging them in the **Document Outline** window.

The steps we provide here help you configure the GUI to appear exactly as shown in Fig. 25.4. When you build your own apps, you should experiment with the many control properties that are available to you.

Step 1: Configuring Row 0

Row 0 consists of the amountTextBlock in column 0 and the amountTextBox in columns 1 and 2—that is, it *spans* two columns. Each time you drop a control onto the GUI designer, the control is placed in the exact location you specify. You'll use the **Properties** window to specify values that place each control into the proper row and column. Perform the following tasks to create row 0's controls:

1. If the **Toolbox** window is not displayed, select **VIEW > Toolbox**.

2. Drag a TextBlock (amountTextBlock) onto the GUI designer.

3. In the **Properties** window's **Common** section, set **Text** to Amount.

4. In the **Properties** window's **Layout** section, set **Row** and **Column** to 0. Set the left **Margin** to 12 and the other **Margin** values to 0. Set the **HorizontalAlignment** to Right (▤) and the **VerticalAlignment** to Center (▐▌▐). All of the TextBlocks in column 0 will have their left **Margin**s set to 12 to ensure that whichever one is the *widest* will align with the app name (Tip Calculator) that's displayed at the top of the GUI.

5. Next, drag a TextBox (amountTextBox) onto the GUI designer.

6. In the **Properties** window's **Common** section, delete the default value of **Text** and set **InputScope** to **Number**—this restricts the TextBox to *numeric input* and ensures that a *numeric keypad* will be displayed when this control has the focus.

7. In the **Layout** section, set **Row** to 0, **Column** to 1 and **ColumnSpan** to 2. Set all **Margin** values to 0. Set the **HorizontalAlignment** to Stretch (▤).

Step 2: Configuring Row 1

Next, you'll add a TextBlock and Slider to the Grid. To do so:

1. Drag a TextBlock (customPercentTextBlock) onto the GUI designer, then set its **Text** (Custom %), **Row** (1), **Column** (0) and **HorizontalAlignment** (Right). For the **Margin**, set the **Top** and **Left** to 12 and the **Bottom** and **Right** to 0.

2. Drag a Slider (customTipPercentSlider) onto the GUI designer, then set its **Row** (1), **Column** (1), **RowSpan** (1), **ColumnSpan** (2), **HorizontalAlignment** (Stretch) and **Margin** (0 for all four sides).

Step 3: Configuring Row 2

Next, you'll add two TextBlocks to the Grid. To do so:

1. Drag a TextBlock (percent15TextBlock) onto the GUI designer, then set its **Text** (15 %), **Row** (2), **Column** (1), **HorizontalAlignment** (Center), **Margin** (0 for all

four sides) and **Padding** (8 for all four sides)—**Padding** adds space around the content *inside* a control's borders, whereas **Margin** adds space *outside* a control's borders. Expand the **Properties** window's **Text** section, select the **Paragraph** (¶) tab and change the **TextAlignment** (≡) to Center.

2. Repeat the preceding instructions for the percentCustomTextBlock but set its **Text** to 18 % and its **Column** to 2.

Step 4: Configuring Row 3
Next, you'll add three TextBlocks and two Borders. TextBlocks are transparent, so we use Borders to add color behind the tip15TextBlock and tipCustomTextBlock. Perform the following tasks:

1. Drag a TextBlock (tipTextBlock) onto the GUI designer, then set its **Text** (Tip), **Row** (3), **Column** (0), **HorizontalAlignment** (Right) and **VerticalAlignment** (Center). For the **Margin**, set **Left** (12) and other **Margin** values to 0.

2. Drag a Border onto the GUI designer, then set its **Row** (3), **Column** (1), **RowSpan** (1), **ColumnSpan** (1), **Margins** (12 on all sides), **HorizontalAlignment** (Stretch) and **VerticalAlignment** (Stretch). In the **Properties** window's **Brush** section, select the Border's **Background** property, then click the **Brush** resources (▭) tab to view a list of predefined *color resources* from the device's *theme*, which defines the look-and-feel of the GUI. Select PhoneAccentBrush as the Border's background color. The actual color is determined at *runtime* based on the theme setting on each device. The default color in the Windows Phone Emulator is red.

3. Drag a TextBlock (tip15TextBlock) onto the GUI designer. Initially, in the **Document Outline** window, tip15TextBlock appears below the Border you just created. We'd like the tip15TextBlock to be *nested* in the Border, so that its background color is displayed *behind* tip15TextBlock. To do so, in the **Document Outline** window, drag tip15TextBlock onto the [Border] node (Fig. 25.8). The tip15TextBlock is now nested in the [Border] node.

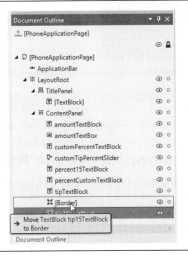

Fig. 25.8 | Dragging tip15TextBlock onto the [Border] node in the **Document Outline**.

4. With tip15TextBlock selected, set its **Margins** (10 for all four sides), **Horizontal-Alignment** (Center), **VerticalAlignment** (Center) and **TextAlignment** (Center).

5. Repeat items 2–4 above for another Border and the tipCustomTextBlock, placing the new Border in row 3 and column 2.

Step 5: Configuring Row 4
Repeat Step 4 to create and configure the last row's controls, but specify row 4 for the totalTextBlock and the two Borders, and set totalTextBlock's **Text** to Total. The GUI and **Document Outline** window should now appear as shown in Fig. 25.9.

a) Final GUI design   b) **Document Outline** window showing all the controls

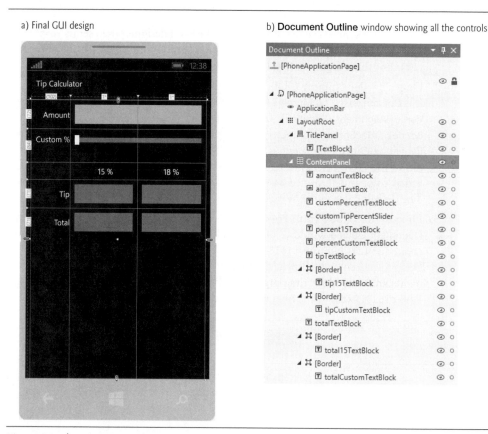

Fig. 25.9 | The GUI and the **Document Outline** window after adding all the controls.

25.7 Adding Functionality to the App with C#

Class MainPage's *code-behind file* (Figs. 25.10–25.18) implements the **Tip Calculator** app's functionality. It calculates the 15% and custom percentage tips and total bill amounts, and displays them in *locale-specific* currency format.

MainPage *Code-Behind File's* using *Statements*

Figure 25.10 shows the using statements in MainPage.xaml.cs. These *namespaces* and several others were added to the code-behind file when you created the TipCalculator project. We deleted the using statements that we did not use in this app.

```
1   // MainPage.xaml.cs
2   // Calculates bills using 15% and custom percentage tips
3   using System; // for classes String and Convert
4   using System.Windows; // for event handler argument classes
5   using System.Windows.Controls; // for event handler argument classes
6   using Microsoft.Phone.Controls; // for base class PhoneApplicationPage
7
```

Fig. 25.10 | MainPage code-behind file's using statements.

MainPage *Derived Class of* PhoneApplicationPage

Class MainPage (Figs. 25.11–25.18) derives from class PhoneApplicationPage (Fig. 25.11) the base class for each page of your app. When you created this app's project, the IDE created this derived class for you.

```
8    namespace TipCalculator
9    {
10      public partial class MainPage : PhoneApplicationPage
11      {
```

Fig. 25.11 | Class MainPage derives from PhoneApplicationPage.

Instance Variables and the MainPage *Constructor*

Lines 12–13 of Fig. 25.12 declare class MainPage's variables. The bill amount entered in amountTextBox will be converted to a decimal (for use in monetary calculations) and stored in billAmount (line 12). The custom tip percentage (a double value limited to the range 0.0–0.3) that the user sets by moving the Slider thumb will be converted to a decimal (Fig. 25.17) for use in tip calculations then stored in customTipPercent (line 13).

```
12        private decimal billAmount = 0.0M; // amount entered by the user
13        private decimal customTipPercent = 0.18M; // custom tip percentage
14
15        // Constructor
16        public MainPage()
17        {
18          InitializeComponent();
19        } // end constructor
20
```

Fig. 25.12 | MainPage class's instance variables and constructor.

PhoneApplicationPage_Loaded *Event Handler*

The PhoneApplicationPage_Loaded event handler (Fig. 25.13) is called by the system after a PhoneApplicationPage's constructor has built the app's GUI. You use this method to perform additional tasks that require the GUI to exist—we use this event handler to display values in the **Tip** and **Total** TextBlocks, and to customize the Slider's settings, and to give the TextBox the focus so that the keyboard is displayed when the app appears on the screen. To create this event handler:

1. Select the **[PhoneApplicationPage]** node in the **Document Outline** window.

2. In the **Properties** window, click the **Event handlers** icon (⚡) to display the list of the page's events.

3. Double click the textbox to the right of the **Loaded** event.

4. Insert the code in lines 25–30.

```
21          // executes when app has loaded
22          private void PhoneApplicationPage_Loaded(object sender,
23              RoutedEventArgs e)
24          {
25              // update GUI based on billAmount and customTipPercent
26              update15PercentTip(); // update the 15% tip TextBlocks
27              updateCustomTip(); // update the custom tip TextBlocks
28              customTipPercentSlider.Value = 0.18; // initial value
29              customTipPercentSlider.Maximum = 0.30; // maximum value
30              amountTextBox.Focus(); // give amountTextBox the focus
31          } // end method PhoneApplicationPage_Loaded
32
```

Fig. 25.13 | MainPage class's PhoneApplicationPage_Loaded event handler.

Displaying Initial Values in the **TextBlocks**
Lines 26–27 call methods update15PercentTip (Fig. 25.14) and updateCustomTip (Fig. 25.15) to display initial values in the tip and total TextBlocks.

Customizing the **Slider**'s *Settings*
Lines 28–29 set the customTipPercentSlider's **Value** property to 0.18 (that is, 18%) and its **Maximum** property to 0.30 (a maximum 30% tip).

Giving **amountTextBox** *the Focus*
Line 30 calls the amountTextBox's **Focus** method to make amountTextBox the *active* control on the screen. When a TextBox *receives the focus*, the system displays an appropriate *soft keyboard* on the screen. In Section 25.6, you set the TextBox's InputScope property to Number, so a keyboard that allows only numeric input is displayed in this app. Giving amountTextBox the *focus* as soon as the app is loaded ensures that the *numeric keyboard* is displayed so that the user can begin interacting with the app immediately.

Method **update15PercentTip** *of Class* **MainPage**
Method update15PercentTip (Fig. 25.14) is called from the amountTextBox's Text-Changed event handler to update the 15% tip and total TextBlocks each time the user *changes* the bill amount. The method uses the billAmount value to calculate the tip amount (line 37) and the total of the bill amount and tip (line 38). Lines 41–43 display the amounts in currency format.

```
33          // updates 15% tip TextBlocks
34          private void update15PercentTip()
35          {
36              // calculate 15% tip and total
37              decimal fifteenPercentTip = billAmount * 0.15M;
38              decimal fifteenPercentTotal = billAmount + fifteenPercentTip;
39
40              // display 15% tip and total formatted as currency
41              tip15TextBlock.Text = String.Format("{0:C}", fifteenPercentTip);
42              total15TextBlock.Text =
43                  String.Format("{0:C}", fifteenPercentTotal);
44          } // end method update15PercentTip
45
```

Fig. 25.14 | MainPage method update15PercentTip calculates and displays the 15% tip and total.

Method *updateCustomTip* of Class *MainPage*

Method updateCustomTip (Fig. 25.15) is called from the customTipPercentSlider's ValueChanged event handler to update the tipCustomTextBlock and totalCustomTextBlock based on the customTipPercent. Lines 50–51 set percentCustomTextBlock's text to the customTipPercent value formatted as a percentage. Lines 54–55 calculate the customTip and customTotal. Then, lines 58–59 display the amounts in currency format.

```
46          // updates the custom tip and total TextBlocks
47          private void updateCustomTip()
48          {
49              // show customTipPercent in percentCustomTextBlock formatted as %
50              percentCustomTextBlock.Text =
51                  String.Format("{0:P0}", customTipPercent);
52
53              // calculate the custom tip and total
54              decimal customTip = billAmount * customTipPercent;
55              decimal customTotal = billAmount + customTip;
56
57              // display custom tip and total formatted as currency
58              tipCustomTextBlock.Text = String.Format("{0:C}", customTip);
59              totalCustomTextBlock.Text = String.Format("{0:C}", customTotal);
60          } // end method updateCustomTip
61
```

Fig. 25.15 | MainPage method updateCustomTip calculates and displays customTip and customTotal.

amountTextBox_TextChanged Event Handler

The amountTextBox_TextChanged event handler (Fig. 25.16) is called whenever the user *modifies* the text in the amountTextBox. To create this event handler, double click the amountTextBox in the GUI designer then add the code in lines 66–78. Line 69 attempts to convert the user input in amountTextBox to a decimal and assign it to billAmount. An exception will occur if the TextBox is *empty*, in which case billAmount is set to 0.0M (line 73). Lines 77–78 call methods update15PercentTip and updateCustomTip to recalculate and display the tips and totals.

```
62          // updates 15% tip and total when user enters text in amountTextBox
63          private void amountTextBox_TextChanged(object sender,
64             TextChangedEventArgs e)
65          {
66             // convert amountTextBox's text to a decimal
67             try
68             {
69                billAmount = Convert.ToDecimal(amountTextBox.Text);
70             } // end try
71             catch (FormatException)
72             {
73                billAmount = 0.0M; // default if an exception occurs
74             } // end catch
75
76             // display currency formatted bill amount
77             update15PercentTip(); // update the 15% tip TextBlocks
78             updateCustomTip(); // update the custom tip TextBlocks
79          } // end method amountTextBox_TextChanged
80
```

Fig. 25.16 | MainPage class's amountTextBox_TextChanged event handler.

customTipPercentSlider_ValueChanged *Event Handler*

The customTipPercentSlider_ValueChanged event handler (Fig. 25.17) is called when the user moves customTipPercentSlider's *thumb*. To create this event handler, double click the customTipPercentSlider in the GUI designer, then add the code in lines 85–88. Lines 86–87 get the Slider's current Value, convert it to a decimal and *round* it to two digits after the decimal point. Rounding ensures that customTipPercent always represents a whole number percentage. In this app, the Slider's Value can be *any* value in the range 0.0–0.3, including one like 0.21749567, which would represent 21.749567%. Line 88 calls method updateCustomTip to re-calculate and display the custom tip and total.

```
81          // updates custom tip and total when used changes slider value
82          private void customTipPercentSlider_ValueChanged(object sender,
83             RoutedPropertyChangedEventArgs<double> e)
84          {
85             // sets customTipPercent to position of the Slider's thumb
86             customTipPercent = Math.Round(
87                Convert.ToDecimal(customTipPercentSlider.Value), 2);
88             updateCustomTip(); // update the custom tip TextBlocks
89          } // end method customTipPercentSlider_ValueChanged
90
```

Fig. 25.17 | MainPage class's customTipPercentSlider_ValueChanged event handler.

amountTextBox_LostFocus *Event Handler*

The amountTextBox_LostFocus event handler (Fig. 25.18) is called when the amount-TextBox *loses the focus* because the user touched another control. In this app, this occurs when the user touches the customTipPercentSlider to change its thumb position. Normally, when a TextBox loses the focus, the system *hides* the soft keyboard. In this app, we *force* the keyboard to stay on the screen by calling amountTextBox's Focus method when the TextBox loses the focus. This allows the user to change the bill amount without having to first touch the amountTextBox again. To create this event handler:

1. Select the amountTextBox in the **Document Outline** window or in the GUI.

2. In the **Properties** window, click the **Event handlers** icon to display the list of the TextBox control's events.

3. Double click the textbox to the right of the LostFocus event.

4. Insert the code in line 95.

```
91          // force amountTextBox to keep the focus so keypad remains on screen
92          private void amountTextBox_LostFocus(object sender,
93             RoutedEventArgs e)
94          {
95             amountTextBox.Focus();
96          } // end method amountTextBox_LostFocus
97       } // end class MainPage
98    } // end namespace TipCalculator
```

Fig. 25.18 | MainPage class's amountTextBox_LostFocus event handler.

25.8 WMAppManifest.xml

Each WP8 app project contains the file WMAppManifest.xml. This so-called *manifest file*—located in the project's **Properties** folder in the **Solution Explorer** window—enables you to set various app settings, such as the name and icons that WP8 displays for your app on a device's **Start** screen, a description of your app, device features the app uses (e.g., device sensors, accessing the user's contacts, network connectivity, etc.), hardware requirements for your app (e.g., gyroscope, camera, etc.) and more. None of these settings were required for you to build and test the **Tip Calculator** app. However, you'll need to specify settings in the manifest file for any app you plan to publish in the Windows Phone Store. For more details on the manifest file, visit:

```
bit.ly/WMAppManifest
```

25.9 Windows Phone Dev Center

To test your apps on a Windows phone device and to sell your apps or distribute your free apps through the Windows Phone Marketplace, you'll need to join the **Windows Phone Dev Center** (developer.windowsphone.com/) The website includes development tools, sample code, tips for selling your apps, design guidelines, articles, blogs, videos and forums. In this section we provide an overview of the developer registration process and the websites where you'll find step-by-step guidelines.

25.9.1 Microsoft Account

To get started, you must have a *Microsoft account* (formerly a Windows Live ID). If you do not have an account, you can sign up for free at

```
signup.live.com/signup.aspx?lic=1
```

25.9.2 Windows Phone Dev Center Account

Next, join the Windows Phone Dev Center at dev.windowsphone.com/en-us/register. There's an annual fee of $99, payable by credit card or through your PayPal account. The program is *free* to to MSDN subscribers. As a registered developer you'll have access to tools, sample code, tips for selling your apps, design guidelines and more.

To register, you must provide your country of residence or business. Registration for publishing and getting paid for apps is limited to developers in certain countries:

```
bit.ly/WPCountries
```

You'll also need to select an *account type*—either *company* or *individual.* There's a validation process for company accounts. If you're setting up a company account, you'll receive an e-mail from Symantec with a link that you must click to validate the e-mail account. Symantec may request additional documentation. For more information on validating company accounts, see

```
bit.ly/WPValidateCompanyAcct
```

Next, you'll enter your contact information and create your unique *Publisher Name* which users will see when they download your app. Companies must use their legal company name, which will be checked in the validation process. Individuals may use either their personal name or a "doing business as" name.

Finally, you'll enter either your payment information. Enter your bank account information for electronic deposit or link directly to your PayPal account by providing the mail address associated with it. If you intend to sell your apps or offer in-app purchase, you must also set up a tax profile which contains information such as your social security number or employer tax ID number if you're registering as a corporation. You must also sign the appropriate government tax forms. For more information, see *Getting Paid for Windows Phone* at

```
bit.ly/WPGettingPaid
```

For more information about registering for a Windows Phone Dev Center account, see

```
bit.ly/WPDevCenterAccount
```

25.9.3 Registering a Windows Phone Device for Development

This chapter shows you how to create a WP8 app and test it on an emulator. If you intend to develop apps for distribution in the Windows Phone Store, you should test your apps on a Windows Phone device. To learn how to register a device for testing (and how to un-register the device), see *How to register your phone for development* at

```
bit.ly/WPRegisterPhoneForDev
```

25.10 Selling Your Apps in the Windows Phone Marketplace

You can sell your own Windows Phone apps in the **Windows Phone Marketplace** (www.windowsphone.com/marketplace), similar to other app commerce platforms such as Apple's App Store, Google Play, Facebook's App Center and the Windows Store. You can also earn money by making your apps free for download and selling *virtual goods* (e.g., additional content, game levels, e-gifts and add-on features) using *in-app purchase*.

25.10.1 Free vs. Paid Apps

A recent study by Gartner found that 89% of all mobile apps are free, and that number is likely to increase to 93% by 2016, at which point in-app purchases will account for over 40% of mobile app revenues. [1] Paid WP8 apps range in price from $1.49 (which is higher than the $0.99 starting price for apps in Google Play and Apple's App Store) to $999.99. The average price for mobile apps is generally between $1.50 and $3, depending on the platform. For Windows Phone apps, Microsoft retains 30% of the purchase price and distributes 70% to the app authors. At the time of this writing, there were over 160,000 apps in the Windows Phone Marketplace. [2]

25.10.2 Submitting Your Apps and In-App Products

Before submitting your apps for publication or **In-App Products** (i.e., virtual goods for in-app purchase), make sure that they comply with Microsoft's requirements for Windows Phone apps (Fig. 25.19). Apps that fail to meet the requirements will be rejected by Microsoft—for example if the app includes illegal content, contains pornography or obscene content, encourages harm or violence to others, prevents the user from disabling location services, sells competing mobile services, contains defamatory or threatening content, infringes on trademarks of others and more. This is similar to Apple's strict approval process for iOS apps and different from Google's Android process where apps are *not* vetted, but they could be removed after the fact.

Document	URL
App certification requirements for Windows Phone	bit.ly/WPAppCertificationRequirements
App policies for Windows Phone	bit.ly/WPAppPolicies

Fig. 25.19 | Microsoft's requirements for WP8 apps. (Part 1 of 2.)

---

1. techcrunch.com/2012/09/11/free-apps/.
2. thenextweb.com/microsoft/2013/06/27/microsoft-windows-phones-160000-apps-see-more-than-200-million-downloads-monthly/.

Document	URL
Content policies for Windows Phone	`bit.ly/WPContentPolicies`
App submission requirements for Windows Phone	`bit.ly/WPAppSubmitionRequirements`
Technical certification requirements for Windows Phone	`bit.ly/WPTechnicalCertificationRequirements`
Additional requirements for specific app types for Windows Phone	`bit.ly/WPAdditionalRequirements`

Fig. 25.19 | Microsoft's requirements for WP8 apps. (Part 2 of 2.)

It takes five to seven business days for Microsoft to review a submission for publication in the Windows Phone Store. To learn more about the approval process, see .

> `bit.ly/WPAppApprovalProcess`

25.10.3 Monetizing Apps with Microsoft Advertising pubCenter

Many developers offer free apps monetized with **in-app advertising**—often banner ads similar to those you find on websites. Mobile advertising networks such as **Microsoft Advertising pubCenter** (`adsinapps.microsoft.com/pubcenter`) aggregate advertisers for you and serve relevant ads within your app on the user's device. You can select the advertising categories that are relevant to your users and the size and placement of ads within the app. You earn advertising revenue based on the number of clickthroughs.

Microsoft Advertising pubCenter is available to registered Windows Phone Developers. To register for a pubCenter account, see `pubcenter.microsoft.com/SignUp/WP7`.

25.11 Other Popular Mobile App Platforms

According to ABI Research, 56 billion smartphone apps and 14 billion tablet apps will be downloaded in 2013.[3] By porting your WP8 apps to other mobile app platforms, especially to Android and iOS (for iPhone, iPad and iPod Touch devices) you could reach an even larger audience (Fig. 25.20). The Windows Phone Dev Center also provides information for porting existing iOS, Android and XAML apps to Windows Phone at

> `bit.ly/WPPorting`

Platform	URL	Worldwide app downloads market share
Android	`developer.android.com`	58% of smartphone apps 17% of tablet apps

Fig. 25.20 | Popular mobile app platforms. (`www.abiresearch.com/press/android-will-account-for-58-of-smartphone-app-down`). (Part 1 of 2.)

---

3. `www.abiresearch.com/press/android-will-account-for-58-of-smartphone-app-down`.

Platform	URL	Worldwide app downloads market share
iOS (Apple)	developer.apple.com/ios	33% of smartphone apps 75% of tablet apps
Windows Phone 8	developer.windowsphone.com	4% of smartphone apps 2% of tablet apps
BlackBerry	developer.blackberry.com	3% of smartphone apps
Amazon Kindle	developer.amazon.com	4% of tablet apps

Fig. 25.20 | Popular mobile app platforms. (www.abiresearch.com/press/android-will-account-for-58-of-smartphone-app-down). (Part 2 of 2.)

25.12 Developer Documentation

Figure 25.21 lists some of the key Windows Phone developer documentation.

Document	URL
Windows Phone development	bit.ly/WPDevelopment
Visual Studio Express 2012 for Windows Phone	bit.ly/WPVSExpress
Windows Phone Emulator	bit.ly/WPEmulator
How to create your first app for Windows Phone	bit.ly/WPCreateFirstApp
How to create a new app project from a template for Windows Phone	bit.ly/WPNewAppProject
Design library for Windows Phone	bit.ly/WPDesignLibrary
How to deploy and run a Windows Phone app	bit.ly/WPDeployApp
Windows Phone samples: learn through code	bit.ly/WPSampleCode
Testing apps for Windows Phone	bit.ly/WPTestingApps
Windows Phone Store Test Kit	bit.ly/WPStoreTestKit
App certification requirements for Windows Phone	bit.ly/WPAppCertificationRequirements
Monetizing apps for Windows Phone	bit.ly/WPMonetizing

Fig. 25.21 | Some key Microsoft Windows Phone documentation.

25.13 Additional Windows Phone 8 Resources

Microsoft Guides, Blogs and Tutorials

msdn.microsoft.com/en-us/library/windowsphone/develop/ff402529(v=vs.105).aspx
The Microsoft guide, *Getting started with developing for Windows Phone*, discusses building your first app and testing it on a device.

msdn.microsoft.com/en-us/library/windowsphone/develop/ff402526(v=vs.105).aspx
The Microsoft guide, *How to create your first app for Windows Phone*, walks you through the development of a simple web browser app.

`msdn.microsoft.com/en-us/library/windowsphone/develop/jj206958(v=vs.105).aspx`
The Microsoft Guide, *Speech for Windows Phone 8*, discusses voice commands, speech recognition and text-to-speech and handling errors in speech apps for WP8.

`blogs.msdn.com/b/matthiasshapiro/archive/2013/03/21/10-great-windows-phone-8-code-samples-no-wait-30.aspx`
The MSDN blog, "10 Great Windows Phone 8 Code Samples," by Matthias Shapiro, highlights 10 of the authors favorite sample apps from the Microsoft Windows Phone 8 Samples collection.

`msdn.microsoft.com/en-US/library/windowsphone/develop/hh394031(v=vs.105).aspx`
The guide, *Porting your app to Windows Phone*, from the Windows Phone Dev Center, provides instructions and API mapping tools for porting existing XAML, iOS and Android apps to Windows Phone.

`channel9.msdn.com/Series/Building-Apps-for-Windows-Phone-8-Jump-Start/Building-Apps-for-Windows-Phone-8-Jump-Start-01a-Introducing-Windows-Phone-8-Development-Part-1`
The video tutorial, "Building Apps for Windows Phone 8 Jump Start: Introducing Windows Phone 8 Development Part 1," by Andy Wigley and Rob Tiffany. Topics include WP8 APIs and app development models. The second part of the tutorial discusses designing and building apps, app lifecycle, tiles and lock screen notifications and more.

Other Online Tutorials

`www.youtube.com/watch?v=blU9rBiVURM`
The free video tutorial, "Windows Phone 8 Development—Tutorial 1—New Application."

`codeproject.tv/video/5036055/setting_up_a_command_mvvm_in_windows_phone_8`
The video tutorial, "Setting up a Command (Model View View-Model) in Windows Phone 8," by Michael Crump—a Microsoft MVP.

`www.codeproject.com/Articles/521530/A-Windows-Phone-8-Run-Tracking-App-in-100-Lines-of`
The tutorial, "A Windows Phone 8 Run Tracking App in 100 Lines of Code," by Colin Eberhardt. Topics include the new WP8 map control, tracking the user's location, using live tiles and more.

`www.lynda.com/Visual-Studio-tutorials/Up-Running-Windows-Phone-8-Development/117545-2.html`
The fee-based online training course, "Up and Running with Windows Phone 8 Development," by Doug Winnie. This course teaches introductory WP8 app development. You'll learn how to set up the Visual Studio tools, build a simple tip calculator app in C# and XAML and how to submit your app to the Windows Store.

Nokia Windows Phone Resources

`www.developer.nokia.com/Develop/Windows_Phone/Code_examples/`
Nokia's Windows Phone code examples site includes samples of several fully implemented WP8 apps.

`www.developer.nokia.com/Community/Wiki/Speech_Enabled_Calculator_For_Windows_Phone_8`
The tutorial, "Speech Enabled Calculator For Windows Phone 8." This app uses several APIs including Voice Commands, Speech Recognition and Text To Speech. The tutorial walks you through the development of a calculator app that accepts input and provides output via both touch and speech commands.

Open-Source Windows Phone Tools

`coding4fun.codeplex.com`
Coding4Fun Toolkit includes controls, audio, network and storage wrappers for XAML based apps.

`phone.codeplex.com`
Windows Phone Toolkit from Microsoft's Windows Phone developer platform team includes components for building WP8 apps. The site also includes open source code samples.

`wptools.codeplex.com`
Windows Phone Power Tools—Includes tools for testing updates to existing apps, and a GUI for interacting with your apps.

25.14 Wrap-Up

In this chapter, you created an interactive WP8 app—the **Tip Calculator**. We overviewed the app's capabilities, then you test-drove it to calculate tips based on the bill amount and tip percentage entered. You followed detailed step-by-step instructions to build the app's GUI using the Visual Studio Express 2012 for Windows Phone IDE. In the app's GUI, you used a `Grid` to arrange the controls into rows and columns. You displayed text in `Text-Blocks` and received input from a `TextBox` and a `Slider`. Using the IDE's GUI designer, **Document Outline** window and **Properties** window, you built the app's GUI without manipulating XAML directly.

We also walked through the code of the `PhoneApplicationPage` derived class `Main-Page`, which defines the app's functionality. You responded to its `Loaded` event to customize various controls after they've been created. You handled a `TextBox`'s `TextChanged` event so the app could calculate new tips and totals as the user changed the text in the `TextBox`. You also handled a `Slider`'s `ValueChanged` event so the app could calculate a new custom tip and total as the user changed the custom tip percentage by moving the `Slider`'s *thumb*.

We walked through the registration process for Windows Phone Dev Center so you can test your WP8 apps and distribute them free or for a fee in the Windows Phone Store. We discussed how to prepare apps and in-app products for submission to the Windows Phone Store, including testing them on the emulator and following Microsoft's requirements for Windows Phone apps. We discussed pricing your apps, and resources for monetizing them with in-app advertising and in-app products.

26

Asynchronous Programming with async and await

Objectives
In this chapter you'll:

- Understand what asynchronous programming is and how it can improve the performance of your apps.
- Use the `async` modifier to indicate that a method is asynchronous.
- Use an `await` expression to wait for an asynchronous task to complete execution so that an `async` method can continue its execution.
- Take advantage of multicore processors by executing tasks asynchronously via features of the Task Parallel Library (TPL).
- Use `Task` method `WhenAll` to wait for multiple tasks to complete before an `async` method can continue its execution.
- Time multiple tasks running on single-core and dual-core systems (with the same processor speeds) to determine the performance improvement when these tasks are run on a dual-core system.
- Use a `WebClient` to invoke a web service asynchronously.

26.1 Introduction

It would be nice if we could focus our attention on performing only one action at a time and performing it well, but that's usually difficult to do. The human body performs a great variety of operations *in parallel*—or **concurrently**. Respiration, blood circulation, digestion, thinking and walking, for example, can occur concurrently, as can all the senses—sight, touch, smell, taste and hearing.

Computers, too, can perform operations concurrently. It's common for your computer to compile a program, send a file to a printer and receive electronic mail messages over a network concurrently. Tasks like these that proceed independently of one another are said to execute asynchronously and are referred to as **asynchronous tasks**.

Only computers that have multiple processors or cores can *truly* execute multiple asynchronous tasks concurrently. Visual C# apps can have multiple **threads of execution**, where each thread has its own method-call stack, allowing it to execute concurrently with other threads while sharing with them application-wide resources such as memory and processors. This capability is called **multithreading**. Operating systems on single-core computers create the illusion of concurrent execution by rapidly switching between activities (threads), but on such computers only a *single* instruction can execute at once. Today's multicore computers, smartphones and tablets enable computers to perform tasks truly concurrently.

To take full advantage of multicore architecture you need to write applications that can process tasks *asynchronously*. **Asynchronous programming** is a technique for writing apps containing tasks that can execute asynchronously, which can improve app performance and GUI responsiveness in apps with long-running or compute-intensive tasks. At first, concurrency was implemented with operating system primitives available only to experienced systems programmers. Then programming languages (such as C#) began enabling app developers to specify concurrent operations. Initially these capabilities were complex to use, which led to frequent and subtle bugs. Although the human mind can perform functions concurrently, people find it difficult to jump between parallel trains of thought.

To see why concurrent programs can be difficult to write and understand, try the following experiment: Open three books to page 1 and try reading the books concurrently. Read a few words from the first book, then a few from the second, then a few from the third, then loop back and read the next few words from the first book, and so on. After this experiment, you'll appreciate many of the challenges of multithreading—switching between the books, reading briefly, remembering your place in each book, moving the book you're reading closer so that you can see it and pushing the books you're not reading aside—and, amid all this chaos, trying to comprehend the content of the books!

Visual C# 2012 introduces the async modifier and await operator to greatly simplify asynchronous programming, reduce errors and enable your apps to take advantage of the processing power in today's multicore computers, smartphones and tablets. In .NET 4.5, many classes for web access, file processing, networking, image processing and more have been updated with new methods that return Task objects for use with async and await, so you can take advantage of this new asynchronous programming model.

This chapter presents a simple introduction to asynchronous programming with async and await. It's designed to help you evaluate and start using these capabilities. Our async and await resource center

```
http://www.deitel.com/async
```

provides links to articles and other resources that will help you get a deeper understanding of these capabilities.

26.2 Basics of async and await

Before async and await, it was common for a method that was called *synchronously* (i.e., performing tasks one after another in order) in the calling thread to launch a long-running task *asynchronously* and to provide that task with a *callback method* (or, in some cases, register an event handler) that would be invoked once the asynchronous task *completed*. This style of coding is simplified with async and await.

async *Modifier*

The **async modifier** indicates that a method or lambda expression (introduced in Section 20.5) contains at least one await expression. An async method executes its body in the same thread as the calling method. (Throughout the remainder of this discussion, we'll use the term "method" to mean "method or lambda expression.")

await *Expression*

An **await expression**, which can appear *only* in an async method, consists of the **await operator** followed by an expression that returns an *awaitable entity*—typically a Task object (as you'll see in Section 26.3), though it is possible to create your own awaitable entities. Creating awaitable entities is beyond the scope of our discussion. For more information, see

```
http://blogs.msdn.com/b/pfxteam/archive/2011/01/13/10115642.aspx
```

When an async method encounters an **await** expression:

- If the asynchronous task has already completed, the async method simply continues executing.

- Otherwise, program control returns to the async method's caller until the asynchronous task completes execution. This allows the caller to perform other work that does not depend on the results of the asynchronous task.

When the asynchronous task completes, control returns to the async method and continues with the next statement after the await expression.

The mechanisms for determining whether to return control to the async method's caller or continue executing the async method, and for continuing the async method's execution when the asynchronous task completes are handled entirely by code that's written for you by the compiler.

async, await *and Threads*

The async and await mechanism does *not* create new threads. If any threads are required, the method that you call to start an asynchronous task on which you await the results is responsible for creating the threads that are used to perform the asynchronous task. For example, we'll show how to use class Task's Run method in several examples to start new threads of execution for executing tasks asynchronously. Task method Run returns a Task on which a method can await the result.

26.3 Executing an Asynchronous Task from a GUI App

This section demonstrates the benefits of executing compute-intensive tasks asynchronously in a GUI app.

26.3.1 Performing a Task Asynchronously

Figure 26.1 demonstrates executing an asynchronous task from a GUI app. Consider the GUI at the end of Fig. 26.1. In the GUI's top half, you can enter an integer then click **Calculate** to calculate that integer's Fibonacci value using a compute-intensive recursive implementation (Section 26.3.2). Starting with integers in the 40s (on our test computer), the recursive calculation can take seconds or even minutes to calculate. If this calculation were to be performed *synchronously*, the GUI would *freeze* for that amount of time and the user would not be able to interact with the app (as we'll demonstrate in Fig. 26.2). We launch the calculation *asynchronously* and have it execute on a *separate* thread so the GUI remains *responsive*. To demonstrate this, in the GUI's bottom half, you can click **Next Number** repeatedly to calculate the next Fibonacci number by simply adding the two previous numbers in the sequence. For the screen captures in Fig. 26.1, we used the top-half of the GUI to calculate Fibonacci(45), which took over a minute on our test computer. While that calculation proceeded in a separate thread, we clicked **Next Number** repeatedly to demonstrate that we could still interact with the GUI. Along the way, we were able to demonstrate that the iterative Fibonacci calculation is much more efficient.

```
1   // Fig. 26.1: FibonacciForm.cs
2   // Performing a compute-intensive calculation from a GUI app
3   using System;
4   using System.Threading.Tasks;
5   using System.Windows.Forms;
6
```

Fig. 26.1 | Performing a compute-intensive calculation from a GUI app. (Part 1 of 3.)

```csharp
7   namespace FibonacciTest
8   {
9      public partial class FibonacciForm : Form
10     {
11        private long n1 = 0; // initialize with first Fibonacci number
12        private long n2 = 1; // initialize with second Fibonacci number
13        private int count = 1; // current Fibonacci number to display
14
15        public FibonacciForm()
16        {
17           InitializeComponent();
18        } // end constructor
19
20        // start an async Task to calculate specified Fibonacci number
21        private async void calculateButton_Click(
22           object sender, EventArgs e )
23        {
24           // retrieve user's input as an integer
25           int number = Convert.ToInt32( inputTextBox.Text );
26
27           asyncResultLabel.Text = "Calculating...";
28
29           // Task to perform Fibonacci calculation in separate thread
30           Task< long > fibonacciTask =
31              Task.Run( () => Fibonacci( number ) );
32
33           // wait for Task in separate thread to complete
34           await fibonacciTask;
35
36           // display result after Task in separate thread completes
37           asyncResultLabel.Text = fibonacciTask.Result.ToString();
38        } // end method calculateButton_Click
39
40        // calculate next Fibonacci number iteratively
41        private void nextNumberButton_Click( object sender, EventArgs e )
42        {
43           // calculate the next Fibonacci number
44           long temp = n1 + n2; // calculate next Fibonacci number
45           n1 = n2; // store prior Fibonacci number in n1
46           n2 = temp; // store new Fibonacci
47           ++count;
48
49           // display the next Fibonacci number
50           displayLabel.Text = string.Format( "Fibonacci of {0}:", count );
51           syncResultLabel.Text = n2.ToString();
52        } // end method nextNumberButton_Click
53
54        // recursive method Fibonacci; calculates nth Fibonacci number
55        public long Fibonacci( long n )
56        {
57           if ( n == 0 || n == 1 )
58              return n;
```

Fig. 26.1 | Performing a compute-intensive calculation from a GUI app. (Part 2 of 3.)

```
59              else
60                  return Fibonacci( n - 1 ) + Fibonacci( n - 2 );
61          } // end method Fibonacci
62      } // end class FibonacciForm
63  } // end namespace FibonacciTest
```

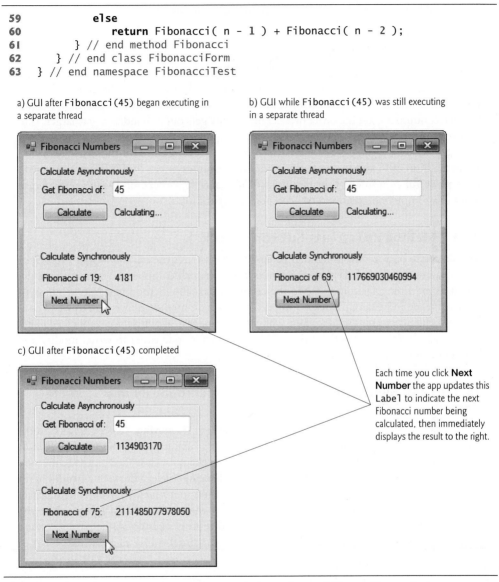

a) GUI after `Fibonacci(45)` began executing in a separate thread

b) GUI while `Fibonacci(45)` was still executing in a separate thread

c) GUI after `Fibonacci(45)` completed

Each time you click **Next Number** the app updates this `Label` to indicate the next Fibonacci number being calculated, then immediately displays the result to the right.

Fig. 26.1 | Performing a compute-intensive calculation from a GUI app. (Part 3 of 3.)

A Compute-Intensive Algorithm: Calculating Fibonacci Numbers Recursively

The powerful technique of recursion was introduced in Section 7.15. The examples in this section and in Sections 26.4–26.5 each perform a compute-intensive *recursive* Fibonacci calculation (defined in the `Fibonacci` method at lines 55–61). The Fibonacci series

> 0, 1, 1, 2, 3, 5, 8, 13, 21, ...

begins with 0 and 1 and has the property that each subsequent Fibonacci number is the sum of the previous two Fibonacci numbers.

The Fibonacci series can be defined *recursively* as follows:

```
Fibonacci(0) = 0
Fibonacci(1) = 1
Fibonacci(n) = Fibonacci(n – 1) + Fibonacci(n – 2)
```

A word of caution is in order about recursive methods like the one we use here to generate Fibonacci numbers. The number of recursive calls that are required to calculate the nth Fibonacci number is on the order of 2^n. This rapidly gets out of hand as n gets larger. Calculating only the 20th Fibonacci number would require on the order of 2^{20} or about a million calls, calculating the 30th Fibonacci number would require on the order of 2^{30} or about a billion calls, and so on. This **exponential complexity** can humble even the world's most powerful computers! Calculating just Fibonacci(47)—even on today's most recent desktop and notebook computers—can take many minutes.

26.3.2 Method `calculateButton_Click`

The **Calculate** button's event handler (lines 21–38) initiates the call to method `Fibonacci` in a separate thread and displays the results when the call completes. The method is declared `async` (line 21) to indicate to the compiler that the method will initiate an asynchronous task and `await` the results. In effect, an `async` method allows you to write code that looks like it executes sequentially, while the compiler deals with the complicated issues of managing asynchronous execution. This makes your code easier to write, modify and maintain, and reduces errors.

26.3.3 Task Method Run: Executing Asynchronously in a Separate Thread

Lines 30–31 create and start a **Task** (namespace **System.Threading.Tasks**). A Task promises to return a result *at some point* in the future. Class Task is part of .NET's *Task Parallel Library (TPL)* for asynchronous programming. The version of class Task's `static` method **Run** used in line 31 receives a **Func<TResult> delegate** (delegates were introduced in Section 14.3.3) as an argument and executes a method in a *separate thread*. The delegate Func<TResult> represents any method that takes *no arguments* and returns a *result*, so the name of any method that takes no arguments and returns a result can be passed to Run. However, Fibonacci requires an argument, so line 31 use the *lambda expression*

```
() => Fibonacci( number )
```

which takes *no arguments* to encapsulate the call to Fibonacci with the argument number. The lambda expression *implicitly* returns the result of the Fibonacci call (a long), so it meets the Func<TResult> delegate's requirements. In this example, Task's `static` method Run creates and returns a Task<long> that represents the task being performed in a separate thread. The compiler *infers* the type long from the return type of method Fibonacci.

26.3.4 `await`ing the Result

Next, line 34 `await`s the result of the `fibonacciTask` that's executing asynchronously. If the `fibonacciTask` is *already complete*, execution continues with line 37. Otherwise, control returns to `calculateButton_Click`'s caller (the GUI event handling thread) until the result of the fibonacciTask is available. This allows the GUI to remain *responsive* while the Task executes. Once the Task completes, calculateButton_Click continues execution at line 37, which uses Task property **Result** to get the value returned by Fibonacci and display it on asyncResultLabel.

It's important to note that an async method can perform other statements between those that launch an asynchronous Task and await the Task's results. In such a case, the method continues executing those statements after launching the asynchronous Task until it reaches the await expression.

Lines 30–34 can be written more concisely as

```
long result = await Task.Run( () => Fibonacci( number ) );
```

In this case, the await operator unwraps and returns the Task's result—the long returned by method Fibonacci. You can then use the long value directly without accessing the Task's Result property.

26.3.5 Calculating the Next Fibonacci Value Synchronously

When you click **Next Number**, the event handler registered in lines 41–52 executes. Lines 44–47 add the previous two Fibonacci numbers stored in instance variables n1 and n2 to determine the next number in the sequence, update n1 and n2 to their new values and increment instance variable count. Then lines 50–51 update the GUI to display the Fibonacci number that was just calculated. The code in the **Next Number** event handler is performed in the GUI thread of execution that processes user interactions with controls. Handling such short computations in this thread does *not* cause the GUI to become unresponsive. Because the longer Fibonacci computation is performed in a *separate thread,* it's possible to get the next Fibonacci number *while the recursive computation is still in progress.*

26.4 Sequential Execution of Two Compute-Intensive Tasks

Figure 26.2 uses the recursive Fibonacci method that we introduced in Section 26.3. The example sequentially performs the calculations fibonacci(46) (line 22) and Fibonacci(45) (line 37) when the user clicks the **Start Sequential Fibonacci Calls** Button. Before and after each Fibonacci call, we capture the time so that we can calculate the total time required for *that* calculation and the total time required for *both* calculations.

The first two outputs show the results of executing the app on a *dual-core* Windows 7 computer. The last two outputs show the results of executing the app on a single-core Windows 7 computer. In all cases, the cores operated at the same speed. The app *always* took longer to execute (in our testing) on the single-core computer, because the processor was being *shared* between this app and all the others that happened to be executing on the computer at the same time. On the dual-core system, one of the cores could have been handling the "other stuff" executing on the computer, reducing the demand on the core that's doing the synchronous calculation. Results may vary across systems based on processor speeds, the number of cores, apps currently executing and the chores the operating system is performing.

```
 1   // Fig. 26.2: SynchronousTestForm.cs
 2   // Fibonacci calculations performed sequentially
 3   using System;
 4   using System.Windows.Forms;
 5
 6   namespace FibonacciSynchronous
 7   {
 8      public partial class SynchronousTestForm : Form
 9      {
10         public SynchronousTestForm()
11         {
12            InitializeComponent();
13         } // end constructor
14
15         // start sequential calls to Fibonacci
16         private void startButton_Click( object sender, EventArgs e )
17         {
18            // calculate Fibonacci (46)
19            outputTextBox.Text = "Calculating Fibonacci(46)\r\n";
20            outputTextBox.Refresh(); // force outputTextBox to repaint
21            DateTime startTime1 = DateTime.Now; // time before calculation
22            long result1 = Fibonacci( 46 ); // synchronous call
23            DateTime endTime1 = DateTime.Now; // time after calculation
24
25            // display results for Fibonacci(46)
26            outputTextBox.AppendText(
27               String.Format( "Fibonacci(46) = {0}\r\n", result1 ) );
28            outputTextBox.AppendText( String.Format(
29               "Calculation time = {0:F6} minutes\r\n\r\n",
30               endTime1.Subtract( startTime1 ).TotalMilliseconds /
31               60000.0 ) );
32
33            // calculate Fibonacci (45)
34            outputTextBox.AppendText( "Calculating Fibonacci(45)\r\n" );
35            outputTextBox.Refresh(); // force outputTextBox to repaint
36            DateTime startTime2 = DateTime.Now;
37            long result2 = Fibonacci( 45 ); // synchronous call
38            DateTime endTime2 = DateTime.Now;
39
40            // display results for Fibonacci(45)
41            outputTextBox.AppendText(
42               String.Format( "Fibonacci( 45 ) = {0}\r\n", result2 ));
43            outputTextBox.AppendText( String.Format(
44               "Calculation time = {0:F6} minutes\r\n\r\n",
45               endTime2.Subtract( startTime2 ).TotalMilliseconds /
46               60000.0 ) );
47
48            // show total calculation time
49            outputTextBox.AppendText( String.Format(
50               "Total calculation time = {0:F6} minutes\r\n",
51               endTime2.Subtract( startTime1 ).TotalMilliseconds /
52               60000.0 ) );
53         } // end method startButton_Click
```

Fig. 26.2 | Fibonacci calculations performed sequentially. (Part 1 of 2.)

```
54
55        // Recursively calculates Fibonacci numbers
56        public long Fibonacci( long n )
57        {
58            if ( n == 0 || n == 1 )
59                return n;
60            else
61                return Fibonacci( n - 1 ) + Fibonacci( n - 2 );
62        } // end method Fibonacci
63    } // end class SynchronousTestForm
64 } // end namespace FibonacciSynchronous
```

a) Outputs on a Dual Core Windows 7 Computer

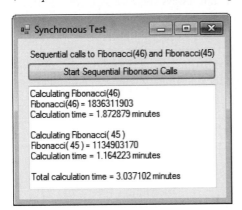
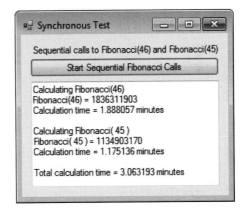

b) Outputs on a Single Core Windows 7 Computer

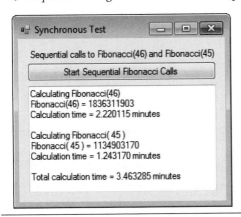
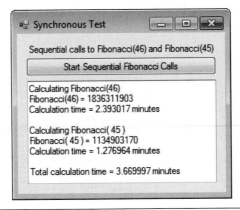

Fig. 26.2 | Fibonacci calculations performed sequentially. (Part 2 of 2.)

26.5 Asynchronous Execution of Two Compute-Intensive Tasks

When you run any program, your program's tasks compete for processor time with the operating system, other programs and other activities that the operating system is running on your behalf. When you execute the next example, the time to perform the Fibonacci calculations can vary based on your computer's processor speed, number of cores and what else is running on your computer. It's like a drive to the supermarket—the time it takes can vary based on traffic conditions, weather, timing of traffic lights and other factors.

Figure 26.3 also uses the recursive Fibonacci method, but the two initial calls to Fibonacci execute in *separate threads*. The first two outputs show the results on a *dual-core* computer. Though execution times varied, the total time to perform both Fibonacci calculations (in our tests) was typically *significantly less* than the total time of the sequential execution in Fig. 26.2. Dividing the compute-intensive calculations into threads and running them on a dual-core system does *not* perform the calculations *twice* as fast, but they'll typically run *faster* than performing the calculations *in sequence* on one core. Though the total time was the compute time for the longer calculation, this is not always the case as there's overhead inherent in using threads to perform separate Tasks.

The last two outputs show that executing calculations in multiple threads on a single-core processor can actually take *longer* than simply performing them synchronously, due to the overhead of sharing *one* processor among the app's threads, all the other apps executing on the computer at the same time and the chores the operating system was performing.

```
 1   // Fig. 26.3: AsynchronousTestForm.cs
 2   // Fibonacci calculations performed in separate threads
 3   using System;
 4   using System.Threading.Tasks;
 5   using System.Windows.Forms;
 6
 7   namespace FibonacciAsynchronous
 8   {
 9      public partial class AsynchronousTestForm : Form
10      {
11         public AsynchronousTestForm()
12         {
13            InitializeComponent();
14         } // end constructor
15
16         // start asynchronous calls to Fibonacci
17         private async void startButton_Click( object sender, EventArgs e )
18         {
19            outputTextBox.Text =
20               "Starting Task to calculate Fibonacci(46)\r\n";
21
22            // create Task to perform Fibonacci(46) calculation in a thread
23            Task< TimeData > task1 =
24               Task.Run( () => StartFibonacci( 46 ) );
25
26            outputTextBox.AppendText(
27               "Starting Task to calculate Fibonacci(45)\r\n" );
28
29            // create Task to perform Fibonacci(45) calculation in a thread
30            Task< TimeData > task2 =
31               Task.Run( () => StartFibonacci( 45 ) );
```

Fig. 26.3 | Fibonacci calculations performed in separate threads. (Part 1 of 3.)

```csharp
32
33          await Task.WhenAll( task1, task2 ); // wait for both to complete
34
35       // determine time that first thread started
36       DateTime startTime =
37          ( task1.Result.StartTime < task2.Result.StartTime ) ?
38          task1.Result.StartTime : task2.Result.StartTime;
39
40       // determine time that last thread ended
41       DateTime endTime =
42          ( task1.Result.EndTime > task2.Result.EndTime ) ?
43          task1.Result.EndTime : task2.Result.EndTime;
44
45       // display total time for calculations
46       outputTextBox.AppendText( String.Format(
47          "Total calculation time = {0:F6} minutes\r\n",
48          endTime.Subtract( startTime ).TotalMilliseconds /
49          60000.0 ) );
50    } // end method startButton_Click
51
52    // starts a call to fibonacci and captures start/end times
53    TimeData StartFibonacci( int n )
54    {
55       // create a TimeData object to store start/end times
56       TimeData result = new TimeData();
57
58       AppendText( String.Format( "Calculating Fibonacci({0})", n ) );
59       result.StartTime = DateTime.Now;
60       long fibonacciValue = Fibonacci( n );
61       result.EndTime = DateTime.Now;
62
63       AppendText( String.Format( "Fibonacci({0}) = {1}",
64          n, fibonacciValue ) );
65       AppendText( String.Format(
66          "Calculation time = {0:F6} minutes\r\n",
67          result.EndTime.Subtract(
68             result.StartTime ).TotalMilliseconds / 60000.0 ) );
69
70       return result;
71    } // end method StartFibonacci
72
73    // Recursively calculates Fibonacci numbers
74    public long Fibonacci( long n )
75    {
76       if ( n == 0 || n == 1 )
77          return n;
78       else
79          return Fibonacci( n - 1 ) + Fibonacci( n - 2 );
80    } // end method Fibonacci
81
82    // append text to outputTextBox in UI thread
83    public void AppendText( String text )
84    {
```

Fig. 26.3 | Fibonacci calculations performed in separate threads. (Part 2 of 3.)

```
85              if ( InvokeRequired ) // not GUI thread, so add to GUI thread
86                  Invoke( new MethodInvoker( () => AppendText( text ) ) );
87              else // GUI thread so append text
88                  outputTextBox.AppendText( text + "\r\n" );
89          } // end method AppendText
90      } // end class AsynchronousTestForm
91  } // end namespace FibonacciAsynchronous
```

a) Outputs on a Dual Core Windows 7 Computer

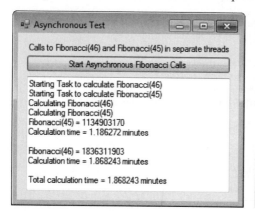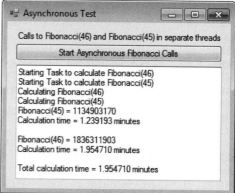

b) Outputs on a Single Core Windows 7 Computer

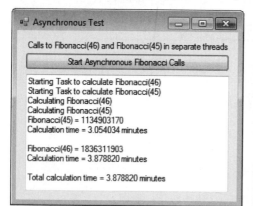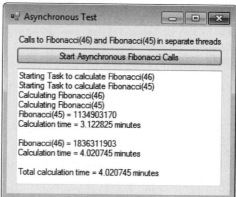

Fig. 26.3 | Fibonacci calculations performed in separate threads. (Part 3 of 3.)

26.5.1 Method startButton_Click: awaiting Multiple Tasks with Task Method WhenAll

In method `startButton_Click`, lines 23–24 and 30–31 use Task method Run to create and start Tasks that execute method `StartFibonacci` (lines 53–71)—one to calculate Fibonacci(46) and one to calculate Fibonacci(45). To show the total calculation time, the app must wait for *both* Tasks to complete *before* executing lines 36–49. You can wait for *multiple* Tasks to complete by awaiting the result of Task static method **WhenAll** (line 33), which returns a Task that waits for *all* of WhenAll's argument Tasks to complete and places *all* the results in an array. In this app, the Task's Result is a TimeData[], because both of WhenAll's argument Tasks execute methods that return TimeData objects. This array can be used to iterate through the results of the awaited Tasks. In this example, we have only two Tasks, so we interact with the task1 and task2 objects directly in the remainder of the event handler.

26.5.2 Method StartFibonacci

Method StartFibonacci (lines 53–71) specifies the task to perform—in this case, to call Fibonacci (line 60) to perform the recursive calculation, to time the calculation (lines 59 and 61), to display the calculation's result (lines 63–64) and to display the time the calculation took (lines 65–68). The method returns a TimeData object (defined in this project's TimeData.cs file) that contains the time before and after each thread's call to Fibonacci. Class TimeData contains public auto-implemented properties StartTime and EndTime, which we use in our timing calculations.

26.5.3 Method AppendText: Modifying a GUI from a Separate Thread

Lines 58, 63 and 65 in StartFibonacci call our AppendText method (lines 83–89) to append text to the outputTextBox. GUI controls are designed to be manipulated *only* by the GUI thread—modifying a control from a non-GUI thread can corrupt the GUI, making it unreadable or unusable. When updating a control from a non-GUI thread, you *must schedule* that update to be performed by the GUI thread. To do so in Windows Forms, you check the **InvokeRequired property** of class Form (line 85). If this property's value is true, the code is executing in a non-GUI thread and *must not* update the GUI directly. Instead, you call the **Invoke** method of class Form (line 86), which receives as an argument a Delegate representing the update to perform in the GUI thread. In this example, we pass a MethodInvoker (namespace System.Windows.Forms), which is a Delegate that invokes a method with no arguments and a void return type. The MethodInvoker is initialized here with a *lambda expression* that calls AppendText. Line 86 *schedules* this MethodInvoker to execute in the GUI thread. When that occurs, line 88 updates the outputTextBox. (Similar concepts also apply to GUIs created with WPF and Windows 8 UI.)

26.5.4 awaiting One of Several Tasks with Task Method WhenAny

Similar to WhenAll, class Task also provides static method **WhenAny**, which enables you to wait for any one of several Tasks specified as arguments to complete. WhenAny returns the Task that completes first. One use of WhenAny might be to initiate several Tasks that perform the same complex calculation on computers around the Internet, then wait for any one of those computers to send results back. This would allow you to take advantage of computing power that's available to you to get the result as fast as possible. In this case, it's up to you to decide whether to cancel the remaining Tasks or allow them to continue executing. For details on how to do this, see

> http://msdn.microsoft.com/en-us/library/vstudio/jj155758.aspx

Another use of WhenAny might be to download several large files—one per Task. In this case, you might want all the results eventually, but would like to immediately start processing the results from the first Task that returns. You could perform a new call to WhenAny for the remaining Tasks that are still executing.

26.6 Invoking a Flickr Web Service Asynchronously with `WebClient`

In this section, we present a **Flickr Viewer** app (Fig. 26.4) that allows you to search for photos on the photo-sharing website Flickr then browse through the results. The app uses an asynchronous method to invoke a Flickr web service. A **web service** is software that can receive method calls over a network using standard web technologies. Flickr provides a so-called REST web service that can receive method calls via standard web interactions, just like you'd use to access a web page in a web browser. (You'll learn more about REST web services in Chapter 28.) Because there can be unpredictably long delays while `awaiting` a web-service response, asynchronous `Tasks` are frequently used in GUI apps that invoke web services (or perform network communication in general) to ensure that the apps remain responsive.

Our **Flickr Viewer** app allows you to search by *tag* for photos that users worldwide have uploaded to Flickr. *Tagging*—or labeling content—is part of the collaborative nature of social media. A tag is any user-supplied word or phrase that helps organize web content. Tagging items with self-chosen words or phrases creates a strong identification of the content. Flickr uses tags on uploaded files to improve its photo-search service, giving the user better results. *To run this example on your computer, you must obtain your own Flickr API key at*

> `http://www.flickr.com/services/apps/create/apply`

and use it to replace the words YOUR API KEY HERE inside the quotes in line 18. This key is a unique string of characters and numbers that enables Flickr to track the usage of its APIs.

```
 1   // Fig. 26.4: FickrViewerForm.cs
 2   // Invoking a web service asynchronously with class WebClient
 3   using System;
 4   using System.Drawing;
 5   using System.IO;
 6   using System.Linq;
 7   using System.Net;
 8   using System.Threading.Tasks;
 9   using System.Windows.Forms;
10   using System.Xml.Linq;
11
12   namespace FlickrViewer
13   {
14      public partial class FickrViewerForm : Form
15      {
16         // Use your Flickr API key here--you can get one at:
17         // http://www.flickr.com/services/apps/create/apply
18         private const string KEY = "YOUR API KEY HERE";
19
20         // object used to invoke Flickr web service
21         private WebClient flickrClient = new WebClient();
22
23         Task<string> flickrTask = null; // Task<string> that queries Flickr
24
```

Fig. 26.4 | Invoking a web service asynchronously with class `WebClient`. (Part 1 of 4.) [Photos used in this example courtesy of Paul Deitel. All rights reserved.]

```
25      public FickrViewerForm()
26      {
27         InitializeComponent();
28      } // end constructor
29
30      // initiate asynchronous Flickr search query;
31      // display results when query completes
32      private async void searchButton_Click( object sender, EventArgs e )
33      {
34         // if flickrTask already running, prompt user
35         if ( flickrTask != null &&
36            flickrTask.Status != TaskStatus.RanToCompletion )
37         {
38            var result = MessageBox.Show(
39               "Cancel the current Flickr search?",
40               "Are you sure?", MessageBoxButtons.YesNo,
41               MessageBoxIcon.Question );
42
43            // determine whether user wants to cancel prior search
44            if ( result == DialogResult.No )
45               return;
46            else
47               flickrClient.CancelAsync(); // cancel current search
48         } // end if
49
50         // Flickr's web service URL for searches
51         var flickrURL = string.Format( "http://api.flickr.com/services" +
52            "/rest/?method=flickr.photos.search&api_key={0}&tags={1}" +
53            "&tag_mode=all&per_page=500&privacy_filter=1", KEY,
54            inputTextBox.Text.Replace( " ", "," ) );
55
56         imagesListBox.DataSource = null; // remove prior data source
57         imagesListBox.Items.Clear(); // clear imagesListBox
58         pictureBox.Image = null; // clear pictureBox
59         imagesListBox.Items.Add( "Loading..." ); // display Loading...
60
61         try
62         {
63            // invoke Flickr web service to search Flick with user's tags
64            flickrTask =
65               flickrClient.DownloadStringTaskAsync( flickrURL );
66
67            // await flickrTask then parse results with XDocument and LINQ
68            XDocument flickrXML = XDocument.Parse( await flickrTask );
69
70            // gather information on all photos
71            var flickrPhotos =
72               from photo in flickrXML.Descendants( "photo" )
73               let id = photo.Attribute( "id" ).Value
74               let title = photo.Attribute( "title" ).Value
75               let secret = photo.Attribute( "secret" ).Value
```

Fig. 26.4 | Invoking a web service asynchronously with class WebClient. (Part 2 of 4.) [Photos used in this example courtesy of Paul Deitel. All rights reserved.]

```
76              let server = photo.Attribute( "server" ).Value
77              let farm = photo.Attribute( "farm" ).Value
78              select new FlickrResult
79              {
80                  Title = title,
81                  URL = string.Format(
82                      "http://farm{0}.staticflickr.com/{1}/{2}_{3}.jpg",
83                      farm, server, id, secret )
84              };
85          imagesListBox.Items.Clear(); // clear imagesListBox
86          // set ListBox properties only if results were found
87          if ( flickrPhotos.Any() )
88          {
89              imagesListBox.DataSource = flickrPhotos.ToList();
90              imagesListBox.DisplayMember = "Title";
91          } // end if
92          else // no matches were found
93              imagesListBox.Items.Add( "No matches" );
94      } // end try
95      catch ( WebException )
96      {
97          // check whether Task failed
98          if ( flickrTask.Status == TaskStatus.Faulted )
99              MessageBox.Show( "Unable to get results from Flickr",
100                 "Flickr Error", MessageBoxButtons.OK,
101                 MessageBoxIcon.Error );
102         imagesListBox.Items.Clear(); // clear imagesListBox
103         imagesListBox.Items.Add( "Error occurred" );
104     } // end catch
105 } // end method searchButton_Click
106
107 // display selected image
108 private async void imagesListBox_SelectedIndexChanged(
109     object sender, EventArgs e )
110 {
111     if ( imagesListBox.SelectedItem != null )
112     {
113         string selectedURL =
114             ( ( FlickrResult ) imagesListBox.SelectedItem ).URL;
115
116         // use WebClient to get selected image's bytes asynchronously
117         WebClient imageClient = new WebClient();
118         byte[] imageBytes = await imageClient.DownloadDataTaskAsync(
119             selectedURL );
120
121         // display downloaded image in pictureBox
122         MemoryStream memoryStream = new MemoryStream( imageBytes );
123         pictureBox.Image = Image.FromStream( memoryStream );
124     } // end if
125 } // end method imagesListBox_SelectedIndexChanged
126 } // end class FlickrViewerForm
127 } // end namespace FlickrViewer
```

Fig. 26.4 | Invoking a web service asynchronously with class `WebClient`. (Part 3 of 4.) [Photos used in this example courtesy of Paul Deitel. All rights reserved.]

Fig. 26.4 | Invoking a web service asynchronously with class `WebClient`. (Part 4 of 4.) [Photos used in this example courtesy of Paul Deitel. All rights reserved.]

As shown in the screen captures of Fig. 26.4, you can type one or more tags (e.g., "pde-itel flowers") into the TextBox. When you click the **Search** Button, the application invokes the Flickr web service that searches for photos, which returns an XML document containing links to the first 500 (or fewer if there are not 500) results that match the tags you specify. We use LINQ to XML (Chapter 22) to parse the results and display a list of photo titles in a ListBox. When you select an image's title in the ListBox, the app uses another asynchronous Task to download the full-size image from Flickr and display it in a PictureBox.

Using Class `WebClient` to Invoke a Web Service

This app uses class **WebClient** (namespace System.Net) to interact with Flickr's web service and retrieve photos that match the tags you enter. Line 21 creates object flickr-Client of class WebClient that can be used, among other things, to download data from a website. Class WebClient is one of many .NET classes that have been updated with new methods in .NET 4.5 to support asynchronous programming with `async` and `await`. In the searchButton_Click event handler (lines 32–105), we'll use class WebClient's DownloadStringTaskAsync method to start a new Task in a separate thread. When we create that Task, we'll assign it to instance variable flickrTask (declared in line 23) so that we can test whether the Task is still executing when the user initiates a new search.

Method `searchButton_Click`

Method searchButton_Click (lines 32–105) initiates the *asynchronous* Flickr search, so it's declared as an async method. First lines 35–48 check whether you started a search previously (i.e., flickrTask is not null and the prior search has not completed) and, if so, whether that search has already completed. If an existing search is still being performed, we display a dialog asking if you wish to cancel the search. If you click **No**, the event handler simply returns. Otherwise, we call the WebClient's **CancelAsync** method to terminate the search.

Invoking the Flickr Web Service's `flickr.photos.search` Method

Lines 51–54 create the URL required for invoking the Flickr web service's method flickr.photos.search. You can learn more about this web-service method's parameters and the format of the URL for invoking the method at

```
http://www.flickr.com/services/api/flickr.photos.search.html
```

In this example, we specify values for the following parameters:

- api_key—Your Flickr API key that you obtained from www.flickr.com/services/apps/create/apply.

- tags—A comma-separated list of the tags for which to search. In our sample executions it was "pdeitel,flowers".

- tag_mode—all to get results that match *all* the tags you specified in your search (or any to get results that match *one or more* of the tags).

- per_page—The maximum number of results to return (up to 500).

- privacy_filter—The value 1 indicates that only *publicly accessible* photos should be returned.

Lines 64–65 call class WebClient's **DownloadStringTaskAsync** method using the URL specified as the method's string argument to request information from a web server. Because this URL represents a call to a web service method, calling `DownloadStringTaskAsync` will invoke the Flickr web service to perform the search. `DownloadStringTaskAsync` creates and starts a *new thread* for you and returns a `Task<string>` representing a promise to eventually return a `string` containing the search results. The app then `await`s the results of the `Task` (line 68). At this point, if the `Task` is complete, method `searchButton_Click`'s execution continues at line 71; otherwise, program control returns to method `searchButton_Click`'s caller until the results are received. This allows the GUI thread of execution to handle other events, so the GUI remains *responsive* while the search is ongoing. Thus, you could decide to start a *different* search at any time (which cancels the original search in this app).

Processing the XML Response

When `Task` completes, program control continues in method `searchButton_Click`. Lines 71–84 process the search results, which are returned in XML format. A sample of the XML is shown in Fig. 26.5.

```
 1   <rsp stat="ok">
 2     <photos page="1" pages="1" perpage="500" total="5">
 3       <photo id="2608518370" owner="8832668@N04" secret="0099e12778"
 4         server="3076" farm="4" title="Fuscia Flowers" ispublic="1"
 5         isfriend="0" isfamily="0"/>
 6       <photo id="2608518732" owner="8832668@N04" secret="76dab8eb42"
 7         server="3185" farm="4" title="Red Flowers 1" ispublic="1"
 8         isfriend="0" isfamily="0"/>
 9       <photo id="2607687273" owner="8832668@N04" secret="4b630e31ba"
10         server="3283" farm="4" title="Red Flowers 2" ispublic="1"
11         isfriend="0" isfamily="0"/>
12       <photo id="2608518890" owner="8832668@N04" secret="98fcb5fb42"
13         server="3121" farm="4" title="Yellow Flowers" ispublic="1"
14         isfriend="0" isfamily="0"/>
15       <photo id="2608518654" owner="8832668@N04" secret="57d35c8f64"
16         server="3293" farm="4" title="Lavender Flowers" ispublic="1"
17         isfriend="0" isfamily="0"/>
18     </photos>
19   </rsp>
```

Fig. 26.5 | Sample XML response from the Flickr APIs.

Once the app receives the XML response from Flickr, line 68 converts the XML `string` returned by the `await` expression into an `XDocument` that we can use with LINQ to XML. The LINQ query (lines 71–84) gathers from each `photo` element in the XML the `id`, `title`, `secret`, `server` and `farm` attributes, then creates an object of our class `FlickrResult` (located in this project's `FlickrResult.cs` file). Each `FlickrResult` contains:

- A `Title` property—initialized with the `photo` element's `title` attribute.
- A `URL` property—assembled from the `photo` element's `id`, `secret`, `server` and `farm` (a *farm* is a collection of servers on the Internet) attributes.

The format of the URL for each image is specified at

```
http://www.flickr.com/services/api/misc.urls.html
```

We use these URLs in the `imagesListBox_SelectedIndexChanged` event handler to download an image that you select from the `ListBox` at the left side of the app.

Binding the Photo Titles to the *ListBox*

If there are any results, lines 87–91 clear any prior results from the `ListBox`, then *bind* the titles of all the new results to the `ListBox`. You cannot bind a LINQ query's result directly to a `ListBox`, so line 89 invokes `ToList` on the `flickrPhotos` LINQ query to convert it to a `List` first, then assigns the result to the `ListBox`'s `DataSource` property. This indicates that the `List`'s data should be used to populate the `ListBox`'s `Items` collection. The `List` contains `FlickrResult` objects, so line 90 sets the `ListBox`'s `DisplayMember` property to indicate that the `Title` property of a `FlickrResult` should be displayed for each item in the `ListBox`.

Method *imagesListBox_SelectedIndexChanged*

Method `imagesListBox_SelectedIndexChanged` (lines 108–125) is declared `async` because it `await`s an *asynchronous* download of a photo. Lines 113–114 get the URL property of the selected `ListBox` item. Line 117 creates a `WebClient` object for downloading the selected photo from `Flickr`. Lines 118–119 invoke the `WebClient`'s **Download-DataTaskAsync** method to get a `byte` array containing the photo and `await` the results. The method uses the URL specified as the method's `string` argument to request the photo from Flickr and returns a `Task<byte[]>`—a promise to return a `byte[]` once the task completes execution. The event handler then `await`s the result. When the `Task` completes, the `await` expression returns the `byte[]`, which is then assigned to `imageBytes`. Line 122 creates a `MemoryStream` from the `byte[]` (which allows reading `bytes` as a stream from an array in memory), then line 123 uses the `Image` class's `static` `FromStream` method to create an `Image` from the byte array and assign it to the `PictureBox`'s `Image` property to display the selected photo.

26.7 Wrap-Up

In this chapter, you learned how to use the `async` modifier, `await` operator and `Tasks` to perform long-running or compute-intensive tasks asynchronously. You learned that tasks that proceed independently of one another are said to execute asynchronously and are referred to as asynchronous tasks.

We showed that multithreading enables threads to execute concurrently with other threads while sharing application-wide resources such as memory and processors. To take full advantage of multicore architecture, we wrote applications that processed tasks asynchronously. You learned that asynchronous programming is a technique for writing apps containing tasks that can execute asynchronously, which can improve app performance and GUI responsiveness in apps with long-running or compute-intensive tasks.

To provide a convincing demonstration of asynchronous programming, we presented several apps:

- The first showed how to execute a compute-intensive calculation asynchronously in a GUI app so that the GUI remained responsive while the calculation executed.

- The second app performed two compute-intensive calculations synchronously (sequentially). When that app executed, the GUI froze because the calculations were performed in the GUI thread. The third app executed the same compute-intensive calculations asynchronously. We executed these two apps on single-core and dual-core computers to demonstrate the performance of each program in each scenario.

- Finally, the fourth app used class WebClient to interact with the Flickr website to search for photos. You learned that class WebClient is one of many built-in .NET Framework classes that can initiate asynchronous tasks for use with async and await.

In the next chapter, we continue our discussion of ASP.NET that began in Chapter 21.

27

Web App Development with ASP.NET: A Deeper Look

Objectives

In this chapter you'll:

- Use the **Web Site Administration Tool** to modify web app configuration settings.
- Restrict access to pages to authenticated users.
- Create a uniform look-and-feel for a website using master pages.
- Use ASP.NET Ajax to improve the user interactivity of your web apps.

27.1 Introduction

In Chapter 21, we introduced ASP.NET and web app development. In this chapter, we introduce several additional ASP.NET web-app development topics, including:

- master pages to maintain a uniform look-and-feel across a web app's pages

- creating a password-protected website with registration and login capabilities

- using the **Web Site Administration Tool** to specify which parts of a website are password protected

- using ASP.NET Ajax to quickly and easily improve the user experience for your web apps, giving them responsiveness comparable to that of desktop apps.

As in Chapter 21, we used Visual Studio Express 2012 for Web to build this chapter's apps.

27.2 Case Study: Password-Protected Books Database App

This case study presents a web app in which a user logs into a password-protected website to view a list of publications by a selected author. The app consists of several ASPX files. For this app, we'll use the **ASP.NET Web Forms Application** template, which is one of several *starter kit*s for ASP.NET-based website development. The templates use Microsoft's recommended practices for organizing a website and separating the website's style (that is, its look and feel) from its content. The default site has three primary pages—**Home, About** and **Contact**—and is pre-configured with *login* and *registration* capabilities. The template also provides so-called master pages for both desktop and mobile web browsers—these provide a common look-and-feel for all the pages in the website.

  We begin by examining some features of the default **ASP.NET Web Forms Application** that the IDE generates when you choose this template. Next, we test drive the completed website to demonstrate the changes we made. Then, we provide step-by-step instructions to guide you through building the website.

There are many additional features in the default website that we do not use in this app. To learn more about the IDE's ASP.NET templates visit:

```
bit.ly/ASPNETtemplates
```

27.2.1 Examining the ASP.NET Web Forms Application Template

To test the default website, you'll begin by creating it. In Chapter 21, you created a new website by selecting **FILE > New Web Site...**. To be able to take advantage of future new ASP.NET features, Microsoft recommends that you use **FILE > New Project...** instead:

1. Select **FILE > New Project...** to display the **New Project** dialog.

2. In the dialog's left column, ensure that **Visual C#** is expanded in the **Templates** node, then select **Web** to display the list of ASP.NET templates.

3. In the dialog's middle column, select **ASP.NET Web Forms Application**.

4. Choose a location for your website, name it Bug2Bug and click **OK** to create it.

Fig. 27.1 shows the website's contents in the **Solution Explorer**. We expanded the Account folder to show you the pages for registration, login and account management.

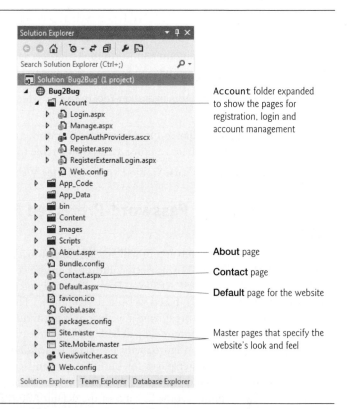

Fig. 27.1 | ASP.NET Web Forms Application in the **Solution Explorer**.

Executing the Website
You can now execute the website. Select the `Default.aspx` page in the **Solution Explorer**, then type *Ctrl + F5* to display the default page shown in Fig. 27.2.

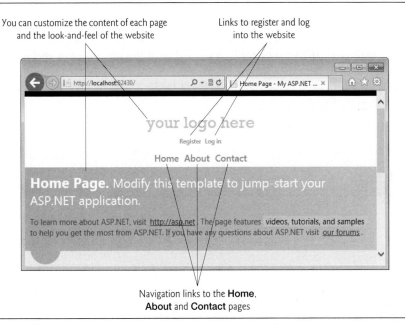

You can customize the content of each page and the look-and-feel of the website

Links to register and log into the website

Navigation links to the **Home**, **About** and **Contact** pages

Fig. 27.2 | Default **Home** page of a website created with the **ASP.NET Web Forms Application** template.

Navigation and Pages
The default website contains **Home**, **About** and **Contact** pages—so-called **content pages**—that you'll customize in subsequent sections. The **Home**, **About** and **Contact** links near the top of the page allow you navigate to each of the site's pages. In Section 27.2.7, you'll add another link to the navigation bar to allow users to browse book information. If you make your browser window wider, the page dynamically adjusts to the new width and reposition the **Register**, **Log in**, **Home**, **About** and **Contact** links to the upper-right corner of the page, and the text **Your Logo Here** to the upper-left corner.

As you navigate between the pages, notice that each page has the same look and feel, with the text **Your Logo Here**, and the **Register**, **Log in**, **Home**, **About** and **Contact** links at the top of the page. This commonality is typical of professional websites. The default site uses a **master page** and cascading style sheets (CSS) to achieve this. A master page defines common GUI elements that are displayed by each page in a set of content pages. Just as C# classes can inherit instance variables and methods from existing classes, content pages can inherit elements from master pages—this is a form of visual inheritance.

Login and Registration Support
Websites commonly provide "membership capabilities" that allow users to register at a website and log in. The default **ASP.NET Web Forms Application** is pre-configured to sup-

port registration and login capabilities. The default website has a pre-configured registration database that stores usernames and passwords. In addition, ASP.NET websites now provide capabilities for logging in with OAuth and OpenID services like Facebook, Twitter and Google. You can learn more about this at

    bit.ly/ASPNETOAuthOpenID

At the top of each page are **Register** and **Log in** links. You can log in only if you've previously registered. If you are already registered with the site, you can click the **Log In** link then log in with your username and password. Since this is the first time the site has been executed, you'll need to register to be able to log in. Click the **Register** link to display the **Register** page (Fig. 27.3).

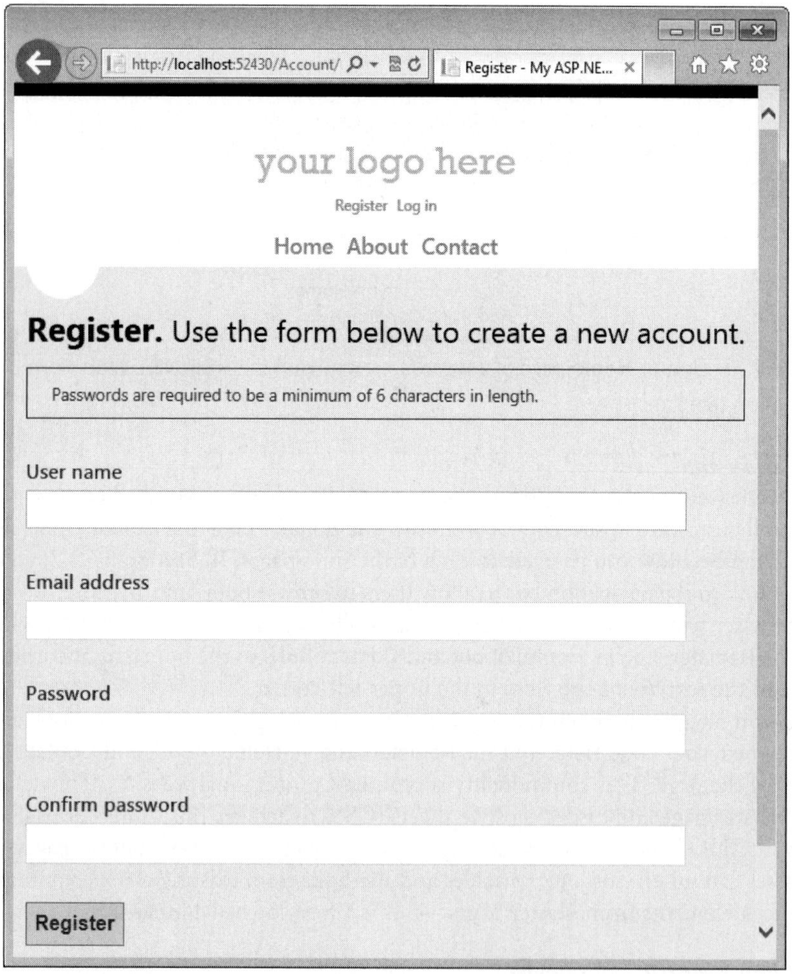

Fig. 27.3 | Registration page.

For the purpose of this case study, we created an account with the username `testuser1` and the password `testuser1`. When you're logged into the site, the **Log in** link changes to a **Log off** link and the **Register** link is replaced with

Hello, *YourUserName*

where *YourUserName* is a link to a page where you can manage your account (e.g., to change your password). You do not need to be registered or logged into the default website to view the **Home**, **About** and **Contact** pages, but you will need to log into the final version of the Bug2Bug website to view the **Books** page.

27.2.2 Test-Driving the Completed App

This example uses *authentication* to protect a page so that only registered users who are logged into the website can access the page. Such users are known as the site's members. Authentication is a crucial tool for a site that allows only members to view protected or premium content. In this app, website visitors must log in before they're allowed to view the publications in the Books database.

Let's open the completed Bug2Bug website and execute it so that you can see the authentication functionality in action. Perform the following steps:

1. Close the app you created in Section 27.2.1—you'll reopen this website so that you can customize it in Section 27.2.3.

2. Open the Bug2Bug.sln file located in the Bug2Bug folder with this chapter's examples.

The website appears as shown in Fig. 27.4. We modified the site's master page so that the top of the page displays an image. Also, the navigation bar contains a link for the **Books** page that you'll create later in this case study.

Fig. 27.4 | **Home** page for the completed Bug2Bug website.

Try to visit the **Books** page by clicking the **Books** link in the navigation bar. Because this page is password protected in the Bug2Bug website, the website automatically redirects you to the **Login** page instead—you cannot view the **Books** page without logging in first. If you've not yet registered at the completed Bug2Bug website, click the **Register** link to create a new account. If you have registered, log in now.

If you are logging in, when you click the **Log in** Button on the **Log In** page, the website attempts to validate your username and password by comparing them with the usernames and passwords that are stored in a database on the server—this database is created for you with the **ASP.NET Web Forms Application** template. If there's a match, you are **authenticated** (that is, your identity is confirmed) and you're redirected to the **Books** page (Fig. 27.5). If you're registering for the first time, the server ensures that you've filled out the registration form properly, then logs you in and redirects you to the **Books** page.

Fig. 27.5 | Books.aspx displaying a drop-down list for selecting an author.

The **Books** page provides a drop-down list of authors and a table containing the ISBNs, titles, edition numbers and copyright years of books in the database. By default, the page displays only the drop-down list until you make a selection. Links appear at the bottom of the table that allow you to access additional pages of data—we configured the table to display only four rows of data at a time. When the user chooses an author, a postback occurs, and the page is updated to display information about books written by the selected author (Fig. 27.6).

Logging Out of the Website
When you're logged in, the **Log In** link is replaced in each page with the message "Hello, *username*" where *username* is your log in name, and a **Log off** link. When you click **Log off**, the website redirects you to the **Home** page (Fig. 27.4).

Fig. 27.6 | `Books.aspx` displaying books by Paul Deitel.

27.2.3 Configuring the Website

Now that you're familiar with how this app behaves, you'll modify the default website you created in Section 27.2.1. Thanks to the default website's rich functionality, the only C# code you'll write for this example is in the code-behind file for the new Books page that you'll add to the site. The **ASP.NET Web Forms Application** template hides the details of authenticating users against a database of user names and passwords, displaying appropriate success or error messages and redirecting the user to the correct page based on the authentication results. We now discuss the steps you must perform to create the password-protected books database app.

Step 1: Opening the Website
Open the default website that you created in Section 27.2.1.

Step 2: Setting Up Website Folders
For this website, you'll create a new folder for the password-protected page. Such parts of your website are typically placed in one or more separate folders. As you'll see shortly, you can control access to specific folders in a website.

You can choose any name you like for the new folder—we chose `ProtectedContent` for the folder that will contain the password-protected **Books** page. To create the folder, right click the project name in the **Solution Explorer**, select **Add > New Folder** and type the name ProtectedContent.

Step 3: Importing the Website Header Image
At the top of each page in the final Bug2Bug website, you saw a header image. Next, you'll add that image to the project's Images folder:

1. In Windows Explorer, locate the folder containing this chapter's examples.

2. Drag the image bug2bug.png from the images folder in Windows Explorer into the Images folder in the **Solution Explorer** to copy the image into the website.

Step 4: Opening the Web Site Administration Tool
In this app, we want to ensure that only authenticated users are allowed to access Books.aspx (which you'll create in Section 27.2.5) to view the information in the database. Previously, we created all of our ASPX pages in a website's root directory. By default, any website visitor (regardless of whether the visitor is authenticated) can view pages in the root directory. ASP.NET allows you to restrict access to particular folders of a website. We do not want to restrict access to the root of the website, however, because users won't be able to view any pages of the website except the login and registration pages. To restrict access to the **Books** page, we place it in a folder other than the project's root folder, then restrict access to that folder. You'll now configure the website to allow only authenticated users (that is, users who have logged in) to view the pages in the ProtectedContent folder. Perform the following steps:

1. Select **PROJECT > ASP.NET Configuration** to open the **Web Site Administration Tool** in a web browser (Fig. 27.7). This tool allows you to configure various options that determine how your site behaves.

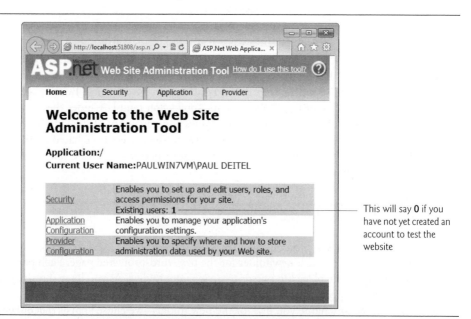

Fig. 27.7 | **Web Site Administration Tool** for configuring a web app.

2. Click either the **Security** link or the **Security** tab to open a web page in which you can set security options (Fig. 27.8), such as the type of authentication the app should use. By default, website users are authenticated by entering username and password information in a web form.

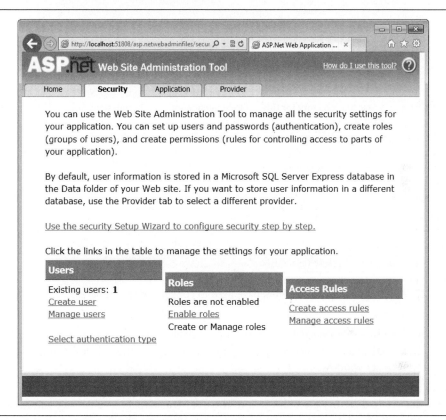

Fig. 27.8 | **Security** page of the **Web Site Administration Tool**.

Step 5: Configuring the Website's Security Settings

Next, you'll configure the ProtectedContent folder to grant access only to authenticated users—anyone who attempts to access pages in this folder without first logging in will be redirected to the **Login** page. Perform the following steps:

1. Click the **Create access rules** link in the **Access Rules** column of the **Web Site Administration Tool** (Fig. 27.8) to view the **Add New Access Rule** page (Fig. 27.9). This page is used to create an **access rule**—a rule that grants or denies access to a particular directory for a specific user or group of users.

2. Select the ProtectedContent directory in the left column of the page to identify the directory to which our access rule applies.

3. In the middle column, select the radio button marked **Anonymous users** to specify that the rule applies to users who have not been authenticated.

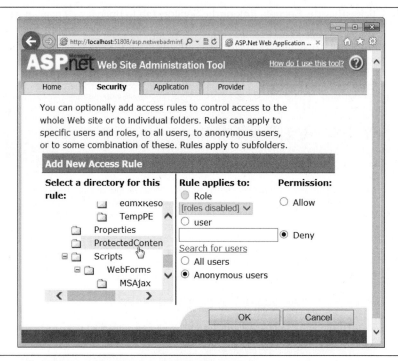

Fig. 27.9 | **Add New Access Rule** page used to configure directory access.

4. Finally, select **Deny** (the default) in the **Permission** column to prevent unauthenticated users from accessing pages in this directory, then click **OK** and close the browser window.

By default, unauthenticated (anonymous) users who attempt to load a page in the ProtectedContent directory are redirected to the Login.aspx page so that they can identify themselves. Because we did not set up any access rules for the Bug2Bug root directory, anonymous users may still access pages there.

27.2.4 Modifying the Home and About Pages

We modified the **Home** (Default.aspx) and **About** (About.aspx) pages to replace the default content. For this example, we did not modify the default content in the **Contact** page but you should edit the page if you intend to make your website publicly accessible.

Modifying the Home Page
For the **Home** page, perform the following steps:

1. Double click Default.aspx in the **Solution Explorer** to open it, then switch to **Design** view (Fig. 27.10). As you move the cursor over the page, you'll notice that sometimes the cursor displays as ⊘ to indicate that you cannot edit the part of the page behind the cursor. Any part of a content page that is defined in a master page can be edited only in the master page.

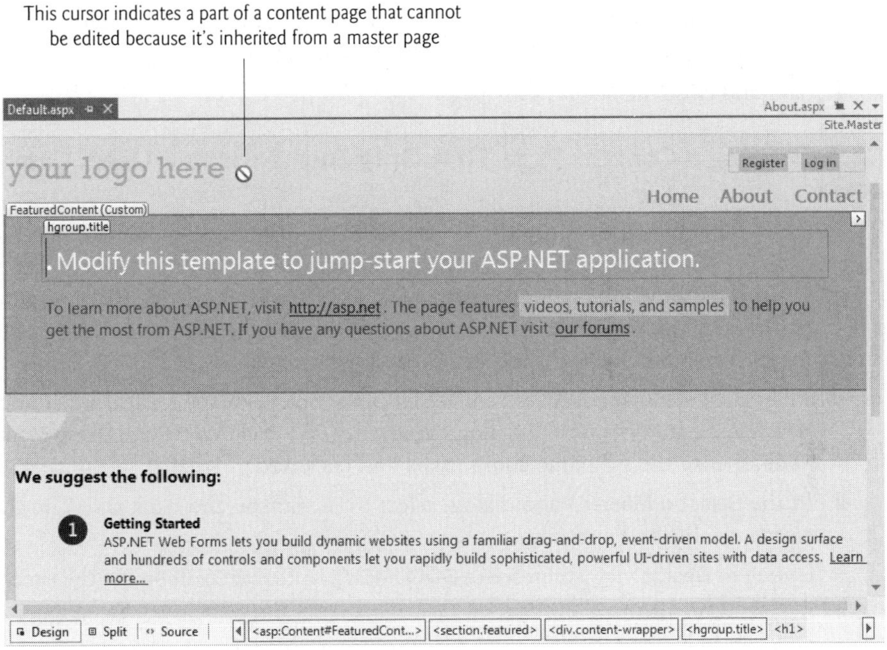

This cursor indicates a part of a content page that cannot
be edited because it's inherited from a master page

Fig. 27.10 | Default.aspx page in **Design** view.

2. There are two predefined content areas that you can change in Default.aspx—
   FeaturedContent (light blue background just below the page header) and Main-
   Content (light gray background). For this example, we deleted the content in
   MainContent.

3. In the FeaturedContent section, change the text "Modify this template to
   jump-start your ASP.NET application." to "Welcome to Our Password-
   Protected Book Information Site."

4. Select the text of the other paragraph in the FeaturedContent section and replace
   it with "To learn more about our books, click here or click the Books tab in
   the navigation bar above. You must be logged in to view the Books page."
   In a later step, you'll link the words "click here" to the **Books** page.

5. Save and close the Default.aspx page.

Modifying the About Page
For the **About** page, perform the following steps:

1. Open About.aspx and switch to **Design** view. There are two predefined content
   areas that you can change in About.aspx—named MainContent and aside (located at the right side of the page). For this example, we deleted the content in
   aside.

2. In the MainContent section of the page, change the text "Your app description
   page." to "Bug2Bug password-protected book information example."

3. Replace the text of the next three paragraphs with, "This database-driven example demonstrates how to use the ASP.NET Web Forms Application template and how to password protect portions of your site."

4. Save and close the About.aspx page.

27.2.5 Creating a Content Page That Only Authenticated Users Can Access

We now create the Books.aspx file in the ProtectedContent folder—the folder for which we set an access rule denying access to anonymous users. If an unauthenticated user requests this file, the user will be redirected to Login.aspx. From there, the user can either log in or create a new account, both of which will authenticate the user, then redirect back to Books.aspx. To create the page, perform the following steps:

1. Right click the ProtectedContent folder in the **Solution Explorer** and select **Add > New Item....** In the resulting dialog's **Web** category, select **Web Form Using Master Page**, specify the file name Books.aspx and click **Add**.

2. In the **Select a Master Page** dialog, select Site.master and click **OK**. The IDE creates the file and opens it.

3. Switch to **Design** view, then select **DOCUMENT** from the ComboBox in the **Properties** window.

4. Change the Title property to Books, then save and close the page.

You'll customize this page and create its functionality shortly.

27.2.6 Linking from the Default.aspx Page to the Books.aspx Page

Next, you'll add a hyperlink from the text "click here" in the Default.aspx page to the Books.aspx page. To do so, perform the following steps:

1. Open the Default.aspx page and switch to **Design** view.

2. Select the text "click here".

3. Select **FORMAT > Convert to Hyperlink** to display the **Hyperlink** dialog. You can enter a URL here, or you can link to another page within the website.

4. Click the **Browse...** Button to display the **Select Project Item** dialog, which allows you to select another page in the website.

5. In the left column, select the ProtectedContent directory.

6. In the right column, select Books.aspx, then click **OK** to dismiss the **Select Project Item** dialog and click **OK** again to dismiss the **Hyperlink** dialog.

When browsing the website, users can now click the **click here** link in the Default.aspx page to browse to the Books.aspx page. If a user is not logged in, clicking this link will redirect the user to the **Login** page.

27.2.7 Modifying the Master Page (Site.master)

Next, you'll modify the website's master page, which defines the common elements we want to appear on each page. A master page is like a base class in an inheritance hierarchy, and content pages are like derived classes. The master page contains placeholders for custom content created in each content page. The content pages visually inherit the master page's content, then add content in the areas designated by the master page's placeholders.

For example, it's common for every page in a website to include navigation links for navigating to other pages on the site. If a site encompasses a large number of pages, adding markup to create the navigation bar for each page can be time consuming. Moreover, if you subsequently modify the navigation bar, every page on the site that uses it must be updated. By creating a master page, you can specify the navigation-bar in one file and have it appear on all the content pages. If the navigation links change, you need to modify only the master page—any content pages that use it are updated the next time the page is requested.

In the final version of this website, we modified the master page to include the Bug2Bug logo in the header at the top of every page.

Inserting an Image in the Header

To display the logo, you'll replace the text "your logo here" with an image in the header of the master page. Each content page based on this master page will include the logo. Perform the following steps to add the image:

1. Open Site.master and switch to **Design** view.

2. Delete the text "your logo here" at the top of the page.

3. In the **Toolbox**, double click **Image** to add an Image control where the text used to be.

4. Edit the Image control's ImageUrl property to point to the bug2bug.png image in the Images folder.

Adding a **Books** Link to the Navigation Links

Next, you'll add a link to the **Books** page. This will appear with the other links at the top of the each page. The easiest way to do this is to edit the master page's markup directly. Perform the following steps:

1. Switch to **Source** view to edit the master page's markup.

2. Locate the following line of code:

   ```
   <li><a runat="server" href="~/About">About</a></li>
   ```

   This represents the link to the site's **About** page. Copy this line of code and paste the copy *above* the existing line.

3. In the new copy, replace "~/About" with "~/ProtectedContent/Books" and About with Books. This creates a link to the Books.aspx page in the website's ProtectedContent folder. The new line of code should now appear as follows:

   ```
   <li><a runat="server" href="~/ProtectedContent/Books">Books
   </a></li>
   ```

4. Save and close the Site.master to complete the changes to the master page.

27.2.8 Customizing the Password-Protected Books.aspx Page

You're now ready to customize the Books.aspx page to display the book information for a particular author. The Books.aspx page will provide a DropDownList containing authors' names and a GridView displaying information about books written by the author selected in the DropDownList. A user will select an author from the DropDownList to cause the GridView to display information about only the books written by the selected author.

Creating the Entity Data Model for the *Books* Database

To work with the Books database through LINQ, first you need to generate the Entity Data Model classes based on the Books database that you used in Chapter 20—Books.mdf is provided in the databases directory of this chapter's examples folder. Perform the following steps:

1. Right click the project name in the Solution Explorer and select **Add > Add New Item...** to display the **Add New Item** dialog.

2. Select the **Data** category in the left column, then **ADO.NET Entity Data Model** in the middle column. Change the **Name** to BooksModel.edmx and click **Add**.

3. In the **Entity Data Model Wizard**'s **Choose Model Contents** step, select **Generate from Database** and click **Next >**.

4. In the **Choose Your Data Connection** step, click **New Connection....**

5. In the **Connection Properties** dialog, click **Browse...** then select the Books.mdf file (located in the databases folder with this chapter's examples) and click **Open**. Click **OK** to dismiss the **Connection Properties** dialog and click **Next >** in the **Entity Data Model Wizard**.

6. A dialog appears indicating that the data file (Books.mdf) is not in the project. Click **Yes** to copy it to the project.

7. In the **Entity Data Model Wizard** dialog's **Choose Your Database Objects and Settings** step, check the **Tables** node so that all three database tables (AuthorISBN, Authors and Titles) will be part of the Entity Data Model. By default, the IDE names the model BooksModel. Ensure that **Pluralize or singularize generated object names** is checked, keep the other default settings and click **Finish**. The IDE displays the BooksModel in the editor. Save the Entity Data Model then select **BUILD > Build Solution** to ensure that the model's new classes are compiled.

Adding a *DropDownList* to Display the Authors' First and Last Names

Now that you've created the model, you'll add controls to Books.aspx that will display the data on the web page. First, you'll add a DropDownList for selecting an author. Normally, only one database column's value can be displayed in a DropDownList. For that reason, you'll configure a custom query to display each author's full name.

1. Open Books.aspx in **Design** mode, then add the text Select author: and a DropDownList control named authorsDropDownList in the page's MainContent area. The DropDownList initially displays the text Unbound. In this app, you'll programmatically bind the results of a LINQ to Entities query to the authorsDropDownList.

2. Set the authorsDropDownList control's **AutoPostBack** property to True. This property indicates that a postback occurs each time the user selects an item in the DropDownList. As you'll see shortly, this enables us to populate the GridView with new data based on the user's selection.

3. Double click the `authorsDropDownList` control to create its `SelectedIndex-Changed` event handler, which is called when the user makes a new selection in the `DropDownList`.

Creating a GridView to Display the Selected Author's Books

Next, you'll add a `GridView` to `Books.aspx` for displaying the book information for the author selected in the `authorsDropDownList`.

1. Insert the cursor to the right of the `authorsDropDownList` then press *Enter* to create a new paragraph.

2. Add a `GridView` named `titlesGridView` to the new paragraph.

3. In the `GridView`'s smart tasks menu, click **Auto Format....** In the dialog that appears, select **Professional** and click **OK** to give the `GridView` a nicer look and feel.

Code-Behind File for the Books Page

Figure 27.11 shows the code for the completed code-behind file. Line 12 defines the `DbContext` object that's used in the LINQ queries that are bound to the `Books` page's controls.

```
1   // Fig. 27.11: Books.aspx.cs
2   // Code-behind file for the password-protected Books page.
3   using System;
4   using System.Data.Entity;
5   using System.Linq;
6
7   namespace Bug2Bug.ProtectedContent
8   {
9      public partial class Books : System.Web.UI.Page
10     {
11        // Entity Framework DbContext
12        BooksEntities dbcontext = new BooksEntities();
13
14        // Load event handler for Books page
15        protected void Page_Load(object sender, EventArgs e)
16        {
17           // if this is the first time the page is loading
18           if (!IsPostBack)
19           {
20              dbcontext.Authors.Load(); // load Authors table into memory
21
22              // LINQ query that populates authorsDropDownList
23              var authorsQuery =
24                 from author in dbcontext.Authors.Local
25                 orderby author.LastName, author.FirstName
26                 select new
27                 {
28                    Name = author.LastName + ", " + author.FirstName,
29                    author.AuthorID
30                 };
31
```

Fig. 27.11 | Code-behind file for the password-protected **Books** page. (Part 1 of 2.)

```
32                    // specify the field used as the selected value
33                    authorsDropDownList.DataValueField = "AuthorID";
34
35                    // specify the field displayed in the DropDownList
36                    authorsDropDownList.DataTextField = "Name";
37
38                    // set authorsQuery as the authorsDropDownList's data source
39                    authorsDropDownList.DataSource = authorsQuery;
40
41                    authorsDropDownList.DataBind(); // displays query results
42                } // end if
43            } // end method Page_Load
44
45            // display selected author's books
46            protected void authorsDropDownList_SelectedIndexChanged(
47                object sender, EventArgs e)
48            {
49                dbcontext.Authors.Load(); // load Authors table into memory
50
51                // use LINQ to get Author object for the selected author
52                Author selectedAuthor =
53                    (from author in dbcontext.Authors.Local
54                     where author.AuthorID ==
55                         Convert.ToInt32(authorsDropDownList.SelectedValue)
56                     select author).First();
57
58                // query to get books for the selected author
59                var titlesQuery =
60                    from book in selectedAuthor.Titles
61                    orderby book.Title1
62                    select book;
63
64                // set titlesQuery as the titlesGridView's data source
65                titlesGridView.DataSource = titlesQuery;
66                titlesGridView.DataBind(); // displays query results
67            } // end method authorsDropDownList_SelectedIndexChanged
68        } // end class Books
69    } // end namespace Bug2Bug.ProtectedContent
```

Fig. 27.11 | Code-behind file for the password-protected **Books** page. (Part 2 of 2.)

Page_Load *Event Handler*

When the Page_Load event handler (lines 15–43) executes, it first determines whether the
Load event was due to a *postback*. If not, line 20 loads the database's Authors table so that
we can query it to populate the authorsDropDownList. Lines 23–30 define a LINQ query
that combines the author names so that they're can be displayed in the format *LastName,
FirstName* in the DropDownList. The query's results are anonymous objects that each con-
tain a Name and an AuthorID property. Line 33 indicates that the value of the authors-
DropDownList's selected item will be the author's AuthorID, and line 36 indicates that the
the authorsDropDownList will display the authors Name. Line 39 sets authorsDropDown-
List's data source to the results of the LINQ query. Calling DataBind on the authors-
DropDownList loads the query results.

authorsDropDownList_SelectedIndexChanged *Event Handler*

When the user selects an author from the authorsDropDownList, the authorsDropDown-List_SelectedIndexChanged event handler (lines 46–67) loads the author's books into the titlesGridView. First, line 49 loads the database's Authors table so that we can get the selected author's Author object (lines 52–56). There can be only one match for the selected author's AuthorID, so we use LINQ extension method First to get the Author object from the LINQ query result. The titlesQuery (lines 59–62) sorts the author's books by title. Line 65 sets the query as titlesGridView's data source, then line 66 calls Data-Bind to populate the GridView with the author's books.

27.3 ASP.NET Ajax

In this section, you learn the difference between a traditional web app and an **Ajax (Asynchronous JavaScript and XML) web app**. You also learn how to use **ASP.NET Ajax** to quickly and easily improve the user experience for your web apps. To demonstrate ASP.NET Ajax capabilities, you enhance the validation example of Section 21.6 by displaying the submitted form information without reloading the entire page. The only modifications to this web app appear in the Validation.aspx file. You use Ajax-enabled controls to add this feature.

27.3.1 Traditional Web Apps

Figure 27.12 presents the typical interactions between the client and the server in a traditional web app, such as one that uses a user registration form. The user first fills in the form's fields, then submits the form (Fig. 27.12, *Step 1*). The browser generates a request to the server, which receives the request and processes it (*Step 2*). The server generates and sends a response containing the exact page that the browser renders (*Step 3*), which causes the browser to load the new page (*Step 4*) and temporarily makes the browser window blank. The client *waits* for the server to respond and *reloads the entire page* with the data

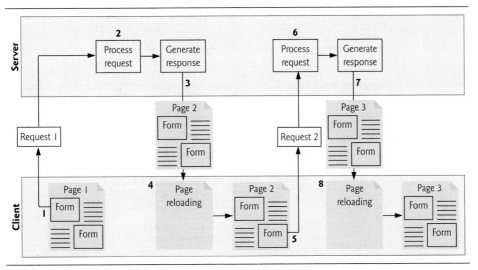

Fig. 27.12 | Traditional web app reloading the page for every user interaction.

from the response (*Step 4*). While such a **synchronous request** is being processed on the server, the user cannot interact with the web page for an indeterminate period of time. If the user interacts with and submits another form, the process begins again (*Steps 5–8*).

This model was designed for a web of hypertext documents—what some people called the "brochure web." As the web evolved into a full-scale apps platform, the model shown in Fig. 27.12 yielded "choppy" user experiences. Every full-page refresh required users to reload the full page. Users began to demand a more responsive model.

27.3.2 Ajax Web Apps

Ajax web apps add a layer between the client and the server to manage communication between the two (Fig. 27.13). When the user interacts with the page, the client requests information from the server (*Step 1*). The request is intercepted by the ASP.NET Ajax controls and sent to the server as an **asynchronous request** (*Step 2*)—the user can continue interacting with the app in the client browser while the server processes the request. Other user interactions could result in additional requests to the server (*Steps 3 and 4*). Once the server responds to the original request (*Step 5*), the ASP.NET Ajax control that issued the request calls a client-side function to process the data returned by the server. This function—known as a **callback function**—uses **partial-page updates** (*Step 6*) to display the data in the existing web page *without reloading the entire page*. At the same time, the server may be responding to the second request (*Step 7*) and the client browser may be starting another partial-page update (*Step 8*). The callback function updates only a designated part of the page. Such partial-page updates help make web apps more responsive, making them feel more like desktop apps. The web app does not load a new page while the user interacts with it. In the following section, you use ASP.NET Ajax controls to enhance the `Validation.aspx` page.

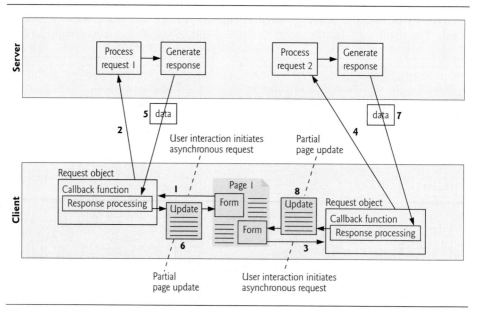

Fig. 27.13 | Ajax-enabled web app interacting with the server asynchronously.

27.3.3 Testing an ASP.NET Ajax App

To demonstrate ASP.NET Ajax capabilities, you'll enhance the **Validation** app from Section 21.6 by adding ASP.NET Ajax controls. There are no C# code modifications to this app—all of the changes occur in the `.aspx` file.

Testing the App in Your Default Web Browser
To test this app in your default web browser, perform the following steps:

1. Open the **Validation** app's project by double clicking its `Validation.sln` file (located in the `Validation` folder with this chapter's examples).

2. Select `Validation.aspx` in the **Solution Explorer**, then type *Ctrl + F5* to execute the web app in your default web browser.

Figure 27.14 shows a sample execution of the enhanced app. In Fig. 27.14(a), we show the contact form split into two tabs via the `TabContainer` Ajax control. You can switch between the tabs by clicking the title of each tab. Fig. 27.14(b) shows a `ValidatorCalloutExtender` control, which displays a validation error message in a callout that points to the control in which the validation error occurred, rather than as text in the page. Fig. 27.14(c) shows the updated page with the data the user submitted to the server.

a) Entering a name on the **Name** tab then clicking the **Contact** tab

b) Entering an e-mail address in an incorrect format and pressing the *Tab* key to move to the next input field causes a callout to appear informing the user to enter an e-mail address in a valid format

Fig. 27.14 | **Validation** app enhanced by ASP.NET Ajax. (Part 1 of 2.)

c) After filling out the form properly and clicking **Submit**, the submitted data is displayed at the bottom of the page with a partial page update

Fig. 27.14 | **Validation** app enhanced by ASP.NET Ajax. (Part 2 of 2.)

27.3.4 The ASP.NET Ajax Control Toolkit

There's a tab of basic **AJAX Extensions** controls in the **Toolbox**. Microsoft also provides the **ASP.NET Ajax Control Toolkit** that contains many more Ajax-enabled, rich GUI controls. In this section, you'll open the original Validation example from Chapter 21, use Visual Studio's *NuGet package manager* to add the Ajax Control Toolkit to the project, then incorporate the toolkit's controls into your **Toolbox**. In subsequent sections, you'll then use the toolkit's TabContainer control to enhance the Validation example with Ajax capabilities. To learn more about the toolkit's many other extenders and controls, visit:

```
www.asp.net/ajaxlibrary/ajaxcontroltoolkitsamplesite
```

Using NuGet to Download the Ajax Control Toolkit and Add It to the Project
To download the Ajax Control Toolkit and add it to the project:

1. Open the original Validation example, which is located in the folder named CopyOfValidationExample provided with this chapter's examples. We provided a solution (.sln) file so that you can double click it to open the project in Visual Studio Express 2012 for Web (or your full version of Visual Studio).

2. Right click the solution name at the top of the **Solution Explorer** window and select **Manage NuGet Packages for Solution.**

3. In the dialog that appears, locate AjaxControlToolkit—you can find this quickly by selecting the **Online** tab at the left side of the dialog, then typing ajax in the dialog's **Search Online** field.

4. Select AjaxControlToolkit, then click **Install**. In the **Select Projects** dialog, ensure that the Validation project is selected and click **OK**.

This will download the toolkit and place its files into the Bin folder within your project. When the installation is complete, close the **Manage NuGet Packages** window.

Adding the ASP.NET Ajax Controls to the Toolbox
Next, you'll add the toolkit's controls to the **Toolbox**, so you can drag and drop them onto your Web Forms. To do so, perform the following steps:

1. Right click inside the **Toolbox** and choose **Add Tab**, then type AjaxControlToolkit in the new tab.

2. Right click in the new **AjaxControlToolkit** tab and select **Choose Items…** to open the **Choose Toolbox Items** dialog.

3. Click **Browse…** then locate the Bin folder within the Validation project.

4. Select the file AjaxControlToolkit.dll then click **Open**. All of the toolkit's controls will automatically be selected in the .NET Framework Components tab.

5. Click **OK** to close dialog. The toolkit's controls now appear in the **Toolbox**'s **AjaxControlToolkit** section.

6. If the control names are not in alphabetical order, you can sort them alphabetically, by right clicking in the list of Ajax Control Toolkit controls and selecting **Sort Items Alphabetically**.

27.3.5 Using Controls from the Ajax Control Toolkit
You'll now enhance the Validation app by adding ASP.NET Ajax controls. The key control in every ASP.NET Ajax-enabled app is the **ScriptManager** (in the **Toolbox**'s **AJAX Extensions** tab), which manages the JavaScript client-side code (called scripts) that enable asynchronous Ajax functionality. A benefit of using ASP.NET Ajax is that you do not need to know JavaScript to be able to use these scripts. The ScriptManager is meant for use with the controls in the **Toolbox**'s **AJAX Extensions** tab. There can be only one ScriptManager per page.

27.3.6 ToolkitScriptManager
The Ajax Control Toolkit comes with an enhanced ScriptManager called the **ToolkitScriptManager**, which manages the scripts for the Ajax Control Toolkit's controls. This one should be used in any page with controls from the ASP. NET Ajax Toolkit. Drag a ToolkitScriptManager from the **AjaxControlToolkit** tab in the **Toolbox** to the top of the page—a script manager must appear *before* any controls that use the scripts it manages.

Common Programming Error 27.1
More than one ScriptManager and/or ToolkitScriptManager control on a Web Form causes the app to throw an InvalidOperationException when the page is initialized.

27.3.7 Grouping Information in Tabs Using the TabContainer Control
The **TabContainer control** enables you to group information into tabs that are displayed only if they're selected. The information in an unselected tab won't be displayed until the user selects that tab. To demonstrate a TabContainer control, let's split the form into two tabs—one in which the user can enter the name and one in which the user can enter the e-mail address and phone number. Perform the following steps:

1. In **Design** view, click to the right of the text **Please fill in all the fields in the following form:** and press *Enter* to create a new paragraph.

2. Drag a `TabContainer` control from the **AjaxControlToolkit** tab in the **Toolbox** into the new paragraph. This creates a container for hosting tabs. Set the `TabContainer`'s `Width` property to 450px.

3. To add a tab, open the **TabContainer Tasks** smart-tag menu and select **Add Tab Panel**. This adds a **TabPanel object**—representing a tab—to the `TabContainer`. Do this again to add a second tab. In **Design** view, you can navigate between tabs by clicking the tab headers. You can drag-and-drop elements into each tab as you would anywhere else on the page.

4. Next, change each `TabPanel`'s text label by clicking the tab, then selecting the text and typing the new text. Change `TabPanel1` to `Name` and `TabPanel2` to `Contact`.

5. Select the **Name** tab, then click in its body and insert a one row and two column table. Take the text and controls that are currently in the **Name:** row of the original table and move them to the table in the **Name** tab.

6. Switch to the **Contact** tab, click in its body, then insert a two-row-by-two-column table. Take the text and controls that are currently in the **E-mail:** and **Phone:** rows of the original table and move them to the table in the **Contact** tab.

7. Delete the original table that is currently below the `TabContainer`.

27.3.8 Partial-Page Updates Using the UpdatePanel Control

The **UpdatePanel control** eliminates full-page refreshes by isolating a section of a page for a *partial* page update. You'll now use a partial-page update to display the user's information that is submitted to the server. Perform the following steps:

1. Insert an `UpdatePanel` control (located in the **Toolbox**'s **AJAX Extensions** tab) before the **Submit** `Button`.

2. Partial page updates require the control(s) to update and the control that triggers the update to be placed in the `UpdatePanel`. For this reason, drag the paragraph elements containing the `submitButton` and `outputLabel` into the `UpdatePanel`.

Now, when the user clicks the **Submit** button, the `UpdatePanel` intercepts the request and makes an asynchronous request to the server instead. Then the response is inserted in the `outputLabel` element, and the `UpdatePanel` reloads the label to display the new text without refreshing the entire page.

27.3.9 Adding Ajax Functionality to ASP.NET Validation Controls Using Ajax Extenders

Several controls in the Ajax Control Toolkit are **extenders**—components that enhance the functionality of regular ASP.NET controls. In this example, we use **ValidatorCallout-Extender controls** that enhance the ASP.NET validation controls by displaying error messages in small yellow callouts next to the input fields, rather than as text in the page.

You can create a `ValidatorCalloutExtender` by opening any validator control's smart-tag menu and clicking **Add Extender....** In the **Extender Wizard** dialog (Fig. 27.15), choose

`ValidatorCalloutExtender` from the list of available extenders. The extender's ID is chosen based on the ID of the validation control you're extending, but you can rename it if you like. Click **OK** to create the extender. Do this for each of the validation controls in this example.

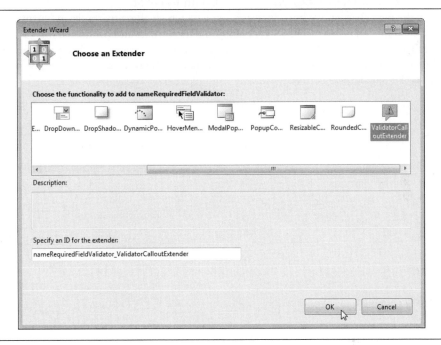

Fig. 27.15 | Creating a control extender using the **Extender Wizard**.

27.3.10 Changing the Display Property of the Validation Controls

The `ValidatorCalloutExtenders` display error messages with a nicer look-and-feel, so we no longer need the validator controls to display these messages on their own. For this reason, set each validation control's `Display` property to `None`.

27.3.11 Running the App

When you run this app, the `TabContainer` will display whichever tab was last displayed in the ASPX page's **Design** view. Ensure that the **Name** tab is displayed, then select `Valida-tion.aspx` in the **Solution Explorer** and type *Ctrl* + *F5* to execute the app.

27.4 Wrap-Up

In this chapter, we presented a case study in which we built a password-protected web app that requires users to log in before accessing information from the `Books` database. You used the **Web Site Administration Tool** to configure the app to prevent anonymous users from accessing the book information. We used the **ASP.NET Web Forms Application** template, which provides preconfigured login and registration capabilities for a website. You also modified a master page that defined the website's uniform look-and-feel.

Finally, you learned the difference between a traditional web app and an Ajax web app. We introduced ASP.NET Ajax and the Ajax Control Toolkit. You learned how to build an Ajax-enabled web app by using a `ScriptManager` and the Ajax-enabled controls of the Ajax Extensions package and the Ajax Control Toolkit.

In the next chapter, we introduce web services, which allow methods on one machine to call methods on other machines via common data formats and protocols, such as XML and HTTP. You will learn how web services promote software reusability and interoperability across multiple computers on a network such as the Internet.

Web Services

Objectives

In this chapter you'll:

- Create WCF web services.
- Understand how XML, JSON and Representational State Transfer Architecture (REST) enable WCF web services.
- Learn the elements that comprise WCF web services, such as service references, service endpoints, service contracts and service bindings.
- Create a client that consumes a WCF web service.
- Use WCF web services.

28.1 Introduction

This chapter introduces **Windows Communication Foundation (WCF)** services. WCF is a set of technologies for building distributed systems in which system components communicate with one another over networks. In earlier versions of .NET, the various types of communication used different technologies and programming models. WCF uses a common framework for all communication between systems, so you need to learn only one programming model to use WCF.

This chapter focuses on WCF web services, which promote software reusability in distributed systems that typically execute across the Internet. A **web service** is a class that allows its methods to be called by apps on other computers via common data formats and protocols, such as XML (see Chapter 22), JSON (Section 28.5) and HTTP.

In .NET, the over-the-network method calls are commonly implemented through **Simple Object Access Protocol (SOAP)** or the **Representational State Transfer (REST)** architecture. SOAP—the original technology for communicating with web services—is an XML-based protocol describing how to mark up requests and responses so that they can be sent via protocols such as HTTP. SOAP uses a standardized XML-based format to enclose data in a message that can be sent between a client and a server. REST is a network architecture that uses the web's traditional request/response mechanisms such as get and post requests. REST-based systems do *not* require data to be wrapped in a special message format. Though SOAP is still in use today, most web services are developed using REST, as we'll do in this chapter.

You'll build this chapter's web services using Visual Studio Express 2012 for Web. To interact with the web services, you'll build Windows Forms client apps using Visual Studio Express 2012 for Windows Desktop. Full versions of Visual Studio 2012 include the functionality of both Express editions. Though we demonstrate only Windows Forms client apps, the techniques you'll learn here can be used in any type of app you've implemented in this book.

28.2 WCF Services Basics

Windows Communication Foundation (WCF) was created as a single platform to encompass many existing communication technologies. WCF increases productivity, because you learn only one straightforward programming model. Each WCF service has three key components—addresses, bindings and contracts (usually called the ABCs of a WCF service):

- An **address** represents the service's *location* (also known as its **endpoint**), which includes the protocol (for example, HTTP) and host (e.g., `www.deitel.com`) used to access the service.

- A **binding** specifies how a client *communicates* with the service (e.g., SOAP, REST, etc.). Bindings can also specify other options, such as security constraints.

- A **contract** is an *interface* representing the service's methods and their return types. The service's contract allows clients to interact with the service.

The computer on which the web service resides is referred to as a **web service host**. The client app that accesses the web service sends a method call over a network to the web service host, which processes the call and returns a response over the network to the app. This kind of *distributed computing* benefits systems in various ways. For example, an app without direct access to data on another system might be able to retrieve this data via a web service. Similarly, an app lacking the processing power necessary to perform specific computations could use a web service to take advantage of another system's superior resources.

28.3 HTTP get and post Requests

The two most common **HTTP request types** (also known as **request methods**) are `get` and `post`. A **get request** typically gets (or retrieves) information from a server. Common uses of `get` requests are to retrieve a document or an image, or to fetch search results based on a user-submitted search term. A **post request** typically posts (or sends) data to a server. Common uses of `post` requests are to send form data or documents to a server.

An HTTP request often sends data to a **server-side form handler** that processes the data. For example, when a user performs a search or participates in a web-based survey, the web server receives the information specified in the HTML form as part of the request. *Both* types of requests can be used to send form data to a web server, yet each request type sends the information differently.

Sending Data in a get Request
A get request sends information to the server in the URL. For example, in the URL

```
www.google.com/search?q=deitel
```

search is the name of Google's server-side form handler, q is the name of a *variable* in Google's search form and deitel is the search term. A ? separates the **query string** from the rest of the URL in a request. A *name/value* pair is passed to the server with the *name* and the *value* separated by an equals sign (=). If more than one *name/value* pair is submitted, each pair is separated by an ampersand (&). The server uses data passed in a query string to retrieve an appropriate resource from the server. The server then sends a **response** to the client. A get request may be initiated by submitting an HTML form whose method attribute is set to "get", or by typing the URL (possibly containing a query string) directly into the browser's address bar.

*Sending Data in a **post** Request*

A post request sends form data as part of the HTTP message, not as part of the URL. A get request typically limits the query string (that is, everything to the right of the ?) to a specific number of characters. For example, Internet Explorer restricts the entire URL to no more than 2083 characters. Typically, large amounts of information should be sent using the post method. The post method is also sometimes preferred because it *hides* the submitted data from the user by embedding it in an HTTP message. If a form submits hidden input values along with user-submitted data, the post method might generate a URL like www.searchengine.com/search. The form data still reaches the server for processing, but the user does not see the exact information sent.

28.4 Representational State Transfer (REST)

Representational State Transfer (REST) refers to an architectural style for implementing web services. Such web services are often called **RESTful web services**. Though REST itself is not a standard, RESTful web services are implemented using web standards. Each operation in a RESTful web service is identified by a unique URL. Thus, when the server receives a request, it immediately knows what operation to perform. Such web services can be used in a program or directly from a web browser. In browser-based apps, the results of a particular REST operation may be *cached* locally by the browser when the service is invoked with a get request. This can make subsequent requests for the same operation faster by loading the result directly from the browser's cache. REST web services typically return data in XML (Chapter 22) or JSON (Section 28.5) format, but can return other formats, such as HTML, plain text and media files.

28.5 JavaScript Object Notation (JSON)

JavaScript Object Notation (JSON) is an alternative to XML for representing data. JSON is a text-based data-interchange format used to represent objects in JavaScript as collections of name/value pairs represented as strings. It's commonly used in Ajax apps. JSON is a simple format that makes objects easy to read, create and parse, and allows programs to transmit data efficiently across the Internet because it is much less verbose than XML. Each JSON object is represented as a list of property names and values contained in curly braces, in the following format:

```
{ propertyName1 : value1, propertyName2 : value2 }
```

Arrays are represented in JSON with square brackets in the following format:

```
[ value1, value2, value3 ]
```

Each value in an array can be a string, a number, a JSON object, true, false or null. To appreciate the simplicity of JSON data, examine this representation of an array of address-book entries:

```
[ { first: 'Cheryl', last: 'Black' },
  { first: 'James', last: 'Blue' },
  { first: 'Mike', last: 'Brown' },
  { first: 'Meg', last: 'Gold' } ]
```

Many programming languages now support the JSON data format.

28.6 Publishing and Consuming REST-Based XML Web Services

This section presents our first example of **publishing** (enabling for client access) and **consuming** (using) a web service using REST architecture.

28.6.1 WCF Web Service Project

To build your web service, you'll create a **WCF Service Application** project. The IDE will generate various files, including an **SVC file** (`Service1.svc`, which provides access to the service) and a **Web.config** file (which specifies the service's binding and behavior). The IDE will also generate code files for the **WCF service class** and any other code that's part of the WCF service's implementation. In the service class, you'll define the methods that your web service makes available to client apps.

28.6.2 Implementing a REST-Based XML WCF Web Service

Figures 28.1 and 28.2 present the code-behind files for the `WelcomeRESTXMLService` WCF web service that you'll build in Section 28.6.3. When creating services, you work almost exclusively in the code-behind files. The service that you'll build in the next few sections provides a method that takes a name (represented as a `string`) as an argument and appends it to the welcome message that is returned to the client. You'll use a parameter in the method definition to demonstrate that a client can send data to a web service.

Web Service Interface
Figure 28.1 is the service's interface, which describes the service's *contract*—the set of methods and properties the client uses to access the service. The **ServiceContract** attribute (line 9) exposes a class that implements this interface as a WCF web service. The **OperationContract** attribute (line 13) exposes the `Welcome` method to clients for remote calls. Both of these attributes are defined in namespace `System.ServiceModel` (line 4).

```
1   // Fig. 28.1: IWelcomeRESTXMLService.cs
2   // WCF web service interface. A class that implements this interface
3   // returns a welcome message through REST architecture and XML data format
4   using System.ServiceModel;
5   using System.ServiceModel.Web;
6
7   namespace WelcomeRESTXMLService
8   {
9      [ServiceContract]
10     public interface IWelcomeRESTXMLService
11     {
12        // returns a welcome message
13        [OperationContract]
14        [WebGet( UriTemplate = "/welcome/{yourName}" )]
15        string Welcome( string yourName );
16     } // end interface IWelcomeRESTXMLService
17  } // end namespace WelcomeRESTXMLService
```

Fig. 28.1 | WCF web-service interface. A class that implements this interface returns a welcome message through REST architecture and XML data format.

WebGet Attribute

The `Welcome` method's `WebGet` attribute (line 14; from namespace `System.Service-Model.Web`) maps a method name and its parameters to a unique URL that can be accessed via an HTTP get operation programmatically or in a web browser. WebGet's `UriTemplate` property (line 14) specifies the URI format that is used to invoke the method. You access the `Welcome` method in a web browser by appending text that matches the `UriTemplate` to the end of the service's location, as in

```
http://localhost:portNumber/WelcomeRESTXMLService.svc/welcome/Paul
```

Web Service Implementation

`WelcomeRESTXMLService` (Fig. 28.2) is the class that implements the `IWelcomeRESTXML-Service` interface that was declared as the `ServiceContract`. Lines 9–14 define the method `Welcome`, which returns a `string` welcoming you to WCF web services. As you'll soon see, the `string` object will be serialized to XML—that is, it will be converted to an XML representation—then returned to the client. In the next section, you'll build the web service from scratch.

```
 I   // Fig. 28.2: WelcomeRESTXMLService.svc.cs
 2   // WCF web service that returns a welcome message using REST architecture
 3   // and XML data format.
 4   namespace WelcomeRESTXMLService
 5   {
 6      public class WelcomeRESTXMLService : IWelcomeRESTXMLService
 7      {
 8         // returns a welcome message
 9         public string Welcome( string yourName )
10         {
11            return string.Format(
12               "Welcome to WCF Web Services with REST and XML, {0}!",
13               yourName );
14         } // end method Welcome
15      } // end class WelcomeRESTXMLService
16   } // end namespace WelcomeRESTXMLService
```

Fig. 28.2 | WCF web service that returns a welcome message using REST architecture and XML data format.

28.6.3 Building a REST WCF Web Service

In the following steps, you create a **WCF Service Application** project for the `WelcomeREST-XMLService` and test it using the IIS Express web server that comes with Visual Studio Express 2012 for Web.

Step 1: Creating the Project

To create a project of type **WCF Service Application**, select **File > Project...** to display the **New Project** dialog (Fig. 28.3). Select the **WCF Service Application** template in the **Visual C# > WCF** templates category. By default, Visual Studio Express 2012 for Web places files on the local machine in a directory named `WcfService1`. Rename this folder to `Welcome-RESTXMLService`, specify where you'd like to save the project, then click **OK** to create it.

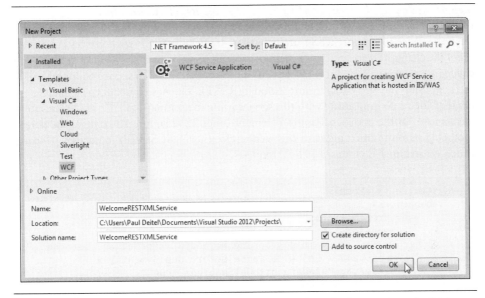

Fig. 28.3 | Creating a **WCF Service Application** in Visual Studio Express 2012 for Web.

Step 2: Examining the Newly Created Project

After creating the project, the code-behind file Service1.svc.cs, which contains code for a simple web service, is displayed by default. If it's not displayed, double-click Service1.svc in the **Solution Explorer**—the IDE opens the service's code-behind file Service1.svc.cs. By default, the code-behind file implements an interface named IService1. This interface (located in IService1.cs) is marked with the ServiceContract and OperationContract attributes that we introduced in Section 28.6.2. In addition, the IService1.cs file defines a class named CompositeType with a DataContract attribute (discussed in Section 28.7). The IService1 interface contains two sample service methods named GetData and GetDataUsingContract. The Service1.svc.cs file defines these methods.

Step 3: Modifying and Renaming the Code-Behind File

To create the WelcomeRESTXMLService service developed in this section, first use the IDE's refactoring capabilities to rename the IService1 interface and the Service1 class:

1. In IService1.cs, right click the interface name IService1, then select **Refactor > Rename...**, specify IWelcomeRESTXMLService as the new name and click **OK**. In the next dialog, click **Apply** to change the interface's name throughout the project.

2. Repeat the preceding step in Service1.svc.cs to rename the class Service1 as WelcomeRESTXMLService.

You should also modify the corresponding file names. In the **Solution Explorer**, rename IService1.cs and Service1.svc to IWelcomeRESTXMLService.cs and WelcomeRESTXMLService.svc, respectively. When you rename the SVC file the IDE automatically renames the code-behind file. Next, replace the code in WelcomeRESTXMLService.svc.cs with the code in Fig. 28.2.

Step 4: Modifying the `Web.config` *File to Enable REST Architecture*

Figure 28.4 shows part of the default `Web.config` file reformatted and modified to enable the web service to support REST architecture—by default WCF web services use SOAP. All of the changes are located in the `Web.config` file's `system.serviceModel` element. The **endpointBehaviors** element (lines 16–20) indicates that this web service endpoint will be accessed using the web programming model (REST). The nested **webHttp** element specifies that clients communicate with this service using the standard HTTP request/response mechanism. In the `protocolMapping` element (lines 22–25), line 23 changes the default protocol for communicating with this web service (normally SOAP) to **webHttpBinding**, which is used for REST-based HTTP requests.

```
 I   <system.serviceModel>
 2     <behaviors>
 3       <serviceBehaviors>
 4         <behavior>
 5           <!-- To avoid disclosing metadata information, set the
 6                values below to false before deployment -->
 7           <serviceMetadata httpGetEnabled="true"
 8             httpsGetEnabled="true"/>
 9           <!-- To receive exception details in faults for debugging
10                purposes, set the value below to true.  Set to false
11                before deployment to avoid disclosing exception
12                information -->
13           <serviceDebug includeExceptionDetailInFaults="false"/>
14         </behavior>
15       </serviceBehaviors>
16       <endpointBehaviors>
17         <behavior>
18           <webHttp/>
19         </behavior>
20       </endpointBehaviors>
21     </behaviors>
22     <protocolMapping>
23       <add binding="webHttpBinding" scheme="http" />
24       <add binding="basicHttpsBinding" scheme="https" />
25     </protocolMapping>
26     <serviceHostingEnvironment aspNetCompatibilityEnabled="true"
27       multipleSiteBindingsEnabled="true"/>
28   </system.serviceModel>
```

Fig. 28.4 | The modified `system.serviceModel` element of the `WelcomeRESTXMLService` project's `Web.config` file.

28.6.4 Deploying the WelcomeRESTXMLService

Choose **Build Solution** from the **Build** menu to ensure that the web service compiles without errors. To deploy the web service on IIS Express for testing, simply right click the web service's SVC file, then select **View in Browser**. A browser window opens and displays information about the service (Fig. 28.5), which is your confirmation that the service was deployed and can now receive requests. The information shown in the web browser is generated dynamically when the `WelcomeRESTXMLService.svc` file is requested.

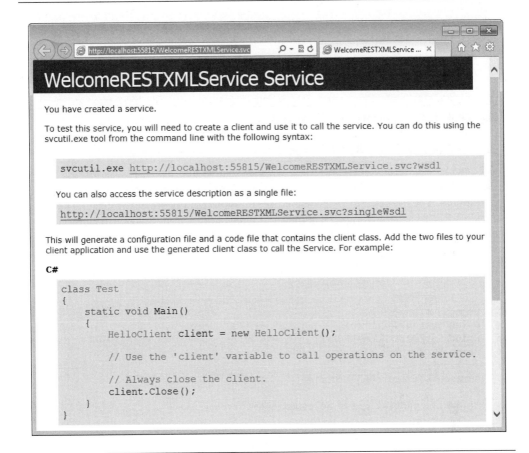

Fig. 28.5 | SVC file rendered in a web browser.

Once the service is running, you can access the SVC page from any web browser on your computer by typing a URL of the following form in a web browser:

```
http://localhost:portNumber/SVCFileName
```

(See the actual URL in Fig. 28.5.) By default, IIS Express assigns a random port number to each website or web service it hosts.

Testing the Web Service
To test the web service's Welcome method, add

```
/welcome/YourName
```

to the end of the URL in Fig. 28.5, then press *Enter*. Figure 28.6 shows the result. This change to the URL uses the UriTemplate (line 14 of Fig. 28.1) to invoke method Welcome with the argument Paul. The browser displays the XML response from the web service. In Section 28.6.5, you'll learn how to consume this service from an app.

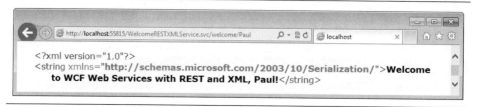

Fig. 28.6 | Response from `WelcomeRESTXMLService` in XML data format.

28.6.5 Consuming a REST-Based XML WCF Web Service

`WelcomeRESTXMLClient` (Fig. 28.7) is a Windows Forms app that uses class **HttpClient** (line 13) from namespace System.Net.Http (line 4) to invoke the web service and receive its response. The System.Net.Http namespace is not part of the project by default. To add a reference to its assembly, right click the References folder in the **Solution Explorer**, select **Add Reference...** to display the **Reference Manager** dialog, place a check in the checkbox for System.Net.Http then click **OK**.

```
 1  // Fig. 28.7: WelcomeRESTXML.cs
 2  // Client that consumes the WelcomeRESTXMLService.
 3  using System;
 4  using System.Net.Http;
 5  using System.Windows.Forms;
 6  using System.Xml.Linq;
 7
 8  namespace WelcomeRESTXMLClient
 9  {
10     public partial class WelcomeRESTXML : Form
11     {
12        // object to invoke the WelcomeRESTXMLService
13        private HttpClient client = new HttpClient();
14
15        private XNamespace xmlNamespace = XNamespace.Get(
16           "http://schemas.microsoft.com/2003/10/Serialization/" );
17
18        public WelcomeRESTXML()
19        {
20           InitializeComponent();
21        } // end constructor
22
23        // get user input, pass it to web service, and process response
24        private async void submitButton_Click( object sender, EventArgs e )
25        {
26           // send request to WelcomeRESTXMLService
27           string result = await client.GetStringAsync( new Uri(
28              "http://localhost:55815/WelcomeRESTXMLService.svc/welcome/" +
29              textBox.Text ) );
30
31           // parse the returned XML
32           XDocument xmlResponse = XDocument.Parse( result );
```

Fig. 28.7 | Client that consumes the `WelcomeRESTXMLService`. (Part 1 of 2.)

```
33
34              // get the <string> element's value
35              MessageBox.Show( xmlResponse.Element(
36                 xmlNamespace + "string" ).Value, "Welcome" );
37          } // end method submitButton_Click
38       } // end class WelcomeRESTXML
39    } // end namespace WelcomeRESTXMLClient
```

a) User inputs name   b) Message sent from **WelcomeRESTXMLService**

Fig. 28.7 | Client that consumes the `WelcomeRESTXMLService`. (Part 2 of 2.)

Recall that we introduced C#'s async/await mechanism in Chapter 26. This mechanism is ideal for invoking web services. In this example, we declare the **Submit** button's event handler async then await a call to HttpClient's method **GetStringAsync**, which invokes the web service and returns its response. The method's argument (i.e., the URL to invoke the web service) must be specified as an object of class **Uri**. Class Uri's constructor receives a string representing a uniform resource identifier. The URL's port number must match the one issued to the web service by IIS Express—*this might be different on your computer*, so you might need to modify the port number in line 28. When the call to the web service completes, the event handler continues executing at line 32, which parses the XML response using XDocument method Parse. In lines 15–16, we specify the XML message's namespace (the value of xmlns in Fig. 28.6). This is required to access the elements in the service's XML response so that we can display the welcome string in a MessageBox (lines 35–36).

28.7 Publishing and Consuming REST-Based JSON Web Services

You'll now reimplement the example from Section 28.6 to build a RESTful web service that returns data in JSON format.

28.7.1 Creating a REST-Based JSON WCF Web Service

By default, a web-service method with the WebGet attribute returns data in *XML format*. In Fig. 28.8, we modify the WelcomeRESTXMLService to return data in *JSON format* by setting WebGet's **ResponseFormat** property to WebMessageFormat.Json (line 15)—the default is WebMessageFormat.XML. For JSON serialization to work properly, the objects being converted to JSON must have *properties* with both set and get accessors. This enables the JSON serialization to create name/value pairs representing each property and its corresponding value. The previous example returned a string object containing the response. Even though strings are objects, they do not have any properties that represent their contents. So, lines 21–27 define a TextMessage class that encapsulates a String value and defines a Public property Message to access that value. The **DataContract** attribute (line 21) exposes the TextMessage class to the client. Similarly, the **DataMember** attribute (line 25) exposes a property of this class to the client. This property will appear in the JSON object as a name/value pair. Only DataMembers of a DataContract are serialized.

```
 1    // Fig. 28.8: IWelcomeRESTJSONService.cs
 2    // WCF web service interface that returns a welcome message through REST
 3    // architecture and JSON format.
 4    using System.Runtime.Serialization;
 5    using System.ServiceModel;
 6    using System.ServiceModel.Web;
 7
 8    namespace WelcomeRESTJSONService
 9    {
10       [ServiceContract]
11       public interface IWelcomeRESTJSONService
12       {
13          // returns a welcome message
14          [OperationContract]
15          [WebGet( ResponseFormat = WebMessageFormat.Json,
16             UriTemplate = "/welcome/{yourName}" )]
17          TextMessage Welcome( string yourName );
18       } // end interface IWelcomeRESTJSONService
19
20       // class to encapsulate a string to send in JSON format
21       [DataContract]
22       public class TextMessage
23       {
24          // automatic property message
25          [DataMember]
26          public string Message { get; set; }
27       } // end class TextMessage
28    } // end namespace WelcomeRESTJSONService
```

Fig. 28.8 | WCF web-service interface that returns a welcome message through REST architecture and JSON format.

Figure 28.9 shows the implementation of the interface of Fig. 28.8. The Welcome method (lines 9–17) returns a TextMessage object, reflecting the changes we made to the interface class. This object is automatically serialized in JSON format (as a result of line 15 in Fig. 28.8) and sent to the client.

```
 1    // Fig. 28.9: WelcomeRESTJSONService.cs
 2    // WCF web service that returns a welcome message through REST
 3    // architecture and JSON format.
 4    namespace WelcomeRESTJSONService
 5    {
```

Fig. 28.9 | WCF web service that returns a welcome message through REST architecture and JSON format. (Part 1 of 2.)

```
 6      public class WelcomeRESTJSONService : IWelcomeRESTJSONService
 7      {
 8         // returns a welcome message
 9         public TextMessage Welcome( string yourName )
10         {
11            // add welcome message to field of TextMessage object
12            TextMessage message = new TextMessage();
13            message.Message = string.Format(
14               "Welcome to WCF Web Services with REST and JSON, {0}!",
15               yourName );
16            return message;
17         } // end method Welcome
18      } // end class WelcomeRESTJSONService
19   } // end namespace WelcomeRESTJSONService
```

Fig. 28.9 | WCF web service that returns a welcome message through REST architecture and JSON format. (Part 2 of 2.)

We can once again test the web service using a web browser, by accessing the Service.svc file (`http://localhost:49745/WelcomeRESTJSONService/Service.svc`) and appending the URI template (welcome/*yourName*) to the address. The response prompts you to download a file called *yourName*.json, which is a text file that contains the JSON formatted data. By opening the file in a text editor such as Notepad (Fig. 28.10), you can see the service response as a JSON object. Notice that the property named Message has the welcome message as its value.

Fig. 28.10 | Response from WelcomeRESTJSONService in JSON data format.

28.7.2 Consuming a REST-Based JSON WCF Web Service

Objects of class types that are sent as arguments to or returned from a REST web service are converted to XML or JSON data format—known as **XML serialization** or **JSON serialization**, respectively. In Fig. 28.11, we consume the WelcomeRESTJSONService service using an object of the System.Runtime.Serialization.Json namespace's **DataContractJsonSerializer** class (lines 31–32). (You must add a reference to the System.Runtime.Serialization assembly.) DataContractJsonSerializer deserializes the JSON response and assigns its fields to an object of the TextMessage class (lines 43–47). The **Serializable** attribute (line 43) indicates that TextMessage objects can be converted to and from JSON format. Class TextMessage on the client must have public data or properties that match the public data or properties in the corresponding class from the web service. Since we want to convert the JSON response into a TextMessage object, we set the DataContractJsonSerializer's type parameter to TextMessage (line 32). In lines 33–35, we use the System.Text namespace's Encoding.Unicode.GetBytes method to convert the JSON response to a Unicode encoded byte array, then encapsulate the array in a MemoryStream object so we can read data from the array using stream semantics. The bytes in the MemoryStream object are read by the DataContractJsonSerializer and deserialized into a TextMessage object.

```csharp
 1   // Fig. 28.11: WelcomeRESTJSONForm.cs
 2   // Client that consumes the WelcomeRESTJSONService.
 3   using System;
 4   using System.IO;
 5   using System.Net.Http;
 6   using System.Runtime.Serialization.Json;
 7   using System.Text;
 8   using System.Windows.Forms;
 9
10   namespace WelcomeRESTJSONClient
11   {
12      public partial class WelcomeRESTJSONForm : Form
13      {
14         // object to invoke the WelcomeRESTJSONService
15         private HttpClient client = new HttpClient();
16
17         public WelcomeRESTJSONForm()
18         {
19            InitializeComponent();
20         } // end constructor
21
22         // get user input and pass it to the web service
23         private void submitButton_Click( object sender, EventArgs e )
24         {
25            // send request to WelcomeRESTJSONService
26            string result = await client.GetStringAsync( new Uri(
27               "http://localhost:56429/WelcomeRESTJSONService.svc/welcome/" +
28               textBox.Text ) );
29
30            // deserialize response into a TextMessage object
31            DataContractJsonSerializer JSONSerializer =
32               new DataContractJsonSerializer( typeof( TextMessage ) );
33            TextMessage message =
34               ( TextMessage ) JSONSerializer.ReadObject( new
35               MemoryStream( Encoding.Unicode.GetBytes( e.Result ) ) );
36
37            // display Message text
38            MessageBox.Show( message.Message, "Welcome" );
39         } // end method submitButton_Click
40      } // end class WelcomeRESTJSONForm
41
42      // TextMessage class representing a JSON object
43      [Serializable]
44      public class TextMessage
45      {
46         public string Message;
47      } // end class TextMessage
48   } // end namespace WelcomeRESTJSONClient
```

Fig. 28.11 | Client that consumes the WelcomeRESTJSONService. (Part 1 of 2.)

a) User inputs name.

b) Message sent from `WelcomeRESTJSONService`.

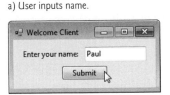

Fig. 28.11 | Client that consumes the `WelcomeRESTJSONService`. (Part 2 of 2.)

28.8 Equation Generator: Returning User-Defined Types

The web services we've demonstrated so far each receive simple `strings` as arguments. It's also possible to process instances of programmer-defined class types in a web service. These types can be passed to or returned from web-service methods.

This section presents an `EquationGenerator` web service that generates random arithmetic equations of type `Equation`. The client is a math-tutoring app that inputs information about the mathematical question that the user wishes to attempt (addition, subtraction or multiplication) and the skill level of the user (1 specifies equations using numbers from 0 to 9, 2 specifies equations involving numbers from 10 to 99, and 3 specifies equations containing numbers from 100 to 999). The web service then generates an equation consisting of random numbers in the proper range. The client app receives the `Equation` and displays the sample question to the user.

Defining Class Equation

We define class `Equation` in Fig. 28.12. Lines 35–55 define a constructor that takes three arguments—two `int`s representing the left and right operands and a `string` that represents the arithmetic operation to perform. The constructor sets the `Equation`'s properties, then calculates the appropriate result. The parameterless constructor (lines 28–32) calls the three-argument constructor (lines 35–55) and passes default values.

```
1   // Fig. 28.12: Equation.cs
2   // Class Equation that contains information about an equation.
3   using System.Runtime.Serialization;
4
5   namespace EquationGeneratorServiceXML
6   {
7      [DataContract]
8      public class Equation
9      {
10        // automatic property to access the left operand
11        [DataMember]
12        private int Left { get; set; }
13
14        // automatic property to access the right operand
15        [DataMember]
16        private int Right { get; set; }
```

Fig. 28.12 | Class `Equation` that contains information about an equation. (Part 1 of 3.)

```
17
18      // automatic property to access the result of applying
19      // an operation to the left and right operands
20      [DataMember]
21      private int Result { get; set; }
22
23      // automatic property to access the operation
24      [DataMember]
25      private string Operation { get; set; }
26
27      // default constructor
28      public Equation()
29         : this( 0, 0, "add" )
30      {
31         // empty body
32      } // end default constructor
33
34      // three-argument constructor for class Equation
35      public Equation( int leftValue, int rightValue, string type )
36      {
37         Left = leftValue;
38         Right = rightValue;
39
40         switch ( type ) // perform appropriate operation
41         {
42            case "add": // addition
43               Result = Left + Right;
44               Operation = "+";
45               break;
46            case "subtract": // subtraction
47               Result = Left - Right;
48               Operation = "-";
49               break;
50            case "multiply": // multiplication
51               Result = Left * Right;
52               Operation = "*";
53               break;
54         } // end switch
55      } // end three-argument constructor
56
57      // return string representation of the Equation object
58      public override string ToString()
59      {
60         return string.Format( "{0} {1} {2} = {4}", Left, Operation,
61            Right, Result );
62      } // end method ToString
63
64      // property that returns a string representing left-hand side
65      [DataMember]
66      private string LeftHandSide
67      {
68         get
69         {
```

Fig. 28.12 | Class Equation that contains information about an equation. (Part 2 of 3.)

```
70                  return string.Format( "{0} {1} {2}", Left, Operation, Right );
71              } // end get
72           set
73           {
74               // empty body
75           } // end set
76        } // end property LeftHandSide
77
78        // property that returns a string representing right-hand side
79        [DataMember]
80        private string RightHandSide
81        {
82           get
83           {
84              return Result.ToString();
85           } // end get
86           set
87           {
88               // empty body
89           } // end set
90        } // end property RightHandSide
91     } // end class Equation
92  } // end namespace EquationGeneratorService
```

Fig. 28.12 | Class Equation that contains information about an equation. (Part 3 of 3.)

Class Equation defines properties LeftHandSide (lines 66–76), RightHandSide (lines 80–90), Left (line 12), Right (line 16), Result (line 21) and Operation (line 25). The web service client does not need to modify the values of properties LeftHandSide and RightHandSide. However, a property can be serialized only if it has both a get and a set accessor—even if the set accessor has an empty body. Each property is preceded by the DataMember attribute to indicate that it should be serialized. LeftHandSide (lines 66–76) returns a string representing everything to the left of the equals (=) sign in the equation, and RightHandSide (lines 80–90) returns a string representing everything to the right of the equals (=) sign. Left (line 12) returns the int to the left of the operator (known as the left operand), and Right (lines 16) returns the int to the right of the operator (known as the right operand). Result (line 21) returns the solution to the equation, and Operation (line 25) returns the operator in the equation. The client in this case study does not use the RightHandSide property, but we included it in case future clients choose to use it. Method ToString (lines 58–62) returns a string representation of the equation.

28.8.1 Creating the REST-Based XML EquationGenerator Web Service

Figures 28.13 and 28.14 present the interface and class for the EquationGenerator-Service web service, which creates random, customized Equations. This web service contains only method GenerateEquation (lines 11–28 of Fig. 28.14), which takes two parameters—a string representing the mathematical operation ("add", "subtract" or "multiply") and a string representing the difficulty level. When line 27 of Fig. 28.14 returns the Equation, it is serialized as XML by default and sent to the client. We'll do this with JSON as well in Section 28.8.3. Recall from Section 28.6.3 that you must modify the Web.config file to enable REST support as well.

```csharp
1   // Fig. 28.13: IEquationGeneratorService.cs
2   // WCF REST service interface to create random equations based on a
3   // specified operation and difficulty level.
4   using System.ServiceModel;
5   using System.ServiceModel.Web;
6
7   namespace EquationGeneratorServiceXML
8   {
9      [ServiceContract]
10     public interface IEquationGeneratorService
11     {
12        // method to generate a math equation
13        [OperationContract]
14        [WebGet( UriTemplate = "equation/{operation}/{level}" )]
15        Equation GenerateEquation( string operation, string level );
16     } // end interface IEquationGeneratorService
17  } // end namespace EquationGeneratorService
```

Fig. 28.13 | WCF REST service interface to create random equations based on a specified operation and difficulty level.

```csharp
1   // Fig. 28.14: EquationGeneratorService.cs
2   // WCF REST service to create random equations based on a
3   // specified operation and difficulty level.
4   using System;
5
6   namespace EquationGeneratorServiceXML
7   {
8      public class EquationGeneratorService : IEquationGeneratorService
9      {
10        // method to generate a math equation
11        public Equation GenerateEquation( string operation, string level )
12        {
13           // calculate maximum and minimum number to be used
14           int maximum =
15              Convert.ToInt32( Math.Pow( 10, Convert.ToInt32( level ) ) );
16           int minimum = Convert.ToInt32(
17              Math.Pow( 10, Convert.ToInt32( level ) - 1 ) );
18
19           Random randomObject = new Random(); // generate random numbers
20
21           // create Equation consisting of two random
22           // numbers in the range minimum to maximum
23           Equation newEquation = new Equation(
24              randomObject.Next( minimum, maximum ),
25              randomObject.Next( minimum, maximum ), operation );
26
27           return newEquation;
28        } // end method GenerateEquation
29     } // end class EquationGeneratorService
30  } // end namespace EquationGeneratorServiceXML
```

Fig. 28.14 | WCF REST service to create random equations based on a specified operation and difficulty level.

28.8.2 Consuming the REST-Based XML EquationGenerator Web Service

The MathTutor app (Fig. 28.15) calls the EquationGenerator web service's Generate-Equation method to create an Equation object. The tutor then displays the left-hand side of the Equation and waits for user input.

```
1   // Fig. 28.15: MathTutor.cs
2   // Math tutor using EquationGeneratorServiceXML to create equations.
3   using System;
4   using System.Net.Http;
5   using System.Windows.Forms;
6   using System.Xml.Linq;
7
8   namespace MathTutorXML
9   {
10     public partial class MathTutor : Form
11     {
12        private string operation = "add"; // the default operation
13        private int level = 1; // the default difficulty level
14        private string leftHandSide; // the left side of the equation
15        private int result; // the answer
16        private XNamespace xmlNamespace = XNamespace.Get(
17           "http://schemas.datacontract.org/2004/07/" +
18           "EquationGeneratorServiceXML" );
19
20        // object used to invoke service
21        private HttpClient service = new HttpClient();
22
23        public MathTutor()
24        {
25           InitializeComponent();
26        } // end constructor
27
28        // generates new equation when user clicks button
29        private async void generateButton_Click(
30           object sender, EventArgs e )
31        {
32           // send request to EquationGeneratorServiceXML
33           string xmlString = await service.DownloadStringAsync( new Uri(
34              "http://localhost:56770/EquationGeneratorService.svc/" +
35              "equation/" + operation + "/" + level ) );
36
37           // parse response and get LeftHandSide and Result values
38           XDocument xmlResponse = XDocument.Parse( e.Result );
39           leftHandSide = xmlResponse.Element(
40              xmlNamespace + "Equation" ).Element(
41              xmlNamespace + "LeftHandSide" ).Value;
42           result = Convert.ToInt32( xmlResponse.Element(
43              xmlNamespace + "Equation" ).Element(
44              xmlNamespace + "Result" ).Value );
45
```

Fig. 28.15 | Math tutor using EquationGeneratorServiceXML to create equations. (Part 1 of 4.)

```
46              // display left side of equation
47              questionLabel.Text = leftHandSide;
48              okButton.Enabled = true; // enable okButton
49              answerTextBox.Enabled = true; // enable answerTextBox
50          } // end method generateButton_Click
51
52          // check user's answer
53          private void okButton_Click( object sender, EventArgs e )
54          {
55              if ( !string.IsNullOrEmpty( answerTextBox.Text ) )
56              {
57                  // get user's answer
58                  int userAnswer = Convert.ToInt32( answerTextBox.Text );
59
60                  // determine whether user's answer is correct
61                  if ( result == userAnswer )
62                  {
63                      questionLabel.Text = string.Empty; // clear question
64                      answerTextBox.Clear(); // clear answer
65                      okButton.Enabled = false; // disable OK button
66                      MessageBox.Show( "Correct! Good job!", "Result" );
67                  } // end if
68                  else
69                  {
70                      MessageBox.Show( "Incorrect. Try again.", "Result" );
71                  } // end else
72              } // end if
73          } // end method okButton_Click
74
75          // set the operation to addition
76          private void additionRadioButton_CheckedChanged( object sender,
77              EventArgs e )
78          {
79              if ( additionRadioButton.Checked )
80                  operation = "add";
81          } // end method additionRadioButton_CheckedChanged
82
83          // set the operation to subtraction
84          private void subtractionRadioButton_CheckedChanged( object sender,
85              EventArgs e )
86          {
87              if ( subtractionRadioButton.Checked )
88                  operation = "subtract";
89          } // end method subtractionRadioButton_CheckedChanged
90
91          // set the operation to multiplication
92          private void multiplicationRadioButton_CheckedChanged(
93              object sender, EventArgs e )
94          {
95              if ( multiplicationRadioButton.Checked )
96                  operation = "multiply";
97          } // end method multiplicationRadioButton_CheckedChanged
```

Fig. 28.15 | Math tutor using EquationGeneratorServiceXML to create equations. (Part 2 of 4.)

```
98
99       // set difficulty level to 1
100      private void levelOneRadioButton_CheckedChanged( object sender,
101         EventArgs e )
102      {
103         if ( levelOneRadioButton.Checked )
104            level = 1;
105      } // end method levelOneRadioButton_CheckedChanged
106
107      // set difficulty level to 2
108      private void levelTwoRadioButton_CheckedChanged( object sender,
109         EventArgs e )
110      {
111         if ( levelTwoRadioButton.Checked )
112            level = 2;
113      } // end method levelTwoRadioButton_CheckedChanged
114
115      // set difficulty level to 3
116      private void levelThreeRadioButton_CheckedChanged( object sender,
117         EventArgs e )
118      {
119         if ( levelThreeRadioButton.Checked )
120            level = 3;
121      } // end method levelThreeRadioButton_CheckedChanged
122   } // end class MathTutor
123 } // end namespace MathTutorXML
```

a) Generating a level 1 addition equation

b) Answering the question incorrectly

Fig. 28.15 | Math tutor using `EquationGeneratorServiceXML` to create equations. (Part 3 of 4.)

c) Answering the question correctly

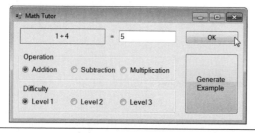

Fig. 28.15 | Math tutor using `EquationGeneratorServiceXML` to create equations. (Part 4 of 4.)

Difficulty Level and the Arithmetic Operation to Perform

The default setting for the difficulty level is 1, but the user can change this by choosing a level from the `RadioButtons` in the `GroupBox` labeled **Difficulty**. This invokes the corresponding `RadioButton`'s `CheckedChanged` event handler (lines 100–121), which sets integer `level` to the level selected by the user. The default question type is **Addition**, which the user can change by selecting one of the `RadioButtons` in the `GroupBox` labeled **Operation**. This invokes the corresponding operation's event handler in lines 76–97, which assigns to `string operation` the string corresponding to the user's selection.

Invoking the EquationGeneratorService

Line 21 defines the `HttpClient` that is used to invoke the web service. Event handler `generateButton_Click` (lines 29–50), which is declared `async`, invokes `EquationGenerator-atorService` method `GenerateEquation` (line 33–35) using the web service's `UriTemplate` specified at line 14 in Fig. 28.13.

Processing the XML Response

When the response arrives, the `await` keyword unwraps the XML `string`. Next, line 38 parses the XML response, then lines 39–41 use `XDocument`'s `Element` method to obtain the equation's left side, and lines 42–44 perform the same task to get the equation's result. As in the `WelcomeRESTXMLClient` example, we define the XML response's namespace (lines 16–18) as an `XNamespace` so that we can use it when extracting data from the XML. Then, the handler displays the left-hand side of the equation in `questionLabel` (line 47) and enables `okButton` and `answerTextBox` so that the user can enter an answer.

Checking Whether the User Entered the Correct Answer

When the user clicks **OK**, `okButton_Click` (lines 53–73) checks whether the user provided the correct answer.

28.8.3 Creating the REST-Based JSON WCF EquationGenerator Web Service

You can set the web service to return JSON data instead of XML. Figure 28.16 is a modified `IEquationGeneratorService` interface for a service that returns an `Equation` in JSON format. The `ResponseFormat` property (line 14) is added to the `WebGet` attribute and set to `WebMessageFormat.Json`. We don't show the implementation of this interface here, because it is identical to that of Fig. 28.14. This shows how flexible WCF can be.

```
 1   // Fig. 28.16: IEquationGeneratorService.cs
 2   // WCF REST service interface to create random equations based on a
 3   // specified operation and difficulty level.
 4   using System.ServiceModel;
 5   using System.ServiceModel.Web;
 6
 7   namespace EquationGeneratorServiceJSON
 8   {
 9      [ServiceContract]
10      public interface IEquationGeneratorService
11      {
12         // method to generate a math equation
13         [OperationContract]
14         [WebGet( ResponseFormat = WebMessageFormat.Json,
15            UriTemplate = "equation/{operation}/{level}" )]
16         Equation GenerateEquation( string operation, string level );
17      } // end interface IEquationGeneratorService
18   } // end namespace EquationGeneratorServiceJSON
```

Fig. 28.16 | WCF REST service interface to create random equations based on a specified operation and difficulty level.

28.8.4 Consuming the REST-Based JSON WCF EquationGenerator Web Service

A modified MathTutor app (Fig. 28.17) accesses the URI of the EquationGenerator web service to get the JSON object (lines 30–32). We define class Equation (Fig. 28.18) to use with JSON serialization, so that the Equation object sent from the web service can be deserialized into an Equation object on the client. The JSON object is deserialized using the System.Runtime.Serialization.Json namespace's DataContractJsonSerializer (created at lines 35–36) and converted into an Equation object (line 37–39). We use the LeftHandSide field of the deserialized object (line 42) to display the left side of the equation and the Result field (line 53) to obtain the answer.

```
 1   // Fig. 28.17: MathTutor.cs
 2   // Math tutor using EquationGeneratorServiceJSON to create equations.
 3   using System;
 4   using System.IO;
 5   using System.Net;
 6   using System.Runtime.Serialization.Json;
 7   using System.Text;
 8   using System.Windows.Forms;
 9
10   namespace MathTutorJSON
11   {
12      public partial class MathTutor : Form
13      {
14         private string operation = "add"; // the default operation
15         private int level = 1; // the default difficulty level
16         private Equation currentEquation;  // represents the Equation
```

Fig. 28.17 | Math tutor using EquationGeneratorServiceJSON. (Part 1 of 4.)

```
17
18       // object used to invoke service
19       private HttpClient service = new HttpClient();
20
21       public MathTutor()
22       {
23          InitializeComponent();
24       } // end constructor
25
26       // generates new equation when user clicks button
27       private async void generateButton_Click(object sender, EventArgs e)
28       {
29          // send request to EquationGeneratorService
30          string jsonString = await service.GetStringAsync( new Uri(
31             "http://localhost:57184/EquationGeneratorService.svc/" +
32             "equation/" + operation + "/" + level ) );
33
34          // deserialize response into an Equation object
35          DataContractJsonSerializer JSONSerializer =
36             new DataContractJsonSerializer( typeof( Equation ) );
37          currentEquation =
38             ( Equation ) JSONSerializer.ReadObject(new MemoryStream(
39             Encoding.Unicode.GetBytes( jsonString ) ) );
40
41          // display left side of equation
42          questionLabel.Text = currentEquation.LeftHandSide;
43          okButton.Enabled = true; // enable okButton
44          answerTextBox.Enabled = true; // enable answerTextBox
45       } // end method generateButton_Click
46
47       // check user's answer
48       private void okButton_Click( object sender, EventArgs e )
49       {
50          if ( !string.IsNullOrEmpty( answerTextBox.Text ) )
51          {
52             // determine whether user's answer is correct
53             if ( currentEquation.Result ==
54                Convert.ToInt32( answerTextBox.Text ) )
55             {
56                questionLabel.Text = string.Empty; // clear question
57                answerTextBox.Clear(); // clear answer
58                okButton.Enabled = false; // disable OK button
59                MessageBox.Show( "Correct! Good job!", "Result" );
60             } // end if
61             else
62             {
63                MessageBox.Show( "Incorrect. Try again.", "Result" );
64             } // end else
65          } // end if
66       } // end method okButton_Click
67
```

Fig. 28.17 | Math tutor using EquationGeneratorServiceJSON. (Part 2 of 4.)

```
68          // set the operation to addition
69          private void additionRadioButton_CheckedChanged( object sender,
70             EventArgs e )
71          {
72             if ( additionRadioButton.Checked )
73                operation = "add";
74          } // end method additionRadioButton_CheckedChanged
75
76          // set the operation to subtraction
77          private void subtractionRadioButton_CheckedChanged( object sender,
78             EventArgs e )
79          {
80             if ( subtractionRadioButton.Checked )
81                operation = "subtract";
82          } // end method subtractionRadioButton_CheckedChanged
83
84          // set the operation to multiplication
85          private void multiplicationRadioButton_CheckedChanged(
86             object sender, EventArgs e )
87          {
88             if ( multiplicationRadioButton.Checked )
89                operation = "multiply";
90          } // end method multiplicationRadioButton_CheckedChanged
91
92          // set difficulty level to 1
93          private void levelOneRadioButton_CheckedChanged( object sender,
94             EventArgs e )
95          {
96             if ( levelOneRadioButton.Checked )
97                level = 1;
98          } // end method levelOneRadioButton_CheckedChanged
99
100         // set difficulty level to 2
101         private void levelTwoRadioButton_CheckedChanged( object sender,
102            EventArgs e )
103         {
104            if ( levelTwoRadioButton.Checked )
105               level = 2;
106         } // end method levelTwoRadioButton_CheckedChanged
107
108         // set difficulty level to 3
109         private void levelThreeRadioButton_CheckedChanged( object sender,
110            EventArgs e )
111         {
112            if ( levelThreeRadioButton.Checked )
113               level = 3;
114         } // end method levelThreeRadioButton_CheckedChanged
115      } // end class MathTutorForm
116   } // end namespace MathTutorJSON
```

Fig. 28.17 | Math tutor using `EquationGeneratorServiceJSON`. (Part 3 of 4.)

a) Generating a level 2 multiplication equation

b) Answering the question incorrectly

c) Answering the question correctly

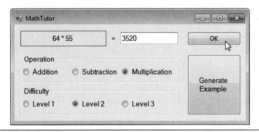

Fig. 28.17 | Math tutor using `EquationGeneratorServiceJSON`. (Part 4 of 4.)

```
1   // Fig. 28.18: Equation.cs
2   // Equation class representing a JSON object.
3   using System;
4
5   namespace MathTutorJSON
6   {
7      [Serializable]
8      class Equation
9      {
10        public int Left = 0;
11        public string LeftHandSide = null;
12        public string Operation = null;
13        public int Result = 0;
14        public int Right = 0;
15        public string RightHandSide = null;
16     } // end class Equation
17  } // end namespace MathTutorJSON
```

Fig. 28.18 | Equation class representing a JSON object.

28.9 Wrap-Up

This chapter introduced WCF—a set of technologies for building distributed systems in which system components communicate with one another over networks. You used WCF to build web services. You learned that a web service is a class that allows client software to call the web service's methods remotely via common data formats and protocols, such as XML, JSON, HTTP, SOAP and REST. We also discussed several benefits of distributed computing with web services.

We discussed how WCF facilitates publishing and consuming web services. You learned how to define web services and methods using REST architecture, and how to return data in both XML and JSON formats. You consumed REST-based web services using class HttpClient in Windows Forms apps.

29

Building a Windows Azure™ Cloud Computing App

Objectives

In this chapter you'll:

- Learn what cloud computing is.
- Learn about Windows Azure's cloud computing capabilities.
- Be introduced to Windows Azure security, privacy and reliability.
- Download the tools you'll need to start developing Azure apps and learn how to register for a free Windows Azure trial.
- Code an app that uses Windows Azure Table Storage.
- Test your app using the Storage Emulator that comes with the Windows Azure SDK.
- Learn about other popular cloud app platforms.

29.1 Introduction

As we discussed in Chapter 1, *cloud computing* allows you to use software and data stored in the "cloud"—i.e., accessed on remote computers (or servers) via the Internet and available on demand—rather than having it stored on your desktop, notebook computer or mobile device. Cloud computing allows you to instantaneously scale your computing resources (e.g., storage and processing power) to meet their occasional peak levels, making it more cost effective than purchasing expensive hardware. Using cloud computing services also saves money by shifting the burden of *managing* these apps to the service provider. Microsoft's Windows Azure is a cloud computing platform that allows you to develop, manage and distribute your apps in the cloud. With Windows Azure, your apps can store their data in the cloud so that the data is available at all times from any of your desktop computers and mobile devices. Windows Azure also provides scalable, flexible and cost effective infrastructure. Figure 29.1 describes the key use cases for Windows Azure cloud computing.

Use case	Description
Big data	The amount of data produced worldwide is enormous and growing quickly. Windows Azure enables you to scale your computing and storage capacity as needed, giving you flexibility and saving you the expense of buying hardware that's needed only occasionally. You can also use the additional computing power to process the data (e.g., performing analytics to track customer behavior and find trends).
Testing and development	Use multiple virtual machines to develop and test your apps in a variety of scenarios rather than buying additional hardware and software and setting up a variety of platforms.
Websites and web apps	Host your websites and web apps on Windows Azure which can handle varying demand and shifts the administrative burden (e.g., security and reliability) to Microsoft.

Fig. 29.1 | Windows Azure use cases (`www.windowsazure.com/en-us`). (Part 1 of 2.)

Use case	Description
Mobile apps	Use Windows Azure to support your mobile apps across a variety of platforms (e.g., Windows Phone 8, iOS, Android)—for example, authenticating app users, storing data and sending push notifications to users' devices.
Infrastructure	Set up servers in the cloud and scale your infrastructure (e.g., processor cycles, memory and secondary storage) as needed, paying for only what you use rather than purchasing additional costly hardware.
Storage, Backup and Recovery	Use Windows Azure's secure, reliable storage space to back up your data. The data is stored on servers in multiple locations worldwide to ensure that it's safe and accessible even in the case of a local disaster.
Identity and access management	Enable single sign-on to authenticate users just once to access multiple apps. Control access to apps or other data by setting up rules.
Media	Distribute media (e.g., stream video on demand) to several devices and platforms such as Windows, Android, iOS and others. You can also use Windows Azure to manage and protect your media content.

Fig. 29.1 | Windows Azure use cases (`www.windowsazure.com/en-us`). (Part 2 of 2.)

Figure 29.2 lists several other popular cloud computing platforms and apps.

Platform or app	URL	Description
Infrastructure		
Amazon Cloud Computing services	`aws.amazon.com`	Infrastructure, compute engine, database, big data, content delivery, storage, app deployment and more.
Google Drive™	`cloud.google.com`	Data storage, compute engine, infrastructure, app and web site development, big data analysis and more.
Hosting and sharing services		
NaviSite®	`navisite.com`	Infrastructure hosting.
Rackspace®	`www.rackspace.com`	Internet hosting.
Dropbox	`dropbox.com`	File hosting.
Microsoft SkyDrive®	`windows.microsoft.com/en-us/skydrive/download`	File hosting.
Box	`www.box.com`	File sharing.

Fig. 29.2 | Popular cloud computing platforms and apps. (Part 1 of 2.)

Platform or app	URL	Description
Media		
Audiobox	`audiobox.fm`	Media library management, synchronization and streaming.
Spotify®	`www.spotify.com`	Music streaming.
App delivery		
Cloudbees®	`www.cloudbees.com`	Web- and mobile-app delivery.
Heroku	`www.heroku.com`	App delivery.
Data storage and backup		
iCloud®	`www.apple.com/icloud`	Data storage and backup.
PrimaDesk	`www.primadesk.com`	Data backup, file sharing and single sign on.
SOS Online Backup	`www.sosonlinebackup.com/`	Online backup.
Miscellaneous cloud apps		
Evernote	`www.evernote.com`	Note taking.
Salesforce®	`www.salesforce.com`	Customer Relationship Management (CRM).
Waze	`www.waze.com`	GPS navigation.

Fig. 29.2 | Popular cloud computing platforms and apps. (Part 2 of 2.)

29.2 Installing the Windows Azure SDK for Visual Studio 2012

To install the **Windows Azure SDK for Visual Studio 2012**, go to

```
www.windowsazure.com/en-us/downloads/?sdk=net
```

and follow these steps:

1. Under **Languages** on the left side of the page, click **.NET**.

2. Next, click **VS 2012** under **.NET SDKs** in the middle of the page to download the executable file to your computer.

3. Open the executable file and click **Yes**.

4. In the **Web Platform Installer** window, click **Install**.

29.3 Windows Azure Cloud Services Accounts

The example that you'll build in this chapter uses the **Windows Azure Storage Emulator** on your local computer rather than connecting to the fee-based Windows Azure cloud services. By doing this, we're able to show you the basics of working with Windows Azure cloud-based storage without the need for a Windows Azure account.

29.3.1 Signing Up for a Windows Azure Cloud Services Account

To build real-world Azure apps, you'll need a Windows Azure cloud services account. To sign up for a free one-month trial,[1] visit

```
www.windowsazure.com/en-us/pricing/free-trial/
```

You must provide a credit card number even though it's a free trial.

29.3.2 Windows Azure Educator Grant

Instructors teaching Windows Azure in college courses may apply for an educator grant of **Windows Azure academic passes** at

```
academicpass.cloudapp.net
```

The grant provides students enrolled in the course with six months of access to Windows Azure cloud services. Educators receive 12 months of access. *No credit card information is required to use these services.* To learn more about the program, visit

```
www.windowsazure.com/en-us/community/education
```

Educators teaching Windows Azure should also check out the *Introduction to Cloud Computing: Faculty Resource Kit* provided by Microsoft's Faculty Connection. The kit includes:

- Cloud computing curriculum materials for computer science courses, such as course presentations, labs, tutorials, demos, papers from faculty who have taught Azure and more.

- Links to developer resources, forums, videos and sample code.

- Numerous presentations (videos and PDFs) from the Cloud Futures conference.

To access the Faculty Resource Kit, visit

```
www.facultyresourcecenter.com/curriculum/resourcekits/cloudv3/
```

29.3.3 Windows Azure for MSDN Subscribers

At the time of this writing, MSDN (Microsoft Developer Network) subscribers who sign up for Windows Azure receive $200 of Windows Azure credits for the first month after activation, then $50 to $150 of credits per month thereafter, depending on their MSDN subscription level. To learn more about the Windows Azure benefits included in the MSDN subscription, see

```
www.windowsazure.com/en-us/pricing/member-offers/msdn-benefits
```

29.4 Favorite Twitter Searches: Introduction

Twitter's search mechanism makes it easy to follow the trending topics being discussed by the more than 500 million Twitter users. Searches can be fine tuned using Twitter's *search operators* (we overview several of these in Section 29.6), often resulting in lengthy search strings that are time consuming and cumbersome to enter. The **Favorite Twitter Searches**

---

1. This Microsoft offer is subject to change.

app saves your favorite Twitter search queries with short tag names that are easy to remember. You can then select from your saved searches to quickly and easily follow tweets on your favorite topics.

Your favorite searches are saved using **Windows Azure Table Storage**, which we'll discuss in more detail in Section 29.6. If you use an actual Windows Azure account, rather than the Storage Emulator, your saved searches will be available on any computer running the app.

29.5 Favorite Twitter Searches: Test-Drive

Opening the Completed Application
In this chapter's examples folder, open the FavoriteTwitterSearches folder and double click FavoriteTwitterSearches.sln to open the project.

Running the Windows Azure Storage Emulator
The Windows Azure Storage Emulator lets you test the Azure storage capabilities of your apps locally before you connect your apps to live Azure accounts in the cloud. To run the emulator on Windows 7, go to **Start > All Programs > Windows Azure > Emulator** and select **Windows Azure Storage Emulator**. On Windows 8, click **Windows Azure Storage Emulator** on your **Start** screen. Once the emulator is up and running the icon ▓ will appear in the task tray of your Windows task bar. You can right click the icon to manage the emulator.

Running the App
In the IDE, select **Debug > Start Debugging** to run the app (Fig. 29.3). The TextBoxes in the **Add a Search** GroupBox allow you to enter new searches, and the ListBox in the **Tagged Searches** GroupBox displays previously saved searches (in this case, none yet). When the app first executes both GroupBoxes (and their contents) are disabled.

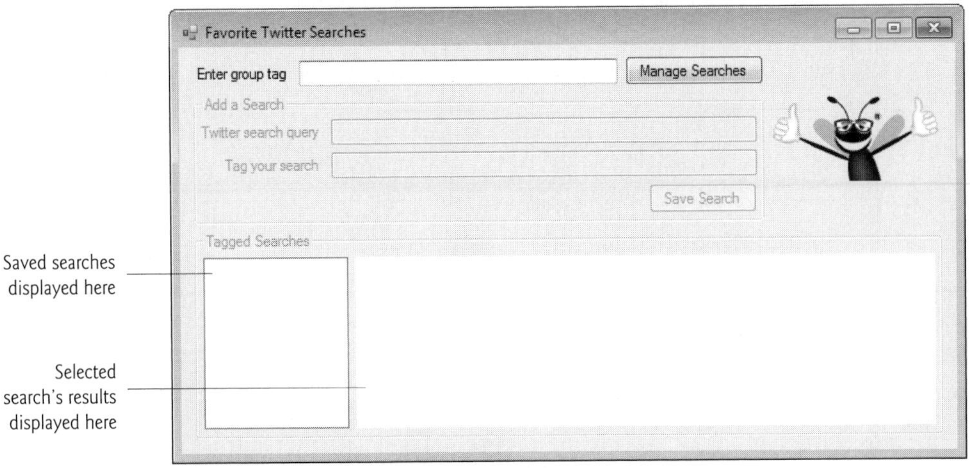

Fig. 29.3 | **Favorite Twitter Searches** app when it first executes.

Entering a Group Tag

The app enables you to store *groups of searches*. For example, you might have groups for different areas of interest, like books, music, movies stars, etc. Before you can enter any searches, you must specify a *group tag*. The app uses that to store and load the searches in that group. Enter the group tag deitel, then press **Manage Searches** to enable the rest of the app's GUI.

Adding a New Favorite Search

In the **Twitter search query** TextBox, enter from:deitel since:2013-08-16 as the search query (Fig. 29.4). The from: operator locates tweets from a specified Twitter account and the since: operator specifies a date in the format yyyy-mm-dd—tweets before that date will not appear in the search results. This query will return only tweets from the @deitel Twitter account that occurred on or after August 16, 2013. Figure 29.5 shows several Twitter search operators. A complete list can be found at

```
http://bit.ly/TwitterSearchOperators
```

In the **Tag your search** TextBox, enter deiteltweets as the tag for the search query. This will be the *short name* displayed in the ListBox at the **Tagged Searches** GroupBox's left side. Click **Save Search** to save the search into the Windows Azure Table Storage—the tag name for the new search appears in the ListBox at the **Tagged Searches** GroupBox's left side.

Fig. 29.4 | Entering a Twitter search.

Example	Finds tweets containing
`deitel iOS6`	Implicit *logical and* operator—find tweets containing `deitel` *and* `iOS6`.
`deitel OR iOS6`	Logical `OR` operator—find tweets containing `deitel` *or* `iOS6` *or both*.
`"how to program"`	String in quotes(`""`)—find tweets containing the exact phrase `"how to program"`.
`deitel ?`	`?` (question mark)—find tweets asking questions about `deitel`.
`deitel -mervyn`	`-` (minus sign)—find tweets containing `deitel` but not `mervyn`.
`deitel :)`	`:)` (happy face)—find *positive attitude* tweets containing `deitel`.
`deitel :(`	`:(` (sad face)—find *negative attitude* tweets containing `deitel`.
`since:2012-08-12`	`since:`—find tweets that occurred *on or after* the specified date, which must be in the form YYYY-MM-DD.
`from:deitel`	`from:`—find tweets from the Twitter account `@deitel`.
`to:deitel`	`to:`—find tweets to the Twitter account `@deitel`.

Fig. 29.5 | Some Twitter search operators.

Viewing Twitter Search Results

We rebind the `ListBox`'s `DataSource` to the list of searches when a new search is added. This selects the `ListBox`'s first item and displays its search results. Since `deiteltweets` is the only item in the `ListBox` at the moment, it's search results are displayed automatically. After adding more than one saved search, you can select your new search in the `ListBox` to see its results in the `WebBrowser` control on the right (Fig. 29.6).

Fig. 29.6 | Viewing search results.

29.6 Favorite Twitter Searches: Technologies Overview

This section overviews the Windows Azure technologies used in the **Favorite Twitter Searches** app.

Windows Azure Table Storage Service
Windows Azure provides three primary storage services:

- BLOB (Binary Large OBject)—Stores arbitrary binary data, such as images, audio and video.

- Table—Stores unstructured data (known as *entities*) that does not require complex manipulations like those that can be performed on data in a SQL database.

- SQL Database—Stores structured relational database data using techniques like those you learned in Chapter 20.

The **Favorite Twitter Searches** app demonstrates the Table service. Classes required for using these services are located in namespace `Microsoft.WindowsAzure.Storage`. To use these classes, you must add the Windows Azure Storage NuGet package to your app. After creating a project, right click the project name in **Solution Explorer**, then select **Manage NuGet Packages...**. In the dialog that appears, select the **Online** category, then use the **Search Online** field in the dialog's top-right corner to search for `Windows Azure Storage`. When the search completes, select **Windows Azure Storage** in the dialog's center column, then click **Install**. Once the installation is complete, click the dialog's **Close** button. Your project now contains the features required for accessing Windows Azure Storage services.

Storage Account
When you sign up for Windows Azure, you get your own *storage account*. Each storage account is currently limited to a maximum of 100 Terabytes of data across all three storage services. In this example, you'll use the so-called *development storage account*, which allows you to locally test your apps that use Windows Azure Storage services before attaching them to a paid Azure account. You specify the storage account in an app with an instance of class **CloudStorageAccount** (namespace `Microsoft.WindowsAzure.Storage`).

Table
For each storage account, the Windows Azure Table service can manage any number of *tables* provided that they all have unique names. For this app, you'll create a table named "FTS" that will store the information for groups of tagged Twitter searches.

TableEntity
To use Table Storage, you first create a subclass of **TableEntity** (namespace `Microsoft.WindowsAzure.Storage.Table`) that defines up to 252 properties to store, each with a *name* and a *value*. The total storage space for an entity cannot exceed one megabyte. Property values can have various types, including `byte` arrays, `bool`, `DateTime`, `double`, `int`, `long` and `string`. Both `byte` arrays and `strings` are limited to 64KB size.

In addition, every `TableEntity` has three inherited properties:

- **PartitionKey**—A unique string that's used by the Windows Azure Table Storage service to partition a table across multiple servers. This service is designed for fast access to massive amounts of data. Partitioning a table into pieces helps the

Windows Azure Table Storage service perform *load balancing*—a technique that distributes massive numbers of web requests across multiple servers so that all requests can receive better response times. Operations on entities that have the same PartitionKey are more efficient than those with different PartitionKeys.

- **RowKey**—A unique name that identifies an entity within a partition.
- **TimeStamp**—A DateTime value (maintained by Windows Azure) that represents when the entity was last modified.

Together, an entity's PartitionKey and RowKey are the primary key that uniquely identifies the entity in the table. Entities in a table are *not* required to have the same properties.

Complete details of the Windows Azure Table Storage service's restrictions on tables, entities and properties can be found at:

```
http://msdn.microsoft.com/en-us/library/windowsazure/dd179338.aspx
```

29.7 Favorite Twitter Searches: Code

The following subsections discuss the code for classes TaggedSearchEntity and FTSForm.

29.7.1 TableEntity for Storing Data in Windows Azure Table Storage

Figure 29.7 presents the TaggedSearchEntity subclass of TableEntity for storing tagged Twitter searches using the Windows Azure Table Storage service. (Recall that you can right click your project name in **Solution Explorer** and select **Add > Class...** to add a new class to your project.) The inherited property PartitionKey stores the name for a group of saved searches. Thus, all saved searches in a group will be stored on the same Azure Table storage server. The inherited RowKey property stores the short tag name that you specify for a Twitter search. The Query property (line 10) stores the search to submit to Twitter. Each subclass of TableEntity is required to provide a no-argument constructor so that the Windows Azure Table Storage service can serialize objects. We defined an empty no-argument constructor, because the compiler will not provide a default constructor if you define any constructors of your own (as we did in lines 16–26).

```
1   // Fig. 29.7: TaggedSearchEntity.cs
2   // TableEntity that stores tagged Twitter searches
3   using Microsoft.WindowsAzure.Storage.Table;
4
5   namespace FavoriteTwitterSearches
6   {
7      // class to represent a tagged search
8      public class TaggedSearchEntity : TableEntity
9      {
10        public string Query { get; set; } // Twitter query to perform
11
12        public TaggedSearchEntity()
13        {
14        } // end constructor
15
```

Fig. 29.7 | TableEntity that stores tagged Twitter searches. (Part 1 of 2.)

```
16          public TaggedSearchEntity( string groupname, string tag,
17             string query )
18          {
19             Query = query; // query to submit to Twitter
20
21             // set partition key to group name for group of tagged searches
22             PartitionKey = groupname;
23
24             // set row key to tag for specific search
25             RowKey = tag;
26          } // end constructor
27       } // end class TaggedSearchEntity
28    } // end namespace FavoriteTwitterSearches
```

Fig. 29.7 | TableEntity that stores tagged Twitter searches. (Part 2 of 2.)

29.7.2 Storing and Retrieving TableEntity Objects

Figures 29.8–29.12 present class FTSForm, which enables you to store your tagged Twitter searches and view search results.

FTSForm Instance Variables and Constructor
Figure 29.8 contains class FTSForm's instance variables and constructor. The string groupTag (line 14) is used as the PartitionKey in each TaggedSearchEntity.

```
1    // Fig. 29.8: FTSForm.cs
2    // Storing tagged Twitter searches in Azure Table Storage
3    using Microsoft.WindowsAzure.Storage;
4    using Microsoft.WindowsAzure.Storage.Table;
5    using System;
6    using System.Linq;
7    using System.Web;
8    using System.Windows.Forms;
9
10   namespace FavoriteTwitterSearches
11   {
12      public partial class FTSForm : Form
13      {
14         private string groupTag; // used to manage group of searches
15
16         CloudStorageAccount storageAccount; // used to access Azure account
17         CloudTableClient tableClient; // gives access to Azure tables
18         CloudTable ftsTable; // used to interact with specific Azure table
19
20         public FTSForm()
21         {
22            InitializeComponent();
23
24            // gives access to the Azure storage emulator
25            storageAccount = CloudStorageAccount.DevelopmentStorageAccount;
26
```

Fig. 29.8 | FTSForm instance variables and constructor. (Part 1 of 2.)

```
27              // create Azure table storage client
28              tableClient = storageAccount.CreateCloudTableClient();
29
30              // get reference to Contacts table
31              ftsTable = tableClient.GetTableReference( "FTS" );
32
33              // create the Contacts table if it does not already exist
34              ftsTable.CreateIfNotExists();
35          } // end constructor
36
```

Fig. 29.8 | FTSForm instance variables and constructor. (Part 2 of 2.)

CloudStorageAccount

The CloudStorageAccount (line 16) specifies the Azure storage account in which to store the TaggedSearchEntity objects. We use the *local storage emulator* in this app for demonstration purposes. To connect to the local storage emulator, line 25 in the constructor initializes variable storageAccount to CloudStorageAccount.DevelopmentStorageAccount. The setup to use *online* storage requires additional steps that are discussed in detail at

www.windowsazure.com/en-us/develop/net/how-to-guides/table-services/

CloudTableClient

The **CloudTableClient** (line 17) provides access to the Windows Azure Table Storage service from a client app. Class CloudStorageAccount's **CreateCloudTableClient** method (line 28 in the constructor) returns a CloudTableClient that's properly configured for the CloudStorageAccount on which it's called. You use the CloudTableClient to get the table that the app manipulates.

CloudTable

The **CloudTable** (line 18) provides access to a specific table that's managed by the Windows Azure Table Storage service. Class CloudTableClient's **GetTableReference** method (line 31 in the constructor) returns a CloudTable that you can use to interact with a specified table. Class CloudTable's **CreateIfNotExists** method checks whether the table specified in line 31 ("FTS") exists and, if not, creates it.

manageSearchesButton_Click Event Handler

The manageSearchesButton_Click event handler (Fig. 29.9) removes the data from the tagsListBox (lines 55–56), clears the webBrowser control (line 57), stores the group name entered by the user (line 60) and loads the searches for the new group name that was just entered. WebBrowser method **Navigate** (line 57) loads the specified web page into the control. Specifying the argument string.Empty clears the control's current contents.

```
37          // get group tag, enable capabilities for adding searches
38          // and load existing searches into the app
39          private void manageSearchesButton_Click(
40              object sender, EventArgs e )
41          {
```

Fig. 29.9 | manageSearchesButton_Click event handler. (Part 1 of 2.)

```
42                  // check whether groupTagTextBox is empty
43                  if ( string.IsNullOrEmpty( groupTagTextBox.Text ) )
44                  {
45                      MessageBox.Show( "Enter group tag " );
46                  } // end if
47                  else
48                  {
49                      addSearchGroupBox.Enabled = true;
50                      taggedSearchesGroupBox.Enabled = true;
51
52                      // if new groupTag does not equal previous groupTag
53                      if ( !groupTagTextBox.Text.Equals( groupTag ) )
54                      {
55                          tagsListBox.DataSource = null; // remove data source
56                          tagsListBox.Items.Clear(); // clear tasListBox
57                          webBrowser.Navigate( string.Empty ); // clear webBrowser
58
59                          // get groupTag for use as Azure PartitionKey
60                          groupTag = groupTagTextBox.Text;
61
62                          LoadSearches(); // Load group of searches
63                      } // end if
64                  } // end else
65              } // end method manageSearchesButton_Click
66
```

Fig. 29.9 | manageSearchesButton_Click event handler. (Part 2 of 2.)

LoadSearches *Method—Querying the Table Storage Service*
Method LoadSearches (Fig. 29.10) creates a **TableQuery** that locates TaggedSearchEntity objects with a specified PartitionKey value. A TableQuery provides capabilities for selecting and filtering table contents. Method Where applies a filter condition. TableQuery static method GenerateFilterCondition requires three arguments:

- A string representing the property to compare—in this case, the PartitionKey.

- A constant from the QueryComparisons class indicating the type of comparison to perform—in this case, we create a filter that checks whether the value of the property in the first argument is *equal* to the value in the third argument. You can also perform *not equal, less than, less than or equal to, greater than* or *greater than or equal to* comparisons.

- A value to compare to the value of the property in the first argument—in this case the groupTag entered by the user.

Lines 80–81 call CloudTable method **ExecuteQuery** to perform the query. The method returns an IEnumerable<TaggedSearchEntity> containing the query results. Lines 84–85 sort the results into ascending alphabetical order. Line 87 specifies that the value of the TaggedSearchEntity property RowKey will be displayed in the tagsListBox and line 88 binds a List representation of the sorted TaggedSearchEntity objects to the ListBox's DataSource property, which displays the tags in the ListBox.

```
67        // access Azure table storage to load group of search
68        private void LoadSearches()
69        {
70           try
71           {
72              // create TableQuery to get group of searches
73              TableQuery<TaggedSearchEntity> query =
74                 new TableQuery<TaggedSearchEntity>().
75                    Where( TableQuery.GenerateFilterCondition(
76                       "PartitionKey", QueryComparisons.Equal,
77                       groupTag ) );
78
79              // execute query to get group of searches
80              var searches =
81                 ftsTable.ExecuteQuery<TaggedSearchEntity>( query );
82
83              // Sort tags (RowKeys) alphabetically
84              var sortedSearches =
85                 searches.OrderBy( search => search.RowKey.ToLower() );
86
87              tagsListBox.DisplayMember = "RowKey";
88              tagsListBox.DataSource = sortedSearches.ToList();
89           } // end try
90           catch ( Exception exception )
91           {
92              MessageBox.Show(
93                 String.Format( "Load Failed: {0}", exception ) );
94           } // end catch
95        } // end method LoadSearches
96
```

Fig. 29.10 | LoadSearches method.

saveSearchButton_Click *Event Handler*

Method saveSearchButton_Click (Fig. 29.11) inserts a new TaggedSearchEntity into the table. Lines 104–105 create the TaggedSearchEntity. TableOperation static method **Insert** creates a TableOperation that can insert the specified entity. Line 111 calls class CloudTable's **Execute** method to perform the insertSearch TableOperation. We then reload the saved searches.

```
97        // save a search into the Azure table for this app
98        private void saveSearchButton_Click( object sender, EventArgs e )
99        {
100          // try to save a search
101          try
102          {
103             // create a new TaggedSearchEntity to insert
104             TaggedSearchEntity search = new TaggedSearchEntity(
105                groupTag, tagTextBox.Text, queryTextBox.Text );
106
```

Fig. 29.11 | saveSearchButton_Click event handler. (Part 1 of 2.)

```
107              // create TableOperation to insert TaggedSearchEntity
108              TableOperation insertSearch = TableOperation.Insert( search );
109
110              // execute the TableOperation to insert the new search
111              ftsTable.Execute( insertSearch );
112
113              LoadSearches(); // Reload searches and select new one
114
115              queryTextBox.Text = string.Empty; // clear queryTextBox
116              tagTextBox.Text = string.Empty; // clear tagTextBox
117           } // end try
118           catch ( Exception exception )
119           {
120              MessageBox.Show(
121                 String.Format( "Insert Failed: {0}", exception ) );
122           } // end catch
123        } // end method saveSearchButton_Click
124
```

Fig. 29.11 | saveSearchButton_Click event handler. (Part 2 of 2.)

tagsListBox_SelectedIndexChanged *Event Handler*

Method tagsListBox_SelectedIndexChanged (Fig. 29.12) performs the selected search. Lines 136–138 create a string representing the Twitter search to perform. Some Twitter search operators use characters that are special in URLs, so line 138 encodes those characters in the selected search's Query property by calling static method **UrlEncode** of class HttpUtility (namespace System.Web). Line 140 calls WebBrowser method Navigate to load the search results into the webBrowser control.

```
125        // display search results in the webBrowser control
126        private void tagsListBox_SelectedIndexChanged(
127           object sender, EventArgs e )
128        {
129           // get selected item from tagsListBox
130           TaggedSearchEntity selectedSearch =
131              ( TaggedSearchEntity ) tagsListBox.SelectedItem;
132
133           if ( selectedSearch != null )
134           {
135              // create URL representing search
136              String urlString = String.Format(
137                 "https://twitter.com/search?q={0}",
138                 HttpUtility.UrlEncode( selectedSearch.Query ) );
139
140              webBrowser.Navigate( urlString ); // show results
141           } // end if
142        } // end method tagsListBox_SelectedIndexChanged
143     } // end class
144  } // end namespace FavoriteTwitterSearches
```

Fig. 29.12 | tagsListBox_SelectedIndexChanged event handler.

29.8 Security, Privacy and Reliability

Cloud services can be vulnerable to denial-of-service (DoS) attacks and security breaches. Many of the largest cloud computing services have been the targets of cyber attacks that have interrupted service to users or compromised their data. Much of the security and reliability burden is on the service provider; however, there are steps you can take to ensure the privacy and security or your data—particularly protecting identity and access (Fig. 29.13). Microsoft's *Windows Azure Security Guidance* guide (www.windowsazure.com/en-us/develop/net/best-practices/security) lists several identity and access scenarios and provides best practices for handling each.

Microsoft Global Foundation Services (GFS) manages data centers for Windows Azure which comply with industry standards for security (see www.iso.org/iso/catalogue_detail?csnumber=42103). Microsoft uses internal checks and third-party auditors to ensure that Windows Azure is compliant with the security, privacy and reliability standards and policies.

Visit the Windows Azure Trust Center (www.windowsazure.com/en-us/support/trust-center/) to learn more about Azure security, privacy and compliance. For additional cloud security information and research, check out the Cloud Security Alliance (cloudsecurityalliance.org).

Solution	Description
Windows Identity Foundation (WIF)	Verify identity and grant access rather than programming your own solution.
Windows Azure AD Access Control	Single sign on across multiple applications.
Active Directory Federation Services	Allows the user's organization to verify identity so the user can access web apps from trusted business partners.
Windows Azure Shared Access Signatures	Allow restricted access to blobs, tables, containers and queues for a set time period.

Fig. 29.13 | Windows Azure identity access mechanisms (www.windowsazure.com/en-us/develop/net/best-practices/security).

29.9 Microsoft Windows Azure Resources

Figure 29.14 lists some of the key Microsoft Windows Azure resources.

Resource	URL	Description
Reference		
Windows Azure home page	www.windowsazure.com/en-us/documentation	Includes links to Windows Azure news, blogs, videos and documentation.

Fig. 29.14 | Some key Microsoft Windows Azure resources. (Part 1 of 3.)

Resource	URL	Description
Introducing Windows Azure	`www.windowsazure.com/en-us/ develop/net/fundamentals/ intro-to-windows-azure`	Discusses the fundamentals of Windows Azure including the components, execution models, data management, networking, business analytics, messaging, caching, identity, high-performance computing, media, commerce and SDKs.
Windows Azure Execution Models	`www.windowsazure.com/en-us/ develop/net/fundamentals/ compute`	Discusses three execution models for running Windows Azure apps—virtual machines, web sites and cloud services—and provides examples of when to use each.
Videos		
Windows Azure Developer Experience Videos	`channel9.msdn.com/Blogs/ Windows-Azure-Developer- Experience-Videos`	Several introductory Windows Azure videos that demonstrate how to build a simple app.
Official YouTube Channel for Windows Azure	`www.youtube.com/user/ windowsazure`	Microsoft's Windows Azure channel includes numerous video tutorials and presentations.
Code samples, labs and demos		
Windows Azure code samples	`code.msdn.microsoft.com/ windowsazure`	Hundreds of code samples from Windows Azure team members and from the community.
Windows Azure Training Kit	`www.windowsazure.com/en-us/ develop/net/other-resources/ training-kit`	Presentations, demos, labs and code samples that show you how to build Windows Azure apps.
Documentation		
Reference	`www.windowsazure.com/en-us/ develop/net/reference`	Includes links to the various cloud computing feature guides and the .NET and REST API references.
Guidance (best practices)	`www.windowsazure.com/en-us/ develop/net/guidance`	Best practices for designing, deployment, troubleshooting, security, and performance.
App Services	`www.windowsazure.com/en-us/ develop/net/app-services`	Guides and tutorials for Windows Azure app services.
Data Services	`www.windowsazure.com/en-us/ develop/net/data`	Guides and tutorials for Windows Azure data services.
Mobile Services	`www.windowsazure.com/en-us/ develop/mobile/`	Documentation, tutorials, forums and code samples for Windows Azure mobile services.

Fig. 29.14 | Some key Microsoft Windows Azure resources. (Part 2 of 3.)

Resource	URL	Description
News and forums		
Windows Azure Blog	www.windowsazure.com/en-us/community/blog	News and tutorials from Microsoft Windows Azure team members and the Azure community.
Windows Azure Newsletter	www.windowsazure.com/en-us/community/newsletter	Stay up-to-date with the latest Windows Azure developments and events.
Forums	www.windowsazure.com/en-us/support/forums	Ask questions and get answers from other Windows Azure developers.

Fig. 29.14 | Some key Microsoft Windows Azure resources. (Part 3 of 3.)

29.10 Microsoft Windows Azure Code Samples

Microsoft's All-In-One Code Framework (blogs.msdn.com/b/onecode) is a library of free sample apps designed to help developers address real-world issues. Developers can use the samples available on the website and submit requests for new solutions to be posted. Figure 29.15 lists some of the Microsoft sample apps. Visit the websites for each to find the source code and a tutorial that shows you how to build the app.

Code Example	URL
Windows Azure Access Control for Single Sign-On	code.msdn.microsoft.com/windowsazure/Windows-Azure-Access-d01d282b
Azure + Bing Map Sample Application	code.msdn.microsoft.com/windowsazure/CSAzureBingMaps-bab92df1
Access Azure Table Storage via WCF Data Services	code.msdn.microsoft.com/windowsazure/CSAzureTableStorageWCFDS-2355159b
Host and use WCF Services in Windows Azure	code.msdn.microsoft.com/windowsazure/CSAzureWCFServices-20c7d9c5
Geolocation Sample End-to-End using Windows Azure Mobile Services	code.msdn.microsoft.com/windowsapps/Geolocation-sample-end-to-5d9ee245
Windows Azure Mobile Services— Doto Sample (to do list app)	code.msdn.microsoft.com/windowsapps/doto-a-simple-social-todo-7e6ba464
Create a Game Leaderboard using Windows Azure Mobile Services	code.msdn.microsoft.com/windowsapps/Adding-a-Leaderboard-to-1f9d216d
Authenticate Microsoft Account, Facebook, Twitter and Google with Mobile Services	code.msdn.microsoft.com/windowsapps/Authenticate-Account-827dd37b
How to use Bing Search API	code.msdn.microsoft.com/windowsazure/How-to-use-bing-search-API-4c8b287e

Fig. 29.15 | A few Microsoft Windows Azure sample apps.

29.11 Additional Web Resources

Web-Based Training

channel9.msdn.com/Series/Windows-Azure-Cloud-Services-Tutorials
A series of eight short online courses that introduce you to Windows Azure Cloud Services, ending with a tutorial that shows you how to build a Windows Azure trivia game.

www.microsoftvirtualacademy.com/training-courses/introduction-to-windows-azure
The Microsoft Virtual Academy training course, "Introduction to Windows Azure Training." The course provides an introduction to Windows Azure and discusses deploying, managing and monitoring Azure apps.

Feature Overviews

msdn.microsoft.com/en-us/library/windowsazure/gg441573.aspx
"What's New in Windows Azure," from Microsoft. Discusses the Management Portal, infrastructure as a service (IaaS) support, platform as a service (PaaS) support, high-density hosting of websites, health monitoring for apps and services, linked resources, scaling, single portal for all key workloads, in-portal help and information, easy transitions, integrated developer experience, and more.

weblogs.asp.net/scottgu/archive/2012/06/07/meet-the-new-windows-azure.aspx
Blog: "Meet the New Windows Azure," by Scott Guthrie. Discusses the new Admin portal and command line tools, virtual machines, websites, cloud services and distributed caching, and the new SDKs and tooling support.

hwww.windowsazure.com/en-us/overview/what-is-windows-azure/
Windows Azure features including mobile services, web sites, virtual machines, cloud services, data management, business analytics, caching, networking, identity, messaging, media services and marketplace.

www.windowsazure.com/en-us/home/features/mobile-services/
Azure Mobile Services include creating a backend for Windows 8 client apps, saving data to the cloud, adding users to an app, and quickly integrating push notifications.

How-To Articles

msdn.microsoft.com/en-us/library/windowsazure/gg433055.aspx
"Use the Windows Azure SDK Tools to Package, Run, and Deploy an Application," from Microsoft. Discusses the Windows Azure Compute Emulator for running your app locally, the Windows Azure Storage Emulator for storage services, packaging a Windows Azure application, uploading certificates and encrypting passwords for remote desktop connections, testing applications in the Compute Emulator, reducing the number of running instances for testing, debugging and collecting diagnostic data.

www.windowsazure.com/en-us/manage/services/cloud-services/how-to-create-and-deploy-a-cloud-service/
"How to Create and Deploy a Cloud Service," from Microsoft's Windows Azure documentation. Topics include how to create a cloud service using Quick Create, upload a certificate for a cloud service, deploy a cloud service

Fundamentals

blogs.msdn.com/b/acoat/archive/2012/06/03/excellent-windows-azure-intro-videos.aspx
The blog post, "Excellent Windows Azure Intro Videos," by Andrew Coates of Microsoft. The post includes four short, animated videos that explain the basics of Windows Azure, SQL Azure, Access Control and Service Bus.

www.windowsazure.com/en-us/develop/net/fundamentals/identity/
"Windows Azure Identity," discusses running and using Windows Server Active Directory to manage identities in Windows Azure.

www.windowsazure.com/en-us/develop/net/fundamentals/cloud-storage/
"Data Management and Business Analytics," from Microsoft. Discusses storing data in blobs and tables, running a database management system in a virtual machine and SQL database data sync and reporting.

www.windowsazure.com/en-us/develop/net/fundamentals/networking/
"Windows Azure Networking," from Microsoft. Discusses the Windows Azure Virtual Network, Windows Azure Connect and Windows Azure Traffic Manager.

www.windowsazure.com/en-us/develop/net/fundamentals/hybrid-solutions/
Discusses the benefits of hybrid, service bus relay, service bus queries and topics, SQL data sync, access control services (ACS) paired with Active Directory Federation Services (AD FS), and Windows Azure Connect.

Reference Guides

msdn.microsoft.com/en-us/library/windowsazure/ee460799.aspx
"Windows Azure Service Management REST API Reference," from Microsoft. Discusses the Service Management API, versioning, addressing service management resources, authenticating requests, tracking asynchronous requests, status and error codes, operations on storage accounts, operations on hosted services, operations on service certificates, operations on affinity groups, operations on locations, operations on tracking asynchronous requests, retrieving operating systems information, retrieving subscription history, management certificates, the traffic manager, virtual machines, virtual machine images, virtual machine disks, virtual networks, and virtual network gateways.

Tutorials

www.windowsazure.com/en-us/develop/net/tutorials/get-started/
The Microsoft tutorial, "Deploying an ASP.NET Web Application to a Windows Azure Web Site," shows you build a simple web app that runs in the cloud using Visual Studio ASP.NET MVC 4 and Windows Azure.

www.windowsazure.com/en-us/develop/net/how-to-guides/twilio-voice-and-sms-service/
The Microsoft tutorial, "How to Use Twilio for Voice and SMS Capabilities from Windows Azure," shows you how to use the Twilio API on Windows Azure to make phone calls and send an SMS (Short Message Service) text message. Includes sample code.

www.windowsazure.com/en-us/develop/net/tutorials/web-site-with-sql-database/
The tutorial, "Deploy a Secure ASP.NET MVC App with Membership, OAuth, and SQL Database to a Windows Azure Web Site," by Rick Anderson and Tom Dykstra.

www.windowsazure.com/en-us/manage/services/hdinsight/get-started-hdinsight/
The tutorial, "Getting Started with Windows Azure HDInsight Service," by Microsoft shows you how to start using HDInsight to manage and store your data in Windows Azure.

Tools and Resources

vmdepot.msopentech.com/List/Index
VM Depot includes open-source virtual machine images for use with Windows Azure.

29.12 Wrap-Up

In this chapter, we introduced cloud computing and Windows Azure. We discussed some popular cloud computing apps. We discussed how to sign up for a free Windows Azure trial and download the tools you'll need to build Windows Azure apps.

You created the **Favorite Twitter Searches** app to demonstrate Windows Azure Table Storage. We overviewed the app's capabilities, then you test-drove it. Next, we presented the app's code implementation, which showed the features you needed to create a table, insert items into the table and query the table's contents.

GUI with Windows Presentation Foundation

Objectives

In this chapter you'll:

- Define a WPF GUI with Extensible Application Markup Language (XAML).

- Handle WPF user-interface events.

- Use WPF's commands feature to handle common tasks such as cut, copy and paste.

- Customize the look-and-feel of WPF GUIs using styles and control templates.

- Use data binding to display data in WPF controls.

30.1 Introduction

In Chapters 14–15, you built GUIs using Windows Forms. In this chapter, you'll build GUIs using **Windows Presentation Foundation** (WPF)—one of Microsoft's two newer frameworks for GUI, graphics, animation and multimedia (the other is Windows 8 UI). In Chapter 31, WPF Graphics and Multimedia, you'll learn how to incorporate 2D graphics, 3D graphics, animation, audio and video in WPF apps.

We begin with an introduction to WPF. Next, we discuss an important tool for creating WPF apps called **XAML** (pronounced "zammel")—**Extensible Application Markup Language**. XAML is an XML vocabulary for defining and arranging GUI controls without any C# code. Because XAML is an XML vocabulary, you should understand the basics of XML before learning XAML and WPF. We introduce XML in Sections 22.2–22.4.

Section 30.3 demonstrates how to define a WPF GUI with XAML. Sections 30.4–30.7 demonstrate the basics of creating a WPF GUI—layout, controls and events. You'll also learn capabilities of WPF controls and event handling that are different from those in Windows Forms. WPF allows you to easily customize the look-and-feel of a GUI beyond what is possible in Windows Forms. Sections 30.8–30.11 demonstrate several techniques for manipulating the appearance of your GUIs. WPF also allows you to create data-driven GUIs that interact with many types of data. We demonstrate this in Section 30.12.

30.2 Windows Presentation Foundation (WPF)

Before WPF, you often had to use multiple technologies to build client apps. If a Windows Forms app required video and audio capabilities, you needed to incorporate an additional technology such as Windows Media Player. Likewise, if your app required 3D graphics capabilities, you had to incorporate a separate technology such as Direct3D. WPF provides a single platform capable of handling both of these requirements, and more. It enables you to use one technology to build apps containing GUI, images, animation, 2D or 3D graphics, audio and video capabilities. In this chapter and Chapter 31, we demonstrate each of these capabilities.

WPF can interoperate with existing technologies. For example, you can include WPF controls in Windows Forms apps to incorporate multimedia content (such as audio or video) without converting the entire app to WPF, which could be a costly and time-consuming process. You can also use Windows Forms controls in WPF apps.

WPF can use your computer's graphics hardware acceleration capabilities to increase your apps' performance. In addition, WPF generates **vector-based graphics** and is **resolution independent**. Vector-based graphics are defined not by a grid of pixels as **raster-based graphics** are, but rather by mathematical models. An advantage of vector-based graphics is that when you change the resolution, there's no loss of quality. Hence, the graphics become portable to a great variety of devices. Moreover, your apps won't appear smaller on higher-resolution screens. Instead, they'll remain the same size and display sharper. Chapter 31 presents more information about vector-based graphics and resolution independence.

Building a GUI with WPF is similar to building a GUI with Windows Forms—you drag-and-drop predefined controls from the **Toolbox** onto the design area. Many WPF controls correspond directly to those in Windows Forms. Just as in a Windows Forms app, the functionality is event driven. Many of the Windows Forms events you're familiar with are also in WPF. A WPF Button, for example, is similar to a Windows Forms Button, and both raise Click events.

There are several important differences between the two technologies, though. The WPF layout scheme is different. WPF properties and events have more capabilities. Most notably, WPF allows designers to define the appearance and content of a GUI without any C# code by defining it in XAML, a descriptive **markup** language (that is, a text-based notation for describing something).

Introduction to XAML

In Windows Forms, when you use the designer to create a GUI, the IDE generates code statements that create and configure the controls. In WPF, it generates XAML markup. Because XML is designed to be readable by both humans and computers, you can also manually write XAML markup to define GUI controls. When you compile your WPF app, a XAML compiler generates code to create and configure controls based on your XAML markup. This technique of defining *what* the GUI should contain without specifying *how* to generate it is an example of **declarative programming**.

XAML allows designers and programmers to work together more efficiently. Without writing any code, a graphic designer can edit the look-and-feel of an app using a design tool, such as Microsoft's **Blend for Visual Studio**—a XAML graphic design program. A programmer can import the XAML markup into Visual Studio and focus on coding the logic that gives an app its functionality. Even if you're working alone, however, this separation of front-end appearance from back-end logic improves your program's organization and makes it easier to maintain. XAML is an essential component of WPF programming.

30.3 Declarative GUI Programming Using XAML

A XAML document defines the appearance of a WPF app. Figure 30.1 is a simple XAML document that defines a window that displays Welcome to WPF! A XAML document consists of many nested elements, delimited by start tags and end tags. As with any other XML document, each XAML document must contain a single root element. Just as in XML, data is placed as nested content or in attributes.

```
 1   <!-- Fig. 30.1: XAMLIntroduction.xaml -->
 2   <!-- A simple XAML document. -->
 3
 4   <!-- the Window control is the root element of the GUI -->
 5   <Window x:Class="XAMLIntroduction.MainWindow"
 6      xmlns="http://schemas.microsoft.com/winfx/2006/xaml/presentation"
 7      xmlns:x="http://schemas.microsoft.com/winfx/2006/xaml"
 8      Title="A Simple Window" Height="150" Width="250">
 9
10      <!-- a layout container -->
11      <Grid Background="Gold">
12         <!-- a Label control -->
13         <Label Content="Welcome to WPF!" HorizontalAlignment="Center"
14            VerticalAlignment="Center"/>
15      </Grid>
16   </Window>
```

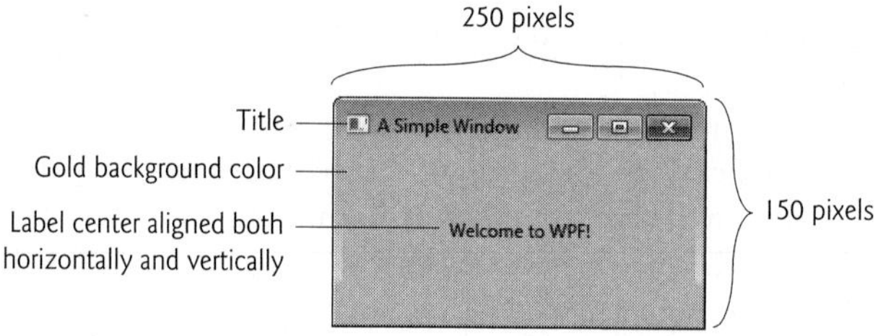

Fig. 30.1 | A simple XAML document.

Presentation XAML Namespace and Standard XAML Namespace

Two standard namespaces must be defined in every XAML document so that the XAML compiler can interpret your markup—the **presentation XAML namespace**, which defines WPF-specific elements and attributes, and the **standard XAML namespace**, which defines elements and attributes that are standard to all types of XAML documents. Usually, the presentation XAML namespace (`http://schemas.microsoft.com/winfx/2006/xaml/presentation`) is defined as the default namespace (line 6), and the standard XAML namespace (`http://schemas.microsoft.com/winfx/2006/xaml`) is mapped to the namespace prefix x (line 7). These are both automatically included in the `Window` element's start tag when you create a WPF app.

Window Control

WPF **controls** are represented by elements in XAML markup. The root element of the XAML document in Fig. 30.1 is a **Window** control (lines 5–16), which defines the app's window—this corresponds to the `Form` control in Windows `Forms`.

The `Window` start tag **x:Class** attribute (line 5) specifies the class name of the associated *code-behind* class that provides the GUI's functionality. The x: signifies that the `Class` attribute is located in the standard XAML namespace. A XAML document must have an associated code-behind file to handle events.

Using attributes, you can define a control's properties in XAML. For example, the `Window`'s `Title`, `Width` and `Height` properties are set in line 8. A `Window`'s `Title` specifies the text that's displayed in the title bar. The Width and Height properties specify a control's width and height, respectively, using machine-independent pixels.

Content Controls

Window is a **content control** (a control derived from class **ContentControl**), meaning it can have exactly one child element or text content. You'll almost always set a **layout container** (a control derived from the **Panel** class) as the child element so that you can host multiple controls in a Window. A layout container such as a Grid (lines 11–15) can have many child elements, allowing it to contain many controls. In Section 30.5, you'll use content controls and layout containers to arrange a GUI.

Label Control

Like Window, a **Label** (lines 13–14) is also a ContentControl. Labels are generally used to display text.

30.4 Creating a WPF App

To create a new WPF app, select **File > New Project...** to display the **New Project** dialog (Fig. 30.2) and select **WPF Application** from the list of template types under **Visual C# > Windows**. Specify a name and location for your app, then click **OK** to create the project. The IDE for a WPF app looks nearly identical to that of a Windows Forms app. You'll recognize the familiar **Toolbox**, **Design** view, **Solution Explorer** and **Properties** window.

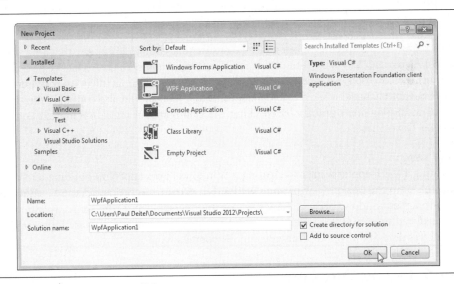

Fig. 30.2 | New Project dialog.

XAML View

There are differences in the IDE, however. One is the new **XAML view** (Fig. 30.3) that appears below the design area when you open a XAML document that represents a window. The **XAML** view is linked to the **Design** view and the **Properties** window. When you edit content in the **Design** view, the **XAML** view automatically updates, and vice versa. Likewise, when you edit properties in the **Properties** window, the **XAML** view automatically updates, and vice versa.

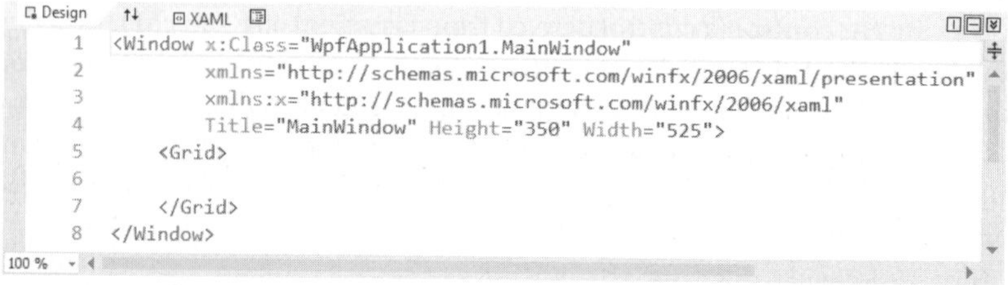

```
□ Design   ↑↓   □ XAML  □                                                  □□☑
  1  <Window x:Class="WpfApplication1.MainWindow"                           ⊕
  2          xmlns="http://schemas.microsoft.com/winfx/2006/xaml/presentation" ▲
  3          xmlns:x="http://schemas.microsoft.com/winfx/2006/xaml"
  4          Title="MainWindow" Height="350" Width="525">
  5     <Grid>
  6
  7     </Grid>
  8  </Window>
100 %  ▾ ◄                                                                 ►
```

Fig. 30.3 | **XAML** view.

Generated Files
When you create a WPF app, several files are generated and can be viewed in the **Solution Explorer**. **App.xaml** defines the Application object and its settings. The most noteworthy setting is the Application element's **StartupUri** attribute, which defines the XAML document that executes first when the app loads (MainWindow.xaml by default). **App.xaml.cs** contains App.xaml's code-behind class and handles application-level events. MainWindow.xaml defines the app's window, and MainWindow.xaml.cs contains its code-behind class, which handles the window's events. The file name of the code-behind class is always the file name of the associated XAML document followed by the .cs file-name extension.

Setting XAML Indent Size and Displaying Line Numbers
We use three-space indents in our code. To ensure that your code appears the same as the book's examples, change the tab spacing for XAML documents to three spaces (the default is four). Select **Tools > Options...** to display the **Options** dialog, then in **Text Editor > XAML > Tabs** change the **Tab size** and **Indent size** to 3. You should also configure the **XAML** editor to display line numbers by checking the **Line numbers** checkbox in **Text Editor > XAML > General**.

GUI Design
Creating a WPF app is similar to creating a Windows Forms app. You can drag-and-drop controls onto the **Design** view of your WPF GUI. A control's properties can be edited in the **Properties** window. Because XAML is easy to understand and edit, some programmers manually edit their GUIs' XAML markup directly rather than doing everything through the IDE's drag-and-drop GUI designer and **Properties** window.

30.5 Laying Out Controls

In Windows Forms, a control's size and location are specified explicitly. In WPF, a control's size should be specified as a *range* of possible values rather than fixed values, and its location specified *relative* to those of other controls. This scheme, in which you specify how controls share the available space, is called **flow-based layout**. Its advantage is that it enables your GUIs, if designed properly, to be aesthetically pleasing, no matter how a user might *resize* the app. Likewise, it enables your GUIs to be resolution independent.

30.5.1 General Layout Principles

Layout refers to the *size* and *positioning* of controls. The WPF layout scheme addresses both of these in a flow-based fashion and can be summarized by two fundamental principles with regard to a control's size and position.

Size of a Control

Unless necessary, a control's size should *not* be defined *explicitly*. Doing so often creates a design that looks pleasing when it first loads, but deteriorates when the app is resized or the content updates. In addition to the Width and Height properties associated with every control, all WPF controls have the **MinWidth**, **MinHeight**, **MaxHeight** and **MaxWidth** properties. If the Width and Height properties are both Auto (which is the default when they are not specified in the XAML code), you can use MinWidth, MinHeight, MaxWidth and MaxHeight to specify a *range* of acceptable sizes for a control as it's resized with its container.

Position of a Control

A control's position should *not* be defined in absolute terms. Instead, it should be specified based on its position *relative* to the layout container in which it's included and the other controls in the same container. All controls have three properties for this purpose—Margin, HorizontalAlignment and VerticalAlignment. **Margin** specifies how much space to put around a control's edges. The value of Margin is a comma-separated list of four integers, representing the left, top, right and bottom margins. Additionally, you can specify two integers—the first represents the value for the left and right margins and the second for the top and bottom margins. If you specify just one integer, it uses the same margin on all four sides.

HorizontalAlignment and **VerticalAlignment** specify how to align a control within its layout container. Valid options of HorizontalAlignment are Left, Center, Right and Stretch. Valid options of VerticalAlignment are Top, Center, Bottom and Stretch. Stretch means that the object will occupy as much space as possible.

Other Layout Properties

A control can have other layout properties specific to the layout container in which it's contained. We'll discuss these as we examine the specific layout containers. WPF provides many controls for laying out a GUI. Figure 30.4 lists several of them.

Control	Description
Layout containers (derived from Panel)	
Grid	Layout is defined by a *grid of rows and columns*, depending on the RowDefinitions and ColumnDefinitions properties. Elements are placed into *cells*.
Canvas	Layout is *coordinate based*. Element positions are defined explicitly by their distance from the *top* and *left* edges of the Canvas.
StackPanel	Elements are arranged in a *single row or column*, depending on the Orientation property.

Fig. 30.4 | Common controls used for layout. (Part 1 of 2.)

Control	Description
DockPanel	Elements are positioned based on which edge they're *docked* to. If the LastChild-Fill property is True, the last element gets the remaining space in the middle.
WrapPanel	A wrapping StackPanel. Elements are arranged *sequentially in rows or columns* (depending on the Orientation), each row or column wrapping to start a new one when it reaches the WrapPanel's right or bottom edge, respectively.
Content controls (derived from ContentControl)	
Border	Adds a background or a border to the child element.
GroupBox	Surrounds the child element with a titled box.
Window	The app's window. Also the root element.
Expander	Puts the child element in a titled area that collapses to display just the header and expands to display the header and the content.

Fig. 30.4 | Common controls used for layout. (Part 2 of 2.)

30.5.2 Layout in Action

Figure 30.5 shows the XAML document and the GUI display of a painter app. Note the use of Margin, HorizontalAlignment and VerticalAlignment throughout the markup. This example introduces several WPF controls that are commonly used for layout, as well as a few other basic controls like Buttons and RadioButtons.

This app's controls look similar to Windows Forms controls. WPF **RadioButton**s function as *mutually exclusive* options, just like their Windows Forms counterparts. However, a WPF RadioButton does not have a Text property. Instead, it's a ContentControl, meaning it can have *exactly one child* or *text content*. This makes the control more versatile, enabling it to be labeled by an image or other item. In this example, each RadioButton is labeled by plain text specified with the Content attribute (for example, lines 31, 33, 35 and 37). A WPF **Button** behaves like a Windows Forms Button but is a ContentControl. As such, a WPF Button can display any single element as its content, not just text. Lines 58–59 and 62–63 define the two buttons seen in the Painter app. You can drag and drop controls onto the WPF designer and create their event handlers, just as you do in the Windows Forms designer.

```
 1    <!-- Fig. 30.5: MainWindow.xaml -->
 2    <!-- XAML of a painter app. -->
 3    <Window x:Class="Painter.MainWindow"
 4       xmlns="http://schemas.microsoft.com/winfx/2006/xaml/presentation"
 5       xmlns:x="http://schemas.microsoft.com/winfx/2006/xaml"
 6       Title="Painter" Height="340" Width="350" Background="Beige">
 7
 8       <!-- creates a Grid -->
 9       <Grid>
10          <Grid.ColumnDefinitions>
11             <ColumnDefinition Width="Auto" /> <!-- defines a column -->
12             <ColumnDefinition Width="*" />
13          </Grid.ColumnDefinitions>
```

Fig. 30.5 | XAML of a painter app. (Part 1 of 3.)

```
14
15          <!-- creates a Canvas -->
16          <Canvas x:Name="paintCanvas" Grid.Column="1" Background="White"
17              Margin="0" MouseMove="paintCanvas_MouseMove"
18              MouseLeftButtonDown="paintCanvas_MouseLeftButtonDown"
19              MouseLeftButtonUp="paintCanvas_MouseLeftButtonUp"
20              MouseRightButtonDown="paintCanvas_MouseRightButtonDown"
21              MouseRightButtonUp="paintCanvas_MouseRightButtonUp" />
22
23          <!-- creates a StackPanel-->
24          <StackPanel Margin="3">
25              <!-- creates a GroupBox for color options -->
26              <GroupBox Header="Color" Margin="3">
27                  <StackPanel Margin="3" HorizontalAlignment="Left"
28                      VerticalAlignment="Top">
29
30                      <!-- creates RadioButtons for selecting color -->
31                      <RadioButton x:Name="redRadioButton" Content="Red"
32                          Margin="3" Checked="redRadioButton_Checked" />
33                      <RadioButton x:Name="blueRadioButton" Content="Blue"
34                          Margin="3" Checked="blueRadioButton_Checked" />
35                      <RadioButton x:Name="greenRadioButton" Content="Green"
36                          Margin="3" Checked="greenRadioButton_Checked" />
37                      <RadioButton x:Name="blackRadioButton" Content="Black"
38                          IsChecked="True" Margin="3"
39                          Checked="blackRadioButton_Checked" />
40                  </StackPanel>
41              </GroupBox>
42
43              <!-- creates GroupBox for size options -->
44              <GroupBox Header="Size" Margin="3">
45                  <StackPanel Margin="3" HorizontalAlignment="Left"
46                      VerticalAlignment="Top">
47                      <RadioButton x:Name="smallRadioButton" Content="Small"
48                          Margin="3" Checked="smallRadioButton_Checked" />
49                      <RadioButton x:Name="mediumRadioButton" IsChecked="True"
50                          Checked="mediumRadioButton_Checked" Content="Medium"
51                          Margin="3" />
52                      <RadioButton x:Name="largeRadioButton" Content="Large"
53                          Margin="3" Checked="largeRadioButton_Checked" />
54                  </StackPanel>
55              </GroupBox>
56
57              <!-- creates a Button-->
58              <Button x:Name="undoButton" Content="Undo" Width="75"
59                  Margin="3,10,3,3" Click="undoButton_Click"/>
60
61              <!-- creates a Button-->
62              <Button x:Name="clearButton" Content="Clear" Width="75"
63                  Margin="3,10,3,3" Click="clearButton_Click"/>
64          </StackPanel>
65      </Grid>
66  </Window>
```

Fig. 30.5 | XAML of a painter app. (Part 2 of 3.)

Fig. 30.5 | XAML of a painter app. (Part 3 of 3.)

GroupBox Control

A WPF **GroupBox** arranges controls and displays just as a Windows Forms GroupBox would, but using one is slightly different. The **Header** property replaces the Windows Forms version's Text property. Also, a GroupBox is a ContentControl, so to place *multiple* controls in it, you must place them in a layout container such as a StackPanel (lines 27–40).

StackPanel Control

In the Painter app, we organized each GroupBox's RadioButtons by placing them in **StackPanel**s (for example, lines 27–40). A StackPanel is the *simplest* of layout containers. It arranges its content either *vertically* or *horizontally*, depending on its **Orientation** property's setting. The default Orientation is Vertical, which is used by every StackPanel in the Painter example.

Grid Control

The Painter Window's contents are contained within a **Grid**—a flexible, all-purpose layout container. A Grid organizes controls into a user-defined number of *rows* and *columns* (one row and one column by default). You can define a Grid's rows and columns by setting its **RowDefinitions** and **ColumnDefinitions** properties, whose values are a collection of **Row-Definition** and **ColumnDefinition** objects, respectively. Because these properties do not take string values, they cannot be specified as attributes in the Grid tag. Another syntax is used instead. A class's property can be defined in XAML as a *nested* element with the name *ClassName.PropertyName*. For example, the Grid.ColumnDefinitions element in lines 10–13 sets the Grid's ColumnDefinitions property and defines two columns, which separate the options from the painting area, as shown in Fig. 30.5.

You can specify the Width of a ColumnDefinition and the Height of a RowDefinition with an *explicit size*, a *relative size* (using *) or Auto. Auto makes the row or column only as big as it needs to be to fit its contents. The setting * specifies the size of a row or column with respect to the Grid's other rows and columns. For example, a column with a Height of 2* would be twice the size of a column that's 1* (or just *). A Grid first allocates its space to the rows and columns whose sizes are defined explicitly or determined automatically. The remaining space is divided among the other rows and columns. By default, all Widths and Heights are set to *, so every cell in the grid is of equal size. In the Painter app, the first column is just wide enough to fit the controls, and the rest of the space is allotted to the painting area (lines 11–12). If you resize the Painter window, you'll notice that only the width of the paintable area increases or decreases.

If you click the ellipsis button next to the RowDefinitions or ColumnDefinitions property in the **Properties** window, the **Collection Editor** window will appear. (If you cannot find a property, type its name in the **Search Properties** text box at the top of the **Properties** window or view the properties by **Name** rather than **Category**.) This tool can be used to add, remove, reorder, and edit the properties of rows and columns in a Grid. In fact, any property that takes a collection as a value can be edited in a version of the **Collection Editor** specific to that collection. For example, you could edit the Items property of a ComboBox (that is, drop-down list) in such a way. The ColumnDefinitions **Collection Editor** is shown in Fig. 30.6.

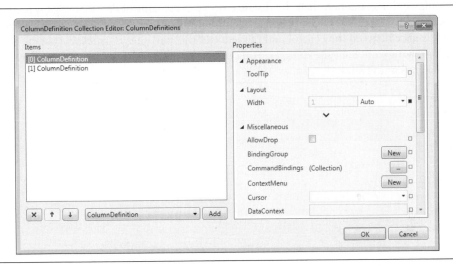

Fig. 30.6 | Using the **Collection Editor**.

The control properties we've introduced so far look and function just like their Windows Forms counterparts. To indicate which cell of a Grid a control belongs in, however, you use the **Grid.Row** and **Grid.Column** properties. These are known as **attached properties**—they're defined by a *different* control than that to which they're applied. In this case, Row and Column are defined by the Grid itself but applied to the controls contained in the Grid (for example, line 16 in Fig. 30.5). To specify the number of rows or columns that a control spans, you can use the **Grid.RowSpan** or **Grid.ColumnSpan** attached properties, respectively. By default, a control spans the entire Grid, unless the Grid.Row or Grid.Column property is set, in which case the control spans only the specified row or column by default.

Canvas Control
The painting area of the Painter app is a **Canvas** (lines 16–21), another layout container. A Canvas allows users to position controls by defining explicit coordinates. Controls in a Canvas have the attached properties, **Canvas.Left** and **Canvas.Top**, which specify the control's coordinate position based on its distance from the Canvas's *left* and *top* borders,

respectively. If two controls *overlap*, the one with the *greater* **Canvas.ZIndex** displays in the *foreground*. If this property is not defined for the controls, then the *last* control added to the canvas displays in the foreground. When you provide a name for a control via the Properties window, the IDE adds an x:Name attribute to the controls XAML. This name is used in the C# code as the control's variable name.

Layout in Design Mode

As you're creating your GUI in **Design** mode, you'll notice many helpful layout features. For example, as you *resize* a control, its width and height are displayed. In addition, *snaplines* appear as necessary to help you align the edges of elements. These lines will also appear when you move controls around the design area.

When you select a control, *margin lines* that extend from the control to the edges of its container appear, as shown in Fig. 30.7. If a solid line containing a number extends to the edge of the container, then the distance between the control and that edge is *fixed*. If a dashed line appears between the edge of the control and the edge of the container, then the distance between the control and that edge of the container is *dynamic*—the distance changes as the container size changes. You can toggle between the two by clicking the icons at the ends of the lines.

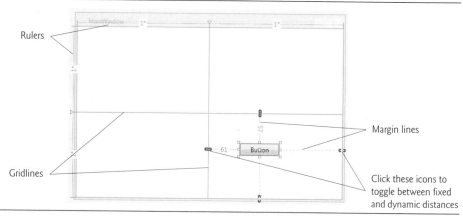

Fig. 30.7 | Margin lines and gridlines in **Design** view.

Furthermore, the **Design** view also helps you use a Grid. As shown in Fig. 30.7, when you select a control in a Grid, the Grid's rulers appear to the *left* and on *top* of it. The widths and heights of each column and row, respectively, appear on the rulers. Gridlines that outline the Grid's rows and columns also appear, helping you align and position the Grid's elements. You can also create more rows and columns by clicking where you want to separate them on the ruler.

30.6 Event Handling

Basic event handling in WPF is almost identical to Windows Forms event handling, but there is a fundamental difference, which we'll explain later in this section. We'll use the Painter example to introduce WPF event handling. Figure 30.8 provides the code-behind class for the Painter Window. As in Windows Forms GUIs, when you double click a control, the IDE automatically generates an event handler for that control's primary event. The IDE also adds an attribute to the control's XAML element specifying the event name and the name of the event handler that responds to the event. For example, in line 32 of Fig. 30.5, the attribute

Checked="redRadioButton_Checked"

specifies that the redRadioButton's Checked event handler is redRadioButton_Checked.

```csharp
// Fig. 30.8: MainWindow.xaml.cs
// Code-behind for MainWindow.xaml.
using System.Windows;
using System.Windows.Controls;
using System.Windows.Input;
using System.Windows.Media;
using System.Windows.Shapes;

namespace Painter
{
   public partial class MainWindow : Window
   {
      private int diameter = (int) Sizes.MEDIUM; // diameter of circle
      private Brush brushColor = Brushes.Black; // drawing color
      private bool shouldErase = false; // specify whether to erase
      private bool shouldPaint = false; // specify whether to paint

      private enum Sizes // size constants for diameter of the circle
      {
         SMALL = 4,
         MEDIUM = 8,
         LARGE = 10
      } // end enum Sizes

      // constructor
      public MainWindow()
      {
         InitializeComponent();
      } // end constructor

      // paints a circle on the Canvas
      private void PaintCircle( Brush circleColor, Point position )
      {
         Ellipse newEllipse = new Ellipse(); // create an Ellipse

         newEllipse.Fill = circleColor; // set Ellipse's color
         newEllipse.Width = diameter; // set its horizontal diameter
         newEllipse.Height = diameter; // set its vertical diameter

         // set the Ellipse's position
         Canvas.SetTop( newEllipse, position.Y );
         Canvas.SetLeft( newEllipse, position.X );
```

Fig. 30.8 | Code-behind for MainWindow.xaml. (Part 1 of 4.)

```
44              paintCanvas.Children.Add( newEllipse );
45      } // end method PaintCircle
46
47      // handles paintCanvas's MouseLeftButtonDown event
48      private void paintCanvas_MouseLeftButtonDown( object sender,
49          MouseButtonEventArgs e )
50      {
51          shouldPaint = true; // OK to draw on the Canvas
52      } // end method paintCanvas_MouseLeftButtonDown
53
54      // handles paintCanvas's MouseLeftButtonUp event
55      private void paintCanvas_MouseLeftButtonUp( object sender,
56          MouseButtonEventArgs e )
57      {
58          shouldPaint = false; // do not draw on the Canvas
59      } // end method paintCanvas_MouseLeftButtonUp
60
61      // handles paintCanvas's MouseRightButtonDown event
62      private void paintCanvas_MouseRightButtonDown( object sender,
63          MouseButtonEventArgs e )
64      {
65          shouldErase = true; // OK to erase the Canvas
66      } // end method paintCanvas_MouseRightButtonDown
67
68      // handles paintCanvas's MouseRightButtonUp event
69      private void paintCanvas_MouseRightButtonUp( object sender,
70          MouseButtonEventArgs e )
71      {
72          shouldErase = false; // do not erase the Canvas
73      } // end method paintCanvas_MouseRightButtonUp
74
75      // handles paintCanvas's MouseMove event
76      private void paintCanvas_MouseMove( object sender,
77          MouseEventArgs e )
78      {
79          if ( shouldPaint )
80          {
81              // draw a circle of selected color at current mouse position
82              Point mousePosition = e.GetPosition( paintCanvas );
83              PaintCircle( brushColor, mousePosition );
84          } // end if
85          else if ( shouldErase )
86          {
87              // erase by drawing circles of the Canvas's background color
88              Point mousePosition = e.GetPosition( paintCanvas );
89              PaintCircle( paintCanvas.Background, mousePosition );
90          } // end else if
91      } // end method paintCanvas_MouseMove
92
93      // handles Red RadioButton's Checked event
94      private void redRadioButton_Checked( object sender,
95          RoutedEventArgs e )
96      {
```

Fig. 30.8 | Code-behind for MainWindow.xaml. (Part 2 of 4.)

```
97              brushColor = Brushes.Red;
98           } // end method redRadioButton_Checked
99
100          // handles Blue RadioButton's Checked event
101          private void blueRadioButton_Checked( object sender,
102             RoutedEventArgs e )
103          {
104             brushColor = Brushes.Blue;
105          } // end method blueRadioButton_Checked
106
107          // handles Green RadioButton's Checked event
108          private void greenRadioButton_Checked( object sender,
109             RoutedEventArgs e )
110          {
111             brushColor = Brushes.Green;
112          } // end method greenRadioButton_Checked
113
114          // handles Black RadioButton's Checked event
115          private void blackRadioButton_Checked( object sender,
116             RoutedEventArgs e )
117          {
118             brushColor = Brushes.Black;
119          } // end method blackRadioButton_Checked
120
121          // handles Small RadioButton's Checked event
122          private void smallRadioButton_Checked( object sender,
123             RoutedEventArgs e )
124          {
125             diameter = ( int ) Sizes.SMALL;
126          } // end method smallRadioButton_Checked
127
128          // handles Medium RadioButton's Checked event
129          private void mediumRadioButton_Checked( object sender,
130             RoutedEventArgs e )
131          {
132             diameter = ( int ) Sizes.MEDIUM;
133          } // end method mediumRadioButton_Checked
134
135          // handles Large RadioButton's Checked event
136          private void largeRadioButton_Checked( object sender,
137             RoutedEventArgs e )
138          {
139             diameter = ( int ) Sizes.LARGE;
140          } // end method largeRadioButton_Checked
141
142          // handles Undo Button's Click event
143          private void undoButton_Click( object sender, RoutedEventArgs e )
144          {
145             int count = paintCanvas.Children.Count;
146
```

Fig. 30.8 | Code-behind for MainWindow.xaml. (Part 3 of 4.)

```
147              // if there are any shapes on Canvas remove the last one added
148              if ( count > 0 )
149                  paintCanvas.Children.RemoveAt( count - 1 );
150          } // end method undoButton_Click
151
152          // handles Clear Button's Click event
153          private void clearButton_Click( object sender, RoutedEventArgs e )
154          {
155              paintCanvas.Children.Clear(); // clear the canvas
156          } // end method clearButton_Click
157      } // end class MainWindow
158  } // end namespace Painter
```

Fig. 30.8 | Code-behind for `MainWindow.xaml`. (Part 4 of 4.)

The `Painter` app "draws" by placing colored circles on the `Canvas` at the mouse pointer's position as you drag the mouse. The `PaintCircle` method (lines 32–45 in Fig. 30.8) creates the circle by defining an `Ellipse` object (lines 34–38), and positions it using the **Canvas.SetTop** and **Canvas.SetLeft** methods (lines 41–42), which change the circle's `Canvas.Left` and `Canvas.Top` attached properties, respectively.

The **Children** property stores a list (of type **UIElementCollection**) of a layout container's child elements. This allows you to edit the layout container's child elements with C# code as you would any other implementation of the `IEnumerable` interface. You can add an element to the container by calling the **Add** method of the `Children` list (for example, line 44). The **Undo** and **Clear** buttons work by invoking the **RemoveAt** and **Clear** methods of the `Children` list (lines 149 and 155), respectively.

Just as with a Windows Forms RadioButton, a WPF RadioButton has a Checked event. Lines 94–140 handle the **Checked** event for each of the RadioButtons in this example, which change the color and the size of the circles painted on the Canvas. The Button control's **Click** event also functions the same in WPF as it did in Windows Forms. Lines 143–156 handle the **Undo** and **Clear** Buttons. The event-handler declarations look almost identical to how they would look in a Windows Forms app, except that the event-arguments object (e) is a `RoutedEventArgs` object instead of an `EventArgs` object. We'll explain why later in this section.

Mouse and Keyboard Events

WPF has built-in support for keyboard and mouse events that's nearly identical to the support in Windows Forms. Painter uses the **MouseMove** event of the paintable Canvas to paint and erase (lines 76–91). A control's MouseMove event is triggered whenever the mouse moves within the boundaries of the control. Information for the event is passed to the event handler using a **MouseEventArgs** object, which contains mouse-specific information. The **GetPosition** method of MouseEventArgs, for example, returns the current position of the mouse relative to the control that triggered the event (for example, lines 82 and 88). MouseMove works the same as it does in Windows Forms. [*Note:* Much of the functionality in our sample Painter app is already provided by the WPF InkCanvas control. We chose not to use this control so we could demonstrate various other WPF features.]

WPF has additional mouse events. Painter also uses the **MouseLeftButtonDown** and **MouseLeftButtonUp** events to toggle painting on and off (lines 48–59), and the **Mouse-RightButtonDown** and **MouseRightButtonUp** events to toggle erasing on and off (lines 62–73). All of these events pass information to the event handler using the **MouseButtonEvent-Args** object, which has properties specific to a mouse button (for example, ButtonState or ClickCount) in addition to mouse-specific ones. These events are new to WPF and are more specific versions of MouseUp and MouseDown (which are still available in WPF). A summary of commonly used mouse and keyboard events is provided in Fig. 30.9.

Common mouse and keyboard events	
Mouse Event with an Event Argument of Type MouseEventArgs	
MouseMove	Raised when you move the mouse within a control's boundaries.
Mouse Events with an Event Argument of Type MouseButtonEventArgs	
MouseLeftButtonDown	Raised when the left mouse button is pressed.
MouseLeftButtonUp	Raised when the left mouse button is released.
MouseRightButtonDown	Raised when the right mouse button is pressed.
MouseRightButtonUp	Raised when the right mouse button is released.
Mouse Event with an Event Argument of Type MouseWheelEventArgs	
MouseWheel	Raised when the mouse wheel is rotated.
Keyboard Events with an Event Argument of Type KeyEventArgs	
KeyDown	Raised when a key is pressed.
KeyUp	Raised when a key is released.

Fig. 30.9 | Common mouse and keyboard events.

Routed Events

WPF events have a significant distinction from their Windows Forms counterparts—they can travel either up (from child to parent) or down (from parent to child) the containment hierarchy—the hierarchy of nested elements defined within a control. This is called **event routing**, and all WPF events are **routed events**.

The event-arguments object that's passed to the event handler of a WPF Button's Click event or a RadioButton's Check event is of the type **RoutedEventArgs**. All event-argument objects in WPF are of type RoutedEventArgs or one of its subclasses. As an event travels up or down the hierarchy, it may be useful to stop it before it reaches the end. When the **Handled** property of the RoutedEventArgs parameter is set to true, event handlers ignore the event. It may also be useful to know the source where the event was first triggered. The **Source** property stores this information. You can learn more about the benefits of routed events at bit.ly/RoutedEvents.

Demonstrating Routed Events

Figures 30.10 and 30.11 show the XAML and code-behind for a program that demonstrates event routing. The program contains two GroupBoxes, each with a Label inside (lines 15–27 in Fig. 30.10). One group handles a left-mouse-button press with Mouse-LeftButtonUp, and the other with PreviewMouseLeftButtonUp. As the event travels up or down the containment hierarchy, a log of where the event has traveled is displayed in a **TextBox** (line 29). The WPF TextBox functions just like its Windows Forms counterpart.

```
 I   <!-- Fig. 30.10: MainWindow.xaml -->
 2   <!-- Routed-events example (XAML). -->
 3   <Window x:Class="RoutedEvents.MainWindow"
 4      xmlns="http://schemas.microsoft.com/winfx/2006/xaml/presentation"
 5      xmlns:x="http://schemas.microsoft.com/winfx/2006/xaml"
 6      Title="Routed Events" Height="300" Width="300"
 7      x:Name="routedEventsWindow">
 8      <Grid>
 9         <Grid.RowDefinitions>
10            <RowDefinition Height="Auto" />
11            <RowDefinition Height="Auto" />
12            <RowDefinition Height="*" />
13         </Grid.RowDefinitions>
14
15         <GroupBox x:Name="tunnelingGroupBox" Grid.Row="0" Header="Tunneling"
16            Margin="5" PreviewMouseLeftButtonUp="Tunneling">
17            <Label x:Name="tunnelingLabel" Margin="5"
18               HorizontalAlignment="Center"
19               PreviewMouseLeftButtonUp="Tunneling" Content="Click Here"/>
20         </GroupBox>
21
22         <GroupBox x:Name="bubblingGroupBox" Grid.Row="1" Header="Bubbling"
23            Margin="5" MouseLeftButtonUp="Bubbling">
24            <Label x:Name="bubblingLabel" Margin="5"
25               MouseLeftButtonUp="Bubbling" HorizontalAlignment="Center"
26               Content="Click Here"/>
27         </GroupBox>
28
29         <TextBox x:Name="logTextBox" Grid.Row="2" Margin="5" />
30      </Grid>
31   </Window>
```

Fig. 30.10 | Routed-events example (XAML).

```
 1   // Fig. 30.11: MainWindow.xaml.cs
 2   // Routed-events example (code-behind).
 3   using System.Windows;
 4   using System.Windows.Controls;
 5   using System.Windows.Input;
 6
 7   namespace RoutedEvents
 8   {
 9      public partial class MainWindow : Window
10      {
11         int bubblingEventStep = 1; // step counter for Bubbling
12         int tunnelingEventStep = 1; // step counter for Tunneling
13         string tunnelingLogText = string.Empty; // temporary Tunneling log
14
15         public RoutedEventsWindow()
16         {
17            InitializeComponent();
18         } // end constructor
19
20         // PreviewMouseUp is a tunneling event
21         private void Tunneling( object sender, MouseButtonEventArgs e )
22         {
23            // append step number and sender
24            tunnelingLogText = string.Format( "{0}({1}): {2}\n",
25               tunnelingLogText, tunnelingEventStep,
26               ( ( Control ) sender ).Name );
27            ++tunnelingEventStep; // increment counter
28
29            // execution goes from parent to child, ending with the source
30            if ( e.Source.Equals( sender ) )
31            {
32               tunnelingLogText = string.Format(
33                  "This is a tunneling event:\n{0}", tunnelingLogText );
34               logTextBox.Text = tunnelingLogText; // set logTextBox text
35               tunnelingLogText = string.Empty; // clear temporary log
36               tunnelingEventStep = 1; // reset counter
37            } // end if
38         } // end method Tunneling
39
40         // MouseUp is a bubbling event
41         private void Bubbling( object sender, MouseButtonEventArgs e )
42         {
43            // execution goes from child to parent, starting at the source
44            if ( e.Source.Equals( sender ) )
45            {
46               logTextBox.Clear(); // clear the logTextBox
47               bubblingEventStep = 1; // reset counter
48               logTextBox.Text = "This is a bubbling event:\n";
49            } // end if
50
```

Fig. 30.11 | Routed-events example (code-behind). (Part 1 of 2.)

```
51              // append step number and sender
52              logTextBox.Text = string.Format( "{0}({1}): {2}\n",
53                 logTextBox.Text, bubblingEventStep,
54                 ( ( Control ) sender ).Name );
55              ++bubblingEventStep;
56          } // end method Bubbling
57      } // end class MainWindow
58   } // end namespace RoutedEvents
```

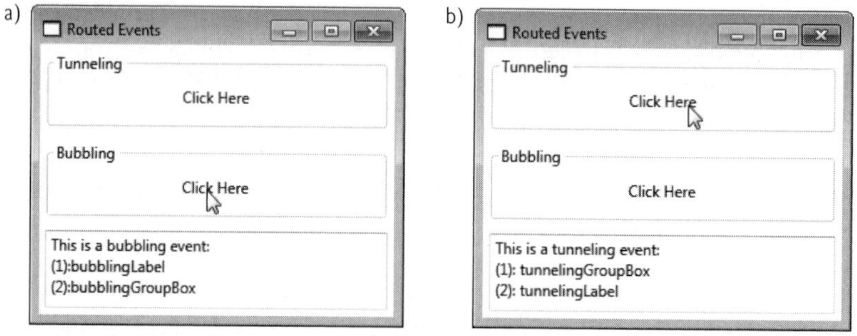

Fig. 30.11 | Routed-events example (code-behind). (Part 2 of 2.)

There are three types of routed events—**direct events**, **bubbling events** and **tunneling events**. *Direct events* are like ordinary Windows Forms events—they do *not* travel up or down the containment hierarchy. Bubbling events start at the Source and travel *up* the hierarchy ending at the root (Window) or until you set Handled to true. *Tunneling events* start at the top and travel *down* the hierarchy until they reach the Source or Handled is true. To help you distinguish tunneling events from bubbling events, WPF prefixes the names of tunneling events with Preview. For example, **PreviewMouseLeftButtonDown** is the tunneling version of MouseLeftButtonDown, which is a bubbling event.

If you click the **Click Here** Label in the **Tunneling** GroupBox, the click is handled first by the GroupBox, then by the contained Label. The event handler that responds to the click handles the **PreviewMouseLeftButtonUp** event—a tunneling event. The Tunneling method (lines 21–38 in Fig. 30.11) handles the events of both the GroupBox and the Label. An event handler can handle events for many controls. Simply select each control then use the events tab in the **Properties** window to select the appropriate event handler for the corresponding event of each control. If you click the other Label, the click is handled first by the Label, then by the containing GroupBox. The Bubbling method (lines 41–56) handles the MouseLeftButtonUp events of both controls.

30.7 Commands and Common Application Tasks

In Windows Forms, event handling is the only way to respond to user actions. WPF provides an alternate technique called a **command**—an action or a task that may be triggered by many different user interactions. In Visual Studio, for example, you can cut, copy and paste code. You can execute these tasks through the **Edit** menu, a toolbar or keyboard shortcuts. To program this functionality in WPF, you can define a single command for each task, thus centralizing the handling of common tasks—this is not easily done in Windows Forms.

Commands also enable you to synchronize a task's availability to the state of its corresponding controls. For example, users should be able to copy something only if they have content selected. When you define the copy command, you can specify this as a requirement. As a result, if the user has no content selected, then the menu item, toolbar item and keyboard shortcut for copying are all automatically disabled.

Commands are implementations of the **ICommand** interface. When a command is executed, the **Execute** method is called. However, the command's execution logic is not defined in its Execute method. You must specify this logic when implementing the command. An ICommand's **CanExecute** method works the same way. The logic that specifies when a command is enabled and disabled is not determined by the CanExecute method and must instead be specified by responding to an appropriate event. Class RoutedCommand is the standard implementation of ICommand. Every RoutedCommand has a Name and a collection of **InputGestures** (that is, keyboard shortcuts) associated with it. RoutedUICommand is an extension of RoutedCommand with a Text property, which specifies the default text to display on a GUI element that triggers the command.

WPF provides a command library of built-in commands. These commands have their standard keyboard shortcuts already associated with them. For example, Copy is a built-in command and has *Ctrl-C* associated with it. Figure 30.12 provides a list of some common built-in commands, separated by the classes in which they're defined.

Common built-in commands from the WPF command library			
ApplicationCommands properties			
New	Open	Save	Close
Cut	Copy	Paste	
EditingCommands properties			
ToggleBold	ToggleItalic	ToggleUnderline	
MediaCommands properties			
Play	Stop	Rewind	FastForward
IncreaseVolume	DecreaseVolume	NextTrack	PreviousTrack

Fig. 30.12 | Common built-in commands from the WPF command library.

Figures 30.13 and 30.14 are the XAML markup and C# code for a simple text-editor app that allows users to format text into bold and italics, and also to cut, copy and paste text. The example uses the **RichTextBox** control (line 49), which allows users to enter, edit and format text. We use this app to demonstrate several built-in commands from the command library.

A command is executed when it's triggered by a *command source*. For example, the Close command is triggered by a MenuItem (line 23 in Fig. 30.13). The Cut command has two sources, a MenuItem and a ToolBar Button (lines 26 and 39, respectively). A command can have many sources.

To make use of a command, you must create a **command binding**—a link between a command and the methods containing its logic. You can declare a command binding by creating a **CommandBinding** object in XAML and setting its Command property to the name of the associated command (line 10). A command binding raises the **Executed** and **PreviewExecuted** events (*bubbling* and *tunneling* versions of the same event) when its associated command is executed. You program the command's functionality into an event handler for one of these events. In line 10, we set the Executed attribute to a method name, telling the program that the specified method (closeCommand_Executed) handles the command binding's Executed event.

```xml
 1   <!-- Fig. 30.13: MainWindow.xaml -->
 2   <!-- Creating menus and toolbars, and using commands (XAML). -->
 3   <Window x:Class="TextEditor.MainWindow"
 4      xmlns="http://schemas.microsoft.com/winfx/2006/xaml/presentation"
 5      xmlns:x="http://schemas.microsoft.com/winfx/2006/xaml"
 6      Title="Text Editor" Height="300" Width="300">
 7
 8      <Window.CommandBindings> <!-- define command bindings -->
 9         <!-- bind the Close command to handler -->
10         <CommandBinding Command="Close" Executed="closeCommand_Executed" />
11      </Window.CommandBindings>
12
13      <Grid> <!-- define the GUI -->
14         <Grid.RowDefinitions>
15            <RowDefinition Height="Auto" />
16            <RowDefinition Height="Auto" />
17            <RowDefinition Height="*" />
18         </Grid.RowDefinitions>
19
20         <Menu Grid.Row="0"> <!-- create the menu -->
21            <!-- map each menu item to corresponding command -->
22            <MenuItem Header="File">
23               <MenuItem Header="Exit" Command="Close" />
24            </MenuItem>
25            <MenuItem Header="Edit">
26               <MenuItem Header="Cut" Command="Cut" />
27               <MenuItem Header="Copy" Command="Copy" />
28               <MenuItem Header="Paste" Command="Paste" />
29               <Separator /> <!-- separates groups of menu items -->
30               <MenuItem Header="Bold" Command="ToggleBold"
31                  FontWeight="Bold" />
32               <MenuItem Header="Italic" Command="ToggleItalic"
33                  FontStyle="Italic" />
34            </MenuItem>
35         </Menu>
36
37         <ToolBar Grid.Row="1"> <!-- create the toolbar -->
38            <!-- map each toolbar item to corresponding command -->
39            <Button Command="Cut">Cut</Button>
40            <Button Command="Copy">Copy</Button>
41            <Button Command="Paste">Paste</Button>
42            <Separator /> <!-- separates groups of toolbar items -->
43            <Button FontWeight="Bold" Command="ToggleBold">Bold</Button>
```

Fig. 30.13 | Creating menus and toolbars, and using commands (XAML). (Part 1 of 2.)

```
44                <Button FontStyle="Italic" Command="ToggleItalic">
45                   Italic</Button>
46           </ToolBar>
47
48           <!-- display editable, formattable text -->
49           <RichTextBox Grid.Row="2" Margin="5" />
50        </Grid>
51     </Window>
```

Fig. 30.13 | Creating menus and toolbars, and using commands (XAML). (Part 2 of 2.)

```
 1    // Fig. 30.14: MainWindow.xaml.cs
 2    // Code-behind class for a simple text editor.
 3    using System.Windows;
 4    using System.Windows.Input;
 5
 6    namespace TextEditor
 7    {
 8       public partial class MainWindow : Window
 9       {
10          public MainWindow()
11          {
12             InitializeComponent();
13          } // end constructor
14
15          // exit the app
16          private void closeCommand_Executed( object sender,
17             ExecutedRoutedEventArgs e )
18          {
19             Application.Current.Shutdown();
20          } // end method closeCommand_Executed
21       } // end class MainWindow
22    } // end namespace TextEditor
```

a) When the app loads

b) After selecting some text

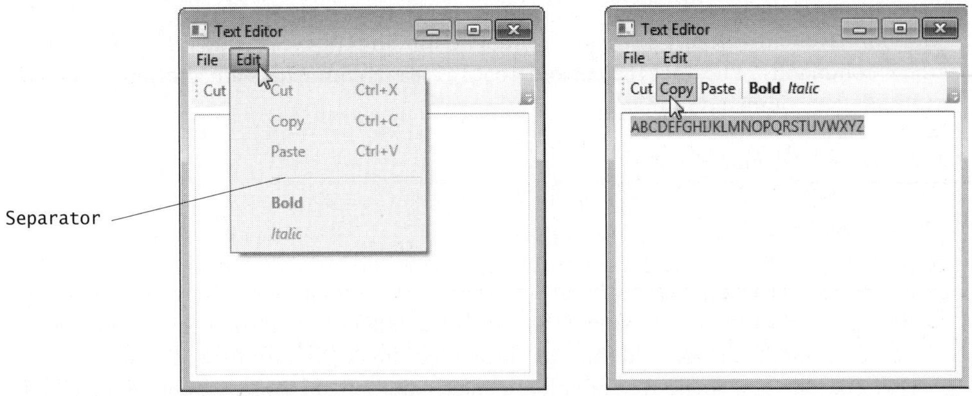

Separator

Fig. 30.14 | Code-behind class for a simple text editor. (Part 1 of 2.)

c) After copying some text

Fig. 30.14 │ Code-behind class for a simple text editor. (Part 2 of 2.)

In this example, we demonstrate the use of a *command binding* by implementing the Close command. When it executes, it shuts down the app. The method that executes this task is **Application.Current.Shutdown**, as shown in line 19 of Fig. 30.14.

You can also use a command binding to specify the logic for determining when a command should be *enabled* or *disabled*. You can do so by handling either the **CanExecute** or **PreviewCanExecute** (*bubbling* and *tunneling* versions of the same events) events in the same way that you handle the Executed or PreviewExecuted events. Because we do not define such a handler for the Close command in its command binding, it's always enabled. Command bindings should be defined within the **Window.CommandBindings** element (for example, lines 8–11 in Fig. 30.13).

The only time a command binding is *not* necessary is when a control has built-in functionality for dealing with a command. A Button or MenuItem linked to the Cut, Copy, or Paste commands is an example (for example, lines 26–28 and lines 39–41). As Fig. 30.14(a) shows, all three commands are disabled when the app loads. If you select some text, the Cut and Copy commands are enabled, as shown in Fig. 30.14(b). Once you have copied some text, the Paste command is enabled, as evidenced by Fig. 30.14(c). We did not have to define any associated command bindings or event handlers to implement these commands. The ToggleBold and ToggleItalic commands are also implemented without any command bindings.

Menus and Toolbars
The text editor uses menus and toolbars. The **Menu** control creates a menu containing **MenuItem**s. MenuItems can be top-level menus such as **File** or **Edit** (lines 22 and 25 in Fig. 30.13), submenus, or items in a menu, which function like Buttons (for example, lines 26–28). If a MenuItem has nested MenuItems, then it's a top-level menu or a submenu. Otherwise, it's an item that executes an action via either an event or a command. MenuItems are content controls and thus can display any single GUI element as content.

A **ToolBar** is a single row or column (depending on the Orientation property) of options. A ToolBar's Orientation is a *read-only* property that gets its value from the parent

ToolBarTray, which can host multiple ToolBars. If a ToolBar has no parent ToolBarTray, as is the case in this example, its Orientation is Horizontal by default. Unlike elements in a Menu, a ToolBar's child elements are not of a specific type. A ToolBar usually contains Buttons, CheckBoxes, ComboBoxes, RadioButtons and Separators, but any WPF control can be used. ToolBars overwrite the look-and-feel of their child elements with their own specifications, so that the controls look seamless together. You can override the default specifications to create your own look-and-feel. Lines 37–46 define the text editor's ToolBar.

Menus and ToolBars can incorporate **Separators** (for example, lines 29 and 42) that differentiate groups of MenuItems or controls. In a Menu, a Separator displays as a horizontal bar—as shown between the **Paste** and **Bold** menu options in Fig. 30.14(a). In a horizontal ToolBar, it displays as a short vertical bar—as shown in Fig. 30.14(b). You can use Separators in any type of control that can contain multiple child elements, such as a StackPanel.

30.8 WPF GUI Customization

One advantage of WPF over Windows Forms is the ability to customize controls. WPF provides several techniques to customize the look and behavior of controls. The simplest takes full advantage of a control's properties. The value of a control's **Background** property, for example, is a *brush* (i.e, Brush object). This allows you to create a *gradient* or an *image* and use it as the background rather than a solid color. For more information about brushes, see Section 31.5. In addition, many controls that allowed only text content in Windows Forms are ContentControls in WPF, which can host any type of content—including other controls. The caption of a WPF Button, for example, could be an *image* or even a *video*.

In Section 30.9, we demonstrate how to use styles in WPF to achieve a uniform look-and-feel. In Windows Forms, if you want to make all your Buttons look the same, you have to manually set properties for every Button, or copy and paste. To achieve the same result in WPF, you can define the properties once as a style and apply the style to each Button. This is similar to the CSS/HTML implementation of styles. HTML specifies the content and structure of a website, and CSS defines styles that specify the presentation of elements in a website. For more information on CSS and HTML, see our Resource Centers at www.deitel.com/ResourceCenters.html.

Styles are limited to modifying a control's look-and-feel through its properties. In Section 30.11, we introduce control templates, which offer you the freedom to define a control's appearance by modifying its visual structure. With a custom control template, you can completely strip a control of all its visual settings and rebuild it to look exactly the way you like, while maintaining its existing functionality. A Button with a custom control template might look structurally different from a default Button, but it still functions the same as any other Button.

If you want to change only the appearance of an element, a style or control template should suffice. However, you can also create entirely new custom controls that have their own functionality, properties, methods and events.

30.9 Using Styles to Change the Appearance of Controls

Once defined, a **WPF style** is a collection of property-value and event-handler definitions that can be reused. Styles enable you to eliminate repetitive code or markup. For example, if you want to change the look-and-feel of the standard Button throughout a section of your app, you can define a style and apply it to all the Buttons in that section. Without styles, you have to set the properties for each individual Button. Furthermore, if you later decided that you wanted to tweak the appearance of these Buttons, you would have to modify your markup or code several times. By using a style, you can make the change only once in the style and it's automatically be applied to any control which uses that style.

Styles are **WPF resources**. A resource is an object that's defined for an entire section of your app and can be reused multiple times. A resource can be as simple as a property or as complex as a control template. Every WPF control can hold a collection of resources that can be accessed by any element down the containment hierarchy. In a way, this is similar in approach to the concept of variable scope that you learned about in Chapter 7. For example, if you define a style as a resource of a Window, then any element in the Window can use that style. If you define a style as a resource of a layout container, then only the elements of the layout container can use that style. You can also define application-wide resources for an Application object in the App.xaml file. These resources can be accessed in any file in the app.

Color Chooser App

Figure 30.15 provides the XAML markup and Fig. 30.16 provides the C# code for a color-chooser app. This example demonstrates styles and introduces the Slider user input control.

```
1   <!-- Fig. 30.15: MainWindow.xaml -->
2   <!-- Color chooser app showing the use of styles (XAML). -->
3   <Window x:Class="ColorChooser.MainWindow"
4      xmlns="http://schemas.microsoft.com/winfx/2006/xaml/presentation"
5      xmlns:x="http://schemas.microsoft.com/winfx/2006/xaml"
6      Title="Color Chooser" Height="150" Width="500">
7
8      <Window.Resources> <!-- define Window's resources -->
9         <Style x:Key="SliderStyle"> <!-- define style for Sliders -->
10
11            <!-- set properties for Sliders -->
12            <Setter Property="Slider.Width" Value="256" />
13            <Setter Property="Slider.Minimum" Value="0" />
14            <Setter Property="Slider.Maximum" Value="255" />
15            <Setter Property="Slider.IsSnapToTickEnabled" Value="True" />
16            <Setter Property="Slider.VerticalAlignment" Value="Center" />
17            <Setter Property="Slider.HorizontalAlignment" Value="Center" />
18            <Setter Property="Slider.Value" Value="0" />
19            <Setter Property="Slider.AutoToolTipPlacement"
20               Value="TopLeft" />
21
22            <!-- set event handler for ValueChanged event -->
23            <EventSetter Event="Slider.ValueChanged"
24               Handler="slider_ValueChanged" />
25         </Style>
26      </Window.Resources>
27
```

Fig. 30.15 | Color-chooser app showing the use of styles (XAML). (Part 1 of 2.)

```
28      <Grid Margin="5"> <!-- define GUI -->
29          <Grid.RowDefinitions>
30              <RowDefinition />
31              <RowDefinition />
32              <RowDefinition />
33              <RowDefinition />
34          </Grid.RowDefinitions>
35          <Grid.ColumnDefinitions>
36              <ColumnDefinition Width="Auto" />
37              <ColumnDefinition Width="Auto" />
38              <ColumnDefinition Width="50" />
39              <ColumnDefinition />
40          </Grid.ColumnDefinitions>
41
42          <!-- define Labels for Sliders -->
43          <Label Grid.Row="0" Grid.Column="0" HorizontalAlignment="Right"
44              VerticalAlignment="Center" Content="Red:"/>
45          <Label Grid.Row="1" Grid.Column="0" HorizontalAlignment="Right"
46              VerticalAlignment="Center" Content="Green:"/>
47          <Label Grid.Row="2" Grid.Column="0" HorizontalAlignment="Right"
48              VerticalAlignment="Center" Content="Blue:"/>
49          <Label Grid.Row="3" Grid.Column="0" HorizontalAlignment="Right"
50              VerticalAlignment="Center" Content="Alpha:"/>
51
52          <!-- define Label that displays the color -->
53          <Label x:Name="colorLabel" Grid.RowSpan="4" Grid.Column="3"
54              Margin="10" />
55
56          <!-- define Sliders and apply style to them -->
57          <Slider x:Name="redSlider" Grid.Row="0" Grid.Column="1"
58              Style="{StaticResource SliderStyle}"
59              Value="{Binding Text, ElementName=redBox}" />'
60          <Slider x:Name="greenSlider" Grid.Row="1" Grid.Column="1"
61              Style="{StaticResource SliderStyle}"
62              Value="{Binding Text, ElementName=greenBox}"/>
63          <Slider x:Name="blueSlider" Grid.Row="2" Grid.Column="1"
64              Style="{StaticResource SliderStyle}"
65              Value="{Binding Text, ElementName=blueBox}"/>
66          <Slider x:Name="alphaSlider" Grid.Row="3" Grid.Column="1"
67              Style="{StaticResource SliderStyle}"
68              Value="{Binding Text, ElementName=alphaBox}" />
69
70          <TextBox x:Name="redBox" Grid.Row="0" Grid.Column="2"
71              Text="{Binding Value, ElementName=redSlider}"/>
72          <TextBox x:Name="greenBox" Grid.Row="1" Grid.Column="2"
73              Text="{Binding Value, ElementName=greenSlider}"/>
74          <TextBox x:Name="blueBox" Grid.Row="2" Grid.Column="2"
75              Text="{Binding Value, ElementName=blueSlider}"/>
76          <TextBox x:Name="alphaBox" Grid.Row="3" Grid.Column="2"
77              Text="{Binding Value, ElementName=alphaSlider}"/>
78      </Grid>
79  </Window>
```

Fig. 30.15 | Color-chooser app showing the use of styles (XAML). (Part 2 of 2.)

```
 1    // Fig. 30.16: MainWindow.xaml.cs
 2    // Color chooser app showing the use of styles (code-behind).
 3    using System.Windows;
 4    using System.Windows.Media;
 5
 6    namespace ColorChooser
 7    {
 8       public partial class MainWindow : Window
 9       {
10          public MainWindow()
11          {
12             InitializeComponent();
13             alphaSlider.Value = 255; // override Value from style
14          } // constructor
15
16          // handles the ValueChanged event for the Sliders
17          private void slider_ValueChanged( object sender,
18             RoutedPropertyChangedEventArgs< double > e )
19          {
20             // generates new color
21             SolidColorBrush backgroundColor = new SolidColorBrush();
22             backgroundColor.Color = Color.FromArgb(
23                ( byte ) alphaSlider.Value, ( byte ) redSlider.Value,
24                ( byte ) greenSlider.Value, ( byte ) blueSlider.Value );
25
26             // set colorLabel's background to new color
27             colorLabel.Background = backgroundColor;
28          } // end method slider_ValueChanged
29       } // end class MainWindow
30    } // end namespace ColorChooser
```

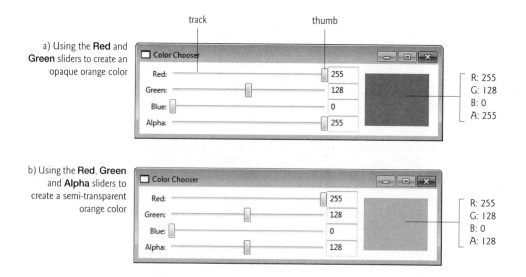

a) Using the **Red** and **Green** sliders to create an opaque orange color

b) Using the **Red**, **Green** and **Alpha** sliders to create a semi-transparent orange color

Fig. 30.16 | Color-chooser app showing the use of styles (code-behind).

RGBA Colors

This app uses the RGBA color system. Every color is represented by its red, green and blue color values, each ranging from 0 to 255, where 0 denotes no color and 255 full color. For example, a color with a red value of 0 would contain no red component. The alpha value (A)—which also ranges from 0 to 255—represents a color's *opacity*, with 0 being completely *transparent* and 255 completely *opaque*. The two colors in Fig. 30.16's sample outputs have the same RGB values, but the color displayed in Fig. 30.16(b) is *semitransparent*.

Slider Controls

The color-chooser GUI uses four **Slider** controls that change the RGBA values of a color displayed by a Label. Next to each Slider is a TextBox that displays the Slider's current value. You can also type a number in a TextBox to update the value of the corresponding Slider. A Slider is a numeric user input control that allows users to drag a "thumb" along a track to select the value. Whenever the user moves a Slider, the app generates a new color, the corresponding TextBox is updated and the Label displays the new color as its background. The new color is generated by using class Color's FromArgb method, which returns a color based on the four RGBA byte values you pass it (Fig. 30.16, lines 22–24). The color is then applied as the Background of the Label. Similarly, changing the value of a TextBox updates the thumb of the corresponding Slider to reflect the change, which then updates the Label with the new color. We discuss the updates of the TextBoxes shortly.

Style for the Sliders

Styles can be defined as a resource of any control. In the color-chooser app, we defined the style as a resource of the entire Window. We also could have defined it as a resource of the Grid. To define resources for a control, you set a control's Resources property. Thus, to define a resource for a Window, as we did in this example, you would use Window.Resources (lines 8–26 in Fig. 30.15). To define a resource for a Grid, you'd use Grid.Resources.

Style objects can be defined in XAML using the **Style** element. The x:Key attribute (i.e., attribute Key from the standard XAML namespace) must be set in every style (or other resource) so that it can be referenced later by other controls (line 9). The children of a Style element set properties and define event handlers. A **Setter** sets a property to a specific value (e.g., line 12, which sets the styled Slider's Width property to 256). An **EventSetter** specifies the method that responds to an event (e.g., lines 23–24, which specifies that method slider_ValueChanged handles the Slider's ValueChanged event).

The Style in the color-chooser example (SliderStyle) primarily uses Setters. It lays out the color Sliders by specifying the Width, VerticalAlignment and HorizontalAlignment properties (lines 12, 16 and 17). It also sets the Minimum and Maximum properties, which determine a Slider's range of values (lines 13–14). In line 18, the default Value is set to 0. IsSnapToTickEnabled is set to True, meaning that only values that fall on a "tick" are allowed (line 15). By default, each tick is separated by a value of 1, so this setting makes the styled Slider accept only integer values. Lastly, the style also sets the AutoToolTip-Placement property, which specifies where a Slider's tooltip should appear, if at all.

Although the Style defined in the color-chooser example is clearly meant for Sliders, it can be applied to any control. Styles are not control specific. You can make all controls of one type use the same default style by setting the style's **TargetType** attribute to the control type. For example, if we wanted all of the Window's Sliders to use a Style, we would add TargetType="Slider" to the Style's start tag.

Using a Style
To apply a style to a control, you create a **resource binding** between a control's Style property and the Style resource. You can create a resource binding in XAML by specifying the resource in a **markup extension**—an expression enclosed in curly braces ({}). The form of a markup extension calling a resource is {*ResourceType ResourceKey*} (for example, {StaticResource SliderStyle} in Fig. 30.15, line 58).

Static and Dynamic Resources
There are two types of resources. **Static resources** are applied only at initialization time. **Dynamic resources** are applied every time the resource is modified by the app. To use a style as a *static* resource, use StaticResource as the type in the markup extension. To use a style as a *dynamic* resource, use DynamicResource as the type. Because styles don't normally change during runtime, they are usually used as static resources. However, using one as a dynamic resource is sometimes necessary, such as when you wish to enable users to customize a style at runtime.

In this app, we apply SliderStyle as a static resource to each Slider (lines 58, 61, 64 and 67). Once you apply a style to a control, the **Design** view and **Properties** window update to display the control's new appearance settings. If you then modify the control through the **Properties** window, the control itself is updated, not the style.

Element-to-Element Bindings
In this app, we use a new feature of WPF called **element-to-element binding** in which a property of one element is always equal to a property of another element. This enables us to declare in XAML that each TextBox's Text property should always have the value of the corresponding Slider's Value property, and that each Slider's Value property should always have the value of the corresponding TextBox's Text property. Once these bindings are defined, changing a Slider updates the corresponding TextBox and vice versa. In Fig. 30.15, lines 59, 62, 65 and 68 each use a Binding markup extension to bind a Slider's Value property to the Text property of the appropriate TextBox. Similary, lines 71, 73, 75 and 77 each use a Binding markup extension to bind a TextBox's Text property to the Value property of the appropriate Slider.

Programmatically Changing the **Alpha** *Slider's Value*
As shown in Fig. 30.17, the Slider that adjusts the alpha value in the color-chooser example starts with a value of 255, whereas the R, G and B Sliders' values start at 0. The Value property is defined by a Setter in the style to be 0 (line 18 in Fig. 30.15). This is why the R, G and B values are 0. The Value property of the alpha Slider is programmat-

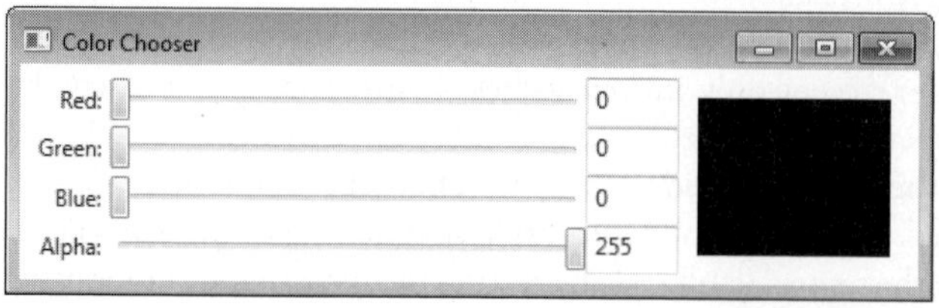

Fig. 30.17 | GUI of the color-chooser app at initialization.

ically defined to be 255 (line 13 in Fig. 30.16), but it could also be set locally in the XAML. Because a local declaration takes precedence over a style setter, the alpha Slider's value would start at 255 when the app loads.

Dependency Properties

Most WPF properties, though they might look and behave exactly like ordinary ones, are in fact **dependency properties**. Such properties have built-in support for change notification—that is, an app knows and can respond to changes in property values. In addition, they support inheritance down the control-containment hierarchy. For example, when you specify FontSize in a Window, every control in the Window inherits it as the default FontSize. You can also specify a control's property in one of its child elements. This is how *attached properties* work.

A control's properties may be set at many different levels in WPF, so instead of holding a fixed value, a *dependency property's value* is determined during execution by a value-determination system. If a property is defined at several levels at once, then the current value is the one defined at the level with the highest precedence. A style, for example, overwrites the default appearance of a control, because it takes higher precedence. A summary of the levels, in order from highest to lowest precedence, is shown in Fig. 30.18.

Levels of value determination system	
Animation	The value is defined by an active animation. For more information about animation, see Chapter 31.
Local declaration	The value is defined as an attribute in XAML or set in code. This is how ordinary properties are set.
Trigger	The value is defined by an active trigger. For more information about triggers, see Section 30.11.
Style	The value is defined by a setter in a style.
Inherited value	The value is inherited from a definition in a containing element.
Default value	The value is not explicitly defined.

Fig. 30.18 | Levels of value determination from highest to lowest precedence.

30.10 Customizing Windows

For over a decade, the standard design of an app window has remained practically the same—a framed rectangular box with a header in the top left and a set of buttons in the top right for minimizing, maximizing and closing the window. Cutting-edge apps, however, have begun to use *custom windows* that diverge from this standard to create a more interesting look.

WPF lets you do this more easily. To create a custom window, set the **WindowStyle** property to None. This removes the standard frame around your Window. To make your Window irregularly shaped, you set the **AllowsTransparency** property to True and the Background property to Transparent. If you then add controls, only the space within the boundaries of those controls behaves as part of the window. This works because a user cannot interact with any part of a Window that's *transparent*. You still define your Window as a rectangle with a width and a height, but when a user clicks in a transparent part of the Window, it behaves as if the user clicked *outside* the Window's boundaries—that is, the window does not respond to the click.

Figure 30.19 is the XAML markup that defines a GUI for a circular digital clock. The Window's WindowStyle is set to None and AllowsTransparency is set to True (line 7). In this example, we set the background to be an image using an ImageBrush (lines 10–12). The background image is a *circle* with a *drop shadow* surrounded by *transparency*. Thus, the Window appears *circular*.

```
 1    <!-- Fig. 30.19: MainWindow.xaml -->
 2    <!-- Creating a custom window and using a timer (XAML). -->
 3    <Window x:Class="Clock.MainWindow"
 4       xmlns="http://schemas.microsoft.com/winfx/2006/xaml/presentation"
 5       xmlns:x="http://schemas.microsoft.com/winfx/2006/xaml"
 6       Title="Clock" Name="clockWindow" Height="118" Width="118"
 7       WindowStyle="None" AllowsTransparency="True"
 8       MouseLeftButtonDown="clockWindow_MouseLeftButtonDown">
 9
10       <Window.Background> <!-- Set background image -->
11          <ImageBrush ImageSource="images/circle.png" />
12       </Window.Background>
13
14       <Grid>
15          <TextBox x:Name="timeTextBox" Margin="0,42,0,0"
16             Background="Transparent" TextAlignment="Center"
17             FontWeight="Bold" Foreground="White" FontSize="16"
18             BorderThickness="0" Cursor="Arrow" Focusable="False" />
19       </Grid>
20    </Window>
```

Fig. 30.19 | Creating a custom window and using a timer (XAML).

The time is displayed in the center of the window in a TextBox (lines 15–18). Its Background is set to Transparent so that the text displays directly on the circular background (line 16). We configured the text to be size 16, bold, and white by setting the FontSize, FontWeight, and Foreground properties. The Cursor property is set to Arrow, so that the mouse cursor doesn't change when it moves over the time (line 18). Setting Focusable to False disables the user's ability to select the text (line 18).

When you create a custom window, there's no built-in functionality for doing the simple tasks that normal windows do. For example, there is no way for the user to move, resize, minimize, maximize, or close a window unless you write the code to enable these features. You can move the clock around, because we implemented this functionality in the Window's code-behind class (Fig. 30.20). Whenever the left mouse button is held down on the clock (handled by the MouseLeftButtonDown event), the Window is dragged around using the **DragMove** method (lines 27–31). Because we did not define how to close or minimize the Window, you can shut down the clock by pressing *Alt-F4*—this is a feature built into Windows—or by right clicking its icon on the taskbar and selecting **Close window**.

```csharp
// Fig. 30.20: MainWindow.xaml.cs
// Creating a custom window and using a timer (code-behind).
using System;
using System.Windows;
using System.Windows.Input;

namespace Clock
{
   public partial class MainWindow : Window
   {
      // create a timer to control clock
      private System.Windows.Threading.DispatcherTimer timer =
         new System.Windows.Threading.DispatcherTimer();

      // constructor
      public MainWindow()
      {
         InitializeComponent();

         timer.Interval = TimeSpan.FromSeconds( 1 ); // tick every second
         timer.IsEnabled = true; // enable timer

         timer.Tick += timer_Tick;
      } // end constructor

      // drag Window when the left mouse button is held down
      private void clockWindow_MouseLeftButtonDown( object sender,
         MouseButtonEventArgs e )
      {
         this.DragMove(); // moves the window
      } // end method clockWindow_MouseLeftButtonDown

      // update the time when the timer ticks
      private void timer_Tick( object sender, EventArgs e )
      {
         DateTime currentTime = DateTime.Now; // get the current time

         // display the time as hh:mm:ss
         timeTextBox.Text = currentTime.ToLongTimeString();
      } // end method timer_Tick
   } // end class MainWindow
} // end namespace Clock
```

Fig. 30.20 | Creating a custom window and using a timer (code-behind).

The clock works by getting the current time every second and displaying it in the TextBox. To do this, the clock uses a **DispatcherTimer** object (of the Windows.Threading namespace), which raises the **Tick** event repeatedly at a prespecified time interval. Since the DispatcherTimer is defined in the C# code rather than the XAML, we need to specify the method to handle the Tick event in the C# code. Line 23 assigns method timer_Tick to the Tick event's delegate. This adds the timer_Tick method as an EventHandler for the specified event. After it's declared, you must specify the interval between Ticks by setting the **Interval** property, which takes a TimeSpan as its value. **TimeSpan** has several class methods for instantiating a TimeSpan object, including FromSeconds, which defines a TimeSpan lasting the number of seconds you pass to the method. Line 20 creates a one-second TimeSpan and sets it as the DispatcherTimer's Interval. A DispatcherTimer is disabled by default. Until you enable it by setting the **IsEnabled** property to true (line 21), it will not Tick. In this example, the Tick event handler gets the current time and displays it in the TextBox.

You may recall that the Timer component provided the same capabilities in Windows Forms. A similar object that you can drag-and-drop onto your GUI doesn't exist in WPF. Instead, you must create a DispatcherTimer object, as illustrated in this example.

30.11 Defining a Control's Appearance with Control Templates

We now update the clock example to include buttons for minimizing and closing the app. We also introduce **control templates**—a powerful tool for customizing the look-and-feel of your GUIs. As previously mentioned, a custom control template can redefine the appearance of any control *without* changing its functionality. In Windows Forms, if you want to create a round button, you have to create a new control and simulate the functionality of a Button. With control templates, you can simply redefine the visual elements that compose the Button control and still use the preexisting functionality.

All WPF controls are **lookless**—that is, a control's properties, methods and events are coded into the control's class, but its *appearance* is *not*. Instead, the appearance of a control is determined by a *control template*, which is a hierarchy of visual elements. Every control has a built-in default control template. All of the GUIs discussed so far in this chapter have used these default templates.

The hierarchy of visual elements defined by a control template can be represented as a tree, called a control's **visual tree**. Figure 30.21(b) shows the visual tree of a default Button (Fig. 30.22). This is a more detailed version of the same Button's **logical tree**, which is shown in Fig. 30.21(a). A logical tree depicts how a control is a defined, whereas a visual tree depicts how a control is graphically rendered.

A control's logical tree always mirrors its definition in XAML. For example, you'll notice that the Button's logical tree, which comprises only the Button and its string caption, exactly represents the hierarchy outlined by its XAML definition, which is

```
<Button>
    Click Me
</Button>
```

To actually render the Button, WPF displays a ContentPresenter with a Border around it. These elements are included in the Button's visual tree. A **ContentPresenter** is an object used to display a single element of content on the screen. It's often used in a template to specify where to display content.

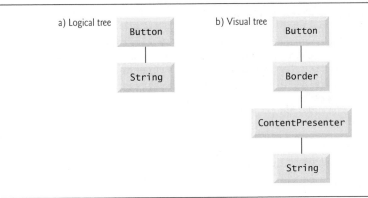

Fig. 30.21 | The logical and visual trees for a default Button.

Click Me

Fig. 30.22 | The default Button.

In the updated clock example, we create a custom control template (named ButtonTemplate) for rendering Buttons and apply it to the two Buttons in the app. The XAML markup is shown in Fig. 30.23. Like a style, a control template is usually defined as a resource, and applied by binding a control's **Template** property to the control template using a *resource binding* (for example, lines 47 and 52). After you apply a control template to a control, the **Design** view will update to display the new appearance of the control. The **Properties** window remains unchanged, since a control template does *not* modify a control's properties.

```xml
1    <!-- Fig. 30.23: MainWindow.xaml -->
2    <!-- Using control templates (XAML). -->
3    <Window x:Class="Clock.MainWindow"
4       xmlns="http://schemas.microsoft.com/winfx/2006/xaml/presentation"
5       xmlns:x="http://schemas.microsoft.com/winfx/2006/xaml"
6       Title="Clock" Name="clockWindow" Height="118" Width="118"
7       WindowStyle="None" AllowsTransparency="True"
8       MouseLeftButtonDown="clockWindow_MouseLeftButtonDown">
9
10      <Window.Resources>
11         <!-- control template for Buttons -->
12         <ControlTemplate x:Key="ButtonTemplate" TargetType="Button">
13            <Border Name="Border" BorderThickness="2" CornerRadius="2"
14               BorderBrush="RoyalBlue">
15
16               <!-- Template binding to Button.Content -->
17               <ContentPresenter Margin="0" Width="8"
18                  Content="{TemplateBinding Content}" />
19            </Border>
20
```

Fig. 30.23 | Using control templates (XAML). (Part 1 of 2.)

```
21          <ControlTemplate.Triggers>
22             <!-- if mouse is over the button -->
23             <Trigger Property="IsMouseOver" Value="True">
24                <!-- make the background blue -->
25                <Setter TargetName="Border" Property="Background"
26                   Value="LightBlue" />
27             </Trigger>
28          </ControlTemplate.Triggers>
29       </ControlTemplate>
30    </Window.Resources>
31
32    <Window.Background> <!-- Set background image -->
33       <ImageBrush ImageSource="images/circle.png" />
34    </Window.Background>
35
36    <Grid>
37       <Grid.RowDefinitions>
38          <RowDefinition Height="Auto" />
39          <RowDefinition />
40       </Grid.RowDefinitions>
41
42       <StackPanel Grid.Row="0" Orientation="Horizontal"
43          HorizontalAlignment="Right">
44
45          <!-- these buttons use the control template -->
46          <Button x:Name="minimizeButton" Margin="0" Focusable="False"
47             IsTabStop="False" Template="{StaticResource ButtonTemplate}"
48             Click="minimizeButton_Click">
49             <Image Source="images/minimize.png" Margin="0" />
50          </Button>
51          <Button x:Name="closeButton" Margin="1,0,0,0" Focusable="False"
52             IsTabStop="False" Template="{StaticResource ButtonTemplate}"
53             Click="closeButton_Click">
54             <Image Source="images/close.png" Margin="0"/>
55          </Button>
56       </StackPanel>
57
58       <TextBox x:Name="timeTextBox" Grid.Row="1" Margin="0,30,0,0"
59          Background="Transparent" TextAlignment="Center"
60          FontWeight="Bold" Foreground="White" FontSize="16"
61          BorderThickness="0" Cursor="Arrow" Focusable="False" />
62    </Grid>
63 </Window>
```

a) Templated minimize and close buttons

Templated Buttons

b) Minimize button with light blue background

Fig. 30.23 | Using control templates (XAML). (Part 2 of 2.)

To define a control template in XAML, you create a **ControlTemplate** element. Just as with a style, you must specify the control template's x:Key attribute so you can reference it later (line 12). You must also set the **TargetType** attribute to the type of control for which the template is designed (line 12). Inside the ControlTemplate element, you can build the control using any WPF visual element (lines 13–19). In this example, we replace the default Border and ContentPresenter with our own custom ones.

Sometimes, when defining a control template, it may be beneficial to use the value of one of the templated control's properties. For example, if you want several controls of different sizes to use the same control template, you may need to use the values of their Width and Height properties in the template. WPF allows you to do this with a **template binding**, which can be created in XAML with the markup extension, {TemplateBinding *PropertyName*}. To *bind* a property of an element in a control template to one of the properties of the templated control (that is, the control that the template is applied to), you need to set the appropriate markup extension as the value of that property. In ButtonTemplate, we bind the **Content** property of a ContentPresenter to the Content property of the templated Button (line 18). The nested element of a ContentControl is the value of its Content property. Thus, the images defined in lines 49 and 54 are the Content of the Buttons and are displayed by the ContentPresenters in their respective control templates. You can also create template bindings to a control's events.

Often you'll use a combination of control templates, styles and local declarations to define the appearance of your app. Recall that a control template defines the default appearance of a control and thus has a lower precedence than a style in dependency property-value determination.

Triggers
The control template for Buttons used in the updated clock example defines a **trigger**, which changes a control's appearance when that control enters a certain state. For example, when your mouse is over the clock's minimize or close Buttons, the Button is highlighted with a light blue background. This simple change in appearance is caused by a trigger that fires whenever the IsMouseOver property becomes True.

A trigger must be defined in the **Style.Triggers** or **ControlTemplate.Triggers** element of a style or a control template, respectively (for example, lines 21–28). You can create a trigger by defining a **Trigger** object. The **Property** and **Value** attributes define the state when a trigger is active. Setters *nested* in the Trigger element are carried out when the trigger is fired. When the trigger no longer applies, the changes are removed. A Setter's **TargetName** property specifies the name of the element that the Setter applies to (for example, line 25).

Lines 23–27 define the IsMouseOver trigger for the minimize and close Buttons. When the mouse is over the Button, **IsMouseOver** becomes True, and the trigger becomes active. The trigger's Setter makes the background of the Border in the control template temporarily light blue. When the mouse exits the boundaries of the Button, IsMouseOver becomes False. Thus, the Border's background returns to its *default setting*, which in this case is transparent.

Functionality
Figure 30.24 shows the code-behind class for the clock app. Although the custom control template makes the Buttons in this app look different, it doesn't change how they behave.

Lines 3–40 remain unchanged from the code in the first clock example (Fig. 30.20). The functionality for the minimize and close Buttons is implemented in the same way as any other button—by handling the Click event (lines 43–47 and 50–53 of Fig. 30.24, respectively). To minimize the window, we set the **WindowState** of the Window to **WindowState.Minimized** (line 46).

```csharp
 1   // Fig. 30.24: MainWindow.xaml.cs
 2   // Using control templates (code-behind).
 3   using System;
 4   using System.Windows;
 5   using System.Windows.Input;
 6
 7   namespace Clock
 8   {
 9      public partial class MainWindow : Window
10      {
11         // creates a timer to control clock
12         private System.Windows.Threading.DispatcherTimer timer =
13            new System.Windows.Threading.DispatcherTimer();
14
15         // constructor
16         public MainWindow()
17         {
18            InitializeComponent();
19
20            timer.Interval = TimeSpan.FromSeconds( 1 ); // tick every second
21            timer.IsEnabled = true; // enable timer
22
23            timer.Tick += timer_Tick;
24         } // end constructor
25
26         // drag Window when the left mouse button is held down
27         private void clockWindow_MouseLeftButtonDown( object sender,
28            MouseButtonEventArgs e )
29         {
30            this.DragMove();
31         } // end method clockWindow_MouseLeftButtonDown
32
33         // update the time when the timer ticks
34         private void timer_Tick( object sender, EventArgs e )
35         {
36            DateTime currentTime = DateTime.Now; // get the current time
37
38            // display the time as hh:mm:ss
39            timeTextBox.Text = currentTime.ToLongTimeString();
40         } // end method timer_Tick
41
42         // minimize the app
43         private void minimizeButton_Click( object sender,
44            RoutedEventArgs e )
45         {
```

Fig. 30.24 | Using control templates (code-behind). (Part 1 of 2.)

```
46                    this.WindowState = WindowState.Minimized; // minimize window
47            } // end method minimizeButton_Click
48
49            // close the app
50            private void closeButton_Click( object sender, RoutedEventArgs e )
51            {
52               Application.Current.Shutdown(); // shut down app
53            } // end method closeButton_Click
54         } // end class MainWindow
55      } // end namespace Clock
```

Fig. 30.24 | Using control templates (code-behind). (Part 2 of 2.)

30.12 Data-Driven GUIs with Data Binding

Often, an app needs to edit and display data. WPF provides a comprehensive model for allowing GUIs to interact with data.

Bindings
A **data binding** is a pointer to data, represented by a **Binding** object. WPF allows you to create a *binding* to a broad range of data types. At the simplest level, you could create a binding to a single property. Often, however, it's useful to create a binding to a data object—an object of a class with properties that describe the data. You can also create a binding to objects like arrays, collections and data in an XML document. The versatility of the WPF data model even allows you to bind to data represented by LINQ statements.

Like other binding types, a *data binding* can be created declaratively in XAML markup with a *markup extension*. To declare a data binding, you must specify the data's *source*. If it's another element in the XAML markup, use property **ElementName**. Otherwise, use **Source**. Then, if you're binding to a specific data point of the source, such as a property of a control, you must specify the **Path** to that piece of information. Use a comma to separate the binding's property declarations. For example, to create a binding to a control's property, you would use {Binding ElementName=*ControlName*, Path=*PropertyName*}.

Figure 30.25 presents the XAML markup of a book-cover viewer that lets the user select from a list of books, and displays the cover of the currently selected book. The list of books is presented in a **ListView** control (lines 15–24), which displays a set of data as items in a selectable list. Its current selection can be retrieved from the **SelectedItem** property. A large image of the currently selected book's cover is displayed in an Image control (lines 27–28), which automatically updates when the user makes a new selection. Each book is represented by a Book object, which has four string properties:

1. ThumbImage—the full path to the small cover image of the book.

2. LargeImage—the full path to the large cover image of the book.

3. Title—the title of the book.

4. ISBN—the 10-digit ISBN of the book.

Class Book also contains a constructor that initializes a Book and sets each of its properties. The full source code of the Book class is not presented here but you can view it in the IDE by opening this example's project.

```xaml
1   <!-- Fig. 30.25: MainWindow.xaml -->
2   <!-- Using data binding (XAML). -->
3   <Window x:Class="BookViewer.MainWindow"
4      xmlns="http://schemas.microsoft.com/winfx/2006/xaml/presentation"
5      xmlns:x="http://schemas.microsoft.com/winfx/2006/xaml"
6      Title="Book Viewer" Height="400" Width="600">
7
8      <Grid> <!-- define GUI -->
9         <Grid.ColumnDefinitions>
10           <ColumnDefinition Width="Auto" />
11           <ColumnDefinition />
12        </Grid.ColumnDefinitions>
13
14        <!-- use ListView and GridView to display data -->
15        <ListView x:Name="booksListView" Grid.Column="0" MaxWidth="250">
16           <ListView.View>
17              <GridView>
18                 <GridViewColumn Header="Title" Width="100"
19                    DisplayMemberBinding="{Binding Path=Title}" />
20                 <GridViewColumn Header="ISBN" Width="80"
21                    DisplayMemberBinding="{Binding Path=ISBN}" />
22              </GridView>
23           </ListView.View>
24        </ListView>
25
26        <!-- bind to selected item's full-size image -->
27        <Image Grid.Column="1" Source="{Binding ElementName=booksListView,
28           Path=SelectedItem.LargeImage}" Margin="5" />
29     </Grid>
30  </Window>
```

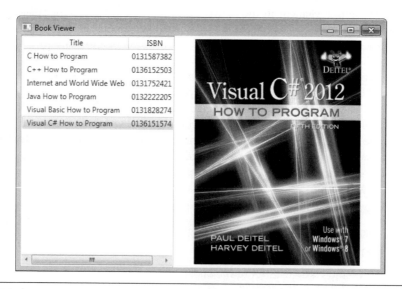

Fig. 30.25 | Using data binding (XAML).

To *synchronize* the book cover that's being displayed with the currently selected book, we bind the Image's Source property to the file location of the currently selected book's large cover image (lines 27–28). The Binding's ElementName property is the name of the selector control, booksListView. The Path property is SelectedItem.LargeImage. This indicates that the binding should be linked to the LargeImage property of the Book object that's currently booksListView's SelectedItem.

Some controls have built-in support for data binding, and a separate Binding object doesn't need to be created. A ListView, for example, has a built-in **ItemsSource** property that specifies the *data source* from which the items of the list are determined. There is no need to create a binding—instead, you can just set the ItemsSource property as you would any other property. When you set ItemsSource to a collection of data, the objects in the collection automatically become the items in the list. Figure 30.26 presents the code-behind class for the book-cover viewer. When the Window is created, a collection of six Book objects is initialized (lines 17–29) and set as the ItemsSource of the booksListView, meaning that each item displayed in the selector is one of the Books.

```csharp
 1   // Fig. 30.26: MainWindow.xaml.cs
 2   // Using data binding (code-behind).
 3   using System.Collections.Generic;
 4   using System.Windows;
 5
 6   namespace BookViewer
 7   {
 8      public partial class MainWindow : Window
 9      {
10         private List< Book > books = new List< Book >();
11
12         public MainWindow()
13         {
14            InitializeComponent();
15
16            // add Book objects to the List
17            books.Add( new Book( "C How to Program", "013299044X",
18               "images/small/chtp.jpg", "images/large/chtp.jpg" ) );
19            books.Add( new Book( "C++ How to Program", "0133378713",
20               "images/small/cpphtp.jpg", "images/large/cpphtp.jpg" ) );
21            books.Add( new Book(
22               "Internet and World Wide Web How to Program", "0132151006",
23               "images/small/iw3htp.jpg", "images/large/iw3htp.jpg" ) );
24            books.Add( new Book( "Java How to Program", "0132940949",
25               "images/small/jhtp.jpg", "images/large/jhtp.jpg" ) );
26            books.Add( new Book( "Visual Basic How to Program", "0133406954",
27               "images/small/vbhtp.jpg", "images/large/vbhtp.jpg" ) );
28            books.Add( new Book( "Visual C# How to Program", "0133379337",
29               "images/small/vcshtp.jpg", "images/large/vcshtp.jpg" ) );
30
31            booksListView.ItemsSource = books; // bind data to the list
32         } // end constructor
33      } // end class MainWindow
34   } // end namespace BookViewer
```

Fig. 30.26 | Using data binding (code-behind).

Displaying Data in the ListView

For a ListView to display objects in a useful manner, you must specify how. For example, if you don't specify how to display each Book, the ListView simply displays the result of the item's ToString method, as shown in Fig. 30.27.

Fig. 30.27 | ListView display with no data template.

There are many ways to format the display of a ListView. One such method is to display each item as a row in a *tabular grid*, as shown in Fig. 30.25. This can be achieved by setting a **GridView** as the View property of a ListView (lines 16–23). A GridView consists of many **GridViewColumns**, each representing a property. In this example, we define two columns, one for **Title** and one for **ISBN** (lines 18–19 and 20–21, respectively). A GridViewColumn's Header property specifies what to display as its header. The values displayed in each column are determined by its **DisplayMemberBinding** property. We set the **Title** column's DisplayMemberBinding to a Binding object that points to the Title property (line 19), and the **ISBN** column's to one that points to the ISBN property (line 21). Neither of the Bindings has a specified ElementName or Source. Because the ListView has already specified the data source (line 31 of Fig. 30.26), the two data bindings inherit this source, and we do not need specify it again.

Data Templates

A much more powerful technique for formatting a ListView is to specify a template for displaying each item in the list. This template defines how to display bound data and is called a **data template**. Figure 30.28 is the XAML markup that describes a modified version of the book-cover viewer GUI. Each book, instead of being displayed as a row in a table, is represented by a small thumbnail of its cover image with its title and ISBN. Lines 11–32 define the data template (that is, a **DataTemplate** object) that specifies how to display a Book object. Note the similarity between the structure of a data template and that of a control template. If you define a data template as a resource, you apply it by using a resource binding, just as you would a style or control template. To apply a data template to items in a ListView, use the **ItemTemplate** property (for example, line 43).

A data template uses data bindings to specify how to display data. Once again, we can omit the data binding's ElementName and Source properties, because its source has already been specified by the ListView (line 31 of Fig. 30.26). The same principle can be applied in other scenarios as well. If you bind an element's **DataContext** property to a data source, then its child elements can access data within that source without your having to specify it again. In other words, if a binding already has a context (i.e, a DataContext has already been defined by a parent), it automatically inherits the data source. For example, if you bind a data source to the DataContext property of a Grid, then any data binding created in the Grid uses that source by default. You can, however, *override* this source by explicitly defining a new one when you define a binding.

```xaml
 1  <!-- Fig. 30.28: MainWindow.xaml -->
 2  <!-- Using data templates (XAML). -->
 3  <Window x:Class="BookViewer.MainWindow"
 4     xmlns="http://schemas.microsoft.com/winfx/2006/xaml/presentation"
 5     xmlns:x="http://schemas.microsoft.com/winfx/2006/xaml"
 6     Title="Book Viewer" Height="400" Width="600" Name="bookViewerWindow">
 7
 8     <Window.Resources> <!-- Define Window's resources -->
 9
10         <!-- define data template -->
11         <DataTemplate x:Key="BookTemplate">
12           <Grid MaxWidth="250" Margin="3">
13              <Grid.ColumnDefinitions>
14                 <ColumnDefinition Width="Auto" />
15                 <ColumnDefinition />
16              </Grid.ColumnDefinitions>
17
18              <!-- bind image source -->
19              <Image Grid.Column="0" Source="{Binding Path=ThumbImage}"
20                 Width="50" />
21
22              <StackPanel Grid.Column="1">
23                 <!-- bind Title and ISBN -->
24                 <TextBlock Margin="3,0" Text="{Binding Path=Title}"
25                    FontWeight="Bold" TextWrapping="Wrap" />
26                 <StackPanel Margin="3,0" Orientation="Horizontal">
27                    <TextBlock Text="ISBN: " />
28                    <TextBlock Text="{Binding Path=ISBN}" />
29                 </StackPanel>
30              </StackPanel>
31           </Grid>
32         </DataTemplate>
33     </Window.Resources>
34
35     <Grid> <!-- define GUI -->
36        <Grid.ColumnDefinitions>
37           <ColumnDefinition Width="Auto" />
38           <ColumnDefinition />
39        </Grid.ColumnDefinitions>
40
41        <!-- use ListView and template to display data -->
42        <ListView x:Name="booksListView" Grid.Column="0"
43           ItemTemplate="{StaticResource BookTemplate}" />
44
45        <!-- bind to selected item's full-size image -->
46        <Image Grid.Column="1" Source="{Binding ElementName=booksListView,
47           Path=SelectedItem.LargeImage}" Margin="5" />
48     </Grid>
49  </Window>
```

Fig. 30.28 | Using data templates (XAML). (Part 1 of 2.)

a) App showing the ListView with the DataTemplate applied to its items

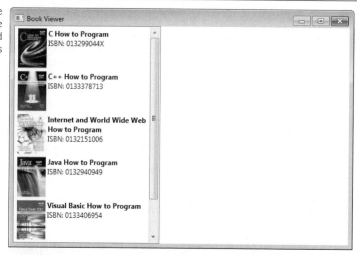

b) Selecting an item from the ListView

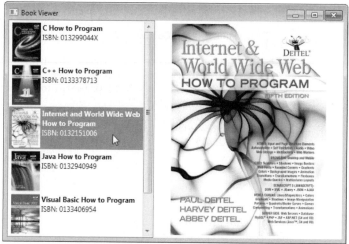

Fig. 30.28 | Using data templates (XAML). (Part 2 of 2.)

In the BookTemplate data template, lines 19–20 of Fig. 30.28 define an Image whose Source is bound to the Book's ThumbImage property, which stores the relative file path to the thumbnail cover image. The Book's Title and ISBN are displayed to the right of the book using **TextBlocks**—lightweight controls for displaying text. The TextBlock in lines 24–25 displays the Book's Title because the Text property is bound to it. Because some of the books' titles are long, we set the TextWrapping property to Wrap (line 25) so that, if the title is too long, it will wrap to multiple lines. We also set the FontWeight property to Bold. Lines 26–29 display two additional TextBlocks, one that displays ISBN:, and another that's bound to the Book's ISBN property.

Figure 30.28(a) shows the book-viewer app when it first loads. Each item in the List-View is represented by a thumbnail of its cover image, its title and its ISBN, as specified in the data template. As illustrated by Fig. 30.28(b), when you select an item in the List-

View, the large cover image on the right automatically updates, because it's bound to the SelectedItem property of the list.

Collection Views

A **collection view** (of class type **CollectionView**) is a *wrapper* around a collection of data and can provide multiple "views" of the data based on how it's filtered, sorted and grouped. A *default view* is created in the background every time a *data binding* is created. To retrieve the collection view, use the **CollectionViewSource.GetDefaultView** method and pass it the source of your data binding. For example, to retrieve the default view of bookListView, you'd use CollectionViewSource.GetDefaultView(bookListView.ItemsSource).

You can then modify the view to create the exact view of the data that you want to display. The methods of filtering, sorting and grouping data are beyond the scope of this book. For more information, see msdn.microsoft.com/en-us/library/ms752347.aspx# what_are_collection_views.

Asynchronous Data Binding

Sometimes you may wish to create *asynchronous data bindings* that don't hold up your app while data is being transmitted. To do this, you set the **IsAsync** property of a data binding to True (it's False by default). Often, however, it's not the transmission but the instantiation of data that's the most expensive operation. An asynchronous data binding does not provide a solution for instantiating data asynchronously. To do so, you must use a **data provider**, a class that can create or retrieve data. There are two types of data providers, **Xml-DataProvider** (for XML) and **ObjectDataProvider** (for data objects). Both can be declared as resources in XAML markup. If you set a data provider's **IsAsynchronous** property to True, the provider will run in the background. Creating and using data providers is beyond the scope of this book. See msdn.microsoft.com/en-us/library/ aa480224.aspx for more information.

30.13 Wrap-Up

Many of today's commercial apps provide GUIs that are easy to use and manipulate. The demand for sophisticated and user-friendly GUIs makes GUI design an essential programming skill. In Chapters 14–15, we showed you how to create GUIs with Windows Forms. In this chapter, we demonstrated how to create GUIs with WPF. You learned how to design a WPF GUI with XAML markup and how to give it functionality in a C# code-behind class. We presented WPF's new flow-based layout scheme, in which a control's size and position are both defined relatively. You learned not only to handle events just as you did in a Windows Forms app, but also to implement WPF commands when you want multiple user interactions to execute the same task. We demonstrated the flexibility WPF offers for customizing the look-and-feel of your GUIs. You learned how to use styles, control templates and triggers to define a control's appearance. The chapter concluded with a demonstration of how to create data-driven GUIs with data bindings and data templates.

But WPF is not merely a GUI-building platform. Chapter 31 explores some of the many other capabilities of WPF, showing you how to incorporate 2D and 3D graphics, animation and multimedia into your WPF apps.

31

WPF Graphics and Multimedia

Objectives

In this chapter you'll:

- Manipulate fonts.

- Draw basic WPF shapes.

- Use WPF brushes to customize the `Fill` or `Background` of an object.

- Use WPF transforms to reposition or reorient GUI elements.

- Customize the look of a control while maintaining its functionality.

- Animate the properties of a GUI element.

- Use speech synthesis and recognition.

31.1 Introduction

This chapter overviews WPF's graphics and multimedia capabilities, including two-dimensional and three-dimensional shapes, fonts, transformations, animations, audio and video. The graphics system in WPF is designed to use your computer's graphics hardware to reduce the load on the CPU.

WPF graphics use *resolution-independent* units of measurement, making apps more uniform and portable across devices. The size properties of graphic elements in WPF are measured in **machine-independent pixels**, where one pixel typically represents 1/96 of an inch—however, this depends on the computer's DPI (dots per inch) setting. The graphics engine determines the correct pixel count so that all users see elements of the same size on all devices.

Graphic elements are rendered on screen using a **vector-based** system in which calculations determine how to size and scale each element, allowing graphic elements to be preserved across any rendering size. This produces smoother graphics than the so-called **raster-based** systems, in which the precise pixels are specified for each graphical element. Raster-based graphics tend to degrade in appearance as they're *scaled* larger. Vector-based graphics appear *smooth* at any scale. Graphic elements other than images and video are drawn using WPF's vector-based system, so they look good at any screen resolution.

The basic 2-D shapes are Lines, Rectangles and Ellipses. WPF also has controls that can be used to create *custom* shapes or curves. *Brushes* can be used to fill an element with solid *colors*, complex *patterns*, *gradients*, *images* or *videos*, allowing for unique and interesting visual experiences. WPF's robust animation and transform capabilities allow you to further customize GUIs. *Transforms* reposition and reorient graphic elements. The chapter ends with an introduction to speech synthesis and recognition.

31.2 Controlling Fonts

This section introduces how to control fonts by modifying the font properties of a **Text-Block** control in the XAML code. Figure 31.1 shows how to use TextBlocks and how to change the properties to control the appearance of the displayed text. When building this example, we removed the StackPanel's HorizontalAlignment, Height, VerticalAlignment and Width attributes from the XAML so that the StackPanel would occupy the entire window. Some of the font formatting in this example was performed by editing the XAML markup because some TextDecorations are not available via the **Properties** window.

```
 1   <!-- Fig. 31.1: MainWindow.xaml -->
 2   <!-- Formatting fonts in XAML code. -->
 3   <Window x:Class="UsingFonts.MainWindow"
 4      xmlns="http://schemas.microsoft.com/winfx/2006/xaml/presentation"
 5      xmlns:x="http://schemas.microsoft.com/winfx/2006/xaml"
 6      Title="UsingFonts" Height="120" Width="400">
 7
 8      <StackPanel>
 9         <!-- make a font bold using the FontWeight -->
10         <TextBlock TextWrapping="Wrap" Text="Arial 14 bold."
11            FontFamily="Arial" FontSize="14" FontWeight="Bold"/>
12
13         <!-- if no font size is specified, default size is used -->
14         <TextBlock TextWrapping="Wrap"
15            Text="Times New Roman plain, default size."
16            FontFamily="Times New Roman"/>
17
18         <!-- specifying a different font size and using FontStyle -->
19         <TextBlock TextWrapping="Wrap"
20            Text="Courier New 16 bold and italic."
21            FontFamily="Courier New" FontSize="16"
22            FontStyle="Italic" FontWeight="Bold"/>
23
24         <!-- using Overline and Baseline TextDecorations -->
25         <TextBlock TextWrapping="Wrap"
26            Text="Default font with overline and baseline.">
27            <TextBlock.TextDecorations>
28               <TextDecoration Location="Overline"/>
29               <TextDecoration Location="Baseline"/>
30            </TextBlock.TextDecorations>
31         </TextBlock>
32
33         <!-- using Strikethrough and Underline TextDecorations -->
34         <TextBlock TextWrapping="Wrap"
35            Text="Default font with strikethrough and underline.">
36            <TextBlock.TextDecorations>
37               <TextDecoration Location="Strikethrough"/>
38               <TextDecoration Location="Underline"/>
39            </TextBlock.TextDecorations>
40         </TextBlock>
41      </StackPanel>
42   </Window>
```

Fig. 31.1 | Formatting fonts in XAML code.

The text that you want to display in the TextBlock is specified either via the Text-Block's Text property (line 10) or by placing the text between a TextBlock's start and end tags. The **FontFamily** property defines the font of the displayed text. This property can be set to any available font. Lines 11, 16 and 21 define the first three TextBlock fonts to be Arial, Times New Roman and Courier New, respectively. If the font is not specified or is not available, the *default font* (Segoe UI) is used.

The **FontSize** property defines the text size measured in machine-independent pixels unless the value is qualified by appending in (inches), cm (centimeters) or pt (points). When no FontSize is specified, the property is set to the default value of 12 (this is actually determined by System.MessageFontSize). The font sizes are defined in lines 11 and 21.

TextBlocks have various font-related properties. Lines 11 and 22 set the **FontWeight** property to Bold to make the font thicker. This property can be set either to a numeric value (1–999) or to a predefined descriptive value—such as Light or UltraBold (msdn.microsoft.com/en-us/library/system.windows.fontweights.aspx)—to define the thickness of the text. You can use the **FontStyle** property to make the text either Italic (line 22) or Oblique—which is simply a more emphasized italic.

You can also define **TextDecorations** for a TextBlock to draw a horizontal line through the text. **Overline** and **Baseline**—shown in the fourth TextBlock of Fig. 31.1—create lines above the text and at the base of the text, respectively (lines 28–29). **Strikethrough** and **Underline**—shown in the fifth TextBlock—create lines through the middle of the text and under the text, respectively (lines 37–38). The Underline option leaves a small amount of space between the text and the line, unlike the Baseline. The **Location** property of the **TextDecoration** class defines which decoration you want to apply.

31.3 Basic Shapes

WPF has several built-in shapes. The BasicShapes example (Fig. 31.2) shows you how to display Lines, Rectangles and Ellipses on a WPF Canvas object. When building this example, we removed the Canvas's HorizontalAlignment, Height, VerticalAlignment and Width attributes from the XAML so that the StackPanel would occupy the entire window. By default, the shape elements are *not* displayed in the WPF **Toolbox**, so all the shape elements in this example were added via the XAML editor—this will be the case for many other examples in this chapter.

```xml
 1   <!-- Fig. 31.2: MainWindow.xaml -->
 2   <!-- Drawing basic shapes in XAML. -->
 3   <Window x:Class="BasicShapes.MainWindow"
 4      xmlns="http://schemas.microsoft.com/winfx/2006/xaml/presentation"
 5      xmlns:x="http://schemas.microsoft.com/winfx/2006/xaml"
 6      Title="BasicShapes" Height="200" Width="500">
 7      <Canvas>
 8         <!-- Rectangle with fill but no stroke -->
 9         <Rectangle Canvas.Left="90" Canvas.Top="30" Width="150" Height="90"
10            Fill="LightBlue" />
11
12         <!-- Lines defined by starting points and ending points-->
13         <Line X1="90" Y1="30" X2="110" Y2="40" Stroke="Black" />
14         <Line X1="90" Y1="120" X2="110" Y2="130" Stroke="Black" />
15         <Line X1="240" Y1="30" X2="260" Y2="40" Stroke="Black" />
16         <Line X1="240" Y1="120" X2="260" Y2="130" Stroke="Black" />
```

Fig. 31.2 | Drawing basic shapes in XAML. (Part 1 of 2.)

```
17
18        <!-- Rectangle with stroke but no fill -->
19        <Rectangle Canvas.Left="110" Canvas.Top="40" Width="150"
20           Height="90" Stroke="Black" />
21
22        <!-- Ellipse with fill and no stroke -->
23        <Ellipse Canvas.Left="280" Canvas.Top="75" Width="100" Height="50"
24           Fill="Orange" />
25        <Line X1="380" Y1="55" X2="380" Y2="100" Stroke="Black" />
26        <Line X1="280" Y1="55" X2="280" Y2="100" Stroke="Black" />
27
28        <!-- Ellipse with stroke and no fill -->
29        <Ellipse Canvas.Left="280" Canvas.Top="30" Width="100" Height="50"
30           Stroke="Black" />
31     </Canvas>
32  </Window>
```

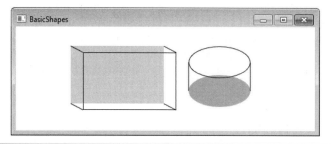

Fig. 31.2 | Drawing basic shapes in XAML. (Part 2 of 2.)

The first shape drawn uses the **Rectangle** object to create a filled rectangle in the window. The layout control is a Canvas, which allows us to use coordinates to position the shapes. To specify the upper-left corner of the Rectangle at lines 9–10, we set the Canvas.Left and Canvas.Top properties to 90 and 30, respectively. We then set the Width and Height properties to 150 and 90, respectively, to specify the size. To define the Rectangle's color, we use the **Fill** property (line 10). You can assign any Color or Brush to this property. Rectangles also have a **Stroke** property, which defines the color of the *outline* of the shape (line 20). If either the Fill or the Stroke is not specified, that property will be rendered *transparently*. For this reason, the light blue Rectangle in the window has no outline, while the second Rectangle drawn has only an outline (with a transparent center). Shape objects have a **StrokeThickness** property which defines the *thickness* of the outline. The default value for StrokeThickness is 1 pixel.

A **Line** is defined by its two *endpoints*—X1, Y1 and X2, Y2. Lines have a Stroke property that defines the *color* of the line. In this example, the lines are all set to have black Strokes (lines 13–16 and 25–26).

To draw a circle or ellipse, you can use the **Ellipse** control. The placement and size of an Ellipse is defined like a Rectangle—with the Canvas.Left and Canvas.Top properties for the *upper-left corner*, and the Width and Height properties for the size (line 23). Together, the Canvas.Left, Canvas.Top, Width and Height of an Ellipse define a *bounding rectangle* in which the Ellipse touches the center of each side of the rectangle. To draw a circle, provide the same value for the Width and Height properties. As with

Rectangles, having an unspecified `Fill` property for an `Ellipse` makes the shape's fill *transparent* (lines 29–30).

31.4 Polygons and Polylines

There are two shape controls for drawing *multisided shapes*—**Polyline** and **Polygon**. `Polyline` draws a series of connected lines defined by a set of points, while `Polygon` does the same but connects the start and end points to make a closed figure. The app DrawPolygons (Fig. 31.3) allows you to click anywhere on the `Canvas` to define points for one of three shapes. You select which shape you want to display by selecting one of the RadioButtons in the second column. The difference between the **Filled Polygon** and the **Polygon** options is that the former has a `Fill` property specified while the latter does not.

```xml
1   <!-- Fig. 31.3: MainWindow.xaml -->
2   <!-- Defining Polylines and Polygons in XAML. -->
3   <Window x:Class="DrawPolygons.MainWindow"
4      xmlns="http://schemas.microsoft.com/winfx/2006/xaml/presentation"
5      xmlns:x="http://schemas.microsoft.com/winfx/2006/xaml"
6      Title="DrawPolygons" Height="400" Width="450" Name="mainWindow">
7      <Grid>
8         <Grid.ColumnDefinitions>
9            <ColumnDefinition />
10           <ColumnDefinition Width="Auto" />
11        </Grid.ColumnDefinitions>
12
13        <!-- Canvas contains two polygons and a polyline -->
14        <!-- only the shape selected by the radio button is visible -->
15        <Canvas Name="drawCanvas" Grid.Column="0" Background="White"
16           MouseDown="drawCanvas_MouseDown">
17           <Polyline Name="polyLine" Stroke="Black"
18              Visibility="Collapsed" />
19           <Polygon Name="polygon" Stroke="Black" Visibility="Collapsed" />
20           <Polygon Name="filledPolygon" Fill="DarkBlue"
21              Visibility="Collapsed" />
22        </Canvas>
23
24        <!-- StackPanel containing the RadioButton options -->
25        <StackPanel Grid.Column="1" Orientation="Vertical"
26           Background="WhiteSmoke">
27           <GroupBox Header="Select Type" Margin="10">
28              <StackPanel>
29                 <!-- Polyline option -->
30                 <RadioButton Name="lineRadio" Content="Polyline"
31                    Margin="5" Checked="lineRadio_Checked"/>
32
33                 <!-- unfilled Polygon option -->
34                 <RadioButton Name="polygonRadio" Content="Polygon"
35                    Margin="5"Checked="polygonRadio_Checked"/>
36
```

Fig. 31.3 | Defining Polylines and Polygons in XAML. (Part 1 of 2.)

```
37                         <!-- filled Polygon option -->
38                         <RadioButton Name="filledPolygonRadio"
39                             Content="Filled Polygon" Margin="5"
40                             Checked="filledPolygonRadio_Checked"/>
41                     </StackPanel>
42                 </GroupBox>
43
44                 <!-- Button clears the shape from the canvas -->
45                 <Button Name="clearButton" Content="Clear"
46                     Click="clearButton_Click" Margin="5"/>
47             </StackPanel>
48         </Grid>
49     </Window>
```

a) App with the Polyline option selected

b) App with the Filled Polygon option selected

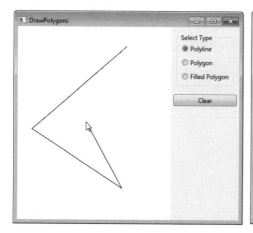

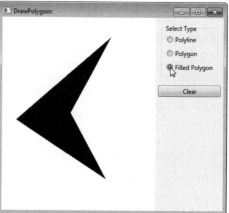

Fig. 31.3 | Defining Polylines and Polygons in XAML. (Part 2 of 2.)

The XAML defines a two-column GUI (lines 9–10). The first column contains a Canvas (lines 15–22) that the user interacts with to create the points of the selected shape. Embedded in the Canvas are a Polyline (lines 17–18) and two Polygons—one with a Fill (lines 20–21) and one without (line 19). The **Visibility** of a control can be set to **Visible**, **Collapsed** or **Hidden**. This property is initially set to Collapsed for all three shapes (lines 18, 19 and 21), because we'll display only the shape that corresponds to the selected RadioButton. The difference between Hidden and Collapsed is that a Hidden object occupies space in the GUI but is *not visible*, while a Collapsed object has a Width and Height of 0. As you can see, Polyline and Polygon objects have Fill and Stroke properties like the simple shapes we discussed earlier.

The RadioButtons (lines 30–40) allow you to select which shape appears in the Canvas. There is also a Button (lines 45–46) that clears the shape's points to allow you to start over. The code-behind file for this app is shown in Fig. 31.4.

To allow the user to specify a variable number of points, line 12 in Fig. 31.4 declares a **PointCollection**, which is a collection that stores Point objects. This keeps track of each mouse-click location. The collection's **Add** method adds new points to the end of the

```csharp
 1  // Fig. 31.4: MainWindow.xaml.cs
 2  // Drawing Polylines and Polygons.
 3  using System.Windows;
 4  using System.Windows.Input;
 5  using System.Windows.Media;
 6
 7  namespace DrawPolygons
 8  {
 9     public partial class MainWindow : Window
10     {
11        // stores the collection of points for the multisided shapes
12        private PointCollection points = new PointCollection();
13
14        // initialize the points of the shapes
15        public MainWindow()
16        {
17           InitializeComponent();
18
19           polyLine.Points = points; // assign Polyline points
20           polygon.Points = points; // assign Polygon points
21           filledPolygon.Points = points; // assign filled Polygon points
22        } // end constructor
23
24        // adds a new point when the user clicks on the canvas
25        private void drawCanvas_MouseDown( object sender,
26           MouseButtonEventArgs e )
27        {
28           // add point to collection
29           points.Add( e.GetPosition( drawCanvas ) );
30        } // end method drawCanvas_MouseDown
31
32        // when the clear Button is clicked
33        private void clearButton_Click( object sender, RoutedEventArgs e )
34        {
35           points.Clear(); // clear the points from the collection
36        } // end method clearButton_Click
37
38        // when the user selects the Polyline
39        private void lineRadio_Checked( object sender, RoutedEventArgs e )
40        {
41           // Polyline is visible, the other two are not
42           polyLine.Visibility = Visibility.Visible;
43           polygon.Visibility = Visibility.Collapsed;
44           filledPolygon.Visibility = Visibility.Collapsed;
45        } // end method lineRadio_Checked
46
47        //  when the user selects the Polygon
48        private void polygonRadio_Checked( object sender,
49           RoutedEventArgs e )
50        {
51           // Polygon is visible, the other two are not
52           polyLine.Visibility = Visibility.Collapsed;
53           polygon.Visibility = Visibility.Visible;
```

Fig. 31.4 | Drawing Polylines and Polygons. (Part 1 of 2.)

```
54          filledPolygon.Visibility = Visibility.Collapsed;
55       } // end method polygonRadio_Checked
56
57       // when the user selects the filled Polygon
58       private void filledPolygonRadio_Checked( object sender,
59          RoutedEventArgs e )
60       {
61          // filled Polygon is visible, the other two are not
62          polyLine.Visibility = Visibility.Collapsed;
63          polygon.Visibility = Visibility.Collapsed;
64          filledPolygon.Visibility = Visibility.Visible;
65       } // end method filledPolygonRadio_Checked
66    } // end class MainWindow
67 } // end namespace DrawPolygons
```

Fig. 31.4 │ Drawing Polylines and Polygons. (Part 2 of 2.)

collection. When the app executes, we set the **Points** property (lines 19–21) of each shape to reference the PointCollection instance variable created in line 12.

We created a MouseDown event handler to capture mouse clicks on the Canvas (lines 25–30). When the user clicks the mouse on the Canvas, the mouse coordinates are recorded (line 29) and the points collection is updated. Since the Points property of each of the three shapes has a reference to our PointCollection object, the shapes are automatically updated with the new Point. The Polyline and Polygon shapes connect the Points based on the ordering in the collection.

Each RadioButton's Checked event handler sets the corresponding shape's Visibility property to Visible and sets the other two to Collapsed to display the correct shape in the Canvas. For example, the lineRadio_Checked event handler (lines 39–45) makes polyLine Visible (line 42) and makes polygon and filledPolygon Collapsed (lines 43–44). The other two RadioButton event handlers are defined similarly in lines 48–55 and lines 58–65.

The clearButton_Click event handler erases the stored collection of Points (line 35). The **Clear** method of the PointCollection points erases its elements.

31.5 Brushes

Brushes change an element's graphic properties, such as the Fill, Stroke or Background. A SolidColorBrush fills the element with the specified color. To customize elements further, you can use ImageBrushes, VisualBrushes and gradient brushes. Run the Using-Brushes app (Fig. 31.5) to see Brushes applied to TextBlocks and Ellipses.

```
1  <!-- Fig. 31.5: MainWindow.xaml -->
2  <!-- Applying brushes to various XAML elements. -->
3  <Window x:Class="UsingBrushes.MainWindow"
4     xmlns="http://schemas.microsoft.com/winfx/2006/xaml/presentation"
5     xmlns:x="http://schemas.microsoft.com/winfx/2006/xaml"
6     Title="UsingBrushes" Height="470" Width="720">
```

Fig. 31.5 │ Applying brushes to various XAML elements. (Part 1 of 4.)

```
 7      <Grid>
 8         <Grid.RowDefinitions>
 9            <RowDefinition />
10            <RowDefinition />
11            <RowDefinition />
12         </Grid.RowDefinitions>
13
14         <Grid.ColumnDefinitions>
15            <ColumnDefinition />
16            <ColumnDefinition />
17         </Grid.ColumnDefinitions>
18
19         <!-- TextBlock with a SolidColorBrush -->
20         <TextBlock TextWrapping="Wrap" Text="Color" FontSize="100"
21            FontWeight="999">
22            <TextBlock.Foreground>
23               <SolidColorBrush Color="#FF5F2CAE" />
24            </TextBlock.Foreground>
25         </TextBlock>
26
27         <!-- Ellipse with a SolidColorBrush (just a Fill) -->
28         <Ellipse Grid.Column="1" Width="300" Height="100" Fill="#FF5F2CAE"/>
29
30         <!-- TextBlock with an ImageBrush -->
31         <TextBlock TextWrapping="Wrap" Text="Image" Grid.Row="1"
32            FontSize="100" FontWeight="999">
33            <TextBlock.Foreground>
34               <!-- Flower image as an ImageBrush -->
35               <ImageBrush ImageSource="flowers.jpg"
36                  Stretch="UniformToFill"/>
37            </TextBlock.Foreground>
38         </TextBlock>
39
40         <!-- Ellipse with an ImageBrush -->
41         <Ellipse Grid.Row="1" Grid.Column="1" Width="300" Height="100">
42            <Ellipse.Fill>
43               <ImageBrush ImageSource="flowers.jpg"
44                  Stretch="UniformToFill"/>
45            </Ellipse.Fill>
46         </Ellipse>
47
48         <!-- TextBlock with a MediaElement as a VisualBrush -->
49         <TextBlock TextWrapping="Wrap" Text="Video" Grid.Row="2"
50            FontSize="100" FontWeight="999">
51            <TextBlock.Foreground>
52               <!-- VisualBrush with an embedded MediaElement-->
53               <VisualBrush Stretch="UniformToFill">
54                  <VisualBrush.Visual>
55                     <MediaElement Source="media.mp4"/>
56                  </VisualBrush.Visual>
57               </VisualBrush>
58            </TextBlock.Foreground>
59         </TextBlock>
```

Fig. 31.5 | Applying brushes to various XAML elements. (Part 2 of 4.)

```
60
61          <!-- Ellipse with a MediaElement as a VisualBrush -->
62          <Ellipse Grid.Row="2" Grid.Column="1" Width="300" Height="100">
63             <Ellipse.Fill>
64                <VisualBrush Stretch="UniformToFill">
65                   <VisualBrush.Visual>
66                      <MediaElement Source="media.mp4" IsMuted="True"/>
67                   </VisualBrush.Visual>
68                </VisualBrush>
69             </Ellipse.Fill>
70          </Ellipse>
71       </Grid>
72    </Window>
```

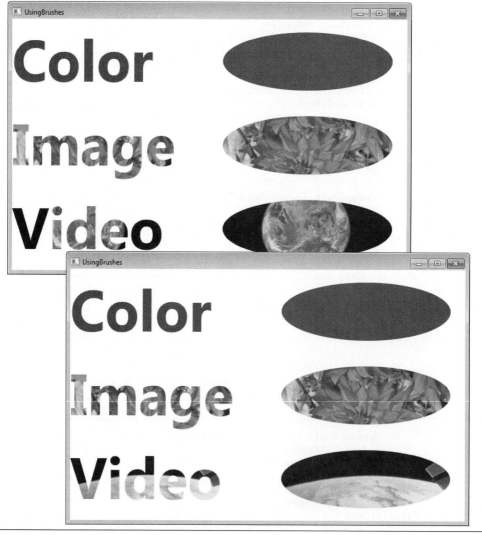

Fig. 31.5 | Applying brushes to various XAML elements. (Part 3 of 4.)

Fig. 31.5 | Applying brushes to various XAML elements. (Part 4 of 4.)

ImageBrush

An **ImageBrush** paints an image into the property it's assigned to (such as a Background). For instance, the TextBlock with the text "Image" and the Ellipse next to it are both filled with the same flower picture. To fill the text, we can assign the ImageBrush to the Foreground property of the TextBlock. The **Foreground** property specifies the fill for the text itself while the **Background** property specifies the fill for the area surrounding the text. Lines 33–37 apply the ImageBrush with its **ImageSource** set to the file we want to display (the image file must be included in the project). We can also assign the brush to the Fill of the Ellipse (lines 43–44) to display the image inside the shape. The ImageBrush's **Stretch** property specifies how to stretch the image. The UniformToFill value indicates that the image should fill the element in which it's displayed and that the original image's **aspect ratio** (that is, the proportion between its width and height) should be maintained. Keeping this ratio at its original value ensures that the video does not look "stretched," though it might be cropped.

VisualBrush and MediaElement

This example displays a video in a TextBlock's Foreground and an Ellipse's Fill. To use audio or video in a WPF app, you use the **MediaElement** control. Before using a video file in your app, add it to your Visual Studio project by dragging it from Windows Explorer to your project's folder in the Visual Studio **Solution Explorer**. Select the newly added video in the **Solution Explorer**. Then, in the **Properties** window, change the **Copy to Output Directory** property to **Copy if newer**. This tells the project to copy your video to the project's output directory where it can directly reference the file. You can now set the **Source** property of your MediaElement to the video. In the UsingBrushes app, we used media.mp4 (line 55 and 66), which we downloaded from www.nasa.gov/multimedia/videogallery.

We use the **VisualBrush** element to display a video in the desired controls. Lines 53–57 define the Brush with a MediaElement assigned to its **Visual** property. In this property you can completely customize the look of the brush. By assigning the video to this property, we can apply the brush to the Foreground of the TextBlock (lines 51–58) and the Fill of the Ellipse (lines 63–69) to *play the video inside the controls*. The Fill of the third Row's elements is different in each screen capture in Fig. 31.5, because the video is playing inside the two elements. The VisualBrush's Stretch property specifies how to stretch the video.

Gradients

A **gradient** is a gradual *transition* through two or more colors. Gradients can be applied as the background or fill for various elements. There are two types of gradients in WPF—LinearGradientBrush and RadialGradientBrush. The **LinearGradientBrush** transitions through colors along a straight path. The **RadialGradientBrush** transitions through colors radially outward from a specified point. Linear gradients are discussed in the Using-Gradients example (Figs. 31.6–31.7), which displays a gradient across the window. This was created by applying a LinearGradientBrush to a Rectangle's Fill. The gradient starts white and transitions linearly to black from left to right. You can set the RGBA values of the start and end colors to change the look of the gradient. The values entered in the TextBoxes must be in the range 0–255 for the app to run properly. If you set either color's alpha value to less than 255, you'll see the text "Transparency test" in the background, showing that the Rectangle is *semitransparent*. The XAML code for this app is shown in Fig. 31.6.

The GUI for this app contains a single Rectangle with a LinearGradientBrush applied to its Fill (lines 21–31). We define the **StartPoint** and **EndPoint** of the gradient in line 23. You must assign **logical points** to these properties, meaning the *x*- and *y*-coordinates take values between 0 and 1, inclusive. *Logical points* are used to reference locations in the control *independent* of the actual size. The point (0,0) represents the top-left corner

```
 1    <!-- Fig. 31.6: MainWindow.xaml -->
 2    <!-- Defining gradients in XAML. -->
 3    <Window x:Class="UsingGradients.MainWindow"
 4       xmlns="http://schemas.microsoft.com/winfx/2006/xaml/presentation"
 5       xmlns:x="http://schemas.microsoft.com/winfx/2006/xaml"
 6       Title="UsingGradients" Height="200" Width="450">
 7       <Grid>
 8          <Grid.RowDefinitions>
 9             <RowDefinition />
10             <RowDefinition Height="Auto" />
11             <RowDefinition Height="Auto" />
12             <RowDefinition Height="Auto" />
13          </Grid.RowDefinitions>
14
15          <!-- TextBlock in the background to show transparency -->
16          <TextBlock TextWrapping="Wrap" Text="Transparency Test"
17             FontSize="30" HorizontalAlignment="Center"
18             VerticalAlignment="Center"/>
19
20          <!-- sample rectangle with linear gradient fill -->
21          <Rectangle>
```

Fig. 31.6 | Defining gradients in XAML. (Part 1 of 3.)

```
22          <Rectangle.Fill>
23            <LinearGradientBrush StartPoint="0,0" EndPoint="1,0">
24              <!-- gradient stop can define a color at any offset -->
25              <GradientStop x:Name="startGradient" Offset="0.0"
26                Color="White" />
27              <GradientStop x:Name="stopGradient" Offset="1.0"
28                Color="Black" />
29            </LinearGradientBrush>
30          </Rectangle.Fill>
31        </Rectangle>
32
33        <!-- shows which TextBox corresponds with which ARGB value-->
34        <StackPanel Grid.Row="1" Orientation="Horizontal">
35          <TextBlock TextWrapping="Wrap" Text="Alpha:"
36            Width="75" Margin="5">
37          <TextBlock TextWrapping="Wrap" Text="Red:"
38            Width="75" Margin="5">
39          <TextBlock TextWrapping="Wrap" Text="Green:"
40            Width="75" Margin="5">
41          <TextBlock TextWrapping="Wrap" Text="Blue:"
42            Width="75" Margin="5">
43        </StackPanel>
44
45        <!-- GUI to select the color of the first GradientStop -->
46        <StackPanel Grid.Row="2" Orientation="Horizontal">
47          <TextBox Name="fromAlpha" TextWrapping="Wrap" Text="255"
48            Width="75" Margin="5"/>
49          <TextBox Name="fromRed" TextWrapping="Wrap" Text="255"
50            Width="75" Margin="5"/>
51          <TextBox Name="fromGreen" TextWrapping="Wrap" Text="255"
52            Width="75" Margin="5"/>
53          <TextBox Name="fromBlue" TextWrapping="Wrap" Text="255"
54            Width="75" Margin="5"/>
55          <Button Name="fromButton" Content="Start Color" Width="75"
56            Margin="5" Click="fromButton_Click"/>
57        </StackPanel>
58
59        <!-- GUI to select the color of second GradientStop -->
60        <StackPanel Grid.Row="3" Orientation="Horizontal">
61          <TextBox Name="toAlpha" TextWrapping="Wrap" Text="255"
62            Width="75" Margin="5"/>
63          <TextBox Name="toRed" TextWrapping="Wrap" Text="0"
64            Width="75" Margin="5"/>
65          <TextBox Name="toGreen" TextWrapping="Wrap" Text="0"
66            Width="75" Margin="5"/>
67          <TextBox Name="toBlue" TextWrapping="Wrap" Text="0"
68            Width="75" Margin="5"/>
69          <Button Name="toButton" Content="End Color" Width="75"
70            Margin="5" Click="toButton_Click"/>
71        </StackPanel>
72      </Grid>
73    </Window>
```

Fig. 31.6 | Defining gradients in XAML. (Part 2 of 3.)

a) The app immediately after it's loaded

b) The app after changing the start and end colors

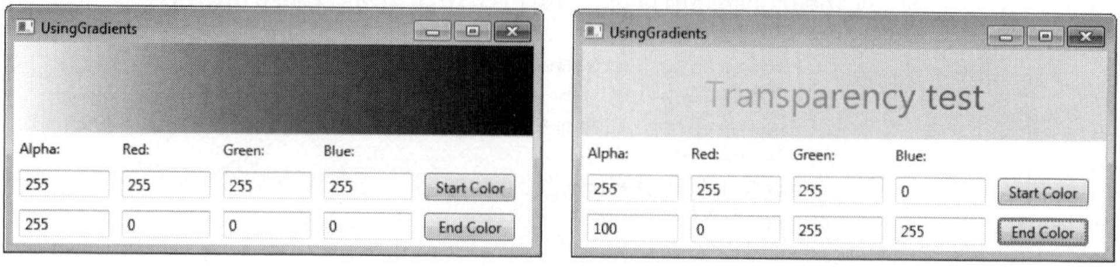

Fig. 31.6 | Defining gradients in XAML. (Part 3 of 3.)

while the point (1,1) represents the bottom-right corner. The gradient will transition linearly from the start to the end—for RadialGradientBrush, the StartPoint represents the *center* of the gradient. The values in line 23 indicate that the gradient should start at the left and be displayed horizontally from left to right.

A gradient is defined using GradientStops. A **GradientStop** defines a single color along the gradient. You can define as many *stops* as you want by embedding them in the brush element. A GradientStop is defined by its Offset and Color properties. The **Color** property defines the color you want the gradient to transition to—lines 25–26 and 27–28 indicate that the gradient transitions through white and black. The **Offset** property defines where along the linear transition you want the color to appear. You can assign any double value between 0 and 1, inclusive, which represent the start and end of the gradient. In the example we use 0.0 and 1.0 offsets (lines 25 and 27), indicating that these colors appear at the start and end of the gradient (which were defined in line 23), respectively. The code in Fig. 31.7 allows the user to set the Colors of the two stops.

When fromButton is clicked, we use the Text properties of the corresponding Text-Boxes to obtain the RGBA values and create a new color. We then assign it to the Color property of startGradient (Fig. 31.7, lines 21–25). When the toButton is clicked, we do the same for stopGradient's Color (lines 32–36).

```
1   // Fig. 31.7: MainWindow.xaml.cs
2   // Customizing gradients.
3   using System;
4   using System.Windows;
5   using System.Windows.Media;
6
7   namespace UsingGradients
8   {
9      public partial class MainWindow : Window
10     {
11        // constructor
12        public MainWindow()
13        {
14           InitializeComponent();
15        } // end constructor
16
```

Fig. 31.7 | Customizing gradients. (Part 1 of 2.)

```
17        // change the starting color of the gradient when the user clicks
18        private void fromButton_Click( object sender, RoutedEventArgs e )
19        {
20           // change the color to use the ARGB values specified by user
21           startGradient.Color = Color.FromArgb(
22              Convert.ToByte( fromAlpha.Text ),
23              Convert.ToByte( fromRed.Text ),
24              Convert.ToByte( fromGreen.Text ),
25              Convert.ToByte( fromBlue.Text ) );
26        } // end method fromButton_Click
27
28        // change the ending color of the gradient when the user clicks
29        private void toButton_Click( object sender, RoutedEventArgs e )
30        {
31           // change the color to use the ARGB values specified by user
32           stopGradient.Color = Color.FromArgb(
33              Convert.ToByte( toAlpha.Text ),
34              Convert.ToByte( toRed.Text ),
35              Convert.ToByte( toGreen.Text ),
36              Convert.ToByte( toBlue.Text ) );
37        } // end method toButton_Click
38     } // end class MainWindow
39  } // end namespace UsingGradients
```

Fig. 31.7 | Customizing gradients. (Part 2 of 2.)

31.6 Transforms

A **transform** can be applied to any UI element to *reposition* or *reorient* the graphic. There are several types of transforms. Here we discuss **TranslateTransform**, **RotateTransform**, **SkewTransform** and **ScaleTransform**. A TranslateTransform *moves* an object to a new location. A RotateTransform *rotates* the object around a point and by a specified RotationAngle. A SkewTransform *skews* (or *shears*) the object. A ScaleTransform scales the object's *x*- and *y*-coordinate points by different specified amounts. See Section 31.7 for an example using a SkewTransform and a ScaleTransform.

The next example draws a star using the Polygon control and uses RotateTransforms to create a circle of randomly colored stars. Figure 31.8 shows the XAML code and a sample output. Lines 10–11 define a Polygon in the shape of a star. The Polygon's Points property is defined here in a new syntax. Each Point in the collection is defined with a comma separating the *x*- and *y*- coordinates. A single space separates each Point. We defined ten Points in the collection. The code-behind file is shown in Fig. 31.9.

```
1  <!-- Fig. 31.8: MainWindow.xaml -->
2  <!-- Defining a Polygon representing a star in XAML. -->
3  <Window x:Class="DrawStars.MainWindow"
4     xmlns="http://schemas.microsoft.com/winfx/2006/xaml/presentation"
5     xmlns:x="http://schemas.microsoft.com/winfx/2006/xaml"
6     Title="DrawStars" Height="330" Width="330" Name="DrawStars">
```

Fig. 31.8 | Defining a Polygon representing a star in XAML. (Part 1 of 2.)

```
7     <Canvas Name="mainCanvas"> <!-- Main canvas of the app -->
8
9        <!-- Polygon with points that make up a star -->
10       <Polygon Name="star" Fill="Green" Points="205,150 217,186 259,186
11          223,204 233,246 205,222 177,246 187,204 151,186 193,186" />
12    </Canvas>
13 </Window>
```

Fig. 31.8 | Defining a `Polygon` representing a star in XAML. (Part 2 of 2.)

```
1    // Fig. 31.9: MainWindow.xaml.cs
2    // Applying transforms to a Polygon.
3    using System;
4    using System.Windows;
5    using System.Windows.Media;
6    using System.Windows.Shapes;
7
8    namespace DrawStars
9    {
10      public partial class MainWindow : Window
11      {
12         // constructor
13         public MainWindow()
14         {
15            InitializeComponent();
16
17            Random random = new Random(); // get random values for colors
18
19            // create 18 more stars
20            for ( int count = 0; count < 18; ++count )
21            {
22               Polygon newStar = new Polygon(); // create a polygon object
23               newStar.Points = star.Points; // copy the points collection
24
25               byte[] colorValues = new byte[ 4 ]; // create a Byte array
26               random.NextBytes( colorValues ); // create four random values
```

Fig. 31.9 | Applying transforms to a `Polygon`. (Part 1 of 2.)

```
27              newStar.Fill = new SolidColorBrush( Color.FromArgb(
28                 colorValues[ 0 ], colorValues[ 1 ], colorValues[ 2 ],
29                 colorValues[ 3 ] ) ); // creates a random color brush
30
31              // apply a rotation to the shape
32              RotateTransform rotate =
33                 new RotateTransform( count * 20, 150, 150 );
34              newStar.RenderTransform = rotate;
35              mainCanvas.Children.Add( newStar );
36           } // end for
37        } // end constructor
38     } // end class MainWindow
39  } // end namespace DrawStars
```

Fig. 31.9 | Applying transforms to a `Polygon`. (Part 2 of 2.)

In the code-behind, we replicate `star` 18 times and apply a different `RotateTransform` to each to get the circle of `Polygon`s shown in the screen capture of Fig. 31.8. Each iteration of the loop duplicates `star` by creating a new `Polygon` with the same set of points (Fig. 31.9, lines 22–23). To generate the random colors for each star, we use the `Random` class's **NextBytes** method, which assigns a random value in the range 0–255 to each element in its `Byte` array argument. Lines 25–26 define a four-element `Byte` array and supply the array to the `NextBytes` method. We then create a new `Brush` with a color that uses the four randomly generated values as its RGBA values (lines 27–29).

To apply a rotation to the new `Polygon`, we set the **RenderTransform** property to a new `RotateTransform` object (lines 32–34). Each iteration of the loop assigns a new rotation-angle value by using the control variable multiplied by 20 as the `RotationAngle` argument. The first argument in the `RotateTransform`'s constructor is the angle by which to rotate the object. The next two arguments are the *x*- and *y*-coordinates of the point of rotation. The center of the circle of stars is the point (150,150) because all 18 stars were rotated about that point. Each new shape is added as a new `Child` element to `mainCanvas` (line 35) so it can be rendered on screen.

31.7 WPF Customization: A Television GUI

In Chapter 30, we introduced several techniques for customizing the appearance of WPF controls. We revisit them in this section, now that we have a basic understanding of how to create and manipulate 2-D graphics in WPF. You'll learn to apply combinations of shapes, brushes and transforms to define every aspect of a control's appearance and to create graphically sophisticated GUIs.

This case study models a television. The GUI depicts a 3-D-looking environment featuring a TV that can be turned on and off. When it's on, the user can play, pause and stop the TV's video. When the video plays, a *semitransparent reflection* plays simultaneously on what appears to be a flat surface in front of the screen (Fig. 31.10).

The TV GUI may appear overwhelmingly complex, but it's actually just a basic WPF GUI built using controls with modified appearances. This example demonstrates the use of **WPF bitmap effects** to apply simple visual effects to some of the GUI elements. In addition, it introduces **opacity masks**, which can be used to hide parts of an element. Other

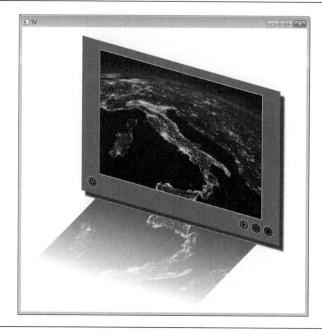

Fig. 31.10 | GUI representing a television.

than these two new concepts, the TV app is created using only the WPF elements and concepts that you've already learned. Figure 31.11 presents the XAML markup and a screen capture of the app when it first loads. The video used in this case study is a public-domain video from `www.nasa.gov/multimedia/videogallery/index.html`.

```
 1   <!-- Fig. 31.11: MainWindow.xaml -->
 2   <!-- TV GUI showing the versatility of WPF customization. -->
 3   <Window x:Class="TV.MainWindow"
 4      xmlns="http://schemas.microsoft.com/winfx/2006/xaml/presentation"
 5      xmlns:x="http://schemas.microsoft.com/winfx/2006/xaml"
 6      Title="TV" Height="720" Width="720">
 7      <Window.Resources>
 8         <!-- define template for play, pause and stop buttons -->
 9         <ControlTemplate x:Key="RadioButtonTemplate"
10            TargetType="RadioButton">
11            <Grid>
12               <!-- create a circular border -->
13               <Ellipse Width="25" Height="25" Fill="Silver" />
14
15               <!-- create an "illuminated" background -->
16               <Ellipse Name="backgroundEllipse" Width="22" Height="22">
17                  <Ellipse.Fill> <!-- enabled and unchecked state -->
```

Fig. 31.11 | TV GUI showing the versatility of WPF customization. (Part 1 of 5.)

```
18              <RadialGradientBrush> <!-- red "light" -->
19                  <GradientStop Offset="0" Color="Red" />
20                  <GradientStop Offset="1.25" Color="Black" />
21              </RadialGradientBrush>
22          </Ellipse.Fill>
23        </Ellipse>
24
25        <!-- display button image -->
26        <ContentPresenter Content="{TemplateBinding Content}" />
27      </Grid>
28
29      <!-- change appearance when state changes -->
30      <ControlTemplate.Triggers>
31        <!-- disabled state -->
32        <Trigger Property="RadioButton.IsEnabled" Value="False">
33          <Setter TargetName="backgroundEllipse" Property="Fill">
34            <Setter.Value>
35              <RadialGradientBrush> <!-- dim "light" -->
36                  <GradientStop Offset="0" Color="LightGray" />
37                  <GradientStop Offset="1.25" Color="Black" />
38              </RadialGradientBrush>
39            </Setter.Value>
40          </Setter>
41        </Trigger>
42
43        <!-- checked state -->
44        <Trigger Property="RadioButton.IsChecked" Value="True">
45          <Setter TargetName="backgroundEllipse" Property="Fill">
46            <Setter.Value>
47              <RadialGradientBrush> <!-- green "light" -->
48                  <GradientStop Offset="0" Color="LimeGreen" />
49                  <GradientStop Offset="1.25" Color="Black" />
50              </RadialGradientBrush>
51            </Setter.Value>
52          </Setter>
53        </Trigger>
54      </ControlTemplate.Triggers>
55    </ControlTemplate>
56  </Window.Resources>
57
58  <!-- define the GUI -->
59  <Canvas>
60    <!-- define the "TV" -->
61    <Border Canvas.Left="150" Height="370" Width="490"
62      Canvas.Top="20" Background="DimGray">
63      <Grid>
64        <Grid.RowDefinitions>
65          <RowDefinition />
66          <RowDefinition Height="Auto" />
67        </Grid.RowDefinitions>
68
```

Fig. 31.11 | TV GUI showing the versatility of WPF customization. (Part 2 of 5.)

```
69                  <!-- define the screen -->
70                  <Border Margin="0,20,0,10" Background="Black"
71                     HorizontalAlignment="Center" VerticalAlignment="Center"
72                     BorderThickness="2" BorderBrush="Silver" CornerRadius="2">
73                     <MediaElement Height="300" Width="400"
74                        Name="videoMediaElement" Source="Video/future_nasa.wmv"
75                        LoadedBehavior="Manual" Stretch="Fill" />
76                  </Border>
77
78                  <!-- define the play, pause, and stop buttons -->
79                  <StackPanel Grid.Row="1" HorizontalAlignment="Right"
80                     Orientation="Horizontal">
81                     <RadioButton Name="playRadioButton" IsEnabled="False"
82                        Margin="0,0,5,15"
83                        Template="{StaticResource RadioButtonTemplate}"
84                        Checked="playRadioButton_Checked">
85                        <Image Height="20" Width="20"
86                           Source="Images/play.png" Stretch="Uniform" />
87                     </RadioButton>
88                     <RadioButton Name="pauseRadioButton" IsEnabled="False"
89                        Margin="0,0,5,15"
90                        Template="{StaticResource RadioButtonTemplate}"
91                        Checked="pauseRadioButton_Checked">
92                        <Image Height="20" Width="20"
93                           Source="Images/pause.png" Stretch="Uniform" />
94                     </RadioButton>
95                     <RadioButton Name="stopRadioButton" IsEnabled="False"
96                        Margin="0,0,15,15"
97                        Template="{StaticResource RadioButtonTemplate}"
98                        Checked="stopRadioButton_Checked">
99                        <Image Height="20" Width="20"
100                          Source="Images/stop.png" Stretch="Uniform" />
101                    </RadioButton>
102                 </StackPanel>
103
104                 <!-- define the power button -->
105                 <CheckBox Name="powerCheckBox" Grid.Row="1" Width="25"
106                    Height="25" HorizontalAlignment="Left"
107                    Margin="15,0,0,15" Checked="powerCheckBox_Checked"
108                    Unchecked="powerCheckBox_Unchecked">
109                    <CheckBox.Template> <!-- set the template -->
110                       <ControlTemplate TargetType="CheckBox">
111                          <Grid>
112                             <!-- create a circular border -->
113                             <Ellipse Width="25" Height="25"
114                                Fill="Silver" />
115
116                             <!-- create an "illuminated" background -->
117                             <Ellipse Name="backgroundEllipse" Width="22"
118                                Height="22">
119                                <Ellipse.Fill> <!-- unchecked state -->
```

Fig. 31.11 | TV GUI showing the versatility of WPF customization. (Part 3 of 5.)

```
120                          <RadialGradientBrush> <!-- dim "light" -->
121                             <GradientStop Offset="0"
122                                Color="LightGray" />
123                             <GradientStop Offset="1.25"
124                                Color="Black" />
125                          </RadialGradientBrush>
126                       </Ellipse.Fill>
127                    </Ellipse>
128
129                    <!-- display power-button image-->
130                    <Image Source="Images/power.png" Width="20"
131                       Height="20" />
132                 </Grid>
133
134                 <!-- change appearance when state changes -->
135                 <ControlTemplate.Triggers>
136                    <!-- checked state -->
137                    <Trigger Property="CheckBox.IsChecked"
138                       Value="True">
139                       <Setter TargetName="backgroundEllipse"
140                          Property="Fill">
141                          <Setter.Value> <!-- green "light" -->
142                             <RadialGradientBrush>
143                                <GradientStop Offset="0"
144                                   Color="LimeGreen" />
145                                <GradientStop Offset="1.25"
146                                   Color="Black" />
147                             </RadialGradientBrush>
148                          </Setter.Value>
149                       </Setter>
150                    </Trigger>
151                 </ControlTemplate.Triggers>
152              </ControlTemplate>
153           </CheckBox.Template>
154        </CheckBox>
155     </Grid>
156
157     <!-- skew "TV" to give a 3-D appearance -->
158     <Border.RenderTransform>
159        <SkewTransform AngleY="15" />
160     </Border.RenderTransform>
161
162     <!-- apply shadow effect to "TV" -->
163     <Border.Effect>
164        <DropShadowEffect Color="Gray" ShadowDepth="15" />
165     </Border.Effect>
166  </Border>
167
168  <!-- define reflection -->
169  <Border Canvas.Left="185" Canvas.Top="410" Height="300"
170     Width="400">
171     <Rectangle Name="reflectionRectangle">
172        <Rectangle.Fill>
```

Fig. 31.11 | TV GUI showing the versatility of WPF customization. (Part 4 of 5.)

```
173                     <!-- create a reflection of the video -->
174                     <VisualBrush
175                       Visual="{Binding ElementName=videoMediaElement}">
176                       <VisualBrush.RelativeTransform>
177                         <ScaleTransform ScaleY="-1" CenterY="0.5" />
178                       </VisualBrush.RelativeTransform>
179                     </VisualBrush>
180                   </Rectangle.Fill>
181
182                   <!-- make reflection more transparent the further it gets
183                     from the screen -->
184                   <Rectangle.OpacityMask>
185                     <LinearGradientBrush StartPoint="0,0" EndPoint="0,1">
186                       <GradientStop Color="Black" Offset="-0.25" />
187                       <GradientStop Color="Transparent" Offset="0.5" />
188                     </LinearGradientBrush>
189                   </Rectangle.OpacityMask>
190                 </Rectangle>
191
192                 <!-- skew reflection to look 3-D -->
193                 <Border.RenderTransform>
194                   <SkewTransform AngleY="15" AngleX="-45" />
195                 </Border.RenderTransform>
196               </Border>
197           </Canvas>
198     </Window>
```

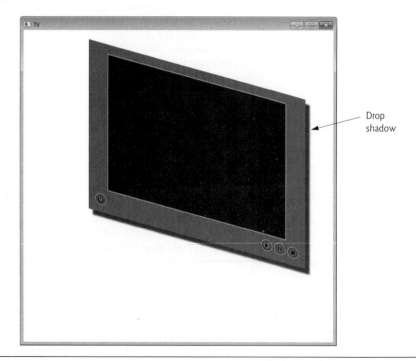

Drop shadow

Fig. 31.11 | TV GUI showing the versatility of WPF customization. (Part 5 of 5.)

WPF Effects

WPF allows you to apply graphical effects to *any* GUI element. There are two predefined effects—the **DropShadowEffect**, which gives an element a shadow as if a light were shining at it (Fig. 31.11, lines 163–165), and the **BlurEffect**, which makes an element's appearance *blurry*. The System.Windows.Media.Effects namespace also contains the more generalized ShaderEffect class, which allows you to build and use your own custom shader effects. For more information on the ShaderEffect class, visit Microsoft's developer center:

```
bit.ly/shadereffect
```

You can apply an effect to any element by setting its Effect property. Each Effect has its own unique properties. For example, DropShadowEffect's ShadowDepth property specifies the distance from the element to the shadow (line 164), while a BlurEffect's KernelType property specifies the type of blur filter it uses and its Radius property specifies the filter's size.

Creating Buttons on the TV

The representations of TV buttons in this example are not Button controls. The play, pause, and stop buttons are RadioButtons, and the power button is a CheckBox. Lines 9–55 and 110–152 define the ControlTemplates used to render the RadioButtons and CheckBox, respectively. The two templates are defined similarly, so we discuss only the RadioButton template in detail.

In the background of each button are two circles, defined by Ellipse objects. The larger Ellipse (line 13) acts as a border. The smaller Ellipse (lines 16–23) is colored by a RadialGradientBrush. The gradient is a light color in the center and becomes black as it extends farther out. This makes it appear to be a source of light. The content of the RadioButton is then applied on top of the two Ellipses (line 26).

The images used in this example are transparent outlines of the play, pause, and stop symbols on a black background. When the button is applied over the RadialGradientBrush, it appears to be *illuminated*. In its default state (*enabled* and *unchecked*), each playback button glows *red*. This represents the TV being on, with the playback option not active. When the app first loads, the TV is off, so the playback buttons are disabled. In this state, the background gradient is *gray*. When a playback option is *active* (i.e., RadioButton is *checked*), it glows *green*. The latter two deviations in appearance when the control changes states are defined by *triggers* (lines 30–54).

The power button, represented by a CheckBox, behaves similarly. When the TV is off (i.e., CheckBox is unchecked), the control is *gray*. When the user presses the power button and turns the TV on (i.e., CheckBox becomes checked), the control turns *green*. The power button is *never disabled*.

Creating the TV Interface

The TV panel is represented by a beveled Border with a gray background (lines 61–166). Recall that a Border is a ContentControl and can host only one direct child element. Thus, all of the Border's elements are contained in a Grid layout container. Nested within the TV panel is another Border with a black background containing a MediaElement control (lines 70–76). This portrays the TV's screen. The power button is placed in the bottom-left corner, and the playback buttons are bound in a StackPanel in the bottom-right corner (lines 79–154).

Creating the Reflection of the TV Screen

Lines 169–196 define the GUI's video *reflection* using a Rectangle element nested in a Border. The Rectangle's Fill is a VisualBrush that's bound to the MediaElement (lines 172–180). To *invert* the video, we define a ScaleTransform and specify it as the RelativeTransform property, which is common to all brushes (lines 176–178). You can *invert* an element by setting the **ScaleX** or **ScaleY**—the amounts by which to scale the respective coordinates—property of a ScaleTransform to a negative number. In this example, we set ScaleY to -1 and CenterY to 0.5, inverting the VisualBrush vertically centered around the midpoint. The **CenterX** and **CenterY** properties specify the point from which the image expands or contracts. When you *scale* an image, most of the points move as a result of the altered size. The center point is the *only* point that stays at its original location when ScaleX and ScaleY are set to values other than 1.

To achieve the *semitransparent* look, we applied an *opacity mask* to the Rectangle by setting the **OpacityMask** property (lines 184–189). The mask uses a LinearGradientBrush that changes from black near the top to transparent near the bottom. When the gradient is applied as an opacity mask, the gradient translates to a range from completely opaque, where it's black, to completely transparent. In this example, we set the Offset of the black GradientStop to -0.25, so that even the opaque edge of the mask is slightly transparent. We also set the Offset of the transparent GradientStop to 0.5, indicating that only the top half of the Rectangle (or bottom half of the movie) should display.

Skewing the GUI Components to Create a 3-D Look

When you draw a three-dimensional object on a two-dimensional plane, you are creating a 2-D *projection* of that 3-D environment. For example, to represent a simple box, you draw three adjoining parallelograms. Each face of the box is actually a flat, skewed rectangle rather than a 2-D view of a 3-D object. You can apply the same concept to create simple 3-D-looking GUIs without using a 3-D engine.

In this case study, we applied a SkewTransform to the TV representation, skewing it vertically by 15 degrees clockwise from the *x*-axis (lines 158–160). The reflection is then skewed (lines 193–195) vertically by 15 degrees clockwise from the *x*-axis (using AngleY) and horizontally by 45 degrees clockwise from the *y*-axis (using AngleX). Thus the GUI becomes a 2-D **orthographic projection** of a 3-D space with the axes 105, 120, and 135 degrees from each other, as shown in Fig. 31.12. Unlike a **perspective projection**, an *orthographic projection* does not show depth. Thus, the TV GUI does not present a realistic 3-D view, but rather a graphical representation.

Examining the Code-Behind Class

Figure 31.13 presents the code-behind class that provides the functionality for the TV app. When the user turns on the TV (i.e., checks the powerCheckBox), the reflection is made visible and the playback options are *enabled* (lines 16–26). When the user turns off the TV, the MediaElement's Close method is called to close the media. In addition, the reflection is made invisible and the playback options are *disabled* (lines 29–45).

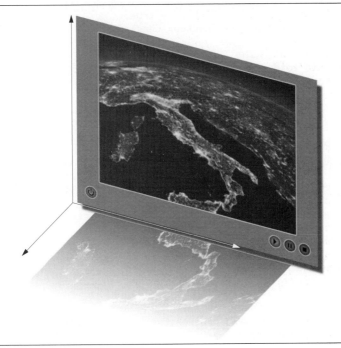

Fig. 31.12 | The effect of skewing the TV app's GUI components.

```
1   // Fig. 31.13: MainWindow.xaml.cs
2   // TV GUI showing the versatility of WPF customization (code-behind).
3   using System.Windows;
4
5   namespace TV
6   {
7      public partial class MainWindow : Window
8      {
9         // constructor
10        public MainWindow()
11        {
12           InitializeComponent();
13        } // end constructor
14
15        // turns "on" the TV
16        private void powerCheckBox_Checked( object sender,
17           RoutedEventArgs e )
18        {
19           // render the reflection visible
20           reflectionRectangle.Visibility = Visibility.Visible;
21
22           // enable play, pause, and stop buttons
23           playRadioButton.IsEnabled = true;
24           pauseRadioButton.IsEnabled = true;
```

Fig. 31.13 | TV GUI showing the versatility of WPF customization (code-behind). (Part 1 of 2.)

```
25          stopRadioButton.IsEnabled = true;
26       } // end method powerCheckBox_Checked
27
28       // turns "off" the TV
29       private void powerCheckBox_Unchecked( object sender,
30          RoutedEventArgs e )
31       {
32          // shut down the screen
33          videoMediaElement.Close();
34
35          // hide the reflection
36          reflectionRectangle.Visibility = Visibility.Hidden;
37
38          // disable the play, pause, and stop buttons
39          playRadioButton.IsChecked = false;
40          pauseRadioButton.IsChecked = false;
41          stopRadioButton.IsChecked = false;
42          playRadioButton.IsEnabled = false;
43          pauseRadioButton.IsEnabled = false;
44          stopRadioButton.IsEnabled = false;
45       } // end method powerCheckBox_Unchecked
46
47       // plays the video
48       private void playRadioButton_Checked( object sender,
49          RoutedEventArgs e )
50       {
51          videoMediaElement.Play();
52       } // end method playRadioButton_Checked
53
54       // pauses the video
55       private void pauseRadioButton_Checked( object sender,
56          RoutedEventArgs e )
57       {
58          videoMediaElement.Pause();
59       } // end method pauseRadioButton_Checked
60
61       // stops the video
62       private void stopRadioButton_Checked( object sender,
63          RoutedEventArgs e )
64       {
65          videoMediaElement.Stop();
66       } // end method stopRadioButton_Checked
67    } // end class MainWindow
68 } // end namespace TV
```

Fig. 31.13 | TV GUI showing the versatility of WPF customization (code-behind). (Part 2 of 2.)

Whenever one of the RadioButtons that represent each playback option is *checked*, the MediaElement executes the corresponding task (lines 48–66). The methods that execute these tasks are built into the MediaElement control. Playback can be modified *programmatically* only if the LoadedBehavior is Manual (line 75 in Fig. 31.11).

31.8 Animations

An animation in WPF apps simply means a *transition of a property from one value to another in a specified amount of time.* Most graphic properties of a control can be animated. The UsingAnimations example (Fig. 31.14) shows a video's size being animated. A MediaElement along with two input TextBoxes—one for Width and one for Height—and an animate Button are created in the GUI. When you click the animate Button, the video's Width and Height properties animate to the values typed in the corresponding TextBoxes by the user.

```
1   <!-- Fig. 31.14: MainWindow.xaml -->
2   <!-- Animating graphic elements with Storyboards. -->
3   <Window x:Class="UsingAnimations.MainWindow"
4      xmlns="http://schemas.microsoft.com/winfx/2006/xaml/presentation"
5      xmlns:x="http://schemas.microsoft.com/winfx/2006/xaml"
6      Title="UsingAnimations" Height="400" Width="500">
7      <Grid>
8         <Grid.ColumnDefinitions>
9            <ColumnDefinition />
10           <ColumnDefinition Width="Auto" />
11        </Grid.ColumnDefinitions>
12
13        <MediaElement Name="video" Height="100" Width="100"
14           Stretch="UniformToFill" Source="media.mp4" />
15
16        <StackPanel Grid.Column="1">
17           <!-- TextBox will contain the new Width for the video -->
18           <TextBlock TextWrapping="Wrap" Text="Width:" Margin="5,0,0,0"/>
19           <TextBox Name="widthValue" Width="75" Margin="5">100</TextBox>
20
21           <!-- TextBox will contain the new Height for the video -->
22           <TextBlock TextWrapping="Wrap" Text="Heigh:" Margin="5,0,0,0"/>
23           <TextBox Name="heightValue" Width="75" Margin="5">100</TextBox>
24
25           <!-- When clicked, rectangle animates to the input values -->
26           <Button Content="Animate" Width="75" Margin="5">
27              <Button.Triggers> <!-- Use trigger to call animation -->
28                 <!-- When button is clicked -->
29                 <EventTrigger RoutedEvent="Button.Click">
30                    <BeginStoryboard> <!-- Begin animation -->
31                       <Storyboard Storyboard.TargetName="video">
32                          <!-- Animates the Width -->
33                          <DoubleAnimation Duration="0:0:2"
34                             Storyboard.TargetProperty="Width"
35                             To="{Binding ElementName=widthValue,
36                             Path=Text}" />
37
38                          <!-- Animates the Height -->
39                          <DoubleAnimation Duration="0:0:2"
40                             Storyboard.TargetProperty="Height"
41                             To="{Binding ElementName=heightValue,
42                             Path=Text}" />
43                       </Storyboard>
```

Fig. 31.14 | Animating graphic elements with Storyboards. (Part 1 of 2.)

```
44                      </BeginStoryboard>
45                    </EventTrigger>
46                  </Button.Triggers>
47              </Button>
48          </StackPanel>
49      </Grid>
50  </Window>
```

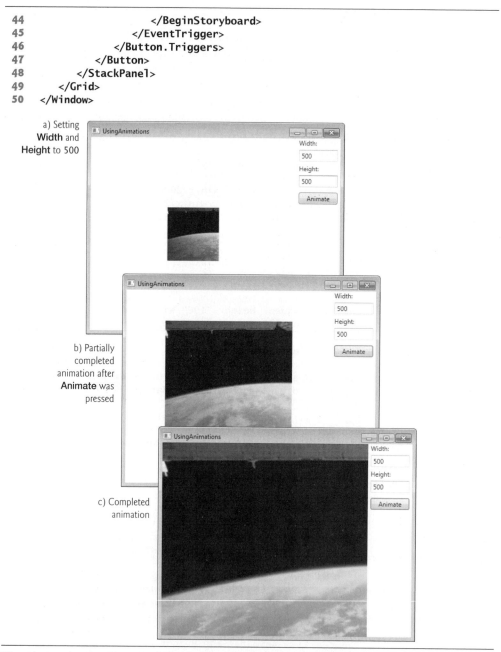

a) Setting **Width** and **Height** to 500

b) Partially completed animation after **Animate** was pressed

c) Completed animation

Fig. 31.14 | Animating graphic elements with Storyboards. (Part 2 of 2.)

As you can see, the animations create a smooth transition from the original Height and Width to the new values. Lines 31–43 define a **Storyboard** element embedded in the Button's click event Trigger. A Storyboard contains embedded animation elements. When the Storyboard begins executing (line 30), all embedded animations execute. A

Storyboard has two important properties—**TargetName** and **TargetProperty**. The TargetName (line 31) specifies which control to animate. The TargetProperty specifies which property of the animated control to change. In this case, the Width (line 34) and Height (line 40) are the TargetProperties, because we're changing the size of the video. Both the TargetName and TargetProperty can be defined in the Storyboard or in the animation element itself.

To animate a property, you can use one of several *animation classes* available in WPF. We use the DoubleAnimation for the size properties—PointAnimations and Color-Animations are two other commonly used animation classes. A **DoubleAnimation** animates properties of type Double. The Width and Height animations are defined in lines 33–36 and 39–42, respectively. Lines 35–36 define the **To** property of the Width animation, which specifies the value of the Width at the end of the animation. We use data binding to set this to the value in the widthValue TextBox. The animation also has a **Duration** property that specifies how long the animation takes. Notice in line 33 that we set the Duration of the Width animation to 0:0:2, meaning the animation takes 0 hours, 0 minutes and 2 seconds. You can specify fractions of a second by using a decimal point. Hour and minute values must be integers. Animations also have a **From** property which defines a constant starting value of the animated property.

Since we're animating the video's Width and Height properties separately, it's not always displayed at its original width and height. In line 14, we define the MediaElement's Stretch property. This is a property for graphic elements and determines how the media *stretches* to fit the size of its enclosure. This property can be set to **None, Uniform, UniformToFill** or **Fill**. None allows the media to stay at its native size regardless of the container's size. Uniform resizes the media to its largest possible size while maintaining its native aspect ratio. UniformToFill resizes the media to completely fill the container while still keeping its *aspect ratio*—as a result, it could be **cropped**. When an image or video is *cropped*, the pieces of the edges are cut off from the media in order to fit the shape of the container. Fill forces the media to be resized to the size of the container (aspect ratio is *not* preserved). In the example, we use Fill to show the changing size of the container.

31.9 Speech Synthesis and Speech Recognition

Speech-based interfaces make computers easier to use for people with disabilities (and others). **Speech synthesizers,** or **text-to-speech (TTS) systems,** read text out loud and are an ideal method for communicating information to sight-impaired individuals. **Speech recognizers,** or **speech-to-text (STT) systems,** transform human speech (input through a microphone) into text and are a good way to gather input or commands from users who have difficulty with keyboards and mice. .NET provides powerful tools for working with speech synthesis and recognition. The program shown in Figs. 31.15–31.16 provides explanations of the various kinds of programming tips found in this book using an STT system (and the mouse) as input and a TTS system (and text) as output.

Our speech app's GUI (Fig. 31.15) consists of a vertical StackPanel containing a TextBox, a Button and a series of horizontal StackPanels containing Images and Text-Blocks that label those Images.

```
1   <!-- Fig. 31.15: MainWindow.xaml -->
2   <!-- Text-To-Speech and Speech-To-Text -->
3   <Window x:Class="SpeechApp.MainWindow"
4      xmlns="http://schemas.microsoft.com/winfx/2006/xaml/presentation"
5      xmlns:x="http://schemas.microsoft.com/winfx/2006/xaml"
6      Title="Speech App" Height="580" Width="350">
7      <Grid>
8         <StackPanel Orientation="Vertical">
9            <TextBox x:Name="SpeechBox" Text="Enter text to speak here"/>
10           <Button x:Name="SpeechButton"
11              Content="Click to hear the text above."
12              Click="SpeechButton_Click" />
13           <StackPanel Orientation="Horizontal"
14              HorizontalAlignment="center">
15              <Image Source="images/CPE_100h.gif" Name="ErrorImage"
16                 MouseDown="Image_MouseDown" />
17              <Image Source="images/EPT_100h.gif" Name="PreventionImage"
18                 MouseDown="Image_MouseDown" />
19              <Image Source="images/GPP_100h.gif"
20                 Name="GoodPracticesImage" MouseDown="Image_MouseDown" />
21           </StackPanel>
22           <StackPanel Orientation="Horizontal"
23              HorizontalAlignment="Center">
24              <TextBlock Width="110" Text="Common Programming Errors"
25                 TextWrapping="wrap" TextAlignment="Center"/>
26              <TextBlock Width="110" Text="Error-Prevention Tips"
27                 TextWrapping="wrap" TextAlignment="Center" />
28              <TextBlock Width="110" Text="Good Programming Practices"
29                 TextWrapping="wrap" TextAlignment="Center"/>
30           </StackPanel>
31           <StackPanel Orientation="Horizontal"
32              HorizontalAlignment="center">
33              <Image Source="images/GUI_100h.gif"
34                 Name="LookAndFeelImage" MouseDown="Image_MouseDown" />
35              <Image Source="images/PERF_100h.gif"
36                 Name="PerformanceImage" MouseDown="Image_MouseDown" />
37              <Image Source="images/PORT_100h.gif"
38                 Name="PortabilityImage" MouseDown="Image_MouseDown" />
39           </StackPanel>
40           <StackPanel Orientation="Horizontal"
41              HorizontalAlignment="Center">
42              <TextBlock Width="110" Text="Look-and-Feel Observations"
43                 TextWrapping="wrap" TextAlignment="Center"/>
44              <TextBlock Width="110" Text="Performance Tips"
45                 TextWrapping="wrap" TextAlignment="Center" />
46              <TextBlock Width="110" Text="Portability Tips"
47                 TextWrapping="wrap" TextAlignment="Center"/>
48           </StackPanel>
49           <Image Source="images/SEO_100h.gif" Height="100" Width="110"
50              Name="ObservationsImage" MouseDown="Image_MouseDown" />
51           <TextBlock Width="110" Text="Software Engineering
52              Observations" TextWrapping="wrap" TextAlignment="Center" />
```

Fig. 31.15 | Text-To-Speech and Speech-To-Text. (Part 1 of 2.)

```
53          <TextBlock x:Name="InfoBlock" Margin="5"
54              Text="Click an icon or say its name to view details."
55              TextWrapping="Wrap"/>
56      </StackPanel>
57  </Grid>
58 </Window>
```

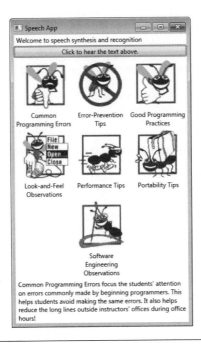

Fig. 31.15 | Text-To-Speech and Speech-To-Text. (Part 2 of 2.)

Figure 31.16 provides the speech app's functionality. The user either clicks an Image or speaks its name into a microphone, then the GUI displays a text description of the concept which that image or phrase represents, and a speech synthesizer speaks this description. To use .NET's speech synthesis and recognition classes, you must add a reference to System.Speech to the project as follows:

1. Right click the project name in the **Solution Explorer** then select **Add Reference....**

2. In the **Reference Manager** dialog under **Assemblies > Framework**, locate and select System.Speech and click **OK**.

You must also import the **System.Speech.Synthesis** and **System.Speech.Recognition** namespaces (lines 5–6).

```
1  // Fig. 31.16: MainWindow.xaml.cs
2  // Text-To-Speech and Speech-To-Text
3  using System;
```

Fig. 31.16 | Text-To-Speech and Speech-To-Text code-behind file. (Part 1 of 4.)

```
4   using System.Collections.Generic;
5   using System.Speech.Synthesis;
6   using System.Speech.Recognition;
7   using System.Windows;
8   using System.Windows.Controls;
9
10  namespace SpeechApp
11  {
12     public partial class MainWindow : Window
13     {
14        // listens for speech input
15        private SpeechRecognizer listener = new SpeechRecognizer();
16
17        // gives the listener choices of possible input
18        private Grammar myGrammar;
19
20        // sends speech output to the speakers
21        private SpeechSynthesizer talker = new SpeechSynthesizer();
22
23        // keeps track of which description is to be printed and spoken
24        private string displayString;
25
26        // maps images to their descriptions
27        private Dictionary< Image, string > imageDescriptions =
28           new Dictionary< Image, string >();
29
30        // maps input phrases to their descriptions
31        private Dictionary< string, string > phraseDescriptions =
32           new Dictionary< string, string >();
33
34        public MainWindow()
35        {
36           InitializeComponent();
37
38           // define the input phrases
39           string[] phrases = { "Good Programming Practices",
40              "Software Engineering Observations", "Performance Tips",
41              "Portability Tips", "Look-And-Feel Observations",
42              "Error-Prevention Tips", "Common Programming Errors" };
43
44           // add the phrases to a Choices collection
45           Choices theChoices = new Choices( phrases );
46
47           // build a Grammar around the Choices and set up the
48           // listener to use this grammar
49           myGrammar = new Grammar( new GrammarBuilder( theChoices ) );
50           listener.Enabled = true;
51           listener.LoadGrammar( myGrammar );
52           myGrammar.SpeechRecognized += myGrammar_SpeechRecognized;
53
```

Fig. 31.16 | Text-To-Speech and Speech-To-Text code-behind file. (Part 2 of 4.)

```
54      // define the descriptions for each icon/phrase
55      string[] descriptions = {
56         "Good Programming Practices highlight " +
57            "techniques for writing programs that are clearer, more " +
58            "understandable, more debuggable, and more maintainable.",
59         "Software Engineering Observations highlight " +
60            "architectural and design issues that affect the " +
61            "construction of complex software systems.",
62         "Performance Tips highlight opportunities " +
63            "for improving program performance.",
64         "Portability Tips help students write " +
65            "portable code that can execute on different platforms.",
66         "Look-and-Feel Observations highlight " +
67            "graphical user interface conventions. These " +
68            "observations help students design their own graphical " +
69            "user interfaces in conformance with industry standards.",
70         "Error-Prevention Tips tell people how to " +
71            "test and debug their programs. Many of the tips also " +
72            "describe aspects of creating programs that " +
73            "reduce the likelihood of 'bugs' and thus simplify the " +
74            "testing and debugging process.",
75         "Common Programming Errors focus the " +
76            "students' attention on errors commonly made by " +
77            "beginning programmers. This helps students avoid " +
78            "making the same errors. It also helps reduce the long " +
79            "lines outside instructors' offices during " +
80            "office hours!" };
81
82      // map each image to its corresponding description
83      imageDescriptions.Add( GoodPracticesImage, descriptions[ 0 ] );
84      imageDescriptions.Add( ObservationsImage, descriptions[ 1 ] );
85      imageDescriptions.Add( PerformanceImage, descriptions[ 2 ] );
86      imageDescriptions.Add( PortabilityImage, descriptions[ 3 ] );
87      imageDescriptions.Add( LookAndFeelImage, descriptions[ 4 ] );
88      imageDescriptions.Add( PreventionImage, descriptions[ 5 ] );
89      imageDescriptions.Add( ErrorImage, descriptions[ 6 ] );
90
91      // loop through the phrases and descriptions and map accordingly
92      for ( int index = 0; index <= 6; ++index )
93         phraseDescriptions.Add( phrases[ index ],
94            descriptions[ index ] );
95
96      talker.Rate = -4; // slows down the speaking rate
97   } // end constructor
98
99   // when the user clicks on the speech-synthesis button, speak the
100  // contents of the related text box
101  private void SpeechButton_Click( object sender, RoutedEventArgs e )
102  {
103     talker.SpeakAsync( SpeechBox.Text );
104  } // end method SpeechButton_Click
105
```

Fig. 31.16 | Text-To-Speech and Speech-To-Text code-behind file. (Part 3 of 4.)

```
106     private void Image_MouseDown( object sender,
107         System.Windows.Input.MouseButtonEventArgs e )
108     {
109         // use the image-to-description dictionary to get the
110         // appropriate description for the clicked image
111         displayString = imageDescriptions[ (Image) sender ];
112         DisplaySpeak();
113     } // end method Image_MouseDown
114
115     // when the listener recognizes a phrase from the grammar, set the
116     // display string and call DisplaySpeak
117     void myGrammar_SpeechRecognized(
118         object sender, RecognitionEventArgs e )
119     {
120         // Use the phrase-to-description dictionary to get the
121         // appropriate description for the spoken phrase
122         displayString = phraseDescriptions[ e.Result.Text ];
123
124         // Use the dispatcher to call DisplaySpeak
125         this.Dispatcher.BeginInvoke(
126             new Action( DisplaySpeak ) );
127     } // end method myGrammar_SpeechRecognized
128
129     // Set the appropriate text block to the display string
130     // and order the synthesizer to speak it
131     void DisplaySpeak()
132     {
133         InfoBlock.Text = displayString;
134         talker.SpeakAsync( displayString );
135     } // end method DisplaySpeak
136 } // end class MainWindow
137 } // end namespace SpeechApp
```

Fig. 31.16 | Text-To-Speech and Speech-To-Text code-behind file. (Part 4 of 4.)

Instance Variables

You can now add instance variables of types **SpeechRecognizer**, **Grammar** and **Speech-Synthesizer** (lines 15, 18 and 21). The SpeechRecognizer class has several ways to recognize input phrases. The most reliable involves building a Grammar containing the exact phrases that the SpeechRecognizer can receive as spoken input. The SpeechSynthesizer object speaks text, using one of several *voices*. Variable displayString (line 24) keeps track of the description that will be displayed and spoken. Lines 27–28 and 31–32 declare two objects of type **Dictionary** (namespace System.Collections.Generic). A Dictionary is a collection of key–value pairs, in which each key has a corresponding value. The Dictionary imageDescriptions contains pairs of Images and strings, and the Dictionary phraseDescriptions contains pairs of strings and strings. These Dictionary objects associate each input phrase and each clickable Image with the corresponding description phrase to be displayed and spoken.

Constructor

In the constructor (lines 34–97), the app initializes the input phrases and places them in a **Choices** collection (lines 39–45). A Choices collection is used to build a Grammar (lines 49–51). Line 52 registers the listener for the Grammar's SpeechRecognized event. Lines 55–80 create an array of the programming-tip descriptions. Lines 83–89 add each image and its corresponding description to the imageDescriptions Dictionary. Lines 92–94 add each programming-tip name and corresponding description to the phraseDescriptions Dictionary. Finally, line 96 sets the SpeechSynthesizer object's Rate property to -4 to slow down the default rate of speech.

*Method **SpeechButton_Click***

Method SpeechButton_Click (lines 101–104) calls the SpeechSynthesizer's Speak-Async method to speak the contents of SpeechBox. SpeechSynthesizers also have a Speak method, which is not asynchronous, and SpeakSsml and SpeakSsmlAsynch, methods specifically for use with *Speech Synthesis Markup Language (SSML)*—an XML vocabulary created particularly for TTS systems. For more information on SSML, visit www.xml.com/pub/a/2004/10/20/ssml.html.

*Method **Image_MouseDown***

Method Image_MouseDown (lines 106–113) handles the MouseDown events for all the Image objects. When the user clicks an Image, the program casts sender to type Image, then passes the results as input into the imageDescriptions Dictionary to retrieve the corresponding description string. This string is assigned to displayString (line 111). We then call DisplaySpeak to display displayString at the bottom of the window and cause the SpeechSynthesizer to speak it.

*Method **myGrammar_SpeechRecognized***

Method myGrammar_SpeechRecognized (lines 117–127) is called whenever the Speech-Recognizer detects that one of the input phrases defined in myGrammar was spoken. The Result property of the RecognitionEventArgs parameter contains the recognized text. We use the phraseDescriptions Dictionary object to determine which description to display (line 122). We cannot call DisplaySpeak directly here, because GUI events and the SpeechRecognizer events operate on different **threads**—they are processes being executed in parallel, independently from one another and without access to each other's methods. Every method that modifies the GUI must be called via the GUI thread of execution. To do this, we use a **Dispatcher** object (lines 125–126) to invoke the method. The method to call must be wrapped in a so-called *delegate object*. An Action delegate object represents a method with no parameters.

*Method **DisplaySpeak***

Method DisplaySpeak (lines 131–135) outputs displayString to the screen by updating InfoBlock's Text property and to the speakers by calling the SpeechSynthesizer's SpeakAsync method.

31.10 Wrap-Up

In this chapter you learned how to manipulate graphic elements in your WPF app. We introduced how to control fonts using the properties of TextBlocks. You learned to change the TextBlock's FontFamily, FontSize, FontWeight and FontStyle in XAML. We also demonstrated the TextDecorations Underline, Overline, Baseline and Strikethrough. Next, you learned how to create basic shapes such as Lines, Rectangles and Ellipses. You set the Fill and Stroke of these shapes. We then discussed an app that created a Polyline and two Polygons. These controls allow you to create multisided objects using a set of Points in a PointCollection.

You learned that there are several types of brushes for customizing an object's Fill. We demonstrated the SolidColorBrush, the ImageBrush, the VisualBrush and the LinearGradientBrush. Though the VisualBrush was used only with a MediaElement, this brush has a wide range of capabilities (msdn.microsoft.com/library/ms749021.aspx).

We explained how to apply transforms to an object to reposition or reorient any graphic element. You used transforms such as the TranslateTransform, the RotateTransform, the SkewTransform and the ScaleTransform to manipulate various controls.

The television GUI app used ControlTemplates and BitmapEffects to create a completely customized 3-D-looking television set. You saw how to use ControlTemplates to customize the look of RadioButtons and CheckBoxes. The app also included an opacity mask, which can be used on any shape to define the opaque or transparent regions of the control. Opacity masks are particularly useful with images and video where you cannot change the Fill to directly control transparency.

We showed how animations can be applied to transition properties from one value to another. Common 2-D animation types include DoubleAnimations, PointAnimations and ColorAnimations.

Finally, we introduced the speech synthesis and speech recognition APIs. You learned how to make computers speak text and receive voice input. You also learned how to create a Grammar of phrases that the user can speak to control the program.

32

ATM Case Study, Part 1: Object-Oriented Design with the UML

Objectives

In this chapter you'll:

- Learn a simple object-oriented design methodology.

- Learn what a requirements document is.

- Identify classes and class attributes from a requirements document.

- Identify objects' states, activities and operations from a requirements document.

- Determine the collaborations among objects in a system.

- Work with various UML diagrams to graphically model an object-oriented system.

32.1 Introduction

Now we begin the optional portion of our object-oriented design and implementation case study. In this chapter and Chapter 33, you'll design and implement an object-oriented automated teller machine (ATM) software system. The case study provides you with a concise, carefully paced, complete design and implementation experience. In Sections 32.2–32.7 and 33.2–33.3, you'll perform the steps of an object-oriented design (OOD) process using the UML while relating these steps to the concepts discussed in Chapters 3–12. In this chapter, you'll work with six popular types of UML diagrams to graphically represent the design. In Chapter 33, you'll tune the design with inheritance, then fully implement the ATM in a C# console app (Section 33.4).

This is not an exercise; rather, it's an end-to-end learning experience that concludes with a detailed walkthrough of the complete C# code that implements our design.

32.2 Examining the ATM Requirements Document

We begin our design process by presenting a **requirements document** that specifies the overall purpose of the ATM system and *what* it must do. Throughout the case study, we refer to the requirements document to determine precisely what functionality the system must include.

Requirements Document
A small local bank intends to install a new automated teller machine (ATM) to allow users (i.e., bank customers) to perform basic financial transactions (Fig. 32.1). For simplicity, each user can have only one account at the bank. ATM users should be able to view their account balance, withdraw cash (i.e., take money out of an account) and deposit funds (i.e., place money into an account).

The user interface of the automated teller machine contains the following hardware components:

- a screen that displays messages to the user
- a keypad that receives numeric input from the user
- a cash dispenser that dispenses cash to the user
- a deposit slot that receives deposit envelopes from the user

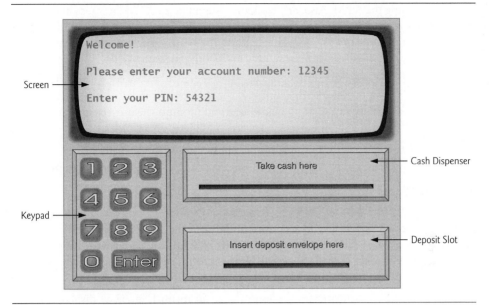

Fig. 32.1 | Automated teller machine user interface.

The cash dispenser begins each day loaded with 500 $20 bills. [*Note:* Owing to the limited scope of this case study, certain elements of the ATM described here simplify various aspects of a real ATM. For example, a real ATM typically contains a device that reads a user's account number from an ATM card, whereas this ATM asks the user to type an account number on the keypad (which you'll simulate with your personal computer's keypad). Also, a real ATM usually prints a paper receipt at the end of a session, but all output from this ATM appears on the screen.]

The bank wants you to develop software to perform the financial transactions initiated by bank customers through the ATM. The bank will integrate the software with the ATM's hardware at a later time. The software should simulate the functionality of the hardware devices (e.g., cash dispenser, deposit slot) in software components, but it need not concern itself with how these devices perform their duties. The ATM hardware has not been developed yet, so instead of writing your software to run on the ATM, you should develop a first version of the software to run on a personal computer. This version should use the computer's monitor to simulate the ATM's screen and the computer's keyboard to simulate the ATM's keypad.

An ATM session consists of authenticating a user (i.e., proving the user's identity) based on an account number and personal identification number (PIN), followed by creating and executing financial transactions. To authenticate a user and perform transactions, the ATM must interact with the bank's account information database. [*Note:* A database is an organized collection of data stored on a computer.] For each bank account, the database stores an account number, a PIN and a balance indicating the amount of money in the account. [*Note:* The bank plans to build only one ATM, so we do not need to worry about multiple ATMs accessing the database at the same time. Furthermore, we assume that the bank does not make any changes to the information in the database while a user is accessing the ATM. Also, any business system like an ATM faces reasonably complicated security issues that go well beyond the scope of this book. We make the simplifying assumption, however, that the bank trusts the ATM to access and manipulate the information in the database without significant security measures.]

Upon approaching the ATM, the user should experience the following sequence of events (see Fig. 32.1):

1. The screen displays a welcome message and prompts the user to enter an account number.

2. The user enters a five-digit account number, using the keypad.

3. For authentication purposes, the screen prompts the user to enter the PIN (personal identification number) associated with the specified account number.

4. The user enters a five-digit PIN, using the keypad.

5. If the user enters a valid account number and the correct PIN for that account, the screen displays the main menu (Fig. 32.2). If the user enters an invalid account number or an incorrect PIN, the screen displays an appropriate message, then the ATM returns to *Step 1* to restart the authentication process.

After the ATM authenticates the user, the main menu (Fig. 32.2) displays a numbered option for each of the three types of transactions: balance inquiry (option 1), withdrawal (option 2) and deposit (option 3). The main menu also displays an option that allows the user to exit the system (option 4). The user then chooses either to perform a transaction (by entering 1, 2 or 3) or to exit the system (by entering 4). If the user enters an invalid option, the screen displays an error message, then redisplays the main menu.

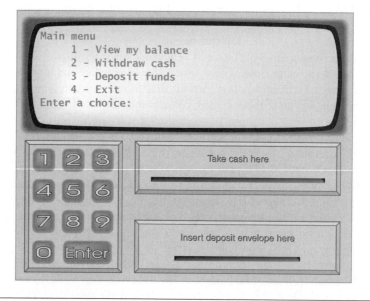

Fig. 32.2 | ATM main menu.

If the user enters 1 to make a balance inquiry, the screen displays the user's account balance. To do so, the ATM must retrieve the balance from the bank's database.

The following actions occur when the user enters 2 to make a withdrawal:

1. The screen displays a menu (shown in Fig. 32.3) containing standard withdrawal amounts: $20 (option 1), $40 (option 2), $60 (option 3), $100 (option 4) and $200 (option 5). The menu also contains option 6, which allows the user to cancel the transaction.

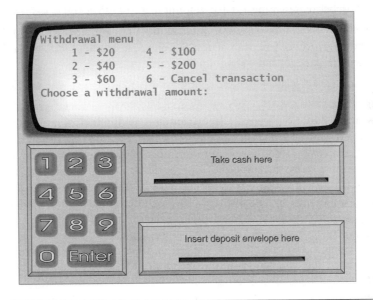

Fig. 32.3 | ATM withdrawal menu.

2. The user enters a menu selection (1–6) using the keypad.

3. If the withdrawal amount chosen is greater than the user's account balance, the screen displays a message stating this and telling the user to choose a smaller amount. The ATM then returns to *Step 1*. If the withdrawal amount chosen is less than or equal to the user's account balance (i.e., an acceptable withdrawal amount), the ATM proceeds to *Step 4*. If the user chooses to cancel the transaction (option 6), the ATM displays the main menu (Fig. 32.2) and waits for user input.

4. If the cash dispenser contains enough cash to satisfy the request, the ATM proceeds to *Step 5*. Otherwise, the screen displays a message indicating the problem and telling the user to choose a smaller withdrawal amount. The ATM then returns to *Step 1*.

5. The ATM debits (i.e., subtracts) the withdrawal amount from the user's account balance in the bank's database.

6. The cash dispenser dispenses the desired amount of money to the user.

7. The screen displays a message reminding the user to take the money.

The following actions occur when the user enters 3 (from the main menu) to make a deposit:

1. The screen prompts the user to enter a deposit amount or to type 0 (zero) to cancel the transaction.

2. The user enters a deposit amount or 0, using the keypad. [*Note:* The keypad does not contain a decimal point or a dollar sign, so the user cannot type a real dollar amount (e.g., $147.25). Instead, the user must enter a deposit amount as a number of cents (e.g., 14725). The ATM then divides this number by 100 to obtain a number representing a dollar amount (e.g., $14725 \div 100 = 147.25$).]

3. If the user specifies a deposit amount, the ATM proceeds to *Step 4*. If the user chooses to cancel the transaction (by entering 0), the ATM displays the main menu (Fig. 32.2) and waits for user input.

4. The screen displays a message telling the user to insert a deposit envelope into the deposit slot.

5. If the deposit slot receives a deposit envelope within two minutes, the ATM credits (i.e., adds) the deposit amount to the user's account balance in the bank's database. [*Note:* This money is not immediately available for withdrawal. The bank first must verify the amount of cash in the deposit envelope, and any checks in the envelope must clear (i.e., money must be transferred from the check writer's account to the check recipient's account). When either of these events occurs, the bank appropriately updates the user's balance stored in its database. This occurs independently of the ATM system.] If the deposit slot does not receive a deposit envelope within two minutes, the screen displays a message that the system has canceled the transaction due to inactivity. The ATM then displays the main menu and waits for user input.

After the system successfully executes a transaction, the system should redisplay the main menu (Fig. 32.2) so that the user can perform additional transactions. If the user chooses to exit the system (by entering option 4), the screen should display a thank-you message, then display the welcome message for the next user.

Analyzing the ATM System

The preceding statement presented a simplified requirements document. Typically, such a document is the result of a detailed process of **requirements gathering** that might include interviews with potential users of the system and specialists in fields related to the system. For example, a systems analyst who is hired to prepare a requirements document for banking software (e.g., the ATM system described here) might interview financial experts and people who have used ATMs to gain a better understanding of *what* the software must do. The analyst would use the information gained to compile a list of **system requirements** to guide systems designers.

The process of requirements gathering is a key task of the first stage of the software life cycle. The **software life cycle** specifies the stages through which software evolves from the time it's conceived to the time it's retired from use. These stages typically include analysis, design, implementation, testing and debugging, deployment, maintenance and retirement. Several software life-cycle models exist, each with its own preferences and specifications for when and how often software engineers should perform the various stages. **Waterfall models** perform each stage once in succession, whereas **iterative models** may repeat one or more stages several times throughout a product's life cycle.

The analysis stage of the software life cycle focuses on precisely defining the problem to be solved. When designing any system, one must certainly *solve the problem right*, but of equal importance, one must *solve the right problem*. Systems analysts collect the requirements that indicate the specific problem to solve. Our requirements document describes our simple ATM system in sufficient detail that you do not need to go through an extensive analysis stage—it has been done for you.

To capture what a proposed system should do, developers often employ a technique known as **use case modeling**. This process identifies the **use cases** of the system, each of which represents a different capability that the system provides to its clients. For example, ATMs typically have several use cases, such as "View Account Balance," "Withdraw Cash," "Deposit Funds," "Transfer Funds Between Accounts" and "Buy Postage Stamps." The simplified ATM system we build in this case study requires only the first three use cases (Fig. 32.4).

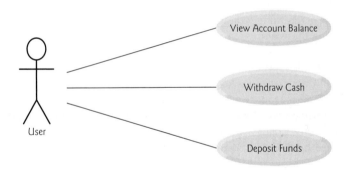

Fig. 32.4 | Use case diagram for the ATM system from the user's perspective.

Each use case describes a typical scenario in which the user uses the system. You have already read descriptions of the ATM system's use cases in the requirements document; the lists of steps required to perform each type of transaction (i.e., balance inquiry, withdrawal and deposit) actually described the three use cases of our ATM—"View Account Balance," "Withdraw Cash" and "Deposit Funds."

Use Case Diagrams

We now introduce the first of several UML diagrams in our ATM case study. We create a **use case diagram** to model the interactions between a system's clients (in this case study, bank customers) and the system. The goal is to show the kinds of interactions users have with a system without providing the details—these are shown in other UML diagrams (which we present throughout the case study). Use case diagrams are often accompanied by informal text that describes the use cases in more detail—like the text that appears in the requirements document. Use case diagrams are produced during the analysis stage of the software life cycle. In larger systems, use case diagrams are simple but indispensable tools that help system designers focus on satisfying the users' needs.

Figure 32.4 shows the use case diagram for our ATM system. The stick figure represents an **actor**, which defines the roles that an external entity—such as a person or another system—plays when interacting with the system. For our automated teller machine, the actor is a User who can view an account balance, withdraw cash and deposit funds using the ATM. The User is not an actual person, but instead comprises the roles that a real person—when playing the part of a User—can play while interacting with the ATM. A use case diagram can include multiple actors. For example, the use case diagram for a real bank's ATM system might also include an actor named Administrator who refills the cash dispenser each day.

We identify the actor in our system by examining the requirements document, which states, "ATM users should be able to view their account balance, withdraw cash and deposit funds." The actor in each of the three use cases is simply the User who interacts with the ATM. An external entity—a real person—plays the part of the User to perform financial transactions. Figure 32.4 shows one actor, whose name, User, appears below the actor in the diagram. The UML models each use case as an oval connected to an actor with a solid line.

Software engineers (more precisely, systems designers) must analyze the requirements document, or a set of use cases, and design the system before programmers implement it in a particular programming language. During the analysis stage, systems designers focus on understanding the requirements document to produce a high-level specification that describes *what* the system is supposed to do. The output of the design stage—a **design specification**—should specify *how* the system should be constructed to satisfy these requirements. In the next several sections, we perform the steps of a simple OOD process on the ATM system to produce a design specification containing a collection of UML diagrams and supporting text. Recall that the UML is designed for use with any OOD process. Many such processes exist, the best known being the Rational Unified Process™ (RUP) developed by Rational Software Corporation (now a division of IBM). RUP is a rich process for designing "industrial-strength" apps. For this case study, we present a simplified design process.

Designing the ATM System

We now begin the design stage of our ATM system. A **system** is a set of components that interact to solve a problem. For example, to perform the ATM system's designated tasks, our ATM system has a user interface (Fig. 32.1), contains software that executes financial transactions and interacts with a database of bank-account information. **System structure** describes the system's objects and their interrelationships. **System behavior** describes how the system changes as its objects interact with one another. Every system has both structure and behavior—designers must specify both. There are several distinct types of system structures and behaviors. For example, the interactions among objects in the system differ from those between the user and the system, yet both constitute a portion of the system behavior.

The UML 2 specifies 13 diagram types for documenting system models. Each diagram type models a distinct characteristic of a system's structure or behavior—six relate to system structure and seven to system behavior. We list here only the six types of diagrams used in our case study—of which one (the class diagram) models system structure and five model system behavior. We overview the remaining seven UML diagram types in Appendix E, UML 2: Additional Diagram Types.

1. **Use case diagrams**, such as the one in Fig. 32.4, model the interactions between a system and its external entities (actors) in terms of use cases (system capabilities, such as "View Account Balance," "Withdraw Cash" and "Deposit Funds").

2. **Class diagrams**, which you'll study in Section 32.3, model the classes, or "building blocks," used in a system. Each noun, or "thing," described in the requirements document is a candidate to be a class in the system (e.g., "account," "keypad"). Class diagrams help us specify the structural relationships between parts of the system. For example, the ATM system class diagram will, among other things, specify that the ATM is physically composed of a screen, a keypad, a cash dispenser and a deposit slot.

3. **State machine diagrams**, which you'll study in Section 32.5, model the ways in which an object changes state. An object's **state** is indicated by the values of all its attributes at a given time. When an object changes state, it may subsequently behave differently in the system. For example, after validating a user's PIN, the ATM transitions from the "user not authenticated" state to the "user authenticated" state, at which point the ATM allows the user to perform financial transactions (e.g., view account balance, withdraw cash, deposit funds).

4. **Activity diagrams**, which you'll also study in Section 32.5, model an object's **activity**—the object's workflow (sequence of events) during program execution. An activity diagram models the actions the object performs and specifies the order in which it performs them. For example, an activity diagram shows that the ATM must obtain the balance of the user's account (from the bank's account-information database) before the screen can display the balance to the user.

5. **Communication diagrams** (called collaboration diagrams in earlier versions of the UML) model the interactions among objects in a system, with an emphasis on *what* interactions occur. You'll learn in Section 32.7 that these diagrams show which objects must interact to perform an ATM transaction. For example, the ATM must communicate with the bank's account-information database to retrieve an account balance.

6. **Sequence diagrams** also model the interactions among the objects in a system, but unlike communication diagrams, they emphasize *when* interactions occur. You'll learn in Section 32.7 that these diagrams help show the order in which interactions occur in executing a financial transaction. For example, the screen prompts the user to enter a withdrawal amount before cash is dispensed.

In Section 32.3, we continue designing our ATM system by identifying the classes from the requirements document. We accomplish this by extracting key nouns and noun phrases from the requirements document. Using these classes, we develop our first draft of the class diagram that models the structure of our ATM system.

Web Resources

We've created an extensive UML Resource Center that contains many links to additional information, including introductions, tutorials, blogs, books, certification, conferences, developer tools, documentation, e-books, FAQs, forums, groups, UML in Java, podcasts, security, tools, downloads, training courses, videos and more. We encourage you to browse our UML Resource Center at www.deitel.com/UML/ to learn more.

Self-Review Exercises

32.1 Suppose we enabled a user of our ATM system to transfer money between two bank accounts. Modify the use case diagram of Fig. 32.4 to reflect this change.

32.2 _____ model the interactions among objects in a system with an emphasis on *when* these interactions occur.
  a) Class diagrams
  b) Sequence diagrams
  c) Communication diagrams
  d) Activity diagrams

32.3 Which of the following choices lists stages of a typical software life cycle in sequential order?
  a) design, analysis, implementation, testing
  b) design, analysis, testing, implementation
  c) analysis, design, testing, implementation
  d) analysis, design, implementation, testing

32.3 Identifying the Classes in the ATM Requirements Document

Now we begin designing the ATM system. In this section, we identify the classes that are needed to build the ATM system by analyzing the nouns and noun phrases that appear in the requirements document. We introduce UML class diagrams to model the relationships between these classes. This is an important first step in defining the structure of our system.

Identifying the Classes in a System

We begin our object-oriented design (OOD) process by identifying the classes required to build the ATM system. We'll eventually describe these classes using UML class diagrams and implement these classes in C#. First, we review the requirements document of Section 32.2 and find key nouns and noun phrases to help us identify classes that comprise the ATM system. We may decide that some of these nouns and noun phrases are attributes of other classes in the system. We may also conclude that some of the nouns and noun phrases do not correspond to parts of the system and thus should not be modeled at all. Additional classes may become apparent to us as we proceed through the design process. Figure 32.5 lists the nouns and noun phrases in the requirements document.

Nouns and noun phrases in the requirements document		
bank	money / funds	account number
ATM	screen	PIN
user	keypad	bank database
customer	cash dispenser	balance inquiry

Fig. 32.5 | Nouns and noun phrases in the requirements document. (Part 1 of 2.)

Nouns and noun phrases in the requirements document		
transaction	$20 bill / cash	withdrawal
account	deposit slot	deposit
balance	deposit envelope	

Fig. 32.5 | Nouns and noun phrases in the requirements document. (Part 2 of 2.)

We create classes only for the nouns and noun phrases that have significance in the ATM system. We do not need to model "bank" as a class, because the bank is not a part of the ATM system—the bank simply wants us to build the ATM. "User" and "customer" also represent entities outside of the system—they're important because they interact with our ATM system, but we do not need to model them as classes in the ATM system. Recall that we modeled an ATM user (i.e., a bank customer) as the actor in the use case diagram of Fig. 32.4.

We do not model "$20 bill" or "deposit envelope" as classes. These are physical objects in the real world, but they're not part of what is being automated. We can adequately represent the presence of bills in the system using an attribute of the class that models the cash dispenser. (We assign attributes to classes in Section 32.4.) For example, the cash dispenser maintains a count of the number of bills it contains. The requirements document does not say anything about what the system should do with deposit envelopes after it receives them. We can assume that simply acknowledging the receipt of an envelope—an **operation** performed by the class that models the deposit slot—is sufficient to represent the presence of an envelope in the system. (We assign operations to classes in Section 32.6.)

In our simplified ATM system, representing various amounts of "money," including the "balance" of an account, as attributes of other classes seems most appropriate. Likewise, the nouns "account number" and "PIN" represent significant pieces of information in the ATM system. They're important attributes of a bank account. They do not, however, exhibit behaviors. Thus, we can most appropriately model them as attributes of an account class.

Though the requirements document frequently describes a "transaction" in a general sense, we do not model the broad notion of a financial transaction at this time. Instead, we model the three types of transactions (i.e., "balance inquiry," "withdrawal" and "deposit") as individual classes. These classes possess specific attributes needed to execute the transactions they represent. For example, a withdrawal needs to know the amount of money the user wants to withdraw. A balance inquiry, however, does not require any additional data if the user is authenticated. Furthermore, the three transaction classes exhibit unique behaviors. A withdrawal involves dispensing cash to the user, whereas a deposit involves receiving a deposit envelope from the user. [*Note:* In Section 33.3, we "factor out" common features of all transactions into a general "transaction" class using the object-oriented concepts of abstract classes and inheritance.]

We determine the classes for our system based on the remaining nouns and noun phrases from Fig. 32.5. Each of these refers to one or more of the following:

• ATM

- screen

- keypad

- cash dispenser

- deposit slot

- account

- bank database

- balance inquiry

- withdrawal

- deposit

The elements of this list are likely to be classes we'll need to implement our system, although it's too early in our design process to claim that this list is complete.

We can now model our system's classes based on the list we've created. We capitalize class names in the design process—a UML convention—as we'll do when we write the C# code that implements our design. If the name of a class contains more than one word, we run the words together and capitalize each word (e.g., `MultipleWordName`). Using these conventions, we create classes `ATM`, `Screen`, `Keypad`, `CashDispenser`, `DepositSlot`, `Account`, `BankDatabase`, `BalanceInquiry`, `Withdrawal` and `Deposit`. We construct our system using all of these classes as building blocks. Before we begin building the system, however, we must gain a better understanding of how the classes relate to one another.

Modeling Classes

The UML enables us to model, via **class diagrams**, the classes in the ATM system and their interrelationships. Figure 32.6 represents class `ATM`. In the UML, each class is modeled as a rectangle with three compartments. The top compartment contains the name of the class, centered horizontally and appearing in boldface. The middle compartment contains the class's attributes. (We discuss attributes in Sections 32.4–32.5.) The bottom compartment contains the class's operations (discussed in Section 32.6). In Fig. 32.6, the middle and bottom compartments are empty, because we've not yet determined this class's attributes and operations.

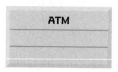

Fig. 32.6 | Representing a class in the UML using a class diagram.

Class diagrams also show the relationships between the classes of the system. Figure 32.7 shows how our classes `ATM` and `Withdrawal` relate to one another. For the moment, we choose to model only this subset of the ATM classes for simplicity. We present a more complete class diagram later in this section. Notice that the rectangles representing classes in this diagram are not subdivided into compartments. The UML allows the suppression of class attributes and operations in this manner, when appropriate, to create more readable diagrams. Such a diagram is said to be an **elided diagram**—one in which some information, such as the contents of the second and third compartments, is not modeled. We'll place information in these compartments in Sections 32.4–32.6.

Fig. 32.7 | Class diagram showing an association among classes.

In Fig. 32.7, the solid line that connects the two classes represents an **association**—a relationship between classes. The numbers near each end of the line are **multiplicity** values, which indicate how many objects of each class participate in the association. In this case, following the line from one end to the other reveals that, at any given moment, one ATM object participates in an association with either zero or one Withdrawal objects—zero if the current user is not performing a transaction or has requested a different type of transaction, and one if the user has requested a withdrawal. The UML can model many types of multiplicity. Figure 32.8 explains the multiplicity types.

Symbol	Meaning
0	None
1	One
m	An integer value
0..1	Zero or one
m, n	m or n
$m..n$	At least m, but not more than n
*	Any nonnegative integer (zero or more)
0..*	Zero or more (identical to *)
1..*	One or more

Fig. 32.8 | Multiplicity types.

An association can be named. For example, the word Executes above the line connecting classes ATM and Withdrawal in Fig. 32.7 indicates the name of that association. This part of the diagram reads "one object of class ATM executes zero or one objects of class Withdrawal." association names are directional, as indicated by the filled arrowhead—so it would be improper, for example, to read the preceding association from right to left as "zero or one objects of class Withdrawal execute one object of class ATM."

The word currentTransaction at the Withdrawal end of the association line in Fig. 32.7 is a **role name**, which identifies the role the Withdrawal object plays in its relationship with the ATM. A role name adds meaning to an association between classes by identifying the role a class plays in the context of an association. A class can play several roles in the same system. For example, in a college personnel system, a person may play the role of "professor" when relating to students. The same person may take on the role of "colleague" when participating in a relationship with another professor, and "coach" when coaching student athletes. In Fig. 32.7, the role name currentTransaction indicates that the Withdrawal object participating in the Executes association with an object of class ATM represents the transaction currently being processed by the ATM. In other contexts, a Withdrawal object may take on other roles (e.g., the previous transaction). Notice that we do not specify a role name for the ATM end of the Executes association. Role names are often omitted in class diagrams when the meaning of an association is clear without them.

In addition to indicating simple relationships, associations can specify more complex relationships, such as objects of one class being composed of objects of other classes. Consider a real-world automated teller machine. What "pieces" does a manufacturer put together to build a working ATM? Our requirements document tells us that the ATM is composed of a screen, a keypad, a cash dispenser and a deposit slot.

In Fig. 32.9, the **solid diamonds** attached to the association lines of class ATM indicate that class ATM has a **composition** relationship with classes Screen, Keypad, CashDispenser and DepositSlot. Composition implies a whole/part relationship. The class that has the composition symbol (the solid diamond) on its end of the association line is the whole (in this case, ATM), and the classes on the other end of the association lines are the parts—in this case, classes Screen, Keypad, CashDispenser and DepositSlot. The compositions in Fig. 32.9 indicate that an object of class ATM is formed from one object of class Screen, one object of class CashDispenser, one object of class Keypad and one object of class DepositSlot—the ATM "has a" screen, a keypad, a cash dispenser and a deposit slot. The **has-a relationship** defines composition. (We'll see in Section 33.3 that the *is-a* relationship defines inheritance.)

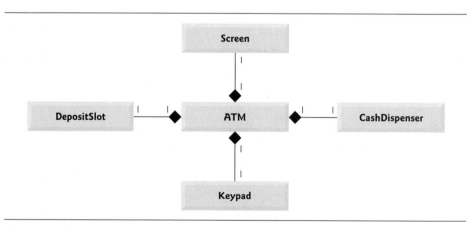

Fig. 32.9 | Class diagram showing composition relationships.

According to the UML specification, composition relationships have the following properties:

1. Only one class in the relationship can represent the whole (i.e., the diamond can be placed on only one end of the association line). For example, either the screen is part of the ATM or the ATM is part of the screen, but the screen and the ATM cannot both represent the whole in the relationship.

2. The parts in the composition relationship exist only as long as the whole, and the whole is responsible for creating and destroying its parts. For example, the act of constructing an ATM includes manufacturing its parts. Furthermore, if the ATM is destroyed, its screen, keypad, cash dispenser and deposit slot are also destroyed.

3. A part may belong to only one whole at a time, although the part may be removed and attached to another whole, which then assumes responsibility for the part.

The solid diamonds in our class diagrams indicate composition relationships that fulfill these three properties. If a *has-a* relationship does not satisfy one or more of these criteria, the UML specifies that hollow diamonds be attached to the ends of association lines to indicate **aggregation**—a weaker form of composition. For example, a personal computer and a computer monitor participate in an aggregation relationship—the computer "has a" monitor, but the two parts can exist independently, and the same monitor can be attached to multiple computers at once, thus violating the second and third properties of composition.

Figure 32.10 shows a class diagram for the ATM system. This diagram models most of the classes that we identified earlier in this section, as well as the associations between them that we can infer from the requirements document. [*Note:* Classes BalanceInquiry and Deposit participate in associations similar to those of class Withdrawal, so we've chosen to omit them from this diagram for simplicity. In Section 33.3, we expand our class diagram to include all the classes in the ATM system.]

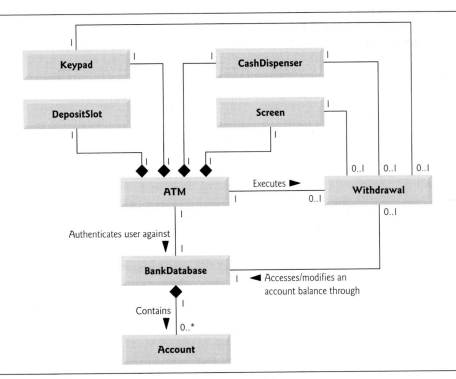

Fig. 32.10 | Class diagram for the ATM system model.

Figure 32.10 presents a graphical model of the structure of the ATM system. This class diagram includes classes BankDatabase and Account and several associations that were not present in either Fig. 32.7 or Fig. 32.9. The class diagram shows that class ATM has a **one-to-one relationship** with class BankDatabase—one ATM object authenticates users against one BankDatabase object. In Fig. 32.10, we also model the fact that the bank's database contains information about many accounts—one object of class BankDatabase participates in a composition relationship with zero or more objects of class Account. Recall from Fig. 32.8 that the multiplicity value 0..* at the Account end of the association between class BankDatabase and class Account indicates that zero or more objects of class Account take part in the association. Class BankDatabase has a **one-to-many relationship** with class Account—the BankDatabase can contain many Accounts. Similarly, class Account has a **many-to-one relationship** with class BankDatabase—there can be many Accounts in the BankDatabase. Recall from Fig. 32.8 that the multiplicity value * is identical to 0..]

Figure 32.10 also indicates that if the user is performing a withdrawal, "one object of class Withdrawal accesses/modifies an account balance through one object of class Bank-Database." We could have created an association directly between class Withdrawal and class Account. The requirements document, however, states that the "ATM must interact with the bank's account-information database" to perform transactions. A bank account contains sensitive information, and systems engineers must always consider the security of personal data when designing a system. Thus, only the BankDatabase can access and manipulate an account directly. All other parts of the system must interact with the database to retrieve or update account information (e.g., an account balance).

The class diagram in Fig. 32.10 also models associations between class Withdrawal and classes Screen, CashDispenser and Keypad. A withdrawal transaction includes prompting the user to choose a withdrawal amount and receiving numeric input. These actions require the use of the screen and the keypad, respectively. Dispensing cash to the user requires access to the cash dispenser.

Classes BalanceInquiry and Deposit, though not shown in Fig. 32.10, take part in several associations with the other classes of the ATM system. Like class Withdrawal, each of these classes associates with classes ATM and BankDatabase. An object of class Balance-Inquiry also associates with an object of class Screen to display the balance of an account to the user. Class Deposit associates with classes Screen, Keypad and DepositSlot. Like withdrawals, deposit transactions require use of the screen and the keypad to display prompts and receive inputs, respectively. To receive a deposit envelope, an object of class Deposit associates with an object of class DepositSlot.

We've identified our ATM system's classes, although we may discover others as we proceed with the design and implementation. In Section 32.4, we determine each class's attributes, and in Section 32.5, we use these attributes to examine how the system changes over time.

Self-Review Exercises

32.4   Suppose we have a class Car that represents a car. Think of some of the different pieces that a manufacturer would put together to produce a whole car. Create a class diagram (similar to Fig. 32.9) that models some of the composition relationships of class Car.

32.5 Suppose we have a class `File` that represents an electronic document in a stand-alone, non-networked computer represented by class `Computer`. What sort of association exists between class `Computer` and class `File`?

 a) Class `Computer` has a one-to-one relationship with class `File`.
 b) Class `Computer` has a many-to-one relationship with class `File`.
 c) Class `Computer` has a one-to-many relationship with class `File`.
 d) Class `Computer` has a many-to-many relationship with class `File`.

32.6 State whether the following statement is *true* or *false*. If *false*, explain why: A UML class diagram in which a class's second and third compartments are not modeled is said to be an elided diagram.

32.7 Modify the class diagram of Fig. 32.10 to include class `Deposit` instead of class `Withdrawal`.

32.4 Identifying Class Attributes

In the previous section, we began the first stage of an object-oriented design (OOD) for our ATM system—analyzing the requirements document and identifying the classes needed to implement the system. We listed the nouns and noun phrases in the requirements document and identified a separate class for each one that plays a significant role in the ATM system. We then modeled the classes and their relationships in a UML class diagram (Fig. 32.10). Classes have attributes (data) and operations (behaviors). Class attributes are implemented in C# programs as instance variables and properties, and class operations are implemented as methods and properties. In this section, we determine many of the attributes needed in the ATM system. In Section 32.5, we examine how these attributes represent an object's state. In Section 32.6, we determine the operations for our classes.

Identifying Attributes

Consider the attributes of some real-world objects: A person's attributes include height, weight and whether the person is left-handed, right-handed or ambidextrous. A radio's attributes include its station setting, its volume setting and its AM or FM setting. A car's attributes include its speedometer and odometer readings, the amount of gas in its tank and what gear it is in. A personal computer's attributes include its manufacturer (e.g., Dell, HP, Apple or IBM), type of screen (e.g., LCD or CRT), main memory size and hard-disk size.

We can identify many attributes of the classes in our system by looking for descriptive words and phrases in the requirements document. For each one we find that plays a significant role in the ATM system, we create an attribute and assign it to one or more of the classes identified in Section 32.3. We also create attributes to represent any additional data that a class may need, as such needs become clear throughout the design process.

Figure 32.11 lists the words or phrases from the requirements document that describe each class. For example, the requirements document describes the steps taken to obtain a "withdrawal amount," so we list "amount" next to class `Withdrawal`.

Figure 32.11 leads us to create one attribute of class `ATM`. Class `ATM` maintains information about the state of the ATM. The phrase "user is authenticated" describes a state of the ATM (we discuss states in detail in Section 32.5), so we include `userAuthenticated` as a `bool` **attribute** (i.e., an attribute that has a value of either `true` or `false`). This attribute indicates whether the ATM has successfully authenticated the current user—user-Authenticated must be `true` for the system to allow the user to perform transactions and

Class	Descriptive words and phrases
ATM	user is authenticated
BalanceInquiry	account number
Withdrawal	account number
	amount
Deposit	account number
	amount
BankDatabase	[no descriptive words or phrases]
Account	account number
	PIN
	balance
Screen	[no descriptive words or phrases]
Keypad	[no descriptive words or phrases]
CashDispenser	begins each day loaded with 500 $20 bills
DepositSlot	[no descriptive words or phrases]

Fig. 32.11 | Descriptive words and phrases from the ATM requirements document.

access account information. This attribute helps ensure the security of the data in the system.

Classes BalanceInquiry, Withdrawal and Deposit share one attribute. Each transaction involves an "account number" that corresponds to the account of the user making the transaction. We assign integer attribute accountNumber to each transaction class to identify the account to which an object of the class applies.

Descriptive words and phrases in the requirements document also suggest some differences in the attributes required by each transaction class. The requirements document indicates that to withdraw cash or deposit funds, users must enter a specific "amount" of money to be withdrawn or deposited, respectively. Thus, we assign to classes Withdrawal and Deposit an attribute amount to store the value supplied by the user. The amounts of money related to a withdrawal and a deposit are defining characteristics of these transactions that the system requires for them to take place. Recall that C# represents monetary amounts with type decimal. Class BalanceInquiry does not need additional data to perform its task—it requires only an account number to indicate the account whose balance should be retrieved.

Class Account has several attributes. The requirements document states that each bank account has an "account number" and a "PIN," which the system uses for identifying accounts and authenticating users. We assign to class Account two integer attributes: accountNumber and pin. The requirements document also specifies that an account maintains a "balance" of the amount of money in the account, and that the money the user deposits does not become available for a withdrawal until the bank verifies the amount of cash in the deposit envelope and any checks in the envelope clear. An account must still record the amount of money that a user deposits, however. Therefore, we decide that an account should represent a balance using two decimal attributes—availableBalance and `totalBalance`. Attribute `availableBalance` tracks the amount of money that a user can withdraw from the account. Attribute `totalBalance` refers to the total amount of money that the user has "on deposit" (i.e., the amount of money available, plus the amount of cash deposits waiting to be verified or the amount of checks waiting to be cleared). For example, suppose an ATM user deposits $50.00 in cash into an empty account. The `totalBalance` attribute would increase to $50.00 to record the deposit, but the `availableBalance` would remain at $0 until a bank employee counts the amount of cash in the envelope and confirms the total. [*Note:* We assume that the bank updates the `availableBalance` attribute of an `Account` soon after the ATM transaction occurs, in response to confirming that $50 worth of cash was found in the deposit envelope. We assume that this update occurs through a transaction that a bank employee performs using a bank system other than the ATM. Thus, we do not discuss this transaction in our case study.]

Class `CashDispenser` has one attribute. The requirements document states that the cash dispenser "begins each day loaded with 500 $20 bills." The cash dispenser must keep track of the number of bills it contains to determine whether enough cash is on hand to satisfy withdrawal requests. We assign to class `CashDispenser` integer attribute `count`, which is initially set to 500.

For real problems in industry, there is no guarantee that requirements documents will be rich enough and precise enough for the object-oriented systems designer to determine all the attributes, or even all the classes. The need for additional classes, attributes and behaviors may become clear as the design process proceeds. As we progress through this case study, we too will continue to add, modify and delete information about the classes in our system.

Modeling Attributes

The class diagram in Fig. 32.12 lists some of the attributes for the classes in our system—the descriptive words and phrases in Fig. 32.11 helped us identify these attributes. For simplicity, Fig. 32.12 does not show the associations among classes—we showed these in Fig. 32.10. Systems designers commonly do this. Recall that in the UML, a class's attributes are placed in the middle compartment of the class's rectangle. We list each attribute's name and type separated by a colon (:), followed in some cases by an equal sign (=) and an initial value.

Consider the `userAuthenticated` attribute of class `ATM`:

```
userAuthenticated : bool = false
```

This attribute declaration contains three pieces of information about the attribute. The **attribute name** is `userAuthenticated`. The **attribute type** is `bool`. In C#, an attribute can be represented by a simple type, such as `bool`, `int`, `double` or `decimal`, or a class type. We have chosen to model only simple-type attributes in Fig. 32.12—we discuss the reasoning behind this decision shortly.

We can also indicate an initial value for an attribute. Attribute `userAuthenticated` in class `ATM` has an initial value of `false`. This indicates that the system initially does not consider the user to be authenticated. If an attribute has no initial value specified, only its name and type (separated by a colon) are shown. For example, the `accountNumber` attribute of class `BalanceInquiry` is an `int`. Here we show no initial value, because the value of this attribute is a number that we do not yet know. This number will be determined at execution time based on the account number entered by the current ATM user.

Fig. 32.12 | Classes with attributes.

Figure 32.12 does not contain attributes for classes Screen, Keypad and DepositSlot. These are important components of our system for which our design process simply has not yet revealed any attributes. We may discover some, however, in the remaining phases of design or when we implement these classes in C#. This is perfectly normal.

Software Engineering Observation 32.1

Early in the design process, classes often lack attributes (and operations). Such classes should not be eliminated, however, because attributes (and operations) may become evident in the later phases of design and implementation.

Fig. 32.12 also does not include attributes for class BankDatabase. We have chosen to include only simple-type attributes in Fig. 32.12 (and in similar class diagrams throughout the case study). A class-type attribute is modeled more clearly as an association (in particular, a composition) between the class with the attribute and the attribute's own class. For example, the class diagram in Fig. 32.10 indicates that class BankDatabase participates in a composition relationship with zero or more Account objects. From this composition, we can determine that when we implement the ATM system in C#, we'll be required to create an attribute of class BankDatabase to hold zero or more Account objects. Similarly, we'll assign attributes to class ATM that correspond to its composition relationships with classes Screen, Keypad, CashDispenser and DepositSlot. These composition-based attributes would be redundant if modeled in Fig. 32.12, because the compositions modeled in Fig. 32.10 already convey the fact that the database contains information about zero or more accounts and that an ATM is composed of a screen, keypad, cash dispenser and deposit slot. Software developers typically model these whole/part relationships as composition associations rather than as attributes required to implement the relationships.

The class diagram in Fig. 32.12 provides a solid basis for the structure of our model, but the diagram is not complete. In Section 32.5 we identify the states and activities of the objects in the model, and in Section 32.6 we identify the operations that the objects perform. As we present more of the UML and object-oriented design, we'll continue to strengthen the structure of our model.

Self-Review Exercises

32.8 We typically identify the attributes of the classes in our system by analyzing the _____ in the requirements document.
    a) nouns and noun phrases
    b) descriptive words and phrases
    c) verbs and verb phrases
    d) All of the above

32.9 Which of the following is not an attribute of an airplane?
    a) length
    b) wingspan
    c) fly
    d) number of seats

32.10 Describe the meaning of the following attribute declaration of class `CashDispenser` in the class diagram in Fig. 32.12:

```
count : int = 500
```

32.5 Identifying Objects' States and Activities

In the previous section, we identified many of the class attributes needed to implement the ATM system and added them to the class diagram in Fig. 32.12. In this section, we show how these attributes represent an object's state. We identify some key states that our objects may occupy and discuss how objects change state in response to various events occurring in the system. We also discuss the workflow, or **activities**, that various objects perform in the ATM system. We present the activities of `BalanceInquiry` and `Withdrawal` transaction objects in this section.

State Machine Diagrams

Each object in a system goes through a series of discrete states. An object's state at a given point in time is indicated by the values of its attributes at that time. **State machine diagrams** model key states of an object and show under what circumstances the object changes state. Unlike the class diagrams presented in earlier case study sections, which focused primarily on the *structure* of the system, state machine diagrams model some of the *behavior* of the system.

Figure 32.13 is a simple state machine diagram that models two of the states of an object of class `ATM`. The UML represents each state in a state machine diagram as a **rounded rectangle** with the name of the state placed inside it. A **solid circle** with an attached stick arrowhead designates the **initial state**. Recall that we modeled this state information as the `bool` attribute `userAuthenticated` in the class diagram of Fig. 32.12. This attribute is initialized to `false`, or the "User not authenticated" state, according to the state machine diagram.

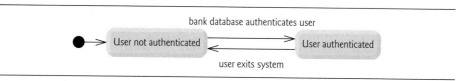

bank database authenticates user

User not authenticated   User authenticated

user exits system

Fig. 32.13 | State machine diagram for some of the states of the `ATM` object.

The arrows with stick arrowheads indicate **transitions** between states. An object can transition from one state to another in response to various events that occur in the system. The name or description of the event that causes a transition is written near the line that corresponds to the transition. For example, the `ATM` object changes from the "User not authenticated" state to the "User authenticated" state after the bank database authenticates the user. Recall from the requirements document that the database authenticates a user by comparing the account number and PIN entered by the user with those of the corresponding account in the database. If the database indicates that the user has entered a valid account number and the correct PIN, the `ATM` object transitions to the "User authenticated" state and changes its `userAuthenticated` attribute to the value `true`. When the user exits the system by choosing the "exit" option from the main menu, the `ATM` object returns to the "User not authenticated" state in preparation for the next ATM user.

Software Engineering Observation 32.2

Software designers do not generally create state machine diagrams showing every possible state and state transition for all attributes—there are simply too many of them. State machine diagrams typically show only the most important or complex states and state transitions.

Activity Diagrams

Like a state machine diagram, an activity diagram models aspects of system behavior. Unlike a state machine diagram, an activity diagram models an object's workflow (sequence of tasks) during app execution. An activity diagram models the actions to perform and in what order the object will perform them. The activity diagram in Fig. 32.14 models the actions involved in executing a `BalanceInquiry` transaction. We assume that a `BalanceInquiry` object has already been initialized and assigned a valid account number (that of the current user), so the object knows which balance to retrieve. The diagram includes the actions that occur after the user selects a balance inquiry from the main menu and before the ATM returns the user to the main menu—a `BalanceInquiry` object does not perform or initiate these actions, so we do not model them here. The diagram begins with the retrieval of the available balance of the user's account from the database. Next, the `BalanceInquiry` retrieves the total balance of the account. Finally, the transaction displays the balances on the screen.

The UML represents an action in an activity diagram as an action state, which is modeled by a rectangle with its left and right sides replaced by arcs curving outward. Each

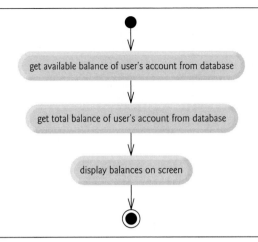

Fig. 32.14 | Activity diagram for a `BalanceInquiry` transaction.

action state contains an action expression—for example, "get available balance of user's account from database"—that specifies an action to perform. An arrow with a stick arrowhead connects two action states, indicating the order in which the actions represented by the action states occur. The solid circle (at the top of Fig. 32.14) represents the activity's initial state—the beginning of the workflow before the object performs the modeled actions. In this case, the transaction first executes the "get available balance of user's account from database" action expression. Second, the transaction retrieves the total balance. Finally, the transaction displays both balances on the screen. The solid circle enclosed in an open circle (at the bottom of Fig. 32.14) represents the final state—the end of the workflow after the object performs the modeled actions.

Figure 32.15 shows an activity diagram for a `Withdrawal` transaction. We assume that a `Withdrawal` object has been assigned a valid account number. We do not model the user selecting a withdrawal from the main menu or the ATM returning the user to the main menu, because these are not actions performed by a `Withdrawal` object. The transaction first displays a menu of standard withdrawal amounts (Fig. 32.3) and an option to cancel the transaction. The transaction then inputs a menu selection from the user. The activity flow now arrives at a decision symbol. This point determines the next action based on the associated guard conditions. If the user cancels the transaction, the system displays an appropriate message. Next, the cancellation flow reaches a merge symbol, where this activity flow joins the transaction's other possible activity flows (which we discuss shortly). A merge can have any number of incoming transition arrows, but only one outgoing transition arrow. The decision at the bottom of the diagram determines whether the transaction should repeat from the beginning. When the user has canceled the transaction, the guard condition "cash dispensed or user canceled transaction" is true, so control transitions to the activity's final state.

If the user selects a withdrawal amount from the menu, `amount` (an attribute of class `Withdrawal` originally modeled in Fig. 32.12) is set to the value chosen by the user. The transaction next gets the available balance of the user's account (i.e., the `availableBalance` attribute of the user's `Account` object) from the database. The activity flow then arrives at another decision. If the requested withdrawal amount exceeds the user's available balance, the system displays an appropriate error message informing the user of the

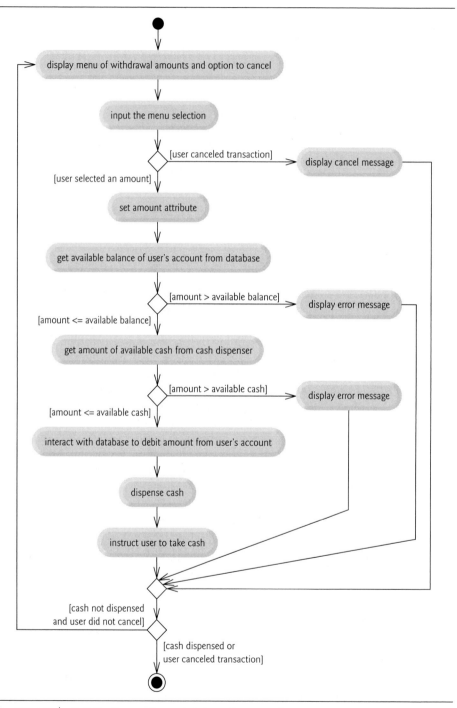

Fig. 32.15 | Activity diagram for a `Withdrawal` transaction.

problem. Control then merges with the other activity flows before reaching the decision at the bottom of the diagram. The guard condition "cash not dispensed and user did not cancel" is true, so the activity flow returns to the top of the diagram, and the transaction prompts the user to input a new amount.

If the requested withdrawal amount is less than or equal to the user's available balance, the transaction tests whether the cash dispenser has enough cash to satisfy the withdrawal request. If it does not, the transaction displays an appropriate error message and passes through the merge before reaching the final decision. Cash was not dispensed, so the activity flow returns to the beginning of the activity diagram, and the transaction prompts the user to choose a new amount. If sufficient cash is available, the transaction interacts with the database to debit the withdrawal amount from the user's account (i.e., subtract the amount from *both* the availableBalance and totalBalance attributes of the user's Account object). The transaction then dispenses the desired amount of cash and instructs the user to take the cash.

The main flow of activity next merges with the two error flows and the cancellation flow. In this case, cash was dispensed, so the activity flow reaches the final state.

We've taken the first steps in modeling the behavior of the ATM system and have shown how an object's attributes affect the object's activities. In Section 32.6, we investigate the operations of our classes to create a more complete model of the system's behavior.

Self-Review Exercises

32.11 State whether the following statement is *true* or *false*, and if *false*, explain why: State machine diagrams model structural aspects of a system.

32.12 An activity diagram models the _____ that an object performs and the order in which it performs them.
  a) actions
  b) attributes
  c) states
  d) state transitions

32.13 Based on the requirements document, create an activity diagram for a deposit transaction.

32.6 Identifying Class Operations

In the preceding sections, we performed the first few steps in the object-oriented design of our ATM system. In this section, we determine some of the class operations (or behaviors) needed to implement the ATM system.

Identifying Operations

An operation is a service that objects of a class provide to clients of the class. Consider the operations of some real-world objects. A radio's operations include setting its station and volume (typically invoked by a person adjusting the radio's controls). A car's operations include accelerating (invoked by the driver pressing the accelerator pedal), decelerating (invoked by the driver pressing the brake pedal or releasing the gas pedal), turning, and shifting gears. Software objects can offer operations as well—for example, a software graphics object might offer operations for drawing a circle, drawing a line and drawing a square. A spreadsheet software object might offer operations like printing the spreadsheet, totaling the elements in a row or column and graphing information in the spreadsheet as a bar chart or pie chart.

We can derive many of the operations of the classes in our ATM system by examining the verbs and verb phrases in the requirements document. We then relate each of these to particular classes in our system. The verbs and verb phrases in Fig. 32.16 help us determine the operations of our classes.

Class	Verbs and verb phrases
ATM	executes financial transactions
BalanceInquiry	[none in the requirements document]
Withdrawal	[none in the requirements document]
Deposit	[none in the requirements document]
BankDatabase	authenticates a user, retrieves an account balance, credits an account, debits an account
Account	retrieves an account balance, credits a deposit amount to an account, debits a withdrawal amount to an account
Screen	displays a message to the user
Keypad	receives numeric input from the user
CashDispenser	dispenses cash, indicates whether it contains enough cash to satisfy a withdrawal request
DepositSlot	receives a deposit envelope

Fig. 32.16 | Verbs and verb phrases for each class in the ATM system.

Modeling Operations

To identify operations, we examine the verb phrases listed for each class in Fig. 32.16. The "executes financial transactions" phrase associated with class ATM implies that class ATM instructs transactions to execute. Therefore, classes BalanceInquiry, Withdrawal and Deposit each need an operation to provide this service to the ATM. We place this operation (which we have named Execute) in the third compartment of the three transaction classes in the updated class diagram of Fig. 32.17. During an ATM session, the ATM object will invoke the Execute operation of each transaction object to tell it to execute.

The UML represents operations (which are implemented as methods in C#) by listing the operation name, followed by a comma-separated list of parameters in parentheses, a colon and the return type:

> *operationName(parameter1, parameter2, ..., parameterN) : returnType*

Each parameter in the comma-separated parameter list consists of a parameter name, followed by a colon and the parameter type:

> *parameterName : parameterType*

For the moment, we do not list the parameters of our operations—we'll identify and model the parameters of some of the operations shortly. For some of the operations, we do not yet know the return types, so we also omit them from the diagram. These omissions are perfectly normal at this point. As our design and implementation proceed, we'll add the remaining return types.

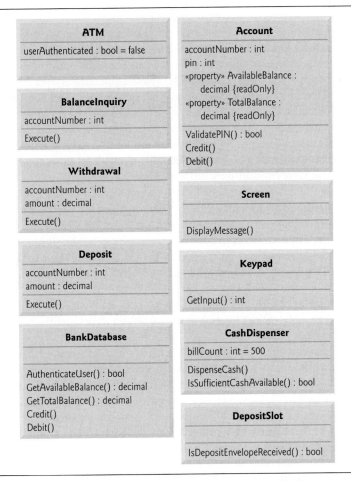

Fig. 32.17 | Classes in the ATM system with attributes and operations.

Operations of Class BankDatabase and Class Account

Figure 32.16 lists the phrase "authenticates a user" next to class BankDatabase—the database is the object that contains the account information necessary to determine whether the account number and PIN entered by a user match those of an account at the bank. Therefore, class BankDatabase needs an operation that provides an authentication service to the ATM. We place the operation AuthenticateUser in the third compartment of class BankDatabase (Fig. 32.17). However, an object of class Account, not class BankDatabase, stores the account number and PIN that must be accessed to authenticate a user, so class Account must provide a service to validate a PIN obtained through user input against a PIN stored in an Account object. Therefore, we add a ValidatePIN operation to class Account. We specify a return type of bool for the AuthenticateUser and ValidatePIN operations. Each operation returns a value indicating either that the operation was successful in performing its task (i.e., a return value of `true`) or that it was not successful (i.e., a return value of `false`).

Figure 32.16 lists several additional verb phrases for class `BankDatabase`: "retrieves an account balance," "credits an account" and "debits an account." Like "authenticates a user," these remaining phrases refer to services that the database must provide to the ATM, because the database holds all the account data used to authenticate a user and perform ATM transactions. However, objects of class `Account` actually perform the operations to which these phrases refer. Thus, class `BankDatabase` and class `Account` both need operations that correspond to each of these phrases. Recall from Section 32.3 that, because a bank account contains sensitive information, we do not allow the ATM to access accounts directly. The database acts as an intermediary between the ATM and the account data, preventing unauthorized access. As we'll see in Section 32.7, class `ATM` invokes the operations of class `BankDatabase`, each of which in turn invokes corresponding operations (which are `get` accessors of read-only properties) in class `Account`.

The phrase "retrieves an account balance" suggests that classes `BankDatabase` and `Account` each need an operation that gets the balance. However, recall that we created two attributes in class `Account` to represent a balance—`availableBalance` and `totalBalance`. A balance inquiry requires access to both balance attributes so that it can display them to the user, but a withdrawal needs to check only the value of `availableBalance`. To allow objects in the system to obtain these balance attributes individually from a specific `Account` object in the `BankDatabase`, we add operations `GetAvailableBalance` and `GetTotalBalance` to the third compartment of class `BankDatabase` (Fig. 32.17). We specify a return type of `decimal` for each of these operations, because the balances that they retrieve are of type `decimal`.

Once the `BankDatabase` knows which `Account` to access, it must be able to obtain each balance attribute individually from that `Account`. For this purpose, we could add operations `GetAvailableBalance` and `GetTotalBalance` to the third compartment of class `Account` (Fig. 32.17). However, in C#, simple operations such as getting the value of an attribute are typically performed by a property's `get` accessor (at least when that particular class "owns" the underlying attribute). This design is for a C# app, so, rather than modeling operations `GetAvailableBalance` and `GetTotalBalance`, we model `decimal` properties `AvailableBalance` and `TotalBalance` in class `Account`. Properties are placed in the second compartment of a class diagram. These properties replace the `available-Balance` and `totalBalance` attributes that we modeled for class `Account` previously. Recall that a property's accessors are implied—thus, they're not modeled in a class diagram. Figure 32.16 does not mention the need to set the balances, so Fig. 32.17 shows properties `AvailableBalance` and `TotalBalance` as read-only properties (i.e., they have only `get` accessors). To indicate a read-only property in the UML, we follow the property's type with "`{readOnly}`."

You may be wondering why we modeled `AvailableBalance` and `TotalBalance` *properties* in class `Account`, but modeled `GetAvailableBalance` and `GetTotalBalance` *operations* in class `BankDatabase`. Since there can be many `Account` objects in the `BankDatabase`, the ATM must specify which `Account` to access when invoking `BankDatabase` operations `GetAvailableBalance` and `GetTotalBalance`. The ATM does this by passing an account-number argument to each `BankDatabase` operation. The `get` accessors of the properties you've seen in C# code cannot receive arguments. Thus, we modeled

`GetAvailableBalance` and `GetTotalBalance` as operations in class `BankDatabase` so that we could specify parameters to which the ATM can pass arguments. Also, the underlying balance attributes are not owned by the `BankDatabase`, so get accessors are not appropriate here. We discuss the parameters for the `BankDatabase` operations shortly.

The phrases "credits an account" and "debits from an account" indicate that classes `BankDatabase` and `Account` must perform operations to update an account during deposits and withdrawals, respectively. We therefore assign `Credit` and `Debit` operations to classes `BankDatabase` and `Account`. You may recall that crediting an account (as in a deposit) adds an amount only to the `Account`'s total balance. Debiting an account (as in a withdrawal), on the other hand, subtracts the amount from both the total and available balances. We hide these implementation details inside class `Account`. This is a good example of encapsulation and information hiding.

If this were a real ATM system, classes `BankDatabase` and `Account` would also provide a set of operations to allow another banking system to update a user's account balance after either confirming or rejecting all or part of a deposit. Operation `ConfirmDepositAmount`, for example, would add an amount to the `Account`'s available balance, thus making deposited funds available for withdrawal. Operation `RejectDepositAmount` would subtract an amount from the `Account`'s total balance to indicate that a specified amount, which had recently been deposited through the ATM and added to the `Account`'s total balance, was invalidated (or checks may have "bounced"). The bank would invoke operation `RejectDepositAmount` after determining either that the user failed to include the correct amount of cash or that any checks did not clear (i.e., they "bounced"). While adding these operations would make our system more complete, we do not include them in our class diagrams or implementation because they're beyond the scope of the case study.

Operations of Class *Screen*

Class `Screen` "displays a message to the user" at various times in an ATM session. All visual output occurs through the screen of the ATM. The requirements document describes many types of messages (e.g., a welcome message, an error message, a thank-you message) that the screen displays to the user. The requirements document also indicates that the screen displays prompts and menus to the user. However, a prompt is really just a message describing what the user should input next, and a menu is essentially a type of prompt consisting of a series of messages (i.e., menu options) displayed consecutively. Therefore, rather than provide class `Screen` with an individual operation to display each type of message, prompt and menu, we simply create one operation that can display any message specified by a parameter. We place this operation (`DisplayMessage`) in the third compartment of class `Screen` in our class diagram (Fig. 32.17). We do not worry about the parameter of this operation at this time—we model the parameter momentarily.

Operations of Class *Keypad*

From the phrase "receives numeric input from the user" listed by class `Keypad` in Fig. 32.16, we conclude that class `Keypad` should perform a `GetInput` operation. Because the ATM's keypad, unlike a computer keyboard, contains only the numbers 0–9, we specify that this operation returns an integer value. Recall from the requirements document that in different situations, the user may be required to enter a different type of number (e.g., an account number, a PIN, the number of a menu option, a deposit amount as a number of cents). Class `Keypad` simply obtains a numeric value for a client of the class—

it does not determine whether the value meets any specific criteria. Any class that uses this operation must verify that the user entered appropriate numbers and, if not, display error messages via class Screen. [*Note:* When we implement the system, we simulate the ATM's keypad with a computer keyboard, and for simplicity, we assume that the user does not enter nonnumeric input using keys on the computer keyboard that do not appear on the ATM's keypad.]

Operations of Class *CashDispenser* and Class *DepositSlot*

Figure 32.16 lists "dispenses cash" for class CashDispenser. Therefore, we create operation DispenseCash and list it under class CashDispenser in Fig. 32.17. Class CashDispenser also "indicates whether it contains enough cash to satisfy a withdrawal request." Thus, we include IsSufficientCashAvailable, an operation that returns a value of type bool, in class CashDispenser. Figure 32.16 also lists "receives a deposit envelope" for class DepositSlot. The deposit slot must indicate whether it received an envelope, so we place the operation IsDepositEnvelopeReceived, which returns a bool value, in the third compartment of class DepositSlot. [*Note:* A real hardware deposit slot would most likely send the ATM a signal to indicate that an envelope was received. We simulate this behavior, however, with an operation in class DepositSlot that class ATM can invoke to find out whether the deposit slot received an envelope.]

Operations of Class *ATM*

We do not list any operations for class ATM at this time. We're not yet aware of any services that class ATM provides to other classes in the system. When we implement the system in C#, however, operations of this class, and additional operations of the other classes in the system, may become apparent.

Identifying and Modeling Operation Parameters

So far, we have not been concerned with the parameters of our operations—we have attempted to gain only a basic understanding of the operations of each class. Let's now take a closer look at some operation parameters. We identify an operation's parameters by examining what data the operation requires to perform its assigned task.

Consider the AuthenticateUser operation of class BankDatabase. To authenticate a user, this operation must know the account number and PIN supplied by the user. Thus we specify that operation AuthenticateUser takes int parameters userAccountNumber and userPIN, which the operation must compare to the account number and PIN of an Account object in the database. We prefix these parameter names with user to avoid confusion between the operation's parameter names and the attribute names that belong to class Account. We list these parameters in the class diagram in Fig. 32.18, which models only class BankDatabase. [*Note:* It is perfectly normal to model only one class in a class diagram. In this case, we're most concerned with examining the parameters of this particular class, so we omit the other classes. In class diagrams later in the case study, parameters are no longer the focus of our attention, so we omit the parameters to save space. Remember, however, that the operations listed in these diagrams still have parameters.]

Recall that the UML models each parameter in an operation's comma-separated parameter list by listing the parameter name, followed by a colon and the parameter type. Figure 32.18 thus specifies, for example, that operation AuthenticateUser takes two parameters—userAccountNumber and userPIN, both of type int.

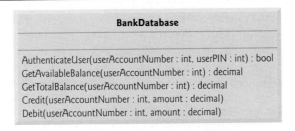

BankDatabase
AuthenticateUser(userAccountNumber : int, userPIN : int) : bool GetAvailableBalance(userAccountNumber : int) : decimal GetTotalBalance(userAccountNumber : int) : decimal Credit(userAccountNumber : int, amount : decimal) Debit(userAccountNumber : int, amount : decimal)

Fig. 32.18 | Class BankDatabase with operation parameters.

Class BankDatabase operations GetAvailableBalance, GetTotalBalance, Credit and Debit also each require a userAccountNumber parameter to identify the account to which the database must apply the operations, so we include these parameters in the class diagram. In addition, operations Credit and Debit each require a decimal parameter amount to specify the amount of money to be credited or debited, respectively.

The class diagram in Fig. 32.19 models the parameters of class Account's operations. Operation ValidatePIN requires only a userPIN parameter, which contains the user-specified PIN to be compared with the PIN associated with the account. Like their counterparts in class BankDatabase, operations Credit and Debit in class Account each require a decimal parameter amount that indicates the amount of money involved in the operation. Class Account's operations do not require an account-number parameter—each can be invoked only on the Account object in which they're executing, so including a parameter to specify an Account is unnecessary.

Account
accountNumber : int pin : int «property» AvailableBalance : decimal {readOnly} «property» TotalBalance : decimal {readOnly}
ValidatePIN(userPIN: int) : bool Credit(amount : decimal) Debit(amount : decimal)

Fig. 32.19 | Class Account with operation parameters.

Figure 32.20 models class Screen with a parameter for operation DisplayMessage. This operation requires only string parameter message, which is the text to be displayed.

Screen
DisplayMessage(message : string)

Fig. 32.20 | Class Screen with an operation parameter.

The class diagram in Fig. 32.21 specifies that operation DispenseCash of class Cash-Dispenser takes decimal parameter amount to indicate the amount of cash (in dollars) to be dispensed. Operation IsSufficientCashAvailable also takes decimal parameter amount to indicate the amount of cash in question.

CashDispenser
billCount : int = 500
DispenseCash(amount : decimal) IsSufficientCashAvailable(amount : decimal) : bool

Fig. 32.21 │ Class CashDispenser with operation parameters.

We don't discuss parameters for operation Execute of classes BalanceInquiry, With-drawal and Deposit, operation GetInput of class Keypad and operation IsDepositEn-velopeReceived of class DepositSlot. At this point in our design process, we cannot determine whether these operations require additional data to perform their tasks, so we leave their parameter lists empty. As we progress through the case study, we may decide to add parameters to these operations.

In this section, we have determined many of the operations performed by the classes in the ATM system. We have identified the parameters and return types of some of the operations. As we continue our design process, the number of operations belonging to each class may vary—we might find that new operations are needed or that some current operations are unnecessary—and we might determine that some of our class operations need additional parameters and different return types. Again, all of this is perfectly normal.

Self-Review Exercises

32.14 Which of the following is not a behavior?
    a) reading data from a file
    b) displaying output
    c) text output
    d) obtaining input from the user

32.15 If you were to add to the ATM system an operation that returns the amount attribute of class Withdrawal, how and where would you specify this operation in the class diagram of Fig. 32.17?

32.16 Describe the meaning of the following operation listing that might appear in a class diagram for an object-oriented design of a calculator:

```
Add( x : int, y : int ) : int
```

32.7 Identifying Collaboration Among Objects

When two objects communicate with each other to accomplish a task, they're said to **collaborate**. A **collaboration** consists of an object of one class sending a **message** to an object of another class. Messages are sent in C# via method calls. In this section, we concentrate on the collaborations (interactions) among the objects in our ATM system.

In the previous section, we determined many of the operations of the classes in our system. In this section, we concentrate on the messages that invoke these operations. To identify the collaborations in the system, we return to the requirements document of Section 32.2. Recall that this document specifies the activities that occur during an ATM session (e.g., authenticating a user, performing transactions). The steps used to describe how the system must perform each of these tasks are our first indication of the collaborations in our system. As we proceed through this and the remaining ATM Case Study sections, we may discover additional collaborations.

Identifying the Collaborations in a System

We begin to identify the collaborations in the system by carefully reading the sections of the requirements document that specify what the ATM should do to authenticate a user and to perform each transaction type. For each action or step described in the requirements document, we decide which objects in our system must interact to achieve the desired result. We identify one object as the sending object (i.e., the object that sends the message) and another as the receiving object (i.e., the object that offers that operation to clients of the class). We then select one of the receiving object's operations (identified in Section 32.6) that must be invoked by the sending object to produce the proper behavior. For example, the ATM displays a welcome message when idle. We know that an object of class Screen displays a message to the user via its DisplayMessage operation. Thus, we decide that the system can display a welcome message by employing a collaboration between the ATM and the Screen in which the ATM sends a DisplayMessage message to the Screen by invoking the DisplayMessage operation of class Screen. [*Note:* To avoid repeating the phrase "an object of class…," we refer to each object simply by using its class name preceded by an article (e.g., "a," "an" or "the")—for example, "the ATM" refers to an object of class ATM.]

Figure 32.22 lists the collaborations that can be derived from the requirements document. For each sending object, we list the collaborations in the order in which they're discussed in the requirements document. We list each collaboration involving a unique sender, message and recipient only once, even though the collaboration may occur several times during an ATM session. For example, the first row in Fig. 32.22 indicates that the ATM collaborates with the Screen whenever the ATM needs to display a message to the user.

An object of class...	sends the message...	to an object of class...
ATM	DisplayMessage	Screen
	GetInput	Keypad
	AuthenticateUser	BankDatabase
	Execute	BalanceInquiry
	Execute	Withdrawal
	Execute	Deposit
BalanceInquiry	GetAvailableBalance	BankDatabase
	GetTotalBalance	BankDatabase
	DisplayMessage	Screen

Fig. 32.22 | Collaborations in the ATM system. (Part 1 of 2.)

An object of class...	sends the message...	to an object of class...
Withdrawal	DisplayMessage	Screen
	GetInput	Keypad
	GetAvailableBalance	BankDatabase
	IsSufficientCashAvailable	CashDispenser
	Debit	BankDatabase
	DispenseCash	CashDispenser
Deposit	DisplayMessage	Screen
	GetInput	Keypad
	IsDepositEnvelopeReceived	DepositSlot
	Credit	BankDatabase
BankDatabase	ValidatePIN	Account
	AvailableBalance (get)	Account
	TotalBalance (get)	Account
	Debit	Account
	Credit	Account

Fig. 32.22 | Collaborations in the ATM system. (Part 2 of 2.)

Let's consider the collaborations in Fig. 32.22. Before allowing a user to perform any transactions, the ATM must prompt the user to enter an account number, then a PIN. It accomplishes each of these tasks by sending a DisplayMessage message to the Screen. Both of these actions refer to the same collaboration between the ATM and the Screen, which is already listed in Fig. 32.22. The ATM obtains input in response to a prompt by sending a GetInput message to the Keypad. Next the ATM must determine whether the user-specified account number and PIN match those of an account in the database. It does so by sending an AuthenticateUser message to the BankDatabase. Recall that the Bank-Database cannot authenticate a user directly—only the user's Account (i.e., the Account that contains the account number specified by the user) can access the user's PIN to authenticate the user. Figure 32.22 therefore lists a collaboration in which the Bank-Database sends a ValidatePIN message to an Account.

After the user is authenticated, the ATM displays the main menu by sending a series of DisplayMessage messages to the Screen and obtains input containing a menu selection by sending a GetInput message to the Keypad. We have already accounted for these collaborations. After the user chooses a type of transaction to perform, the ATM executes the transaction by sending an Execute message to an object of the appropriate transaction class (i.e., a BalanceInquiry, a Withdrawal or a Deposit). For example, if the user chooses to perform a balance inquiry, the ATM sends an Execute message to a BalanceInquiry.

Further examination of the requirements document reveals the collaborations involved in executing each transaction type. A BalanceInquiry retrieves the amount of money available in the user's account by sending a GetAvailableBalance message to the BankDatabase, which sends a get message to an Account's AvailableBalance property to access the available balance. Similarly, the BalanceInquiry retrieves the amount of money on deposit by sending a GetTotalBalance message to the BankDatabase, which sends a get message to an Account's TotalBalance property to access the total balance on deposit. To display both measures of the user's balance at the same time, the BalanceInquiry sends DisplayMessage messages to the Screen.

A `Withdrawal` sends `DisplayMessage` messages to the `Screen` to display a menu of standard withdrawal amounts (i.e., $20, $40, $60, $100, $200). The `Withdrawal` sends a `GetInput` message to the `Keypad` to obtain the user's menu selection. Next, the `Withdrawal` determines whether the requested withdrawal amount is less than or equal to the user's account balance. The `Withdrawal` obtains the amount of money available in the user's account by sending a `GetAvailableBalance` message to the `BankDatabase`. The `Withdrawal` then tests whether the cash dispenser contains enough cash by sending an `IsSufficientCashAvailable` message to the `CashDispenser`. A `Withdrawal` sends a `Debit` message to the `BankDatabase` to decrease the user's account balance. The `BankDatabase` in turn sends the same message to the appropriate `Account`. Recall that debiting an `Account` decreases both the total balance and the available balance. To dispense the requested amount of cash, the `Withdrawal` sends a `DispenseCash` message to the `CashDispenser`. Finally, the `Withdrawal` sends a `DisplayMessage` message to the `Screen`, instructing the user to take the cash.

A `Deposit` responds to an `Execute` message first by sending a `DisplayMessage` message to the `Screen` to prompt the user for a deposit amount. The `Deposit` sends a `GetInput` message to the `Keypad` to obtain the user's input. The `Deposit` then sends a `DisplayMessage` message to the `Screen` to tell the user to insert a deposit envelope. To determine whether the deposit slot received an incoming deposit envelope, the `Deposit` sends an `IsDepositEnvelopeReceived` message to the `DepositSlot`. The `Deposit` updates the user's account by sending a `Credit` message to the `BankDatabase`, which subsequently sends a `Credit` message to the user's `Account`. Recall that crediting an `Account` increases the total balance but not the available balance.

Interaction Diagrams

Now that we have identified a set of possible collaborations between the objects in our ATM system, let us graphically model these interactions. The UML provides several types of **interaction diagrams** that model the behavior of a system by modeling how objects interact with one another. The **communication diagram** emphasizes *which objects* participate in collaborations. [*Note:* Communication diagrams were called **collaboration diagrams** in earlier versions of the UML.] Like the communication diagram, the **sequence diagram** shows collaborations among objects, but it emphasizes *when* messages are sent between objects.

Communication Diagrams

Figure 32.23 shows a communication diagram that models the `ATM` executing a `BalanceInquiry`. Objects are modeled in the UML as rectangles containing names in the form `objectName : ClassName`. In this example, which involves only one object of each type, we disregard the object name and list only a colon followed by the class name. Specifying the name of each object in a communication diagram is recommended when modeling multiple objects of the same type. Communicating objects are connected with solid lines, and messages are passed between objects along these lines in the direction shown by arrows with filled arrowheads. The name of the message, which appears next to the arrow, is the name of an operation (i.e., a method) belonging to the receiving object—think of the name as a service that the receiving object provides to sending objects (its "clients").

Fig. 32.23 | Communication diagram of the ATM executing a balance inquiry.

The filled arrow in Fig. 32.23 represents a message—or **synchronous call**—in the UML and a method call in C#. This arrow indicates that the flow of control is from the sending object (the ATM) to the receiving object (a BalanceInquiry). Since this is a synchronous call, the sending object cannot send another message, or do anything at all, until the receiving object processes the message and returns control (and possibly a return value) to the sending object. The sender just waits. For example, in Fig. 32.23, the ATM calls method Execute of a BalanceInquiry and cannot send another message until Execute finishes and returns control to the ATM. [*Note:* If this were an **asynchronous call**, represented by a stick arrowhead, the sending object would not have to wait for the receiving object to return control—it would continue sending additional messages immediately following the asynchronous call.]

Sequence of Messages in a Communication Diagram

Figure 32.24 shows a communication diagram that models the interactions among objects in the system when an object of class BalanceInquiry executes. We assume that the object's accountNumber attribute contains the account number of the current user. The collaborations in Fig. 32.24 begin after the ATM sends an Execute message to a BalanceInquiry (i.e., the interaction modeled in Fig. 32.23). The number to the left of a message name indicates the order in which the message is passed. The **sequence of messages** in a communication diagram progresses in numerical order from least to greatest. In this diagram, the numbering starts with message 1 and ends with message 3. The BalanceInquiry first sends a GetAvailableBalance message to the BankDatabase (message 1), then sends a GetTotalBalance message to the BankDatabase (message 2). Within the parentheses following a message name, we can specify a comma-separated list of the names of the arguments sent with the message (i.e., arguments in a C# method call)—the BalanceInquiry passes attribute accountNumber with its messages to the BankDatabase to indicate which Account's balance information to retrieve. Recall from Fig. 32.18 that operations GetAvailableBalance and GetTotalBalance of class BankDatabase each require a parameter to identify an account. The BalanceInquiry next displays the available balance and the total balance to the user by passing a DisplayMessage message to the Screen (message 3) that includes a parameter indicating the message to be displayed.

Figure 32.24 models two additional messages passing from the BankDatabase to an Account (message 1.1 and message 2.1). To provide the ATM with the two balances of the user's Account (as requested by messages 1 and 2), the BankDatabase must send get messages to the Account's AvailableBalance and TotalBalance properties. A message passed within the handling of another message is called a **nested message**. The UML recommends using a decimal numbering scheme to indicate nested messages. For example, message 1.1 is the first message nested in message 1—the BankDatabase sends the get message to the Account's AvailableBalance property during BankDatabase's processing of a GetAvailableBalance message. [*Note:* If the BankDatabase needed to pass a second nested message while processing message 1, it would be numbered 1.2.] A message may

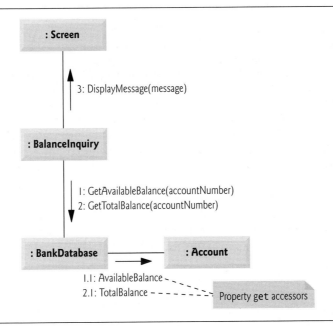

Fig. 32.24 | Communication diagram for executing a BalanceInquiry.

be passed only when all the nested messages from the previous message have been passed. For example, the BalanceInquiry passes message 3 to the Screen only after messages 2 and 2.1 have been passed, in that order.

The nested numbering scheme used in communication diagrams helps clarify precisely when and in what context each message is passed. For example, if we numbered the five messages in Fig. 32.24 using a flat numbering scheme (i.e., 1, 2, 3, 4, 5), someone looking at the diagram might not be able to determine that BankDatabase passes the get message to an Account's AvailableBalance property (message 1.1) *during* the BankDatabase's processing of message 1, as opposed to *after* completing the processing of message 1. The nested decimal numbers make it clear that the get message (message 1.1) is passed to an Account's AvailableBalance property within the handling of the GetAvailable-Balance message (message 1) by the BankDatabase.

Sequence Diagrams

Communication diagrams emphasize the participants in collaborations but model their timing a bit awkwardly. A sequence diagram helps model the timing of collaborations more clearly. Figure 32.25 shows a sequence diagram modeling the sequence of interactions that occur when a Withdrawal executes. The dotted line extending down from an object's rectangle is that object's **lifeline**, which represents the progression of time. Actions typically occur along an object's lifeline in chronological order from top to bottom—an action near the top happens before one near the bottom.

Message passing in sequence diagrams is similar to message passing in communication diagrams. An arrow with a filled arrowhead extending from the sending object to the receiving object represents a message between two objects. The arrowhead points to an activation on the receiving object's lifeline. An **activation**, shown as a thin vertical rect-

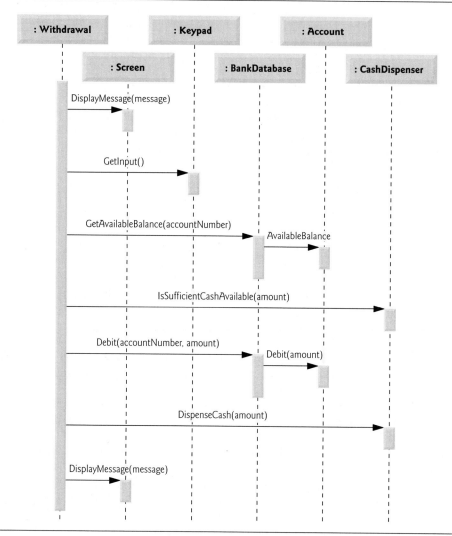

Fig. 32.25 | Sequence diagram that models a Withdrawal executing.

angle, indicates that an object is executing. When an object returns control, a return message, represented as a dashed line with a stick arrowhead, extends from the activation of the object returning control to the activation of the object that initially sent the message. To eliminate clutter, we omit the return-message arrows—the UML allows this practice to make diagrams more readable. Like communication diagrams, sequence diagrams can indicate message parameters between the parentheses following a message name.

The sequence of messages in Fig. 32.25 begins when a Withdrawal prompts the user to choose a withdrawal amount by sending a DisplayMessage message to the Screen. The Withdrawal then sends a GetInput message to the Keypad, which obtains input from the user. We have already modeled the control logic involved in a Withdrawal in the activity diagram of Fig. 32.15, so we do not show this logic in the sequence diagram of Fig. 32.25.

Instead, we model the best-case scenario, in which the balance of the user's account is greater than or equal to the chosen withdrawal amount, and the cash dispenser contains a sufficient amount of cash to satisfy the request. You can model control logic in a sequence diagram with UML frames (which are not covered in this case study). For a quick overview of UML frames, visit www.agilemodeling.com/style/frame.htm.

After obtaining a withdrawal amount, the `Withdrawal` sends a `GetAvailableBalance` message to the `BankDatabase`, which in turn sends a `get` message to the `Account`'s `AvailableBalance` property. Assuming that the user's account has enough money available to permit the transaction, the `Withdrawal` next sends an `IsSufficientCashAvailable` message to the `CashDispenser`. Assuming that there is enough cash available, the `Withdrawal` decreases the balance of the user's account (both the total balance and the available balance) by sending a `Debit` message to the `BankDatabase`. The `BankDatabase` responds by sending a `Debit` message to the user's `Account`. Finally, the `Withdrawal` sends a `DispenseCash` message to the `CashDispenser` and a `DisplayMessage` message to the `Screen`, telling the user to remove the cash from the machine.

We have identified collaborations among objects in the ATM system and modeled some of these collaborations using UML interaction diagrams—communication diagrams and sequence diagrams. In the next chapter, we enhance the structure of our model to complete a preliminary object-oriented design; then we begin implementing the ATM system in C#.

Self-Review Exercises

32.17 A(n) _____ consists of an object of one class sending a message to an object of another class.
- a) association
- b) aggregation
- c) collaboration
- d) composition

32.18 Which form of interaction diagram emphasizes *what* collaborations occur? Which form emphasizes *when* collaborations occur?

32.19 Create a sequence diagram that models the interactions among objects in the ATM system that occur when a `Deposit` executes successfully. Explain the sequence of messages modeled by the diagram.

32.8 Wrap-Up

In this chapter, you learned how to work from a detailed requirements document to develop an object-oriented design. You worked with six popular types of UML diagrams to graphically model an object-oriented automated teller machine software system. In Chapter 33, we tune the design using inheritance, then completely implement the design in a C# console app.

Answers to Self-Review Exercises

32.1 Figure 32.26 contains a use case diagram for a modified version of our ATM system that also allows users to transfer money between accounts.

32.2 b.

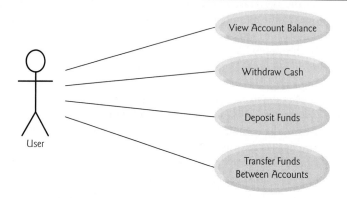

Fig. 32.26 | Use case diagram for a modified version of our ATM system that also allows users to transfer money between accounts.

32.3 d.

32.4 Figure 32.27 presents a class diagram that shows some of the composition relationships of a class Car.

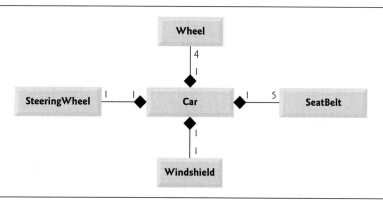

Fig. 32.27 | Class diagram showing some composition relationships of a class Car.

32.5 c. In a computer network, this relationship could be many-to-many.

32.6 True.

32.7 Figure 32.28 presents a class diagram for the ATM including class Deposit instead of class Withdrawal (as in Fig. 32.10). Class Deposit does not associate with class CashDispenser but does associate with class DepositSlot.

32.8 b.

32.9 c. Fly is an operation or behavior of an airplane, not an attribute.

32.10 This declaration indicates that attribute count is an int with an initial value of 500; count keeps track of the number of bills available in the CashDispenser at any given time.

32.11 False. State machine diagrams model some of the behaviors of a system.

32.12 a.

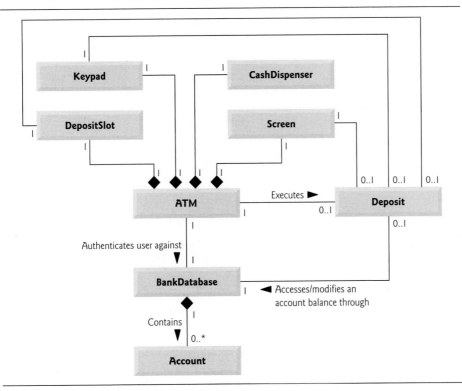

Fig. 32.28 | Class diagram for the ATM system model including class `Deposit`.

32.13 Figure 32.29 presents an activity diagram for a deposit transaction. The diagram models the actions that occur after the user chooses the deposit option from the main menu and before the ATM returns the user to the main menu. Recall that part of receiving a deposit amount from the user involves converting an integer number of cents to a dollar amount. Also recall that crediting a deposit amount to an account involves increasing only the `totalBalance` attribute of the user's `Account` object. The bank updates the `availableBalance` attribute of the user's `Account` object only after confirming the amount of cash in the deposit envelope and after the enclosed checks clear—this occurs independently of the ATM system.

32.14 c.

32.15 An operation that retrieves the `amount` attribute of class `Withdrawal` would typically be implemented as a `get` accessor of a property of class `Withdrawal`. The following would replace attribute `amount` in the attribute (i.e., second) compartment of class `Withdrawal`:

    «property» Amount : decimal {readOnly}

32.16 This is an operation named `Add` that takes `int` parameters `x` and `y` and returns an `int` value. This operation would most likely sum its parameters `x` and `y` and return the result.

32.17 c.

32.18 Communication diagrams emphasize *what* collaborations occur. Sequence diagrams emphasize *when* collaborations occur.

32.19 Figure 32.30 presents a sequence diagram that models the interactions between objects in the ATM system that occur when a `Deposit` executes successfully. It indicates that a `Deposit` first

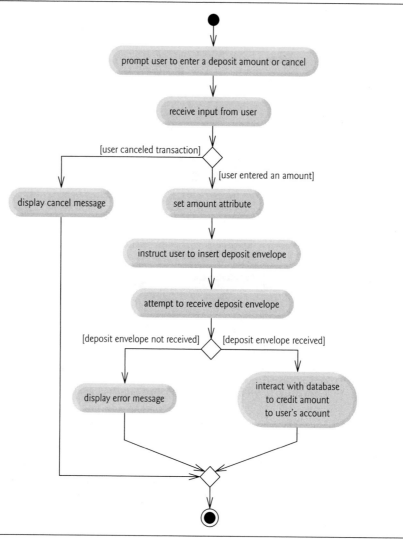

Fig. 32.29 | Activity diagram for a `Deposit` transaction.

sends a `DisplayMessage` message to the `Screen` (to ask the user to enter a deposit amount). Next, the `Deposit` sends a `GetInput` message to the `Keypad` to receive the amount the user will be depositing. The `Deposit` then prompts the user (to insert a deposit envelope) by sending a `DisplayMessage` message to the `Screen`. The `Deposit` next sends an `IsDepositEnvelopeReceived` message to the `DepositSlot` to confirm that the deposit envelope has been received by the ATM. Finally, the `Deposit` increases the total balance (but not the available balance) of the user's `Account` by sending a `Credit` message to the `BankDatabase`. The `BankDatabase` responds by sending the same message to the user's `Account`.

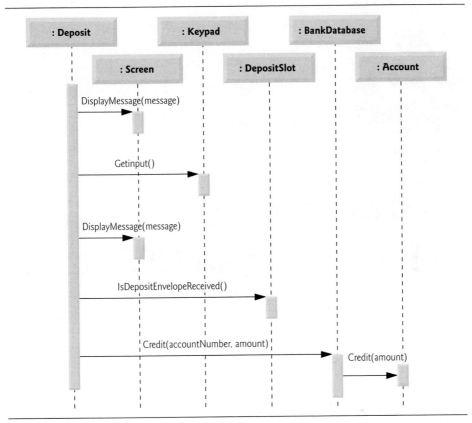

Fig. 32.30 | Sequence diagram that models a `Deposit` executing.

33

ATM Case Study, Part 2: Implementing an OO Design

Objectives

In this chapter you'll:

- Incorporate inheritance into the design of the ATM.

- Incorporate polymorphism into the design of the ATM.

- Fully implement in C# the UML-based object-oriented design of the ATM software.

- Study a detailed code walkthrough of the ATM software system that explains the implementation issues.

33.1 Introduction

In Chapter 32, we developed an object-oriented design for our ATM system. In this chapter, we take a deeper look at the details of programming with classes. We now begin implementing our object-oriented design by converting class diagrams to C# code. In the final case study section (Section 33.3), we modify the code to incorporate the object-oriented concepts of inheritance and polymorphism. We present the full C# code implementation in Section 33.4.

33.2 Starting to Program the Classes of the ATM System

Visibility

We now apply access modifiers to the members of our classes. In Chapter 4, we introduced access modifiers `public` and `private`. Access modifiers determine the **visibility**, or accessibility, of an object's attributes and operations to other objects. Before we can begin implementing our design, we must consider which attributes and methods of our classes should be `public` and which should be `private`.

In Chapter 4, we observed that attributes normally should be `private` and that methods invoked by clients of a class should be `public`. Methods that are called only by other methods of the class as "utility functions," however, should be `private`. The UML employs **visibility markers** for modeling the visibility of attributes and operations. Public visibility is indicated by placing a plus sign (+) before an operation or an attribute; a minus sign (–) indicates private visibility. Figure 33.1 shows our updated class diagram with visibility markers included. [*Note:* We do not include any operation parameters in Fig. 33.1. This is perfectly normal. Adding visibility markers does not affect the parameters already modeled in the class diagrams of Figs. 32.18–32.21.]

Navigability

Before we begin implementing our design in C#, we introduce an additional UML notation. The class diagram in Fig. 33.2 further refines the relationships among classes in the ATM system by adding navigability arrows to the association lines. **Navigability arrows** (represented as arrows with stick arrowheads in the class diagram) indicate in which direction an association can be traversed and are based on the collaborations modeled in communication and sequence diagrams (see Section 32.7). When implementing a system designed using the

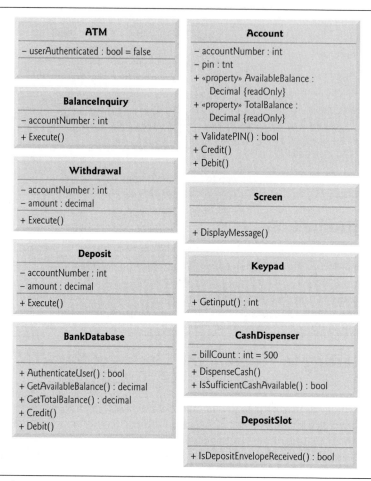

Fig. 33.1 | Class diagram with visibility markers.

UML, programmers use navigability arrows to help determine which objects need references to other objects. For example, the navigability arrow pointing from class ATM to class Bank-Database indicates that we can navigate from the former to the latter, thereby enabling the ATM to invoke the BankDatabase's operations. However, since Fig. 33.2 does not contain a navigability arrow pointing from class BankDatabase to class ATM, the BankDatabase cannot access the ATM's operations. Associations in a class diagram that have navigability arrows at both ends or do not have navigability arrows at all indicate **bidirectional navigability**—navigation can proceed in either direction across the association.

The class diagram of Fig. 33.2 omits classes BalanceInquiry and Deposit to keep the diagram simple. The navigability of the associations in which these classes participate closely parallels the navigability of class Withdrawal's associations. Recall that Balance-Inquiry has an association with class Screen. We can navigate from class BalanceInquiry to class Screen along this association, but we cannot navigate from class Screen to class BalanceInquiry. Thus, if we were to model class BalanceInquiry in Fig. 33.2, we would place a navigability arrow at class Screen's end of this association. Also recall that class

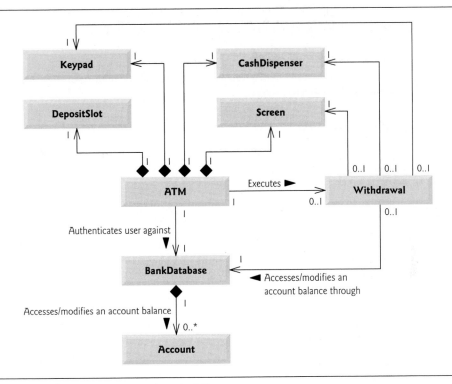

Fig. 33.2 | Class diagram with navigability arrows.

Deposit associates with classes Screen, Keypad and DepositSlot. We can navigate from class Deposit to each of these classes, but not vice versa. We therefore would place navigability arrows at the Screen, Keypad and DepositSlot ends of these associations. [*Note:* We model these additional classes and associations in our final class diagram in Section 33.3, after we have simplified the structure of our system by incorporating the object-oriented concept of inheritance.]

Implementing the ATM System from Its UML Design

We're now ready to begin implementing the ATM system. We first convert the classes in the diagrams of Fig. 33.1 and 33.2 into C# code. This code will represent the "skeleton" of the system. In Section 33.3, we modify the code to incorporate the object-oriented concept of inheritance. In Section 33.4, we present the complete working C# code that implements our object-oriented design.

As an example, we begin to develop the code for class Withdrawal from our design of class Withdrawal in Fig. 33.1. We use this figure to determine the attributes and operations of the class. We use the UML model in Fig. 33.2 to determine the associations among classes. We follow these four guidelines for each class:

1. Use the name located in the first compartment of a class in a class diagram to declare the class as a public class with an empty parameterless constructor—we include this constructor simply as a placeholder to remind us that most classes will need one or more constructors. In Section 33.4.10, when we complete a working

version of this class, we add any necessary arguments and code to the body of the constructor. Class Withdrawal initially yields the code in Fig. 33.3.

```
 1   // Fig. 33.3: Withdrawal.cs
 2   // Class Withdrawal represents an ATM withdrawal transaction
 3   public class Withdrawal
 4   {
 5      // parameterless constructor
 6      public Withdrawal()
 7      {
 8         // constructor body code
 9      } // end constructor
10   } // end class Withdrawal
```

Fig. 33.3 | Initial C# code for class Withdrawal based on Figs. 33.1 and 33.2.

2. Use the attributes located in the class's second compartment to declare the instance variables. The private attributes accountNumber and amount of class Withdrawal yield the code in Fig. 33.4.

```
 1   // Fig. 33.4: Withdrawal.cs
 2   // Class Withdrawal represents an ATM withdrawal transaction
 3   public class Withdrawal
 4   {
 5      // attributes
 6      private int accountNumber; // account to withdraw funds from
 7      private decimal amount; // amount to withdraw from account
 8
 9      // parameterless constructor
10      public Withdrawal()
11      {
12         // constructor body code
13      } // end constructor
14   } // end class Withdrawal
```

Fig. 33.4 | Incorporating private variables for class Withdrawal based on Figs. 33.1 and 33.2.

3. Use the associations described in the class diagram to declare references to other objects. According to Fig. 33.2, Withdrawal can access one object of class Screen, one object of class Keypad, one object of class CashDispenser and one object of class BankDatabase. Class Withdrawal must maintain references to these objects to send messages to them, so lines 10–13 of Fig. 33.5 declare the appropriate references as private instance variables. In the implementation of class Withdrawal in Section 33.4.10, a constructor initializes these instance variables with references to the actual objects.

4. Use the operations located in the third compartment of Fig. 33.1 to declare the shells of the methods. If we have not yet specified a return type for an operation, we declare the method with return type void. Refer to the class diagrams of Figs. 32.18–32.21 to declare any necessary parameters. Adding the public operation Execute (which has an empty parameter list) in class Withdrawal yields the

code in lines 23–26 of Fig. 33.6. [*Note:* We code the bodies of the methods when we implement the complete ATM system.]

Software Engineering Observation 33.1

Many UML modeling tools can convert UML-based designs into C# code, considerably speeding up the implementation process.

```csharp
1   // Fig. 33.5: Withdrawal.cs
2   // Class Withdrawal represents an ATM withdrawal transaction
3   public class Withdrawal
4   {
5      // attributes
6      private int accountNumber; // account to withdraw funds from
7      private decimal amount; // amount to withdraw
8
9      // references to associated objects
10     private Screen screen; // ATM's screen
11     private Keypad keypad; // ATM's keypad
12     private CashDispenser cashDispenser; // ATM's cash dispenser
13     private BankDatabase bankDatabase; // account-information database
14
15     // parameterless constructor
16     public Withdrawal()
17     {
18        // constructor body code
19     } // end constructor
20  } // end class Withdrawal
```

Fig. 33.5 | Incorporating `private` reference handles for the associations of class `Withdrawal` based on Figs. 33.1 and 33.2.

```csharp
1   // Fig. 33.6: Withdrawal.cs
2   // Class Withdrawal represents an ATM withdrawal transaction
3   public class Withdrawal
4   {
5      // attributes
6      private int accountNumber; // account to withdraw funds from
7      private decimal amount; // amount to withdraw
8
9      // references to associated objects
10     private Screen screen; // ATM's screen
11     private Keypad keypad; // ATM's keypad
12     private CashDispenser cashDispenser; // ATM's cash dispenser
13     private BankDatabase bankDatabase; // account-information database
14
15     // parameterless constructor
16     public Withdrawal()
17     {
```

Fig. 33.6 | C# code incorporating method `Execute` in class `Withdrawal` based on Figs. 33.1 and 33.2. (Part 1 of 2.)

```
18          // constructor body code
19      } // end constructor
20
21      // operations
22      // perform transaction
23      public void Execute()
24      {
25          // Execute method body code
26      } // end method Execute
27  } // end class Withdrawal
```

Fig. 33.6 | C# code incorporating method `Execute` in class `Withdrawal` based on Figs. 33.1 and 33.2. (Part 2 of 2.)

This concludes our discussion of the basics of generating class files from UML diagrams. In the next section, we demonstrate how to modify the code in Fig. 33.6 to incorporate the object-oriented concepts of inheritance and polymorphism, which we presented in Chapters 11 and 12, respectively.

Self-Review Exercises

33.1   State whether the following statement is *true* or *false*, and if *false*, explain why: If an attribute of a class is marked with a minus sign (-) in a class diagram, the attribute is not directly accessible outside of the class.

33.2   In Fig. 33.2, the association between the ATM and the Screen indicates:
  a) that we can navigate from the Screen to the ATM.
  b) that we can navigate from the ATM to the Screen.
  c) Both a and b; the association is bidirectional.
  d) None of the above.

33.3   Write C# code to begin implementing the design for class Account.

33.3 Incorporating Inheritance and Polymorphism into the ATM System

We now revisit our ATM system design to see how it might benefit from inheritance and polymorphism. To apply inheritance, we first look for commonality among classes in the system. We create an inheritance hierarchy to model similar classes in an elegant and efficient manner that enables us to process objects of these classes polymorphically. We then modify our class diagram to incorporate the new inheritance relationships. Finally, we demonstrate how the inheritance aspects of our updated design are translated into C# code.

In Section 32.3, we encountered the problem of representing a financial transaction in the system. Rather than create one class to represent all transaction types, we created three distinct transaction classes—BalanceInquiry, Withdrawal and Deposit—to represent the transactions that the ATM system can perform. The class diagram of Fig. 33.7 shows the attributes and operations of these classes. They have one private attribute (accountNumber) and one public operation (Execute) in common. Each class requires attribute accountNumber to specify the account to which the transaction applies. Each class contains operation Execute, which the ATM invokes to perform the transaction. Clearly, BalanceInquiry, Withdrawal and Deposit represent *types of* transactions.

Figure 33.7 reveals commonality among the transaction classes, so using inheritance to factor out the common features seems appropriate for designing these classes. We place the common functionality in base class Transaction and derive classes BalanceInquiry, Withdrawal and Deposit from Transaction (Fig. 33.8).

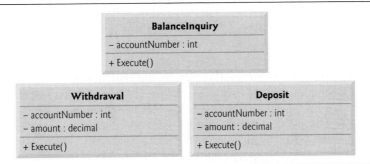

Fig. 33.7 | Attributes and operations of classes BalanceInquiry, Withdrawal and Deposit.

The UML specifies a relationship called a **generalization** to model inheritance. Figure 33.8 is the class diagram that models the inheritance relationship between base class Transaction and its three derived classes. The arrows with triangular hollow arrowheads indicate that classes BalanceInquiry, Withdrawal and Deposit are derived from class Transaction by inheritance. Class Transaction is said to be a generalization of its derived classes. The derived classes are said to be **specializations** of class Transaction.

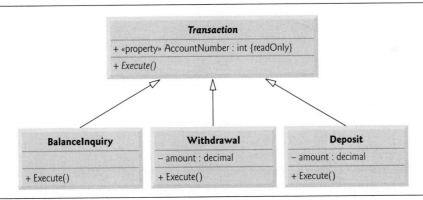

Fig. 33.8 | Class diagram modeling the generalization (i.e., inheritance) relationship between the base class Transaction and its derived classes BalanceInquiry, Withdrawal and Deposit.

As Fig. 33.7 shows, classes BalanceInquiry, Withdrawal and Deposit share private int attribute accountNumber. We'd like to factor out this common attribute and place it in the base class Transaction. However, recall that a base class's private attributes are not accessible in derived classes. The derived classes of Transaction require access to attribute accountNumber so that they can specify which Account to process in the BankDatabase. A derived class can access the public and protected members of its base class. However, the derived classes in this case do not need to modify attribute accountNumber—they need only to access its value. For this reason, we have chosen to replace private attribute accountNumber in our model with the public read-only property AccountNumber. Since this is a read-only property, it provides only a get accessor to access the account number. Each derived class inherits this property, enabling the derived class to access its account number as needed to execute a transaction. We no longer list accountNumber in the second compartment of each derived class, because the three derived classes inherit property AccountNumber from Transaction.

According to Fig. 33.7, classes BalanceInquiry, Withdrawal and Deposit also share operation Execute, so base class Transaction should contain public operation Execute. However, it does not make sense to implement Execute in class Transaction, because the functionality that this operation provides depends on the specific type of the actual transaction. We therefore declare Execute as an **abstract operation** in base class Transaction—it will become an abstract method in the C# implementation. This makes Transaction an abstract class and forces any class derived from Transaction that must be a concrete class (i.e., BalanceInquiry, Withdrawal and Deposit) to implement the operation Execute to make the derived class concrete. The UML requires that we place abstract class names and abstract operations in italics. Thus, in Fig. 33.8, Transaction and Execute appear in italics for the Transaction class; Execute is not italicized in derived classes BalanceInquiry, Withdrawal and Deposit. Each derived class overrides base class Transaction's Execute operation with an appropriate concrete implementation. Fig. 33.8 includes operation Execute in the third compartment of classes BalanceInquiry, Withdrawal and Deposit, because each class has a different concrete implementation of the overridden operation.

A derived class can inherit interface and implementation from a base class. Compared to a hierarchy designed for implementation inheritance, one designed for interface inheritance tends to have its functionality lower in the hierarchy—a base class signifies one or more operations that should be defined by each class in the hierarchy, but the individual derived classes provide their own implementations of the operation(s). The inheritance hierarchy designed for the ATM system takes advantage of this type of inheritance, which provides the ATM with an elegant way to execute all transactions "in the general" (i.e., polymorphically). Each class derived from Transaction inherits some implementation details (e.g., property AccountNumber), but the primary benefit of incorporating inheritance into our system is that the derived classes share a common interface (e.g., abstract operation Execute). The ATM can aim a Transaction reference at any transaction, and when the ATM invokes the operation Execute through this reference, the version of Execute specific to that transaction runs (polymorphically) automatically (due to polymorphism). For example, suppose a user chooses to perform a balance inquiry. The ATM aims a Transaction reference at a new object of class BalanceInquiry, which the C# compiler allows because a BalanceInquiry *is a* Transaction. When the ATM uses this reference to invoke Execute, BalanceInquiry's version of Execute is called (polymorphically).

This polymorphic approach also makes the system easily extensible. Should we wish to create a new transaction type (e.g., funds transfer or bill payment), we would simply create an additional Transaction derived class that overrides the Execute operation with a version appropriate for the new transaction type. We would need to make only minimal changes to the system code to allow users to choose the new transaction type from the main menu and for the ATM to instantiate and execute objects of the new derived class. The ATM could execute transactions of the new type using the current code, because it executes all transactions identically (through polymorphism).

An abstract class like Transaction is one for which the programmer never intends to (and, in fact, cannot) instantiate objects. An abstract class simply declares common attributes and behaviors for its derived classes in an inheritance hierarchy. Class Transaction defines the concept of what it means to be a transaction that has an account number and can be executed. You may wonder why we bother to include abstract operation Execute in class Transaction if Execute lacks a concrete implementation. Conceptually, we include this operation because it is the defining behavior of all transactions—executing. Technically, we must include operation Execute in base class Transaction so that the ATM (or any other class) can invoke each derived class's overridden version of this operation polymorphically via a Transaction reference.

Derived classes BalanceInquiry, Withdrawal and Deposit inherit property Account-Number from base class Transaction, but classes Withdrawal and Deposit contain the additional attribute amount that distinguishes them from class BalanceInquiry. Classes Withdrawal and Deposit require this additional attribute to store the amount of money that the user wishes to withdraw or deposit. Class BalanceInquiry has no need for such an attribute and requires only an account number to execute. Even though two of the three Transaction derived classes share the attribute amount, we do not place it in base class Transaction—we place only features common to *all* the derived classes in the base class, so derived classes do not inherit unnecessary attributes (and operations).

Figure 33.9 presents an updated class diagram of our model that incorporates inheritance and introduces abstract base class Transaction. We model an association between class ATM and class Transaction to show that the ATM, at any given moment, either is executing a transaction or is not (i.e., zero or one objects of type Transaction exist in the system at a time). Because a Withdrawal is a type of Transaction, we no longer draw an association line directly between class ATM and class Withdrawal—derived class Withdrawal inherits base class Transaction's association with class ATM. Derived classes BalanceInquiry and Deposit also inherit this association, which replaces the previously omitted associations between classes BalanceInquiry and Deposit, and class ATM. Note again the use of triangular hollow arrowheads to indicate the specializations (i.e., derived classes) of class Transaction, as indicated in Fig. 33.8.

We also add an association between Transaction and BankDatabase (Fig. 33.9). All Transactions require a reference to the BankDatabase so that they can access and modify account information. Each Transaction derived class inherits this reference, so we no longer model the association between Withdrawal and BankDatabase. The association between class Transaction and the BankDatabase replaces the previously omitted associations between classes BalanceInquiry and Deposit, and the BankDatabase.

We include an association between class Transaction and the Screen because all Transactions display output to the user via the Screen. Each derived class inherits this association. Therefore, we no longer include the association previously modeled between Withdrawal and the Screen. Class Withdrawal still participates in associations with the CashDispenser and the Keypad, however—these associations apply to derived class Withdrawal but not to derived classes BalanceInquiry and Deposit, so we do not move these associations to base class Transaction.

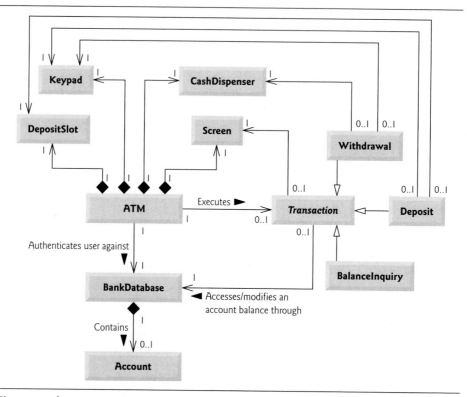

Fig. 33.9 | Class diagram of the ATM system (incorporating inheritance). Abstract class name Transaction appears in italics.

Our class diagram incorporating inheritance (Fig. 33.9) also models classes Deposit and BalanceInquiry. We show associations between Deposit and both the DepositSlot and the Keypad. Class BalanceInquiry takes part in only those associations inherited from class Transaction—a BalanceInquiry interacts only with the BankDatabase and the Screen.

The modified class diagram in Fig. 33.10 includes abstract base class Transaction. This abbreviated diagram does not show inheritance relationships (these appear in Fig. 33.9), but instead shows the attributes and operations after we have employed inheritance in our system. Abstract class name Transaction and abstract operation name Execute in class Transaction appear in italics. To save space, we do not include those attributes shown by associations in Fig. 33.9—we do, however, include them in the C# implementation. We also omit all operation parameters—incorporating inheritance does not affect the parameters already modeled in Figs. 32.18–32.21.

Software Engineering Observation 33.2

A complete class diagram shows all the associations among classes, and all the attributes and operations for each class. When the number of class attributes, operations and associations is substantial (as in Figs. 33.9 and 33.10), a good practice that promotes readability is to divide this information between two class diagrams—one focusing on associations and the other on attributes and operations.

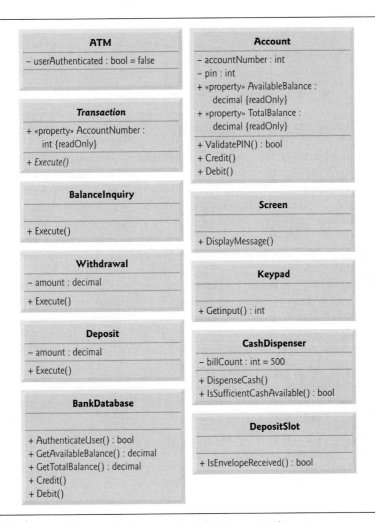

Fig. 33.10 | Class diagram after incorporating inheritance into the system.

Implementing the ATM System Design Incorporating Inheritance

In the previous section, we began implementing the ATM system design in C#. We now incorporate inheritance, using class Withdrawal as an example.

1. If a class A is a generalization of class B, then class B is derived from (and is a specialization of) class A. For example, abstract base class Transaction is a generalization of class Withdrawal. Thus, class Withdrawal is derived from (and is a specialization of) class Transaction. Figure 33.11 contains the shell of class Withdrawal, in which the class definition indicates the inheritance relationship between Withdrawal and Transaction (line 3).

2. If class A is an abstract class and class B is derived from class A, then class B must implement the abstract operations of class A if class B is to be a concrete class. For example, class Transaction contains abstract operation Execute, so class Withdrawal

```
1   // Fig. 33.11: Withdrawal.cs
2   // Class Withdrawal represents an ATM withdrawal transaction.
3   public class Withdrawal : Transaction
4   {
5      // code for members of class Withdrawal
6   } // end class Withdrawal
```

Fig. 33.11 | C# code for shell of class `Withdrawal`.

must implement this operation if we want to instantiate `Withdrawal` objects. Figure 33.12 contains the portions of the C# code for class `Withdrawal` that can be inferred from Figs. 33.9 and 33.10. Class `Withdrawal` inherits property `Account-Number` from base class `Transaction`, so `Withdrawal` does not declare this property. Class `Withdrawal` also inherits references to the `Screen` and the `BankDatabase` from class `Transaction`, so we do not include these references. Figure 33.10 specifies attribute amount and operation `Execute` for class `Withdrawal`. Line 6 of Fig. 33.12 declares an instance variable for attribute amount. Lines 17–20 declare the shell of a method for operation `Execute`. Recall that derived class `Withdrawal` must provide a concrete implementation of the `abstract` method `Execute` from base class `Transaction`. The keypad and cash-`Dispenser` references (lines 7–8) are instance variables whose need is apparent from class `Withdrawal`'s associations in Fig. 33.9—in this class's C# implementation (Section 33.4.10), a constructor initializes these references to actual objects.

We discuss the polymorphic processing of `Transactions` in Section 33.4.1 of the ATM implementation. Class ATM performs the actual polymorphic call to method `Execute` at line 99 of Fig. 33.26.

```
1    // Fig. 33.12: Withdrawal.cs
2    // Class Withdrawal represents an ATM withdrawal transaction.
3    public class Withdrawal : Transaction
4    {
5       // attributes
6       private decimal amount; // amount to withdraw
7       private Keypad keypad; // reference to keypad
8       private CashDispenser cashDispenser; // reference to cash dispenser
9
10      // parameterless constructor
11      public Withdrawal()
12      {
13         // constructor body code
14      } // end constructor
15
16      // method that overrides Execute
17      public override void Execute()
18      {
19         // Execute method body code
20      } // end method Execute
21   } // end class Withdrawal
```

Fig. 33.12 | C# code for class `Withdrawal` based on Figs. 33.9 and 33.10.

Self-Review Exercises

33.4 The UML uses an arrow with a _____ to indicate a generalization relationship.
  a) solid filled arrowhead
  b) triangular hollow arrowhead
  c) diamond-shaped hollow arrowhead
  d) stick arrowhead

33.5 State whether the following statement is *true* or *false*, and if *false*, explain why: The UML requires that we underline abstract class names and abstract operation names.

33.6 Write C# code to begin implementing the design for class Transaction specified in Figures 33.9 and 33.10. Be sure to include private references based on class Transaction's associations. Also, be sure to include properties with public get accessors for any of the private instance variables that the derived classes must access to perform their tasks.

33.4 ATM Case Study Implementation

This section contains the complete working implementation of the ATM system. The implementation comprises 655 lines of C# code. We consider the 11 classes in the order in which we identified them in Section 32.3 (with the exception of Transaction, which was introduced in Section 33.3 as the base class of classes BalanceInquiry, Withdrawal and Deposit):

- ATM
- Screen
- Keypad
- CashDispenser
- DepositSlot
- Account
- BankDatabase
- Transaction
- BalanceInquiry
- Withdrawal
- Deposit

We apply the guidelines discussed in Sections 33.2–33.3 to code these classes based on how we modeled them in the UML class diagrams of Figs. 33.9–33.10. To develop the bodies of class methods, we refer to the activity diagrams presented in Section 32.5 and the communication and sequence diagrams presented in Section 32.6. Our ATM design does not specify all the program logic and may not specify all the attributes and operations required to complete the ATM implementation. This is a normal part of the object-oriented design process. As we implement the system, we complete the program logic and add attributes and behaviors as necessary to construct the ATM system specified by the requirements document in Section 32.2.

We conclude the discussion by presenting a test harness (ATMCaseStudy in Section 33.4.12) that creates an object of class ATM and starts it by calling its Run method. Recall that we are developing a first version of the ATM system that runs on a personal computer and uses the keyboard and monitor to approximate the ATM's keypad and screen. Also, we simulate the actions of the ATM's cash dispenser and deposit slot. We attempt to implement the system so that real hardware versions of these devices could be integrated without significant code changes. [*Note:* For the purpose of this simulation, we have provided two predefined accounts in class BankDatabase. The first account has the account number 12345 and the PIN 54321. The second account has the account number 98765 and the PIN 56789. You should use these accounts when testing the ATM.]

33.4.1 Class ATM

Class ATM (Fig. 33.13) represents the ATM as a whole. Lines 5–11 implement the class's attributes. We determine all but one of these attributes from the UML class diagrams of Figs. 33.9–33.10. Line 5 declares the bool attribute userAuthenticated from Fig. 33.10. Line 6 declares an attribute not found in our UML design—int attribute currentAccountNumber, which keeps track of the account number of the current authenticated user. Lines 7–11 declare reference-type instance variables corresponding to the ATM class's associations modeled in the class diagram of Fig. 33.9. These attributes allow the ATM to access its parts (i.e., its Screen, Keypad, CashDispenser and DepositSlot) and interact with the bank's account information database (i.e., a BankDatabase object).

Lines 14–20 declare an enumeration that corresponds to the four options in the ATM's main menu (i.e., balance inquiry, withdrawal, deposit and exit). Lines 23–32 declare class ATM's constructor, which initializes the class's attributes. When an ATM object is first created, no user is authenticated, so line 25 initializes userAuthenticated to false. Line 26 initializes currentAccountNumber to 0 because there is no current user yet. Lines 27–30 instantiate new objects to represent the parts of the ATM. Recall that class ATM has composition relationships with classes Screen, Keypad, CashDispenser and DepositSlot, so class ATM is responsible for their creation. Line 31 creates a new BankDatabase. As you'll soon see, the BankDatabase creates two Account objects that can be used to test the ATM. [*Note:* If this were a real ATM system, the ATM class would receive a reference to an existing database object created by the bank. However, in this implementation, we are only simulating the bank's database, so class ATM creates the BankDatabase object with which it interacts.]

```
1    // ATM.cs
2    // Represents an automated teller machine.
3    public class ATM
4    {
5       private bool userAuthenticated; // true if user is authenticated
6       private int currentAccountNumber; // user's account number
7       private Screen screen; // reference to ATM's screen
8       private Keypad keypad; // reference to ATM's keypad
9       private CashDispenser cashDispenser; // ref to ATM's cash dispenser
10      private DepositSlot depositSlot; // reference to ATM's deposit slot
11      private BankDatabase bankDatabase; // ref to account info database
12
13      // enumeration that represents main menu options
14      private enum MenuOption
15      {
```

Fig. 33.13 | Class ATM represents the ATM. (Part 1 of 4.)

```
16            BALANCE_INQUIRY = 1,
17            WITHDRAWAL = 2,
18            DEPOSIT = 3,
19            EXIT_ATM = 4
20      } // end enum MenuOption
21
22      // parameterless constructor initializes instance variables
23      public ATM()
24      {
25            userAuthenticated = false; // user is not authenticated to start
26            currentAccountNumber = 0; // no current account number to start
27            screen = new Screen(); // create screen
28            keypad = new Keypad(); // create keypad
29            cashDispenser = new CashDispenser(); // create cash dispenser
30            depositSlot = new DepositSlot(); // create deposit slot
31            bankDatabase = new BankDatabase(); // create account info database
32      } // end constructor
33
34      // start ATM
35      public void Run()
36      {
37            // welcome and authenticate users; perform transactions
38            while ( true ) // infinite loop
39            {
40                  // loop while user is not yet authenticated
41                  while ( !userAuthenticated )
42                  {
43                        screen.DisplayMessageLine( "\nWelcome!" );
44                        AuthenticateUser(); // authenticate user
45                  } // end while
46
47                  PerformTransactions(); // for authenticated user
48                  userAuthenticated = false; // reset before next ATM session
49                  currentAccountNumber = 0; // reset before next ATM session
50                  screen.DisplayMessageLine( "\nThank you! Goodbye!" );
51            } // end while
52      } // end method Run
53
54      // attempt to authenticate user against database
55      private void AuthenticateUser()
56      {
57            // prompt for account number and input it from user
58            screen.DisplayMessage( "\nPlease enter your account number: " );
59            int accountNumber = keypad.GetInput();
60
61            // prompt for PIN and input it from user
62            screen.DisplayMessage( "\nEnter your PIN: " );
63            int pin = keypad.GetInput();
64
65            // set userAuthenticated to boolean value returned by database
66            userAuthenticated =
67                  bankDatabase.AuthenticateUser( accountNumber, pin );
68
```

Fig. 33.13 | Class ATM represents the ATM. (Part 2 of 4.)

```
69          // check whether authentication succeeded
70          if ( userAuthenticated )
71             currentAccountNumber = accountNumber; // save user's account #
72          else
73             screen.DisplayMessageLine(
74                "Invalid account number or PIN. Please try again." );
75       } // end method AuthenticateUser
76
77       // display the main menu and perform transactions
78       private void PerformTransactions()
79       {
80          Transaction currentTransaction; // transaction being processed
81          bool userExited = false; // user has not chosen to exit
82
83          // loop while user has not chosen exit option
84          while ( !userExited )
85          {
86             // show main menu and get user selection
87             int mainMenuSelection = DisplayMainMenu();
88
89             // decide how to proceed based on user's menu selection
90             switch ( ( MenuOption ) mainMenuSelection )
91             {
92                // user chooses to perform one of three transaction types
93                case MenuOption.BALANCE_INQUIRY:
94                case MenuOption.WITHDRAWAL:
95                case MenuOption.DEPOSIT:
96                   // initialize as new object of chosen type
97                   currentTransaction =
98                      CreateTransaction( mainMenuSelection );
99                   currentTransaction.Execute(); // execute transaction
100                  break;
101               case MenuOption.EXIT_ATM: // user chose to terminate session
102                  screen.DisplayMessageLine( "\nExiting the system..." );
103                  userExited = true; // this ATM session should end
104                  break;
105               default: // user did not enter an integer from 1-4
106                  screen.DisplayMessageLine(
107                     "\nYou did not enter a valid selection. Try again." );
108                  break;
109            } // end switch
110         } // end while
111      } // end method PerformTransactions
112
113      // display the main menu and return an input selection
114      private int DisplayMainMenu()
115      {
116         screen.DisplayMessageLine( "\nMain menu:" );
117         screen.DisplayMessageLine( "1 - View my balance" );
118         screen.DisplayMessageLine( "2 - Withdraw cash" );
119         screen.DisplayMessageLine( "3 - Deposit funds" );
120         screen.DisplayMessageLine( "4 - Exit\n" );
121         screen.DisplayMessage( "Enter a choice: " );
```

Fig. 33.13 | Class ATM represents the ATM. (Part 3 of 4.)

```
122          return keypad.GetInput(); // return user's selection
123     } // end method DisplayMainMenu
124
125     // return object of specified Transaction derived class
126     private Transaction CreateTransaction( int type )
127     {
128         Transaction temp = null; // null Transaction reference
129
130         // determine which type of Transaction to create
131         switch ( ( MenuOption ) type )
132         {
133             // create new BalanceInquiry transaction
134             case MenuOption.BALANCE_INQUIRY:
135                 temp = new BalanceInquiry( currentAccountNumber,
136                     screen, bankDatabase);
137                 break;
138             case MenuOption.WITHDRAWAL: // create new Withdrawal transaction
139                 temp = new Withdrawal( currentAccountNumber, screen,
140                     bankDatabase, keypad, cashDispenser);
141                 break;
142             case MenuOption.DEPOSIT: // create new Deposit transaction
143                 temp = new Deposit( currentAccountNumber, screen,
144                     bankDatabase, keypad, depositSlot);
145                 break;
146         } // end switch
147
148         return temp;
149     } // end method CreateTransaction
150 } // end class ATM
```

Fig. 33.13 | Class ATM represents the ATM. (Part 4 of 4.)

Implementing the Operation

The class diagram of Fig. 33.10 does not list any operations for class ATM. We now implement one operation (i.e., public method) in class ATM that allows an external client of the class (i.e., class ATMCaseStudy; Section 33.4.12) to tell the ATM to run. ATM method Run (Fig. 33.13, lines 35–52) uses an infinite loop (lines 38–51) to repeatedly welcome a user, attempt to authenticate the user and, if authentication succeeds, allow the user to perform transactions. After an authenticated user performs the desired transactions and exits, the ATM resets itself, displays a goodbye message and restarts the process for the next user. We use an infinite loop here to simulate the fact that an ATM appears to run continuously until the bank turns it off (an action beyond the user's control). An ATM user can exit the system, but cannot turn off the ATM completely.

Inside method Run's infinite loop, lines 41–45 cause the ATM to repeatedly welcome and attempt to authenticate the user as long as the user has not been authenticated (i.e., the condition !userAuthenticated is true). Line 43 invokes method Display-MessageLine of the ATM's screen to display a welcome message. Like Screen method DisplayMessage designed in the case study, method DisplayMessageLine (declared in lines 14–17 of Fig. 33.14) displays a message to the user, but this method also outputs a newline after displaying the message. We add this method during implementation to give class Screen's clients more control over the placement of displayed messages. Line 44

(Fig. 33.13) invokes class ATM's private utility method AuthenticateUser (declared in lines 55–75) to attempt to authenticate the user.

Authenticating the User

We refer to the requirements document to determine the steps necessary to authenticate the user before allowing transactions to occur. Line 58 of method AuthenticateUser invokes method DisplayMessage of the ATM's screen to prompt the user to enter an account number. Line 59 invokes method GetInput of the ATM's keypad to obtain the user's input, then stores this integer in local variable accountNumber. Method AuthenticateUser next prompts the user to enter a PIN (line 62), and stores the PIN in local variable pin (line 63). Next, lines 66–67 attempt to authenticate the user by passing the accountNumber and pin entered by the user to the bankDatabase's AuthenticateUser method. Class ATM sets its userAuthenticated attribute to the bool value returned by this method—userAuthenticated becomes true if authentication succeeds (i.e., the accountNumber and pin match those of an existing Account in bankDatabase) and remains false otherwise. If userAuthenticated is true, line 71 saves the account number entered by the user (i.e., accountNumber) in the ATM attribute currentAccountNumber. The other methods of class ATM use this variable whenever an ATM session requires access to the user's account number. If userAuthenticated is false, lines 73–74 call the screen's DisplayMessageLine method to indicate that an invalid account number and/or PIN was entered, so the user must try again. We set currentAccountNumber only after authenticating the user's account number and the associated PIN—if the database cannot authenticate the user, currentAccountNumber remains 0.

After method Run attempts to authenticate the user (line 44), if userAuthenticated is still false (line 41), the while loop body (lines 41–45) executes again. If userAuthenticated is now true, the loop terminates, and control continues with line 47, which calls class ATM's private utility method PerformTransactions.

Performing Transactions

Method PerformTransactions (lines 78–111) carries out an ATM session for an authenticated user. Line 80 declares local variable Transaction, to which we assign a BalanceInquiry, Withdrawal or Deposit object representing the ATM transaction currently being processed. We use a Transaction variable here to allow us to take advantage of polymorphism. Also, we name this variable after the role name included in the class diagram of Fig. 32.7—currentTransaction. Line 81 declares another local variable—a bool called userExited that keeps track of whether the user has chosen to exit. This variable controls a while loop (lines 84–110) that allows the user to execute an unlimited number of transactions before choosing to exit. Within this loop, line 87 displays the main menu and obtains the user's menu selection by calling ATM utility method DisplayMainMenu (declared in lines 114–123). This method displays the main menu by invoking methods of the ATM's screen and returns a menu selection obtained from the user through the ATM's keypad. Line 87 stores the user's selection, returned by DisplayMainMenu, in local variable mainMenuSelection.

After obtaining a main menu selection, method PerformTransactions uses a switch statement (lines 90–109) to respond to the selection appropriately. If mainMenuSelection is equal to the underlying value of any of the three enum members representing transaction types (i.e., if the user chose to perform a transaction), lines 97–98 call utility method

CreateTransaction (declared in lines 126–149) to return a newly instantiated object of the type that corresponds to the selected transaction. Variable currentTransaction is assigned the reference returned by method CreateTransaction, then line 99 invokes method Execute of this transaction to execute it. We discuss Transaction method Execute and the three Transaction derived classes shortly. We assign to the Transaction variable currentTransaction an object of one of the three Transaction derived classes so that we can execute transactions. For example, if the user chooses to perform a balance inquiry, (MenuOption) mainMenuSelection (line 90) matches the case label MenuOption.BALANCE_INQUIRY, and CreateTransaction returns a BalanceInquiry object (lines 97–98). Thus, currentTransaction refers to a BalanceInquiry and invoking currentTransaction.Execute() (line 99) results in BalanceInquiry's version of Execute being called polymorphically.

Creating Transactions

Method CreateTransaction (lines 126–149) uses a switch statement (lines 131–146) to instantiate a new Transaction derived class object of the type indicated by the parameter type. Recall that method PerformTransactions passes mainMenuSelection to method CreateTransaction only when mainMenuSelection contains a value corresponding to one of the three transaction types. So parameter type (line 126) receives one of the values MenuOption.BALANCE_INQUIRY, MenuOption.WITHDRAWAL or MenuOption.DEPOSIT. Each case in the switch statement instantiates a new object by calling the appropriate Transaction derived class constructor. Each constructor has a unique parameter list, based on the specific data required to initialize the derived class object. A BalanceInquiry (lines 135–136) requires only the account number of the current user and references to the ATM's screen and the bankDatabase. In addition to these parameters, a Withdrawal (lines 139–140) requires references to the ATM's keypad and cashDispenser, and a Deposit (lines 143–144) requires references to the ATM's keypad and depositSlot. We discuss the transaction classes in detail in Sections 33.4.8–33.4.11.

After executing a transaction (line 99 in method PerformTransactions), userExited remains false, and the while loop in lines 84–110 repeats, returning the user to the main menu. However, if a user does not perform a transaction and instead selects the main menu option to exit, line 103 sets userExited to true, causing the condition in line 84 of the while loop (!userExited) to become false. This while is the final statement of method PerformTransactions, so control returns to line 47 of the calling method Run. If the user enters an invalid main menu selection (i.e., not an integer in the range 1–4), lines 106–107 display an appropriate error message, userExited remains false (as set in line 81) and the user returns to the main menu to try again.

When method PerformTransactions returns control to method Run, the user has chosen to exit the system, so lines 48–49 reset the ATM's attributes userAuthenticated and currentAccountNumber to false and 0, respectively, to prepare for the next ATM user. Line 50 displays a goodbye message to the current user before the ATM welcomes the next user.

33.4.2 Class Screen

Class Screen (Fig. 33.14) represents the screen of the ATM and encapsulates all aspects of displaying output to the user. Class Screen simulates a real ATM's screen with the computer monitor and outputs text messages using standard console output methods

Console.Write and Console.WriteLine. In the design portion of this case study, we endowed class Screen with one operation—DisplayMessage. For greater flexibility in displaying messages to the Screen, we now declare three Screen methods—DisplayMessage, DisplayMessageLine and DisplayDollarAmount.

```
1   // Screen.cs
2   // Represents the screen of the ATM
3   using System;
4
5   public class Screen
6   {
7      // displays a message without a terminating carriage return
8      public void DisplayMessage( string message )
9      {
10        Console.Write( message );
11     } // end method DisplayMessage
12
13     // display a message with a terminating carriage return
14     public void DisplayMessageLine( string message )
15     {
16        Console.WriteLine( message );
17     } // end method DisplayMessageLine
18
19     // display a dollar amount
20     public void DisplayDollarAmount( decimal amount )
21     {
22        Console.Write( "{0:C}", amount );
23     } // end method DisplayDollarAmount
24  } // end class Screen
```

Fig. 33.14 | Class Screen represents the screen of the ATM.

Method DisplayMessage (lines 8–11) takes a string as an argument and prints it to the screen using Console.Write. The cursor stays on the same line, making this method appropriate for displaying prompts to the user. Method DisplayMessageLine (lines 14–17) does the same using Console.WriteLine, which outputs a newline to move the cursor to the next line. Finally, method DisplayDollarAmount (lines 20–23) outputs a properly formatted dollar amount (e.g., $1,234.56). Line 22 uses method Console.Write to output a decimal value formatted as currency with a dollar sign, two decimal places and commas to increase the readability of large dollar amounts.

33.4.3 Class Keypad

Class Keypad (Fig. 33.15) represents the keypad of the ATM and is responsible for receiving all user input. Recall that we are simulating this hardware, so we use the computer's keyboard to approximate the keypad. We use method Console.ReadLine to obtain keyboard input from the user. A computer keyboard contains many keys not found on the ATM's keypad. We assume that the user presses only the keys on the computer keyboard that also appear on the keypad—the keys numbered 0–9 and the *Enter* key.

```
 1   // Keypad.cs
 2   // Represents the keypad of the ATM.
 3   using System;
 4
 5   public class Keypad
 6   {
 7      // return an integer value entered by user
 8      public int GetInput()
 9      {
10         return Convert.ToInt32( Console.ReadLine() );
11      } // end method GetInput
12   } // end class Keypad
```

Fig. 33.15 | Class Keypad represents the ATM's keypad.

Method GetInput (lines 8–11) invokes Convert method ToInt32 to convert the input returned by Console.ReadLine (line 10) to an int value. [*Note:* Method ToInt32 can throw a FormatException if the user enters non-integer input. Because the real ATM's keypad permits only integer input, we simply assume that no exceptions will occur. See Chapter 13 for information on catching and processing exceptions.] Recall that ReadLine obtains all the input used by the ATM. Class Keypad's GetInput method simply returns the integer input by the user. If a client of class Keypad requires input that satisfies some particular criteria (i.e., a number corresponding to a valid menu option), the client must perform the appropriate error checking.

33.4.4 Class CashDispenser

Class CashDispenser (Fig. 33.16) represents the cash dispenser of the ATM. Line 6 declares constant INITIAL_COUNT, which indicates the number of $20 bills in the cash dispenser when the ATM starts (i.e., 500). Line 7 implements attribute billCount (modeled in Fig. 33.10), which keeps track of the number of bills remaining in the CashDispenser at any time. The constructor (lines 10–13) sets billCount to the initial count. [*Note:* We assume that the process of adding more bills to the CashDispenser and updating the billCount occur outside the ATM system.] Class CashDispenser has two public methods—DispenseCash (lines 16–21) and IsSufficientCashAvailable (lines 24–31). The class trusts that a client (i.e., Withdrawal) calls method DispenseCash only after establishing that sufficient cash is available by calling method IsSufficientCashAvailable. Thus, DispenseCash simulates dispensing the requested amount of cash without checking whether sufficient cash is available.

```
 1   // CashDispenser.cs
 2   // Represents the cash dispenser of the ATM
 3   public class CashDispenser
 4   {
 5      // the default initial number of bills in the cash dispenser
 6      private const int INITIAL_COUNT = 500;
 7      private int billCount; // number of $20 bills remaining
```

Fig. 33.16 | Class CashDispenser represents the ATM's cash dispenser. (Part 1 of 2.)

```
 8
 9      // parameterless constructor initializes billCount to INITIAL_COUNT
10      public CashDispenser()
11      {
12         billCount = INITIAL_COUNT; // set billCount to INITIAL_COUNT
13      } // end constructor
14
15      // simulates dispensing the specified amount of cash
16      public void DispenseCash( decimal amount )
17      {
18         // number of $20 bills required
19         int billsRequired = ( ( int ) amount ) / 20;
20         billCount -= billsRequired;
21      } // end method DispenseCash
22
23      // indicates whether cash dispenser can dispense desired amount
24      public bool IsSufficientCashAvailable( decimal amount )
25      {
26         // number of $20 bills required
27         int billsRequired = ( ( int ) amount ) / 20;
28
29         // return whether there are enough bills available
30         return ( billCount >= billsRequired );
31      } // end method IsSufficientCashAvailable
32   } // end class CashDispenser
```

Fig. 33.16 | Class `CashDispenser` represents the ATM's cash dispenser. (Part 2 of 2.)

Method `IsSufficientCashAvailable` (lines 24–31) has a parameter amount that specifies the amount of cash in question. Line 27 calculates the number of $20 bills required to dispense the specified amount. The ATM allows the user to choose only withdrawal amounts that are multiples of $20, so we convert amount to an integer value and divide it by 20 to obtain the number of `billsRequired`. Line 30 returns true if the `CashDispenser`'s `billCount` is greater than or equal to `billsRequired` (i.e., enough bills are available) and `false` otherwise (i.e., not enough bills). For example, if a user wishes to withdraw $80 (i.e., `billsRequired` is 4), but only three bills remain (i.e., `billCount` is 3), the method returns `false`.

Method `DispenseCash` (lines 16–21) simulates cash dispensing. If our system were hooked up to a real hardware cash dispenser, this method would interact with the hardware device to physically dispense the cash. Our simulated version of the method simply decreases the `billCount` of bills remaining by the number required to dispense the specified amount (line 20). It is the responsibility of the client of the class (i.e., `Withdrawal`) to inform the user that cash has been dispensed—`CashDispenser` does not interact directly with `Screen`.

33.4.5 Class `DepositSlot`

Class `DepositSlot` (Fig. 33.17) represents the deposit slot of the ATM. This class simulates the functionality of a real hardware deposit slot. `DepositSlot` has no attributes and only one method—`IsDepositEnvelopeReceived` (lines 7–10)—which indicates whether a deposit envelope was received.

```
 I   // DepositSlot.cs
 2   // Represents the deposit slot of the ATM
 3   public class DepositSlot
 4   {
 5      // indicates whether envelope was received (always returns true,
 6      // because this is only a software simulation of a real deposit slot)
 7      public bool IsDepositEnvelopeReceived()
 8      {
 9         return true; // deposit envelope was received
10      } // end method IsDepositEnvelopeReceived
11   } // end class DepositSlot
```

Fig. 33.17 | Class DepositSlot represents the ATM's deposit slot.

Recall from the requirements document that the ATM allows the user up to two minutes to insert an envelope. The current version of method IsDepositEnvelopeReceived simply returns true immediately (line 9), because this is only a software simulation, so we assume that the user inserts an envelope within the required time frame. If an actual hardware deposit slot were connected to our system, method IsDepositEnvelopeReceived would be implemented to wait for a maximum of two minutes to receive a signal from the hardware deposit slot indicating that the user has indeed inserted a deposit envelope. If IsDepositEnvelopeReceived were to receive such a signal within two minutes, the method would return true. If two minutes were to elapse and the method still had not received a signal, then the method would return false.

33.4.6 Class Account

Class Account (Fig. 33.18) represents a bank account. Each Account has four attributes (modeled in Fig. 33.10)—accountNumber, pin, availableBalance and totalBalance. Lines 5–8 implement these attributes as private instance variables. For each of the instance variables accountNumber, availableBalance and totalBalance, we provide a property with the same name as the attribute, but starting with a capital letter. For example, property AccountNumber corresponds to the accountNumber attribute modeled in Fig. 33.10. Clients of this class do not need to modify the accountNumber instance variable, so AccountNumber is declared as a read-only property (i.e., it provides only a get accessor).

```
 I   // Account.cs
 2   // Class Account represents a bank account.
 3   public class Account
 4   {
 5      private int accountNumber; // account number
 6      private int pin; // PIN for authentication
 7      private decimal availableBalance; // available withdrawal amount
 8      private decimal totalBalance; // funds available + pending deposit
 9
10      // four-parameter constructor initializes attributes
11      public Account( int theAccountNumber, int thePIN,
12         decimal theAvailableBalance, decimal theTotalBalance )
13      {
```

Fig. 33.18 | Class Account represents a bank account. (Part I of 2.)

```
14            accountNumber = theAccountNumber;
15            pin = thePIN;
16            availableBalance = theAvailableBalance;
17            totalBalance = theTotalBalance;
18        } // end constructor
19
20        // read-only property that gets the account number
21        public int AccountNumber
22        {
23            get
24            {
25                return accountNumber;
26            } // end get
27        } // end property AccountNumber
28
29        // read-only property that gets the available balance
30        public decimal AvailableBalance
31        {
32            get
33            {
34                return availableBalance;
35            } // end get
36        } // end property AvailableBalance
37
38        // read-only property that gets the total balance
39        public decimal TotalBalance
40        {
41            get
42            {
43                return totalBalance;
44            } // end get
45        } // end property TotalBalance
46
47        // determines whether a user-specified PIN matches PIN in Account
48        public bool ValidatePIN( int userPIN )
49        {
50            return ( userPIN == pin );
51        } // end method ValidatePIN
52
53        // credits the account (funds have not yet cleared)
54        public void Credit( decimal amount )
55        {
56            totalBalance += amount; // add to total balance
57        } // end method Credit
58
59        // debits the account
60        public void Debit( decimal amount )
61        {
62            availableBalance -= amount; // subtract from available balance
63            totalBalance -= amount; // subtract from total balance
64        } // end method Debit
65    } // end class Account
```

Fig. 33.18 | Class Account represents a bank account. (Part 2 of 2.)

Class Account has a constructor (lines 11–18) that takes an account number, the PIN established for the account, the initial available balance and the initial total balance as arguments. Lines 14–17 assign these values to the class's attributes (i.e., instance variables). Account objects would normally be created externally to the ATM system. However, in this simulation, the Account objects are created in the BankDatabase class (Fig. 33.19).

public Read-Only Properties of Class Account

Read-only property AccountNumber (lines 21–27) provides access to an Account's accountNumber instance variable. We include this property in our implementation so that a client of the class (e.g., BankDatabase) can identify a particular Account. For example, BankDatabase contains many Account objects, and it can access this property on each of its Account objects to locate the one with a specific account number.

Read-only properties AvailableBalance (lines 30–36) and TotalBalance (lines 39–45) allow clients to retrieve the values of private decimal instance variables available-Balance and totalBalance, respectively. Property AvailableBalance represents the amount of funds available for withdrawal. Property TotalBalance represents the amount of funds available, plus the amount of deposited funds pending confirmation of cash in deposit envelopes or clearance of checks in deposit envelopes.

public Methods of Class Account

Method ValidatePIN (lines 48–51) determines whether a user-specified PIN (i.e., parameter userPIN) matches the PIN associated with the account (i.e., attribute pin). Recall that we modeled this method's parameter userPIN in the UML class diagram of Fig. 33.9. If the two PINs match, the method returns true; otherwise, it returns false.

Method Credit (lines 54–57) adds an amount of money (i.e., parameter amount) to an Account as part of a deposit transaction. This method adds the amount only to instance variable totalBalance (line 56). The money credited to an account during a deposit does not become available immediately, so we modify only the total balance. We assume that the bank updates the available balance appropriately at a later time, when the amount of cash in the deposit envelope has be verified and the checks in the deposit envelope have cleared. Our implementation of class Account includes only methods required for carrying out ATM transactions. Therefore, we omit the methods that some other bank system would invoke to add to instance variable availableBalance to confirm a deposit or to subtract from attribute totalBalance to reject a deposit.

Method Debit (lines 60–64) subtracts an amount of money (i.e., parameter amount) from an Account as part of a withdrawal transaction. This method subtracts the amount from both instance variable availableBalance (line 62) and instance variable totalBalance (line 63), because a withdrawal affects both balances.

33.4.7 Class BankDatabase

Class BankDatabase (Fig. 33.19) models the bank database with which the ATM interacts to access and modify a user's account information. We determine one reference-type attribute for class BankDatabase based on its composition relationship with class Account. Recall from Fig. 33.9 that a BankDatabase is composed of zero or more objects of class Account. Line 5 declares attribute accounts—an array that will store Account objects—to implement this composition relationship. Class BankDatabase has a parameterless constructor (lines 8–

15) that initializes accounts with new Account objects (lines 13–14). The Account constructor (Fig. 33.25, lines 11–18) has four parameters—the account number, the PIN assigned to the account, the initial available balance and the initial total balance.

```
1   // BankDatabase.cs
2   // Represents the bank account information database
3   public class BankDatabase
4   {
5      private Account[] accounts; // array of the bank's Accounts
6
7      // parameterless constructor initializes accounts
8      public BankDatabase()
9      {
10        // create two Account objects for testing and
11        // place them in the accounts array
12        accounts = new Account[ 2 ]; // create accounts array
13        accounts[ 0 ] = new Account( 12345, 54321, 1000.00M, 1200.00M );
14        accounts[ 1 ] = new Account( 98765, 56789, 200.00M, 200.00M );
15     } // end constructor
16
17     // retrieve Account object containing specified account number
18     private Account GetAccount( int accountNumber )
19     {
20        // loop through accounts searching for matching account number
21        foreach ( Account currentAccount in accounts )
22        {
23           if ( currentAccount.AccountNumber == accountNumber )
24              return currentAccount;
25        } // end foreach
26
27        // account not found
28        return null;
29     } // end method GetAccount
30
31     // determine whether user-specified account number and PIN match
32     // those of an account in the database
33     public bool AuthenticateUser( int userAccountNumber, int userPIN)
34     {
35        // attempt to retrieve the account with the account number
36        Account userAccount = GetAccount( userAccountNumber );
37
38        // if account exists, return result of Account function ValidatePIN
39        if ( userAccount != null )
40           return userAccount.ValidatePIN( userPIN ); // true if match
41        else
42           return false; // account number not found, so return false
43     } // end method AuthenticateUser
44
45     // return available balance of Account with specified account number
46     public decimal GetAvailableBalance( int userAccountNumber )
47     {
```

Fig. 33.19 | Class BankDatabase represents the bank's account information database. (Part 1 of 2.)

```
48          Account userAccount = GetAccount( userAccountNumber );
49          return userAccount.AvailableBalance;
50      } // end method GetAvailableBalance
51
52      // return total balance of Account with specified account number
53      public decimal GetTotalBalance( int userAccountNumber )
54      {
55          Account userAccount = GetAccount(userAccountNumber);
56          return userAccount.TotalBalance;
57      } // end method GetTotalBalance
58
59      // credit the Account with specified account number
60      public void Credit( int userAccountNumber, decimal amount )
61      {
62          Account userAccount = GetAccount( userAccountNumber );
63          userAccount.Credit( amount );
64      } // end method Credit
65
66      // debit the Account with specified account number
67      public void Debit( int userAccountNumber, decimal amount )
68      {
69          Account userAccount = GetAccount( userAccountNumber );
70          userAccount.Debit( amount );
71      } // end method Debit
72  } // end class BankDatabase
```

Fig. 33.19 | Class BankDatabase represents the bank's account information database. (Part 2 of 2.)

Recall that class BankDatabase serves as an intermediary between class ATM and the actual Account objects that contain users' account information. Thus, methods of class BankDatabase invoke the corresponding methods and properties of the Account object belonging to the current ATM user.

private Utility Method *GetAccount*

We include private utility method GetAccount (lines 18–29) to allow the BankDatabase to obtain a reference to a particular Account within the accounts array. To locate the user's Account, the BankDatabase compares the value returned by property AccountNumber for each element of accounts to a specified account number until it finds a match. Lines 21–25 traverse the accounts array. If currentAccount's account number equals the value of parameter accountNumber, the method returns currentAccount. If no account has the given account number, then line 28 returns null.

public Methods

Method AuthenticateUser (lines 33–43) proves or disproves the identity of an ATM user. This method takes a user-specified account number and a user-specified PIN as arguments and indicates whether they match the account number and PIN of an Account in the database. Line 36 calls method GetAccount, which returns either an Account with userAccountNumber as its account number or null to indicate that userAccountNumber is invalid. If GetAccount returns an Account object, line 40 returns the bool value returned by that object's ValidatePIN method. BankDatabase's AuthenticateUser method does not perform the PIN comparison itself—rather, it forwards userPIN to the Account object's Validate-PIN method to do so. The value returned by Account method ValidatePIN (line 40) indicates whether the user-specified PIN matches the PIN of the user's Account, so method AuthenticateUser simply returns this value (line 40) to the client of the class (i.e., ATM).

The BankDatabase trusts the ATM to invoke method AuthenticateUser and receive a return value of true before allowing the user to perform transactions. BankDatabase also trusts that each Transaction object created by the ATM contains the valid account number of the current authenticated user and that this account number is passed to the remaining BankDatabase methods as argument userAccountNumber. Methods GetAvailableBalance (lines 46–50), GetTotalBalance (lines 53–57), Credit (lines 60–64) and Debit (lines 67–71) therefore simply retrieve the user's Account object with utility method GetAccount, then invoke the appropriate Account method on that object. We know that the calls to GetAccount within these methods will never return null, because userAccountNumber must refer to an existing Account. GetAvailableBalance and GetTotalBalance return the values returned by the corresponding Account properties. Also, methods Credit and Debit simply redirect parameter amount to the Account methods they invoke.

33.4.8 Class Transaction

Class Transaction (Fig. 33.20) is an abstract base class that represents the notion of an ATM transaction. It contains the common features of derived classes BalanceInquiry, Withdrawal and Deposit. This class expands on the "skeleton" code first developed in Section 33.2. Line 3 declares this class to be abstract. Lines 5–7 declare the class's private instance variables. Recall from the class diagram of Fig. 33.10 that class Transaction contains the property AccountNumber that indicates the account involved in the Transaction. Line 5 implements the instance variable accountNumber to maintain the AccountNumber property's data. We derive attributes screen (implemented as instance variable userScreen in line 6) and bankDatabase (implemented as instance variable database in line 7) from class Transaction's associations, modeled in Fig. 33.9. All transactions require access to the ATM's screen and the bank's database.

Class Transaction has a constructor (lines 10–16) that takes the current user's account number and references to the ATM's screen and the bank's database as arguments. Because Transaction is an abstract class (line 3), this constructor is never called directly to instantiate Transaction objects. Instead, this constructor is invoked by the constructors of the Transaction derived classes via constructor initializers.

Class Transaction has three public read-only properties—AccountNumber (lines 19–25), UserScreen (lines 28–34) and Database (lines 37–43). Derived classes of Transaction inherit these properties and use them to gain access to class Transaction's private instance variables. We chose the names of the UserScreen and Database properties for clarity—we wanted to avoid property names that are the same as the class names Screen and BankDatabase, which can be confusing.

Class Transaction also declares abstract method Execute (line 46). It does not make sense to provide an implementation for this method in class Transaction, because a generic transaction cannot be executed. Thus, we declare this method to be abstract, forcing each Transaction concrete derived class to provide its own implementation that executes the particular type of transaction.

```
1   // Transaction.cs
2   // Abstract base class Transaction represents an ATM transaction.
3   public abstract class Transaction
4   {
5      private int accountNumber; // account involved in the transaction
6      private Screen userScreen; // reference to ATM's screen
7      private BankDatabase database; // reference to account info database
8
9      // three-parameter constructor invoked by derived classes
10     public Transaction( int userAccount, Screen theScreen,
11        BankDatabase theDatabase )
12     {
13        accountNumber = userAccount;
14        userScreen = theScreen;
15        database = theDatabase;
16     } // end constructor
17
18     // read-only property that gets the account number
19     public int AccountNumber
20     {
21        get
22        {
23           return accountNumber;
24        } // end get
25     } // end property AccountNumber
26
27     // read-only property that gets the screen reference
28     public Screen UserScreen
29     {
30        get
31        {
32           return userScreen;
33        } // end get
34     } // end property UserScreen
35
36     // read-only property that gets the bank database reference
37     public BankDatabase Database
38     {
39        get
40        {
41           return database;
42        } // end get
43     } // end property Database
44
45     // perform the transaction (overridden by each derived class)
46     public abstract void Execute(); // no implementation here
47  } // end class Transaction
```

Fig. 33.20 | abstract base class Transaction represents an ATM transaction.

33.4.9 Class BalanceInquiry

Class BalanceInquiry (Fig. 33.21) inherits from Transaction and represents an ATM
balance inquiry transaction (line 3). BalanceInquiry does not have any attributes of its
own, but it inherits Transaction attributes accountNumber, screen and bankDatabase,

which are accessible through Transaction's public read-only properties. The BalanceInquiry constructor (lines 6–8) takes arguments corresponding to these attributes and forwards them to Transaction's constructor by invoking the constructor initializer with keyword base (line 8). The body of the constructor is empty.

Class BalanceInquiry overrides Transaction's abstract method Execute to provide a concrete implementation (lines 11–27) that performs the steps involved in a balance inquiry. Lines 14–15 obtain the specified Account's available balance by invoking the GetAvailableBalance method of the inherited property Database. Line 15 uses the inherited property AccountNumber to get the account number of the current user. Line 18 retrieves the specified Account's total balance. Lines 21–26 display the balance information on the ATM's screen using the inherited property UserScreen. Recall that DisplayDollarAmount takes a decimal argument and outputs it to the screen formatted as a dollar amount with a dollar sign. For example, if a user's available balance is 1000.50M, line 23 outputs $1,000.50. Line 26 inserts a blank line of output to separate the balance information from subsequent output (i.e., the main menu repeated by class ATM after executing the BalanceInquiry).

```
1   // BalanceInquiry.cs
2   // Represents a balance inquiry ATM transaction
3   public class BalanceInquiry : Transaction
4   {
5      // five-parameter constructor initializes base class variables
6      public BalanceInquiry( int userAccountNumber,
7         Screen atmScreen, BankDatabase atmBankDatabase )
8         : base( userAccountNumber, atmScreen, atmBankDatabase ) {}
9
10     // performs transaction; overrides Transaction's abstract method
11     public override void Execute()
12     {
13        // get the available balance for the current user's Account
14        decimal availableBalance =
15           Database.GetAvailableBalance( AccountNumber );
16
17        // get the total balance for the current user's Account
18        decimal totalBalance = Database.GetTotalBalance( AccountNumber );
19
20        // display the balance information on the screen
21        UserScreen.DisplayMessageLine( "\nBalance Information:" );
22        UserScreen.DisplayMessage( " - Available balance: " );
23        UserScreen.DisplayDollarAmount( availableBalance );
24        UserScreen.DisplayMessage( "\n - Total balance: " );
25        UserScreen.DisplayDollarAmount( totalBalance );
26        UserScreen.DisplayMessageLine( "" );
27     } // end method Execute
28  } // end class BalanceInquiry
```

Fig. 33.21 | Class BalanceInquiry represents a balance inquiry ATM transaction.

33.4.10 Class Withdrawal

Class Withdrawal (Fig. 33.22) extends Transaction and represents an ATM withdrawal transaction. This class expands on the "skeleton" code for this class developed in

Fig. 33.11. Recall from the class diagram of Fig. 33.9 that class Withdrawal has one attribute, amount, which line 5 declares as a decimal instance variable. Figure 33.9 models associations between class Withdrawal and classes Keypad and CashDispenser, for which lines 6–7 implement reference attributes keypad and cashDispenser, respectively. Line 10 declares a constant corresponding to the cancel menu option.

```csharp
1   // Withdrawal.cs
2   // Class Withdrawal represents an ATM withdrawal transaction.
3   public class Withdrawal : Transaction
4   {
5      private decimal amount; // amount to withdraw
6      private Keypad keypad; // reference to Keypad
7      private CashDispenser cashDispenser; // reference to cash dispenser
8
9      // constant that corresponds to menu option to cancel
10     private const int CANCELED = 6;
11
12     // five-parameter constructor
13     public Withdrawal( int userAccountNumber, Screen atmScreen,
14        BankDatabase atmBankDatabase, Keypad atmKeypad,
15        CashDispenser atmCashDispenser )
16        : base( userAccountNumber, atmScreen, atmBankDatabase )
17     {
18        // initialize references to keypad and cash dispenser
19        keypad = atmKeypad;
20        cashDispenser = atmCashDispenser;
21     } // end constructor
22
23     // perform transaction, overrides Transaction's abstract method
24     public override void Execute()
25     {
26        bool cashDispensed = false; // cash was not dispensed yet
27
28        // transaction was not canceled yet
29        bool transactionCanceled = false;
30
31        // loop until cash is dispensed or the user cancels
32        do
33        {
34           // obtain the chosen withdrawal amount from the user
35           int selection = DisplayMenuOfAmounts();
36
37           // check whether user chose a withdrawal amount or canceled
38           if ( selection != CANCELED )
39           {
40              // set amount to the selected dollar amount
41              amount = selection;
42
43              // get available balance of account involved
44              decimal availableBalance =
45                 Database.GetAvailableBalance( AccountNumber );
46
```

Fig. 33.22 | Class Withdrawal represents an ATM withdrawal transaction. (Part 1 of 3.)

```
47              // check whether the user has enough money in the account
48              if ( amount <= availableBalance )
49              {
50                  // check whether the cash dispenser has enough money
51                  if ( cashDispenser.IsSufficientCashAvailable( amount ) )
52                  {
53                      // debit the account to reflect the withdrawal
54                      Database.Debit( AccountNumber, amount );
55
56                      cashDispenser.DispenseCash( amount ); // dispense cash
57                      cashDispensed = true; // cash was dispensed
58
59                      // instruct user to take cash
60                      UserScreen.DisplayMessageLine(
61                          "\nPlease take your cash from the cash dispenser." );
62                  } // end innermost if
63                  else // cash dispenser does not have enough cash
64                      UserScreen.DisplayMessageLine(
65                          "\nInsufficient cash available in the ATM." +
66                          "\n\nPlease choose a smaller amount." );
67              } // end middle if
68              else // not enough money available in user's account
69                  UserScreen.DisplayMessageLine(
70                      "\nInsufficient cash available in your account." +
71                      "\n\nPlease choose a smaller amount." );
72          } // end outermost if
73          else
74          {
75              UserScreen.DisplayMessageLine( "\nCanceling transaction..." );
76              transactionCanceled = true; // user canceled the transaction
77          } // end else
78      } while ( ( !cashDispensed ) && ( !transactionCanceled ) );
79  } // end method Execute
80
81  // display a menu of withdrawal amounts and the option to cancel;
82  // return the chosen amount or 6 if the user chooses to cancel
83  private int DisplayMenuOfAmounts()
84  {
85      int userChoice = 0; // variable to store return value
86
87      // array of amounts to correspond to menu numbers
88      int[] amounts = { 0, 20, 40, 60, 100, 200 };
89
90      // loop while no valid choice has been made
91      while ( userChoice == 0 )
92      {
93          // display the menu
94          UserScreen.DisplayMessageLine( "\nWithdrawal options:" );
95          UserScreen.DisplayMessageLine( "1 - $20" );
96          UserScreen.DisplayMessageLine( "2 - $40" );
97          UserScreen.DisplayMessageLine( "3 - $60" );
98          UserScreen.DisplayMessageLine( "4 - $100" );
99          UserScreen.DisplayMessageLine( "5 - $200" );
```

Fig. 33.22 | Class `Withdrawal` represents an ATM withdrawal transaction. (Part 2 of 3.)

```
100          UserScreen.DisplayMessageLine( "6 - Cancel transaction" );
101          UserScreen.DisplayMessage(
102             "\nChoose a withdrawal option (1-6): " );
103
104          // get user input through keypad
105          int input = keypad.GetInput();
106
107          // determine how to proceed based on the input value
108          switch ( input )
109          {
110             // if the user chose a withdrawal amount (i.e., option
111             // 1, 2, 3, 4, or 5), return the corresponding amount
112             // from the amounts array
113             case 1: case 2: case 3: case 4: case 5:
114                userChoice = amounts[ input ]; // save user's choice
115                break;
116             case CANCELED: // the user chose to cancel
117                userChoice = CANCELED; // save user's choice
118                break;
119             default:
120                UserScreen.DisplayMessageLine(
121                   "\nInvalid selection. Try again." );
122                break;
123          } // end switch
124       } // end while
125
126       return userChoice;
127    } // end method DisplayMenuOfAmounts
128 } // end class Withdrawal
```

Fig. 33.22 | Class Withdrawal represents an ATM withdrawal transaction. (Part 3 of 3.)

Class Withdrawal's constructor (lines 13–21) has five parameters. It uses the constructor initializer to pass parameters userAccountNumber, atmScreen and atmBankDatabase to base class Transaction's constructor to set the attributes that Withdrawal inherits from Transaction. The constructor also takes references atmKeypad and atmCash-Dispenser as parameters and assigns them to reference-type attributes keypad and cash-Dispenser, respectively.

Overriding **abstract** *Method* **Execute**
Class Withdrawal overrides Transaction's abstract method Execute with a concrete implementation (lines 24–79) that performs the steps involved in a withdrawal. Line 26 declares and initializes a local bool variable cashDispensed. This variable indicates whether cash has been dispensed (i.e., whether the transaction has completed successfully) and is initially false. Line 29 declares and initializes to false a bool variable transactionCanceled to indicate that the transaction has not yet been canceled by the user.

Lines 32–78 contain a do...while statement that executes its body until cash is dispensed (i.e., until cashDispensed becomes true) or until the user chooses to cancel (i.e., until transactionCanceled becomes true). We use this loop to continuously return the user to the start of the transaction if an error occurs (i.e., the requested withdrawal amount is greater than the user's available balance or greater than the amount of cash in the cash dispenser). Line 35 displays a menu of withdrawal amounts and obtains a user selection by calling private utility method DisplayMenuOfAmounts (declared in lines 83–127). This method displays the menu of amounts and returns either an int withdrawal amount or an int constant CANCELED to indicate that the user has chosen to cancel the transaction.

Displaying Options With **private** *Utility Method* **DisplayMenuOfAmounts**

Method DisplayMenuOfAmounts (lines 83–127) first declares local variable userChoice (initially 0) to store the value that the method will return (line 85). Line 88 declares an integer array of withdrawal amounts that correspond to the amounts displayed in the withdrawal menu. We ignore the first element in the array (index 0), because the menu has no option 0. The while statement at lines 91–124 repeats until userChoice takes on a value other than 0. We will see shortly that this occurs when the user makes a valid selection from the menu. Lines 94–102 display the withdrawal menu on the screen and prompt the user to enter a choice. Line 105 obtains integer input through the keypad. The switch statement at lines 108–123 determines how to proceed based on the user's input. If the user selects 1, 2, 3, 4 or 5, line 114 sets userChoice to the value of the element in the amounts array at index input. For example, if the user enters 3 to withdraw $60, line 114 sets user-Choice to the value of amounts[3]—i.e., 60. Variable userChoice no longer equals 0, so the while at lines 91–124 terminates, and line 126 returns userChoice. If the user selects the cancel menu option, line 117 executes, setting userChoice to CANCELED and causing the method to return this value. If the user does not enter a valid menu selection, lines 120–121 display an error message, and the user is returned to the withdrawal menu.

The if statement at line 38 in method Execute determines whether the user has selected a withdrawal amount or chosen to cancel. If the user cancels, line 75 displays an appropriate message to the user before control is returned to the calling method—ATM method PerformTransactions. If the user has chosen a withdrawal amount, line 41 assigns local variable selection to instance variable amount. Lines 44–45 retrieve the available balance of the current user's Account and store it in a local decimal variable availableBalance. Next, the if statement at line 48 determines whether the selected amount is less than or equal to the user's available balance. If it is not, lines 69–71 display an error message. Control then continues to the end of the do...while statement, and the loop repeats because both cashDispensed and transactionCanceled are still false. If the user's balance is high enough, the if statement at line 51 determines whether the cash dispenser has enough money to satisfy the withdrawal request by invoking the cash-Dispenser's IsSufficientCashAvailable method. If this method returns false, lines 64–66 display an error message, and the do...while statement repeats. If sufficient cash is available, the requirements for the withdrawal are satisfied, and line 54 debits the user's account in the database by amount. Lines 56–57 then instruct the cash dispenser to dispense the cash to the user and set cashDispensed to true. Finally, lines 60–61 display a message to the user to take the dispensed cash. Because cashDispensed is now true, control continues after the do...while statement. No additional statements appear below the loop, so the method returns control to class ATM.

33.4.11 Class **Deposit**

Class Deposit (Fig. 33.23) inherits from Transaction and represents an ATM deposit transaction. Recall from the class diagram of Fig. 33.10 that class Deposit has one attribute, amount, which line 5 declares as a decimal instance variable. Lines 6–7 create reference attributes keypad and depositSlot that implement the associations between class Deposit and classes Keypad and DepositSlot, modeled in Fig. 33.9. Line 10 declares a constant CANCELED that corresponds to the value a user enters to cancel a deposit transaction.

```
1   // Deposit.cs
2   // Represents a deposit ATM transaction.
3   public class Deposit : Transaction
4   {
5      private decimal amount; // amount to deposit
6      private Keypad keypad; // reference to the Keypad
7      private DepositSlot depositSlot; // reference to the deposit slot
8
9      // constant representing cancel option
10     private const int CANCELED = 0;
11
12     // five-parameter constructor initializes class's instance variables
13     public Deposit( int userAccountNumber, Screen atmScreen,
14        BankDatabase atmBankDatabase, Keypad atmKeypad,
15        DepositSlot atmDepositSlot )
16        : base( userAccountNumber, atmScreen, atmBankDatabase )
17     {
18        // initialize references to keypad and deposit slot
19        keypad = atmKeypad;
20        depositSlot = atmDepositSlot;
21     } // end five-parameter constructor
22
23     // perform transaction; overrides Transaction's abstract method
24     public override void Execute()
25     {
26        amount = PromptForDepositAmount(); // get deposit amount from user
27
28        // check whether user entered a deposit amount or canceled
29        if ( amount != CANCELED )
30        {
31           // request deposit envelope containing specified amount
32           UserScreen.DisplayMessage(
33              "\nPlease insert a deposit envelope containing " );
34           UserScreen.DisplayDollarAmount( amount );
35           UserScreen.DisplayMessageLine( " in the deposit slot." );
36
37           // retrieve deposit envelope
38           bool envelopeReceived = depositSlot.IsDepositEnvelopeReceived();
39
40           // check whether deposit envelope was received
41           if ( envelopeReceived )
42           {
43              UserScreen.DisplayMessageLine(
44                 "\nYour envelope has been received.\n" +
45                 "The money just deposited will not be available " +
46                 "until we \nverify the amount of any " +
47                 "enclosed cash, and any enclosed checks clear." );
```

Fig. 33.23 | Class Deposit represents an ATM deposit transaction. (Part 1 of 2.)

```
48
49                    // credit account to reflect the deposit
50                    Database.Credit( AccountNumber, amount );
51               } // end inner if
52               else
53                  UserScreen.DisplayMessageLine(
54                     "\nYou did not insert an envelope, so the ATM has " +
55                     "canceled your transaction." );
56            } // end outer if
57            else
58               UserScreen.DisplayMessageLine( "\nCanceling transaction..." );
59         } // end method Execute
60
61         // prompt user to enter a deposit amount to credit
62         private decimal PromptForDepositAmount()
63         {
64            // display the prompt and receive input
65            UserScreen.DisplayMessage(
66               "\nPlease input a deposit amount in CENTS (or 0 to cancel): " );
67            int input = keypad.GetInput();
68
69            // check whether the user canceled or entered a valid amount
70            if ( input == CANCELED )
71               return CANCELED;
72            else
73               return input / 100.00M;
74         } // end method PromptForDepositAmount
75      } // end class Deposit
```

Fig. 33.23 | Class Deposit represents an ATM deposit transaction. (Part 2 of 2.)

Class Deposit contains a constructor (lines 13–21) that passes three parameters to base class Transaction's constructor using a constructor initializer. The constructor also has parameters atmKeypad and atmDepositSlot, which it assigns to the corresponding reference instance variables (lines 19–20).

Overriding abstract Method Execute

Method Execute (lines 24–59) overrides abstract method Execute in base class Transaction with a concrete implementation that performs the steps required in a deposit transaction. Line 26 prompts the user to enter a deposit amount by invoking private utility method PromptForDepositAmount (declared in lines 62–74) and sets attribute amount to the value returned. Method PromptForDepositAmount asks the user to enter a deposit amount as an integer number of cents (because the ATM's keypad does not contain a decimal point; this is consistent with many real ATMs) and returns the decimal value representing the dollar amount to be deposited.

Getting Deposit Amount with private Utility Method PromptForDepositAmount

Lines 65–66 in method PromptForDepositAmount display a message asking the user to input a deposit amount as a number of cents or "0" to cancel the transaction. Line 67 receives the user's input from the keypad. The if statement at lines 70–73 determines whether the user has entered a deposit amount or chosen to cancel. If the user chooses to cancel, line 71 returns constant CANCELED. Otherwise, line 73 returns the deposit amount after converting the int number of cents to a dollar-and-cents amount by dividing by the decimal literal 100.00M. For example, if the user enters 125 as the number of cents, line 73 returns 125 divided by 100.00M, or 1.25—125 cents is $1.25.

The if statement at lines 29–58 in method Execute determines whether the user has chosen to cancel the transaction instead of entering a deposit amount. If the user cancels, line 58 displays an appropriate message, and the method returns. If the user enters a deposit amount, lines 32–35 instruct the user to insert a deposit envelope with the correct amount. Recall that Screen method DisplayDollarAmount outputs a decimal value formatted as a dollar amount (including the dollar sign).

Line 38 sets a local bool variable to the value returned by depositSlot's IsDepositEnvelopeReceived method, indicating whether a deposit envelope has been received. Recall that we coded method IsDepositEnvelopeReceived (lines 7–10 of Fig. 33.17) to always return true, because we are simulating the functionality of the deposit slot and assume that the user always inserts an envelope in a timely fashion (i.e., within the two-minute time limit). However, we code method Execute of class Deposit to test for the possibility that the user does not insert an envelope—good software engineering demands that programs account for all possible return values. Thus, class Deposit is prepared for future versions of IsDepositEnvelopeReceived that could return false. Lines 43–50 execute if the deposit slot receives an envelope. Lines 43–47 display an appropriate message to the user. Line 50 credits the user's account in the database with the deposit amount. Lines 53–55 execute if the deposit slot does not receive a deposit envelope. In this case, we display a message stating that the ATM has canceled the transaction. The method then returns without crediting the user's account.

33.4.12 Class ATMCaseStudy

Class ATMCaseStudy (Fig. 33.24) simply allows us to start, or "turn on," the ATM and test the implementation of our ATM system model. Class ATMCaseStudy's Main method (lines 6–10) simply instantiates a new ATM object named theATM (line 8) and invokes its Run method (line 9) to start the ATM.

```
1   // ATMCaseStudy.cs
2   // App for testing the ATM case study.
3   public class ATMCaseStudy
4   {
5      // Main method is the app's entry point
6      public static void Main( string[] args )
7      {
8         ATM theATM = new ATM();
9         theATM.Run();
10     } // end method Main
11  } // end class ATMCaseStudy
```

Fig. 33.24 | Class ATMCaseStudy starts the ATM.

33.5 Wrap-Up

In this chapter, you used inheritance to tune the design of the ATM software system, and you fully implemented the ATM in C#. Congratulations on completing the entire ATM case study! We hope you found this experience to be valuable and that it reinforced many of the object-oriented programming concepts that you've learned.

Answers to Self-Review Exercises

33.1 True. The minus sign (–) indicates private visibility.

33.2 b.

33.3 The design for class Account yields the code in Fig. 33.25. We used public auto-implemented properties AvailableBalance and TotalBalance to store the data that methods Credit and Debit, will manipulate.

```
 1   // Fig. 33.25: Account.cs
 2   // Class Account represents a bank account.
 3   public class Account
 4   {
 5      private int accountNumber; // account number
 6      private int pin; // PIN for authentication
 7
 8      // automatic read-only property AvailableBalance
 9      public decimal AvailableBalance { get; private set; }
10
11      // automatic read-only property TotalBalance
12      public decimal TotalBalance { get; private set; }
13
14      // parameterless constructor
15      public Account()
16      {
17         // constructor body code
18      } // end constructor
19
20      // validates user PIN
21      public bool ValidatePIN()
22      {
23         // ValidatePIN method body code
24      } // end method ValidatePIN
25
26      // credits the account
27      public void Credit()
28      {
29         // Credit method body code
30      } // end method Credit
31
32      // debits the account
33      public void Debit()
34      {
35         // Debit method body code
36      } // end method Debit
37   } // end class Account
```

Fig. 33.25 | C# code for class Account based on Figs. 33.1 and 33.2.

33.4 b.

33.5 False. The UML requires that we italicize abstract class names and operation names.

33.6   The design for class `Transaction` yields the code in Fig. 33.26. In the implementation, a constructor initializes `private` instance variables `userScreen` and `database` to actual objects, and read-only properties `UserScreen` and `Database` access these instance variables. These properties allow classes derived from `Transaction` to access the ATM's screen and interact with the bank's database. We chose the names of the `UserScreen` and `Database` properties for clarity—we wanted to avoid property names that are the same as the class names `Screen` and `BankDatabase`, which can be confusing.

```
1   // Fig. 33.26: Transaction.cs
2   // Abstract base class Transaction represents an ATM transaction.
3   public abstract class Transaction
4   {
5      private int accountNumber; // indicates account involved
6      private Screen userScreen; // ATM's screen
7      private BankDatabase database; // account info database
8
9      // parameterless constructor
10     public Transaction()
11     {
12        // constructor body code
13     } // end constructor
14
15     // read-only property that gets the account number
16     public int AccountNumber
17     {
18        get
19        {
20           return accountNumber;
21        } // end get
22     } // end property AccountNumber
23
24     // read-only property that gets the screen reference
25     public Screen UserScreen
26     {
27        get
28        {
29           return userScreen;
30        } // end get
31     } // end property UserScreen
32
33     // read-only property that gets the bank database reference
34     public BankDatabase Database
35     {
36        get
37        {
38           return database;
39        } // end get
40     } // end property Database
41
42     // perform the transaction (overridden by each derived class)
43     public abstract void Execute();
44  } // end class Transaction
```

Fig. 33.26 | C# code for class `Transaction` based on Figures 33.9 and 33.10.

Operator Precedence Chart

Operators are shown in decreasing order of precedence from top to bottom with each level of precedence separated by a horizontal line. The associativity of the operators is shown in the right column.

Operator	Type	Associativity
.	member access	left-to-right
()	method call	
[]	element access	
++	postfix increment	
--	postfix decrement	
new	object creation	
typeof	get System.Type object for a type	
sizeof	get size in bytes of a type	
checked	checked evaluation	
unchecked	unchecked evaluation	
+	unary plus	right-to-left
-	unary minus	
!	logical negation	
~	bitwise complement	
++	prefix increment	
--	prefix decrement	
(*type*)	cast	

Fig. A.1 | Operator precedence chart (Part 1 of 2.).

Operator	Type	Associativity
*	multiplication	left-to-right
/	division	
%	remainder	
+	addition	left-to-right
-	subtraction	
>>	right shift	left-to-right
<<	left shift	
<	less than	left-to-right
>	greater than	
<=	less than or equal to	
>=	greater than or equal to	
is	type comparison	
as	type conversion	
!=	is not equal to	left-to-right
==	is equal to	
&	logical AND	left-to-right
^	logical XOR	left-to-right
|	logical OR	left-to-right
&&	conditional AND	left-to-right
||	conditional OR	left-to-right
??	null coalescing	right-to-left
?:	conditional	right-to-left
=	assignment	right-to-left
*=	multiplication assignment	
/=	division assignment	
%=	remainder assignment	
+=	addition assignment	
-=	subtraction assignment	
<<=	left shift assignment	
>>=	right shift assignment	
&=	logical AND assignment	
^=	logical XOR assignment	
|=	logical OR assignment	

Fig. A.1 | Operator precedence chart (Part 2 of 2.).

Simple Types

Type	Size in bits	Value range	Standard
bool	8	true or false	
byte	8	0 to 255, inclusive	
sbyte	8	−128 to 127, inclusive	
char	16	'\u0000' to '\uFFFF' (0 to 65535), inclusive	Unicode
short	16	−32768 to 32767, inclusive	
ushort	16	0 to 65535, inclusive	
int	32	−2,147,483,648 to 2,147,483,647, inclusive	
uint	32	0 to 4,294,967,295, inclusive	
float	32	*Approximate negative range:* −3.4028234663852886E+38 to −1.40129846432481707E−45 *Approximate positive range:* 1.40129846432481707E−45 to 3.4028234663852886E+38 *Other supported values:* positive and negative zero positive and negative infinity not-a-number (NaN)	IEEE 754 IEC 60559
long	64	−9,223,372,036,854,775,808 to 9,223,372,036,854,775,807, inclusive	
ulong	64	0 to 18,446,744,073,709,551,615, inclusive	

Fig. B.1 | Simple types. (Part 1 of 2.)

Type	Size in bits	Value range	Standard
double	64	*Approximate negative range:* –1.7976931348623157E+308 to –4.94065645841246544E–324 *Approximate positive range:* 4.94065645841246544E–324 to 1.7976931348623157E+308 *Other supported values:* positive and negative zero positive and negative infinity not-a-number (NaN)	IEEE 754 IEC 60559
decimal	128	*Negative range:* –79,228,162,514,264,337,593,543,950,335 (–7.9E+28) to –1.0E–28 *Positive range:* 1.0E–28 to 79,228,162,514,264,337,593,543,950,335 (7.9E+28)	

Fig. B.1 | Simple types. (Part 2 of 2.)

Additional Simple Type Information

- This appendix is based on information from Sections 4.1.4–4.1.8 of Microsoft's version of the *C# Language Specification* and Sections 11.1.4–11.1.8 of the ECMA-334 (the ECMA version of the *C# Language Specification*). These documents are available from the following websites:

  msdn.microsoft.com/en-us/vcsharp/aa336809.aspx
  www.ecma-international.org/publications/standards/Ecma-334.htm

- Values of type float have seven digits of precision.

- Values of type double have 15–16 digits of precision.

- Values of type decimal are represented as integer values that are scaled by a power of 10. Values between –1.0 and 1.0 are represented exactly to 28 digits.

- For more information on IEEE 754 visit grouper.ieee.org/groups/754/. For more information on Unicode, see Appendix F.

C

ASCII Character Set

	0	1	2	3	4	5	6	7	8	9
0	nul	soh	stx	etx	eot	enq	ack	bel	bs	ht
1	nl	vt	ff	cr	so	si	dle	dc1	dc2	dc3
2	dc4	nak	syn	etb	can	em	sub	esc	fs	gs
3	rs	us	sp	!	"	#	$	%	&	'
4	(	)	*	+	,	-	.	/	0	1
5	2	3	4	5	6	7	8	9	:	;
6	<	=	>	?	@	A	B	C	D	E
7	F	G	H	I	J	K	L	M	N	O
8	P	Q	R	S	T	U	V	W	X	Y
9	Z	[	\	]	^	_	'	a	b	c
10	d	e	f	g	h	i	j	k	l	m
11	n	o	p	q	r	s	t	u	v	w
12	x	y	z	{			}	~	del		

Fig. C.1 | ASCII Character Set.

The digits at the left of the table are the left digits of the decimal equivalent (0–127) of the character code, and the digits at the top of the table are the right digits of the character code. For example, the character code for "F" is 70, and the character code for "&" is 38.

Most users of this book are interested in the ASCII character set used to represent English characters on many computers. The ASCII character set is a subset of the Unicode character set used by C# to represent characters from most of the world's languages. For more information on the Unicode character set, see Appendix F.

Number Systems

Objectives

In this appendix you'll:

- Learn number systems concepts, such as base, positional value and symbol value.
- Work with numbers represented in the binary, octal and hexadecimal number systems.
- Abbreviate binary numbers as octal numbers or hexadecimal numbers.
- Convert octal numbers and hexadecimal numbers to binary numbers.
- Convert between decimal, binary, octal and hexadecimal.
- Learn binary arithmetic and representing negative binary numbers using two's complement notation.

D.1 Introduction

In this appendix, we introduce the key number systems that programmers use, especially when they're working on software projects that require close interaction with machine-level hardware. Projects like this include operating systems, computer networking software, compilers, database systems and applications requiring high performance.

When we write an integer such as 227 or –63 in a program, the number is assumed to be in the decimal (base 10) number system. The digits in the decimal number system are 0, 1, 2, 3, 4, 5, 6, 7, 8 and 9. The lowest digit is 0 and the highest digit is 9—one less than the base of 10. Internally, computers use the binary (base 2) number system. The binary number system has only two digits, namely 0 and 1. Its lowest digit is 0 and its highest digit is 1—one less than the base of 2.

As we'll see, binary numbers tend to be much longer than their decimal equivalents. Programmers who work in assembly languages and in high-level languages like C# that enable programmers to reach down to the machine level, find it cumbersome to work with binary numbers. So two other number systems—the octal number system (base 8) and the hexadecimal number system (base 16)—are popular primarily because they make it convenient to abbreviate binary numbers.

In the octal number system, the digits range from 0 to 7. Because both the binary number system and the octal number system have fewer digits than the decimal number system, their digits are the same as the corresponding digits in decimal.

The hexadecimal number system poses a problem because it requires 16 digits—a lowest digit of 0 and a highest digit with a value equivalent to decimal 15 (one less than the base of 16). By convention, we use the letters A through F to represent the hexadecimal digits corresponding to decimal values 10 through 15. Thus in hexadecimal we can have numbers like 876 consisting solely of decimal-like digits, numbers like 8A55F consisting of digits and letters and numbers like FFE consisting solely of letters. Occasionally, a hexadecimal number spells a common word such as FACE or FEED—this can appear strange to programmers accustomed to working with numbers. The digits of the binary, octal, decimal and hexadecimal number systems are summarized in Fig. D.1–Fig. D.2.

Each of these number systems uses positional notation—each position in which a digit is written has a different positional value. For example, in the decimal number 937 (the 9, the 3 and the 7 are referred to as symbol values), we say that the 7 is written in the ones position, the 3 is written in the tens position and the 9 is written in the hundreds position. Each of these positions is a power of the base (base 10) and that these powers begin at 0 and increase by 1 as we move left in the number (Fig. D.3).

Binary digit	Octal digit	Decimal digit	Hexadecimal digit
0	0	0	0
1	1	1	1
	2	2	2
	3	3	3
	4	4	4
	5	5	5
	6	6	6
	7	7	7
		8	8
		9	9
			A (decimal value of 10)
			B (decimal value of 11)
			C (decimal value of 12)
			D (decimal value of 13)
			E (decimal value of 14)
			F (decimal value of 15)

Fig. D.1 | Digits of the binary, octal, decimal and hexadecimal number systems.

Attribute	Binary	Octal	Decimal	Hexadecimal
Base	2	8	10	16
Lowest digit	0	0	0	0
Highest digit	1	7	9	F

Fig. D.2 | Comparing the binary, octal, decimal and hexadecimal number systems.

Positional values in the decimal number system			
Decimal digit	9	3	7
Position name	Hundreds	Tens	Ones
Positional value	100	10	1
Positional value as a power of the base (10)	10^2	10^1	10^0

Fig. D.3 | Positional values in the decimal number system.

For longer decimal numbers, the next positions to the left would be the thousands position (10 to the 3rd power), the ten-thousands position (10 to the 4th power), the hundred-thousands position (10 to the 5th power), the millions position (10 to the 6th power), the ten-millions position (10 to the 7th power) and so on.

In the binary number 101, the rightmost 1 is written in the ones position, the 0 is written in the twos position and the leftmost 1 is written in the fours position. Each position is a power of the base (base 2) and these powers begin at 0 and increase by 1 as we move left in the number (Fig. D.4). So, $101 = 1 * 2^2 + 0 * 2^1 + 1 * 2^0 = 4 + 0 + 1 = 5$.

Positional values in the binary number system			
Binary digit	1	0	1
Position name	Fours	Twos	Ones
Positional value	4	2	1
Positional value as a power of the base (2)	2^2	2^1	2^0

Fig. D.4 | Positional values in the binary number system.

For longer binary numbers, the next positions to the left would be the eights position (2 to the 3rd power), the sixteens position (2 to the 4th power), the thirty-twos position (2 to the 5th power), the sixty-fours position (2 to the 6th power) and so on.

In the octal number 425, we say that the 5 is written in the ones position, the 2 is written in the eights position and the 4 is written in the sixty-fours position. Each of these positions is a power of the base (base 8) and that these powers begin at 0 and increase by 1 as we move left in the number (Fig. D.5).

Positional values in the octal number system			
Decimal digit	4	2	5
Position name	Sixty-fours	Eights	Ones
Positional value	64	8	1
Positional value as a power of the base (8)	8^2	8^1	8^0

Fig. D.5 | Positional values in the octal number system.

For longer octal numbers, the next positions to the left would be the five-hundred-and-twelves position (8 to the 3rd power), the four-thousand-and-ninety-sixes position (8 to the 4th power), the thirty-two-thousand-seven-hundred-and-sixty-eights position (8 to the 5th power) and so on.

In the hexadecimal number 3DA, we say that the A is written in the ones position, the D is written in the sixteens position and the 3 is written in the two-hundred-and-fifty-sixes position. Each of these positions is a power of the base (base 16) and that these powers begin at 0 and increase by 1 as we move left in the number (Fig. D.6).

For longer hexadecimal numbers, the next positions to the left would be the four-thousand-and-ninety-sixes position (16 to the 3rd power), the sixty-five-thousand-five-hundred-and-thirty-sixes position (16 to the 4th power) and so on.

Positional values in the hexadecimal number system			
Decimal digit	3	D	A
Position name	Two-hundred-and-fifty-sixes	Sixteens	Ones
Positional value	256	16	1
Positional value as a power of the base (16)	16^2	16^1	16^0

Fig. D.6 | Positional values in the hexadecimal number system.

D.2 Abbreviating Binary Numbers as Octal and Hexadecimal Numbers

The main use for octal and hexadecimal numbers in computing is for abbreviating lengthy binary representations. Figure D.7 highlights the fact that lengthy binary numbers can be expressed concisely in number systems with higher bases than the binary number system.

Decimal number	Binary representation	Octal representation	Hexadecimal representation
0	0	0	0
1	1	1	1
2	10	2	2
3	11	3	3
4	100	4	4
5	101	5	5
6	110	6	6
7	111	7	7
8	1000	10	8
9	1001	11	9
10	1010	12	A
11	1011	13	B
12	1100	14	C
13	1101	15	D
14	1110	16	E
15	1111	17	F
16	10000	20	10

Fig. D.7 | Decimal, binary, octal and hexadecimal equivalents.

A particularly important relationship that both the octal number system and the hexadecimal number system have to the binary system is that the bases of octal and hexadecimal (8 and 16 respectively) are powers of the base of the binary number system (base 2). Consider the following 12-digit binary number and its octal and hexadecimal equivalents. See if you can determine how this relationship makes it convenient to abbreviate binary numbers in octal or hexadecimal. The answer follows the numbers.

Binary number	Octal equivalent	Hexadecimal equivalent
100011010001	4321	8D1

To see how the binary number converts easily to octal, simply break the 12-digit binary number into groups of three consecutive bits each and write those groups over the corresponding digits of the octal number as follows:

100	011	010	001
4	3	2	1

The octal digit you have written under each group of three bits corresponds precisely to the octal equivalent of that 3-digit binary number, as shown in Fig. D.7.

The same kind of relationship can be observed in converting from binary to hexadecimal. Break the 12-digit binary number into groups of four consecutive bits each and write those groups over the corresponding digits of the hexadecimal number as follows:

1000	1101	0001
8	D	1

Notice that the hexadecimal digit you wrote under each group of four bits corresponds precisely to the hexadecimal equivalent of that 4-digit binary number as shown in Fig. D.7.

D.3 Converting Octal and Hexadecimal Numbers to Binary Numbers

In the previous section, we saw how to convert binary numbers to their octal and hexadecimal equivalents by forming groups of binary digits and simply rewriting them as their equivalent octal digit values or hexadecimal digit values. This process may be used in reverse to produce the binary equivalent of a given octal or hexadecimal number.

For example, the octal number 653 is converted to binary simply by writing the 6 as its 3-digit binary equivalent 110, the 5 as its 3-digit binary equivalent 101 and the 3 as its 3-digit binary equivalent 011 to form the 9-digit binary number 110101011.

The hexadecimal number FAD5 is converted to binary simply by writing the F as its 4-digit binary equivalent 1111, the A as its 4-digit binary equivalent 1010, the D as its 4-digit binary equivalent 1101 and the 5 as its 4-digit binary equivalent 0101 to form the 16-digit 1111101011010101.

D.4 Converting from Binary, Octal or Hexadecimal to Decimal

We are accustomed to working in decimal, and therefore it is often convenient to convert a binary, octal, or hexadecimal number to decimal to get a sense of what the number is "really" worth. Our diagrams in Section D.1 express the positional values in decimal. To convert a number to decimal from another base, multiply the decimal equivalent of each digit by its positional value and sum these products. For example, the binary number 110101 is converted to decimal 53, as shown in Fig. D.8.

Converting a binary number to decimal					
Postional values:	32	16	8	4	2	1
Symbol values:	1	1	0	1	0	1
Products:	1*32=32	1*16=16	0*8=0	1*4=4	0*2=0	1*1=1
Sum:	= 32 + 16 + 0 + 4 + 0s + 1 = 53					

Fig. D.8 | Converting a binary number to decimal.

To convert octal 7614 to decimal 3980, we use the same technique, this time using appropriate octal positional values, as shown in Fig. D.9.

Converting an octal number to decimal				
Positional values:	512	64	8	1
Symbol values:	7	6	1	4
Products	7*512=3584	6*64=384	1*8=8	4*1=4
Sum:	= 3584 + 384 + 8 + 4 = 3980			

Fig. D.9 | Converting an octal number to decimal.

To convert hexadecimal AD3B to decimal 44347, we use the same technique, this time using appropriate hexadecimal positional values, as shown in Fig. D.10.

Converting a hexadecimal number to decimal				
Postional values:	4096	256	16	1
Symbol values:	A	D	3	B
Products	A*4096=40960	D*256=3328	3*16=48	B*1=11
Sum:	= 40960 + 3328 + 48 + 11 = 44347			

Fig. D.10 | Converting a hexadecimal number to decimal.

D.5 Converting from Decimal to Binary, Octal or Hexadecimal

The conversions in Section D.4 follow naturally from the positional notation conventions. Converting from decimal to binary, octal, or hexadecimal also follows these conventions.

Suppose we wish to convert decimal 57 to binary. We begin by writing the positional values of the columns right to left until we reach a column whose positional value is greater than the decimal number. We do not need that column, so we discard it. Thus, we first write:

Positional values: 64   32   16   8   4   2   1

Then we discard the column with positional value 64, leaving:

Positional values: 32   16   8   4   2   1

Next we work from the leftmost column to the right. We divide 32 into 57 and observe that there is one 32 in 57 with a remainder of 25, so we write 1 in the 32 column. We divide 16 into 25 and observe that there is one 16 in 25 with a remainder of 9 and write 1 in the 16 column. We divide 8 into 9 and observe that there is one 8 in 9 with a remainder of 1. The next two columns each produce quotients of 0 when their positional values are divided into 1, so we write 0s in the 4 and 2 columns. Finally, 1 into 1 is 1, so we write 1 in the 1 column. This yields:

Positional values:	32	16	8	4	2	1
Symbol values:	1	1	1	0	0	1

and thus decimal 57 is equivalent to binary 111001.

To convert decimal 103 to octal, we begin by writing the positional values of the columns until we reach a column whose positional value is greater than the decimal number. We do not need that column, so we discard it. Thus, we first write:

Positional values: 512   64   8   1

Then we discard the column with positional value 512, yielding:

Positional values: 64   8   1

Next we work from the leftmost column to the right. We divide 64 into 103 and observe that there is one 64 in 103 with a remainder of 39, so we write 1 in the 64 column. We divide 8 into 39 and observe that there are four 8s in 39 with a remainder of 7 and write 4 in the 8 column. Finally, we divide 1 into 7 and observe that there are seven 1s in 7 with no remainder, so we write 7 in the 1 column. This yields:

Positional values:	64	8	1
Symbol values:	1	4	7

and thus decimal 103 is equivalent to octal 147.

To convert decimal 375 to hexadecimal, we begin by writing the positional values of the columns until we reach a column whose positional value is greater than the decimal number. We do not need that column, so we discard it. Thus, we first write:

Positional values: 4096   256   16   1

Then we discard the column with positional value 4096, yielding:

Positional values: 256   16   1

Next we work from the leftmost column to the right. We divide 256 into 375 and observe that there is one 256 in 375 with a remainder of 119, so we write 1 in the 256 column. We divide 16 into 119 and observe that there are seven 16s in 119 with a remainder of 7 and write 7 in the 16 column. Finally, we divide 1 into 7 and observe that there are seven 1s in 7 with no remainder, so we write 7 in the 1 column. This yields:

Positional values:	256	16	1
Symbol values:	1	7	7

and thus decimal 375 is equivalent to hexadecimal 177.

D.6 Negative Binary Numbers: Two's Complement Notation

The discussion so far in this appendix has focused on positive numbers. In this section, we explain how computers represent negative numbers using *two's complement notation*. First we explain how the two's complement of a binary number is formed, then we show why it represents the negative value of the given binary number.

Consider a machine with 32-bit integers. Suppose

```
int value = 13;
```

The 32-bit representation of `value` is

```
00000000 00000000 00000000 00001101
```

To form the negative of `value` we first form its *one's complement* by applying C#'s bitwise complement operator (~):

```
onesComplementOfValue = ~value;
```

Internally, `~value` is now `value` with each of its bits reversed—ones become zeros and zeros become ones, as follows:

```
value:
00000000 00000000 00000000 00001101

~value (i.e., value's ones complement):
11111111 11111111 11111111 11110010
```

To form the two's complement of `value`, simply add 1 to `value`'s one's complement. Thus

```
Two's complement of value:
11111111 11111111 11111111 11110011
```

Now if this is in fact equal to −13, we should be able to add it to binary 13 and obtain a result of 0. Let us try this:

```
  00000000 00000000 00000000 00001101
 +11111111 11111111 11111111 11110011
 ------------------------------------
  00000000 00000000 00000000 00000000
```

The carry bit coming out of the leftmost column is discarded and we indeed get 0 as a result. If we add the one's complement of a number to the number, the result would be all 1s. The key to getting a result of all zeros is that the two's complement is one more than the one's complement. The addition of 1 causes each column to add to 0 with a carry of 1. The carry keeps moving leftward until it is discarded from the leftmost bit, and thus the resulting number is all zeros.

Computers actually perform a subtraction, such as

```
x = a - value;
```

by adding the two's complement of `value` to a, as follows:

```
x = a + (~value + 1);
```

Suppose a is 27 and `value` is 13 as before. If the two's complement of `value` is actually the negative of `value`, then adding the two's complement of value to a should produce the result 14. Let us try this:

```
a (i.e., 27)       00000000 00000000 00000000 00011011
+(~value + 1)     +11111111 11111111 11111111 11110011
                  ------------------------------------
                   00000000 00000000 00000000 00001110
```

which is indeed equal to 14.

UML 2: Additional Diagram Types

E.1 Introduction

If you read the optional Software Engineering Case Study in Chapters 32–33, you should now have a comfortable grasp of the UML diagram types that we use to model our ATM system. For simplicity, we limit our discussion to a concise subset of the UML. The UML 2 provides a total of 13 diagram types. The end of Section 32.2 summarizes the six diagram types that we use in the case study. This appendix lists and briefly defines the seven remaining diagram types.

E.2 Additional Diagram Types

The following are the seven diagram types that we have chosen not to use in our Software Engineering Case Study.

- *Object diagrams* model a "snapshot" of the system by modeling a system's objects and their relationships at a specific point in time. Each object represents an instance of a class from a class diagram, and several objects may be created from one class. For our ATM system, an object diagram could show several distinct Account objects side by side, illustrating that they're all part of the bank's account database.

- *Component diagrams* model the *artifacts* and *components*—resources (which include source files)—that make up the system.

- *Deployment diagrams* model the system's runtime requirements (such as the computer or computers on which the system will reside), memory requirements, or other devices the system requires during execution.

- *Package diagrams* model the hierarchical structure of *packages* (which are groups of classes) in the system at compile time and the relationships that exist between the packages.

- *Composite structure diagrams* model the internal structure of a complex object at runtime. UML 2 allows system designers to hierarchically decompose a complex object into smaller parts. Composite structure diagrams are beyond the scope of our case study. They're more appropriate for larger industrial applications, which exhibit complex groupings of objects at execution time.

- *Interaction overview diagrams* provide a summary of control flow in the system by combining elements of several types of behavioral diagrams (e.g., activity diagrams, sequence diagrams).

- *Timing diagrams* model the timing constraints imposed on stage changes and interactions between objects in a system.

To learn more about these diagrams and advanced UML topics, please visit www.uml.org.

F

Unicode®

F.1 Introduction

The use of inconsistent character **encodings** (i.e., numeric values associated with characters) in the developing of global software products causes serious problems, because computers process information as numbers. For instance, the character "a" is converted to a numeric value so that a computer can manipulate that piece of data. Many countries and corporations have developed their own encoding systems that are incompatible with the encoding systems of other countries and corporations. For example, the Microsoft Windows operating system assigns the value 0xC0 to the character "A with a grave accent"; the Apple Macintosh operating system assigns that same value to an upside-down question mark. This results in the misrepresentation and possible corruption of data when it is not processed as intended.

In the absence of a widely implemented universal character-encoding standard, global software developers had to **localize** their products extensively before distribution. Localization includes the language translation and cultural adaptation of content. The process of localization usually includes significant modifications to the source code (such as the conversion of numeric values and the underlying assumptions made by programmers), which results in increased costs and delays releasing the software. For example, some English-speaking programmers might design global software products assuming that a single character can be represented by one byte. However, when those products are localized for Asian markets, the programmer's assumptions are no longer valid; thus, the majority, if not the entirety, of the code needs to be rewritten. Localization is necessary with each release of a version. By the time a software product is localized for a particular market, a newer version, which needs to be localized as well, may be ready for distribution. As a result, it is cumbersome and costly to produce and distribute global software products in a market where there is no universal character-encoding standard.

In response to this situation, the **Unicode Standard**, an encoding standard that facilitates the production and distribution of software, was created. The Unicode Standard outlines a specification to produce consistent encoding of the world's characters and symbols. Software products that handle text encoded in the Unicode Standard need to be localized, but the localization process is simpler and more efficient, because the numeric values need not be converted and the assumptions made by programmers about the character encoding are universal. The Unicode Standard is maintained by a nonprofit organization called the **Unicode Consortium**, whose members include Apple, IBM, Microsoft, Oracle, Sybase and many others.

When the Consortium envisioned and developed the Unicode Standard, they wanted an encoding system that was **universal, efficient, uniform** and **unambiguous**. A universal encoding system encompasses all commonly used characters. An efficient encoding system allows text files to be parsed easily. A uniform encoding system assigns fixed values to all characters. An unambiguous encoding system represents a given character in a consistent manner. These four terms are referred to as the Unicode Standard **design basis**.

F.2 Unicode Transformation Formats

Although Unicode incorporates the limited ASCII character set (i.e., a collection of characters), it encompasses a more comprehensive character set. In ASCII each character is represented by a byte containing 0s and 1s. One byte is capable of storing the binary numbers from 0 to 255. Each character is assigned a number between 0 and 255; thus, ASCII-based systems can support only 256 characters, a tiny fraction of world's characters. Unicode extends the ASCII character set by encoding the vast majority of the world's characters. The Unicode Standard encodes all of those characters in a uniform numerical space from 0 to 10FFFF hexadecimal. An implementation will express these numbers in one of several transformation formats, choosing the one that best fits the particular application at hand.

Three such formats are in use, called **UTF-8**, **UTF-16** and **UTF-32**, depending on the size of the units—in bits—being used. UTF-8, a variable-width encoding form, requires one to four bytes to express each Unicode character. UTF-8 data consists of 8-bit bytes (sequences of one, two, three or four bytes depending on the character being encoded) and is well suited for ASCII-based systems, where there is a predominance of one-byte characters (ASCII represents characters as one byte). Currently, UTF-8 is widely implemented in UNIX systems and in databases.

The variable-width UTF-16 encoding form expresses Unicode characters in units of 16 bits (i.e., as two adjacent bytes, or a short integer in many machines). Most characters of Unicode are expressed in a single 16-bit unit. However, characters with values above FFFF hexadecimal are expressed with an ordered pair of 16-bit units called **surrogates**. Surrogates are 16-bit integers in the range D800 through DFFF, which are used solely for the purpose of "escaping" into higher-numbered characters. Approximately one million characters can be expressed in this manner. Although a surrogate pair requires 32 bits to represent characters, it is space efficient to use these 16-bit units. Surrogates are rare characters in current implementations. Many string-handling implementations are written in terms of UTF-16. [*Note:* Details and sample code for UTF-16 handling are available on the Unicode Consortium website at www.unicode.org.]

Implementations that require significant use of rare characters or entire scripts encoded above FFFF hexadecimal should use UTF-32, a 32-bit, fixed-width encoding form that usually requires twice as much memory as UTF-16 encoded characters. The major advantage of the fixed-width UTF-32 encoding form is that it expresses all characters uniformly, so it is easy to handle in arrays.

There are few guidelines that state when to use a particular encoding form. The best encoding form to use depends on computer systems and business protocols, not on the data itself. Typically, the UTF-8 encoding form should be used where computer systems and business protocols require data to be handled in 8-bit units, particularly in legacy systems being upgraded, because it often simplifies changes to existing programs. For this reason, UTF-8 has become the encoding form of choice on the Internet. Likewise, UTF-16 is the encoding form of choice on Microsoft Windows applications. UTF-32 is likely to become more widely used in the future, as more characters are encoded with values above FFFF hexadecimal. Also, UTF-32 requires less sophisticated handling than UTF-16 in the presence of surrogate pairs. Figure F.1 shows the different ways in which the three encoding forms handle character encoding.

Character	UTF-8	UTF-16	UTF-32
Latin Capital Letter A	0x41	0x0041	0x00000041
Greek Capital Letter Alpha	0xCD 0x91	0x0391	0x00000391
CJK Unified Ideograph-4e95	0xE4 0xBA 0x95	0x4E95	0x00004E95
Old Italic Letter A	0xF0 0x80 0x83 0x80	0xDC00 0xDF00	0x00010300

Fig. F.1 | Correlation between the three encoding forms.

F.3 Characters and Glyphs

The Unicode Standard consists of characters, written components (i.e., alphabetic letters, numerals, punctuation marks, accent marks, and so on) that can be represented by numeric values. Examples of characters include: U+0041 Latin capital letter A. In the first character representation, U+*yyyy* is a **code value**, in which U+ refers to Unicode code values, as opposed to other hexadecimal values. The *yyyy* represents a four-digit hexadecimal number of an encoded character. Code values are bit combinations that represent encoded characters. Characters are represented with **glyphs**, various shapes, fonts and sizes for displaying characters. There are no code values for glyphs in the Unicode Standard. Examples of glyphs are shown in Fig. F.2.

The Unicode Standard encompasses the alphabets, ideographs, syllabaries, punctuation marks, **diacritics**, mathematical operators and so on that comprise the written languages and scripts of the world. A diacritic is a special mark added to a character to distinguish it from another letter or to indicate an accent (e.g., in Spanish, the tilde "~" above the character "n"). Currently, Unicode provides code values for 94,140 character representations, with more than 880,000 code values reserved for future expansion.

Fig. F.2 | Various glyphs of the character A.

F.4 Advantages/Disadvantages of Unicode

The Unicode Standard has several significant advantages that promote its use. One is its impact on the performance of the international economy. Unicode standardizes the characters for the world's writing systems to a uniform model that promotes transferring and sharing data. Programs developed using such a schema maintain their accuracy, because each character has a single definition (i.e., *a* is always U+0061, % is always U+0025). This enables corporations to manage all characters in an identical manner, thus avoiding any confusion caused by different character-code architectures. Moreover, managing data in a consistent manner eliminates data corruption, because data can be sorted, searched and manipulated via a consistent process.

Another advantage of the Unicode Standard is portability (i.e., the ability to execute software on disparate computers or with disparate operating systems). Most operating systems, databases, programming languages and web browsers currently support, or are planning to support, Unicode. Additionally, Unicode includes more characters than any other character set in common use (although it does not yet include all of the world's characters).

A disadvantage of the Unicode Standard is the amount of memory required by UTF-16 and UTF-32. ASCII character sets are 8 bits in length, so they require less storage than the default 16-bit Unicode character set. However, the **double-byte character set** (**DBCS**) and the **multibyte character set** (**MBCS**) that encode Asian characters (ideographs) require two to four bytes, respectively. In such instances, the UTF-16 or the UTF-32 encoding forms may be used with little hindrance to memory and performance.

F.5 Using Unicode

Visual Studio uses Unicode UTF-16 encoding to represent all characters. Figure F.3 uses C# to display the text "Welcome to Unicode!" in eight different languages: English, French, German, Japanese, Portuguese, Russian, Spanish and Traditional Chinese.

The first welcome message (lines 19–23) contains the hexadecimal codes for the English text. The **Code Charts** page on the Unicode Consortium website contains a document that lists the code values for the **Basic Latin** block (or category), which includes the English alphabet. The hexadecimal codes in lines 19–21 equate to "Welcome." When using Unicode characters in C#, the format \u*yyyy* is used, where *yyyy* represents the hexadecimal Unicode encoding. For example, the letter "W" (in "Welcome") is denoted by \u0057.

```
1   // Fig. F.3: UnicodeForm.cs
2   // Unicode enconding demonstration.
3   using System;
4   using System.Windows.Forms;
5
6   namespace UnicodeDemo
7   {
8      public partial class UnicodeForm : Form
9      {
10        public UnicodeForm()
11        {
12           InitializeComponent();
13        }
14
15        // assign Unicode strings to each Label
16        private void UnicodeForm_Load( object sender, EventArgs e )
17        {
18           // English
19           char[] english = { '\u0057', '\u0065', '\u006C',
20              '\u0063', '\u006F', '\u006D', '\u0065', '\u0020',
21              '\u0074', '\u006F', '\u0020' };
22           englishLabel.Text = new string( english ) +
23              "Unicode" + '\u0021';
24
```

Fig. F.3 | Unicode enconding demonstration. (Part 1 of 3.)

```
25              // French
26              char[] french = { '\u0042', '\u0069', '\u0065',
27                  '\u006E', '\u0076', '\u0065', '\u006E', '\u0075',
28                  '\u0065', '\u0020', '\u0061', '\u0075', '\u0020' };
29              frenchLabel.Text = new string( french ) +
30                  "Unicode" + '\u0021';
31
32              // German
33              char[] german = { '\u0057', '\u0069', '\u006C',
34                  '\u006B', '\u006F', '\u006D', '\u006D', '\u0065',
35                  '\u006E', '\u0020', '\u007A', '\u0075', '\u0020' };
36              germanLabel.Text = new string( german ) +
37                  "Unicode" + '\u0021';
38
39              // Japanese
40              char[] japanese = { '\u3078',  '\u3087', '\u3045',
41                  '\u3053', '\u305D', '\u0021' };
42              japaneseLabel.Text = "Unicode" + new string( japanese );
43
44              // Portuguese
45              char[] portuguese = { '\u0053', '\u0065', '\u006A',
46                  '\u0061', '\u0020', '\u0062', '\u0065', '\u006D',
47                  '\u0020', '\u0076', '\u0069', '\u006E', '\u0064',
48                  '\u006F', '\u0020', '\u0061', '\u0020' };
49              portugueseLabel.Text = new string( portuguese ) +
50                  "Unicode" + '\u0021';
51
52              // Russian
53              char[] russian = { '\u0414', '\u043E', '\u0431',
54                  '\u0440', '\u043E', '\u0020', '\u043F', '\u043E',
55                  '\u0436', '\u0430', '\u043B', '\u043E', '\u0432',
56                  '\u0430', '\u0442', '\u044A', '\u0020', '\u0432', '\u0020' };
57              russianLabel.Text = new string( russian ) +
58                  "Unicode" + '\u0021';
59
60              // Spanish
61              char[] spanish = { '\u0042', '\u0069', '\u0065',
62                  '\u006E', '\u0076', '\u0065', '\u006E', '\u0069',
63                  '\u0064', '\u006F', '\u0020', '\u0061', '\u0020' };
64              spanishLabel.Text = new string( spanish ) +
65                  "Unicode" + '\u0021';
66
67              // Simplified Chinese
68              char[] chinese = { '\u6B22', '\u8FCE', '\u4F7F',
69                  '\u7528', '\u0020' };
70              chineseLabel.Text = new string( chinese ) +
71                  "Unicode" + '\u0021';
72          } // end method UnicodeForm_Load
73      } // end class UnicodeForm
74  } // end namespace UnicodeDemo
```

Fig. F.3 | Unicode enconding demonstration. (Part 2 of 3.)

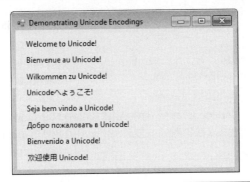

Fig. F.3 | Unicode enconding demonstration. (Part 3 of 3.)

Line 20 contains the hexadecimal for the *space* character (\u0020). The hexadecimal value for the word "to" is on line 21, and the word "Unicode" is on line 23. "Unicode" is not encoded because it is a registered trademark and has no equivalent translation in most languages. Line 23 also contains the \u0021 notation for the exclamation mark (!).

The remaining welcome messages (lines 26–71) contain the hexadecimal codes for the other seven languages. The code values used for the French, German, Portuguese and Spanish text are located in the **Basic Latin** block, the code values used for the Traditional Chinese text are located in the **CJK Unified Ideographs** block, the code values used for the Russian text are located in the **Cyrillic** block and the code values used for the Japanese text are located in the **Hiragana** block.

[*Note:* To render the Asian characters in an application, you need to install the proper language files on your Windows computer. To do this, open the **Regional Options** dialog from the **Control Panel** (**Start > Settings > Control Panel**). At the bottom of the **General** tab is a list of languages. Check the **Japanese** and the **Traditional Chinese** checkboxes and press **Apply**. Follow the directions of the install wizard to install the languages. For more information, visit www.unicode.org/help/display_problems.html.]

F.6 Character Ranges

The Unicode Standard assigns code values, which range from 0000 (**Basic Latin**) to E007F (**Tags**), to the written characters of the world. Currently, there are code values for 94,140 characters. To simplify the search for a character and its associated code value, the Unicode Standard generally groups code values by **script** and function (i.e., Latin characters are grouped in a block, mathematical operators are grouped in another block, and so on). As a rule, a script is a single writing system that is used for multiple languages (e.g., the Latin script is used for English, French, Spanish, and so on). The **Code Charts** page on the Unicode Consortium website lists all the defined blocks and their respective code values. Figure F.4 lists some blocks (scripts) from the website and their range of code values.

Script	Range of code values
Arabic	U+0600–U+06FF
Basic Latin	U+0000–U+007F
Bengali (India)	U+0980–U+09FF
Cherokee (Native America)	U+13A0–U+13FF
CJK Unified Ideographs (East Asia)	U+4E00–U+9FAF
Cyrillic (Russia and Eastern Europe)	U+0400–U+04FF
Ethiopic	U+1200–U+137F
Greek	U+0370–U+03FF
Hangul Jamo (Korea)	U+1100–U+11FF
Hebrew	U+0590–U+05FF
Hiragana (Japan)	U+3040–U+309F
Khmer (Cambodia)	U+1780–U+17FF
Lao (Laos)	U+0E80–U+0EFF
Mongolian	U+1800–U+18AF
Myanmar	U+1000–U+109F
Ogham (Ireland)	U+1680–U+169F
Runic (Germany and Scandinavia)	U+16A0–U+16FF
Sinhala (Sri Lanka)	U+0D80–U+0DFF
Telugu (India)	U+0C00–U+0C7F
Thai	U+0E00–U+0E7F

Fig. F.4 | Some character ranges.

Index